ERNIE SHIMANO

85 ST. ANDREWS

WESTON ONT.

2476589.

care & TRAINING OF THE TROTTER & PaceR

CARE and TRAINING of

the *TROTTER* and *PACER*

written by JAMES C. HARRISON

in conjunction with

RALPH N. BALDWIN

DR. EDWIN A. CHURCHILL

STANLEY F. DANCER

FRANK ERVIN

ROBERT G. FARRINGTON

HARRY M. HARVEY

WILLIAM R. HAUGHTON

DELVIN MILLER

GEORGE B. NOBLE

JOSEPH C. O'BRIEN

HARRY POWNALL

SANDERS RUSSELL

JOHN F. SIMPSON, SR.

T. WAYNE SMART

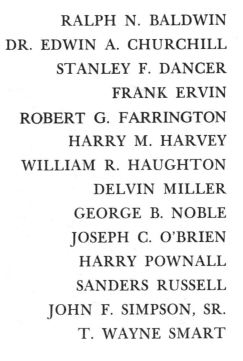

Plus a special section on nutrition
by DR. WILLIAM J. TYZNIK

Illustrated by WILLIAM A. ORR

THE UNITED STATES TROTTING ASSOCIATION

Published by

THE UNITED STATES TROTTING ASSOCIATION
750 Michigan Avenue
Columbus, Ohio 43215

Library of Congress Catalog Card Number: 68-17295

Printed and bound in the United States of America
by the Telegraph Press, Harrisburg, Pennsylvania

PHOTO CREDITS: All photographs by ED KEYS, *USTA Photography Department*, with the following exceptions: pages 366-67 by GEORGE SMALLSREED, *USTA Photography Department;* page 675 by LUBITSH & BUNGARZ, Wilmington, Del.; and Chapter 14 by COLIN L. W. BERRY, Christchurch, New Zealand.

Table of Contents

Foreword

Until now, the literature of harness racing has suffered from the lack of a single, comprehensive volume devoted to the technical, track-side aspects of the sport. Indeed, with the rare exception of an occasional article in one of the trade publications, there has been nowhere to turn for anyone seeking detailed information on such subjects as training, driving, shoeing and balancing.

With the publication by The United States Trotting Association of *Care and Training of the Trotter and Pacer,* I believe this void has been substantially filled. In the pages that follow, some of the most famous figures in harness racing have offered their thoughts on a wide variety of technical subjects some of which have never been explored in such specific detail in any book anywhere in the world.

Here, many will learn for the first time what is actually involved in the complicated process of shoeing and balancing the trotter and pacer as well as the proper methods of conditioning horses of all ages. Day-to-day training charts are laid out and the proper and improper use of bits, bridles, boots and equipment of all kinds is explained in painstaking detail. There is a chapter on the care of horses, one on bloodlines and breeding, another on lameness and still others on such wide-ranging subjects as nutrition and feeding, stable management, colt-breaking, race driving, stock farm management and even one on training methods used in New Zealand and Australia. In addition, the work is profusely illustrated and contains a number of excellent photographs as well as more than 200 original illustrations by the distinguished equine artist William A. Orr.

On behalf of the U.S. Trotting Association and speaking as well, I am sure, for everyone in harness racing, I wish to express my thanks to those men who participated in this worthwhile project by contributing chapters. They served without remuneration and were motivated solely by a desire to serve their sport by passing on to others some of the knowledge they have acquired. This marks the first time that the leading figures in any national sport have banded together to produce a book of this type and harness racing owes these men a great and lasting debt.

The book was actually written by Jim Harrison, the USTA'S Director of Racing Information, who spent more than two years crisscrossing the country and taping lengthy conversations with each of the chapter authors. From these tapes came the finished product that is this book and which has all the earmarks of becoming a "bible" for the harness racing sport.

To Jim Harrison, congratulations and thanks for a book we all need.

Walter J. Michael, President
The United States Trotting Association

January, 1968

Introduction and Acknowledgements

When I agreed to write this book, I had in mind a slender volume of perhaps a hundred pages requiring no more than six months to prepare and publish. The finished product, I thought then, would be a useful handbook that would skim the highlights involved in training and driving the harness horse. I had no sooner sketched out a rough framework than it became obvious that it would not be possible to do justice to the assignment without enlarging the scope of the work considerably. There were simply too many other related aspects that deserved consideration in a book of this type and it was important that each be included. Therefore, the subject matter was expanded, the hundred pages grew into a thousand and the time stretched from six months to almost three years. And, yet, the completed work still does nothing more than skim the highlights. For the one lesson that was driven forcibly home to me as I worked with the various chapter authors was that there was no way in which the sum total of their vast knowledge could be presented in so limited a space. As so many of them said, and rightfully, "You could write a whole book on my subject alone."

The original plan was for Delvin Miller and I to collaborate. He would describe how to train and drive trotters and pacers and I would put his thoughts on paper. But when this was proposed to him, he immediately, and typically, rejected the idea and suggested instead that a number of leading trainers be asked to participate. "We ought to have the thoughts of a lot of men instead of just one," was the way he put it. The book, therefore, does represent the thoughts of many men and, naturally, some of their opinions conflict. But no effort was made to avoid or gloss over these occasional differences of opinion and, indeed, it is a healthy sign that even among the best trainers there is no single cut and dried system that is applicable to every horse or every phase.

The selection of the men who contributed to the book was

made basically by Miller and, for the most part, he assigned their subjects. He and I regret sincerely that not more leading trainers could have been included but the limited range of subjects rendered this impossible. Each of the contributing authors participated without remuneration of any kind and as far as I am able to determine it is the first time in history that the leading figures in any nationally prominent sport have ever banded together in a project of this type. Everyone in harness racing can be proud of these men and of the unselfish contribution they have made toward a better understanding of the intricacies of their profession.

Background material concerning the authors follows each chapter. I feel their very names speak sufficiently for them but I would be remiss if I did not add a few lines summing up their impact on the sport. Through the end of the 1966 season, for instance, they had won 11 Hambletonians (including six of the last eight); 14 of the 21 Little Brown Jugs that have been raced; the last 17 national money-winning titles in succession; 13 of the last 17 heat-winning crowns; 15 of the last 17 Grand Circuit driving championships; and 13 of the last 17 UDRS (batting average) titles. They have also won 10 of the 11 Horseman of the Year awards in polls conducted annually since 1956 by *The Horseman and Fair World.* In addition, nine of the authors are among the living top 10 in the matter of total drives in 2:00 or faster and their names appear a total of 80 times in the current world record tables. I do not feel that it is out of line to call them, as a group, the cream of the nation's crop.

A word of caution about the book itself. It is not intended for casual reading; indeed, the going becomes rather heavy at times. That is because so much of the subject matter is extremely complex and has never been treated in such detailed fashion in any existing literature anywhere in the world. Basically it is a text book, and while I have made every effort to present the thoughts of the authors in smooth, free-flowing form, I have not been afraid, where necessary, to sacrifice narrative quality for the sake of specific and even, at times, repetitious detail. In this respect, the course I had to chart was clear from the very beginning. I was not writing for the trainer who was already well-established in the profession, although there are very few, indeed, who will not learn something from these men. I was aiming, rather, at young men who aspire to be trainers, drivers and grooms and at thousands of owners who have a general understanding of the various subjects but whose technical knowledge is limited. If such people can read this book and say, "Now, at last, I know what it's all about," then we who produced it can honestly claim to have done our job well.

As Johnny Simpson says in his chapter, "I know that a book of this type would have been helpful to me when I was starting out. It wouldn't have made a horse trainer out of me but I know it would have showed me some shortcuts and saved me some time and headaches."

Aside from the authors, acknowledgements are due many others, foremost among whom is Lawrence T. Evans, USTA publicity director. Mr. Evans read and edited the manuscript in highly professional fashion and, frankly speaking, rescued me from a number of glaring errors of both omission and commission.

Stanley F. Bergstein, USTA vice president and executive secretary of HTA, was a prime mover in the development of the idea and format of the book and rendered sage advice and wise counsel at all stages. The same applies for Don R. Millar, former executive vice president of the USTA and now a vice president at Hanover Shoe Farms.

Richard P. Conley, USTA director of officials and a former trainer-driver of considerable skill, provided valuable technical assistance. My secretary, Carol Sattelberg, transcribed the many hours of tape recordings and her technical knowledge of the sport proved invaluable in this respect. Grand Circuit blacksmith William Wick gave generously of his time in helping to set up the various shoeing illustrations. Pearson's Harness Horse Equipment Co., of Muncie, Ind. furnished the bits from which the illustrations in Joe O'Brien's chapter were made. Edwin Koch of Copenhagen, Denmark, provided information on European breeding for my own chapter and in this area Bowman Brown, Jr., and Les Ford of *The Harness Horse* and Bob Hackett and Elizabeth Rorty of *The Horseman & Fair World* also were helpful as were the various trotting control bodies in Australia and New Zealand. I should also like to point out that it is not technically correct to say that I wrote the entire book. The section on

Nutrition in Chapter 17 was written by Dr. William J. Tyznik himself.

The illustrations were done by William A. Orr of Maitland, Fla., a gifted artist whose work in this book will stand out as a harness racing landmark. When the need for illustrations became apparent, a careful search of racing literature brought home the fact that virtually nothing of the type required had ever been done before and that almost everything would have to be entirely original. Nowhere, for instance, could there be found examples indicating the proper placement of shadow rolls, head poles, bridles, bits, hobbles and the like. Undaunted, Mr. Orr worked closely with the authors involved to produce the illustrations in this book, all of them technically correct and many in intricate and astonishing detail. In addition, he designed and illustrated the cover and dust jacket and provided the sketches accompanying the chapter heading pages.

Mr. Orr is well-known for his portraits of horses, having done Ayres, Elma and Speedy Scot among others. He has also been commissioned to do the famous Hanover Shoe Farms stallions, Star's Pride and Tar Heel. What is less well-known is that he has also been active in painting individual and group portraits of many persons prominently involved in the U.S. space program at Cape Kennedy. He is the only artist, for instance, who has painted portraits of all seven of the original Astronauts. His contribution to this book is a unique and very important one.

For my own part, it remains only to say that the assignment was both pleasant and rewarding; pleasant because it gave me an opportunity to work closely with the finest group of men I have ever known and rewarding because it enabled me to discover how much more complicated it all is than it appears on the surface. I know now why these men are the leaders in their field. They are the thinkers and the innovators and the planners and they all have that instinctive "horse sense" with which all great horsemen are born. It was a pleasure to have worked with them on this project.

James C. Harrison
Columbus, Ohio

January, 1968

1

BLOODLINES and BREEDING

JAMES C. HARRISON

T HE American harness horse emerges in the declining years of the twentieth century as a unique animal whose officially recorded breeding history spans something less than a hundred years but whose prowess and popularity have grown all out of proportion to its humble beginnings.

In the rugged formative years that antedated the first stud book (1871) by many decades, it was linked historically and romantically to the social and economic patterns of the young nation that nurtured it and which, in scope and origin, it resembled so much. And, like the land of its birth, it rapidly outgrew the limitations placed upon or predicted for it and evolved into a swift race horse whose ability to generate early and extreme speed at either the trotting or pacing gait is patronized by thrill-seeking millions.

The breed comes down to us today as a direct male line legacy from a purely Thoroughbred horse who never raced on the trot and who never had a son that did. This was the immortal Messenger, a blue-blooded member of the English Stud Book and the great grandsire of a horse named Hambletonian. From four distinguished sons of Hambletonian, all present-day trotting and pacing blessings flow.

But despite the luster of its present and the undisguised quality of the male line from which it sprung, much of its breeding past is still shrouded in mystery. There was no official "scorekeeper" in the formative days and the exact identity of many of the more remote ancestors that made a contribution to it— as well as a surprisingly large number that are not so remote in the pedigrees of the foundation horses—is and will remain forever unknown.

But even these horses, the ones whose pedigrees were on the shadow side, possessed certain distinctive traits that enabled them to help establish a new breed when their unknown or unverified blood was intermingled with that of Messenger and, later, with that of Hambletonian and his sons. These traits included such basic ones as substance, disposition and endurance but they were overshadowed in the infant breed by the inborn ability of the immediate ancestors to reproduce the trotting gait in their offspring.

While the breed itself marked time in the early 1800's and waited on nature to confirm the accuracy of the novel compass heading she had set, the individual horses performed plebeian tasks uncommonly well. They worked early American farm fields and transported families to places of worship, merchants to business appointments and physicians on rounds of mercy. And, as if to indicate the grandeur that lay ahead, they also engaged in brief contests of speed over crude country roads.

As the breed began to mature and eventually reached a point where it became obvious that something new and startling had burst upon the equine world, it was given a name. For want of something better, the American trotter became the Standardbred because sire and dam were mated to produce a horse capable of trotting or pacing a mile within the prescribed limits of a certain standard of time.

The original Standard, (establishing a record of 2:30 for the mile distance as a base) was adopted by the National Association of Trotting Horse Breeders in 1879 and appeared in Volume 4 of John H. Wallace's American Trotting Register, the breed registry and predecessor of the U. S. Trotting Association's *Sires & Dams Book*. Volume 4 was published in 1882 and was the first in which stallions were assigned numbers to provide positive identification. Hambletonian was assigned No. 10. His sire, Abdallah, was No. 1.

Wallace, a fiercely independent and scrupulously honest Iowa farmer, had first tried his hand as a recorder of pedigrees in 1867 when he published Wallace's American Stud Book for Thoroughbreds. Almost as an afterthought, he had gathered together those trotting horse pedigrees he could find and incorporated them into a separate section in the back of the book. The Thoroughbred book fell flat on its face, but the trotting horse section was greeted enthusiastically by the leading owners and breeders of the day. Wallace then decided to concentrate on the trotting breed and published Volume 1 of his Trotting Register in 1871.

The popularity of the work spread and soon Wallace had a thriving business on his hands. He became the final authority on pedigrees and he ruled with an iron hand. It was probably just as well that he did. He made mistakes but he checked out pedigrees with a rigid singleness of purpose and his integrity was unquestioned. He had no qualms whatsoever about throwing out dubious crosses and eventually he became so domineering that he was bought out by the leading breeders who took over the Register. But by that time (1891), he had laid a proper groundwork that is recognized today for exactly what it was: a constant searching out for the truth, the whole truth and nothing but the truth.

Only in two ways could Wallace have been said to have deviated even slightly from the straight and narrow path. Aside from Messenger, he had an abiding hatred of Thoroughbred crosses in the trotting horse—some said because of his unfortunate experience in attempting to establish a Thoroughbred Stud Book—and expurgated or refused to accept a great many such crosses, some of which were doubtless valid. In addition, he held that "speed at the trot comes from speed at the pace" and in pursuing that theory admitted to the Register a large number of pacing crosses that were backed by relatively flimsy evidence. Neither of these shortcomings was important enough to have any lasting effect on the great and valuable work to which he devoted his life.

All that led to this and all that came afterward has been described in flowing rhetoric and rich detail by the late John Hervey in his classic work, *The American Trotter,* published in 1947. I do not propose here to cover exactly the same ground but intend, rather, to initiate a more intimate and specific discussion relative to the current status and structure of a proud breed. But in order to accomplish this purpose, it is necessary that I establish a solid base. For that reason I must go back and raise the shade on the window of the past.

This would put us back in the very early 1700's where a new breed of horses was in the process of being established in England. The foundation sires of this new breed hailed from the desert countries of North Africa and the Middle East and, according to their place of origin, were called Arabians, Barbs or Turks. There were numerous such stallions. Some were purchased, others arrived as gifts of reigning monarchs courting favor with the British crown and the remainder were the spoils of war. Mares of similar type and breeding also were imported.

Crossed with their own kind and with native English stock, some of which dated back to William The Conqueror, these horses founded the Thoroughbred breed. In time, the male line influence of all except three of these stallions disappeared. Those three were the Godolphin Arabian (classed as a Barb by some authorities), the Darley Arabian and the Byerly Turk. Every Thoroughbred living today traces to one of them in the direct male line. The exact dates of their birth and arrival in England vary with the authority quoted but, roughly speaking, they span the period from 1680 to 1725.

For our immediate purposes, only the Darley Arabian is of interest. It was he who founded the line that led to Messenger and thence to Hambletonian. The connecting link was the Darley Arabian's brilliant son, the undefeated Flying Childers, one of the great race horses of all time and still a legend on the British turf. (In passing, it is of interest to note that Bartlett's Childers, a full brother to Flying Childers that did not race because he was a bleeder, founded the dominant Thoroughbred line through Eclipse that leads to the vast majority of classic American runners. There are three basic male line Thoroughbred families, those of Eclipse, Herod and Matchem. Eclipse traces to the Darley Arabian through Bartlett's Childers, Herod to the Byerly Turk and Matchem to the Godolphin Arabian.)

The direct line from Messenger to the Darley Arabian runs through Mambrino, Messenger's sire, to Engineer, Sampson, Blaze and Flying Childers. Messenger's pedigree is carried in Volume I of the English Stud Book and I have taken the liberty of reproducing it in full (Fig. 1) because I do not know of any authoritative harness racing work (certainly none of recent origin) in which it has been set out on this fashion. The pedigree includes crosses to all three of the Thoroughbred foundation sires.

The question then arises as to why a trotting influence should develop among the descendents of a horse (Flying Childers) who carried in his veins uncounted generations of the purest desert blood and in which horses no inclination to trot had ever been observed. For even though none of these English ancestors of our own breed ever raced on the trot, certain of them were capable of showing extreme speed (for that time) at the trotting gait. As an example, Lord Grosvenor, the owner of Mambrino, sire of Messenger, offered to wager a thousand guineas that his horse could trot 14 miles in an hour. There were no takers.

When the Messenger family began to spread its trotting wings in America, the street corner critics, who could not tolerate the thought of a completely Thoroughbred background, began taking long-range potshots at Messenger's ancestors. It was alleged, for instance, that Sampson was not by Blaze but by a Lincolnshire coach horse that trotted. Under these assaults, the towering authenticity of the English Stud Book stood firm and in time the criticism waned and disappeared.

It is true that Sampson was a different type than most of the fine-boned descendents of the Oriental breeds. He was black—an off color for the burgeoning English breed—and he was large and coarse. But in addition to Sampson, Blaze also sired Old Shales, the foundation horse of the English Norfolk-Hackney breed and thus the lie was given to those who insisted that the trotting inheritance could not have come from him.

Whether there actually was a trespass of cold blood and whether it occurred at Blaze's generation or Sampson's is not very important at this stage. What is of interest to all authorities is that somewhere in this two-generation span the first flickering light of a trotting inheritance appeared. It was to remain relatively dormant through several more generations until it reappeared among the American descendents of Messenger.

Messenger was foaled in 1780 and, like his sire and grandsire, was a grey. He was out of an unnamed mare by Turf, he by Matchem, a grandson of the Godolphin Arabian. His second dam was by Regulus, a son of the Godolphin Arabian. The female line traced to a mare by the Byerly Turk. All the signposts of the pedigree pointed to Africa and the Middle East.

Messenger raced at three, four and five and won eight of 14 starts. He was not as good a race horse as his sire, but since he lost only one of the match races in which he engaged and gained forfeit in two others, it may be assumed that he was better than his record showed. During that time, large amounts were wagered on match races and the truest line on a horse was obtained by referring to the results of the match races in which he competed.

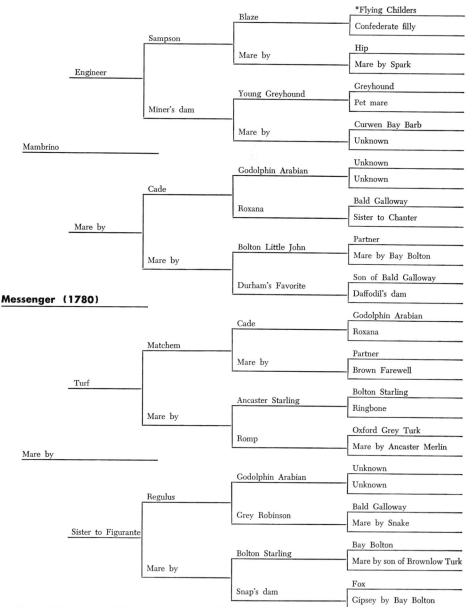

Messenger (1780)

Mambrino
- Engineer
  - Sampson
    - Blaze
      - °Flying Childers
      - Confederate filly
    - Mare by
      - Hip
      - Mare by Spark
  - Miner's dam
    - Young Greyhound
      - Greyhound
      - Pet mare
    - Mare by
      - Curwen Bay Barb
      - Unknown
- Mare by
  - Cade
    - Godolphin Arabian
      - Unknown
      - Unknown
    - Roxana
      - Bald Galloway
      - Sister to Chanter
  - Mare by
    - Bolton Little John
      - Partner
      - Mare by Bay Bolton
    - Durham's Favorite
      - Son of Bald Galloway
      - Daffodil's dam

Mare by
- Turf
  - Matchem
    - Cade
      - Godolphin Arabian
      - Roxana
    - Mare by
      - Partner
      - Brown Farewell
  - Mare by
    - Ancaster Starling
      - Bolton Starling
      - Ringbone
    - Romp
      - Oxford Grey Turk
      - Mare by Ancaster Merlin
- Sister to Figurante
  - Regulus
    - Godolphin Arabian
      - Unknown
      - Unknown
    - Grey Robinson
      - Bald Galloway
      - Mare by Snake
  - Mare by
    - Bolton Starling
      - Bay Bolton
      - Mare by son of Brownlow Turk
    - Snap's dam
      - Fox
      - Gipsey by Bay Bolton

° Flying Childers was a full brother to Bartlett's Childers who founded the male line through Eclipse which dominates modern Thoroughbred breeding. Both were by the Darley Arabian from Betty Leeds by Careless, he by Spanker, he by D'Arcy's Yellow Turk. Careless was out of a Barb mare. Spanker was out of a mare by the Morocco Barb from Bald Peg, she by a Barb horse from a Barb mare. Betty Leeds was out of a sister to Leeds by Leeds' Arabian, next dam the Spanker mare by Spanker (see above) from a mare by the Morocco Barb.

6th dam by Newcastle Turk.
7th dam by Byerly Turk.
8th dam by Taffolet Barb.
9th dam by Place's White Turk.
10th dam, Tragonwell's Natural Barb Mare.

Fig. 1

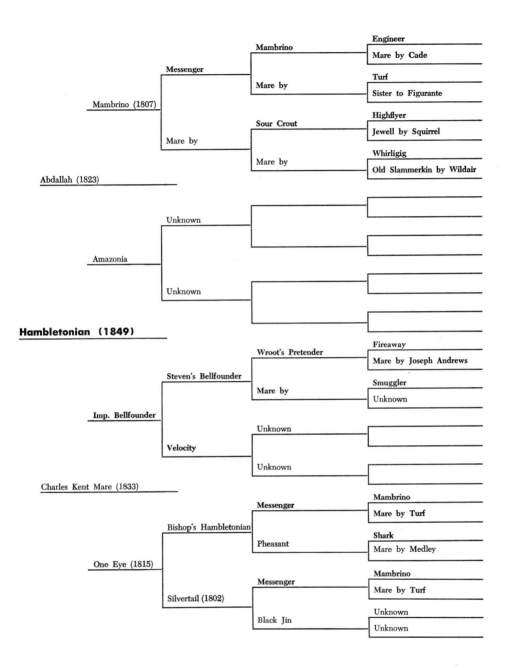

Hambletonian 10 (his registry number) was bred by Jonas Seely of Sugar Loaf, Orange County, New York, and foaled his property on May 5, 1849, at Sugar Loaf. He was sold that fall, along with his dam, for $125 to William Rysdyk of Chester, N. Y., and remained Rysdyk's property thereafter. He died March 27, 1876.

Horses in **bold face** were foaled in England.

Fig. 2

After his last start on November 1, 1785, Messenger disappears from view until his arrival in Philadelphia in May of 1788. He stood that year in Philadelphia at a fee of $15 and for the next 20 years made stud seasons in Pennsylvania, New York and New Jersey. He died in January, 1808, and was buried on Long Island.

In America, Messenger was bred to mares of every type, description and variety. Many were Thoroughbreds and while he sired a number of very fine runners he established no lasting dynasty. In running horse circles, he is probably best known as the sire of the dam (Miller's Damsel) of American Eclipse. His name is preserved today through The Messenger Stakes, a rich 3-year-old pacing event contested annually at Roosevelt Raceway not far from where the old horse died.

I will bridge the gap between the death of Messenger (1808) and the birth of Hambletonian (1849) as quickly as possible.

The first recognized trotting performance in America was credited to Yankey, a horse of unknown breeding, who went a mile in 2:59 in 1806 over a half mile track at Harlaam, N. Y. (For the record, an English horse with a Norfolk background is reported to have trotted in 2:58 under saddle that same year.) Yankey was rapidly followed into the 3:00 ranks by two others of unknown breeding, the Boston Horse, alleged to have trotted in 2:48½ in Philadelphia in 1810, and then by Boston Blue with a mile in 3:00 at Jamaica, N. Y. in 1818.

Thereafter, the descendents of Messenger began to take over. They were led by such horses as Whalebone, Screwdriver, Top Gallant, Betsy Baker and Dutchman all of whom were second or third generation offspring of the old horse and most of whom had more than one cross to him.

The Messenger banner was already flying high in the 1840's when there appeared on the trotting turf Lady Suffolk, the grey mare of Long Island. Lady Suffolk became the first 2:30 trotter in harness when at the age of 12 in 1845 she went a mile in 2:29½. She had previously trotted in 2:26 under saddle. There was nothing strange about this since many if not most of the early trotting races were to saddle.

With Lady Suffolk, the Messenger fever reached peak proportions and perhaps it would be best here to retreat and identify the opposition. It consisted of a number of bloodline channels but we will ignore all except two, those which fought hardest against the Messengers and lasted longest.

The first would be the Morgan horses. Descendents of a New England horse named Justin Morgan whose breeding has never been established satisfactorily but who was conceded to be strongly Thoroughbred, the Morgans produced a great many fine trotters. Their best was Ethan Allen, a son of Vermont Blackhawk and a great grandson of Justin Morgan, an outstanding race horse in the 1850's and 60's, who made a pass at establishing a lasting line through his son Daniel Lambert. The Morgans were good-looking, game horses but they had two fatal flaws. They were much too small—most of them barely topped 14 hands (four inches to a hand) and many were not that tall—and they were trappy-gaited, trotting with virtually a straight up and down action.

The third major trotting family of the mid-19th century was the Clays. The Clays descended from a Barb stallion that was imported from Tripoli in 1820. He was called Grand Bashaw. From a mare of basically Thoroughbred blood including at least one cross to Messenger, Grand Bashaw sired Young Bashaw (1822) who, in turn, from a mare of unknown blood, sired Andrew Jackson. From this horse descended the various Clay stallions such as Harry Clay, Henry Clay, Cassius M. Clay and a number of Cassius M. Clay Jr.'s.

The Clay family prospered roughly in the period from 1850 to 1880. It was represented by such outstanding trotters as American Girl, Lucy and George M. Patchen. For a fleeting instant, it appeared that it might emerge as the leading family. But the Clays had an intolerable fault. They would quit. Gradually, the wheel of fate turned against them and Robert Bonner, publisher of the *New York Ledger* and owner of many of the great harness horses of the day, wrote their epitaph in a sentence of scorn: "Clay blood is sawdust in the trotter." The Clays were out of business.

Whatever their other faults, the Morgans and Clays helped to establish the gait of the new trotting breed. The Messengers were low-going, long-gaited horses. They had some action in front but not a great deal. Their strong suit was a ground-devouring stride along with substance and courage. The high-gaited Morgans and the medium-gaited Clays helped to establish a trotting gait that is typified now by the round, slashing front action of the modern trotter who has the extension of the Messengers as well as the more rounded action of the Morgans and Clays. The front stroke of the modern trotter is closer to that of the Clays than either of the other two.

Another Messenger branch was also active in those days. It descended through Mambrino, a Thoroughbred son of Messenger who sired Mambrino Paymaster. (The name Mambrino always causes some confusion in discussing Messenger who was sired by Mambrino and whose most famous son was Mambrino. Some authorities refer to one as English Mambrino and the other as American Mambrino.) Mambrino Paymaster, in turn, sired Mambrino Chief who established a line of his own (he was the sire of the great trotting mare Lady Thorn) and then kept it going for a time through his son Mambrino Patchen and his grandson Mambrino King. Eventually, the Mambrinos established their niche on the brood mare side by providing many of the best females that were bred to Hambletonian stallions to produce trotting champions.

All these families were living on borrowed time. They were soon to be overwhelmed by a tribe that sprang from the loins of a horse foaled at Sugar Loaf, N. Y., on May 5, 1849. This was Hambletonian 10 and as his pedigree indicates (Fig. 2), he was intensely inbred to Messenger.

His sire, Abdallah, was a foul-tempered, rat-tailed horse who could trot himself and who was the first horse to sire two 2:30 trotters. He was by Mambrino, the strictly Thoroughbred horse mentioned above as the founder of the Mambrino Chief line. Abdallah's dam, Amazonia, was a fast road mare of absolutely unknown breeding. She has been given occasionally as by a son of Messenger and while it is plausible that she was, there is no evidence to support the contention.

Hambletonian's dam, the Charles Kent mare, was a cripple. She had a hip down and had changed hands several times before she foaled the "great father of trotters." But she and her dam, and grand dam had all been owned by the Seely family of Sugar Loaf, Jonas and his father Jonas Sr., and thus their breeding could be verified.

The Charles Kent mare was by imported Bellfounder, a horse that was a descendent of the famed Norfolk trotters of England.

He was foaled in 1816 and was the first English Hackney of which there is any reliable record in this country. In tail-male he traced through famed Norfolk and Hackney names—Stevens' Bellfounder, Wroot's Pretender, Fireaway and Driver—to Old Shales (1755) the foundation sire of the Norfolk-Hackney breed. Old Shales was a son of Blaze, the son of Flying Childers who set the trotting line of Messenger in motion.

Bellfounder's dam was a mare of unknown breeding who was alleged to have trotted 16 miles in an hour on an English road in 1806. Her son arrived in this country in 1822 and his sole major contribution to the trotting horse breed was to sire the dam of Hambletonian.

Hambletonian's second and third dams were of Messenger blood as was his sire. The second dam, One Eye, was by Bishop's Hambletonian, a Thoroughbred son of Messenger. The third dam, Silvertail, was by Messenger himself. The fourth dam, Black Jin, was of unknown blood. In later years it was reported that she was a pacer, but this may only have been Wallace attempting to enhance his previously related doctrine concerning the value of pacing crosses.

In the fall of the year he was foaled, Hambletonian was sold, along with his dam, to William Rysdyk of Chester, N. Y., who worked for Jonas Seely as a farmhand. The price for mare and foal was $125. Hambletonian was never raced but is reported to have trotted in 2:48½ in a trial as a 3-year-old. In keeping with the Messenger-Abdallah tradition, he was not a handsome horse. He had a very plain head and there was nothing refined about his conformation. It reeked of brute power with massive quarters, strong bone and heavily-muscled forearms setting off the trotting pitch which he and so many of his descendents possessed. In the old horse himself, this was emphasized by a two-inch slope from rump to withers. He stood 15-1¼ at the withers and 15-3¼ behind.

The stars of the 1850's were non-Hambletonian horses. The victories went to Flora Temple, Tacony, Highland Maid, Ethan Allen, Lady Moscow and a mare who was known as the Adams Filly, then the Billings Mare, then Topsey and finally Princess. In later years, Princess was to become the dam of one of Hambletonian's greatest sons.

In the sixties the tide turned. The immortal Dexter, a son of

Hambletonian out of a mare by the Thoroughbred stallion American Star (tracing in the male line to Diomed, winner of the first English Derby in 1780) appeared on the turf and ravaged it for four years, reducing the trotting record to 2:17¼ before Robert Bonner bought him for $25,000 and took him out of competition. Bonner never raced horses. He drove them solely for pleasure and owned many of the greatest. The evening he bought Dexter in Buffalo, N. Y., he wired a friend, "I came here to see the two great American wonders, Niagara Falls and Dexter. I could not buy the falls so I bought Dexter."

As Dexter departed the racing scene, other Hambletonians arrived to carry on the name. They included Goldsmith Maid, the great mare who raced triumphantly through the sixties and seventies, George Wilkes, St. Julien and many, many others. George Wilkes was by Hambletonian himself but it was The Maid and St. Julien who gave the first evidence that Hambletonian was a horse that would pass on lasting greatness into future generations. Goldsmith Maid was a daughter of Alexander's Abdallah whom Hambletonian sired when he was two. St. Julien was by Volunteer, another son of the old horse.

Since it is my purpose here to relate breeding rather than racing history, I will leave the racing scene with the Hambletonians in full command and concentrate on the four sons of Hambletonian who founded the sire lines that lead to virtually all trotters and pacers racing in this country today. Chronologically, they were George Wilkes (1856), Dictator and Happy Medium (1863) and Electioneer (1868).

George Wilkes was the only one of the four that engaged in an extensive racing career. He made his first start as a 4-year-old, raced until he was 16 and at one time was the world champion trotting stallion with a record of 2:22 taken at the age of 12. He retired absolutely sound. He was a tool of gamblers and was denounced as a quitter. No horse that raced as long, hard and successfully as Wilkes could have been a quitter. It appears more likely that he was a sulker, much as certain of the get of Adios are known to sulk today. Of one of his races, an admirer wrote: "Through the stretch, George Wilkes was seen to relax his efforts." Of the same race, a critic of the horse wrote: "George Wilkes quit like a dog."

George Wilkes is also responsible for the wide-gaited characteristic that we still observe today in so many of our trotters. Hiram Woodruff, a famous trainer of the period, described it as follows: "His hind leg, when straightened out in action when he went at his best pace, reminded me of that of a duck in swimming." This is the duck stroke that comes down to us through Axtell, Axworthy and Mr. McElwyn to many of their descendents.

Wilkes was not quite 15 hands high and when he was finally retired to Kentucky in his 17th year his potential as a stock horse was not highly regarded. His foes called him "Eph Simmons's baked-up pony." His services were not in demand.

But like all great horses that have been properly endowed by nature, George Wilkes rose above it all. Year after year he sent out tough, game horses and he sired sons who sired not only race winners but more sons who sired more winners. These sons and grandsons scattered to the best farms in the land and his line and that of Electioneer ruled the trotting roost.

In time, the Wilkes line came down to two male branches. One was headed by McKinney, a grandson of George Wilkes through Alcyone. The other was headed by Axworthy. Only it survived. The Axworthy line, most prominently identified today in the trotting sires Florican and Hickory Smoke and in the pacing sires Knight Dream, Duane Hanover and Torpid, lived on through a sheer fluke.

In 1885, an Iowa farmer named C. W. Williams wanted to breed Lou, a cheap inbred Mambrino Boy mare, to either Baron Wilkes or Red Wilkes, the leading sons of George Wilkes standing in Kentucky. He could not afford the service fees for those horses and for less than the advertised fee of $50 settled instead on William L., a crippled and unraced full brother to the successful stallion Guy Wilkes.

From this mating came Axtell, who established the world's 3-year-old trotting record at 2:12 in 1889 and who was sold that evening for $105,000. Axtell, in turn, sired Axworthy and Axworthy, sold for $500 when he was five, sired Guy Axworthy. The latter horse became the leading futurity sire of the early twentieth century and his son Guy McKinney was the first Hambletonian winner.

George Wilkes, the founder of the Axworthy line, was out of a mare named Dolly Spanker whose pedigree was and is unknown. Wallace carried her in The Register for many years as by Henry Clay. This was later proved incorrect and was stricken from the official record in 1895.

Among the foundation sires, Electioneer stands out as a paradox. He was the divining instrument in a carefully calculated, boldly implemented and fabulously successful plan to develop colt trotters at a time when it was considered almost sacrilegious to send horses to the races until they were at least four years old.

The experiment was carried out at Palo Alto Farm in California between 1876 and 1893. The instigators were Leland Stanford, the farm owner, who believed it could be done, and his trainer, Charles Marvin, who shared Stanford's enthusiasm and thus became the first of the great colt trainers.

The paradox arises from the fact that while Stanford would not tolerate a pacer on the farm, immediately culling the rare one that appeared, (Electioneer is credited with 158 standard record trotters and two pacers) the horse that permitted him to enjoy a measure of success beyond his wildest dreams lives today only as the ancestor of a pacing family. Even the fact that the male line from Electioneer has culminated in as great a horse as Adios would not have appeased Stanford. The man who was Governor of California, U. S. Senator and whose name is borne by the great University he founded, would have cringed at the very thought.

Electioneer was bred by Charles Backman of Stony Ford Farm near Goshen, N. Y. He was out of a mare named Green Mountain Maid, she by Harry Clay, a descendent of the Barb horse from Tripoli. Green Mountain Maid's dam was Shanghai Mary, but her breeding is officially unknown. Most authorities agree that she was by Iron's Cadmus, a Thoroughbred, but it could never be proved.

Electioneer had never raced and was eight years old when Stanford visited Stony Ford in 1876 in search of a stallion. It was assumed that he would try to purchase Messenger Duroc, also at Stony Ford, but for reasons of his own he asked instead for a price on Electioneer and bought him for $12,500.

Stanford purchased the best mares available and began breeding them to Electioneer. Marvin began training the foals according to the Palo Alto "brush" system. The young horses were rarely asked to go full miles. Instead, they brushed eighths, quarters and halves. The results electrified the harness racing world.

In 1881, Hinda Rose, a daughter of Electioneer-Beautiful Bells, went for a record as a yearling and trotted in 2:43, later reducing it to 2:36½. Ten years later, Bell Bird, a product of the identical breeding lowered the mark to 2:26¼.

In 1880, Fred Crocker lowered the 2-year-old record to 2:25¼. Within 10 years, three other Palo Alto products reduced it almost 15 seconds, Wildflower to 2:21, Sunol to 2:18 and Arion to 2:10¾. All were by Electioneer.

As 3-year-olds, Hinda Rose, Sunol and Arion were world record holders, the latter two going in 2:10½ and Sunol wresting the crown from Axtell who was the same age and who had trotted in 2:12 after she had registered 2:13¾.

Stanford also believed that Thoroughbred blood could be mingled successfully with trotting horse blood and conducted experiments along that line. Sunol, for instance, had for her second dam the Thoroughbred mare Waxy by Lexington, and Dame Winnie, an out and out Thoroughbred (Wallace insisted that Waxy was not Thoroughbred and the battle raged for 20 years before definite proof emerged) became the third dam of the very successful stallion Belwin.

But Stanford's greatest accomplishment in his experimental program involving Thoroughbreds stemmed from the brood mare Esther. Bred to Mendocino, a son of Electioneer, Esther produced the filly Mendocita. Mendocita was bred to San Francisco and a daughter of that mating, Cita Frisco, comes down to us as the dam of Volomite, one of the all-time great Standardbred sires.

Bred to Electioneer, Esther produced the good race mare Expressive who, when bred to Bellini (a grandson of Hambletonian through his son Artillery) produced Atlantic Express. Atlantic Express, in turn, sired the world champion trotting mare, Nedda 1:58¼, as well as the dams of Dean Hanover 3, 1:58½, and Spintell 1:58¾. Nedda, in turn, is the third dam of Good Time and since his dam, On Time, is by Volomite, it means that he is inbred to a Thoroughbred mare.

Eastern breeders were anxious to sample the Electioneer blood and for a long price, C. J. Hamlin, owner of The Village Farm at East Aurora, N. Y., bought Chimes, an unraced son of Electioneer and the great matron Beautiful Bells. From a Clay line mare, Chimes sired The Abbe who took a trotting record of

2:10¾ at three in 1903. But the horse wanted to pace and the following year Ed (Pop) Geers raced him at that gait and gave him a record of 2:03½.

With this horse, the basic Electioneer trotting line died and the pacing line came to life. The Abbe sired Abbedale and Bert Abbe. Abbedale sired Hal Dale and he sired Adios and Good Time. Bert Abbe sired Gene Abbe.

One other branch of the Electioneer family made a pass at keeping the trotting line alive, but it, too, failed. This was the Bingen line through Electioneer's son May King. In the 1920's it was still one of four currently popular trotting families (the others were Axworthy, Peter The Great and McKinney) and its bright shining light was Uhlan 1:58. But Uhlan was a gelding and Bingen never sired anything else good enough to warrant consideration by the leading farms. Another trotting family fell by the wayside.

If, at the dawn of the twentieth century, it was considered a sure thing that Electioneer would found a lasting trotting family, and it was, the odds would have been long indeed against the possibility of Happy Medium doing it.

A successful sire himself, Happy Medium appeared incapable of passing on to future generations the greatness of the Hambletonian blood. His sons were denounced as quitters, much as George Wilkes had been many years before, and none of them stood at major farms. Just as they were about to toll the final count, there appeared in 1895 a horse named Peter The Great, a grandson of Happy Medium. He was to change the course of harness racing history and live to establish the most prominent trotting line the sport has ever known.

Happy Medium was out of the celebrated trotting mare Princess who was mentioned earlier and who once trotted and won two 10-mile races to wagon on consecutive days in California for a stake of $35,000. Despite the fact that she bore at least four names in her lifetime, her ancestry was traced to Messenger through her sire Andrus's Hambletonian and thence to Judson's Hambletonian and Messenger's son Bishop's Hambletonian.

Happy Medium was raced only lightly and made a handful of starts at four, five and six. His record of 2:32½ was taken when he was six. Despite this unimpressive record, he was sold on the strength of his breeding for $25,000 as a potential sire, standing first in Philadelphia and then in Kentucky.

He was a successful sire but his get were criticized as lacking in courage and they were noted for having bad feet as well, specifically navicular disease which was alleged to have been inherited from Princess who was constantly lame in her feet during her racing days.

In his last year in Pennsylvania, Happy Medium sired a grey colt from a Pilot Jr. mare Tackey, who was also known as Polly. The foal was a cripple (he had a hip down) and never raced. His name was Pilot Medium. He was purchased in Williamsport, Pa., by Walter Clark of Battle Creek, Michigan, and taken to that state to head Clark's farm. This was literally a graveyard for a stallion since very few of the mares to whom he was bred possessed any kind of Standard pedigree.

One of these mares was Santos, owned by D. D. Streeter, of Kalamazoo, Michigan. She was by Grand Sentinel, he by Sentinel, a full brother to Hambletonian's son, Volunteer, the sire of Goldsmith Maid. But beyond that the pedigree was as short as an eight-day candle on the ninth day. As a matter of fact, it required more than 20 years to clear it up to the satisfaction of the Registry authorities and even then it revealed nothing aside from the most common of ancestors. The foal of this mating was Peter The Great.

Peter The Great wanted to pace from the start and only great effort on the part of his trainer Peter V. Johnston, for whom he was named, kept him from doing it. But Johnston persisted and Peter The Great became a successful race horse. When he was eight years old he was sold at auction for $5,000 to Patchen Wilkes Farm in Kentucky and there sired Peter Volo and Peter Scott. It is doubtful that any stallion ever sired two horses that did as much for the harness horse breed.

Peter Volo sired Volomite and Peter Scott sired Scotland. From these two horses descend most of the leading trotting sires of the day, the exceptions being those few (Florican and Hickory Smoke are the prime examples) that come down to us through George Wilkes. All other prominent male line trotting blood in America descends from Peter The Great.

The fourth son of Hambletonian to establish a sire line was Dictator, the handsomest of the four foundation sires. Dictator was a full brother to Dexter, the first and most famous of the sons of Hambletonian. His dam was Clara by the Thoroughbred stallion American Star and his second dam the McKinstry mare, pedigree unknown.

Because of the reputation of his brother, Dictator was sold as a yearling for a long but undisclosed price to Harrison Durkee, a very wealthy New York sportsman who did not race him. Durkee said, however, that Dictator showed a high turn of speed. When he was 13, Dictator was sent to Kentucky on a two-year agreement where he stood at a service fee of $200 which was twice that of George Wilkes, then in his prime. His patronage was extremely limited and after two years he was returned to New York without regret.

But from the few mares to which he was bred in those years he sired Jay-Eye-See, the first 2:10 trotter; Phallas, who reduced the stallion record to 2:13¾ and Director who won two $10,000 races and trotted in 2:17. Dictator was syndicated for $25,000 in 1884 and returned to Kentucky where he stood successfully for another nine years before his death, siring among others the dam of the immortal Nancy Hanks.

Director sired Direct, a double-gaited horse that was extremely game and who waged some memorable races against Hal Pointer, the pride of the Tennessee Hals. After his retirement, Direct stood a year (1895) in Tennessee and was bred to mares of the Hal blood. From one of them, Bessie Hal, he sired Direct Hal and thus founded the line that comes down to us today through Billy Direct, the former world champion pacer.

Direct Hal sired Walter Direct and his son Napoleon Direct sired Billy Direct. Billy Direct, of course, sired Tar Heel who currently heads the sole line of speed descent leading back to the brother to Dexter.

The pedigrees of some of the leading exponents of these four Hambletonian sire lines appear in the appendix.

Having established the source and traced the lineal descent of the American trotter, it is time to give additional consideration to his poor cousin grown rich, the pacer. So popular have pacers become in the modern harness racing concept that very frequently eight of nine races on a major pari-mutuel track card are devoted to them. Fitted with hobbles that enable them to maintain gait in tight situations that would send trotters into a flying break, the sidewheeler is the darling of the American wagering public. And yet, men still live who remember the days when pacers were scorned and leading Grand Circuit trainers wore buttons that read, "No Hobbles," meaning that they would drive a pacer if necessary but only if he did not wear the leg straps which were anathema to the leading horseman of that day. These observations, however, are offered only as general background and will not be pursued further since they have no bearing on the nature of the breed which is the sole considera- tion of this chapter.

As has already been established, the modern American pacer is tightly-bred to Hambletonian and Messenger, basically through Electioneer and Dictator but also including links to Happy Medium and George Wilkes. This is a fortunate happenstance for those breeding buffs who prefer their bloodlines neat and well- defined. For the truth is that the origin of the pacing blood that preceded the linkage to the Hambletonian line constitutes a blend of the unknown and the unfathomable. All pacing roads prior to the advent of the Hambletonian influence reach dead ends. It is a maze without an exit.

The pacers have been with us almost as long as the trotters and the first performance, recorded long afterward in Wallace's Register, was two miles in 5:04½ in 1829 by Bowery Boy, a horse of unknown breeding. He was followed by Oneida Chief who paced in 2:31 to a sulky in 1835 and then by the first 2:30 pacer, Aggie Down, who went in 2:29 in 1844. The first pacer to capture national interest was the great mare Pocahantas who obtained a record of 2:17¼ in 1855. She was also the first with any recognized breeding, her sire being Iron's Cadmus, a horse of Thoroughbred descent.

The breakthrough for the pacers occurred in 1879 when the Big Four consisting of Sleepy Tom, Rowdy Boy, Mattie Hunter and Lucy engaged in some brilliant battles on the newly-founded Grand Circuit. In that year, Sleepy Tom lowered the pacing record to 2:12¾. From that time on, the pacers were tolerated. They had few champions among the leading sportsmen of the day but they needed none. Their speed spoke for them and in 1897 Star Pointer, a pacer, became the first two-minute horse when he went in 1:59¼ at Readville, Mass.

Star Pointer represented the male line of the Tennessee Hal family which reached its high and low point with him. He was never able to establish a male line nor were any of his fellow Hals. As a rule, the Hals were stiff-legged pacers and it remained for the Hambletonian line horses, notably Direct, to introduce the frictionless gait of the modern pacer.

The Hal family undoubtedly had its origins in Canada, although no positive evidence to that effect has ever been uncovered. French Canada was a mecca for gaited horses and many of them were pacers. The first known horses arrived in the Montreal area about 1608 after having been introduced four years earlier in Nova Scotia by their importer, a French lawyer named L'Escarbot. They were alleged to have been descendents of the Norman horses of France.

At any rate, in the early 1800's the French-Canadian horses were well-known in America. Their specific locale was usually given as being "about 30 miles below Montreal on the St. Lawrence." The severe climate stamped their type. Their hair was coarse, their manes and tails heavy and full flowing and displayed a wave or curl. They grew shaggy growths around the fetlocks and had thick necks, heavy around the windpipe and throat. They were closely built and quite muscular and displayed the sloping rump that characterizes the pacer of today.

The original Tom Hal, founder of the Hal family, was purchased in Philadelphia about 1824 and was identified as a Canadian. He went to Kentucky where he was variously known as Mason's, Boswell's, West's and Shropshire's Tom Hal.

He was a roan and when bred to a mare by Chinn's Copperbottom, a light chestnut and a son of the original Copperbottom, who also came from Canada, produced a chestnut colt known as Bald Stockings and also called Lail's Tom Hal and Clark's Tom Hal. From a mare of Thoroughbred blood, Bald Stockings sired Kittrell's Tom Hal, a bay, who went to Tennessee in 1850 as the property of Major M. B. Kittrell. From the pacing mare Julia Johnson, whose mixed blood was principally Thoroughbred, Kittrell's Tom Hal sired Gibson's Tom Hal, the true foundation horse of the Hal breed.

Bred to Lizzie, a great granddaughter of Kittrell's Tom Hal, Gibson's Tom Hal sired the full brothers Little Brown Jug and Brown Hal. Little Brown Jug, a gelding, was the first world champion of the Hal line pacing in 2:11¾ in 1881. Brown Hal was the champion pacing stallion with a record of 2:12. Lizzie's antecedents combined Thoroughbred and pacing blood, much of the former tracing to the Virginia stallion Sir Archy, a son of Diomed. (Incidentally, Sir Archy, the leading American running horse sire of his day, deserves more credit for his contribution to the harness horse breed than the early historians have given him. I have counted at least 20 separate sons whose names may be found in early Standardbred pedigrees. Obviously, he was a horse who suffered as a result of Wallace's antipathy to non-Messenger Thoroughbred blood.)

Sweepstakes, another great granddaughter of Kittrell's Tom Hal, and, like Lizzie, bred along pacing and Thoroughbred lines maternally, also produced two world champions. The first was Hal Pointer by Gibson's Tom Hal that Geers raced so successfully on the Grand Circuit and who was matched against Direct in the early nineties in a pair of the keenest contests ever waged. The second of Sweepstakes' championship foals was Star Pointer himself, he by Brown Hal the son of Gibson's Tom Hal and Lizzie. Thus, the Hal breed, at its apogee, was woven around two stallions, Gibson's Tom Hal and his son Brown Hal, and two mares, Lizzie and Sweepstakes, all of whom traced in the direct male line to Kittrell's Tom Hal.

Star Pointer, an unnatural pacer, a puller, and a confirmed knee-knocker was a failure at the stud and eventually the Hal family disappeared from view in this country except in very rare collateral crosses. In Australia and New Zealand, Logan Pointer, a son of Star Pointer, made a more strenuous effort to establish a male line, but apparently has failed although his blood is prominent and popular on the female side.

The demise of the Hal line actually began in 1895 when the owner of Direct, the Hambletonian-line grandson of Dictator, was encouraged by Pop Geers to stand the horse in Tennessee where breeders there remembered his thrilling battles with Hal Pointer. From Bessie Hal, a daughter of Gibson's Tom Hal as previously related, Direct sired Direct Hal who was campaigned by Geers and who went on to establish the line that led to Billy Direct and Tar Heel.

The only other Canadian horse that left any lasting imprint on the modern Standardbred was a black horse known as Old Pilot and who resembled in type and conformation the French-Canadian pacer. He was purchased in New Orleans in 1832 where he was said to have paced a mile in 2:26 to wagon. He could also trot. In Kentucky, he sired Pilot Jr. from a mare of mixed saddle and Thoroughbred blood and Pilot Jr., a grey, sired the dam of Pilot Medium, also a grey and the sire of Peter the Great. The blood of Pilot Jr. is also found in a number of the key mares of the leading maternal families.

Aside from the Hals, the only pacing tribe that ever mounted any kind of a challenge to The Hambletonians was the Blue Bull family that was prominent in Indiana in the late 1800's. Blue Bull, the family founder, was by a horse known as Pruden's Blue Bull, a chestnut with a dark stripe running the length of his back, and he by Merring's Blue Bull. Little or nothing else is known of their breeding. Strangely, Blue Bull, although a pacer himself, sired trotters. As a matter of fact, in 1884 Blue Bull momentarily dethroned Hambletonian as the leading sire of Standard performers with 40 to 38 for the Hero of Chester. But the Blue Bulls were a passing fancy. Although trotters, they were manufactured to go at the gait. Actually, they were natural pacers and they could not meet the test of either trotting or pacing speed as it moved upward and onward. The Blue Bulls soon disappeared from the scene.

There were also other pacing tribes that accounted for a performer here and there such as the Hiatogas, Red Bucks, Tom Crowders and Davy Crocketts. They were mostly of Canadian origin, although Hiatoga descended from Virginia Thoroughbreds. There is no evidence that the Narragansett Pacer, the horse that provided transportation for the Rhode Island colony in the 17th century, played any part in the evolution of the American pacer. It is quite possible that they did through descendents taken to Virginia but there is nothing to support the theory.

The United States is not the only country in which harness racing prospers. It is extremely popular in virtually every European country including Russia. In Europe there are no pacing races, activity being limited exclusively to trotters. Harness racing has recently been introduced into England, the last major holdout among the great nations of the world, and is or has been popular in such widely-scattered geographic areas as Japan, North Africa and South America. In Australia and New Zealand, it is a leading sport.

The blood of Hambletonian plays a major part in the success of harness horses throughout the world. As a matter of fact, male lines descending from Hambletonian dominate all countries except France and Russia and even there American blood is quite prominent. From a bloodline standpoint, it might be worthwhile to comment briefly on the world-wide exceptions to the rule of Hambletonian descendency.

The most important non-Hambletonian line in the world today exists in France where the Stud Book has been closed to American horses since 1937. France has developed its own breeding lines and while three American sires who were involved before the Stud Book was closed—Sam Williams, The Great McKinney and Net Worth—still play a relatively prominent part through their descendents, the French have also established vital male lines of their own which descend from sources other than Hambletonian.

In the appendix, there will be found a chart which traces the French sire lines. Aside from the one leading to Hambletonian, the French have two additional lines that descend from Thoroughbred horses that were crossed with native French stock as well as horses imported from Denmark, Germany and other countries. One of these lines traces back to the Godolphin Arabian through the Thoroughbred Rattler and his half-Thoroughbred son, Young Rattler, he the sire of Imperieux and Xerces. The Imperieux line was kept alive by the great horse Fuschia and his sons Bemecourt and Narquois. Through Bemecourt's son Intermede, we get such horses as Jamin, winner of the Roosevelt International in 1959, Tornese, another International competitor and the fine sire Tigre Royal. Through Bemecourt's son Ontario and his son Hernani III, we get the great mares Roquepine and Infante II as well as horses like The Prix d'Amerique winner Masina, Oscar R. L. and the fabulous Toscan, considered the coming European champion as this is written.

Through Narquois via Koenigsberg comes Oriolo, currently the leading sire in Italy, and Querido II, a great race horse, and his sire Fandango.

The other major non-Hambletonian line comes down through the Thoroughbred stallion Eclipse, previously identified as the tail-male ancestor of the majority of the world's great running horses. In France, this inheritance comes through the half-breed (not pure Thoroughbred) horse Phaeton down to present-day horses such as the champion mare Ozo as well as Icare IV and Kracovie.

Despite all this non-Hambletonian blood, the leading sire in France in 1966 was Carioca II, a grandson of Sam Williams, he a purely American-bred son of Peter Scott. The lines from The Great McKinney descend through the full brothers Kairos and Ogaden (both are out of the French-bred mare Uranie by Intermede) with Kairos standing out as the better of the two. He has sired Hermes D., Hairos II, Pick Wick, Gelinotte and is the grandsire of Mick D'Angerieux.

In addition to the male-line chart, I am also reproducing in the appendix the pedigrees of two of the very greatest French race horses, the outstanding mare Roquepine and her apparent successor, the horse Toscan. French crosses predominate these pedigrees, although Roquepine is out of a mare by Kairos who traces to American lines. It is of interest also to note that Jalna IV, the dam of Roquepine, is a half sister to Infante II, 1:14 9/10 (2:00⅗), the fastest mare ever bred in Europe as this is written, and a full sister to Hermes D, one of the leading sires in France and the sire of Pluvier III, the winner of the 1965 Roosevelt International.

Jamin, the French trotter who opened American eyes to that country's breeding when he appeared here several years ago, is linebred to Bemecourt (his dam, Dladys, is by Hernani III) and his second dam, Gladys, is a purely Thoroughbred mare.

In Russia, the foundation stock is the Orloff. The Orloff trotter resulted from a breeding experiment conducted by Count Alexey Orlow-Tschmenskoi. In the mid-1700's, Count Orlow imported a pure-blooded Arabian stallion named Smetanka. He bred this horse to a large-boned Danish mare and got Polkan I, who was larger than his sire. Polkan I was, in turn, bred to a large Dutch mare that had a trotting background to produce Bars I, a foal of 1784. The Orloff breed descends from Dobry, Lebed I and Lubenzy, all sons of Bars I.

The Orloff breed runs to large, grey horses that have considerable size and stamina but very little quick or extreme speed. In the later part of the 19th century and the early part of the 20th, several drafts of American horses were imported in an effort to improve the breed but this traffic ceased with the Revolution of

1917 and it was not until recent years that any further effort was made to improve the Orloff type. The importation within the last half dozen years of such well-bred stallions as Lowe Hanover and Apex Hanover (Star's Pride) and Bill Hanover (Hoot Mon) indicates that the Russians are aware of the shortcomings of the Orloff trotter and are attempting to improve the type. The man responsible for this trend is Yevgeniy Dolmotov, who is in charge of the Moscow Hippodrome and a keen student of breeding and racing matters. Dolmotov has visited the United States on a number of occasions and has made many friends in this country.

In other European countries the leading sires are basically of American blood although the French lines are enjoying some success. According to Edwin Koch of Denmark, one of the most prominent European breeding authorities, the top sires of the various European countries, aside from France and Russia are as follows:

AUSTRIA: The two leading sires are the French-bred Gentil Kaiqui, a son of Kairos; and the Austrian-bred Kahlenberg, a son of the American horse Vansandt, he a son of San Francisco.

BELGIUM: The leading sire is a French horse, Ottarus who is by either Hernani III or Salam.

DENMARK: Joe's Pride, a son of Volomite, is the best sire in Denmark. Two other American sires, the deceased Lloyd Hanover by Dean Hanover and Victory Mon by Hoot Mon were next in the most recent ratings.

HUNGARY: The French-bred Uniforme, tracing to Bemecourt, is currently the leading Hungarian sire. The deceased American sire The Skipper (Volomite-The Worthy Miss Morris and thus a full brother to Speed King, 2:00, a successful sire in Sweden) has had a great influence on Hungarian breeding.

ITALY: More good American horses have been exported to Italy than to all other European countries combined. The former great stars of the breed were Prince Hall and Doctor Spencer and, to a somewhat lesser degree, McLin Hanover and De Sota, all American-bred. The current leaders are Oriolo, Scotch Thistle and Mighty Ned, the latter two American. Oriolo is French-bred on the top line but his dam is of purely American blood. As a matter of fact, his dam, Heluan, is by the Italian-bred Floridoro, he by The Laurel Hall-Alma Lee. Alma Lee is, of course, the dam of Rosalind, 1:56¾, world champion trotting mare, Alma

Lee was exported to Italy before Rosalind became famous.

HOLLAND: The sire list is headed by the French-bred Double Six M (who traces to Intermede), Enterprise, a grandson of Scotland (sired by the American-bred Locomotive), and Stüermann, a German-bred son of Calumet Butler, winner of the 1931 Hambletonian.

NORWAY: The latest Norwegian lists are headed by Saint Protector, a son of the American stallion Protector, and Khedive by Bulwark, the latter a son of Volomite and the most prominent Swedish sire. One of the chief foundation sires in Norway was Senator Ford by The Senator, a son of Peter The Great.

SWEDEN: Two American sires, both now dead, left a lasting impression on harness horse breeding in this country. They were Bulwark by Volomite and Sir Walter Scott by Peter Scott. The most recent lists have been headed by Scotch Nibs (Nibble Hanover), Fibber (Dean Hanover) and Iran Scott (Sir Walter Scott).

WEST GERMANY: The great names in German pedigrees have been Walter Dear, the 1929 Hambletonian winner; and Epilog, by the American sire Legality and out of a half French, half American mare. The leading sire now is Permit, a son of Epilog out of a mare by The Great Midwest, a brother to Peter Volo. Two other prominent sires, both of American breeding, are Worthy Pride (Worthy Boy) and Bibijunge (Brother Hanover).

In contrast to the European scene where no pacing races are permitted, lateral-gaited horses are very popular in Australia and New Zealand where only a smattering of trotting races are scheduled. The bloodlines are basically American and in recent years this emphasis has been increased with the importation of large numbers of well-bred American stallions.

Through the 1966-67 season, only 17 horses have taken 2:00 records in either Australia or New Zealand and in the appendix I have listed the male line descendency of these animals. Since they principally involve either major U. S. lines or produced only a single performer, I am not going to discuss any of them except the one that descends through Hambletonian's son Strathmore and which is known as the Globe Derby line. Because of the major contribution it has made through horses of the caliber of Lawn Derby (the first 2:00 horse "down under") Ribands,

Johnny Globe and the current star Lordship, it is worthy of more than passing mention.

Strathmore was the only prominent son of Hambletonian that was a pacer. There may have been others, but, if so, they have passed into history without attracting attention. Strathmore never raced but it was widely known that he was a natural pacer. Ironically, he was responsible in the male line for the appearance of America's first 2:00 trotter, Lou Dillon, who went in 1:58½ in 1903. She was by Sidney Dillon by Sidney by Santa Claus by Strathmore.

Strathmore also sired Steinway, a horse that lowered the 3-year-old trotting record to 2:25¾ in 1879. Steinway, in turn, sired Klatawah who set the 3-year-old pacing record at 2:05½ in 1893 and comes down to us today as the sire of the fifth dam of Romeo Hanover. In addition, Steinway also sired Charles Derby and he, in turn sired Owyhee, who won in 2:11 on the trot before being exported to Australia. Owyhee sired Mambrino Derby and from Springheel, a mare of purely American blood, Mambrino Derby sired Globe Derby, a foal of 1910.

Globe Derby established a sire line through his sons Springfield Globe, Robert Derby, Walla Walla and Logan Derby. Three of the four, all except Walla Walla, appear on the 2:00 descendency chart. Robert Derby's Australian-bred son Lawn Derby became the first 2:00 horse "down under" when he went in 1:59⅖ in New Zealand in 1938 and he sired the 2:00 horses Ribands p, 1:58 7/10 and Avian Derby p, 2:00. Logan Derby sired Johnny Globe p, 1:59⅘ and he sired Lordship p, 1:58⅗. Springfield Globe sired Tactician p, 1:59⅘.

Earlier, I mentioned that a son of Star Pointer, Logan Pointer, had been exported to New Zealand and failed in an effort to establish a sire line that would have kept the Tennessee Hals alive. But his blood lives on prominently in the female line. For instance, Logan Pointer is the sire of the dam of Springfield Globe and Logan Derby and is the sire of the second dam of the 2:00 horses Caduceus, Highland Fling, Tobias, Haughty and Gold Bar.

Now that we have girdled the world and established the basic bloodline patterns, it is time to sit back and take a good long look at what we have accomplished in this country in the past hundred years, the direction we are headed and methods by which we can improve the breed.

First of all, I do not believe that we have established a definitive type of Standardbred. I think that we have taken but a tiny step along the evolutionary path in that direction and that while we have passed the dawn we are still in the early morning hours.

I am led to this conclusion by stepping into the forest and taking a good close look at the trees. I cannot conceive that nature will permit the establishment of a breed of horses that are required to trot and pace and yet constantly hit their shins, cross-fire and rap their knees. I envision, instead, trotters that will never hit their shins, pacers that will never cross-fire and horses of both gaits that will never touch their knees.

In order to establish these desirable characteristics, we must probe for a type. The type is a long-barrelled trotter that will permit positive clearance between the legs on the same side. The type is a pacer that will be wider-bodied and will never cross-fire. The type is a horse, either trotter or pacer, that will pick his front foot up and lay it down again in an absolutely straight line thus eliminating the knee-knockers.

Only when we have achieved these ends will we have perfected the type. It lays far in the future but evolution will bring it about, probably within the next hundred years and just as surely as she brought the present breed out of the wilderness to its current status in the last hundred.

While I am on the subject of breed type, let me also offer the observation that the Standardbred has not yet achieved, in the overall sense, the regal, refined bloodlike appearances that characterizes other breeds, such as the Thoroughbreds. There are many exceptions, of course, and when I see a horse looking like Adios followed by a son as handsome as Bullet Hanover, I know we are on the right track. We have made exceptional progress in this direction in the past 20 years alone, but there is still a long way to go. For all our progress, I still see in the leading stud barns and brood mare paddocks a great many plain individuals who would not create much of a stir in the show ring.

The reason for this is quite obvious. Speaking very frankly, Messenger and many other of the foundation ancestors were not good looking horses. Hambletonian was an extremely plain horse personifying strength and power rather than beauty. The Messenger line through Mambrino Chief and Mambrino Patchen, which is found in many of the best maternal pedigrees, consisted principally of very homely horses, although strangely enough, Mambrino King, a son of Mambrino Patchen, was very handsome.

Peter The Great was a relatively awkward looking horse with poor hind legs and his sons Peter Volo and Peter Scott were quite plain, the former having a pronounced Roman nose which he has passed on to many of his descendents. Scotland took after his sire, Peter Scott, and was masculine rather than handsome. But Volomite, who had a Thoroughbred mare for a third dam, was quite refined. Eventually, the breed will become refined and evolve into a type. Great improvement is noted along this line with each succeeding generation. But it will take a long time before the early ancestors are completely bred out. The truth is that the handsome horses did not, for the most part, sire the early champions and the sires that were to succeed them. The plain horses did. It was a case of speed before beauty.

I have always felt that this was a factor that could be used to good advantage in buying yearlings and brood mares. It has been my experience that the plain horses sell much cheaper than they should; that too great a premium is placed on beauty for beauty's sake alone.

I reached this conclusion after studying carefully the appearance of perhaps 50 outstanding mares that had produced exceptional horses. I found that a disproportionate number of these mares could be classified as "plain" in appearance. I soon came to realize that this was no knock against them and that, actually, they were simply conforming to the breed pattern which has not completely evolved and which thus provides a number of bargain yearlings at the various sales.

The proper type of horse, both as to overall beauty and conformation is what we hope to establish. What we have already established is very simple to define. Beyond any shadow of doubt, we have developed in the United States an early speed breed by producing horses that are capable of rattling off miles at a breath-taking clip literally before they are weaned. Early speed is, of course, natural speed and to that extent we have worked wonders with the tools that nature has furnished us. As I watch the 2-year-olds perform their speed miracles these days, I am thankful that we do not permit races or trials for yearlings. I am sure that if we did, yearlings would be beating 2:10.

But at the same time, I think it is equally obvious that we have not been able to milk an excessive amount of additional speed out of our breed although we may be on the threshold of doing so. At first glance and in an era when Bret Hanover has gone in 1:53⅗ and Noble Victory has trotted in 1:55⅗, this observation might appear entirely out of line. But I do not believe it is.

Almost 60 years ago Dan Patch went a mile in 1:55¼. We have chipped less than two seconds from that time. In 1903, Lou Dillon became the first 2:00 trotter and went in 1:58½. The current world record for a trotting mare is 1:56¾ (Rosalind) and even that was established more than 30 years ago. Once again, less than two seconds is involved.

The world record for trotters is Greyhound's 1:55¼. It was established almost 30 years ago and since then only two trotters have ever beaten 1:56 (Noble Victory and Matastar, 1:55⅘) and Greyhound is still the champion.

I will concede that our present-day horses are not prepped as religiously for fast miles as were those of earlier generations, nor do they see mile track action as frequently. But I also submit that no horse that I ever considered capable of challenging either the world's trotting or pacing record was ever denied the opportunity of racing over a mile track.

This is not a critical appraisal and is offered only to emphasize that our greatest progress in recent years has been directed into early speed rather than extreme speed channels. Our horses can go almost as fast at two as they can at four. I have no doubt that as our breed type solidifies and evolves that we will once again begin shaking full seconds off the overall as well as the juvenile world records. In order that the general reduction rate may be studied, I have charted in Fig. 3 the various championship records by age and gait by decade intervals from 1890 to the present.

The other point that I think should be made with respect to breed progress is the obvious one that we have today so many more horses that can do so much. We are breeding larger numbers of faster horses and consequently the 2-year-old stake fields are very frequently overloaded to the extent that two and sometimes even three divisions are required. This is despite the fact that more stake opportunities are available than ever before

REDUCTION OF THE WORLD RECORDS BY DECADES SINCE 1890

	ALL AGE		4-YEAR-OLDS		3-YEAR-OLDS		2-YEAR-OLDS	
	Trot	Pace	Trot	Pace	Trot	Pace	Trot	Pace
1890	2:08¾	2:06¼	2:10½	2:11¼	2:10½	2:14	2:18	2:16½
1900	2:03¼	1:59¼	2:05¼	2:04	2:08¾	2:05½	2:10¾	2:07¾
1910	1:58½	1:55¼	2:05¼	2:04	2:04¾	2:05½	2:07¾	2:07¾
1920	1:58	1:55¼	2:02	2:00	2:02¾	2:00¾	2:04¼	2:06½
1930	1:56¾	1:55¼	1:58¾	2:00	1:59½	1:59½	2:02	2:04¼
1940	1:55¼	1:55	1:57¼	1:55	1:58½	1:57¾	2:02	2:00¾
1950	1:55¼	1:55	1:57¼	1:55	1:58	1:57¾	2:00	2:00⅖
1960	1:55¼	1:54⅗	1:57¼	1:54⅗	1:58	1:55⅗	1:59⅘	1:57
1967	1:55¼	1:53⅗	1:55⅗	1:53⅗	1:56⅘	1:55	1:58⅖	1:57

Fig. 3

and that at most tracks overnight events are also carded. This is a sign of general progress and is highly desirable despite the traffic problems that occasionally arise on the race track.

Having dispensed with these few general observations, let me get into the area of specific bloodlines and give consideration to those that are charting the present day course. In any such discussion it is necessary to separate the trotter from the pacer because they are beginning to have very little in common except for mutual ancestors. Let me consider the trotter first because he poses the more pressing problem as his lines diminish either by disappearing in tail male or by switching over into the pace.

A good starting point would be about 40 years ago when we still had four prominent male line families and the first sounds of fear began to echo through the land.

In 1926, the male line trotting families were Peter The Great, Axworthy, McKinney (which, like the Axworthy family, traced to George Wilkes) and Bingen. The latter traced to Electioneer.

The Bingen line, as it developed, was in the process of expiring and the McKinney line, although held together for a number of years thereafter through Belwin, Bunter and San Francisco, was also on the way out. The breeding authorities who sensed this protested that there would be nothing left except Axworthy and Peter The Great. What, they asked, would happen to the breed then?

The authorities proved correct in assuming the demise of Bingen and McKinney but the trotting breed has still prospered although it has undergone a very subtle change. This change is best illustrated by referring to the roster of Hambletonian winners. From 1926, when the stake was introduced, until 1935, six of the 10 Hambletonian winners traced their male line ancestry to Axworthy. Four traced to Peter The Great. But of the 11 Hambletonian winners from 1957 through 1967, only one Axworthy line horse (Hickory Smoke in 1957) has won the race. The last 10 in a row have been won by horses tracing to Peter The Great.

In other words, Axworthy is going down hill and Peter The Great is rising. The Axworthy trotting line is held up today principally by Florican and Hickory Smoke. If neither of those two horses fan the family flames, the Axworthy trotting family is in danger of disappearing in the tail-male line. There were a number of other Axworthy horses that were capable of siring notable trotting sons to carry on for them but none did. Included among these would be Mr. McElwyn, Dean Hanover, Nibble Hanover and Spencer to name but a few. It is possible that the early death of Demon Hanover, Dean's greatest son, cost the breed a sire line.

As the male line influence of Axworthy declined, slowly at first and then drastically in the past 20 years, the influence of Peter The Great rose. His son Peter Scott sired Scotland and his son Peter Volo sired Volomite. From Scotland and Volomite came such horses as Spencer Scott, Rodney, Hoot Mon, Star's Pride and Victory Song. All were very successful and each has left at least one son that appears capable of carrying on the line.

The shifting tides of trotting blood thereupon created a new "Golden Cross" just as Axworthy-Peter The Great was so described more than a quarter of a century earlier. This cross consisted of Scotland on Volomite or vice versa and today we consider it the epitome of good breeding to mate a Hoot Mon mare to Star's Pride. Yet, both trace within four generations (three for Hoot Mon) to Peter The Great. We have inbred, of course, but we have also produced a better horse. To say otherwise would be to criticize the likes of Ayers 1:56⅘, Armbro Flight 3, 1:59 and Nevele Pride 2, 1:58⅖ who are the prime examples of the cross.

My point is that whenever it seems that we are in danger of breeding ourselves into a corner something new and marvelous appears on the horizon. The most desirable step, of course, would be for one of the Axworthy line horses to produce a really spectacular sire that could take advantage of all the Volomite-Scotland blood floating around. An ideal trotting sire in this respect might be, for instance, a son of Florican and Ilo Hanover, she the dam of the world champion 2-year-old trotting filly Impish 2, 1:58⅗. The third generation male line ancestors of such a horse would consist of four different Axworthy line sires, Guy Axworthy, Spencer, Calumet Chuck and Dillon Axworthy. This horse would stand out as a natural cross to Volomite and Scotland blood.

Failing that, an acceptable horse would be one that linked up in the two male lines (through sire and sire of the dam) to either Volomite or Scotland, so that he could take advantage not only of the available Axworthy blood but also of the other Peter The Great line to which he did not trace. Noble Victory, who is linked to Volomite through Victory Song and Star's Pride, is such a horse and one by Speedster, for instance, out of a Hoot Mon mare, (both tracing to Scotland) would be another.

No, there is no reason yet to fear for the trotting breed. It is still in the formative stage and, in my opinion, is still going through the shakedown cruise of infancy. Remember, we are only a hundred years removed from the tap root. In evolution, that is nothing but a finger snap! I feel that the greatest danger confronting the trotter lies not in the breeding paddocks but on the race track where it seems that fewer and fewer races are offered for trotters each year. But as long as the stakes and futurities continue to carry trotting divisions, there will still be sufficient opportunities for horses of that gait.

Taking the long-range view, I am certain that in time American and French blood will meld somehow to produce a trotting sire that will startle the world. The reason that it has not been done successfully to date (I speak of the United States, of course, because Oriolo, the leading sire of Italy, is a product of this cross) is that we breed for early speed and the French breed for stamina and neither is very enthused about the other's goals. It is inconceivable that eventually these two lines will not join to produce a horse that will shake the foundation of the breed. I would rather see it done by using a French sire on American mares because I think our broodmares are superior to any in the world. But it would have to be a brave American breeder indeed who would risk the possibility of losing his early speed market to prove a technical point. Perhaps, after all, it will simply develop as a matter of random chance as so many things have in the past hundred years of breeding history.

From trotting horse lines, we move on to the pacer who enjoys a built-in breeding advantage because he is still being produced from four bloodline sources instead of two. The pacers not only have their own two major families (Electioneer and Dictator), but they also have encroached on the basic trotting lines and boast prominent avenues of descent from both Peter The Great and Axworthy.

(With respect to the breeding of trotters and pacers, I want to take a moment here, as any knowing harness horseman could, to correct a statement that I still see carried occasionally in scientific journals to the effect that the trotting gait is dominant over the pace. This theory undoubtedly emerged in the late 1800's when pacing blood was being employed to produce better trotters and apparently nobody has ever bothered to correct the record. Quite obviously, while it is not an absolute dominant, the pacing gait is almost completely so over the trotting gait. With rare exceptions, when a pacer is bred to a trotter, the resulting foal is a pacer. Bred to each other, pacers produce pacers 99% of the time. And, as we all know so well, a trotter bred to a trotter very often produces a pacer. This, incidentally, is the reason that trotting families are beginning to produce pacing branches without intent to do so on the part of the breeders involved. On the other hand, neither of the two major pacing families has ever produced a leading trotting sire.)

The No. 1 pacing family in the world today is that descending from Electioneer through The Abbe and thence to Adios and Good Time through Hal Dale, and Gene Abbe through Bert Abbe. The other basic pacing family is that which comes to us through Dictator and the combination of Direct-Tennessee Hal blood that is anchored today by Tar Heel and his sons.

On the trotting side, there is evidence that Volomite, a grandson of Peter The Great, will remain active, at least for the present, through horses such as Poplar Byrd, Bye Bye Byrd, Sampson Hanover and King's Counsel. The Axworthy trotting line was the last to switch and this came about when Nibble Hanover, a trotting sire who wanted to pace, was bred to a double-gaited mare and gave us Knight Dream and his sons Duane Hanover and Torpid.

Nevertheless, if the signposts the breed has laid out over the past hundred years are accurate, I believe there is a strong possibility that within the next 50 years Adios and his descendents stand a good chance of dominating all pacing blood just as Hambletonian dominates all harness racing blood today. I visualize entire new families spreading out along the trail he has blazed, sucking up the blood of other lines like a giant sponge and converting it to the new breed picture. This will require a number of generations and perhaps 50 years is too brief a period. Perhaps it will not even come to pass; but when Adios and his accomplishments are viewed from every conceivable angle and as it becomes obvious that his sons are also sires as well as race horses, it does not seem an unreasonable conclusion.

There is no question that Adios has exercised the most powerful influence on the Standardbred breed of any horse since Hambletonian. This bay son of Hal Dale-Adioo Volo (Ped. No. 37) has sent forth literally showers of champions and through the end of the 1966 season had sired 75 2:00 performers, more than twice as many as his nearest rival.

Adios was selected as a stallion by Del Miller and purchased by him for $21,000 at public auction in 1948. Seven years later he was sold for $500,000 to Hanover Shoe Farms with Miller and Max Hempt later buying equal one third interests. Adios stood at Miller's Meadowlands Farm and died in 1965 at the age of 25. In assessing his contribution, I think it is best summed up by saying simply that only four harness horses have ever negotiated a mile in 1:55 or faster and that three of them are by Adios —Bret Hanover p, 4, 1:53⅗, Adios Butler p, 4, 1:54⅗ and Adios Harry p, 4, 1:55.

From the actual breeding lines themselves, we move logically to the appearance on the scene of successful sires and seek an understanding of why some horses succeed and others fail. This has troubled men since the dawn of time and probably always will. I cannot provide answers but I think I can clarify what is involved.

In breeding successful race horses, I believe that the family is greater than the individual and that, in the long run, the man who concentrates on well-bred mares from the leading maternal families and breeds them to the best available sires will produce the most colt racing champions. However, I have a qualification to that rule which I believe just as firmly and which I have never heard espoused by anyone else. My rule is: "The family is greater than the individual except in the case of the sire."

I believe that the successful sire rises or falls strictly as an individual and that while family may be an important consideration it is definitely a secondary one. I reached that conclusion long ago and have never had any occasion to change my mind. All the foundation sires of the breed were relatively short-bred maternally in the sense that none of the female families that produced them ever established lasting maternal lines of their own.

As I look about today I observe the same thing. Star's Pride, for instance, is the only 2:00 horse in his maternal family. Gene Abbe, great sire that he is, never took a 2:00 record and neither did any other member of his maternal family. Volomite's maternal family, although it has produced additional 2:00 horses, is not one of the strongest in the book.

It is also apparent that the identity of the sire of the dam is not absolutely crucial to the success of a sire. San Francisco (Volomite), Protector (Rodney), Adioo Guy (Adios) and Guy Abbey (Hoot Mon,) are not among those horses that will go down in history as great sires. Their contribution to the breed —aside from the fact that Guy Abbey sired Greyhound—is that they sired the dams of great sires. All these facts make it quite obvious, to me at least, that the successful sire is strictly an individual, equipped by nature in some miraculous and as yet unfathomable way with a genetic factor that enables him to rise beyond the others who possess similar or even better breeding.

At the same time, I do not know of any way in which the sire potential of a horse can be assessed positively in advance. I suppose I have probably devoted more time to this problem than any living person. I have spent hundreds of hours running up charts and laying out check lists covering the factors of speed, early speed, gait, disposition, size, general conformation, breeding, racing manners, courage, endurance, opportunity and other items of interest covering page after close-typed page. In the end, nothing came of it. I recall that on one occasion I proved conclusively that Volomite could not be a successful sire. It was then that I gave it up as a bad job and reverted to the basic philosopy or so many of the most successful breeders, "Breed the best to the best and hope for the best."

In essence, this is the philosophy of Lawrence B. Sheppard, master of Hanover Shoe Farms and, in my opinion, the greatest harness horse breeder that ever lived. I was complimenting him once on his shrewd selection of sires when he interrupted me: "There hasn't been a day since this farm was founded," he said, "that I haven't had at least one mistake in that stud barn." He then went on to tell me that he was fortunate to have learned relatively early in his career that only a fool put all his eggs in one breeding basket and dared the world to prove him wrong. The horse that taught him the basic lesson, he said, was Lawrence

Hanover, a great race horse himself, exquisitely bred (Peter Volo-Miss Bertha Dillon-Dillon Axworthy) and a full brother to three mares with 2:00 records. Lawrence was a monumental failure and Mr. Sheppard soon discarded him.

In this connection, it is also interesting to note that Mr. Sheppard is quick to dispose of brood mares by unsuccessful sires. Except for the rare exception that makes the rule, mares by such stallions contribute nothing to the future of a brood mare band.

That observation provides an opportunity to make a quick and what I believe quite decisive point relative to brood mare sires, or sires of the dams. I am frequently asked whether I think such and such a horse will make a brood mare sire. My answer is always the same: the horses that are the leading sires of this generation will invariably be the leading brood mare sires of the next. It was ever thus and will always be. For that reason, no good purpose will be served here by pursuing the matter further.

The reason that there is no means by which the success of a stallion can be guaranteed in advance is that there is no absolute relationship between a horse's ability on a race track and his performance in the stud. The important word is "absolute." There is a relationship, of course, because all of the great sires of the past 50 years have also been great race horses. But the grave-yards and boneyards are full of horses that were superb on the race track and ineffective in the stud.

The answer to this riddle lies in the complex world of genetics. The combination of genes that blends to make a race horse is not the same combination that enables him to sire animals as good or better than he. These reproductive genes lay dormant during a racing career and do not expose themselves until the horse is called on to reproduce his like. They are linked to the ones that made him a race horse but they are not identical.

There are many glaring examples of this and one of the most prominent is the comparison of Adios and King's Counsel. I do not hesitate to make it because King's Counsel was not a failure as a sire. He was a very successful one but he was simply over-whelmed by Adios. Yet, on the race track they were as near being equal as any two horses that ever lived. They raced against each other in 67 heats with King's Counsel being victorious on 34 occasions.

Yet, in the breeding ranks there was no comparison. Indeed,

in my opinion, there is no comparison between Adios and any Standardbred sire that ever lived with the exception of Hambletonian himself. But the Adios-King's Counsel comparison affords an opportunity to view at first hand the prominent part that genetic makeup plays in the reproductive ability of a stallion.

Genetically, Adios carried an overpowering factor that was not visible to the eye nor apparent during his racing career but that enabled him upon retirement to the stud ranks to reproduce early and extreme speed in super-consistent fashion and, even more important, to pass that trait on, through his sons, to succeeding generations. To anyone familiar with bloodlines, it has become obvious in recent years that certain sons of Adios whose performance and/or breeding never approached classic proportions are endowed with the capacity to reproduce beyond the apparent limits of their own qualifications. This has been passed on to them by their sire and there is no doubt in my mind that they in turn are passing it on to their own sons.

All of this is wrapped up in heredity, the process by which the traits of the parents are transmitted to their offspring. It is an uncertain process at best because some traits that are not present or apparent in the phenotype (the visible horse) may be present in the genotype (the genetic makeup which is not visible to the eye) and just as capable of being passed on. These invisible genetic factors can and often do result in inferior horses being produced by outstanding parents and, occasionally, in a superior horse being produced by very ordinary parents. To put it briefly, Adios's phenotype was not superior to King's Counsel's; his genotype was far superior.

All inheritable characteristics are carried by the parents in the form of genes which are attached to chromosomes and lodged in the nucleus of a body cell. Each body cell of a horse, and there are millions, contains 60 chromosomes consisting of 30 matched pairs. The number of chromosomes varies with the species but is constant for it. A human body cell, for instance, contains 46 chromosomes. Under a microscope, each of these chromosomes appears in the form of a long, thread-like strand and surrounding the chromosome, like beads on a string, are the genes, the carriers of inheritance. The exact number of genes is unknown but there are probably at least a thousand associated with each chromosome. Thus there are millions of random possibilities in-

volved in the genetic makeup of any single horse and aside from
identical twins the chance of any two horses being exactly alike
is virtually nil.

When a sex cell (gamete) divides for reproductive purposes,
the number of chromosomes in the male sperm cell and the
female egg cell are halved by some miraculous process with each
contributing 30 to the new organism which is then assured of
its normal complement of 60.

At the moment of conception, the genes establish the genetic
makeup of the horse. The exact manner in which they function
is still unknown although vast research programs are currently
underway in the field and great progress has been made. Certain
things are known. It is known that some genes are dominant and
that they overpower the corresponding gene for the same hereditary factor contributed by the other parent. Those that are over-
powered are called recessive genes and while the factor they
represent will not appear in the specific horse created by the
union of the sex cells, it can and does appear in descendents of
that horse.

Other genes are neither dominant nor recessive—most of them
fall in this category—but, rather, blend with each other to establish the makeup of the new organism. Just as blue, when mixed
with yellow, produces green, a high-gaited gene from one parent
may blend with a low-gaited gene from the other parent to produce a medium-gaited horse.

The existence of dominant and recessive genes and the manner
in which they function was set forth in a brilliant paper published
in 1865 by Gregor Mendel, an Austrian monk. Mendel's work
went unrecognized until 1900 but it stands today as the basic
text on elementary genetics.

Mendel worked with tall peas and short peas to prove his
theory relative to dominant and recessive genes. First, he developed a strain of tall peas that, when bred within themselves, always produced tall peas. He did the same thing with short peas
until he had established completely pure strains for the genetic
factor of size.

Then he crossed a tall pea with a short pea. All the offspring
were tall peas. He had thus proved beyond any shadow of doubt
that the genetic factor for tallness was dominant over the factor
for shortness. (If these two factors had been "blenders" rather

than dominant and recessive, Mendel would have produced a medium-sized pea.)

But when Mendel cross-bred succeeding generations of his new hybrid, he discovered variations which I will translate into horse language by substituting coat color for size and working with a pure bay stallion (tall pea) and a pure chestnut mare (short pea). The coat color bay (also brown and black) is dominant over the coat color chestnut just as the tall pea is over the short pea. The pure bay stallion inherits a pure bay factor from both sire and dam and thus is represented genetically by the symbol BB (one B for the pure bay color from each parent). The chestnut mare is pure for that color and since it is a recessive factor it is represented genetically by the lower case symbol bb.

The pure bay horse (BB) is then bred to the chestnut mare (bb) and although there are four possible genetic combinations that may result (either of the factors of the BB sire may be coupled at random with either of the factors of the bb dam) each resulting foal will carry the genetic factor Bb, and thus will be a hybrid. However, all horses of this mating will be bay because they carry the B factor which is dominant over the b.

But these Bb horses are *not* pure for the color bay as their sire was. When two of these Bb horses are mated, there are again four possible genetic combinations that will appear with mathematical regularity in any sufficiently large sample. These combinations are one BB (pure bay), two Bb's (which will be bay themselves but which are genetically hybrid and carry the recessive factor for chestnut) and one bb that will be an actual chestnut horse. (When two chestnuts are mated, the offspring will always be chestnut since bb is the only genetic color code that can be reproduced.)

In applying this knowledge as a practical matter in horse breeding, we look at a bay horse (or brown or black) and ask ourselves whether he is BB pure, or Bb hybrid carrying the recessive gene for chestnut. The answer is, of course, that BB horses can *never* sire a chestnut while Bb horses will sire a certain number of chestnuts when bred to Bb (one out of four) or bb (one out of two) mares.

To sum it up, the following prominent horses are among those who have never, to my knowledge, sired a chestnut and thus must be considered to be BB from a genetic standpoint: Peter

Volo, Volomite, Worthy Boy, Star's Pride, Rodney, Dean Hanover, Knight Dream, Tar Heel, Victory Song and Good Time. On the other hand, the following horses, although not chestnuts themselves, have sired chestnuts and therefore must be Bb horses genetically: Adios, Gene Abbe, Hoot Mon, Scotland, Nibble Hanover and Florican. All bay, brown or black stallions, of course, fall in one of these two categories, and a check of a sufficient sampling of the colors of a sire's foals as carried in *The USTA Sires & Dams Book* will indicate which. The colors grey and roan, incidentally, are also dominant over chestnut. Two grey parents will not always produce a grey foal but one parent must be a grey in order for the foal to be a grey.

None of this will help a single person breed a better horse because color has nothing whatsoever to do with reproductive ability. But I think it serves to demonstrate how Mendel's Law, as it has come to be known, functions with regard to coat color in horses and how recessive factors that do not appear in a specific offspring may suddenly reappear in later generations.

One genetic factor that is obviously neither dominant nor recessive but which develops, rather, under the blend rule of genetics is speed. Factors for speed are inherited in equal parts, although not necessarily in equal quality, from both sire and dam and it might be of interest if I simplified the manner in which I believe the factor of inherited speed develops genetically.

I believe that every sire (and broodmare as well) has a gametic range that he acquires at conception and that governs his ability to reproduce speed. A horse is thus capable of siring performers whose speed potential falls within the limits of this range or, to a limited degree, in excess of it if sufficiently modified by a superior factor inherited from the other parent. I also believe that this gametic range is linked to but not identical with the horse's own ability to trot or pace at a certain speed. That there is a difference in the ability to achieve speed and the ability to reproduce it is amply demonstrated by the fact that certain great race horses fail as sires while others of equal or lesser racing ability are extremely successful.

To make it easy to understand, let us assume that every sire has a gametic range that spans 13 separate and distinct speed rates, any one of which he is capable of reproducing. This range extends from a high of a potential mile in 1:53 down to a low of 2:17. Then let us convert these 13 ranges into one suit of a deck of ordinary playing cards and say that a sire has a gametic speed range that runs from ace (1:53) down to two (2:17). The medium point would be an eight card equivalent to a reproductive speed factor of 2:05.

Since the brood mare possesses a similar gametic range, when stallion and mare are mated each contributes by chance (or through random selection as it is technically known) a gametic range "card" to the new foal. The two "cards" that the foal thus draws by chance and which are matched or "blended" at the instant of conception govern that foal's lifetime speed potential. There is no way that he can ever exceed that potential. But very often, for reasons having to do with care, training, soundness, environment etc., he will never actually achieve this potential.

If a stallion possessing an all-inclusive gametic range from ace through two (Fig. 4, Column I) is bred to a similarly endowed mare, the two could produce a world champion if the two aces in their decks (each carrying a potential speed factor of 1:53) were linked by chance at conception. By the same token, the very same parents could produce a complete dud if their two deuces were linked. Taking the law of average into consideration, however, it is much more likely that these two parents would produce a foal carrying a playing card blend of 8-8 (the medium point) and thus a 2:05 speed potential. This 2:05 potential would develop not only from an actual 8-8 combination but also as a "blend" from, for instance, an A-2 (1:53-2:17) or Q-4 (1:57-2:13) combination.

It is my contention, however—and the reader must bear in mind that I take great liberties here in attempting to condense the entire realm of genetics as it applies to inherited speed into anything as simple as a deck of cards—that very few stallions and fewer mares have an ace in their deck at all. I think that the vast majority of our best sires (Column II) are probably working with decks headed by a Queen (1:57) or possibly a King (1:55). I also doubt that the leading sires have any extremely low cards and that the limit of the gametic range of a leading sire might be something like Q-4 as I have indicated on the chart. Since the number of gametic range factors must always remain constant at 13, the Q-4 sire has four additional factors that fall within that range and that replace the missing A-K-3-2. In ad-

justing this, I have assigned the good sire an additional credit
for each of the factors from jack through eight and thus he has
two of each of those cards.

Now let us say that our Q-4 stallion is bred to a mare whose
gametic range is a very weak one, (Column III) running from
an eight high to a two low with double factors from seven
through two to provide the necessary 13. Shuffle the 13-card
decks for sire and dam separately and lay them face down on
opposite sides of the table. Take one card at random from each
deck and pair the two. In this fashion, the speed inheritance
of the foal is established. The best random chance draw that
could be made from these two decks would be a queen (1:57)
from the sire and an eight (2:05) from the dam. This combination would "blend" into a foal with a speed potential of 2:01.

But you must remember that this is the *best* foal that these
two parents could produce. Any chance pairing of two cards
from Columns II and III would run closer to the average value
of the available cards, say a 9-5 combination. This would produce
an absolute speed potential of 2:05.

In a sense, this also demonstrates the manner in which the
occasional "freak" horse appears; the one with fabulous speed
that is all out of proportion to the breeding and racing qualities
of both sire and dam. In this case, each parent happened to
possess one superior (ace) gametic range factor and 12 poor
ones (twos through fives). In the "freak" horse, the two superior
factors matched up by chance. Since the odds against another
pairing of these superior gametic range factors are astronomical,
there is little likelihood that these parents will ever produce
anything except duds even if they are mated repeatedly thereafter as is usually the case.

Then, of course, we encounter a sire like Adios and it is
necessary to explain why he, of all horses in the breed, was able
to reproduce as he did. To me, it is quite simple. I think Adios
worked from a gametic range deck that was topped by an ace
and didn't have a card in it lower than a ten. Since he still
retained the 13 separate speed stops, he possessed at least two
of each of those high range cards and in Column IV of the
chart I have set him up to indicate what his gametic range might
have looked like.

When you start shuffling the deck for Adios and intermingling

GAMETIC RANGE FOR SPEED INHERITANCE

| | I | II | III | IV | V |
	BASIC RANGE (Or MARE)	GOOD SIRE (Or MARE)	POOR SIRE (Or MARE)	ADIOS	TOP MARE
Ace (1:53)	1	None	None	2	1
King (1:55)	1	None	None	3	1
Queen (1:57)	1	1	None	3	1
Jack (1:59)	1	2	None	3	3
Ten (2:01)	1	2	None	2	2
Nine (2:03)	1	2	None	None	2
Eight (2:05)	1	2	1	None	1
Seven (2:07)	1	1	2	None	1
Six (2:09)	1	1	2	None	1
Five (2:11)	1	1	2	None	None
Four (2:13)	1	1	2	None	None
Three (2:15)	1	None	2	None	None
Two (2:17)	1	None	2	None	None

The number in the columns represents the number of factors for that particular speed rate carried by the stallion or mare.

FIG. 4

it with other decks representing mares, you can see what is going to happen. It is like playing poker with a pinochle deck!

When you play with the Adios deck and the basic range deck in Column I of the chart, the worst foal you can get is one with a 10-2 speed inheritance which is a 2:07 horse. But your average horse from these two decks is going to be Q-8 which is a blended speed potential of 2:01. You can also tell just by glancing at the available cards that there are going to be a lot of horses with a speed potential from 1:57 to 1:59.

Working with Adios and the good mare in Column II, the average genetic blend, Q-9, represents a horse with a speed potential of 2:00. And this is just about exactly what you could expect any time you bred a good mare to Adios.

In Column V, I have added another gametic range example, this one for a top brood mare. The average inheritance here is better than 2:00 since the A-K factors which do not appear for the good mare in Column II are present. This is where the Bret Hanovers, Adios Butlers, Bullet Hanovers and Adios Harrys come from. The aces, kings and queens combine to make them.

Now that we have discussed the origin of the breed, fixed the sire lines and dabbled in genetics, the next step is to consider means by which we produce better horses. This leads naturally to the brood mare herself for no matter how you slice it, she contributes 50% to the foal. Simple genetics, as previously explained, accounts for this since a horse inherits an equal number of genes from each parent. But I think that everyone interested in breeding goes through a period when he credits an exaggerated influence either to sire or dam. I know that I did when I first began studying breeding patterns. I was inclined then to credit the dam with too much. Later, I swung over to the sire and gave him too much. It was not long before I conceded the obvious—that each contributes equally.

This, of course, is a generalized statement. Among individual horses, you will find those that exhibit virtually all of the phenotypical (the genotypical, of course, cannot be determined by sight) traits of the sire and none of the dam, or vice versa. I think, also, that certain characteristics—the obvious ones are strength and stamina—derive principally from one or the other of the parents, in this case the sire. But for the most part, I think the contribution is an equal one.

The three things that everyone looks for in a brood mare are performance, conformation and pedigree. I think we would all agree that the ideal brood mare would be able to go in 1:55, would be a conformation class winner in the show ring and would have a pedigree made up of names that had nothing but 2:00 credits for all sires and dams in the first three generations at least. Unfortunately, there are no mares like this and if there were, you and I could not afford them. We must therefore begin accepting the kind of compromises that Johnny Simpson writes about in his fine chapter on Shoeing and Balancing.

We now get into an area where even the experts disagree and I can only speak for myself on the basis of observations I have made over a long period of time. I rate pedigree the highest. I know that in saying this I will run afoul of those who insist that conformation is the most important factor and of those who value racing performance in the brood mare above all else. But I have always felt this way and am sure that I always will.

I have seen too many fast-record mares that did not have the pedigree to back them up fail as brood mares. I have seen far too many "beautiful" mares turn out foal after eye-catching foal that were duds on the race track. On the other hand, I have seen mare after well-bred mare that could do little or nothing on the race track produce far beyond the anticipated limits of her own ability. There are hundreds of these and I will name but two just to make my point. One was Beverly Hanover, the dam of Blaze Hanover. Gene Cray, who raced her, told me that she was on her life to win as a 3-year-old in 2:13. The other was Tisma Hanover who was trained for two years by Hanover Shoe Farms and could do absolutely nothing. Yet she produced the first 2:00 2-year-old trotter, Titan Hanover, as well as Tassel Hanover, p, 1:57 4/5. And these are not isolated instances by any means. I know a very successful sire, for instance, whose dam was, in the words of a famous trainer who drove her, "just about the commonest thing I ever sat behind." But this mare had breeding as did Beverly Hanover and Tisma Hanover and the breeding came through.

In using pedigree as the primary consideration in acquiring brood mares, attention must be given to maternal families. Certain families produce two-minute horses and stakes winners much more often than others. These families are well known. They are led by the Jessie Pepper, Thompson and Medio families and in the appendix I have reproduced key pedigrees and fastest performers from the top seven of these families.

I recommend that brood mares be purchased from these families and from other high-ranking ones but at the same time I caution against buying mares that come from a leading family but from a weak branch or that are by an unsuccessful sire. These are weak links and should be avoided.

There are also maternal families that produce a large number of decent race horses, but which come up a little light when the two-minute and stakes wins are passed around. These are good mares to buy if you are looking for a raceway horse but dangerous if you are a market breeder. People will buy their foals, but they will not pay the big money for them. This is why I have always maintained that while the sire sells the foal, the brood mare sells the high-priced foal. If you breed an ordinarily-bred mare to a top stallion, even to Adios when he was in his prime, you stand the danger of failing to regain the stud fee when you sell. But when you breed a top-bred mare to a leading sire, even if this mare does not have a record, you will realize more than the normal expectancy for the foal.

What, then, is the best way for a "little fellow" to acquire a brood mare with the potential of producing a champion without having to spend a fortune? To me, this has always been a relatively simple thing. I think the best brood mare buys are found at the yearling sales of the major farms.

Every year, for $5,000 or less, I see yearling fillies with tremendous brood mare potential go through the sales rings at the major auctions. Usually, there is a little something wrong with top-bred mares that fall in this price range, but you must remember that the big buyers want perfection, or as close to it as they can get, for they are buying race horses rather than brood mares. I would be looking for the mare with the splint right up in her knee, or the big ankle, or the scar that indicates she went through the fence—items that are going to limit her value as a race mare but which will have no effect on her brood mare future.

This, in my opinion, is the ideal way to buy a brood mare and I would rather pay from $3,000 to $5,000 for one like this than to buy five cheap mares at $1,000 each. Quantity never made anybody any money in this business and never will. Quality produces the champions and makes the money, and quality is attainable at the yearling auctions of the top farms.

One other thing that I consider a plus in the selection of brood mares is the one that could show a quarter in better than 30 seconds, either training or racing but was never able to take a record at a mile in keeping with this ability and may have an actual mark somewhere between 2:06 and 2:10. I have found that as a group these mares will produce all out of proportion to their mile ability and more in keeping with what they could show for a quarter of a mile. It is because many such mares have been outstanding producers that I have concluded that strength and stamina derive basically through the stallion. That is also the reason that I consider a stallion that was a little short on the end of a mile a very poor risk.

I also do not have any objection to sour or mean mares as brood mares. I have known a number of them and have found that as a rule, providing that they have the pedigree to back them up, they will produce just as well, and in some cases better, than their well-mannered full sisters and near-relatives.

After acquiring a mare, the next step in breeding a successful horse is to mate her to a proper stallion. The obvious move, of course, is to breed her to an Adios. But we cannot all breed to an Adios. For one thing, the book is limited and for another the service fee is too high. We have to cast about for an available stallion whose service fee is within our price range.

First of all, we search for a stallion type. If our mare is very small, we do not want to breed her to a small horse (I do not like small mares because a small mare bred to a big horse is much more likely to produce a small foal than is a big mare bred to a small horse). If she was bad-gaited on the turns, we do not want to breed her to a horse that was not noted for his fluid gait. If she has an obvious conformation fault—perhaps she stands quite straight or is sickle-hocked or has weak sesamoids —we do not want to breed her to a horse that had similar problems.

If our financial resources are limited, we explore two stallion areas. We look for horses just entering the stallion ranks or for the horse who has had a couple of crops without setting the world on fire but whose "figures" run up well.

The reason we look for a young horse is that we are breeding a larger number of high class horses these days than ever before and thus we have a greater availability of good young sires. Even though certain horses do and will continue to dominate the winning scene, I think there is a greater opportunity for the smaller breeder to do well than ever before. Many of these fine young horses enter the breeding ranks at relatively moderate service fees. This is one of the prime areas in which I think a small breeder of moderate means should concentrate his efforts.

Horses that have not yet made it but that have a good chance to do so, can also be picked out with relative accuracy. It is a fact of life that some horses go through two or three disappointing seasons before they hit their stride. Star's Pride is a good current example of this and so was his great grandsire, Peter Volo, many years ago. The lists of two and 3-year-old winners credited to stallions should be studied closely. The horse you are looking for is the one who has a substantial percentage of winners in proportion to his number of registered foals and whose mares have not been the very best, or whose progress has been contained or limited by small crops. In making this study, guard against those stallions who show up with a large number of relatively slow time trial performers. Search, rather, for the half mile track race records. But the really important thing here is not to be misled by a horse that has produced a single world champion but whose percentage is very poor. These are the horses that are not going to make it.

In summing up, if I had only a moderate budget, I would prefer first of all to breed to young stallions that did not have foals at the races and whose service fees were competitive or to a slow-starting sire whose "figures" I liked. There has never been such a wide variety of good young horses available as there is at present and small breeders should capitalize on the fact.

The next step in breeding a successful horse is to decide which of the theoretical bloodline approaches should be followed. There are a number of these but for the sake of this discussion I am going to limit myself to the two basic types which I will label outcrossing and close-breeding. The latter has three categories which I call linebreeding, inbreeding or incest according to a numerical rating.

The numerical rating is obtained by assigning a number to each generation and correlating these numbers to each other when the same horse appears more than once in a pedigree. The sire and dam of a horse (or of a potential foal) appear in the first or No. 1 generation. There are four ancestors in the second or No. 2 generation, eight in No. 3, 16 in No. 4 etc. Referring to Noble Victory's pedigree (No. 26 in the appendix), Volomite appears as a common ancestor in the second (No. 2) generation as the sire of Victory Song and in the fourth (No. 4) generation as the grandsire of Star's Pride. Thus, Noble Victory is 2x4 to Volomite and therefore inbred to that horse since the sum of the two numbers, six, is an inbred number on my scale.

I consider any generation numbers that add up to nine or more (4x5, 5x5 or higher relationships) to be too far back to make any appreciable difference in a pedigree and to that extent a horse so bred would be considered an outcross. A Star's Pride foal out of a Hoot Mon mare would carry a 5x5 relationship to Peter The Great and thus, as far as I am concerned, would be an outcross provided there was no closer trespass of other lines.

I consider any generation numbers that add up to seven or eight (3x4, 4x4, 3x5) to be linebred horses within the framework of the three categories of close-breeding. (Mathematically, we could also have 1x6, 1x7, 2x5 or 2x6 but from a practical standpoint of the age of the horses involved this rarely happens although it is observed in the case of Adios Vic (Ped. No. 60) who is 2x5 to Hal Dale.)

I consider horses bearing generation numbers that add up to five or six (2x3, 3x3, 2x4) to be inbred and thus I would consider Noble Victory (2x4 to Volomite) to be an inbred horse. Any horse whose generation count is four or less (1x3, 2x2) I consider incestuously bred.

Having established the numerical ground rules, let me go back and consider each of the types individually.

Outcrossing is the matching up of two horses (sire and dam) that have relatively little in common as far as bloodlines are concerned. It is one of the two (linebreeding is the other) most common, practical and successful forms of breeding. The proponents of outcross breeding hold that the blending of relatively unlike lines will produce "hybrid vigor" in the foal and that great champions will result.

In considering this theoretical approach, we should bear in mind that it is virtually impossible to breed a true hybrid from American stock. All American harness horses trace in virtually every line of their pedigree directly to Hambletonian, a horse that is not yet dead a hundred years. Thus, we can outcross but we cannot produce a true hybrid. A true hybrid would result if an American trotter was crossed with one of pure French blood.

From an American standpoint, an outcross would be a horse that did not have a common ancestor within four generations and whose lowest numerical count was nine (4x5) representing a common ancestor at the fourth and fifth generation levels. From a technical standpoint, it would be better if a horse did not have a common ancestor within five generations in order to qualify as a true outcross but as a practical matter it is all but impossible to get five free generations in a top American Standardbred. The leading sire Gene Abbe is about as solid an example of an outcross that American breeding has to offer. Within five generations embracing 62 horses, only one, Onward, appears more than once, both times at the fifth generation level. It is almost impossible to outcross an American harness horse any more distant.

The pedigree of Gene Abbe (No. 15 in the appendix) serves also to emphasize that even the apparent outcross is actually no such thing. For instance, of the 16 male line ancestors in Gene Abbe's fifth generation, 11 trace directly in tail-male to Hambletonian. Of the remaining five, two trace to Mambrino Chief (also a descendent of Messenger), and two to the Clay line while the male line of descent of the remaining one is unknown.

There is a much better opportunity to produce outcross pacers in this country than trotters. That is because the pacers are still working from four basic sire lines while the trotters have been reduced to two. A typical pacing outcross is a Billy Direct line mare on an Abbedale line stallion. In addition, it is still possible to cross back and forth the pacing lines emanating from Volomite and Scotland (the latter basically in brood mares only) as well as those from the Axworthy line centering around Nibble Hanover.

Among trotters, it is not as easy. We have now reached the stage where we consider Scotland line mares, such as those by Rodney and Hoot Mon, to be excellent outcross material for

Volomite line stallions such as Star's Pride and, while he was living, Victory Song, to name just two. And yet, Volomite and Scotland have the same grandsire, Peter The Great. What we have done in this case is to reduce the common denominator by about 50 years by leaping from Hambletonian (1849) to Peter The Great (1895).

This is where horses that were successful sires but which, for one reason or another, failed to found a male line do so much to help the breed. Among the more recent in this category have been Mr. McElwyn and Dean Hanover. Their contribution to the breed has been and will be exceedingly meritorious despite the fact that they left no sons to carry on for them.

Outcrossing is an extremely sound form of breeding. It has produced a great number of harness racing champions and successful sires. Limiting ourselves to those horses whose pedigrees are carried in the appendix, outcross horses (no reappearing name in the first four generations) include Adios, Volomite, Scotland, Tar Heel, Dean Hanover, Good Time, Billy Direct, Gene Abbe, Thorpe Hanover, Hoot Mon, Bret Hanover, Bullet Hanover, Bye Bye Byrd, Adios Harry, Peter Manning, Nevele Pride and Tarport Lib. The advantages of being able to join the best of two existing lines is quite obvious and there are no drawbacks.

The next theoretical type to consider is linebreeding which, as I have already explained, involves a common ancestor in the fourth (4x4) or third and fourth (3x4) generations. In my opinion, it is just as effective as outcrossing and breeding to these number combinations permits the linkage of popular sires without actually becoming involved in inbreeding. The great trotting sires Star's Pride and Rodney are examples of linebreeding, each in a compound manner, under my numerical formula. Star's Pride (Ped. No. 11) is 4x4 to Axworthy and 4x4x4 to Peter The Great who appears three times in the fourth generation. Rodney (Ped. No. 35) is bred almost identically, but in reverse. He is 4x4 to Peter The Great and 4x4x4 to Axworthy's son, Guy Axworthy. Despite the overlap of similar blood, these horses fall within the acceptable limits of my definition of linebreeding. They are not technically inbred but at the same time I consider the relationships close enough to have an effect on the horses.

I think I should also explain here that I use the word "linebred" loosely in the context that I am employing the word as a theoretical breeding pattern. By proper definition, a linebred horse is one whose connection to a common ancestor is through the male line of the sire and the sire of the dam only. However, for purposes of using my numerical formula, I do not limit the relationship in this manner but extend it to refer to any numerical generation no matter what the exact bloodline arrangement might be. Rodney, for instance, is actually linebred to Peter The Great and only technically linebred to Guy Axworthy although the degree of relationship is the same, or would be if he had two crosses to Guy Axworthy instead of three.

Linebred horses also appear with regularity among the ranks of leading sires and great race horses. In addition to Star's Pride and Rodney, other linebred horses in the appendix are Florican, Hickory Smoke, Peter The Great, Speedster, Blaze Hanover, Greyhound, Matastar, Scott Frost, Mr. McElwyn, Armbro Flight, Ayres, Speedy Scot, Rosalind, Impish, Meadow Skipper Overtrick, Sampson Direct, Duane Hanover, Adios Butler, Torpid, Best of All, Direct Rhythm, Abbedale, Dan Patch and True Duane.

The reader may draw his own conclusion as to whether the best sires have been outcrossed or linebred horses. What is quite obvious is that among the outcross horses there are more pacers and among the linebred horses more trotters which is natural in view of the previously related fact that the pacers are working from four sire lines and the trotters from only two.

This leads to the even more intricate matter of inbreeding (any horse whose generation count adds up to five or six—2x3, 3x3, 2x4) and I can honestly say that if I have learned anything in a lifetime devoted to the study of harness horse pedigrees it is that more people are interested in and know less about this aspect of the inexact science of horse breeding than any other. For that reason, I will discuss it in some detail.

Inbreeding, with all its advantages and disadvantages, was explained to me in depth long, long ago by a very wonderful man who, next to Mr. Sheppard, I consider the greatest authority on harness horse breeding that I have ever known. His name was Charles W. Phellis and working from a modest brood mare band he bred the Hambletonian winners Miss Tilly, Hoot Mon and Emily's Pride (the dam of Noble Victory) and recommended to his good friend David Look that he mate May Spencer to

Scotland and, when Mr. Look demurred, promised to buy the foal when it was a weanling. This was Spencer Scott, Hambletonian winner, world champion trotting stallion and the sire of Rodney before his untimely death at a relatively early age. Mr. Phellis and Mr. Sheppard are the only two men I have ever known that I could honestly classify as experts on breeding.

Many years ago, Mr. Phellis was kind enough to spend countless hours lecturing me on harness horse breeding as we sat beneath the shade of the giant oak trees at Goshen's Good Time Park. It was he who instilled in me the firm belief that strong maternal families are required to produce the great champions. He worked from two such families, the Thompson Sisters (whence came Hoot Mon and Miss Tilly) and the Emily Ellen family (Emily's Pride, Spencer Scott and Noble Victory). Incidentally, he preferred the Thompson family and to this day I have a greater liking for that blood than for any other.

It was natural that in the course of these discussions the subject of inbreeding should arise. Let me paraphrase what I learned from him.

In the basic sense, there is absolutely nothing wrong with inbreeding. You can breed a mare to her own sire and produce a world champion just as easily as any other way. The only thing that two animals can reproduce are the factors they carry in their own genes. Therefore, the good will be multiplied. But the danger lies in the fact that the bad, especially that which is present but may not show in the phenotype, is also multiplied and, therefore, if you are not breeding to absolutely superior parents it is likely that you will produce inferior horses.

It is true that if you consistently inbreed the same stock by piling on generation after generation of identical blood that in the long run you may well create an inferior strain. But if you think of inbreeding only in terms of producing "a" superior horse rather than a completely inbred network of horses, your chances of success are reasonably good.

One of the biggest complaints against inbreeding is that it affects stamina. This was quite laughable to Mr. Phellis who pointed out, when I asked him about it, that two breeds that required great stamina, fighting cocks and homing pigeons, were incestuously inbred in many instances. He even went so far as

to give me a book on the inbreeding of homing pigeons to emphasize this fact.

I finally got around to asking Mr. Phellis why he didn't practice
inbreeding himself. He smiled and told me that he would when
he finally produced two outstanding animals whose blood he
thought should be joined. He emphasized again that inbreeding
should only be employed with superior horses. "It's like playing
catch with a jar of nitro-glycerin," he said, "you must be extremely careful."

I asked him about a specific inbreeding cross and he told me
he thought Hoot Mon (Ped. No. 36) would produce his best performer from a mare by Spencer, the sire of his second dam. A
few years later Mr. Phellis confided that he was going to breed
his Hambletonian winner Miss Tilly to Hoot Mon in an effort to
take advantage of the additional infusion of Spencer blood that
this mating would offer. Miss Tilly was out of Tilly Tonka (by
Spencer-Minnetonka) and Tilly Tonka was Hoot Mon's second
dam. This not only provided the additional Spencer blood but
linked Tilly Tonka herself as a 2x3 cross in the pedigree.

I would like to be able to report that the foal of this mating was
a world champion. Unfortunately, this was not the case. The
horse was Gang Awa (Ped. No. 50) and while he did win in
2:03⅗ as a 3-year-old, he was not the horse that Mr. Phellis
(who died before the colt raced) hoped he would be or the
horse that trainer Fred Egan thought he was through his 2-year-
old and early 3-year-old form. Egan, incidentally, told me in the
spring of 1958 that he thought Gang Awa would win The
Hambletonian. He had the Hambletonian winner in his stable all
right but it was Emily's Pride, another one bred by Mr. Phellis.

The interesting thing about this is that Mr. Phellis made the
decision to breed Miss Tilly to Hoot Mon in 1953 and the mating
was consummated in 1954. That very year there appeared on the
Grand Circuit a great 2-year-old that swept the boards clean and
went on to capture The Hambletonian and become the sport's
first Triple Crown winner. This was Scott Frost (Ped. No. 28)
who was by Hoot Mon and out of a Spencer mare, thus carrying
a 2x4 relationship to that horse. Even though Mr. Phellis was
unsuccessful in his own experiment with returning Spencer blood
to Hoot Mon, he hit the nail right on the head when he told me

that Hoot Mon's greatest performer would be out of a Spencer mare.

The closest form of inbreeding is, of course, the mating of sire and daughter (or a form thereof) which would represent a 1x2 cross. This is incest and except where nearly perfect horses are involved should be avoided. It is probably just as well to say that it should be avoided altogether because the instances in which I believe it would succeed are so few that they are not worth mentioning. The next step would be a 2x2 or 1x3 cross and, in my opinion, these too are incestuous and except in specific instances should be avoided.

What I like to see is what I call a "touch up" of the blood of an outstanding ancestor. To me, this represents a 3x3 cross— or its equivalent such as the 2x4 crosses of Scott Frost and Noble Victory—and while I consider it inbreeding, I do not consider it undesirable providing that the ancestor inbred to is an exceptional one. In actual practice, there is not very much 3x3 breeding at the major farms these days. But I do believe successful results can be achieved although I do not recommend that it be followed up with another infusion of the same blood. That is, I think a stallion so bred should be given mares that are deep in other bloodlines and that mare so bred should be outcrossed.

Let me relate by example what I mean. I think I can explain it best by referring to my experiences at Hanover Shoe Farms. During the seven years I was there, all the matings of farm mares and mares owned by members of the Sheppard family were arranged by Mr. Sheppard and me. I did my "homework" throughout the year and then Mr. Sheppard and I would sit down and, during sessions that lasted for hours on end, I would recommend that a mare be bred to a specific stallion and Mr. Sheppard would make the final decision. (It was during these sessions, incidentally, that I learned to appreciate Mr. Sheppard's vast knowledge and came to understand why he is the world's greatest breeder. I would recommend a mating and from an astonishing array of facts stored for as long as fifty years in a computer-like mind, he would bring forth some little thing about one of that mare's ancestors that indicated that she should not be bred to the stallion of my choice but should go to another. I made notes on these observations and discovered that as a result a large number of top horses that otherwise might never have seen the light of day were bred.)

Because I did help plan the Hanover matings, I run across people who say it must be a matter of great pride to me to have participated in the decision that led to the breeding of Bret Hanover. Nothing could be farther from the truth. Anyone with any sense at all would have booked Brenna Hanover, a truly outstanding Tar Heel mare, to Adios. I do not recall that Mr. Sheppard and I spent more time on the mating than for me to have said, "Brenna Hanover to Adios" and he to reply, "O.K., next mare."

The ones I do take pride in are those that were brought about through careful thought and planning and which involved a delicate blending of bloodlines at the third generation level. There are a number of examples, but the two that stand out in my mind are the pacing full brothers Romeo Hanover and Romulus Hanover and the great trotting mare Elma. Romeo (Ped. No. 43) and Romulus represent a 3x3 cross to Hal Dale. On the top line, he is their great grandsire through Adios and Dancer Hanover and has the same relationship on the bottom line as the sire of their second dam, Romola Hal. Elma (Ped. No. 44) is bred a little differently, but has the same degree of relationship. Her sire and dam are both out of Dean Hanover mares. In each case, the relationship is 3x3. In passing, it is interesting to note that Bowman Brown, Sr. applied the same principle in breeding Hickory Pride as was used to produce Elma. Hickory Pride's sire, (Star's Pride) is out of a Mr. McElwyn mare and his dam (Misty Hanover, who is also the dam of Hickory Smoke) is also out of a Mr. McElwyn mare and thus the relationship is 3x3.

I do not mean to imply that this type of breeding should be practiced promiscuously. Indeed, unless a superior ancestor is involved and unless the pedigrees are far above average, the results will be uniformly disastrous. What I am saying as plainly as I know how is that this type of breeding can be a most useful tool when properly employed by an intelligent breeder.

In departing this subject, I cannot resist one additional observation. I once called attention in print to the fact that Alma Lee, (Ped. No. 51) dam of the world champion trotting mare, Rosalind 1:56¾, second dam of Worthy Boy (sire of Star's Pride), and the third dam of Scott Frost, was quite inbred to Guy Axworthy being 2x3 to him and, through an additional cross, 3x4x4 to his sire, Axworthy. A friend chided me for doing this and accused me of citing the exception rather than the rule. I told him that I had only mentioned Alma Lee because she was involved in a pedigree that I was discussing and that if I had wanted to make a case for 3x3 broodmares I would simply have referred my readers to the pedigrees of the two greatest 2:00 producing mares of all time, Evensong and Maggie Counsel. Evensong (Ped. No. 47) is the dam of six in 2:00. She is inbred 3x3 to Axworthy. Maggie Counsel (Ped. No. 48) is also the dam of six in 2:00. She is inbred 3x3 to Guy Axworthy and, in addition, is linebred 3x4 to Peter The Great.

Perhaps an even more interesting example of a highly-successful brood mare with intertwining blood lines is Helen Hanover (Ped. No. 52). Here is a mare that is about as deeply inbred as you will ever find coming off a major farm. Not only is she inbred 2x3 to Dillon Axworthy but she is also 3x3 to Peter The Great. Helen Hanover not only produced three in 2:00 herself (Ensign Hanover, Hayes Hanover and Atlantic Hanover) but through her daughter Norette Hanover, she by a son of Peter The Great, is the third dam of Bullet Hanover and the fourth dam of Overtrick.

When the exceptions among brood mares stand out as strongly as Alma Lee, Evensong, Maggie Counsel and Helen Hanover, they are worthy of being called to the attention of the serious student of breeding.

In summing it all up, the practical approach is to fuse lines that are relative outcrosses to each other. This is the policy that has been successfully followed by the majority of the leading breeders of this and other generations and is the simplest and safest way as a study of the pedigrees carried in the appendix well indicates. But, at the same time, I do not believe it is sound to reject a mating out of hand just because there happens to be a common ancestor as close as the third generation. This is where the knowledge, skill and natural instincts of a good horse breeder come into play. It is a more dangerous form of the breeding game but it is also a more exciting one.

In attempting, as I have, to lay out some of the basic guidelines that may be applied to the breeding of better horses, I hope that I have neither confused the issue nor oversimplified the subject. I have tried to chart a practical course somewhere between these two extremes by citing specific examples of the various types of breeding theories that have been employed to produce the trotting and pacing champions. These patterns stand out in the numerous pedigrees carried in the appendix. It is my recommendation that they be contemplated at leisure for there are lessons to be learned therein.

As breeders, we are no better than the tools with which we work. And if we can improve our knowledge by studying the successful methods of those who preceded us, then we, too, are in a position to make a contribution to what I firmly believe to be the greatest breed of animals that nature has ever produced. And as the crowds gather and the lights go up and the horses are called to the post, we should never for a moment lose sight of the fact that all this is but a means to an end and that each of us, in one way or another, is dedicated to the common cause of improving the breed.

The names over the remaining chapters belong to others, but the man who took their words from hundreds of tape recordings and converted the raw material into the finished product that is *Care and Training of the Trotter and Pacer* was James C. Harrison, Director of Racing Information for the United States Trotting Association. Acknowledged as the leading technical writer in the sport today, Harrison has inherited the robes worn by the late John Hervey as harness racing's most articulate and authoritative chronicler and thus was the logical choice for this tremendous undertaking. He was born in Port Jervis, N. Y. on February 26, 1921 and went to work as  a sports writer for the Middletown, N. Y. *Times-Herald* after graduation from high school in 1938. After World War II service as a B-26 aerial gunner in the 12th Air Force, he returned to the *Times-Herald* and became sports editor before a lifelong interest in and intimate knowledge of harness racing gained the upper hand—it could not have been otherwise for one raised so near Goshen's Cradle of The Trotter —and led him to join the USTA publicity staff in 1949. He subsequently became USTA Public Relations Director and in 1958 went with Hanover Shoe Farms as assistant to the president. In that capacity, he managed the day-to-day operation of that vast enterprise and worked closely with Lawrence B. Sheppard in the selection and mating of farm mares until 1965, when he returned to the USTA in his present role. Since that time, his monthly articles on bloodlines and other racing subjects in *Hoof Beats* magazine have been must reading in the sport in this country and abroad, and his advice on breeding is sought internationally wherever Standardbreds are raised and raced.

2

SELECTING the YEARLING

WILLIAM R. HAUGHTON

A number of stock farm managers have told me I examine more yearlings and do it in greater detail than any other trainer. Although I have never thought much about it, I suppose this is true. But it isn't really surprising because I am sure I buy more yearlings than anybody else, and I would guess that I bid on four times as many as I buy.

On the last day of any given year, I will have between 50 and 60 yearlings in my public stable. Some of them, of course, have been bred and raised by my owners but most of them have been purchased by me at public auctions held between August and November.

It is true that I spend a great deal of time studying the conformation and pedigrees of yearlings. But why shouldn't I? Harness racing is my profession and yearlings are my bread and butter. They are my stake colts and raceway performers of the future. If the ones I select do well, I prosper and my owners prosper; if they do badly, I suffer and my owners suffer.

In my approach to buying yearlings, I am no different from any other business man who exercises a professional judgment culminating in the purchase of a given product. My product happens to be the yearling trotter and pacer and if the rate of failure is appreciably higher, the rewards are proportionately greater. If you don't believe the latter is true, just ask the people who have dipped into the annual yearling pool and come up with horses like Bret Hanover and Noble Victory, just to mention the two that were later sold for $1,000,000 or more.

It is true that later on, when the splints and curbs start popping and the bows, bogs and bone chips have me talking to myself, I sometimes think the yearling market is nothing more than a giant lottery and that I would do just as well if I simply reached in blind-folded and picked a number. But that feeling quickly passes because deep down I know it is not true and that if I continue to do my homework I am going to accomplish far more good than harm for myself and my owners.

Nobody, of course, and that includes me, bats 1.000 or anywhere close to it in the selection of yearlings. It is a frustrating business and rough on the nervous system. I remember, for instance, an October afternoon in 1963 when George Sholty and I were examining yearlings at Hanover Shoe Farms. We had looked at scores of them and had made bundles of notes and observations. I had been through this routine many times before and wasn't thinking too much about it, but George must have been. Suddenly he threw his catalog in the air and said, "I'll be damned if I can separate them. I'll give $10,000 to anybody in the world for the name of the best horse in this consignment."

We all got a good laugh out of it because it pointed up the frustrations involved. But the funny thing is that George was standing practically in front of Bret Hanover's stall when he said it. I could have made myself an easy $10,000 right there, but if I had known for sure that Bret was going to be as good as he turned out to be I would have been the last bidder instead of tangling with Vernon Dancer for the dubious runner-up honor. Hindsight wears well on Monday Morning Quarterbacks but it fits a horse trainer poorly.

The one thing I know I can do by studying my lesson faithfully and preparing my homework carefully is to steer my owners away from yearlings which, in my opinion, for reasons of conformation or pedigree or a combination of the two, have only a remote chance of making good. I have done this successfully enough for a sufficient number of years to have confidence in my ability in this respect.

On the other hand, I am a long way from mastering the opposite end of the scale. On too many occasions I have selected and purchased a yearling which I considered outstanding in every way—and I mean in *every* way, conformation, gait and breeding —only to wind up six months later with an absolute dud. It makes you a little sick when this happens, especially if a good owner has extended himself pretty well financially on your recommendation. But that's the way the ball bounces and you might as well take your best hold and go on.

The reason I try to examine every yearling at every major sale and many of the minor ones is that I have patrons with pocketbooks fitting every price range and a free hand from many of them to exercise my own judgment. I have bought yearlings that cost more than $50,000 and others that cost less than $1,000. Most of my purchases, however, fall in the $5,000-$20,000 bracket.

Stanley Dancer, for instance, doesn't examine nearly as many yearlings as I do because he buys fewer and concentrates in the upper price ranges. I don't mean to say that Stanley tries to pay more for a yearling; he's like the rest of us, he wants to get one as cheaply as possible. But the type of horse Stanley buys almost always brings a top price because he's keying his search strictly to yearlings with absolute A-1 factors of conformation, pedigree and gait. Because of this, Stanley is less likely to let one go and wait for the next one. He's willing to pay more for the one horse he has rated tops.

Many other trainers know their owners can't pay more than $10,000 and their limit may even be $5,000 or less. So they don't bother to take more than a passing look at the ones we all know are going to be the real tops in any sale. But my own buying range is a very broad one and I feel that I am better prepared if I have looked at every yearling.

One of the most important things about having something written down on every yearling is that occasionally you will run across a "bargain" colt or filly. The truth is that nobody knows for certain whether he has a "bargain" for at least six months and price is not a determining factor. Bret Hanover was just as much a bargain for Frank Ervin at $50,000 as Belle Acton was for me at $1,600, Speedy Count at $2,200, or Nardin's Byrd at $2,500. I guess maybe I better explain what I mean by this.

Let's say I'm at ringside and a colt that looks like he ought to be bringing $10,000 to $15,000 is hanging at $3,500. For some unexplained reason, this will actually happen every once in a while, maybe a dozen times during a lengthy sale. Farm managers will tell you the same thing.

Whenever this situation arises, you'll see owners and trainers scurrying about and whispering to each other, trying to figure what's going on. They, too, have marked this youngster in a higher price bracket but now, unless they have examined him closely, they are beginning to second guess their own judgment and to think that maybe there's a big hole in him they missed. They think they ought to bid but they're a little hesitant.

This is where my practice of screening every yearling carefully comes in handy. I glance at my catalog markings and I know immediately whether, in my own professional opinion, there is anything wrong with the colt. If there isn't; if he's one of those true "sleepers" or "overlays" that pop up every once in a while, I throw in a bid. I have acquired a number of darn good horses this way, horses I didn't intend to bid on but which I thought weren't bringing nearly the price their potential indicated.

Strangely enough, my most rewarding experience in this field involved a high-priced rather than a low-priced yearling. This was Romulus Hanover whom I bought for $35,000 at the 1965 Harrisburg auction. Because he was a full brother to Romeo Hanover, I had looked Romulus over very carefully before the sale and had given him high marks as indicated by my comments on the catalog page as reproduced in Fig. 5. I thought Romulus would bring at least $50,000 and I remember saying to myself that I wouldn't have been surprised if he brought $60,000 or $70,000. I didn't have any owners who wanted to go that high so I forgot about him.

But when Romulus entered the ring, he wasn't greeted by the frenzied bidding that I expected. I really don't know why. Perhaps they thought Dancer Hanover and Romola Hanover couldn't do it twice in a row or maybe they were concerned because his pasterns were a trifle long or because he had a slightly dished foot. But in my mind, Romulus was a far better individual than Romeo and I had already discounted the length of the pastern and the dished foot as minor faults that would not bother him.

The bidding moved up to $25,000 at a fairly rapid clip but then it suddenly lagged. I couldn't believe my ears, but for all his pleading George Swinebroad couldn't coax another bid from the crowd. At the last second, I threw up my hand and bid $27,000. He went to $30,000, I bid $32,000; he went to $33,000 and I bid $35,000. That was how Romulus Hanover became the property of John Froehlich.

Here was a horse that I wouldn't have had if I hadn't looked him over carefully beforehand and considered him a "bargain" at the price he was bringing. It is true, of course, that Romulus Hanover might not have been a "bargain" at all; but in my opinion the knowledge that I rated the colt much higher than what he was selling for gave me a little edge on the game. And believe me, in buying yearlings you need all the edge you can get.

I am in a position to do this more readily than most other

trainers because I have more owners than most and, as I said before, a number of them have given me virtual "carte blanche" in selecting one or more yearlings for them.

Before a sale, I will go over the general picture with my owners at which time they might say something like, "Bill, see if you can find me a nice trotting colt in the $7,500-$10,000 range." The order might be a little more detailed for a certain owner who has a specific preference as to gait, sex, or sire. But other than that, I am pretty much on my own with a number of my patrons and some of them don't even bother to come to the sales. I have been able to achieve generally good results this way because it gives me much more maneuverability at a sale.

I have another advantage, too, over many trainers. If I happen to buy a colt that for one reason or another none of my owners wants, I can pay for him myself and race him in my own name. This doesn't happen very often, but it is always good to know that you won't have to turn one back for lack of financing, as occasionally happens.

I ran into a situation something like this a few years ago at Lexington. I had purchased a Good Time colt out of the Castleton Farm consignment because I liked him a great deal even though his knees were a little questionable. I paid $19,000 for him and didn't have a specific patron in mind when I bought him. I talked to several of my owners, pointing out that I liked him an awful lot but that I was a little suspicious of his knees. For one reason or another, each of them turned him down and it looked as though I was going to be racing him myself. I didn't really mind that, although I must confess that I am not in the habit of buying $19,000 yearlings for my own account.

The next morning I ran into Ralph Baldwin, the Castleton trainer. He asked me for whom I had bought the colt. I told him that as yet I didn't have an owner and he mentioned that he didn't have a pacing colt in his string and might be interested in this one if we could work something out. We talked it over and a few days later I gave Castleton an option on the colt at $25,000. Subsequently the option was picked up and that's how Castleton got Race Time p, 1:57. He went on to win $486,955 and is now a Castleton stallion. The last time I saw him race his knees were still holding up quite well and my owners and myself were out a pretty penny. But that's the yearling business for you.

Doesn't pace on lead. Very nice head Looks more like thoroughbred

No. 647 **ROMULUS HANOVER** (3rd Foal)

CHESTNUT COLT BY DANCER HANOVER Great body

Full brother to the 1965 star, Romeo Hanover, p, 2, 1:59-2:01h winner of $100,000 L. B. Sheppard, $50,000 Fox Stake, and $100,000 at two; also won $18750 Star Pointer, Arden Downs Stake 2:03⅘h; three-quarter brother to the free-legged Rarest (Rarest Hanover) p, 2, 2:08⅖f.

Third foal from the swift young Tar Heel mare, Romola Hanover p, 2,T1:59⅘, 3,T1:59, second in the Hanover Filly Stakes at two, and winner of $18,104 in her juvenile campaigns before retirement to the broodmare band.

Out of a full sister to the fast stakes winning young mare, Ritzy Hanover p, 2, 2:00, record in Hanover Filly Stake, 2:02⅘h, record in Delaware Filly Stake, winner of more than $100,000.

Out of a full sister to the fast Rebel Hanover p, 2,T2:05⅘, 3, 2:04⅖h, 4, 2:03⅖h, Romantic Hanover p, 3, 2:05⅕h, and to Rochelle Hanover p, 2,T2:03⅘f; half-sister to the extremely fast Newport Ali p, 3,T1:58; the top Canadian Stake winner Senator Spangler p, 2, 2:06⅗h, 3, 2:03⅘h, 4, 2:00⅘h, Rome Hanover p, 2:03⅖h, Newport Senator p, 2:09⅘h, etc.

Out of a daughter of Romola Hal p, 2, 2:10, 3,T2:00⅗, winner of the Hanover Filly Stake, only mare in Register which has produced two 2:00 2-year-olds; dam also of 7 in 2:05, 9 in 2:10, five 2:07 2yos.

Out of a granddaughter of the great mare Romola, dam of 2 in 2:00, 7 in 2:05, 11 in 2:10; grandam of the $100,000 winner Senator Byrd p, 2:02h, Romola Girl p, 2:02⅗, Poplar Glen p, 3, 2:02⅗, Will Romola p, 2,T2:03⅖, 3, 2:03⅖h, Wilellen p, 3, 2:04⅖h, Glen Byrd p, 2,T2:04⅘, 18 in 2:05, 33 in 2:10 including nine 2:10 2-year-olds, etc.

The family of the great free-for-all pacing stars Stephen Smith p, 4, 1:58⅘ and Irvin Paul p, 4, 1:58⅗, Country Don p, 3, 1:57⅘, Way Dream p, 3, 2:00⅕, the World's Champion Adora p, 2, 2:03⅕h, 3, 2:02⅖h, (the dam of Adora's Dream p, 2, 2:04⅖h, 3, 2:00⅕h, 4, 1:58⅕).

Bred by The Hanover Shoe Farms, Inc., Hanover, Pa. Foaled April 17, 1964.
Marks: Left hind coronet white.

CHESTNUT COLT	DANCER HANOVER, Ref. Sire 9	Adios	Hal Dale
			Adioo Volo
		The Old Maid	Guy Abbey
			Spinster
	Romola Hanover	Tar Heel	Billy Direct
			Leta Long
		Romola Hal	Hal Dale
			Romola

Hocks much better than Romeo

3rd Foal	11 Foals	11 Foals
2 2:09 2yo	9 Winners	2 in 2:00
1 2:04h 2yo	4 Stake Winners	7 in 2:05
	3 in 2:00	11 in 2:10
	7 in 2:04	
	9 in 2:10	

Right front foot slight dish
Pasterns long but sloped right.

1st dam, Romola Hanover p, 2,T1:59⅘, 3,T1:59 .... by Tar Heel
Her first foal the free-legged Rarest (Rarest Hanover) p, 2, 2:08⅖f in 1964, her second Romeo Hanover p, 2, 1:59-2:01h in 1965, this the third foal from a young mare which took a record faster than 2:00 during both of her campaigns as a juvenile. Second in the Hanover Filly Stake at 2, and winner of $18,104 before retired to the broodmare band following her 3-year-old season. By Tar Heel p, 4,T1:57, sire of 26 in 2:00 and the dams of 5 in 2:00.

2nd dam, Romola Hal p, 2, 2:10, 3,T2:00⅗ .... by Hal Dale
One of the great broodmares, she is the dam of Newport Ali p, 3,T1:58, Romola Hanover p, 2,T1:59⅘, 3,T1:59, Senator Spangler p, 2, 2:06⅗h, 4, 2:00⅘h, Ritzy Hanover p, 2, 2:00-2:02⅘h, season's champion on both mile and half-mile tracks, Rebel Hanover p, 2,T2:05⅘, 3, 2:04⅖h, 4, 2:03⅖h, Rome Hanover p, 3, 2:05⅘h, 2:03⅖h, Romantic Hanover p, 3, 2:05⅕h, Rochelle Hanover p, 2,T2:03⅘ in 1963 and Newport Senator p, 2:09⅘h. By Hal Dale p, 2:02¼, sire of 13 and the dams of 18 in 2:00.

796

Should bring $50,000 or more

Fig. 5. Catalog pages bearing the author's comments on two yearlings he bought at public auction are reproduced. At the left is the page for Romulus Hanover purchased for $35,000 at Harrisburg in 1965. Among the comments is one to the effect that the colt should bring $50,000 or more. At the right is the page for Carlisle purchased for $5,500 at Lexington in 1964. The author noted that the fact

This anecdote illustrates another policy I have and which I will always follow as long as I am in the horse business. I always tell my owners the absolute truth. I know there are trainers who don't always lay it on the line with their owners. It is my opinion that this might work all right for a time but that eventually it has got to catch up with you. It costs you once in a while as in the case of Race Time—I know I could have found a customer for him in my own stable if I hadn't mentioned my feeling about his knees—but over the long run you and your owners are better off if you level with them and they level with you.

As I was saying, there is no way you can really beat the yearling game and there's no way you should be able to beat it. I hope the time never comes that yearlings can be appraised like diamonds with the best being sold to the man with the most money. That would take all the fun out of it and it is fun despite all the trials and tribulations and fears and frustrations that go with it.

It also seems to me that our breeders are putting out a better product than they did 10 years ago and that's good for the business, too. I know that until just a few years ago I could narrow the catalog down to a dozen or so horses that I thought were outstanding in any given sale. Now I will have 25 to 35 in that same category. There are also fewer "trash" yearlings than there were and that's good, too.

The natural result of this upgrading is that you now must have a pacer with 2:00 2-year-old potential, if not the actual record, to do any good in the stakes. The trotters are not far behind. Each year it seems there are more 2-year-olds that can go faster than the year before. It's a good sign regarding improvement of the breed, but it sure makes it tough on us fellows who are trying to pick "the one."

Perhaps I ought to pause here and explain my philosophy concerning the type of yearling I am trying to buy. I would, naturally, like every yearling to develop into a stake colt. But I am always happy to settle for a trotter or pacer that will eventually become a good raceway winner.

As the purse structure has risen in recent years, excellent earnings opportunities have developed in the metropolitan areas where I race for good, sound 3, 4 and 5-year-old horses. Solid horses in those categories can win from $20,000 to $40,000 a year

Leads good XXXX

nice individual

5,500

could be a shade starter

Hip No. 190

nice round stroke

Carlisle

Consigned by

CHESTNUT FARM, George Alexander, Sugar Grove, Ill.

First foal of Good Note 2, 2:07⅘, 3, 2:04⅕; sister to the Kentucky Futurity winner and 2:05 sire, Sharp Note 3, 2:00, Bank Note 2:02⅕, The Bethel Boy 2:03⅘ (2:05 sire), and Grand Note 2, 2:04⅕.

Out of a daughter of Rosemary Hanover 4, 2:07¾h, dam of 1 in 2:00, 5 in 2:05; grandam of 8 in 2:10, incl. Brod Hanover 3, T2:03⅘, Blazer Hanover p, 2:05⅘h, Knotty Pine 3, 2:05⅘, etc.; half-sister to 6 in 2:10, incl. American Hanover 2:03¾, Invader Hanover 4, 2:06⅗h, Victor Hanover 2:06½.

Out of a granddaughter of Isonta Hanover 3, T2:08¼, dam of 1 in 2:05, 7 in 2:10; grandam of 1 in 2:00, 17 in 2:10; sister to Zombro Hanover p, 2:00, Irene Hanover 4, T2:01 (dam of Sampson Hanover p, 4, T1:56⅘, Bettyjane Hanover p, 3, 2:04, Saint Claire 3, 2:04⅗, etc.), Isabel Hanover T2:04, the 2:00 sire DeSota Hanover p, 3, T2:04½.

The famous "Isotta" maternal family of Sampson Hanover p, 4, T1:56⅘, Impish 2, 1:58⅗, Kimberly Kid 4, 1:59, Duke Rodney 3, 1:59, Frost Ridge 3, 1:59⅕, Demon's Kim p, 4, 1:59⅗, etc.

BROWN COLT. Foaled May 16, 1963.

CARLISLE

- HICKORY PRIDE T1:59⅖ — Winner of $166,622 — Oldest foals now yearlings
  - STAR'S PRIDE 1:57⅕ (Reference Sire)
    - WORTHY BOY 3, 2:02½
    - STARDRIFT 2:03
  - MISTY HANOVER 2:08⅗h — Dam of 6 in 2:10, incl. Hickory Smoke 4, T1:58⅖, Hickory Pride T1:59⅖, Hickory Fire 4, 2:04⅗h, Hickory Star 2:06⅕, Hickory Bill 4, 2:07⅖h
    - DEAN HANOVER 3, T1:58½ (Reference Sire)
    - TWILIGHT HANOVER — Great broodmare
- GOOD NOTE 3, 2:04⅕ (First foal)
  - PHONOGRAPH 4, T1:59¼ — Sire of 24 in 2:05, incl. Sharp Note 3, 2:00, Bank Note 2:02⅕, Gratis p, 2:02⅘; Dams of 20 in 2:05, incl. Expresson 3, T1:58, Galophone 4, T1:58⅕, Record Mat 3, T2:00⅕
    - VOLOMITE 3, 2:03¼ (Reference Sire)
    - SYMPHONIA 2:03 by Guy Axworthy 2:08¾
  - ROSEMARY HANOVER 4, 2:07¾h — Dam of 5 in 2:05, incl. Sharp Note 3, 2:00, Bank Note 2:02⅕, The Bethel Boy 2:03⅘, Grand Note 2, 2:04⅕, Good Note 3, 2:04⅕; Grandam of 8 in 2:10, incl. Brod Hanover 3, T2:03⅘, Blazer Hanover p, 2:05⅘h, Knotty Pine 3, 2:05⅘
    - GUY McKINNEY 4, T1:58¾ — Sire of 16 in 2:05, incl. Dale Hanover 4, 2:01; Dams of 5 in 2:00, incl. Dudley Hanover p, T1:57⅘
    - ISONTA 3, T2:08¼ by Dillon Axworthy 3, 2:10¼ — Dam of 7 in 2:10, incl. American Hanover 2:03¾, Invader Hanover 4, 2:06⅗h; Grandam of 17 in 2:10, incl. Sharp Note 3, 2:00, Bank Note 2:02⅕

exceptionally sharp and alert

I rubbed Rosemary was good trotter

should bring $5000–$8000

4th dam—Isotta 3, T2:09¼ (dam of 13 in 2:10, incl. Zombro Hanover p, 2:00, Irene Hanover 4, T2:01, Melba Hanover 4, T2:03¾, Isabell Hanover T2:04, Dillon Hanover p, 2:04, DeSota Hanover p, 3, T2:04½, Gilt Hanover p, 2, T2:04¾; grandam of 19 in 2:05, incl. Sampson Hanover p, 4, 1:56⅘, Orpha p, 2:00)----by Peter the Great 4, 2:07¼

ENGAGEMENTS

American-National Stake 16
Arden Downs Stake 9
Batavia Downs Colt & Filly Stake 14
Battle of Saratoga Stake 4
Bloomsburg Fair Stake 20
Buckeye Futurity 18
Castleton Farm–McMahon Memorial Stake 20
Champaign County Futurity 17
Dexter Cup 7
Excelsior Stake 5
Great Mid-West Trot & Pace Stake 66
Hambletonian Stake 41
Hanover & Hempt Farms Stake 6
Hanover Colt Stake 1
Hoosier Futurity 29
Horseman Futurity 57
Horseman Stake 28
Kentucky Futurity 74th Renewal
Matron Stake 57
Ohio Standardbred 23
Dr. H. M. Parshall Memorial Futurity 13
Quad Futurities 9
Reading Fair Futurity 41
Realization Stake for 1967
Review Futurity 70
W. N. Reynolds Stake 15
Roosevelt Raceway Futurity for 1965

(Delvin + Mrs Lloyd both like)

that he had rubbed (been the groom for) Carlisle's second dam, Rosemary Hanover, and that she had been a good mare. He also indicated a price range and jotted down the fact that both Mrs. Lloyd Lloyds and Delvin Miller liked the colt. Haughton bought the colt for Mr. and Mrs Lloyds and Miller and his wife Mary Lib.

and this is the kind you need as the base for your large public stable.

So while I am trying to get a stake horse, I am not in the same position as some trainers and owners who seek only stake horses and dispose of their yearlings at the end of their two or 3-year-old form if they do not measure up to that standard. I like and need good raceway horses and am always grateful to have them. Most of the ones I race are graduates of my yearling buying sessions.

Having dispensed with some of the preliminary observations, it is probably time that I got into the specific whys and where-fores of selecting a yearling. I want to emphasize at this point that the views I express here are strictly my own and I am glad to accept the responsibility for them. I know very well that there are going to be areas of honest disagreement because no two trainers look at a horse alike or think alike in selecting one. What appeals to one man may be a cause of rejection by another. What I have learned and the opinions I have formed and am expressing here come as a result of many years of looking at thousands of horses.

I also want to say that what follows is not going to be an ultra-technical discussion laced with a lot of fancy words and terms that only a few people will understand. I read a book once that devoted almost an entire chapter to the proper slope of a horse's shoulder. It was interesting reading at first but, frankly, it got boring after a while. I don't propose to do anything like that. I propose, rather, to set forth in language as simple and explicit as I can make it the good and bad points to consider in the selec-tion of yearlings based on my experience in this field. I will leave the theories and the long words to the scholars.

Before we get into the conformation of a yearling, let me review a couple of points pertaining to pedigree. I am, of course, like everybody else in that I want yearlings by the top sires. Who wouldn't want a barnful by Adios if he could get them? I am also completely willing to take a shot at the first crop by any sire if he was a horse I knew and admired.

On the female side, I like a yearling to have a strong maternal family and I also prefer the first or second foal, or the first stud colt if a mare's first three or four foals have been fillies. My experience has been that a great many of our top trotters and pacers come from these categories and I consider it worthwhile to concentrate in this area. You see very few brood mares coming up with top foals as they get old.

I am not the same way about stallions. There is plenty of evidence to support the opposite theory. Adios certainly didn't slow down and neither did Volomite or Scotland or any of the other top studs. So while I will willingly buy a yearling by an aging sire, I rarely become interested in the produce of an aging mare.

In judging yearlings on pedigree, full brothers and sisters have to stand on their own with me. I never buy a yearling simply because he is fully related to another outstanding horse. I learned that lesson the hard way 10 years ago and have never been caught since.

I bought Bonnie Belle for $19,000 strictly because she was Belle Acton's full sister. She was much coarser than Belle and if she hadn't been her sister I'm sure I never would have made a bid. But I was carried away by the relationship and wound up with the filly. She wasn't anything like Belle as far as ability went either and I learned the folly of the brother-sister lesson real well from that. I have also seen many other brothers and sisters sold over the years that didn't measure up to the relationship.

On the other hand, I suppose this can create a mental block in the opposite direction. I don't believe there ever was a yearling I liked more than Baron Hanover, the first foal of Adios-Brenna Hanover and a full brother to Bret. I went past $50,000 on this colt and Johnny Simpson outbid me at $55,000. The colt didn't stay sound and never amounted to much, although I understand he had high speed.

Bret was sold the following year and I liked him almost as much. Mr. Froehlich and I went past $45,000 on him and then quit. I know that if he had been the first foal we would have gone on. But I could also remember that Baron had gone lame and I know that subconsciously that was affecting my thinking when I advised Mr. Froehlich to sign off. Fortunately, as I have previously related, Mr. Froehlich and I didn't let the full brother relationship stop us when we bought Romulus Hanover. Full brothers and sisters must be judged individually with neither too much nor too little emphasis placed on the relationship.

I have also had very good luck racing colts and fillies out of mares that I trained myself. But this, too, can work against you. In the fall of 1964, I was very much interested in a Star's Pride

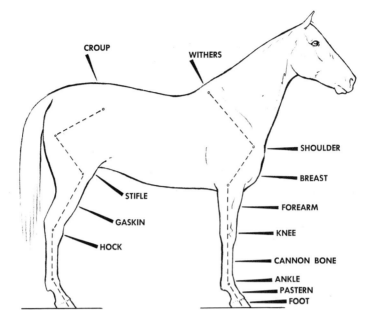

Fig. 6. This profile view illustrates the author's idea of the representative Standardbred type. Various anatomical points are identified. The shoulder actually runs upward from the point where it is indicated roughly along the dotted line toward the withers.

filly out of the mare Beloved which I had raced. I had given the filly outstanding marks on conformation and gait and, of course, her breeding was excellent.

I was bidding on her and as the action got past $10,000 I recalled more and more about Beloved. Believe it or not, this was a mare that had only gone one mile completely flat in all the times I'd raced her. The more I got to thinking about this, the more I decided that I didn't want anything out of Beloved that bad so I let her go.

Frank Ervin bought her for $16,000. That was Kerry Way, the 2-year-old Trotter of the Year in 1965 with earnings in excess of $100,000, and who went on to win The Hambletonian in 1966 and be named 3-year-old Trotter of the Year.

Size in a yearling is a factor, but it is not an especially important one with me. I would say the average yearling would run about 15 hands but if a horse has the kind of breeding I like and otherwise measures up, I don't believe I would knock him out because of size unless he were a real pony or an ungainly giant.

The sire has quite a bit to do with my decision in this respect. I never liked undersized Rodneys because Rodney was a big horse and most of his good sons and daughters were good-sized horses. On the other hand, if you're interested in a Good Time you're most likely going to get a little horse. He was that way and so are his get. But as far as I'm concerned the little Good Times can pace enough and the big Rodneys could trot enough for me.

I always figured that an average Rodney would run from 15-2 to 15-3 hands and an average Good Time from 14-2 to 14-3. In those size ranges, I would be willing to buy all I could get if they were otherwise acceptable.

In examining yearlings (Fig. 6), the first thing I look at is the head. I like to see a horse with a lot of width between the eyes. To me this indicates that the horse has good sense. You very seldom see a good horse that has manners and a good disposition with a little narrow head.

Then I look at the nostrils carefully. I like to see a nice wide nostril so there is plenty of room for air to pass through. A wide nostril indicates a bigger air intake capacity and this, of course, can affect racing ability. I have seen some pretty fair horses that have not had wide nostrils, but I'd rather have that width if there is a choice.

While I am studying the head, I always check the eyes. Of course, most consignors guarantee the sight of yearlings, but I check the eyes anyway. Actually the only thing you can observe in a visual examination is whether there's a spot there or not. Once in a while you run across a horse whose eyes look good but who is handling himself strangely and shying when he shouldn't be. In a case like this, you should have a veterinarian examine the eyes. A horse that has eye trouble will often show it as he walks in and out of his stall or goes through an entry way of some kind. He may either shy away from an imagined object or bump into something that he doesn't realize is there.

Like most trainers, I also check the size of the ear but it doesn't really mean a great deal to me. I know a couple of top trainers who will automatically turn down a horse with long ears. But Belle Acton had long ears and so did Charming Barbara and Speedy Count, two others which I selected and bought. And Speedy Scot and Armbro Flight didn't exactly have the smallest ears in the world either. So while I like to see a nice medium-sized ear that fits proportionately to the head, I certainly wouldn't knock a yearling out because he didn't have that kind.

Standing directly in front of the horse, I then observe the depth of his chest and the width between his front legs (Fig. 7-1). I like a good wide chest because that indicates a superior lung capacity, which is one thing a good horse must have. I like width between the legs because it is an indication that the horse will go clear and will not hit himself.

Of course, that doesn't mean that a narrow horse is going to hit himself because this depends on how they stand and how the foot breaks over as it leaves the ground, not how wide they are in front. Nevertheless, it is a preferable factor and I definitely grade it.

Still in front of the horse, I take a real good look now at how he stands. I want those feet flat on the ground and pointing straight ahead of him. For him to get an A-1 rating at this point, I don't want to see either foot pointing either to the right or left.

If either foot turns outward (Fig. 7-2), you can be pretty sure that this is a horse that will hit his knees and with me that is an automatic rejection. We call this "toeing out" and it is a bad thing. I do know of a couple of horses that toed out and did not hit their knees, but you can put all of them in one small barn.

I do not give a yearling that "toes in" or is "pigeon toed" (Fig. 7-3) an A-1 rating, but this is distinctly preferable to toeing out. Such a horse won't hit his knees but he could wind up putting an unnecessary strain on the tendons and ligaments and this can lead to lameness. Trotters that toe in will usually "paddle" and thus are more likely to hit their hind shins. Johnny Simpson explains this in his chapter.

In examining a horse that toes in or out, you should try to determine the cause. I always check to see if the leg itself is crooked or whether the trouble is from the ankle down. Most of the time the leg itself is perfectly straight with the trouble developing in the ankle. It isn't a desirable characteristic no matter what the cause. You must always remember that it's how the foot swings from the ankle, not necessarily the way a horse stands, that determines whether he will hit his knees or not.

Every once in a while you will run across a yearling that appears to be toeing out but you find upon examining the foot that it has been improperly trimmed and that the cause can be eliminated. I always make a note on something like that, especially if

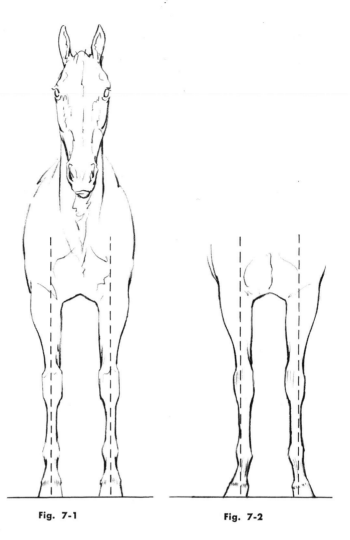

Fig. 7-1   **Fig. 7-2**

Fig. 7. The horse in Fig. 7–1 has ideal conformation with respect to width of chest and straight-line placement of both front legs. In Fig. 7–2, the horse has sufficient chest width but toes out. This is a bad fault. In Fig. 7–3, the horse toes in. This is a fault but is not nearly as bad as toeing out. The horse in Fig. 7–4 is narrow at the chest, base-wide at the ground and toes out slightly. Because of his lack of chest width in conjunction with his other faults, this horse is an even riskier proposition than the one in Fig. 7–2. In Fig. 7–5, the horse is narrow but his legs and feet are straight and thus he probably will not interfere. However, this is not a desirable type. The horse in Fig. 7–6 is the very worst kind, in the author's opinion. Not only does he toe out excessively, but he is very narrow in the chest and is almost certain to interfere badly.

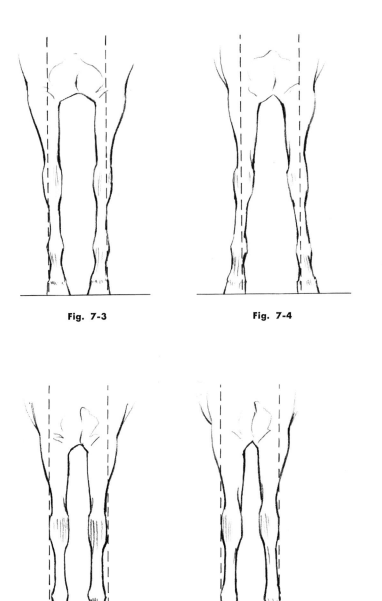

Fig. 7-3   Fig. 7-4

Fig. 7-5   Fig. 7-6

it's an otherwise top colt that might be getting a complete "toes out-turn down" from a lot of people. You do not run into this very often at the top farms where they are constantly working on the feet, but you will run into it occasionally in a small consignment where the regular services of a good blacksmith have not been employed.

As I move away from the front of the yearling and walk around to the side, I always examine first the shape and general angle of the foot. The normal angle in front, formed by the sole of the foot and the toe, would be about 47-48 degrees (Fig. 10-1). However, you must bear in mind that yearling angles can be and sometimes are considerably more or less than this norm, especially with yearlings from a farm that does not do a good trimming job. What you have to determine is whether the faulty angle is caused by an improperly trimmed foot, in which case it can be remedied, or by faulty conformation which is much more of a problem. The subject of angles is covered thoroughly by Johnny Simpson in his chapter on shoeing and balancing and I refer you to that for more detailed information.

Observing the front of the foot, I don't like to see a "dish" or a concave growth to it. A dish indicates pressure against the bones inside the foot and this can cause lameness within the foot. However, if the dish is a very slight one, as it was in Romulus Hanover's case, it can be discounted. At the other end, I don't like to see a contracted heel, that is, a narrow, pinched-together heel. That can give you an awful lot of trouble, especially with trotters because they hit the ground harder. A trotter will sore up very quickly on contracted heels.

Either a contracted heel or a dished foot, or, in the extreme, a combination of both means that the shell of the hoof is crowding the bones and that the bones inside the hoof don't have room to grow and develop in their normal position. This is one of the prime sources of navicular and coffin bone trouble.

I also check a hoof for fever rings. These are rings—something like those which determine the age of a tree—that you will find from time to time encircling the hoof. This is a sign that the horse at some time or other has had a touch of fever and it could indicate a slight touch of or a predisposition to founder. Founder, of course, is the dropping down of the soles of the feet and is something nobody wants to fool with.

Fig. 8. This is a seedy foot and horses that have seedy feet should be avoided, according to the author. He points out that in addition to causing unsoundness of one type or another, a seedy foot will not hold a shoe properly.

Of course, you do want to remember that with virus sweeping through young horses the way it does these days, the fever rings could indicate only that the yearling has had a mild touch of virus. But you must examine the sole to make certain it hasn't dropped and that the horse isn't foundered.

I have heard a lot of talk over the years about horses with white feet and I guess it's been going on ever since Dexter, the first world champion by Hambletonian and a white-footed horse, appeared on the track. Maybe before that for all I know. Anyway, I am one of those trainers who doesn't like white feet. I won't knock a horse out completely because of a white foot, but you're more apt to have trouble with them. I have noticed that quarter cracks and other ailments of this type seem to go with white-footed horses. And yet that's a funny thing because the first good horse I ever had, Ankaway, did have two white feet. On the other hand, he had quarter cracks, too. Matter of fact, that's where I learned my lesson about quarter cracks.

There is one type of foot that I will definitely rule out and that's a seedy foot (Fig. 8). This is much worse than a white foot. A seedy foot is where the shell of the foot itself, the outside covering, is seedy and cracking out. You notice it especially in the point of the toes. Sometimes it will be almost like sawdust there. It's a dead growth and while you can cut it out you will find that it will grow back the same way every time. You just don't get any new life there. A foot like this, in addition to causing unsoundness, won't even hold a shoe the way it should. And that's the foundation of the whole thing.

Also from the side of the horse, I observe the jowls, the flesh that surrounds either side of the jaw. I just don't like coarse, thick-jowled horses. I don't know anybody else who does either. These, too, are horses that are likely to choke down on you. Stay away from them.

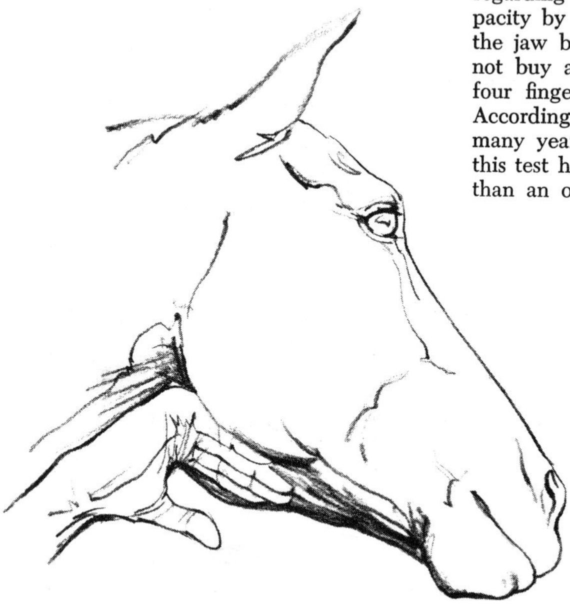

Fig. 9.   The author satisfies himself regarding a yearling's air intake capacity by placing his fingers between the jaw bones as illustrated. He will not buy a yearling if he cannot get four fingers between the jaw bones. According to records he has kept for many years, no horse that has failed this test has ever been anything more than an ordinary raceway performer.

At the same time I am observing the jowls, I conduct a little test on every yearling I examine (Fig. 9). Some years ago I read that the late Sunny Jim Fitzsimmons, the running horse trainer, said he always wanted to be able to get four fingers between the jaws of any yearling he ever bought. He said that if he couldn't do that they didn't have sufficient space there for proper air intake. I have been practicing this myself for a number of years now and I have found it to be generally true. I have marked this in my catalog for quite a few years and in checking back I haven't found a single horse that failed this "finger test" that ever amounted to anything more than an ordinary raceway horse.

In making this test, you simply hold your four fingers straight out together, and insert them between the jaw bones of the horse. If they fit smoothly and easily the horse passes the test. But if you can't get those fingers in, he fails the test and, as I say, I am still looking for the first yearling that flunked this test and then went on to become a top horse.

After concluding this examination, my next move is to study

the neck. I like a good long neck on a horse. I have rarely seen a good horse with a short neck. They're not nearly as easy to control as a long-necked horse and they're very apt to choke down if they take hold at all, because they double up their neck and don't get their air. Consequently, I steer pretty clear of short-necked horses.

Moving backward from the neck, I next observe the shoulder and heart girth. I like a good deep shoulder with a symmetrical slope to it. A shoulder should have a powerful look and should be well-muscled. The shoulder is the prime area of driving power in front; it is a weapon of propulsion and as such it must have both power and strength. A sloping shoulder indicates a bolder, longer stroke which is especially desirable in a trotter. A straighter shoulder usually means that a horse will hit the ground straighter and harder and go lame more quickly for that reason. A straight shoulder is often accompanied by straight pasterns.

The heart girth is the measurement around the horse directly behind the front legs right where your saddle and girth go. I probably attach much more significance to this measurement than most other trainers. Experience has taught me that this area, which encompasses the heart and lungs of the horse, is a very vital one and that it must be roomy in order for these organs to perform their important functions properly.

I had a big horse in my barn once that I thought quite a bit of as a 2-year-old. He stood almost 16 hands and the same groom that had him had a filly called Good Little Girl by Good Time, who stood about 14′1. He told me one day that the filly girthed one hole larger than the big horse. Since I hadn't bought the big colt as a yearling, I hadn't paid much attention to this but I watched him from then on. Sure enough, his 2-year-old form was something of a flash in the pan and he never developed into the trotter I thought he was going to be. I attribute this completely to the lack of heart girth. He just didn't have the capacity to go on after his early promise. All the good horses I have had including such top horses as Belle Acton, Duke Rodney, Charming Barbara, Speedy Count, Duane Hanover, Romulus Hanover, and Trader Horn had real deep heart girths.

After looking over the shoulder, neck, and heart girth I go to the knees of the yearling (Fig. 10). This is a critical area, one of the most critical of them all. It seems to me that in the last few

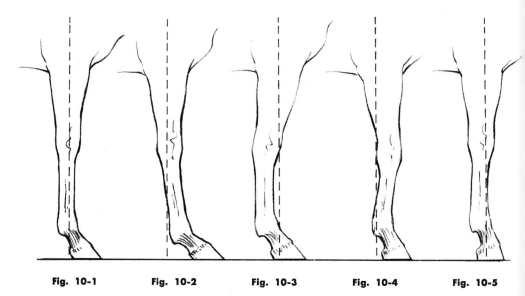

Fig. 10-1   **Fig. 10-2**   **Fig. 10-3**   **Fig. 10-4**   **Fig. 10-5**

Fig. 10.   The normal front leg, as viewed from the side, is shown in Fig. 10–1. The others are faulty for one reason or another. The horse in Fig. 10–2 is not only calf-kneed (back on his knee) but has long, sloping pasterns which compound the basic fault. In Fig. 10–3, the horse is calf-kneed but has a normal pastern. This is undesirable conformation but not as bad as Fig. 10–2. The horse in Fig. 10–4 is buck-kneed or over on his knees. This is a fault but not a serious one in the opinion of the author. The pastern of the horse in Fig. 10–5 is too straight and thus will not provide the proper shock absorber action for the front leg.

years we have had more knee trouble than ever before. I don't know what the cause is and the veterinarians don't either. We used to call them "running horse knees" but lately we seem to have about as much knee trouble as they do.

First of all, you like to see a horse straight in his knees. He can be little forward on them, or buck-kneed as it is called, but I sure don't want him back on his knees. This condition is known as calf-kneed and it is very undesirable.

A calf-kneed horse is a prime candidate for lameness. Very often this lameness develops in the tendons. It's a weak attachment there and usually there is trouble in the knee itself. Generally, you'll find a deep crease in the knee of a calf-kneed horse which is an indication of improper bone development. A good many times calcium will form in such knees and you get bone chips.

I did turn down one good colt that was a little calf-kneed and had what I considered a weak tendon attachment. That was Thorpe Hanover. He wasn't real bad, but yet he did have that weak attachment and he was back on his knees a little. But Del Miller took a chance on him and he sure was great for him, on the race track as well as in the stud.

When I examine a knee I always pick the foot up and fold the leg back until the foot touches the elbow. If they don't fold up, if they're tight and can't get up to the elbow, then trouble is quite apt to develop. If you can't make the fold, it means the knee joint isn't functioning properly, its conformation is preventing it from folding completely. And a horse that is calf-kneed, of course, just can't fold that far because the joint is turned too much in the other direction.

Observing the horse from the side, you should note carefully the angle of the pastern bone. The pastern runs from the bottom of the ankle to the coronary band at the top of the hoof. The size, shape and angle of the pastern is a very important consideration in the selection of a yearling. Depending on the angle of this bone, a yearling might be referred to as short-pasterned or "up on his ankles" or long and sloping-pasterned and thus "down on his fetlocks."

The angle of the pastern also affects the angle of the foot. A short-pasterned horse will usually have more heel and less toe. A long-pasterned horse would be just the opposite. Both conditions are undesirable (Figs. 10-2 and 10-5).

It has been my experience that many calf-kneed horses also have short pasterns and thus are "up in their ankles." The same holds for straight-shouldered horses. I do not like a horse that stands straight and is calf-kneed as well. Bachelor Hanover stood quite straight on his ankles as a yearling but I took a chance on him anyway and he never had a bit of trouble with his ankles and raced very well for me. If he had been a shade calf-kneed along with this, I am sure I would not have bought him. On the other hand, Romulus Hanover had fairly long pasterns, but they had the proper slope and thus were not objectionable to me.

In considering the consequences of long and short pasterns, you have to remember that the pastern is the bone that acts as

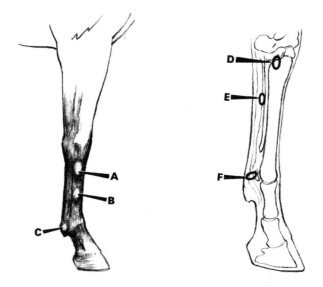

Fig. 11.   Splints of various types and prominent sesamoid bones are illustrated in these two drawings. The two splints on the horse at the left probably will not bother him. One (A) is not up into the knee and is forward on the shin bone, The other (B) is also forward on the shin bone and unlikely to cause trouble. The sesamoid (C) is prominent and the author considers this a fault in a yearling. The illustration at the right shows the prominent sesamoid again (F) as well as two dangerous types of splits. One (D) is a knee splint and will interfere with proper action of the knee joint. The other (E) is located on the back side of the shin bone and will rub against the suspensory ligament which it can damage.

the shock absorber when the horse hits the track. When the foot hits the ground, the pastern bone "gives" and acts as a spring to help absorb the shock of impact.

If the pastern bone is too straight, horses don't get this normal spring to help relieve the strain as they hit the ground. This tends to jam the bones in the foot and leg all up together and this is what causes osselets and sesamoid trouble and things like that.

When the pastern is too long and sloping, you don't get the jar that comes with a short-pasterned horse, but what you do get is an extra strain on the tendons both above and below the ankle. The tendons have to stretch too far to accommodate the slope of the pastern and after a while something just has to give. And any way you spell bowed tendon you are spelling big trouble.

In checking the ankle area, you also like to see that the sesamoids (Fig. 11) aren't too prominent. The sesamoids are tiny pyramid-shaped bones at each side of the back of the ankle bone. They are delicate and fracture relatively easy. You are most likely to have trouble with those that are most prominent.

I passed one filly in the fall of 1964 that I guess I made a big mistake on and that was Bonjour Hanover, Bret Hanover's sister. She was very prominent in her sesamoids and a little pigeon-toed as well, which would tend to throw all the strain on the outside sesamoid as she hit the ground. A few years before this, I had a filly called Romantic Hanover by Tar Heel out of Romola Hal that stood that way and I never did get her to the races as a 2-year-old. She had trouble with her ankles and sesamoids all her life.

Despite Bonjour Hanover, I consider that a sesamoid that sticks out is a definite conformation weakness. It doesn't neces-sarily indicate a weakness in the sesamoid itself, but it is a con-formation weakness that predisposes to trouble and could cause damage as such horses race on.

With all the attention I am giving to the front end of the horse, you can probably tell by this time that I consider it the vital area for lameness. Horses do get off behind, but I have found that the vast majority of lameness is in front. And much of our lameness behind comes as a result of a horse being a little off in front and favoring the ailment to a degree that it eventually affects him behind. That's why I spend as much time as I do studying and examining the front end of a yearling.

I have been mentioning tendons here and there and as every-body knows, they are a vital checkpoint in any yearling. The thing I like to see on a yearling is a nice, tight tendon that stands out and looks like a whipcord. What I don't like to see is a fat, beefy, fleshy tendon. This is not only an eyesore on a horse but it practically guarantees trouble later on.

That brings me to splints (Fig. 11). We all know that a splint is a bony growth that appears on the splint bone or between the splint bone and the cannon bone. You can get a splint on a hind leg but they are rare. I would guess that 95% of all splints appear in front.

I think I am echoing the sentiments of all professional horse trainers when I say that a splint, taken by itself, means ab-solutely nothing. It depends on where it is and what other areas it is affecting. I have seen splints as big as ping pong balls that

Fig. 12. In order to examine a yearling for the possible presence of a small splint in behind the suspensory ligament, it is necessary to pick up the leg thus relaxing the ligament so that the area beneath it may be palpated. In this illustration, the author demonstrates the proper method, picking up the right front leg with the left hand and making the examination with the right hand.

were nothing more than unsightly. Carmel Boy, a horse that I raced successfully for many years, had a couple like that and they never gave him a minute's trouble, and I never did a thing about them. On the other hand, I have had them no bigger than the tip of your little finger give me troubles that took a long time to cure.

A splint can be as big as a hen's egg but if it's forward on the shin bone and not tight to the knee it doesn't bother me a bit. I don't want a splint that runs into the knee. I always pick up the leg of a horse with a splint and when I flex the knee back I can tell whether the splint will run into the knee joint. If it does, count me out. If it doesn't, I do not worry about it.

When you flex the knee to examine for a splint, always be sure that you check for splints on the back side of the splint bone. With the leg up, you have released the tension on the suspensory ligament and this enables you to feel in under there to determine whether a little splint is starting to grow (Fig. 12).

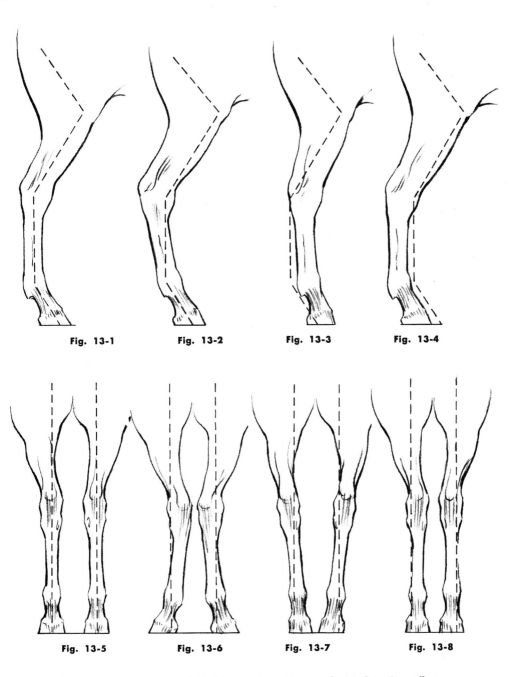

Fig. 13-1 Fig. 13-2 Fig. 13-3 Fig. 13-4

Fig. 13-5 Fig. 13-6 Fig. 13-7 Fig. 13-8

Fig. 13. Various types of hind leg conformation are depicted in these illustrations. In the upper panel, Fig. 13–1 shows a horse with normal hind leg conformation as viewed from the side. Fig. 13–2 demonstrates the sickle-hocked condition. In Fig. 13–3, the hock is too straight and thus too far forward while in Fig. 13–4 it is set too far back. In the lower panel, normal conformation, as viewed from the rear, is indicated in Fig. 13–5. The horse is cow-hocked in Fig. 13–6, bowed at the hocks and too narrow at the base in Fig. 13–7, and too narrow at both top and bottom in Fig. 13–8.

The ones I am afraid of are those little splints on the back side of the splint bone growing toward the suspensory ligament. They're the ones that can really give you trouble. And if they have started to grow at all, you can feel them by flexing the knee and getting in behind the suspensory. When they enlarge, they will rub on the suspensory ligament and irritate it seriously.

As I have said, I am not as critical of the hind end of a horse as I am the front. The first thing I look at behind is the hock (Fig. 13).

I like a nice normal curve to the hock (Fig. 13-1) and so does everybody else. But I will not knock out a horse just because he is sickle-hocked (Fig. 13-2). A sickle hock is one that has too much curve to it and is shaped something on the order of a sickle. I have seen quite a few fast horses that have had quite a bit of curve to their hocks. If I excluded sickle-hocked horses, I certainly wouldn't have bought Charming Barbara. But while Charming Barbara was sickle-hocked, she wasn't curby. Usually the two go together and I do not like to see that.

I don't think curbs (Fig. 14), taken by themselves are a major problem. A curb is a little tendon that runs underneath the main tendon on the back of the hock, just below the cap. If there is any sort of weakness there—and there is in a great many horses— the tendon will most likely spring and cause some lameness at some time during a horse's career.

However, I don't consider curbs or a predisposition toward them to be a serious fault with yearlings. Unless it's a real bad one, I feel that you always have a good chance to treat a curb and tighten it up with no great harm to the horse. I don't rate curbs nearly as bad as a lot of other weaknesses.

While the ideal hind leg is straight from the hock down, you will often find sickle-hocked horses, and every once in a while you will find a hind leg that I consider too straight, from the stifle to the point of the hock (Fig. 13-3). An example of this type of conformation was the Rodney mare Sandalwood which Ralph Baldwin bought and raced successfuly several years ago. I have seen a couple of others like this and I never knew it to hurt one. I would not reject a yearling just because of this defect in conformation but I think it should be mentioned.

I never fault a horse for a capped hock, unless there is other damage involved. A capped hock (Fig. 14) is just what the

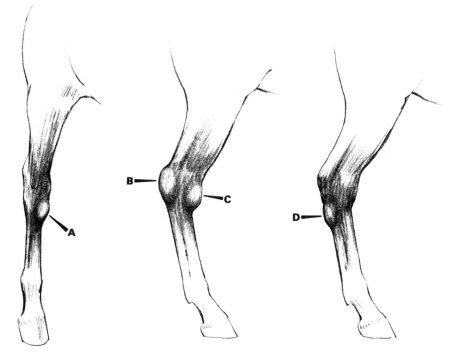

Fig. 14 In this series of illustrations of the hind leg, a bone spavin (A) is indicated at the left, a capped hock (B) and a bog spavin (C) at the center and a curb (D) at the right.

name implies, a cap or bulge at the back and top of the hock. It usually develops as a result of a horse kicking a fence or the wall of his stall or something like that. It is a big swelling and it certainly is unsightly but in itself it means nothing.

A cow-hocked yearling (Fig. 13-6) is a relatively poor risk, although every once in a while you will see a decent cow-hocked pacer. You rarely see a good cow-hocked trotter. The cow-hocked condition is where the hocks point in toward each other and, naturally, the horse toes out behind.

Such horses are very apt to hit themselves behind because they don't carry their hind legs straight. They carry them out and there is a predisposition toward interference, especially in the case of trotters. I think the condition also predisposes toward other hind end trouble later because every time such a horse hits the ground he is twisting those hocks and putting abnormal pressure on them.

A horse that is just a shade cow-hocked will not stop me, but I don't like horses in which the condition is extremely pronounced. I do remember one two-minute pacing filly who was very cow-hocked, but I never saw a good cow-hocked trotter.

Moving down the hind leg to the ankle area, I naturally prefer a horse with a normal angle and an average pastern. But I will accept ankle faults behind that I would reject in front. For instance, I don't mind a horse being fairly straight in his ankles behind because you don't get the same concussion on impact as you do in the front. At the same time, I will fault a horse quicker behind for long sloping pasterns and low heels. That puts a strain on the suspensory ligament and I have found that this is a critical lameness area behind.

Another thing you run into quite a bit with yearlings, especially in the last week before the sale when they have quit leading them, is stocked ankles behind. This occurs as a direct result of lack of exercise and/or too much feed and means nothing. A stocked ankle is a puffed ankle that has filled and appears swollen.

The thing you must determine here is that the condition is that of a stocked ankle and that there is no other underlying trouble. You've got to make sure that there hasn't been an injury to the suspensory ligament in this area.

I check this by picking up the leg and feeling the cord itself, the actual ligament. You have to run your fingers down into the swollen area and feel the ligament through the thickness and the filling. If there was any trouble other than the basic stocked ankle, you would feel a knot in the cord itself and the ligament would be swollen.

Naturally, you should devote some time to an examination of the hock joint (Fig. 14). You are looking for bogs and spavins which are generally apparent in a visual examination. The hock joint, of course, is the joint formed by the upper and lower extremities of the hind leg.

A bog is caused by a strain on the hock and results in leakage of fluid from the joint capsule. This fluid permeates the area and a puffiness and swelling develops. In a real bad case, I have seen the swelling almost completely encircle the joint.

But let me say this and let me make it as clear and plain as possible. I have never had any trouble with a bog and when I

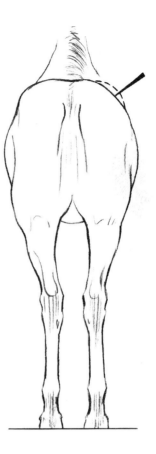

Fig. 15. The author is always on the lookout for a yearling with a hip down and will
reject one for this fault. The hip-down condition is indicated by the arrow. The dotted line
is where the hip should be.

say this, I mean *never!* I've had a few that we've had to drain
and maybe use a little cortisone or something like that but they've
all healed, without exception, and raced sound. And I have had
a lot of yearlings with bogs. As far as I am concerned, a bog in
a yearling is a fault you can ignore.

On the other hand, if I ever ran across a yearling with a true
bone spavin, that is, a calcification of the bones in the hock area,
I'd have to turn him down. Bone grating against bone can only
mean big trouble. I must confess, though, that I don't believe I
have ever seen a true bone spavin in a yearling; that is, one that
you could see and put your finger on. I suppose you might find
one if you X-rayed the hocks of every yearling but at that age I
don't believe their bones have developed to a point where true
calcification, which is necessary for a bone spavin, is involved.

After examining the hock area, I next move to a point directly behind and several feet in back of the yearling. At this point I am making a routine examination to determine if he has a hip down (Fig. 15). I almost missed this on a yearling once and since that time I have added it to my list of "automatic" checks.

From this vantage point, you are making sure that both hips are even. You can determine this by looking up over the hips, making sure that they are the same height. A good many times a colt will run into a fence or a door and knock the cap off one of his hip bones. This results in the hip down condition. And I would certainly have to pass a horse with this kind of trouble unless he was a truly great bred one that was going at a give-away price. A horse with a hip down will almost immediately develop lameness behind. He will get to hiking, going bad-gaited, and going crooked as he carries his hind end away from the side where the hip is down.

The next thing I do is to walk up toward the shoulder of the horse and then work my way backward running my hand over his body as I go. I am not necessarily checking anything when I do this, but I am getting ready to examine the hock area from behind more closely and I want to grasp his tail and pull it aside in order to accomplish this.

I approach from the front because I don't want to startle the horse by suddenly grabbing his tail—this is a great way to get kicked—and in taking hold of the tail I am performing two functions. I am pulling it to the side to give me a clearer view of the hock area, which the tail covers, and I am also determining the type of tail the horse has. I don't know how many trainers do this, but it's a very important point with me.

I like a horse with a good stiff tail, a good stiff dock as we say. I hate to see a horse with a tail like a dish mop. Now don't ask me to go into any details on this because I can't do it. Some years ago I began making notes on tails as I grasped them; were they stiff or were they soft and wishy-washy? Pretty soon my notes began to add up to something. Yearlings with dish-mop tails just weren't appearing in the ranks of top horses. Every good horse I have ever had had a good stiff dock to his tail. I don't know, maybe other trainers can refute this, but as far as I'm concerned it's actual fact and I depend on it a great deal in assessing a yearling.

Incidentally, a horse is much less likely to kick you when you have hold of his tail. It is always a good practice to stay in very close to a horse when you are examining him behind or to get completely out of kicking range. And when you have hold of a horse's tail, you will get a little warning if he starts thinking about kicking.

With the tail in my hand, I run my eyes down over the rear of the hock area and get a look at the inside of the hocks from another angle. At the same time, I also glance through the hind legs to see from that angle how he is standing in front. Very often this will disclose something about the stance or the way he carries a foot or a leg that you had not noticed from the front or side.

After this, I step back and take another good broadside look at the yearling. I am going now from the ears back to the tail taking in the general conformation. In making this inspection you will find that yearlings vary greatly. Some are high over the withers, others are high over the croup. Neither one is an especially important factor to me.

Some trainers say they don't like a horse to be too high behind, but I have never faulted a yearling on this unless it was an exceptional case. I am inclined to believe that a little height behind is, as many old timers used to say, a sign of speed.

A quick sloping off of the hips behind in a trotting-bred colt is said by some trainers to be an indication that the horse will pace. I think that as a general rule there is probably enough truth in it to warrant a notation to that effect in your catalog, but I don't really pay too much attention to it myself. If I did, I wouldn't have bought one of the best trotters I ever raced and who sloped off quite a bit behind. This horse did jog on the pace, but in a race he was all trot.

There is one other thing I always check on a stud colt and that is to make sure that he has both testicles down. I missed this once and almost bought a colt with a testicle up. At the last minute, I heard another trainer talking about it and I passed the colt. Ever since then, I have made it a routine practice to check every stud colt.

A colt with a testicle up is almost certainly going to be trouble. Like everything else in harness racing, there is nothing absolute about it but I'd like to be the one making book against their becoming top horses. A good many times if the testicle doesn't come down you have to remove it and this in itself is a serious operation. Then, too, with a testicle up, the cord is often very short and the testicle withered up and there are sometimes adhesions that cause a colt to go bad-gaited. Oh, sure, you might take a chance on it with a great-bred horse that was going real cheap. But I figure the yearling market is gamble enough without asking for this kind of trouble.

The next thing to do is to ask that the yearling be led up and down so that you can see him in motion. Maybe 50 feet one way and then back toward you. You look at him from behind as he moves away and then you stand directly in front of him when he is coming toward you.

You can't tell anything about gait this way, but you can tell the way he handles his feet. I am looking principally to see that a colt is picking his front feet up right and that he isn't swinging them in toward his knees. A good many times I've observed that a colt will stand absolutely straight but that as soon as you lead him off in a walk he'll start bending that ankle and swinging that foot in toward his knees. That means a black mark in my catalog.

It is preferable, of course, to see yearlings led alongside the pony or better still to have them broken so that they can be driven to a cart. You can get a much better idea of their gait that way. But I want to say right here that as far as making speed alongside the pony is concerned it doesn't mean a darn thing to me. I've seen too many yearlings that could literally out-trot or out-pace the pony when leading but that couldn't do anything when hooked up.

I remember so distinctly the year that Ebby Hanover and Harlan were yearlings. Ebby Hanover was perhaps the fastest leading colt I ever saw and Harlan could just barely keep up with the slowest pony around. But when it came time to race, Harlan was the one.

The things I am interested in when a colt is being led are gait and manners. Generally speaking, if a colt is going toward his knees when he is being led and if his foot is properly trimmed, he's going to do it when you train him. You can also tell whether a colt is going to go to his shins. You can see that quite readily when they are being led. Again, later shoeing may correct this, but if he's a short-coupled trotting colt and appears to be going to his shins pretty good, you wouldn't be very smart to give a lot of money for him.

I like a long-barreled trotter as every other trainer does and maybe I should have mentioned this earlier because it's something I check when I run my eye over the overall conformation of the horse. A short-barreled pacer is fine and gives you no trouble, but a short-barreled trotter is predisposed toward shin-hitting. This will run in sire families. It is not uncommon to find it in some yearlings by Worthy Boy and Star's Pride, two of our greatest stallions, because both of them, father and son, were short-barreled horses and many of their get are, too.

Around the stall and out on the track when they are being led, it is always good to make some kind of a note regarding the disposition of a colt or filly. Fillies, especially, are sometimes inclined to be mean and sour. They pin their ears, roll their eyes and switch their tails. Alongside the pony they want to fight, balk and bite. I like yearlings to be cheerful and interested in their surroundings, ears pricked and alert, head up high.

Of course, a sour filly can be a good race mare and a great many of them make real good brood mares. And if I had to buy a sour one, I'd certainly take a trotter over a pacer. When you take one of these sour fillies and then put the hobbles on her and they start burning her, you are in pretty deep.

In watching a horse lead, you can get confused by the get of certain pacing sires, such as those by Adios and Tar Heel, very few of which are natural pacers. Most of them, especially the Tar Heels, lead on the trot. I look for the same evidence and make the same notes regarding the possibility of this type of colt going to his knees as I would for a trotter. I have found that the pacing-bred colt that leads on the trot and goes toward his knees will very likely do the same thing when you break him and he goes off on the pace.

Over a period of years, I have observed an interesting thing about horses that go on their knees. I have seen a number of horses that hit their knees badly on the pace but that went clean when they were converted to the trot. On the other hand, I have seen quite a few trotters that went clean at that gait and then became bad knee-knockers when they were switched to the pace. In my mind, that pretty well establishes the fact that if a horse goes toward his knees while he is trotting he will do it to a greater degree on the pace.

I think this pretty well sums up my approach to the yearling selection business. The main things I will reject a yearling for are a testicle up, a crooked front leg which causes a horse to toe out badly, weak knees, badly calf-kneed horses, especially one that also stands straight on his ankles, and a splint that is growing back into the suspensory ligament or into the knee.

After you've eliminated yearlings with these faults you have to be lucky, extremely lucky. And you have to remember something that I first heard Sanders Russell say years ago.

We were looking at a yearling and Sanders suddenly turned to me and said, "If only there was some way we could look inside him and see his heart."

And Sanders was and is so right. So often I have wished I could.

Sanders didn't mean the actual size or shape of the heart. He was talking about the courage which this yearling might or might not show in the heat of battle as it is waged on Hamble-tonian or Little Brown Jug day. A horse can have everything else but if he doesn't have heart—courage, stamina, great desire— you might as well steer clear of the tops because they'll choke you to death every time.

Unfortunately, nobody has ever established a method of assessing this quality or the lack of it. Breeding can give you a clue but it still falls in the finger-crossing category. It is the greatest of the imponderables.

But when you get a horse that has breeding and conformation and gait and the heart to go with it, it is worth all the headaches and heartaches that line the yearling selection path.

It makes everything worthwhile.

Since the U. S. Trotting Association began keeping such records in 1939, William R. (Billy) Haughton has won more money (in excess of $11,000,000) and more races (2,800 plus) than any other harness horse driver. The man who has thus earned his way to the top of the harness racing ranks is an intelligent, soft-spoken and tremendously talented individual who will tell you that working an 18-hour day, which he usually does, is just as important to success as being born with a light driving touch and sharp reflexes, which he was. Haughton was born on Nov. 2, 1923 in Gloversville, N. Y. and gained his first practical driving experience at the age of eight when he hitched a pony named Betty to a makeshift sulky he had constructed and drove her confidently up and down the streets of Fonda, N. Y. where he was then living. At 14, he was grooming horses at New York county fairs; at 15 he was training a couple after school and during summer vacation; at 17 he drove his first race and at 18, in 1942, he registered his first win. He drove at Saratoga Raceway during and after the war—a knee injury suffered in a racing spill kept him out of service—and then moved his headquarters to the metropolitan New York area in 1950. He has won the national race-winning title six times (consecutively from 1953 through 1958) and the national money-winning crown a total of 10 times. In the last 16 years (1950 through 1966) he has never ranked lower than third in this category and has four second place finishes and two thirds to go with his 10 championships. This is the most remarkable money-winning record ever compiled by any driver. His great horses have included such as Romulus Hanover, Duke Rodney, Belle Acton, Trader Horn, Charming Barbara, Speedy Count and Duane Hanover among others. He is a director of the U. S. Trotting Association and was voted Harness Horseman of The Year in 1958.

3

BREAKING the YEARLING

DELVIN MILLER

THE process of breaking a trotter or pacer does not begin when he is hitched for the first time as a yearling, but during the first two weeks of his life. The lessons a foal learns then will stand him in good stead when the time comes to introduce him to the more complicated procedures involved in hitching, checking and driving.

So, in writing a chapter on breaking colts, I think I should immediately emphasize the importance of this stage and offer a few suggestions regarding these very early lessons. Of course, if you are breaking a horse that has been raised by one of the leading farms, you will not have to be concerned about this. All such nurseries employ skilled personnel to handle these chores.

But if you are raising a colt of your own and have not had any experience along this line, these introductory remarks might be of interest to you and help you avoid trouble later on. A horse will never forget what he is taught in the first weeks of his life and, therefore, it is important that he be taught correctly. You can work with a new-born foal for two weeks and teach him a few little things that he will still remember if you then turn him out and don't pick him up again for five years.

The first thing you should do after a horse is born is teach him to lead properly. I recommend that the colt's training in this respect begin the day after he is foaled and continue for at least two weeks and even longer if that is possible. If the weather is fair, the colt should be led to and from a paddock during this two-week period, If it is not, the colt should be led up and down the aisle of the barn each day.

In teaching a colt to lead, you don't snap a shank into the halter and walk off and try to force the colt to follow you. For one thing, he simply won't do it. He'll brace his front legs and get just as stubborn as a mule. And if you persist, you'll only teach him a bad habit that someone else will have to correct later.

The proper way to teach a colt to lead is to use a "rump rope."

Fig 16. Harry Harvey demonstrates the manner in which a rump rope is properly adjusted in teaching a young foal to lead. The author points out that a little time spent at this stage in teaching a colt to lead properly and in mannering him can pay big dividends later on.

(Fig. 16) This is nothing more than a long piece of clothesline rope that is knotted, roughly in the middle, and thus has a loop at one end. The loop should be big enough to fit down over the horse's rump, beneath the tail, and lay in the natural contour of the hind leg, about where the hobbles would go. The knot in the rope lays in the middle of the horse's back and the two loose ends of the line are brought up on each side of the neck and go through the bottom halter ring.

When you start off with the colt, you take the two loose ends of the line in one hand and pull on them gently but firmly. Since this applies a certain amount of pressure on the hind legs above the hock, the colt's natural inclination is to follow right along.

In doing this, you must always remember that a young foal wants to be with his mother and will naturally follow her. So don't try to lead the colt while leaving the mare in the stall. This won't work at all. Have someone lead the mare out and then follow along with the colt, leading him by the "rump rope." The combination of this piece of equipment and the colt's natural desire to follow his dam will simplify the job for you.

I think this is probably a good place to insert a thought that you must always bear in mind whenever you are working around a horse. It applies whether the horse is one day old or 20 years. Always work from the horse's left side. Anyone who is experienced in working with horses knows this, but every once in a while I run across someone who doesn't realize its importance. Horses are creatures of habit and are accustomed to just about everything being done from their left side. If you suddenly reverse that procedure, I guarantee that you will upset any horse of any age.

The first weeks of life are also the best time to teach a colt to pick up his feet. A trotter or a pacer spends a good deal of his life with one or more feet off the ground, either in the blacksmith shop or in the stall when the groom is cleaning and packing the feet. The sooner the colt becomes accustomed to this, the better off he is.

I recommend that during the first two weeks you are working with a new-born foal you reach down every day and pick up each foot at least once. In this manner, you are teaching him that this is a natural thing that he should come to expect as a routine procedure throughout his life. Then when it comes time to start trimming him as a baby and shoeing him later on, he will know what it is all about and give you very little trouble.

There is one other thing I ought to mention here about young horses. I strongly urge that nobody make a pet of one. I have had a few of these and they are much more difficult to break and handle. You can make pets out of some young horses without too much trouble. But I think that such horses tend to lose some of their respect for human beings and as a result will not respond as they should later on. They are much more inclined to be stubborn and to want their own way in everything. And, of course, between the horse trainer and the horse there can be only one boss—the trainer.

Now let's take a big jump from the first few weeks of a colt's life to the stage where he has been picked up as a yearling and is ready to be broken to harness. He is, roughly, a year and a half old; he's strong and willing but he also has a mind of his own and can cause trouble if a trainer isn't careful.

That's why I have always said that patience is the primary virtue involved in breaking a horse. Patience is a requirement that is necessary in all phases of training and driving harness horses, but I think more of it is needed in these early stages of breaking than at any other time.

Try to keep in mind when you are starting to break a colt that 99 out of 100 want to learn what you are teaching them. If they aren't learning, it's usually because you aren't teaching them right. And harsh words, slaps around the head and punches in the ribs aren't going to make your job any easier. In most instances, they will lengthen the period of time necessary to break a colt.

The first thing to do in breaking a colt is to teach him to stand in the crossties. Crossties may be made of rope or chain link or even chain-link covered with plastic. There are two crossties and one end of each is snapped into separate screw eyes on the wall of the stall. The other ends are snapped into the halter rings on each side of the horse's head. Their purpose is to keep the horse in a fairly stationary position while he is harnessed, handled or treated in any way by the groom, trainer, veterinarian or whoever might be in the stall with him. A horse will spend a great deal of his life in crossties.

Actually, in most instances I employ a preliminary step to get a horse used to crossties and I recommend it if you are going to break a colt that has not come from one of the major farms and thus probably has not been crosstied.

What I do is take a piece of ordinary clothesline rope, fasten one end to the halter ring and tie the other end close to or on the hay rack or near the feed tub (Fig. 17–1). In this manner, I am getting the horse used to being tied but I am doing it at a time he can occupy himself with feeding and thus is not as likely to be concerned with it and cause trouble.

The reason I prefer the clothesline rope is that a horse might rear up and get over the tie. If you were using a chain crosstie, the horse could be injured. A rope would probably break in the same situation but, in any event, there would be less likelihood of injury. This is also the reason I like to tie this rope a little high.

When I first tie a horse in this manner, I usually stand there myself and pull the horse toward me a time or two just to show him that he is tied. If you don't do that, once in a while you will find a horse that will become startled for some reason while he is eating hay and start to walk away only to find that he cannot. A horse might panic under these circumstances. But if you have

Fig. 17-1

Fig. 17-2

Fig. 17-3

Fig. 17-4

Fig. 17. The author employs three steps in getting young horses accustomed to chain crossties. The first step (Fig. 17–1) is to use a piece of clothesline rope to tie the horse near the hay rack or feed tub. The second step (Fig. 17–2) is to use rope crossties until the colt has become completely accustomed to them after which he will be broken to stand calmly (Fig. 17–3) in the chain ties. A length of clothesline rope dangling from the halter (Fig. 17–4) is recommended for colts that are a little flighty in the stall and difficult to catch for that reason.

already reminded him that he is tied he will remember it. A horse has a marvelous memory for such things.

After a horse is broken to stand tied in this manner, you can then crosstie him. The first few times I do this I use rope ties (Fig. 17-2) instead of chain ties because there is less chance of a horse injuring himself if he does become scared and reacts suddenly. Once the horse is broken to the crossties, you can substitute the regular chain ties (Fig. 17-3) for the rope ties. I do not recommend, however, that you leave chain crossties hanging in the stall when they are not in use. A horse can pull a tooth or hurt his mouth on one. I always instruct my grooms to snap the crossties into both screw eye and halter when they begin to work on the horse and to remove them from the stall when they are finished.

Some horses are harnessed up outside their stalls and are crosstied there while being harnessed. I do not advocate that this be done until the horse is well broken to crossties. If he is not, he might rear up, break the ties and either fall over backwards or get away. He cannot do this in the stall. In a stall, he will usually back into a wall before the ties break.

While I am on the general subject, let me say that I think it is a good idea to leave a halter on a horse at all times. The principal reason is that if there is a fire, you can grab hold of a halter quite readily and lead a horse out of his stall. If he isn't wearing a halter there is virtually no chance that you can get hold of him to lead him to safety. If something like this should happen, a horse wearing a halter also is easier to catch later. You don't necessarily have to buy a costly leather halter. There are very reasonably-priced web halters on the market that will fill the bill admirably. You should also make certain that there are no protrusions on the walls of the stall, such as nails, on which a halter might get caught.

Another thing to keep in mind is that if you have a colt that is a little flighty and hard to catch in the stall, it is not a bad idea to take a piece of clothesline rope about two or three feet long and let it hang from the bottom halter ring (Fig. 17-4). You will be surprised how much easier it is to catch a horse if he has this length of rope hanging from his halter.

In approaching a colt at this stage—or at any stage for that matter—you should not walk up to him and suddenly grab at the halter. A sudden movement like this will upset a colt. The recommended procedure is to walk up toward the colt on his left side, raise your hand slowly and pat him gently along the neck or even over the rump. Then work your way gradually up to his head and let your hand slide up to the halter and grasp it. Going easy with a horse at this stage can pay big dividends by making him that much easier to break and manner.

When you are breaking colts and you have one man taking care of four or five head—this is usually at a farm rather than in a racing stable—you are much better off to use two men with eight or 10 head and have them work together on all the yearlings. If you can avoid it, you should never have one man working alone in a stall with a colt. With two men, one can put the harness on while the other holds the colt's head. You will get along a lot better this way and while it is desirable in any case, it is especially important if you have a colt that is inclined to be nervous or excitable.

In a case like this, one man can hold the colt and talk to him while the other is putting on the harness. The first man can even cup his hand over the colt's left eye so the colt can't see the second man, and he will gradually become accustomed to his being there. In addition, it isn't a bad idea just before you put the harness on for one man to rub his hands over much of the colt's body and perhaps give him a little slap that will tend to lessen his fear when the harness does drop over him.

One other important point is that a colt should never be harnessed in the crossties until he is well broken. If you are by yourself, the best thing to do is to put a lead shank on him and steady the colt with one hand while you gently lay the harness on yourself. If you don't want to do that, I suggest you tie the horse to the hay rack with a rope. But for the first two or three times, never harness the colt in the crossties. No matter how gentle he appears, he might rear back and hurt himself.

I always make it a practice to put on the bridle before the harness. I use a blind bridle to start my colts out and the reason I put the bridle on first is that the blinds prevent the horse from seeing what is going on behind him while the harness is being put on and he is much less likely to shy or jump during the process.

The first few times I put on the bridle, I remove the overcheck

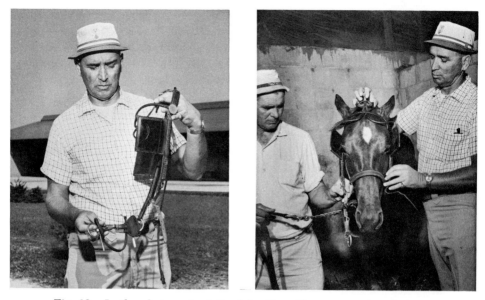

Fig. 18. In the photograph at the left, Aime Choquette, Del Miller's chief assistant, displays the blind bridle and the Frisco June colt bit which are used in breaking all colts in the author's stable. At the right, the bridle is put on for the first time. Note that one side has been unbuckled at the bit. This is done the first few times because some colts have a tendency to be fussy about the ears and will resent the ear being folded down as it must be if the bridle is to be put on without being unbuckled.

(or check rein) before I do. I am not going to use an overcheck bit until I get the colt well-broken and thus the overcheck would just be in the way.

The normal way to put a bridle on is to put the bit in the horse's mouth and then pull the bridle back over the top of the head. Usually, you have to pull the horse's ears down to do this. Because some colts are quite fussy about the ears, especially when you are just starting out with them, I make it a practice to unbuckle one side of the bit and let it hang down (Fig. 18). Then the bridle may be slipped over the colt's ears without having to bend them or getting the colt excited or upset. After you do this, you slip the bit in the mouth and buckle the side that was loose.

Once in a while, you will run across a colt that doesn't like the bit or doesn't seem to realize what it is for. In a case like this, I will usually put a bit in the colt's mouth and snap it fast in the halter rings. Then I will let him wear it around the stall for a while to get accustomed to it. I find that colts will roll the bit in their mouth, play with it and even eat hay while wearing it. After a couple of sessions like this, they will usually respond and you will not have any more trouble. They find it is not going to hurt them and they will not bother with it any more.

I mentioned before that I do not use an overcheck bit when I break colts. I use what is known as the Frisco June Colt Breaking Bit (Fig. 18) and I recommend it. This bit is a combination leather-covered snaffle bit and chin strap. The chin strap serves as an overcheck bit in the sense that it usually exerts enough pressure to keep a colt from hogging down too hard. This is a relatively soft, mild bit and is ideal for breaking colts.

If you do not have a Frisco June bit or one similar to it, you can hook the check rein directly into the driving bit when you

Fig. 19.   If an overcheck (the strap running from between the colt's ears to the top of the saddle) is used when a colt is being broken, or when it is used for the first time, it should be adjusted very loosely as in this illustration. This also demonstrates the manner in which the long lines (the white web lines) are snapped into the bit and pass through the harness loops rather than the terrets and how the "third line" (held by the groom) is snapped into the bottom halter ring.

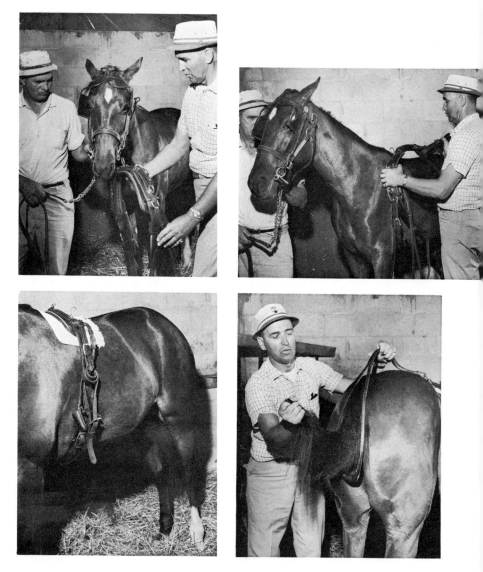

Fig. 20. Here are four of the most important steps involved in hitching a colt for the first time. At the upper left, the colt is permitted to smell the harness and look it over. The next step, upper right, is for the harness to be rubbed slowly and smoothly against the colt's side. Then, lower left, the harness is adjusted properly on the colt's back and is loosely cinched. As a final step, lower right, the crupper is unfastened from the harness, the tail is lifted gently and the crupper inserted beneath it.

are a little further advanced in the breaking process and this will provide whatever check bit pressure is necessary.

Incidentally, during these early sessions and for about a month after a colt is broken, I always leave the halter on and put the bridle on over it as shown in the various illustrations. A halter is a strong piece of equipment and there are times when you will probably be glad to have it during the early part of the breaking period.

If you use an overcheck at the beginning, or when you do go to it after the first few sessions, be sure that you do not check the colt up too high. The check should be let out so that it is long enough to allow the top of the colt's head to be level with his back (Fig. 19).

Now it is time to harness the colt and there is a proper procedure to follow. Immediately we come to one of the first "Don'ts" in connection with harnessing the colt for the first time or the first few times. Don't walk right up to the colt and abruptly throw the harness over his back. He has never had this done before and is bound to be suspicious. Before you put the harness on, let the colt smell it and look it over (Fig. 20). Then rub it against his hide slowly and smoothly so that he gets accustomed to the feel of it. After that, slip it gently over his back and fasten the girth loosely. Fast or rough movements should be avoided at all times.

Now that you have the harness on the colt's back, the next step is to get the crupper placed under his tail without getting him fussed or excited. The preferred way to do this the first few times is to remove the crupper from the harness and put a snap in the end of the crupper so that it may be snapped back into the harness after it has been placed properly beneath the tail. After the crupper has been removed from the harness, gradually lift up the tail and bring the crupper up slowly and gently beneath the tail. Now hold the crupper up under the tail with one hand and with the other pull it gently forward and snap it into the harness. In doing all this, there are two very important things to remember. The first is to leave the crupper very loose. The second is not to cinch the girth too tightly for the first few minutes. Just tighten it enough to keep the harness from turning on the colt's back.

If you have one available, a split crupper is a good thing to use when first harnessing the colt. This is a crupper that instead of having a continuous loop for the tail has a buckle on the loop so that it may be opened up. If you use a split crupper, you can lightly cinch your girth when you first put the harness over the

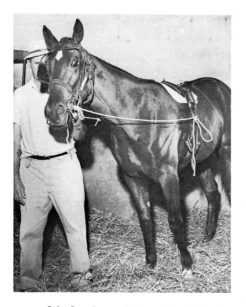

Fig. 21. The "short lines" that run from the bit to the harness are shown in this illustration. When properly adjusted, there will be a slight amount of pressure on the bit when the colt turns his head either to the left or right.

colt's back and then buckle the crupper under the tail. In this way, it is not necessary to lift the colt's tail high at first, and it keeps from scaring him. It also does away with any chance of the harness falling off the colt's back while you are putting on the crupper.

I am still in the process of harnessing the colt in the stall for the first time, and the last step, now that he is harnessed and bitted, is to adjust the "short lines" (Fig. 21). These are lines that run from each side of the bit to the harness in the middle of the back. They are adjusted so that when the horse turns his head to the left or right, a slight amount of pressure is put on the bit. This is the way I teach the colt what the bit is and how it operates in his mouth. You may purchase a set of "short lines" in a harness shop or you can use a couple of pieces of clothesline rope, as in the illustration.

The horse is now harnessed for the first time, and what I want to do on this first day is let him walk around the stall for a couple of hours and get used to the equipment. Before I turn him loose, I walk him around several times myself to show him he has nothing to be afraid of. Then I turn him loose in the stall for about two hours. I will usually do this for a couple of days before going on to the next stage. I always make sure the colt's groom is close by if not watching him every minute.

The next stage in the breaking process is known as "line driv-

Fig. 22.   Before line-driving a colt for the first time, it is a good idea to have the groom lead him around for about 20 minutes on the "third line" as in the top photograph. This will get the colt accustomed to the procedure after which the long lines can be snapped in place and the actual line-driving begun as in the center photograph. Two men are required to line-drive a colt properly. One handles the long lines and is positioned behind the colt. The other handles the "third line" and walks to the left and usually a little forward of the other man. If the colt is well-mannered during his first lesson, it is usually safe for one man to line-drive him thereafter as in the lower photograph. This man will hold the "third line" as well as the long lines.

ing" and consists of harnessing and bitting the colt and walking along behind him while teaching him the basic commands such as Stop, Go, Stand, and Turn. This period lasts from a week to 10 days after which the colt is hitched.

In order to line drive a colt properly, you will need a set of "long lines" and an extra line, which is called the "third" line. This line is usually, although not necessarily, the same type as the regular long lines. Two men are required to line drive a colt properly. One handles the driving lines and is positioned behind the colt. The second man handles the third line and is stationed to the left and usually a little forward of the other man (Fig. 22).

When you start line driving a colt, never attempt to do it with the lines you would use to drive a horse. These lines are absolutely too short and you will be much too close to the colt. You can get kicked, and if the colt starts up suddenly you will not have enough line to "give him a little rope" and enable you to circle him a time or two until you can get him back under control.

The long lines you should use are about twice as long as the regulation driving lines and may be purchased in any harness shop. They are usually webbed lines about an inch wide and are quite light. They are also much easier on a colt's mouth than the heavier, regulation lines, and that is an important consideration at this stage. If you cannot afford a set of long lines, you can make a set out of some similar web material.

The long lines are snapped into the bit rings on each side and run back through the tugs, which are the loops on the harness through which the cart or sulky shafts usually go (Fig. 19). Do not run the lines through the terrets on the harness. The driving lines run through the terrets but the long lines do not. By running the long lines through the tugs, you will have sufficient control over the horse and they will be down around his sides where he can feel them. The tugs also will keep the lines from flopping around and scaring the colt.

The third line is snapped into the bottom halter ring and is handled by the man who is assisting in the line driving process (Fig. 19). It is important that this line be snapped into the halter ring and not one of the bit rings. The man driving the colt has his lines snapped in the bit rings and that is enough for him to handle.

The duty of the man handling the third line is to make certain that the colt does not break away if he becomes scared. You will find that many colts will get a little scared the first time or two they are line driven, and if you don't have the third line they can easily get away after breaking a bridle or something like that. The halter, however, will withstand a great deal of pressure and usually will not break.

At the same time, it is presumed that the colt has been broken to lead to halter, and until he begins to understand the commands from the driver as applied by the long lines and the bit, the third line will be used to stop him. A little tug on this line puts pressure on the halter and the colt already knows that this is a signal for him to stop. By gradually introducing the "line and bit" control along with the "halter and shank" control, a trainer will soon teach a colt to stop.

The first day I am going to line drive a colt, I have the assistant take the colt out of the stall and lead him around on the third line for about 20 minutes (Fig. 22). This gets the colt somewhat accustomed to moving about outside with the rigging on. Then I will bring the colt back, fasten the long lines in the bit and move off behind him myself while the assistant accompanies me holding the third line.

I will usually line drive a colt about a half hour the first day. I gently use my own lines to turn him but I always make certain the assistant is pulling the colt a little bit in that direction too. Always be certain to turn the colt as often to the right as you do to the left. If you make all your turns in the same direction, your colt might develop a sore mouth on one side, and that's too early in life for a colt to start going with his head off to one side.

After about 10 or 15 minutes of walking along behind the colt and perhaps turning him a little to the left and right a few times, I will stop the colt. This is when I teach him to stop and stand. When I stop him I will do so by saying "Whoa" very gently and putting a little pressure on my own lines while the assistant puts pressure on the halter.

Then I usually like to have my assistant walk slowly up to the colt, pat him a few times and talk to him a little. I am teaching the colt to stand, and it is a very important thing. A lot of people will just take a colt out and line drive him and never stop him during that time. This is wrong. A colt has to be taught to stand quietly because he must do this while he is being hitched and unhitched. The sooner you teach him, the better off you are.

I like to stop a colt and let him stand about three times each day he is line driven. This means that he will stop and stand from

21 to 30 times while he is being line driven, and by the time you are ready to hitch him he knows what to do and how to do it.

On the second day, you may have your assistant lead the colt off again, and if he is not causing any trouble, you can then take him by yourself (Fig. 22). However, if you have plenty of help, it is best to have someone along with you until the colt is well broken.

The length of time you should line drive a colt depends on the individual. If he responds well and learns to turn in both directions and to stop and stand after being line driven a half-dozen times, he is probably ready to be hooked to the cart. If not, you should go longer with him in the lines. It is safer to be sure that the colt responds well to the lines rather than to hitch him too soon. If a colt is skittish in any way, it is best to line drive him a few more days until he is no longer frightened. However, a colt will become bored with the whole thing and will be spoiled if line driven for too long a time. He should, therefore, be hooked after he becomes manageable and responsive to the lines.

In the last couple of days of line driving, I usually start the colts up on a little trot or pace two or three times during each session and run along behind them. This gets them accustomed to the idea of what will be expected when you hook them.

If there is a paddock available, I recommend that colts be turned out every day during the breaking stage so that they get plenty of exercise. Not only does the exercise help to keep them in condition, but by taking some of the play out of them it makes them easier to handle while they are being broken.

Before going on to the next phase, there is one other point relative to line driving that I would like to emphasize. Never start a colt off with a real sharp click or chirping sound. These sounds are relatively harsh and might startle a colt. I much prefer a soft, tender word such as "Come" or "Now." I learned this from my grandfather years ago. He was a great horseman and he told me that the main thing in starting a colt out was not to upset him in any way. He said this could be done just as easily by tone of voice as anything else. I have always remembered that and have used a soft sound in starting my colt up.

At the same time that I give the command, I shift the bit slightly in the colt's mouth to teach him that the two things go

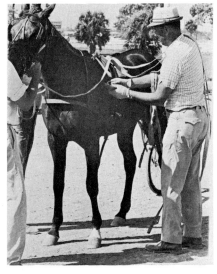

Fig. 23. The colt has been line-driven and is now ready to be hitched for the first time as shown in these two photographs. See text for details of the process. Note that it is done on the track with plenty of room on all sides.

together. A colt will catch on quickly in this respect, and it has been my experience that after a horse is well broken it is seldom necessary to say anything at all when you start up. I know I don't have to very often. Usually the command from the lines to the bit is sufficient.

The next step is to hitch and drive the colt for the first time. I will be using a training cart rather than a sulky, of course, and I always make certain that I have a rubber-tired cart that is well-oiled and free from rattles and noises of any kind. You might think I am being a little cranky about keeping everything as quiet as possible in the early stages of breaking, but if you do, you have never had much experience with colts. If you have, you know that it doesn't take very much to get them excited and to start doing things that it will take weeks or even months to straighten out. A little attention to this kind of detail at this stage will pay for itself many times over.

I don't recommend hitching a colt for the first time in the barn area. I don't like the idea of having to drive one through a draw gate the first time or two. In other words, I want all the wide open space I can get the first time I hitch a colt. If I am at a race track, I never hitch one for the first time in the morning. That is when all the training activity is taking place and that is no place for a colt like this to be. I break my colts in the afternoon, and I hitch them for the first time right out in the middle of the track as far from the fences and gates as I can get.

Fig. 24. As soon as he has been hitched for the first time, the colt is led off by the caretaker, left, with the driver in the cart. After leading the colt for about an eighth of a mile, the caretaker comes back and sits on the cart, above. He keeps a line in his hand so that he can exercise some control over the colt in an emergency.

On the afternoon I am going to hitch my colt, I will line drive him as usual for about 15 minutes and I like to follow this procedure the first three or four times he is driven. After this, I will take him out on the track and hitch him there (Fig. 23).

It is best to have three men on hand when this is done the first time and be sure to caution them to work quietly and not get excited themselves. If they communicate this feeling to the colt, he will respond by acting up.

One man stands directly in front of and at the head of the colt. He takes hold of a rein in each hand and also grasps a long line, which is fastened to the halter, in his right hand. The driver stands on the left side of the colt with the lines in his hands. He will help to hitch the colt on that side. The other assistant stands on the right side and will hook that side.

Now we are ready to hitch the colt. The cart is in position behind the colt, but the colt cannot see it because he is wearing a blind bridle. The driver, still holding the lines, moves back and raises the cart and brings it forward. The shafts pass through the tugs and the safety girth is immediately hooked. This reverses the normal hitching procedure in which the traces are adjusted first, but it is important at this stage that the safety girth be fastened in the event the colt starts acting up. As long as the safety girth is fastened, the cart will remain in position and the colt is less likely to injure himself.

As soon as this is done, the driver gets on the cart quickly and quietly and the colt is ready for his first driving lesson. The assistant, who is holding the long line fastened to the halter, leads the colt forward very quietly (Fig. 24). I like the assistant to lead the colt for at least an eighth of a mile. Then he can come back and sit on the side of the cart with the trainer. He will still have the long line in his hand and will be able to exercise control over the colt if necessary.

If a trainer is experienced in breaking colts, he can and will drive the colt right off by himself the first time. But if this is not the case, I highly recommend that an assistant be used the first few times. It is just another instance of taking a precaution that costs nothing and could mean quite a lot.

Now the colt is on his way, and one of the important things this first time out is to let him have his own way and jog along if he wants to. Some young men seem to have the idea that they should walk the colt a little bit at this stage, but I have found this to be impractical unless the colt indicates he wants to start out that way. If he indicates that he wants to jog right off, let him go. It is actually good for him to get into the jogging routine right away.

The first lesson in my stable usually amounts to a mile and a half of jogging. I then halt the colt in the middle of the track somewhere past the draw gate and unhitch him there. The assistant then leads him back to the barn.

These lessons continue each day until the colt is well-broken and ready to enter the training routine. I will hitch the colt on the track and in the afternoon until he indicates to me that he is ready to be hitched at the barn and driven to the track. You can judge this best by the way the colt acts. If he is the scary, flighty type, continue with the afternoon-on-the-track routine until it is obvious that he is ready to be hitched at the barn.

You also want to be certain your colt is broken to turn well before you start driving him from the barn to the track. He may have to make a fairly sharp turn when he enters the track through a draw gate and should be ready to do it before it becomes part of his regular schedule.

You will recall that when I discussed line driving I made a point of the fact that the colt should be encouraged to stop and

stand several times during the course of each such training session. You do not want to do this, however, once you have your
colt out on the track and are beginning his driving lessons. I don't
advocate it at all during the first two weeks. Keep the colt on the
move until he is unhitched. A colt that tries to stop in the middle
of his early driving sessions is learning a very bad habit that can
be difficult to break.

I am very careful about this and always hustle the colt along
a little any time he acts like he wants to stop. What happens is
that if there is no assistant handy and the colt stops, he thinks he
should be unharnessed and when he finds he isn't going to be,
he will often get balky and cause you trouble.

I didn't mention it before but when I am line driving colts I
always carry an extra long whip with me. I never hit the colt with
it but, instead, use it to shake over his nose in the event he starts
to make a wrong turn or something like that. This whip is also
used when you start to drive the colt and you should shake it
around his nose if he acts like he wants to stop and stand on the
track.

If a colt starts to trot off a little too fast the first time or two, I
will pull very gently on the lines and at the same time say "Whoa"
in a soft voice. This is the same word I have been using to stop
him during his line driving lessons and he probably understands
what it means by now, especially when it is said in conjunction
with a slight pressure on the lines. I never stop a colt abruptly
at this stage. I always make certain I do it slowly and smoothly.

Here is one very important point I want to make with respect
to driving colts the first few times they are on the track. I have
told many people this, but I still see trainers who do it wrong and
get in trouble every year.

If you are driving along and your colt suddenly starts to turn
to the left and head in toward the fence, don't yank on the right
line to try to get him straightened away. When you do this, the
blind bridle prevents the horse from seeing the fence and he will
run right into it. Instead, pull a little on the left line so that he
has an unobstructed view of the obstacle in his path (Fig. 25).
I never saw a colt yet that would run into a fence or anything
else intentionally. If you will notice colts running loose in fields,
you will observe that they will run helter skelter toward a fence,
but will always turn just before they get there.

Fig. 25. If a newly-broken colt heads toward a fence as shown in this photograph, the author cautions strongly against yanking on the right line which will only complicate the problem. Instead, turn the colt toward the fence as in the photograph and avoid trouble. The author says that colts that run into fences are those whose drivers have been trying to pull them in the opposite direction.

It is the same thing when you are driving one. Maybe it doesn't sound right to pull on the left line of a colt that is veering left, but it is the easiest and best way to get him to stop and straighten up. If you pull the other way, you are probably going to go through or over the fence.

Incidentally, this tendency that colts have to shy rather quickly to either the right or left in the early stages is one of the reasons I like to drive them out away from the rail as far as I can. After a few lessons, they usually overcome this fault and you can then handle them in the normal way.

Now, suppose you have trouble starting the colt up after you have hitched him, or any other kind of trouble getting him to go around the track. Do not fight the colt and cause him to throw himself on the track. A good solution here is to use a lead pony and have your assistant ride the pony and lead the colt. In fact, if there is a gentle lead pony or riding horse available, we always use this method to get a colt started. Another advantage of using a lead pony is that if the colt starts up too fast, the rider can help slow him down without the driver having to put too much pressure on the bit and taking a chance on hurting the colt's mouth.

A phase of breaking which requires as much patience as skill is teaching the colt to turn on the track. Do not be in too great a hurry to turn the colt. Wait until he is well broken, and then make a wide arc when you turn him. Another point is to adjust the length of the shafts so they won't stick in the colt's neck when he turns. This can cause trouble. In the first stages of breaking, it is advisable to hook the colt as far forward as possible in the cart to lessen the danger of this happening.

Generally speaking, you can increase the jogging distance after about a week to 10 days. I start out at a mile and a half and after two weeks I usually have the colt up to three miles.

After the first 10 days or so, you do not have to be as cautious about keeping your colt on the move as you were in the early stages. If he wants to walk a little bit while he is being jogged, that is all right as long as you do not let it become a habit. It is also important that you jog the colt both ways of the track so that he grows accustomed to turning in different directions.

There is one item of equipment that I think I ought to comment on with respect to breaking colts. That is a kicking strap. A kicking strap is a leather strap that goes over the horse's rump and is fastened to the sides of the shaft. Its purpose is to keep a colt that kicks from getting his feet up over the shafts or the cross bar of the cart. As you can imagine, a colt could be injured quite seriously in this manner.

I don't use a kicking strap myself, and I don't think one is necessary for a person that has had a lot of experience breaking colts. I do think one is necessary for a young trainer who has not had a great deal of experience along this line, and I recommend its use in such cases (Fig. 58).

A word of caution, however. The great danger in using a kicking strap is in fastening it too tightly. A colt has a natural inclination to kick a little, and I have found that some people will tighten the kicking strap the first time a colt does this. Well, what happens is that the colt resents this strap either because it is too tight or it tickles him—yes, horses are ticklish just as humans are and as with humans some horses are more ticklish than others—and he kicks harder than ever. This is a bad habit for a horse to get into.

If you decide you want to use a kicking strap, I suggest you put one over the colt's rump the last three or four days he is line driven prior to being hitched. This will give him an idea of what the strap is all about and he is not as likely to resent it when he is hitched. But be certain that it is adjusted fairly loose.

At this stage, I never concern myself about shoes for the colt. I usually start them out without any shoes and continue this way through the entire line-driving phase and the first few times they are hooked. If the colt's feet are worn down, or if they are shelly or broken out at all, you might put a light plate on in front and let him go bare-footed behind. He probably won't need any more than that for the first three weeks to a month. By that time, he'll be a little easier to shoe since he will have had extra handling and work and it will be a lot easier on the blacksmith and everybody else when the time comes. If you think a trotter needs a little weight, you can use a pair of bell boots and they will help balance him. If you do use shoes, make certain they are not too long because a colt might go sideways and grab one and pull it off. When I shoe a colt for the first time, I usually put on a bell boot or a rubber scalper which will keep him from pulling a shoe right away.

About the only other thing you have to remember during the early breaking stage is that a colt isn't getting as much exercise as he has been out in the field, or as he will later on when you start to train him, and thus he must be fed lightly. During this period, I will feed the colts twice a day instead of three times and if a colt is quite fat and a little hard to handle I might even cut off his grain ration entirely and feed only hay.

Now we have advanced to the point where the colt is just about broken and ready to go on with. After the first two weeks, if he is acting good, you can start hooking him at the barn and driving him to the track. Do not insist on making the colt walk to the track at this time. It is important that he learn this later but right now you are more interested in encouraging him to get from the barn to the track by the quickest, shortest route. Jog him right on out.

As you started doing when you first hooked the colt, continue going both ways of the track in order to prevent him from starting to go with his head crooked. You may go one way of the track one day and the other way the next. Or, if you wish, you may give him part of his jog the wrong way of the track and then turn him and jog him the right way. In going only one way, the colt begins to carry his head with the contour of the track. By going in both directions, he learns to carry his head straight.

I usually brush a colt three or four times while jogging him, and in between times I permit him to slow down and catch his breath. This is a good time to teach the colt to walk. I let him walk awhile and then start him up and brush him again.

When I talk about brushing a colt at this stage, I don't mean a 2:20 shot or even a three-minute shot. When you are jogging a colt along slowly, as you are now, a "brush" is anything faster than the relatively moderate jog that is his regular work. There is an old saying that "You have to learn to walk before you can fly," and I think this applies to colts.

Maybe you are jogging a mile at about a five-minute rate and the first time you brush your horse you speed him up to a four-minute rate. I will grant you that I'm not talking about much speed here, but to the colt, who hasn't been faster than a five-minute jog rate, it is a brush and it is teaching him how to brush.

You can brush a colt in stages from perhaps a four-minute shot to a 3:40 shot for a little ways, but you want to be sure to do it gradually. I would never drop a colt from a 4:00 shot to more than a 3:30 shot, even if he could obviously go much more.

If you will let colts work up their brush speed gradually, they won't be starting up quickly on you and hitting themselves and becoming afraid and making breaks. I think this is the ideal stage of the game to teach your colts not to make breaks. If you will just let them brush on their own, find their own way, instead of extending them, they will respond better and may never make that first break.

When I was younger, it was always a great sight to see Ben White, Fred Egan and Tom Berry training colts at this stage. They would brush a colt along pretty good, but they were always trying to keep the colt from making a break. They were artists at it, and I like to think I learned a lot from the way they did it.

I have seen a great many colts spoiled because their trainers went too fast and too far with them before the colts were able to sustain the rate. If a colt shows you he can trot fast, leave it in him. I wouldn't even go a sixteenth of a mile, much less an eighth, at top brush speed. I don't care if they have the capability of brushing a 2:40 shot. It's all right for a few steps but no more than that. What I am writing about applies to the very early stages of training but, actually, I never let any of my colts brush as fast as they can for even a sixteenth of a mile at any stage, even later on.

When he has been jogging like this for a couple of weeks, it is then time to teach the colt to walk to and from the track, instead of trotting in and out at a brisk gait. Walking a horse like this always makes a better mannered one, and he will even jog more quietly as a result. If the colt will walk without causing any trouble, walk him at least an eighth of a mile before starting to jog him. Then, when returning to the barn, slow him down and walk him about an eighth of a mile again.

It has now been a month since the colt was first hooked. At this stage, I even go 3½ to four miles a day every once in a while, especially if the colt is a good feeling one. Sometimes, it takes this extra distance to get such a colt to make an effort to stay on a gait.

Now we have reached the stage where we have to start giving a little thought to the shoeing and balancing of our colt. You will recall that I recommended that you either let the horse go barefooted for the first few weeks or perhaps wear a light plate on him in front and nothing behind.

If this has been the case, the colt has probably worn his foot down in front and has a toe that measures 3½ inches or less. When you get the toe down this short, quite a few trotting colts will not be able to balance themselves and will need some help.

I like to start my trotting colts out with a light shoe. If they have acted very natural, I will try a half-inch half-round which will weigh between five and six ounces. If they act as though they need a little more, I will use a 5/8ths half-round which is a couple of ounces heavier.

I always like to start my colts out as light as possible and add weight as I need it. If you have the right weight in the shoe you will not have nearly as much trouble balancing the colt. If a colt is trotting along unbalanced, the trainer has to take too much hold to steady him and this will lead to a sore mouth. Shoes of the proper weight have a great deal to do with this. My rule of thumb is that I should be applying just enough pressure on the lines to let the colt know I am sitting behind him. If I have to apply more than that, my colt is not balanced. If I am applying less, I am driving my colt on too loose a line.

I am also a great believer in bell boots and rubber scalpers at this stage of a colt's career. Both types provide protection, and the bell boots, as I said before, also help balance a young trotter quite a bit.

Another thing I like to do is to start all my colts out, pacers as well as trotters, with a half-round shoe behind. As a matter of fact, I shoe them with a half-round shoe on all four feet. A half-round shoe is not normally worn by a horse behind, but I think that it is helpful at this stage because it doesn't have the sharp edges that a flat shoe does, and if it does touch a colt someplace it isn't as likely to cut him as a flat shoe is. It also quickens his gait up all around. I am also very careful to make certain when a horse is first shod that all the sharp edges are rasped off the sides of the hind shoes. This applies any time a horse is shod, of course, but is especially important at this time.

You also can use a loaded quarter boot of some kind on a trotting colt in front to get him started, but the truth is that I hate to advocate any kind of loaded boot unless a colt absolutely has to have the weight. Unfortunately, we all know that there are certain colts that simply must have the weight to get them gaited right, and in such cases I will use loaded boots reluctantly. As soon as the colt starts developing a gait, the boots should be removed.

I think weight is one of the principal causes of splints in young horses. I have found that there are more splints among trotting colts that have to carry weight in front than among those that don't. That is why I am always trying to cut back on weight. When a colt is reshod for the first time, I invariably have the blacksmith put the same front shoes back on him. Whatever they weighed when I started, they weigh less now, and if the horse is trotting well with them, I am satisfied and do not want new shoes.

Another thing I am quite particular about with my trotting colts is that they wear scalpers behind as soon as they are shod the first time. Even if you can't find any marks that indicate the colt is scalping, it is a good idea to use scalpers for a while at first. In the early stages of a colt's development, when he isn't quite as strong and well-muscled as he will be later on, he will scalp just a little bit, and it is better to be safe than sorry. The scalpers, of course, are in addition to the shin boot with the speedy cut attachment that I automatically put on all my trotting colts right at the start.

I would judge that 75% or more trotting colts start off on a natural trot. The remainder may be inclined to be double-gaited. If a colt is double-gaited, do not decide immediately to make a pacer out of him, because he may not be balanced quite right to trot or be as quick to get on the trot as others. I have had colts that could trot a 2:40 shot in the first stages of training and others that could just barely hit a trot and, by the end of six weeks, have had the slow learning ones catch and pass the natural colt trotters.

I do not say that all trotting bred colts will make trotters, but there are many that will make good ones if you give them plenty of time. Even though a colt finally makes a pacer, you will not lose much progress at this stage of his training if you keep him on the trot, because all the slow work he will be getting will be developing his wind and muscles. If you do not get impatient and shift him to a pace, then you will at least have given him a chance to trot and there will be nothing lost.

In the case of a colt that is pacing bred but will not pace, I either leave the front shoes off or put on a pair of the lightest weight shoes possible. Then I add weight to his hind shoes, sometimes as much as 12 to 14 ounces. The weight behind will assist him in learning to swing over into a pace and help him balance himself. Sometimes, I add a five- or six-ounce toe weight on the outside of each hind foot instead of putting the weight in the shoes.

If the colt will not hit a pace with this added weight behind, you will probably have to resort to hobbles in order to help establish his gait. However, if at all possible, I like to have a colt going free-legged before I go to the hobbles. If he hits a pace naturally, the hobbles will not burn nearly as much when they are first put on.

When you do put on the hobbles for the first time, you have to exercise a little caution so that they don't burn the colt too badly. I usually put the hobbles on a colt and walk him around the barn area for a few minutes so he has a chance to get accustomed to them and realize they are there.

If you are working with a colt that doesn't have a natural pacing gait, it is logical that the hobbles will sting him pretty good the first day. However, this is not a bad thing if you don't force him too much, because this tends to encourage him to develop the proper pacing gait. Many colts discover they can relieve the stinging sensation by swinging over into the pace, and they do so promptly.

If the colt doesn't hit a decent pace after jogging a couple of miles the first day he wears the hobbles, I wouldn't go any farther. Sometimes you will find that the colt catches on the second day and moves off. He has had a little chance to think about the hobbles and realizes what they are. If I have a colt that is not coming along the way I think he should at this stage, I will take the hobbles off for a few days and then try them again later.

You will have to determine the length of the hobbles from the way the colt paces in them. I keep them tight enough so that the colt cannot trot in them and as soon as he hits a good pace I let them out until they seem comfortable on him.

It is a good practice at this stage to put hobbles on a pacing colt, even though he has developed a natural pacing gait without their help. This will get him used to them and even if you go back then and train him free-legged, you will always be assured that he will know what the hobbles are in the event that you have to resort to them.

In commenting on this point, I think I can safely say that 80% of the pacing colts that are broken today are broken in hobbles that are too tight for them. Most of these colts are going to wind up racing the rest of their lives in tight hobbles, and their full potential may never be realized. So my advice is to start your colts out in loose hobbles and keep the hobbles as loose as you can as long as you can. Your colt will go farther and faster.

About a month has passed now since we started to line break our colt and he is beginning to learn what it is all about. At this point, I would stop brushing the colt while jogging him. Instead, I would jog him two or three miles the wrong way of the track and then turn the right way and let him trot a mile at a very moderate rate and brush him a little at the end of it.

If I was working with a playful colt that was full of life, I would probably brush him a quarter of a mile or so the wrong way of the track before I turned him. By this time, I would assume the colt would be brushing anywhere between a 4:00 and a 2:40 shot.

As soon as the colt learns to trot somewhere between a 3:00-3:30 mile, I would stop brushing him every day and resort to turning him around every other day instead. I would then work him a slow mile and brush him a little at the end of it. I would be merely jogging parts of such a mile.

When you first turn a colt, great care should be exercised not to tire him. If he is a natural trotter or pacer and would go a fast mile if you would let him, be sure that you don't give in to the temptation. It is all right if he takes off during the mile and trots a little piece, but don't let him carry it very far. Bring him back to you and keep him within the range you have set up. The important thing is not to let the colt get so tired that he gets discouraged or that his gait is affected.

I think this covers the breaking operation. In certain areas, Ralph Baldwin and I have overlapped a bit, but not to any great extent. In the next chapter Ralph will explain the proper techniques used from this point on in training a 2-year-old.

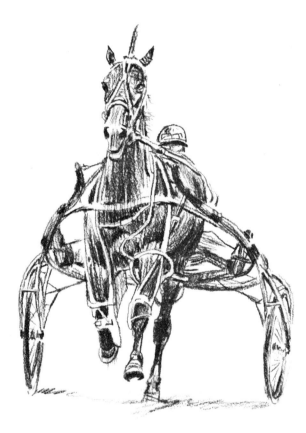

Delvin Miller wears more hats than any man in harness racing. He is—though not necessarily in this order—one of the sport's greatest trainer-drivers, an owner, breeder (Meadowlands Farm where the great Adios stood), track official (president, The Meadows), president of the Grand Circuit, director of the U.S. Trotting Association, Harness Tracks of America and the Standardbred Owner's Association and, last but certainly not least in this case, the man who suggested that this book be written and then helped write it while successfully encouraging other well-known horsemen to participate in the venture. Miller was born in Woodland, California  on July 5, 1913 and inherited his interest in harness racing from his paternal grandfather who was a horseman and who raised him on the Miller homestead near Avella, Pa. after his father's early death. He won his first race in 1930 and has been winning ever since—with time out for World War II service as a First Sergeant in the India-Burma Theater—even though he has cut back his training activities in recent years. He has won more than 1,500 races, in excess of $4,500,000 and has more than 80 2:00 miles to his credit. His notable victories have included a 1950 sweep of The Hambletonian (Lusty Song) and The Little Brown Jug (Dudley Hanover). In addition, he trained the winners but gave the mounts to others in the 1951 (Tar Heel) and 1952 (Meadow Rice) Jugs and the 1953 (Helicopter) and 1961 (Harlan Dean) Hambletonians. He has been the leading Grand Circuit driver on three occasions and was the nation's leading money-winning and UDRS (batting average) driver in 1950. He won the *Horseman & Fair World's* inaugural Horseman of the Year award in 1956 but despite all the honors and titles that have been heaped upon him he is still best known among horsemen as the man to turn to in time of need—whether it be a loan, a job or advice concerning a foul-gaited trotter.

4

TRAINING the 2-YEAR-OLD

RALPH N. BALDWIN

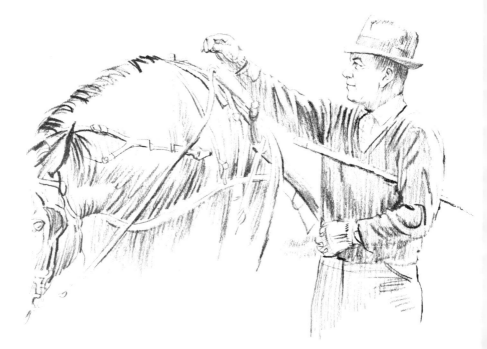

I suppose everyone has his own ideas about training colts. I know I have mine. I don't know whether my methods are exactly right, but I do know that the way I learned was by watching some of the more successful colt trainers and trying to pattern my methods after theirs.

From time to time, as I gained more experience, I adopted innovations of my own and consequently my present system is a blend of what I learned by watching and talking to others and what I picked up myself. I consider it a privilege to be able to pass on some of that knowledge by means of this chapter devoted to the training of 2-year-olds.

I think the man I learned the most from was the late Fred Egan, in my opinion one of the greatest colt trainers that ever lived. I also learned a great deal from the late Tom Berry, who was also a top colt man, although he didn't use the same training methods Mr. Egan did. I tried to pick the best from each of them and use what I learned to my advantage.

The training techniques I am going to describe apply to 2-year-olds being conditioned in the warmer climate of the south, but, except for certain minor adjustments necessitated by differing climates, they are just as applicable to horses being trained anywhere in the country. A good colt is a good colt and whether he is trained in the north or the south he will still win the stakes if he is bred to win them and if he is properly trained and driven.

At the end of this chapter, you will find two daily training charts for 2-year-olds that are being trained to race in the stakes and whose first start is scheduled for about May 15th. One (Chart No. 1) is for colts that are being trained over a mile track in Florida and the other (Chart No. 2) is for colts that are being trained over a half mile track in the north.

I have never trained any 2-year-olds in the north so I have prevailed on my friend Stanley Dancer to furnish that schedule. He has obliged by providing the actual training schedule followed by Bonjour Hanover when that great filly was a 2-year-old. The other schedule is one I have drawn up myself, but I do want to say that I have done so with reservations. The fact is that I don't train 2-year-olds by a set pattern that requires a colt to meet a certain time bracket every week. Rather, I work out my schedule for individual horses as I go along. I do more with some colts at the same stage than I do with others and it is the colt himself that tells me when to go on and when to hold back a little.

Some colts will train real good one day and the next time the wind might be blowing or some other little thing isn't just right and they won't train on schedule. They might go two or three bad training sessions in a row for no apparent reason. A trotting colt will very often throw in a poor work just after he has been shod and it might take him a week or more to get straightened away. If you tried to train every 2-year-old according to a rigid schedule of timed miles, you could easily get into trouble because a slow-developing colt might start making breaks and things like that if you asked him to go more than he was able to at a particular stage.

So, in studying my training schedule, please remember that I have set it up for a perfectly average colt, one that is neither a star pupil nor a laggard, but one that was lucky and went every training mile just as it was planned. In actual practice, you will not find very many exactly like this.

I have set up my schedule for southern-trained colts to begin in mid-October, which is when I start with most of mine. I am aware, however, that many colts cannot even be broken until after the Harrisburg sale the last week of October and therefore an allowance in the schedule should be made for that. I think you will find, however, that since the Harrisburg colts have been led and/or handled longer than colts sold at earlier sales they are actually about two-thirds broken when you get them. You can move along a little faster with these colts and by the first of the year they would be at about the same notch as mine are, that is, about a mile in 2:50.

When I start out with colts fresh from the farm or from a sale, I devote about a week to 10 days to ground breaking. After that they are ready to hook and I spend the next week to 10 days teaching them to drive. This two-stage initial period takes from two to three weeks depending on the colt and after that he is ready to be introduced to the normal jogging routine which represents the beginning of his training.

These first two stages are very important because if you do your job well it keeps you out of trouble later on when you start to do more with your colt. A little extra time spent mannering and gentling colts during this period can pay big dividends.

When a colt comes to me to be broken, the first thing I do is to take his grain away from him. Most of these colts have been grained on the farm and the ones that have been through a sales ring have had a lot of grain. Most of them are usually too fat but that isn't the only reason I do this. I have found that if their grain is removed they are much easier to break. If you grain a colt good before you break him, a lot of times he will do bad things that he wouldn't ordinarily do. The grain sort of sets him up to get a little tough.

I think that taking it away from them is good for their systems because they're not doing much anyway and thus are getting virtually no exercise during the breaking period. I give them about all the hay they want and when they do go back on grain, which is when I start to jog them daily, I start out light with two feeds a day and a couple of quarts of grain at each feeding.

I won't devote any more space to the breaking of colts because Del Miller is handling that in another chapter. I will go right ahead and pick them up at the end of that initial two or three week period when I begin to jog them. Before I do that, I think it would be appropriate if I reviewed a couple of other basic subjects which are also being covered elsewhere but which have specific application to the training of a 2-year-old and which I do not think I should ignore completely.

Proper shoeing is such a category and with Johnny Simpson and Frank Ervin covering the subject in detail I will limit myself to some general observations as to the basic shoes I use on my 2-year-olds.

Most of my trotting colts will wear a 5/8ths half-round shoe in front. This is not a heavy shoe but it has enough weight in it to make most of them trot. However, I flatten this shoe down so that it doesn't snap their ankles too much and thus isn't as hard on their front legs as the standard half-round.

You have to bear in mind that the leg bones of a 2-year-old—and all his bones for that matter—are not as set as those of an older horse. In my opinion, the quick snapping action of the standard half-round shoe is pretty hard on them. I believe it is especially hard on the ankle bones.

When you start out, you'll usually find that most of the colts don't fold their knees enough and are inclined, as a result, to speedy cut a little bit. To help them learn to fold their knees and begin to acquire the proper trotting gait in front you really need a shoe with a rounded front edge that will break them over a little quicker and thus encourage the folding action.

What I do is take a standard 5/8ths half-round shoe, heat it, place it on the anvil and pound it down all the way around. This flattens the surface that hits the track but still leaves rounded edges, both in front and on the sides. Then I have a shoe that doesn't snap them over as quickly and thus eases the strain on the bones and muscles. At the same time, the edges are still rounded enough so that if a colt does interfere a little with the hind leg on the same side the rounded edge doesn't cut him, it just sort of slides off. I find this is a very nice shoe with which to start a trotting colt.

I start my trotting colts out behind with a plain 3/16ths by a half shoe. I switch most of them over to a full swedge shoe when they get down around 2:40 in their training routine. When I used to train over the clay track at Orlando, I let them go until they were down around 2:20 before switching to the swedge and I recommend this to those who are training over a clay track which has a superior holding action.

But the surface at Pompano is a little sandier and I have found that their feet begin to slip a little around the 2:40 notch. This is a sign that it is time to go to swedge shoes and I do. If you are training over a track that has sand or stone dust mixed in with the clay, you will probably find that you will want to go to the swedge shoe a little sooner.

I start my pacers out with a light half-inch half-round shoe in front and a 3/16ths by a half plain shoe behind, the same one I use to start my trotters. In addition, it is my usual procedure to run a short trailer and turn a heel calk on the outside end of each hind shoe. This tips the pacers up a little bit and helps to keep them off their front quarters when they are just starting out. One of the main things, of course, is to make sure that the foot is absolutely level all around.

In connection with the shoeing of 2-year-olds, I think it is vital that a trainer be in the blacksmith shop every time one of his colts is shod. Not only are you supervising one of the most important areas involved in colt training, but you also get a chance to see so many other things that you might otherwise miss. It is one of the few times that you really have a chance to sit down and look your colt over carefully from every angle. Occasionally this policy will pay big dividends.

I recall an incident of this type involving Dartmouth when he was still a yearling. Mr. and Mrs. Van Lennep had purchased him at the Walnut Hall Farm sale for $25,000. I had watched him lead and he was a perfect-gaited horse. I was elated to have him.

After he was broken and I had started to jog him, I discovered that he was snatching one hind leg. This certainly didn't go with the colt I had seen lead so well prior to the sale and I couldn't understand it. This went on for a week or ten days with no improvement and I began to think I had made a big mistake in recommending him and that Mr. and Mrs. Van Lennep had made another by following my advice. Every trainer knows that there isn't much you can do with one of those trotters that snatches a hind leg.

One day when I was standing in the shop while he was being shod I suddenly noticed a very tiny rough spot in the heel of his left hind foot right in the coronary band. It didn't really look like anything, in fact it was hardly visible, but I reached down anyway and put a little finger pressure on it. Dartmouth really jumped when I touched it and I could tell it was very sore. It turned out to be a pus pocket. We opened it up right on the spot, put a little disinfectant in it and he was a new horse within 24 hours. From that moment on he was perfect in every way.

What had happened was that when we jogged the colt we put the scalpers on and the scalper rubbed against this sore spot and made it very painful. He kept trying to get away from this pain and that was causing him to stab and jab with that hind leg. If I hadn't been standing in the blacksmith shop looking him over very carefully, I might have missed that sore spot and it might have stayed with him long enough for him to have developed a habit of gait that he would never have overcome. It just proves that it pays to be around when your colts are being shod.

There are other reasons why it it important that you be there when your colt has an appointment with the horseshoer. As you know, every colt that goes to the shop has a little card showing the length of toe, angle, etc. that goes with him. You are dealing here in fractions of inches and any competent trainer will tell you that even the tiniest variations of these fractional measurements can make a major difference in the gait of a colt.

If you take as little as an eighth of an inch too much off the front toe of a trotting colt you can change his gait entirely and get him completely out of kilter. The same thing can happen to a pacer by leaving the toe an eighth of an inch too long.

This can happen accidentally despite all the precautions you take. Let's say, for instance, that the card calls for a 3⅝-inch front toe on a trotting colt. And maybe between trips to the shop you have had some wet weather or something like that and this colt's toe has grown more than you anticipated. On previous trips you have only had to take off an eighth of an inch but this time you find that you have to take off a quarter of an inch to get him down to the 3⅝ you want.

The next time you go out with that colt he could miss that extra eighth of an inch so much that he would train badly. His gait would be completely different than it had been. This might continue for a week to 10 days until that foot grew out a little.

If you hadn't been at the shop, or even if you had been at the shop and were visiting with somebody when this colt was trimmed, you might have missed this. You would be looking for other reasons for his poor showing and trying to change things to make him trot better. You'd be doing wrong. The first thing you know, you would be all mixed up and the colt would be all mixed up and you would be in real trouble.

But if you'd been in the shop and watching the horseshoer as he worked, you would have noticed this and consequently would not have been concerned when your colt didn't train properly the next time out. Actually, what I would do in a case like this and what I would recommend is that you train your colt in a pair of hinge quarter boots or something like that for two or three workouts or until the colt's foot has had a chance to grow out a little. This will not only help compensate for the lack of foot but might also prevent your colt from developing a bad habit of some kind.

So it's important to know not only that the toe is the proper length but how much had been trimmed off to get it that way. A lot of races are won or lost in the blacksmith shop.

If you don't have your own horseshoer and are dealing with different ones all the time, it is probably a good idea to measure the toe yourself before the horseshoer starts to work on it and place a little mark there indicating the proper length. Some horseshoers make their measurements from slightly different places and it can make a difference. I don't do this because I have my own horseshoer and he and I measure exactly the same. But if this weren't the case, I am sure I would adopt the practice.

Another thing to examine closely while you are in the shop is the condition of your colt's feet. I pack my horse's feet with clay and in the shop I can tell whether the boys are putting in too much or too little. If the feet are hard and brittle, they are not using enough clay. If they are inclined to be soft and mushy they are probably using too much.

A lot of young trainers don't realize that you can get a horse's feet too soft as well as too hard. This is especially true of the hind feet. A horse's hind feet are inclined to stay a little softer because they stand in the wet part of the stall and they will get manure in them while the front feet won't.

If the hind feet get too soft, the heels are inclined to mash down and you lose your angle. You may have a colt that should be carrying a 53 or 54-degree angle and he might lose as much as two or three degrees this way without your realizing it. This will put a lot of strain on your colt's hind ankles and hocks and he'll begin to knuckle over. This will very quickly lead to stifle and whirlbone trouble if not corrected immediately.

So it pays to look the feet over while you are in the shop. If they are too soft they will start getting mushy and they will either spread out or curl down under and mash into the wall of the foot. You can tell when the horseshoer trims the colt's feet whether this is taking place or not. You should always be on the lookout for it.

Another thing I like to do before I go along very far with my colts is to have the dentist come in and go over their teeth. I try to have this done as soon as possible after the colts arrive to be broken. Of course, a dentist can't really do too much with horses that young but he certainly can round off the rough edges so that the colts aren't cutting their cheeks. This is the kind of thing that if left unattended can get a colt to carrying his head to one side or the other and no horse trainer wants that.

I also like to have the dentist extract the wolf teeth of every one of my colts if he can. The wolf teeth are small, pointed teeth that grow right in front of the molars on each side. They serve no useful purpose and are a prime source of mouth trouble.

Occasionally I will find that some of the wolf teeth haven't grown out far enough at this stage for the dentist to get hold of them. I like to have them through the gums pretty well so that I can make sure they aren't broken off. If I run across a colt like this, I will make a note of it and have him treated at a later date when the teeth come through.

If a wolf tooth gets broken off, it act like a sliver in a horse's mouth and can cause trouble for years. I have run into this with older horses that have had their wolf teeth broken off as colts and have sore mouths because of this. They will carry their head to one side or the other and fuss with their mouth.

Once in a while even a good dentist will break a wolf tooth off when he tries to extract it. Something like this can't be helped, but a trainer has to remember that it is there and keep watching it, hoping that what is left will grow out enough that it can be removed later. If it doesn't, you'll probably have to go in there and extract it anyway. This is pretty rough but it is a lot better to do that and get it over with than to have your colt develop a sore mouth.

The mouth of a young horse is very tender and apt to become sore at the slightest provocation. That is why I am always careful to use soft bits on my colts in the early stages. I use snaffle bits for the most part but I usually cover them with leather or with a self-sticking rubbery substance that gives them a pretty good cushion to bite into. If you use this material, you have to change it every couple of weeks or sooner if a colt chews it up as some will. Believe me, anything you can do to keep a colt from developing a sore mouth is a plus for you as a trainer.

I usually start my colts by breaking them in a blind bridle and then I will switch over to whatever I think is best for the individual colt. Not everybody breaks a colt in a blind bridle and I wouldn't say whether it is the right or wrong way, but I always thought it was a little easier to break them that way.

For one thing, if they are wearing a blind bridle they aren't spending as much time trying to go out a gate. Most colts have what I call "gateitis." They seem to feel they have to go out every gate they see. A blind bridle is a big help in this respect.

If I have a colt that is wearing a blind bridle and acts a little scared when another horse comes up alongside, I will switch to a Kant-See-Bak bridle. This enables him to see another colt alongside and works very well.

With a nervous colt, you are probably better off training him in an open bridle. I have one like that as I write this. I had a blind bridle on him and he was so nervous he wouldn't relax enough even to hit a trot. He would just canter and rack along. He also wanted to go out every gate he came to so I had a compound problem.

I decided he'd be better off in an open bridle and I rigged him that way. The first couple of times after that he was still nervous but you could see improvement each time. He was seeing what was going on and what was making all those noises behind him and he became content and satisfied. In virtually no time at all he calmed down, stopped trying to go out every gate he saw and became an absolutely perfect colt. There is no set pattern. You have to treat each case individually.

When I get my colts to the races, I wear a lot of blind bridles on my studs, especially those that aren't on the iron too much. The ones that are just a little bit on the lazy side seem to race a little gamer in a blind bridle. On the other hand, after they have raced a little, many colts will start to take more hold than you like and then you have to go to an open or a Kant-See-Bak bridle. You have to weigh the circumstances and exercise your own judgment.

Now let me go back and pick up my colt at the beginning. From two to three weeks have passed since I started with him. He has been ground broken, hooked, and taught the rudiments of responding to basic driver commands. He is ready to enter training. The first phase consists of nothing but jogging and it is a period which will last for about five weeks. He will not be asked to go any actual training miles until this phase is satisfactorily completed.

My colts are jogged every day except Sunday. As a matter of

fact, Sunday is a complete day off for all colts in my stable throughout the colt training period which is until they get to the races and even then I give them Sunday off unless there are extenuating circumstances. I believe colts are just like people. I think they know when it is Sunday. I know that on a Sunday morning you can walk through my stable and I'll guarantee that at least half the colts will be down at the same time taking a good rest. They are all stretched out and snoring and really enjoying themselves. A day off doesn't hurt a colt at all and in my opinion a Sunday off freshens them up for the start of a new week.

I start jogging my colts two miles a day and gradually work it up to three. In practice, I usually have them up to two miles by the end of the 10-day to two week period during which they were hooked and taught to drive. Therefore, most of them are up to three miles a day when I start them on their five-week jogging phase. I have found that you have to jog a colt at least two miles a day or he doesn't know he's been out of the barn. The colt himself will let you know when he is ready to switch over to three miles. If he is still playing and full of life at the end of two, it's time to start going three.

However, as in anything having to do with the conditioning of harness horses, there are exceptions to these general rules. For instance, if you run across a colt that is inclined to be fussy and nervous when you first start to jog him, he might take off at a pretty good clip with you. If you go too far with this kind they will just get hot and start losing their minds, so to speak, and acting a lot worse. What I will usually do with one like this is to go only about a mile the first few days. This is far enough for them to know they have been hooked and it really isn't a bad idea at all. Most of the time it works.

On the other hand, every once in a while you will get a big tough colt and if you only went two miles you would probably never get anything done with him. You would actually get into trouble because this type of colt would get worse instead of better. When I get a colt like this I will go more jog miles. I have gone as high as five miles with a real high strung colt that didn't want to settle down. But I don't go fast with them, just enough so that they will get a little tired. It is only after they get a little tired that they start learning anything.

You can tell when a colt is getting tired by the way he acts. He will start hanging his head a little in the check and stop seeing things around the race track that had caused him to make a jump or veer with you the last time he passed them. He wasn't really afraid of these things but when he was still full of life they gave him an excuse to make a little trouble for you.

At this time, I will usually be working with from 15 to 20 2-year-olds and I have two assistant trainers helping me. In my stable the grooms do not begin to jog these colts until they start to train two heats. Until then, all the jogging is done by me and my assistants.

Even after the colts have started to go two training heats I still try to do as much of the jogging as I can. The reason for this is that very often you can spot faults while colts are being jogged, little things that a groom might not notice. They might be starting to carry their heads off to one side or something like that and if you are doing the jogging you can pinpoint the moment they started to go wrong and work from there. Actually, you are getting as much done as if you were training them that day.

During the five-week jogging period, I will jog a colt both the right and wrong way of the track. But even though he is going the right way of the track he is still going at a jog rate. I turn him around to give him a little change of scenery, to let him know there is more than just one way around a race track and to keep him from developing any bad habits that he might fall into if he went the same way every time.

I am not trying to train the colt during this period but at the same time I don't hold him to the same slow jog rate all the way around. After a colt is broken, I don't believe it is right to maintain the same jog speed all the time. I think that if a colt wants to trot on a little he should be permitted to do so. This will change his gait and he will start developing more of the gait he is going to have to use later on and he is doing it on his own.

At the end of five weeks, my colts are being jogged three miles a day, six days a week and they are ready to enter training. This is the beginning of the next stage of their conditioning program. During this stage, they will start by training a mile around 3:20

and then work their way down to 2:50. This stage lasts about four weeks.

I will train the colts a single mile on Monday, Wednesday and Friday. When I start with them, I don't carry a watch, but I would guess the first timing mile would be at about the 3:20 rate I just mentioned. That is really just a good, fast jog. At the end of the mile I will let them move on a little faster. I don't mean that I am brushing them, but just letting them move along a little bit more than they have been. This teaches them to move out a little at the end of the mile.

The colts are jogged three miles before they go their single training mile. At this stage I will run across an occasional colt that will get a little tired after three jog miles and a training mile. By the time you are ready to go the training mile he has lost a little of his edge and will start going bad-gaited. I will back a colt like this off and jog him two miles instead of three.

On the days off, which for this set of colts would be Tuesday, Thursday and Saturday, each colt will be jogged three miles. As I said before, I feel that it is important that I do this jogging or that one of my assistants does it.

This 3:20 to 2:50 stage is the one in which you concentrate on getting your colts hung up right. You can see the way their feet are growing and what sort of gait they are going to have and you also find out whether a colt wants to go light or whether he needs a little more weight. This is the best time for experimentation of this type because you can do it much easier at this stage than you can if you have to wait and then force them later on.

You are trying to establish a rhythm in their gait. Any fast colt has to have a rhythmic gait or he won't go very far. Rhythm in gait is an easy way of going with every muscle coordinated. You can help colts by shoeing, by length of toe and by the kind of boots they wear.

For the first month or so, a lot of colts will be nervous and I find that this very often causes them to become racky-gaited. Because of this, some trotters will even act like pacers for the first month or six weeks. With this kind, you have to have patience and work quietly with them. Many of them will come around if you don't go overboard and try to force them too much. Very often with a trotter you will find that you can put on a pair of hinge quarter boots and this will change his gait in front and make him fold his knees and start getting a gait like a trotter should have.

This is also a good time to teach your colts to turn properly. A lot of colts will get in trouble when they start turning. They get their neck around and the fill of the cart will bump them in the side of the neck and they will get so they don't want to turn at all.

The draw gate at Pompano, where my colts enter the track, is above the finish line. I always turn to the left when I go out this gate to go my two jogging miles. When I am ready to go my training miles, I always bring the colts back up above this draw gate before turning them. In this way, they are turning back toward the gate which leads to the stable area and they will always have the idea in their mind that maybe they are going back to the barn and they will turn more readily. It is very seldom that one won't learn to turn properly if you follow this procedure and I recommend it. Even if the draw gate at the track where you are training is placed differently, you can usually figure out some little variation that will help you in this respect.

If I run across one that is giving me a little trouble, I will also work on the problem after he completes his training mile. When I come back with him I will walk him past the gate to the spot where I turned him before to start his training mile. This time I will turn him slowly and let him walk on out the gate. The next time he comes up there he will remember this and will usually turn because he thinks you're going to let him walk out the gate again. It's just a little psychological feeling you give the colt and it changes his mind. After you've done this a few times, the colt will have learned to turn properly and you shouldn't have any more trouble.

I have been talking about balky colts and this is as good a place as any to mention fillies. Anybody who is training 2-year-olds is training fillies as well as colts and there is a big difference between them. Most colts can be worked on a little bit if necessary and if you do use a little pressure the average colt will go ahead and take it and probably be a better horse for it.

It isn't the same way with fillies. They are like women. They get their feelings hurt real easy and they get a little sulky. So you have to treat them a little easier and try to train them so that they feel they are doing it on their own.

They can get so they don't like anything very well and I've found it's pretty hard to force them when they get this way. Usually if you try to force them they get silly. If you get one that doesn't do the right thing, about all I can advise is that you try to make everything as nice and as pleasant for her as you can and give her lots and lots of time.

Working fillies like this in plenty of company seems to help a great deal. Sometimes when you work one alone, she apparently thinks she's the only one that has to perform this chore and she resents it and lets you know about it. Fillies are much more of a problem than colts and patience and understanding are a trainer's best weapons.

After about a month of my every-other-day schedule, I will find that certain colts are going miles in 2:50 like it was nothing more than a good brisk jog. When they reach this point they are ready to enter the next stage during which they will start to train two miles a day twice a week. Now they are said to be "repeating."

At the same time, I should point out that you will find some colts that are not as comfortable and as easy at 2:50. These continue in this bracket until they are ready to move on. That is why I say it is impossible to lay out a schedule of training miles that will cover all colts.

But with the ones that are ready to advance, I adopt a new system. Let's say that our colt is going to be trained on Monday and Thursday. On the first Monday that we switch over to two heats our colt goes a mile in 2:50, goes back to the barn for forty minutes and then returns and goes another mile in 2:50 (week of Dec. 14, Chart No. 1, page 180).

On Thursday he comes back and goes two more miles in 2:50. The next week we will drop him two or three seconds in his second mile on Monday and Thursday and during each of the next two or three weeks thereafter he will drop another two or three seconds a week until he reaches the 2:40 stage.

I figure that two or three seconds a week is plenty until we reach 2:40. At the same time they are dropping, these colts are developing leg muscles and manners, both of which are very important. They are acquiring the foundation they will need later on when I ask a lot more of them.

You will find at this stage that some of your colts, especially the trotters, will make a break from time to time. Don't worry too much about that if it isn't a persistent fault. Colts are like children and they have to go through their grades. All of them will make occasional breaks. After a while, if they are good colts, they will get so they don't make breaks. But don't punish them at this stage just because they do.

Now that we have started to repeat, it is important that every colt be completely stripped between trips and that he be allowed a full forty minutes before he returns for his second heat. All boots and hobbles should be taken off and cleaned. Dirt will get in boots and pack down and make them heavy. This chafes the colt and he will not train as he should. In addition to boots, you also have to be especially careful at this stage with chafing that is caused by hobbles. Everyone knows that tight hobbles will chafe a horse. But very often a loose, swinging hobble will also cause a horse to chafe. If the hobbles were that loose the trainer would know the cause and could work on the problem.

One of the troubles you can get into here is with sticky hobble chafe. When you put it on, you think you are helping the horse but actually you are not. This sticky hobble chafe is like glue and it gets on the hobbles and pulls the skin. They really chafe worse than if you didn't use anything at all. You should use a hobble chafe that feels smooth when you put it on and one which will dry out quickly on a horse's leg.

This is why I always caution my grooms to be especially careful about cleaning the hobbles between heats. I use a lot of talcum powder on both the colt's leg and the hobbles. It pays off and good common sense will tell you that if you keep the hobbles clean and smooth they aren't going to chafe like they will if they get gummed up with dirt and sweat.

I've got my colts down around 2:40 now and I'm beginning to find out that I like some of them a lot better than others. Some act like they could go in 2:30 without any trouble while others look like 2:40 is going to suit them for a while. These are the ones that have developed a few problems such as putting in extra steps and the like and I hold these where they are until I can iron out their difficulties.

The others are ready to go on to 2:35 which is the next stage. I realize this is only a five-second drop, but it is an important one for two reasons. One is that when I reach 2:35 I start to go three training trips instead of two and the other is that for some reason it is right here, where you are getting ready to beat 2:35, that you run into a lot of problems.

I have noticed, for instance, that at about this level some colts will begin to develop fillings in their legs and ankles. I am always watching for this, but I am especially cautious about it when I reach the 2:40-2:35 stage. If you are doing just a little bit too much with a colt, bringing him down just a little quicker than he is able to come, it will usually show in the legs first. His physical condition may be fine and it wouldn't give you a clue that you were moving too fast. But those legs will.

Any time a colt shows me a little strain or a little filling I will do him up. They are only in light training at this stage, but you have to remember that this is the first time in their lives that they have been at this rate and it might be harder on them than we think. It certainly is for some of them.

Most of these fillings develop in front and when they appear I will do the colt up in alcohol. I use alcohol because it isn't hot and doesn't burn his legs. If you put something warm on the leg, a stronger liniment or something like that, it will scurf and start to itch. The colt is very apt to tear his bandages off and do more damage to himself.

I use alcohol, four sheets of cotton and a bandage. I never use a string bandage on a colt because he might grab the string in his teeth and tighten the bandage around his leg which could cause additional trouble. As a matter of fact, I have seen this cause a bowed tendon.

The procedure I usually follow when I do a colt up for the first time is to mix up some soap, red pepper, hot sauce and anything else that a colt might not like or that has a disagreeable odor and spread this on the outside of the bandage. You might spoil a couple of sets of bandages this way but it will teach a colt not to fool with bandages and he will soon learn to wear them and not try to pull them off.

When we are doing our colts up as a precautionary measure

after these light training sessions, I usually see that it's done right after they've been cooled out. I don't let them stand around for two or three hours and let the leg begin to fill again. I get them when the filling has been worked out, put the alcohol on and do them up right away. The alcohol doesn't have any particular medicinal qualities, it just wets the hair a little and feels good on the leg. About 90% of the time you will find that when you take the bandage off the next morning the leg is just as clean as the day the colt was born.

If a filling like this doesn't respond to such treatment after a day or two, it is an indication that there is more there than meets the eye and I usually call in a veterinarian to take a look at it with me.

At this same stage, you will also find that colts begin to pop curbs and splints. Curbs don't bother me too much and unless they are those big, juicy ones that require extra treatment I usually apply a light blister and continue to train the colt. Splints are something else again. Some of them are as big as golf balls and don't mean a thing while others are barely visible and can cause you all kinds of trouble.

For the past month I have been watching some of my colts that show signs of being a little curby and hoping that curbs don't develop because they are something of a nuisance to deal with. But now some of them begin to fill and I have to do something with them.

Mine is not the only way to treat curbs because all of us think a little differently. But I can tell you what I do. If the curb isn't too bad, I will paint it every day for ten days with M.A.C. and continue to train the colt, although a little lighter than usual. It's very unlikely that you will hurt a colt this way. He may be a little stiff on the scab but very often that curb will straighten right out within a 10-day period after the scab comes off.

What you must be careful of is that you train the colt lightly while he is being treated. A blister is inclined to make a colt a little bad-gaited and he could start making breaks if he's hurting too much. At the same time, such a colt might possibly pick up some bad habits like getting on one line and doing a lot of other things you don't like to see a colt do. Once a colt starts getting on one line it's a problem to get him off. Even after a colt gets sound again he may still cling to that habit of hanging on one line and anyone who's raced horses knows what it's like when you are driving a horse on one line. It's a big handicap. So while you can continue to train a colt that has been blistered for a small curb, take it very easy with him and be sure he doesn't develop any bad habits as a result.

If you run into a colt that uses his hind quarters a lot, or is sickle hocked or a little crooked to start with, you can be pretty sure that the curb this colt develops is going to be one of those big juicy ones and a blister isn't going to get it. With a colt like this, I would probably fire him right away and forget about the blister.

If you do this, you will have to lay your colt off for about three weeks, which is about how long it takes for the soreness to disappear. He should be jogged three to four miles daily during this period but not trained.

When a colt like this returns to training, you can work him a couple of times around 3:00 and then start dropping back toward the 2:40-2:35 bracket. You can drop him quicker than you did the first time around but it still ought to take about three weeks before you get him back to where he was.

You might think you are losing a lot of valuable time with this colt, but you have to remember that his whole life is ahead of him. What difference does it make if it takes three or four extra weeks to get him ready? In relation to the racing career that lies ahead of him, it means nothing. It might not be absolutely necessary to do it this way, but it's a good type of insurance and it always makes me feel good to know that I at least tried to do the right thing and didn't break the colt down or get him bad-mannered by going too much with him before he was ready.

Splints also begin popping at this stage and they can be much more difficult to treat than curbs. They can really be a thorn in a colt trainer's side. Size means nothing. The big one on the front side of the shin bone will probably never bother him. But those little ones the size of a pea on the inside of the leg and back around the ligaments are really bad. You will look at an innocent little splint like this and wonder how in the world it can make a horse as sore as it does.

Sometimes these dangerous splints are so small that you can't see or feel them. These are known as blind splints. But the ligaments start riding over them, the splint is a little rough around the edges and the next thing you know you have suspensory trouble or even a bowed tendon.

I usually treat a splint by painting it. I am reluctant to fire one because if it is brand new, or a "green splint" as we say, it will, many times, mushroom out and get much bigger and more bothersome than if you hadn't touched it at all.

I use a soft leg paint that doesn't make a hard crust on a colt's leg. It peels off like tobacco peelings. I've had a lot of luck doing this. It doesn't cure them, but as a general rule it will keep the soreness out. If the colt is well-advanced in his training, I may go all summer just painting that splint and watching it closely. In the fall, when the splint is well set up and has reached its full growth, I'll fire it.

It is not my intention to write a veterinary section in this chapter because that phase is handled very capably by Dr. Churchill. But I think it is important that a colt trainer be aware of some of the common signs of approaching unsoundness and from that standpoint I do not think it would be out of order for me to review a few of the obvious indicators.

For instance, one of the first signs of an approaching splint is that a colt, especially a trotter, will not be folding his knee quite right. He will be handling the leg as though it were a little stiff and then he will probably start hanging on one line. Such a colt will also begin to stumble from time to time, but in using this as a sign, you have to be certain you know your horse since some colts have a natural tendency to stumble a little and it doesn't mean a thing.

If you suspect that a colt might be starting to get a little off in front, it is a good idea to jog him from the barn to the track yourself. In the first stages, colts will warm out of such trouble quickly, and very often, if the groom jogs them to the track, they will have warmed out of it before they get there without the trainer ever knowing the warning sign existed. This is one of the reasons, as I explained earlier, that my assistant trainers and I do as much of the jogging as we can.

The first sign of knee trouble is when a colt starts to arc the foot outward on the side where he is hurting. That is, he begins to put all his weight on the inside heel of the foot and arcs the sore leg outward as he walks. He will walk around the stall this way and will jog in the same manner. When he first starts up on the track, he will not be going straight but will be edging off to one side or the other. When you train him, he will be landing on the inside heel of the foot on the sore side and the shoe will soon begin to show wear in this area. A knee does not have to appear puffy or give other outward indications of trouble at this stage, although some puffiness, however slight, is usually visible on close examination.

When I spot these symptoms, I use a knee paint that is stronger than a regular leg paint because the skin around the knee is much thicker and it requires a stronger paint to get through it and do the job properly. When you paint a knee, it might blow up quite a bit the first few days, but that is actually a good sign because it shows that you are getting something done with the paint.

It is not necessary to lay up a colt like this unless he is actually lame. You can go right on and train him as usual. He will be a little stiff when you start him up but will work out of it quickly. Of course, if he does not work out of it, the best and only policy is to stop with him right away and X-ray the knee. There may be more there than meets the eye.

A horse's tail will usually give you the first inkling that unsoundness is developing behind. This applies to all hind end trouble including curbs, hocks and stifles. The colt will tell you there is something wrong by starting to carry his tail stiff. He will begin holding his tail very rigid and usually a slight kink will develop. Once again, you have to know your colt because some of them tend naturally to carry their tails stiff and you should be familiar with their normal bearing in this respect.

Another sign is when a colt starts knuckling over behind and this is especially indicative of stifle trouble. If the trouble is going to develop on the left side, the colt will then usually start edging over toward the right side of the cart. These are all signs of unsoundness developing behind. The one to watch for because it is usually the very first is the rigid tail that begins to show a kink.

Now I am ready to beat 2:35 with my advanced set of colts (week of Feb. 1, Chart No. 1) and I am going to start training them three trips instead of two. This stage goes on for about a month until I reach the 2:25 level.

The way I go my three trips is the first one in 2:50, the second in 2:40 and the third or fastest trip at the level where I have decided to drop the colt. This might be 2:33 or 2:32 the first week and around 2:30 the next week.

I am also going my Monday and Thursday trips alike as to the fastest mile. If my fastest mile on Monday is 2:32, my fastest Thursday mile is also 2:32. This way I am keeping my colt up to something and I am making him a little stronger and tougher. After all, 2:35 isn't very fast and the more miles like that you can get into your colt the better off you are.

When I am working my colts twice a week, as I am at this stage, I jog them three miles a day on the days off, that is Tuesday, Wednesday, Friday and Saturday for the Monday-Thursday set I have been writing about.

I know some trainers will jog four miles the day before they are scheduled to work and only two miles the day after they work. But I find that at Pompano Park, where I train, you are better off to go three every day.

The reason for that is that if you jog a colt four miles at Pompano you are getting him almost as hot as if you'd worked him and if you do that twice a week there are actually four days a week that he is getting lathered up pretty good. They have to be cooled out just about as much after a four-mile jog as they do after a workout. I find that three miles does not get them nearly as hot and that there is all the difference in the world between three and four. This applies even though we get our joggers out early in the morning before it is too hot.

On training days, I will jog my colts three miles before I go my first trip if I am training two heats and cut it back to two miles when I start to go three heats around the first of February. This is only a general rule and might vary according to the individual horse or even weather conditions. For instance, I might jog a gross horse an extra mile or I might go an extra mile on a raw, chilly day. Depending on how many heats I am training on a day like that, I might go three or four jog miles instead of two or three.

The technique of cooling a horse out is also an important one, especially at Pompano. I have two horses to a groom and if the boys do their jobs right they are busy all day long. I try to spend some extra time explaining to them the importance of cooling a colt out thoroughly.

After I work a colt, I have found that he can't be properly cooled out in less than an hour and actually I think it takes longer than that. Even though the weather is hot and they have maybe one or two coolers on, they will dry out very fast while they are walking if you don't watch them. In fact, they sometimes dry out too fast. I always try to make sure they are well cooled out before the blankets are removed. There is usually a little draft down there and as everybody knows there is nothing worse than a draft on a hot horse.

In cooling a horse out, it is my policy, and the policy of most trainers, to have the groom offer the horse a half-dozen mouthfuls of water at ten-minute intervals. Usually after about an hour or an hour and fifteen minutes, the horse will refuse the water. If he has stopped blowing and his skin is dry and cool beneath the blanket, I usually have the groom make a few extra turns and offer him water again to be sure he doesn't want any and then I consider him cooled out.

This watering out process can get real tricky. I have seen horses that wouldn't take any water at all while they were being cooled out. You have to watch this kind very carefully. They can go back in the stall and be considered cooled out after the usual time has passed and they have stopped blowing and feel cool and dry. But where you can get into trouble is by putting a pail of water in this horse's stall. I have seen them go back to the stall, take a mouthful of hay and then walk over and drink a full bucket of water. This is how you get foundered horses.

In a case like this, the groom has to water the horse out in the stall. He doesn't put a bucket in the stall but offers the horse several mouthfuls at a time at the usual ten minute intervals. Usually this type of horse will drink in this manner after he is back in the stall. He still has to be watered out by degrees. It makes the groom's job a little more difficult, but it is worth the effort.

And then there are the horses that act like they never want to stop drinking while they are being cooled out. They just keep drinking water and after you have walked them for an hour and a half they are still thirsty. With this kind, I usually start giving them a larger quantity of water after about an hour and fifteen minutes. I stick to the 10-minute interval but give them more at a time. You can usually water them out quickly after that. However, I have seen days—those real hot days at Springfield or Du Quoin—when it took two to two and one-half hours to cool out a horse like this.

In order to be cooled out properly, a horse in my stable must refuse water and his body must feel both dry and cool to the touch. I do not consider that a horse is cooled out properly unless each of these requirements is met.

I know there is a lot of talk to the effect that we spend too much time cooling our horses out and I am aware that my good friend Curly Smart is advising in another chapter of this book that it is not necessary to spend as much time cooling a horse out as we do. I have a great deal of respect for Curly and his opinions because everybody knows he is one of the country's master horsemen. But I am afraid I would not want to take the chance.

I also know that the foreigners don't spend nearly as much time cooling a horse out as we do and that some of them don't really cool them out at all. To tell the truth, I am amazed that they get away with it. I am sure that if I tried this way I'd probably founder everything in the barn the first week. I think one of the reasons they are successful is that their horses are accustomed to it and have known nothing else since they entered training. It may be an area in which we can improve our methods, but I don't want to be the one doing the experimenting.

One of the big problems you run into in cooling a horse out is that some of them, especially when the weather is real hot, will "bake" out before they cool out. That is, their body will feel completely dry but when you run your hand over them they will feel "hot dry" instead of "cool dry."

Many horses of this type will have refused water, indicating that they are cooled out. In fact, the ones that water out real easy are the ones that usually bake out. But you can tell that they are not cooled out because they feel hot to the touch and invariably they are still blowing. What you must do with a horse like this is take him back in the stall and go over his whole body lightly with a cold water sponge, just enough to dampen the hair. Then you cover him up and you will find that he will break out and start to sweat again. He will then cool out normally.

Now let me get back to my colts that have moved in easy stages from 2:35 to 2:25. The pacers are probably doing this a little easier than the trotters because you don't have to be quite so careful with them to keep them on gait. But there is no reason to think that just because they are doing it easier you should move on with them. As a matter of fact, when my colts get to 2:25, I ease up on them a little and go at that notch for about three weeks.

At the same time, I start going a "fast" workout and a "slow" workout. I try to schedule my fast work early in the week and the slow work late in the week. This gives my colts an extra day of rest before their fast work. However, I don't consider this a vital thing and you will usually find that sickness, lameness, and track conditions cause the "fast" work day to be juggled back and forth during the lengthy training period from November to May. When I start to do this, the fast work is completed with a mile in 2:25 and the fastest mile in the slow workout is maybe three seconds slower or something like 2:28.

At this stage, I am getting down into another danger area where, if I go a little too much with some colts, it will start to affect their manners, disposition and general condition. So I sit there and drill at the 2:25 level for about three weeks.

I remember the year Race Time was a 2-year-old. I held him at the 2:25 level for the longest time. He wasn't exactly the soundest colt in the world—he had a knee problem as most horsemen know—and I was kind of holding my breath with him. I wanted to get a lot of good miles in him, miles that would leg him up and toughen him up before I went on.

I was training with another fellow and he had a nice colt, too. We kept going in 2:25 with a couple of colts that could easily go in 2:15 or maybe even 2:12, because they were just jogging where we were training them. One day the other trainer looked over at me and said, "Say, do you suppose we'll ever beat 2:25 or are we just going to stay here all summer?" I had to laugh because maybe it did look a little silly, but I knew that Race Time needed those extra miles and I like to think maybe this was one of the things that helped make him the horse he turned out to be.

I don't mean to say that I train every mile at exactly 2:25. I might go the mile in 2:26 and maybe come the last eighth in 16 or 17 seconds, instead of going a mile in 2:25 and coming a last eighth in :15. That kind of an eighth is probably more than my colt would want and he might get bad-gaited going there. I don't want any of that at this stage.

I would sooner miss a second on my watch and have the colt do it right. Maybe I'll get down to the half a little quick and, if I do, I will come my mile in 2:23 or 2:24 rather than try to back the colt up the last end. Slowing at the end is a bad thing to do with colts. They should always be going on in that last sixteenth. If they get in the habit of doing this, they will try a little harder for you when they begin racing.

When Speedy Scot was a 2-year-old and going in 2:25, I am sure that he could have gone just as easily in 2:15. He was a big strong colt and had a great way of going. But I kept him at 2:25 for his own good. Even though he looked big and strong he was still a baby and his bones hadn't developed. This applies to any colt. Some are more developed than others physically but their bones still aren't hard and the longer you keep the pressure off them the better chance you have of getting them to the races.

That's what I think, and that's why I spend a lot of time around 2:25. I am waiting for the colt to develop and harden up so that when I do drop him he will drop easily. That way I don't get a lot of sore muscles and I know my colts are better off.

I want to mention again the importance of teaching a colt to brush but not tip-toeing him at any stage. I let my colts brush a little even on the end of their slowest miles. It is important to develop the habit of making the last end of any mile a little quicker, even if it is a slow mile. They'll soon learn that you expect them to do this and won't cause trouble for you later on. You won't have to be hitting them and knocking them around to get them to move out at the end.

What I usually do is reach up about the eighth pole and tap them and speak to them at the same time, just enough to wake them up and let them know that when I do speak it is the signal to move on. Maybe you won't even have to tap them every time. Possibly all you will have to do after you've touched them a few times and spoken at the same time is to speak to them from then on to get them to move out.

As I reach the 2:25 level, I am also starting to teach my colts to brush the last quarter a little, maybe in 33 or 34 seconds. But when I start doing this, I never, never put them on their toes, even for an eighth of a mile. Everything they do has to be well within them or I won't let them do it or ask them to do it.

I never try to see how fast a colt can go an eighth of a mile. If you do, you are liable to get a really generous response from your colt, especially a good willing one, but you're not accomplishing a single thing by doing it. People talk about making speed, but I find that speed will come as a natural result if they are trained progressively.

If you ask for a real fast eighth from your colt, you are putting a terrific strain on him. An eighth doesn't sound far, but when they are going all they can go they are really straining themselves. The longer you can hold off doing this the longer your colt will last. Now and then everyone misjudges a colt and thinks he is up to more than he really is. It always makes me feel bad to see a colt get tired and stop a little in the last eighth.

I make it a practice to train my colts in sets of three. It is a wonderful experience for them and teaches them a great deal. I like to train with one colt on top, one colt in behind him and the third on the outside. When we are going three heats, we switch the order of position each heat so that each colt trains in a different position each time. I think it is good for a colt to sit on the outside for a mile. They have to learn some time in their lives that even though they are going the long route they have to keep up and go on. It is good for them as long as they are being trained within their limits. It also keeps them from thinking that the rail is the only place to go.

I don't work my colts right in tight against the rail. If you always work them along the rail, you will find that after they get to the races they think they belong at the rail and if you are parked out they will be inclined to bear in with you and try to get next to the rail. Obviously, this can get you in trouble. When my colts get to the races, they know what it is like to be parked out.

After I have been sitting for about three weeks at the 2:25 level, I will start to move my colts on down. I am heading for 2:15 now and there is still a lot to be done. I will drop from 2:25 to 2:22 and then somewhere in the next two or three weeks, depending on the individual colt, I will pass the 2:20 barrier. I say pass 2:20 because I've never worked a colt in 2:20 in my life. I always work one in 2:21 or 2:19. Fred Egan told me years ago that he never worked one in 2:20 because about half of them will stop right there. He always went in either 2:21 or 2:19 and so do I. I know it's just a superstition but I still do it.

At about the time I reach this stage (week of March 29, Chart No. 1) I begin to work my colts four trips. I know a lot of trainers don't go four trips any more, but I think it is good for a colt and I continue to do it. A lot of my colts have to race heats and I think the extra trip helps them in this respect.

But even if I were training 2-year-olds that were only going to race one dash, I believe I would still go four trips. These colts can go the second heat of a race just as fast or faster than the first, so they have to have just as much muscle strength in their legs to go that dash as they would if they went that second heat.

From 2:19 (or 2:20 for anybody else) to within about a month of a colt's first race, a period of about three weeks, I will use the fourth heat as a cooling out heat on my "fast" work day with the third heat being my fastest one. I will go my first mile in 2:50, my second in 2:35, my third in 2:19 and my fourth mile will be around 2:25.

By scheduling the heats in this manner, I am assured that my colt is good and fresh for his fast mile, which is the third one. If the fourth heat was my fastest at this stage, the colt might get a little tired on the end of his fast mile, which is actually when I want him at his best. What I am doing in this fourth heat is putting legs under my colt. It isn't too fast for him but it is muscling him up and laying the foundation that a stake colt has to have.

The fourth heat, when I introduce it at this stage and when I make it my fastest training trip a little later on, tends to take the edge off colts at the same time that it lays a foundation. Colts that are going four trips don't want to buck and play as much while they are warming up. They are still fresh and vigorous but they are more settled in their ways. I think they are better off by being stronger from going four training trips.

I am sure a colt would go just as fast if he was only trained three trips, but I think he would have to strain himself harder to do it than the colt that has been trained four trips and is tighter and toughened up more. In other words, I believe the fourth heat provides the foundation for the strength and stamina that a stake colt needs.

The way I feel about it is that when you are ready to really put a strain on them, that is, ready to race them against other stake horses, they are better off if they have the edge knocked off them a little, but with plenty of legs under them where they can't get hurt that way. They may not look quite as quick because they won't be quite as fresh, but after they race a week or so they will start going on like good horses should because you have built a solid foundation under them.

Now we have gradually moved on down to 2:15 and the men are pretty well separated from the boys. Some colts have already been turned out, others are lagging behind and probably aren't going to make it, others are unsound and you are left with the cream of the crop, so to speak. You may soon find out that your cream isn't quite good enough, but that's what horse racing is all about.

At this stage, I start moving the colts out and going faster halves. I also start brushing them over to the eighth and teaching them to leave a little.

Maybe I'll brush a colt away from the wire pretty good and then back him off, planning to reach the half in 1:10. I might go the first eighth in 16 seconds and the quarter in 33 seconds. Then I would go a slow second quarter in 37 seconds. From there, I will come my last half in 1:05. When I first start going halves in 1:05 I will go both quarters pretty much alike. In that way, I'm giving my colt a pretty good workout, but I'm not putting too much strain on him in either of the last two quarters.

My third heat is still my fastest one. I go in 2:50, drop the second mile to 2:30, go my mile in 2:15 and then come back with a fourth mile in 2:25. This last one is still my "leg and muscle builder."

This might be a good time to go through a full week of training (week of April 12th on Chart No. 1) so that you will understand exactly what I am doing and how I am doing it. I have just worked the colt in 2:15 on a Monday according to the pattern in the preceding paragraph.

On Tuesday and Wednesday this colt will jog three miles.

On Thursday, I will go four trips with him, the last two pretty much alike, let's say 2:23. The first trip would have been in 2:50 and the second in 2:35. The last two miles were pretty evenly rated, except that I brushed the colt just a little away from the wire and again coming home. On Friday and Saturday the colt jogged three miles a day. He rests on Sunday and now he is ready for his fast work again on Monday.

During this period, I am working on sharpening up his racing reflexes by brushing him pretty good eighths and I am gradually reducing the final quarter. I am pretty well content to race him off a mile in 2:12 with a last quarter in 31 seconds.

Now we are within a month of the colt's racing debut and the following week I switch my third and fourth trips, making the fourth trip the fastest one. The colt has been going four trips for about a month now and he is legged up pretty good and is fresh for the last mile so that I am no longer afraid to make that my fastest one.

While I am going four trips with these colts, I want to explain that it doesn't mean that they have to go four trips week in and week out. At this stage, some colts, even the top ones, may start to show signs of getting a little dull and tired and if one starts acting like this you have to use your own judgment and maybe cut out the fourth trip and only go three. At the same time, you might only walk the colt the day after his fast work instead of jogging him. The main thing is that at this time of year you want your colt fresh and eager in all his training miles. He has a long season ahead of him and he has to race heats so you don't want to wear him out. You want him fresh so that his work always appears easy for him.

When I say I want my colts "fresh and eager," I don't mean to imply that this is indicated by a colt that has his tail up over his back and is bucking and playing around when you warm him up. As I said before, my fourth heat is intended to take this kind of edge off a colt. Where I want him "fresh and eager" is during the training miles themselves. There is a big difference between the two.

In actual practice, I find that the initial signs that a colt is getting a little tired or dull will not show up in his training miles at all. By this time, all the colts are getting keyed up a little and they will go on whether they are tired or not. Most of the time

I will pick this up by the way they look or the way they stand around in the stall. If I am beginning to overdo things with a particular colt, he will start to tuck up and maybe begin backing away from the feed tub. So I always look for the initial signs of dullness off the track rather than on it. At this stage, I don't want a colt to look stodgy and dull as if he'd been at the races six months instead of still getting ready. The time to catch a colt like this and to ease up on him is when he shows these off-track signs and before it begins to show up in his work, as it will eventually if you don't back off a little.

Some horses just naturally require more or less training than others. The only way you can find out is by experience and by watching the signs such as physical condition and feeding habits. A lot of times a big stout horse doesn't need as much training as a little frail horse.

If I run across a colt that is the least bit chicken-hearted, I will always train him harder than an ordinary horse. As soon as a horse like this gets the least bit tired he will simply quit on you. You have to have a horse like this real tight so that he never gets that tired feeling. He really has to have legs under him. This means plenty of training for him.

By now I have gradually worked my top colts down to 2:12 with a last quarter in 31 seconds as shown on Chart No. 1. They are now ready to race.

Before the race, I will usually warm my colt up three heats, but again that depends on the individual. I try to warm them up just enough to take the edge off them. Usually three trips does this and when they get in behind the gate they have their mind on their business instead of watching the other horses and things like that. You will also find that if you take the edge off in warming them up they aren't nearly as likely to become frightened by every little thing they see. I go my first trip in 2:50, the second in 2:35 and the last one in 2:25.

If I am warming up a very nervous horse or a frail little filly, I might go only two warmup trips instead of three. In that case, I would go the first trip in 2:50 and the second around 2:30 or maybe a shade faster.

Later on, I would be going my third warmup trip quite a bit faster than I am here at the beginning of the season. A good rugged colt racing two heats on the Grand Circuit would go his last trip around 2:16 or 2:17 to get the edge off him. I would probably brush him the last eighth around 16 seconds. Others might warm up a little slower than that. I would jog the horse two miles before I went my first warmup heat.

I would like it if that first race went around 2:10. But I have found that it usually goes around 2:08 and sometimes faster than that. I usually open my season at Lexington over the mile track and I remember very well the year Speedy Scot was a 2-year-old.

He won in 2:06 the first time he started. He had only been in 2:12 and I was scared to death. They have races exclusively for 2-year-olds at Lexington now but in those days you had to race your colts against aged horses and you could never tell what you might run into. I didn't start him after that for several weeks because I was afraid he might get the idea he could beat those aged horses every time and keep going all he could. I got by with it all right that time, but I'd never try it again. It was all those slow miles around 2:25 that helped hold him together for that 2:06 mile.

Anyway, our colt makes his first start off a mile in 2:12 and the race goes in 2:08. He races well and finishes third, even though he got charged up and came that last quarter and eighth more than I wanted. His last quarter was in :30⅖ and the last eighth in 15 seconds flat.

I sat in the hole with him most of the way and then let him ramble a little through the stretch. I would have preferred to have gone in 2:10 but he was keyed up and wanted to move on a little so I let him. Even though I went two seconds more than I wanted, I knew he had plenty of foundation miles in him and that it wouldn't hurt him any.

Let's say I raced this colt on Tuesday night. Now let's take him through the following week leading up to a race the next Tuesday night. On Wednesday morning he was walked for about 30 minutes. I don't walk them too long, just enough to let them know they have been out of the barn and to limber them up a little. Once they know they have been out of the stall for the day they won't stand around at the door waiting for you to hook them. They will be more inclined to lie down and rest and even go to sleep, which is good for them.

On Thursday I will jog the colt either three or four miles. I won't do any more than I have to, I want the colt fresh and feeling good. If he is still fresh and up on his toes at the end of the three miles I will go four. Otherwise, three is enough.

On Friday I will train him. How I train him depends on a number of things. If he raced well, acted real sharp and I think a good mile might not hurt him, I might go my fastest mile in 2:17. I'll probably be training him four heats although, as I said before, this depends on the horse. My first three miles would be in 2:50, 2:40 and 2:30. All miles would be evenly rated.

On the other hand, if the colt hadn't raced up to my expectations and if I thought he might be better if I let up on him between races I would try that. If I had been working him in 2:17 or 2:18 on his slow work day, maybe I'd be content to go a couple of miles around 2:25 which would just be some good leg work for him and might freshen him up. The first two miles would be in 2:50 and 2:35. This would be a nice, easy workout with no brush work and I would just be trying to keep his muscles toned up and his legs under him.

How much or how little to train a colt between races is a matter that only a competent horse trainer in full possession of all the facts concerning a particular colt is qualified to determine. It depends to a great extent on how the colt has been racing. He might need faster or slower workouts between races or more or fewer heats. I have provided a couple of simple examples but in the final analysis it is strictly a judgment matter and it is impossible for me or anybody else to prescribe a specific pattern for a particular horse.

There is one thing that I know for sure: The quickest way for a trainer to get in a rut is to start training every colt exactly alike between races. It simply won't work. You'll never know whether you're getting the best out of your colt unless you move around and try different things. And the time to start trying something else is when he hasn't responded in a race the way you think he should have and there is no other reason you can think of that would cause it.

On Saturday, our colt that raced the preceding Tuesday would be jogged three miles. I wouldn't go four because he had been worked the day before. On Sunday he would either spend the day in the stall or he might get out for a little walk.

On Monday, I would jog him four miles. I would do this whether his Tuesday race was scheduled for afternoon or evening. In either event, it is going to be more than 24 hours before anything is done with him again and the extra mile will be good for him.

Tuesday is race day and sometimes I think horses can read the overnight sheet and know it as well as I do. I don't know how, but some of them seem to have a sixth sense about it and they get worried and keyed up. It is a policy in my stable to walk almost all horses on the morning of the day they race. It gives them a little relaxation and in many cases it makes them think the day's work is done and they will settle down in the stall. I don't walk them for more than 30 minutes and usually not that long. With a horse that appears especially worried and upset, I will even put the harness on him and jog him a real slow mile to try to fool him and make him think it's just a normal day.

In exhibiting these "race day" symptoms, some horses will back off their feed while others will just mope around in the stall. The funny thing is that it isn't necessarily the naturally nervous horses that act this way. Even usually well-mannered horses can become affected. They seem to know they are going to race and for some reason it bothers them. I guess it is like the fellow who knows he has to make a speech that night and gets worked up about it. And like the fellow with the speech facing him, these colts are all right once they get on the track and the starter says "Go." It's the waiting that bothers them.

I have had horses that I took out and jogged and then even walked for a few minutes afterward to make them think they were being cooled out. But they still knew better and wouldn't touch their feed no matter how hard I tried to make it appear an ordinary day. A funny thing about this is that in my stable top horses were never affected. Horses like Speedy Scot, Dartmouth, Race Time and others of that caliber never got worked up in advance on race day.

Since I have mentioned that this pre-race tension can affect feeding habits, let me review the feeding practices followed in my stable on race day. The colt we are going to race that night gets his normal feed in the morning and all the hay he wants throughout the day unless he is one of those that gorges himself. If that is the case, I would take his hay away around noon.

The colt gets his normal noon time grain ration and a half

feed at about five o'clock, which is regular feeding time. If he is in an early race he will get the half feed about 4:30. After he races and is cooled out, he gets a full feed. This consists of a bran mash and whatever other supplements you want to put with it.

If the colt is going to race in the afternoon, he usually stays on a regular feeding schedule. He would get his morning feed and even his usual noon time feed because he won't be getting that extra feed that the one racing at night gets. Actually, a colt like this is racing between meals.

While I am on the subject of feeding, let me review my program in a general way even though it is being covered in detail elsewhere. In the beginning, I feed twice a day at 5 a.m. and 4:30 p.m., keeping them off the noon time feed as long as I can. This helps a great deal when you have so many colts on the go. Sometimes you won't get a colt cooled out until after 1:30 and it might be 2 p.m. before he got fed. Then he would have another feed coming up at too close an interval.

As soon as my colts reach the 2:35 level and start going three trips, I begin to give them a little grain at noon and back the evening feeding time up to 5 p.m. At first I only give them about a half feed at noon and then work it up to a full feed when they start to go four trips.

On a twice-a-day feeding schedule, my colts get three quarts of oats in the morning with a pellet supplement mixed in. In the evening, I feed a mash made up of three quarts of oats, some bran and a little blood tonic. The noon feed, when I go to it, consists of a quart and a half of oats which I gradually build up to three quarts for those that will eat that much.

Once in a while I will get a colt that isn't a "good doer" and I will usually feed this kind four times a day. I don't give them any more but I spread it out so they don't have too much at any one time. It's usually the fillies that will be this way, although some colts will also.

Now my colt is ready to make his second start and I will soon know whether he is any stock or not. Some of them will fool me by not measuring up when the going gets tough while others will suddenly catch on to the hang of things and come real fast.

I am not going to attempt to carry a training schedule for 2-year-olds any further than this. The colt is at the races and from that time on every trainer has to be on his own.

Probably the main thing you should be on the lookout for as your colt races his way through a tough stakes campaign is that he doesn't start to tail off and get a little dull. You will notice this most in the latter part of the mile. At this stage of the season, all colts have reached a point where they will really boil away from the gate and that won't tell you anything. But if you notice that a colt is beginning to soften up a bit on the last end of it and doesn't seem to have his usual lick, then maybe it's time he had a little rest.

Usually there will be a week somewhere along the line that the colt doesn't have a stake and this is when you let up on him. Let's say you race on a Wednesday and your next race is exactly two weeks away. What I do is jog this colt every day except one during that two-week period, Sundays excluded. I would only train him once and that would be on the Wednesday between his two races. And I wouldn't train him too fast, either, maybe three trips with the fastest around 2:25.

On the other days I would jog him lightly, say two miles the first couple of days and three miles thereafter except the day before his work, when I would jog him four. I would also try to get him out to jog early in the morning before it got too hot. Even though you're easing up on the colt, he'll feel better than if he stood around in the stall and that wouldn't be doing him any good anyway. What you actually have done here is to eliminate two slow works and substituted a relatively slow work on what would normally have been his race day. A program like this will often freshen a horse up and restore his finishing lick.

Another good thing for a horse like this is to give him as much grass as possible. Green grass seems to freshen a horse up and cool him out inside. The best time to grass them is the day after they've raced, if they're racing at night, or in the afternoon while cooling them out if they are racing then. Just take them out and give them 30 to 45 minutes on the grass. It really helps them.

I think I have covered about everything with the possible exception of the procedures to be followed in the event you lose one or more training sessions, either because of weather or a brief spell of sickness. This is an important area and I want to devote some space to it in closing.

If you miss a workout because of track conditions, the best

policy is to train the following day and adjust your schedule accordingly for the remainder of the week. By that, I mean if you are rained out on Monday, train as usual on Tuesday and set your Thursday training session back to Friday. The only other change I would make under these circumstances is that I would probably jog my colt an extra mile before training him on Tuesday and possibly a little stiffer than usual.

Now, let's say a trainer is rained out for an entire week and that he is able to do nothing more than jog his colt during that period. To make it easier to follow, let's assume that this has happened and that I have lost the week of April 19th on Chart No. 1. My colt had been in 2:15 for the first time the week before and was scheduled to work in 2:15 again on his "fast" day of the week that was rained out.

On the Monday following the rained out week, I would give my colt an "in between" work of 2:20, which is neither as fast as his usual "fast" work nor as slow as his usual "slow" work. This trip in 2:20 is designed to get my colt back into the training routine as smoothly as possible without either taking too much out of him after the layoff or going so slow that he will not regain any of the lost ground. On Thursday, I would train right back in 2:15 and go on from there. I would figure that the week off had not hurt my colt a bit and that it actually might have been quite beneficial to him in the respect that it would have freshened him up a little.

Sickness is the other factor, in addition to weather and unsoundness, that can interfere with a regular training schedule. This is quite common, actually, since most colts will come up with some kind of a virus bug some time during their training program. For the sake of discussion, let's say I have a colt that shows up with a temperature on Monday morning of the same week (April 19th) on the training chart.

The temperature stays with the colt for three straight days and breaks on the fourth day, which is Thursday. The colt has not left his stall from Monday through Thursday and I cannot over-emphasize the importance of such a colt being laid up. A colt that is running a temperature should not even be jogged, let alone trained. I think every good horseman is aware of that.

The colt's temperature is normal on Thursday night and again on Friday morning. I jog the colt three easy miles on Friday and take his temperature when he returns to the stall and throughout the remainder of the day, maybe as often as at noon, in the early evening and again late at night. If the temperature stays down, I jog the colt three miles again on Saturday and keep checking the temperature the same way. If it remains normal, I will assume the colt is ready to return to his regular training schedule Monday morning.

On Monday, I will work the colt in 2:30, which is plenty for one that has only been jogged two of the past seven days. At the same time, I will only go three training heats even though my regular schedule calls for four. Four heats is just a little too rough for the first day back. On Thursday, if the colt acts cheerful and seems like his old self, I will train him between 2:20 and 2:25 and will return to my four-heat schedule.

On the following Monday, I would train my fastest mile in 2:18 and then on Thursday, instead of scheduling the usual slow workout, I would train a mile in 2:15, which is where the colt was before he got sick. This would result in two "fast" works the same week, but I would feel the colt was up to it because of the foundation miles I had already put in him, and for that reason the extra "fast" work would not concern me. On the following Monday I would schedule my usual "slow" work and follow it up with the regular "fast" work on Thursday. Thus, I would be back on a normal schedule although my "fast" work would now be on Thursday instead of Monday. As I said earlier, the day of the week in which the "fast" work is scheduled is not a really vital factor.

That just about brings me to the end of the line. Whether your 2-year-old is going to be a top colt, a champion, depends to a very great extent—in addition to his natural ability, of course, over which no trainer has any control—on what you did with him from the time you broke him until he made his first start. If you laid the proper foundation and resisted the temptation to do too much with him just because he was obviously precocious and could do it, you may have made yourself a stake colt right there.

The stakes you win in August and September can almost invariably be traced back to the little things you did properly or, even more important, the foolish things you refrained from doing back in February and March. That's where the colt champions are made. The man who makes them is the man who has skill, patience and a lot of luck.

TRAINING SCHEDULE

(For southern-trained 2-year-olds on mile track)

DATE Week of	MONDAY	TUESDAY	WEDNESDAY	THURSDAY	FRIDAY	SATURDAY
Oct. 12	J3	J3	J3	J3	J3	J3
Oct. 19	J3	J3	J3	J3	J3	J3
Oct. 26	J3	J3	J3	J3	J3	J3
Nov. 2	J3	J3	J3	J3	J3	J3
Nov. 9	J3	J3	J3	J3	J3	J3
Nov. 16	J3 3:20	J3	J3 3:20	J3	J3 3:15	J3
Nov. 23	J3 3:15	J3	J3 3:10	J3	J3 3:05	J3
Nov. 30	J3 3:05	J3	J3 3:00	J3	J3 2:55	J3
Dec. 7	J3 2:55	J3	J3 2:50	J3	J3 2:50	J3
Dec. 14	J3 2:50 2:50	J3	J3	J3 2:50 2:50	J3	J3
Dec. 21	J3 2:50 2:47	J3	J3	J3 2:50 2:47	J3	J3
Dec. 28	J3 2:50 2:45	J3	J3	J3 2:50 2:45	J3	J3
Jan. 4	J3 2:50 2:42	J3	J3	J3 2:50 2:42	J3	J3
Jan. 11	J3 2:50 2:40	J3	J3	J3 2:50 2:40	J3	J3
Jan. 18	J3 2:50 2:37	J3	J3	J3 2:50 2:37	J3	J3
Jan. 25	J3 2:50 2:35	J3	J3	J3 2:50 2:35	J3	J3
Feb. 1	J2 2:50 2:40 2:32	J3	J3	J2 2:50 2:40 2:32	J3	J3
Feb. 8	J2 2:50 2:40 2:30	J3	J3	J2 2:50 2:40 2:30	J3	J3
Feb. 15	J2 2:50 2:40 2:27	J3	J3	J2 2:50 2:40 2:27	J3	J3
Feb. 22	J2 2:50 2:40 2:25	J3	J3	J2 2:50 2:40 2:27	J3	J3

DATE Week of	MONDAY	TUESDAY	WEDNESDAY	THURSDAY	FRIDAY	SATURDAY
March 1	J2 2:50 2:40 2:25	J3	J3	J2 2:50 2:40 2:28	J3	J3
March 8	J2 2:50 2:40 2:25-1:10- 34-17	J3	J3	J2 2:50 2:40 2:28	J3	J3
March 15	J2 2:50 2:40 2:23-1:10- 34-17	J3	J3	J2 2:50 2:40 2:26	J3	J3
March 22	J2 2:50 2:35 2:21-1:07- 33.3-16	J3	J3	J2 2:50 2:35 2:25	J3	J3
March 29	J2 2:50 2:35 2:19-1:06- 33.2-16 2:25	J3	J3	J2 2:50 2:35 2:25 2:25	J3	J3
April 5	J2-3 2:50 2:35 2:17-1:06- 33-16 2:25	J3	J3	J2-3 2:50 2:35 2:25 2:25	J3	J3
April 12	J2-3 2:50 2:30 2:15-1:05- 32-16 2:25	J3	J3	J2-3 2:50 2:35 2:23 2:23	J3	J3
April 19	J2-3 2:50 2:30 2:25 2:15-1:05- 32-16	J3	J3	J2-3 2:50 2:35 2:23 2:23	J3	J3
April 26	J2-3 2:50 2:30 2:25 2:14-1:05- 32-15.3	J3	J3	J2-3 2:50 2:35 2:21 2:21	J3	J3
May 3	J2-3 2:50 2:35 2:25 2:13-1:04- 32-15.2	J3	J3	J2-3 2:50 2:35 2:21 2:21	J3	J3
May 10	J2-3 2:50 2:35 2:25 2:12-1:04- 31-15	J3	J3	J2-3 2:50 2:35 2:19 2:19	J3	J3

TRAINING SCHEDULE

(For northern-trained 2-year-olds on half-mile track)
(Actual schedule followed by Bonjour Hanover as 2-year-old)

DATE Week of	MONDAY	TUESDAY	WEDNESDAY	THURSDAY	FRIDAY	SATURDAY
Nov. 16	J1½	J1½	J1½	J1½	J1½	J1½
Nov. 23	J2	J2	J2	J2	J2	J2
Nov. 30	J2½	J2½	J2½	J2½	J2½	J2½
Dec. 7	J3	J3	J3	J3	J3	J3
Dec. 14	J2 3:30	J3	J2 3:20	J3	J2 3:10	J3
Dec. 21	J2 3:00	J3	J2 3:00	J3	J2 3:00	J3
Dec. 28	J2 2:55	J3	J3	J2 2:55	J3	J3
Jan. 4	J2 2:50	J3	J3	J2 2:50-40	J3	J3
Jan. 11	J2 2:50	J3	J3	J2 2:47-18	J3	J3
Jan. 18	J2 2:45	J3	J3	J2 2:45 2:43-38-18	J3	J3
Jan. 25	J2 2:55 2:42	J3	J3	J2 2:55 2:40-36-17	J3	J3
Feb. 1	J2 2:55 2:40	J3	J3	J2 °2:50	J3	J3
Feb. 8	J2 2:55 2:37-35-17	J3	J3	J2 2:55 2:45	J3	J3
Feb. 15	J2 2:55 2:35-35-17	J3	J3	J2 2:55 2:45	J3	J3
Feb. 22	J2 2:55 2:35-35-17	J3	J3	J2 2:55 2:40	J3	J3
March 1	J2 2:55 2:32-34-16.2	J3	J3	J2 2:55 2:40	J3	J3
March 8	J2 2:55 2:40 2:30-34-16.2	J3	J3	J2 2:55 2:40	J3	J3
March 15	J2 2:55 2:40 2:30	J3	J3	J2 2:55 2:40	J3	J3
March 22	J2 2:55 2:40 2:27-33	J3	J3	J2 2:55 2:35	J3	J3

DATE Week of	MONDAY	TUESDAY	WEDNESDAY	THURSDAY	FRIDAY	SATURDAY
March 29	J2 2:55 2:35 2:25-33-16	J3	J3	J2 2:55 2:35	J3	J3
April 5	J2 2:55 2:35 2:22-33-16	J3	J3	J3 ° °	J3	J3
April 12	J2 2:55 2:35 2:20-32-15.3	J3	J3	J2 2:55 2:35 2:30	J3	J3
April 19	J2 2:55 2:35 2:18-32-15.3	J3	J3	J2 2:55 2:35 2:30	J3	J3
April 26	J2 2:50 2:25 2:16-32-15.2	J3	J3	J3 ° °	J3	J3
May 3	J2 2:50 2:20 2:14-1:06-32	J3	J3	J2 2:50 2:30 2:25	J3	J3
May 10	J2 2:50 2:20 2:12-1:04-31	J3	J3	J2 2:50 2:30 2:25	J3	J3
May 17			RACE 2:45 2:20 Won in 2:09⅖h			

° Second mile is skipped, just for a change in routine.
°° Slow work is skipped to freshen horse up.

Each harness racing generation produces a limited number of horsemen who are recognized universally as superior "colt trainers," men who are especially proficient at the delicate art of gaiting, balancing and conditioning two and 3-year-old trotters and pacers. One who stands out in this category is Ralph N. Baldwin, head trainer for the vast Castleton Farm operation which campaigns principally on harness racing's Grand Circuit. In recent years his name has been linked with such Castleton champions as Speedy Scot, Race Time and Dartmouth, all of whom have graduated from Baldwin's stable to the stallion ranks at the home farm in Kentucky. Baldwin was born on  February 25, 1916 in Lloydminster, Saskatchewan, but his roots are not nearly as Canadian as his birth place would indicate, a fact which is little known in the sport. Actually, Ralph's father came from central Ohio where he farmed, raced harness horses and, among other things, operated a barber shop across the street from Ohio State University. In 1912 the elder Baldwin emigrated to Canada and Ralph was the only member of the family born in that country. He drove and won his first race at Dufferin Park, Toronto, in 1933 with a horse in his father's stable and has been a harness horseman ever since with time out for service as a U. S. Infantryman in Europe in World War II. He is also unique in that he has never operated a public stable. After he left his father, he worked privately for Art Sherrier in Wisconsin and was employed both by the Saunders Mills Stable and Two Gaits Farm before accepting the Castleton post in 1960. He was the nation's leading money-winning driver in 1948, topped the Grand Circuit list that same year and won the 1963 Hambletonian with Speedy Scot. He is consistently among the leading average drivers in the country and was voted Horseman of The Year in 1963.

5

TRAINING and CONDITIONING

STANLEY F. DANCER

I am a horse trainer rather than a public speaker and whenever I attend a banquet I duck the head table if I possibly can. But there are times when you have to respond to a presentation or something like that and can't get out of saying a few words. I recall an incident of this nature that happened several years ago.

This was an awards banquet for people in the sports world and I was among those at the head table. While I was sitting there trying to think of something to say that might be appropriate to the occasion, I glanced down the line and saw Ralph Houk, manager of the New York Yankees. I thought about him and about my friend Whitey Ford, who pitched for the Yankees, and I suddenly knew what I was going to say.

When my turn came, I got up and told the people that I sure wished harness racing was like baseball. Then I pointed out that whenever Ford got a little tired, Houk came out of the dugout, patted him on the shoulder and summoned a fresh pitcher to come in and save the day.

It was too bad, I said, that I couldn't do the same thing in harness racing. What I wouldn't give to be able to reach the three-quarter pole with a tiring horse and suddenly raise my hand and stop all the action while I took my horse off the track and replaced him with a nice fresh one for that drive to the wire.

Well, the people got a real kick out of that and it drew a big laugh. I was pleased with the reaction and driving home that night I thought about how it sure would be a great thing if I could only do in fact what I had described in jest.

But horse racing isn't like baseball—or football or basketball or any other sport for that matter. Substitutes are strictly prohibited once the action is under way. You have to play the whole "game" with the same horse and he'd better be in shape to go the full distance.

That's why the conditioning of horses plays such an important part in harness racing and why I am happy to be able to discuss it in a chapter of this book.

You can be the greatest driver in the world but if your horse isn't conditioned properly, if he isn't ready to go the distance demanded and be at his best in that last sixteenth of a mile, you might as well stay home. No amount of driving talent can convert an improperly trained horse into a winner.

I am going to write at length about conditioning programs for all types of horses. I have every kind in my stable. I have trotters and pacers; colts, fillies, and geldings; youngsters and aged stock; raceway horses that can't beat 2:05 and Grand Circuit stock than can better 1:58; sound horses, lame horses and some that are just race horse sound.

It takes all kinds to make up a stable like mine and I know a little something about every type. I'm going to try to pass on some of that knowledge and I am going to lay out specific training schedules for every type of horse except a 2-year-old. My good friend Ralph Baldwin, in my opinion one of the very best colt trainers our sport has ever known, is going to handle that end of it in another chapter while I concentrate on the remaining classes.

But first of all, even though I am going to be referring to them only in a general way, I want to say that I definitely prefer to train colts. There is just no feeling like the one you get when a horse you have selected, broken, and trained all his life goes on to win the big stakes in the two and 3-year-old divisions. As far as I am concerned there is nothing in the world that can equal this thrill.

People frequently ask me about my favorite horse and some of them seem surprised when I name Noble Victory rather than SuMac Lad. I think the world of SuMac Lad, who is retired now with earnings of more than $850,000, but I didn't break Sumie, I wasn't with him from the start.

On the other hand, I consider Noble Victory in the same light as my own children. He grew up in my house, so to speak, and consequently has a special place in my affections. I selected him as a yearling, bought him, broke him and trained him for Mr. K. D. Owen. A neighbor boy might come to live with me and I would treat him just as kindly as if he were my own child, but the feeling would never be quite the same. That's the way it is with a colt you break, train and race yourself.

I also don't think very much of the trend toward catch drivers for trotters and pacers. I hear it said that some day we will be like the running horse sport where a few top jockeys get all the mounts on the best horses. I hope that day never comes in harness racing and I know it never will for me.

I like to know my horses and to think that I should and do know every little thing my horse might do both in training and in a race. I think I know better than any catch driver how my horse should act behind the gate, how he should carry his head and how he should respond. I just don't feel that a catch driver, no matter how many times he drives a horse, can know as much about him. I think a man should train and drive his own horses unless his driving ability is so poor that he has to use someone else.

A man who is training a horse is the only one who can really know if the horse is rigged right. But a horse that is rigged just right for a trainer may not suit the man who is catch-driving and he might want to make changes that would not correspond with the trainer's thinking. This sometimes creates problems that affect the horse's racing efficiency. At the same time, there are a number of horses that do not act the same way in training and warming up as they do in races. Competition changes a horse's habits. A trainer who hires catch drivers has no way of knowing this and very often it results in he and the catch driver being on different wave lengths with respect to something that might be troubling the horse. If you are both the trainer and driver, you are alert to these subtle changes and can make the necessary adjustments that might be called for. Very often this can make the difference in winning and losing a race.

There is just no way that a catch driver can recommend ways to hang a horse up as a result of sitting behind him for two minutes and a few seconds. On the other hand, there is no way that a trainer can really understand what a catch driver is talking about when he tries to describe something that the horse is doing only in a race and not when he is being trained or warmed up. A lot of people think this is the coming thing in harness racing, but I'm sure not one of them.

Now that I have that out of my system, let me get back to my basic subject and say that the conditioning of a horse covers a lot of territory in addition to the actual time spent on the training track with him. It covers such things as turning a horse out properly, cooling him out the right way, the manner in which he is cared for between training heats and even the way he goes to the training track, enters it and so on.

On the track itself, there is more to it than just turning him around and going a mile at a certain speed. The factors that enter into the conditioning picture here include such things as jogging the horse properly, teaching him to turn, rating the mile the way you want it, and teaching horses to train in company and to follow a starting gate.

The human element, aside from the trainer himself, is also directly involved and one of the most important factors in the success of any racing stable is the quality of the caretakers. The best efforts of a leading trainer and a great horse can be completely wasted if a poor caretaker is involved. This is a continuing problem with all stables and for my part I am constantly on the lookout for sober, reliable young men who are genuinely interested in becoming grooms.

I have found that the best way to train a caretaker and to find out whether he can be expected to amount to anything is to put him alongside an experienced man who can teach him the ropes. Horses can be ruined by inexperienced caretakers who do things improperly around the stall and the best way to avoid this is to have a reliable groom looking over the new man's shoulder. Young men who really want to be good caretakers appreciate this system and if I find one who resents it I can be quite sure that the fellow wasn't going to amount to much anyway.

I have also found that husband-wife teams make excellent caretakers and as I write this I have three such teams working for me. The wives do as good a job as the men and, to tell the truth, I believe they probably think a little more of their horses than the men do.

All these things must be placed in their proper perspective and attention must be given to each one of them in developing a sound conditioning program. You can do nine things right with a horse and yet if you do just one thing wrong you can ruin him.

Accompanying this chapter are a number of training charts that I use myself and that I have laid out to cover different types of horses and different racing situations. I think charts like this will make it much easier for the reader to follow along as I discuss conditioning programs.

Although I have laid out quite a few charts, I feel that in addition to 2-year-olds there are actually only four classes of horses involved. They are green (inexperienced) 3-year-olds, stakes caliber 3-year-olds, raceway horses and horses that are not entirely sound and have to be conditioned just a little differently. I plan to discuss each of these categories in some detail.

In laying out these schedules, I have also borne in mind that we are in the midst of a major change in the way we race horses. That is, harness racing has now become a year-round proposition and thus it is no longer enough to say that we are going to start training a horse on January first to get him ready to race on May first.

Now we start racing some horses in January or February while others will not start, for one reason or another, until April or May. I think this is an important consideration in setting up training charts and I have tried to cater to the trend by varying the dates on which the various types of horses quit racing the previous year and are scheduled to return the next year.

With respect to these schedules, it is also important to remember that I am talking about a normal horse and not the one that is the exception to the rule. No two horses can be trained exactly alike and a trainer will determine by experience which ones he has to go a little more or a little less with. But the schedules I have laid out are, in my opinion, generally acceptable ones and should prove of value to anyone planning a racing campaign.

I think it is very important to set up training schedules for horses and to follow them as closely as you can. I am going to emphasize this in my presentation because the area in which it has the least application—the training of 2-year-olds—is being handled separately by Ralph Baldwin and he has explained that you have to be careful about setting up any kind of schedule for horses of this age. There is a lot more difference among them than there is among older horses and they are less likely to be able to follow a rigid schedule.

While I am not writing about the training of 2-year-olds, there is one thought that I want to leave with all trainers and I am sure that Ralph will agree. The worst thing you can do with a 2-year-old is to get him tired and not finishing his mile strongly and willingly.

A colt will learn a lot quicker when he is feeling good. For that reason, I never go all I can with a colt at any time. If you are training off a schedule and are set to go in 2:17 while the colt has had all he could do to go in 2:20 the week before, back off and go again in 2:20. Maybe he just needed an extra week at that stage. I know for sure that if you go on and the colt gets tired he is going to start shifting his weight around and the next thing you know you are going to have a leg problem or a gait problem. I always insist that whatever 2-year-olds do must be done cheerfully and within themselves. I would rather quit on one and try again the next year than to force him to do what he isn't capable of doing.

But with the horses I am writing about, raceway horses, 3-year-olds that are to race in the stakes and green 3-year-olds that are to go to the raceways, you fairly well know what you can expect from them and can plan accordingly. The only class I have under discussion in which you might find a variance would be the green 3-year-old category. Some of these horses might not have been trained any faster than 2:15 the year before and some probably weren't even that far advanced when you quit with them. You might find that when you get around that 2:15 notch again some of them will begin to hang a little. If I find this to be the case, I simply back off as I would with a 2-year-old until they are ready to go on or until I am convinced they do not have the potential to go on.

But for the most part, the horses I am dealing with have been to the races and have demonstrated their qualifications. Therefore, I can set up a schedule for them with confidence. What I do is to sit down and figure out when I want to start them and map out a schedule that fits this plan. In the charts I have made to accompany this chapter, I have taken different types of horses and broken them into groups that quit at different times the previous year and which are going to start racing again at different times the next year. I am sure that one of these charts will cover just about any horse in the country, either as it stands or by adjusting the actual training schedule to a different starting date.

When I plan my schedule, I do so with the idea that I will always be ahead of myself and never behind. It doesn't hurt to be an hour early at the airport but if you're a minute late you're in trouble. It's the same way with horses. Under the schedules I have drawn up, I have taken into account the fact that we might get a bad snow storm that would shut us down for several days—although this rarely happens where I train—or my horse might develop a touch of virus or get just a little off and have to miss a week of training. I am set up so that a horse can miss a week, or even two in most cases, and still not be in any trouble at all.

I have seen fellows who will get in trouble like this and drop a horse from 2:40 to 2:15 with no ill effects. I know it can be done but I have never done it and doubt that I ever will. The percentage says that such a horse isn't ready for a drop like this and while you might get away with it once, if you kept doing it you would get in trouble. An airplane can fly on one engine but all of us would rather not if we didn't have to.

As far as dropping horses is concerned, I feel that any horse except a 2-year-old is capable of dropping five seconds a week until he reaches 2:20. The faster class raceway horses can even be dropped 10 seconds a week when you are on a short training schedule. But once I get to 2:20 with my slower class horses and my green 3-year-olds, I make the drops less drastic, say two or three seconds a week. As I said before, some of these horses are approaching a plateau they have not passed before, and I want to take a little more time with them. Schedules are great things and I rely on them a lot, but the horse will soon tell you whether the schedule is meeting with his approval and, if it is not, you had better listen to the horse or you are in trouble.

In addition to planning a "loose" schedule, there is one other thing I do to cope with weather problems when I run into them and they prevent me from training. I double up on my jog miles. Let's take a radical instance that has never actually happened with me but which, I imagine, could happen elsewhere in the north, and say that we have had a bad snow storm and that I missed a full week of training.

Every day that week I would jog my horse eight miles instead of the usual four. And after I had jogged seven miles at a moderate clip, I would step him along the last mile at about a 3:00 rate. Even if I had to do this for an entire week, I would not feel that it had thrown my training schedule off and I would go right back the next week to whatever miles I had scheduled.

Even though I train in the North, I don't have much trouble with snow and one of the reasons is that I don't have a hub rail around my track. Instead I have pieces of rubber hose two feet high placed along the inside edge of the track at intervals of about 100 feet. These lengths of rubber fit into hollow pipes which are encased in cement about three inches below the surface. They can be and are removed when we get a snow storm. If a horse should accidentally hit one of these pieces of rubber, the rubber simply bends backward and causes no trouble.

I like this setup for two reasons. One is that it enables us to plow all our snow into the center field. The center field is lower than the track and provides excellent drainage which Curly Smart will tell you in his chapter is the main thing you need in a race track. When it snows, we remove the pieces of rubber and just plow the snow right into the infield and push it back quite a distance. We couldn't do this if we had a hub rail.

The other reason is that if I am having a little trouble with a colt, I don't ever have to worry about one getting into the hub rail as some of them will. If they do shy off sideways, I can let them go and even drive them around in the center field if I have to and back on the track. It provides a great deal of maneuverability in this respect and I am glad to have it.

When people visit my track for the first time they always ask me if I don't run into a lot of trouble when my colts go to the races and see a hub rail for the first time. I can honestly say that no colt that has ever been trained at my track has ever had a particle of trouble with a hub rail once he got to a raceway. I don't want to suggest that no training track should have a hub rail because that would be a foolish thing to say. But I feel it is far more important to me not to have one than to have one. I am very pleased with the setup and plan to retain it.

In addition to missing work because of inclement weather, there are bound to be days when the track is fit enough to train over but when you cannot train as much as your schedule calls for. In cases like this, you must adjust your schedule to compensate for how much your track is off.

Let's say your schedule calls for a mile in 2:20 and from your experience with your own track you know it is eight seconds off. You would work a mile in 2:28 and call it 2:20 on your schedule. You have to know your track to be able to do this, but most trainers can come up with an approximate figure.

Another point worth mentioning is that while I start most of my horses in training with a 2:50 mile, it can actually be anywhere between 2:50 and 3:00. I like to leave myself 10 seconds to play with and I am not exact about it. Maybe I want to go in 3:00 but when the horse leaves he is full of life and going a little more than a 3:00 shot would call for. Rather than double this horse up to keep at the 3:00 rate and possibly have him hit a quarter, I will let him roll on out a little and go my mile in 2:50.

This horse has been jogged for a minimum of four weeks and 2:50 isn't going to hurt him a bit. A mile in 2:40 probably wouldn't hurt him, but I think 2:50 is enough and anywhere between 2:50 and 3:00 is satisfactory. This applies to the first two or three weeks a horse is in training, but it is always a good thing to keep in mind. If a horse is startled by a tractor or a harrow or something like that, don't take a chance on an injury by doubling him up. Let him step on a little even though the mile won't be exact. This isn't the case, of course, if he is going his last mile on his "fast" work day late in the training season which would be the fastest he has been that year. You want to rate that one where you have it scheduled. The slowest mile I have listed on any of my training charts is 2:50. These are the miles that can go from 2:50 to 3:00.

As a general rule, a big rugged horse can stand and will probably need more training than a narrow-waisted horse, a nervous horse, or a filly that doesn't eat for a day or two after she races. But there are rules within rules that defy even these broad outlines. Noble Victory is an example of that. While he is a well-made horse, I would not describe him as a big, rugged one. And yet, I found through experience that as a two and 3-year-old he was a horse that took quite a bit of work, especially in getting him ready for a race. At four, he was just the opposite as I will explain later.

Horses aren't like people. They can't tell you they are ready and at peak form. A boxer training for a championship bout might tell his handlers a week before the fight that he was as fit as he could get and that it would be better if he backed off in his training during the last week. If he didn't do this, he might over-train and it might cost him the fight. A horse can't tell you this. You have to figure it out for yourself.

One of the most important things in training a horse is to lay the proper foundation. This is why baseball players go south for winter training. This is where they build the muscles, harden the legs, and strengthen the wind. I remember one year the Yankees had Mickey Mantle working out all winter because they thought he might stay "sounder" if he didn't "let down," to use race horse parlance. In one of his last active years, Stan Musial did the same thing, worked out with weights and things like that long before he went into training. He had a real good year, too. The same thing applies to horses. They need a real foundation before they can race. Sometimes I actually think certain horses would be better off if we never let them down, kept them doing a little something all year round. This, again, is just another way of laying the foundation.

Sandy Koufax could probably have pitched a good game if he hadn't touched a baseball or done a lick of exercise for six months, just as I could take a horse that had only been in 2:50 and work him in 2:10. Although each would be quite tired at the finish, Sandy would pitch one good game and my horse would go one good mile. But I wouldn't have bet any money on either one of them for a couple of months after that. Neither had the proper foundation for such an effort and would suffer as a result.

Training patterns must also be modified to accommodate changing conditions. Years ago we had four, five and even six-heat races. Now, only our two and 3-year-old stake horses go more than one heat and even many of the stakes are single-heat affairs. Single dash races and a lengthening season that now covers the entire year have resulted in a lightening of the basic training schedule for a horse.

As recently as 20 years ago, almost all horses were trained four heats and many went five. Now I think you would find that the vast majority of raceway horses are trained no more than three heats and a goodly number go only two. This is nothing more than a case of making the training program fit the racing circumstances.

I am sure that if a lot of the old time trainers came back and saw harness racing the way it is today they would say it was unbelievable. I can just imagine what they would say if they saw us racing over a muddy track during a snow storm in the month of January. But that's commonplace now and it is the way progress is measured. Why, I can remember old-time trainers telling me they would never race behind a starting gate because it wasn't right for an automobile to be on a race track with horses. And just think what the gate has done for our sport. It's revolutionized it!

I think I have laid sufficient ground work now to begin discussing actual conditioning methods. Some of the practices I am going to describe may sound very routine for anyone who has had any experience training horses. But I know that a great many of our owners and new, young people, who have not yet become familiar with harness racing, are not completely aware of the generally accepted training procedures and for that reason I think I should review them briefly.

Generally speaking—and again I must emphasize that I am referring here to the normal horse and not the one that is the exception to the rule—trotters and pacers are trained twice a week before they get to the races.

These two training days are as evenly spaced as possible for a seven day week and the accepted combinations are Monday-Thursday, Tuesday-Friday, and Wednesday-Saturday. In my own stable, half the horses are trained on Mondays and Thursdays and the other half on Tuesdays and Fridays.

I do not schedule any regular training sessions for Wednesdays and Saturdays for two reasons. One is that if I run into a rainy day I can move my schedule back a day and not lose any training. I cannot set a Wednesday-Saturday group back because I do not train on Sunday, nor does any other trainer except in an emergency.

The other reason is that I like to reserve Wednesday and Saturday for tardy colts and problem horses. We all have some of these. They need extra lessons for one reason or another and I always schedule these horses for those two days so I can devote extra time to their problems.

At the start of my training program, the workouts on the two training days will go at about the same speed. But as I progress, one of these days will be designated as my "fast work" day and the other as my "slow work" day. I always try to schedule my fast workouts for Monday or Tuesday because that gives the horse an extra day of rest before his fast work. It is just a little thing, but I think it is worthwhile. Depending on which days he trains, a horse works "fast" on Monday or Tuesday and "slow" on Thursday or Friday.

The fast work is the one in which the horse goes his fastest mile of the week. The slow work is actually the work which helps lay the foundation, keeps the horse up to something and builds legs, wind and muscle. In my stable, the fastest mile on a horse's slow work day is seldom faster than 2:20, no matter what class of horse I am dealing with. In a good many cases, a mile in 2:25 is plenty. I am not looking for speed in this work-out but, rather, am using it as a conditioning exercise.

Once a horse gets to the races, he stays roughly on the same type of schedule providing he is racing once a week. His race is considered his "fast work" and between races he gets his "slow work." I will go into more detail regarding this later.

I think it would probably be best to establish at this point that all the horses I am going to train in this chapter are on a Mon-day-Thursday schedule unless I indicate otherwise. This will save having to explain it each time.

I train my horses in "sets" of two, three or even more. Most of the time there will be three horses in a set. By one o'clock of each day, I post a training schedule for the following day, thus giving the caretakers ample time to schedule their own work for that day. The schedule identifies the horses in the various sets, lists the driver, tells how fast the training miles are to be and designates the times at which that set will be trained. The care-takers are expected to have their horses at the track and ready to go precisely at the times indicated. I train many horses each day and I insist that these schedules be followed to the minute. An operation like mine can only function smoothly if such a schedule is prepared and enforced.

Keeping that in mind, a training session will consist of one, two, three, or four workout miles or heats spaced at intervals of ap-proximately 40 minutes. It is only in the very early stages of his conditioning program that a horse is trained just one or two heats. Most of my horses are trained three heats although an occasional 2-year-old and my top stake 3-year-olds are some-times trained four on their "fast work" day only. These heats are known as "singles." If you asked a horseman how he planned to train his horse on a certain day he might say, "I'm going three singles with him." This means he plans to work the horse three one-mile heats with an interval of approximately 40 min-utes between heats.

Whether a horse trains three or four heats, depends on the type of horse and the trainer. I used to train all my horses four heats and so did most of the other trainers. I stopped that several years ago and now train them all three heats with the exceptions noted in the preceding paragraph. Most other trainers do the same.

I think the advent of year-round racing will probably result in further modifications of training methods. I know that I have changed a number of my own methods over the years and am not afraid to make changes if I feel they will help my horses.

For instance, I used to train far more double headers than I do now. A double header is when you train a horse two single miles without leaving the track. I will write more about that later. Double headers used to be routine with me. I would sometimes go a double header with a horse and then train him three singles. Now, the only time I double head a horse is in the fall of the year when I am short of help and just getting under way with green, coming 3-year-olds that I am planning to campaign as raceway horses rather than stake horses. I do not go double headers with any other class of horse. I never go double headers after the first of the year.

I think the tendency is to train horses lighter than we used to and I am in favor of it. I go fewer training heats with my raceway horses than I did when I was just starting out. I do less with them between races, I warm them up fewer heats and slower on race nights and I don't brush them nearly as much as I used to. All of this has to do with the fact that raceway horses are going a single dash and that they are campaigning for longer periods each year. If you want to race them as long as we do these days, you have to ease up somewhere along the line or they will not last.

I hardly ever go a fast warmup mile with a raceway horse any more and I do very little brushing. I find that these fast eighths and quarters at either the beginning or end of a warmup mile take something out of a horse and since they only have so many of these in their systems I think it's best to leave them there.

I see raceway horses that are warmed up routinely in 2:10 to 2:12. I have found that it is much better to warm them up from 2:17 to 2:20 in their fastest mile and make it an evenly rated one. I only go two warmup miles, one around 2:45 to the cart and the second one to the sulky at the rate I just mentioned. There are, of course, as in everything involved in training harness horses, certain exceptions. Some horses might have to be warmed up faster to get them on edge for a race. But aside from a few like that, I see absolutely no reason why a horse has to be warmed up fast or brushed fast on the end of a warmup mile. I will warm up a real top horse in 2:40 and 2:20 with both miles evenly rated. If it was to be a two-heat race, I might go my second mile around 2:17 or so.

Probably the best way for me to begin to discuss specific conditioning methods is to select one of the training chart categories and follow it through from the time I start out with a horse until he gets to the races. For that purpose, I will pick the "green 3-year-old" category which is made up of horses which were raced either lightly or not at all as 2-year-olds and which are picked up earlier than any of the other groups. These are not my stake 3-year-olds, but the ones that I expect to race in overnight events, or in a limited number of early closers.

I should also establish at the outset that I train over my own half mile track at New Egypt, N. J., and have about 90 horses in my stable. I am also very fortunate to have as my second trainer a great horseman named Dick Baker, who, in my opinion, is the strongest right hand man any harness horse trainer ever had. I always consult with him when training problems arise and his vast knowledge and experience have helped me over a number of rough spots.

Incidentally, if you are a young trainer and have a problem you haven't encountered before, don't be afraid to go to a more experienced trainer and ask for advice. I did this when I was starting out and a lot of good trainers helped me. I have never forgotten this and have always been willing to do anything I could to help somebody out. Most other experienced trainers feel the same way about it.

This also might be as good a place as any to say that I believe a horse can be prepped just as well in the north as in the south. There is nothing wrong with training in the warmer climate of the south—I trained there one year myself—and there are times, when it is bitter cold and a stiff wind is blowing, that I wish I were there. But I know now from experience that I can get my horses just as ready in New Jersey as anywhere else.

The thing that will slow you down in the north is weather and this boils down, for the most part, to snow storms that might keep a trainer off his race track for a week or longer. The answer to this lies in having proper track maintenance equipment. I have this and consequently I rarely lose a day of training.

Actually, I think I have a little edge over southern-trained raceway horses early in the year. There is no question that a horse moving up from the south to begin racing in the north has to go through a brief period of acclimatization in the early stages if the transition is made roughly prior to mid-May.

The year I trained in the south I maintained the same training schedule as when I was in the north with one exception. In the south, I began repeating my 2-year-olds about the first of January as most of the other trainers down there do. But in the north I do not begin repeating, that is training more than one mile on any one day, until February first. I do not like to repeat colts when it is bitter cold—one session on the track is enough on such days. Instead, I would rather train them a mile a day three times a week than two miles a day twice a week. If we were having an especially severe winter, I might not begin repeating 2-year-olds until the middle of February.

This does not apply to older horses. I repeat them throughout the winter no matter what the conditions are. They are veterans and are accustomed to the weather and the training pattern. The only difference between north and south for these horses is that the time interval between heats is about 40 minutes in the north and perhaps an hour in the south.

As to whether one area has an advantage over the other, I think I have only to point out that of the two fastest race horses of all time, Bret Hanover and Noble Victory, one was trained in the north and the other in the south. A few other great northern-trained champions that are racing as I write this are Best of All, Romulus Hanover, True Duane and Bonjour Hanover. I do not consider that where they are trained is very important; what is important is how they are trained.

Green horses that I am going to race in February or later are picked up on or after October first depending on when I plan to start them. I like to jog horses four full weeks before I begin to train them. I like to have between 75 and 100 timing miles (actual training miles as opposed to jogging miles) in a green horse before he goes to the races. You will not get this many miles into raceway horses these days, but these are usually horses you have quit with late in the season and which you plan to race early the next season. These horses have not really been let all the way down from the previous campaign so obviously they don't need as many miles to get them back in shape.

The green horses I am going to start training on October first have usually been turned out all summer, so let me lead off by explaining my feeling about that. Horses that are turned out should be able to get as much exercise as possible and should be in a paddock with a shed or enclosure of some type that will provide shelter for a horse if he needs it. My turnouts are grained twice a day and get all the hay they will eat. As a rule, horses will not eat much hay if good, green grass is available but I keep it before them anway. Turnouts should also have their feet trimmed once a month. I think it is very important that horse's feet not be allowed to get out of shape.

Now it is October first and we bring these horses in and start jogging them. These are the ones that are going to make their first start on February 15th and you can follow their progress on Chart No. 2. Charts Nos. 1 and 3 are also for green three-year-olds but these are slated to begin racing at different dates, January 2nd (Chart No. 1) and April 15th (Chart No. 3). These charts begin on page 262.

As a rule, a horse that has been turned out isn't nearly as soft as one that has been standing up in a stall so I begin by jogging these horses two miles a day. I continue this for a week and advance to three miles a day the second week. During the third and fourth weeks I jog them four miles a day. All jogging, of course, is done the wrong way of the track (clockwise) and as close to the outer rim as practical. That portion of any track from the rail out at least to the center should be reserved for horses that are actually being trained and thus going the right way (counter clockwise) of the track.

My rule of thumb—and I think it is a good one—is that every horse must be jogged for a period of four full weeks before I start to go training miles with him. Of course, that is neither possible or necessary with certain types of raceway horses that raced late and are going to start again early, but for green horses and horses that have been laid off a long time, it is a solid rule with me and I follow it religiously. A full month of jogging gets a horse started off on the proper conditioning path and is the first step in laying the foundation that all race horses require.

In some cases, I will go more jog miles during this four-week period than I have indicated. For instance, if a horse is hog fat as a result of having been turned out for an extended period. I would start going five miles a week with him in the fourth week if he hadn't shaped up the way I thought he should have. I would do the same thing with a horse that indicated to me that he was a little weak in his stifles.

A little extra jogging is the best thing in the world for a horse that shows a weakness in the stifle area. You must not overdo it to the point where the horse starts to lose a lot of weight, but if he holds his flesh it is a good idea at this stage to step up the number of jog miles to as many as six in the fourth week and to jog him as much as six miles a day on his jogging days even after you start to train him. I will write a little more about training horses with stifle trouble a little later on. Medication is good, but extra jogging is the best thing in the world for such a horse.

Extra jogging, that is an extended period of jogging, is also called for in the case of a horse that is a little sore from the effects of firing or blistering and that needs additional time before he is exposed to a full-fledged training routine.

I have had a number of horses that fit in this category and I will review one of them briefly to make my point. One year I had a 2-year-old that showed stake horse potential but that developed knee lameness in May. I quit with the colt and had the knee fired in September. (Incidentally, I prefer to have my firing done, especially when it involves the knees, tendons or ankles, in the fall of the year. Horses that have been fired do better when the weather is a little cooler).

I held this colt in the stall for ten days after he was fired and during that period limited his exercise to a short walk each morning. On the 11th day, I started to jog him and went two miles since he was a horse that had been turned out prior to the firing and was in good physical condition.

The colt was a little sore in the knee and showed it when he jogged by not bending the knee the way he should have. He remained that way throughout the first week so I had the knee

X-rayed to make certain that he had not chipped a bone or something like that. The X-rays were negative indicating that the soreness was a result of the firing itself and that the horse would eventually work out of it. But at the same time I re-scheduled this colt's prep program to accommodate the condition.

I held him at two miles a day for an additional two weeks, making a total of three weeks that he was not jogged more than that distance. He kept getting a little better each week and in the fourth week he was jogging sound.

Normally, a colt would now be ready to enter serious training, but in this case I felt that because of the trouble he had had that he required additional jogging. Therefore, I increased the jog rate to four miles a day the fifth week and then stepped it up to five miles a day in the sixth and seventh weeks. Only after that did I begin to train him.

I gave this colt plenty of extra jogging not only because I thought he had stake potential but also because I felt that he had missed some miles in the first few weeks and that he should have these and more under his belt before he went on. I wanted to be absolutely sure that he had recovered from the firing and that he had been properly legged up before he went into training.

All horses should be jogged to the outside of the track and caretakers should be cautioned to be on the lookout for such things as harrows, tractors, the starting gate, other horses turning and especially for 2-year-olds that might shy and veer suddenly in or out. In other words, they should act like a cautious driver on any heavily traveled highway and be on the alert at all times.

I am also very particular never to let any of my horses be jogged through a draw gate. As a matter of fact, my instructions are that a horse leaving the track is to be stopped briefly about a hundred yards from the draw gate and then again at the gate where he is made to stand for few seconds before he goes through it and back to the barn. The same holds true when the horses enter the track. They are taught to stop for a few seconds before going out on the track.

There are a lot of reasons for this. I find that if you don't stop them at the gate going in either direction they will get in the habit of running through the gate to get on or off the track. I want to teach them manners and this is a good place to do it.

At the same time, a horse running through a draw gate can start making sharp turns and fall or, on entering the track, run right into another horse or the starting gate or a tractor or something like that. In effect, there is a big STOP sign at my draw gate in both directions. A horse is *never* jogged through a draw gate at my track. I just don't permit it.

There are certain procedures that I insist that my caretakers and assistant trainers follow with respect to bringing horses to the track and jogging them. Dick Baker and I are constantly on the lookout for violations and when we see them we let the boys know what they are doing wrong.

For instance, I insist that my horses be walked from the barn to the track. And when they reach the track, I insist that they be walked at least a sixteenth of a mile before they begin to jog. I think this is real important for a couple of reasons. For one thing, it limbers them up a bit, loosens their muscles before they start their work. For another, it teaches them manners and manners are so important in horses.

When a child sits down at a table to eat, does he grab a spoon and dig right in or should he wait and have his food passed to him? He should wait, of course, but if an adult doesn't teach him to wait he'll never know any better. It's the same way with a horse. Unless you teach him to wait, he'll dash out of the barn and dash to the track and keep right on going. I've heard people say that horses can't be taught manners. Well, I don't know about that but I do know they can be taught *bad* manners.

I know, for instance, that they can be taught to jog too fast. I've seen trainers jog horses at a faster clip than I train my first or second mile. That's why Dick and I are always on the lookout for boys who do this. Sometimes they have to be taught just as the horse must be.

I would say that a proper jog clip would be a mile in about 4½ to five minutes. You don't want to poke along because this is just as bad for a horse as jogging him at a 3:00 clip which is too fast. Jogging is intended to leg a horse up and build strength and muscle. It is not intended to train him. That's why it should be neither too fast nor too slow. You can tell if you are jogging too slow in many cases because the horse will have a tendency to stumble and knuckle over or even break a check.

I believe four miles a day is enough jogging for the average horse. There are very few horses that I will ever jog more than that with the exceptions I noted earlier. After four weeks of jogging, I will turn the horse for the first time and go a slow mile the right way of the track on Monday and Thursday as shown on Chart No. 2. I cut out one of my jog miles when I do this. I jog the horse three miles and then turn and go my mile the right way.

I think I should also insert here that the number of jog miles on a training day is in proportion to the number of miles being trained. As I just wrote, when a horse is being trained one mile, he goes three jog miles prior to that for a total of four. If he is being trained two heats, he jogs three miles prior to going his first heat for a total of five miles. When it gets to the stage where he is being trained three heats, he goes two jog miles before going his first training mile. In addition to this, my horses are always jogged a half mile before starting any training mile after the first one. I might as well preserve the continuity by explaining my reason for that right now.

In training green horses, such as I am writing about now, or any horses except 2-year-olds for that matter, I try to eliminate scoring as much as possible. I believe a lot of scoring has a tendency to develop bad habits in horses. If you score them a lot, it doesn't take them long to learn you're going to pull them up at a certain point and they get so they want to pull up there when you are going training miles.

I compensate for not scoring by having the groom jog the horse a half mile when he brings him to the track for a training mile. He enters the track, jogs the horse a half mile the wrong way and then hands him over to the trainer who turns the horse and goes his mile. He does not score at all. When the horse is turned the right way of the track, he goes his mile and that is it.

There is one other policy I follow in this respect that I think is worth mentioning. After the horse has finished his training mile, he turns and comes back up past the starting line where he is picked up by his caretaker and jogged a half mile, or once around the track, before he goes back to the barn. I think this extra turn around the track serves two useful purposes. It builds muscle and helps lay the foundation and at the same time it gives the horse a chance to blow out a little before he goes back to the barn. It is a good policy and I recommend it although I do not continue to do this once the horse is at the races. By that time, I do not feel the horse needs this extra half mile of jogging.

There is one exception I make to my no-scoring policy and this is when I start to train horses behind the starting gate. I think training behind a gate is a very important thing and that a trainer should do as much of it as he can. There is a proper procedure involved as it applies to green horses that have not had any gate experience and I will describe how I do it.

I like to introduce my green horses to a starting gate on days that they jog, not on training days. This would be prior to the time I start to train them three heats. On days that these horses are scheduled to jog, I will bring the gate out and have it circle the track slowly while they follow it along. At first I will not let them get too close to the gate, say maybe five lengths or so off it. Horses are no different than children in this respect. Some of them will take to it right away and others will be a little scared of it. But after a couple of weeks, you will find that almost every one of them will be completely accustomed to the gate and will be willing to move right in behind it.

The next step is to introduce them to the gate in training miles. I don't do this until they are up to a little something, along about 2:35 to 2:40. They are going three heats and I will use the gate for the last heat and maybe for the second heat as well.

When I start doing this, which is usually around the first of the year, I will have the horses I am training line up behind the gate and trail it once around the track before starting my training mile. I like to have as many horses as possible doing this and sometimes there will be five or six involved. But even if it is only one horse it is better than nothing.

The gate is stationed at the three-quarter pole just as it is at all race tracks and the horses line up behind it. The gate takes off slowly and the horses follow it for three quarters of a mile. Now they have gone one and a half times around the track and as the gate approaches the starting line the driver picks up a little speed and moves off. He doesn't bust the gate out of there; he just picks up speed gradually because I don't want my horses getting all tangled up and making breaks. What I am trying to do is to teach them manners and to get them accustomed to the gate.

After I have done it this way a few times, maybe four such sessions over a two-week period, I usually find that the horses are accustomed to the gate and are relaxed behind it. Now I am ready for the next step in starting gate education.

In this stage, I have the gate stationed at the three-quarter pole and this is where I make my only exception to the scoring rule that is in force in my operation. After their caretakers have jogged the horses once around, the trainers pick them up and score them down. But instead of coming back to go their mile, they are scored right on down the backstretch to where the starting gate is positioned at the three-quarter pole. This is exactly the procedure that is followed when the horse gets to the races and the sooner he learns it the better.

We let them look the gate over a little, turn them and go back up the track two or three hundred feet. Then we get them together, turn them and head back toward the gate. Again we let them stop and look the gate over and then I have the driver start it up at a slow rate. He picks up a little speed as he goes on, but not much the first few times. At the starting line he gradually pulls away and the horses go their training mile. I will do this for the third heat and if time and weather permit, I will do it for the second heat as well. After a few such lessons, the horses are all pretty well broken to the gate and I rarely have any trouble.

Your reaction might be that this is a fine thing for a fellow like Stanley Dancer who has a big operation and a fancy starting gate and all that but what about the poor little fellow who can't afford this type of thing? My answer has to be that I was doing this long before I got to be well-known in harness racing and I think it is one of the principal reasons that my horses were good in the early racing when I was just starting out.

For years, I used an old, second-hand jeep. And after that, I went to a pickup truck. But I always had something that would teach my horse what a gate was all about. It doesn't really take much to rig up a gate or something that will pass for a gate. You can use two by fours or aluminum pipe for a cross bar and attach wire to it for the horses to get their heads against. You can construct something like this very reasonably and set it into the platform of a pickup truck or on the back of a jeep. There really isn't any excuse for a fellow not to have some kind of starting gate if he really wants one badly enough.

A starting gate also comes in handy if you have a horse with a bad gate problem and you have to work on it. Frosty Hanover was a horse like that and the story is worth telling because it might help someone with the same kind of problem.

Frosty Hanover was owned by M. J. Duer of Exmore, Virginia, and I trained him some as a 2-year-old. By the time I got him he could trot fairly well, but he was bad at the gate and would run off and make breaks. I got along fairly well with him that year but he was still a problem and at the end of the season Mr. Duer took him home and trained him himself. The next year, when he was a 3-year-old, several trainers had him and Billy Haughton gave him a record of 1:59⅘ at Lexington against the fence. But he still had bad gate manners and race secretaries and track officials weren't exactly enthused when he showed up.

That fall, Mr. Duer asked me if I would take him again. I thought about it a little and said that I would if I could keep him for the whole season because I had a plan I wanted to try with him. Mr. Duer agreed and sent him to me.

I put him down to train on Wednesdays and Saturdays which, as I have explained, are the days I reserve for problem horses. From the day I started with him until the next spring when he made his first start at Roosevelt, Frosty Hanover went every single mile behind the starting gate. And I mean *every* step of *every* mile!

When I started to jog the horse, I put a boy in the gate and told him how fast I wanted him to drive it. I stuck Frosty Hanover's nose against the gate and we went our jog miles all the way around the track that way.

Then, when I started to train him, I put one of my assistant trainers in the gate and told him how fast I wanted to go. I didn't even carry a watch. I would tell my assistant I wanted to go a mile in 2:40 and he would time the mile as he drove the gate. All I did was sit behind Frosty and guide him.

I didn't have any problem when I was jogging him, but when I first started to train him the right way of the track he tried to ram the gate and go over it or under it. But my gate was built so that he'd have to jump pretty high to get over it and there was no way he could get under it. It didn't take him long to learn there wasn't anything he could do about that gate and finally he grew content and would follow it. But I never varied the pattern. Every training mile and every jog mile that Frosty Hanover went that winter was with his nose on the gate every step of every mile.

Finally we went to Roosevelt for our first start. I will confess that I was a little nervous when they folded the wings with the money on the line but he went out of there trotting and raced well. I quit training him that way then. I figured that from then on he had to make it on his own and he did. He won several races in a row, earned more than $25,000 and was a good horse. Mr. Duer sold him for a good price to go abroad that fall.

This is an example of a horse that developed a bad habit but that was cured of it. I believe Frosty Hanover was afraid of the gate and that was what was bothering him. Those hundreds of training and jogging miles all the way around the track behind the gate taught him he had nothing to fear from it and when he learned that he became a good horse.

Getting back to the conditioning of green 3-year-olds (Chart No. 2), I have now jogged them for the prescribed four weeks and they are ready to enter training. I put them on a regular Monday-Thursday schedule but for the first two weeks I only go one heat on each training day. The first week I jog three miles and go a heat around 2:50 and the second week I go around 2:45.

What I am doing is introducing them to the training routine in easy stages. On the "off" days, which are Tuesday, Wednesday, Friday and Saturday, the horses are being jogged four miles daily. Sunday, of course is a day off.

In the seventh week, I start to train the horses two heats instead of one, and the progress may be followed on the chart. This is also when I will double-head horses if I am going to do it.

At this time of the year, when we are busy breaking and mannering 2-year-olds and when help is a problem, I will occasionally go double headers and continue to do so until I start training three trips. As I said before, these green 3-year-olds are the only ones in my stable that ever go double headers and while my charts are not set up in this manner, the adjustment can be made by jogging two miles instead of three and going in the indicated time brackets.

In going a double header, the horse is brought to the track by his caretaker who jogs him two miles. He is then turned over to the trainer who turns the horse the right way of the track and goes a mile in 2:45. The horse is pulled up at about the quarter pole, turned and walked or jogged very slowly back to the seven-eighths pole above the starting line. There he is turned again and goes a mile in 2:40.

This is nothing but a time and labor saving device. It has the same conditioning effect as if a horse went a mile in 2:45 and then went back to the barn and waited 40 minutes before coming out and going another mile in 2:40. You can see how much time and labor it saves. I am not in favor of double headers and most of my horses have never even been a double header but at this time of year I do not feel they will hurt these green 3-year-olds and I have found that under these circumstances they can serve a very useful purpose. Even when I am forced to go double headers, I stop doing it when I start to go three training miles or earlier than that after we get to the first of the year and the 2-year-olds are pretty well settled and worked into the training program.

It used to be that you saw a lot of double headers. Old-time trainers not only went one double header, they very often went two and occasionally three. It is my own opinion that singles are easier on a horse. I think a horse that is not going double headers will hold his flesh better and that is why I don't train that way except for green 3-year-olds in the very beginning and under the circumstances I have described. Horses will get legged up just as well going singles.

The fastest mile any of my horses go in a double header is 2:35 and the miles are always evenly rated. I don't feel that this is doing them any harm and it is building up muscles and getting legs under them at a time when this is important. I would never go a double header in hot weather.

There is one other time that double headers can still be used to advantage and I would not hesitate to recommend that a young trainer try it. This is when you have a big, fat horse that is carrying a lot of flesh and you have to get it off him before you can really start training him. In a case like this, I would not be afraid to go a double header every other day or two double headers a day twice a week. I see no harm in this unless you tried to go too fast. I would say that if you were going two double headers you should go at the same rate in each. That is, the first double header would consist of a mile from 2:50 to

3:00, and the second between 2:38 and 2:42. After 45 minutes, you could bring the horse back and go another double header the same way. But you must remember to walk your horse slowly back up to the starting point so that he can blow out a little between double header heats and never, never go anything except evenly rated miles.

With my green horses that are scheduled to start on February 15th, I have now had four weeks of jogging, two weeks in which they were trained a single mile on Monday and Thursday and have entered the stage where they are going two training heats on their work days.

This continues for four full weeks through the week of December 5th, (Chart No. 2) and I have them down to a mile in 2:35. The time schedule is identical on Monday and Thursday. The first week their fastest mile was in 2:40. I held them there for three weeks (or six training sessions) and then dropped them to 2:35.

During the week of December 12th, I start going three single trips. I do this by going the usual 2:45 and 2:35 miles and then adding a third one in 2:30. At the same time, I start to time my final quarters and make them about 35 seconds on both Monday and Thursday. Until now, my miles have been evenly rated except for a very slight acceleration at both start and finish. No matter what stage of training you are in, it is always a good practice to go a little more at both the beginning and the end of the mile, even if it is only for a couple of hundred feet. Horses must be taught that they are expected to respond automatically at the start and finish of the race.

I don't believe in going fast quarters off slow miles at this stage of training. I move the final quarters down in accordance with the speed of my fastest mile. I drop to about 34 at the 2:25 notch and maybe a quarter in 33 seconds off a mile in 2:20. What I am doing is teaching my horse to extend himself at the end of the mile without asking him to do anything that is not within his capability.

I would never think of tip-toeing a horse by going a mile in 2:20 and a quarter in 30 seconds. That is asking too much of him. When I get horses down around 2:12 and have a good foundation and a little time left before they have to start, I will search them a little by going over to the half in 1:07 with the last half in 1:05 and the last quarter in 32 seconds. These are nice miles and help a horse a lot. After a trainer gets two or three workouts like this under his horse's belt, it is a good idea then to work a mile in 2:12 with the first half in 1:10 and the last half in 1:02 with each of the last two quarters in 31 seconds. An ideal final workout, which we can't always get, is a mile in 2:12 with the last half in 1:02 and the last quarter in 30 seconds. That sets one up pretty good.

Now that we have reached the three-heat stage, I think it is probably time that I discussed what happens between heats. This is a very critical period and is just as important as the actual training. Every horse I train goes to his stall between heats where his equipment is completely removed and he is permitted to rest and "blow out." This period usually involves about 40 minutes. Why 40 minutes? Well, let's take extreme examples. Ten minutes would be too brief because the horse would still be blowing from the previous heat, that is, he wouldn't have his wind back, and it would be injurious to his system if he returned to the track that soon. Two hours would be too long because the horse would probably have cooled out completely and when he returned for the next heat it would be the same as starting to train him again on another day.

Keeping these reasons in mind, you might get by with 30 minutes on the short end and an hour and a quarter on the long end. But a period of approximately 40 minutes is just about right because experience has taught us that horses blow out properly in this length of time but do not start to cool out. This period is usually extended to an hour during the hot weather months when it naturally takes a horse longer to blow out. Conversely, a horse will blow out quicker on a cold day and might be brought back sooner. But a factor here is that it takes a good 40 minutes to do the job of stripping and refreshing the horse properly.

Removal of equipment between heats is very important. I want my horses to be comfortable and to feel good at all times and there is no way in the world a horse can feel comfortable between heats if he has any part of his equipment left on him. In addition, the removal of equipment gives the caretaker an opportunity to check the horse closely. For instance, in picking up the foot to remove a hobble, the caretaker might notice that the horse had picked up a tiny stone in his foot or even a nail. These things can be important. So between trips all my horses are stripped, sponged off very lightly and covered with a blanket.

During the week of January 2nd, (Chart No. 2) I switch over and begin to go a "fast" work and a "slow" work. This system is in keeping with the way a horse is to race and is designed to set one up to race once a week and to maintain condition between starts. Although he is still in training, the "fast" work is the horse's "race day" for that week and the slow work that follows three days later is used to build strength and stamina but does not ask the horse for speed. When the horse begins campaigning, his weekly race is substituted for his "fast" work and he continues to receive his "slow" work between races. This, of course, is nothing more than a broad outline and must be refined to suit individual horses and specific racing circumstances.

I designate Monday as my "fast" work day and drop my horse to 2:20 for his fastest mile. On Thursday, I back off and go my fastest mile in 2:30 and train two heats at that notch. This is roughly the pattern I will follow from now on. The "fast" work sharpens my horse up and will eventually bring him to racing pitch. The "slow" work lays the foundation of strength and stamina.

Because 2:20 is a pretty good clocking for some of these horses and since I am not pressed for time, I hold them at this level for another full week. Thus, my training schedules for the weeks of January 2nd and 9th are identical. I drop my horse again the week of January 16th, but this time it is only two seconds as he goes a mile in 2:18. In this same week, I bring the fastest mile of my slow work down to 2:25 which is where it will remain from now on. Training miles on "slow" work days are always evenly rated.

In the next training session, I drop my horse to 2:15 and start brushing him along a little since he is scheduled to start in about three weeks. I go the last half in 1:05 and come my last quarter in 32 seconds. The day after this workout I only jog him three miles instead of four and I also cut his number of jog miles back to three after his Thursday work. He is getting sharp now and I do not feel he needs as many jog miles on these days. I want to keep him as fresh as I can.

It is at this stage that I start going certain training trips to a sulky instead of a cart. It is my policy not to hook horses to a sulky until approximately three weeks before they are to race. I will then hook them to a sulky for their last two miles on their "fast" work day. I don't think it is necessary to use a sulky any more than that. This policy applies to 2-year-olds as well as aged horses.

I think it also goes without saying that this is a time where you may have to start making some adjustments that will not show up on a charted schedule. Most of these horses haven't been in 2:15 before and you may find right here that some of them don't care for it too much, or aren't ready for it. In that case, you must back off with that horse instead of going on. I hope that as I continue to describe the progress of a horse that is responding to all my demands at this stage that you will bear in mind that all horses do not and that training schedules must be adjusted to meet these conditions.

In addition to those that just don't have the ability, a typical horse of the type I am talking about might be the one that is a little sulky or a little lazy. He goes in 2:15 all right, but he acts like he doesn't want to go any more; not that he can't but that he doesn't want to. I will race one like this off 2:15. These are the ones that usually whittle down after a while and of whom you will hear a trainer say, "Why, he never woke up until after I'd raced him two or three times."

You might put a horse like this in a qualifying race and only go in 2:13. Then the next time he might hit 2:11. If that's enough to qualify him, he's entered in a regular race and the lights and the crowd and the other horses charging up around him wake him up and shake him loose and the first thing you know your horse is going in 2:07 and liking it. He suddenly got interested. As I said, it is usually the lazy ones or maybe those that are just a little sulky that will act like this.

The week after I go in 2:15, I work my horse in 2:12 on his "fast" day. This time I ramble a pretty good half in 1:03 and come my last quarter in 31 seconds. The day after this work, I walk the horse instead of jogging him. He is also cut back to three jog miles the following day. Now, the only day he is being jogged four miles is Saturday which is the only day of the week that he either has not been trained the day before or will train the next day. The reason I lighten up on the off days is that the horse is getting tight and doesn't need as much of the routine jogging as he once did. His jogging now is more or less to give him a little exercise. To keep a horse fresh, I also walk him on days after he has his fast works and after he races. You will notice this throughout my charts. I recommend that a horse be walked from 20 to 30 minutes.

The training schedule for the week of February 6th is identical to the preceding week. My horse is about ready to race and 2:12 is enough for him. What I am doing here is tightening him up. In actual practice, you will probably find that this is the week you have to take your green horse to the raceway and qualify him. I have not made allowance for that in my schedule but it must be kept in mind. These qualifying races are actually no more than good training sessions and I pretty well follow my own training plans when I enter this type of horse.

Just before I load the horse up and ship him off to the races, let me comment a little on the proper way of cooling a horse out which I have not mentioned before but which is an important phase of the conditioning program. You have to remember, of course, that there is a great deal of difference between cooling out a horse in the winter in New Egypt, N. J. and out on the Grand Circuit on those hot summer afternoons.

During the winter training period, my horses are cooled out in the cross ties in the stall. When they come in from the track after their last training mile, they are not bathed but rather are rubbed off with a towel. On occasion, the caretakers might use a damp sponge if necessary. Depending on the severity of the weather, from one to three coolers are put on them—most of the time I use two coolers—and the horse is tied to the hay rack.

The horse is permitted all the hay he wants and at about 10-minute intervals he is offered water. As a rule, a horse will take eight to twelve swallows. About every 15 minutes the caretaker pulls the coolers back, first at one end and then the other, takes his rub rag and goes over the horse good. The length of time required to cool a horse out depends to some extent on how much of a coat of hair the horse has, but I would say that after three training trips it would require two hours for a normal horse to be cooled out and put away. By "put away," I mean that the horse is completely dry and his hair brushed out, his feet and legs have been washed, his hoofs have been greased, his feet packed with clay, his stable sheets or blankets put on and he has been turned loose in his stall for the rest of the day.

There is a wide difference of opinion as to whether horses should wear stable sheets or stable blankets while at rest in the stall. My own preference is for stable sheets and I use two of them all the time if it is cold or one in the daytime and two at night if it is not quite so severe. It's a pretty difficult thing to say whether a horse needs a blanket or a sheet. But I like my horses to look good and to have slick coats so that I can be proud of them when I show them to anybody. Stable sheets are great for this.

While I am in this general area, let me say that I am opposed to clipping horses. First of all, I think it is against nature's way and I like to keep things as close to nature as I can. Nature intended that horses should have heavy coats in the winter and shed out in the summer.

When we start repeating horses, that is going two or more miles with them on their scheduled training days, I think it is easier for a horse that has been clipped to pick up a cold or tie up while walking from the barn to the track. I don't like to take the chance myself.

The second reason I am opposed to clipping is that I find clipped horses tend to break out in a skin rash. This is a known fact and I am sure this is why we rarely ever have any skin rashes in my stable. Sometimes when you clip a horse, the clippers have a tendency to pull the hair which in turn starts a fungus that spreads over different parts of the horse's body. And, as is well known, things like this will spread from one horse to another.

Now I have my green horse up to a race and he is ready to make his first start in actual competition. Keep in mind that this horse has qualified at the track and is used to the surroundings so I do not have anything special to worry about there. The only thing that might concern me is that he is making his first appearance under the lights. Whenever possible, I like to try to get in a special training trip of some kind under the lights with a green horse or a top two-year-old. It isn't an absolute must, of course, but it is one of those little things that might prove helpful, and if I can arrange to do it I will.

During the early and late parts of the season, when the weather is cold, I make it a practice to jog all my horses a mile on the morning of race day. It is a long time from morning to night and I think this mile is a good thing because it loosens them up and tends to freshen them a little. In addition, I know that the horse has been out of the stall, that he has been cleaned up and that his feet have been picked out, his shoes checked, etc.

During the summer months, I don't jog the horses on race day, but insist that they be walked about 20 minutes instead. I don't jog them because I don't want them to get heated up. I have found that no matter how early you hook a horse up on a summer morning, he will get hot. The only exception to this is that horses being raced Monday night will be jogged Monday morning rather than walked since they were not jogged on Sunday and I do not like to let horses go more than 24 hours without being jogged.

I give my horse a fairly normal feed before he races. I know I like to have something in my stomach when I go to work and I figure a horse feels the same way. I don't want to stuff him, but I want him to get pretty near a regular feed. He is in the first race and has to be in the paddock at six o'clock. About four o'clock, therefore, he gets about four quarts of either mixed feed or oats. He has had water before him all day and all the hay he wanted, unless he was one of those real hogs in which case I might muzzle him. I don't believe very much in that, however, and seldom do it.

At six o'clock, he goes to the paddock and I begin the routine of warming him up. At about 6:30 he is jogged two miles, turned and goes his first trip in 2:45 to a training cart. Usually, my chief assistant, Dick Baker, takes him his first mile. I know my horse is going to be called out of the paddock to race at about eight o'clock so I schedule his next and last warmup mile for 7:15 which will leave me from 40 to 45 minutes between his last trip and his call to the post. During the summer months this period between warmup miles and between the last mile and the race is extended to about an hour since horses need longer to blow out in hot weather.

I will go the last warmup mile myself. I do not warm many horses up faster than 2:20 and that is what I have scheduled for this one. If it is a green horse, as this one is, I may brush him a little on the last end, but not very much at all. I think the idea of brushing horses, as I have said, takes something out of them that is better left in them. So I would probably come a last quarter in about 32 seconds with this particular horse on the end of his mile in 2:20.

The procedure of warming a horse up two heats has come to be more or less the accepted thing in recent years. We used to warm up three heats and what we have done now is to eliminate the middle heat. I used to warm a horse up in 2:45, 2:30 and 2:20. Now I go the 2:45 and 2:20 miles and skip the one in 2:30. You have to bear in mind that these are not stake horses which are warmed up more by some trainers, including me. These are raceway horses that only have to go one heat and I think this kind will stay in better shape and hold their flesh better with fewer warmup miles.

The warmup policy is also controlled to some degree by the gait of the horse. All of us have pacers that are not good-gaited when they are going slow in the hobbles and these are not the easiest horses in the world to warm up. With this kind, I will usually go four jog miles instead of two and call that the first warming up heat. Some trainers will go five miles under these circumstances, but I recommend four.

If I feel that a horse like this needs two pretty decent warmup trips, I would go four jog miles as I have described and then come back in 40 minutes, put the hobbles on and go a mile in 2:30. Then I would come back 40 minutes later with a mile in 2:20.

With horses that tend to chafe themselves in the hobbles when they go slow because they are racking or single-footing rather than pacing, I think it is a definite advantage to go the first warmup session free legged. You can then go either one or two warmup trips at a faster rate depending on how many you feel the horse should have.

This brings up a point that I have heard discussed pro and con for a number of years—whether it is absolutely necessary to go warmup miles before a race. There are those who hold that it is enough to jog a horse a couple of miles and then go on and race him off that without any warmup miles at all.

I know this can be done successfully because I have done it

myself. On a real muddy night when the track is very bad, I have done nothing more than jog horses a couple of miles and raced them off that. And I have had these horses go wonderful races, just as good as if I had followed the usual routine.

But the point is that while you might get away with that a time or two, I am afraid that if you followed the practice week after week you would find your horse tailing off and losing form. Horses are just like athletes and they need a certain amount of training to keep them in shape to produce a maximum effort week after week.

For that reason, it is my contention that a horse should be warmed up before a race; not that he must have it for that specific race but, rather, to maintain condition for all the races that he will be called on to go.

Using the formula that the horse is trained twice a week to maintain condition, his race is actually the last heat of one of those training sessions. I do not believe that he should go his fastest heat of the week—which is what his race mile would be—without a couple of additional slow miles under his belt. These warmup miles not only tone a horse up for the race that night but, more importantly, they keep him in shape for week-to-week racing.

You must bear in mind, of course, that there are exceptions to all rules and that there is the occasional horse that races routinely without warming up, just as there are horses that race well without being trained at all between starts. I have this kind myself and so do all other trainers. But they are the exception rather than the rule and the test of a good trainer is to be able to determine which horses need more or less work. This is the key to being a successful conditioner. If a horse will race at his best and maintain a consistent form without ever being turned the right way of the track except when he faces a starting gate in a race, then that is the way to train him. After all, results are what count.

At any rate, the green 3-year-old that I have been writing about races and is returned to the barn and cooled out. Now, let me take this horse through an additional week to explain what I will do with him between races. Let's say he raced on a Wednesday night and that I expect to race him again the following Wednesday night.

The first thing that happens on Thursday morning is that he is fed and watered and his stall cleaned out. His bandages are removed and he is left to rest for awhile. His caretaker probably has another horse to work on and also has to eat his breakfast. After that he returns and takes the horse out of the stall and walks him for a half hour or so. The caretaker might not get around to this until 10 o'clock if he has another horse, but meantime our horse is getting a nice rest. This is his day of vacation.

On Friday, the horse will be hooked up and jogged three miles. Then he will be done up and put away for the day. Saturday is a day the trainer has to do a little thinking. What he does depends on a number of things. Personally, if the horse raced well and I was satisfied with his performance, I would jog him four miles and that would be all. In that event, he would be walked on Sunday because that is a day that we don't jog or train any horses unless there are special circumstances involved.

With a race scheduled for Wednesday night, the horse would be trained lightly on Monday, going three trips in 2:45, 2:30, and 2:20. All would be evenly rated. On Tuesday morning the horse would be jogged three miles and on Wednesday morning he would be jogged a mile since this is mid-February. That completes a normal routine for an average horse that has raced well and has no problems.

But let's say, for the sake of argument, that the first night our horse raced, he made breaks or didn't race well and that for one reason or another I wasn't at all satisfied with his performance. I would still walk him on Thursday and jog him on Friday, but I would do a little something different on Saturday instead of jogging him.

For one thing, since the box usually closes on Saturday morning for the next Wednesday's races, I would have to train the horse earlier if I really wanted to decide whether he should start back or not. In actual practice, I would probably let a horse like this go and not plan to start him again on Wednesday. But let's say we are involved in a series of early closers and that I want to start him if I can.

What I would probably do on Saturday under those circumstances would be to train him four heats instead of three. The reason for the fourth trip would be that I was making some kind of an equipment change and wanted to give myself ample opportunity to determine whether it was making a difference in the way my horse performed. Maybe he was a trotter that was hitting his shins or touching his elbows or maybe he was a pacer that was jumping over things or rolling around in the hobbles or something like that. At any rate, he would be a horse that required some kind of equipment or shoeing change and that would be my reason for training him on Saturday instead of Monday with the Wednesday race in view. As I will explain later, I will step a horse along pretty good when I have a problem like this. I will even go a quarter in 30 seconds because I feel it is important under these circumstances to simulate actual racing speed.

While I am not afraid to make an equipment change in a situation like this, I want to make clear that I have never believed a horse should wear a piece of equipment unless he absolutely had to have it. I like to stay as close to nature as I can. I don't believe every pacer needs a shadow roll, tendon boots and a high head. Nor do I believe every trotter needs hinged quarter boots and a ring martingale, which is the way a lot of old-time trainers used to rig them almost automatically. I like to start out with an open bridle and a simple bit and work from there.

If a horse starts jumping over shadows, he needs a shadow roll. But I don't put one on just because I look at the horse paper and see where a lot of pacers are wearing them. If he starts getting too close to his knees, you have to use knee boots, but don't put them on just because somebody else does. Precautionary equipment in the boot line is important but only if you have a specific need.

I guess maybe every trainer has personal feelings regarding certain pieces of equipment. I know in my case I don't care for tendon boots and use them only when I absolutely have to. I have a funny theory about them; I think they can cause bowed tendons. If you will notice the way they are buckled on a horse, you will see that they put pressure on the tendon and I think this is a bad thing. I do have pacers that wear them and that didn't get bowed tendons as a result, but that is still the way I feel about them and I know I always will.

If you will go back to Chart No. 2, which we are working with, you will note that I have laid out five starts for this horse in the first month. A green horse probably won't get that many

starts at a major track but this is a consensus program so I want
to cover all the ground I can. I have spaced the five races on this
chart and on all the charts at intervals of approximately seven,
ten, five and seven days so you will get an idea of how I adjust
my schedule for a horse that has more or fewer days between
races.

I have already described what takes place during the seven-
day interval between the horse's first two races. Assuming that
he is a normal horse and has no problems, let me go on and
consider the ten-day interval between his second and third starts
(Feb. 23rd and March 5th). He races Wednesday night, is
walked on Thursday, jogged three miles Friday, four miles
Saturday and rests on Sunday. Since he is not going to race until
Saturday night, I will probably train him twice that week but
I do not want to go too much. Therefore, I will go three little
trips in 2:45, 2:30 and 2:25 on Monday, jog him on Tuesday
and Wednesday and train him two light trips on Thursday in
2:45 and 2:30. This should blow him out just about right for
his Saturday race.

He races well Saturday and has to come back the following
Thursday night. In a situation like this, he rests Sunday, jogs
Monday and Tuesday and goes a single "blow-out" mile in 2:45
on Wednesday, the day before his race. With only a five-day
interval, he doesn't need much between starts, but I feel I have
to do a little something to keep him on his toes and the 2:45
mile is enough for that purpose in my opinion.

After his Thursday race, we are back to a normal one-week
interval and he returns to his regular schedule. He gets his
slow work on Monday consisting of three miles in 2:45, 2:30 and
2:20 and that sets him up to race on Thursday. You will note
that except for the fact that the Monday and Thursday schedule
is reversed, this is the same routine I have been following at
the farm.

I hope that in presenting this basic conditioning program for
a green 3-year-old that I have been able to explain how I do
things and, what is even more important, why I do them. This
is the system I have followed for a number of years and I have
had quite a bit of success with it. My horses are ready to race
off a schedule like this and as a general rule they keep on racing
well. That is really the important thing, not that they go one

good race but that they hold their condition and race well throughout the season.

I also hope I did not make all this sound too easy. While it is true that I have a great many green horses that have followed this schedule—or one like it depending on when the horse was slated to make his first start—I have had others that have given me all kinds of fits. One of these was a trotter named Speedy Play, a son of Speedster-Gentle Play, and perhaps it would be of interest if I described my problem with him and what I went through to get him to the races and make a decent horse out of him. He ties in with the class of horse I have been discussing and shows what the other side of the coin is like.

Speedy Play was a tall, gangly 2-year-old who didn't fill out or develop very well. I trained him down to 2:25 and he showed me that while he wasn't a stake horse he had the makings of a very nice raceway trotter. I stopped making stake payments on him, turned him out and had him gelded in preparation for his 3-year-old season which would be in 1965.

He moved through the routine training program for a green 3-year-old and trained so perfectly that I had very high hopes for him. I figured he was capable of trotting in 2:06 in March, although I knew he wouldn't have to at that time of the year.

I shipped him to Yonkers to qualify him. In his first try he won in 2:10⅗, but made a break and thus failed to qualify. I tried him again a week later and he qualified by winning in 2:10⅖ without a break. I entered him in a race and he made two breaks, winding up on the steward's list.

Now he had me wondering a little because he was showing speed in his races but he wasn't set. I didn't want to make any drastic changes at this stage but I did go to a blind bridle and a standing Martingale. In addition, I plugged his ears because I thought that perhaps the noise of the racing action was bothering him. I put him in another qualifier two weeks later and he made another break.

Now I was beginning to worry. I had spent the better part of two training years getting this horse ready and I thought I had a nice green trotter only to find myself suddenly sailing up a blind river. I didn't know whether I had a horse, a dud or what.

I had a little time to experiment so I made a couple of additional changes. I went back to an open bridle, switched from a flat shoe behind to a full swedge and lightened him up a little in front.

I think all of us have a tendency to make the same mistake with a trotter that is making breaks by adding weight in front by means of a toe weight or a weighted heel boot or a quarter boot or something like that. Most of the time this isn't the right thing to do and it would have been especially harmful in the case of Speedy Play who didn't get off the ground much in front anyway. I thought weight would definitely impair him so I squared his front toes instead. I trained him after making these changes and he was fine.

He stayed flat in a qualifying race at Yonkers and then I sent him to Rosecroft where he had been named in a series of early closers. He won his first start there in 2:08⅕ and I was congratulating myself. I should have known better. He made a break in his very next start.

The following week I pulled his hind shoes before I began warming him up for his race. Sometimes a trotter will go better bare-footed behind. But I didn't like the way he warmed up without his shoes so I had them tacked back on before he raced. I also sent his groom back to the barn at the last minute for a set of brace bandages and replaced the horse's hind shin boots with these. Once in a while you will find that this will help a trotter by slowing him down a little behind. But the only way you can find these things out is by experimenting and a trainer should never be afraid to. If a horse isn't racing well, you have to do something; make some kind of a change or changes. I never hesitate. I will try anything, especially if a horse has shown me the potential that Speedy Play had.

At any rate, he went out and raced well that night, even though he was interfered with and made a break when it looked like I was going to win. Again I thought I had the problem licked and again I was wrong. He made a break in his next start. Three days later I qualified him at Rosecroft by winning in 2:09 but four days after that he made another break.

It was with mixed emotions that I shipped the horse from Rosecroft to Liberty Bell. I was quite frustrated, but I wasn't about to give up. I knew I had plenty of horse if I could only straighten him away. Speedy Play had begun to fuss with his head a little so at Liberty Bell I went to a chin strap instead of a check bit and to a standing Martingale with a nose band. And just when it seemed darkest, Speedy Play began to come to himself. He won five out of six at Liberty Bell, the fastest in 2:04⅗ and then went on to Brandywine where he won in 2:04⅕ the first week of September.

I had also changed the horse's conditioning program after I reached Liberty Bell. In making the various changes I have described, I had been working Speedy Play an extra mile on nights that he made a break and had been giving him an additional mile on his regular work day. He had begun to lose a little condition so after he started racing well at Liberty Bell I changed his training routine.

Instead of going three trips between races as I had been, I went only two with the fastest mile in 2:25. He trained and raced very well that way and after he won at Brandywine in early September I was satisfied that he had found himself and I quit with him.

In 1966, he was an outstanding trotter, winning 17 of 35 starts and was 29 times among the first three with earnings of $94,555. That year I returned to a check bit instead of a chin strap and he wore a Murphy blind on the right side, a gaiting strap on the same side and a tongue tie as well as the standing Martingale with a nose band. He trotted in an open bridle and a rubber snaffle bit and wore bell boots in front and rubber scalpers and brace bandages behind. He was shod with a half inch, half-round square-toed shoe in front and wore a flat aluminum shoe behind. I trained him the same way I did in the latter part of the 1965 season, working him two miles between races with the fastest in 2:25.

My purpose in discussing Speedy Play in such great detail is to point out that a trainer shouldn't be afraid to experiment, especially if he feels the horse has some definite potential if he, the trainer, can just find the key. In so doing, I touched on one thing that I want to go back now and discuss some more.

I said that Speedy Play had begun to get a little out of condition because I had been going extra trips with him both in regular training sessions and in bringing him back for an additional fast trip on nights that he raced and made breaks. I don't like to take more out of a horse than I have to because any kind of a training trip is a mile that the horse has had to perform and it takes something out of him.

But in order to find out if the changes I had been making were doing any good, I felt it was necessary to go pretty sharp miles to determine this. Sometimes you won't find out what you want to know unless you simulate racing conditions as much as possible, as I mentioned earlier.

For instance, let's say I had a pacer that rolled or tumbled when I pulled him out of the hole in a race or, if it was a trotter, one that was all right at an even rate of speed but made a break or got all tangled up when I moved with him. At any rate, he wasn't smooth and good at speed. I feel that a horse like this has to be stepped along a little after you make an equipment or shoeing change in order for you to be able to tell if it did any good. And when I say stepped along, I mean a quarter in 30 seconds. If he performed that chore satisfactorily, I would feel that I had accomplished something in making the change.

This is what I had been doing with Speedy Play and as a result he had begun to tuck up and lose a little condition. Since I thought I had finally got him straightened away, I decided to send him home and wait for another year rather than race him when he was not in tip-top physical shape.

It took me a long time to get Speedy Play the way I wanted him. Training a horse like this and trying to determine his trouble is a lot different from having a car break down and sending it to the garage. In that case, the mechanic simply reaches under the hood, locates the bad part and replaces it. You can't do this with a horse. About all you can do is to experiment within the bounds of common sense and good judgment and hope that the next thing you try will solve the problem. It is a procedure that is sometimes fruitful, sometimes frustrating, but always interesting and exciting.

I feel that pretty well covers the conditioning of green 3-year-olds and that I can go on now and talk about 3-year-old stake colts. I have laid out two training charts for this class of horse. I think two charts are necessary because there are actually two different types of horses involved even though both are of stakes caliber.

The horses in one of these groups will be campaigning almost entirely at the raceways and their stakes will be single dash affairs. Only rarely will they be going more than one heat and never three or four.

These horses will be ready to race a little earlier and I have set them down to make their first start on May first. Since I quit with them as 2-year-olds on November first and they have had two full months out before entering training on January first, they could be prepped for an April first opening by starting a month earlier and following the same schedule. The month they would be turned out would be enough for them.

I do not think it would be necessary or desirable to get stakes horses ready for a first start earlier than April first. At least I hope it never will be, because in my opinion that would be rushing things along too much. The training schedule for these horses is laid out on Chart No. 4.

The other stake chart (No. 5) is for horses of absolutely top quality that are being pointed specifically for the heat racing classics such as The Hambletonian for trotters and The Little Brown Jug for pacers as well as the other multi-heat races on the western circuit. When these horses get into the heart of their season, they will be going two heats almost every week and occasionally three or four. They are the ones that really need a good foundation.

I have set these horses down to make their first start on June first. They, too, can be backed up a month if necessary by curtailing the length of time they were turned out between campaigns, but I would be less likely to do that with this group than I would with the other one. What has to affect your thinking along this line is that from time to time one of the really big races over an eastern pari-mutuel track is scheduled to be raced in May. When that happens, you have to adjust your schedule to accommodate the race unless you are willing to skip it, which is unlikely.

The principal difference in the two training schedules is that those horses that are being prepped for an extensive heat racing campaign are trained four heats instead of three on their fast work day beginning about two months before they make their first start.

I am not very much in favor of training horses four heats, but if you are going to participate actively in a Grand Circuit campaign that stacks one heat race right on top of another, you'd better have a real foundation in your horse. Some time, some place, that foundation will pay off in the fourth heat of a big race.

I guess I am fairly well qualified to talk about that even though the occasion was a day that was as heart-breaking for me on the one hand as it was heart-warming on the other. I am referring, of course, to the 1965 Hambletonian which went four heats and was won by Egyptian Candor, a very game horse that I trained for my wife, Rachel, and that Del Cameron drove so well.

That was the heart-warming part. The heart-breaking part was what happened to Noble Victory, a horse that I confidently thought would win The Hambletonian easily. I have never made any excuses in my life and I am not going to start making them now. Anybody who saw the race knows that Noble Victory wasn't himself that day, that he simply couldn't handle the muddy going. But horses can't carry their race tracks around with them so I'm not going to alibi what happened.

Even though it was obviously the track condition that hampered him—he was much better in the third heat as the track surface improved than he was in the first or second—I still might have thought I had trained him wrong except that Egyptian Candor was trained exactly the same way.

They were prepped almost identically throughout the season and their workouts prior to The Hambletonian were just about the same. The foundation I had laid by training them four heats served Egyptian Candor in good stead when the time came to dig into him as it did in the fourth heat. Noble Victory would have responded in the same fashion and, in my opinion, would have gone faster than Egyptian Candor did or could have. But that's the way the ball bounces in harness racing.

Getting back to the training of these top 3-year-olds, let me refer to Chart No. 5 and point out that I begin by jogging these horses four full weeks, start their training with two single miles in a week and then go to two singles a day twice a week for five weeks. These workouts are identical and I take them down about five seconds a week until I reach the 2:30 level.

At this stage I start going three trips, make my Monday work my fast one and do not drop them as quickly. I go in 2:25 the first week, 2:22 the next and then in 2:20 the following week. The week after that, I train them exactly the same way which is a foundation workout and sets them up to begin going four heats the following week.

When I start training four heats (week of April 10th on Chart No. 5) I stick at 2:20 for a week and train my two fastest Monday miles at that notch. On Thursday I go another mile in 2:20 but I only go three heats instead of four. I do not go four heats on my slow workout day. This, of course, varies with the individual horse. With Noble Victory and Egyptian Candor, for instance, I went four trips on both days because I thought each of them needed the work. But I would train most horses three heats on the "slow" day which is why I have set the chart up that way.

After I start training four heats, I always hold my fastest mile on the slow workout day to 2:20 because I think that is enough. I am using this day to hold condition and build muscle, and I do not think there is any necessity to go more than 2:20. On the fast workout days, I start to drop the horse, first to about 2:16 and then two or three seconds a week.

When I reach the 2:15 level I start brushing these horses halves and quarters, moderately at first and then increasingly faster until in their last workout before they race, they go a mile in 2:05 with a half in 1:01 and a quarter in 30 seconds.

There is one other procedural change I make with respect to horses of this caliber. You will note on the chart that they are warmed up three heats instead of two. As I have already related, I believe two warmup miles are enough for most horses, but we are dealing here with stakes horses racing heats and I think they need an extra one. The last warmup mile is at the usual speed for a fast horse—between 2:17 and 2:20—but I throw in an extra one at 2:35.

In getting specific horses ready for certain races, I will even vary this procedure as I did when I was prepping Noble Victory and Egyptian Candor for The Hambletonian. Both had raced at Springfield, Illinois, and the following week were scheduled to go one dash in the American-National Stake at Sportsman's Park with the Hambletonian exactly a week off. Each of them had warmed up three heats and raced two at Springfield and normally they would warm up three and race one at Sportsman's. But I felt that I had to get them ready for a possible split heat race so I warmed them up four heats apiece and went along pretty brisk with them the last two. I started with trips in 2:45 and 2:30 and then followed up with trips in 2:11 and 2:07, give or take a fraction of a second. I thought then that they were ready to race four heats if they had to, even though I thought I would win it in two with Noble Victory. I am sure that this method contributed a little something to Egyptian Candor's Hambletonian victory.

After I start racing my top stakes horses, I do not train them four heats between races, unless there is a blank week on their schedule. You will note also that in going three trips between races I do not as a rule go a mile faster than 2:20. Specific circumstances might dictate otherwise on occasion, but I am dealing here with a top stakes horse that has no problems that might force me to switch plans. Actually, by warming up three heats and then racing, the horse is still going four heats on his "fast" day.

The stake horse that is picked up the first of the year and that is going to race May first and will be going single dashes is handled a little differently. First of all, he will never be trained more than three heats and since he is going to the races earlier he won't have as many timing miles in him. The exact number as listed on Chart No. 4 is 68 as contrasted to almost 100 for the other stake group. If these were horses that had not campaigned through most of the previous season, I would like to have more than that. But if they had only light campaigns I would consider them to be green 3-year-olds and would train them according to the schedules I have already reviewed for horses in that class.

Aside from the difference in the number of heats they are trained, these horses are also moved along a little faster, dropping to 2:20 in the 10th week of their training (including four weeks of jogging) as contrasted to the 13th week for the other group. Until they reach 2:25, they train the same in both workouts, after which their slow work holds at 2:25 an additional week and then drops to 2:20. I do not train these horses a mile faster than 2:20 on their slow work days from then on. Since I am moving them along pretty quickly on their fast days, I do not want to take any more out of them than I have to on the other training day. This, of course, is their foundation work.

The last week of April I will work these horses a mile in 2:05 with a half in 1:01 and a last quarter in 30 seconds. They have been gradually led into this kind of a mile and are ready for it. I should emphasize again at this point that if any of them indicate to me for any reason that they are not ready to meet the schedule I have laid out, I discard the schedule and train the horse in accordance with the situation that has developed. The mile in 2:05 that I have trained these horses might sound a little fast but you must remember that we are talking about stakes horses and presumably all of them in this class demonstrated the previous year their ability to go at this rate or even much faster. These horses, incidentally, are warmed up two heats on race night just as my other raceway horses are.

Before getting into the conditioning of other classes of horses, I want to take a little time right here to emphasize through specific example that not all horses can or should be trained alike and that, in some cases, even individual horses will vary from year to year as to conditioning requirements.

I have already gone into some detail explaining how I trained Noble Victory and Egyptian Candor, pointing out that Noble Victory in particular was a horse that, as a two and 3-year-old, seemed to require a great deal of work between races to keep him on edge and in top form.

Egyptian Candor was retired at the end of his 3-year-old form, but I planned to race Noble Victory again and conditioned him in much the same manner as I began preparing him for his 4-year-old campaign. Before going to the races I worked him a mile in 1:59⅘ in company with Bonjour Hanover and Cardigan Bay and was confident that he was fit and ready. I thought I had the right number of miles in him, that he wasn't over-trained and that there was no way that I could have conditioned him better.

But Noble Victory raced in a disappointing manner in his first few starts. He didn't finish back up the track by any means and in his first four starts he had a first, a second and two thirds, but I thought he should have done better. In his fifth start, he got in a mixup in the first turn and made a break, finishing eighth. He came out of that race with a big ankle and I was afraid he might not remain sound. Consequently, I trained him very lightly between races and he came back exactly seven days later at Roosevelt Raceway and equalled the world's record of 2:31⅖ for a mile and a quarter in winning The American Trotting Championship. He then went back on his regular training schedule and turned in two very poor races. One was The Roosevelt International in which he did not seem to have his lick at all, even though he finished third, and the other was The Gold Cup the following week in which he was only beaten a nose, but in the relatively slow time of 3:07⅘ for a mile and a half.

Right there I sat down and did some thinking. There was nothing wrong with my horse, but at the same time he wasn't the Noble Victory I knew so well. I racked my brain in an effort to figure out what I might be doing wrong. One of the things that came to mind was that Noble Victory had gone his best race of the season the week before The International when he had trained less between races than ever before. As I have repeatedly said, I am not afraid to experiment, even with top horses, when I know they are not producing up to their potential and no horse in my stable, not even one as great as Noble Victory, is an exception to this rule.

I decided to let up on Noble Victory between races and after his last Roosevelt start, which was on July 16th, I didn't do a thing with him except jog him three miles a day until his next race which was at Brandywine Raceway on July 23rd, exactly a week later. Normally, I would have trained him three miles in 2:45, 2:25 and 2:20 three days prior to the race.

Noble Victory responded to this type of conditioning by scoring a 3¾ length victory at Brandywine in track record time of 2:00⅖. Six days later, without any training between races, he won at Saratoga in a world record 1:59. Eight days later, again without being trained between starts, he went to Sportsman's Park and won by two lengths in a track record 1:59⅖.

He had three weeks off after that and was trained once a week instead of twice a week with the fastest mile each week in 2:10 before coming back to equal the stake record in winning a mile and a quarter event in 2:31⅘ at Yonkers. He was scheduled to race at Du Quoin exactly a week later and since I knew that I might be going for a world's record if conditions were right, I took the liberty of working him one trip in 2:45 three days before he raced. He responded with a mile in 1:55⅗ and exactly a week later, again without being trained, won the $100,000 Empire at Yonkers by more than two lengths.

To my way of thinking, this is a perfect example of the need for a trainer to make a change in conditioning techniques under

certain circumstances. The trainer who adopts a single conditioning system for all horses and follows it blindly is riding for a
fall.

The experience I had with Noble Victory is almost identical
to one I ran into several years earlier with Worth Seein, a really
high class trotting mare owned by Lou and Hilda Silverstein. She,
too, was a 4-year-old at the time and had just won handily in
2:02⅕ at Liberty Bell. The American-National Stake for $63,639
was exactly two weeks off at Sportsman's Park and I thought
she was a lead pipe cinch to win it. I figured that all I had to
do was to sharpen her up a little and collect the money.

Exactly a week before the stake, I trained her four trips with
the third mile in 2:07 and the last one in 2:02. She felt like she
could have beaten 2:00 for fun. That was on a Friday and the following Tuesday I trained her three routine trips with the fastest
in 2:20. She then proceeded to go a terrible race in The American-National, one of the worst she ever went in her life.

I went over everything I could think of and came up with a
blank. She was sound, eating well, looked good and had no
temperature. The more I thought about it, the more I came back
to the way I had dug into her between races. I decided to back
off on her training and see what happened.

The next time I raced her I didn't train her at all beforehand
and she went a real fine race. That convinced me she didn't want
a lot of work between races and I began conditioning her that
way.

If she raced on a Friday and had to go back on Wednesday,
I wouldn't train her at all. If she had to go back on Thursday, I
would go one heat with her between races, maybe a mile in 2:40
on Tuesday. If her races were scheduled on Friday and exactly
a week apart I would train her two little heats on Monday, something like 2:45 and 2:30. If there was a two-week period between
races, I would train her three heats with the fastest between
2:10 and 2:12 exactly a week between the races and otherwise
would not train her at all. I also warmed her up about as slowly
as I could on race night. I would go my first mile in 2:45 and
then one around 2:25. Of course, she was jogged three miles a
day except on Sunday.

But despite the fact that I eased up with excellent results on
both Noble Victory and Worth Seein, I want to emphasize and

point out by example that just the opposite could be true for another horse. I have had a number of horses that really had to be drilled hard between races to be at their very best and while I could cite a half dozen of them I will content myself with using Bonjour Hanover, a very great pacing filly, as an example.

During the 1966 season, Bonjour Hanover rattled off a long string of victories and was obviously the best in her division. But I was never satisfied that she was performing as well as I knew she could and after she won at Sportsman's Park in late August for her 12th win in 14 starts I decided that she was acting like a filly that could stand more work.

She had raced on a Tuesday at Sportsman's and was scheduled to race at Du Quoin on a Thursday, nine days later. Normally I would have trained her three light trips on Monday, the fastest in 2:20. But I decided to dig into her and trained her four heats in 2:40, 2:20, 2:10 and 2:06, all evenly rated. From the way she had been acting, I thought this should set her up perfectly for her Thursday race and I was right. She went out and won by 15 lengths in 1:57 and came back in 1:59⅕ for a one and two-heat world record performance. She had never been better in her life and I am sure that the extra work I gave her on Monday set her up for her Thursday race.

I had planned to do the same thing Little Brown Jug week, but the weather fouled me up to some extent, although I was still very satisfied with her showing. I entered her in the filly stake on Monday and planned to come back in The Jug on Thursday. A lot of people thought this was too close, but I knew Bonjour very well and was sure it would help her rather than hurt her. Unfortunately, the track was very bad on Monday and we only went one heat, which I won in 2:11⅗. I figured that was equivalent to a 2:03 mile over a fast track but was sorry that I couldn't get a second mile into her.

At any rate, she was very sharp on Jug Day although she could not beat Romeo Hanover. She finished 4-3, but I felt she was second best except for poor racing luck. I know for sure that no horse ever went a tougher trip than she did in the second heat when she was parked out the entire mile over a track that was not good and still hung on to be third in 1:59⅗.

These are examples of individuality in horses. I know that if I tried to train Bonjour Hanover the way I did Noble Victory and Worth Seein, she would have been way short. And I also know that if I had drilled the other two between races the way I did Bonjour that they would have been dull on race day. These are things that a horse trainer has to figure out for himself. The only guideline is the sure and certain fact that no two horses are exactly alike and that the smart trainer is the one who is not afraid to experiment when he knows there is room for improvement in the performance of a specific horse.

Incidentally, writing about Worth Seein reminds me of another incident involving her that serves as an illustration of the little things a horse trainer has to be constantly on the lookout for. It doesn't apply directly to the conditioning of a horse but it involves a situation that any trainer might run up against at any time and is worth mentioning for that reason.

Worth Seein was three at the time, had won at Lexington and Washington, Pa., where the Arden Downs Stakes used to be raced, and I had her in a big stake in New York for around $50,000. I warmed her up the night of the race and she was terribly foul-gaited. This bothered me because I couldn't figure what could possibly be wrong with her. After her last warmup mile, I began to tick off possibilities in my mind and the only thing that was at all different was that she was wearing a new pair of hind shoes. She had worn the same set in her three previous races and I had had her re-shod for this race.

It was a terrible decision to have to make at that stage but I finally decided that this had to be the reason she was acting the way she was, so between her last warmup mile and the race I pulled her hind shoes. I raced her bare-footed behind and she went a great race, was perfectly gaited and won easily. You can imagine that I breathed a sigh of relief when that was over.

What had happened, of course, was that the previous set of shoes had worn down real thin and she was set and all right in them. But the new ones were heavier and shaped differently and it affected her gait. If the old shoes had been available I would have tacked them on and I am sure she would have been just as good, but I didn't have them so I had to take a chance and make a spot decision. Anybody who says the little things don't count in training trotters and pacers has a lot to learn.

Now I will return to general conditioning techniques and discuss some of the other classes of horses that trainers have to deal

with. One of these is the older raceway horse that has been to
the wars and knows something about how to conduct himself
under battlefield conditions. As such, he is an entirely different
conditioning proposition than either the green 3-year-old or the
stake horse.

You rarely have to teach this horse anything. All you have to
do is to condition him. I thought originally of setting up a single
training chart for the raceway horse but after considering the
matter I decided that I was actually dealing with two different
types of horses as well as a number of possibilities regarding
the length of time required to get them ready. Since my overall
purpose in this chapter is to provide as much general information on conditioning horses as I possibly can, I have expanded
these charts in two ways.

I have broken the horses down into two principal categories,
those that will race between 2:01 and 2:05 and those that will
go from 2:06 to 2:10. They will be conditioned approximately
alike except that the faster class will go more in the later stages
of the training program. For that reason I decided it would
be best to separate them.

The other factor is that horses quit racing and start up again on
many different dates. We have raceway horses now that quit
December first and start again a month later. But at the same
time, we still have those that get anywhere from two to six
months off. To accommodate this variance, I have laid out a
number of different schedules with the time away from the races
ranging from 30 days to six months. What I hope I have accomplished in doing this is that any trainer in the country will be able
to find "his" horse and "his" training period on one of these charts.

For the purpose of specific discussion, I am going to limit myself to the older, fast class (2:01-2:05) raceway horse that quits
on December 15th and is going back to the races on February
15th, just two short months later (Chart No. 6). I selected this
category because it is one of the newest we have to contend with
in the face of an expanding harness racing season, and, since it is
new, I thought it might be of the most interest.

Our horse came home from the races on December 15th. He
is turned out for two weeks. I think that turning a horse out,
even for a brief period and even when, as in this case, we are
faced with a short prep time, is vital. I think a horse that is

turned out tends to take a new view of life. Just the idea of getting away from the same old routine is as important as the fact that he is being turned out. Horses are like people. They get tired of the same old thing all the time. If they can be turned out for as little as two weeks, they seem to take a new lease on life and come back refreshed and ready.

When I first turn a horse out, I do him up in leg bandages and bell boots. Many horses, when turned out for the first time in a long while, will buck and jump and play. This is when they are likely to strike a quarter or a tendon or something like that and injure themselves. In most instances, I will only turn a horse out a little while each day for the first week so that he can get acclimated. I might give him 15 minutes in the morning and 15 minutes in the evening the first day and then gradually extend that.

With the raceway horse I am writing about that will be back in training in two weeks, I would probably give him an hour both morning and evening the first day, extend that to two hours morning and evening the second day and then all day after that. It depends on his reaction and, to some degree, on the weather.

This also brings up the subject of letting a horse down after a long season of racing. Whether to let one down by continuing to train him for a stipulated period at an increasingly slower rate, is really nothing more than a matter of opinion. Some trainers turn horses out immediately without letting them down at all, others jog their horses daily but do not train them while the remainder do let their horses down by training them at an increasingly slower rate for perhaps three weeks after they are through racing.

Years ago, it was fairly routine to let a horse down by training him lightly. The principle was that a horse that had been racing fast miles every week for a number of months should not immediately be turned out thus exposing him to a sudden and drastic change.

Personally, I do not let horses down. I just turn them out and let them enjoy a little freedom. I feel that they have had enough of the harness and the cart and the routine of training and that what they really need is some rest. In my opinion, horses do not have to be trained to let them down.

I think it is also important that such horses be turned out

twice a day rather than once and the longer each time the better. You have to remember that these horses are tight and that they do need exercise. They will take the exercise themselves if you will give them the opportunity.

The exception—and there are always exceptions in the horse-training business—is that if you have a real lazy horse that won't take any exercise, it would be preferable to jog him a couple of miles a day for the first week and then turn him out after that, making certain that you waited about an hour after he was jogged before turning him out. Of course, if you are located where you can't turn a horse out, then you definitely should jog him daily to make certain he gets some exercise.

Now let me get back to the raceway horse (Chart No. 6) that I quit with on December 15th. Considering that I have only eight full weeks to get this horse back to the races I have to pick him up and start jogging him after two weeks. Because he has to return to the races so quickly, I will only jog this horse two weeks instead of four before I begin to train him. But this horse has never really been let down. He is in racing condition and is just being given a lengthy breather between campaigns.

When I pick this horse up to begin jogging him, I will go two miles a day the first two days, 2½ the next two and three on Friday and Saturday of that week. I will move him up to 3½ the following Monday and to four on Thursday.

The next week I will put him on a regular training schedule and go two miles in 2:40 on Monday. On Thursday, I will go my first mile in 2:45 and then drop to 2:30. The following week I will go two heats on Monday with the fastest in 2:25, and then start training three heats on Thursday with the fastest in 2:20. I am dropping this horse quite rapidly, but he still has a foundation from the previous season and can stand it without any trouble.

Now I have only two full weeks and part of another before he starts and if he is a fast class horse, one that will race between 2:01 and 2:05, as this one is, I have to start digging into him even more abruptly. On January 30th, I work him in 2:15 and go a half in 1:05 and a quarter in 32 seconds. I make Thursday his slow work day and hold him at 2:25 for his fastest mile that day, although I do reduce his middle mile from 2:35 to 2:30. I cut his jog miles back to two after his fast work and to three on Friday.

The following Monday, with his racing debut scheduled in

nine days, I work him in 2:10 and come a half in 1:03 and a quarter in 31 seconds. He will race off this. He walks the day after this work and his Wednesday jogging is cut back to three miles. He has a normal slow work on Thursday and since he is scheduled to race the following Wednesday, I give him an identical slow work again on Monday. I jog him three miles on Tuesday and race him on Wednesday. You will notice that his last warmup mile before he races is in 2:18. This is a little better than the 2:20 which the green horses go and is a routine figure for raceway horses. Both warmup miles are evenly rated.

The training procedure for a slower class horse (2:06-2:10) with the same schedule will be found on Chart No. 7. The routine is the same through the week of January 23rd, but from that time on, I do not drop the slower class horse as quickly. I will race him off a mile in 2:15 and his last warmup mile on race night will be in 2:22 rather than 2:18. You can observe the difference in the two schedules by studying the charts. Between races, I will train the two types (fast class and slow class) much the same except that I will go an extra heat with the fast class horse the day before his race, the week of March 6th. I feel that I have to do a little more under the circumstances with a horse that might have to race in 2:02 than with one that I expect to go in 2:09.

I have trained quite a few horses in this manner and they have raced exactly in their class and have gone exactly where I thought they should go. On a number of occasions, my fast class raceway horses have raced between 2:01 and 2:03 off a prep of this type.

I think I should probably comment briefly on the raceway horse that quits on December 15th and is going to start again on January 15th. We are starting to get some like this these days and I have laid out two charts (Nos. 8 and 9) covering the two classes of raceway horses I have been writing about. These horses don't get turned out at all.

How long horses can last under a program like this is a question I cannot answer. But I certainly don't believe you can race a horse 11 months out of the year and expect him to keep his form over that period. It is simply asking too much of him. Sooner or later you are going to have to give him a prolonged vacation.

I do think that the slower class horses will outlast the free-for-all type. The slow class horse isn't going as fast and doesn't have to contend with distance races as the free-for-allers do. I think the free-for-all horses and our stake horses that engaged in heat races extensively at two and three will show the effects first. But experience is going to be the only teacher and time will provide the only answer.

There are two other types of horses that will benefit appreciably from being turned out at regular intervals. They are the sore horses that are "race horse sound" and the poor doers that don't eat well, and fret and worry every time you put the harness on them.

What I have done with horses like this is to send them back to the farm for a week and race them off nothing, no training and no jogging in between. I will only warm the horse up one heat around 2:25 and go with him. You have to remember that I am not talking about lame horses, but horses that are just a little sore. The state vet won't let you race a lame horse and I wouldn't race one anyway. But I do race horses that are just a little sore and I have found that this is an ideal way to do it.

When they are turned out back on the farm, the poor doers will eat and will take on flesh. In each of these instances, the horses must be turned out so that they can exercise. It doesn't do a bit of good just to send them away from the race track and put them in a box stall. They have to get out and move around.

What it all boils down to is that the sore horse will race better if he is relatively sound and a little short than if he is tight and lame. By the same token, the poor feeder will feel stronger rather than weaker when he races. Again, experience is the only teacher but I have had success doing this and I know that other trainers have, too.

The trotter or pacer that is "race horse sound" and that I have just referred to, is the only other type of horse whose conditioning program requires any explanation among those for which I have laid out training charts. This horse is not actually lame but he is a little off, usually as a result of a chronic ailment of one type or another that makes him a prime candidate for lameness if he is pushed too hard. I have already described the training principle involved which is that the horse is better off "short (of work) and sound" rather than "tight and lame." Training Chart No. 10 covers this type.

I have laid out this chart for a horse in the 2:06-2:10 raceway class, but there would not be much variance whatever his capability. I do not feel that I can give this horse any very fast training miles and I am especially careful not to brush him any fast halves or quarters. I also feel that I must train him a little bit lighter all the way around.

With that in mind, you will note on the chart that I do not train him faster than 2:15 and do not drill him any fast fractions. While I drop this horse to 2:20 a week earlier than a completely sound horse in the same class (See Chart No. 12), I only go two trips instead of three on his slow work day and do not beat 2:30 on that day at any time during the pre-racing conditioning period. On his slow work day, I jog this horse an extra mile and I neither walk him after a workout nor decrease the non-training day jog miles until after he gets to the races.

What I am trying to do is to get him to the races with enough work under him to establish a solid foundation but without ever having asked him for his limit, or anywhere near his limit, at any time during the conditioning program. A horse of this type should maintain a consistent racing form off this kind of prep. On race night, I warm him up two miles but the second one is not quite as fast as my usual final warmup miles, perhaps 2:22 to 2:25 instead of from 2:17 to 2:20.

As I mentioned previously, some horses like this are not trained at all between races and hold up very well this way. Unless the horse is a borderline case between "race horse sound" and "unsound," I would much prefer to get a little work in him because slow miles can be very beneficial and are not likely to bring about lameness. In most instances, horses of this type finally go lame after being called on to go at top speed, especially if that speed has to be maintained over any appreciable distance. These are the horses that you have to save ground with in a race and cannot use as boldly as you would others. Whatever they have in them must be conserved, both in training and in actual competition.

As our racing season lengthens and our horses are called on to race for longer and longer periods, I think all trainers have to start giving some thought to letting up on horses sometime during the year. Horses are flesh and blood and if you don't let up on them occasionally something will have to give. When this happens, the trainer, the horse, and the owner will suffer.

As in other areas, trainers are going to have to experiment. But I am sure that one of the things that will happen is that some of us will start giving our horses a little time off during the campaign. It seems to me that if a man planned to race a horse ten months out of the year he would be wise if he raced the horse five months, gave him a month off and then raced him another five. After that, I would think any horse ought to have two or three months off before repeating that pattern.

I have thought quite a bit about this and have laid out a training chart (No. 13) for a horse that is slated for a month off from the races during the peak of the season. I have set it up for the month of July. The horse races on July first and will make his next start on August 3rd.

First of all, I think it would be most advantageous if the horse was turned out for two full weeks. There is no question in my mind that horses get sick and tired of the same old surroundings after a while and that two weeks spent running out in a pasture or a large paddock is much superior to standing up in a stall. It's just like a man who works hard all year and goes on vacation for two weeks. He wants to get away from anything that reminds him of that daily grind and the farther the better.

So I would start my horse off on his "vacation" with two full weeks as a turnout. He should have room to run and play; he should be grained twice a day and have all the hay and fresh water he wants. Other than that he should be on his own. Depending on the circumstances and the type of horse he was, I might do him up in bandages and bell boots, but whether I did that or not I know I would pull his shoes during this period.

After two full weeks out, I would pick the horse up and begin jogging him. I would jog him two miles the first day, three miles the second and four miles the third. I can get him right up to a four-mile jog because he hasn't really been let down and is still in race horse condition. On Thursday of this third week, I would jog him two miles, work him a mile in 2:50 and then come back from 50 minutes to an hour later (the time between heats is longer because of the hot weather) with a mile in 2:40. I would jog him four miles on Friday and work him three moderate trips with the fastest in 2:30 on Saturday.

The following week I would work him a mile in 2:15 on Tuesday and in either 2:05 or 2:10 on Friday, depending on his class. If he were a 2:01-2:05 horse I would work him in 2:05-1:02-:30, whereas if he were a 2:06-2:10 horse I would train him in 2:10-1:03-:31. The horses is just a week away from racing now and I feel I have to get one decent work into him.

I would walk the horse on Saturday, train him back three miles on Tuesday with the last one in 2:20 evenly rated and figure he was ready to race on Friday. The only change I would make in his normal routine on race day is that I would jog him a mile that morning instead of walking him. Since he had been off a month, I would feel that this would do him a little more good than a walk, even though, as I have already explained, I do not normally jog horses on race day morning during the hot weather months.

I would consider that this horse would race right back to where he had a month earlier when I stopped with him. And in view of the two weeks that he had had to run out, I would also feel that I had done the horse a lot of good and that he would be much more likely to race for another four or five months than if I had not freshened him up this way.

In addition to those training charts which I have now discussed in some detail, I have prepared a number of others that cover varying periods of training and time away from the races. By now, I imagine that my training routines and the reasons I do or do not do certain things are familiar to the reader. Therefore, I do not feel it is necessary to comment further on these additional charts which will be found at the end of this chapter.

As everyone knows, American training methods differ greatly from those in use in other parts of the world. I have never been in Europe so I cannot comment authoritatively on what they do over there, but I have been in New Zealand and Australia and have observed their methods at close hand. I know that George Noble, a prominent New Zealand horseman, is doing a chapter on training in that country but I do not think it would be out of order if I, as an American trainer, reported what I saw there, my reaction to it and how I went about converting one well-known horse, Cardigan Bay, to the American training system. In view of the large number of horses that are being shipped to this country from New Zealand and Australia each year, I think this might be of interest.

I went to New Zealand in February of 1964 and bought Cardigan Bay. I saw things in the way of training techniques that I had never seen before and never thought I would see. But I want to say right here that they are quite successful using these methods and I was quite impressed by them.

For instance, I saw a trainer jogging one horse and leading two others behind the cart. This is done to save time and labor and it seemed to work quite well. The horses that were being led were well-mannered and accustomed to this system and it didn't seem to bother them a bit.

They place a lot of stress on jogging and do it by the watch rather than by distance. They may jog a horse for an hour or an hour and a half. They jog the right way of the track and usually on the run rather than on the trot or pace.

Cardigan Bay had had a hip knocked down when he was younger so they jogged him on the trot rather than on the run. Two days before he was scheduled to race, I saw Cardigan Bay jogged 15 miles after which they took him to a little shed, something like one of our paddocks, and tied him to a rail much like the hitching rails you see on front of saloons in old western movies. Then they put the hobbles and boots on him and brought him right back and trained him two miles without stopping. I timed the first mile in 2:20 and the second in 2:02⅗.

The temperature was right at 100 degrees and as soon as Cardigan Bay left the track he was brought back to the "paddock," his gear was removed and he was washed down with a hose and cold water. Then they put a cooler on him and walked him for about five minutes. Now he was cooled out. They put him on a trailer and hauled him about three miles to where he was stabled. This was like a garage in your back yard. He was fed in this stable and then turned out in a paddock.

I rode along in the trailer, which they call a "float," with his trainer, Peter Wolfenden, a very nice fellow who was extremely cooperative and helpful to me. He told me how he had trained the horse in the past and how he was getting him ready for the race the next night.

He said that on the following day the horse would be hauled back to the track and jogged from 15 to 20 miles. Some horses, he told me, are "breezed" on the morning of the race. They jog five miles and then are turned and trained a mile and a half with the first mile in 2:20 and the last half in 1:05.

Cardigan Bay raced cold out of the paddock that night. I saw it or I wouldn't have believed it. He was brought to the track with the harness on and when the race was called he went out on the track for the first time that evening. I did notice that they scored their horses farther and faster than we do. This warmed them up and they were ready to race.

Cardigan Bay started with a big handicap but he just circled the field and kept on going to win around 2:02. He looked like a lot of horse and after I completed the negotiations leading to his purchase for $100,000 I sat back and did some serious thinking.

I finally decided that if I continued to train him in our country under their system that he would not hold up. I considered that their horses don't race as often, that their season is much shorter and that their climate is a lot different, much hotter than ours as a rule. I had two months to decide what to do.

The first thing I did with Cardigan Bay when he arrived in this country was to turn him out for 10 days. He was used to that because they believe in turning a horse out all they can and he usually got out every day which is a good thing for a horse. They would turn him out in a paddock with maybe 10 other geldings.

When I started to train him, I knew I wanted to cut back on his jogging but I was afraid to cut it back too far so I started by jogging him about seven miles a day. He learned quickly to jog the wrong way of the track and I didn't have any trouble in that respect.

Then I put him on my regular twice-a-week training schedule and was pleased to observe that he adapted readily. At first he would want to go a little bit more than I would want him to or when I would want him to pull up at the end of a mile he would want to go on. But he soon got over that and those were the only problems I had relative to changing him over.

I worked him in 2:05 before I left home and when he got to Yonkers I qualified him for the judges in 2:02 after warming him up in 2:40 and 2:20. He felt like he could have gone in 2:00 and he went on that year to earn $160,000 and won in 1:58⅕ at Yonkers which is the world's record for a gelding. Between races he was trained just like my other horses, three trips in 2:40, 2:30 and 2:20.

At the beginning of the 1965 season, I ran into trouble with him. He prepped well and went an average race in his first start. In his second start he raced badly. I had a vet look him over but we couldn't find anything wrong so I raced him a third time. He raced badly again.

Now I began to think that maybe my training methods were wrong and that I had better go back to the New Zealand system which I had copied down in detail before I left that country. I started jogging him long distances, 15 to 20 miles, training him one two-mile heat, warming him up the morning of his race and racing him cold. But he still raced badly. I finally brought him home after another month of this and blistered a front leg which looked a little suspicious. The blister didn't come down like it should have so we X-rayed the leg and it showed a broken splint bone.

Dr. Churchill removed the splint bone and I started jogging the horse six days later on an American schedule. He got back to the races in six weeks and was his old self again. I sure was glad to find out that it was unsoundness that was bothering him and that the training methods didn't have anything to do with it.

In my opinion, a comparison of training methods used in different countries boils down to just one thing: A great horse is a great horse regardless of the training system you use. I think you have to use a little common sense and hit a happy medium somewhere but aside from that a trainer is pretty much on his own. Cardigan Bay is a perfect example of that. He was a champion while racing under two different systems. I did not think the horse would stand up to a long and arduous campaign in this country if I used the New Zealand system. But for the type of campaign laid out for him in his own country, the training method was fine.

Cardigan Bay also ties in naturally with another subject I want to discuss with reference to the proper conditioning of horses. That is distance racing. I might add that I am not in favor of distance races because I think our horses would last a lot longer if we didn't have them but most of the purses involved are so worthwhile that we have to shoot for them and prepare our horses for them.

My advice is that if a horse is sound he should be trained a little extra distance but at a moderate rate. I have to feel that if you are going to race a mile and a quarter, you should go at least one mile and a quarter heat the last time you train him before the race or maybe the last couple times if your schedule will permit it. As far as I am concerned, it would be all right to train two of the three heats at a mile and a quarter. If the race were at a mile and a half, I would train my horse that distance. But at no time would I recommend training a fast mile and a quarter or a mile and a half. This would do your horse more harm than good and as you read on you will find that on the lone occasion that I violated this rule myself the results were not satisfactory.

SuMac Lad was a horse that could go any distance over any footing. He didn't require a lot of fast miles between races. Sometimes I wouldn't beat 2:25 with him between races or maybe my best mile would be around 2:20 depending on when he last raced and when he was scheduled to race again. When he was scheduled to race a mile and a half, I would train him one heat at a mile, the second heat at a mile and a half but at a very slow rate and the third heat at a mile and a half in something like 3:33. I recall that this is the way I trained him prior to the Gotham trot which he won in 3:11 at Yonkers in 1960. You can see that he was not trained faster than 22 seconds of where he raced. I gave him the distance but not the speed. His fastest mile was fast enough and yet not too fast. I think it set him up very well.

I usually worked Cardigan Bay the same way in prepping him for distance races but I ran into late-season problems both in 1965 and 1966 and had to revamp his usual conditioning program both years. Each time it worked out quite well and I think it might be worthwhile if I reviewed what I did.

In 1965, Cardigan Bay had raced in California and had won three out of four at Hollywood Park including a world record trip in 1:57⅖. He was extremely sharp. I shipped him back to Roosevelt Raceway and he had a three-week layoff before his last two starts which were the $50,000 National Pacing Derby at a mile and a quarter and the $50,000 Nassau Pace at a mile and a half. These races were spaced a week apart in December.

I trained him a fairly slow mile and a quarter in preparation for the first race and he won quite handily coming the last quarter in 29 seconds. But he pulled up a little sore and I had a problem about what to do with him to prep him for the mile and a half race a week later. Normally, I would have trained him a mile and a half and while I realized that he needed a little work I didn't want to press him by going that distance when he wasn't 100% right. So I crossed my fingers and worked him two light miles three days before the race, one in 2:40 and the other in 2:30. Both were evenly rated. The old horse raced exceptionally well off those two miles and won the Nassau, coming the last half of his mile and a half in a minute, the last quarter in 29 seconds breezing.

Just a year later, I was faced with the same kind of a conditioning problem for the same horse but under slightly different circumstances. Once again, Cardigan Bay had raced in California and was coming back to Roosevelt to wind up his campaign.

The difference this time was that while Cardigan Bay was sound he hadn't raced up to what I thought was his potential in California. He shipped back east and I had two weeks before the first of three races which, in order, would be the $25,000 Adios Butler at a mile, the $50,000 National Pacing Derby at a mile and a quarter and, once again, the $50,000 Nassau at a mile and a half.

I let him skip a workout the first week he was home and then decided that although his next race was at a mile, he had two races at longer distances following immediately and that I'd better tie into him pretty good. I was on the shelf at the time with a neck injury and I asked my brother Vernon to work him three trips, the first two in 2:40 and 2:20 and the last one a pretty good mile and a half. Vernon went the first mile in 2:10 and the last half in a minute for a mile and a half in 3:10. He said the horse trained great and felt good. I felt that since he hadn't been racing as well as he should have in California that maybe he needed a good trip to jar him loose. As it turned out, it was the wrong decision and I shouldn't have violated my own rule about not working a horse fast when going an extra distance.

I didn't see the Adios Butler, which was the one mile race, but I heard the call over the phone and talked to Vernon later. The horse was parked to the half but he had good cover and never showed any high speed. He wasn't the Cardigan Bay I knew. He had raced just as he had in California and I had to decide how to prepare for the mile and a quarter and mile and a half races that were coming up.

One of the things I did was to talk to Joe Wideman, Cardigan

Bay's caretaker. Now I don't recommend that trainers consult with caretakers about the conditioning of horses because you can get in all kinds of trouble that way. But it is a little different story with a fellow like Joe Wideman. He is one of the all-time great caretakers and had spent virtually all his time with Cardigan Bay since the horse came to this country. He knows the horse better than anyone else in the world.

The actual question I asked him was whether he thought the horse was better with more work or less work. Joe hesitated before replying and I could tell that he didn't feel it was his position to be offering advice to the trainer. But I assured him that in this case his opinion would be helpful to me and he then told me he thought Cardigan Bay was better off with less work. I had been getting around to this view myself so I decided to let up on the horse for his last two starts.

Cardigan Bay had raced on Saturday and was scheduled to go a mile and a quarter the following Saturday. From Monday through Wednesday, he was jogged five miles each morning and turned out in the afternoon. On Thursday, I had Joe jog him five miles and then I trained one trip, just about as slow as I could, a mile in 2:30, but I stepped the last quarter in 29 seconds. He was jogged five miles on Friday and shipped to Roosevelt that evening. On Saturday morning he was jogged a mile and that evening I warmed him up differently than I ever had before. Instead of going two warmup miles, I jogged him two miles after the third race and warmed him up a mile in 2:22 free-legged after the fourth. The horse went a spectacular race; I don't think he ever went a better one, although the time wasn't outstanding, 2:34⅖ for the mile and a quarter. I went to the front with him three different times and he won quite handily. I was very pleased.

Now he had one race remaining, the Nassau nine nights later. I had already decided that he didn't need much between these two races, but I wanted to be exact about it and the interval between races was two days longer than the usual seven. I went over everything carefully and decided to jog him five miles a day and to work him one heat at a mile and a half on Thursday with the race scheduled for the following Monday. After he was jogged on Thursday, I had him geared up just as though he was going to race and I trained him the mile and a half in 3:28. I went a very slow first mile, in exactly 2:28 and then went the last half in a minute evenly rated.

Once again, I didn't know whether I had done right or not but I was fully committed. Cardigan Bay was jogged five miles a day on Friday and Saturday and shipped on Sunday. He was jogged a mile Monday morning and warmed up that night the same as the week before. He came through again with an outstanding performance and won in 3:09⅗ in much simpler fashion than his neck margin at the end indicated. In his last two races he had truly been the Cardigan Bay of old and I am sure that the manner in which he was conditioned had a great deal to do with the way he raced.

Writing about SuMac Lad as I was a few paragraphs back, reminds me of the number of times people have come up to me and said, "Don't you wish SuMac Lad hadn't been gelded? What a loss to the breed that was." Well, it might have been a loss to the breed but I'll tell you one thing for sure: In my opinion, you probably would never have heard of SuMac Lad if he hadn't been gelded. Because the gelding of horses plays a part in the conditioning and training picture, let me offer my thoughts on it.

First of all, let me discuss SuMac Lad. He was a horse that tended to be nervous and flighty even after he was gelded and at certain times I think it would even be proper to describe him as verging on the hysterical.

For one thing, he wouldn't wear a mud apron. A mud apron is a little piece of canvas that comes down from the horse's back and fastens to the sulky. It keeps the mud off the driver. I tried one on SuMac Lad and he kicked and got all sweaty and worked himself up to a point where I thought he might get hurt. I tried it a couple of times but I finally had to discard it and take a beating myself every time he raced in the mud.

Another thing about him was that when you would get him around water trucks or harrows and things like that he would be worse than the greenest 2-year-old. He'd be all over the track and acting scared to death of them. And when you'd start training him in the spring, he'd want to kick all the time and get sideways in the shafts. He wasn't mean and you didn't have to worry about him that way, but he acted nervous and worried all the time. I think his disposition was such that if he'd been left entire nobody would ever have heard of him.

Generally speaking, I am in favor of gelding horses that are not of stakes caliber and thus have no stallion potential. I think the proper time to geld such a horse is when you quit with him at the end of his 2-year-old form. The type of horse that I will almost always geld under these circumstances is the one that is acting like a "bully" around the track or barn, one that pins his ears or even one that has speed and sulks on you, doesn't give his best. I also like to geld the ones that act mean and miserable around the stall and are apt to hurt themselves or somebody else.

I don't usually geld a horse whose only fault is that he is lazy because this will sometimes tend to make him even lazier. An exception to this line of thinking was William Time, a good pacer by Good Time-Direct Win that I bought for Mr. Irving Berkemeyer for $26,000 as a yearling. This colt was a disappointment to me from the time I broke him. If I wanted to train him in 2:20 and the others in his set went in that notch he would tag along and go in 2:22 or something like that. I finally got him to the races as a 2-year-old but it was the same thing all over again. If they went in 2:15 he would go in 2:16, if they went in 2:10 he went in 2:11. I was thoroughly disgusted.

As I said, I would not normally geld a colt like this because his only fault was that he was lazy and just wouldn't try. But I finally decided he'd never make any more than a county fair horse unless I did something and at this point I was willing to try just about anything in an effort to recoup something for the owner. I had the horse gelded when I quit with him as a 2-year-old.

When I started to train him the next year, it didn't appear that the change had made any difference. There was a little improvement but not very much. I wasn't very happy when I sent him to the races off a 2:15 mile, but I was still hoping for the best.

He won two of his first five starts, the second in 2:12⅕ and the fourth in 2:08⅕. But he never really tried very hard and while he had shown improvement he still didn't act like much horse. But the sixth time I raced him he showed me something. He really barreled out from behind the gate and showed me high speed going into the first turn. I backed him off and let a couple of horses go but he was a heavy favorite off his two wins and I didn't want to get trapped with him so I moved him out early and roughed him pretty good from the half to the head of the stretch. He came home like a good horse and won in 2:05⅕. It had taken him six starts to wake up but I knew then that I had made the right move in gelding him. He races consistently between 2:01 and 2:03 over a half mile track and has won over $150,000.

At the same time I gelded William Time, I gelded another 2-year-old for another reason and he also went on and became a top horse. This was Egyptian Pride who was bred to trot but who developed too many legs at that gait when he got down around 2:20. I converted him to the pace as a 2-year-old and sent him to Saratoga where he won four in a row before cracking a bone in his foot. When he was going along at a decent rate on the pace, he always gave me the feeling that he wanted to get a little too firey and that he would eventually learn to get on the bit and become very hard to rate. For that reason, I gelded him, and he went on the next year to win 11 of 15 starts, including the first eight in a row, and paced a world record mile of 1:59 at Liberty Bell. I doubt very much that he would have been this kind of horse if I had left him entire. In fact, I think he would have been just the opposite—not very much stock at all.

In this day and age when broken bones are relatively common and horses are required, as a result, to stand up in stalls for long periods of time, I think it would be worthwhile to discuss this type as a group and to mention some of my thoughts regarding their subsequent return to racing.

Let's say you have a horse with a broken bone and your veterinarian has instructed you to keep him in the stall from six to ten weeks. In the first place, you should remember that such a horse should be grained very little if at all when he is standing up. Such a horse is getting absolutely no exercise and grain will certainly make him fat and could lead to colic or founder. If I fed a horse like this any grain at all, it would not be more than a quart twice a day. He could have all the hay and water he wanted, but I would go very light on the grain.

When the period of confinement is over for such a horse, I think it is downright dangerous to turn him right out in a paddock. After standing up so long, he will feel so good that he will buck and play and run and kick and it is very possible that he might re-fracture the same bone. A horse like this should be jogged instead of being turned out.

But at the same time, you have to be careful how you jog him. When you return him to training, I don't think you should jog him more than a mile a day for the first week to 10 days. And I wouldn't jog him when there were other horses on the track, either. My main concern would be in wanting to jog him at a very moderate clip and not to get him excited in any way. After the first week or ten days, I would step the horse up at the rate of about a mile a week until I got him up to four miles a day. I would continue to jog him for at least six weeks and would prefer to make it two months if I could. After that, if the horse acts sound and all right, you can begin to train him just as you would any other horse. I would think that it would take five months to get a horse like this back to the races as compared to 90 days for a normal horse.

When you begin to jog this horse, you start then to restore his grain ration. He is working now and even though it is only light work he needs a little more to sustain him and the danger of founder or colic is diminished as he begins to get exercise. I would increase the grain in proportion to the increase in his exercise.

This seems an appropriate place to return to the subject of stifle soreness, a common ailment which I mentioned briefly earlier in the chapter. There are a number of indications of stifle trouble, but probably the most prominent one is that the horse's muscles in the stifle area are trembling and shaking when he comes off the track after jogging. A horse with stifle trouble will also tend to knuckle over behind and begin to get his hind end over toward one cart shaft or the other.

There are a number of causes, but I am going to defer to Dr. Churchill on this point because he knows a lot more about those things than I do and will discuss the subject at length in his chapter. However, I do want to mention one specific and relatively uncommon instance that occurred in my own stable because it emphasizes the importance of trainers always being alert for the little things that can cause so much trouble.

I had a horse that had been shipped to another track and was accidentally trained in a pair of hobbles measuring 52 inches.

The horse wore a 57½ inch set of hobbles. The trainer only went one slow heat because he knew something was wrong although he could not pinpoint it. The horse sored up badly in the stifles and it took him quite a while to get straightened out. This was the first time this had ever happened in my stable and I felt quite badly about it. But I do think it taught everybody who works for me a good lesson and I pass it on here with the idea that it might help remind all trainers that they should always make certain the hobbles are the right size for the horse.

This particular horse will also serve as an example of how I condition horses that have stifle trouble. The important thing is that they get plenty of work so that the muscles tighten up. At the same time, all of their work is evenly-rated and there is absolutely no brushing.

It is my practice to train horses like this three times a week until the stifle regains its strength and is tight again. I might do this for one, two or three weeks depending on how the horse is progressing.

On Monday, I might train the horse three miles in 2:45, 2:30 and 2:20. I would jog him two miles before he went the first mile. On Tuesday, I would jog the horse four miles. On Wednesday and Friday, I would repeat exactly what I had done on Monday and would jog the horse four miles on Thursday and Saturday.

I would hope that one week of this would be enough to cure the stifle trouble, but if it was not, I would go on for a second and even a third week in this manner. It is rarely necessary to go more than three weeks and usually one, or two at the most, is enough.

If, for any reason, I wanted to hold the horse on a twice-a-week training schedule, I would step up the number of jog miles to six on the four off days. I am trying to build up the muscles in the stifle area and this is the way it is done.

If a horse has stifle trouble, I never increase the speed of his training miles from what they were when he developed it. I hold him there with no brushing while I try to restore strength to the muscles.

Sometimes stifle weakness will develop as a result of a horse being laid up for a brief period, such as a bout with the virus. You put him back in training and if he is a trotter he is hitching and hiking and if a pacer, he is fumbling in the hobbles and doesn't want to hit a true pace. This is an indication that the forced rest has brought about a muscle weakness that must be overcome. Extra jogging and/or extra training at a moderate rate with no brushing is indicated.

I guess every horse trainer knows the proper way to convert a horse from the trot to the pace. It is a very common thing and all of us have our own methods. These will not vary a great deal except in minor details.

I will review my own methods, but before I do, I want to say that I think a lot of trainers are too hasty about making the switch. A great many trotters are inclined to be a little pacey, especially when you are just starting out with them and a trainer should not be too discouraged when he is faced with this. Very often a liberal amount of patience on the part of a trainer can make a trotter out of a horse that shows pacing tendencies. In his chapter, Johnny Simpson has gone into detail concerning this and what he has written on the subject is well worth reading.

But there are also horses that you could fool with until they were ten or twelve years old and never get anything done on the trot. These are the ones you should convert and must convert.

The basic principle in converting from the trot to the pace is less weight and a shorter toe in front and more weight behind. The first step is to remove the front shoes and take the horse's toes down fairly short.

To be specific, let's say the horse has been trotting in a 3¾-inch toe in front. You would probably have this much toe because the horse has undoubtedly been showing some pacing tendencies, and you have been lengthening the toe to compensate for it as you tried to keep him trotting. For this reason, it is doubtful that the horse you were planning to convert would be wearing a 3½ inch toe, which is a more natural one for a trotter.

I would probably take the toe down to 3⅜ inches or a scant 3½ at the most. Then I would remove the hind shoes and replace them with a sideweight shoe. A sideweight shoe is one in which all the weight is pulled to the outside, as described by Simpson, and which tends to encourage the swinging motion of the pacing gait. Some trainers will use rattlers or even toe weights on the outside wall of each hind foot to accomplish the same purpose. However, I prefer the sideweight shoe.

If you were converting a horse that had the habit of swinging over into the pace as you were jogging him along, I don't believe it would be necessary to go to the sideweight shoe because the horse has already indicated that he will pace. With one like this, I would remove his front shoes, cut the front toes down, boot him up and take him to the track.

As to boots, I always use bell boots in front because when you start out with a converted pacer, there is a possibility that he might get on a quarter as he fumbles around trying to establish himself on his new gait. I would use tendon boots if he was a close-going horse in front but would not use knee boots unless he really needed them. Sometimes I will also use a pair of bell boots behind, depending on how the horse is gaited.

The next step is to put the hobbles on. When you do, make certain they are loose. If you find when you begin working the horse that the hobbles are too loose, you can always take them up a notch. But if they are too tight in the beginning, they will chafe a horse badly and you will be off to a poor start. Joe O'Brien has explained the proper adjustment of hobbles when you are starting out.

When I put the hobbles on a horse for the first time, I like to walk him around for about 15 minutes to let him know they are there. Then I take the horse to the track and jog him a mile or so. If I think it is a horse that might not take too kindly to the hobbles, I will take another man along with me to help out in case the horse starts to buck or rear. During this first jog session, I will also be observing the fit of the hobbles with an eye toward adjusting them if necessary. The main thing here is not to have them too tight.

If the horse indicates he is going to make the conversion smoothly, I will shoe him in front and begin training him on the pace. If the horse appears to be a fairly natural pacer, I will probably shoe him with a half-round aluminum shoe in front because this will reduce the possibility of cross-firing. At the same time, I will remove the weight behind—sideweight shoe, rattlers, toe weight, etc.—as soon as possible. I don't like to leave the extra weight on any longer than necessary and usually it will not be long before I have the horse pacing in a light half-round, half swedge shoe behind.

Now, let me take a specific horse and explain how I would

switch him over into the training routine for a pacer. Let's say it's one of those green 3-year-olds I discussed earlier. I get him down to 2:15 on the trot and that's all he can go. Not only that, but once or twice he has broken into a pace when I urged him on at the trot and it is obvious that he is a prime candidate to be converted.

I think one of the biggest mistakes a trainer can make is to go too much too soon with a horse that has been converted. Very often, a converted horse might feel so good that you would think you could turn him and train him the second day you had the hobbles on him. Maybe on the third day you could go out and go a mile in 2:30. But I would resist the temptation and jog such a horse four miles a day for a full week without ever turning him. I want to make sure he is absolutely accustomed to the hobbles before I start training him.

On Monday of the following week, I would turn the horse and train him two miles. The first would be in 2:45 and the second between 2:25 and 2:30. The horse would pretty well tell you how fast that second mile should be. If he was slick and clean-gaited and went "cheerful", I might go in 2:25. However, in most instances, I would prefer not to beat 2:30 the first time because the main thing is that I don't want the horse to start making breaks and sticking his toes in. This comes about if you go just a little faster than you should the first time or two you train him. And if he does do something wrong, he might remember it the next time and start making a habit of it. The main thing is to make certain he is solid and set before you go with him.

If the horse trained well on Monday, I would give him his usual slow work of three heats on Thursday and drop him into the regular training routine the following Monday with three heats, the last one in 2:25. The following Monday I would probably drop him to 2:20 if he was training smoothly. If not, I would back off and govern myself by the horse's ability to adapt to the new gait. That is really just about all there is to it.

I don't think I have to spend much time reviewing some of the routine practices that every trainer should be following with respect to the health of his horses. I believe that blood counts and fecal checks should be taken every 30 days if possible and every 60 days without fail. I know that in my own stable fecal checks have determined that certain horses that appeared in excellent flesh were actually heavily infested with blood worms. If you wait for the appearance of the horse to tell you this, it may be too late. By that time, the horse will probably have fallen off to a point where you will have to quit with him in order to bring him back to form.

One thing I consider especially important is that temperatures be taken twice a day when horses are in training. All of us have had trouble with the virus and the best way to combat it is not to train a horse that has a temperature. That tends to run the temperature up, whereas, if the horse is left in the stall and treated by a veterinarian and permitted to rest he will soon recover.

A normal temperature will range anywhere from 99 to 100⅔ degrees. If you check temperatures daily, you will soon determine the normal range for each horse and will be able to spot a departure from this range immediately. If a horse has a mild temperature, something like 102, you can treat it yourself. But if it gets over that, you should call a veterinarian. It's just like your own child; if he has a little cold and a sniffle you can treat him, but if he's real sick you'd better call the doctor. The best treatment I know for a mild temperature is rest and a couple of aspirins. I usually crush the aspirins in a little water and give it to the horse by syringe. You can also break the aspirin tablets up and pull the horse's tongue out and place the aspirins on it.

In winding up this chapter, I am going to refrain from the normal procedure of summing up my thoughts on the conditioning of horses. I have written at great length on a variety of related subjects and I am afraid that whatever I might try to add at this point would only prove repetitious. But I don't want to close without saying a little something about the unsung heroes of harness racing, the ones who make it possible for people like me to be successful and who provide the horses that put on the show that thrills millions of fans every year. I am referring, of course, to the owners.

If the odds are still stacked against any group in our sport today, they are stacked against the owner. Even in this present period of escalating purses and stretched-out racing seasons, the owner is still the least likely to show a profit. I think trainers and track officials alike should show more consideration for them and cater more to them. Without them, fellows like me would never be where we are and the landscape would be dotted with housing developments where race tracks are now located.

I think every race track should have an attractive winner's circle and attach a little more pomp and ceremony to the presentation of awards to owners. For many of them a victory in a major event is the biggest day or night of their lives, the one thing they really look forward to more than anything else. I think they are deserving of more recognition than they get at some tracks today. Many tracks do a good job in this respect but others still fall short in my opinion.

I also think trainers should be more courteous to their owners and take more pains to keep them informed of what is going on with regard to their horses. When an owner sends a horse to a trainer, he is entitled to periodic reports concerning the progress of that horse or even the lack of progress, if that is the case. A trainer whose only contact with an owner is a bill that goes out once a month isn't fostering an ideal relationship.

In one of his chapters, Del Miller is describing the proper liaison between a trainer and an owner. I will not go into the subject further and will sign off by saying simply that whatever success I have enjoyed in harness racing I owe to my owners and I appreciate the opportunities they have given me to demonstrate whatever talent I might have.

CHART NO. 1

TRAINING SCHEDULE

Green 3-year-old. Quit between April and June; raced a couple of times or not at all and turned out for minor unsoundness or lack of top colt speed. Being trained now as a raceway horse. Picked up for jogging Sept. 5th.

To race on Jan. 2nd, 9th, 18th, 23rd, and 30th.

DATE Week of	MONDAY	TUESDAY	WED.	THURSDAY	FRIDAY	SATURDAY
Sept. 5	J2	J2	J2	J2	J2	J2
Sept. 12	J3	J3	J3	J3	J3	J3
Sept. 19	J4	J4	J4	J4	J4	J4
Sept. 26	J4	J4	J4	J4	J4	J4
Oct. 3	J3 2:50	J4	J4	J3 2:50	J4	J4
Oct. 10	J3 2:45	J4	J4	J3 2:45	J4	J4
Oct. 17	J3 2:45 2:40	J4	J4	J3 2:45 2:40	J4	J4
Oct. 24	J3 2:45 2:35	J4	J4	J3 2:45 2:35	J4	J4
Oct. 31	J2 2:45 2:35 2:30-35	J4	J4	J2 2:45 2:35 2:30-35	J4	J4
Nov. 7	J2 2:45 2:30 2:25-34	J4	J4	J2 2:45 2:30 2:25-34	J4	J4
Nov. 14	J2 2:45 2:25 2:22-34	J4	J4	J2 2:45 2:25 2:25	J4	J4
Nov. 21	J2 2:45 2:25 2:20-33	J4	J4	J2 2:45 2:25 2:25	J4	J4
Nov. 28	J2 2:45 2:25 2:20-33	J4	J4	J2 2:45 2:25 2:25	J4	J4
Dec. 5	J2 2:45 2:25 2:17-1:06-32	J3	J4	J2 2:45 2:25 2:25	J4	J4
Dec. 12	J2 2:45 2:25 2:15-1:05-32	J2	J4	J2 2:45 2:25 2:25	J4	J4
Dec. 19	J2 2:45 2:25 2:12-1:04-31	WALK	J3	J2 2:45 2:25 2:25	J3	J4

CHART NO. 1 Continued

DATE Week of	MONDAY	TUESDAY	WED.	THURSDAY	FRIDAY	SATURDAY
Dec. 26	J2 2:45 2:25 2:12-1:04-31	WALK	J3	J2 2:45 2:25 2:25	J3	J4
Jan. 2	RACE J2 2:45 2:20-32	WALK	J3	J4	J2 2:45 2:30 2:20	J3
Jan. 9	RACE J2 2:45 2:20	WALK	J3	J4	J2 2:45 2:30 2:20	J3
Jan. 16	J4	J3 2:45 2:35	RACE J2 2:45 2:20	WALK	J3	J4
Jan. 23	RACE J2 2:45 2:18	WALK	J3	J4	J2 2:45 2:35 2:20	J3
Jan. 30	RACE J2 2:45 2:18	WALK	J3	J4	J2 2:45 2:35 2:20	J3

CHART NO. 2

TRAINING SCHEDULE

Green 3-year-old. Quit between April and June; raced a couple of times or not at all and turned out for minor unsoundness or lack of top colt speed. Being trained now as a raceway horse. Picked up for jogging October 3rd.

To race on Feb. 15th, 22nd, March 4th, 9th, and 16th.

DATE Week of	MONDAY	TUESDAY	WED.	THURSDAY	FRIDAY	SATURDAY
Oct. 3 Oct. 10 Oct. 17 Oct. 24 Oct. 31 Nov. 7 Nov. 14	During the first seven weeks beginning Oct. 3 and continuing through the week of Nov. 14, the schedule for this horse is identical to the first seven weeks (Weeks of Sept. 5 through Oct. 17) for the horse on Chart No. 1.					
Nov. 21 (8th week)	J3 2:45 2:40	J4	J4	J3 2:45 2:40	J4	J4
Nov. 28	J3 2:45 2:40	J4	J4	J3 2:45 2:40	J4	J4
Dec. 5	J3 2:45 2:35	J4	J4	J3 2:45 2:35	J4	J4
Dec. 12	J2 2:45 2:35 2:30-35	J4	J4	J2 2:45 2:35 2:30-35	J4	J4
Dec. 19	J2 2:45 2:30 2:25-34	J4	J4	J2 2:45 2:30 2:25-34	J4	J4
Dec. 26	J2 2:45 2:30 2:25-34	J4	J4	J2 2:45 2:30 2:25-34	J4	J4
Jan. 2	J2 2:45 2:25 2:20-33	J4	J4	J2 2:45 2:30 2:30	J4	J4
Jan. 9	J2 2:45 2:25 2:20-33	J4	J4	J2 2:45 2:30 2:30	J4	J4
Jan. 16	J2 2:45 2:25 2:18-33	J4	J4	J2 2:45 2:30 2:25	J4	J4
Jan. 23	J2 2:45 2:25 2:15-1:05-32	J3	J4	J2 2:45 2:30 2:25	J3	J4
Jan. 30	J2 2:45 2:25 2:12-1:03-31	WALK	J3	J2 2:45 2:30 2:25	J3	J4

CHART NO. 2 Continued

DATE Week of	MONDAY	TUESDAY	WED.	THURSDAY	FRIDAY	SATURDAY
Feb. 6	J2 2:45 2:25 2:12-1:03-31	WALK	J3	J2 2:45 2:30 2:25	J3	J4
Feb. 13	J2 2:45 2:35 2:25	J3	RACE J2 2:45 2:20-32	WALK	J3	J4
Feb. 20	J2 2:45 2:30 2:20	J3	RACE J2 2:45 2:20	WALK	J3	J4
Feb. 27	J2 2:45 2:30 2:25	J3	J4	J3 2:45 2:30	J3	RACE J2 2:45 2:20
Mar. 6	J3	J4	J3 2:45	RACE J2 2:45 2:20	WALK	J3
Mar. 13	J2 2:45 2:30 2:20	J3	J4	RACE J2 2:45 2:20		

CHART NO. 3

TRAINING SCHEDULE

Green 3-year-old. Quit between April and June; raced a couple of times or not at all and turned out for minor unsoundness or lack of top colt speed. Being trained now as a raceway horse. Picked up for jogging December 12th.

To race on April 15th, 22nd, May 2nd, 8th, and 15th.

DATE Week of	MONDAY	TUESDAY	WED.	THURSDAY	FRIDAY	SATURDAY
Dec. 12 Dec. 19 Dec. 26 Jan. 2 Jan. 9 Jan. 16 Jan. 23 Jan. 30 Feb. 6 Feb. 13	During the first 10 weeks beginning Dec. 12 and continuing through the week of Feb. 13, the schedule for this horse is identical to the first 10 weeks (Weeks of Sept. 5 through Nov. 7) for the horse on Chart No. 1.					
Feb. 20 (11th week)	J2 2:45 2:30 2:25-34	J4	J4	J2 2:45 2:35 2:30	J4	J4
Feb. 27	J2 2:45 2:25 2:22-34	J4	J4	J2 2:45 2:35 2:30	J4	J4
Mar. 6	J2 2:45 2:25 2:20-33	J4	J4	J2 2:45 2:35 2:30	J4	J4
Mar. 13	J2 2:45 2:25 2:18-1:06-33	J3	J4	J2 2:45 2:35 2:25	J3	J4
Mar. 20	J2 2:45 2:25 2:15-1:05-32	J2	J3	J2 2:45 2:35 2:25	J3	J4
Mar. 27	J2 2:45 2:25 2:12-1:04-31	WALK	J3	J2 2:45 2:30 2:25	J3	J4
Apr. 3	J2 2:45 2:25 2:12-1:03-31	WALK	J3	J2 2:45 2:30 2:25	J3	J4
Apr. 10	J2 2:45 2:25 2:15	J3	J4	J3 2:45 2:25	J3	RACE J2 2:45 2:20-32
Apr. 17	J3	J4	J2 2:45 2:30 2:20	J3	J4	RACE J2 2:45 2:20
Apr. 24	J3	J3 2:45 2:30	J3	J4	J2 2:45 2:30 2:15	J3

CHART NO. 3 Continued

DATE Week of	MONDAY	TUESDAY	WED.	THURSDAY	FRIDAY	SATURDAY
May 1	J4	RACE J2 2:45 2:20	WALK	J3	J4	J3 2:45 2:30
May 8	RACE J2 2:45 2:20	WALK	J3	J4	J2 2:45 2:30 2:20	J3
May 15	RACE J2 2:45 2:20					

CHART NO. 4

TRAINING SCHEDULE

Top Stake 3-year-old. Quit sound Nov. 1st.
Picked up for jogging on Jan. 2nd.
To race May 1st, 8th, 18th, 23rd, and 30th.

DATE Week of	MONDAY	TUESDAY	WED.	THURSDAY	FRIDAY	SATURDAY
Jan. 2	J2	J2	J2	J2	J2	J2
Jan. 9	J3	J3	J3	J3	J3	J3
Jan. 16	J4	J4	J4	J4	J4	J4
Jan. 23	J4	J4	J4	J4	J4	J4
Jan. 30	J3 2:50	J4	J4	J3 2:50	J4	J4
Feb. 6	J3 2:50 2:45	J4	J4	J3 2:45 2:40	J4	J4
Feb. 13	J3 2:45 2:35	J4	J4	J3 2:45 2:35	J4	J4
Feb. 20	J3 2:45 2:30	J4	J4	J3 2:45 2:30	J4	J4
Feb. 27	J2 2:45 2:25 2:25	J4	J4	J2 2:45 2:30 2:25	J4	J4
Mar. 6	J2 2:45 2:25 2:20	J4	J4	J2 2:45 2:30 2:25	J4	J4
Mar. 13	J2 2:45 2:20 2:16-33	J3	J4	J2 2:45 2:30 2:20	J3	J4
Mar. 20	J2 2:45 2:20 2:14-1:06-32	J3	J4	J2 2:45 2:30 2:20	J3	J4
Mar. 27	J2 2:45 2:20 2:12-1:05-32	J3	J4	J2 2:45 2:30 2:20	J3	J4
Apr. 3	J2 2:45 2:20 2:10-1:04-32	WALK	J3	J2 2:45 2:30 2:20	J3	J4
Apr. 10	J2 2:45 2:20 2:08-1:03-31	WALK	J3	J2 2:45 2:30 2:20	J3	J4
Apr. 17	J2 2:45 2:20 2:06-1:02-30	WALK	J3	J2 2:45 2:30 2:20	J3	J4

CHART NO. 4 Continued

DATE Week of	MONDAY	TUESDAY	WED.	THURSDAY	FRIDAY	SATURDAY
Apr. 24	J2 2:45 2:20 2:05-1:01-30	WALK	J3	J2 2:45 2:30 2:20	J3	J4
May 1	RACE J2 2:45 2:18	WALK	J3	J4	J2 2:45 2:25 2:20	J2
May 8	RACE J2 2:45 2:18	WALK	J3	J4	J2 2:45 2:25 2:20	J2
May 15	J3	J2 2:45 2:30 2:25	J3	RACE J2 2:45 2:18	WALK	J3
May 22	J3 2:45	RACE J2 2:45 2:18	WALK	J3	J4	J2 2:45 2:25 2:20
May 29	J3	RACE J2 2:45 2:18				

CHART NO 5

TRAINING SCHEDULE

Top Stake 3-year-old. Quit sound Nov. 1st.
Picked up for jogging on Jan. 2nd.

To race June 1st, 8th, 17th, 22nd and 29th.

DATE Week of	MONDAY	TUESDAY	WED.	THURSDAY	FRIDAY	SATURDAY
Jan. 2 Jan. 9 Jan. 16 Jan. 23 Jan. 30	During the first five weeks beginning Jan. 2 and continuing through the week of Jan. 30, the schedule for this horse is identical to the first five weeks (weeks of Jan. 2 through Jan. 30) for the horse on Chart No. 4.					
Feb. 6 (6th week)	J3 2:50 2:45	J4	J4	J3 2:50 2:45	J4	J4
Feb. 13	J3 2:50 2:40	J4	J4	J3 2:50 2:40	J4	J4
Feb. 20	J3 2:50 2:40	J4	J4	J3 2:50 2:40	J4	J4
Feb. 27	J3 2:45 2:35	J4	J4	J3 2:45 2:35	J4	J4
Mar. 6	J3 2:45 2:30	J4	J4	J3 2:45 2:30	J4	J4
Mar. 13	J2 2:45 2:35 2:25	J4	J4	J2 2:45 2:35 2:30	J4	J4
Mar. 20	J2 2:45 2:35 2:22	J4	J4	J2 2:45 2:35 2:30	J4	J4
Mar. 27	J2 2:45 2:35 2:20	J4	J4	J2 2:45 2:30 2:30	J4	J4
Apr. 3	J2 2:45 2:35 2:20	J4	J4	J2 2:45 2:30 2:30	J4	J4
Apr. 10	J2 2:45 2:35 2:20 2:20	J4	J4	J2 2:45 2:30 2:20	J4	J4
Apr. 17	J2 2:45 2:35 2:20 2:16-33	J4	J4	J2 2:45 2:30 2:20	J4	J4
Apr. 24	J2 2:45 2:35 2:17 2:14-1:06-32	J3	J4	J2 2:45 2:30 2:20	J4	J4

CHART NO. 5 Continued

DATE Week of	MONDAY	TUESDAY	WED.	THURSDAY	FRIDAY	SATURDAY
May 1	J2 2:45 2:35 2:19 2:11-1:04-31	J2	J3	J2 2:45 2:30 2:20	J4	J4
May 8	J2 2:45 2:35 2:17 2:09-1:03-31	WALK	J3	J2 2:45 2:30 2:20	J4	J4
May 15	J2 2:45 2:35 2:17 2:07-1:02-30	WALK	J3	J2 2:45 2:30 2:20	J4	J4
May 22	J2 2:45 2:30 2:17 2:05-1:01-30	WALK	J3	J2 2:45 2:30 2:20	J3	J4
May 29	J2 2:45 2:30 2:20	J3	J4	RACE J2 2:45 2:35 2:17	WALK	J3
June 5	J2 2:45 2:30 2:20	J3	J4	RACE J2 2:45 2:35 2:17	WALK	J3
June 12	J2 2:45 2:30 2:20	J3	J4	J3 2:45 2:30	J3	RACE J2 2:45 2:35 2:17
June 19	J3	J3 2:45 2:25	J3	RACE J2 2:45 2:35 2:17	WALK	J3
June 26	J2 2:45 2:30 2:20	J3	J4	RACE J2 2:45 2:35 2:17		

CHART NO. 6

TRAINING SCHEDULE

Raceway Horse, 2:01 to 2:05 class. Quit sound Dec. 15th. To race again on Feb. 15th. Turned out Dec. 15th and picked up for jogging Jan. 2nd.

To race on Feb. 15th, 22nd, March 4th, 9th and 16th.

DATE Week of	MONDAY	TUESDAY	WED.	THURSDAY	FRIDAY	SATURDAY
Jan. 2	J2	J2	J2½	J2½	J3	J3
Jan. 9	J3½	J3½	J3½	J4	J4	J4
Jan. 16	J3 2:40 2:40	J4	J4	J3 2:45 2:30	J4	J4
Jan. 23	J3 2:45 2:25	J4	J4	J2 2:45 2:35 2:20	J4	J4
Jan. 30	J2 2:45 2:25 2:15-1:05-32	J2	J4	J2 2:45 2:30 2:25	J3	J4
Feb. 6	J2 2:45 2:25 2:10-1:03-31	WALK	J3	J2 2:45 2:30 2:25	J3	J4
Feb. 13	J2 2:45 2:30 2:25	J3	RACE J2 2:45 2:18	WALK	J3	J4
Feb. 20	J2 2:45 2:30 2:25	J3	RACE J2 2:45 2:18	WALK	J3	J4
Feb. 27	J2 2:45 2:25 2:20	J2	J3	J2 2:45 2:30 2:25	J3	RACE J2 2:45 2:18
Mar. 6	J3	J4	J3 2:45 2:30	RACE J2 2:45 2:18	WALK	J3
Mar. 13	J2 2:45 2:30 2:25	J3	J4	RACE J2 2:45 2:18		

CHART NO. 7
TRAINING SCHEDULE

Raceway Horse, 2:06 to 2:10 class. Quit sound Dec. 15th. To race again on Feb. 15th. Turned out Dec. 15th and picked up for jogging Jan. 2nd.

To race Feb. 15th, 22nd, March 4th, 9th and 16th.

DATE Week of	MONDAY	TUESDAY	WED.	THURSDAY	FRIDAY	SATURDAY
Jan. 2 Jan. 9 Jan. 16 Jan. 23	During the first four weeks beginning Jan. 2 and continuing through the week of Jan. 23, the schedule for this horse is identical to the first four weeks (weeks of Jan. 2 through Jan. 23) for the horse on Chart No. 6.					
Jan. 30 (5th Week)	J2 2:45 2:25 2:20-1:07-33	J3	J4	J2 2:45 2:30 2:25	J3	J4
Feb. 6	J2 2:45 2:25 2:15-1:05-32	WALK	J3	J2 2:45 2:30 2:25	J3	J4
Feb. 13	J2 2:45 2:30 2:25	J3	RACE J2 2:45 2:22	WALK	J3	J4
Feb. 20	J2 2:45 2:30 2:25	J3	RACE J2 2:45 2:22	WALK	J3	J4
Feb. 27	J2 2:45 2:25 2:20	J2	J3	J2 2:45 2:30 2:25	J3	RACE J2 2:45 2:22
Mar. 6	J3	J4	J3 2:45	RACE J2 2:45 2:22	WALK	J3
Mar. 13	J2 2:45 2:30 2:25	J3	J4	RACE J2 2:45 2:22		

CHART NO. 8

TRAINING SCHEDULE

Raceway Horse, 2:01 to 2:05 class. Quit sound Dec 15th. Not turned out.

To race on Jan. 16th, 23rd, Feb. 2nd, 7th and 14th.

DATE Week of	MONDAY	TUESDAY	WED.	THURSDAY	FRIDAY	SATURDAY
Dec. 12				RACED	WALK	J3
Dec. 19	J3 2:45 2:30	J2	J3	J3 2:45 2:30	J2	J3
Dec. 26	J3 2:45 2:30	J2	J3	J3 2:45 2:30	J2	J3
Jan. 2	J2 2:45 2:30 2:15-1:05-32	J2	J3	J2 2:45 2:25 2:20	J2	J3
Jan. 9	J2 2:45 2:25 2:10-1:03-30	J2	J3	J2 2:45 2:25 2:20	J2	J3
Jan. 16	RACE J2 2:45 2:18	WALK	J3	J4	J2 2:45 2:25 2:20	J2
Jan. 23	RACE J2 2:45 2:18	WALK	J3	J4	J2 2:45 2:25 2:20	J2
Jan. 30	J4	J3 2:45 2:25	J3	RACE J2 2:45 2:18	WALK	J3
Feb. 6	J3 2:45	RACE J2 2:45 2:18	WALK	J3	J4	J2 2:45 2:30 2:20
Feb. 13	J3	RACE J2 2:45 2:18				

CHART NO. 9

TRAINING SCHEDULE

Raceway Horse, 2:06 to 2:10 class. Quit sound Dec. 15th. Not turned out.

To race Jan. 16th, 23rd, Feb. 2nd, 7th and 14th.

DATE Week of	MONDAY	TUESDAY	WED.	THURSDAY	FRIDAY	SATURDAY
Dec. 12				RACED	WALK	J3
Dec. 19	J3 2:45 2:30	J2	J3	J3 2:45 2:30	J2	J3
Dec. 26	J3 2:45 2:30	J2	J3	J3 2:45 2:30	J2	J3
Jan. 2	J2 2:45 2:30 2:20	J2	J4	J2 2:45 2:30 2:25	J2	J4
Jan. 9	J2 2:45 2:25 2:15-1:05-31	WALK	J3	J2 2:45 2:30 2:25	J2	J4
Jan. 16	RACE J2 2:45 2:22	WALK	J3	J4	J2 2:45 2:30 2:25	J2
Jan. 23	RACE J2 2:45 2:22	WALK	J3	J4	J2 2:45 2:30 2:25	J2
Jan. 30	J4	J3 2:45 2:30	J3	RACE J2 2:45 2:22	WALK	J3
Feb. 6	J3 2:45	RACE J2 2:45 2:22	WALK	J3	J4	J2 2:45 2:30 2:25
Feb. 13	J3	RACE J2 2:45 2:22				

CHART NO. 10

TRAINING SCHEDULE

Raceway Horse, 2:06 to 2:10 class (Racehorse Sound). Quit Dec. 15th.
Turned out until Jan. 16th and picked up for jogging.

To race April 1st, 8th, 18th, 24th and May 1st.

DATE Week of	MONDAY	TUESDAY	WED.	THURSDAY	FRIDAY	SATURDAY
Jan. 16	J2	J2	J2	J2	J2	J2
Jan. 23	J3	J3	J3	J3	J3	J3
Jan. 30	J4	J4	J4	J4	J4	J4
Feb. 6	J3 2:50 2:45	J4	J4	J3 2:50 2:40	J4	J4
Feb. 13	J3 2:45 2:35	J4	J4	J3 2:45 2:35	J4	J4
Feb. 20	J3 2:45 2:30	J4	J4	J3 2:45 2:35	J4	J4
Feb. 27	J2 2:45 2:30 2:25	J4	J4	J3 2:45 2:30	J4	J4
Mar. 6	J2 2:45 2:30 2:20	J4	J4	J3 2:45 2:30	J4	J4
Mar. 13	J2 2:45 2:30 2:15	J4	J4	J3 2:45 2:30	J4	J4
Mar. 20	J2 2:45 2:30 2:15	J4	J4	J3 2:45 2:30	J4	J4
Mar. 27	J4	J2 2:45 2:30 2:20	J3	J4	J4	RACE J2 2:45 2:22
Apr. 3	J4	J4	J2 2:45 2:30 2:20	J3	J4	RACE J2 2:45 2:22
Apr. 10	J4	J4	J2 2:45 2:30 2:20	J3	J4	J2 2:45 2:30 2:17
Apr. 17	J4	RACE J2 2:45 2:22	WALK	J3	J4	J3 2:45 2:30
Apr. 24	RACE J2 2:45 2:22	WALK	J3	J4	J2 2:45 2:30 2:25	J3
May 1	RACE J2 2:45 2:22					

CHART NO. 11

TRAINING SCHEDULE

Raceway Horse, 2:01 to 2:05 class. Quit sound Dec. 15th. Turned out until
Jan. 16th and picked up for jogging.

To race April 1st, 8th, 18th, 24th and May 1st.

DATE Week of	MONDAY	TUESDAY	WED.	THURSDAY	FRIDAY	SATURDAY
Jan. 16	J2	J2	J2	J2	J2	J2
Jan. 23	J3	J3	J3	J3	J3	J3
Jan. 30	J4	J4	J4	J4	J4	J4
Feb. 6	J3 2:45	J4	J4	J3 2:45 2:40	J4	J4
Feb. 13	J3 2:45 2:35	J4	J4	J3 2:45 2:35	J4	J4
Feb. 20	J2 2:45 2:35 2:30	J4	J4	J2 2:45 2:35 2:30	J4	J4
Feb. 27	J2 2:45 2:30 2:25	J4	J4	J2 2:45 2:30 2:30	J4	J4
Mar. 6	J2 2:45 2:25 2:20-1:07-33	J3	J4	J2 2:45 2:30 2:25	J3	J4
Mar. 13	J2 2:45 2:25 2:18-1:06-32	J2	J3	J2 2:45 2:30 2:25	J3	J4
Mar. 20	J2 2:45 2:25 2:15-1:05-31	WALK	J3	J2 2:45 2:30 2:25	J3	J4
Mar. 27	J2 2:45 2:25 2:10-1:03-30	WALK	J3	J3 2:45 2:30	J3	RACE J2 2:45 2:18
Apr. 3	J3	J4	J2 2:45 2:20 2:20	J2	J3	RACE J2 2:45 2:18
Apr. 10	J3	J4	J2 2:45 2:30 2:20	J3	J4	J2 2:45 2:20 2:10
Apr. 17	J4	RACE J2 2:45 2:18	WALK	J3	J4	J3 2:45 2:30
Apr. 24	RACE J2 2:45 2:18	WALK	J3	J2 2:45 2:20 2:20	J2	J3
May 1	RACE J2 2:45 2:18					

CHART NO. 12

TRAINING SCHEDULE

Raceway Horse, 2:06 to 2:10 class. Quit sound Dec. 15th.
Turned out until Jan. 16th and picked up for jogging.
To race April 1st, 8th, 18th, 24th and May 1st.

DATE Week of	MONDAY	TUESDAY	WED.	THURSDAY	FRIDAY	SATURDAY
Jan. 16 Jan. 23 Jan. 30 Feb. 6	During the first four weeks beginning Jan. 16 and continuing through the week of Feb. 6, the schedule for this horse is identical to the first four weeks (Weeks of Jan. 16 through Feb. 6) for the horse on Chart No. 11.					
Feb. 13 (5th week)	J3 2:45 2:40	J4	J4	J3 2:45 2:40	J4	J4
Feb. 20	J3 2:45 2:35	J4	J4	J3 2:45 2:35	J4	J4
Feb. 27	J2 2:45 2:30 2:30	J4	J4	J2 2:45 2:30 2:30	J4	J4
Mar. 6	J2 2:45 2:30 2:25-1:10-34	J4	J4	J2 2:45 2:30 2:30	J4	J4
Mar. 13	J2 2:45 2:25 2:20-1:07-33	J3	J4	J2 2:45 2:30 2:25	J3	J4
Mar. 20	J2 2:45 2:25 2:15-1:05-32	WALK	J3	J2 2:45 2:25 2:25	J3	J4
Mar. 27	J2 2:45 2:25 2:15-1:05-31	WALK	J3	J2 2:45 2:30 2:25	J3	RACE J2 2:45 2:22
Apr. 3	J3	J4	J2 2:45 2:30 2:25	J2	J3	RACE J2 2:45 2:22
Apr. 10	J3	J4	J2 2:45 2:30 2:25	J2	J3	J2 2:45 2:25 2:15
Apr. 17	J3	RACE J2 2:45 2:22	WALK	J3	J4	J3 2:45 2:30
Apr. 24	RACE J2 2:45 2:22	WALK	J3	J4	J2 2:45 2:25 2:20	J3
May 1	RACE J2 2:45 2:22					

TRAINING SCHEDULE

Raceway Horse getting 30-day layoff during racing season.

DATE Week of	MONDAY	TUESDAY	WED.	THURSDAY	FRIDAY	SATURDAY
July 1	RACE	TURN OUT ENTIRE WEEK				
July 8		TURN OUT ENTIRE WEEK				
July 15	J2	J3	J4	J2 2:50 2:40	J4	J2 2:50 2:40 2:30
July 22	J4	J2 2:45 2:30 2:15	J3	J3	J2 2:45 2:25 2:10-1:03-31* 2:05-1:02-30§	WALK
July 29	J4	J2 2:45 2:30 2:20	J4	J4	RACE J2 2:40 2:18	

*2:06-2:10 Horse.
§2:01-2:05 Horse.

CHART NO. 14

TRAINING SCHEDULE

Raceway Horse, 2:01 to 2:05 class. Quit sound Oct. 1st.
Turned out until Oct. 31st and picked up for jogging.

To race Jan. 2nd, 9th, 19th, 24th and 31st.

DATE Week of	MONDAY	TUESDAY	WED.	THURSDAY	FRIDAY	SATURDAY
Oct. 31	J2	J2	J2½	J2½	J3	J3
Nov. 7	J3½	J3½	J3½	J4	J4	J4
Nov. 14	J3 2:45 2:40	J4	J4	J3 2:45 2:40	J4	J4
Nov. 21	J2 2:45 2:35 2:30	J4	J4	J2 2:45 2:35 2:30	J4	J4
Nov. 28	J2 2:45 2:30 2:25	J4	J4	J2 2:45 2:30 2:30	J4	J4
Dec. 5	J2 2:45 2:25 2:20-1:08-33	J3	J4	J2 2:45 2:30 2:30	J3	J4
Dec. 12	J2 2:45 2:20 2:15-1:06-32	J3	J4	J2 2:45 2:25 2:25	J4	J4
Dec. 19	J2 2:45 2:20 2:10-1:04-31	WALK	J3	J2 2:45 2:25 2:20	J3	J4
Dec. 26	J2 2:45 2:20 2:08-1:03-30	WALK	J3	J2 2:45 2:25 2:20	J2	J4
Jan. 2	RACE J2 2:45 2:18	WALK	J3	J4	J2 2:45 2:25 2:20	J3
Jan. 9	RACE J2 2:45 2:18	WALK	J3	J4	J2 2:45 2:25 2:20	J3
Jan. 16	J4	J2 2:45 2:30 2:25	J3	RACE J2 2:45 2:18	WALK	J3
Jan. 23	J3 2:45	RACE J2 2:45 2:18	WALK	J3	J4	J2 2:45 2:30 2:20
Jan. 30	J4	RACE J2 2:45 2:18				

CHART NO. 15

TRAINING SCHEDULE

Raceway Horse, 2:06 to 2:10 class. Quit sound Oct. 1st.
Turned out until Oct. 31st and picked up for jogging.

To race Jan. 2nd, 9th, 19th, 24th and 31st.

DATE Week of	MONDAY	TUESDAY	WED.	THURSDAY	FRIDAY	SATURDAY
Oct. 31	J2	J2	J2½	J2½	J3	J3
Nov. 7	J3½	J3½	J3½	J4	J4	J4
Nov. 14	J3 2:45 2:40	J4	J4	J3 2:45 2:40	J4	J4
Nov. 21	J3 2:45 2:35	J4	J4	J3 2:45 2:35	J4	J4
Nov. 28	J2 2:45 2:30 2:30	J3	J4	J2 2:45 2:35 2:30	J3	J4
Dec. 5	J2 2:45 2:30 2:25	J3	J4	J2 2:45 2:30 2:30	J3	J4
Dec. 12	J2 2:45 2:25 2:20-1:08-33	J3	J4	J2 2:45 2:30 2:30	J3	J4
Dec. 19	J2 2:45 2:25 2:17-1:07-32	J2	J4	J2 2:45 2:25 2:25	J3	J4
Dec. 26	J2 2:45 2:25 2:15-1:05-31	WALK	J3	J2 2:45 2:25 2:25	J2	J4
Jan. 2	RACE J2 2:45 2:22	WALK	J3	J4	J2 2:45 2:30 2:45	J2
Jan. 9	RACE J2 2:45 2:22	WALK	J3	J4	J2 2:45 2:30 2:25	J2
Jan. 16	J2 2:45 2:30 2:15	WALK	J3	RACE J2 2:45 2:22	WALK	J3
Jan. 23	J3 2:45	RACE J2 2:45 2:22	WALK	J3	J4	J2 2:45 2:30 2:25
Jan. 30	J4	RACE J2 2:45 2:22				

CHART NO. 16

TRAINING SCHEDULE

Raceway Horse, 2:01 to 2:05 class. Quit sound Oct. 1st.
Turned out until Dec. 12th and picked up for jogging.

To race March 1st, 8th, 18th, 23rd and 30th.

DATE Week of	MONDAY	TUESDAY	WED.	THURSDAY	FRIDAY	SATURDAY
Dec. 12	J2	J2	J2	J2	J2	J2
Dec. 19	J3	J3	J3	J3	J3	J3
Dec. 26	J4	J4	J4	J4	J4	J4
Jan. 2	J3 2:45	J4	J4	J3 2:45	J4	J4
Jan. 9	J3 2:45 2:40	J4	J4	J3 2:45 2:35	J4	J4
Jan. 16	J2 2:45 2:35 2:30	J4	J4	J2 2:45 2:35 2:30	J4	J4
Jan. 23	J2 2:45 2:25 2:20	J4	J4	J2 2:45 2:35 2:30	J4	J4
Jan. 30	J2 2:45 2:20 2:20-1:07-32	J4	J4	J2 2:45 2:30 2:25	J4	J4
Feb. 6	J2 2:45 2:20 2:15-1:05-31	J3	J4	J2 2:45 2:30 2:25	J3	J4
Feb. 13	J2 2:45 2:20 2:12-1:04-31	WALK	J3	J2 2:45 2:25 2:25	J3	J4
Feb. 20	J2 2:45 2:20 2:08-1:03-30	WALK	J3	J2 2:45 2:25 2:20	J2	J4
Feb. 27	J2 2:45 2:30 2:25	J3	RACE J2 2:45 2:18	WALK	J3	J4
Mar. 6	J2 2:45 2:30 2:25	J3	RACE J2 2:45 2:18	WALK	J3	J4
Mar. 13	J4	J2 2:45 2:25 2:15	WALK	J3	J4	RACE J2 2:45 2:18
Mar. 20	J3	J4	J3 2:45	RACE J2 2:45 2:18	WALK	J3
Mar. 27	J4	J2 2:45 2:30 2:25	J3	RACE J2 2:45 2:18		

CHART NO. 17

TRAINING SCHEDULE

Raceway Horse, 2:06 to 2:10 class. Quit sound Oct. 1st.
Turned out until Dec. 12th and picked up for jogging.
To race March 1st, 8th, 18th, 23rd and 30th.

DATE Week of	MONDAY	TUESDAY	WED.	THURSDAY	FRIDAY	SATURDAY
Dec. 12 19 26 Jan. 2	During the first four weeks beginning Dec. 12 and continuing through the week of Jan. 2, the schedule for this horse is identical to the first four weeks (Weeks of Dec. 12 through Jan. 2) for the horse on Chart No. 16.					
Jan. 9 (5th Week)	J3 2:45 2:40	J4	J4	J3 2:45 2:40	J4	J4
Jan. 16	J2 2:45 2:35 2:30	J4	J4	J3 2:45 2:35 2:30	J4	J4
Jan. 23	J2 2:45 2:35 2:30	J4	J4	J2 2:45 2:35 2:30	J4	J4
Jan. 30	J2 2:45 2:30 2:25	J4	J4	J2 2:45 2:30 2:30	J4	J4
Feb. 6	J2 2:45 2:30 2:22-1:10-33	J3	J4	J2 2:45 2:30 2:25	J3	J4
Feb. 13	J2 2:45 2:25 2:20-1:08-32	J3	J4	J2 2:45 2:30 2:25	J3	J4
Feb 20	J2 2:45 2:25 2:15-1:05-31	WALK	J4	J2 2:45 2:30 2:25	J3	J4
Feb. 27	J2 2:45 2:30 2:30	J3	RACE J2 2:45 2:22	WALK	J3	J4
Mar. 6	J2 2:45 2:30 2:30	J3	RACE J2 2:45 2:22	WALK	J3	J4
Mar. 13	J2 2:45 2:30 2:25	J2	J4	J3 2:45 2:30	J3	RACE J2 2:45 2:22
Mar. 20	J3	J4	J3 2:45	RACE J2 2:45 2:22	WALK	J3
Mar. 27	J4	J2 2:45 2:30 2:30	J3	RACE J2 2:45 2:22		

CHART NO. 18

TRAINING SCHEDULE

Raceway Horse, 2:01-2:05 class. Quit sound Oct. 1st.
Turned out until Jan. 2nd and picked up for jogging.
To race May 1st, 8th, 18th, 23rd and 30th.

DATE Week of	MONDAY	TUESDAY	WED.	THURSDAY	FRIDAY	SATURDAY
Jan. 2	J2	J2	J2	J2	J2	J2
Jan. 9	J3	J3	J3	J3	J3	J3
Jan. 16	J4	J4	J4	J4	J4	J4
Jan. 23	J4	J4	J4	J4	J4	J4
Jan. 30	J3 2:50	J4	J4	J3 2:50	J4	J4
Feb. 6	J3 2:45 2:45	J4	J4	J3 2:45 2:40	J4	J4
Feb. 13	J3 2:45 2:40	J4	J4	J3 2:45 2:40	J4	J4
Feb. 20	J3 2:45 2:35	J4	J4	J3 2:45 2:35	J4	J4
Feb. 27	J2 2:45 2:35 2:30	J4	J4	J2 2:45 2:35 2:30	J4	J4
Mar. 6	J2 2:45 2:35 2:30	J4	J4	J2 2:45 2:35 2:30	J4	J4
Mar. 13	J2 2:45 2:30 2:25	J4	J4	J2 2:45 2:30 2:30	J4	J4
Mar. 20	J2 2:45 2:30 2:20	J4	J4	J2 2:45 2:30 2:25	J4	J4
Mar. 27	J2 2:45 2:30 2:20-1:07-33	J4	J4	J2 2:45 2:30 2:25	J4	J4
Apr. 3	J2 2:45 2:25 2:16-1:06-32	J4	J4	J2 2:45 2:30 2:25	J4	J4
Apr. 10	J2 2:45 2:20 2:14-1:05-32	J4	J4	J2 2:45 2:30 2:25	J3	J4
Apr. 17	J2 2:45 2:20 2:10-1:04-31	WALK	J3	J2 2:45 2:30 2:25	J3	J4

CHART NO. 18 Continued

DATE Week of	MONDAY	TUESDAY	WED.	THURSDAY	FRIDAY	SATURDAY
Apr. 24	J2 2:45 2:20 2:08-1:03-30	WALK	J3	J2 2:45 2:30 2:25	J3	J4
May 1	RACE J2 2:45 2:18	WALK	J3	J4	J2 2:45 2:30 2:20	J2
May 8	RACE J2 2:45 2:18	WALK	J3	J4	J2 2:45 2:30 2:20	J2
May 15	J4	J2 2:45 2:30 2:25	J3	RACE J2 2:45 2:18	WALK	J3
May 22	J3 2:45	RACE J2 2:45 2:18	WALK	J3	J4	J2 2:45 2:30 2:25
May 29	J3	RACE J2 2:45 2:18				

CHART NO. 19

TRAINING SCHEDULE

Raceway Horse, 2:06 to 2:10 class. Quit sound Oct. 1st.
Turned out until Jan. 2nd and picked up for jogging.
To race May 1st, 8th, 18th, 23rd, and 30th.

DATE Week of	MONDAY	TUESDAY	WED.	THURSDAY	FRIDAY	SATURDAY
Jan. 2 9 16 23 30 Feb. 6 13 20 27 March 6	During the first 10 weeks beginning Jan. 2 and continuing through the week of March 6, the schedule for this horse is identical to the first 10 weeks (Weeks of Jan. 2 through March 6) for the horse on Chart No. 18.					
Mar. 13 (11th week)	J2 2:45 2:30 2:30	J4	J4	J2 2:45 2:30 2:30	J4	J4
Mar. 20	J2 2:45 2:30 2:25	J4	J4	J2 2:45 2:30 2:25	J4	J4
Mar. 27	J2 2:45 2:30 2:25	J4	J4	J2 2:45 2:30 2:25	J4	J4
Apr. 3	J2 2:45 2:25 2:20-1:07-33	J4	J4	J2 2:45 2:30 2:25	J4	J4
Apr. 10	J2 2:45 2:20 2:18-1:06-32	J3	J4	J2 2:45 2:30 2:25	J3	J4
Apr. 17	J2 2:45 2:20 2:15-1:05-31	WALK	J3	J2 2:45 2:30 2:25	J3	J4
Apr. 24	J2 2:45 2:20 2:15-1:05-31	WALK	J3	J2 2:45 2:30 2:25	J3	J4
May 1	RACE J2 2:45 2:22	WALK	J3	J4	J2 2:45 2:30 2:25	J3
May 8	RACE J2 2:45 2:22	WALK	J3	J4	J2 2:45 2:30 2:25	J3
May 15	J4	J2 2:45 2:30 2:25	J3	RACE J2 2:45 2:22	J3	J4

CHART NO. 19 Continued

DATE Week of	MONDAY	TUESDAY	WED.	THURSDAY	FRIDAY	SATURDAY
May 22	J3 2:45	RACE J2 2:45 2:22	WALK	J3	J4	J2 2:45 2:30 2:25
May 29	J3	RACE J2 2:45 2:22				

CHART NO. 20

TRAINING SCHEDULE

Raceway Horse, 2:01 to 2:05 class. Quit sound Dec. 15th.
Turned out until Jan. 16th and picked up for jogging.
To race May 1st, 8th, 18th, 23rd, and 30th.

DATE Week of	MONDAY	TUESDAY	WED.	THURSDAY	FRIDAY	SATURDAY
Jan. 16	J2	J2	J2	J2	J2	J2
Jan. 23	J3	J3	J3	J3	J3	J3
Jan. 30	J4	J4	J4	J4	J4	J4
Feb. 6	J3 2:45	J4	J4	J3 2:45	J4	J4
Feb. 13	J3 2:45 2:40	J4	J4	J3 2:45 2:40	J4	J4
Feb. 20	J3 2:45 2:35	J4	J4	J3 2:45 2:35	J4	J4
Feb. 27	J2 2:45 2:35 2:30	J4	J4	J2 2:45 2:35 2:30	J4	J4
Mar. 6	J2 2:45 2:35 2:30	J4	J4	J2 2:45 2:35 2:30	J4	J4
Mar. 13	J2 2:45 2:35 2:25	J4	J4	J2 2:45 2:30 2:30	J4	J4
Mar. 20	J2 2:45 2:35 2:25	J4	J4	J2 2:45 2:30 2:30	J4	J4
Mar. 27	J2 2:45 2:25 2:20-1:07-33	J3	J4	J2 2:45 2:35 2:30	J3	J4
Apr. 3	J2 2:45 2:25 2:17-1:07-33	J3	J4	J2 2:45 2:35 2:30	J3	J4
Apr. 10	J2 2:45 2:25 2:15-1:06-32	J3	J4	J2 2:45 2:30 2:25	J3	J4
Apr. 17	J2 2:45 2:25 2:12-1:04-31	WALK	J3	J2 2:45 2:30 2:25	J3	J4
Apr. 24	J2 2:45 2:25 2:10-1:03-30	WALK	J3	J2 2:45 2:30 2:25	J3	J4

CHART NO. 20 Continued

DATE Week of	MONDAY	TUESDAY	WED.	THURSDAY	FRIDAY	SATURDAY
May 1	RACE J2 2:45 2:18	WALK	J3	J4	J2 2:45 2:35 2:25	J3
May 8	RACE J2 2:45 2:18	WALK	J3	J4	J2 2:45 2:35 2:25	J4
May 15	J3	J2 2:45 2:30 2:20	J3	RACE J2 2:45 2:18	WALK	J3
May 22	J4	RACE J2 2:45 2:18	WALK	J3	J4	J2 2:45 2:30 2:20
May 29	J3	RACE J2 2:45 2:18				

CHART NO. 21

TRAINING SCHEDULE

Raceway Horse, 2:06 to 2:10 class. Quit sound Dec. 15th.
Turned out until Jan. 16th and picked up for jogging.
To race May 1st, 8th, 18th, 23rd, and 30th.

DATE Week of	MONDAY	TUESDAY	WED.	THURSDAY	FRIDAY	SATURDAY
Jan. 16 23 30 Feb. 6 13 20 27 March 6 13 20	During the first 10 weeks beginning Jan. 16 and continuing through the week of March 20, the schedule for this horse is identical to the first 10 weeks (Weeks of Jan. 16 through March 20) for the horse on Chart No. 20.					
Mar. 27 (11th week)	J2 2:45 2:25 2:20	J3	J4	J2 2:45 2:35 2:30	J3	J4
Apr. 3	J2 2:45 2:25 2:20-1:07-33	J3	J4	J2 2:45 2:35 2:30	J3	J4
Apr. 10	J2 2:45 2:25 2:18-1:06-32	J2	J4	J2 2:45 2:30 2:25	J3	J4
Apr. 17	J2 2:45 2:25 2:15-1:05-31	WALK	J3	J2 2:45 2:30 2:25	J3	J4
Apr. 24	J2 2:45 2:25 2:15-1:05-31	WALK	J3	J2 2:45 2:30 2:25	J3	J4
May 1	RACE J2 2:45 2:22	WALK	J3	J4	J2 2:45 2:30 2:25	J2
May 8	RACE J2 2:45 2:22	WALK	J3	J4	J2 2:45 2:30 2:25	J2
May 15	J3	J2 2:45 2:30 2:25	J3	RACE J2 2:45 2:22	WALK	J3
May 22	J4	RACE J2 2:45 2:22	WALK	J3	J4	J2 2:45 2:30 2:25
May 29	J3	RACE J2 2:45 2:22				

In 1947, a young man named Stanley Dancer made two good moves. He married his childhood sweetheart, Rachel Young, and the newlyweds used her $250 nest egg to buy an aged trotting gelding named Candor. The young couple went off to the races in a battered trailer and in 1948 Dancer began demonstrating with Candor the training and driving talent that was to lead to the position of great prominence he presently occupies on the American harness racing scene. That progress has been relatively swift. In 1947 his earnings were so meager that the U. S. Trotting Association did not even bother to record them. In 1964 he became the first harness racing  driver to earn more than a million dollars ($1,051,538) in a single year. Two years later he established another all-time high of $1,218,-403. Dancer does it by concentrating on quality horses and developing them into great racing champions such as Nevele Pride, Noble Victory, Su Mac Lad, Cardigan Bay, Henry T. Adios, Egyptian Candor (1965 Hambletonian), Lehigh Hanover and others. He has won four national money-winning titles, two Grand Circuit crowns and for five consecutive years (1962-66) has compiled the leading UDRS (batting average) rating among drivers making 300 or more starts. He was born on an Edinburg, N. J. farm on July 25, 1927, not far from New Egypt, N. J. where his home and training plant are now located. He comes naturally by his harness racing talent with two brothers and two nephews actively involved in the sport plus a son, Ronnie, who has designs on a harness racing career. With career earnings of close to ten million dollars, he ranks second only to Billy Haughton and has won more than 2,100 races, trailing only Haughton and Joe O'Brien in that department. He is a director of the U. S. Trotting Association and was voted Horseman of the Year in 1962.

6

The THEORY
of SHOEING and BALANCING

JOHN F. SIMPSON, SR.

THE shoeing and balancing of trotters and pacers is a delicate science of inches and ounces. A trotter might be perfectly gaited and absolutely balanced with a front toe 3⅝ inches long. With a 3½-inch toe, that same trotter might switch over into a pace. At 3¾ inches he might start interfering behind.

More or less weight, width or thickness in a shoe can make as much difference. Ayres wore a front shoe that was 9/16ths of an inch wide. The standard shoe of the type he wore comes ready-made in widths of a half-inch (8/16ths) and five-eighths (10/16ths) of an inch. But in my professional judgment Ayres was better gaited and better balanced in a shoe 9/16ths of an inch wide and I had Bill Wick, my blacksmith, make a special set for him.

At this point you might be saying to yourself, "Is Johnny Simpson trying to tell me that a sixteenth of an inch in width and an ounce in weight made a difference in the way Ayres trotted?"

Johnny Simpson can and is telling you this. I don't pretend to be omnipotent and I can make just as many mistakes as the next fellow. But man and boy I have been training horses for more than 30 years and you have my word that I thought Ayres was a better trotter with a front shoe that was 9/16ths of an inch wide than he was at 8/16ths or 10/16ths. A little later I will explain why.

You have probably gathered that my subject matter is rather complicated. As I said at the outset, I am dealing with inches and ounces and there is very little margin for error. But while I intend to treat the subject of shoeing and balancing completely, and in detail, I am going to try very hard not to get ultra-technical.

I recently glanced through a book on shoeing and balancing, written more than 50 years ago. The author went into mathematical formulae, involved pictorial sequences applicable to gait and motion and other assorted trivia. In my opinion, a book like this would do nothing but confuse a reader unless he was especially well versed in mathematics and science.

My intention, on the other hand, is to attempt to explain in clear-cut, everyday language that any layman can understand the basic principles of shoeing and balancing.

I will be dealing with trotters and pacers, animals that are making speed at artificial gaits unnatural to them. The natural gait of the horse is the run or gallop and it has been for thousands of years. I am sure the process of evolution will eventually develop trotters and pacers that will never leave the gait they are bred for from the moment they are born until they die. I have seen great progress in this respect in my own lifetime. Present-day trotters and pacers are much more natural than they were when I was a youngster. They come to their gaits more quickly and they go lighter and interfere less.

On the other hand, the very nature of modern harness racing has created problems that didn't exist 15 years ago. From the standpoint of my own subject, for instance, the development of all-weather pari-mutuel tracks has made rainouts virtually a thing of the past and is a measure of our progress. But at the same time, the abrasive surfaces of some of these tracks have made shoeing and balancing a more difficult chore and adjustments very often have to be made on a week-to-week basis.

When we used to race the whole season over those great clay tracks, you could make a slight change in a shoeing or balancing adjustment, have it show instant results and never be required to make any other change the rest of the season.

But now you very often have to make one change to accommodate the surface of one track and then either change back or try something else at the next track the next week because the surface is completely different. It has created quite a problem for those of us charged with keeping a horse properly shod and balanced.

So, despite the progress the breed has made, we are still a long way from the utopian day when we can discard boots and toe weights and special shoes altogether. As long as trotters and pacers interfere or require any human help to establish a perfect gait, and as long as track surfaces continue to vary as much as they do, there is need for knowledge of the proper methods of shoeing and balancing.

I also realize that no man is going to become a horse trainer simply by reading this chapter or even by reading the entire book. A horse trainer can tell things by the feel of the lines or by the attitude and actions of his horse that just can't be expressed in writing.

Sometimes, even a good horse trainer makes changes in rigging or shoeing or conditioning that even he can't explain in detail. He just "knows" it's the right thing to do. This is the type of "horse sense" that every good horse trainer has. A good trainer is born with a certain amount of this intuition and the rest comes with experience. Not only is experience the best teacher, but in training horses it is just about the only teacher.

What I think I can do and intend to do to the very best of my ability is to establish certain guidelines that can point a man in the right direction. I can lay down general rules that should help young men avoid some of the pitfalls that confronted me when I was starting out. I know a book of this type would have been helpful to me. It wouldn't have a made a horse trainer out of me but I know it would have showed me some shortcuts and saved me some time and headaches.

I am also going to try to keep in mind that my subject will likewise be of interest to thousands of owners who have no aspirations to train or drive but who would like to acquire a basic knowledge of the principles of shoeing and balancing. For that reason, I will be going into greater detail concerning some of the elementary phases than I would if I were writing only for horse trainers.

Since the two gaits involved are really as different as night and day, I think I should take a little time here to describe them and to establish what I consider to be the ideal for each.

The trotting gait is that in which the diagonal legs move forward at the same time and strike the ground at the same time. The left front foot hits the ground at the exact instant the right hind foot does. It is a rhythmical one-two beat involving the alternate pairs of legs.

A proper trotting gait conserves muscle and strength and increases endurance. It is built around an even and equal extension backward and forward of the four moving legs. An irregular extension of any leg or combination of legs brings about a faulty gait, usually accompanied by interference, and affects both speed and endurance. In many instances, such irregularities can be overcome by proper shoeing and balancing.

When the trotter is at speed, the hind legs act as giant pistons and provide the driving power that propels the horse forward. The front legs, rolling over in a fluid, rhythmical manner, act as balance wheels and establish the basic nature of the gait.

I believe the late trainer-driver Thomas W. Murphy described the ideal trotting gait best when he said, "A good-gaited trotter resembles nothing as much as a barrel rolling down a hill."

To establish properly the rolling nature of the trotting gait in front, I believe it is desirable for a trotter to go within an inch or two of his elbows (Fig. 26). A trotter that goes close to his elbows while not actually touching them is less likely to interfere with the hind leg on the same side and at the same time is establishing the momentum to roll the front leg properly in its forward stroke.

A good-gaited trotter must have a certain amount of knee action and, generally speaking, the more the better. A stiff-legged trotter, one that doesn't fold his knees or folds them only slightly, not only fails to develop that round, rolling gait in front but he is almost sure to interfere with his hind legs.

On the other hand, there also must be a certain amount of extension in front in conjunction with the proper knee action. A trotter that is folding his knees properly but is going straight up and down without any noticeable forward extension is sacrificing reach and range and is wasting energy. I want my trotters reaching out with a bold round stroke and at all times resembling as nearly as possible Mr. Murphy's barrel rolling down the hill.

An ideal gait behind is one in which the trotter goes fairly close to the ground thus achieving maximum driving power. A trotter with an extremely high "hocky" action behind is wasting energy and cannot and will not trot to the limit of his potential speed.

Because the folding action of the knee and hock joints is exactly opposite, it is natural that the trotter will go a little higher in front than he will behind. For the same reason, the hind leg will reach forward with greater ease and when I begin discussing interference in gait you will find that it is sometimes just as necessary to decrease the extension of the hind legs as it is to increase the extension of the forelegs to overcome the problem.

Trotters can be either line-gaited or passing-gaited (Fig. 26).

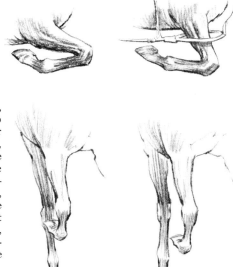

Fig. 26. The ideally-gaited trotter, upper left, goes within an inch or two of his elbows in making the proper front stroke. The pacer, upper right, should come within about the same distance of his hobbles. The two basic gait types among trotters are illustrated below. The line-gaited trotter, left, carries his legs on the same side in a direct line as viewed from front or rear. The passing-gaited trotter, right, places the hind leg slightly outside the front leg. Both views are from the front.

The line-gaited trotter is one whose front and hind feet on the same side are in a direct line with each other, viewed either from the front or rear when the horse is in motion. The passing-gaited trotter is one whose hind feet land outside the front feet.

Some people have the mistaken impression that the passing-gaited trotter extends his hind legs farther forward than the line-gaited trotter. This is not the case. In both instances, the hind legs have the same degree of forward extension. The only difference is that the hind legs of the passing-gaited trotter land farther to the outside.

Every trainer has his own preference as to these gaits. Frankly, I prefer passing-gaited trotters. It has been my experience that they come to their speed quicker, carry it farther and are less likely to show double-gaited tendencies.

Very often you will find that when you start out with a passing-gaited trotter he is inclined to be quite sprawly behind. I have found, however, that as you go on, good colts will close up behind and soon develop an outstanding gait. Ayres was like this. He was quite wide and sprawly when I started with him but closed up and became perfect-gaited as I went on.

The gait of the trotter behind is basically a family trait. The Axworthy family, which descends from Hambletonian's son George Wilkes, is a passing-gaited family. The Peter The Great horses, descending from Hambletonian's son Happy Medium, tend to be line-gaited. However, the sire-to-sire relationship will not always indicate this because some trotters will inherit the trait from other ancestors and these days you will find male-line Axworthys that are line-gaited and Peter The Greats that are passing-gaited.

The pacing gait is the opposite of the trotting gait. The legs on the same side move forward and backward in unison. The ideal one-two beat is the same. The trot is a straight up and down gait while the pace is a rolling gait. If you will stop to think of the difference in the way each goes you will recognize this.

The trotter lands alternately on the left front and the right hind and right front and left hind legs. Thus his body is always balanced in the center and he does not roll from side to side. The pacer lands with both feet on the same side and his weight is constantly bearing from the right side to the left side and back again. Thus, he has a rolling, rocking motion.

The basic interference in a trotter occurs when the front foot comes in contact with the hind leg on the same side. With the pacer, it is just the opposite and takes place when the hind foot on one side comes in contact with the front foot on the other side at the peak of stride. This is known as cross-firing.

To overcome this, pacers are generally shod and balanced so that their gait is widened out behind and the chance of cross-firing interference thus minimized. This naturally tends to over-emphasize the rolling gait.

In front, the pacer does not have or need as much folding action as the trotter. He goes lower to the ground and thus usually wears a lighter shoe and a shorter toe. However, although he does not usually fold as high, he does need a good round stroke to help develop the rolling action of the pacing gait. At the same time it is just as disadvantageous for a pacer to fold his knee properly, yet fail to establish reach and extension, as it is for a trotter.

I have found that most of the great pacers had knee action very similar to a good-gaited trotter except that they didn't go quite as high. Earlier, I wrote that I liked my trotters to be gaited so that they went within an inch or two of their elbows. By the same token, I like my pacers to go within an inch or two of the bottom of their hobbles (Fig. 26).

Many of the great pacing champions went this way. Billy Direct was free-legged but if he had worn hobbles he would have come very close to the bottom of them. Bullet Hanover, Torpid, Adios Harry, Adios Butler and even Bret Hanover either touched their hobbles slightly or came within an inch of them.

I know there have been exceptions and that a lot of fast pacers went very low and were "daisy-cutters" as we call them. But if I had my choice, everything else being equal, I would take the pacer that was gaited to go within an inch of his hobbles.

Before you can successfully shoe and balance a horse you must have two things going for you. Your horse must be sound and he must be carrying his head and body straight. I never knew a trainer who could shoe a horse sound, that is overcome a lameness through shoeing. And I never knew anyone who could properly balance a horse that had his head or his hind end way off to one side.

In another chapter, Joe O'Brien has discussed the reasons why a horse will go with his head or his hind end crooked and has advised what to do to straighten that horse up. At the same time, Dr. Churchill has explored the various areas of lameness and has set forth causes, symptoms and treatments. In all except a few isolated instances, therefore, I will be talking about a horse that is sound, is going straight between the shafts and is carrying his head straight out in front of him.

Given such a horse, the next thing a trainer must have in order to properly shoe and balance him is infinite patience. This applies to any horse but is especially true of 2-year-olds that haven't been through the training mill before. I have always thought that too many of us are in too much of a hurry with our colts. We have a race for a young horse in the middle of May and we are in a big hurry to get there just because we've made a payment to keep him eligible.

If that colt is not perfectly shod and balanced, you are much better off to wait a couple of additional months with him. This lack of patience with young horses that do not immediately respond to efforts to shoe and balance them probably puts more 2-year-olds on the shelf each year than anything else.

A young horse that is hurried before he is properly balanced just has to begin interfering and eventually will go unsound. When you ask about this colt later you hear something like, "Oh, he went lame early and I had to quit with him." The truth is that the colt very likely wouldn't have gone lame at all if the trainer had taken his time and made sure the colt was balanced properly before going on with him.

In this respect, you must also keep in mind that some horses simply aren't meant to be good 2-year-olds and there is nothing in the world that a horse trainer, even the most experienced one, can do about it. In such cases, you are doing yourself and the horse a big favor if you quit with him early and hold him over a year. Many horses that raced well when they grew older were relatively helpless as 2-year-olds. The point is that you can spoil such a horse if you persist in training him when he should be turned out and permitted to mature both physically and mentally.

In a situation like this, there are a number of indicators to observe. A typical horse in this category is the big growthy one that is growing so fast you can almost see a day-to-day change. Nature never intended such a horse to be trained stiffly as a 2-year-old. All this colt's energy is being channelled into the growing process and he doesn't have much left for anything else.

Then there is the type I call the "mental case." This one either isn't willing about his work or isn't trying. No matter what the reasons might be, he shows a complete lack of interest and you are better off to turn him out and try again the next year.

There is also a third type, probably the most common of all, and the one that can cause any horse trainer a lot of grief. He seems to be shod and balanced exactly right except for some little imperfection in his gait that can't be cleared up no matter what the trainer does. All trainers get colts like this. After working with them awhile those of us who have had experience along this line soon realize that our skills are to no avail and that we are dealing with a horse that simply lacks maturity. A horse like this should be turned out right away because this is the one that can be ruined most easily by a trainer who persists in going on with him.

In short, you simply can't force an issue with a young horse you are trying to gait properly if his problem is lack of physical or mental maturity. If you do force him, he is bound to start

Fig. 27. The length of a horse's toe is measured with a caliper, left. The angle is measured with a foot level, right. Accurate toe and angle measurements are vital in balancing the harness horse as explained in the text.

interfering and, if you persist, he will go lame.

I also think the reports on colt training progress that appear in the weekly turf publications sometimes tend to become a psychological factor in this regard. A young fellow reads where so and so trained his colt in 2:25 while he has only been in 2:45 and he begins to think, "Gee, I'm way behind, I'd better hurry and catch up." This man is sending himself on a fool's errand.

I have never in my life known of a horse that lost a big race because he didn't go fast enough in winter training. You can drop colts fairly rapidly once you have given them the solid foundation of slow miles so necessary to condition them for the stakes. And those foundation miles are the ones you utilize to shoe and balance your colt properly.

I have always said that, on the first day of March, I would rather have a colt trot a good-gaited mile in 3:00 than a bad-gaited one in 2:30. All other things being equal, the 3:00 colt will win the stakes and the 2:30 colt will wind up in the pasture. If I can be said to have a basic philosophy about shoeing and balancing 2-year-olds, that is it.

When I get a colt fresh from the farm or from a sale, the first thing I do is check the angle and the length of toe preparatory to shoeing him. The angle and length of toe are probably the two most important measurements a harness horse trainer will ever have to deal with and I want to go into some detail relative to each.

The length of a horse's toe is measured from the center of the top of the hoof to the point where the toe touches the ground. This measurement is made with a caliper (Fig. 27) which is then placed on a ruler or yardstick to determine the exact length. Since toes are usually lengthened or shortened by either an eighth or a quarter of an inch, an exact measurement is of vital importance.

As a rule of thumb, you like a trotting colt to go with a 3½-inch toe in front. This is ideal but you don't get many like that. In order to establish balance, you will find that many trotting colts require a front toe that is 3⅝ or 3¾ inches long. A 3⅞-inch toe is not uncommon and you find some four-inch toes. A toe longer than four inches is uncommon. I would say that more trotters wear a 3⅝-inch toe than a 3½, especially 2-year-olds. I like to start with 3½ because it is ideal, but I don't have too many that stay that way. Most of them usually carry a little more.

A trotter will go with a little shorter toe behind than in front. The usual length of toe for a trotter behind is 3¼ inches.

An average pacer will wear a little shorter toe all around than a trotter. In front, a typical pacer may wear a 3¼-inch toe, but 3⅛, or even three inches, is not uncommon. The measurement of a pacer's toe behind is usually shorter than in front but there are instances when it might be the same or even longer, especially if a pacer is carrying a very short toe in front.

What does the length of toe do in a harness horse? It affects balance principally and is a factor in whether or not a horse is going to interfere. A longer toe provides a little additional weight on the end of a horse's foot and has a tendency to steady his gait. This is why a trotter will often need a longer toe. If the front toe of a trotter is too short, the horse will be unsteady and will be "struggling" in an effort to balance himself as he makes his forward stride. By increasing the length of the toe by even as little as an eighth of an inch, a trainer can very often overcome a deficiency of this sort and establish proper balance.

Maybe I could simplify it a little if I likened a trotter's foot to a fishing line. If you threw an ordinary fishing line out into a stream it would wave and wiggle before it hit its mark. But if you put a little weight on the end of the line, it would go straight and true and would not waver. In a way, this is what a little extra toe does for a trotter. It adds weight and steadies the action of the foot, just as a sinker steadies the action of a fishing line. A little later I will be discussing toe weights and in general terms this is also the way they serve as a means of improving balance.

One of the principal reasons trainers like their trotters to go with as short a toe as possible is that a longer toe puts more strain on muscles, ligaments and bones and leads to possible unsoundness. And, of course, the shorter the toe the less likelihood of interference with the hind leg.

When a horse's foot hits the ground, a certain amount of leverage is required for it to break over and begin the next stride. With a 3½-inch toe, for instance, less leverage is required than with a four-inch toe because a smaller overall area is involved.

A longer toe thus results in more strain when a foot breaks over. We are dealing here with something that is accomplished in a minute fraction of a second, but if you multiply the additional strain by the number of times the foot hits the ground in training miles and in a race, you are getting into an area of considerable consequence. That's one of the reasons all trainers like a short toe.

Despite this, I have always contended that a horse that needed a four-inch toe to balance him was better off than if you cut his toe to 3½ inches and had him making breaks while you tried to teach him to trot. Running and making breaks just don't contribute to keeping a horse sound. We are all striving to get a horse to go with as short a toe and as little weight as possible, but you simply can't sacrifice balance to accomplish this.

I have one other thought regarding length of toe that I think is well worth mentioning. When a trainer takes a horse to the blacksmith shop, he should never estimate how long the toe has grown since the last shoeing and tell the blacksmith to take off an eighth of an inch or a quarter of an inch or any stated length.

The normal growth of a toe will vary with the weather. In a dry spell in mid-summer, it will not grow as rapidly as it will in the spring when there is a lot of rain and more moisture in the ground. The proper procedure is to have the correct toe length measurement made on the foot with a caliper and a mark put there. The blacksmith should then be instructed to trim to that mark.

The measurement that always correlates with the length of the horse's toe is his angle. The angle is formed by the sole of the foot and the toe and is measured at the front of the foot where the sole and toe come together. In essence, the size of the angle is determined by length of toe and height of heel measured on a foot that is level on the ground.

An angle is measured by using an instrument called a foot level (Fig. 27), also known as a hoof level. The bottom part of the foot level is in the shape of a horseshoe and is placed beneath the foot exactly as a horseshoe would be.

Attached to the front of the foot level is a moveable stem which extends upward. With the horseshoe-shaped part of the level in position beneath the foot, push the stem back against the front of the foot until it lays level against it from toe to hairline. The angle thus formed and measured automatically by means of a radius on the foot level is the horse's angle.

The importance of the angle is that it is a factor in the way a horse stands and consequently in the way a foot comes in contact with the ground and how it breaks over after it does. The

Fig. 28. The front foot at the left is a completely natural one and demonstrates the proper toe and angle combination as defined in the text. A horse with a long, sloping pastern, center, usually carries a lower natural angle and the angle must be raised by trimming the foot in the manner indicated by the dotted line. If the toe length must be maintained, then the angle may be changed by growing more heel. A horse with a straight, stubby pastern, right above, often grows too much heel which must be trimmed down (dotted line) to establish the proper angle.

angle is just as important in the proper balancing of a trotter or pacer as the length of toe or type, size or weight of shoe. The natural angle of a horse depends to a great extent on his conformation and, within limitations, a trainer may raise or lower this angle to accomplish a specific purpose with regard to balancing and gaiting.

Now let's see if I can't simplify that. An ideal trotter might wear a 3½-inch toe and a 48-degree angle in front. If this combination of length of toe and angle is the right one, the horse will stand naturally under himself and when trotting will break over quickly enough so that he will not interfere with his hind leg on the same side. In addition, he will fold to within an inch or two of his elbows and the concussion, as his foot hits the ground, will be held to an absolute minimum (Fig. 28).

Now, for the sake of argument, let's say that I didn't measure my angle before starting out with this same trotter, that he still has his 3½-inch toe but that the unmeasured angle is 54 degrees.

Since the length of toe remains the same and the foot is trimmed level, the only way this horse can have a higher angle is to have a higher heel. With a higher heel and the same length toe, the horse hits the ground straighter and thus sets up a more severe concussion as he hits. At the same time, he breaks over quicker and thus shortens his stride. He will also fold a little higher in his stroke and since he had been a horse that was just missing his elbows, he now begins to hit them.

On top of all that, he simply isn't natural, doesn't have good balance and is beginning to go bad-gaited. All of this has occurred because his angle is faulty.

If the same horse carried a 3½-inch toe and a lower heel, thus cutting his angle down to perhaps 44 degrees, things begin to happen in the opposite direction. He breaks over more slowly when he hits because there is more leverage than with a higher heel. This puts excessive strain on ligaments, muscles and bones and leads to unsoundness. His stride is extended, but he loses that sharp, folding action so necessary for a good trotter. And since he is breaking over slower, the front foot does not get out of the way of the hind foot on the same side and he begins to interfere.

In either of the two cases I have cited, a horse trainer is asking for trouble. He must, therefore, achieve the proper angle before going on.

You change a horse's angle by cutting down or rasping off the foot either at the heel or the toe. The blacksmith does this with his nippers and/or rasp. If you cut down the length of toe and leave the heel alone, you automatically raise the angle. If you cut down the heel and leave the toe alone, you automatically lower the angle.

You must always remember that if you want to change the angle you have to take more off either the heel or the toe. If you cut the same amount off both, you will have a shorter toe and a lower heel but you will wind up with exactly the same angle. In making such changes, a trainer must always be sure that when he is through and the angle measurement is made that the horse is standing level on the ground.

With an average horse, wearing a normal toe, the rule of thumb is that a lower heel (thus a lower angle) will result in a longer stride and a lower folding action and will cause the horse to break over slower, thus slowing up his action in front. If the same horse has a higher heel (thus a higher angle) he will stride shorter, break over quicker and fold up higher.

Let me cite a couple of other quick examples. With a trotter that carried a 52-degree angle and was hitting his elbows, I might want to reduce that angle either by lowering the heel only or by taking a little off the toe and more off the heel if I thought the latter was more desirable. The lower angle would shorten his folding arc and would help to get him off his elbows.

If a trotter was carrying a 47-degree angle and wasn't breaking over fast enough to clear his hind leg and thus was interfering, I might want to raise that angle to quicken his action in front. To accomplish this, I would let him grow more heel.

You will often run across a naturally high-going pacer that will be hitting the bottom of his hobbles. With a horse like this I might lower his angle by cutting his heel down to get him to stride a little more and fold a little lower so that he missed the hobbles.

Carrying the same angle, the trotter would tend to fold a little higher than most pacers because of the difference in the gaits. The trotting gait usually involves more folding action than the pace. For that reason a pacer will usually carry an angle about two degrees higher than a trotter.

One thing to watch for when you are taking an angle is whether your horse has a dished toe. A dished toe is one that dishes away from the tip to the coronary band. An angle measurement on a horse of this type would naturally show a much lower angle than the horse actually has and could confuse you and lead to trouble if you weren't aware of it.

You have to use your eye and your good judgment in a case like this. I always instruct the blacksmith to rasp away as much toe as he can to a point where he can lay the rasp flat against the surface of the foot. If the other foot is normal, which it usually is, I keep checking the dished foot against the good one by eye until I am satisfied they look alike. If you depend on the actual measurement of the angle without compensating for the dish, either by eye or by rasping away the toe, you could be off by as much as three to five degrees and wind up with mis-matched feet and a bad-gaited horse.

I have often said that taking an angle without making a preliminary check to see if a horse has a dished foot is one of the most foolish things a trainer can do.

Actually, I've never yet seen a horse that didn't have some slight variation in the size of his front feet. I've never checked the hind feet that closely but usually in front one foot will be a little larger than the other. If the angles of the front feet were maybe one degree off it wouldn't bother me a great deal. But if you start talking about two, three and four degrees, then I think there could be problems. This is where your own eyesight and a good blacksmith can be very helpful.

Another type of horse that you can have angle trouble with is a club footed horse, one that tends naturally to grow a lot more heel than toe. With a horse like this you are constantly trying to cut the heel down and grow some toe. In such cases, I think it is a good idea and recommend the use of a light blister around the coronary bands to stimulate growth. A horse's foot is like a finger nail. It grows and must be cut from time to time. It takes about a year to grow a completely new foot on a horse. By using a light blister you can probably grow a new foot in eight months or so and in the meantime you are constantly working to get that heel down.

I usually use Reducine during winter training and will apply it daily for two weeks and then back off for several weeks before starting another two-week round if necessary. If you haven't had any experience along this line, it's a good idea to consult with your blacksmith or veterinarian before beginning such treatment. You have to be careful, for instance, with a white-haired or white-footed horse. A white-footed horse just can't take a blister the way a black-footed or black-haired one can.

You also have to be sure to take time and exercise caution in lowering the angle of a club-footed horse or one with a short, stubby pastern that tends to be clubby. If you lower it too much at one time by taking off more heel than you should, you can easily cause unsoundness because this puts so much extra strain on the tendons.

This ties in with a very important point that a trainer should always keep in mind when he is taking an angle. Very often when you pick up a colt out of the pasture or from a sale, his angle may be four or five degrees off what would be natural for that particular horse. This is not uncommon because farm blacksmiths are not as technical about such things.

In such cases, I am always careful not to take off more than two degrees at a time when I am setting an angle. If the colt comes to me with 54 degrees in front and I want to get him down to 50 or 48, I will take him down to 52 the first time and then when he is re-shod three weeks later I will take off another couple of degrees and keep doing that until I have him where I want him.

If you take off too much at once, you are making a drastic change in the angle this colt has been carrying and it could affect his performance or even cause unsoundness. The rule of not reducing an angle more than two degrees at a time is a very good one to follow.

An angle is one of the most important measurements a horse trainer has to deal with. It isn't something to be changed every day like a pair of sox. In affecting changes in gait and balance, both shoeing and adjustment of the length of toe take precedence over it.

Summing up my thoughts regarding length of toe and angle, I think the word that comes most quickly to mind is "natural." A horse that carries the proper length of toe and the proper angle, stands, looks and goes naturally. There is nothing forced about his carriage or action. Viewed while standing at ease, he doesn't look propped up on his ankles nor is he tilted forward or backward. He stands, looks, acts and goes just one way—naturally.

Before moving on to the next step in shoeing and balancing, I think it might be a good idea if I set up a little chart that can be used as a general guide. In studying it, you must remember that each horse is different and each may require a little different toe and angle. The specific toe and angle figures are the ones I use to start an average horse of normal conformation and gait.

TOE & ANGLE GUIDE CHART

	Inches Length of Toe		Degrees Angle	
	Average	Normal Range	Average	Range
Trotter in Front	3½	3½-4	48	45-52
Trotter Behind	3¼	3⅛-3⅝	54	50-56
Pacer in Front	3¼	3 -3⅞	50	46-52
Pacer Behind	3⅛	3 -3⅝	54	50-56

After establishing what I believe to be a proper and reasonable starting point for both length of toe and angle, I have to begin thinking about a shoe for that foot. A horseshoe serves two purposes. In all instances it provides protection for the foot. In many instances, it provides sufficient weight to balance a horse properly and, by its shape or type, quickens or slows down his action. The basic shoes worn by trotters and pacers are illustrated in Fig. 29.

Before I get too deeply into this subject, I want to mention the fact that there has been a recent development that may possibly revolutionize the shoeing of trotters and pacers. This was the introduction in late 1967 of a plastic shoe designed and marketed by Jonel Chyriacos, the internationally-known Greek trainer who makes his headquarters near Paris, France. I have used the Chyriacos shoes with some remarkable results that I will describe in detail later on. However, since these shoes have not been tested sufficiently for me to be able to state categorically that they will replace steel shoes, I am going to write this chapter as though they did not exist. Only time will tell whether they are as good as they appear to be and while I have been quite encouraged with the results to date, much more testing will be required before a final decision can be reached.

Almost all trotters and pacers are shod all the way around, that is they have shoes on all four feet every time they race. However, I cannot say that this is an absolute rule because occasionally you might want to pull the front shoes off a knee-hitting pacer or the hind shoes off a trotter racing over the new Tartan composition track. I will comment on each of these situations later.

Harness horses wear one of three basic types of shoes. Both

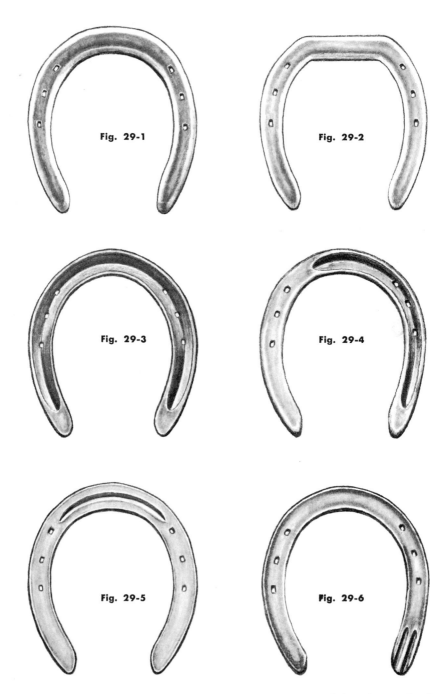

Fig. 29-1

Fig. 29-2

Fig. 29-3

Fig. 29-4

Fig. 29-5

Fig. 29-6

Fig. 29. The basic shoes worn by trotters and pacers and described in detail in the text are illustrated. Beginning at the upper left, Fig. 29–1 is a half-round shoe; Fig. 29–2, half-round with squared toe; Fig. 29–3, full swedge; Fig. 29–4, half-round, half-swedge; Fig. 29–5, flat shoe with toe crease; Fig. 29–6, half-round with double heel crease; Fig. 29–7, flat shoe with a grab; Fig. 29–8,

Fig. 29-7

Fig. 29-8

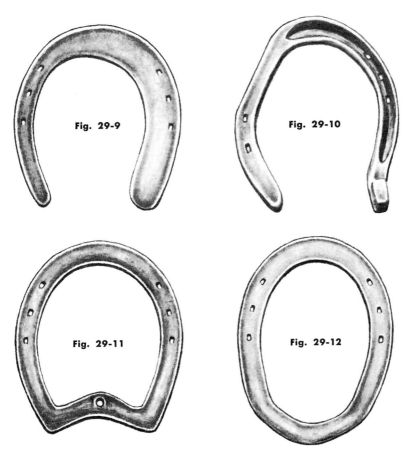

Fig. 29-9

Fig. 29-10

Fig. 29-11

Fig. 29-12

flat shoe with jar calks (without the grab or calks, both Fig. 29–7 and Fig. 29–8 would be standard flat or plain shoes); Fig. 29–9, sideweight shoe; Fig. 29–10, diamond-toed half-round, half-swedge with trailer and heel calk; Fig. 29–11, standard bar shoe; and Fig. 29–12, egg-bar shoe.

trotters and pacers wear flat shoes, half-round shoes and swedge shoes. (For the time being I am just going to mention the swedge shoes in passing and will return to them later.) These shoes are usually made of steel although quite a few pacers wear aluminum shoes in front. Trotters, because they usually require more weight, rarely wear an aluminum shoe.

The flat shoe is, as the name indicates, flat on both sides (Fig. 29-7). It comes from the factory in two basic thicknesses and a number of widths. Some trainers will also refer to this shoe as a plain shoe. I do myself sometimes. But in this chapter I am going to call it a flat shoe throughout.

The two standard thicknesses for a flat shoe are a quarter of an inch and 3/16ths of an inch. The quarter-inch stock comes in strips that are a half-inch, 5/8ths of an inch and three-quarters of an inch wide. The 3/16ths steel comes in widths of 3/8ths, 1/2, 9/16ths, 5/8ths and three quarters of an inch. The width of the shoe is also known as the web.

The weight of the shoe is determined by the width and thickness and by the size of the horse's foot. A shoe for a horse with an average-size foot is made from a piece of steel about 13 inches long. The average weight for the various flat shoes is indicated on the chart that follows. Please remember that a shoe for a pacer would probably weigh an ounce or two less than the same shoe on a trotter because the pacer usually goes with a shorter toe and thus it takes less steel to go around his foot.

In examining the chart you will note that the heaviest flat shoe I could order would be a "quarter by three quarters" which would weigh about 12 ounces. Some trainers will say "three quarters by a quarter" in referring to the same shoe, but since the thickness is either one-quarter or 3/16ths and there are no shoes of these widths, there is never any question concerning the type shoe they are talking about. The lightest flat shoe I could get would be a "3/16ths by 3/8ths." It would weigh five ounces, and probably a little less if I was using it on a pacer.

The half-round shoe differs from the flat shoe in that the surface that bears on the track is rounded. The bottom of the shoe, or the part that lays against the horse's foot, is flat, as it must be to fit the wall of the foot.

The half-round shoe (Fig. 29-1) usually comes ready-made from the factory and when it does the standard widths are 1/2,

SIZES & WEIGHTS OF FLAT (PLAIN) SHOES

Thickness	Width (Web)	Average Weight
	1/2 inch	7 oz.
1/4 inch	5/8 inch	9 oz.
	3/4 inch	12 oz.
	3/8 inch	5 oz.
	1/2 inch	6½ oz.
3/16 inch	9/16 inch	8 oz.
	5/8 inch	9-10 oz.
	3/4 inch	10-11 oz.

STOCK SIZES FOR HALF-ROUND SHOES

	Width	Average Weight
	1/2 inch	7 oz.
*	5/8 inch	9 oz.
	3/4 inch	11 oz.

* The half-round shoe has no technical thickness measurement since it is round in shape. Actually a half-round shoe is made from stock a quarter of an inch thick.

5/8ths and three quarters of an inch as shown on the chart. A half-round shoe is often made by a blacksmith. Because of its rounded edge, this shoe has no technical thickness measurement. Actually, it is made from quarter-inch thick stock. So when you talk about a half-round shoe, the figure you are using in conjunction with it is always the width or the web.

You might tell your blacksmith, "Shoe him with a 'half-inch, half-round.'" This means that the shoe will be a half-inch wide. Similarly, a "three-quarter, half-round" would be three quarters of an inch wide.

If you aren't a horse trainer, I may have confused you a little with this description of a half-round shoe. Let's see if I can't make it a little simpler.

Take a round piece of steel a half-inch in diameter and approximately 13 inches long. Now cut that piece of steel in half, lengthways, right down the middle. Then you have two pieces of steel, each 13 inches long, round on one side and flat on the other, thus the name "half-round." Heat the steel, form it into the shape of the horse's foot and you are ready to shoe him with a half-inch half-round. The flat part of the shoe goes against the wall of the horse's foot and the round part bears on the ground.

You will recall that I said the half-rounds come ready-made from the factory in three widths; half-inch, 5/8ths and three-quarters. Occasionally you will find that you want a half-round shoe of a slightly different width, perhaps a 9/16ths half-round.

What you do in a case like this is to have your blacksmith make one for you by taking a 3/16ths by 9/16ths strip of flat steel and running it through a half-round block. This is a block of steel with a pattern running the length of its surface at the top. One of these special patterns is a half-round, 9/16ths of an inch wide. The blacksmith heats the flat shoe, runs it through the block to change its shape to a half-round and you have a 9/16ths half-round shoe. In addition to a half-round block, blacksmiths also have a swedging block (Fig. 30) for converting to that type of shoe.

Earlier I mentioned that I used this type shoe on Ayres. I found by experimenting that Ayres went best that way. With a five-eighths (10-16ths) half-round shoe, he acted as though he was laboring just a trifle, that is carrying just a little too much weight. With a half-inch, half-round (8/16ths) he felt just a little light, so I had the 9/16th half-round made and he was perfect. There was probably just an ounce of difference and maybe for another trainer he would have trotted just as well in one of the other shoes, but I thought this suited him best and I used it on him in front.

I don't think I need to spend a great deal of time discussing aluminum shoes. They can be flat, swedged or half-round. They are worn principally by a pacer in front and occasionally by a trotter behind. Their one big advantage is that they are lighter than steel shoes. An aluminum shoe will weigh from two to five ounces and is fine for a pacer that doesn't require any special weight to balance him, or for a trotter that needs a very light shoe behind.

The principal difference between flat and half-round shoes is that the half-round has a rounded edge and thus has a roller motion that breaks a horse over quicker when his foot hits the ground. I think you can see why this would be so. When the foot with the half-round shoe hits the ground it tends to roll

Fig. 30 Blacksmiths use steel blocks of the type at the left to convert flat steel into half-round or full or half-swedge shoes. A swedging block is illustrated. At the right is a toe weight (A), often used as an aid in balancing a trotter. A toe weight may either be fastened directly to the foot or attached by means of a spur into which it slides as illustrated. It is important to remember that in order for a toe weight to function properly it should not be placed either too high or too low on the foot. This illustration also indicates (B) the manner in which the shoe may be underset at the inside near the toe to lessen the impact of interference with the hind leg on the same side. This is the left front foot of a trotter. For another view of the undersetting process see Fig. 36.

forward and come over quicker. A foot shod with a flat shoe will not break over quite as fast because the shoe presents a blunt front edge instead of a rounded one.

The importance of whether the front edge of a shoe is flat or rounded is tied in with the basic rule governing the shoeing of harness horses to eliminate interference. The rule is that, except in rare instances, you must "quicken him up in front and slow him down behind." While equal attention must be given to both the front and hind ends, the contrasting action of the principal joints involved, the knee in front and the hock and stifle behind, make it much easier to speed up a horse's action in front and to slow it down behind.

Thus a half-round shoe quickens a horse up in front by breaking him over faster as his foot hits the ground and prepares to begin the next stride. But it has one disadvantage that must always be borne in mind. Because it does have a quick, snapping action, it is harder on a horse's legs, especially his ankles, than a flat shoe.

I like to start all my colts off in half-round shoe because I want to have them breaking over and establishing a gait as quickly as possible. But very often I will flatten the top of a half-round shoe, that is the portion that comes in contact with the track, to lessen the snap of breaking over. This is done by having the blacksmith heat the shoe and pound it down on top all the way round.

A horse should never be permitted to go more than four weeks without being either re-shod or re-set, although I never let one go more than three weeks in my own stable. When a horse is re-shod, his shoes are replaced by new ones. When a blacksmith re-sets a horse, he removes the shoes, trims the feet, adjusts the angle and length of toe in accordance with the trainer's instructions and puts the same shoes back on.

A three-week period is my outside limit, but in many cases it is necessary to re-shoe the horse or re-set his shoes more often. This is especially true when you are racing over the abrasive surfaces of some of our all-weather tracks. Shoes simply will not hold up on these surfaces and your horse may have to be re-shod as often as once a week. When you are racing over a good clay track, you don't have to re-shoe a horse nearly as often and many times the same shoes can be re-set over and over again.

In shoeing a horse for the first time, a trainer should always examine the foot carefully to determine the width of the wall, which is the solid outside edge of the bottom of the foot. This is important because the width of the wall governs the way the nail holes will be punched in the shoe.

There are three nail holes on each side of a standard horseshoe. From front to back, they are identified as the toe, middle and heel nail holes and, in the same order, are sometimes called the first, second and third nail holes. If a horse has a good wide, solid wall, the nail holes should be punched in the middle of the shoe or perhaps even a little to the inside. But if a horse has a narrow wall, the holes must be punched much closer to the outside edge or you run the risk of driving a nail into the quick and coming up with a lame horse.

It is possible to buy shoes with the nail holes already punched. But I don't believe in this and have never permitted a blacksmith to use such shoes for horses in my stable. There is too much difference in the width of the walls of horses feet for this to be practical. I always insist on the nail holes being punched in accordance with the width of the wall.

Now I am ready to describe the techniques involved in the

actual shoeing and balancing of a horse and I will concentrate for a while on the trotter. He is much more difficult to shoe and balance than the pacer for three basic reasons: (1) because of the nature of his gait he usually requires more weight to help him maintain his balance, (2) he is more likely to interfere behind and thus should always be shod to clear the hind leg on the same side and (3) he doesn't have any hobbles to help steady him on his gait as he moves along at speed.

I start most of my trotters out with a 5/8ths half-round shoe in front, a 3½-inch toe and a 50-degree angle. (I consider a 48-degree angle a more normal one for a trotter in front, but colts that are fresh from sales or pasture fields usually carry a higher natural angle and for that reason, as I have already explained, I do not like to take too much off at once. I will start most trotters at 50 degrees and cut them down within the next month to six weeks if it is indicated.) I start them behind with a 3¼-inch toe, a 54-degree angle and a flat 9/16ths by 3/16ths shoe.

If there is any possible way I can do it, I want to keep that front toe at 3½ inches. Very simply put, a horse will go faster, stay sounder and race longer with a 3½-inch toe than he will with a four-inch toe.

But I find that in one way training horses is a great deal like being involved in politics. You may brag about your principles and cherished ideals but sooner or later a situation will develop where you'll probably have to make some kind of a concession to expediency to get something done that has to be done. Shoeing and balancing horses is a series of such concessions and compromises.

If I can't balance that colt in a 3½-inch toe, I have no hesitation at all about going to a longer one. Maybe that colt isn't going to go quite as fast or last quite as long with a four-inch toe, but at least he will be racing. He obviously isn't going any place at all at 3½ inches and I have to accept the lesser of two evils if I want to do any good. I accept the compromise as cheerfully as I can and continue on my way.

I start to train my colt. He is perfect. He never makes a mistake. He has flawless action, terrific speed and Emily Post manners. He doesn't touch a boot behind, misses his elbows by an inch and goes in 1:55 carrying a glass of water on his back.

Just as I cross the finish line in that 1:55 mile I wake up. I have been dreaming again. There just aren't any horses like that. There is no such thing as a perfect horse. And if you insist on perfection you'll never have a horse in your stable.

When you are trying to shoe and balance horses, you will find that sooner or later you will have to make some kind of an adjustment with every one of them. You will have to start compromising. That's what I'm going to write about now.

When I start my trotter off, there are four things I am especially watchful for. Does he have good overall balance, is he interfering behind, is he hitting his knees or paddling, is he hitting his elbows? Since it is the least complicated of all, let us consider the last fault first.

As I have already said, I like a horse that trots close to his elbows. The ideally-gaited trotter will just miss them by an inch or two (Fig. 26). Horses that go that way seldom interfere behind. If a horse is just barely nicking his elbows I will put a pair of elbow boots on him and keep going. A great many of our best trotters wore elbow boots. There is nothing wrong with them. But I never use them just for decoration. I use them on a horse that is just barely touching once in a while as a protection for him. I would rather have him touching there than banging away at his hind shins.

The elbow of a horse is a very tender area, just as your own is. So while I can stand a horse nicking his elbows, I can't have him walloping them every time he takes a step. I find that my colt is hitting his elbows too hard. I must try to "shoe him off his elbows."

The reason my colt is hitting his elbows is that he is folding his front feet too high when he breaks over and raises the foot to begin the next stride. I have to stop these front feet from coming up so high.

The first thing I will consider is the possibility of changing his angle. Occasionally I can correct this condition by lowering the angle of the front feet slightly. As you know, a horse will not fold as high if he is carrying a lower angle. It may be that I started this horse out with a little higher-than-normal angle because I thought it might suit his conformation better and in that case I would probably lower it by trimming the heel down a little. But in most cases I have already correlated the angle with the length of toe and I don't want to change it unless I absolutely have to. At any rate, let us assume that that is the case and that I don't want to change the angle.

The next step will be to try my horse in a flat shoe instead of a half-round. Actually, I have no objection to a flat shoe on a trotter in front. If I had my choice, I would use a flat shoe in front in preference to the half-round. A flat shoe doesn't snap the foot over the way a half-round does and thus there is less strain involved.

I have also found that a flat shoe of the same weight will usually have a little wider web than the comparable half-round shoe and thus provides added protection for the bottom of a horse's foot. Such things contribute to keeping a horse sound. However, a great many of our trotters will require a half-round to break them over fast enough to avoid interference behind.

Since the flat shoe will slow the breaking action, my horse will not fold up as high and I may be able to get him off his elbows that way. My horse is well-balanced and I don't want to change the amount of weight he is carrying so I am careful when I make the switch that I go to the flat shoe that has the equivalent weight of the 5/8ths half-round he is wearing. If you will check back on the weight chart you will find that a quarter by 5/8ths flat shoe is the equivalent at nine ounces.

I make the change and hold my breath, hoping that in slowing down the front action I haven't set the horse up to begin interfering behind as will sometimes happen when you switch from a half-round to a flat shoe.

My horse doesn't interfere behind, but he doesn't get off his elbows either. He isn't hitting them as hard as he was but he is still touching them enough that I feel there is room for improvement. I must try something else.

In the distant racing past there lived a man to whom all present-day trainers owe a great and lasting debt. He invented the swedge shoe. A swedge shoe is a very common thing and is one of the three basic types I mentioned earlier. It cures a number of ills for both trotters and pacers. A swedge shoe or a variation of it is often used with elbow hitters.

A swedge is nothing more than a deep valley in a shoe. The outside edges of the web of the shoe remain as they are and make the first contact with the surface of the track when the foot hits the ground. But the area between these edges is hollowed out and makes its contact with the track an instant later.

A standard swedge begins about an inch and a half above the trailing edge of the shoe (Fig. 29-3) at the heel and runs all the way around the surface to the same point on the opposite side. However, in a great many cases I extend the swedge all the way through the heel of a front shoe so that the shoe is completely swedged. It has always been my feeling and one of my theories that a pacer goes better with a completely swedged front shoe. The additional swedge seems to provide a little extra traction. I always use this type of shoe on pacers that require a full swedge in front and occasionally on trotters. Either one of these shoes is known as a full swedge.

Very often, for reasons that I will go into later, a trainer will want to use a half-swedge shoe (Fig. 29-4) instead of a full swedge. This swedge, which may be either on the inside or outside half of the shoe depending on what you are using it for, runs from the same point back near the heel around to the center of the toe. The other half of the shoe is always half-round, never flat. On a half-swedge shoe I never extend the swedge all the way back to the end of the heel because I rarely use a half-swedge shoe in front.

The purpose of the swedge is to slow or hesitate the action of the foot on which it is placed. When a swedge shoe hits the ground, the surface of the track fills the swedge, or hollowed-out area of the shoe, and works a holding effect on that foot. Thus the action of the foot is slowed or "hesitated" as I like to put it.

A full swedge shoe will hesitate the front action of a horse that is hitting his elbows and very often will lower his arc enough so that he misses them. However, this is a fairly radical change and I would prefer to take an intermediate step before resorting to a full swedge. In most cases, with a horse that was going to his elbows, my first choice would be a crease which is a variation of a swedge.

A crease (Fig. 29-5) is an indentation punched into the toe of the shoe. It is usually about three inches long and perhaps an eighth of an inch deep and is shaped a little bit like a new moon. It doesn't amount to a great deal in the overall gait of the horse and is a very common thing. But it does hesitate the horse's stride a tiny bit. Many times it is just enough to get a trotter off his elbows.

You usually put a crease in a flat shoe rather than a half-round shoe. You are using a half-round shoe to get a horse to break over quicker in front and if you crease that shoe you are actually working against yourself by trying to quicken and slow the action at the same time. I will say that there have been occasions when I have used a crease in a half-round shoe. Perhaps I have a horse that needs a half-round shoe to break him over the way I want but that is breaking just a trifle too quick and I know he wouldn't break over quick enough in a flat shoe. Under these circumstances I might crease a half-round, but this is very rare.

The colt I am discussing now doesn't have this problem and he is gaited all right in a flat shoe. So I put a crease in his toe and it hesitates his stride just enough to get him off his elbows. The problem is solved.

Wait just a minute. Where did I put that crease? Right in the center of the toe where you might normally think any crease would go? Maybe you're right and maybe you're 100% wrong.

This brings me to another phase of shoeing and balancing and there is no way I can over-emphasize its importance. It concerns the fact that, except in special circumstances that I will describe later, a horse's foot should always land level when it hits the ground. You will recall that when I set the length of toe and angle for the first time I made sure that the horse's foot was level while I was taking these measurements.

A horse whose foot is not hitting the ground absolutely level is a prime candidate for lameness. If he hits on the outside or the inside of his foot, all his weight is being jammed into that one area instead of being distributed evenly over the entire surface of the foot. The constant pounding of training and racing miles is bad enough on a foot that is level, but it is especially harsh on a horse that is hitting on one side or the other.

How can you tell whether a horse is hitting level? By examining the shoes when he is re-shod or re-set. Pick up the shoe and take a good look at it. If it shows excessive wear on the outside half, have your blacksmith trim the outside of the horse's foot down a little. If it shows wear on the inside half, trim the foot a little lower on the inside. In other words, trim directly in accordance with the wear of the shoe.

What is happening is that your horse is standing level on the ground when he is not in motion, but his gait at speed, dictated by conformation or the natural way he carries and handles his foot, is such that he tends to land a little to the inside or the outside of that foot. This is quite common with horses and, if you stop to think about it, it is the same way with people.

Men and women are all gaited a little differently and when we walk we are inclined to wear out our shoes in slightly different places. Very often, a man will wear down the outside or inside heel of one shoe quicker than any place else. It is natural for him to do this because he is "gaited" to wear down his shoes this way. Sometimes, when he buys a new pair of shoes, he is uncomfortable in them until he gets that heel worn down to fit his natural gait. If you don't believe this is true, take off your shoes right now and see if you aren't wearing down the heels, or even the soles, more in one place than elsewhere.

It is the same way with horses. But it isn't a bad thing at all if a trainer will just study that shoe every time the horse goes to the shop and have the blacksmith trim the foot to accommodate the natural gait of the horse. This is one of the most important things involved in the shoeing and balancing of trotters and pacers.

Occasionally, you will find you have to trim a horse to such an extent on one side of his foot or the other that he will not look natural when he is standing or walking. This is the exception to the level-standing horse I wrote about earlier. Such a horse might look a little pigeon-toed or even unbalanced. But you don't care how he looks or acts when he walks. He'll never go lame walking! What you are interested in is that his foot is hitting the ground level when he is at speed and that is what you are accomplishing by trimming the foot in accordance with the natural way he is wearing his shoes.

There is one word of caution I want to insert about this principle of trimming a horse according to the way he wears his shoes. Be absolutely certain that you are not being deceived by a horse that is wearing his shoes a certain way because of unsoundness. Horses will do this as you will find when you read Dr. Churchill's chapter on lameness. If they are unsound, they will start hitting on a certain part of the foot to escape the pain they feel when they land on another part. If you trim in accordance with this type of wear, you are only compounding

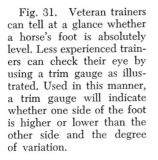

Fig. 31. Veteran trainers can tell at a glance whether a horse's foot is absolutely level. Less experienced trainers can check their eye by using a trim gauge as illustrated. Used in this manner, a trim gauge will indicate whether one side of the foot is higher or lower than the other side and the degree of variation.

your trouble. This is where a trainer's knowledge of his horse and his common sense come into play.

There is also one other point that I feel I should make in this regard. Experienced trainers can tell at a glance whether a horse's foot is level or whether it is a little high or low on the inside or outside. I can stand several feet away in the blacksmith shop and call these slight variations without fail. So can other veteran horsemen. But I do not recommend that young trainers try to do this. I suggest that, until they develop an eye for this sort of thing, they rely on an instrument which, for want of a better name, I call a trim gauge.

The basic part of a trim-gauge is nothing more than a straight piece of steel that curves slightly at the lower end. It is placed along the back of the leg (Fig. 31) and runs from approximately the middle of the shin bone down to the heel. There is a steel loop at the top that fits around the contour of the leg and holds the gauge in place. A straight, flat piece of steel about four inches long and an inch wide is affixed at right angles to the bottom end. The leg is then picked up and the flat end of the trim gauge is laid along the width of the heel. If either side of the foot is high or low, the gauge will show you which and how much. If the foot is level the gauge will also indicate that.

My son, John Jr., who works with me, uses a trim gauge to test his own eye. He looks at a foot, decides in his own mind whether it is high, low or level, and then checks himself with the gauge. It has been useful to him from this standpoint. In using a trim gauge, you must be very careful that the horse has an absolutely straight leg, ankle and foot. If any anatomical deviation is present, it will automatically throw the gauge off.

I was discussing creasing the toe of a trotter's front shoe to get him off his elbows and I had asked where the crease went? Where it goes, is tied in with the way the horse is wearing his shoe at the toe. Some trotters will break over at the center of the foot and thus the crease belongs right in the middle of the toe. But most trotters will break over more to the outside of the toe and, if this is the case, the crease should be placed there so that it coincides with the horse's action in breaking over.

(There are also trotters that break over on the inside of the toe but they almost never hit their elbows and thus there would be no necessity for a crease. The horses that break over on the inside are the ones that toe in or stand "pigeon-toed." In breaking over, the natural action of the foot is to whip outward as it makes its upward arc and thus the foot will rarely interfere with the elbow. It might get up as high as the elbow but it would go outside it. Such horses are known as "paddlers" and will be discussed later.)

If you had a horse that was breaking over on the outside of the toe and you creased the shoe in the middle, you would be working against yourself. The horse would be wanting to break over one way naturally and your crease would be taking action in another direction thus setting up an additional strain that would certainly lead to a faulty gait and could cause unsoundness.

The wear of the shoe at the toe will show you where the horse is breaking over. Unless the way a horse is breaking over is causing interference, you do not want to change it. This is his natural way and you want to keep him as natural as possible. However, you also want to remember that you do not trim the toe down to accommodate the natural breakover as you would on the sides of the feet. If you did this you would be affecting the length of the toe and you can't afford to take too many liberties with a measurement as vital as this.

Now let's forget about elbow hitters for a while and get back to that trotting colt we are starting out with. In addition to the half-round shoe and the 3½-inch toe, I also start all my trotting colts out with hinged quarter boots (Fig. 72).

These are boots that fit around the back of the foot just above and below the heel. They weigh about four ounces apiece and encourage trotting colts to fold their feet. In order to develop the smooth round stroke that is necessary to become a good trotter, a horse must fold up high enough to establish the momentum for that stroke.

A trotter that goes low and doesn't fold properly, usually doesn't establish the interference-free gait desired in the trotter and probably won't go very far. He is also a likely candidate to become a pacer.

Because of their weight and placement back on the heel, hinged quarter boots encourage greater folding of the front feet and thus help to bring about the increased action which is so important to a trotter. Whether it is obtained in the form of a heavier shoe, a hinged quarter boot, a loaded heel boot (similar to the hinged boot but not providing as much protection) or a longer toe and thus a heavier foot, weight will make a horse go higher.

In and by itself, weight is detrimental. Too much of it will break a horse down. That's why I keep saying I like a short toe and a light shoe. But horse trainers have to keep making those compromises I have mentioned and the fact that a certain amount of weight is essential in establishing the proper trotting gait falls in this category.

This is contrasted to the pacing gait where weight is not nearly as important. The lighter a horse goes in front the more likely he is to pace. That's why pacers wear short toes and light shoes, including aluminum shoes which are the lightest of all.

So while the hinged quarter boots do add weight, it is more important to me that I establish the folding action necessary to the trotting gait. That's why I use them. I like the action they give a baby trotter in front. They help roll him up and you start from there to establish the bold, round stroke you want. However, I rarely race a horse in hinged quarter boots. Once you start asking a horse for top speed, the weight of the boot becomes a definite handicap. I will usually discard them about a month before I go to the races. By that time, colts have usually developed their gait to the point where they can go without them.

This is also true with respect to many other factors involved in the shoeing and balancing of harness horses. As colts learn and mature, as they grow smarter about knowing what you want and as their muscles become better developed, they are able to do what they are supposed to with less mechanical help.

This applies not only to hinged quarter boots, but to weight in shoes, toe weights, length of toe and everything else. Once a colt establishes the gait you want, you will often find that you can gradually cut down on all these things and actually derive a beneficial effect as a result.

But it must be done carefully and by stages. It's just as though you suddenly found yourself in a cold room. If you took your clothes off all at once, your teeth would start chattering and you'd be freezing. But if you stayed in that room long enough and took your overcoat off first and then waited awhile before taking your suit coat off, you would find that you would be more conditioned to the cold and it wouldn't bother you nearly as much. Applying this to a trotter and extending it over a period of several months, you would find that you could gradually remove items of shoeing and balancing equipment without any negative effect and that in most instances the horse's performance would actually improve.

In training certain trotters, for example, you might have to use a heavier shoe to get them started but as they progress they will often learn to go in a lighter shoe without any change in their gait. Sometimes I will leave the same shoes on them for months and these shoes will weigh from two to four ounces less than they did when they were new because they have worn down that much. But in the meantime, the colt has learned to trot in a lighter shoe and he doesn't miss the weight.

Years ago it was much more common to find horses racing in hinged quarter boots than it is today. Ben White, one of the great colt trainers of all time, raced many of his trotters that way. Volo Song, a horse that many experts consider the greatest trotter of the first half of this century, wore hinged quarter boots all his life and won The Hambletonian in them.

I raced Ford Hanover in hinged quarter boots and he was undefeated as a three-year-old and won The Kentucky Futurity in 1951. He wore a 3¾-inch toe and hinged boots in front. He might have trotted just as well in a four-inch toe and no boots but I always felt there was more chance of his staying sound with the hinged boots than if I went to the four-inch toe and created that extra strain in breaking over. In this case I didn't feel the boot would affect his soundness and it didn't. I never experimented with the longer toe.

Some trainers will use a bell boot (Fig. 73) instead of a hinged quarter boot and there is nothing wrong with that. A bell boot is a rubber boot which slips over the foot and covers it completely. It will weigh about three ounces. It helps to balance a horse because it has some weight in it and it encourages additional action in his gait.

The hinged boot has more weight in the heel and will make a trotter fold up higher than a bell boot will. The bell boot encircles the entire foot and thus its weight is more evenly distributed.

A bell boot, incidentally, is not a bad piece of equipment for a trotter to wear at any time. In addition to helping balance him it also offers protection for the front heels, quarters and pasterns. Front shin boots, with or without the tendon attachment on the back, serve the same protective purpose for areas between the ankle and the knee.

During the time a trotter is running and trying to get back on the trot after he makes a break, he might hit himself in three or four places on the front leg. Occasionally you will have to double a trotter up in a race and this can cause him to get bad-gaited and hit himself someplace he normally wouldn't. In such cases, shin boots and bell boots, especially the latter, furnish a great deal of protection.

I'm pretty much of a boot man and I don't take too many chances along that line. I have never run across a trotter yet that wouldn't put some kind of a mark on his shin boots someplace along the way. I think boots are a pretty cheap form of insurance.

Now let's go back to my trotting colt. I've been working with him for a few weeks and it is obvious that he isn't balanced. He feels "mixey" gaited, that is, he acts like he might want to pace. I know a great many trainers today would simply put the hobbles on a colt like this and convert him to the pace.

But, frankly, I am much more interested in getting a nice trotting colt and I will do everything I can to keep this colt trotting.

When a trotting colt is trying to pace, you can feel it in the lines. He isn't flat and balanced and is constantly shortening his stride and trying to switch over to the pace and sometimes does.

Assuming that this colt is wearing a 3½-inch toe, a 5/8ths half-round shoe and a pair of hinged quarter boots, the first thing I would do to try to improve him would be to add a pair of toe weights. A toe weight (Fig. 30) is a small piece of metal weighing from two to six ounces. It is fastened to the toe of the foot either directly or by means of a spur into which it slides.

The reason I will go to a toe weight first is that it is a change that can be made easily and quickly and you can usually determine right away whether it is going to help. For instance, I might go a training heat with my colt and then send him to the blacksmith shop between heats to have a pair of three ounce toe weights put on. Some of the other changes are more complicated and require a lot more time.

A toe weight extends stride and aids balance. Very often the toe weights will be all you need to balance your colt and get him trotting right. If this does the job, I am satisfied and will leave the toe weights on him for the time being.

Actually, I would prefer to have a little more foot than a toe weight so after I put the toe weights on I will usually let the foot grow out and in a month or six weeks I will have a 3⅝-inch toe instead of 3½. I will try the colt without the toe weights then and if he goes balanced and is not interfering behind, I will leave the toe at 3⅝ and race him that way. In situations like this, time is also working in my favor because during the period I have been waiting for the toe to grow out my colt has matured somewhat and, as I have explained, that in itself, could be very beneficial in helping him to establish the balance I am after.

Unfortunately, sometimes when you grow a longer toe your horse breaks over a little slower in front and starts to interfere with his hind leg. When this happens and you can't clear up the interference, you are better off to cut the toe back down to where it was and use the toe weight. Again, you must compromise. Very often you will find that after trotters race for two or three

Fig. 32. Pads, indicated by the arrows in the first two illustrations above, are used to lessen the impact on a horse's foot when it hits the ground or to protect an injured area. There are two types of pads; the rim pad, left, which is only as wide as the shoe itself and the full pad, center, which covers the entire sole. A bar shoe, as shown, is usually used with a full pad. A clip (A, right) is sometimes used on thin-walled feet to help hold the shoe in place. A clip is actually a part of the shoe which has been heated and turned up into this position by the blacksmith. In this illustration, the trailing end of the shoe has also been extended slightly (B) to provide a place for the boot to rest so that it will be less likely to fall off.

months, toe weights can be discarded with no ill effects, or at least lighter ones can be used.

If I put toe weights on a colt and he still feels a little mixey-gaited, I will very often go to a full pad as a temporary measure to determine whether a longer toe is going to help him without having to wait a month or six weeks for him to grow the extra toe.

As a matter of fact, I would prefer to use full pads on a trotter in front instead of toe weights if I could. Maybe it's just my idea, but I think any horse will trot a little better without toe weights than he will with them.

Using a pad to extend the horse's toe while you are waiting for the toe to grow to the length that you want it, and using one to help balance a horse by adding weight in the bottom of his foot are two of the three reasons why I use a pad. The third, and probably the most important reason, is that a pad protects a horse's foot.

As long as I have brought them into the picture, let me stay with pads (Fig. 32) for a while.

Pads are made of leather or plastic and they cover the bottom of the foot. They are placed between the foot and the shoe and must be fitted carefully. In effect, a pad is nothing more than extension of the foot and thus you must be sure that it fits smoothly with the contour of the foot all the way around. If a pad doesn't fit flush with the foot and juts out on one side or the other, it simply provides a little additional surface that might be enough to cause a close-going horse to interfere. If it is not flush on the outside of the foot, a trotter might hit his hind shin; if it protruded on the inside, any horse would be more likely to hit his knee.

You can cut a pad to whatever thickness you want. Let's say you decide on an eighth of an inch which is fairly standard. What you are doing is increasing the length of the toe by an eighth of an inch and adding weight in the bottom of the foot. Since the pad extends back to the heel, the length of the heel is also increased by an eighth of an inch and thus the angle remains unchanged.

If you are using a pad for protection only and it is an eighth of an inch thick, you have to remember to trim the foot down an eighth of an inch before you put the pad on. If you don't, you will have extended the length of the toe and as you now know, that would affect the horse's gait.

Pads are worn principally by horses going over hard race tracks. They have some resiliency to them and they "give" a little when a horse's foot hits the track. They are also worn by horses that have flat feet, quarter cracks, corns or some other foot trouble that would be painful to the horse if the shod foot was hitting the track without pads.

Many trotters wear pads in front but you seldom see a trotter wearing a pad behind. A pad is additional weight and usually you don't want weight in a trotter behind because it will tend to make him pacey.

I usually use leather pads instead of plastic, although both are satisfactory. The advantage of a plastic pad is that it doesn't absorb water but I have always felt that a leather pad had a little more give to it and was easier on a horse's foot. There again, it depends on your horse's foot and why you are using the pad. If I am using it for weight, I definitely use a leather pad. Depending on the thickness, a leather pad will weigh from two to four ounces.

You also see a lot of rim pads today, especially with pacers that don't need the added weight of the pad as a trotter usually does. A rim pad is nothing more than a full pad with the center section cut completely away. In other words, a rim pad is just the width of the shoe and no more all the way around. If a trotter is stinging his foot on a hard track and doesn't need the weight of a full pad, I will use a rim pad.

Usually when you use a full pad you use a bar shoe (Fig. 29-11). A bar shoe is one in which a bar extends across the back of the shoe joining the two trailing ends and usually fitting in flush against the heel so that there is no overlap behind the foot.

There is one exception to this general rule of a shoe always fitting flush against the back of the front feet and it applies whether a horse is wearing a bar shoe or an open shoe. If I have a trotter that wears either a hinged quarter boot or an ordinary trotting quarter boot or a pacer that wears a quarter boot or a scalper in front, I make it a practice to extend the trailing end of the shoe back about an eighth to a quarter of an inch on each side so that the boot has a place to rest (Fig. 32). In this manner, the boot is more secure and less likely to fall off. Without this extension, the heel of the boot doesn't have anything to catch on and will come off much easier and quicker. In almost any given race, you will see at least one scalper laying on the track when the race is over. This extension will prevent this in most cases.

Getting back to the standard bar shoe, what you really have is one length of steel completely encircling the foot. The reason I use a bar shoe with a full pad is that the bar keeps dirt and other foreign substances from getting up under the pad. In addition to being a health hazard, dirt will also add weight and you want to keep that from happening. A bar shoe is also useful in front when you want to add a little additional weight in the heel.

When a horse is wearing a full pad, the entire bottom surface of the foot is covered over and you have to put something in there to keep the foot moist and growing. If you don't, the frog, bars and sole will tend to wither and shrivel up. The way to prevent this is to pack the horse's foot beneath the pad.

I think one of the most foolish things a trainer can do is to pack a horse's foot with one of the commercial grease products that are on the market these days. I have always felt that grease closes up the pores of a horse's foot. A horse's foot is spongy and has pores in it just like your skin and it needs moisture to encourage growth. In my opinion grease deprives a horse's foot of moisture and is detrimental to it.

I prefer to use a mixture of tar and oakum. I feel that this combination is beneficial to the horse's foot. It stimulates the natural growth of the sole and frog and if you are using a full pad it is vital that you do this. In packing the tar and oakum, you don't want to put in too much because that will create additional pressure against the sole. Nor do you want to pack too little because that will leave room for dirt to collect. Consult your blacksmith and your veterinarian about the proper proportions which to some degree, of course, will depend on the size of the foot.

The basic reason you use a pad is for protection. But very often the additional weight of the pad and the bar in the shoe will be enough to get a mixey-gaited young trotter going flat and right.

Returning once again to the young trotter that is acting a little mixey-gaited and doesn't feel quite balanced, you can also start adding weight in front by means of a heavier shoe. Very often this will overcome the tendency. Duke of Lullwater was a horse like this. He wanted to pace very obviously as a 2-year-old and one time I even contemplated putting the hobbles on him. But I had a feeling that if I could make a trotter out of him he would be a good one so I decided to give it a real try.

I went to the heaviest shoe in stock, a quarter by three-quarter flat shoe that weighed about 12 ounces. In addition, I went to a hinged quarter boot and a three-ounce toe weight. I was getting up to about 20 ounces on a 2-year-old in February and that is a great deal.

But the weight didn't break the Duke down and he learned to trot. What I did was to let him wear down that quarter by three-quarter shoe until it weighed about the same as a quarter by 5/8ths, say seven or eight ounces. In April or May I was able to discard the toe weights and thus I got about six ounces off him before I started him. He still wore the hinged quarter boots and raced in them. As you will recall, he was the outstanding 2-year-old trotter that year. It would have been very easy to have made a pacer out of him.

Duke of Lullwater was typical of the trotters I mentioned earlier that need quite a lot of weight to get them gaited properly but that will go lighter and better-gaited as soon as they find out what you want them to do and learn how to do it.

Once again, you are taking a calculated risk when you go

to these extremes. Weight, as I have said, can and will break a horse down. At the same time it can cause the front feet to break over slower and result in interference behind. In the Duke's case, it did neither and I was lucky in that respect.

In working with the mixey-gaited horse, if you have extended the toe by means of a pad and are using a toe weight and your colt still acts like he wants to pace, you might try a little heavier boot. For example, a heel-weighted boot will help a mixey-gaited horse. You might even go so far to use a heel-weighted boot and put a bell boot over that to give you a little more weight if it will achieve the balance you are after and still not break your horse down or slow his breakover action too much.

If I find that a longer toe, a heavier shoe and heel weights are slowing up my horse's breakover action to the point where he is beginning to interfere behind, I will usually go just the opposite. I will discard the heel weight boots, shorten the toe and square it and use toe weights.

In doing this, I am aware that I am reducing the amount of weight and that, as a general rule, extra weight will help to balance a mixey-gated horse. But at the same time I know I am in trouble because I have been experimenting for some time with no success and I must try something else if I want to develop a trotter. I am hopeful that during the period of experimentation my horse may have matured a little and developed a little more natural ability that would enable him to trot with less weight. The addition of the toe weights tends to compensate for shortening the toe and losing some of the weight and should help balance my horse.

I think I had better pause right here and explain what I mean by squaring a toe (Fig. 29-2) because this is the first time I have mentioned it and it is quite a common thing. In squaring a toe, you blunt the front edge of the foot much as you might run a file straight across your finger nail to produce a squared nail instead of a pointed or rounded one. A squared toe breaks a horse over faster. In the first place, when you square a toe you automatically raise the angle because you have shortened the toe and that, as you know, will speed the breakover action to a certain extent. In addition, the squared toe has less ground surface to cover when it starts to break over and thus does so quicker. You can square a horse's toe whether he is wearing a flat or a half-round shoe and he will always break over faster.

Actually, you should never square the toe itself until after you have squared the shoe. You have the blacksmith heat the shoe and instruct him how you want it squared. You might have the shoe on and off the foot several times while you are inspecting it to make certain it is exactly as you want it. When you have it just right you nail it on the foot and then rasp the toe down to fit it.

If you worked the other way and started trying to square the toe first, you might get in trouble because you could take a little too much off the toe in attempting to get it just right. You can make a shoe bigger in a few minutes; it takes weeks to grow a new toe.

Returning to the horse whose toe I plan to square in an effort to overcome his mixey-gaited tendencies, at first I would probably square only the shoe and not the toe itself. As you know, I am experimenting and I am not certain that what I am doing is going to solve my problem. Even though I am only squaring the shoe and not the toe, I am still going to get some increased breakover action and there should be enough difference to indicate whether I am on the right track. If I discover that I am, I will go ahead and square the toe. If I find that I did wrong, I still have not committed any great crime because the toe itself has retained its original shape and I am still no worse off than I was when I started.

You must also take the same precaution in squaring a toe that you do in placing a crease. If a horse is breaking over a little to the outside or inside, you must square the toe in accordance with the horse's natural tendency.

Very often the shorter, squared toe, along with toe weights, will be just enough to balance your horse while at the same time eliminating any interference that may have started to develop behind while you were experimenting earlier with the longer toe, heavier shoe, pad, etc.

If necessary, you can also put a crease in a square-toed shoe. Perhaps the square is almost exactly what your horse needed except that it brings him just a shade too close to his elbows. The crease might be just enough to make him go an inch lower. This is not done very often, but there are rare times when it might be just what you need.

Aside from the colt that acts a little mixey-gaited and the one that's a little unsteady and may require more weight, there is one other type of balancing problem you can run into with a trotter in front.

This is the colt that doesn't have that quick, round stroke so necessary to a perfectly-gaited and balanced trotter. He is laboring a little as he trots and it appears almost as though he is going in slow motion. This is a sign that he is carrying too much weight and that you have to take a little off.

With a colt like this, it is usually a good idea to go to a lighter shoe. If you are using a 5/8ths half-round, try a half-inch, half-round. A couple of ounces in weight might make all the difference in the world.

If you find he still labors, or dwells, or is "lonesome-gaited" as we say, go to the lightest shoe you can, a plain 3/16ths by a half or 3/8ths and square the toe. The squared toe and raised angle will break the horse over faster and speed up his action.

You can usually tell the next time you train the horse whether you took off too much weight. If you think you did because he starts to act a little mixey, go to a little more shoe and start aiming for that happy medium again. Don't be afraid to experiment. As I said earlier, experience is really the only teacher.

I like to see any change improve a horse within a relatively short period of time but I wouldn't feel I was on the wrong track simply because my horse didn't show a major improvement in his next workout. I would be satisfied if he showed a little improvement the next time out and I would want to give him at least two or three workouts before deciding I had done wrong, unless it was so immediately obvious that there was no question about it.

Some horses will show a major improvement in the very next workout following a change in shoeing or balancing. But others will show only a slight improvement and these are the ones that I feel are entitled to two or three more workouts before you reach a final decision.

These changes that alter a horse's way of going even to a minor degree are what I have in mind when I say that shoeing and balancing is a science of inches and ounces. A horse that is missing his hind shins by a sixteenth of an inch is just as good as one that is missing them by the proverbial mile. Often times,

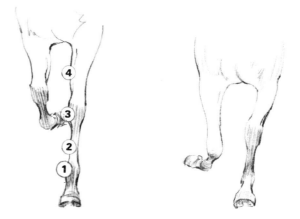

Fig. 33. The illustration at the left indicates the manner in which a horse interferes with one front leg by hitting it with the opposite front leg in passing. Horses that stand toed-out are more likely to interfere in this manner. The horse is shown actually hitting his knee (3), but he may also hit the ankle (1), shin (2) or forearm (4). The manner in which the paddler (the opposite of the knee-knocker) handles his front foot is shown at the right. Horses that toe in are more inclined to paddle although horses that stand straight in front may also paddle or hit their knees. Because of the nature of the gaits, paddling creates an interference problem only with trotters.

a very slight change, one whose effect is measured in tiny fractions of inches, may be absolutely all you need.

There are two other types that you must always be on the lookout for when you are dealing with the front end of a harness horse, either trotter or pacer. These are the horses that hit their knees, and the ones that paddle (Fig. 33).

The ones that hit their knees, and these are the very worst kind, wing their foot inward as they break over. Horses that stand toed out are the ones most likely to do this. Because of the conformation of the foot and leg, such a horse will break over on the outside and as the foot follows this natural path on the way up it will hook in and catch the knee on the opposite leg.

But while horses that toe out are more likely to hit their knees, they don't always do so. I have seen many horses that toed out and did not go to their knees. I have also seen a lot of horses that stood absolutely straight and yet banged their knees with every step they took. The point I am making is that while the way a horse stands may furnish a clue, it is actually the way a horse handles his foot after it breaks over that determines whether he will go to his knees (Fig. 34).

A paddler is just the opposite from a knee-knocker. When his foot leaves the ground, it turns outward instead of inward. A paddler will not hit his knees, but he is much more likely to brush his hind shins. Many paddlers stand naturally toed in but, as I have already said, the way a horse stands is never an absolute indication of how he will handle his foot after it breaks over. You can never be sure until you start training him.

Knee-hitting is a problem with both trotters and pacers. In all instances, you are attempting to shoe the horse so that he goes above or below the knob that sticks out on the inside of the knee and which is where the basic interference occurs.

Occasionally you will want to work on a trotter to get him to go below his knees but that is rare and only when the horse is a naturally low-going trotter. Most of the time you will be trying to get trotters to go above the knee because it is natural for them to go higher. If you are successful, you will sometimes find that a trotter will start interfering with his arm, the area above the knee. This is not desirable, but it is a lot better than having the horse hit his knee. You can put on a little pair of arm boots or a pair of half knee and arm boots and go right on.

Pacers naturally go a little lower than trotters and you can work on them to get them to go either above or below the knee, whichever seems most desirable according to the horse's natural gait.

The first thing I do with a trotter that is hitting his knees is to lower him on the outside. That is, I have the blacksmith rasp the outside of the bottom of that foot down about an eighth of an inch from just above the first nail hole all the way back to the heel.

In doing this you are affecting the direction the foot takes as it breaks over by changing its natural upward arc and encouraging it to follow a new path away from the knee. You might think this would be getting away from the idea of the horse landing with a perfectly level foot and in some cases, with a real bad knee-knocker, this might be true. But once again you must compromise. A horse is much better off landing a little off center than he would be if he hit his knees with every stride. Again you follow the path of least resistance.

Some of the time, however, you will find when you examine the shoe that the horse has been wearing it excessively on the outside anyway and that what you are actually doing is making his foot hit level.

If this does not get a trotter off his knees, I will lengthen his toe. You might have a trotter wearing a 3⅝-inch toe that you had to race in a toe measuring four inches or even longer to get him off his knees. The longer toe provides greater leverage when a horse breaks over and thus will extend the upward arc of his foot and get it above the knee in many cases.

If you had a trotter that suddenly started hitting his knees and you thought the answer lay in a longer toe, the way to get immediate action would be to go to a pad. You could either use a full pad or, if you didn't think the horse needed the extra weight, a rim pad. You might start out with a pad an eighth of an inch thick and if that wasn't enough you could go to a quarter-inch pad or even a thicker one. Meantime, you would be starting to grow more toe on your horse.

Since the paddler is doing just the opposite of what a knee-knocker is, you would naturally go just the opposite with regard to trimming his foot. Instead of lowering him on the outside, you lower him on the inside of the foot he is paddling with.

The paddler is usually interfering by brushing his hind shins and since you are not trying to get him to go higher or lower as you would be if he were hitting his knees, you do not usually have to lengthen or shorten his toe. If he seems to be balanced and gaited properly aside from the paddling fault, I would be satisfied to lower him on the inside which will have a tendency to close up his gait by breaking him over straighter.

There is one other thing I like to do to help a paddler. I will run a double crease on the inside heel of the shoe (Fig. 29-6). This will have a little tendency to hold him as he leaves the ground with that foot and encourage him to carry the foot straighter. I lower paddlers on the inside and use the double crease in the heel of the shoe on the same side.

The greatest cure in the world for a paddler is to be born with a long barrel so that he won't interfere behind. Scott Frost paddled badly all his life, but he was a long-barreled horse and never interfered. Paddling never bothered him a bit. The paddling problem exists, of course, only in the case of trotters. Pacers may paddle but they will not interfere because the legs on the same side never come that close together.

I have written a great deal concerning the problems of a trotter in front because, to a great extent, gait and balance are

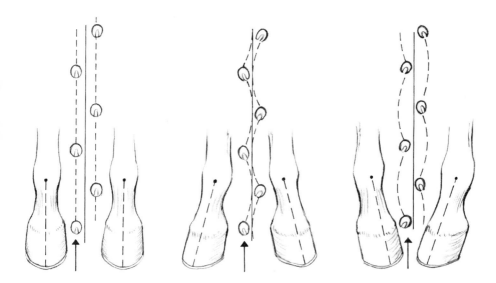

Fig. 34. The line of flight of horses that handle their front feet in one of three basic ways is illustrated. At the left, the horse stands straight, breaks over straight and has an absolutely straight line of flight. The horse in the center toes out and thus the line of flight of his front feet will probably (although not always) be in toward the front leg on the opposite side and he is likely to be a knee-knocker. The horse at the right toes in and thus his line of flight is more likely to be outward and he will be a paddler. Although the way a horse stands in front usually provides a clue as to the anticipated line of flight of the front feet, this is not always a sure sign as explained both by the author and by Billy Haughton in his chapter on the selection of yearlings.

established by the quality of the swift, round stroke of the front legs. Now it is time to start tying the front end and the hind end together.

The problem now becomes one of interference. I hear talk from time to time to the effect that we use too many boots behind and that trotters would be better off if they didn't wear any. I couldn't agree more. But, as I said before, I never knew a trotter yet that didn't brush himself someplace behind sometime during a race and until they start breeding them with a guarantee concerning this I will go on using boots and hoping for the best.

The basic interference in a trotter (Fig. 35) occurs when the front foot, as it leaves the ground to begin its new stroke, ticks, brushes, hits or actually wallops the hind leg on the same side.

The name applied to the interference depends on where it is taking place with respect to the hind leg. Some of this interference will occur on the front of the hind leg. But most of it takes place on the inside of the leg as the front foot touches while passing.

From the bottom of the hind leg upward, the interfering horse is said to be scalping, speedy-cutting, ankle-hitting, shin-hitting, and, in some instances, hock-hitting. The faster a horse goes, the higher up he hits. Roughly speaking, scalping will develop at about a 2:40 rate, speedy-cutting at 2:20 or so, and ankle, shin, and hock-hitting at higher speeds. Forging (Fig. 35) is another type of interference but it differs from the others in that it occurs as a result of the hind foot of the trotter striking the bottom of the front foot on the same side. It usually happens when a horse is jogging. It is actually more of a nuisance type interference than anything else, and if a forging horse is otherwise well-balanced, my remedy is to jog him faster.

It is a very discouraging thing to have your horse perfectly-gaited in front only to find that he is interfering somewhere behind. This means that you have to do something about it; that you may have to make a compromise in that perfect front stroke to overcome the interference.

If you don't eliminate the interference yourself, your horse will start trying to do it for you. He will start changing his gait to get away from the impact he feels with every stride and if you don't do something about it, sooner or later that perfect gait in front will disappear like a shadow at sunset.

Because of the differing natures of the anatomical structure of the principal joints involved—the knee in front and the hock behind—you will find that it is natural for the front leg to break over faster and go higher than the hind leg. Therefore, to eliminate interference it is much easier to speed up the action on the front end and slow it down on the hind end. The extreme folding capacity of the knee joint lends itself naturally to speeding up the action of the front foot in breaking over. It is just the opposite with the hind leg whose action is controlled principally by the hock and to a lesser extent by the stifle joint.

There are only rare occasions when you would want to quicken the action of the hind leg. It is usually much better and much easier to slow down the hind leg. Used separately or in combina-

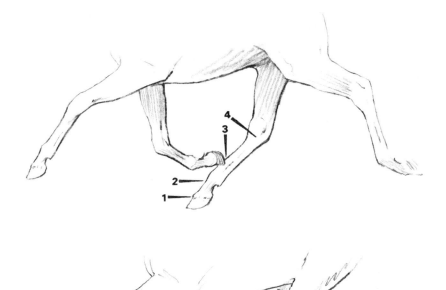

Fig. 35. Basic interference at the trotting gait, top, occurs when the front foot comes in contact with the hind foot on the same side. When the interference takes place at (1) it is known as scalping; at (2) speedy-cutting; at (3) shin-hitting, as illustrated; and at (4) hock-hitting. Except for scalping, the interference usually takes place on the inside of the hind leg. Among pacers, directly above, the basic type of interference between front and hind legs occurs when the hind foot on one side interferes with the front foot on the opposite side. This is known as cross-firing and usually takes place as illustrated but may occur higher up on the front leg such as in the ankle-pastern area or even above it. Forging, opposite, is a type of interference that occurs with trotters when the hind foot strikes the bottom of the front foot on the same side. It usually happens when the horse is jogging and the author's remedy is to jog the horse faster.

tions, methods of speeding up the front leg and slowing down the hind leg are employed to eliminate interference in the trotter.

If you speeded up the action of the hind leg, you would find that the horse would have his hind foot more forwardly placed under his body when he reached the point of maximum extension because you would have lengthened his stride. This would not only upset his natural balance but would also bring the offending foot and leg up into an area where the chance of interfering with the front foot would be increased.

Nature intended that the front foot should break over before the hind foot. If she did not, if she intended the opposite, the hind foot would strike the front foot instead of vice versa. The only time this occurs is when a horse forges which, as I have explained, happens only when he is jogging slowly. As a horse goes faster, the front foot breaks over faster and hits higher up on the hind leg. That is why, to overcome interference, you must "quicken them up in front and slow them down behind."

For these reasons, the shoes and techniques you used to speed a trotter up in front are rarely used behind. Half-round shoes are almost never used. Light flat shoes are preferred and swedges, which slow the action quite a bit, are most preferred.

The reason we usually shoe the trotter light behind is that weight tends to make him pace. As you will discover later when I discuss pacers, the way to encourage a horse to pace is to lengthen his hind toe and use a heavy shoe. So with a trotter behind you usually want a short toe and a light shoe. Whatever weight is required to balance him, goes on the front end. This is where it is used to establish the trotting gait. Used behind, it encourages the pacing action.

Usually a trotter wears a steel shoe, either flat or swedged, behind. But occasionally, with a trotter that has pacing inclinations, an aluminum shoe will be used. The sole purpose of the aluminum shoe is to reduce the amount of weight and thus counteract the pacing tendency. Carrying this a step further, such a trotter might also go in brace bandages and cottons instead of shin boots simply to reduce the amount of weight on the hind leg.

Because it is usually desirable to slow or hesitate the action behind, almost all trotters wear a full swedge shoe (Fig. 29-3). As I have already described, the swedge grips the track and slows the action. This enables the trotter to get his front feet out of the way before the hind feet move forward.

I have always contended that a flat shoe is easier on a horse than a full swedge and for that reason I like to train all my horses, aged stock as well as colts, in a flat shoe until they reach 2:20. I say 2:20 because I train over a good clay track at Orlando, Florida. If I were training over a track with a sandy, all-weather surface, I would probably go to a full swedge at about 2:40. The flat shoe doesn't give you the traction that a swedge does, but I think it is easier on a horse's stifles and I feel he is ready for a swedge somewhere between 2:40 and 2:20 depending on the track surface.

Every once in a while you will find a trotter that will race well in a flat shoe behind. This is fine if he can do it and I am all for it. But mostly you will find that it is beneficial to go to the swedge.

An exception is when you are racing over the Tartan tracks such as we have at The Meadows, Laurel, Tropical Park and Windsor. It has been my experience on such tracks that trotters will race better bare-footed or with a flat shoe than with a swedge. The swedge really grips into the Tartan surface. This was brought home to me by the fact that so many trotters pull their hind shoes off on the Tartan track. What happens is that the Tartan track is holding the hind swedge so much and putting so much traction on it that it is creating enough force to pull the shoe right off the foot. I believe a flat shoe on a Tartan track has about the same holding action that a swedge shoe does on any other track.

Occasionally you will find a trotter that wears a squared toe behind. Since I have already explained that one of the functions of a squared toe in front is to speed the action up, you might think this would be in conflict with the general idea of slowing a trotter down behind. But actually, just the opposite is true. This is only done with a trotter that is wearing a swedge shoe and when you square the toe of a swedge shoe you are presenting a greater area of swedge surface along the front of the shoe and this slows down the horse's breaking action rather than speeding it up.

Personally, I have never enjoyed much success using square toed shoes on trotters behind. I've used them only in rare instances and hardly at all in the past several years. If I thought I needed more holding action behind than the full swedge was giving me, I would prefer to go to a grab around the toe in front. I will discuss grabs a little later.

In order to eliminate interference, it is sometimes necessary to narrow a trotter's gait behind. There are two ways of doing this. The first and easiest way is to lower him a little on the outside of the hind foot. This is similar to the way we lowered the feet of the knee-knockers and paddlers in front. Have the blacksmith rasp off a little bit of the outside of the foot from the center of the toe all the way back to the heel. This will draw the horse in.

I daresay you will find that most trotters are trimmed a little low on the outside behind. They have a natural tendency to wear their feet that way and if you are checking your shoes closely you will find this to be true in most instances.

The other way to narrow a trotter up behind is to go to a half-swedge, half-round shoe (Fig. 29-4) with the swedge on the inside. When we get to pacers you will find that we use a half-round, half-swedge shoe with the swedge on the outside to widen them out and avoid cross-firing interference. With a trotter it is just the opposite. Put the swedge on the inside and draw his gait in, narrow it up. This will also tend to shorten his stride behind which is desirable when you are having interference problems. If a horse is naturally inclined to trot wide behind, the half-round, half-swedge will draw him in more than the full swedge.

Let's take the typical horse that is interfering behind. He is going to his speedy cuts or his shins and rapping them pretty good as he passes. The first thing I will do, of course, is to go to the front end and try to quicken him up so that the front stride is completed and the foot out of the way before the hind leg reaches the area where the interference is occurring.

I've already discussed the ways to quicken a horse's gait in front which amount to nothing more than forcing him to break over faster to get out of the way of the hind leg.

If he's wearing a flat shoe, maybe you want to go to a half-round. If he is already wearing a half-round, perhaps you can shorten his toe or maybe you can go to a lighter shoe or a little higher angle. Any little thing that will speed his action up might help.

I imagine you can see now the kind of trouble a horse trainer can get into. I go to the front end and shorten the toe to break him over faster and eliminate the interference behind. Right away my horse starts to get pacey so I have to add a little weight to compensate for that. The weight slows the action just a little and I am right back where I started with the same interference staring me in the face.

Well, the main thing is that I have to take that front toe back to where it was because if I foul up the gait in front I am completely out of business. How else can I compromise to preserve gait in front and at the same time eliminate interference behind? There are a couple of ways I can juggle the shape of either a flat or a half-round shoe that might give me the "happy medium" I am looking for.

Let's say the horse is wearing a flat shoe in front and is interfering behind. I have tried this horse with a half-round shoe already and for one reason or another it hasn't proved satisfactory. What I need is something in between a flat shoe and a half-round.

What I will do in a case like this is to take a flat shoe, heat it and run the toe of the shoe through a half-round block. Now I have a shoe that is half-round at the toe, which speeds up the breaking action. But the remainder of the shoe is flat and tends to slow the breaking action a trifle because the flat surface on both 'sides of the shoe will hold the foot on the ground an instant longer. Often a little change like this is just what I need.

Let me go one step further and demonstrate another alternative that falls in the same category. The horse is wearing a flat shoe in front and is interfering behind. This time I go to a half-round shoe but instead of disappearing, the interference becomes even more pronounced. The half-round has introduced a shuffling or sliding action as the foot breaks over.

What I do here is to go to the flattened half-round shoe I described earlier. I heat the shoe and pound it down all the way around. Now I have a shoe that is neither completely flat nor completely half-round. It is about "half" half-round over its entire surface. In flattening it, I have given the horse additional surface to break over and the foot is no longer shuffling or sliding. But the shoe maintains enough of its half-round qualities to break the foot over faster and in some cases it will be exactly what I need.

Are you beginning to understand now why horse trainers seem to have a liberal sprinkling of gray in their hair?

By this time, I have just about exhausted all my remedies in front and if none of the shoes or techniques I have described have eliminated the interference behind I have to try something else. Since I cannot accomplish what I want by working on the front end, I shoe and balance my horse so that he is as pure-gaited as I can get him in front and take another look at the hind end. What else can I do there to slow his action down?

Well, if I am not using a swedge shoe I can go to one or maybe I can narrow his gait, if that appears to be the trouble, by lowering him on the outside or going to a half-round, half-swedge shoe as I have already described. But by this time I have probably tried all these or can tell from experience that one or more of them will not do the job. I know I have three choices left.

You will recall I said earlier that a longer toe will slow a horse down because it presents a larger surface for the foot to break over on and thus breaks it over slower. So I will go back and lengthen the hind toe from 3¼ to 3½ inches. That automatically lowers the angle and slows the breakover action of the hind foot.

I hope the longer toe solves the problem for me. But if it doesn't I still have two choices remaining. For one, I can go to a bar shoe. A bar shoe behind is not a bad thing at all, except for the extra weight involved, and when I am in this kind of a situation I am happy to be able to use it.

A bar shoe, which is closed at the back end, gives a foot more bearing surface and slows it down a trifle. I prefer an egg bar shoe (Fig. 29-11) to a straight bar shoe (Fig. 29-12) under these circumstances. The egg bar protrudes outward along the back edge and thus the shoe itself is covering a larger ground surface and providing additional slowing action. I have seen egg bar shoes used in front but I have never used one myself.

When I am using a bar shoe behind, I seldom use a pad with it unless the horse has a sore foot or a wound. In this instance, a pad would be adding weight and as you know by now I am trying to keep weight at a minimum in the hind end of my trotter.

I also find the egg bar shoe beneficial for horses that have a high "hocky-going" action wherein the hind legs seem to move straight up and down rather than backward and forward. An egg bar shoe tends to give them more backward extension.

If the increased length of the toe didn't stop the interference and the bar shoe failed as well, I have one choice left and while I'm not particularly happy about it I will use it if I have to and so will any other good horse trainer. That is a grab.

A grab will really slow a horse's action, either in front or behind. But it is quite severe on the muscles and ligaments and I only use one when I absolutely have to. I have never used a grab on a trotter in front and its primary use on a trotter behind is with a horse that is interfering badly and is starting to stab one hind foot, first to the outside and then to the inside, to keep from hitting himself.

A grab (Fig. 29-7) is a thin strip of metal that is welded to the outside rim of the front of a flat hind shoe or in the channel of a swedge shoe on a trotter that is interfering such as the one we have under discussion. To visualize what a grab is, think of a rifle sight. Take that sight and extend its length to about three inches. Make it from an eighth to a quarter of an inch deep and weld it on the outside rim or in the swedge of the shoe directly at the center in front. A grab that is set in the channel of a swedge shoe will naturally be deeper than one welded to the rim of a flat shoe but the area that comes in contact with the track will be the same depth.

When a shoe that has a grab on it hits the ground, the grab takes hold of the track and slows down the action of the foot as it begins to break over. Grabs are pretty rough on the stifles and the hind legs because the severe holding action puts a real strain on the muscles in these areas. But in certain cases they are necessary if your horse is going to trot good-gaited and I will use them when I have to.

The length of a grab can be more or less than the three inches I have described. An inch and a half is about the minimum length and they can extend either straight across the toe or can be curved to follow the natural contour of the toe. They can be placed a little differently with pacers and I will describe that later.

That just about covers the various ways you can slow a trotter down behind. I think now I should discuss a couple of the principal defects of the trotting gait behind, those first cousins—the hikers and the stabbers.

Occasionally you will find that in going around a turn, a colt will stride farther with the left hind leg than he will with the right hind leg. Now you want to remember that this is a horse that is carrying his head perfectly straight in front of him and is perfectly sound. He simply unbalances just a little in the turns and begins to stride farther with the left hind leg to compensate for that and begins interfering. This is known as hiking.

You can tell this by the way your horse is going and if you close your eyes and listen you won't hear that perfect one-two beat but a one-hup-two. It's like a sour note in a good song. But if there is still any question in your mind, an examination of the shin boots will usually show you that your horse is hitting the left one and not touching the right one.

The answer to this problem doesn't always lie in shoeing and can often be solved by using a gaiting strap (Fig. 58) or a gaiting pole, or a side strap or sidepole as they are also called. What you want to do is to shorten that horse's stride on the left side and the pole or strap will help do this. If you recognize the problem quickly enough and help your horse when he first develops the habit, you will usually find that you can discard the pole or strap after he gets his gait established.

But you want to remember that these things take time and that the worst thing you can do is to hurry a colt like this. The problem usually develops because you are asking a colt for a little more speed than he really has to offer right at the moment. You want to forget about speed and back him off to where he *is* going good-gaited.

Train him awhile at the notch where he is good-gaited and can handle himself. This is what I meant when I said earlier that I would rather have a horse going good-gaited in 3:00 on March first than bad-gaited in 2:30. If you can continue to press for speed under these circumstances, you'll only get a bad-gaited hippity-hoppin' trotter and if you persist you won't have any trotter at all.

You will also find that a lot of perfect-gaited horses that start to get a little sore behind will begin striding like this, or hiking, either with the right or left hind leg, depending on which is hurting. When a horse gets sore on the left side behind, he will usually twist his rear end to the right which will then cause him to stride farther with the right hind leg. This applies to either side and a gaiting strap or pole is indicated. This will straighten a horse up and even his stride.

Hikers usually hike with only one leg. The initial cause of the trouble rarely has anything to do with interference, although interference will develop if no remedial steps are taken.

The stabber, on the other hand, is the worst kind of horse behind and his trouble is almost always interference. The front foot keeps rapping that hind leg in passing and pretty soon the horse becomes tired of this and gets angry just as you would get angry if you kept hitting your thumb nail with a hammer.

In order to escape this constant pain, the stabber begins to move his hind leg to one side and then the other. Instead of striding forward, as his cousin the hiker does, the stabber jabs that hind foot into the ground as quickly as he can in his stride and off to the left or right of where he thinks that front leg is going to be. You will usually find that in one stride he will jab to the right while in the next one he will jab to the left.

If you come up with a real bad stabber it usually means one or two things. Either you haven't been doing your shoeing and balancing job very well or, if you think you have done everything possible, you probably have a colt that has not yet matured and learned to handle himself. A colt like this is probably much better off being turned out for a year.

This is why I say that very often a stabber is made and not born. If you get a colt that is not interfering and is still stabbing, it is usually a sign that he needs more time to develop muscles and legs, that he simply isn't mature enough to handle the chores you have been assigning him.

The most important thing is to slow down with a colt like this just as you did with his cousin the hiker. If he goes good at 3:00 and starts to stab at 2:50, go back and train him at 3:00 and keep training him there until he can show progress without stabbing. If he can't, don't persist with him; turn him out. I have said this often enough now that I imagine my message is clear. I think many potentially good trotters are ruined for just this reason and it actually makes me a little sick when I see a trainer going on with a colt like this.

The technical remedies for a stabber are the same as for any other type of interference behind. You try to quicken the horse up in front and slow him down behind. I think I can safely say that if you have a true stabber, and not one that is a product of immaturity, you will usually wind up with a pretty sharp grab on the hind toe.

Most trainers who get a real bad stabbing trotter these days solve the problem by converting him to the pace and going right on. And maybe they're right, too. But I do believe that age and maturity help more than anything. As a horse grows older and his muscles strengthen, he will have less tendency to interfere, and thus to stab, and can overcome the problem. If I had a colt like this that I thought had the ability to be a top trotter, I would turn him out right away and try him again next year.

Proximity stabbed badly as a 2-year-old but overcame the fault as she matured. She went on and became a champion. She always did stab a little but each year she seemed to get better about it.

I had a colt once that stabbed quite badly and he was a real good horse. We sold him at the end of his 2-year-old form and he went on and won The Yonkers Futurity as a 3-year-old. That was Spunky Hanover. An extra year helped him a great deal.

Even though I have never used calks on a trotter in a race, I want to discuss them here because they do have an application in my thinking concerning a trotter behind. Years ago, almost every horse wore calks of one type or another, but their use these days is pretty well confined to special cases.

A calk (often pronounced "cork") is a piece of steel that protrudes from the bottom of the shoe and comes in contact with the ground. A typical calk is usually worn by a pacer behind and is placed at the end of the outside heel of the shoe. Used this way, it would be called a heel calk (Fig. 29-10).

In making this type of calk, the blacksmith works with a piece of steel that is perhaps a quarter to a half-inch longer than he needs for that particular shoe. When he heats the shoe, he turns this extra length downward from the bottom of the shoe and it cools and hardens in this position. This is what is known as "turning a calk." This kind of calk tips a pacer to the inside and widens his gait behind, which is desirable. I will explain it in more detail later.

The other kind of calks are known as jar calks (Fig. 29-8) and usually consist of four pieces of metal shaped roughly like a small grab and welded on the shoe. For example, there might be one on each side of the toe, and one on each heel. They provide a holding action when the horse's front foot hits the ground and are sometimes used with knee-knockers, especially pacers. I have always felt they would lead to unsoundness because of the severe concussion and holding action they bring about, and have never used them. Other trainers have and apparently with some success.

The theory is that when a horse thus shod begins to pick his foot up, after it hits the ground, the calks will hold it straight and the foot won't turn either to the right or left as it describes its backward arc. I would be afraid that what worked on one track one day might have a very detrimental effect over another track the next week, or even the same track a week later if the surface wasn't exactly the same.

As you can tell, I don't care much for calks, except on cross-firing pacers behind, but I do use them in training certain horses and I wanted to mention them for that reason.

Once in a while when you start out with a colt, you will run into one you think is a little weak in his stifles. He just doesn't appear to have the action there that he should and you suspect that he is not 100% sound in that area. He is what we would call "a little loose in the stifles." What I will do in a case like this, is to turn calks on the heels of both hind shoes and train the horse that way. This applies to either a trotter or a pacer.

There is a ligament that runs across a horse's stifle and it has been my theory, and I've found it to be true, that you can strengthen the stifle by taking pressure off this ligament and, in effect, shortening it.

It is the same with humans. If you walked without a heel on your shoe, you would be putting pressure on the muscles and ligaments in your legs and would strain them. By adding a heel, you relieve this strain. Well, that applies to a horse, too. If you have one that acts weak in the stifle area, try turning a calk on his hind shoes. This raises his angle, relieves the pressure and enables the ligament crossing the stifle to develop strength. Once that ligament appears tight and the horse is going sound, I remove the calks. I have never raced a trotter with a calk and this is the only reason I ever use one. I have had good luck doing it.

I think I have covered quite thoroughly the various causes of interference in a trotter and I have tried to explain in some detail the shoeing and balancing techniques employed to correct these faults. Before I begin writing about pacers and their problems, I do want to make a point about interference that applies to horses of both gaits.

Sometimes you will encounter interference that you either cannot clear up or, if you can, the remedy you will have to use will bring about an even bigger problem. I am not writing now about the horse that hits his shins real hard or really wallops a knee every time he takes a step, because if you don't clear up that kind of interference your horse will soon be on the sidelines. I am writing about minor interference that is more annoying than anything else. The horse races all right despite it, but would be a better horse if the effect of the interference could be minimized in some way.

With this kind of horse, it is usually a good idea to shoe him so that the wall of the foot protrudes slightly over the edge of the shoe in the area where the interference is occurring.

For instance, you might have a trotter that is just barely interfering with his hind shin. The middle of the outside of the front foot is coming in contact with the hind shin during the horse's stride. You either cannot get the horse off his shin, or, if you can, you know that in doing so you would create a bigger problem for yourself in one way or another.

The first thing you do is to examine the shoe carefully to determine exactly where the interference is occurring. You can tell this because the part of the shoe that is touching the hind shin is a little glossy from where it has come in contact with the shin boot. The wall of the foot itself will show the same indication of interference.

After fitting the shoe so that it is flush with the outside wall of the foot, re-heat the shoe and rasp off about a sixteenth of an inch in the area where the interference is occurring. Depending on the circumstances, this area might measure from two to four inches in length (Fig. 36).

When you tack this shoe back on, it is underset beneath the wall of the foot and what interference occurs now will involve

Fig. 36. When it is impossible or impractical to keep a trotter from interfering behind, it is sometimes beneficial to underset the front shoe as illustrated so that only the wall of the foot, rather than the shoe itself, comes in contact with the hind leg. This is the left front shoe and it has been underset as indicated by the shaded area. This is done by having the blacksmith rasp the shoe when it is hot and the process is known as hot-rasping. This may also be done with the shoe of a pacer that is cross-firing or with the shoe of any horse that is interfering anywhere.

the wall of the foot only and not the shoe. I think you can understand that it is a lot easier on a horse if the hind shin is being brushed by the wall of the foot instead of by a steel shoe. Horses will not sore up as much and the shin will not fill as much under these circumstances.

This applies to any type shoe and to other types of interference. You would do the same thing, for instance, on the inside of the front foot of a trotter or pacer that was hitting his knees. If you can't get away from interference, always remember that the shoe is much harder than the foot itself and can do a great deal more damage. If you can eliminate the shoe as an agent of interference you have done yourself and your horse a good turn. This can frequently be accomplished by undersetting the shoe as I have described.

It is much easier to shoe and balance a pacer than a trotter. A pacer doesn't interfere with the legs on the same side and that in itself makes him an easier assignment. Also, while it is true that a pacer must be balanced to go at his best, there is no way you can discount the fact that a set of hobbles is a big help in this respect.

There are really only two serious areas of interference with respect to the proper shoeing and balancing of a pacer. In most cases, a pacer that is interfering is either hitting his knees (Fig. 33) or cross-firing (Fig. 35).

I have already written about knee-knockers and how they rap the opposite knee when they bring the front foot up to begin the next stride.

Cross-firing occurs when the hind foot interferes with the front foot on the opposite side. This interference usually takes place low down in the area of the quarter although in some cases it can be higher. Once in a great while a pacer will rap a hind shin or scalp behind just as a trotter does. In such cases, he hits the hind leg with the front foot on the opposite side.

There is not nearly as much cross-firing these days as there used to be and I am sure that one day there will appear a breed of pacers that won't cross-fire at all.

Let me start at the beginning with a pacer and take him through a shoeing and balancing routine just as I did a trotter.

I usually start my pacers out with a half-inch, half-round in front that weighs about five ounces and is the lightest half-round shoe in stock. It is an eighth of an inch narrower than the 5/8ths, half-round I use to start my trotters and about two ounces lighter.

I usually make the front toe 3¼ inches, which is a quarter of an inch shorter than I use to start my trotting colts. The normal angle in front will be roughly 50 degrees and compares with 48 for most trotters. The higher angle might indicate that the pacer would break over quicker and thus go higher, but you will find that the pacing gait does not naturally lend itself to a front action as high as the trotter. The pacer goes a little lower but, as I wrote earlier, most of the great ones have a round, rolling stroke that brings them within an inch of the bottom of their hobbles.

In discussing the shoeing and balancing of pacers, I think it probably would be best if I took things one step at a time and stayed with the front end for a while.

Let's take the pacer that hits his knees. You have a choice of trying to go over the knuckle of the knee or staying under it. With a pacer, it is usually best to try to get over, although I have seen trainers who have had success going under the knee.

One of the ways to help a pacer that is hitting his knees is to increase the length of his toe. At the same time, you might want to add more weight to the shoe if you could get away with it without upsetting his gait and balance. A heavier shoe and a longer toe tends to make him go higher.

Little Pat, that great pacer of the 1930's, is an example of a horse that went with a long toe to get him over his knees. I know that Charlie Lacey had a four or a 4¼-inch toe on Little Pat and we used to shake our heads every time the horse raced. We didn't think he could hold up, but Little Pat raced on and on, year after year, and was truly a great pacing champion. I know, too, that he wouldn't have been worth a nickel without those long toes because he would have banged knees to a fare-thee-well.

There are other things you can try with a knee-hitting pacer. You can go to a full swedge shoe that provides more traction, lower him a little on the outside or even go to half-round, half-swedge shoe in front with the swedge on the outside. You might even try grabs on the outside of the front feet although I do not recommend the practice because of the additional strain they put on a horse. All these things tend to get the horse over or under the knee or to pull him away from it.

Another thing that is always worth checking is the fit of the hobbles. In some instances, the hobbles might be too tight, causing the horse to shorten his stride which, in turn, might be forcing him into his knees. Perhaps if you let the hobbles out a couple of holes he would go freer and miss his knees.

Some knee-knockers won't stand more weight or a longer toe. If a knee-knocker is naturally a little low-going and doesn't have that round, rolling motion in front, more weight and toe are just going to make him hit his knees that much harder. This is the one you have to widen out through the use of grabs or swedges or by lowering him on the outside.

If you have a pacer that is a real "daisy-cutter" and going very low in front, there is not much chance of shoeing or trimming him to go over his knees. Your best bet in this instance is to go just the opposite way. Trim his feet down just as short as you can get them, almost down to the blood line, and make his foot as small as you possibly can by rasping the walls off. Then shoe him with a full swedge to make him go even lower. This, of course, is drastic action but sometimes it is required with a knee-knocker.

If you happen to be successful in getting your pacer to go below his knees, it is probably a good idea to wear tendon boots (Fig. 71) on him. You have him breaking over now so that he might be low enough to begin rapping his tendon and you don't want that.

If you don't have any luck getting a pacer off his knees and you insist on racing him, it might not be a bad idea to race him bare-footed in front. That, at least, will minimize the damage he does when he raps his knee and I know some horses that have raced successfully this way. Just slip his front shoes off before he goes to the post and tack them back on again after the race.

Of course, none of this is to say that a knee-knocker won't race. A lot of good horses have been knee-knockers and I know one recent free-for-aller that I drove a couple of times that hit his knees constantly. It still didn't keep him from winning a few hundred thousand dollars. But if I had my choice of horses that could go in 2:00, I would always take the one that didn't wear the knee boots.

A fellow trainer once asked me what he should do about a real bad knee-knocker that he couldn't even get to the races. I told him to trade the horse for a dog and get rid of the dog. In some cases that's still the best advice.

The honest truth is that I don't even like to talk about knee-knockers. I just haven't had much luck with them and, when I find that somebody has, I always check it out to see what the fellow did. I usually find that what worked for that particular horse won't work at all for the ones I have.

In working on a pacer in front, the main thing you are trying to develop is a long, smooth stride and a folding action that is usually lower than a trotter, but that brings him to within about an inch of the bottom of his hobbles (Fig. 26). When I find a pacer that is going too high in front, I will resort to the same remedies that we used with the trotter. The first thing I will do is to switch from a half-round to a flat shoe, maybe a 3/16ths by a half which weighs about the same as the half-inch, half-round.

If that doesn't do it, I will go to a crease in his toe, remembering to place the crease in accordance with the way he is breaking over at the toe. My next choice would be a full swedge shoe which is quite common on a pacer in front.

If that still didn't do the job, I would probably go to an aluminum shoe. I don't have anything at all against aluminum shoes and use quite a few myself on pacers in front. They are very light, weighing from two to five ounces, and since a pacer doesn't normally require much weight in front they can often solve the problem for one that goes too high.

Incidentally, if you've got a chronic knee-knocker that absolutely has to have a shoe but that will go light, you are better off to use the aluminum shoe. If he has to wear a shoe and has to hit his knee, an aluminum shoe will cause much less damage than a steel one.

There is one thing about an aluminum shoe that I don't like. When you start racing over these hard race tracks, the so-called all-weather tracks we have today, an aluminum shoe will barely last through one race. That means you're shoeing the horse practically every week and a lot of trainers, including me, would rather go with a light steel shoe than to have their horse shod every week.

After you have worked your high-going pacer down through the flat shoe, the crease, etc., and have come to an aluminum shoe and he is still going too high, you might try a grab across his toe (Fig. 29-7).

This is what I did with Bullet Hanover and it worked very well. He was a high-going horse, as everybody knows, and I thought he even went a little too high with aluminum shoes. So I ran a grab across the front of his toe about an inch and a half in length. It was about an eighth of an inch deep and it provided just enough holding action to gait Bullet Hanover the way I wanted him.

As you know by now, a grab creates quite a bit of strain on a horse's leg. For that reason, I only shod Bullet Hanover with grabs the morning of the day he raced. Those shoes came off immediately after the race and he jogged and went his training miles in flat aluminum shoes. In this manner, I kept the strain on his legs to an absolute minimum and it is a procedure I would recommend that young trainers follow in using grabs.

Indiscriminate use of grabs and other severe devices of this type is extremely ill-advised in the training of harness horses. This is not only true in shoeing but in other areas such as the use of wire driving bits and things like that. If you have to use severe devices, try to limit their use, to actual racing performances.

Because a trotter is sometimes so difficult to gait and balance properly, I think young trainers occasionally lose sight of the fact that it is also very important that a pacer be properly balanced. There is no question that the hobbles play an important part in this type of thinking. It is true that through use of the hobbles you can make a pacer stay on gait while a trotter, under similar circumstances, would go off stride. But hobbles should never be used as a crutch in training pacers.

As a general rule, the looser the hobbles the better off a pacer is. The average pacer wearing loose hobbles will go faster and farther than one wearing tight hobbles. I'm not writing here about the occasional pacer that needs tight hobbles and won't go any other way, because there are some of those and when you run into them there isn't anything you can do except take your best hold and go on.

But in an effort to balance a pacer, I would much rather do a number of other things before I tightened the hobbles. I would prefer to try my horse with a little longer toe or more weight or change the rigging around his head or something like that. Very often it develops that a toe that is an eighth of an inch longer will balance a pacer to the extent that he will be able to go in a looser hobble. I have seen many pacers that, if they were shod in front with a three-quarter half-round or even a three-quarter by quarter flat shoe and permitted to go in loose hobbles, would race better and be a lot better gaited than if they went with a half-inch, half-round and a tight hobble.

Balance in a pacer, or in any horse for that matter, is a funny thing and every once in a while you will run across a case that defies all the rules. Noble Adios, who won The Little Brown Jug in 1956 and who was a full brother to Adios Harry, was such a horse.

Noble Adios was a trappy-gaited pacer who went straight up and down in front and hit the bottom of his hobbles with his feet. His gait would indicate to 99 out of 100 horse trainers that a full swedge shoe was called for to slow his up and down action and make him extend his stride.

But he was absolutely helpless with a full swedge. He was horribly-gaited and, as a matter of fact, would make breaks in the hobbles. I went through every page of the shoeing book and nothing worked. Finally, I tried a 5/8ths half-round shoe with a square toe which, according to the rules, is just what you shouldn't do with a high going horse because it breaks him over that much faster.

But for some strange reason, this made Noble Adios a good-gaited pacer. He didn't hit the bottom of his hobbles and while he remained trappy-gaited he had enough extreme speed to compensate for it.

I really and truthfully don't know the answer as to why he went better that way. The only explanation I can offer is that he felt better balanced, more sure of himself and more confident. I didn't ask any questions at that stage, I just kept on going. It just proves that you can't lay down hard and fast rules about shoeing horses. There are always exceptions.

I usually start my pacers with a 3⅛-inch toe behind, an angle of 54 or 55 degrees and a light flat shoe, maybe a 3/16ths by a half. When I first start to train a young pacer, I am interested in what he wants to do, which will be one of three things—he will slip off into a natural pace, he will be trying to pace but not quite able to make it, or he will be a trotter.

I am opposed to forcing a horse to pace in the beginning if he wants to trot. You will occasionally run across one like this and if you are impatient and force him to pace by using a pair of tight hobbles and a whip, you will often do irreparable damage to his disposition. This is the best way I know to spoil a horse.

I will usually let this kind trot and it has been my experience that when you get down around 2:30 you will go out to train him one morning and he will suddenly slip over into a pace. And that will be the end of that because once they slide over into the pace they rarely ever trot again.

I remember a natural pacer that I spent two years trying to make into a trotter and really had no idea she wanted to pace. This was Trustful Hanover by Titan Hanover out of Little Lie, a fine trotting mare that had been producing trotters.

I tried her as a 2-year-old but she was hiking and bad-gaited and never did get to where she could trot any. I turned her out fairly early figuring a year in the pasture would cure her colt soreness and develop her muscles and make her easy to work with the next year.

As a 3-year-old she wasn't any better. Along in March I was doing my best with her but she was still wearing a heavy shoe, a hinged quarter boot, a four-inch toe and a full pad and still couldn't trot. One day I had her out on the half-mile track and she suddenly switched over into the nicest pace you ever saw.

The next heat I took everything off in front including her shoes and she paced a slick mile in 2:30 which was 10 seconds faster than she had ever trotted in her life. She went on to win in 2:00 that year and her first three foals have been 2:00 pacing performers.

What I'm saying is that if they want to trot let them trot, even if they're pacing-bred. Eventually, 99 out of 100 will switch over into a pace, even if you try to keep them from doing so, which is what my Trustful Hanover story amounts to.

That takes care of the pacing-bred colt that wants to trot when you start out with him. You have no problem with the one that swings off into a natural pace and that leaves those that want to be pacers but can't quite make it. They're hitting the pace for a few strides, then running, then trotting a few steps and in general telling you they can't quite do it yet and need help. Probably three out of four young pacers fall in this category when they enter training.

These are the kind I will immediately have shod behind with a side-weight shoe. A side-weight shoe (Fig. 29-9) is one in which there is more weight on one side than on the other. With a pacer, whose tendency is to swing in as he goes forward, you want the weight on the outside half of the shoe to round out his gait.

What I usually do is to take a quarter by three-quarter flat shoe and have the blacksmith file off about an eighth of an inch from the inside web. That leaves more weight on the outside and tends to roll the colt over into a pace. You can have a side-weight shoe made any way you want. A blacksmith will turn one out to your order and you can make it even heavier than I do on the outside if you think you want more weight there.

I haven't raced a free-legged pacer in many years but whenever I do I will usually race him in a side-weight shoe. I know that Frank Ervin never used anything but a side-weight shoe on the champion filly, Good Counsel, throughout her career.

Frankly, I wish I could race more free-legged pacers but there are two good reasons why I don't. One is that most pacers will need the hobbles to help steady them as they go away and as they go around the turns. The other is that the hobbles these days are so light and airy and are worn so loose that it is just good insurance to have them in case you need them. It isn't like the old days when they were heavy, cumbersome things that made you think you were riding with the brakes on half the time.

Now the time has come to talk about cross-firing pacers. I don't really want to make it sound like such a big deal because there is so much less cross-firing than there was even 20 years ago that the change is very noticeable. We are breeding better-gaited pacers and they are cross-firing less. But along with knee-hitting it is still one of the two primary causes of interference among pacers and is worthy of discussion.

As I have explained, a pacer cross-fires when, at the peak of his stride, the feet on the opposite side come in contact with each other. For instance, the left front foot and the right hind foot will meet. Usually, the hind foot gets into the tender quarter of the front foot but it is also possible for the front foot to interfere higher up on the hind leg as happens with trotters.

Let's consider what you do with a cross-firing pacer. First of all, you work on the front end just as you do with a trotter to try to speed up his action and get the front leg folded out of the way before the hind leg comes up to meet it. You do this by going to a half-round shoe or by squaring the toe as we discussed with trotters.

But because a pacer doesn't have as much natural folding action in front as a trotter, you will very often get your best results by working on the pacer behind. What you try to do is widen out the gait behind so that the hind leg won't reach over far enough to come in contact with the opposite front leg.

The first thing you go to is a half-round, half-swedge shoe (Fig. 29-4) with the swedge on the outside. The swedge, as you know, has a holding action and used on the outside with a pacer it tends to widen out his gait. I start my pacers out with a plain shoe behind but I race 99% of them in a half-round, half swedge and I think everybody else does, too.

The next step is to rasp off a little of the wall on the inside of the hind foot at the point where the hind foot would come in closest contact with the front foot. Depending on how much you rasp away, this can provide from a sixteenth to a quarter of an inch of clearance and in many cases is enough to cure a cross-firing pacer. A horse that goes like this is said to be wearing a diamond toed (or shaped) half-round, half-swedge shoe.

If this doesn't do it, the next step is to run a trailer on the outside heel. A trailer is nothing more than an extension of the shoe. It runs out about an inch or so past the end of the heel and provides additional bearing surface and thus brings about a certain amount of additional holding action for the foot, delaying the stride.

The next step is to turn a calk on the end of the trailer. This will tip the foot up to the outside and again encourages a widening of the gait aimed at keeping the hind foot and the opposite front foot from coming in contact with each other. The diamond toed half-round, half-swedge shoe with trailer and calk is illustrated in Fig. 29-10.

The last step, as with the trotter, is a grab. In severe cases, you could run the grab from the point where the half-round part of the shoe stops at the toe all the way around to the last nail hole on the outside. This will hold a pacer pretty good and will definitely widen his gait.

The severity of the grab I use on a pacer behind usually depends to some extent on his conformation. For instance, if I had a pacer that tended to be curby, I would be careful about using an extreme grab. Perhaps, on a pacer of this type, I might run the grab only from the middle of the toe around to the second nail hole. Often this will be enough to clear up the cross-firing and still keep that curb from flaring up. In any and all of these cases, you can use a bar shoe if you like.

If I find I have to go to a trailer and a calk to prevent a horse from cross-firing, at each subsequent shoeing I will probably try the horse without the calk to see if he will go that way without interfering. I often find that I can get away from the calk after a while and since a calk tips a horse up quite a bit this is a good thing to do.

Once in a while, you will run across a pacer that is so gaited that the front foot interferes with the hind shin or around the coronary band of the opposite hind leg. This is not exactly a common thing but it occurs much more often than most young trainers think.

If your pacer is "doing things in the hobbles," as we say, it's not a bad idea to take a close look at the hind shins to see if you can't find some little mark there that would indicate interference.

If this is the case, I wouldn't have any hesitancy at all about putting a pair of hind shin boots on him. They don't weigh very much, and as far as that goes, that little extra weight might make him pace better. We all know that weight behind is a good thing for a pacer. If he was interfering around the coronary band instead of brushing his shins, you would use a pair of coronet boots or rubber scalpers.

There is one other thing you might want to file away with respect to pacers and their way of going. Every once in a while you will run across one that shows a great deal of the trotting gait in front. He goes high, folds more like a trotter and extends out more than a pacer. Occasionally a three-ounce toe weight will help a horse that is going like this and doesn't feel quite balanced.

If you use a toe weight on a hobbled pacer, you have to be very careful because the horse is much more likely to go to his knees. I have seen toe weights used on pacers to good advantage but it has usually been with free-legged pacers. It is a last resort thing with me but I wouldn't rule it out.

There are also occasions when you can use a toe weight on a pacer behind with considerable success. In this case, the toe weight would be used in conjunction with a side-weighted shoe to provide additional weight on the outside of the foot, thus further widening the gait and promoting the rolling action of the pace. The toe weight, of course, would go on the outside of the foot rather than on the front. You can either install them permanently or use a spur.

Earlier, I mentioned my introduction in late 1967 to plastic shoes and now I want to discuss them at greater length. I am quite pleased by the immediate results I have obtained by using these shoes but, at the same time, I want to caution that it is premature to describe them as a panacea for all shoeing and balancing ills. The concept is quite revolutionary and the shoes must be tested over a long period of time and under all possible track and racing conditions before a final decision regarding their effectiveness can be reached. Offhand, I would say that it appears that they are going to have an extremely beneficial effect in the field of shoeing and balancing, but I have been around much too long to climb too far out on a limb like this. While I am encouraged by what I have observed to date, I am officially adopting a "wait and see" attitude.

As I have already said, the shoe was designed by Jonel Chyriacos, who trains in France and who conditioned Elma for me when that great mare raced in Europe in 1965-66. It comes from the factory in the form of a bar shoe with a wide web as illustrated in Fig. 36A. The basic shoe weighs 4½ ounces, is 5¾ inches long, 5¼ inches wide and 5/16ths of an inch thick. The web is 1½ inches wide at the center on each side and the hollow part is three inches long and 2¼ inches wide at the widest point. The same style shoe is worn on all four feet and for both trotters and pacers.

The present technique in fitting the plastic shoe is to have the horse stand on a piece of paper while the outline of the hoof is traced. That outline is then marked off on the plastic shoe which is trimmed to fit and nailed on. There are no nail holes and thus the nails may be placed as the trainer desires. At first, I used four nails on each side but now I am using three. In an occasional instance, I place an additional nail at the toe. Because there are no nail holes, the nails may be placed to avoid a weak spot in the wall of the foot.

The first horse I used the plastic shoes on was Aztec, a 3-year-old trotter. Aztec was wearing a 5/8ths half-round shoe in front with a rim pad and a three-ounce toe weight. He carried 11½ ounces and, in my opinion, needed that much to balance him. You can imagine that after I cut the plastic shoes to fit and found they weighed 3½ ounces, I was a little concerned. But I decided to go all the way and removed the toe weights as well. Now I had a horse that was wearing eight ounces less and whose toe, because of the absence of the pad, was slightly shorter than it had been the day before. I worked Aztec and he was smooth and free-gaited. He had had a tendency to scalp and speedy cut a little when he was going slow but he did not do it in the plastic shoes.

I started Aztec and he won a good race at Liberty Bell. Then I took him to Lexington, worked him and went against the fence. He had a record of 2:00⅕ taken in a time trial at Du Quoin. At Lexington he trotted in 1:58⅖. The only honest appraisal I could make under the circumstances was that Aztec was a better horse with the plastic shoes (he wore them behind as well) than he had been with steel shoes.

The day after I gave Aztec his record I was scheduled to go

for a record with a 3-year-old pacing colt named Bolger Hanover. I had already tried the shoes on a few pacers back at Liberty Bell and that night I decided I would put them on Bolger Hanover, who had never worn them, the next day. But at the same time I decided that Aztec's shoes might be worn down just enough to suit Bolger Hanover.

The next morning I warmed Bolger Hanover up two trips in his regular shoes. Then I brought him to the shop between his second and third trips, removed Aztec's shoes and put them on Bolger Hanover. Aztec's front shoes weighed three ounces when I took them off and his hind shoes had worn down from three ounces to 2½. Actually, there was very little wear on the shoes and I would guess that the plastics would last about as long as steel shoes.

At any rate, Bolger Hanover went against the fence in Aztec's plastic shoes and paced in 1:58⅖. Believe me, any time you can use the same shoes on a trotter and a pacer and go in 1:58⅖ with each of them you are really accomplishing something.

In a couple of instances I have put the plastic shoes on cross-firing pacers and cleared up the interference. One pacer in my barn wore a cross-firing shoe behind and scalpers in front to protect against the interference. I put on plastic shoes, removed the scalpers and the horse did not interfere.

I do not say that the shoes will work for all horses. I found one that they did not help. This was a trotter that brushed his knees. In plastic shoes he brushed them even more and I went back to steel. I am sure that as I go on I will find other horses that they will not help, but so far they have been in the minority.

I do not think that the plastic shoes, as such, will make a horse go faster. I do think that they will enable certain horses to come closer to achieving their potential speed. That is, if, in plastic shoes, a horse no longer interferes, then he is going to go free and smooth and is going to go faster for that reason; not because he has more speed but because he is able to trot or pace up to his potential. I think the shoes will be especially helpful with a horse that a driver always has to steady through a race because he might interfere and make a break if you let him go too much too soon. These are the ones you are always saying "whoa, whoa" to during a race. I think also that plastic shoes are bound to help horses that are a little sore.

Fig. 36A. The plastic horseshoe which the author describes in the text is shown as it comes from the factory in Fig. 36A-1. The first step in applying the plastic shoe is to trace the outline of the horse's foot (2) after which the pattern is cut (3). As the author looks on, blacksmith Bill Wick lays the paper pattern on the shoe (4) and marks it off. Then he cuts along the pattern line with his nippers (5) as a prelude to making the final cut (6) with a sharp knife. After buffing the shoe (7) to smooth the rough edges, he fits it to the foot (8) and then nails it on (9). The completed job is shown in Fig. 36A-10. The front shoes worn by the trotter Aztec when he took his record of 1:58 2/5 are shown in Fig. 36A-11 and the hind shoes in 36A-12. These shoes had been on two weeks when the photographs were taken and were worn the following day by the pacer Bolger Hanover when he took his record of 1:58 2/5.

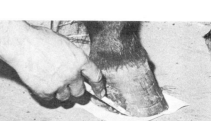

Fig. 36A-2

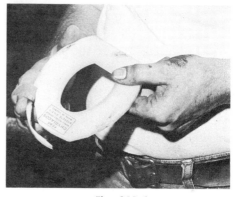

Fig. 36A-1

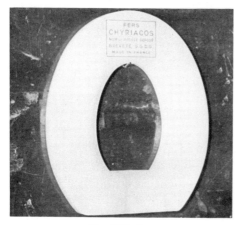

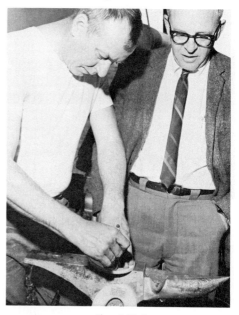

Fig. 36A-4

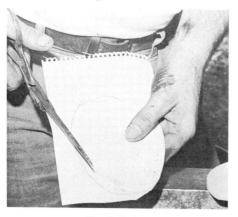

Fig. 36A-3

Fig. 36A-5

Fig. 36A-6

Fig. 36A-7

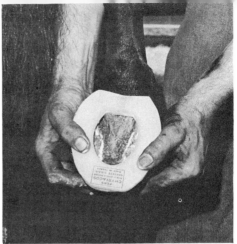

Fig. 36A-8

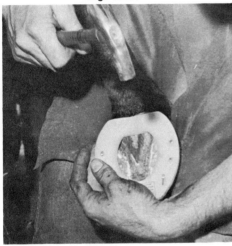

Fig. 36A-9

Fig. 36A-10

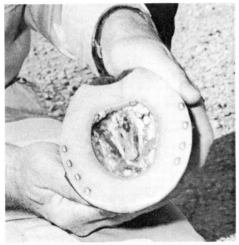

Fig. 36A-11

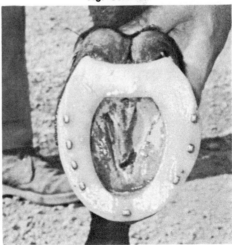

Fig. 36A-12

Frankly, I don't know exactly why the plastic shoes have the beneficial effect they do. I suppose it has something to do with the appreciably wider web, the additional frog pressure thus provided and the natural resiliency of the shoe as compared to steel. The shoes I put on one trotter (not Aztec) had web measurements in front of 1¼ inches at the toe and on the sides and one inch at the heel. The hind shoes on the same horse measured 1 3/16ths inches at the toe (squared) and on the sides, and one inch at the heel. Actual web measurements for a horse would depend on the size of the foot and thus how much had to be trimmed off the basic shoe to make it fit.

Plastic shoes are still in the experimental stage as I write this and we have a great deal to learn about them. It may be that for one reason or another they will not stand the test of time. But they certainly are a refreshing innovation on the shoeing and balancing scene and for that reason alone are worthy of discussion here.

The man who first said, "no foot, no horse," really knew what he was talking about. The problems caused by contracted feet, shelly feet, and thin-walled feet fall principally within the province of the veterinarian and as I begin to close out this chapter, I will confine my comments to the shoeing and balancing of such horses.

One of the most common such ailments a trainer encounters is a quarter crack. A quarter crack (Fig. 37) is a crack in the hoof, usually starting at the coronary band and working down from there. It is like a hang nail on your finger. It will break open and bleed and is very painful. Dr. Churchill is covering quarter cracks in greater detail and I will concern myself only with the basic shoeing technique for a horse so affected.

Fig. 37. A quarter crack usually begins at the coronary band and often runs all the way to the bottom of the hoof as illustrated. In order to relieve the pressure and enable the horse to race, the recommended procedure is to rasp away the wall of the foot all the way back to the heel (arrow) as shown.

Because it is so painful, the thing you have to do with a quarter crack is to relieve the pressure as much as possible so that the horse will not feel that stabbing pain each time the foot comes in contact with the ground. You do this by drawing an imaginary straight line from the point at the hoof line where the quarter crack is located to the bottom of the foot. You then mark this spot for the blacksmith and have him cut or rasp away a portion of the wall of the foot so that the area beneath the quarter crack is not bearing directly on the shoe.

It is also usually a good idea to use a bar shoe on a horse with a quarter crack. If the crack is around toward the front of the foot, you may or may not need a bar and should be guided by the advice of your veterinarian and blacksmith. However, since most quarter cracks appear toward the back of the foot, a bar shoe is usually indicated.

In using a bar shoe on a horse with a quarter crack, fit the bar so that it rests on the frog. In that manner, when the foot hits the ground, the primary pressure is transferred from the wall of the foot to the frog, thus providing relief for the area in which the quarter crack is located.

There is also a new technique in which quarter cracks are "patched." This has been done successfully with both trotters and runners, including SuMac' Lad and Buckpasser. However, this is another field which does not involve shoeing and balancing and I mention it only in passing.

A contracted foot is one in which the heel is pinched together thus preventing the proper frog, bar, and sole pressure when the foot hits the ground. A horse lands heel first with all four feet and if he is landing on feet that have contracted heels and an unsound frog, he is setting up a concussion which not only contributes to unsoundness in the foot but which can and will affect tendons and ligaments as well. In addition, a contracted foot tends to jam the bones in the foot together and hinders circulation. For an animal of his size, the horse has very small blood vessels leading to his extremities and when this circulation is disturbed, unsoundness often develops.

When I get a horse with a contracted foot, the first thing I like to do is go to a tip. A tip (Fig. 38) is a partial shoe. I run a tip around the toe to just below the first nail hole on each side. I take

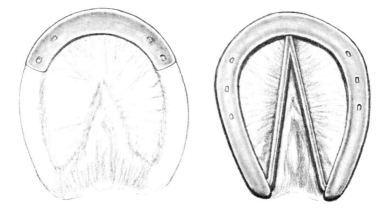

Fig. 38. Use of a tip, upper left, is one means of helping a horse with a contracted foot. A tip is nothing more than a partial shoe and is made so that it permits the horse to land directly on the frog of the foot which helps spread the heels. In using a tip, it is important that it be inserted flush with the foot, opposite, rather than simply tacked on the foot. A V-shaped piece of spring steel, upper right, is often inserted in the foot as an aid in spreading contracted heels. The open ends of the spring create outward pressure at the heels.

all I can off the heels and trim the bars down as far as I can exposing all the frog I can get. What I am trying to do is to let the horse land on the frog because this will spread his heels and help a natural foot set up.

When you use a tip, be certain that you use it as an insert. Don't just lay it on top of the foot and tack it on. You must keep the foot level, so you have to rasp away that area where the tip is to go until the foot is flush with the ground all the way back to the heel. I have seen trainers who failed to do this. They did not have a level foot and the horse was rocking back and forth on it. This is a very bad thing.

If I find that the heel is still not expanding after the horse has been wearing the tips for a while, I will try using springs (Fig. 38). A spring is nothing more than a piece of spring steel that is placed in the foot in such a way that it applies an outward pressure at the heels. It is V-shaped and each of the open ends lays against one of the heels. The closed end goes forward in the foot. Springs will very often bring about the proper expansion of a contracted heel.

You have to be very careful with springs and check them closely. They should be re-set at least every two weeks not only so that you can determine the effect they are having but also so that you can apply more pressure if necessary.

If you are training a trotter with a contracted heel and find that he can't trot in light tips, you will probably have to go to a regular trotting shoe and use springs to try to spread his heels.

If you have a clay track and your training situation will permit it, you can often help this type of horse by letting him go barefooted. This is satisfactory, but I would still prefer a tip. When you turn a horse like this out to pasture, I think it is desirable that you have tips on him. Tips are very beneficial in my opinion.

Thin walls and shelly feet usually go together. On the all-weather tracks that we race over today, a horse of this type usually has to be shod once a week. A set of shoes will generally last through one race and one training session. I usually have my blacksmith make this horse's shoes from a special type of steel that has more carbon in it and thus has greater wearing qualities. With a shoe like this, you will only have to shoe your horse half as often, maybe once every two weeks in the circumstances I have described.

You could also use clips on a thin-walled horse. Horseshoes have a natural tendency to spread as they wear thin; and with a thin-walled horse, the nails will not hold like they will with a normal foot and the shoe will spread and often chip one or more pieces out of the hoof. Clips will help prevent this.

A clip (Fig. 32) is actually a piece of the shoe itself which is turned up by the blacksmith and then pounded in against the outer wall of the hoof to help hold the shoe on. A clip will run up perhaps a half-inch above the level of the shoe and there will be one on each side at about the middle of the foot.

Occasionally, you will run across a thin-walled horse that will cast a shoe and chip off a portion of the outside wall of the foot. When you re-shoe this horse there will be a gap in the wall. This hole can be filled in with a type of wood plastic that all blacksmiths have in stock. Most blacksmiths like to do this and most trainers want it done so it is quite common. But as far as helping the horse goes, I don't think it amounts to very much. It's just that it helps the appearance of the foot.

On that note, I reach the end of my presentation. In an effort to simplify the many complex elements involved in the shoeing and balancing of trotters and pacers, I have ranged over a wide area and touched all the bases I could think of. Undoubtedly I have missed some points that I should have covered. But even that would not have been enough because an entire book could easily have been devoted to this single subject.

But at the same time, as I said in the beginning, nobody will ever learn how to shoe and balance a horse by reading a book. I will be more than satisfied if the guidelines I have established help a young trainer over a few rough spots or provide an interested owner with a basic knowledge of the subject. Those were the only goals I had in mind when I sat down to write this chapter.

It is not possible to sum up my subject in a single paragraph. But if I were to try, I think I would say something like this: The art of gaiting and balancing a harness horse consists of a series of delicate adjustments covering hitching and checking, weight of shoes and length of toe and angle, and designed to bring about with the least expenditure of energy the truest and freest action of gait and, therefore, the greatest speed the horse is capable of producing.

John F. Simpson Sr. is, like Delvin Miller, that rare combination of practicing business executive and talented trainer-driver. As executive vice president and general manager of Hanover Shoe Farms, he guides the destinies of the largest and most successful Standardbred breeding operation the world has ever known. And though his actual driving activities have been curtailed in recent years, he also operates his own training stable which is made up almost exclusively of Hanover horses. In this endeavor he is assisted by his son, John Jr., who has taken over most of the training and driving chores. Simpson Sr. is recognized as one of the great colt trainers in the  sport and specializes in the conditioning, shoeing and balancing of 2-year-old trotters, the most difficult category of them all. He was born in Chester, S. C. on December 26, 1919, the son and grandson of horse trainers. He attended Clemson College for two years but the lure of the trotters was too great and he cast his lot with the harness racing sport. He drove his first race at Myrtle Beach, S. C. in 1938 and his first 2:00 horse in 1942 when he was only 22. After World War II service as an Infantry officer in Europe, he returned to harness racing and at one time or another since then has won all four major driving championships. He has been the leading money-winning driver (1951), dash winner (1950 and 1951), UDRS (1957) and Grand Circuit (1951 and 1957). He has driven 89 2:00 miles (only Frank Ervin and Joe O'Brien have more) and has won The Hambletonian twice (Hickory Smoke and Ayres) and The Little Brown Jug three times (Bullet Hanover, Noble Adios and Torpid). He has won almost 1,500 races—despite the fact that only once has he made more than 500 starts in a season—has career earnings in excess of $4,500,000 and was voted Harness Horseman of The Year in 1957.

7

The PRACTICE
of SHOEING and BALANCING

FRANK ERVIN

N the preceding chapter, Johnny Simpson has reviewed the basic techniques involved in the complicated business of shoeing and balancing the trotter and pacer. I think he has done a fine job and is to be complimented on it. Since he and I are discussing the same general subject, I suggest that if you have not already done so you read his chapter before you read this one so that the proper continuity will be maintained. In a sense, I am picking up where Johnny left off. He has laid down the ground rules and I propose to go on and demonstrate how some of those rules apply to horses that I have trained and driven.

And I have trained and driven a good many since I first pulled a line over a horse back in 1920. I would be less than honest with myself and with my readers if I didn't say that I am mighty proud to have had such horses as Bret Hanover, Good Time, Good Counsel, Adios, Sampson Hanover, Kerry Way, Expresson and Timely Beauty just to name a few of the 34 to whom I already have given 2:00 records. I am also extremely proud of the fact that I have trained and driven four of the nine 2-year-old trotters that have 2:00 records at this writing. These four, all fillies, are Impish, 2, 1:58⅗; Cheer Honey, 2, 1:59⅖; Sprite Rodney, 2, 1:59⅖; and Yankee Lass, 2, 1:59⅘.

I plan to write about all these horses and about many others that are less prominent but taught me lessons about shoeing and balancing that I want to pass on. I think a book of this type is a great thing and I am glad to be able to contribute to it.

For the most part, I am going to be writing about horses that presented problems in shoeing and balancing. For that reason, I won't be saying very much about Bret Hanover, Impish and a few like that who were so natural and so perfect that no real shoeing and balancing problems were involved. That, of course, is one of the reasons why they were such great horses.

But I don't think I could write a chapter of a book or even engage in a lengthy conversation about harness racing without saying at least a little something about Bret Hanover. Bret is retired now after having raced three years, winning 62 of his

68 starts with five seconds and a third, and pacing a mile in 1:53⅗, the fastest in the history of the sport. I will say without hesitation that Bret was the greatest horse of his era and I will leave it to others to express it more strongly if they feel so inclined.

The reason I limit my judgment to the current era is that I do not care to take anything away from great horses out of the past. I do not think, for instance, that it is my place to compare Bret Hanover with Dan Patch nor do I think in all honesty that an accurate comparison could be made any more than Joe Louis could be compared with Jack Dempsey. They competed at different times and under different circumstances, and I am sure that history will rank them properly. The same holds in comparing Bret to super horses of other eras such as Billy Direct, Adios Butler and one of my own favorites, the great pacer Good Time, to name just a few. I am satisfied to let Bret Hanover rest on his laurels and to permit the millions of people who saw him speak for him.

Bret proved to me what a great horse he was on a number of occasions. He proved it as a 2-year-old when he went undefeated in 24 starts; and as a 3-year-old when he won in 1:55 and then came back to set a world half-mile track record of 1:57 in The Little Brown Jug over a track that was still a little off despite a herculean task by my old sidekick, Curly Smart, who converted it from a sea of mud at eleven in the morning into a slick piece of dirt by late afternoon. Bret also demonstrated his championship qualities a number of times as a 4-year-old and before I get into the basic text I want to write a little about some of the highlights of Bret's final year at the races.

There were very few easy races and in the early part of the season those that stood out in my opinion were his victory in the Realization at Roosevelt Raceway and his performance the following week when he beat that great old horse, Cardigan Bay, in 1:59⅘ in what was billed as the "Revenge Pace," Cardigan Bay having beaten Bret earlier.

I also remember an extremely tough race at Brandywine where Bret was parked two and three deep for three quarters of a mile before coming on like a great champion to win in 1:59⅘. At Batavia Downs he won in 1:58⅗ and swept around Cardigan

Bay on a turn as though the old horse were standing still. He was very sharp that night.

He paced in 1:54 at Vernon to lower the world's record and then went on to Lexington where he paced in 1:53⅗ to establish still another record. I had worked Bret in 1:57 on Monday at Lexington and planned to go with him on Saturday. But on Friday the weather forecast for the next day was not favorable and as I began to blow the horse out I became more and more inclined to go that day. I would like to have had the extra day of rest and as a result I didn't make up my mind to go until about an hour before I went. I waited as late in the day as I could and the longer I waited the better the track and weather conditions became. As it turned out, I made the right decision because conditions were poor the next day.

I had to beat 1:54 and I figured that in order to do that I had to be at the three-quarters in 1:24. I went over this with Del Miller and Ike Bailey, who were driving the prompters, and we reached the three-quarters in exactly 1:24. From there on it was up to Bret and he did himself proud coming the last quarter in :29⅗.

In preparing Bret that day I jogged him two miles and then worked him a mile in 2:40. I went the second mile in 2:31 and the third in 2:12, all evenly rated. Bret's first warmup mile was always keyed to the way he felt. Left to my own devices, I would always go the first one in 2:45 but if Bret wanted to go on a little I wouldn't hold him back and the mile would always be somewhere between 2:35 and 2:45.

In rating record miles, such as those that Bret went at Vernon and Lexington, you have to know the strong and weak points of the race tracks and plan accordingly. At Vernon, a three-quarter mile track with a starting chute, it is slightly downhill out of the chute and you have to go the first half at a very fast clip to capitalize on this natural advantage. At Lexington, the third quarter has always been the slowest, for some reason or another, and in rating miles there you have to take that into consideration. I did this when I set up my schedule to reach the three-quarter mark in 1:24.

After his world record performance at Lexington, I took Bret to Canada where he raced on a Sunday afternoon at Blue Bonnets Raceway in Montreal. It was cold and windy that day and almost dark by the time we went to the post. I buzzed Bret out of there and he went to the quarter in 28 seconds. A horse fell down behind him and the next time around I had to go six or seven horses wide. But Bret still went a mile in 1:59 and I thought it was a terrific performance under the circumstances.

I then flew Bret to California where in the first of his two starts there he went the only bad race of his career although he finished second. I could tell warming him up that day that he wasn't good but I didn't know then what was wrong with him and still don't. Maybe it was the long ship or something of that nature.

At any rate, after that race I did a lot of thinking before the next one which would be the last start of his career. I finally decided that perhaps he was beginning to "cheat" a little on me with an open bridle so I warmed him up in an open bridle and put a blind bridle on for the race which was at a mile and an eighth.

I could tell as soon as I turned him behind the gate that I was in trouble, but it was too late to do anything about it then. Normally Bret would just relax and walk up to the gate, but this time he grabbed on and charged the gate. He hit it two or three times before we reached the starting line and I never rode as fast in my life as I did that first sixteenth of a mile after the gate opened. We were two lengths on top at the quarter in 27 seconds and I was just a passenger. At the half in :56 I was busy trying to wrap the lines around my hands, which were numb by this time, in an effort to take Bret off. But there wasn't anything I could do. Bret went right on down the road and he reached the mile in 1:54⅗, the fastest mile ever paced in a race. He tired a little in the last eighth and finished third but I want to say right here that this was one of Bret Hanover's greatest performances. I'll take some of the blame myself because if I hadn't gone to a blind bridle, I might not have had that trouble. But I was a little disappointed about Bret's previous California race and I didn't want him to go two bad races in a row for those people.

When I raced Bret Hanover in a blind bridle in the final start of his career, it was the first time I had done that in his 4-year-old form except in time trial performances. However, I had raced him solely in a blind bridle at two and three and there is an interesting story that goes with it and that I believe I will mention here even though it doesn't have anything specific to do with shoeing and balancing.

As Joe O'Brien has explained in his chapter, some horses have a tendency to grab on in a blind bridle because they can't see the other horses coming up on them and will try to go on when they hear them coming. With an open bridle, on the other hand, most horses will tend to relax and not take as much hold because they can see what's going on around them and can watch the other horses coming up on them.

Strangely, I found that exactly the opposite was true of Bret when I raced him at two and three. I prefer to race horses in an open bridle and I started Bret out that way. But he wanted to grab on, so I switched to a blind bridle whereupon he was perfectly content until I asked him to respond, which he always did with alacrity.

In preparing Bret for his 4-year-old campaign, I trained him in an open bridle and he acted perfectly normal. For that reason, I raced him that way, except in time trials and his very last race.

Now don't ask me why Bret should have reacted as a two and 3-year-old just the opposite of the way most horses would. I don't know why. But I have been around long enough that I don't argue with horses in situations like this. It's like Johnny Simpson wrote about Noble Adios who went so high in front and yet was worse in a full swedge shoe which would normally correct or at least help this fault. My point is that if a horse demonstrates convincingly that he will go naturally and be at his best in some type of shoeing or rigging that the rule book says is all wrong, it's time to throw the rule book away.

As I said earlier, Bret Hanover was never any kind of a shoeing or balancing problem. When I broke him as a yearling I thought he went a mite too high in front for a pacer and I put a crease in his toe. That hesitated his stride just a trifle and was enough to make him perfect-gaited as far as I was concerned.

I don't like my pacers going too high, although I have had some that did and there wasn't a great deal I could do about it. But if I have a choice, I like them to go a little low to the ground. It is the opposite, of course, with trotters. They have to have a good, round stroke and some action in front.

After I got him started, the only change I ever contemplated in

Bret's shoeing was in the middle of his two-year-old form when I thought maybe he ought to have a pad in front to relieve some of the sting from the hard tracks he was racing over.

I tried him with a full pad and he seemed a little too climby-gaited. I tried a rim pad with the same results so I put him back the way he was and never changed anything afterward. In that respect, I am fortunate that he had a good sound foot and never really needed the pads. I packed his feet and used swabs regularly.

Getting back now to the basic theme of this chapter, let me start off by writing a little something about Niles Hanover, another horse who defied the rule book much as Bret Hanover did with regard to his bridle. Niles Hanover was a trotter who interfered terribly when he was a 2-year-old. He was banging his shins so badly it sounded like a bass drum every time he took a step. I tried everything I knew but I couldn't help him a bit.

Finally, I decided I had to defy the rule book again. I took him to the shop and had the blacksmith put the heaviest shoe he could find on his hind feet. Those shoes must have weighed 16 ounces apiece. Then I shod him with a light half inch half-round in front and squared the toe. It was just what he needed. He stopped interfering and took a record of 2:06 that fall.

I think the reason Niles Hanover stopped interfering was that the heavy shoes slowed him down so much behind. It was all foreign to me because I don't like that much weight on a trotter behind. But it did work in this one instance. Niles Hanover was very hocky-gaited, went up quite high behind and when he jabbed his hind feet down toward the ground they would come in contact with the front feet in the speedy cut area. The heavy shoes apparently slowed this jabbing action and eliminated the interference.

But those are the exceptions. I try to shoe my horses as simply and plainly as possible. Despite Niles Hanover and one or two others, you rarely see me racing horses in freak shoes. But don't be throwing any bouquets at me. I've tried all the freak shoes there are. If I have a problem I can't solve, I'll try most anything if I think it will help. But if I don't get results right away I discard them. Whatever I do has to help a horse within a workout or two or it isn't going to help him at all.

Invariably, I will wind up with a free, plainly-shod horse. I find that most of my trotters will go with a fairly short toe and just enough weight to balance them. But you want to remember that with trotting colts you've generally got to put on a little more weight to get them started, to get the proper gait and balance established. Once you've done that, you can start slipping weight off gradually.

In some cases of interference, you have to keep in mind that time and maturity will help more than anything. As colts develop their muscles and their stamina, their gait changes and they can handle themselves better. Very often a year will make a great deal of difference in the gait and balance of a horse.

Martha Doyle, a good little trotter I had years ago, was like that. When she was a 2-year-old, she was speedy cutting and hitting her shins. I couldn't get her off them. But at three she never touched herself and was shod exactly the same way. The difference was that she had developed and matured. She was stronger behind, could handle her hind legs a lot better and didn't get tired and hit her shins when she was in a tough, drawn-out race.

A lot of colts won't have any trouble interfering behind until you start going on with them. As they go faster, they get a little leg weary and their little bodies are not developed enough to handle a full mile. And the faster you go with them, the more likely they are to tire and start hitting their shins.

Some of this also has to do with the fact that our harness horse breed is comparatively young and that we are still working with artificial gaits that are not completely natural to the horse. If you'll just stop and think about it for a minute, I'm sure you'll agree.

It wasn't but a little over a hundred years ago that they started to breed farm mares and buggy mares to an inbred great-grandson of a runner to establish the trotting breed as we know it today. And then some of those trotters got all confused in their new gait and discovered they could do it easier and faster if they shifted their feet around a little and here came the pacers.

My dad, who was a real good horse trainer and a man who thought a lot about gait and things like that, told me I'd live to see a big difference in my own lifetime. What he said was exactly right. Both trotters and pacers are a lot more natural now than they were when I was a boy and it will get better as the breed evolves. I'm glad of that, too, because it means a lot of future horse trainers won't have to go through the worry that some of us old timers did.

When I was a boy, it was fairly common for a trotter to carry from 15 to 20 ounces and a lot of them wore even more than that. I remember a 2-year-old filly that my dad had in 1922 that trotted in 2:12½ on a half mile track which was within a quarter of a second of the world's record and she wore about 24 ounces on each front foot doing it. Early in the season she wasn't training well, and my dad couldn't figure out why. You know what it was? She didn't have enough weight. Hard to believe, isn't it? A pound and a half on each foot and it wasn't enough. Let me tell you about it.

Dad left this filly with me at Springfield, Ill., while he took the rest of the stable to Galesburg, Ill., to race. Then he would come back each week to work her. She was wearing a quarter by three-quarter plain shoe with an X-ray pad, a toe weight, and, a show horse bell boot. This was a big leather boot with sheep's wool around the top.

The filly wasn't doing well and Dad didn't know quite what to make of her. She wanted to make jumps and didn't act good-gaited. I was second trainer then and was real ambitious and liked to keep everything around the barn neat and clean. The night before my dad was due back to work the mare one week, I washed the bell boots and hung them out on the line to dry.

Dad was ready to go early the next morning but, like kids will, I had forgotten to take the boots off the line and we'd had a heavy dew and the sheep's wool hadn't dried out. I put them on the filly anyway and she trained like a piece of machinery with the water flying out of the boots at every stride.

When we were through my dad said, "Son, I'll be back to train that filly next week. The night before, I want you to throw those bell boots in a bucket of water and let them soak all night."

I couldn't grasp what he meant and asked him why. He told me the wet boots had added weight and that it was just what the filly needed to keep her trotting good-gaited.

Just think about that. She had 24 ounces and still needed more. I mention this just to show young trainers the kind of problems we had when I was a boy and how the trotting gait has become more natural. If I put that kind of weight on a young trotter today he'd either break down in a hurry or rap his shins off. That's how evolution is helping us.

My dad also maintained that eventually trotters and pacers would go as fast as the runners which is a mile between 1:30 and 1:35. I thought he was kidding when he told me that 50 years ago, but when I see how fast our two and 3-year-olds are capable of going these days, it wouldn't surprise me if it came to pass. I won't live to see it and probably the next generation won't either, but I wouldn't bet too much against it eventually happening. Our breed is just beginning to develop.

We still need a certain amount of weight to balance our trotters properly but not nearly as much as we did when I was a youngster. And the big thing is to know when a trotter needs weight and when he doesn't.

This is where some trainers will get in trouble once in a while by adding weight to a 2-year-old trotter in an effort to gait and balance him better. You have to know your horse and the circumstances relating to the individual case. Sometimes it is a mistake to add weight even though you might think it is required.

I am going to cite a couple of examples of what I am talking about but before I do I want to discuss another "weight" case that doesn't fit into any of these categories but is interesting for an entirely different reason. It concerns Yankee Lass, 2, 1:59⅘, 3, 1:58, who set world's records at both two and three and who, as I said previously, was one of the four 2:00 2-year-old trotting fillies I have trained.

I was working for Castleton Farm at the time Yankee Lass was a 2-year-old and we had retained her. She was by Florican and out of Yankee Maid, who had won the Hambletonian in 1944 but who hadn't been living up to her brood mare potential. There were always a lot of visitors at Pompano Park where I was training in Florida and for that reason I was especially anxious that this filly be on gait all the time and not making breaks and things like that. Consequently, I had packed weight on her to make certain she would be trotting any time anybody watched her train. I knew this was a foolish reason for doing something like that, but it was very important to me that she show well.

I knew almost as soon as I started to train this filly that I had too much weight on her. She was laboring and I could tell by the way she was going that she was meant to be a light, airy-going mare. It didn't take me long to start dragging the weight off her and she started to improve right away. I think her subsequent performance will bear me out when I say that this was one of the great fillies of all time.

A case that centered more legitimately around weight was that of the good filly Coalition that took a record of 2:03⅕ as a 2-year-old in 1965, reducing it to 2:01⅗ at three. I bred and raised this filly and naturally wanted to do well with her. I started her out in front with a 5/8ths half-round bar shoe with a pad and a four-ounce toe weight. She wore a 3½-inch toe and a 50-degree angle.

I found that this filly would trot and be good-gaited for about three-quarters or 7/8ths of a mile and then would start getting mixey-gaited. I'm afraid some young trainers would have started adding weight at this point—a heavier shoe or a longer toe or something like that—in an effort to overcome this tendency.

But in this particlular case they would have been all wrong. This filly didn't need more weight. She was perfectly balanced the way she was. Her only trouble was that her muscles weren't fully developed and she couldn't carry her speed a full mile. If you had added weight to a filly like this, she would have gotten more leg weary, done it sooner in the mile and started interfering.

So I left her the way she was and started to race her that way. In her first few starts she still got a little tired down toward the wire but eventually she developed her stamina and began to trot the whole mile as I knew from experience she eventually would. As she improved in this respect, I started dropping off some of the weight. I got her toe down to 3⅜ and dropped first to a three-ounce toe weight and then to two ounces and finally discarded the toe weights altogether. This was natural because trotters will generally go with less toe and less weight as they mature and muscle up.

Another filly that I pampered and babied and resisted putting weight on, even though she acted like she needed it, was By Proxy, who was out of a sister to Proximity.

When I broke this filly I found that she could trot over a little piece of ground and go at a decent rate but that as soon as she started going any she would begin stabbing one hind leg.

I had her shod with a half-inch, half-round shoe with a squared toe. She definitely needed more weight but I knew if I put more on she would scalp and speedy cut and begin stabbing again. So I trained her all winter going slow miles in those light front shoes. She learned to trot real well and didn't snatch that hind leg because she was going clean.

I never really tied into that filly as a 2-year-old because she wasn't set yet, but I did give her a record of 2:10 that fall and the following year she won in 2:01⅕. By that time, she had grown and matured and learned to handle herself so that she didn't interfere.

I know I helped this filly considerably by the way I handled her in her 2-year-old form. She eventually developed into a perfect-gaited mare and I think I caught her at just the right time and did just the right thing in waiting for her to develop her speed and gait. I know that if I had put some weight on her she would undoubtedly have trotted faster earlier. But she also would have been chopping herself up behind. All I would have come up with was a flash-in-the-pan early and a bad-gaited trotter later on.

You really have to back off on horses that are snatching a hind leg. Nine out of ten times they are snatching that leg because they have hit before and are trying to avoid hitting again. Once it becomes a habit it is very difficult, if not impossible, to overcome. Even though you get them cleaned up to where they are not interfering, some of them will do things with their hind legs just from habit. The trick is to back off right away and wait for them to develop as I did with By Proxy. This will help in a great many cases.

I mentioned that this filly was out of a full sister to Proximity and since I trained Proximity as a 2-year-old and in her early 3-year-old form, let me say something about her.

Proximity stabbed badly with her left hind leg, but with her it was something more than a defect in gait. Proximity was string-haltered, that is she had a physical defect that caused her to snatch that leg even when she was walking.

She scalped and speedy cut and hit her shins very badly as a 2-year-old. It was Standard Operating Procedure for me to take her to the shop almost every afternoon and have Jack Robinson shoe her a little differently. I was always trying to speed her up in front and slow her down behind in an effort to get her off her hind shins.

I had her shod with a light half-round shoe in front and a real short, squared toe to get her breaking over as quickly as possible. I let her grow a long toe behind with a big grab around it and jar calks on her heels. But she still scalped and hit her speedy cuts.

In the fall of her 2-year-old form, I had Proximity operated on in an effort to correct her stringhaltered condition. I had the leaders clipped where they cross over the hock joint and I think the operation helped her. As a 3-year-old she was still interfering but she was much better than she had been a year earlier. In later years Proximity all but overcame her stabbing tendencies. I think maturity helped her more than anything else.

Now let's get back to the question of weight in starting young trotters out. I have described a couple of cases in which weight was not desirable. Now let me review a couple in which it was proper to add weight.

One of them was the filly, Proud Emily, out of a sister to Emily's Pride. I bought this filly at the Lexington sale because I had seen her lead and she showed quite a lot of trot. But when I broke her she couldn't trot. She was very mixey-gaited and was quite a disappointment to me.

First of all, I loosened the harness because I thought it might be pinching her and making her a little choppy-gaited. Loosening the harness is always a good idea with a filly like this, especially if you have reason to suspect that she ought to be able to trot as I did with this one after having seen her lead. Often the harness will pinch a young horse if it is too tight and he won't try too hard. It's just as though all your clothes were two sizes too small for you. You certainly couldn't be relaxed in a situation like that.

At any rate, that didn't do any good and I knew I would have to go to weight. I really piled quite a bit on this filly. She wore a three-quarter half-round shoe in front, which is the heaviest half-round you can get, a 3¾-inch toe and a five-ounce toe-weight.

I had one good thing going for me with respect to this filly and that was the fact that she was not interfering behind. Often if you pile this much weight on a horse in front you will set up interference, but I didn't get any with her.

Then I trained her evenly-rated miles all winter long. My theory about weight is that if a young horse has to carry a lot of weight to get him on the trot then I don't want to schedule any brush work because fast quarters and eighths will tend to tire him and cause interference behind and can also lead very quickly to unsoundness. I would rather train such horses evenly-rated miles and keep them good-gaited and trotting right, letting them trot well within themselves until they establish their gait.

This is the pattern I followed with Proud Emily. I kept schooling her and went faster miles with her but I never stepped her any eighths or quarters because a filly like this will get in trouble when you try to start her up too quickly.

As I went on into the racing season with Proud Emily and she began to learn what I wanted her to do and how to do it, I started taking the weight off. Eventually, I got her to where she was wearing a 5/8ths half-round bar shoe in front, a 3½-inch toe and no toe weights. She trotted around 2:03 for me and I was very pleased considering the problems I had faced in the beginning.

Another horse that needed weight to make him trot as a 2-year-old was Intrusion. He was owned by the late Lawrence Lake who wanted him to trot. But when I arrived at Pompano Park where my horses were being winter-trained, Monty Moncrief, my assistant, informed me that the colt couldn't do anything but pace. So I had to put a lot of weight on him to get him started trotting flat. I trained him a lot of very slow miles where he could trot flat and good-gaited and didn't attempt to step him at all unless he felt absolutely flat and indicated to me that he wanted to trot a little on his own.

I got him so that he could trot in 3:00 and then, without brushing him or starting him up fast, I gradually worked him down to 2:50 and then to 2:40. He was still good-gaited and then I began easing the weight off him. For a big horse I lightened him up pretty good in front. He wore a three-quarter by a quarter flat shoe with a creased toe because he would go just a little toward his elbows. That isn't too much of a shoe for a horse as big as he was. And I got him down to a 3½-inch toe which was quite short for a horse his size.

He went on and got a good record and became a very good raceway trotter later on. I know that if I hadn't gone all those slow miles with him and resisted the temptation to brush him a little now and then when he was just starting out that he would have been a pacer for sure.

Intrusion and Proud Emily are examples of horses that needed weight to make them trot and that couldn't be brushed. Coalition and By Proxy are trotters that couldn't stand weight, one because she couldn't carry her speed for a full mile in the early stages and the other because it would have established a habit-forming type of interference that might never have been overcome.

The horse trainer hasn't been born who knows the answers to all the shoeing and balancing problems or who is infallible in his judgment. I will stay with the subject of weight on young horses and relate a story to prove the point.

I was at Lexington one fall watching the yearlings lead and I saw a nice colt by Galophone. The first time I saw him he led on the trot and could fly. The next time I saw him he was on the pace and could still fly. That didn't bother me because he was a good-gaited pacer and I bought him with the intention of making a trotter out of him. His name was Frisky Gallie.

I broke him and started training him as a trotter but he didn't show me much. I shod him, as I do all my trotting colts, with a 5/8ths half-round shoe in front and he was very pacey. Like any other trainer, I kept adding weight to overcome this tendency and when I got through I think I had a three-quarter half-round shoe, a leather pad, a four-ounce toe weight, bell boots and maybe even more to try to get him anchored in front so that he would stay on the trot. I must have had 20 ounces on him.

But he kept getting worse. He would show some trot for a quarter of a mile or something like that, but that was it. If you tried to work him a decent mile, he would trot to the half and then switch into a pace. Of course, he wasn't a good-gaited pacer with all that weight on.

I got him down to around 2:35 and that was it. So I decided I might just as well let him pace. I took his front shoes off, discarded all the weight and worked him the next time on the pace bare-footed in front. He was a perfect gaited free-legged pacer.

That lasted for exactly four workouts. When I took him out for the fifth workout he wouldn't pace. He was trying his very best to trot. I figured it was best to let him have his own way and decided to go a slow mile with him on the trot. He came the last half in 1:10 and was good-gaited. It was so much more than he could do a month earlier that I thought maybe I'd better put him back to trotting.

I shod him in front with a set of half-inch half-round shoes that had been used by another trotter and were worn down some. They weighed practically nothing at all, maybe five ounces, and they didn't amount to anything more than a little protection for his foot.

He continued to train like a champion on the trot. I started him in May and the first time he went to the post he trotted in 2:10⅖. He later became sore but I believe he was meant to be a top trotter.

As I said at the beginning, no horse trainer is infallible. There was a colt I kept adding weight on and the more I added the more he wanted to pace. And when he finally did trot he trotted in a light, worn-out shoe. Don't ask me why he was a natural free-legged pacer for four straight workouts and then suddenly wanted to be a trotter. I don't know the answer and I don't think anybody else does.

Often, things that have nothing at all to do with shoeing and balancing can change a horse's gait and make him train or race bad. That wasn't the case with Frisky Gallie but it was with a couple of other horses I had, Instant Hanover and Floriana.

Instant Hanover was a stabby-gaited trotter and would rap his speedy cuts pretty bad. I had to try to hurry him up in front to get him out of the way. He required a little weight but every time I put some on I would get into trouble behind so I had to keep him light and train him within himself.

I had him shod with a 5/8ths half-round in front with a toe as short as I could get it, three inches, and a very high 55-degree angle. I left a lot of foot behind, a 3½-inch toe. It is only rarely that you will find a trotter wearing a half-inch more toe behind than in front. But he needed it to keep from interfering.

I had trained this colt down to about 2:40 and he was going clean-gaited. I hadn't brushed him any but, rather, was trying to establish his gait and I thought I was doing pretty good. Then one day he went out and started interfering behind. I knew I hadn't changed his shoeing so it had to be something else.

Upon examining his hind legs closely, I discovered that his shin boots had been buckled too loose, and had dropped down over his sesamoids and that he had developed two calluses in that area. This soreness had caused him to go sprawly behind and had changed his gait completely.

I quit using shin boots and went to cottons and bandages. The sesamoids healed up, the soreness left and he got over it. He went on from there to take a record of 2:04⅖ as a 2-year-old.

I mention this so that if a young trainer notices a sudden change in the gait of his horse without any corresponding change having been made in shoeing or equipment, it's a good idea to start checking around. You might find, as in Instant Hanover's case, that the boots are chafing him someplace. But it also might be an indication of soreness developing somewhere. This is the time to start checking for splints, curbs, whirlbone trouble, sore shoulders, sore mouths and the like. If any of these things are responsible for a horse going bad-gaited, there isn't anything you can do about it by changing the shoeing or balancing and you have to leave the shoeing alone and try to correct the other trouble.

Then you will occasionally run into another type of horse that doesn't like a certain piece of equipment. Floriana was like this.

I got Floriana the fall she was a 2-year-old. Eddie Wheeler had raced her and Tom Eaton had purchased her from Eddie and turned her over to me. She was a nice filly and didn't require any weight or freak shoeing of any kind but as I went along with her I noticed that she was going awfully close to her knees. I got her up to a mile in 2:20 and decided I'd better put a pair of knee boots on her as a protective measure.

Well, sir, she went all to pieces right away. She got bad-gaited and became very choppy and mixey-gaited in front. I couldn't imagine what had happened and I wasted three workouts puzzling over it. Then I started to think back and remembered that the day she started acting bad was the day I put the knee boots on her. So I removed them and she was a perfect trotter again.

That summer I ran into Eddie Wheeler and he said, "I see you're racing Floriana without knee boots." I told him my story and he laughed and said he'd tried them on her at two with the same results.

Apparently there was something about the tightness of the boots or the suspender straps that held them up that Floriana didn't like. Maybe one of the buckles was pressing on a leader or a muscle or something like that and it bothered her. Whatever it was, she just didn't like them and wasn't going to race or train in them.

This filly was very funny in that her stroke indicated to both Eddie and me that she would hit her knee. But after I had that trouble with the boots I started watching her closely and noticed that when she reached the top of her stroke her foot would turn out instead of in toward the knee as her conformation and breaking action indicated it would. So she didn't really need the knee boots after all. I don't know what I would have done if she had.

Conformation also has an effect on the way trotters and pacers have to be shod and balanced. Several years ago, when I was employed by Castleton Farm, we kept a filly, Floral Girl, that couldn't be sold because she stood so straight in front. She was so bad that I didn't think she would ever stand training, let alone get to the races.

But I started out with her anyway keeping in mind that a straight-ankled horse can't carry any weight. I was lucky in one respect in that I found she didn't need any weight to trot.

The secret with a horse like this is a very short toe and a high angle so that you remove all the tension you can from the ankle. I raced this filly in a three-inch toe and 55-degree angle. This tipped her up quite a bit and relieved the strain on the ankle joint. She went on and trotted in 2:02⅖ over a half mile track as a 3-year-old, which was within a fifth of a second of the world record at that time.

As Johnny Simpson has told you, if you can get a trotter to go in a 3½-inch toe you are way ahead of the game. The three-inch toe I had on Floral Girl was dictated by necessity but every once in a while you will run across a natural trotter that doesn't require very much toe and will also go light in front. When you get one like this you are always quite happy about it. Kerry Way, 3, 1:58⅗, the 1966 Hambletonian winner and the two and 3-year-old Trotter of the Year 1965 and 1966, was this kind of a mare.

She was a natural when I broke her and after training her once or twice I decided she could probably go even lighter and shorter in front than I had her shod. I had started her with a 5/8ths half-round shoe and a 3½-inch toe and it wasn't 30 days until I decided that I could do even better than that. I went to a half-inch half-round bar shoe and shortened her toe to 3¼ inches while raising her angle to 51 degrees. The next time I shod her I squared her front toes and she was better-gaited than ever. That's the way she raced and I know that if a man could do it without breaking her foot to pieces she would trot bare-footed. You don't often get that kind to train.

Kerry Way also had a habit of throwing her head off to the side and if you didn't know her you might think she was side-lining and that her mouth hurt or something like that. But with her, this was nothing more than the fact that when she was training she was uninterested in what she was doing and would start gawking around looking at things in the infield or on the outside of the track. All it ever took to straighten her out was to be trained in company or to race. She'd be all business then. The reason I mention this is that some young trainers might be inclined to start putting things on the head of a horse like this to straighten her up and they would be doing wrong.

Sometimes a trainer will have troubles with both the front and hind end at the same time and will have to work one against the other, experimenting with this and that until he gets just what he wants.

One good mare that I remember I had to work on at both ends was Cheer Honey 2, 1:59⅖. Everybody commented on what a good-gaited mare she was and they were right, but she was a real problem, especially behind.

She was very sprawly-gaited and would throw her hind legs way back and up when she trotted. She would hit way up on her hock and I even sewed an extra inch on the full hock boot she was wearing and padded it with rubber so that she wouldn't hurt herself when she hit back there.

I had to use a high sulky with her and had to make her grip the race track behind all she could. I used a grab on her for this purpose, She was no account at all if she didn't have a good sharp grab around her toe behind.

I had a full swedge bar shoe on her behind and laid my grab in the channel of the swedge around the toe to the first nail hole on each side. This helped her hold the track and improved her gait quite a bit.

It wasn't until the middle of the summer of her 2-year-old form that I got her cleaned up to where she wasn't hitting herself behind. Of course, I don't think a horse trainer does all this. I think, as I have said before, that as a 2-year-old grows and gets stouter—and some of them will do it in the course of a racing season or even part of a racing season—they will establish a gait and get a lot better about interfering.

But even while Cheer Honey was having her troubles behind, she was also causing me some concern up front. I had trained her in a quarter by 5/8ths, which is about as light as you can get on a mare her size and still have any heft or stiffness to the shoe.

To break her over a little more in front and get away from that interference behind, I had squared her toe and this was putting her mighty close to her elbows. I could have gone to elbow boots because I do not mind them and race some horses that way, but I don't like to use them or any other protective boot unless I have to and I never wear them just for decoration.

At any rate, I kept racing her and watching her very closely. As the summer went on her gait started to clean up in front, I ventured to put a little crease in her front toe, just enough to hesitate her a fraction and draw her away from the elbows. When I did this, I had to be concerned with the possibility that she might start interfering behind as a result, but I didn't think she would and she did not. Maybe I might have gotten away without the crease, but I thought it was what she needed and she certainly seemed to race better that way. When you have a 2-year-old trotting filly that goes faster than 2:00, you can be pretty sure that whatever way she is shod is the right way.

A good example of what I mean when I say that I am not opposed to wearing elbow boots on a trotter if they are required, is the good filly Mary Donner. She is owned by Paul Donner and was a season's champion at both two in 1965 (race record of 2:02⅕) and three in 1966 (2:03⅕ over a half mile track).

She is a high class mare in every respect, but she is also a mare that goes to her elbows and while I would love to get her off them I don't think I ever will. Nevertheless, I am not at all discouraged by this because a number of our great trotters wore elbow boots—Speedy Scot, and Hoot Mon as a 2-year-old just to name a couple—and there is absolutely nothing wrong with them.

Mary Donner is a beautifully-gaited mare in front and has what I would call a perfect round, rolling stroke. Actually, she doesn't really go high enough to hit her elbows in the literal meaning of the expression, but at the top of her stroke she flips her toe up and touches the elbow. This is quite a bit different from the normal elbow-hitter that is simply going too high and banging his elbow as a result.

This filly is shod short and light in front. She has a 3¼-inch toe and a 3/16ths by 5/8ths flat shoe with a crease in the toe. I don't know how you would go about shoeing a trotter any lighter to go any lower than that. Once in a while I will add a rim pad over a very hard track but normally she does not wear one.

An inexperienced trainer might be fooled by a filly like Mary Donner because if you worked her alone she might not go to her elbows at all. But when she gets tensed up behind the gate in the excitement of a race, she'll usually touch them as she goes away or in the first turn on a half-mile track. After that she'll probably relax and be all right the rest of the way. Maybe I could race this mare without elbow boots, but I don't think I could and I'm not about to start conducting any experiments with a mare as perfect as she is.

Let me insert right here something that any good trainer will tell you if you talk to him about it. I don't care how great a trotter you have, you will rarely find one that won't brush a hind shin now and then or brush a speedy cut or something like that. Sure, I keep trying to improve on a situation like this because we all want perfection. But sometimes you can't get perfection. Just a little brushing doesn't amount to much, and I wouldn't consider it a bad fault in a horse. That's why I always put hind shin boots on my trotters whether they need them or not. You can never tell when they might suddenly make a misstep and brush a hind shin.

This occasional interference can happen anywhere on the racetrack but will usually occur in one of three places; at or just before the start when a horse gets anxious and "strutty" behind the gate, in the first turn over a half-mile track when the field is traveling pretty fast, or near the finish when a horse begins to get a little tired.

An example of this type of horse is the trotter Spengay that I raced almost 25 years ago. I got this horse when he was four and in studying his past performance I noticed he would make breaks leaving but that he would then settle and usually win his races despite the handicap. I knew that in the class where I was going to race him he couldn't spot his rivals this kind of an edge and beat them, so I started looking him over to see if I couldn't find out what his trouble was.

I noticed that he was a very high-going horse in front although he wasn't actually hitting his elbows. As a precautionary measure, I equipped him with elbow boots and he touched them going away in his first start. But he didn't make a break and won. It was perfectly clear to me then what had been happening the year before. He would get a little anxious leaving and had been banging his elbows and making breaks going away and in the first turn.

The elbow of a horse is just as sensitive as a person's elbow and you can almost be certain that when a trotter hits an elbow he's going to make a break. Spengay raced perfectly for me and never raised his head any place in the mile and never made a break. After a couple of months, the owner decided he wanted to race him in Michigan so he took him home and removed the elbow boots because he didn't like them. Spengay immediately started making breaks again. I told the owner what was wrong but he wouldn't put the boots back on. The horse couldn't do any good in Michigan so the owner finally sent him back to me and all I did was put the elbow boots back on. He started winning again.

The reason I am citing the case of Spengay is that young trainers should be sure to cover any area of interference, even if the interference is just occurring now and then. This applies to all kinds of boots. If a trainer thinks his horse is getting close to himself somewhere he should add boots of some kind.

Some trotters may look as though they'd never hit a knee or an arm, but in the heat of a race when they start to go a little faster and get nervous and keyed up they may touch in one of those places. This isn't necessarily a shoeing or balancing problem but, rather, it is just a question of using boots as insurance.

Trainers really should be trying to figure these things out ahead of time. You can very often tell by how close a horse is going to an elbow or a knee in training whether it might be a good idea to use a pair of boots on him. If you do this and get through several races without a mark of any kind on the boots, maybe then you can remove them.

In such cases, it's much better to be safe than sorry. Interference can result in pouched elbows, big shins and big knees and can cause usually solid-gaited horses to make breaks. In addition, such horses may soon develop bad manners or sour dispositions or become quitters. I have seen horses that became one or all of these for just this reason.

Before I got off into another area, I had been writing quite a bit about young trotters and when you should and shouldn't add weight. There is one type that I haven't discussed that falls in the "don't add weight" category. This is the colt—although I should probably say filly because it happens more often with fillies—that is fractious, nervous, headstrong and/or temperamental and whose problem usually has little to do with gait and balance, although an inexperienced trainer might be led to think it did.

An example of this type of horse was Expresson, 3, 1:58, co-world champion 3-year-old trotting filly. Expresson was a truly great mare, but I had my problems with her.

As a 2-year-old, she did not require any special weight or length of toe to balance her but she was nervous and headstrong and every once in a while, especially if a piece of dirt flew up and struck her or something like that, she would take off and fly into a pace.

When this happened, I didn't run to the barn and put a pair of toe weights or a heavier pair of shoes on her. I used a little TLC—Tender Loving Care—and I like to think one of the reasons I have enjoyed so much success with fillies is that I treat them with kindness. I find they usually respond in kind.

What I did with Expresson, and what I do with all fillies of this type, was to keep her away from other horses and train her all by herself for as long as I could.

In some instances, you can remove the closed bridle and

wear an open bridle on a horse like this. This will often calm them down a little. But Expresson wasn't that way. With the open bridle she would try to run out every draw gate she saw and I had to keep a closed bridle on her.

I trained her alone with a little quarter by 5/8ths flat shoe and a crease in her toe because she went a little close to her elbows. Later in the spring, I gradually settled her into company and finally I was able to get an open bridle on her and she was an outstanding race mare.

Madam Sampson was another that fell in this category. She was from the first crop by Sampson Hanover, and K. D. Owen, who owned and bred her and who owned Sampson Hanover, was interested in showing that his horse could sire trotters.

But the Madam would get excited and fly into a pace. I had to be very careful with her. I gave her slow miles by herself over long distances and she gradually responded. After she learned what it was all about and got her temper under control, she became a good trotter and went on and took a trotting record of 2:02⅗ as a 2-year-old.

There never was a more perfect gaited horse than the 2-year-old trotting champion Impish, 2, 1:58⅗. She was very simply shod, going in a 3/16ths by 5/8ths flat shoe in front with a chrome pad, which is a light leather pad. But she was also one of those temperamental, excitable fillies and I had to take great pains with her.

I didn't break Impish. I got her on December 15th of her yearling form and she had already been broken to harness. She also had a broken tail and I couldn't put a crupper on her so I had to drive her with a back band and without a check. She would want to throw herself if you tried to check her up.

I took a lot of time with Impish, not because she was a shoeing or balancing problem but because she was so temperamental. I never stepped her for months although she could have gone on at any time. But it was mental with her and I wanted to be sure she had manners and disposition before I stuck her in with other horses. Eventually she did develop these manners and went on to become the fastest 2-year-old trotter of all time with a mile in 1:58⅗.

Another problem mare of this type was Willing Rodney that I purchased out of the Walnut Hall Stud consignment at Lexington some years ago. She was a nervous and temperamental filly and wouldn't trot at all. I tried to train her but she wouldn't go more than 100 feet without dancing up and down. Even when she was jogging she was a problem. She would go a little ways and then would start cantering with her head up in the air and wouldn't hit a trot at all.

I fooled with that mare quite some time before I got her the way I wanted her and the way she had to be. But she was a mental problem, not a shoeing or balancing problem.

I would jog this filly as much as eight or nine miles before she would hit a trot and when she did I would let her jog on the trot a couple of miles and then take her back to the barn. After letting her blow out about 30 minutes, I would take her back to the track. This time she would usually go three or four miles before she got tired and hit a trot and then she would stay on gait.

This was the way I trained that filly and the only way I could train her. She got to be a decent kind of a race mare, took a record of 2:03⅖ as a 2-year-old and then was sold to Italy.

Another top filly that might have been a problem if I hadn't gone easy with her in the early stages of her training was Sprite Rodney, 2, 1:59⅖. Sprite Rodney didn't really have a problem but she could have developed one in the hands of a trainer who wanted to rush her along too fast. This would have been a natural thing with a filly like her because she had a lot of extreme speed early if the trainer had wanted to use it.

Sprite Rodney's problem was that she was a likely candidate to interfere behind and I had to resist the impulse to let her show me the extreme speed I knew she had and which she kept wanting to demonstrate. If I had given way and let her go on, she would have started interfering badly and might have become a stabbing trotter.

What I did was to go very slow with her while at the same time getting her as light as I possibly could in front. All miles were evenly-rated during the early part of her training and if she even looked like she was going to touch a shin, I would back off with her. Eventually I got her down to a 3⅜-inch toe, a 51-degree angle and a 3/16ths by 5/8ths bar shoe in front. She was perfect this way and when I finally got her set and did let her ramble she responded just as I knew she would.

I'm not blowing my own horn about these things, but the

point I am trying to make is that some of these fillies I have been writing about, Expresson and Madam Sampson in particular, could very easily have become pacers if I hadn't taken my time and worked them slow and by themselves. These fillies didn't need weight to make them trot. They were mental cases and they had to be handled delicately.

Horses that get nervous and excited generally show it when you first start to train them and that is the time to correct the fault. But every once in a while you will run into a horse that is fine while he is training but that gives you all kinds of trouble when you are racing him in with other horses. Air Pilot, a half brother to Greyhound, was a horse like this.

Harry Whitney had this horse as a 2-year-old but the colt couldn't trot any and Harry, who didn't want to fool with pacers, turned him over to me about the first of April and I converted him. He trained nicely and I went along real slow with him and didn't start him until Du Quoin. I had trained him in 2:07 the week before and thought I had a good chance to win.

I took him away slowly and trailed the field until about the three quarters when I pulled him out. He did real well until he got up alongside the leaders whereupon he started swelling up in the harness, hitting his knees and climbing in the hobbles.

I didn't know what was wrong so I backed him off and waited for the next heat. He did the same thing. I soon discovered that this was a horse that just couldn't stand to have other horses around him. I gave him a record of 2:05½ at Lexington that fall but I couldn't even use a prompter because even that would make him swell up in the harness and get excited and nervous.

When you get a horse that goes clean while training but suddenly begins to hit himself all over in a race, you can bet that you've got a horse with a mental problem rather than one with shoeing or balancing troubles.

A great mare that I raced once and that had a combination of a mental problem and a shoeing and balancing problem was the world champion two and 3-year-old pacing filly Good Counsel. She went free-legged and never made a break in a race in her life. To watch her race, you would never guess she had ever caused me any trouble but she was responsible for a number of sleepless nights before she reached her championship form.

Good Counsel was a wild, fractious mare when I started with

her, especially about hitching. I would have to hitch her out behind the barn and then take her to the race track because if you hitched her where she could see the track she would get wild and want to throw herself.

Because I knew she was a filly that could be spoiled very easily, I never rushed her or pushed her in training. I let her pace in behind horses but never pulled her out and let her ramble, even though I knew she could. She was a natural pacer and I had her going free-legged and wanted to develop her manners before I went on with her.

I had her shod quite naturally in a half-inch, half-round bar shoe in front and a quarter by three-quarter sideweight shoe behind. She wore a 3¼-inch toe all around. She was exceptionally good-gaited and I was well pleased with her progress.

She was coming along so well that I decided to switch her over to a half-round, half-swedge shoe behind which is what I normally use with all my pacers. I made the change and she immediately became foul-gaited. I told myself that no horse in the world was smart enough to know the difference in the weight of those shoes so I weighed both sets. The new shoes weighed one ounce less than the old ones.

I persisted with that mare and lost about four weeks trying to make her pace in those shoes. I started to work on the front and because I thought maybe she was in trouble there. I took as much off her toe as I could and reduced her angle but nothing seemed to help. She was rough-gaited, rolling, tumbling and making breaks.

I was at Goshen by this time and one night in disgust I told the boys to get a set of hobbles out and that we would try her in them the next day. I didn't want to do it because she had been such a natural pacer, but it didn't look like I had much choice.

I got to thinking about it in bed that night and decided I would try one more thing before I put the hobbles on. I got up early the next morning and went to the hardware store and bought a piece of inch-by-quarter steel.

As you know, the widest standard shoe a blacksmith has in stock is three quarters of an inch so I was really thinking in extremes. I told Bill Wick to make a set of shoes out of this piece of steel and to pull the weight to the outside. I would guess those shoes weighed from 16 to 18 ounces apiece.

I worked her that day with her new shoes on and she was as slick and smooth a gaited pacer as you'd ever want to see. She never made a break after that and her disposition cleared up 100%, too.

She wore those inch-by-quarter shoes all that year and paced to her 2-year-old record of 1:58⅕ in them. Naturally she wore them down until they were quite thin and weighed a good deal less, but after the trouble I'd had, I wasn't about to change them and I didn't.

Since there was only an ounce difference in the quarter by three quarter side weight shoe I had started her with and the half-round, half-swedge I went to when I made the original change, I'd have to guess that it was the shape of the new shoe that bothered her and made her go bad-gaited. A half-round, half-swedge shoe is ideal for a pacer behind and it is very seldom that one will react this way. But Good Counsel sure did. The next year I went back to the original quarter by three-quarter side weight shoe and she took her 1:57 record in those.

Good Counsel is an example of the shoeing and balancing problems you can run into with a pacer behind. On the other hand, Timely Story, another fast Good Time pacer I had, needed help on the front end.

Timely Story was a climby-gaited pacer and couldn't go in the hobbles at all. He couldn't beat 2:40 with the hobbles on and he couldn't beat 2:40 with the hobbles off when I tried him that way.

I tried the hind end first. I went to a heavy sideweight shoe and when that didn't work I went to extremes and put a pair of four-ounce toe weights on the side of each of his hind feet. I thought maybe the toe weight, placed on the side as it was, would help him swing into the natural rolling motion of the pacing gait. It didn't work. He was still climby-gaited in front and couldn't get his hind end to track right. I knew my only hope lay up front.

So I took the weight off behind and finally wound up with a flat quarter by three-quarter shoe in front with a pad, five-ounce toe weights and elbow boots. He wore a 3⅝-inch toe. This sounds a little foolish for a pacer but I was interested only in making a race horse out of him and, of course, I didn't do everything at once.

I put the heavy shoe on first and then the pad and then started adding toe weights. I started with a two-ounce weight and gradually got it up to five. I was making him even climbier-gaited in front but he was getting to be a natural pacer so I just added elbow boots and went on.

Once he had established his gait, which he did quite rapidly under the circumstances, I began to take the weight off by stages. In the fall of that year he took a record of 2:01⅘ and I had him going in a quarter by 5/8ths flat shoe with a pad and a three-ounce toe weight. He still wore his elbow boots.

As a 3-year-old, I got rid of the elbow boots, cut the shoe down to a 3/16ths by 5/8ths and the toe weight to two ounces. He took a record of 1:59 and I sold him to Sanders Russell and told him he was a good horse. He proved that by going out and winning his first start for Sanders around 2:03 at Yonkers.

Good Counsel and Timely Story, both free-legged pacers by the same sire, are examples of horses that needed help at opposite ends in order to balance them correctly. Good Counsel needed weight behind, which is relatively normal, and none in front. Timely Story couldn't stand weight behind and needed it in front which is abnormal for a pacer. That's why you have to treat every horse as an individual and why I can safely say that what will work for one horse won't necessarily work for the next one.

Most of the time these days you won't be able to make a free-legged pacer and the only time you have one is when you are fortunate enough to come across a real natural. Otherwise, racing over the half-mile tracks as much as we do, you nearly always need the hobbles if for no other reason than to steady your horse either at the start or going into a turn.

Timely Beauty, p, 2, 1:57⅓, the world champion 2-year-old pacing filly, was one that I thought would make a free-legged mare but I finally had to go to the hobbles with her. This filly could really fly alongside the lead pony when she was a yearling and after Dick Downing bought her for $19,000 I had visions of another Good Counsel. I was right about the speed part of it but wrong about the free-legged end of it.

I didn't know that for quite a while though. I started her out free-legged and she was a natural. She wore a side weight shoe behind and was perfectly gaited. But as soon as I started to school her behind the starting gate she would commence to get nervous and make breaks. She was just over-anxious and trying too hard.

I went to a pair of three-ounce toe weights on her behind, just as I had with Timely Story, but I still couldn't keep her flat. I started her that way in a qualifying race at Lexington that spring and she paced in 2:08⅖ but I had to hang on to her. I could tell by the feel of the lines and the way she was going that she would make a break if I let her pace any.

It was with a great deal of regret that I put the hobbles on that filly. I pulled her sideweight shoes and went to a half-round, half-swedge shoe behind and left her alone in front where she was wearing a half-inch, half-round. She was perfect, as I knew she would be.

I raced her that summer and at Lexington I put her down to go for a record. I knew she would pace fast and decided to try her free-legged. I did and she got within 75 feet of the wire at a 1:58 gait and went into a break. I know what did it. The prompters got too close to her and the noise and excitement got her over-anxious and she tried too hard. I let her blow out about 45 minutes and brought her back and went in 1:57⅕ with the hobbles on.

Toe weights on the side of the hind feet of pacers might sound a little extreme and I described them that way earlier. But very often you will find that they will balance a pacer behind and get him started right. I recommend their use with a colt that isn't good-gaited and maybe acting a little rocky behind. Used in this manner, toe weights will sometimes establish the pacing gait by widening a horse out just a little bit. If you do this, you should work slow miles for a while until the horse becomes adjusted to the change. You will usually find that you can discard them once the horse has learned what the pacing gait is and how to handle it.

I've raced a lot of good horses but the greatest were Bret Hanover, about whom I've written, and Good Time, the sire of Good Counsel, Timely Story and Timely Beauty. Good Time was a perfect horse in every way. He wasn't a big horse but he had a gait and a way of going that made him look and act big.

Good Time's conformation did present something of a shoeing problem but I dealt with it right away and never had any trouble from then on. He was a very flat-footed horse in front and he had undershot heels. That is, his heels grew all right but they grew down and forward instead of straight down. This put him in under himself and gave him a lower angle that would tend to have him landing on his heels and breaking over much too slowly unless it was remedied.

I shod him simply with a little half-round bar shoe in front, but I let the ends of the shoes extend about an inch beyond his heels on both sides. The end of the shoe was where the heel would normally have been if the foot was not growing the way it did. This provided additional ground surface and gave him bearing where he needed it.

Normally, I would not like to have any part of the shoe protruding from the back of the front foot of any horse, trotter or pacer, because a horse would be almost sure to grab it and pull it off. But I had two things going for me with regard to Good Time that would not ordinarily apply to another horse.

In the first place, he was so perfectly-gaited that he never came anywhere near his quarters and was about as far from a cross-firing pacer as you would ever want to see. I never put a boot of any kind on his feet. In addition, while the end of the shoe did protrude, it did not actually extend beyond the end of the foot, if the quarter and the top of the heel can be considered the end of the foot rather than the bottom of the heel. This was because of the undershot angle of his heel.

I raced Good Time that way at two and three and then when he was four he stepped on a stone and punched a big hole in the sole of his foot. This would normally call for a pad, but I was very hesitant to use one because he was flat-footed anyway and I thought a pad might cost me a second or two in speed. I finally had to go to one and selected a vulcan leather pad that wouldn't weigh more than two ounces. The pad never did affect his speed and, if anything, it made him a better horse than he had been.

The idea of letting a shoe extend beyond the heel to compensate for a horse with a low angle, such as Good Time, is not a new one. It's done quite a bit, more often behind than in front, and the first time I saw it was more than 50 years ago when I was just a child and my dad picked up an old pacer for $300 that could go around 2:17 but that dad thought ought to be going in 2:12. You have to bear in mind that 2:12 out in Missouri where we raced, or anywhere else except on the Grand Circuit for that matter, meant a pretty good horse 50 years ago.

My dad shod this horse by letting the front shoe extend a good two inches past his heel on each side. I had never seen such a freak shoeing job even in those days and I asked about it. Dad explained that he had been watching the horse and that he was landing almost straight up and down on his heels and that when he stood in front of him and watched him coming, all he could see was the bottoms of his feet.

He figured that if he could get that horse on the ground a little sooner and thus cause him to break over quicker and improve his stride he could make a horse out of him. So he went to this freak shoe which caused the horse to hit the ground sooner and it worked. The horse, whose name was Buzz, broke over faster, won a dozen or so races for dad and took a record of around 2:10 which was really something for those days.

I've written quite a bit now about pacers that needed help behind and in front and from the hobbles. Let me tell you about one that couldn't be helped by weight in front or behind or by the hobbles and how I finally got her straightened away in time for her to become a season's champion two-year-old.

This was a filly named Tillie Hal. It was most of the winter before I ever got her on the pace and, as a matter of fact, one time I suggested to the owner that he take her home but he wanted to race her so I agreed I would keep trying.

This filly wouldn't do anything but rack and single foot in the hobbles. Those two gaits are variations of the pace. Most of the time she would be single-footing. A single-footing pacer is one that isn't putting the front foot and the hind foot on the same side down at the same time. Instead of the 1-2 beat of the natural pacer you are getting a 1-2-3-4 beat and that isn't conducive to speed, gait or balance.

I tried this filly with weight in front and she was the same way. I tried her with weight behind and it was the same thing. I tightened her hobbles up and it didn't do any good. She wouldn't touch the hobbles no matter how tight I drew them. She would just shorten up and go racky-gaited and make breaks. She never did chafe herself in the hobbles.

Along about the middle of March I was pretty desperate and knew that in some way I had to get her to lean into the hobbles and start acquiring a pacing gait. So I shod her naturally and adjusted the hobbles to medium length. Then I took off with her and let her single foot as far as she wanted to. I had decided to let her get tired and see if she wouldn't lean into the hobbles then.

The first heat, I single-footed her over to the three-quarter pole just as fast as she could go. I never made any effort to get her pacing as I had been doing in the past. Finally, at the three-quarter pole, she got leg-weary and leaned into the hobbles and hit a pace. She only paced a quarter in 45 seconds but for the first time in her life she was on her gait.

I let her blow out for about 30 minutes and brought her back to the track. Again I let her single foot. She went over to the half that way at about a 2:30 shot. Then she got tired again and started leaning into the hobbles. She came the last half, pacing and gaited right.

I followed that routine for about three weeks and at the end of that time she was pacing and she stayed pacing the rest of the year. She took a record of 2:05¼ and was a real good filly.

That was 25 years ago and I was making a mistake with that mare that I wouldn't make today. That's why experience is such a great teacher. What I was doing wrong was trying to get her to leave the wire flat but not giving her enough time to get herself set. I was trying to rush her into the hobbles but she wouldn't reach for them and would get mixed up and start single footing and break into a run. I had to make this mare know the hobbles were there and I finally decided that in order to do this I had to get her tired. That's the procedure I followed and it worked very well.

The first horse that ever raced faster than 2:00 over a half-mile track was Sampson Hanover who won in 1:59⅗ at Delaware, Ohio, in 1951 when he was a 4-year-old. He is a good horse to use as an example of the procedures I follow in switching a horse over from the trot to the pace and at the same time will enable me to comment on unsoundness behind that in some instances appears to be applicable only to horses on the trotting gait.

Sampson Hanover belonged to Mr. Owen and was a natural trotter when I broke him. I shod him in a 5/8ths, half-round shoe in front with a pad and he wore a 3⅝-inch toe. He didn't need any weight to make him trot. He was a natural.

I shipped him to St. Louis that spring where he picked up the virus but he recovered from that and I took him to Saratoga and worked him in 2:09 well out from the rail for the entire mile. He was real sharp and I had an offer of $25,000 for him that morning. Mr. Owen wasn't interested. I shipped the colt to Goshen and told my second trainer, the late George Boggs, to work him around 2:30 and that I would be down early the next week to work him in 2:06 over the mile track.

George worked him and called to tell me the colt was bad-gaited behind. I drove to Goshen and worked him myself. Not only was he bad-gaited but he was lame behind. He would trot a little piece and then commence to lose himself behind. I fooled around with him for about three weeks and after talking to Fred Egan and some of the other trainers, I decided to turn him out for the year.

The following year I picked him up and he was fine until I got down to about 2:18-2:20 with him. Then that old trouble showed up behind. We went over him with a fine-tooth comb as we had done a year earlier and couldn't find a thing. We never did find his trouble. He would trot maybe a half-mile and then get bad-gaited and start throwing his left hind leg away and hitting his shins and speedy cuts.

I fooled around with him until the first of July and he could work around 2:12 but he was still off behind. Mr. Owen suggested that I convert him to the pace and I agreed although I had a few misgivings about it because he didn't carry any weight or wear any toe as is usually the case with a trotter that you have decided to switch over to the pace.

In converting horses to the pace, it is standard procedure with me to work them barefooted in front a few times while I determine what kind of natural gait they have and, therefore, how they should be shod and balanced. I recommend this procedure any place where the track is soft enough that you can get away with it without injuring your horse's feet. You can do it on most clay tracks but on these hard, all-weather tracks you have to be careful.

Sampson had worn a full swedge shoe behind when he was trotting and I substituted a half-round, half-swedge, added a pair of hobbles and put him on the pace. He showed a tendency to cross-fire so I lowered him on the inside behind, turned a heel calk on the outside and diamond-toed his hind feet. This got him off his quarters in good shape.

Meantime, I had been watching his gait in front and since he was inclined to be a little climby, that is going a little too high, I shod him with a pair of full swedge shoes and off he went.

The rest of the story is well-known. He took a record of 1:59⅗ that fall without ever having started in a race and the next year he won in 1:59⅗ at Delaware. A year later he went in 1:56⅘ and one afternoon I even took the hobbles off him and won a heat in 1:58⅗ at Du Quoin.

In converting a horse to the pace, I prefer to try him barefooted in front for a couple of weeks if I can. If that isn't possible because of the surface of the track, I will go to the lightest shoe I can find, usually a half-round which will help break him over more naturally. In addition, I will be watching his gait to determine whether he might need a crease or a swedge in front.

There isn't really much problem in switching most horses over —but remember, I said "most" horses, not "all" horses. Take the weight off in front and add it behind; cut the front toe down, slip the hobbles on and begin normal training procedure.

The other thought I want to bring in relative to Sampson Hanover is that I am convinced that there are certain muscles high up in a horse's back, in the stifle and whirlbone area, that trotters and pacers use differently.

I am just a horse trainer and not a scientist or a veterinarian but I know this has to be true because Sampson Hanover was absolutely sound behind from the day I put the hobbles on him until he was retired. There just can't be any other explanation.

Sampson Hanover isn't the only horse I learned this from. Both Hundred Proof and The Tippler were trotters who got off behind just as Sampson did and stayed that way until I converted them to the pace. And all three of these horses were checked out completely sound from the hock down. So their trouble was up higher.

I never heard of this happening in the case of a horse being converted the other way, from the pace to the trot, but then we don't have many horses that switch gaits in that direction. Most go from the trot to the pace. If we had a larger sampling, I feel that we would probably find the same thing. If you watched the

gait of the trotter and pacer you would soon conclude that the
same muscles were being used in a different way for the two gaits.

It's just like a person. A man who does deep knee bends doesn't
use the same muscles he does in chinning himself. You could
have a muscle soreness that would keep you from doing a knee
bend that wouldn't bother you a bit if you were chinning yourself. To a degree, I think the same thing applies to trotters and
pacers. The example I have just used is an extreme one, of
course, but I think it serves to emphasize the point I am trying
to make.

Writing about trotters that have trouble in the stifle and
whirlbone area reminds me of Princess Rodney, a filly I raced
for Mr. and Mrs. Sherman Jenney a number of years ago. She
was a great big, growthy filly that the Jenneys had retained for
their Walnut Hall Stud and she had been broken in the summer
by the great colt man Hunter Moody.

I had seen Mr. Moody training her and I knew she would be
able to trot a lot because she had a nice gait in front and went
very light and could show speed. But she was very loose in her
stifles and I was afraid she would have stifle or whirlbone trouble.

When I started to go on with her, I found that my suspicions
were correct. She would trot a little ways, say a half mile or so,
and then knuckle over behind. I knew I had to work on her and
I did something I seldom do with a 2-year-old trotter. I cut her
toe as short as I could behind, raised her angle up very high and
squared the toe of the flat shoe I had on her.

My reasoning was that I didn't want a lot of toe on this filly
behind, which is the opposite of the way I usually go with a
trotter. A short toe would tend to make her stand straighter
behind and would keep her from knuckling over. This shoeing
worked perfectly with this mare. She stopped knuckling over and
went on to take a record of 2:01 that fall which at that time
was the world's record. Shortening the hind toe and raising the
angle is a recommended procedure as far as I am concerned
with this type of trotter.

Of course, when you make a change like this that is "against
the book," you always have to be concerned about interference
developing. In shoeing Princess Rodney as I did, I was speeding
up her action behind and this is not in keeping with the general
practice of "speeding them up in front and slowing them down

behind." But I felt emergency measures were necessary and worth the risk.

When you do something like this, it is also a good idea to train your horse very carefully the next time out. I went three or four real slow miles with Princess Rodney to satisfy myself that what I had done was not going to result in interference. I was fortunate that it did not. When I made the change, I thought there was a pretty good chance that I would also have to make some kind of a compensating adjustment in her front shoes but she went clean and I never had to.

Both Simpson and I have talked about lowering horses on the inside or outside of the foot and at the same time have stressed the importance of the horse hitting level when he lands. This can sometimes result in a horse standing awkwardly when you lead him out of the stall to show him, but if he is hitting level on the race track it doesn't matter a bit to me.

High Volo, the first horse I ever raced that I thought had a chance to trot in 2:00, was like this. He had bad ankles and had been foundered in front. Harry Fitzpatrick and Sep Palin had had him before I got him and they couldn't keep him sound. I didn't do anything special with this horse; I just kept his foot hitting the ground level no matter what it looked like when he was standing.

Having been foundered, High Volo wanted to wear his shoes and his feet down on the outside to get away from pressure on the soles. Consequently, he was really landing hard on the outside of his foot. All I really did was to accommodate him. I kept lowering the outside and he kept racing good for me. He won in 2:05 over a half-mile track and 2:03 over a mile track when that really amounted to something.

He had an awful-looking foot on him but that didn't bother me a bit. He was wearing his shoes flat and even and that was what mattered. I knew that if I tried to tilt him back to where that foot would look level I would have had a lame horse on my hands in no time at all.

Yankee Hanover was another horse I raced that had bad feet. I got him in the middle of his 2-year-old form and he had already been foundered. He also had osselets and finally got splints.

But I'll tell you what he was. He was just about the greatest-gaited trotter I have ever had. He didn't need any weight at all to trot. He wore a quarter by 5/8ths flat shoe in front and didn't require a square toe as most trotters that wear a flat shoe in front will.

He was a natural line-gaited trotter that went close to his elbows and I put a crease in his front shoes to hesitate him a mite for that reason. He had a great, round way of going in front, went to within about two inches of his elbows, was line/gaited, stayed close to the ground behind and was just about an ideal horse. I think he was meant for a truly great trotter and if it hadn't been for his front feet I think he would have taken a much faster record than he did.

Of course, I had to use pads with him because if I hadn't, the soles of his feet would have been right on the ground. He stood very straight and I had to trim him low on the outside because of his foot trouble, but I always had him landing level and natural for him at all times.

I had to tub Yankee Hanover every day from the 15th of March until the 15th of October, but he was game and tried his best every time. I would say that he and Impish were the two best-gaited trotters I ever raced.

Bad-footed horses are always a problem for a trainer and once in a while us old timers have to reach down into our bag of tricks to handle a real difficult case. Daring Rodney was like this until I gave him the old Kansas & Oklahoma treatment and made a trotter out of him.

As a 2-year-old, Daring Rodney was a real thin-walled horse, was sore all the time and it looked for sure that he wouldn't make it to the races at all. It was at Lexington that spring that I decided maybe a street pad would do the job.

A street pad is a big thick rubber pad with leather backing. When I was a boy, they were used on horses that pulled beer wagons and milk wagons and everything else on the streets and that's how they got their name. I had used them years earlier on a few trotters but our pads had become more refined since then and our horse's feet were better and there was no need for street pads.

But I knew I had to go to extremes with Daring Rodney so I talked to Bob Tosh, who was the blacksmith at Lexington and who had put on many a street pad in the old Kansas and Oklahoma days. He found a couple of old street pads and we went to work. They were about an inch and a half thick and we trimmed them down to three-quarters of an inch—which was still plenty big in comparison with our present pads—and put them on Daring Rodney's front feet. He wore a tip, which Johnny Simpson has described, around the front of his foot to the second nail hole on each side. The rest of his foot was made up of this heavy rubber street pad. He had a foot that was half shoe and half rubber.

I trained the horse in these and he was sound. There was a little more weight than I really wanted but I had no choice if I wanted to keep the horse racing so I went on with him. He raced well and took a record of 2:03 that fall. Meantime, I was growing a new set of feet on him and by the next year I was able to get rid of the street pads and go to a regular leather pad. He took a record of 2:00⅖ that year and I sold him to go to Italy.

Here was a case in which there was no chance at all of a horse racing if the trainer hadn't done something extreme. I'm not afraid to do something like that if I think it will help my horse. I'm a charter member of the "light weight, short toe, simply shod" school of shoeing and balancing, but once in a while I'll fall out of that bed if I think it will help my horse.

The little leather and plastic pads we use today are very light compared to a street pad and lighter even than the X-ray pad which has been and still is a very popular one, although the demand for it seems to be dying out. The X-ray pad is a rubber pad with a leather backing to it and it will weigh from two to three ounces more than the leather pad. I remember an incident involving an X-ray pad that caused me a lot of discomfort at the time.

That was back in 1944 after Rupe Parker died and I had taken over the training of Adios and Scotland's Comet, among other of his horses. I did not develop either of those horses. Mr. Parker made them and I am very much in his debt because he was a truly great horseman and I was flattered that he asked me to train them when he became ill. After he died, I took them over.

This incident occurred at Cleveland that summer when Scotland's Comet made his first start wearing a quarter by 5/8ths flat shoe in front with a leather pad. I trained him in 2:05, last half in a minute, and he seemed sharp and all right.

When it came time to race, I got Sep Palin to drive the horse because I had The Colonel's Lady in the same stake. When I passed Scotland's Comet in the first turn he was on the pace and half running and I didn't see any more of him. That was the afternoon the barns burned down and that ended the racing at Cleveland. After the excitement died down, I went to see Sep and asked him about the horse. He said he didn't seem flat or balanced at all. I was worried and didn't know what to do.

Rube Armstrong, who had been Mr. Parker's second trainer, had come to work for me in the same capacity. I asked him about it and he told me Mr. Parker had always trained the horse in leather pads but had raced him in the X-ray pads. The next day I went to the blacksmith shop and told Jack Ball to shoe the horse the same way Mr. Parker had him. He did and a couple of weeks later Scotland's Comet won in 2:00 at Old Orchard, Maine, very handily.

The only difference in the two pads was that the X-ray pad weighed almost three ounces more and Scotland's Comet needed this extra weight in order to trot fully balanced. In addition, he wasn't 100% sound and the X-ray with its rubber surface was absorbing more of the sting when he trotted.

In training with the leather pad, Mr. Parker was trying to lighten the horse up because he felt, as I always did and still do, that any horse will trot a little faster with less weight. He was training him that way trying to get him used to the leather pad but hadn't been successful and always went to the X-ray for a race.

I suppose I could have gone to a heavier shoe with a wider web and accomplished the purpose of adding weight and in that way Scotland's Comet might have gone all right in a leather pad. But Mr. Parker had been doing very well with the X-ray pad and I wasn't about to stick my neck out and change it. When a great horseman has a horse set and trotting square and sound, I'm not going to say that I'm smarter than he is and start changing things around.

This story also emphasizes another point that young trainers should always keep in mind. You will recall that I had trained Scotland's Comet in 2:05 with the last half in a minute and that he acted fine for me. But a training mile isn't a race and never will be. A horse is usually relaxed when he is training, even if you are going a relatively fast mile. But it's a lot different in a race, principally because a horse knows he is competing and tries that much harder. That was the story with Scotland's Comet. He was relaxed while training but he got nervous and excited when he raced and under those circumstances needed just a little more weight in the bottom of his foot to help balance him. As I related earlier, the same thing applies to a horse that goes to his elbows. He might never do it in training and yet might never fail to do it in a race.

The other great horse I inherited from Mr. Parker was Adios and I suppose that if for no other reason than the historical significance of having trained the sire of Bret Hanover and many more of the greatest pacers our breed has known, I should offer some comment on him. He also makes a fitting subject to wind up my chapter.

As everyone knows, Mr. Parker developed Adios and raced him at two and three. I took him over in the summer of 1944 when he was a 4-year-old and raced him that year and the next.

Adios was a terrifically fast, slick-gaited horse and in the fall of his 4-year-old form I won two heats with him at Lexington in 1:58¼ to set the world's record. The following year I gave him his record of 1:57½ in a time trial at Du Quoin.

As a race horse, Adios had only two faults. He liked to ramble a little bit on the front end and if you couldn't make the top with him and had to duck in a hole, he would frequently grab hold and try to go on. Once he reached the top, he was fine and easy to control. I raced him in a Crit Davis overcheck bit without a chin strap so that I could control him a little better when these situations arose. That was a little severe but I always felt he needed it.

His only other fault was a well-known one. He was inclined at times to sulk and pull up near the end of the mile. I don't mean that Adios was faint-hearted or would become physically exhausted because when he wanted to be he was as game as any horse I ever drove. When I visited Mr. Parker in the hospital before he died, he went over this very carefully with me and said I should always be on the lookout for it. He said it was a habit Adios had developed and that when he was ready to stop he would and there wasn't much anybody could do about it. I found out that Mr. Parker was right.

Adios was not a shoeing or balancing problem in the normal sense because he did not require anything special to gait and balance him. His trouble was that he had chronic corns and, consequently I always raced him in a plain bar shoe in front with a pad.

(Incidentally, I consider a bar shoe a very, very good thing for any horse that will wear one. It gives more protection than an open heel shoe and if the horse can stand the little extra weight that the bar adds, I like to use it.)

We treated Adios constantly for those corns and would get them cleaned up in the winter. But when he got down around 2:10 they'd flare up and he'd get awfully pinchy. He had bearing on only about half his foot, the rest of it being frog.

I even built up the pads on him, putting leather on leather so that they were higher in the back of his foot to get pressure on his frog and keep him off his heel walls. The extra thicknesses of leather would be from the last nail hole back. If it hadn't been for that, I doubt very much that Adios would ever have gone on to get his record of 1:57½.

That pretty much winds up my contribution on the shoeing and balancing of trotters and pacers. I have been engaged in the business of trying to accomplish this for almost half a century, longer than that if you want to start counting from the time I began accompanying my father to the races and watching him train and drive.

I have seen about everything there is with respect to freak shoes and trick balancing techniques. I have tried a great many of these things myself but in the long run, short toe and light weight are the keys. If you can achieve balance by sticking to that formula, you have the game half-licked.

For my own part, I think I was probably born a century too soon. I am sure that if I could come back a hundred years from now I would find all the trotters trotting and all the pacers pacing and the trainer's role limited to that of conditioner, more like the present-day running horse trainers.

But for all of that, I wouldn't trade the troubles I've had for the thrills that harness racing has given me. It has been and continues to be the greatest sport of them all. I am very proud to have played a part in writing some of its illustrious history.

To modern harness racing fans, Frank Ervin is probably best known as the man who trained and drove the world champion harness horse, Bret Hanover, p, 1:53⅗. But within the harness racing fraternity, Bret Hanover is considered only the most recent, albeit perhaps the best, of the great trotting and pacing champions that have worn the Ervin brand over a period that stretches backward almost 50 years. Ervin was born in Pekin, Ill. on August 12, 1904, the son of a horse-training father. With a grandfather and two uncles also active in the sport, there was never any doubt as to the professional path he would follow. He began as a groom "at about the age of 10" and drove  his first race in 1920 when he was only 15. He spent the better part of the next 20 years sharpening his skills on the old Kansas-Oklahoma circuit by winning hundreds of races which, unfortunately have gone officially unrecorded. The Colonel's Lady and High Volo were his first two top horses and they were followed in rapid succession by the likes of Adios and Scotland's Comet, Good Time, Sampson Hanover, Impish, Sprite Rodney, and the Hambletonian winners, Kerry Way, Speedy Streak (whom he trained but did not drive) and Diller Hanover (whom he drove but did not train.) He operates a small but select public stable, has earned more than $4,000,000 and has been the leading Grand Circuit driver on two occasions and among the top five 11 times. He has driven more 2:00 miles than any other reinsman and with 106 to his credit is the only man with more than 100. He is a member of the Missouri Sports Hall of Fame and is the only man to win the *Horseman & Fair World's* Horseman of the Year award more than once, having gained that honor three times, in 1961, 1965 and 1966.

8

BITS, BOOTS and BRIDLES

JOSEPH C. O'BRIEN

I T is my earnest hope that the information I am about to set down will prove of value to aspiring harness horse trainers. Harness racing has been good to me from the moment I started helping my dad as a youngster some 40 years ago and if I can serve the sport I love so well by passing on some of the knowledge I have acquired, I feel it is only fitting and proper that I do so.

While there is a great deal more information and practical experience necessary before a man can really become a horse trainer, I firmly believe that anyone who can master the technical intricacies of bits, boots, bridles, and the other pieces of equipment covered in this chapter has met one of the basic challenges of the profession and can succeed. I am afraid that the man who cannot, will fail or, at best, will plod along through life as a second or third rate trainer.

To my way of thinking, bits, boots and bridles are a good deal like guns. In the hands of men who understand and appreciate them, they are the tools of a wonderful trade and, as such, can be used to help shape a successful career. But in the hands of people who understand little of either their nature or purpose they can, like guns, be classified as dangerous weapons and, improperly used, subject a horse to many difficult and trying moments.

The subjects I intend to discuss are vast, wide-ranging and complex. But there is a single thread that runs through the entire pattern. That thread is common sense which, in harness racing, can fittingly be described as "horse sense."

A trainer who will stop and think and use a little "horse sense" before embarking blindly on some false trail that will only complicate his problem has escaped the first pitfall that traps so many young horsemen today. The first step, perhaps, is to keep from going to extremes in both the rigging and shoeing of horses.

It is completely accurate to state that the less equipment a horse wears and the more simply he is rigged, the better it is for him and for the man who is training and driving him. All of us are looking for horses that wear an open bridle, a simple bit and no boots. Unfortunately, such horses are very few and far between.

So I want to say right at the outset that while it may be true that head poles and gaiting straps and shadow roles and Murphy blinds are unsightly and detract from the natural beauty of a trotter or pacer in full flight, it is equally true that properly used they do no harm and can accomplish a great deal of good.

If I am convinced that any or all of these things will improve the effective racing capacity of my horse, I will use them without hesitation. I suppose I admire beauty as much as the next man, but as a horse trainer I am concerned mainly with the proposition that my horse deliver 100% of his potential every time I race him.

I also want to mention at the outset one other thing that I will be referring to constantly and examining in greater detail as I go along. That is the importance of a horse holding his head perfectly straight in front of him and going absolutely straight between the shafts. There is no way I can over-emphasize the importance of this single factor.

A horse that is holding his head off to one side or has his hind end over against the sulky shaft is almost sure to hit himself someplace. It is literally impossible to shoe such a horse so that he will not hit himself. So it becomes the job of the horse trainer not only to diagnose the cause, but to provide an effective remedy.

Many times the cause is acute lameness and you have a major problem on your hands. But more often than not the cause is something less drastic, something a trainer can control. Perhaps the teeth need attention, the bit is too severe, the nose band too tight or the shadow roll too high. Maybe your horse is going crooked simply from habit or perhaps he is just a little lame and shows it going into the turns and nowhere else. All these things can and do occur and every one of them can be corrected or compensated for by an alert, diligent horse trainer using his eyes, his mind and a little "horse sense." Like I tell my assistant trainers sometimes, "You have to use something besides your doggone feet!"

I would like to suggest at the very beginning that if you have a horse that is pulling on one line or going sideways, the first thing you should do is to have a competent veterinarian examine

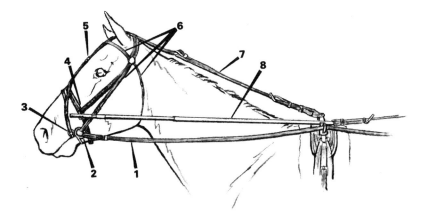

Fig. 39. This illustration indicates basic items of equipment as follows: (1) driving lines, (2) ring of the driving bit with driving lines and bridle buckled into it, (3) overcheck bit, (4) head halter, (5) front part of the check rein, (6) bridle (this is the basic open bridle), (7) back part of the check rein, and (8) head pole. The head pole is not standard equipment for all horses but is illustrated here as a supplement to the closeup views in Fig. 61.

his teeth. Very often this trouble will be caused by the bit pressing the cheek against a sharp tooth or a cap that hasn't come off and is setting up an irritation. If it develops that the horse's teeth are in good shape you can then proceed to check other possibilities, some of which I have mentioned and all of which I will discuss later in greater detail.

Having dispensed with these few generalities, I think the best way to begin is with a discussion of bits. There are two types of bits, the driving bit and the overcheck bit. Because it constitutes the primary link between horse and driver, let's consider the driving bit first.

The driving bit, which is usually made of metal and from 4¼ to 4¾ inches long, is attached to the end of the bridle and usually comes as a part of a regular set of harness. It slides into the horse's mouth, over his tongue, and has circular rings on each side that fall into place outside the mouth (Fig. 39) when the bit is properly positioned. The driving lines, or reins, are buckled into these rings on each side. They pass back through rings on the saddle, which are called terrets, and thence into the driver's hands.

The driving bit is the means of communication between driver and horse. By using the lines to exert pressure on the bit, or by releasing pressure from it, the driver relays his commands to the horse. All driving bits referred to in this chapter are illustrated in Fig. 40.

The secret of successful manipulation of the driving bit in the horse's mouth lies in having light hands. You must teach your horse to respond to the most delicate touch. If you fail in this respect, if you are heavy-handed and always applying undue pressure, your horse will soon come up with a sore mouth or a hard mouth and will be hard to hold back or control.

A horse with a sore mouth will automatically begin turning his head one way or the other to escape the constant pressure against the sore spot. This upsets his natural balance and normal way of going. The next thing you know, your horse is going crooked or bad-gaited and begins to interfere. This path leads to lameness and the possible loss of a horse from your racing stable.

A hard-mouthed horse, one whose mouth has become toughened through constant pressure being applied by a heavy-handed driver, not only is more difficult to control but he simply will not respond to your instantaneous commands as relayed through the lines. Thus he becomes an inferior racing proposition and detracts from his earning capacity as well as yours.

You cannot teach a man to be light-handed. It is a talent he is born with and a driver either has it or he doesn't have it. But even light-handed drivers will come up with sore-mouthed horses. This is something a good trainer can and should control. Much of it lies in the choice of a bit.

It is very, very important that the driving bit be exactly the right type for the horse and that it fit perfectly. Different horses require different types of bits and thus a certain amount of experimentation is necessary.

I think some trainers have a tendency to use too severe a bit. I like to use as easy a bit as a horse will wear without taking too much hold. I know all trainers feel the same way but I think that where some of them go wrong is that as soon as a horse begins to take a little hold they immediately think a more severe bit is required and make a change.

I have found that the more severe bit you put on such a horse the more he is inclined to pull and that many times you are just compounding your problem. The severe bit hurts him and he starts fighting it and the more he fights it the more he pulls. It is an endless circle and such horses have a tendency to get worse instead of better.

I think that if you put the simplest bit you can in a horse's mouth, one that doesn't hurt his mouth at all, the better off you are in the long run. I have found that even pullers, when you start racing them, will gradually get better if there's nothing hurting them. So my advice on this score is for a young trainer to resist the impulse to go to more severe bit just because a horse starts to pull a little. Work with him, gently and patiently. You will find that many such horses will respond to this patience and learn to go in a mild bit.

Of course, if a pulling horse or any other horse is hurting, that is an entirely different story. A hurting horse will usually pull. It's just his nature to set his lower jaw against the bit in an effort to get away from the pain. Maybe one hind leg is hurting him someplace and every time he takes a step he feels a twinge of pain. Well, if you hit him with the whip he also feels a twinge of pain and very soon he begins to associate these twinges with the driver. As a result, he tries to go faster, pulls harder and acts worse. It is my opinion that most pullers are made, not born.

The standard driving bit that comes with every set of harness is a snaffle bit. A snaffle bit (Fig. 40-3) has a joint or hinge in the center. It is made of metal and is sometimes covered with leather or rubber. I find that this standard bit is usually too wide for most horses. It tends to stick out one side of the mouth or the other. A large percentage of horses on the race track are wearing bits that are too wide for them. If they take hold of one line just a trifle, the bit pulls through the mouth about an inch or so and the kind of pressure that will lead to a sore mouth or sore cheek begins to build up. This is especially true of a snaffle bit where the joint sometimes tends to pull over against one cheek instead of being in the center of the mouth. This will eventually result in a horse going with his head to one side and you are bound to come up with a sore-mouthed horse.

I have found that a bit measuring 4¼ to 4½ inches fits most small and medium-sized horses much better than the standard

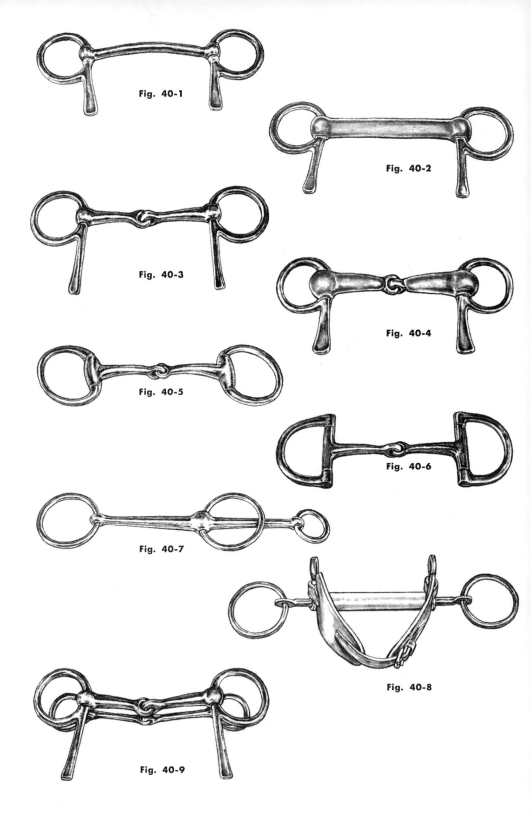

Fig. 40-1

Fig. 40-2

Fig. 40-3

Fig. 40-4

Fig. 40-5

Fig. 40-6

Fig. 40-7

Fig. 40-8

Fig. 40-9

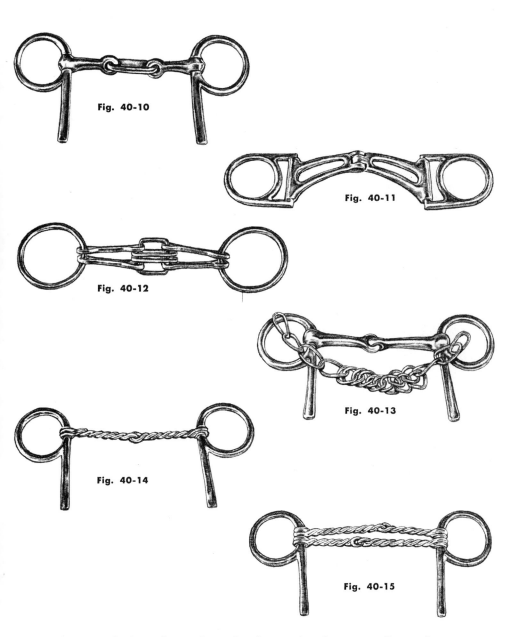

Fig. 40. The basic driving bits referred to in this chapter are illustrated as follows: Fig. 40–1, standard, unjointed driving bit; Fig. 40–2, unjointed bit with rubber covered mouth piece; Fig. 40–3, standard snaffle bit; Fig. 40–4, rubber-covered snaffle bit; Fig. 40–5, barrel-mouth bit; Fig. 40–6, D-ring bit; Fig. 40–7, sidelining bit; Fig. 40-8, slip-mouth sidelining bit; Fig. 40–9, jointed overcheck bit as used in conjunction with snaffle bit; Fig. 40–10, Dr. Bristol bit; Fig. 40–11, Crescendo bit; Fig. 40–12, Simpson bit; Fig. 40–13, snaffle bit with chain link; Fig. 40–14, single wire bit; Fig. 40–15, double wire bit.

4¾-inch bit. I think every horse trainer should make absolutely certain that the bit fits perfectly because an improperly fitted bit is one of the major sources of trouble with horses that are not going absolutely straight.

It is not difficult to determine whether a bit fits properly. Place the bit in the horse's mouth and then stand at his head and see if you can pull the bit either to the left or right so that it sticks out the side of the mouth. If you can do this, it doesn't fit and you need a shorter bit. By the same token, the rings should not be pressing hard against the cheeks because this indicates that the bit is too short. With a properly fitted bit, the rings lay comfortably against the cheek and are neither too snug nor too loose.

There are many kinds of driving bits and they have many uses. There are two basic bits. One is the straight, unjointed bit which is nothing more than a plain, round piece of steel stretching from ring to ring in the horse's mouth (Fig. 40-1). The other is a plain snaffle bit which, as I have previously explained, is the same as a straight bit except that it has a joint in the center permitting it to hinge or bend when the driver applies pressure on the lines.

Both the plain bit and the snaffle bit may be covered with leather or rubber (Figs. 40-2 and 40-4) to make them less severe on a horse's mouth. There are also bits of the same type and style that are wholly rubber or leather and have no metal in them at all, except a small chain in the center for strength. In all these bits there are a number of variations as to size and shape.

I use a plain snaffle bit more than anything else. Because it is jointed, it is a more flexible bit and enables me to exercise just a little more control over a horse than I can with an unjointed bit. A snaffle bit, incidentally, is the oldest known to men and was preferred by the ancient Greeks who were the first great horsemen in history.

While I prefer a bit to be shorter from ring to ring, I prefer one with a comparatively larger diameter, especially out towards the rings where the pressure is applied. The type of bit I like best is what is called a barrel-mouth bit (Fig. 40-5). This is a bit that is smaller in diameter at the center, near the joint, gradually tapering out to a larger diameter, with barrel-shaped cheek

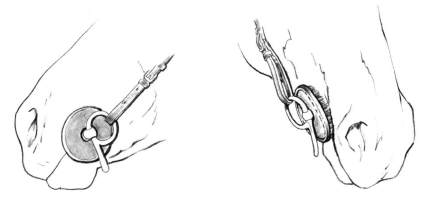

Fig. 41 Rubber bit guards, left, are sometimes used on a tender-mouthed horse to help prevent the bit from pinching the cheek. Some trainers use a bit burr, right, a leather disc with stiff bristles on it, to help encourage a horse to keep his head straight. The author has never found a horse that he helped by using a bit burr.

pieces into which the rings fit. Thus, all the surface touching the horse's cheeks is smooth and cannot pinch. The diameter at the ring ends will be about five-eighths of an inch. I think this type of bit is real comfortable on a horse because of the smoother surface at the cheeks. Rubber bit guards (Fig. 41) can be used on any snaffle bit and help make it more comfortable on a colt's cheeks.

I like the barrel-mouth bit much better than the D-ring bit (Figs. 40-6 and 42) which is also used quite a lot on trotters and pacers. This bit is so named because the rings are shaped like the letter D. It was designed especially for running horses and it has been my experience that it is not a satisfactory bit for harness horses because the angle of the lines pulling on the bit is different than when it is used with a runner. Our lines pull straight back and go through a terret so the pressure on the bit is basically a straight-line pressure (Fig. 39). But a jockey on a horse's back is pulling up on the bit and is exerting pressure at a different angle. The D-ring bit works fine this way but I have found that it pulls at the wrong angle on a Standardbred. For this reason, I like the barrel-mouth bit much better.

I have said that I prefer a snaffle bit, but every once in a while you will run across a horse that is better off with an unjointed bit (Fig. 40-1). The snaffle bit is hinged and tends to press inward on either side of the lower jaw. The harder a horse pulls the

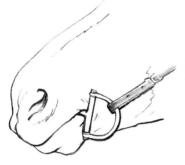

Fig. 42. The author does not recommend use of a D-ring bit, illustrated here, with trotters and pacers. It is his contention that while this bit is a good one for running horses it pulls at the wrong angle on harness horses.

more pressure is exerted. Some horses resent this pinching action and they are better off with a straight bit.

If your horse seems to be pulling on one line a little or shaking his head or holding his head to one side, it might be worthwhile to try him with a straight bit. You can use either a straight metal bit or one that is covered with leather or rubber, depending on how tender your horse's mouth is. I have found that this will sometimes work quite well with a horse that is fighting the pinching action of a snaffle bit.

Another thing that will pinch a horse's cheek and cause him to start pulling on one line and holding his head crooked, is an improperly fitted head halter (Fig. 43). The basic use of a head halter is to keep a horse's mouth closed when he is racing. This is important because a horse is difficult to steer and control when his mouth is open.

The nose band of a standard head halter fits around the horse's muzzle above the bit. It buckles under the jaw and, naturally, is pulled snug to keep the horse's mouth closed. (Incidentally, for purposes of proper identification, a nose *band* encircles the muzzle while a nose *strap* simply goes over the nose and not all the way around the muzzle.)

If the nose band on a head halter isn't up high enough, you run the danger of having it interfere with the action of your driving bit. That is, when you pull back on the bit you pull the cheeks back at the corner of the mouth and they will pinch painfully against the nose band.

A horse has a normal and predictable reaction to this. It hurts him and he gets angry and fights it. Usually one side will begin to hurt before the other and the horse will pull harder on one line in fighting the pain.

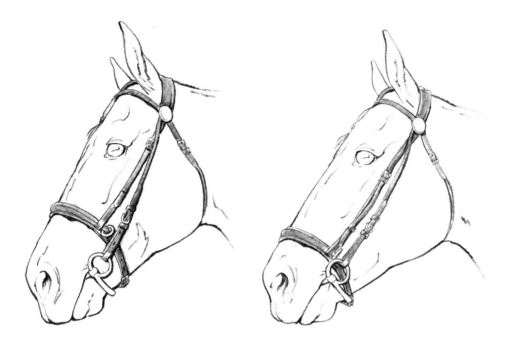

Fig. 43. Properly and improperly fitted head halters are illustrated. The nose band of the properly-fitted halter, left, is up high enough so that it will not interfere with the action of the driving bit when the driver pulls on the lines. In the illustration at the right, the nose band is too low and the horse's cheeks will be pinched against it on both sides when the driver pulls on the lines.

There is also a nose band that fits over the nose similar to a regular head halter (Fig. 44) except that it goes around below the bit instead of above and buckles under the chin. Instead of having the regular adjustable strap that is fastened to the nose band of the head halter on either side and goes over the head behind the ears, this nose band has a strap going from the center of the band, straight up between the horse's ears like a shadow roll strap, to the top or crown of the bridle where there is a buckle into which it is fastened and adjusted as to height. The part I don't like about this type of nose band is that if it is adjusted high enough to be well above the nostrils and tight enough to keep the horse's mouth shut it is inclined to pull the bridle forward on the top of the head. It is also inclined to slip down low enough to interfere with the horse's breathing by pressing on the nostrils.

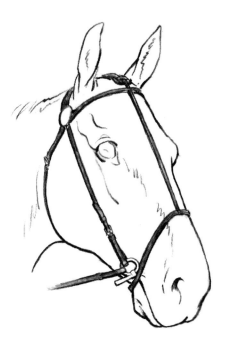

Fig. 44. A nose band with a vertical strap as illustrated here is sometimes used instead of a head halter. The author's objection to it is that if it is adjusted high enough to clear the nostrils and tight enough to keep the horse's mouth shut, it is inclined to pull the bridle forward at the top of the head.

Several years ago I ran across a little polo halter from England that buckles below the bit and I have found that this halter (Fig. 45), with a few minor changes to suit our use, works perfectly on most horses and does not interfere with the fit of the bridle. I find that it has better leverage to keep a horse's mouth shut and, at the same time, there is never any danger of the cheeks being pinched. This halter is on the market and I think it is much superior to the ordinary head halter and recommend its use. I have small rings attached on either side and find that a head pole works very well with this type nose band.

Actually it works on the same principle as the Figure 8 halter (Fig. 46) which also goes below the bit and buckles under the chin. But the Figure 8 crosses over the nose, passes under the eyes and buckles under the jaw, with a strap attached to this part on either side and buckling over the head back of the ears.

The Figure 8 is a good halter but the one I designed is much neater and easier to use. The Figure 8 is more cumbersome, has a lot of excess leather and fastens up around the jaw where it certainly can't do any good because you don't have any leverage up there to keep a horse's mouth closed. If you use either the Figure 8 halter or the little halter I designed, you won't have any trouble with crooked heads caused by pinched cheeks.

Getting back to driving bits, I think the nicest thing you can use to start a yearling is a little leather-covered snaffle bit that buckles under the chin (Fig. 47). This comes in a number of sizes and has leather cheek pieces that help hold it in place. Be especially careful if you are starting with a small colt that you have a small bit that fits him. Again, you do not want any slack in the bit when you stand in front of the horse and try to move the bit from side to side.

One of the reasons this type of bit is so nice for colts is that a colt has a tendency to pull on one line or the other until he learns to steer. A regular bit would be pulling back and forth through his mouth but this bit will not, if you fit it in his mouth properly to begin with, because it buckles under the chin and has larger cheek pieces. The Frisco June is similar except that it has a leather chin strap attached which makes it an especially comfortable bit for most colts. The only advantage to the former is that you can use either a chin strap or a check bit whereas

Fig. 45. The author's choice among head halters is one he redesigned for use with trotters and pacers from an English polo halter. It buckles below the bit and thus not only provides additional leverage to keep the horse's mouth closed (which is the basic purpose of any head halter) but also relieves the danger of the cheeks being pinched. Proper adjustment of this halter is illustrated at the left. At the right, the halter is improperly adjusted above the bit.

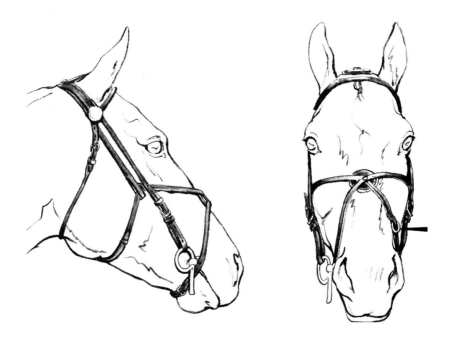

Fig. 46. The Figure 8 head halter, front and side views of which are illustrated, is a good one, but in the author's opinion is much more cumbersome and does not keep the horse's mouth closed as well as the head halter illustrated in Fig 45. The Figure 8 halter does not come with a ring into which a head pole may be fastened and thus some trainers find it necessary to use a standard head halter with a ring on it in addition to the Figure 8 if their horse wears a head pole. To avoid using two head halters in such cases, the author has a ring (arrow) sewn into the Figure 8.

with the Frisco June you have no choice. Another bit that is very often used in breaking colts, or with tender-mouthed horses, is the Stalker bit which comes in a number of styles, one of which is illustrated in Fig. 47. I seldom use this bit on colts because I have found that it is inclined to rub against and irritate a colt's cheeks. Another bit that will not slide through a colt's mouth and which I can recommend is the full cheek bit also illustrated in Fig. 47.

You have to remember, too, that when you are breaking a colt you don't want a head halter on him because he will fight it— at least I don't want one and I don't think any trainer should. Without a head halter, the colt's mouth may come open a little if he becomes scared or frightened, as a colt will occasionally, and you have to take hold of him. In a case like this, a normal bit would either pull through the colt's mouth or pull harshly against one cheek. Of course, you want to avoid this and I find that the leather covered snaffle bit which buckles under the

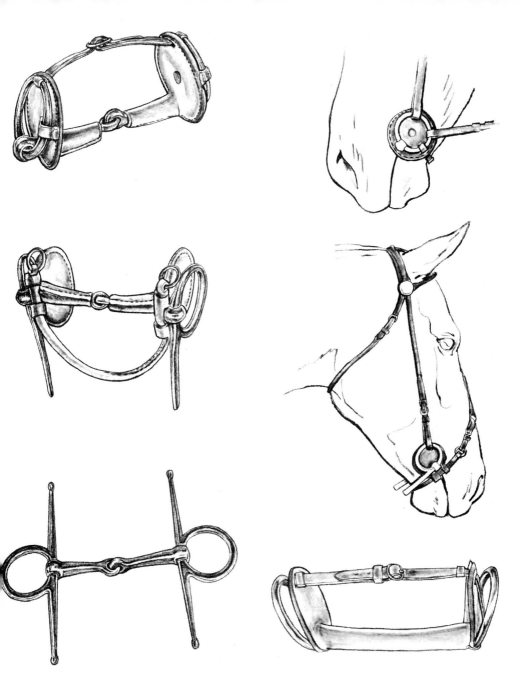

Fig. 47. The basic colt-breaking bits are illustrated. The author prefers the little leather-covered snaffle bit with leather cheek pieces illustrated by itself, top left, and on the horse, top right. The Frisco June bit, center left and right, comes with a chin strap and is a good bit for colts. However, either a chin strap or a check bit may be used with the bit illustrated at the top while the Frisco June can be used only with the chin strap. Thus, it is not quite as versatile. Two other types of colt bits are the full cheek snaffle bit, lower left, which the author recommends and the stalker bit, lower right, which he does not like because it is inclined to rub against and irritate a colt's cheeks.

chin, the Frisco June with the chin strap attached or the full cheek bit do the job real well.

The catalogs are full of different types of driving bits for different purposes. For instance, if a horse is going crooked, you may want to use a side-lining bit. There are a number of such bits, the most prominent being the one which has an extension, a steel bar from two to four inches in length and a quarter of an inch in diameter, extending straight out on one side of the bit (Figs. 40-7 and 48).

The driving line buckles into a ring at the end of this bar and the sideward extension gives you more leverage when you pull the line on that side. If the horse was pulling on the left line for instance, the extension would be on the left side of the bit giving you more leverage on the left line to enable you to straighten his head up.

Some horses, especially those that are hurting a little, will bear in on the turns and out in the stretches. A slip-mouth side-lining bit (Figs. 40-8 and 48) is ideal for such horses. This consists of a plain leather-covered bit which fits in the mouth like any other and buckles under the chin. But the center of this bit is hollow and a bar runs through it and out each side. The lines are fastened into a ring at each end of the bar.

When a horse goes into a turn and starts bearing in, that is, carrying his body in toward the rail, and putting pressure on your right line, the bit slides through and extends outward on the right side giving you the leverage you need on that line. The same holds true on the left side if the horse is bearing out and pulling on the left line.

This might be as good a place as any to explain briefly what I mean when I talk about a horse bearing in and bearing out.

If a horse is perfectly sound and you have him perfectly rigged, he will usually go with his head straight in front of him and with his hind end right in the center of the shafts. But if he is hurting a little he will favor that area and will not go absolutely straight.

This is most noticeable with a horse that is going into a turn on a half mile track and maybe is a little off in the right knee, ankle or pastern. When a horse goes into a turn, the left legs are acting more or less as pivot legs and the pressure is put on the right legs which, because of the angle of the turn and the bank of the track, are pushing harder against the track surface

Fig. 48. Three of the more popular types of sidelining bits are illustrated. At the left, is a sidelining bit with an extension on each side. This is a good bit for a horse that bears in during one stage of the race or workout and out at another since it provides for leverage on either side. In the center, is the slip-mouth sidelining bit which is used with the same type of horse. The difference in the bits is that when the horse pulls on either line with the slip mouth bit (also shown in Fig. 40–8), a bar slides through the hollow part of the bit to the proper side and all the leverage is available on the side where it is most needed. At the right is the basic sidelining bit (also shown in Fig. 40–7) for a horse that pulls on one side only. The horse in the illustration is pulling on the right line and thus the extension is on the right side. If he was pulling on the left line, the same bit would be turned around so that the extension was on the left side.

than the left legs. In other words, he is bracing himself and getting his driving power more from the right legs as he goes around a turn.

Because he is not really lame and is just hurting a little, this is not noticeable and he is not showing it when he goes straight with his weight evenly distributed on all legs. But when he puts that extra pressure on the right legs in a turn it hurts him and he wants to get away from it.

He does this by bearing in, or bearing to the left to get away from the pain which is in his right leg. In order to compensate for this, the driver must put extra pressure on the right line. This pulls the horse's head around to the right and he is going crooked. In order to help straighten his head up, the trainer may have a head pole or Murphy Blind on the left side. It is because of this tendency for most horses to bear in on the turns that you will find head poles and Murphy Blinds on the left side on half mile tracks.

When you have a horse that is going around the turns good and bearing out, or trying to go to the right, in the stretches, it is almost a sure sign that he is hurting somewhere on the left side. The reason he is taking the turns good is that the pressure on the turns is more on the right legs and the pain on the left side is eased as a result. But then when he comes to a straight-away, the pressure is equally distributed and the pain returns and he bears to the right, or outward, to escape it.

The possibility of interference is also increased if you have a horse that is bearing in on the turns. With his body going to the left and his head being pulled around to the right, any horse is more apt to hit a knee and a trotter more likely to hit his shins.

In light of this, I cannot emphasize too strongly the importance of a comfortable bit in helping to keep a horse's head straight. The head must be straight in order for you to extract the maximum potential from your horse whether that potential is a mile in 2:15 or one in 1:55. And even great horses vary widely in the type of bits they require.

Scott Frost, for example, was a perfect race horse and wore nothing but a regular snaffle bit and chin strap. He always went straight. But Sunbelle, who was one of the fastest mares I ever sat behind, was a real problem. She'd bear in on the turns and out in the stretches and was quite difficult to control at times. I found that the slip-mouth side-lining bit worked perfectly on her. Without it I didn't have much control of her, but with it she drove straight and was all right. To make it more comfortable, I covered the mouth piece with elastoplast, a type of spongy material that sticks to itself and gives the bit soft padding.

Aside from horses that turn their heads and pull on one line, the principal problem with driving bits is caused by horses that take hold of the bit and pull. These are horses that want to go more than you want them to and you must slow them down in order to rate them and make them more manageable.

Fig. 49. One of the first things the author will do with a horse that is taking a little hold is to use a jointed overcheck bit in conjunction with the driving bit. If this combination of bits is being used, the important thing to remember is that while the driving lines (A) are buckled into both the driving bit and the jointed overcheck bit (or "minnie bit" as it is sometimes called), the bridle (B) should be buckled into the driving bit only. Some trainers make the mistake of also buckling the bridle into both bits. This combination is also illustrated in Fig. 40–9.

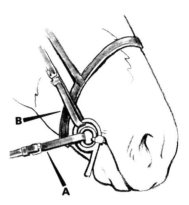

But before I get into that I want to cover a technical point I think might be of interest. In the preceding paragraph, I mentioned horses that "take hold of the bit . . ." Because it is a common expression and all horsemen will know what I mean, I have used it there and probably will elsewhere in this chapter. But actually, horses simply do not take the bit in their teeth and bite down on it as some people seem to think.

The truth is that when a horse is pulling hard, which is when he is most likely to be described as "having the bit in his teeth", he usually has his mouth open. What is actually happening is that the horse has set his lower jaw and when the driver pulls on the bit he is pulling it downward against the teeth in the lower jaw. The teeth in the upper jaw aren't in contact with the bit at all and thus the horse neither has a hold of the bit nor is he biting on it.

Returning now to "pullers", I usually go slowly with such horses and try to get them to race in a normal, mild bit, such as a plain bit or a snaffle. I would much rather take a lot of extra time in an effort to achieve this goal. But if I can't, if they still insist on pulling more than they should, then I will resort to a more severe driving bit. But I only do so when I am absolutely convinced there is no other course.

The first thing I will do is to go to a jointed overcheck bit (or "minnie bit" as it sometimes called) (Figs. 40-9 and 49) and use it in conjunction with the driving bit. I don't know why this bit is called an overcheck bit because it is never used as such. Its only use as far as I am concerned is in conjunction with a driving bit on horses that have a tendency to pull. It isn't as comfortable in the mouth as a plain bit and horses won't pull as hard against it. When I use this bit, I buckle only the lines into the "minnie" bit and not the bridle, the lines, of course, buckling into both the main driving bit and the "minnie" bit. I've had several horses that this bit worked well on.

A Dr. Bristol bit (Fig. 40-10) would probably be my next choice for a horse that was taking a little hold. This bit is much like the plain snaffle except that it has two joints instead of one. A snaffle bit is jointed in the center. The Dr. Bristol has two joints which link to a little plate about an inch and a half in length and a half inch in width and which lies flat in the center of the mouth. Because of the link in the center, the mouthpieces on either side exert pressure at a different angle and give the driver a little more leverage without hurting the horse's mouth. In addition, the Dr. Bristol bit is very good for horses that have a tendency to loll their tongues about in their mouths and start playing with the bit that way.

Another driving bit I have used with "pullers" is the Crescendo (Fig. 40-11). There are different types but the only one with which I have had any success is the one that is jointed like the snaffle with the part of the bit that goes through the mouth made like a half moon with a joint in the center. It is helpful on some horses that pull on one line and because of its shape a horse has trouble setting his jaw against it and thus is less likely to pull while wearing one. It also helps to keep him from getting his tongue over the bit.

Another bit that I have used with much success on certain horses, especially "pullers," is the Simpson bit (Fig. 40-12). This bit consists of several square links joined together and is especially good on a dry-mouthed horse or one that has little or no saliva, making him what is known as a "dead-mouthed" horse. It is also very good to keep a horse from "tongue lolling," that is, rolling his tongue around in his mouth and sometimes getting it over the bit.

Any bit with moving parts, such as the Simpson bit, has a natural tendency to create saliva in a horse's mouth. You can feel the difference when you are driving a horse that has plenty of saliva. The bit is more "alive" and works better and at the same time the horse can't set his lower jaw against it, so you are able to exercise greater control over him.

A very simple thing that is quite effective on some "pullers" that are "dead-mouthed" or "dry-mouthed" is a little piece of chain such as a curb chain tied to each side of the driving bit and hanging loosely in the mouth (Fig. 40-13). The horse will automatically play with the chain with his tongue and increase the saliva in his mouth.

The next step is a wire bit. As a rule, I do not like a wire bit and will use one only when absolutely necessary. But sometimes a horse takes so much hold that you must go to a real severe bit. Wire bits consist of one or more strands of wire in the mouth, running from ring to ring, and each name bit usually has a specific innovation which makes it different from the other wire bits. But they all have the same purpose. They exert quite a lot of pressure on the horse's mouth and tend to render him more tractable and easier to drive.

Twisted wire bits come in two basic styles. The single twisted wire bit (Fig. 40-14) consists of two strands of wire twisted to form a single mouthpiece and jointed in the center. The wire itself is not flexible and when you take hold of the lines the bit hinges at the joint just as the snaffle does and pulls against the corner of the horse's mouth. Naturally, a horse will not pull as hard against this type of bit as he will against a conventional bit.

Even more severe is the double twisted wire bit (Fig. 40-15) which consists of two wire mouthpieces instead of one. However, the joints in these two strands are off center. The joint in one strand is a half inch to the left of center and the joint in the other is a half inch to the right. This bit works like a pair of scissors, in fact we used to call it the "scissor bit." The pressure it exerts is just about twice as much as the single wire bit. It is a maximum control bit for a pulling horse.

Needless to say, such bits can be and are very effective on horses that pull. At the same time, I have found that wire bits are very severe and will usually make a horse's mouth sore. I do not think wire bits should be used day after day. They should be changed off every once in a while for a less severe bit. If you keep training and racing a horse in a wire bit, you are almost bound to come up with a sore-mouthed horse. So if you have to use a wire bit, try to use it only when racing. In other words, use it only when absolutely necessary.

One other piece of equipment you can use on a pulling horse is a lip cord (Fig. 50). I have used lip cords in certain cases and have had good results.

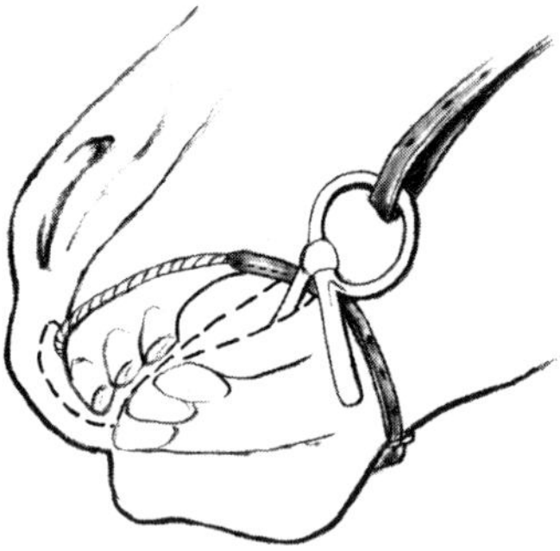

Fig. 50. A lip cord is sometimes used as a control device with a horse that is pulling. The lip cord goes over the gums beneath the upper lip and is buckled beneath the chin as illustrated.

A lip cord is a round cord that goes over the gums beneath the upper lip. The two ends of the cord go behind the driving bit on each side of the mouth and are then brought out and buckled down under the chin.

The first thing to be careful of is that you don't have the cord too small or too hard. I don't like a small cord because it tends to bite into the gums and this is not the purpose of the lip cord. I have seen lip cords that bit into the gums causing them to bleed. This is very severe on a horse and should be avoided. I don't recall that I ever raced a horse with a lip cord that even so much as broke the skin.

When the lip cord is adjusted properly and you pull back on the bit, the bit is pulling against the cord and the cord, in turn, is exerting pressure on the gums. There is a certain nerve in this area and when the cord presses against this nerve it tends to have a quieting effect on the horse. It will often make a horse that is inclined to pull very hard come right back to you and drive quite easily. You will find that you can steer and control the horse much better.

But the most important thing regarding a lip cord is to remember that you must be very light-handed when you are driving a horse that is wearing one. You can still pull hard, because the direct pull will not injure the horse. What you don't want to do is to jerk on one line quickly because that would tend to pull the cord across the gums and make the horse's mouth bleed. If you will remember to be light-handed and to steer as gently as possible, a lip cord can really be used to great advantage at times.

Shadow Wave was a horse that wore a lip cord from time to time. Normally he wore the Simpson bit, but every once in a while he would indicate to me that this wasn't quite enough. On these occasions I would substitute a regular snaffle bit and a lip cord. The results always proved satisfactory and never caused the horse the slightest discomfort.

With a lip cord you can exert every ounce of direct pressure that is at your command and you won't hurt your horse. But be very careful about snatching him in and out. What might appear to you to be a very slight sideward pressure could feel more severe to the horse.

There is one other piece of equipment that I should probably discuss with relation to bits and that is a bit burr. A bit burr (Fig. 41) is a round leather disk made either of bristles which are about a half inch long or metal points, such as rivets. The idea is that if a horse is pulling on one line, you can slip the burr over the bit so that the bristles press against the horse's cheek on the opposite side encouraging him to keep his head straight. Personally, I have never found a horse yet that was helped by using a bit burr, but I know that a lot of trainers do use them and I have to think that they must have had success with them or they wouldn't still be doing it.

From driving bits, we will proceed in our discussion to the subject of overcheck bits. First you must understand what an overcheck bit is and why one is necessary.

The overcheck itself, or check rein, as it is sometimes called, is a strip of leather (Fig. 39) that runs from the saddle in the middle of the horse's back up over the horse's neck where it divides into two straps. Each strap goes through a separate loop provided for it on the headpiece of the bridle between the ears, and then runs down the front of the face and fastens to each side of the check bit or chin strap.

If a horse would trot or pace with his head held at all times in exactly the position you wanted it, there would no necessity for either an overcheck or an overcheck bit. As a matter of fact, there is an occasional horse that will race in this manner and he does not wear an overcheck. But they are so rare that for all practical purposes we may assume that all horses require an overcheck.

The overcheck sets a horse's head at a certain pre-determined height and he is unable to get it any lower. The set of the horse's head is regulated by adjusting the length of the check which can be extended or shortened as the trainer desires.

The angle at which a horse holds his head while racing is very important. The head must not be either too high or too low. If it is too high to suit a particular horse, he may be unable to set himself and give his best effort. If it is too low, he may duck his head and become difficult to control and may sometimes impair his breathing by tucking his chin in and shutting off his wind. This is generally referred to as "choking down," although choking down can also be caused by a horse swallowing his tongue.

The chin strap or overcheck bit completes the overcheck unit. The chin strap is a leather strap that fastens to the two ends of the overcheck on each side of the horse's mouth and runs under his chin. I particularly like a chin strap, especially on colts and tender-mouthed horses as long as they do not require a more severe device to prevent them from ducking their heads or leaning too hard on the check. Scott Frost was one horse that wore nothing but a chin strap throughout his racing career.

There are two types of chin straps. The one I am writing about here is intended for use as a chin strap only and is designed differently than the other whose primary use is in conjunction with an overcheck bit of some kind.

The type that is used as a chin strap only (Fig. 51, left) has a little ring at each end into which the overcheck is buckled. These usually come with a strap that runs from the center at the bottom up beneath the jaw. This strap has a loop in the end and the throat latch passes through this loop to hold the chin strap in place and keep it from falling out when the check is loose.

The other type of chin strap (Fig. 51, right) has a little strap and buckle on each side and, as I said, is used in conjunction with a particular type of overcheck bit whose function is improved

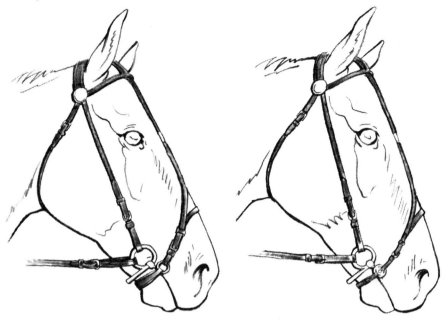

Fig. 51. The two basic types of chin straps are illustrated. At the left is the type used instead of an overcheck bit. It is recommended for use with colts and tender-mouthed horses that do not require anything more severe to keep them from ducking their heads or leaning too hard into the overcheck. Scott Frost raced this way. The other type of chin strap, right, is worn in conjunction with overcheck bits of one type or another and this combination of overcheck bit and chin strap is often very useful in helping to keep a horse's mouth closed. A Speedway overcheck bit, shown in this illustration and by itself in Fig. 52–2, is often used in conjunction with this type of chin strap since the Speedway comes with a little slot on each side designed to accommodate a chin strap.

through the use of a chin strap.

Very often, however, a chin strap will not restrain a horse sufficiently. Many times a horse will start leaning too hard into a chin strap and you will have to make a further adjustment. The next step is a plain overcheck bit.

Before you do that, however, you should be absolutely certain in your own mind that the chin strap will not do the job. I feel the same way about this as I do about advancing to severe driving bits. Don't go on to anything more severe until you are positive it is necessary. Severe driving bits and overcheck bits create problems of their own and the more mild a device you can use the better off you are.

The basic overcheck bit is a straight piece of metal (Fig. 52-1) similar to a straight unjointed driving bit except much smaller. A bit like this comes with most sets of harness. It goes in the horse's mouth along with the driving bit (Fig. 39) and as the horse tends to lower his head in the check, this little bit, held in place by the check rein to which it is fastened, prevents him from lowering his head beyond a predetermined point.

Thus, the purpose of the overcheck bit is as simple as that. It forces the horse to hold his head in the position the trainer has determined in advance is the proper one. The adjustment of the check rein sets that position and the overcheck bit prevents the horse from getting his head any lower.

A chin strap can be used in conjunction with a regular check bit and in some cases this combination is very useful in helping to keep a horse's mouth closed. A lot of horses won't need a head halter if a trainer is using a chin strap-check bit combination. A chin strap can be used with any check bit but it is a little simpler to use with a Speedway overcheck bit (Figs. 52-2 and 51, right) which is especially designed to accommodate a chin strap in that it has a little slot into which the chin strap can be buckled. If you are going to use a chin strap with a check bit, the unit will probably fit the horse's mouth better if you use the Speedway bit.

All that is fine, but what of the horse that neither the chin strap, the ordinary check bit, nor the combination of the two will hold? One that persists in hogging down into the check despite these devices.

The answer lies in using a more severe check bit and, just as with driving bits, there is a wide range and assortment. All serve the same basic purpose and each is designed to meet the problem in a slightly different way.

Some of these bits are named after the horses that wore them or the men who invented them. They carry names like Crit Davis, Crabb, Hutton, Raymond, McKerron and Burch. There are many others but these are a few I have used and that I will discuss here.

From a straight overcheck bit or the overcheck bit-chin strap combination, I usually go to a Burch bit (Fig. 52-3). It is good for a horse that needs a little more than a normal overcheck bit but that still doesn't require any additional leverage to hold

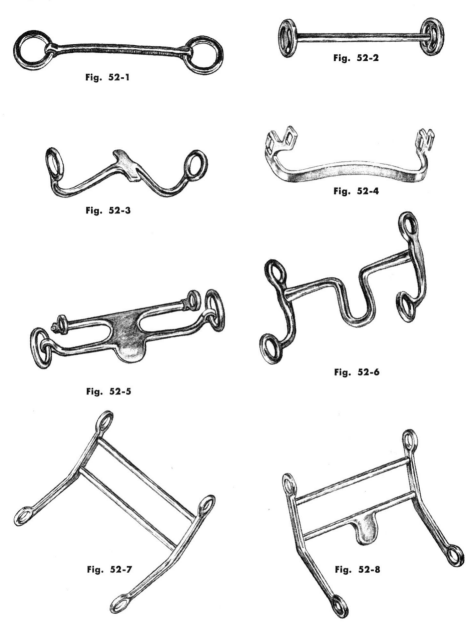

Fig. 52. These are various types of overcheck bits referred to in the text: Fig. 52–1, plain, standard overcheck bit; Fig. 52–2, Speedway; Fig. 52–3, Burch; Fig. 52–4, Hutton; Fig. 52–5, McKerron; Fig. 52–6, Crit Davis; Fig. 52–7, Crabb; and Fig. 52–8, Crabb with spoon. Some of these bits are also illustrated in Fig. 54.

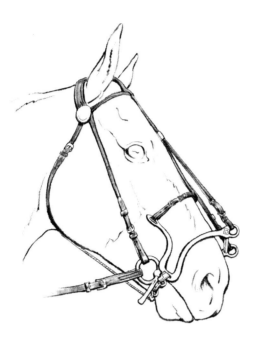

Fig. 53. The Raymond overcheck (it is not called an overcheck bit because there is no bit in the horse's mouth) is a clumsy looking device but is highly recommended by the author who points out that it is especially good with horses that tend to be soremouthed. The Raymond may be used with either a chin strap or, as illustrated, a curb chain.

his head up. The Burch bit is similar to the standard overcheck bit except that it curves upward in the middle and has a little horizontal bar right in the center of the bit. When a horse leans down into a Burch bit, this little bar presses up against the roof of his mouth and the horse tends to relax and move his head back to the normal position. It is a good check bit, but it has no leverage to hold a horse's head up. If you require leverage you must go to another type.

The one I like best of these is the Raymond Leverage. You will notice that I didn't call it an overcheck bit because it isn't. With a Raymond, the only bit in the horse's mouth is the driving bit.

The Raymond is a rather clumsy looking device (Fig. 53), but it does its job well and that is all that really matters to me. The Raymond comes down on each side of the horse's mouth and the steel on each side is shaped roughly like the letter "V" with the lower end of the letter rounded and the upper ends curving outward. On each side, the bottom end of the "V" lays just above and ahead of the driving bit. A strap connects these two ends beneath the chin. The lateral end of the "V" curves up alongside the horse's cheek and another strap goes over the nose connecting these two ends. The other end of the "V" extends upward and forward above the horse's nose about three inches. The ends of the check reins are connected to these two ends of the "V".

When a horse leans his head into a Raymond check, the strap over his nose presses down on the nose and the chin strap lifts up underneath the chin at the same time. This provides a great deal of leverage and will make most horses want to keep their heads up. It is really very comfortable because there isn't anything in the horse's mouth except the driving bit.

If a horse wearing a Raymond tries to hog down a little too much into the chin strap, I will substitute a little curb chin. This chain is similar to those used with curb bits on riding horses. It consists of a series of little chain links which lie flat. They are quite comfortable for a horse but he will not lean down as heavily as with a leather chin strap.

So if you have a horse that's hogging down into the check badly and you decide you need some leverage to stop the habit, don't let anybody talk you out of a Raymond just because it isn't the prettiest thing in the world. It does the job very well and is especially good for horses that tend to be a little soremouthed and might resent a severe overcheck bit.

One of the best and most comfortable check bits and certainly one of the most versatile is the Hutton. (Figs. 52-4 and 54). When used with its own special check and a chin strap, it is a wonderful bit to help get a colt's head set. It is especially good for a horse that keeps his mouth open when he leans a little into the check or takes a little hold. It is also good for a colt that carries his head a little high and fusses a little with the bit. The colt will drop his head into a Hutton and have a better mouth than with most check bits.

The mouthpiece of the bit is made to fit the contour of the mouth. There is a strap that goes over the nose, runs through each side of the bit and up between the eyes and ears and through the top of the bridle to form the front part of the overcheck. When a horse leans down into the check, the strap over the nose presses downward as the bit is pulled up in the mouth. The chin strap that is attached to either side of the bit just a little ahead of the mouthpiece keeps the mouth shut and at the same time provides a certain amount of leverage to help keep the horse from ducking his chin in, thereby impairing his breathing.

Next in line among the overcheck bits would be the McKerron (Figs. 52-5 and 54). The McKerron is a fairly severe bit but not nearly as severe as the Crabb or the Crit Davis. It operates on the same principle but is a little more comfortable in a horse's mouth. The McKerron bit is more comfortable because it is shaped a little better to fit a horse's mouth. It has a spoon right in the center and the sides to which the check fastens are shaped so that they more or less fit around the gums instead of coming up sharply against them as is the case with the Crabb bit. I think that in most instances you can achieve pretty much the same results with it as with the Crabb or Crit Davis and I recommend that it be tried before going to either of the latter two.

I wore a McKerron bit on Diamond Hal. He was almost perfect to drive but he had just one bad habit; he'd hog down into the check just a little too much behind the starting gate. I never did have him checked up very high and he went with a low head. The McKerron was just enough to keep his head just right so that he didn't pull his chin in too much. I tried him without it several times, even when he got to be an older, free-for-all horse. I'd always train him in the winter and spring without it, but when I'd get to the races I'd always have to go back to it. Without it, he would get his head down just a little too much behind the gate and be difficult to take back and tuck in. The leverage provided by the McKerron was just right for him.

The two most severe overcheck bits are the Crit Davis and the Crabb. But before I discuss them, I want to repeat that I am opposed to severe bits on horses whether they be driving bits or overcheck bits. I have used them myself and still do on occasion, but my point is that a trainer should work his way up the scale.

If a horse won't go in a chin strap, try a regular overcheck bit or a combination of the two and then a Burch bit. These apply pressure but not leverage. If you can get by with one of them, you are much better off. And don't give up without being absolutely sure in your own mind that you have to go to a more severe overcheck bit.

The remainder of the bits I have discussed are leverage bits.

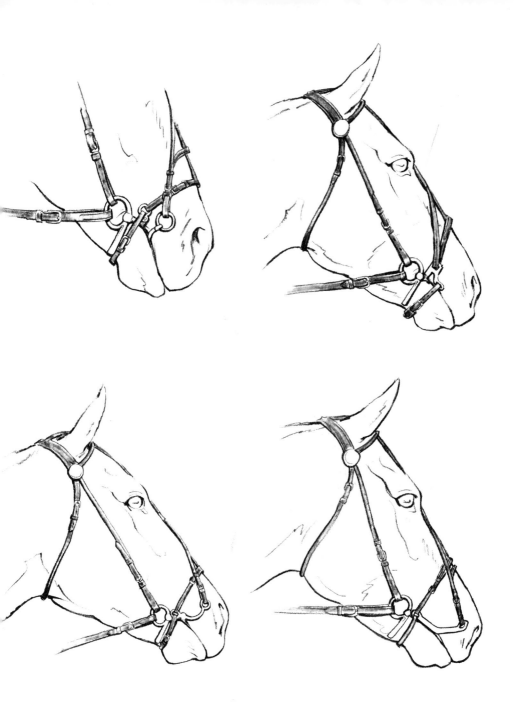

Fig. 54.   Here are four types of overcheck bits that are described in detail in the text and also illustrated by themselves in Fig. 52. Upper left, McKerron; upper right, Hutton; lower left, Crit Davis and lower right, Crabb.

The Hutton is a good bit and very versatile. The Raymond is a fine piece of equipment even though it is clumsy looking. Try those next. Then you can go to a McKerron and if that won't do the job you'll probably have to try a Crabb or a Crit Davis.

The Crabb and the Crit Davis are very severe especially if the check is too short, thereby pulling the horse's head up too high, and they are reserved for use with horses that really hog down in the check. Each exerts a hard pressure on the roof of the horse's mouth. I do not use either unless I absolutely have to and when I do I try to adjust them so they do not press against the roof of the mouth unless the horse hogs down.

The Crit Davis is a single bar bit (Figs. 52-6 and 54), except that instead of the bar running straight through the horse's mouth it is curved in the center roughly in the shape of the letter "U". This curve lies flat against the roof of the horse's mouth with the closed end forward. When the horse lays into the check, the U-bar is forced upward against the roof of the horse's mouth and the resulting pressure is quite severe. All except the most determined horses will back off from this kind of pressure and will hold their heads up rather than go against it.

The Crabb bit (Figs. 52-7 and 54) has two bars, instead of the usual one, running through the horse's mouth. A Crabb bit with a spoon is the same thing with a little piece of metal about an inch square extending forward from the center of the forward bar. This piece of metal is curved to fit the contour of the roof of the mouth. The spoon exerts additional pressure against the roof of the mouth, quite like that of the U-bar on the Crit Davis.

Each side of the Crabb bit consists of a small strip of metal. The back ends of these two strips are connected by a bar which runs through the horse's mouth. About two inches forward of this bar is another one which also runs through the mouth parallel to the first. This is why the Crabb is sometimes referred to as a "double bar" bit.

The metal strips on the side extend forward and upward about another four inches and the check fastens to the ends on each side. As you can understand, this gives the Crabb bit quite a lot of leverage. The spoon, if one is being used, and each of the bars in the mouth are pressing against the roof of the mouth. As with the Crit Davis, very few horses will go up against this kind of pressure.

If you are forced to use either a Crit Davis or a Crabb, it is very, very important that you adjust both the chin strap and the nose band properly. For instance, if you pull the chin strap way down tight, then you are going to force the front end of the spoon on the Crabb or the front end of the U-bar on the Crit Davis right up into the roof of the horse's mouth. This is all wrong.

You must adjust these bits so that after the nose band and the chin strap have been fastened, the spoon and the U-bar will be exactly parallel with the roof of the horse's mouth. The idea of the whole thing is to keep the horse from leaning down into the check, not to force his head higher than necessary or force his mouth open.

Another thing about putting the chin strap on too tight is that it tends to force a horse's mouth open rather than to force him to hold his head up which is the object. It is like any other piece of equipment, you just have to use a little common sense.

If a trainer would just stand back and look at the way a bit fits in the mouth and at the same time remember the purpose of the bit, he'd soon learn to adjust it properly by taking the chin strap up a hole or letting it out a hole. The same goes for the nose band. Adjust them together so that when you have finished the bit is neither pressing against the roof of the mouth nor the tongue, but the part in the mouth is parallel with the contour of the mouth.

I don't like to use a Crabb bit without a spoon. I think it is much less severe on a horse if that primary downward pressure is against the smooth, flat surface of the spoon rather than against the little round bar that runs through the mouth. I have found that bar pressure with a Crabb bit more or less catches a horse on the gums and leads to a sore mouth. With a spoon, this is less likely to happen.

I think another mistake trainers make in using a Crabb or a Crit Davis is that they feel a horse has to be checked way up high with one. This is not always the case. You must remember the purpose of the bit. It is simply to keep a horse from hogging down in the check and there is no good reason why his head has to be checked up especially high. Set the head where you

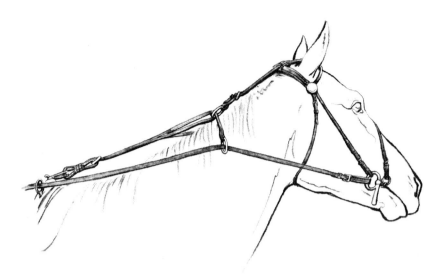

Fig. 55. The 4-ring overcheck is a common type of restraining device used on trotters and pacers. Its basic use is with pulling horses but it is also used with horses that need to have their heads high at certain times (usually just before and after the start) and lower at other times (usually after they have settled into stride in the race).

want it first and then make all your adjustments such as the fit of the bit and the tightening or loosening of the chin strap and nose band from that standpoint.

If you put on a Crabb or a Crit Davis and then get a horse's head checked way up high, he is almost certain to get on one line or the other and start going crooked. There is no sense trying to solve one problem and creating a tougher one for yourself at the same time.

There is one other type of restraining device that falls in the "overcheck" category and which I should probably review at this point. That is the four-ring overcheck (Fig. 55), a fairly common piece of equipment for certain horses and used quite frequently.

Its basic use is with pulling horses but you also wear it on horses that don't like to be checked up too high when they're going slow or parading, or horses that like to hold their heads a little lower after the gate has left and they have settled down somewhat. Indian Land, a free-for-all pacer I drove in the late forties, was like this. It was necessary to have his head higher behind the gate and for the first eighth or so after the gate left in order to exercise any control over him. But for the rest of the mile, especially in the last quarter, he liked to get it down lower.

A four ring check can be adjusted so that the horse can only get his head so low and no lower; but when he pulls, the tension on the lines forces him to raise his head a little higher. A regular front part is used, but the back part of the check is especially made. Instead of buckling to the front part in the usual manner (Fig. 39), there are two short straps two or three inches long that buckle to the front part with rings on the other end. The back parts of the check run through these rings and extend downward several inches. These ends also have rings through which the driving lines pass.

When jogging, going slow miles or parading, the driver can release a little pressure on the lines and let the horse get his head down a little. But in a race, when you want a horse's head in exactly the right position, you put pressure on the lines and that exerts a downward pull on the straps which are attached to the check rein. This tightens the check and raises the head, depending on how hard you pull. It is a very effective check on a lot of horses and is used quite frequently.

I have been writing a great deal about horses that want to lay their heads down in the check and have reviewed at length some of the methods employed to overcome this trouble. This is as good a place as any to mention those horses whose tendency is to throw their heads up all the time, just the opposite of what I have been writing about.

There are fewer of these because a horse's natural inclination is to go the other way, to hog down. But there are still quite a number that do this and the piece of equipment most frequently used to correct this fault is the Martingale.

There are several types of Martingales, almost all of which fasten to the bottom of the girth and come out between the horse's front legs. The most common is the standing Martingale (Fig. 56-1). It is nothing more than a long leather strap. It is fastened to the bottom of the girth, extends between the horse's front legs and is attached to a ring in the center and at the bottom of the head halter. The strap is, of course, adjustable and you make the adjustment to keep the horse's head down to exactly the height you want it.

When a standing Martingale is functioning properly, the horse cannot raise his head beyond a certain point. However, I like a Martingale to have a little slack in it when a horse is traveling at

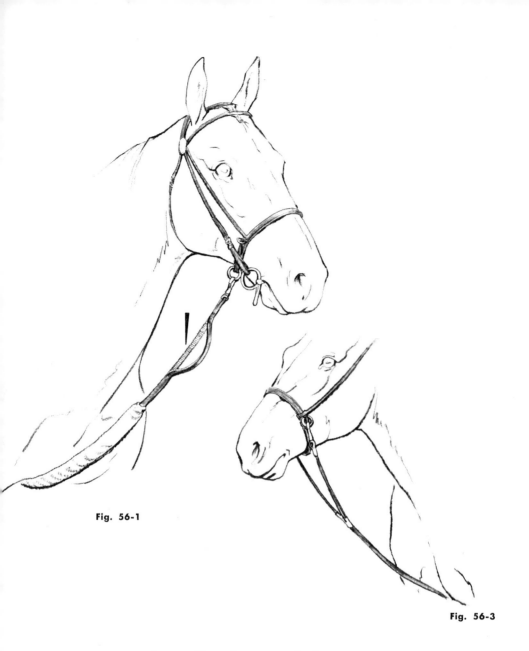

Fig. 56-1

Fig. 56-3

any speed. Usually, a horse needs the Martingale most when he is behind the starting gate or tucked in when the pace slackens some. Its purpose is usually to keep the horse from getting his head higher than the normal position in which he would carry it, not to force him to carry it lower. I know that certain horses require an absolutely tight Martingale, but I prefer to have a little slack if it is at all possible.

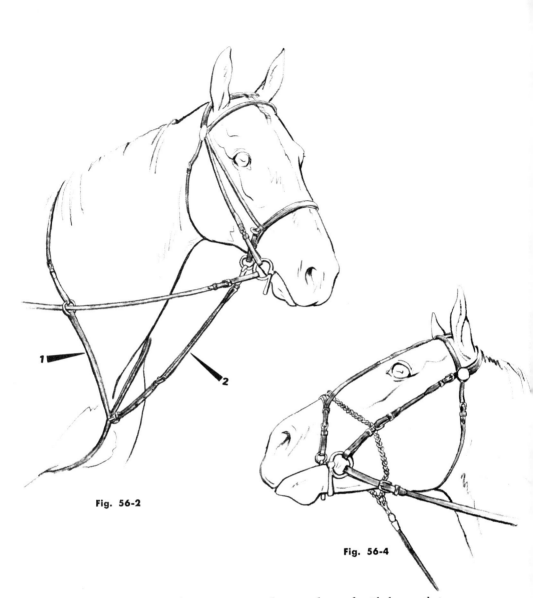

Fig. 56-2

Fig. 56-4

Fig. 56. A Martingale of one type or another may be used with horses that have a tendency to throw their heads up in the air or carry their heads too high. Fig. 56–1 is the basic or standing Martingale which is nothing more than a strap running from the bottom of the girth through the front legs and fastening into the bottom ring of the head halter. The author is also illustrating (arrow) a heavy elastic insert invented by trainer Del Cameron that gives the Martingale a little play to keep the horse from fighting it but which, at the same time, exerts a constant downward pressure. Fig. 56–2 is a combination Martingale, so-called because it combines the functions of a ring Martingale (1) and a standing Martingale (2). Without the basic strap (2), this would be a simple ring or running Martingale. Fig. 56–3 is a split Martingale with separate straps fastening into the rings on each side of the head halter. Fig. 56–4 indicates the manner in which a chain or cord passing over the nose is used in conjunction with a standing Martingale to help keep the horse's head down, especially behind the starting gate.

My general rule in this respect is that there must be enough play so that the horse's head isn't being held in a vice (Fig. 57). If you get your horse's head checked up and then get your Martingale so tight that it's pulling down, you have one working against the other and that is not a satisfactory situation. Eventually, the horse gets in the habit of holding his head to one side and then you have to start all over again with another fault to correct.

A good innovation that I believe was invented by Del Cameron is an insert of heavy elastic (Fig. 56-1) that gives the Martingale a little play and helps to keep a horse from fighting it. At the same time, it exerts a constant downward pressure on his nose. Like the four ring check, it also has a "stopper" that prevents it from stretching beyond a certain point.

We also have what we call the split Martingale (Fig. 56-3). Instead of the strap extending all the way up to the ring of the head halter, it is split down about 18 inches forming two straps, each with a snap on the end. These straps come up and fasten into the rings on each side of the head halter.

In addition to performing the function of the standing Martingale, which is to keep the horse from getting his head too high, the split Martingale also helps to keep the horse's head straight. For instance, if he turns his head to the left the added pressure will be on the right side which will tend to pull his head back toward the center, in other words to straighten his head. Be sure your head halter is high enough that the Martingale isn't pulling it down on the bit, thereby pinching or chafing the horse's mouth or cheeks.

The ring or running Martingale (Fig. 56-2) serves a slightly different purpose. This is made like a split Martingale, branching off into two straps about 18 inches from the end. At the end of each of these straps there is a little ring instead of a snap. The driving lines run back from the bit through these rings, and the Martingale can be adjusted as to length.

This type of Martingale is usually used on a tender-mouthed horse and should be adjusted so that there is just a little downward pull on the lines when the horse is in motion and carrying his head at a normal angle. Instead of pulling up against the tender cheeks, the pull is downward against the teeth and naturally there is less likelihood of a sore mouth developing.

A ring Martingale is also very helpful for a horse that doesn't take enough hold, with the result that the lines keep flopping and jiggling all the time. It helps keep the lines still. When the lines jiggle and bounce around, they jiggle the bit in the horse's mouth. A tender-mouthed horse, especially a colt, minds this.

I use this type of Martingale a lot the first month or two in breaking and driving colts. It helps when colts swing their heads a lot. Sometimes when they do this one of the lines will get caught under the point of the shaft. With a ring Martingale this is less likely to happen.

Another Martingale that I use quite a bit is the combination Martingale (Fig. 56-2). This is a ring Martingale that has a little buckle sewed onto it right in front of the horse's chest slightly below the split in the Martingale. A small strap with a snap on one end fastens to the ring at the bottom of the head halter and the other end fastens into the buckle on the front of the Martingale. This strap can be adjusted separately from the Martingale itself. In this way you can adjust both the ring Martingale and the standing Martingale the exact length you want them. I like this type of Martingale on colts because it helps to set their heads straight in addition to keeping the lines from jiggling around.

Fig. 57. In this illustration, there is no slack in either the check (A) or the Martingale (B) and thus the horse's head is held virtually in a vice. This is undesirable as discussed in the text.

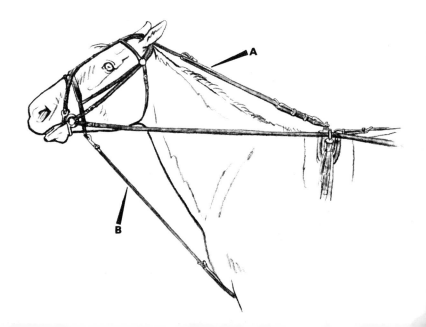

A problem you run into these days is a horse that wears a standing Martingale but still gets his head too high, especially behind the starting gate. What you do in a case like this is to take a piece of cord, something on the order of clothesline rope and run it over the nose (Fig. 56-4), securing the ends to a ring into which the Martingale is fastened. This is more effective than the pressure of the head halter itself on the nose and many times has the desired effect of making the horse keep his head down.

This type of Martingale was very rarely used before we got the starting gate. But at the gate a great many horses get a little anxious and try to get their heads up too high and over the gate. I have found that a little piece of rope is usually adequate to correct this fault. Some trainers even use a piece of wire or a little chain over the nose. These, of course, are even more effective than the rope, but all are serving the same purpose —to keep the horse's head down.

A few paragraphs ago I mentioned using a ring Martingale on colts the first month or two they are being broken because they usually have tender mouths. I realize a kicking strap sounds a little remote when discussing a tender mouth on a colt, but I have found that by its use when breaking colts, I can sometimes prevent a colt from getting a sore mouth, or at least help prevent it. My contention is that without a kicking strap you must snatch a colt every time he looks like he is going to kick, whereas if he has a kicking strap on, you can afford to be more gentle. A kicking strap, of course, is a stout leather strap (Fig. 58) that goes over the horse's rump approximately midway between the hips and the butt of the tail and fastens to the shaft on each side.

I think it is time now to go back and pick up the basic theme of this chapter. That is the premise, which I will emphasize again even at the risk of being repetitious, that in order for the horse to perform at his best his head must be straight and his hind end must be in the center of the shafts. By now, I am sure it has become obvious how important I consider this to be.

I have talked about a horse holding his head crooked because the bit is uncomfortable in his mouth, because he is sore in one or more areas, because his head is checked at an improper angle

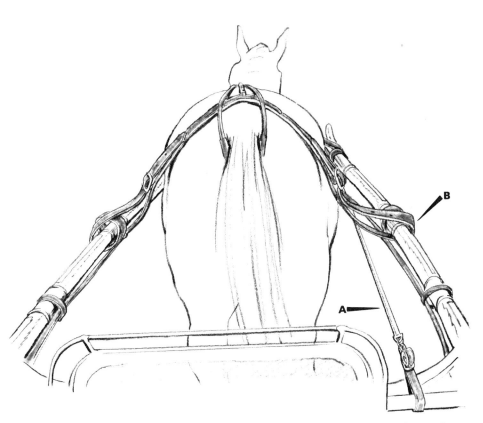

Fig. 58. A gaiting strap (A) or gaiting pole is used with a horse that tends to get his hind end over to one side of the shaft. It may be used on either or both sides depending on the circumstances. A kicking strap (B) is used with horses that have a tendency to kick while hitched to cart or sulky. The author recommends using a kicking strap when breaking colts.

and because the combination of a tight check and a tight Martingale has his head in a virtual vice.

Before I proceed to the remedies for a horse that insists on carrying his head to one side or the other, I want to discuss a couple of other causes and what you can do to correct them.

One of these is improper adjustment of the shadow roll. Any time I see a horse carrying his head crooked, I automatically check the fit of the shadow roll if he is wearing one. Very often a simple adjustment of this piece of equipment will solve the problem. Various types of shadow rolls, properly and improperly adjusted are illustrated in Fig. 59.

A shadow roll is worn principally by pacers and is a vital accessory. Fitted properly, it can convert a potentially dangerous horse into an absolutely safe racing proposition. And yet, I am constantly amazed at the number of trainers who, through inex-

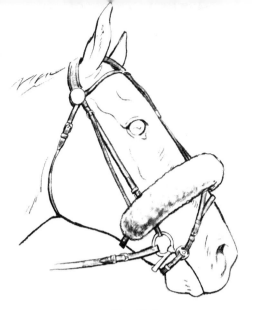

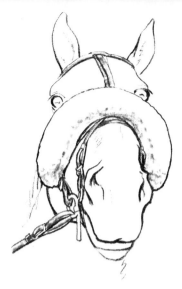

Fig. 59-1   Fig. 59-2

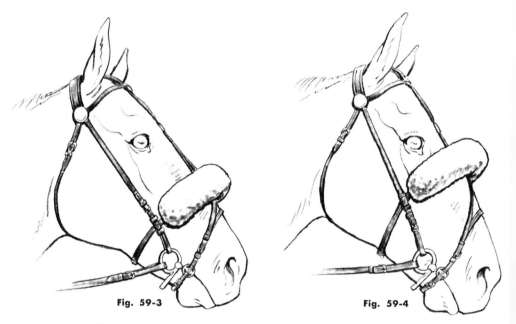

Fig. 59-3   Fig. 59-4

Fig. 59. The author discusses at some length in the text the various types of shadow rolls and their proper and improper adjustment. Some are illustrated here. Fig. 59–1 demonstrates the proper adjustment of a shadow roll that extends beyond the cheek pieces of the bridle. Fig. 59–2 is a head-on view of the same shadow roll indicating that the horse has proper forward vision. Fig. 59–3 is the proper adjustment of a narrow shadow roll, one that does not extend as far as the cheek pieces of the bridle. Fig. 59–4 is an improperly-fitted narrow shadow roll (the same would hold true with the wider shadow roll in Fig. 59–1 as well) in that it is placed too high on the nose thus restricting the horse's vision. Fig. 59–5 is a head-on view of the same shadow roll illustrating the lack of foward vision. Fig. 59–6 is a brush shadow roll, properly adjusted. Fig. 59–7 is the

Fig. 59-5

Fig. 59-6

Fig. 59-7

Fig. 59-8

shadow roll designed by the author. It is narrow at the center to assure proper forward vision and at the same time wide at the sides to prevent the horse from peeking down and seeing objects on the ground. The author prefers this type of shadow roll because he has found that some horses will peek down *behind* a narrow shadow roll (even though it is properly adjusted to prevent them from seeing the track in *front* of them) and step over objects or marks on the track with their *hind* feet. Fig. 59-8 is a head halter with a sheepskin-covered nose band that the author uses to accustom his horses to a shadow roll.

perience or inattention to detail, fit the shadow roll improperly.

There are several types of shadow rolls, the most common of which is the sheepskin roll. It fits across and around the horse's nose below his eyes and buckles under the jaw.

The sole purpose of the shadow roll is to prevent the horse from seeing the *ground* directly in front of him and thus to keep him from observing shadows (hence the name) marks on the track, pieces of paper and other distortions, real and imaginary, which might cause him to shy and go off gait.

Conversely, the purpose of the shadow roll is *not* to prevent the horse from seeing straight ahead. A horse naturally wants to see ahead of him. If an improperly adjusted shadow roll prevents him from doing this, he is just naturally going to start twisting his head around and holding it crooked in an effort to see around the ends of the shadow roll.

Let me review what a trainer might do wrong in adjusting a shadow roll. He decides his horse needs a shadow roll and some morning in the stable area, when the horse is being readied for a training session, he has one put on. The horse, of course, is unchecked and his head is held lower than the angle at which the check will hold it when he is actually training and racing. The trainer puts on the shadow roll, looks over his handiwork, is pleased that everything appears in order and takes his horse to the track. When the horse is checked up, the angle of his head in respect to the ground changes drastically, especially with a horse that is checked up high. His nose comes up and out and in many cases the shadow roll that looked perfectly all right a few minutes earlier is now preventing the horse from seeing anything except the sky. Very often the horse will begin turning his head in an attempt to see over the sides, which are lower when his head is up high.

In my opinion, a trainer should never assume that a shadow roll is adjusted properly until he examines the fit with the horse's head held at the angle he will carry it when he is training or racing.

It is also important to re-examine the fit each time it becomes necessary to check a horse higher. I have seen instances of a shadow roll having been fitted properly in the first place and then causing trouble because the horse was later checked up three or four holes higher without a compensating adjustment being made in the fit of the shadow roll.

Any time I am sitting on the sidelines watching one of my horses warming up, I always make it a point to take a look at the shadow roll, making sure that the horse has proper forward vision.

Not all horses, of course, require a shadow roll. Most trotters do not. Most pacers, however, will need one sooner or later. I think Johnny Simpson has a pretty good idea on this score. He breaks all his 2-year-old pacers to a shadow roll immediately. Since nearly every pacer will eventually need a shadow roll, it is a good idea to have them broken to it.

Generally speaking, the reason pacers need shadow rolls and trotters do not is that the pacers are hobbled. I think pacers are always conscious that their legs are tied together and that they're a little afraid because of it. I think horses are smarter than people realize and that a horse wearing hobbles is more fearful of stepping in a hole or tripping over something than one without hobbles. Consequently, such horses are always looking for things on the track directly in front of them.

On the other hand, I am equally certain that a trotter learns early in life that no great harm can come to him if he does shy from a piece of paper or something and makes a break. His legs are unhindered and he simply goes into a gallop. He does not have the same psychological reaction as a pacer. I seldom use a shadow roll on a trotter.

Several years ago I designed a shadow roll (Fig. 59-7) which I use and recommend. It is round and not too large in the center, over the nose, and the horse always has a clear line of vision out ahead of him. But it is made wider on both sides under his eyes so that he can't peak down over the corners and see something to jump over.

When a horse is racing in an open bridle, I also prefer a shadow roll that is a little longer than the standard one and the one which I designed is made this way. The standard shadow roll comes just to the cheek pieces of the bridle and then is buckled under the jaw with a little strap that joins the sides together. My shadow roll extends back a couple of inches beyond the cheek pieces of the bridle on each side. Instead of running it through the cheek pieces as is the general custom with a regular roll, I just run a little strap from the back corner of the roll on both sides up to the buckles on each side of the bridle. This prevents the shadow roll from sagging down on the sides.

As I mentioned earlier, it is important that you recheck the fit of the shadow roll each time you check your horse any higher. The shadow roll should be lowered to accommodate the change in head posture especially in front over the nose where it might block his vision. When I have a horse that must be checked fairly high, I try to lower the roll on his nose and raise it on the sides. It is sometimes necessary to wrap a little piece of twine around the shadow roll and tie it to the nose band of the head halter to keep the front down.

Of the other varieties of shadow roll, I prefer the brush roll (Fig. 59-6), which has a leather base with bristles glued and sewed into it so that they stick out in front of the horse's nose. The bristles are about four inches long and are always moving in the wind. This type of shadow roll is particularly good for a horse that seems to be generally spooky about little things on the track.

I have had horses like this and I believe their trouble is in their eyes. I think we have more eye trouble than we realize. By that I mean that I think some horses are near-sighted and some far-sighted. The brush shadow roll is ideal for this type of horse. The little bristles keep blowing in the wind and they keep a horse from thinking he sees things on the track in front of him. And if anything does move, a piece of paper or something like that, he probably won't even notice it.

I recently had a mare in my stable that I used this type shadow roll on. She absolutely wouldn't go with any other type. I tried every kind and this was the only one that enabled her to go more than fifty feet without jumping over something.

I think this mare's trouble was that she was near-sighted or far-sighted. She'd be pacing along and all of a sudden she'd make a shying jump even when there wasn't anything on the track that I could see. Sometimes just the footprint of the horse that went ahead of her would startle her and send her into a break. With the brush shadow roll she never took a second look and would go over shadows or anything else on the track. The bristles constantly reminded her that it was natural for something to be moving beneath her eyes.

A horse should be broken to a shadow roll very carefully. I always keep a head halter with the nose band covered with sheepskin around just for this purpose (Fig. 59-8). I use it on a colt as the first step in getting him used to a shadow roll. I buckle it loosely on him in the stall, walk him and cool him out with it on and then graduate to a real small roll, and keep it low on his nose at first. You can then gradually raise it a little higher or use a larger roll.

A shadow roll is an important piece of equipment and an ally of any trainer who uses it properly. Proper adjustment comes naturally if you will just bear in mind the purpose of the shadow roll—to prevent a horse from seeing the track directly in front of him; not to prevent him from seeing straight ahead.

Another thing that will make a horse fight the bit and start carry his head crooked is the fact that he is playing around with his tongue. He lolls his tongue and pulls it back in his mouth. Occasionally he will "swallow" his tongue and choke down for that reason. More often he will get his tongue over the bit.

This is a very painful experience for the horse and is usually disastrous for the driver if it occurs in a race. Even though you may be using the mildest bit in the catalog, the pressure is now being applied against that tender area beneath and at the back edge of the tongue. This makes the horse much more difficult to steer and control and could make the difference between winning or losing a race.

The remedy, of course, is the age-old tongue tie (Fig. 60). I am very much in favor of applying one the minute a horse starts fooling around with his tongue in any way. If he is jogged and trained with one a few times, he will become accustomed to it and never fight it.

As a matter of fact, I like to break my horses to a tongue tie as soon as I can. Very often I will put one on a horse when he is resting in his stall and leave it on for a little while. I also like to introduce horses to a tongue tie while they are being cooled out. I do this to get them used to one in the event it becomes necessary that they wear one later on.

Always make sure the groom takes the tongue tie off as soon as the horse comes off the track and doesn't put it back on until the horse is ready to go out for the next heat. In other words, do not leave it on any longer than necessary. If you are using a leather tongue tie, or tongue strap as it is also called, soak it a few minutes in warm water before putting it on the horse, and between heats drop it into some water until you are ready for it again.

There are many types of tongue ties and the one you select is strictly a matter of choice. The important thing is to put it on properly. A tongue tie can come in the form of a strap, a cord, a piece of cloth or a rubber band and all are satisfactory. Each loops around the tongue and ties beneath the chin. The tongue thus is held in a stationary position and the horse cannot get it over the bit.

Trouble can develop, however, if you apply the tongue tie improperly. First of all you must be certain that you do not tie it so tight that you cut off the circulation. I have seen this happen. A trainer once asked me why his horse's tongue was turning black and was surprised when I told him the tongue tie was too tight. Use a little common sense and discretion in applying a tongue tie. It must be tight enough to hold the tongue in place but must not cut off circulation.

Another thing is to make certain that the tongue is lying flat in the mouth both before and after you apply the tie. Occasionally, when a tongue tie is applied, one side is pulled tighter than the other. This tends to cause the tongue to roll in the mouth and double over. This will cause a horse to fight the tie and shake his head.

An important thing to remember about a tongue tie is that a horse will rarely need one when he is training. A horse will carry his tongue perfectly in all the fast training miles you want to give him and then, all of a sudden, out on the race track in the heat of actual competition you'll find that your perfect pupil has his tongue over the bit.

I am certain that all tongue problems develop as a result of a nervous reaction brought on by a horse's intense desire to compete successfully. A horse that is racing or going to the post for a race gets keyed up and nervous and this is when you have to watch for him getting his tongue over the bit. One of the places he's most likely to do it is behind the starting gate. He is anxious to go and for that reason is taking a little more hold than usual. The next thing you know he has his tongue over the bit.

If you are parading before a race or even if you have started

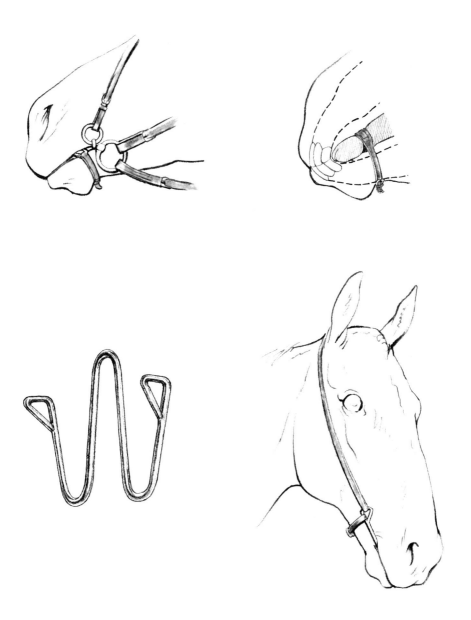

Fig. 60. The author favors using a tongue tie any time a horse starts playing with his tongue in any way. The illustration at the upper left shows the proper outside adjustment. The proper inside adjustment, with the tongue lying flat in the mouth, is illustrated upper right. If a horse does not like a regular tongue tie, a W tongue controller may be used. The W itself is shown left below and properly positioned in the mouth, right.

to go to the gate and it seems there is something wrong with your horse's mouth, you had better check his tongue. The odds are that he has it over the bit.

When I notice this in the parade, I usually ask another driver to take a look for me. You cannot tell from your seat in the sulky and sometimes if you get out to take a look yourself you will find that when you relaxed the pressure on the lines in dismounting the horse got his tongue back under the bit.

As I said, there are many types of tongue ties. I use a flannel material that I buy by the bolt for making stable bandages. I tear a narrow strip off the edge about an inch in width and use it for tongue ties. It is soft yet strong and can be thrown away after a race and a new one applied the next time. Make sure that whatever kind you use is clean and sanitary.

Some people shudder at the thought of a "poor horse" with his tongue tied. This is because they do not know the difference. A tongue tie does not bother a horse in the least, whereas if he has his tongue over the bit and the bit is pulling against the very tender part of his mouth under the tongue it can be very painful. Or if a horse gets his tongue doubled back in his throat and chokes down it can harm both the horse and the driver as well as others in the race.

People who say, "I would never wear a tongue tie on a horse" are just admitting their own ignorance!

Once in a while you will find a horse that does not like a tongue tie but needs one. In cases like this, the W tongue controller can be used with good results. This is a device shaped like the letter "W", and made out of small round steel with a light, adjustable strap running over the top of the head to hold it in place (Fig. 60). The center part of the "W" goes in the mouth, lying loosely on top of the tongue and preventing the horse from getting his tongue over the bit or doubled back in his mouth. The sides are on the outside of the cheeks and the adjustable strap fastens to them. There is also a little adjustable strap attached to the ends that buckles under the jaw to hold the "W" down on the tongue.

If the tongue tie and the shadow roll are being used and have been adjusted properly and if all the other precautions I have discussed have been taken, there are only two reasons why a horse should still be holding his head crooked. One is that he is a little sore and trying to get his weight off a specific area that is hurting him and the other is that he has formed a bad habit. If he is not sore enough to quit with and if you cannot break the habit he has formed, I would advise going to a head pole or a Murphy blind.

Each of these is a common and valuable piece of equipment. I use them both and recommend their use where required. Let me discuss each of them in a little detail.

A head pole is a small pole, about the size of a pool cue that is placed on the side of the horse's head and neck running from the saddle pad up to the head halter (Fig. 39). The purpose of the head pole is to keep the horse's head straighter, to prevent him from turning his head to one side.

If a horse is turning his head to the right, as most horses will do, especially on a half mile track, the head pole is placed on the left side. Since one end of the pole is securely fastened to the saddle pad and the other end to a ring in the side of the head halter it is almost impossible for the horse to turn his head as the center of the pole will come against his neck.

If the horse wants to carry his head to the left, the head pole goes on the right side. Occasionally you will run across a horse that turns his head to the right in the turns and to the left in the stretches. Such a horse might wear two head poles, one on each side.

Until recent years, head poles were shaped like pool cues and, indeed, actual pool cues were used. I used some of them myself. But now they have invented the telescopic pole which is much handier.

The old pool cue type pole used to stick out in front of the horse's head and when starting gates came into use this type of pole would sometimes get caught in the gate. The telescopic pole does not stick out past the horse's nose and cannot get into the gate. It is stationary at both ends and telescopes within itself to adjust to the proper length.

Like anything else, the head pole must be put on properly. It is very simple to put on. The part that holds it to the saddle pad is a leather strap running from the terret (the ring on the saddle pad through which the driving lines pass) through a slot in the end of the head pole and attaching to the overcheck hook on top of the saddle pad (Fig. 61-3).

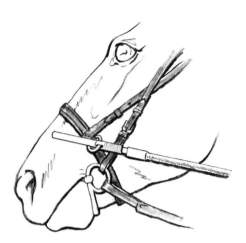

Fig. 61-1

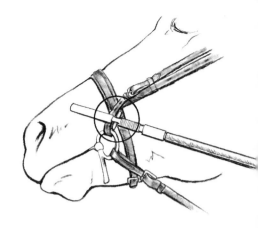

Fig. 61-2

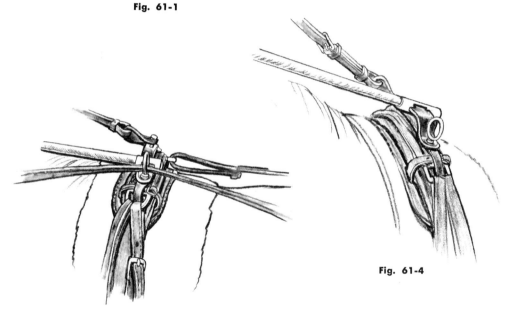

Fig. 61-4

Fig. 61-3

Fig. 61. The head pole (shown as a complete unit in Fig. 39) is a valuable piece of equipment. In adjusting the head pole at the front end, care should be taken that the ring on the head halter to which the head pole is attached is in *front* of the cheek piece of the bridle. The head pole is fastened properly, in Fig. 61–1, and improperly (circled area) in Fig. 61–2. The placing and proper adjustment of the head pole at the saddle is shown in Fig. 61–3. If it is desirable to have the pole closer to the horse's neck, a head pole strap with a shoulder on it, Fig. 61–4, may be used. A head pole burr, Fig. 61–5, or a ball, Fig. 61–6, are sometimes used to prevent a horse from leaning against the head pole.

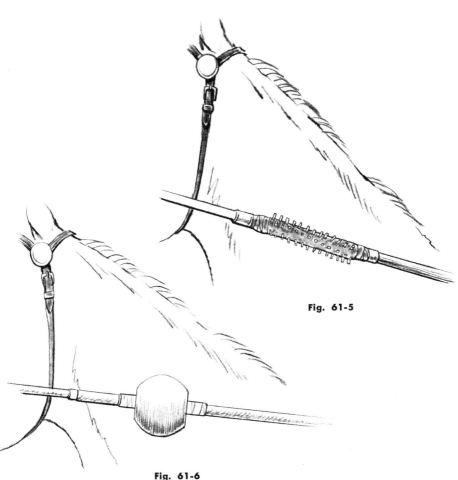

Fig. 61-5

Fig. 61-6

If you want the pole closer to the horse's neck, you can get or make a head pole strap with a shoulder (Fig. 61-4) on it to hold it up. A horse with a little slim neck usually needs one of these straps. If you want the pole closer to the horse's neck without changing the strap, you can wrap a little tape around it at the end nearest the terret.

The most important thing about the adjustment of a head pole is how it is fastened at the other end. The ring in the head halter to which the front end of the head pole is attached should be in front of the cheek piece of the bridle (Fig. 61-1). If you fasten your head pole into a ring which comes out behind the cheek piece, you will be pulling against the end of the pole when you pull on the lines (Fig. 61-2) and that makes your horse very hard to steer and difficult to control. So what you must do is to make sure the bridle is behind the ring of the head halter and that the head pole goes outside the bridle cheek piece and then fastens into the ring.

This is also a good time to check your head halter and make certain that it is not down too low and interfering with the action of your driving bit and pinching your horse's cheek. A good rule of thumb is that the nose band of the head halter should always be at least the width of three fingers above the bit.

If you find, after getting the head pole adjusted properly, that the horse is still leaning against it, bowing his neck and pulling on the opposite line, it is sometimes advisable to put a burr (Fig. 61-5) on the head pole. These burrs can be bought in any harness shop. A burr consists of a length of leather, perhaps six inches long, that wraps around the head pole where it comes in contact with the horse's neck. The outside surface of the leather is studded with little rivets or other metal devices which act as burrs and from which the name is derived. A horse will not lean nearly as hard into a burr as he will into an ordinary head pole and very often a burr will straighten a horse up.

In some cases, a little ball (Fig. 61-6) is good on a head pole when a horse wants to lean into one too much. Just put a little round solid rubber ball, maybe three or four inches in diameter, over the headpole where his neck comes in contact with it.

Some horses that don't like to wear a head pole can be straightened up by means of line burr (Fig 62) which is similar to the burr used on a head pole. It is laced right on the line where the line comes in contact with the horse's neck. Sometimes, in a case like this, I will use a stiff line which is made by taping a piece of aluminum to the line from the bit back to within a few inches of the terret. If you are going to use a line burr, it will probably be better if you use a stiff line because this brings it in more solidly against the horse's neck.

Another excellent device that has been used with marked success for the purpose of straightening a horse's head is a Murphy blind. This was invented by the late trainer-driver Thomas W. Murphy and I use them quite a bit. As a matter of fact, I prefer a Murphy blind to a head pole because it is actually less cumbersome on a horse.

A Murphy blind (Fig. 63) is nothing more than a large piece of stiff leather perhaps eight inches square and cupped in slightly

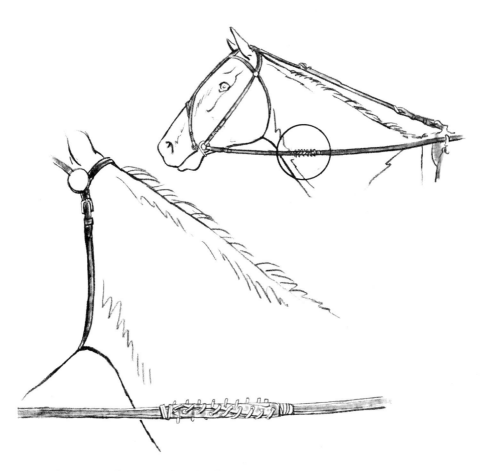

Fig. 62. Horses that carry their heads to one side and do not like to wear a head pole can sometimes be straightened up by means of a line burr as illustrated. It is shown in a closeup below and properly positioned in the circled area above. If a line burr is being used, the author recommends that a piece of aluminum be taped to the line to stiffen it.

toward the eye at the front. It is fastened to the bridle and positioned so that it affects the view out of one eye. Like any other piece of equipment, it must be adjusted properly to serve its purpose.

Let's say you have a horse that is turning his head to the *left*. You put the Murphy blind on the *right* eye. Then, when the horse turns his head to the left, the Murphy blind, if adjusted properly, obstructs the forward vision of the right eye. It is natural for a horse to want to see what is in front of him and consequently the Murphy blind serves as an incentive for him to turn his head back toward the center and hold it straight.

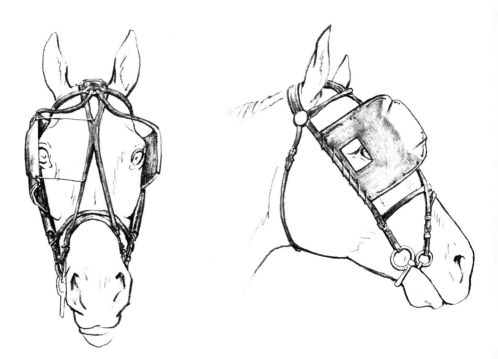

Fig. 63. The Murphy blind is a valuable aid in helping a horse to carry his head straight. The blind, left, (the Murphy blind is on the right eye) must be critically adjusted so that the horse is forced to hold his head absolutely straight out in front of him in order to have completely unrestricted forward vision, which, of course, all horses desire. Illustrated is a horse that is inclined to turn his head to the left and it will be readily observed that if this horse turns his head to the left he will lose forward vision out of the right eye. The proper side adjustment is shown at the right in a drawing that also illustrates a Murphy blind with a "window." The "window" provides backward vision for a horse that requires both a Murphy blind and an open bridle. Shadow Wave, with whom the author won the 1958 Little Brown Jug, was rigged this way.

In putting a Murphy blind on a horse, do not put it on so that the eye is completely blinded because that would be defeating the purpose. If the eye were completely covered and the horse couldn't see straight ahead out of that eye no matter which way he turned his head, he would still turn his head to the left as he had been doing.

The Murphy blind should be adjusted so that it extends out in front of the horse's eye to a point where the horse must keep his head straight in order to have an unobstructed forward view out of that eye. As long as a horse keeps his head straight he has complete forward vision out of both eyes. It does not take a horse long to learn this and most of them will soon be going straight.

A Murphy blind is easier to put on and adjust with an open bridle, but it can be used with any kind of bridle. Always use a nose strap to keep the sides of the bridle from sagging or pulling back when you pull on the lines. Without the nose strap, the sides of the bridle will come back when you pull on the bit and pull the Murphy blind back against the horse's eye.

I always use wire to fasten the upper and lower corners of the front of the blind to the front part of the check. Then I can set the blind at whatever distance I want it from the front of the eye and be sure it will stay there. If you use a shoe lace or something that is not stiff to fasten it to the check, the blind will flop in and out and won't stay at the angle at which you have adjusted it.

Once in a while you will run across a horse that requires an open bridle and a Murphy blind as well. Shadow Wave was such a horse. He needed the blind because he had a habit of turning his head but he also needed the open bridle because he would have a tendency to pace the front end too much if he couldn't see the horses behind him.

So in order to put a Murphy blind on him and still have what amounted to an open bridle, I cut a little window in the Murphy blind (Fig. 63), right behind the eye, so that he could see behind him out of that eye. It worked very well and I recommend it for horses of this type.

If you ever run across a horse that will not go with either a Murphy blind or a head pole, you can always try a King Daphne. A King Daphne (Fig. 64) is a head straightening device which is similar to a head halter except that it has a padded metal band that goes around the horse's nose and a metal bar that sticks out perhaps eight inches, forming a 90 degree angle with the normal position of the head.

If the horse was turning his head to the left, you would put the King Daphne on so that the bar would be on the right side. A strap goes from the end of this bar to the saddle pad where it is fastened. I like to tie a small ring to the thimble on the end of the shaft and let the strap pass through this ring and then fasten to the saddle pad. You would adjust this strap so that when the horse was in motion there would be just enough tension to keep the horse from turning his head to the left.

Sometimes this strap might seem a little tight when you first

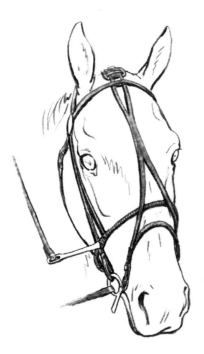

Fig. 64. The King Daphne is a head-straightening device that has a round metal bar extending outward on the side with a taut strap connecting the end of the bar and the saddle pad. The horse in the illustration has a habit of turning his head to the left and thus the bar goes on the right side.

start off, when the horse is just walking; but when he gets in motion and is going along a little, you will find that the strap will slacken.

A King Daphne does not usually work very well with a puller. That is because you have to take a constant hold on a puller and you are bringing his nose down and back toward you. This releases tension on the King Daphne and it will not serve its purpose under these circumstances. On this type of horse, my dad used to replace the strap with a small, strong cord that he would fasten to the bar on the King Daphne and run back through a ring at the point of the shaft to the hand hold on the line. He would run the cord through the metal part of the hand hold along with the line, so that when he pulled on the bit he would also pull on the King Daphne and there would be no slack in the line. This is also a very convenient way to use a King Daphne as far as adjusting it is concerned, since you can lengthen or shorten the cord at the hand hold.

I do not recommend a King Daphne for everyday use. There are very few horses it will work on. I much prefer a Murphy blind or a head pole. But for that occasional horse that does not take too much hold and keeps his head out in front of him, a King Daphne can work very well.

Usually, if you can get a horse to carry his head straight, his hind end will straighten up automatically providing he is not lame or interfering. The latter then becomes a shoeing problem and is being discussed in other chapters of this book.

I think I ought to mention here that in getting a horse to go straight you operate on the same general principle as in shoeing a horse. You work on the front end first and if you are successful there you will generally find that the hind end will take care of itself.

But you will still find some horses that hold their heads perfectly straight but trot or pace with their hind ends over to one side or the other. This can be caused by a number of things, although it is usually unsoundness.

If a horse is sore, he will usually carry his hind end away from the side that is hurting. That is, if he's lame somewhere in the right hind leg he will usually trot or pace with his hind end over toward the left shaft.

The first thing you have to do is determine the cause. If it is lameness, you have to try to alleviate that before you can help him very much. If it is a chronic lameness that you can't cure, you ease him as much as possible and then try to straighten him up by other means such as a gaiting strap or gaiting pole.

A gaiting strap (Fig. 58) is a leather strap that runs from the tip of the shaft back to the crosspiece or arch of the sulky. It must be pulled very tight so that when a horse gets his hind end over against it, it will not sag, but will keep the horse from getting over any farther. A gaiting pole is made of wood and serves the same purpose except that it is naturally stronger than a leather strap. I usually try the strap first and if that is not enough I try the pole.

You will recall that I discussed earlier certain horses that bear in on the turns and out in the stretches. These are the ones on which I use a slip-mouth side-lining bit. Well, this same thing can affect the hind end of a horse. Horses will get their hind ends over toward the left shaft in the turns and against the right shaft in the stretches. In such cases, you can use two gaiting straps, one to hold them straight in the turns and the other to hold them in the stretches. It is the same reason for which you would use two head poles.

I very much dislike putting a gait strap too close to a horse.

When a horse is standing or even jogging, the strap will not look too close, but when he is going faster and the muscles are expanding and contracting he need much more room. This is especially true with a trotter although it causes a lot of pacers to cross-fire or hit their ankles and tendons. If one is put too close to a trotter, you can run into all kinds of problems such as the horse hitting his hind shins, front quarters or pulling his shoes. I believe that gaiting straps that are too close to a horse cause a lot of trotters to break.

There are four basic types of bridles. They are (1) the open bridle which is the most common of all and which permits a horse to see in all directions, (2) the closed or blind bridle which has blinkers on the side so that the horse cannot see behind him or to the side but which provides unobstructed forward vision (3) the "Kant-See-Bak" bridle which permits a horse to see everywhere except directly behind him and (4) the telescope or "Peek-A-Boo" bridle which provides only limited vision straight out in front. The latter bridle comes in several styles and variations.

A normal bridle is nothing more than a leather device that fits over and down each side of the horse's head, and into the open end of which the driving bit is fastened. As a matter of fact, the sole purpose of a standard bridle is to hold the bit and overcheck in place.

Most seasoned race horses wear either an open or a closed bridle. I prefer an open bridle (Fig. 39) with most older horses because if their manners are good it's much more comfortable on a horse. It's especially good on a horse that wants to take hold and go too much. With a closed bridle, a horse can hear the others behind him but cannot see them and he is likely to get excited and want to trot or pace the front end of the race too fast. Usually, an open bridle will relax this type of horse because he can see what's behind him and doesn't get excited.

A closed bridle (Figs. 65-1 and 65-3) is for horses that do too much looking around or are inclined to be lazy. It is perhaps the most widely used bridle, and rightly so, because it suits the majority of horses.

I break most of my colts in an open bridle. I do this so they get used to everything and can see the cart and driver behind them. But it's been my experience that just as soon as you get

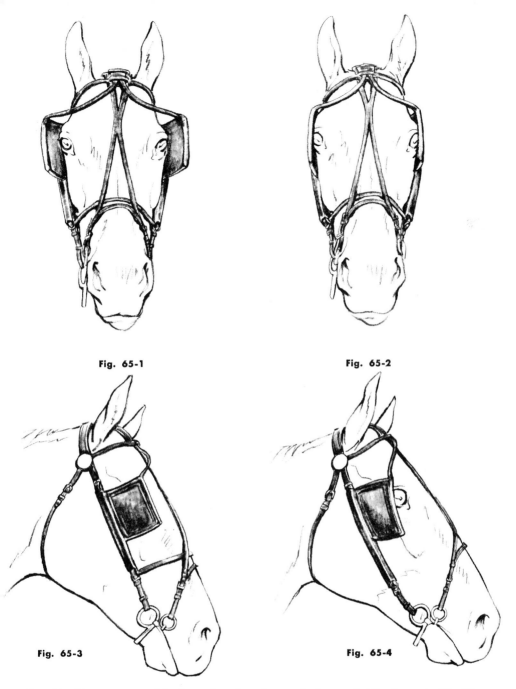

Fig. 65-1

Fig. 65-2

Fig. 65-3

Fig. 65-4

Fig. 65. Various types of bridles, other than the standard open bridle shown in Fig 39, are illustrated here and on the following two pages. Fig. 65–1 is a head-on view of a properly-adjusted blind (or closed) bridle. Fig. 65–2 is an improper illustration of the same bridle in that the blinds are drawn in too tight thus restricting the horse's vision more than necessary. Fig. 65–3 is a profile view of a properly-adjusted blind bridle. Fig. 65–4 is improper in that the trainer has failed to use a nose strap and thus the blind is pulled back out of position and in against the horse's eyes when the driver puts pressure on the lines.

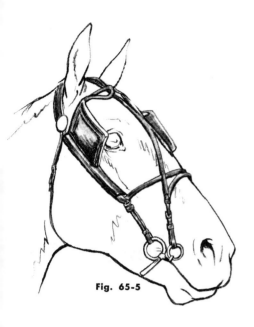

Fig. 65-5

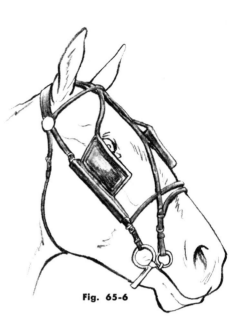

Fig. 65-6

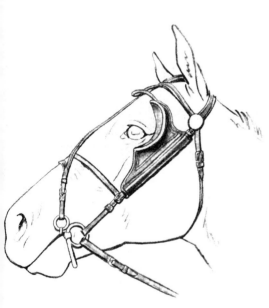

Fig. 65-7

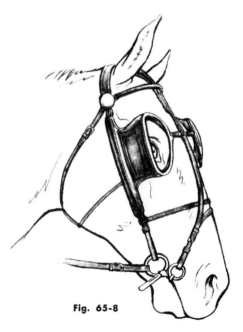

Fig. 65-8

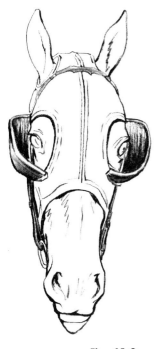

Fig. 65-9

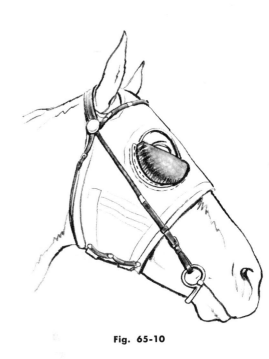

Fig. 65-10

(Continued from page 479)

In Fig. 65–5, the blinds are placed too high and in Fig. 65–6 they are too low. Fig. 65–7 is a properly-adjusted Kant-See-Bak bridle and Fig. 65–8 is a telescope or "Peek-A-Boo" bridle. Figs. 65–9 and 65–10 are front and side views of running horse blinkers with adjustable cups. Fig. 65–11 illustrates the manner in which a sheepskin roll can be used as a satisfactory and economical substitute for a Kant-See-Bak bridle.

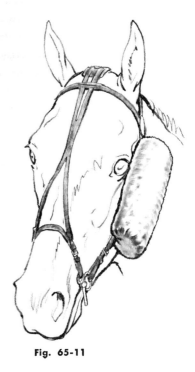

Fig. 65-11

a colt broken he'll start watching you out of one eye and start turning his head a little to one side or the other to watch what you're doing behind him.

So after I reach a certain point with my colts—shortly after they have been broken to drive—I switch to a Kant-See-Bak bridle (Fig. 65-7). Some trainers will go to a blind bridle at this stage but I don't because I have found that with a Kant-See-Bak colts are not nearly as likely to run into a fence or something if they get scared, as colts will, and run sideways. With a Kant-See-Bak, they are much less inclined to run sideways because they can see another horse coming up alongside and at the same time it keeps them from watching the driver behind them. If you do not have a Kant-See-Bak bridle, you can achieve the same result by wrapping a piece of sheepskin around each side of the bridle behind the horse's eyes (Fig. 65-11) to prevent him from seeing back, or by using a hood with blinkers on it.

The telescope bridle (Fig. 65-8) is for use with horses that are inclined to be a little spooky for one reason or another. I used one on Prince Jay. He was a free-for-all pacer but he had one bad habit; he wouldn't go in near the rail. I'd be driving him along in a race and he'd suddenly shy out for no apparent reason—maybe something he saw along the fence or something he thought he saw—and I'd find myself out in second horse position. I always thought he had been frightened by something that jumped out from under a fence and never forgot it. So I put a telescope bridle on him and never did have any trouble with him from then on. He was letter perfect.

I had another horse one time who'd had his legs cut out from under him in a race. After that he was always afraid of wheels getting too close to him and every time a horse came up alongside and a wheel would get near him he would become frightened and jump the other way or shy away from that wheel. I put a telescope bridle on him and this overcame the problem because he couldn't see the wheel down there by his legs.

The telescope bridle has round blinds that fit over the eye and they have to be adjusted exactly. The eye must be right in the center of the little round blinker so that the horse has unlimited forward vision. If the adjustment isn't exact, the angle of the horse's vision could be right or left, up or down and that isn't what you want. You want it straight ahead only.

Another piece of equipment that falls in this category is blinkers. Usually referred to as running horse blinkers because they are worn quite frequently by the runners, a set of blinkers consists of a cloth hood (Figs. 65-9 and 65-10) with two holes at the top where the ears protrude and two holes for the eyes. These hoods come with two adjustable half cups that fit around the eyes.

If your horse was scared of horses coming alongside him in a race, you would put the cups directly behind and over the eye so that he couldn't see back. If he was looking down and trying to find things to jump over and your shadow roll wasn't covering all these points, you would turn the cups at a little angle toward the bottom to cover the open area. Another nice thing about blinkers is that you can adjust each cup on each side at a little different angle if for some reason you might find that necessary.

An important consideration in using blinkers is that they are much more economical than either a Kant-See-Bak or a Peek-A-Boo bridle. If you are careful to adjust the cups properly, you can get the same results for a lot less money. Just as with other items of equipment, you want to be sure, when you adjust the cups, that you don't put them in a position that will leave the horse practically blindfolded when he is checked up. I think blinkers are very good on certain horses and they seem to be getting more and more popular with harness horses.

You can also get blinker hoods that have extensions which cover the ears. It is sometimes very useful to have these ear coverings because they have a lining in them that helps kill the sound of noises outside.

Noise will frequently excite a horse and in a race it will sometimes be enough to start a horse pulling quite hard. I do not usually wear hoods with the ear extensions on pullers, but very often I will stuff a horse's ears with cotton. I don't often find this necessary when training a horse but in a race, especially at the start, amid all the noise, excitement, shouting and whip-slashing, horses will sometimes pull very hard and go the front end of the mile much more than they should. If they have their ears stuffed so they can't hear all this noise, it seems to help them quite a bit.

Some horses don't like to have their ears stuffed and they

will shake their heads and try to throw the cotton out. It is best to wear hoods on horses like this. I would suggest that if you are thinking about doing this, you stuff your horse's ears and put a hood on him while you are cooling him out a few times before you actually do it in a race. This will help him get used to it.

In stuffing a horse's ear, be sure you use one piece of cotton. If you use two or three or more pieces, it's possible that a little piece might get left in the ear and that would lead to trouble. In stuffing the ear, roll the cotton up to what you consider the proper size and then insert it in the ear being careful that there is enough of the cotton showing so that you can get hold of it to pull it out later. Even if you are using but one piece of cotton, it is still a good idea to check the ear after removing the cotton to make sure you get it all out.

With horses that are accustomed to having their ears stuffed and do not resent it, I will put the cotton in place just before I go on the track for the race. I won't use it when I am warming the horse up. But if I have a horse that gets excited and is inclined to pull while warming up, I will stuff his ears for the last warmup mile as well. However, I never stuff a horse's ears until I am going on the track and always take the cotton out as soon as the horse comes off the track. That would be immediately before and after either the warmup mile or the race mile or both. Never leave a horse's ears stuffed between heats.

Returning now to the subject of bridles, a closed or Kant-See-Bak bridle should always have a nose strap, which is a strip of leather that goes across the horse's nose and fastens to the cheek pieces of the bridle on each side. A nose strap does not come on a bridle when you buy a set of harness and many young trainers do not realize its importance. This is especially true with a closed bridle since the blinkers will pull in against the horse's eyes (Fig 65-4) when he takes hold of the bit if there is no nose strap. As I mentioned earlier, a nose "strap" does not encircle the muzzle and differs in that respect only from a nose "band" which does.

Every bridle must be adjusted so that the bit fits comfortably in the mouth. If the bridle is too loose, the bit flops around in the mouth. It is uncomfortable on the horse and he keeps playing with his tongue trying to push the bit back up in his mouth and usually ends up with his tongue over the bit. On the other hand, if the bridle is too tight, it is naturally uncomfortable on the horse because it's pulling up on his cheeks all the time.

It's a simple matter to adjust a bridle properly. It amounts to nothing more than letting out or taking up a hole or two in the cheek pieces. With a closed bridle, you can let it out or take it up both above and below the blinkers so that the blinker fits on the horse's eye properly. I like the blinkers on a closed bridle to be just a little higher than normal; in other words, fitted so that the horse's eye is just a little below the center of the blinker. Then, when his head is checked up, he will not be able to see back over the top of the blinker. If he were able to do this, it would partially defeat the purpose of the closed bridle.

That pretty much concludes my discussion of bits and bridles and leads in a natural way to my third category, that of "boots." In order to treat this subject completely, I am going to expand the category slightly by including certain other items of equipment that, normally, cannot be classified as boots. Such an exception is the first piece of equipment I want to talk about, the hobbles (or hopples).

Hobbles are worn by pacers and their purpose is to steady the horse and help him maintain the pacing gait which, as you know, consists of the legs on the same side of the body moving forward and backward in unison. A hobble is really nothing more than a strap with a loop at each end, each loop encircling a leg on the same side of the body. When the horse moves at speed, his legs "fill" the hobbles which tend to steady him and help him hold his gait.

The pacing gait is an acquired gait rather than a natural one. If you notice horses out loose, they rarely ever pace. They either trot or run. Therefore, it is more difficult to keep a pacer on stride than a trotter. Without the extensive use of hobbles, there would be very few pacers and almost no pacing 2-year-olds.

When I was just a youngster and beginning to help my dad train horses on Prince Edward Island some 35 years ago, hobbles were heavy, cumbersome, awkward devices made out of thick leather. The leather straps were usually from three quarters of an inch to an inch wide with webbing through the center to make them stronger. They were very heavy and must have weighed ten pounds apiece.

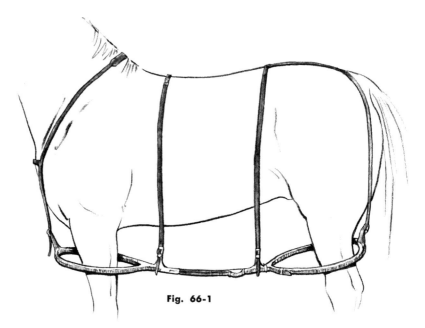

Fig. 66-1

Fig. 66. Proper adjustment of the hobbles, as described in detail in the text, is demonstrated in the illustrations on this and the opposite page. The basic adjustment, indicating the desirable cradle effect, is shown in Fig. 66–1 above. Fig. 66–2 is the proper front leg adjustment and Fig. 66–3 the proper hind leg and back strap adjustment.

In those days, too, horses usually needed a lot tighter hobble because they were of mixed trotting and pacing breeds and did not have too much natural inclination toward the pacing gait. For that reason, horses usually had to wear tight hobbles and these heavy, cumbersome things tired a lot of them very quickly.

In recent years, with the advent of plastic and nylon, hobbles have become lighter and at the same time more durable. A set of plastic hobbles will weigh about 3½ pounds and a horse hardly knows he has them on. At the same time, the breed has improved and pacers go more naturally, so the problem has been helped from that standpoint as well. When I was a boy there were very few natural, free-legged pacers and while we don't have very many today I am sure there would be if it weren't for the circumstances under which we race.

By that, I mean that a lot of our big races for the big money are on half mile tracks and at a single dash rather than three

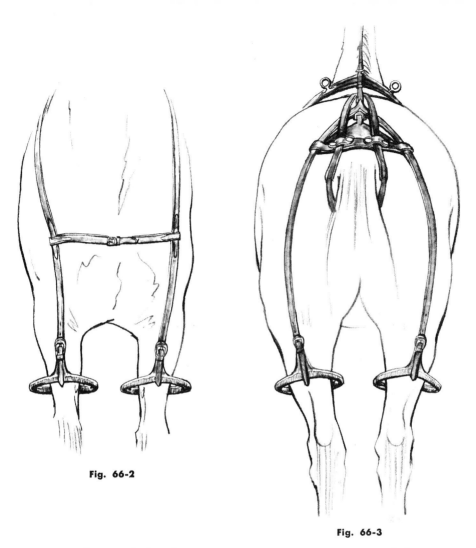

Fig. 66-2

Fig. 66-3

or more heats. Under these circumstances, you pretty much have to put hobbles on your horse whether you want to or not. He has to be steady around the turns; you don't want him to make a break because of the money involved and the track doesn't want you to make a break because the betting public is involved.

In addition, a lot of the big money is hung out for young horses, two and 3-year-olds, and in order to get there and get your share you can't take the time that is necessary to make a free legged pacer. So that variety is just about disappearing from the scene and I, for one, am sorry to see it happen. There is nothing like a good free-legged pacer.

There are three types of hobbles: the regular pacing hobbles, the cross hobbles and the half hobbles. The use of hobbles is limited almost exclusively to the former. They are usually made of leather, plastic or nylon. The leather hobbles usually have a webbing of nylon or cotton in the center to give them added strength and help prevent them from stretching.

I prefer the lightweight plastic hobbles. Actually, the plastic hobbles that I use are nylon in the center, that is the connecting strip between the two loops is nylon, with plastic loops covering the nylon that goes around the leg. They are light and strong and they don't chafe a horse like the old leather hobbles. For those three reasons, I think the plastic hobbles are better for 90% of the horses racing today.

The plastic hobbles are so light that most horses probably feel as though they don't have anything at all around their legs. This occasionally will cause a horse that is not completely steady in his gait to make a mis-step and such a horse probably ought to be wearing leather hobbles. Horses such as these probably need the feel of something a little more substantial on their legs, a little bit of restraining action to help them maintain their gait. Leather hobbles will do this for most horses.

Whether made of leather or some other material, the basic pattern is very much the same. Each hobble (Fig. 66-1) consists of two loops that go around the legs and an adjustable center part between the loops. The loops are oval in shape, stiff enough to hold their shape and smooth on the inside next to the legs to minimize chafing. Each hobble goes around one front leg and one hind leg on the same side. As you can readily understand from this, hobbles force a horse to pace if properly applied and adjusted because actually the legs on the same side of the body are tied together.

The length of the hobbles varies according to the size of the horse, the way he is gaited and the amount he depends on the hobbles to keep him on the pace. Hobbles are measured from the inside of the front loop to the inside of the back loop where the hobbles come against the front of the front leg and the back of the hind leg. They may be anywhere from 42 to 62 inches, but usually are between 52 and 58 inches. The center part that connects the two loops has a buckle or some other similar device so that the hobbles can be lengthened or shortened.

The hobbles should be adjusted so that they ride easily when the horse is in motion. Their length, height, and the way they hang, are important factors and must be considered carefully.

Attached to the front and back of each hobble loop are up-right straps made of leather or other material. These straps are about four inches long and each has a buckle on the end. They are used in conjunction with the hobble hangers. There are four hobble hangers that are used to hold the hobbles up, the front, the rear, and two center hangers. They are usually made of leather but can be made of plastic or any similar material that is both light and strong.

The front hanger goes over the neck, just ahead of the withers, down on each side and is buckled to the uprights on the front of the hobbles (Fig. 66-2). The height of the hobbles on the front legs is adjusted by raising or lowering at this point. An adjustable strap also goes across the chest to hold the hangers the proper distance apart.

The rear hanger buckles into the back strap on the horse's back (Fig. 66-3) and runs back to a point between the horse's coupling and the butt of his tail where it divides, one strap going down each side and buckling into the uprights on the back loops. The height of the rear loops can be adjusted at either or both of two places; at the point where the hanger strap is buckled to the back strap and/or where the hangers are buckled to the uprights on the back loops.

The two center hangers (Fig. 66) complete the set. The forward one attaches to the back strap just behind the saddle, hangs down each side and attaches to the two uprights just back of the front loops. The other one attaches to the backstrap just in front of the hips, hangs down each side and attaches to the upright nearest the back loops. The center of the hobbles can be raised or lowered by adjusting these hangers accordingly.

Some trainers use a different type center hanger consisting of one strap attached to the center of the back strap and hanging down on each side approximately 14 inches with a ring on each end (Fig. 67). Two straps attach to each ring and buckle into the uprights in the center of the hobbles. I prefer the regular type hangers because I think a hobble rides better this way than with the single center strap type. In fact, I insist on the hangers being attached to the harness at points approximately the same distance apart as the uprights on the hobbles to which they attach. In this way, each hanger swings with the hobble like the

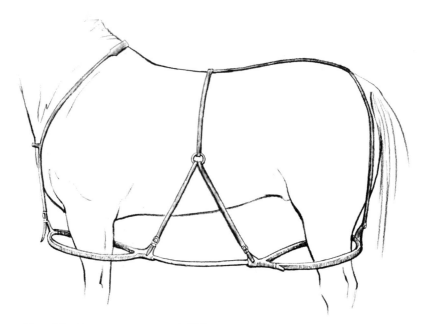

Fig. 67. Some trainers use hobbles with a single-strap center hanger as illustrated. The author does not like this method because the single strap has a tendency to pull the hobbles against the extended leg and chafing is more likely to result.

pendulum of a clock, whereas the other type tends to pull forward on the back legs when they are extended behind the horse and backward on the front legs when they are extended forward. Naturally, any unnecessary friction, even though slight, will tend to tire the muscles as well as chafe the legs.

I guess everyone has a different idea about adjusting hobbles for the first time. I don't think there is any way you can determine the length of hobble a horse should wear just by looking at him. In trying to ascertain the length of hobbles to put on a colt for the first time, or on a horse, if I didn't know what length he was supposed to wear, I use a method my father taught me years ago. He would put a hobble on, adjust it to the proper height and then have the horse stand perfectly natural and adjust the length so that there was four inches between the horse's front leg and the end of the loop when the hobble was pulled snugly forward (Fig. 68). I have done this for many years and consider it a good starting point in most cases.

Of course, as soon as you start training a horse you can tell almost immediately what further adjustment has to be made. For instance, a little, short, rapid-gaited horse probably wouldn't fill the hobbles and they would have to be shortened. A big-gaited horse, on the other hand, would very likely be filling the hobbles and they would be too tight on him at some part of his stride. They would have to be let out, that is lengthened an inch or so.

It is much better to start with the hobbles a little too long than too short. I like to use as loose a hobble as possible and try to balance the horse so he can pace with them loose. Train him as much as you can to go free-legged while balancing him by shoeing and any other means to make him good-gaited. Then he will go better with hobbles and not need them quite so tight. A tight hobble tires a horse's legs and keeps him from taking a good long stride, thereby keeping him from going distance as well as from reaching his top speed potential. If a horse will go with a looser hobble and feel safe and not make any mistakes, then it is just common sense that he will go farther and faster than with a tight hobble.

Lots of times when a horse is going slow, at a 2:30 clip for example, the hobbles might seem awfully loose on him, flopping around and giving the impression that there is too much slack. But when that same horse is at top speed, perhaps going a quarter in 29 seconds, he might be filling his hobbles and they might be fairly snug on him because he would be striding farther. A tight hobble not only could prevent him from reaching his top speed, but could also cause him to tire more quickly.

At the same time, you can't have the hobbles too long because he might start "feeling" for them and start rolling and

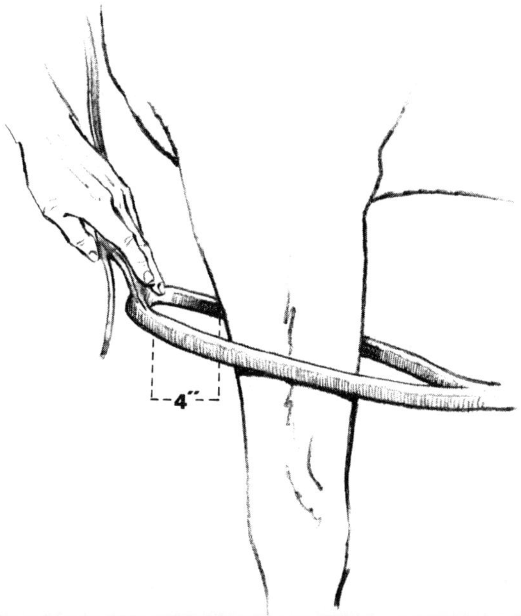

Fig. 68. When the proper hobble length is unknown, the author pulls the hobbles snugly forward as illustrated and adjusts them so that there is four inches between the front leg and the loop of the hobble. He considers this an average starting point for such horses.

tumbling. You can feel this more in the lines than you can see it sometimes. You'll just know that he isn't 100% flat and usually this is the reason. Such a horse will get tired and go bad-gaited just from reaching for the hobbles. If they were just a little shorter they would keep him in good stride and keep him flat.

A horse might also wear his hobbles at different lengths at different times and under different conditions. For example, a horse will usually go with a little looser hobble on a mile track especially if the footing is real good. A horse going from a mile track to a half mile track will very often need his hobbles a little shorter. In many cases, a horse going around the sharper half mile track turns needs just a little tighter hobble to help him navigate the turn. On a track where the footing cups out or where it is muddy, a horse will need a shorter, tighter hobble to help him stay on gait in the bad footing.

Here is another point that I consider very important with regard to hobble length. When I am starting to train my horses in the winter for the next racing season, I always start them out with a little looser hobble than they wore the year before.

For example, if a horse raced the previous year in a 55-inch hobble, I would start him out with a 57 or 57½-inch hobble. I would train him that way and try to get him accustomed to a hobble that is a little longer. Then, gradually, as I get close to race time, if I feel that he still needs them a little shorter I will take them up a little at a time until I have them where I think he needs them.

If you train a horse all fall and all winter in a tight hobble, you just shorten his stride and he gets so he doesn't try to stride out any. But if you will let the hobbles out in the winter when you start training, you will very often find that the horse will begin striding out better and making good use of his increased extension. I think it helps quite a bit to train one this way even though you might have to shorten the hobbles before returning to the races.

Hobbles are inclined to stretch and slip and give a little and consequently they should be measured very carefully before and after each race and workout. On a number of occasions, I have seen horses in a race, sometimes in a big stake race, get rough-gaited and make a break, whereupon the trainer comes back and measures the hobbles and says something like, "Gosh, I just put those hobbles on brand new a few weeks ago and they have stretched two inches already!" What these trainers should have done was to have measured the hobbles *before* the race to make sure they were the exact length they were supposed to be.

Every horse should have an equipment card with all the measurements on it. This card should go to the paddock with the horse every time he races because if you should change grooms you would still have the equipment card that shows what hole the overcheck goes in, what length the hobbles should be, etc. Failure to do so could result not only in losing a big race but, as in the case of improper hobble length, a bad accident.

The height of the hobbles is also important. If they are too low in front they will tire a horse's legs, especially a high going horse. If they are too high, they will not serve their purpose in gaiting a horse and keeping him on stride and at the same time they will bind him in the big muscles where the legs and chest join. A trainer who observes his horse closely and uses a little of that "horse sense" I have been writing about should not have much difficulty finding a happy medium.

In front, the hobble should be fitted (Fig. 66-2) so that it rides just a little higher than halfway between the horse's knee and where his leg and chest join. If a horse had a knee and half arm boot on, then the hobble should be just above the top of the inside of the knee boot. It should also be remembered that when the horse is checked up it will tend to raise the hobbles in front. So they should be adjusted with the horse's head held at the same height that it will be when he is racing.

The rear loops should be adjusted to ride in the hollow or concave part of the hind legs when the horse is in motion (Fig. 66-3). Adjust the top strap first so that the spot where the straps separate to go down each side is in the correct position on the rump. This spot is usually about halfway between the coupling and the butt of the tail, although it varies somewhat according to the conformation of the animal.

It is not a good idea to shorten this top strap too much since this would tend to move the spot on the hanger too far forward. Even though you make the compensating adjustments where the hangers attach to the uprights on the hobbles so that they will be the right height on the legs, they will be continually pulling forward on the hind legs causing a horse to chafe both directly on the back of the legs and on the inside. By the same token, the hobbles will not ride too comfortably if the fork on the hanger is too far back toward the butt of the tail. This will cause them to have a bouncy, jerky movement.

The center of the hobbles should be lower than the ends (Fig. 66), giving a standing side view effect of a cradle or half moon. A hobble swings back and forth and at either extension of the horse's stride the center tends to come up because the straps are swinging instead of hanging straight down. Thus, in order to ride properly when the horse is pacing at any speed, the hobbles will actually look too low in the center when the horse is standing still.

Some horses fold up quite high in front and it sometimes becomes necessary to raise the centers to keep the horse from hitting the bottom of the hobbles near the back part of the front loops with his front feet. But if you have a horse that does not go too high, you will find that the hobbles will ride much better if they are lowered in the center.

The adjustment as to length of hobble is made in the center, between the loops. The leather hobbles have buckles in the center with holes punched in them so that you can shorten the hobbles a hole or lengthen them a hole. The holes are usually an inch and a half apart so that if you shortened a hobble one hole you would be shortening it three quarters of an inch. Of course, you can also punch additional holes as required.

The plastic hobbles come with buckles in the center but there are no holes in the strap. Instead, there is a clamp that may be moved any fraction of an inch to make the proper adjustment.

As I said before, hobbles are usually made of leather, plastic or nylon. The leather ones are still the best on some horses, especially those that need to feel something substantial on their legs to hold them together or to prevent them from going off stride. Hobbles with nylon centers and plastic covered loops are perhaps the most popular at the present time. They are very light, have slip-proof buckles and very little stretch. They are not as likely to chafe a horse and are quite strong. They are also much easier to clean, especially after racing or training on a muddy track.

The loops on either end of the hobbles can be covered with sheepskin to prevent chafing, but once a horse gets chafed, the sheepskin usually does more harm than good. I like to use sheepskin when I put the hobbles on my colts for the first time. I do this for two reasons, primarily because it helps prevents chafing but also because I think that a colt does not mind the feel of the hobbles as much if they are covered with sheepskin and because sheepskin-covered hobbles don't bounce around quite as much.

The cross hobble, the sole purpose of which is to try to keep trotters from making breaks, is very seldom seen any more. I doubt that any manufacturing company even makes them except on special order. I never used a set to race although I have used them in training on rare occasions. They were designed to be used on a trotter and therefore had to go from the left front leg to the right hind leg and vice versa, crossing in the middle under the horse's belly. I have found that they cause a trotter to hit his shins and his knees and do not recommend their use.

In some instances, I have seen the regular pacing hobbles put on this way although the hangers do not fit right in the centers. In fact, if you want to use this type on a trotter, it is better to leave the center hangers off and put a strap like a safety girth from one shaft to the other, passing beneath the center of the hobbles about where they cross. I saw Don Busse use a set in this manner and they seemed to work pretty good.

The half hobble, which can be used on a trotter or a pacer, consists of two loops joined together by a cotton or nylon rope that runs through a pulley. I have seen them used on either end of a horse but they are usually used on the front end of a trotter to try to keep him on the trot.

When used in this manner, the front legs go in the loops with the front carrier of a regular set of hobbles used to hold them up. The pulley, which is padded and which has four straps attached to it, is situated under the horse's belly just behind the girth. The two straps on the sides of the pulley are buckled around the shafts of the cart or sulky directly in line with the pulley. They can be adjusted to raise or lower the pulley to the desired height. The two straps on the back corner of the pulley are taken back and outward at an angle and buckled around the shafts to keep them from slipping forward.

I never thought these hobbles helped a horse much because when the horse takes a little hold the cart or sulky tends to move forward and slackens the tension on the hobbles since the two back straps are the only way to adjust the tightness of the hobbles and they are fastened to the shafts.

I saw my dad take a strap or cord, fasten it to the pulley and run it straight back between the horse's hind legs and fasten it to the sulky in the center of the seat. I also saw him put the hobbles on the hind legs and take the straps from the corners of the pulley, run them between the horse's front legs and fasten them over his neck. At least this way they could be adjusted so that they did not slacken when the horse took hold.

There are many types of boots worn by trotters and pacers. Most are worn for protection although some that are worn by trotters on their front feet are intended primarily to improve balance or gait. Most boots come in three sizes, small, medium and large and usually can be ordered in a fourth size, extra large.

On trotters, the most frequently worn boots are scalpers and shin boots behind and bell boots or quarter boots in front. Trotters will also wear speedy cut or ankle boots behind and elbow boots, knee boots and shin boots in front. Knee boots and front shin boots, however, are not needed as often on trotters as they are on pacers.

Among pacers, the most common boots are knee boots, tendon boots and pacing quarter boots, all worn in front. The latter come in various styles and perhaps the most commonly used is the rubber scalper, primarily made for a trotter's hind feet but turned around and put on a pacer's front feet so that the high part is on the inside and protects the quarters in the event a pacer is cross-firing. This boot is much safer than the old style pacing quarter boot made of leather because there is no danger of it getting caught in a knee boot and tripping the horse. These boots are also much lighter and far more economical and I recommend their use with pacers. Except on very rare occasions, I haven't used a leather pacing quarter boot in years.

Basic interference in the trotter (Fig. 35) consists of the left front foot striking the left hind leg—or the right front foot striking the right hind leg—somewhere between the hairline of the hoof and the hock. The description applied to the interference depends on where the contact is being made.

If the interference is just above the hoof line, that is, if the toe of the left front foot is hitting the hind leg right at or just above the coronary band, the horse is said to be scalping. If the interference is taking place farther up on the pastern bone but still below the ankle, the horse is said to be speedy cutting. Likewise, a trotter may be hitting the ankle itself or—and this is most common of all—his hind shin. In rare instances a trotter may even interfere above the shin bone in the hock area.

In almost all instances, the contact takes place on the inside of the hind legs, and when all four feet are off the ground. In other words, when the horse is trotting, the outside edge of the front hoof hits the inside of the hind leg. There are two minor exceptions to this general rule. Most horses that scalp will hit directly on the front of the hind hoof, and there is the very rare case of the trotter that hits the front of his shins. The latter is usually caused by some abnormality in conformation, some peculiarity in the way he handles his front feet or occurs in the case of a horse that trots with his hind end off to one side, thereby hitting one hind shin in front.

Pacers that are interfering are usually hitting their knees (Fig. 33) or cross-firing (Fig. 35). A horse hits his knee with the front foot on the opposite side. As the front foot comes up and makes its arc, it fails to clear the knee on the opposite side and hits it in passing. (It should also be noted that occasionally a trotter will hit a hind shin with enough force to have the front foot bounce off and hit the opposite knee.) Cross-firing occurs when the hind foot on one side comes in contact with the front foot on the opposite side when the pacer is in motion.

All boots worn by trotters and pacers are adjustable in one or more ways and must be fitted properly from the quarter boots on up in front and from the scalpers on up behind.

Probably the most difficult boot to adjust on a horse is the elbow boot (Fig. 69). This boot is worn by trotters that are high-gaited in front and hit their elbows when the front legs fold to their highest point. The right front foot, for instance, will fold up and touch the right elbow.

The elbow boot has two suspenders that go over the neck and withers to hold the boot up. The front one attaches to the front of the strap going around the horse's leg and goes up over the neck. This suspender is adjustable at both ends and has an ad-

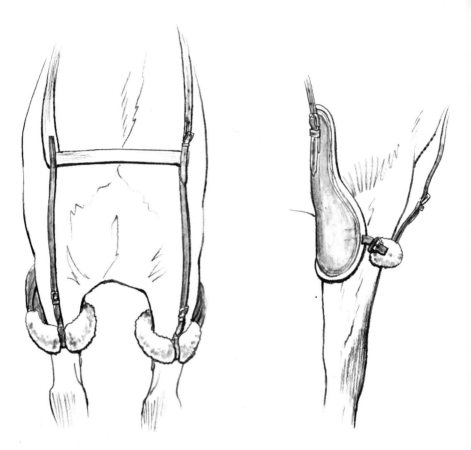

Fig. 69. The elbow boot, worn almost exclusively by trotters, is one of the most difficult to fit properly. The correct adjustment from the front, left, and from the side, right, is illustrated.

justable connecting strap going across the horse's chest. It is very similar to a front hobble carrier. The other suspender is attached to the upper portion of the boot itself. It goes up over the withers and fastens to the check hook on the saddle pad. This suspender is also adjustable so that the boot may be raised or lowered to fit the horse's elbow.

The suspenders and straps must be adjusted properly in order for the boot to fit right and common sense will tell you better than anything whether the adjustments are correct. There is a cup in the boot that fits right over the elbow but in adjusting it you have to take into consideration the fact that when the horse is trotting the foot is in elevation and the elbow moves up and down to a certain extent.

If the boots are adjusted too high, they will chafe a horse up in back of his elbow and if they are too low they will bother a horse when he is in motion because they will drop down too close to his knee.

In checking the adjustment of an elbow boot, stand back away from it and think about what it is supposed to do and how it works. Be certain that it is in the right place and fits over the elbow properly. Make sure that the little strap that goes around the front of the leg is adjusted so that there is enough slack in it to prevent binding when the horse folds his leg. And make certain that the strap that goes over the neck is adjusted to the right height and isn't pulling up on the boot or permitting the strap around the leg to drop down too low. If all these adjustments are made correctly, the boot should fit and ride properly on the horse.

The knee boot (Fig. 70) which, as I said, is worn more often by pacers than by trotters fits right over the inside part of the knee. When buying knee boots I always try to take three or four different styles to the stall and try them on the horse because the style that fits one horse might not fit the next one nearly as well. What you are looking for is a type of boot that on a particular horse gives adequate protection, fits the contour of the knee as perfectly as possible and doesn't stick out at the bottom. Naturally, the more it sticks out, the more likely it is that the horse's foot will hit it. Most knee boots come with a little pad that lies beneath the main buckle. When the boot is buckled on the horse, this pad should fit snugly in the hollow portion of the arm on the outside just above the knee. This makes the boot fit comfortably, prevents it from turning and also helps to keep it from sliding down.

Most knee boots come with suspenders although there are some styles that do not. However, I prefer to use a suspender because then I don't have to buckle the knee boot quite so tight. The suspenders should be adjusted so that they don't lift the boot up off the knee when the horse is in motion. This happens when the suspender is too tight. When it is too loose it just flops around and isn't serving its sole purpose of helping to hold the boot up. Properly adjusted, knee boot suspenders are just barely snug when the horse is standing in a normal position.

Knee boots also come in a number of types that provide protection for the arm as well as the knee. The arm is that part of the front leg between the knee and the elbow. For instance,

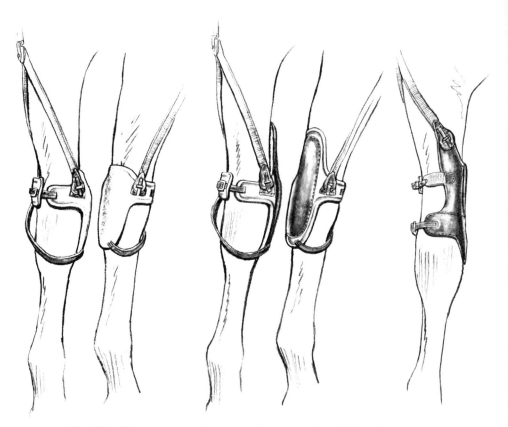

Fig. 70. There are several types and many styles of knee boots. Three of the most commonly used types are illustrated. At the left are plain knee boots which protect the knee only and are for the horse that hits right on the knee itself. In the center are knee and half arm boots which protect the entire knee as well as part of the arm above the knee. Some horses will wear a knee and arm boot (rather than half arm) to provide additional protection, if necessary, for the arm. At the right is an arm and half knee boot fitted properly on the right front leg. This boot is for horses that are higher-gaited and usually hit on the arm above the knee.

there is the knee and arm boot that protects the inside of the entire arm as well as the knee. There is also the knee and half arm boot that has the arm boot portion extending about halfway up the arm as the name indicates. There are several different styles of each of these types.

In addition, there is also the plain arm boot that is worn almost exclusively by trotters. Trotters, as a general rule, go a little higher in front than pacers and a trotter that is inclined to go a little close in front but goes higher than his knee just uses the arm boot. Arm boots are light and don't bother a horse very much and are very good protection. There are quite a few trotters that can get by with an arm boot alone and don't have to wear a knee boot at all.

Personally, I prefer to use the knee and half arm boot on most pacers. The plain knee boot that doesn't have the half arm protection on it is more inclined to stick out at the bottom. The arm part helps to prevent this.

Pacers don't usually go high enough to require a full arm boot. But even if they did it would be very inconvenient because the arm boot suspender comes down and fastens to the arm part of the boot right where the hobbles are. Unless a pacer is free-legged, arm boots are not very satisfactory.

With a pacer that does go a little high, I have found that a knee and half arm boot is usually enough. If they go higher than that, they are going to hit the bottom of the hobbles with their front feet anyway and that's just a little too high for a pacer to go. Besides, you can usually shoe a pacer to go lower. Take the weight off and use a light weight full swedge shoe or an aluminum shoe or, if necessary, an aluminum shoe with a grab around the toe to keep him from going too high.

It is more difficult to shoe a trotter to keep him from going high for two reasons. First, a lot of trotters need a little weight in front, more so than pacers, to balance them and, of course, the weight makes them go a little higher. The other reason is that if you do too much with a trotter to keep him from going high you are slowing his foot up in front and if he's not getting his foot off the ground fast enough he will often start interfering behind and begin hitting either his speedy cuts or his shins.

Farther down on the front leg, trotters and/or pacers may wear front shin boots, tendon boots, and ankle boots (or passing boots as they are also known). These are designed to protect areas where interference occurs.

Some trotters and pacers are inclined to brush their front shins with the opposite front foot, usually when they are traveling at a relatively slow rate of speed. The action is the same as with a horse that is brushing his knees except that it occurs lower down. Such horses would wear a front shin boot (Fig. 71) which covers the inside of the front leg from the bottom of the ankle to the knee, the amount of protection depending on the type of boot. One type ends just below the knee while the

other type, known as the shin and half knee boot, also covers
the lower part of the knee.

(This latter boot, incidentally, is very often used on pacers
behind that are inclined to touch their hind shins with the toe
of the opposite front foot. This type of interference is not easily
detected because the horse does not usually hit hard enough
to make a noticeable mark. But it is enough to make him bad-
gaited or to cause him to make a break. If a trainer has a pacer
that goes rough-gaited or makes an occasional break for no apparent reason, it would probably pay to check the coronary
band on the inside of the hind foot as well as the inside of the
hind shin for tiny marks that might indicate interference. On
rare occasions, a pacer will even touch the lower part of his
hocks in this manner and the shin and half knee boots will
usually cover this area. If not, a trotter's hind shin and half hock
boot without the speedy cut attachment can be used. This
type of interference usually occurs when a horse is pacing at a
very high rate of speed.)

The tendon boot (which is actually a shin boot with an attachment at the rear covering the tendon) protects the inside and
back of the front leg (Fig. 71) and is worn by pacers that cross-

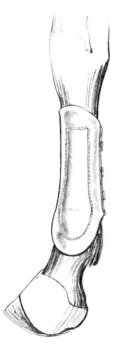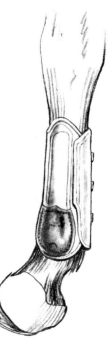

Fig. 71. A front shin boot, left, is
worn by a horse whose front foot interferes with the opposite front leg between
the knee and ankle as illustrated in Fig.
33. The boot at the right is similar except
that it has a back-of-tendon protection
and is usually referred to simply as a
tendon boot. This boot protects against
a horse hitting his tendon with the opposite hind foot and thus is used almost
exclusively by pacers. In the position they
are illustrated here, the rubber scalpers
(on the feet) are for the right front foot
of a pacer to protect against cross-firing.

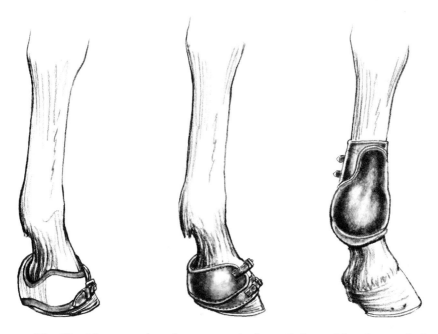

Fig. 72. These are three boots worn in front. Left to right, the standard trotting quarter boot, the hinged quarter boot and the ankle (or passing) boot with behind-the-ankle protection.

fire higher than usual. The hind foot, instead of interfering with the inside of the front hoof on the opposite side, hits up higher in the tendon area and protection is required. The tendon boot provides this protection. Because a trotter does not cross-fire, he seldom wears a tendon boot.

Actually, very few trotters wear either tendon boots or shin boots in front. If a trotter does need a shin boot, it is usually when he is going slow. I have had several trotters that would need shin boots in front while they were jogging or going their slow miles, but as soon as they started trotting at any speed they would not need them because of the higher action of the front feet at speed. I would use shin boots on such horses when they were jogging and going their slow miles and then would remove them for their fast training miles and races.

There are two reasons why I would use tendon boots on a pacer. The first has to do with his gait. Some pacers are gaited so that they come quite close to their tendons and I will use tendon boots on such horses. I will also use tendon boots on young or inexperienced pacers—2-year-olds and green horses—in their first few starts, especially on half mile tracks or on tracks with sharp turns. A horse of this type, especially a fast leaving one, will often make a little mis-step through lack of racing experience and cut a tendon even though he isn't actually gaited to come close. I find that in cases like this tendon boots are a good form of insurance.

Ankle boots, also known as passing boots, provide the same type of protection for the ankle area. There are two basic types and several different styles. One type is the ankle boot that has protection on the inside only. The other type is the ankle boot with "back of the ankle" protection (Fig. 72). This boot comes down quite low on the inside and around the back part of the ankle affording protection in that area.

For reasons previously described in discussing tendon boots and front shin boots, I prefer to use the latter type of ankle boot with pacers and the plain ankle boot with trotters. A pacer that has a tendency to hit a little higher than the hoof area when he cross-fires requires some additional protection and this boot provides it.

If I am certain that my pacer is gaited so that he doesn't require any protection higher than the ankle, I much prefer to use this type of ankle boot instead of a tendon boot. The ankle boot doesn't interfere nearly as much with the natural movement of the horse's leg and thus permits greater freedom in the flexing of the tendons, which is an important consideration.

A plain ankle boot, one without the protection in back, is used with a horse, either trotter or pacer, that brushes an ankle with the opposite front foot, almost always when he is going at a slow rate of speed. These boots buckle around the ankle and are very simple to adjust.

There are a number of boots that are worn on the front feet. Most trotters these days don't wear any boots on their front feet but when they do they usually wear either rubber bell boots or quarter boots of some kind.

When you see a trotter wearing bell boots (Fig. 73) it doesn't necessarily mean he is wearing them for protection. Very often he wears bell boots just to help balance him and get away on the trot. Bell boots do not weigh very much but they are sometimes a big help in balancing a trotter properly.

The bell boot is pulled up over the foot and sets loosely on

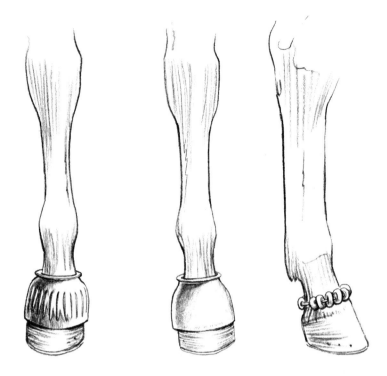

Fig. 73. Bell boots, worn in front by trotters and pacers, are highly regarded by the author. He likes to start his trotting colts out with the ribbed bell boot, left, and uses the plain bell boot, center, on many pacers rather than a rubber scalper or rubber quarter boots. A "rattler," right, is a string of bone or hardwood beads and a set is sometimes used on the hind feet of pacers or the front feet of trotters to help them establish their gait. They should be adjusted loosely. The illustration is of a rattler on the hind foot as it would be used with a pacer.

it. I like these boots very much for getting colts started. Trotting colts seem to like the feel of bell boots flopping around on their feet and I think it helps get them on the trot when they are just jogging and getting started.

Usually, the bell boots are a little too long or a little too deep. If you are using bell boots on your horse and you notice that every time he puts his foot down the bottom of the boot is hitting the track first and sliding the boot up and down the heel, I would suggest you take a pair of scissors and cut a little bit off the bottom of the boot all the way around, say a quarter to a half inch.

When a bell boot is too deep, it can be bad for a couple of reasons. For one thing, as the boot slides up and down it will set up an irritation and cause sore heels. There is also the possibility that the horse might step on the bottom part of a bell boot that is too deep and trip himself. I have seen this happen.

There are two types of bell boots, the ribbed ones which give quite a lot of protection, and which are heavier than the unribbed or plain bell boots. I like these plain bell boots quite a lot because they are very light and unlikely to chafe a horse. An average size plain bell boot will weigh about three ounces.

I usually start my trotting colts out with the ribbed bell boot, because it is a little heavier, and my pacing colts with the plain bell boot. I will usually switch the trotting colts over to the plain bell boot once they have established their gait.

I find the plain bell boot to be a very good boot for a pacer. I use it a lot of times instead of a rubber scalper or a rubber quarter boot. I find that it is not nearly as likely to fly off. This is especially true on a muddy track or a deep track where boots will sometimes push up around the pastern or fly off altogether.

Rubber quarter boots tend to come off under these conditions. Even rubber scalpers will fly off, especially after they have been used for a while and have lost some of their elasticity. This might also happen when they get a little chipped around the bottom where a horse might touch or where they slide down over the shoe and perhaps get torn around the bottom edge. This weakens the boot and it is more likely to come off.

The plain bell boot, on the other hand, usually stays right in place and almost never flies off. If you get a pair of plain bell boots that fit your horse just right and are snug and comfortable on him, they are ideal for a pacer in front. Even if he brushes his knees, there isn't as much danger of the bell boots coming off as there is with the other types of boots.

Trotting quarter boots fit around the front hoof with the protective portion to the rear. The protective portion of a pacing quarter boot, on the other hand, is to the inside and the rear. Actually, the pacing quarter boot is rapidly disappearing from the scene as most trainers, including me, prefer to use rubber scalpers or a pair of bell boots instead.

The basic quarter boot for trotters (Fig. 72) is made of leather or felt. If you want more weight in the boot you use leather. Sometimes a trotter will require this type of boot for balance when he needs just a little weight on his heel. Very often a little leather or white felt quarter boot is just what is required to balance a trotter properly.

Before using a quarter boot, a trainer should always keep in mind that there is a certain amount of expansion in a horse's heel every time it hits the race track. The heels will expand to a certain extent even when a horse is wearing shoes. Since it is necessary for a leather or felt quarter boot to be buckled very snugly in order to fit properly and stay on a horse's foot, I feel that to a certain degree it interferes with the expansion of the horse's heel as the foot hits the ground. Every time the heel expands this way it increases the circulation to the foot and I believe that anything that interferes with this is detrimental to the horse's well being. For that reason, I prefer the bell boot to the quarter boot unless the horse definitely shows that he needs a little weight in the heel.

There are a number of variations in the types of basic quarter boots worn by trotters. One of these is the hinged quarter boot (Fig. 72). It consists of two parts joined together by a piece of leather called a hinge. It is very much like the regular low quarter boot in that the bottom portion fits very snugly around the horse's hoof. But it also has an upper portion that covers the heels and is held in place by the leather hinge in back that fastens it to the lower portion. The upper part has a strap that fastens around the pastern. It is important that this strap be fastened loosely to prevent binding when the horse flexes his ankle while in motion.

Hinged quarter boots are sometimes used on colts to get them started. I don't like them very much myself. I always felt that they would get a colt folding up too high and not striding out enough in front. In addition, as the colt progresses and you want to lighten him up a little in front, it is difficult to remove the quarter boots without the colt missing them, whereas, if the weight were more evenly distributed, as in a bell boot or more weight in the shoe itself, it would not be so noticeable. However, a lot of trainers use hinged quarter boots with success.

Another variation is the small leather quarter boot that has lead sewn in between the layers of leather. These are also called loaded or weighted heel boots and weigh six or eight ounces. These boots are particularly helpful in getting a trotting colt started, especially one that doesn't pick his front feet up the way he should. They help make him pick his front feet up and they also give him a little more action in front.

However, I do not believe in leaving heel weighted quarter boots on a colt for any length of time. I don't like to use them on a horse going fast and I don't like to race a horse in them. I think that at high speed they are hard on a horse's legs and that they make a horse labor when he trots.

You can use heel weighted quarter boots to get a colt started and gaited, but as soon as you accomplish this you should gradually remove the weight so that he can go without it. Usually, a plain leather quarter boot or a bell boot will then be enough for a horse if he does need some weight to balance him.

These boots are also very helpful on occasion in getting a pacing colt started. They would go on the hind feet and you would put them on the same way you would on the front foot of a trotter.

I have also found that the same results can sometimes be obtained by using "rattlers." A "rattler" (Fig. 73) is a string of about 10 or 12 beads, each about three-quarters of an inch in diameter, strung on an adjustable leather strap. These beads are made of various materials. I like the bone or hardwood beads best as the colts seem to like the rattle they make each time the foot hits the ground. A "rattler" is buckled around the pastern and should be adjusted loosely enough so that it can bounce around.

If the same results can be obtained by using "rattlers," instead of heel weighted boots, I would prefer to do so because they are much lighter. You must remember that we are dealing with colts whose legs are not yet fully developed and the use of excess weight in any form can lead to serious trouble. "Rattlers" may be used both on trotters in front and pacers behind.

Some trainers use a real low quarter boot, known as a grab boot (Fig. 74), on a trotter in front. The sole purpose of this boot is to keep a horse from pulling a shoe. Once in a while behind the gate, a horse might get a little over-anxious and over-reach and grab his front shoe with a hind foot and pull it off. These little grab boots prevent this but they do not provide any other protection because they do not cover the horse's heels.

Many pacers wear quarter boots in front because of the danger of cross-firing. These boots are close fitting and are made of leather or rubber. As I said before, I seldom use leather quarter boots on pacers although I do use some rubber quarter boots.

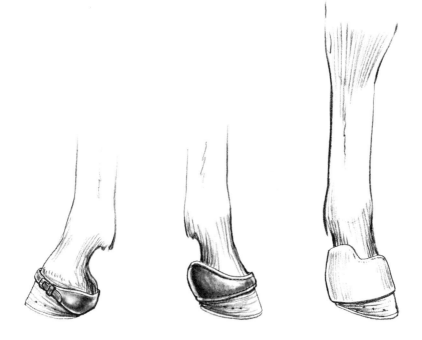

Fig. 74. A grab boot, left, which is actually nothing more than a very low quarter boot, is occasionally worn in front to protect against over-reaching and pulling a shoe with a hind foot. Grab boots may be either leather or rubber. In the center is a coronet boot as it would be fitted on the left hind leg of a pacer that touches the inside of the hind foot with the opposite front foot. Rubber scalpers, right—also fitted here for the left hind foot of a pacer—have almost completely replaced coronet boots as a protection against this type of interference.

Actually, with the vast majority of my horses I prefer to use rubber scalpers or plain bell boots which serve the same protective purpose and are safer and more economical.

A rubber scalper is a very versatile piece of equipment. When used on the front foot of a pacer (Fig. 71), it replaces the old leather pacing quarter boot; when used on the trotter behind (Fig. 75-1 and 75-2) it replaces the much heavier leather scalpers; and when used on the pacer behind (Fig. 74) it replaces the coronet boots. (A coronet boot (Fig 74), by the way, is a narrow leather boot that buckles around the hind hoof of a pacer covering the inside area of the coronary band between the toe and heel. Many pacers touch this area with the opposite front foot and scalpers are now being used almost exclusively in place of coronet boots when this type of interference occurs.)

A scalper (Figs. 71, 74, 75-1, 75-2, and 75-3) is nothing more than a circular piece of rubber that is slipped over the foot. It has no buckles or straps and the rubber itself provides the ten-

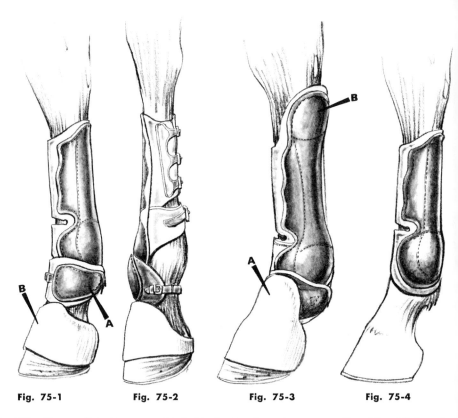

Fig. 75-1   **Fig. 75-2**   **Fig. 75-3**   **Fig. 75-4**

Fig. 75. Almost all trotters wear hind shin boots of one type or another. Figs. 75–1 and 75–2 are the standard hind shin boots with speedy cut connections (A) for the right and left hind leg respectively. Properly positioned rubber scalpers, (B) as worn by trotters behind, also are illustrated. Fig. 75–3 is improper in that there is no need for the high scalper (A) since the speedy cut connection already provides protection for the speedy cut area. All the high scalper does in this case is to provide an additional layer of thickness that might be just enough to cause interference. The high scalper would more properly be used in conjunction

sion that holds it in place. The front part is curved upward in two graduated stages, one being noticeably higher than the other. It is these higher portions that provide the protection for horses that interfere. The remainder of the boot consists of a narrow strip of rubber which encircles the foot and holds the scalper in place. This strip fits in against the heel of a trotter or the front part of a pacer's foot below the coronary band. Scalpers are now a stock item at harness shops although when I was a youngster we used to cut them out of automobile inner tubes.

When used on a trotter, the highest point of the scalper is to the front of the foot, a little to the inside of center, and rises above the hairline of the hoof which is where scalping inter-

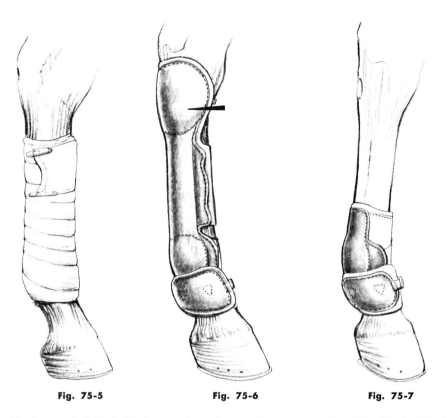

| Fig. 75-5 | Fig. 75-6 | Fig. 75-7 |

with the standard hind shin boot without the speedy cut connection (Fig. 75–4, right hind leg), or with brace bandages, (Fig. 75–5). Fig. 75–3 also illustrates the half hock protection (B), in this case for the right hind leg of a trotter that hits up that high. The occasional trotter that hits even higher than that will wear the longest of shin boots (Fig. 75–6) the one that provides full hock (arrow) protection. Some trotters that do not hit their hind shins will wear only the ankle and speedy cut boot shown in Fig. 75–7 which illustrates the boot as worn on the left hind leg.

ference occurs. A scalping trotter will thus touch the scalper instead of hitting his hind leg just above the hoof. The scalper is also made so that it is a little higher toward the inside of the hind foot—although not as high as the part in front—because this is an area of possible secondary interference for a trotter.

With a passing gaited trotter, that is, one whose hind legs pass outside his front legs, the scalper is often turned a little more to the inside thus offering additional protection for the inside of the hind foot. Because of his gait, this is where scalping interference in this type of trotter is more likely to take place.

From my description, it is obvious that each one of a pair of scalpers is meant for a particular foot. If you put the scalper meant for the left hind foot on the right hind foot, you would still have the highest part in front but the medium high part which provides the secondary protection would be on the outside where it would not do any good because a trotter never interferes there. I have seen trainers put scalpers on the wrong feet.

When you use a scalper on a pacer in front, the one that goes on the right hind foot of the trotter (Fig. 75-1) fits properly on the right front foot of the pacer (Fig. 71). The scalper is then turned so that the highest part covers the inside of the foot where the basic cross-firing interference occurs and the secondary protective part covers the inside heel.

If you put the wrong scalper on a pacer in front and the high part was properly placed, the secondary protective portion would be around toward the front of the foot and there would be no protection at the heel where it is sometimes needed. Used on a pacer behind, the scalper should cover the inside portion of the coronary band all the way back to the heel (Fig. 74). Usually, it is better to put them on the opposite feet so that the higher part covers this area.

In putting a scalper on either a trotter or pacer and making sure that you have the right one on the right foot, nothing helps more than good old common sense.

You will also still find an occasional leather scalper although they have been almost completely replaced now by rubber scalpers which are much lighter, closer fitting, require little or no repair work and are much more economical.

Rubber scalpers come in different heights. The regular one is about four inches high (Fig. 75-1). They also come in six, seven and eight inch heights (Fig. 75-3) and this type of scalper is used when protection is required in the speedy cut area (from coronary band to ankle) and hind shin boots or ankle boots are not being used.

That brings me to the hind shin boot which is the most common boot worn by a trotter. There are very few trotters racing today that do not need either hind shin boots or, as a substitute for them, a set of brace bandages.

Even trotters that do not normally touch their shins usually wear either a hind shin boot or a brace bandage. It is just good common sense to use one or the other on a trotter because you can never tell when a horse might make a mis-step or over-stride or something like that and hit his shins.

There are several types of hind shin boots. The standard one includes a bottom part which covers and protects the ankle (Fig. 75-4). It runs up the hind leg to a point just below the hock.

Since the principal area of interference is on the inside of a trotter's hind leg, the protective portion of the boot is on the inside. However, you can purchase shin boots that also have the front shin protection that protects the inside front of the shin bone. I don't suppose the extra leather involved would weigh over half an ounce and I always order my shin boots with this front shin protection.

The shin part of this boot, running from the ankle to the hock, is fastened around the leg by three straps and buckles (Fig. 75-2), each of which has an elastic insert. When the horse is in motion and the leg is flexed there is a certain amount of "give" to these inserts. Sometimes when a boot gets old and the elasticity goes out of the inserts there isn't any "give" at all. A boot like this should be replaced.

The adjustment of the three shin boot buckles should be made very carefully. If the adjustment is too loose, the boot may slide down and bind a horse's leg over the ankle when he flexes it. At the same time, if they are adjusted too tight they can cord a horse or cause serious damage to a leg. A horse is "corded" when something is fastened too tightly around a leg and causes a rupture in a tendon sheath. It will make a horse very sore and he could wind up with a bowed tendon. The principal causes of cording are boots that are buckled on too tightly and leg bandages that are tied too tight.

A fourth strap on a hind shin boot holds the ankle protection part in place and is buckled around the ankle. There is no elastic insert in this strap. Because there is no "give" to it, extreme care should be taken that it not be buckled too tightly. An improperly buckled shin boot, one that is either too tight or too loose, can cause a horse to become quite sore.

I like to line all my shin boots with a special type of sponge rubber called neoprene. It is a type of rubber that does not absorb moisture. It is glued to the inside of the boot and has a very smooth finish that goes next to the horse's leg. It gives protection by helping to keep the boot from chafing and, at the same time, you can still buckle the boot fairly snug and have some additional "give" from this rubber lining. If you line boots this way, there isn't nearly the danger of cording a horse.

Although all shin boots are made with the ankle protection as part of the boot, they may be ordered with or without the speedy cut connection. This connection (Fig. 75-1) protects the speedy cut area and is fastened to the bottom of the shin boot in one of two ways. One type is fastened by a rivet. The other is attached by two straps which are called hinges and this is called a hinged type speedy cut connection.

I do not like the riveted speedy cut as it is too thick where the speedy cut is riveted to the main boot, making it much easier for the horse to hit it. Also, when the leather wears around the head of the rivet, the speedy cut comes loose. It is very difficult to repair without making it thicker than ever.

I prefer the other type which eliminates the overlap and which hinges and bends quite readily forward and backward by means of the two hinge straps which connect it. The speedy cut on both types has an elastic or rubber strap that goes around the pastern, thereby holding the bottom in close to the leg.

The regular shin boot may also be ordered with additional protection at the top which is the area of the hock. There are two such types and they are known as either the shin boot with the half hock or full hock extension. The boot with the half hock extension (Fig. 75-3) extends upward and flares out to cover the lower half of the hock as well as the shin. The boot with a full hock extension (Fig. 75-6) comes up even higher, covers the entire inside of the hock area and has an elastic strap going around the hock to hold the top of the boot in place and keep it from flopping over. Naturally, these extensions are used on horses that interfere in the hock area.

The longest single-unit hind shin boot a trainer could order would be one that had the full hock extension at the top and the speedy cut connection at the bottom (Fig. 75-6). This would protect the horse from just above the coronary band up to and including the hock.

Some horses do not hit their hind shins but do hit their speedy cuts and touch their ankles a bit. This type of horse might not wear a shin boot but instead would wear an ankle boot with the speedy cut connection (Fig. 75-7).

An ankle boot is nothing more than the ankle protection part of a shin boot. The speedy cut is also the same and is fastened to the ankle boot either by a rivet or by leather hinges.

Some trainers prefer to use a brace bandage (Fig. 75-5) instead of shin boots on a trotter behind. For instance, a horse might be a little sore behind and require the protection and support of a brace bandage. Brace bandages are also lighter and with a horse that doesn't hit his shins or just barely brushes them, they provide enough protection and at the same time permit the horse to trot lighter. Naturally, the lighter you can get a trotter to go behind, the better off you are.

This is usually the type of horse that will wear the high scalper (Fig. 75-3) I described earlier. Let's say you want him to go light and are using brace bandages instead of shin boots, but you find that he tends to brush his speedy cuts. You could go to an ankle boot with the speedy cut connection, but that would also be extra weight because you do not need the ankle boot.

What you do in a case like this is to use the high scalpers that cover the speedy cut area and which are very light. In this manner, you are providing all the protection you need and still keeping weight at an absolute minimum.

Trotters that require the support of a brace bandage, but still need all the protection they can get because they interfere, will wear the bandages beneath the shin boots.

Horses that do not touch their shins but tend to hit their ankles and speedy cuts could wear the bandages with an ankle boot and speedy cut connection over the lower part of the bandage. Any time you are using a speedy cut connection with either an ankle or shin boot, there is no need for a high scalper because one overlaps the other and the horse would be more likely to interfere because of the additional thickness involved. If you use a scalper in conjunction with a speedy cut connection, be sure to use the low scalper, not the high one.

On ending this chapter I realize that I have barely scratched the surface, and I know there are many other ailments and a great many other cures both physical and mechanical, but I will be satisfied if I have in some small way contributed to the success of some young man who is earnest in his desire to become a horse trainer.

I realize that if a man wasn't born with a little of that "horse sense" I have referred to so often, that all the books ever written about horse training would be of no value. The other main ingredient is hard work. Don't ever think that when you have your first good horse or first successful season that you don't need to get up early in the morning.

Led by Hall of Fame immortals Ben F. White and Vic Fleming, some of harness racing's greatest horsemen have come from Canada. One of these is Joseph C. O'Brien who appeared permanently on the American scene some 20 years ago and who has since established himself as one of the finest practitioners of the training and driving art ever produced either by his own or his adopted land. Since the USTA began keeping records in 1939, he has won more races (2,400 plus) than any driver except Billy Haughton, in addition to officially uncounted hundreds registered prior to that in the Maritime provinces where he was born in Alberton, Prince Edward Island, on June 25, 1917.

He learned at the side of his father, an outstanding horseman, and drove his first race in 1930 at the tender age of 13. After World War II service in the Canadian infantry, he began campaigning actively in the United States in 1947 and since that time has sandwiched a public stable operation around a long (1951-1963) association as a private trainer for the S. A. Camp Farm. He has earned more than $5,000,000 in purses and despite the fact that during the Camp years he campaigned a relatively small stable has been among the top five national money (11 times) and race (four times) winners with consistent frequency. He has driven more 2:00 race miles than anyone else (81 through 1966), has led the Grand Circuit drivers on five occasions, has topped the UDRS (batting average) list twice and has "batted" .300 or more on the UDRS scale for 15 consecutive years. He has won two Hambletonians (Scott Frost and Blaze Hanover), a Little Brown Jug (Shadow Wave) and scored with Armbro Flight in 1966 Roosevelt International. He maintains his own training plant at Shafter, Cal., is a member of the Canadian Sports Hall of Fame, was Harness Horseman of The Year in 1959, is a director of the United States Trotting Association and is owner and president of The Champion Turf Equipment Company.

9

The YEAR-ROUND STABLE

ROBERT G. FARRINGTON

I T is my intent in this chapter to discuss in some detail the manner in which my training and racing operation enables me to win 300 races a year. I do not feel that the reasons are particularly complex and I am certain that any competent horseman who patterned his operation after mine could increase his number of annual visits to the winner's circle.

First of all, I should make clear my very simple philosophy about racing a stable of horses. I want to win every time I go to the post and if I can't win I want to finish second or third. There's nothing very startling about that. I suppose every driver feels the same way. The difference probably is that if I don't finish 1-2-3 I definitely do something about it.

The money is up front and that's where I want to be. That's where I have to be to show a profit. I am actually operating a big business and I must run it like a big business. And I have found that I can't make money unless I consistently finish among the top three.

If I have a horse that finishes back of third three times in a row, that horse is not earning his keep and I must do something about it. I do one of three things. I drop him down in class to where I think he can be 1-2-3, I ship him to a smaller track or I send him home.

This means that most of the time when I go to the post I am driving a horse that I have figured, in my own mind, should be first, second or third. Obviously, the actual odds against my winning that race have been shortened appreciably. Instead of those odds being 7-1 against me, as they would in a standard eight-horse race, I figure they are only 2-1 against me. Under these circumstances, it is equally obvious that I am going to win more than my share of races.

I look at it as though I were running a department store and a horse in my stable is comparable to an item on the counter. If that item isn't selling, if it isn't returning a profit to me, (consistently finishing 1-2-3) I have to do something about it.

The first thing I do is to lower the price (drop the horse down in class). If the item still doesn't "sell," I think about sending it to a smaller store (track) in another part of the country where it might have more appeal, even if I have to reduce the price again. And if I don't do any good that way, I can always put the item back in storage for a while (turn the horse out) and maybe change something about it (treat unsoundness, etc.) so that when I do offer it again it is more desirable and once more stands a chance of returning a profit.

I can do a number of things with that piece of merchandise. The one thing I cannot do is leave it out on the original counter where it is only taking up valuable space, gathering dust and making no money for me. I feel this way about the horses in my stable and I operate accordingly.

In racing a stable of horses, therefore, I operate as a business-man with the condition book as my bible, the long racing season as my ally and a smooth-functioning, family-run organization as my ace in the hole.

Expressed as simply as possible, these are the basic reasons why I win 300 races a year. It is not, of course, as easy as all that but I think it sums it up. In saying this, I am not being either naive or modest about my driving ability. I think that God gave me a special talent for which I am very thankful. But at the same time I am also aware that there are a number of my fellow professionals who drive as well or better.

But my success is keyed to much more than driving. The present classification system which emphasizes conditioned and claiming races enables me to act virtually as my own race secretary and to enter my horses where I think they belong. The extension of the racing season to a point where it is a year-round proposition blends perfectly into my picture. And, above all, a smooth operation back at my farm which consistently supplies me with fresh, sharp, ready-to-race horses plays a major part in any success I may have enjoyed.

I will usually have about 50 horses in my racing stable. This isn't a number I picked out of the air. I like to have two or three horses for every class and I have found that in the Chicago area, where I do most of my racing, a string of 50 fits the classification structure almost perfectly. In the middle of the summer, when my young, green horses start to come on, I will sometimes get up to 65 but I would prefer to stay at 50 and usually do.

If I have more than 50 horses at the races, I find that I have too many for certain classes and cannot get them all raced. If I have less than 50, there are classification opportunities available that I am not taking advantage of and I am hurting myself financially by not doing so.

In following this rule of thumb, I find that it is advisable to have one horse at the farm for every one at the track. Those at the farm are going through a conditioning program that will bring them back to me as ready-to-race horses.

Whenever I send a horse back to the farm, he is replaced by one that is ready to race, preferably in the same class so that I do not get out of balance on my classification sheet. No horse remains at the race track with me unless he is fit to race and is racing. If he does not answer that description for any reason whatsoever, he goes home.

So we are talking about a minimum of 100 horses, and with me, taking into consideration that I have a few racing at smaller tracks and around the fairs, the number can get up to about 120.

That sounds like a lot of horses and it is. But if you want to know the honest truth I don't work any harder today than I did when I was breaking in ten years ago with a string of ten. In those days I did all the training and driving, a great deal of the grooming and just about anything else that had to be done around the barn.

Now I concentrate on driving, overall supervision of the training—although very little of the actual training itself—and a daily session with the condition book. I can limit myself to these specific tasks because I think I have an exceptional organization and an outstanding system.

Up to this point, I don't believe there is a horseman in the country who couldn't follow the general pattern I have outlined and improve himself, provided he had the necessary training and driving talent. But I have one big advantage which I don't think anybody else in harness racing can match—a father and three brothers who are directly associated with me in the operation of my stable and without whom I wouldn't stand a ghost of a chance of winning 300 races a year.

We have a 400-acre farm near Richwood, Ohio, which serves as our base of operations. We have a half-mile track, turnout paddocks and everything else that is required for a first class operation. My dad, Louie, who can train a horse very well, is in charge. He takes the horses I send back from the racing stable, supervises their freshening up program and advises me when they are ready to race again, or trains them according to a pre-arranged program that could cover a period of from one to four months.

My brother, Richard, is with me at the races. He has a string of his own in my training system, which I will describe later. He is a good driver and substitutes for me when, for one reason or another, I am unavailable.

Another brother, Brad, uses the farm as his home base but is usually racing a string for me at one of the Ohio mutuel tracks and campaigning around the Ohio fairs. When he is not doing that, he is at the farm helping dad.

Still another brother, Rolland, is the farm manager. He takes care of all the feed, does our trucking and is responsible for a lot of other things which dad or my other brothers are too busy to handle.

It is a great organization and is the real secret of my success. You never have to worry about anybody goofing off or whether the information you are receiving about a horse that is being prepped 500 miles away is accurate. It always is. If dad tells me that one he is freshening up at the farm is ready to go in 2:05 you can bet your last dollar he'll go in 2:05. Or if I talk with Brad and he tells me a horse in his string is ready to move on to Chicago and compete in a certain class there, you can bet the horse is ready and can compete. And I never worry about feed or bedding because Rolland has checked every bushel and bale and eliminated any that don't meet our standards.

Around the racing stable, Richard is on the go all the time, bringing to my attention details he thinks I should handle. Many of the minor things that all too often take up so much of a head trainer's time are handled directly by him. As a result, I can concentrate on the three things I think are so important—driving, general supervision of the training and entering horses.

I mentioned earlier that I do not do a great deal of training myself. Let me explain how that works.

Depending on the number of horses racing, I will have either three or four assistant trainers and each of them is assigned a string of his own. As far as the assistant trainer is concerned, this is his own stable and he is completely responsible for it. A string will consist of from 12 to 16 horses. My brother, Richard, would have one of them.

When I come to the barn in the morning, I talk with each of my assistants. If they are having a problem with a particular horse, I will offer advice. If there is a horse they think I ought to train myself for some specific reason I will do it. But aside from that they are on their own. It is their job to get their string ready and to have their horses in racing condition at all times. If they do not, I replace them. I have good men and there is not much turnover.

In the evening it is the trainer's responsibility to see that his horses get to the paddock and he goes the early warmup miles with them. I take the horse the last warmup mile and race him. He then goes back into the hands of his trainer who sees that he is cooled out properly and returned to his stall.

None of these trainers is concerned with any of the horses in the other fellow's string. They each have their own horses and handle them just as though they were the head trainer in that stable. If a trainer doesn't have any horses in his string scheduled to race, he gets the night off.

This gives me plenty of free time in the morning when a lot of fellows are tied down going training miles with their stock. As a result, I am able to spend a good deal of time looking over horses in their stalls, as they are being walked, and on the track, observing their general condition and making mental notes about them. I also make a daily check of feet and equipment. It is a fine system and I would recommend it to anyone.

I don't know whether any other trainers will adopt this system, but I do think that sooner or later all trainers with large raceway stables are going to have to go to the one-for-one program for their racing stable. That is, one horse back at the farm or "staging area" for every one at the track. For instance, I think a man who wants to race 20 horses ought to have a total of 40 in his string.

With racing on a year-round basis, you just have to rest your horse part of the time and if you can work it out so that you have a replacement for the horse you send home, you haven't lost anything from your stable.

Of course, this won't be as simple for some trainers as it is for

me and that is where I have another great advantage. I own—
that is the Farrington Stable in which my father and brothers
are associated with me own—a great many of the horses I race.
There are many others that I own in partnership with other
people. I would say that four out of five horses in my stable are
wholly or partly owned by me or members of my family. I think
a lot of owners would prefer to be in partnership with their
trainer on a horse. I think it gives them a feeling that they are
getting a real fair shake.

Full or part ownership of a horse creates a tremendous advantage for me. It means that for the most part I do not have
to consult or pacify an owner when I decide to send a horse
home for a rest. I think I am a good judge of when it is time
for a horse to be freshened up and sometimes the condition book
tells me it is time long before the horse ever would. But I know
this system wouldn't work as smoothly and efficiently if I had
to explain my thinking and justify each such move to 50 or more
owners.

There are many reasons why you might want to send a horse
home for a rest. Some horses don't go as well on a half-mile track
and you try to save them for the mile, and five-eighths tracks.
Some race better in the winter or spring while others are at their
best in the summer. I know all these things and I plan accordingly. But I am afraid that if I had a lot of owners I'd have a lot
of minority opinions as well and that isn't a good thing the way
my operation is set up.

I was talking about year-round racing and this seems as good
a place as any to discuss the length of time a horse can hold his
racing condition. As I said before, I am all in favor of year-round
racing because it adapts itself to my type of operation.

You can race a horse a long time if you don't abuse him, but
there is still a limit and a lot of us are still experimenting to
determine that limit. I have had considerable experience with
this over the past few years and I do have a few suggestions to
offer.

In the first place, no two horses are alike. I know there are a
few horses that you could race an entire year on a once-a-week
basis. But I wouldn't consider that an ideal situation. Such a
horse is bound to fall by the wayside sooner or later and when

he does fall he's much more likely to fall harder and stay down longer.

It is difficult to strike any kind of an average, but I would judge that you would have no trouble with a normal, perfectly sound raceway horse if you raced him six months, turned him out for two, raced him another four and turned him out two more. That amounts to ten months of racing over a 14-month period and I would feel that a sound raceway horse going a single dash every week to ten days would stand up to this without too much trouble. Of course, this would not apply to a horse that had to be trained stiffly between races, one that had to undergo a vigorous prep for a series of fast stake races or one that was involved in heat racing. In cases like this you should probably shorten the racing period a little or extend the turnout period.

You can usually tell when a horse needs freshening up. His condition will sometimes show it before it occurs on the track. If he starts to lose weight, check to see how long you have been racing him. Maybe it's time he had a rest.

Very often a horse will show you in a race that he needs to be let down a little. Perhaps he doesn't try at the end of the mile the way you know he should and usually does. This is the time to quit, not after all the danger signs have become so obvious that even a blind man would recognize them. If you get a horse out to pasture before he goes too far down hill you can get him back in a couple of months and still have a high class horse. But if you wait too long, you may lose him altogether.

There is one other guidepost that will sometimes tell you before any of the others that a horse needs to be turned out. That's the condition book. I live with it from day to day and it leads me to many of the decisions I make regarding whether to quit with a horse or to go on with him.

As a specific example, let's say I have a nice 4-year-old that did not race at all at two and was raced lightly and won $4,500 as a 3-year-old. I think this horse has a lot of potential so I don't want to start him in claiming races when I bring him to the track in March. I study the sheet for conditioned races that will fit him.

Let's say I start him first in a race for non-winners of $5,000 and that he wins. It was a $2,500 race and he earned $1,250. Now his total earnings are $5,750 and I have to enter him in a race for non-winners of $6,000. I do this a couple of more times and he wins or is second and piles up some more earnings.

Eventually I wind up racing in a class for non-winners of $10,000 lifetime and the competition is getting a little stiffer. But the meeting has been going on for a couple of months now and the race secretary is starting to write conditions for money winners at this meeting. Perhaps I can find something there or in an age or sex class that is a little softer for him and I enter him accordingly.

If this horse goes on and does well, sooner or later he is going to wind up in a conditioned class that will put him in over his head. I am watching the condition sheet closely. I am fully aware of my horse's capabilities and I will know when he is in too deep. As soon as I see this, I will run for cover with him. Back to the farm he goes. Maybe he's only raced three months instead of six or seven, but he is a nice young horse with plenty of racing opportunity ahead of him and I don't want to ruin him.

Anyway, he goes home for two months. Now you must remember that this horse wasn't sent home because he couldn't compete, but because he was getting in against horses that he shouldn't be racing against. So I tell my dad the story and arrange his training program at the farm on the assumption that he will be back in about two months.

Meantime, I am watching the condition sheets with this horse in mind. Pretty soon the horses he was beating rather handily earlier in the season begin picking up some money and the earnings of the best among these start to approximate what my horse had when I sent him home.

When I see this happening and know that on current money-winning conditions he can get back in with horses I know he can either beat or finish 1-2-3 with, I give my dad the word and we bring him back to the track. Now he is not only ready to pick up some money in this allowance class, but he has had some very useful racing experience and if he is the horse I think he is he can go on now and compete against faster, better horses as soon as he wins his way out of his regular class.

I have lost two months of racing with this horse but as far as I am concerned I am setting him up to win a lot more money than he would have if I had kept him at the track all the time.

He winds up winning as much or more by the end of the year and he also has had a nice rest along the way. Not only that, but while he was turned out, I replaced him in my stable with a horse that fit in the class he was vacating. Sounds a little complicated, maybe, but it really isn't. It's just a question of studying the condition sheet and being able to read between the lines a little.

Let me talk a little more about the condition sheet. In Chicago they usually put one out every three days. The sheet comes out at night and I take it home with me after the races and sit down right then and enter my horses for the next three days. Naturally, I have a little notebook that gives me all the information I need on my horses. I work from this but I also keep a number of other things in mind.

For instance, I think one of the most important things is not to use up a preference date just to get a race for your horse. I would always rather wait an extra three days or so to assure that my horse is racing in a class where he belongs rather than enter him just because there is a race to which he's eligible.

In order to determine this, I have to know not only what my horse can do but what other horses in that class are capable of and even how their trainers think. As an example, let's say I have a horse that is eligible to two races on the condition sheet. One is for non-winners of $10,000 lifetime and another is for non-winners of $5,000 this year.

I know three horses that are eligible to these two classes that can beat my horse. I run them through my mind and try to figure how their trainers will enter them. One of the purses is for $4,000, the other for $3,000. I know from experience that two of these trainers will enter the $4,000 race because they like to shoot for the bigger purse. That leaves only one of the three tough ones for me to beat in the $3,000 race so I enter there. I figure that I am sure to finish second which means that my horse will earn $750. The best I can do in the $4,000 race is to finish third which amounts to $480. Therefore, I stand to win more money in the $3,000 race and I enter accordingly.

You might say, yes, but what if you run into bad racing luck and don't finish second in the $3,000 race? My answer is that I do not consider racing luck when I enter my horses. I figure that racing luck evens up over a period of a year and that I could run into bad luck just as easily in the $4,000 race as in the cheaper one. I enter in the race where I think I stand to earn the most money from the total purse. If there is a "secret" about entering horses in conditioned races, this is it.

There is another thing I watch quite closely; I never like to get more than three horses in one class and it would be better if I just had two. If one of my horses starts to move up and eventually establishes himself pretty solidly in a higher class, then I take the horse in that class that needs freshening up the most and send him home. I must have racing opportunity or I am defeating my purpose.

I like to get a race every week for every horse. That isn't possible, but it is the goal I am shooting for. However, and I cannot emphasize this too strongly, I will always hold a horse over an extra three days or even a full week to get him in the class where he belongs. And where he belongs, as I have said repeatedly, is where I am sure in my own mind that he can finish first, second or third.

If I can't get a race for my horse once a week, I will settle for 10 days if I have to, but if it reaches a point where my horse is not getting a race except every two or three weeks I will send him home to freshen up. A horse like that isn't doing me any good at the track and I might as well let him rest up a little until his classification picture changes to a point where I can get him raced every week or 10 days.

I think that covers conditioned races pretty well and leads me naturally into the subject of claiming races. I am all for claiming races. They tell me we now have 30% claiming races. I wish we had 75%. A claiming race gives a trainer the maximum opportunity to classify his own horse.

I do very well in claiming races and I think one of the reasons for it is that I place a realistic value on the horses I race in this class. Claiming races are relatively new to harness racing and we still have a lot of owners who think their horses are worth much more than they actually are.

Consequently, these owners are opposed to entering their horses in a claiming race at all and if their trainer finally convinces them that it is the only way to get money, they will enter but they will value their horse too high and still won't do any good.

To me, a claimer is worth just exactly what he can win. I have explained before that I want my horses to be able to finish 1-2-3 in any race in which they start. This is especially applicable to claiming horses and I will sometimes move them down after two starts instead of three if it appears they won't get anything. If there's anything I dislike in my stable, it's a horse that isn't winning money.

Let's say that I have claimed a horse for $5,000. In Chicago you have to race him for 30 days in the $5,000 class and I will do this. But at the end of that period if he hasn't demonstrated the capability of being 1-2-3 I will immediately drop him back to the $4,000 class. And if he can't do any good there, he goes into the $3,000 class. I must get him into a class where he can do some good.

I will give you an example of what I mean. I claimed a mare once for $7,000. I started her back in an allowance race and she couldn't get any money. I put her back in a $7,000 claimer and she still couldn't get any money. It looked as though I might have made a bad deal on this mare. But instead of worrying about it, as soon as the month was up I put her in a $4,000 claimer. She won there and kept on winning. At the end of the year she had almost $12,000 on her card. If I hadn't entered her the way I did she wouldn't have won $3,000.

You might ask me why someone didn't claim this mare at $4,000. The answer is that she had bad racing manners and none of the boys wanted her. This is another thing that seems to work for me. I find that I am able to do well with bad-mannered horses, bad post horses, pulling horses and half-sound horses that the other fellows don't want to take a chance with. As a matter of fact I am always on the lookout for this type of horse, figuring that perhaps I can get a little more out of him than the fellow who has him now.

In claiming horses, I am always on the lookout for class horses that have a little something wrong with them, especially a soundness problem. I am not afraid of a horse that has a little suspensory trouble or bad feet or soreness in the shoulders or something like that. I have found that I can deal effectively with such problems. The one type of unsoundness that I steer clear of is bowed tendons. I have never had any luck with bows and

I don't like to see them in my stable. I never claim a horse that has tendon trouble.

One type of horse that I like to claim or buy privately is the front runner that is pulling real hard all the time. I have had a lot of luck with horses like this. I think all good horsemen know that the simpler such a horse is rigged the better off he is. I use a lot of Figure 8 head halters on this kind and usually plug their ears. I have had good results.

I bought a horse one time that ran down on the front end in every race. He was wearing a Crabb bit and a dog chain and I could tell that it was making him mad and that this was the reason he wasn't doing any good and wouldn't stop pulling. I took everything out of his mouth, used a leather bit and plugged his ears and the horse raced real well for me. I taught him to race in the hole and I couldn't have asked for nicer-mannered horse.

Another type of horse that I will take a chance with, either by buying him privately or taking him out of a claiming race, is a knee-knocker. I know a lot of trainers don't want anything to do with a knee-knocker but I've had pretty good luck with them.

There are a lot of things you can do with a knee-knocker but I've enjoyed the greatest success by taking their front shoes off and letting them race barefooted. First I will try a two-ounce aluminum shoe and if that doesn't work I simply remove the shoes altogether. I find they may still hit their knee a little this way but not hard enough to hurt themselves. What we do is warm up the horse with his shoes on and then pull them off just before the race. The next morning we nail his shoes back on so that he doesn't wear his feet off too much and tear them up.

I once had a horse in my own stable that I trained for six months trying to get him off his knees. He was just a 3-year-old that I hadn't raced yet, so I spent a lot of time with him. However, he persisted in hitting his knees and making breaks. I tried everything in the book, but finally I came back to removing his shoes for his racing mile. He won in 2:05 several times and earned quite a bit of money for a green horse. He was a different horse racing without shoes.

Before I go to the races each year, I review my horses and decide which ones I want to start out with. In recent years I have been opening my season at Washington Park, near Chicago, which is a mile track. The season has been opening in February, although it is coming closer to January first each year and, as a matter of fact, I have opened recent campaigns in January at Roosevelt Raceway in New York and Windsor Raceway in Ontario.

But assuming that I am going to open in Chicago, I want to start out with horses that go well in cold weather, over muddy tracks and over a mile track. This usually means that I want with me those horses that do not race well over a half-mile track. I don't have any that don't like a mile track but I do have a certain number that do not prefer the turns on a half-mile track.

Generally speaking, these are the horses that I will be wanting to turn out during the summer to pick up again in the fall. Once again, it's a question of assessing your horses and knowing which ones will race better in certain climatic conditions and over certain types of tracks.

I have heard it said that mares and geldings race better in the fall, winter and spring and that stallions do better in the hot weather but I can't say that I have found this to be true. I think it depends entirely on the individual horse. I have had a number of stallions that have raced very well in cold weather and a lot of mares and geldings that have not.

I do feel that it is a good practice to geld race horses, especially the type that I am racing. As I have pointed out a number of times, I feel that I am a good judge of the ability of my horses and this applies to breeding as well. I am not kidding myself; I know that my horses are not royally bred and consequently I geld practically every one of them.

I don't do this because I think these horses will go faster. On the contrary, it is my opinion that a stallion will race a little faster than a gelding as far as the limit of extreme speed goes. Offhand, I would say a stallion could probably go a second faster than a gelding.

But this is not really important to me since I am not dealing with horses that are going to go in 1:57 or anything like that. I am dealing primarily with raceway horses and it is my experience that geldings will race much more consistently than stallions.

As a stallion, a horse might give you a 2:05 mile. But the next time he might give you a 2:07 mile and the next time a 2:08 mile. I don't like this because this is the kind of horse that doesn't fit into my 1-2-3 picture. Sure, he might win once when you think he ought to be third, but on the other hand he is just as likely to finish sixth or worse.

It has been my experience that after being gelded the same horse will give you a 2:06 mile that you can count on week after week. You won't get 2:05 from him, but you won't get 2:07 or 2:08 either. I am not too interested in extreme speed in a horse like this. I am much more concerned with consistency of form week after week. I will settle for knowing that he will give me that 2:06 mile every time he goes to the post.

There are several other advantages to be derived from gelding a horse. A gelding is easier to take care of around the barn, less likely to injure himself in the stall, and easier to ship and turn out. These are factors which are important in my operation.

A stallion is much more likely to give a groom trouble around the stall, and more prone to suffer injury because of his attitude and conduct. A gelding is much more docile and easier to work with. When you send a stallion back to the farm he requires an individual paddock whereas several geldings can be turned out in a field together if necessary. Very often a stallion will require an extra stall in shipping and he is more likely to cause trouble on a truck. For those reasons I would prefer a gelding.

Of course, if I were campaigning a stable of top stake colts I wouldn't feel that way. I have been asked why I don't specialize in colts. Apparently some people think I don't like colts and would rather have raceway horses. That isn't exactly true and I ought to explain it. I would like to have a top stake colt just as any other trainer would. But over the years I have developed my own pattern of racing and colts just don't fit into it.

They are the most inconsistent of all horses and unless you have a top one there's not much chance of making money with them. We own some mares and raise some colts, but their breeding hasn't been enough to sustain them in the major stakes so I have never entered them. My policy is to break and train 15 to 20 2-year-olds each year. Along about February I turn out all except three or four that look especially precocious and that I will race at the smaller tracks or at the Ohio fairs. In this manner,

I am able to develop a lot of nice young raceway horses that come on good as three and 4-year-olds.

There is another factor, too. If you are going to campaign a stable with a lot of colts in it, you have to move around to the tracks where the colt stakes are. Normally I will drive five or six races every night and each time I had to leave the track where I was campaigning to drive a colt I would be missing four, five or six times as many drives with my raceway horses. To date, I haven't been able to say that this is a desirable thing so I have steered clear of colts.

On the other hand, no leading owner has ever come to me and said, "Bob, I'd like you to go to Harrisburg or Lexington and pick out a couple of real top yearlings and buy them for me." I am sure that if anybody did I would reply affirmatively. I believe I can train and drive colts just as well as I can aged horses. It's just that the situation has never developed.

I was talking about starting my campaign in January or February and perhaps I ought to go on now and explain how I condition my race horses in the winter and what I do differently, if anything, in the summer.

In the winter months, when the weather is cold and the track is usually somewhat off, I warm horses up to race differently than in the summer. In the winter, my horses go only one warmup trip on race night. Actually, they go out on the track twice but the first time they are just jogged three miles the wrong way. About 40 minutes later they come back and go a warmup mile from 2:25 to 2:30. They race off that.

At that time of year, when your horse is cold and the weather is bad, all you can do with a horse anyway is to get him hot, get his blood circulating and get him emptied out. I have found that this is the best way to accomplish that. Occasionally you will find a horse that does not empty out after jogging and going one trip and you will have to go an extra one with him. But this is quite rare and almost all my horses go three jog miles and then a mile between 2:25 and 2:30.

On the end of that mile, I will go a quarter within about four seconds of where I expect the horse to race. If he is a horse that will normally give me a last quarter in a race in 31 seconds, I will go a last quarter in about 35 seconds, maybe a tick or so faster. The last eighth of that quarter will be a little faster than the first eighth. I find that this is sufficient.

When the weather gets better, I change my warmup routine. I jog the horse from three to three and one-half miles and follow that up with two singles at 40-minute intervals. The first warmup mile will be from 2:35 to 2:40 and the last one within 10 to 12 seconds of where the horse has to race.

If a horse is going to race in 2:05, I will warm him up from 2:15 to 2:17 that last trip. The final quarter in the summer will be within two seconds of where I expect him to race. Thus, a horse with a final race quarter expectation of 31 seconds will finish his last warmup mile with a 33-second quarter. Again, the last eighth will be a little faster than the first one.

In the winter, you have to adjust your warmup miles to fit the condition of the track. If the track appears to be eight seconds off, which it occasionally can be in the face of especially bad weather, your warmup mile will be in the 2:33-2:38 range instead of from 2:25 to 2:30. The final quarter and eighth will also be adjusted accordingly.

After the race you have to cool your horse out and there are two ways we do this, the cold weather way and the warm weather way. In the winter time we cool a horse out in his stall. We put three or four blankets on him depending on how cold it is; four if it is real cold, usually three otherwise. We let him stand and eat hay and keep rubbing him beneath the blankets. At regular intervals he is permitted a few swallows of water. Gradually, we take blankets off, maybe one every half hour. It will take from an hour to an hour and a half to cool a horse out this way.

In the summer we walk horses to cool them out. This is a standard procedure and possibly the only way I differ from anybody else is that I almost never walk a horse more than an hour. I've never found one yet that needed to be walked longer than that except in the face of extremely humid conditions at night or if the temperature got up around 100 during the day.

It is important in the winter to make sure your horses get out of the stall and at least get walked every single day. It doesn't make any difference how bad the weather is, you have to get them out. If you don't, you are inviting muscle soreness and tying up. Lack of exercise is what causes this and it is especially prevalent in the winter. I always make sure that every horse gets out of his stall every day of the year.

Let me write a little bit now about conditioning horses between races. I know that this is being covered extensively by Stanley Dancer but I cannot describe my operation fully without going into it.

Let's take for example a horse that has raced in 2:05 on a Tuesday night and is scheduled to race again the following Tuesday. On Wednesday morning, after his race, we walk him a little, maybe a half hour, and keep his legs done up and work on whatever ailments he might have. On Thursday he is jogged three miles and on Friday he is worked three trips in 2:45, 2:30 and 2:16 evenly rated. He is walked on Saturday, stands up on Sunday and is jogged three or four miles on Monday. He is now ready to race again. This schedule applies in winter as well as summer.

There are also certain horses that aren't trained at all between races. I have a number of them, perhaps as many as 25% of my stable. These are horses which either have an unsoundness of some kind or have shown me that they simply won't race as well if they are trained between starts.

If I have a horse that is on my regular training program and he doesn't race well twice in a row and I can't find any reason for it, I will usually try him without training between races and see what happens.

If this horse had raced on a Tuesday night I would walk him on Wednesday and jog him three miles on Thursday. On Friday I would jog him four to five miles and on Saturday five to six miles. He walks on Sunday, and on Monday I would give him a double header, that is two light miles without returning to the barn. One mile would be in 2:50 and the other in 2:40. He would race off that.

You will notice that for horses that are not being trained between races the number of jog miles is stepped up. I feel that this is important to help the horse maintain his racing edge. If you are not going to train a horse between races, you must increase the number of jog miles.

Sometimes you stumble across these things accidentally. I had a mare I was training routinely between races and one day, when it was time for her to train, the track got very muddy and stayed that way for a couple of days. I didn't get to train her and she raced better than she ever had. I put her back on a regular training program but she didn't race well. So I went the other way, didn't train her at all and she got real good. From that time on, I didn't train her at all between races and she thrived on it.

You might think that such horses wouldn't retain their racing edge but they do. The last mare I talked about is a good feeder and those kind usually require more work but she doesn't. I don't know why that would be but I'm certainly not going to quarrel about it.

The other type of horses that I handle this way are those that are a little off, not lame but what all of us call "race horse sound." You probably would be better off to train most horses like this because the majority of them will race better if trained. But they won't last nearly as long. I would much rather race them a little short and almost sound than tight and lame. This is a situation in which you don't really have much choice. If you persist in drilling such horses between races you will tighten them up but they won't last long at all. Working with these horses is also an assignment that I handle personally around the barn each morning. I am able to give them more attention because I don't have to train a string myself.

I have a vet who comes to the barn every morning. I go over all the horses with him and recommend treatment for those that need it. I tell the vet what I think is wrong with the horse and he doctors accordingly.

In the morning I am also checking to see whether the horses have cleaned up their feed and how they are acting. You can tell a great deal about a horse this way. Naturally, I have a routine program for worming and making blood checks and I am careful to see that these procedures are followed faithfully. These are the little things that can sometimes make the difference in a horse and you have to watch them closely.

I am especially interested in seeing that my horses get plenty of good feed. I think that is a very important thing and I am quite particular about it. Horses in the racing stable are fed three times a day and some of them, those that I think could stand a little more, get an extra feed at midnight.

We feed a good grade of mixed alfalfa and timothy hay, much

of which we make at home and haul to the track. My brother, Rolland, is responsible for this and he doesn't deliver anything except top hay. I imagine it would run 50% alfalfa and 50% timothy. In addition to all the hay they can eat, the horses get pellets twice a day as well as oats and corn.

The pellet is a commercial mixture that I buy in Indiana and it contains many of the vitamins and minerals that are so necessary for the well-being of a horse. We feed home-grown oats from our farm and from other locations in Ohio. They are cleaned and dusted and we have better luck with these oats than we do with the top-grade clipped oats that are hard and have been treated.

I believe in feeding corn to horses. I think it is good for them and they really like it. The individual ration varies but I have some horses that would get as many as eight to ten ears a day in the winter. In the summer this would be cut back to six or eight ears daily. About half of the hay, corn and oats fed to my horses is grown on our farm at Richwood.

Horses that leave the racing stable to go back to the farm are cut down to two feeds a day, but whether they are at the track or at the farm they get the pellets twice a day as well as corn and choice hay.

I think it is tremendously important that horses be well-fed and kept in good condition. As the racing season lengthens and horses are asked to race over longer periods, I am sure this factor will become even more important.

I think that pretty well covers my operation at the race track. Perhaps I'd better retrace my steps now and explain how things work back at the farm.

Throughout the racing season, there is a virtual shuttle service running between the farm and the track where I am racing as well as between the farm and mutuel tracks and county fairs in Ohio. At least once a week, and usually twice or more, trucks which I own make the overnight trip between Chicago and Richwood.

My brother, Rolland, handles this end of it. I think it is important that horses ship during the night when it is quieter, cooler in the summer and over roads that are less clogged with traffic.

Rolland will leave Ohio at midnight with a load of horses and

arrive in Chicago at about eight the next morning. He lays over
and then leaves again at midnight with a load going back to the
farm. Between trips he will be trucking other horses to and from
other tracks and the county fairs.

It is advantageous to me to own my own trucks. I save money,
I don't have to worry about waiting to make a load before I
can ship and there aren't two or three other places where the
truck has to stop and unload horses before it gets to me. The
further advantage of having my brother driving the truck and
supervising the loading and unloading is a vital one.

My father and I talk daily about the racing situation and when
I decide to send horses home we make arrangements with
Rolland and he picks them up at the track and delivers them
to the farm.

Now my dad establishes a schedule for them. This schedule
depends on how long they are going to be laid up. Let's say
that they are going to be off the standard two-month period

This is a total of eight weeks and for the first six of these
weeks the schedule is the same. They are turned out about an
hour or two a day in a grass paddock. Then we bring them in,
feed them, do them up and give them whatever special care
they require.

This holds true for six of the seven days in any given week
during that first six-week period. On the seventh day, let's say
every Wednesday, they are trained three easy trips, the fastest
in 2:20. The first two trips are in about 2:45 and 2:30. They are
brushed lightly at the end of the 2:20 mile, maybe a quarter in
33 seconds.

This goes on for six weeks but in the seventh and eighth
weeks, the two just before they are to return to the races, they
are trained twice a week, let's say on Monday and Thursday,
three trips each day. In the last workout before they are to come
back to the track they are trained their fastest mile, within two
or three seconds of where I figure they will have to go in their
race.

If, for one reason or another, a horse is only going to be off
a month, we will follow the daily paddock turnout and once-a-
week training routine for the first three weeks and then train
him twice the last week, stepping him along pretty good in the
last mile of his last training session.

If he is a 2:05 horse, we work the first two trips in 2:40 and 2:25 on Monday followed by a fast mile in 2:12-1:05-:32. On Thursday, his first two miles are in 2:35 and 2:25 and his last mile from 2:07 to 2:08, the last half in 1:03 and the last quarter between 30 and 31 seconds.

If this is a horse that races between 2:08 and 2:10 he will not go quite as much in his fast miles. His last trip on Monday will be around 2:15 and on Thursday he will probably train his last mile in 2:12 with a half in 1:05 and a quarter in 32 seconds. These last workouts are roughly identical for the horse that has been off two months, or for any period of time for that matter.

If a horse is going to be off three or four months, we won't do anything with him the first two weeks he is home except to turn him out every day. On Monday of the third week we pick him up and jog him two or three miles and do the same thing on Tuesday and Wednesday. After we are through jogging him, he is turned out. On Thursday he is trained three trips, the first in 2:50, the second in 2:40 and the third between 2:20 and 2:25. The reason the horse is jogged for three days prior to his first workout is that we don't want to take a chance on him tying up off a 2:20 mile and this brief period of jogging does away with this possibility.

From that time on, the horse falls into the routine conditioning program in effect at the farm. He is turned out every day of the week except one and trained that day as I described earlier until two weeks before he is ready to return to the races. Then he goes on the twice-a-week schedule. I find that a program like this gets a horse back to the races fit and ready. Turning him out every day and not putting the harness on him freshens him up. The single day of training serves to keep him tight.

When I turn horses out at the farm, I leave their shoes on all the way around. Usually they are in separate paddocks so there is no danger of their injuring each other and I find it works better that way than to pull their shoes. Once in a while, when a fractious horse is involved, we will put bell boots on him but normally we don't.

The only time we pull their shoes is when we have horses that are going to be off relatively long periods of time and are unsound or something like that and aren't going to be trained. Then we will turn them out in a big field and let them run. This is also when a number of geldings will be turned out together and is another advantage of having geldings in your stable since a stallion would require an individual paddock.

In the middle of the summer, when flies are at their worst, we turn our horses out very early in the morning or in the late evening. The flies don't get after them as bad that way. We never turn horses out during the day in fly season.

We have a blacksmith who comes to the farm twice a week and keeps the horses trimmed and shod and a vet who is also on call to treat them for whatever ailments they may have. One of the big advantages of having a farm base like this is that it saves so much money. I figure that I can keep a horse at the farm for just about half of what it costs to keep him at the race track. That's why every horse I have at the races has to be ready to race. If he isn't he goes back to the farm because it's so much cheaper to take care of him there.

At the races, I have a groom for two horses while at the farm I usually have a groom for every four horses. This is a big saving in itself and I also save on all other expenses from vet to blacksmith and right on down.

I have explained that sometimes I don't send a horse from my stable to the farm but instead ship him to my brother, Brad, who is racing at one of the Ohio mutuel tracks or at the fairs. This develops when I find myself with a horse that is ready to race and is a halfway decent sort that can do some good but there is no race for him in Chicago. For instance, the lowest claiming price in Chicago is $2,000 and maybe this horse ought to be racing for $1,500 or $1,000. I'll send him to Brad and he will race him in Ohio until we lose him or find out he is good enough to return and race for bigger purses.

The same situation holds for green horses that I expect eventually to become part of my Chicago stable. I like to have Brad race these nice young horses. He works on their manners and when they start to show some potential and begin winning themselves out of their class, he gives me a call and, if I have a spot for them, Rolland will pick them up and deliver them to me.

I talk with Brad once or twice a week during the racing season but I talk to my dad every day of the year that I am away from home. In addition to horses already in the barn, dad, Brad and I are always on the lookout for horses that might suit me and can be purchased privately. Dad and Brad scout Ohio pretty closely in this respect and when they spot something they like we all talk it over. If the horse appears to have quite a bit of potential, or if he fits a class where I might be a little weak, we will buy him.

I would also like to get in here someplace that I really enjoy driving a trotter and I wish there were more races for them. The problem is that there aren't as many trotters as pacers and they just don't get the racing opportunity I think they merit. The public doesn't seem to bet as much on them and I have found that the only kind of trotters I can do any good with are those that are claimers or preferred and invitational horses. Conditioned races for trotters are very limited and you have to be awfully lucky to get a start every 10 days. At that, I would guess that probably 25% of my stable consists of trotters.

That pretty well covers the nature of my operation and I think anybody who reads this will have to agree that it is an ideal setup for a horse trainer. I could hardly wish for anything better and I hope I am able to continue in this fashion for a long, long time.

I have written about a great many things but have said very little about driving. There are two reasons for this. I know that Billy Haughton is doing a chapter for this book on proper driving techniques and I do not want to intrude in his field. At the same time, I feel there is so much more involved in the success of my own stable than simply my ability as a driver that I thought I would go into greater detail on the operational phases.

Nevertheless, I do think there are a few salient points about driving a race that I ought to bring up. In Chicago, I race over a mile track (Washington Park) a half mile track (Maywood Park) and a five-eighths mile track (Sportsman's Park). I race on bitter cold nights over muddy tracks in the winter and on hot humid nights over fast tracks in the summer. I am, in other words, exposed to just about every type of race track condition there is.

I still find that so much of driving a race lies in knowing the capability of your horse and the strengths and weaknesses of the drivers and horses which are opposing you. Certain drivers and certain horses have racing patterns that they follow consistently. If you will learn to recognize and look for these patterns you have an important edge.

On a mile track you can afford to sit and wait. Washington Park has a full quarter mile stretch at the finish and I seldom pull before the five-eighths and usually not until the three-quarters or later. But on the half-mile track you have to be out and gone. Very often I will pull at the quarter-mile mark. I find that sometimes the fellow on top will let you go if you come then, whereas if you wait until just before the half you just have to out-foot him the rest of the way.

Even these things are fairly routine with the top drivers so I don't suppose that anybody is going to learn how to drive a horse from reading what I might set down here. As I am sure Billy Haughton will write, it takes time and experience to become a good driver.

As I think back about what I have written, it occurs to me that one of the most important messages I am leaving is that a trainer should learn how to read a condition sheet.

If a trainer will do that and enter his horses where he is pretty sure they ought to finish first, second or third, he will not only win more races but he will make more money. This I guarantee.

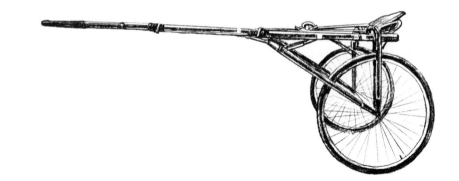

While the name Farrington is a comparatively recent addition to the upper echelons of harness racing, it is becoming increasingly familiar to trotting and pacing fans from coast to coast. Bob Farrington has only been racing horses since 1955, but he has headed the national dash-winning list in five of the past six years (through 1966) and is the only driver in the history of the sport to have registered 300 or more wins in a single season. He did it for the first time in 1964 when he drove 312 winners and then repeated in 1965 and 1966 with 310 and 306. His career total shot past the 2,000 mark in 1967 and he reached that goal earlier in his career than any other driver.

Born on a Richwood, Ohio farm on July 15, 1929, Farrington worked for several years as a farmer and brick mason after graduation from high school in 1948. He embarked on a part-time harness racing career in 1954 by training a few horses after working hours. He drove his first race in 1955 and won 14 of 107 starts. Thereafter he devoted full time to his new profession and moved rapidly up the ladder, hitting the 100 win mark in 1959 and the 200 mark in 1961. He campaigns principally at the Chicago tracks but has also made successful stands on the east and west coasts and in Canada. His lifetime earnings are in excess of $3,000,000 and he has won driving championships at such widely-scattered tracks as Washington Park, Sportsman's Park and Maywood Park (all in the Chicago area), Roosevelt Raceway, (New York), Brandywine Raceway (Delaware), Painesville Raceway (Ohio) and Hollywood Park (California). His single-day record is six wins in six starts at Freehold (N. J.) Raceway in 1963.

10

TIPS on TRAINING

HARRY POWNALL

AS a contributor to this book, I have been assigned the broad subject of horse training in general and asked to discourse at my leisure on whatever comes to mind. A lot of things come to mind because I have been at it for almost half a century and if I haven't learned anything it's my own fault. I think I have.

I am not quite old enough for Social Security, but I am closing in on that milestone and all the memories of my lifetime involve trotters and pacers. I have learned a lot and my teachers have been both men and horses. I would guess the horses have taught me more than the men. For that I thank them.

I differ from most other trainers in that I have only trotters in my barn. I haven't trained a pacer since Tassel Hanover was retired after the 1954 season. That is not to say I don't know anything about pacers. When I was a kid breaking in, and for many years thereafter, I handled just as many pacers as the next fellow and can tell you a lot about them.

But I have a unique situation in that my owners, Mr. and Mrs. E. Roland Harriman and their nephew, E. T. (Ebby) Gerry, prefer not to race pacers and I am perfectly satisfied with that arrangement. I think my owners are the best in harness racing. I have been with them for 30 years now and hope to stay with them until I hang up my silks.

As a result of my relationship with the Harriman family, first as second trainer and race driver and for the past 20 years as head trainer, I have had the good fortune of handling a number of top horses.

In addition to the pacing mare Tassel Hanover, they have included such outstanding trotters as Titan Hanover, Star's Pride, Florican, Florlis and Matastar, to mention just a few that were or still are world champions. I am also quite proud of such trotters as Spud Hanover, Hit Song, Dale Hanover, Sharpshooter, Hanover Maid, Nathaniel and Florimel. The list is a long one and I'd better stop right there or I'll never get started on this chapter.

I am going to scatter my shots and make a fairly broad

presentation in keeping with the general nature of my assignment. But I know what my main point is going to be. I have thought about it all my life and with every passing year I come to believe it more and more.

I honestly and firmly believe that in this country today there is a great tendency to over-train horses. I think this is an especially appropriate subject in that we are just now entering the era of year-round racing and more and more horses are being asked to race over longer and longer periods.

There is no question in my mind that all of us should start thinking about letting up on our horses between races. I think that once you have established a solid foundation for a horse's condition that he can pretty much keep in shape from then on simply by racing each week.

For horses racing every week, I think we should cut down by going less with them between racing assignments and I believe that in many instances such horses shouldn't be trained at all between races. I also think that under these same circumstances there are certain horses that will race better if you do nothing more than blow them out the day before a race without having done anything else except jog them since their last race.

I also think we overdo the proposition of warming a horse up on the day or night of his race. I think a great many more horses than we know are perfectly capable of racing to the best of their ability without any pre-race warmup at all except what they get from the time the post parade is called until the starter says "Go."

I have read about and watched the Europeans and the fellows from Australia and New Zealand train their horses and the more I see of it the more I believe they are on the right track and that our system is the one that has room for improvement.

I am going to go into some detail on this later on, but in general what I will have to say applies to horses of all ages. I qualify this statement only to the extent that it must be borne in mind that all horses are individuals and that what works for one will not necessarily work for the next one. This is one of the fundamental rules of horse training and every trainer worth his salt knows it. If he doesn't know it when he starts, he learns it the first month he is in business.

And before anybody gets the idea that I am going to be

advocating systems and procedures that I wouldn't try myself, let me say that I have done all the things I am going to talk about with large numbers of horses over a long period of time. For many years, I have warmed horses up less and trained them lighter between races than most other trainers.

As a matter of fact, I have even experimented with training 2-year-olds only a single heat. It wasn't successful and I will mention it again later, but I think it proves that I am willing to practice what I preach and also, if the proof were needed, that my owners are willing to go along with me.

But before any young trainer goes rushing off to adopt any of the practices I have mentioned and which I will describe in some detail, let me say that there is one really important consideration involved. Horses that are going to be trained like this must have a solid foundation. They must have had many, many miles between 2:15 and 2:25 to give them the legs and the heart and the muscle that they need to go on with. But once you've established that foundation, I don't believe there is any need to do any more than blow the majority of them out between races if they are racing on a once-a-week basis.

Oh, yes, I understand about the exceptions and, as I have said, I concede they exist. A big, sluggish horse will need extra work and he should have it. But how many big, sluggish horses are there? Not very many. I venture to say that most of the rest will get along a lot better if they are under-trained rather than over-trained.

I am also a firm believer in the axiom that the horse makes the man. I think it's hard to train top horses poorly if you don't go to extremes. On the other hand, I think that any competent, careful trainer will do just as well with a horse that was meant to be a champion as any other trainer. I will concede that really careless men could and probably have spoiled a few top horses, but in my opinion it's not an easy thing to do.

In this respect, I am amused at some of the things that have happened to me to shatter my ego as a horse trainer. A particular case is Matastar and the time I was going for a record with him in 1962. Before I get back to my ideas on conditioning horses, let me tell you about that because it has a direct bearing on what I am writing about.

Matastar, as anybody who saw him will probably remember,

was a terrific trotter but he wasn't easy to control. He had a mind of his own and never would wear a head number on top of his head. It had to be on the side or he would go crazy. He also had a phobia about having horses close to him and wouldn't race in the hole. I got in tight quarters with him a couple of times before I learned this and he would go wild. He was like a crazy man and he had super-human, or maybe I should say "super-horse," strength under these circumstances. He would more or less panic and when he decided it was time to go, he went and you went with him. If there was a horse in front of him he would just as soon run over him as go around him.

Of course, I tried everything with him. I used blinkers and a hood and stuffed his ears and put ear muffs on him, but nothing did any good. He was an intelligent horse and I suppose you could compare him with a human being who has a phobia of one type or another. Under the type of duress brought on by competition he just wasn't normal.

But despite all this, he possessed tremendous speed, even more than either Star's Pride or Florican at their peaks, and I had him at Lexington to go for a record. I had a standard training program mapped out for him, and figured that if I adhered to it faithfully he might have a chance to equal or beat his sire's stallion record of 1:57⅕. In accordance with this schedule, I trained him in 2:02 with the last half in :58⅖ on Friday and planned to go with him on Wednesday of the following week.

Well, the weather came up rainy on Wednesday and the track was no good on Thursday or Friday either. By Saturday, I could tell I was out of the record business for that week so I trained him to a cart over a poor race track in 2:07 with a last half between 1:02 and 1:03.

I didn't figure that was going to help him very much considering the goal I was shooting at, but the season was about over and I didn't have anything to lose so I put him down to go against the fence the following Tuesday. I thought he could probably beat his own record of 1:59, but I was beginning to doubt that he had a shot at Star's Pride's 1:57⅕. After all, it had been 10 days since he had trained in 2:02 with only that 2:07 mile in between. According to the generally accepted training procedures, this was certainly no way to prep a horse for a major effort.

Anyway, I warmed him up that Tuesday at Lexington in an open bridle and just before I was ready to go I went over and slipped the blinds on him. I had raced him a couple of times in a blind bridle as a 2-year-old when I was experimenting with him but I had never done it since. It set him on fire pretty good and he never needed any of that. I did it that day for a psychological reason, figuring that the sudden appearance of the blinds might fire him up for a maximum effort. He scored cheerfully enough but when I turned him around to go he really took off and went out of there like a fast freight on a downhill grade.

Incidentally, let me say here that I think a blind bridle is a partial reason for some of the trouble we have with horses at the gate. If a starter tends to let one or two horses hang back a little and you have a good gate horse that wears a blind bridle and is right on the gate, he will hear those horses coming up from behind him to get in position and will often get over-anxious because he cannot see them and make a break. I have often wished that I could invent something that would permit a driver to convert an open bridle behind the starting gate into a closed one once the field has been released.

But that is another story and I was talking about Matastar going for a record. As I said, he really charged out of there and we were down to the quarter in :29 and to the half in :57⅗. I remember saying to myself, "Oh, boy, this is it. He'll die like a dog off this kind of pace with no work in him." I wasn't driving him; he was driving me. We got to the three quarters in 1:26⅗ and to my surprise he came home strong, finishing his mile in 1:55⅘ which was then the world record for a trotting stallion.

But the thing I remember so well about the mile is that I couldn't get Matastar pulled up until we'd reached the quarter pole. He was still full of trot and I know he could have coasted that last quarter in 31 seconds and set a mile and a quarter record that would probably stand forever.

He was so good that I put him in to go again the next week because I figured he might have a shot at Greyhound's record of 1:55¼. Although he came right back in 1:55⅘, he wasn't quite as sharp as he was the week before. I could tell that because I was able to pull him up long before we reached the quarter pole.

The point I am making is that I had trained Matastar all his life and thought I knew him pretty well. But if I'd had any idea that he was as sharp as he was the day we went that first 1:55⅘ mile, I would have laid my plans a little differently and he might have beaten Greyhound's record. He did beat Greyhound's half-mile track record a year later going in 1:58⅗ against the fence at Delaware, Ohio.

Maybe I should have guessed what he would do. All my life I have been saying that more horses are over-trained than under-trained and that the best thing you can do for any horse is to give him some time off and freshen him up.

I had given Matastar some extra time off, had lightened his work and had accidentally practiced just what I had been preaching. But I just didn't realize how much good the time off and the light work had done him.

Since I am advocating quite forcefully that horses be trained lightly between races, I want to spend some time on the subject and give some examples of what I mean and how I came to believe as I do. I learned my first lesson more than 30 years ago at an upstate New York track where I was racing a big pacer named Hollyrood Knight.

It had rained most of that week and Hollyrood Knight didn't get out of the stall for three days. Not only wasn't I able to train him, but he didn't even get jogged. They finally raced the entire card in one afternoon and Hollyrood Knight won three heats around 2:08 and acted better than he ever had in his life.

I was quite enthused, of course, figuring that my horse had finally found himself and I began laying big plans for him. The next stop was Danbury, Conn., and I figured that all he needed to win easy there was a good tightening. I never gave a thought to the possibility that the three-day layoff might have helped him.

In those days it was routine to train a horse five heats when you worked him between races and that is the procedure I followed with Hollyrood Knight. When I raced him at Danbury, I won the first heat, but just barely, and then dropped the next two. The horse wasn't nearly as sharp as he had been the previous week.

The next stop was Sturbridge, Conn., the last meeting of the year. Everybody was trying to win a bet, of course, to make enough money to last through the winter and I was no exception.

Off what he had showed me two weeks earlier, I thought Holly-rood Knight was just the horse to win such a bet for me and I decided the only thing wrong with him was that he needed to be tightened up a little more. So I trained him five heats again and made them a little faster this time.

He raced awful. He was dull, had no lick and disappointed me terribly, finishing up the race track every heat. That was a long winter for me but it gave me a chance to think about that horse and the way he raced when I hadn't been able to train him. I decided right there that a horse could be trained too much and I have tried to practice training them lightly ever since.

I think a lot of our conditioning methods have simply been handed down from generation to generation and that no really serious effort has ever been made to improve on them. I know that I have made an effort in that direction and I think it has been responsible for some of the success I have enjoyed.

Before I get deeper into this subject I want to emphasize that I am going to be talking about older horses, 3-year-olds and up. I still train my 2-year-olds lighter than most people but I have found you can't train them too lightly before they get to the races and I want to write a little something about that.

Mr. Harriman is always interested in experiments and in ways to improve training methods. A number of years ago he and I discussed the possibility of training our 2-year-olds just as if they were thoroughbreds, that is, just going one trip with them, brushing them a little faster on the end of that one mile as they gained experience, and actually racing them cold. We had a number of nice home-breds and used them to experiment with.

I guess the program lasted about two months. I kept going until I got disgusted and had to give up this method. The colts were simply so full of life that I couldn't even begin to train them going only a single mile. It wasn't until I started repeating them and going the second mile that they learned anything at all.

Going just one heat, they were so full of pep that the slightest little thing would set them off and they would start running, playing and bucking. It was a noble experiment but I just had to give up on it.

I train my 2-year-olds two trips until we start to matinee at Pompano Park in Florida, where I winter, and about that time I will warm them up two little heats and go a heat in the matinee. After that, I will follow about the same procedure on the day of their fast workout. I will just go two heats and then their fast mile. On their other training day, I will just go two heats, unless I run across a real tough colt and then I might give him three. I seldom go four heats with a colt.

As long as I am talking about colts and their early lessons, I might as well spend a little time describing how I break my colts to the starting gate. I think this is an important thing and I like to handle it in a casual way so that the colts get accustomed to a gate early and learn that it isn't anything they have to be concerned about.

At Pompano there is a mile track over which most of the training is done and a half-mile track which is used for some training, but mostly for jogging. Riley Couch, the starter, usually arrives in Florida the latter part of January each year and he is at the half-mile track each morning with his gate. Riley is very cooperative in this respect and tries to help everybody all he can.

What I like to do is take my colts over to the half-mile track and go their jog miles behind the gate. My assistants and I will sit in behind the gate with a set of colts and move along in a very relaxed manner talking back and forth among ourselves and letting the colts put their heads right up against the gate as we jog along.

After we have done this a few times and the colts have grown accustomed to the gate, I will usually ask Riley to speed up to about a three-minute clip for the last mile and we will go along at that rate. At the end of the mile, Riley will speed the gate up just a little and fold the wings as he pulls away. This teaches the colts what they can expect later on when they go away in a race. I have found that this natural, relaxed method is an excellent one and I recommend it a great deal.

Usually the first or second time a colt is behind the gate he will get too close to it and bang his head against it, or something like that, and maybe even make a little break as a result. But when this happens I just go easy with him and let him get back up to the gate in his own good time, which he will, and he soon learns he has nothing to fear. In almost no time, all the colts are marching right along behind the gate and they aren't upset either by the gate itself or by the other horses crowding around them. When I start to repeat my colts, I will very often work them the first mile behind the gate and then will go over to the mile track for my second and fastest mile.

In racing my colts, I only warm them up two heats. I think that is plenty even if they have to race three or even four heats. I'll jog a colt from two to three miles and then go a mile in 2:50. The last warmup mile will be anywhere from 2:15 to 2:25 depending on the colt. If he is a delicate, nervous colt I would be more inclined to go around 2:25. I would brush him the last end of this mile, maybe just the last sixteenth and not very fast at that. Just enough to sharpen him up.

I believe the important thing with colts that are going heats is what happens between heats. I think this period should be used to revive and relieve them and to freshen them up in every way possible.

In this respect, I don't think there's anything better in the world than an alcohol rub. Bring the colt back to the paddock, strip him down, give him a little drink of water, bathe him good using a sponge and buckets of fresh, cool water and then take him out and give him that alcohol rub. Just put the alcohol on your hand and rub it gently over the entire body. A horse is just like a person. You give him a nice massage and he can't help but like it. It refreshes and revives. It makes him ready and willing to go back for the next heat.

Now let me get back to what I was talking about with reference to training horses between races. This principle applies to horses of any age, including 2-year-olds, although you must bear in mind that 2-year-olds are trained differently until they actually get to the races.

Sticking for the moment with older horses, those that are 3-year-olds and up and have had racing experience, your early conditioning program calls for the usual two workouts a week, one "fast" and the other "slow." Eventually, you get your horse down to about 2:10 and race him off that. Assuming that you are able to race him once a week thereafter, you don't vary your pattern. The race is his "fast" work and between races you train him a "slow" work.

When you first get to the races and are going in 2:10, the fastest mile in your slow work is maybe 2:15. As you get down to where you are racing in 2:05, you keep going the same way except that you speed up the fastest mile of the slow work until you are going in 2:12 between races. I don't think this is quite right and never have and I think horses should be freshened up between races instead of drilled unless there is some definite need for it.

Maybe some night your horse doesn't go a good race, lets up a little at the end and you decide he's "short" and drill him pretty hard between races. I think maybe that's exactly wrong and that instead, you might be better off to let up on that be-tween-races training or not train the horse at all.

The first great horse I ever had was Hanover Maid, the second dam of Speedster. She was a natural trotter, perfect-mannered, never took any hold at all and would come out of the middle of the pack and give you everything she had at the end.

The only training Hanover Maid got between races was a blowout mile the day before she raced. She had to race three and four heats, too. Between races I would just jog her a little every day, maybe a couple of miles, and then, on the day be-fore her race, I would jog her a couple of miles, and go a mile around 2:50 or 2:40. That mare raced game, raced her heart out. I know I couldn't have trained her any other way to get any more out of her. And she wasn't an isolated case either. I did that with a lot of good horses and the results were always satis-factory.

I did it with Titan Hanover and with Star's Pride and Florican and every other good horse I ever had at one time or another. When their races were a week apart and they were tight, I would just jog them every day and go one blowout mile the day before the race. Depending on the horse, that mile would be somewhere between 2:35 and 2:50. I pretty well let the horse decide. If he wants to go in 2:35, that's all right with me and if he wants to make it 2:50, I am just as satisfied as he is.

I will also do this with 2-year-olds. Until they get to the races, 2-year-olds generally have to be conditioned differently, but once the foundation has been properly laid and they get to the races, they can be handled the same way in many instances. A case in point is the trotter Pomp, a 2-year-old in 1966. When Pomp was racing on a once-a-week basis, all he got was a blowout mile somewhere between 2:35 and 2:50 the day before the race.

You must remember, though, that it is altogether different if there is more than a week between starts. If you have from 10 days to two weeks between starts, then you obviously have to do a little something with your horse to keep him sharp. It doesn't have to be very much, but it needs to be something more than the blowout mile I have been writing about.

Years ago, there was an old saying, "Rainy days and drunken grooms make the best horses." I think there is a lot in what the saying stood for and that it has a direct application to what I am writing about. Horses couldn't be trained on rainy days and were usually short changed in some part of their conditioning program if the groom was off battling the bottle. Very often, horses were better off in both circumstances, providing the groom didn't make it too long a session.

On the other hand, when you start digging into a horse and really drilling him by racing him regularly and continuing to put the pressure on with stiff workouts between races you are asking for trouble with the vast majority of horses in training today. These are the horses that will start falling off their feed and these are the ones you should start backing off.

If you have conditioned a horse properly by giving him a solid foundation built around a lot of moderate miles over a lengthy period of time, it is pretty hard, in my opinion, ever to say that such a horse is under-trained. I don't see how in the world an occasional rest or a change in the training schedule that gives the horse an easier time between races can do anything except help him.

So if you are having trouble conditioning a horse; if he doesn't act as sharp as he should and you have determined that there is nothing organically wrong, it might be a good idea to let up on that horse a little between races. Don't be afraid to train him as I did Hanover Maid and a great many others by blowing him out the day before the race. You might be surprised at the results.

If you should decide to do this, there is one exception that I want to enter into the record. I think you have to go a little more with an older horse when the weather is very cold.

Many years ago I was racing in Maine at one of the overcoat meetings and it was one of those cold, bitter weeks for which those meetings were named. I had a nice mare that I was racing in the free-for-all class. The weather had been bad for a couple of weeks and I hadn't done much with her. I was sitting around one afternoon when an old fellow sat down alongside me and we started talking about horses.

"You know," he said, "when the weather gets real cold like this late in the year, you have to train an old horse more than you do in the summer."

I thought about this and about my old mare who figured to be as good as any of the others in her race, but certainly no better. Maybe, I thought, this fellow might have something. I decided it was worth experimenting.

The day before the race I brought my mare out and trained her three pretty stiff heats, the fastest in 2:14. This was a mare that would race around 2:07 so I was tying into her pretty good to go a mile within seven seconds of where she could race, and on the day before her race at that. I watched to see if any of the other fellows trained this way but they didn't. The next day my mare went out and knocked the field off for fun. She was real strong at the end and they were letting loose.

I have done this from time to time over the years and it has always worked out fine. So when the weather changes suddenly and it starts getting real cold, it might be a good idea to go pretty good with that old horse the day before his race.

As far as warming up for a race goes, I think we overdo that, too. A long time ago a fellow asked me why we warmed them up so much and I couldn't give him a good answer. You see the Europeans come over here and race their horses cold and do well with them. I don't think our system is any more than a tradition that's been handed down from generation to generation. I don't campaign many actual raceway horses but if I did I would cut down on their warming up routine.

I have raced horses cold with good results. I remember I did this with Walter Spencer when I had him. He was a nervous horse and after he'd race three heats you'd wonder where his middle went. I thought about him for a while and finally decided not to warm him up before his races. I just jogged him a little and went. He raced just as well and held his condition better.

When Roosevelt Raceway opened, there were a number of times when it rained and you couldn't warm your horse up. You'd just have to go cold out of the paddock. I know this never hurt any horse that I had and I thought it was particularly good for those that were inclined to be nervous.

I'm not at all afraid to recommend that a young fellow race an old horse cold, one that has a real solid foundation of training miles and is legged up real good. After all, you get almost 15 minutes on the track before the race goes and that's plenty of time for almost any horse. Just that period of time is more than enough to get him nerved up and sweating pretty good. No sir, don't be afraid to do this just because somebody says it isn't customary.

As I have written, the secret of being able to train a horse lightly or not at all between races lies in having laid a solid foundation. For a horse that is going to trot a mile in 2:05 when he races, a lot of miles around 2:15 will do him more good than anything.

Another very important factor is that when you start to drop a horse from that level, you should begin to concentrate on really brushing the last end of the final mile on the day you give him his fast work. I really believe this sets them up and gets them in condition quicker than anything.

You might start about five weeks before you are scheduled to make your first start and for the first couple of weeks you would only brush the horse an eighth instead of a quarter. The eighth might be in 15⅖ seconds or something like that.

Then, as you start to get down around 2:12, say in the last three weeks of the horse's training program, brush him that last quarter in 30 to 31 seconds. Quarters like this will tighten a horse up real quick.

In doing this, you are better off to train your horse a mile in 2:10 with a last quarter in 30 seconds than a mile in 2:07 with all the quarters pretty much alike. In this way, you are extending your horse to his limit for a quarter of a mile and when the time comes to actually race he is going to be tighter and a lot better off than the one that has not had these fast quarters. And this horse will also tend to stay tighter longer.

Florimel, the dam of Florican, comes to mind as an example of a mare that maintained condition and raced well under a set of adverse circumstances because she had plenty of foundation.

This was back in 1941 when she was a 3-year-old. We were

at Saratoga the week before the Historic meeting at Goshen and were pointing this filly for the Coaching Club Oaks. We wanted her to be good when Mr. and Mrs. Harriman saw her.

About 10 days before the Oaks, she developed a virus and a bad one. The sulfa drugs were just coming out then and we loaded her up with them and they helped her a little but not much. Billy Dickerson was the head trainer for Arden Homestead then and I was his assistant and did the driving.

The filly had typical virus symptoms. We would jog her and she would cough and run a temperature. The next morning the temperature would be gone and we would jog her again whereupon it would return. So we just stopped with her. She stayed in the stall for eight straight days.

The day before the Oaks she was at Goshen and Bill said, "Well, I think we'd better start her if she blows out without running a temperature." I blew her out a little mile around 3:00 and her temperature didn't go up so we declared her in.

That was all she had had in ten days and she went out and won The Oaks the next day. She was a little leg weary at the end but she had raced a little before that and had a solid foundation which was all she needed. This just proved to me again that you don't have to do a great deal with them once they are ready. This particular situation was forced on me, but I have intentionally followed this procedure many times since with good results.

Florimel was a little tired after her race and went to her stall and laid down and rested. We didn't do anything with her the next day, but then we picked her up and went right on into a normal schedule with her. She raced very well and showed no ill effects at all.

So my advice to young trainers is not to be too upset just because a colt picks up a virus and has to miss some training. If you've laid the foundation, he'll bounce back quickly. The main thing is that you shouldn't even take your horse out of the barn until the temperature has disappeared and stayed away for several days. If you jog or train a horse before the virus is out of his system you're just prolonging the illness. But once it's gone, your worries are over and you can come back in a hurry.

I also think horses were better off when we were shipping them from track to track and giving them a change of scenery every week. Horses are like people, they get tired of the same old thing and the same old routine every day. They like a little change.

One of the smartest trainers of all in this respect is my good friend, Jimmy Cruise, whose horsemanship I have always admired. Jimmy has a reputation for doing exceptionally well with half-sound horses and everybody is always shopping around for his secret. Jimmy's main secret is right there for everybody to see. He just takes them away from the race track and gives them a change of scenery. He trains them lightly now and then, but the rest of the time between races they're running out all day in a paddock some place nearby. He's letting Mother Nature do some of his work for him. Not everybody has Jimmy's experience and for that reason not every trainer can expect to duplicate his record. But they'd all do better if they could get their horses away from the track for a few days at a time.

I mentioned earlier that not all horses can be trained the same way and that a trainer has to use his judgment and some common sense. You can't any more train all horses alike than you can put all the 5-year-old children in the world in the same school room and expect them to get identical grades.

I'll give you an example of what I mean. A few years back I was stabled next to a fellow who had two horses that were as different as day and night. One weighed about 1,200 pounds and could go in 2:01. The other weighed around 850 and could go in 2:04. But this fellow trained them the same number of heats at exactly the same speed between races.

It just didn't stand to reason that these two horses, as dissimilar as they were, should be trained alike and it showed when they raced. The big horse raced well but the little horse didn't. I am sure that if the fellow had let up on the little horse he would have raced better in his own class and it is my opinion that the horse actually would have moved up to a faster class if the trainer hadn't drilled him as hard between races.

When Star's Pride and Florican were aged horses they occasionally had to go in distance races. But I never trained them any harder for that kind of race than for any other. As I have said repeatedly, as long as a horse is legged up and has a solid foundation he will go on for you and go any distance right up to and including two miles.

I remember the week before Star's Pride and Florican were going to start in their first distance race, which was scheduled at a mile and a half. It was at Roosevelt Raceway and a trainer asked me how I was going to condition them for distance. I told him I wasn't going to do anything different than I had been, which was to let them go pretty much as they wanted between races.

He insisted on knowing whether I was going to train an extra distance and whether I would train them in 2:10 or faster which is why I recall the occasion so vividly. I can remember saying:

"These horses don't need anything extra, they are in shape. I'm just going to turn them around and let them train where they want. If they want to go in 2:25, that's O.K. and if they want to go in 2:15, that's all right, too."

There was a lot of training traffic when I went with these horses and sometimes this will make a horse want to go more. But Star's Pride and Florican went out there and trained themselves in 2:20 with horses going by them on all sides and they never blinked an eye or pulled a bit.

In the race, Star's Pride set a new world's record for a mile and a half at 3:06⅕ and Florican was right there with him. Believe me, when horses are in shape and are fresh and ready they don't need a lot of extra training.

These horses had entirely different dispositions, too, so you could not say that they should be trained the same way because they were the same kind of horses. About the only thing they really had in common was speed and gait. Star's Pride, for instance, wouldn't stand for the whip. If you touched him with it, he'd try to kick you out of the sulky. But he'd try for his life if you didn't get after him. Florican, on the other hand, would accept the whip and would dig in and go a little more. I never really laid into him, but I would have to keep tapping him all the time and he was better for it.

Naturally, I remember quite a few things about these two horses and it might not be a bad idea to mention some of them, in addition to the distance-training episode I have already related.

I recall, for instance, the only time Florican ever took an unsound step in his life and it highlights something that all trainers should always be on the lookout for because it can happen no matter how careful you are.

This was in 1949 when Florican was a 2-year-old. He was staked in a $10,000 race at Old Orchard in Maine and since Lusty Song wasn't entered, it looked as though I had a pretty good chance to win. I worked Florican lightly before the race and I thought he was a little off behind. But I jogged him the next day and he was all right so I declared him in.

On the day of the race, I started to warm him up but he was sore behind again. I went a slow mile and it was obvious he was favoring his left hind leg. It didn't amount to a great deal but I knew he was a top colt and didn't want to take any chances so I scratched him. I had a good vet look him over but he couldn't find a thing.

The next morning the groom called me into the stall and pointed out a little bunch just above the left hind ankle on the back side of the leg. It was in the exact spot where the hind shin boot separates, above the first buckle and below the wrap-around portion of the boot which has three buckles over an elastic base. The area was very tender and sore and it was obvious that the only way it could have developed was because the boot was too tight and binding.

I told the groom to put brace bandages on him and we would try him out. I went out and trained him in 2:09 and he was sound as a dollar. This was the day after he had been scratched and there was nothing wrong with him except that the boot was pinching. He was wearing a pair of brand new boots which were a little stiff and they had chafed him. Incidentally, I never used shin boots on Florican again.

All horse trainers should always take every possible precaution against boot chafe. It is a very common thing but it usually can be prevented by an alert groom working for an alert trainer. You can never tell when a boot will start to bind or pinch and if it isn't caught right away a horse can go lame. I always tell my grooms never to fasten boots too tightly. I would rather have them a little loose than to take a chance on their pinching and binding.

Over the years, I have heard discussed pro and con the question of whether horses have intelligence. I think they do and I want to relate a couple of stories involving Star's Pride and Florican that demonstrated conclusively to me that horses are intelligent and that a real smart horse will even try to tell you when you are doing something wrong.

My first story concerns Star's Pride, but before I go into details let me say that I don't think every horse is smart. I think horses, in that respect, are just like people. There are smart ones and there are the ones that aren't so smart. But all of the really great horses I had—Star's Pride, Florican, Titan Hanover, Matastar, Florlis—were intelligent horses and showed me they were many times.

I think the classic example was Star's Pride when he was a 4-year-old and was being prepped in Florida for the 1951 racing season.

Along in April I had him up to a mile in 2:17 and trained him there one day. When he came in he had a quarter crack in his left front foot. I took him to the shop and had it burned out and trimmed. He jogged sound so I went with him again on his next training day. He was sound but when he came in he had another quarter crack on the opposite front foot. I doctored him, he jogged sound, I trained him again and he came up with a third quarter crack, this one on the left front foot again.

Naturally, I figured that with three quarter cracks I was out of business. But the horse wasn't sore so I kept training him a little around 2:23. But he got so he didn't want to train. He would go out on the track and wouldn't turn—just get balky and refuse. You can imagine how I felt. Here is a potentially top free-for-all trotter who simply refuses to train even though he is apparently sound.

I hit him with the whip once when he balked, but he just tried to kick me out of the cart so I gave up on that. I would go out there with him and try to make him turn and he wouldn't, and I would bring him back to the barn and do him up without having trained him.

This went on for a couple of weeks and I decided I would try a blind bridle. He had raced in an open bridle since early in his 2-year-old form but I put the blinds on him and finally did get him so that he would turn but he wouldn't really try to trot. The best I ever got out of him after that first quarter crack was a mile in 2:23 and even that was hard work.

Finally we shipped to Goshen without having beaten 2:23

and the horse acted very limber. I had lost about two months by now and I decided I had to train him to start getting ready for the stakes, so I took him out on the track with the idea of trying any way I could to get a mile in 2:20 out of him.

To appreciate this, you have to remember that Star's Pride really knew me and I really knew him. We had been doing battle for more than two months now and he had been resisting me every step of the way.

I hooked him to a cart, took him on the track and he pricked his ears and took off with me. He was down to the half in 1:04 and I had a desperate hold and remember saying, "He'll kill himself sure." I was taking him back all through the last half but he still trotted in 2:09 and when he pulled up he wouldn't have blown out a candle. And remember, he hadn't been a mile in better than 2:23 since early April.

There isn't any question in my mind that on that day Star's Pride was saying to me, "O.K., Mr. Pownall, I'm ready for the races now. Let's go." Nor is there any question that all the time he was balking in Florida he was saying to me, "I know I feel sound to you and that I act sound, but I'm not really sound and because of that I'm not ready to drop down to a faster mile and I'm not going to. When I reach the stage where I know I'm all right on these quarter cracks, I'll let you know."

And he did let me know that day at Goshen. It was an outstanding example of a horse showing his intelligence.

Florican demonstrated his intelligence in a big race in California. He trotted all the way with a broken bit and was absolutely guideless as far as I was concerned. He actually won the race, although he was set back for a lengthy run at the start. That was the cause of all my trouble.

In a similar situation 99 out of 100 horses would have bolted out the nearest draw gate or have run to the outside fence. But Florican didn't panic at all and after he and I got over the first shock of what had happened he went as perfect a race as he ever had in his life. As a matter of fact, I even took the liberty of tapping him a few times in the stretch to keep him going and out of the way of the other horses.

Florican wore a rubber bit with a little chain that runs through it and I discovered later that some water had gotten in there and rusted the bit. Anyway, we were boiling away behind the gate and he made a break, something he seldom did. I grabbed onto him pretty good and when I did the bit broke.

I didn't know at first whether it was a line or the bit, but Florican was running and was guideless and all I could do was yell to the fellows around me that I was in trouble. We were in the first turn at the eighth pole and I thought for sure that Florican would run out the draw gate at the quarter pole when he got there. But he caught just as we passed the eighth pole, trotted right over to the rail, and cut out the race the rest of the way.

He won very comfortably, pulled up with the other horses and stood quietly while I got out and took him by the head to lead him back to the paddock.

Everybody knows that you are in real trouble with a guideless horse and are almost sure to get in some kind of major difficulty. But Florican was so intelligent that as soon as he recovered from his break, he got himself right back in the race, cut out the pace just as nicely as I could have and went on and "won." He probably wonders yet why we didn't go back to the winner's circle that day.

I was perfectly calm while all this was going on but back in the barn area it hit me pretty hard. I got scared thinking about it and decided I needed a drink. I asked my grooms if they had anything laid away for "medicinal purposes" and I'll be darned if the one groom in the whole stable that I would have bet never took a drink didn't go to his trunk and get a bottle.

"Here you are, Harry," he said, "I take two drinks a day for my heart." "By gosh," I replied, "I just better have one for my heart." And I did.

I think a book like this is a good idea because it gives a young fellow an opportunity to profit from some of the lessons the more experienced trainers have learned the hard way. I know that when I was a youngster I would have been glad to shell out a little money, even though I didn't have very much, if some of the leading men in the profession had banded together to turn out such a volume.

In those days, there wasn't much money in harness racing and the successful trainers weren't nearly as inclined to share their knowledge as they are now when there is plenty for everybody.

A fine man who was an exception in this respect was the late

Will Caton, who trained Protector, The Marchioness and so many top colts and aged performers. He was always willing to take the time to try to help a fellow get along and I would like to pass on a couple of little things he told me that might help somebody today. One has to do with pullers and the other concerns a lip cord.

I had a nice little pacing filly that was out of a great race mare, Anna Bradford's Girl, but I was having trouble getting her started. Even at a jog she would pull the heck out of me and I didn't know how I was ever going to get her trained because I couldn't get her slowed down enough to start.

I went to Will and explained my problem and he said, "Did you ever teach her to walk?" I told him I hadn't and he advised me to try it.

I was training at Longwood near Orlando, Fla. at the time and there was a long jog path, maybe two miles long, leading away from the stable area. Will told me to teach her to walk on this path. He said that if I would do this every day for a week that I could then let her jog a little. If she still showed an inclination to pull, I was to quit trying to jog her and walk her another week.

I did this for a week. I walked this filly back and forth once a day. I wouldn't go quite to the end of the path with her, but I was walking her between three and four miles. The first couple of days she acted a little ambitious, but I was patient and just sat there with her and wouldn't let her move into a jog. At the end of the week, I took her to the track and she was perfect. She never pulled an ounce after that.

This filly was just a 2-year-old and I doubt if this would work with an old horse that was used to pulling in races, but I am sure a fellow would have a good chance to straighten out a colt that had this trouble. And as far as I am concerned, you might just as well try it with an old puller, too. You certainly wouldn't have anything to lose.

A lip cord is used with horses that pull, but sometimes when you start to use one a horse will fight it because he is unaccustomed to it. A lip cord can cut a horse along the gums and you don't want them fighting it if you can help it. I had one like this and asked Will what to do.

He told me to take an ordinary piece of chamois and roll it

up until it was about the size of a clothesline rope and use that as a lip cord. He said not to put it on tight and that I would find that this would take enough off the horse's mouth and still wouldn't hurt him. I did it and it proved very successful. After a while, I took the chamois out and substituted an actual lip cord and the horse never knew the difference. It was a sound piece of advice and I pass it on with the thought that perhaps it might help some young fellow somewhere just as it did me more than 30 years ago.

Will was also the man who told me back in the 1920's that I would live to see the day when all the major world's records were held by two and 3-year-olds. It hasn't quite come to that yet but I think everyone will concede that our young horses have made great strides in that direction.

When I see how lightly today's champions are shod, I think of Will Caton and the job he had with Protector, who was the world's champion 3-year-old trotter with a mark of 1:59¼ taken in 1931. Protector wore 27 ounces on each front foot at two. I don't know exactly how much weight he carried at three, undoubtedly less than that, but still a great deal more than the great horses of the present era.

The old-timers also had a lot more trouble with interference than we do now because our horses are much more natural. You never hear of a horse these days having to wear 27 ounces to keep him balanced and the fact that they are going lighter is an indication that the breed is improving.

One of the problems that is still with us, and probably always will be to some degree, is that of knee-knocking. I want to mention the subject because I have a little suggestion that might help. I think it is a good idea to wear felt knee boots instead of leather ones.

Actually, I don't have too much trouble with knee-knockers in my stable. I don't have any pacers and, as everybody knows, a pacer is more likely to hit his knees than a trotter. The last time I had a pair of knee boots on a pacer was when I raced Tassel Hanover and when I took them off she became a better mare. Tassel Hanover was a half-sister to Titan Hanover but she wouldn't trot. She had suffered some kind of a knee injury as a yearling and she had quite a scar there. As a result, she went stiff-legged because that knee wouldn't bend naturally and to be uniform she also went stiff-legged with the other one.

I tried everything with her; toe weights, leaded boots, extra weight in the shoe, but nothing did any good. She was too stiff-legged to be a good trotter. I knew that if I went on that way I would break her down in front so I pulled everything off one day in Florida when she was a 2-year-old and she went off on a natural pace as nice as you'd want. Her disposition changed, too. On the trot she would get angry and want to fight you but on the pace she was perfect.

She jumped off a lot of money as a 2-year-old. She had terrific speed but would tend to fall apart at the finish. I always thought the reason was that she was such a big-gaited mare when she was in high that she couldn't quite handle her gait because she wasn't used to going that way. Of course, you could never train her to the extreme limit of her speed and thus she never got that big-gaited except at the end of a race.

Tassel would tick her knees a little at two so I put a pair of felt knee boots on her at three. She wasn't racing well and at Sedalia in late August I decided to take them off. That seemed to make a big difference with her and she raced very well from that time on. Whether that made all the difference I don't know, but she was a better mare thereafter.

Before I started writing about Tassel Hanover, I had mentioned knee-knockers and in that respect I want to relate why I use felt knee boots instead of leather ones.

A long time ago, before I went to work for the Harrimans, I made a trip to Longwood in Florida and bought a pacer for a friend of mine from Ben White and Mr. W. N. Reynolds. He was a nice little colt but he went to his knees and I wasn't doing any good with him.

When we got to Old Orchard, I went to Ben and explained my problem and he told me to take the colt to his blacksmith, Charlie Snow, and that Charlie would try to fix me up and that it wouldn't cost me a penny.

I went to the shop and while I was sitting there waiting for the colt to be shod an old fellow walked in, watched what was being done, listened to us for a while and then said to me;

"Say, young fellow, what kind of knee boots you got on that horse?"

I told him that I was wearing the standard leather boots.

"Well, let me tell you something," he said, "you take them off and use felt knee boots. And remember this: A horse hears it when he hits a leather knee boot and pretty soon he gets used to that sound and gets to liking it. He'll never quit as long as he hears that sound."

I thought about that a little and decided that he just might have something. So I substituted a pair of felt knee boots and the little colt got off his knees and raced well for me. I am sure Charlie Snow, who was a great mechanic, helped him but I am also sure that the felt boots helped, too. I have never used a pair of leather knee boots since.

A lot of trainers don't use felt knee boots because they don't think they give as much protection. But they do as far as I am concerned and they don't stick out as far either.

Of course, in the old days there were a lot more knee-knockers than there are now. Trainers used to line the knee boots with a piece of aluminum or something like that. You can imagine the jar horses got when they hit that. It didn't hurt just part of the knee, it hurt the whole knee. They also used sheepskin on the outside of the knee boot. That made the boot stick out even more.

I think a long toe will help more than anything with a pacer that goes to his knees. Little Pat was one of the greatest and toughest pacers that ever lived but I don't think you'd ever have heard of him if he hadn't worn a 4¼-inch toe. I think one of the things a young trainer should try with a knee-knocker is lengthening his toe in front.

With a trotting colt, don't ever be afraid to carry a little toe in front. That's one of the lessons I learned from Allie Cornwell, the first trainer for whom I worked when I was just a kid in Brooklyn. I used to go out to the Mineola, N. Y., fairgrounds and work for Allie. That was in the days when it wasn't uncommon for a horse to wear a different type shoe on each foot.

Allie told me that when you had a horse you had to hang on to keep him on stride he wasn't balanced properly. He said that when you reached the stage where you could throw his head away and he would still stay trotting he was balanced right. He told me that the important thing about it was to allow enough toe in front.

This is a little experiment a young trotting horse trainer shouldn't be afraid to try. I'm not trying to encourage anyone to throw a horse's head away in a race because it is a dangerous practice. I'm talking about training. Some day when you are not quite sure whether your trotter is balanced properly, turn his head loose somewhere during a training mile. If he stays steady and flat and keeps on trotting the same way, you've got him balanced. But if he starts fluttering around a little and kind of reaching and feeling his way along, he's probably not set right.

As far as shoeing my trotters is concerned—and pacers too for that matter when I was training them—I am pretty much of a "half-round" man. My preference might very well have something to do with the fact that all the great trotters I've had wore half-round shoes. I have had some trotters that raced in a flat (plain) shoe, but none of my top ones.

The half-round shoe breaks them over quicker in front and usually when I make a change it will be to square the toe and get them over even quicker. A half-round shoe or a half-round with a square toe in my opinion helps as much as anything to eliminate interference behind and while it might be possible that Star's Pride and Florican and some of those horses would have gone just as much in a flat shoe, I wasn't about to make any changes in mid-stream.

I also know a trotter that won the Hambletonian wearing flat shoes in front and the Kentucky Futurity in half-rounds. This was Sharp Note, trained and driven by my old friend, Bi Shively, and I think the story is interesting enough to bear repeating here.

As I said, Sharp Note, who was a truly great colt, won the Hambletonian wearing flat shoes after which we all shipped west to race through what was then known as The Big 5—Springfield, Ill., Sedalia, Mo., Du Quoin, Ill., Indianapolis and Delaware, Ohio. I had won a heat of The Hambletonian with Hit Song and at the first Big 5 stop, Springfield, I won the Review Futurity in three straight heats with Sharp Note second each time.

The following week we were at Sedalia where we got rained out and it happened that Bi and I were in the blacksmith shop at the same time. We started talking about flat and half-round shoes. Bi said he had never had any luck with half-round shoes and I told him that all the best horses I ever had wore half-rounds. We discussed the subject for quite a while. At Du Quoin the following week I won the stake again and it looked as though I had Sharp Note's number.

When I arrived at Indianapolis the next week, an old retired groom who had been present when Bi and I were discussing shoeing at Sedalia was waiting for me at the stable. He said he had some news for me and went on to relate that Bi had had Sharp Note shod in half-rounds the day before. The old fellow seemed happy to pass this information on to me.

The Horseman Futurity was scheduled for the next day and I thought I would wait to see what happened before I said anything to Bi. Sharp Note won the first heat easily so I went to Bi and told him I was going to sue him for using half-rounds. They certainly seemed to help the horse a great deal. Bi laughed and admitted that his horse had trotted better but said that one heat wasn't enough to be sure. But Sharp Note went on and won the second heat just as easily, and then proceeded to beat me in the Kentucky Futurity a month later shod in half-rounds. It tickled me to see a grand old fellow like Bi do well even though it was costing me some pretty big stakes.

Most of your shoeing problems with trotters are in front but a lot of times you will have trouble behind and it can give you gray hairs. I remember the trouble I had with Titan Hanover when he was a 2-year-old, how proud I was when I found the key and how I discovered later that I was just plain lucky and that what applied for one horse sure didn't for another.

When I started training Titan he was stabbing and jabbing terribly with his left hind leg and those kind just don't make trotters.

I tried everything. I tried raising his head way up high, but he was a nervous colt and he didn't like that. He'd fight and break out in a sweat and get all excited. So I finally let his head way down and I guess this is where I got my reputation for doing well with low-headed trotters. I will come back to that in a little while.

My big problem was that left hind leg. I didn't know what to do so I just took his hind shoes off and let him trot bare-footed. I went along real easy with him and with his bare feet and low head he began to like to trot. At the same time, I noticed that he was starting to brush his hind shins a little. This was actually a good sign because horses that are hooking and jabbing will speedy cut and scalp like the devil but they will rarely get up on their shins.

I trained Titan Hanover for about three months with all the quarters alike, never asking him for speed. Finally, along towards the end of March, I brushed him a quarter in 33 seconds and he was good. About two weeks later, maybe the first week of April, I let him ramble on and he gave me a quarter in 31 seconds. I knew I had a top colt but I also knew I was going to have to do something about shoeing him behind because a colt just can't race the whole season bare-footed.

I thought about it for a while and finally decided to try him with plain shoes behind and to put a grab calk straight across the toe of the leg he hooked with. I did this and he was letter perfect. He never hooked that hind leg again and within six weeks I was able to shoe him with a standard full swedge behind.

You can imagine that after he went through his 2-year-old form the way he did and climaxed the season by becoming the sport's first two-minute 2-year-old trotter, I was quite proud of myself. Not only did I have a champion colt but I knew how to cure a stabbing trotter.

The following spring I came up with what looked like another nice colt but when he got down to about 2:35 he started to hook and jab just like Titan had. This time I smiled to myself. I had the answer. I pulled his hind shoes and trained him bare-footed. He still jabbed. I tried the shoe with the grab. He still jabbed. For all I know, he's jabbing yet, and until this day I haven't found another horse that I improved with the method I used with Titan. All that showed me was that Titan Hanover was meant to overcome this handicap. I may have helped him along a little, but he did most of it on his own.

I discovered later that a lot of Titan's sons and daughters trotted the same way. But I never cured any of them. One of the most notable Titans that trotted like this was Hardy Hanover. I remember that when Del Miller won with him in world record time at Delaware as a 2-year-old he took his hind shoes off and raced him bare-footed.

There are a couple of other things regarding Titan Hanover that might be of interest. For one thing, little Titan was strictly a front-runner. He had a tender mouth—that went with the Calumet Chucks, Titan's sire—and I didn't use an overcheck bit on him, just a check and a chin strap along with a snaffle driving bit. He would take a pretty good hold of me until he reached the top. After that he was fine.

I remember in the Horseman Stake, when he was a 2-year-old, I drew the trailing position in the second tier and I couldn't get by anybody. Titan really wanted to move and when I doubled him up he brushed a tendon, just took the hair off like you'd scratched him with a pin, and I knew right then that he'd never race in the hole.

I knew that if I ever tried it again he'd probably cut off a tendon so I always went for the top with him in every race he was in. I was lucky in that he had so much speed there wasn't anything that could go with him and after a while they didn't even try. But I know that I would have been in real trouble if I'd had to race him in the hole.

Titan Hanover had one other problem. As a 2-year-old, he would never empty out when he was being warmed up. This applied for both training and racing days from the moment he stepped out of the stall to start warming up until after he was cooled out.

We tried a lot of things but none of them worked. The next year, when he was three, we found the answer. We discovered that if he was completely stripped and turned loose in his stall between heats he would empty out. We did this throughout the year. We kept a stall bedded down for him and let him walk around in it. We also used some powdered yeast and flax seed in his feed, but I feel that it was the idea of "turning him loose" between heats that cured him.

I mentioned earlier about Titan Hanover and his low head and about my reputation for turning out low-headed trotters. As I said, Titan was a nervous horse anyway and in trying to get him straightened away behind I gradually began letting him go with a lower head until he finally had it way down where the top of his head was virtually parallel with his back. He was balanced very well this way so I let him go. From then on, I was always conscious of a low head and tried to work toward it if I could.

There have been plenty of trotters that have gone very fast with their heads up in the air. But I believe that if a horse can go with his head low, he is a freer-going horse, is better-balanced and can handle himself better in rough going.

When I break my colts, I leave the check very loose. I tie the bits together so that the check bit doesn't fall out and I put a little chin strap on them. In this manner, the colt is permitted to find the right level for his head. You have to have a little more patience, maybe, because you won't have quite as much control in the early going as you would if you had them checked up fairly high. But in time they will settle down and settle their heads where they want them. Most of the time you will find that this position is lower than you had expected. At least, that's my opinion.

When you start doing this, letting your colts have a little bit of their own way and maybe making more training breaks than they should while you try to get them balanced and going with a low head, you need a lot of patience. I believe the first thing a colt trainer has to do is to learn to train himself.

Don't let these colts get you angry and upset and don't fight them. It's very hard to do sometimes because every individual is different and some of them will try you pretty good. But don't try to conquer such colts because in conquering them—and you can probably do it with most of them if you punish them enough —you are breaking their hearts as well. From that time on, they'll never, never try for you. You may have won a battle but you've also lost the war, although you might not realize it at the time.

Horses are a lot like people. As I have already mentioned, I think some of them are very intelligent and others very dumb. I also think they have feelings about their surroundings and the weather and their work just like people have. They like a change of scenery or a little vacation to get away from it all, just as you and I.

I remember one morning at Pompano when it was raw and cold when I went the first heat with my colts. I didn't like the weather at all. I could tell that they didn't either. My own inclination was to go back in the office and stay there but I couldn't because I had horses to train.

I thought about how I felt and how they would feel if I brought them back again in that cold wind and I said, "The heck with it, I'm not going to race until June and missing one heat won't hurt them a bit." So I sent them back to their stalls and I'm sure it was better for them and for me. You can't make me believe the colts liked that kind of weather any better than I did.

You might say to that that you're training in the north where it's cold and raw all the time. The difference is that the northern-trained horse is used to that kind of weather. My colts were not. I wasn't so much getting them away from the cold, windy weather as I was getting them out of weather they weren't used to.

You have to be patient with colts but at the same time there are occasions when you have to be firm. The kind that really bug me are the ones that want to lay down when you start breaking them to harness. I have had them go down for me and I have seen them down with other trainers. I've seen trainers spend a month trying to get a colt to stand up and move off after being harnessed and hooked to the cart for the first time.

This is when a trainer has to be firm. When I get one like this, I usually tie him down and let him lie there while I go about my business. I'll tie all four legs together and forget about him. Or if you don't want to tie his legs down, just sit on his head and hold him down and maybe rap him on the head with a newspaper a few times. If he struggles to get up, don't let him.

Nine times out of ten after a treatment like this, you won't be able to knock that colt off his feet again. You have to be kind and gentle most of the time, but the colt also has to know who the boss is.

A paragraph such as the last one suggesting that a trainer be kind and gentle and at the same time firm, is as good a note as any on which to conclude this chapter. In my opinion, a trainer who heeds this advice, and who also remembers that a horse is better a little under-trained than over-trained, will prosper.

It is unlikely that any man has ever worked with as few horses and left as large an imprint on the trotting breed as Harry Pownall. If he had never done anything other than select, break, train and drive the great trotting sire Star's Pride, his place in harness racing history would be secure. But the handsome veteran who was born in Brooklyn, N. Y. on October 30, 1902 has accomplished far more than that. For the past 30 years, as a contract trainer-driver for the Arden Homestead Stable (the Harriman and Gerry families) of Goshen, N. Y., his assignment has been to produce young trotting champions (the stable does not race pacers) capable of winning

the important Grand Circuit colt stakes. This is the ultimate test of any harness horse trainer's ability and Pownall has acquitted himself in remarkable fashion. For, in addition to Star's Pride, he has also given the breed such outstanding trotters (and sires or potential sires) as Florican, Titan Hanover, Matastar, Florlis, Sharpshooter and Pomp to name just a few. He still carries an accent that betrays his birthplace but despite his big-city origin he came by his love of horses naturally. Both his father and grandfather were horsemen (his brother Gene is also a trainer-driver) and it did not take the young Pownall long to find his way from Brooklyn to the Mineola, N. Y. fairgrounds where trainer Allie Cornwell taught him the rudiments of the harness racing profession. He drove his first race at Mineola in 1919 and his first winner at Goshen a year later. He operated a public stable for many years and was a highly successful young horseman when he went with Arden Homestead in 1937 as assistant to the late Bill Dickerson. His first great Arden horses were Hanover Maid, Spud Hanover and Florimel and he drove harness racing's first 2:00 2-year-old mile behind Titan Hanover in 1944. He won The Hambletonian with Titan the following year and became Arden Homestead's head trainer when Dickerson died in 1947.

11

GENERAL HORSEMANSHIP

T. WAYNE SMART

VERY time somebody starts to tell me how much money horse trainers are making these days I think back to the year I went to Flint, Michigan, to open the season with a string of 12 horses, a loyal wife, two daughters, and $50 in my pocket.

It rained for seven straight days and I was plumb broke before I even got to start a horse. Finally they said "go" and I entered the star of my stable in the feature race on opening day figuring I was a cinch to earn the rent money and maybe even enough to eat on for a week or two. He broke a hobble going down the backstretch the first time around, jumped the outside fence and headed off through a corn field.

"Smart," I said to myself between cuss words as I tried to get him stopped, "you better simmer down and take it easy 'cause it looks like it's gonna be a long summer."

The long summers are shorter now and even the cold suppers and hot horses they talk about are fewer and far between. I race a comparatively small stable and they practically have to stick a gun in my back to get me out of Ohio. But I've got the same wife and a little more money and I've had more fun than anybody. I've also got a few convictions about the right and wrong way to do things with harness horses because I've been training them since 1923.

I haven't been assigned a specific subject and thus I have a broad field to play on. That gives me a free hand to talk about a lot of phases of harness horse training and I plan to do so. For the most part, I pretty well agree with the general practices followed by my fellow trainers and drivers. The truth is that most all horses are trained according to the same pattern, the only real difference being that certain trainers have variations of their own that they toss in.

For my own part, I happen to think that, in general—and I want to stick that qualifier in there right away because the first lesson any horse trainer learns is that no two horses are alike or can be treated or trained alike—horses can and should be trained a little stiffer than most people think.

In addition, I also believe that we don't have to spend nearly

as much time as we do cooling horses out. I don't think a horse
has to be walked to be cooled out unless you are racing on an
extremely hot afternoon or on a hot, muggy night. I know this
will sound like heresy to some of my old friends in the sport,
but I have proved it to myself and there is no doubt in my mind
that it is true.

Since I have taken a firm stand in this regard, let me stay with
the thought for a while and come back to the training of horses
a little later on.

I winter my horses at the Delaware fairgrounds in Delaware,
Ohio, my home town, and with rare exceptions I haven't walked
one or had a blanket on one, unless he was clipped, in a number
of years. I've never had a sick or foundered horse and as far
as I am concerned this is the ideal way to do it. It saves time and
trouble and the results are very satisfactory.

This procedure is followed throughout the training program.
In order to be specific, let's say that we're into the first week of
May and I am training some horses in 2:10 or faster. After their
final heat, these horses are not bathed as is the usual stable
procedure. Instead, we take a damp sponge that has been dipped
in warm water and go over the horse to knock the harness marks
off. Then we scrape the lather off, rub the horse down with a
dry rag and turn him loose in a well-bedded stall without any
cover on at all. At intervals, we give him a few swallows of the
water and this is the way he is cooled out.

Frankly, I think this is a much better method. I have found
that if you follow the normal procedure of bathing a horse and
then wrapping him in blankets and walking him around for an
hour or so that there is much more chance that he will be
exposed to a draft. And that's the big danger in cooling horses
out. If they get in a draft of any kind, they are in trouble.

I start my horses out this way and I have 2-year-olds in my
stable that have never had a blanket on and probably never will
unless it is an emergency of some kind. Horses that don't wear
blankets in the stall are definitely healthier in my opinion. I have
been doing this for the past three years and have had less sickness
among my colts than ever before.

The only covering I use on any of my horses is a light sheet
for one that has been clipped. These horses are cooled out the
same way and the only difference is that as soon as they stop

steaming, something like 15 to 20 minutes after they are back in the stall, we put the sheet back on them. Otherwise, they are treated exactly the same.

There are, of course, exceptions to this as there are for all practices followed by horse trainers. For instance, if we should happen to get a real hot, muggy spell in the middle of May, as we occasionally will, I will turn a horse into the stall for about 15 minutes and then bring him out and walk him awhile until I am certain he is blown out before I put him back in the stall. But the reason is not so much that I think he needs a blanket or to be walked as that he is facing a sudden change in climatic conditions and is therefore subject to catch a cold or something like that just as a person would be.

Now let's go on to the races. If I am racing at night and it is a clear pleasant evening, I will follow exactly the same procedure as I do in training. The horse will be sponged, scraped and turned loose in the stall. He won't be walked unless he was one of those horses that blew extremely hard after a race. In that case, I would probably have him walked anywhere from 15 to 30 minutes depending on the horse. However, if it is one of those hot, muggy, nights, there is just no use kidding yourself. You should walk a horse under these circumstances and you should also walk one if you are racing on a hot, muggy afternoon.

I race quite a lot at Scioto Downs which is about 35 miles from my home base and I very often ship a horse down in the afternoon and bring him home after the races. When I do that, I walk the horse after the race. The reason I walk him is that I don't feel I can take a chance with a horse that is going to have to ride later that night in a trailer or truck. There is too much chance that such a horse will be exposed to a draft and as I have repeatedly said, the big danger to a horse being cooled out is exposure to a draft of any kind.

When I adopted this method of cooling horses out, I watched all the horses very carefully, especially the colts. It was my observation that by the time a horse has been unharnessed, sponged, scraped and rubbed out he is just about through blowing. You give him a few swallows of water and turn him loose in a deep-bedded, draft-free stall. The horse will usually take a few rolls in the straw and then get up and go to the hay rack with absolutely no signs of distress. As far as I am concerned, he is sure a lot better off than he would be walking around with blankets on and the wind blowing up underneath them.

I have only been doing this in recent years, but I had been thinking about it long before that and I can tell you exactly when it first crossed my mind that perhaps we were spending too much time cooling horses out. That was in 1955 when Queen's Adios was a 4-year-old. I had just come off the track with him at Maywood Park in Chicago after winning in 2:01, which was then and still is a pretty snappy performance over a half mile track. Just as we got to the barn, a terrible cloudburst broke and it wouldn't let up. There was no way we could walk the horse to cool him out. So I had the boys bathe him, scrape him and rag him out good right in the stall. Then I threw a light cooler over him and watered him out by giving him a few swallows every 10 minutes or so. I was a little scared when I went to the track the next morning but he was as bright and chipper as he ever had been in his life. I knew right then and there that we could improve our methods of cooling horses out.

The other thing that I believe in quite strongly, as I have already said, is that most horses need a lot of work to keep them sharp. Please note that I said "most" horses. Some don't, as I will point out a little later on because if anybody thinks he can train all horses exactly alike he belongs in some other profession.

I know the trend in training horses is in the opposite direction and that many of them are getting less rather than more work. But all my life I have observed that people that don't work are soft, that horses get soft when they don't work and that the softer you are with a horse the softer he generally is at the end of a mile.

As far as I am concerned, this not only holds true with working horses between races but is equally applicable in warming a horse up on the day or the night of a race. I know that some of the younger trainers and even a few of the old timers just go a dinky little warmup heat or maybe two little ones and race off that. But I want to go three heats warming up and the faster class horse I have the faster I will go my third and final trip. Maybe it's just me but I don't think I could keep a horse going if I just warmed up one or two heats. This might be all right if you had a nervous, high-strung horse but other than that I wouldn't be in favor of it.

The way I warm up a horse for a race is to jog him three miles and then go a mile around 2:35 or 2:40 the first time out. The next trip I'll jog a mile and go in 2:25. The third warmup trip depends on the horse. Some horses will race off a mile in 2:25 and go for their life. With this type I also go my last mile in 2:25. I warm fast class horses up around 2:10 the third time out and let them ramble that last quarter pretty good, say in 30 seconds, because they have to be pretty well thawed out to go against the top stock. The third warmup mile for other horses depends on the individual and is between 2:10 and 2:25.

When we were racing heats like we used to all the time, I would pretty well warm up the last mile in accordance with the way I expected my horse to race. That is, if I had a horse that always showed me he was better in the second or third heat of a race, I would warm him up a little more the last trip. If I had one that was better the first heat than he was in any of the succeeding heats, I would go his last warmup mile a little slower.

Now that we have more dash racing than we used to, I use my training miles as a guide if I don't have a heat-racing line on a horse in my stable. For instance, I train my stake colts four heats. When I find one that goes his fourth heat the best, I will go more his last warmup mile. But if I have one that goes his third training mile better than his fourth, I won't go that last warmup mile as much.

I've found that you've pretty well got to drill horses between races to keep them sharp and if I didn't know it before I had it brought home to me in the fall of 1965 with Tuxedo Hanover. He had been chasing Bret Hanover around all summer and going anywhere between 1:56 and 1:58 and I had just given him a record of 1:58⅗ at Lexington. He didn't have another race until the Messenger at Roosevelt six weeks later and I brought him home to Delaware to get ready for it.

We had run into a lot of rain and bad weather at Delaware and I wasn't able to train him the way I wanted to. As a matter of fact, I hadn't been a mile better than 2:12. About three weeks before The Messenger I had a call from Jim Lynch at Liberty Bell asking me if I would bring Tuxedo over for a $25,000 invitational and race Bret and Rivaltime and the rest of those horses.

I explained to Jim that I had slipped a cog and fell out of

bed with the horse because the weather had thrown a monkey wrench in my training program, but that I wanted to help him anyway and that I would bring the horse. I went out the next day and trained Tuxedo five heats. It was all he could do to go in 2:07 the fourth heat so I brought him back for another and 2:08 was the best I could get. The layoff had affected his ability to carry his speed.

I sure didn't want to go right to the races after that performance, but I had given Jim my word so off we went. Tuxedo Hanover raced the first part of the mile well and it looked like I was going to be second but he got halfway through the stretch and his legs let loose under him and he wound up third.

Lynch asked me to stay over for another race the next week, but I'd heard that they'd put a new track surface in at Roosevelt and I was anxious to get up there and see what it was like so I shipped out. I got Tuxedo in an overnight at Rooesvelt but that new track was a little sandy and he got tired and folded up a couple of hundred feet from the wire when it looked like he was going to win. I went back with him a week later and the same thing happened. This was a Saturday night and The Messenger was scheduled for the next Friday. I was beginning to sweat a little now.

I thought about it and finally decided that I had to tighten that horse up. So I took him out Tuesday morning and worked him five heats. I know they were all saying, "Smart's gonna kill that horse," but I thought I knew what I was doing. I worked him in 2:40, 2:30, 2:15, 2:08 and 2:07.

On Friday night in The Messenger, Tuxedo didn't stop at all and, say, didn't I have my old buddy Frank Ervin strung out at the wire with Bret Hanover. He said he didn't hit Bret but I must have had him a little excited because I know he did and I know I had him stretched out farther than he ever was before and I'd been after him all summer. He beat me a half length because he had the best horse but Tuxedo sure gave him a run for the marbles that night.

The point is that for three weeks after Lexington I hadn't been able to work my horse better than 2:07 and then when I asked him to go pretty good, as I did in that first start at Liberty Bell, he didn't have the legs under him to sustain the speed. It was the same with those first two races at Roosevelt and the new track surface there made it a little tougher, too, because it was sandy and hard for a horse to carry his speed through it. That final preparation three days before the Messenger was just what he needed to put legs under him and enable him to carry his speed the whole mile. It just brought him back to the form he'd been in all summer when he was racing from 1:56 to 1:58.

As far as I am concerned, this isn't an isolated instance. I feel that you have to work horses to keep them tight. Like I said before, I could be wrong about this but I hate to lose a race just because my horse got a little leg weary at the wire. Horses that are worked hard don't do this.

Just to prove that a horse trainer hadn't better start building a mold and fashioning all horses to fit it, let me cite a couple of examples of horses that needed to be trained lightly.

One was Poplar Byrd, a very fast horse that later gained fame as the sire of Bye Bye Byrd. Rex Larkin came to me at Indianapolis in 1947, the year that Poplar Byrd was a 3-year-old, and asked me to take over his training. The horse hadn't been racing well. He was big, fat and saucy but he hadn't been beating anybody. I raced him a couple of heats at Indianapolis where he did a little bit of everything, most of it wrong. I then brought him home to Delaware to prep him for the Jug.

I figured that a big, rugged-looking horse like that needed work and I poured it to him. On his last work day before The Jug I went five or six heats with him, probably six, and worked a mile in 2:03. Man, he acted sharp. I thought I had a chance to win the Jug. But on race day, Poplar Byrd was as stale a horse as I have ever driven. He didn't have any lick at all and I was lucky to get a piece of the money.

I decided then that I'd better go the other way with him since he had a race at Lexington the following week. A couple of days before that race I gave him two or three slow miles, the fastest in 2:25. He breezed in 2:01⅖ and I could have gone in 2:00 had I known I had that much horse.

The following year I trained him the same way—very slow miles between starts and not many of them—and he raced very well. It took him a while to find himself that year but when he did he was an outstanding horse.

I found the same thing to be true once about a mare that I was racing for Walter Michael. Her name was Miss Sarah Abbey and she later was the star of that movie that Charlie Coburn made at Lancaster, Ohio, "The Green Grass of Wyoming." I had been training her at home and she had been in 2:15 but didn't act like much of a trotter to me. They had night racing at Marion, Ohio, then and I planned to take her over there for opening night. It rained for a week before the opening and I wasn't able to train this filly. I raced her anyway and she won in 2:10½ and acted like a real race horse. This opened my eyes a little and I decided to play right along with her. I never trained her again that year. All I did between races was to jog her and she kept winning. She wound up that year with a record of 2:03¾.

So while I believe that, in general, horses need quite a bit of work to keep them on edge, I am also well aware that there are exceptions, such as I have just cited, and that a horse trainer has to be alert to them. The main thing is that if you don't think your horse is racing as well as he should the way you are training him don't be afraid to experiment. You might be pleasantly surprised.

I'll tell you another thing about training raceway horses while I'm on the subject. I learned this a long, long time ago from Pop Geers and you know it has to be a long time ago because Pop was killed in a racing accident in 1924.

We were talking one day about turning horses out and Pop said, "The only time to turn a horse out is when you quit racing him." I thought that made sense and I've followed that idea about all my life because I've always believed that a horse will come back quicker after a hard campaign if you keep him up with a certain amount of light work.

Since I was writing earlier about Tuxedo Hanover, let me use him as an example of what I mean. After the Messenger, which was raced on November 10th, I brought him home and let him down. The way I let a horse down after a tough campaign is to train him once a week for three weeks. The first week I go three trips of, maybe, 2:40, 2:35 and 2:30 with no brush work. The second week I go two trips of 2:40 and 2:30 and the third week I go a single trip in 2:30. Now, as far as I am concerned, the horse has been let down.

All this time I have been jogging him three or four miles a day on the days that I didn't work him. After the three week letdown period, I jog him every day for 60 days from five to seven miles a day. Then he is ready to begin training again. I have found that a horse that is conditioned like this will come back to the races with his hair looking good and that he would have been good all winter long. If I had turned him out instead at that time of year, his hair would probably have gone dead and it would have taken me an extra two months to get him back in the right kind of shape again.

When I start to train a horse like this, he is ready to go in 2:30 the first time I turn him around. For about a month, I will go two trips every other day and then I will put him on a regular twice-a-week schedule with three trips each training day.

When I talk about keeping a horse up between racing campaigns by jogging him instead of turning him out, I don't mean to imply that it isn't a good thing to turn horses out or that I don't do it. I just don't think it's good to turn them out during the off season when you don't have that rich green grass and good sunlight.

As a matter of fact, I've noticed for many years that horses that are turned out for two or three weeks at a time of the year when they do have sun and grass come back with good coats and looking better and acting better. I always knew what did it— the Vitamin C that they get out of the grass and sun.

I often wondered what you could do for a horse that starts to look a little run down and whose coat begins to get a little seedy and the hair starts turning up toward his ears. I talked this over with a veterinarian I know and gave him my thoughts about it and darned if we haven't come up with a liquid product that is doing the job for us. We call it Green Grass. We feed them two ounces once a day in their feed and if they won't eat it we put it in their water and they take it that way.

Frankly, I'm amazed by what is has done for their condition. I'm using it on my colts as well as my aged horses. Where their flanks used to shrink up with work, now they aren't losing any flesh at all. You go a good mile with colts and they don't act as though they've been out at all. Their wind is good and their nostrils are hardly ever open. It's full of Vitamin C and I guess it must give them real good lungs.

In order to race a horse, you've got to have a foundation under him. Sure, you can give a horse a quick 60-day prep and take him to the races. You'll do good too—for a few races. But after about five or six races your horse is bound to run out of smoke and you'll kink him so that he'll never get through the summer and fall. When you kink a horse real good, you might as well turn him out because I never have been able to get the kink out of one until I turned him out to pasture and let him run for five or six months.

A number of years ago I was training in Florida and I came up to New York to race early in the year. A young fellow who lived near me back in Ohio and who had trained at home had his horses sharp and was winning everything in sight the first few weeks. "Jiminy," I thought to myself, "I better find out how this kid's training them because I have to do whatever he's doing." Well, it wasn't but a little while until this fellow came to me and was wondering what had happened to his horses; they were all falling apart on him.

What had happened, of course, was that he had given them one of those quick preps and had gotten them down to racing speed but he hadn't put any bottom under them. They responded by racing well right off the bat because a race horse is very competitive and most of them will try every time they go. But after a bit, their legs started to wobble and they couldn't keep up. They were going backwards while the horses that had been prepped properly were coming on.

I'm a great believer in jogging horses a lot to establish a foundation. I think it works wonders as far as getting them in shape is concerned. I was saying earlier that after I had jogged an aged horse 60 days I put him in training and went two heats a day, both in 2:35, three days a week, say Monday, Wednesday and Friday. This goes on for three or four weeks until I put him on a twice a week schedule with three heats on each workout day.

But during that three-times-a-week period, I am also doing a lot of jogging. On Monday I'm going two miles in 2:35. Before the first mile, I will jog my horse three to 3½ miles. Before the second mile I will jog him two miles. That's seven miles with that horse that day and it is the same three days a week for three or four weeks. On the off days, Tuesday, Thursday and Saturday, the horse will be jogged five miles. That's another 15 miles so this horse is getting about 30 jog miles a week. This is the way you lay a foundation.

When I go to a twice a week training schedule and start to train three trips, I will still jog three to 3½ miles before the first heat and two miles before the second and third. That horse is getting a total of 10 miles a day twice a week and five jog miles a day on the other four which is giving him about 40 miles a week, approximately 34 jogging and six training.

When I start training a fourth heat, as I do with most of my colts and some of my real fast aged horses, I will cut the jogging down to one mile before the fourth heat but he is still getting three, two and two before the first three heats. That's the only way I've ever found that us fellows in the north can stay even with those boys in the south at the beginning of the year. It evens up later on, of course, but you have to have that foundation to tackle the southern-trained horses early in the year.

It's much the same way with 2-year-olds. Oh, it might take me a little longer to catch up but I never noticed that there was a great deal of difference when the chips were down. I know I'm usually going in 2:50 when they're going in 2:25 down there, but I'm getting a lot of miles in my colt, even though they aren't fast ones, and that's what really counts.

Let's say the weather stacks you up for a week and you can't train. Well, even if you just jog for a whole week you're getting almost as many miles as the boys down south are. I will jog my colts from four to five miles a day under those circumstances and I am getting 25-30 miles in that week. Sure, they aren't fast miles but they are foundation miles. I know fellows who train in the south who will jog one day, train the next and then let the colts lay around the next two days. Maybe they are in the barn two days out of the six. It all evens up in the end.

A fellow might say, "Well, that's fine but I'll never learn whether I've got a good colt or not that way." Shucks, that isn't so at all. Any time I have a half way decent fall in Delaware and get my colts gaited and start to get some legs under them it doesn't take long to find out whether a colt amounts to anything.

Unless some illness overtakes him or he doesn't like the hobbles or something like that, a colt will show you something in the first 30 days that will be a definite indication of whether he is stock or not. He'll get scared and rip off a sixteenth of a mile at a perfect gait and man doesn't that make you feel good. No, it doesn't take six months to find that out.

And I'll tell you something else, too. If he hasn't got any ability and if he hasn't shown you a flash of something like that at least once in the first 60 days, you are better off to quit with him and wait for another year. Those good ones don't have to work at it. They show you right off. If you get a sloppy-going trotter that doesn't show any interest or one of those pacers that keeps trying to step out of the hobbles and is cross-firing and hitting his knees, you might as well give him back to the Indians because he won't do you any good.

Colts are like kids going to school. Some kids learn faster than others and the ones that learn fast are the ones that will win the colt races for you. Of course, I'm just as guilty as anybody else about not practicing what I preach in this respect. I've got a colt right now that I've had for three years and I know he isn't going to amount to anything. But every time I get ready to sell him or give him away he shows me a little something and I decide to try him once more. I know deep down it isn't going to happen, but I keep feeding him anyway because I'm just like all the other horse trainers. I think maybe the lightning will strike. I know it won't and can't but I keep hoping it will and that I'll be wrong. The only way I'm wrong is in sending good money after bad with a colt like this.

The one thing that can put a horse trainer out of business quicker than anything else is lameness. There is nothing as frustrating as to have a slick, good-gaited trotter or pacer with 2:00 potential go unsound. I've had a lot of lame horses in my time and I'll be interested in reading Dr. Churchill's chapter because none of us are ever too old to learn something and I'm sure he'll teach me a little. I'm willing to learn, too.

I guess I've seen all the lamenesses there are and tried most of the cures in the book as well as a few that aren't there, including inserting a dime in a horse's shoulder. It didn't work but it sure proves a trainer will try anything to get a lame horse sound.

That dime incident happened a long time ago but I can place it pretty well historically because it was about the time Johnny Simpson was breaking in. I later sold the horse to him and I always wanted to ask him for my dime back but I never did.

The horse was a pacer named Chestnut Lucky Boy and one afternoon he won a heat at an Ohio fair and walked off the track dead lame. It looked as though he had a broken leg but I soon discovered it was only shoulder trouble. I started working on him with a hot blanket to open the pores in his shoulder and then mixed up a big conconction of Smith's Oil and Tuttles and started to rub it to him. My, how he did dance when that hot stuff touched him.

I was still giving him this treatment when I remembered that I'd heard when I was a kid that you could cure lameness by putting a dime under the horse's skin in the area involved. So I cut a little notch up there on the inside of the shoulder and placed the dime beneath the skin.

It didn't work of course but I was sure trying. The horse got sound enough to race after a while but he was pretty raw where I had blistered him and I got some red oil and slapped it on him one day just before he went to the post. It ran all down his leg and some woman was raising the dickens because we were being inhumane to the horse. She thought the red oil was blood and I guess it did look pretty bad if you didn't know what it was.

As I said, I later sold this horse to Simpson and he called me after a while and said he was having trouble hanging him up in the hobbles and wanted to know what to do about him. I thought then about asking for my dime back but I was afraid he would want to give me the horse back instead so I told him how to hang him up and away he went. He's come a long way since then, too.

Diagnosing lameness in a horse is a tough thing. Sometimes some of these vets aren't much help either. You call one in and the first thing he asks you is "Where is he lame?" Heck, if I knew where he was lame I sure wouldn't have called the vet to find it for me.

I used to use Tuttles to determine where the lameness was. You would rub the Tuttles on and wherever the fever was, water blisters as big as your thumb would pop out. Then you would treat the lameness.

Once in a while, if you're not careful, you get caught up in some tide that's sweeping the country. About a dozen years ago it was fractured fibula lameness. It seemed that every horse had a fractured fibula bone and the only treatment was immobilization. I even got roped in but I didn't stay hooked for long.

I had a horse named Philip Frost in Chicago and he won The American-National Stake and came out of it real lame. The next morning I went out to get him X-rayed and had to wait in a long line in front of the vet's office. I asked the fellow in front of me what they were doing there and he said they were X-raying fibulas. When my turn came they took a picture and the vet told me later that the horse had a fractured fibula and would have to stand up in a stall for a couple of months. I was fit to be tied.

I knew Philip Frost didn't have any fibula lameness. A horse with that kind of trouble usually has his stifle out or the muscles in that area have let loose to the point where the stifle is so sore he can't go on it. The horse knuckles over a lot behind when he is jogging. The stifles are weak and they fill up with fluid and the more fluid they get in there the more they fall down behind and the sorer they get. Philip Frost didn't have any of these symptoms so I knew his trouble couldn't be up high.

I took him home while I thought it over. My original thought was that he had ankle trouble so I injected the ankle and in ten days he was sound and never took a lame step thereafter.

While he was recovering, I did some thinking about fibula trouble and remembered an old veterinarian I'd known years ago who had come out one time with a little black box with a battery connection that let you look right into and through a horse's leg. It was some kind of a portable X-ray deal and it was the darnedest thing I ever saw. I had this fellow come over to Delaware one time to look at some of my lame horses and I looked through the thing with him. He would show me where he thought they were lame and we would treat accordingly. We had good results, too. I wonder what ever happened to that little box? It sure was a handy gadget.

Anyway, I remembered that every horse I had looked at through that little black box had had a broken fibula bone, or at least they all looked like they were broken. But all of them were lame somewhere else and some of them were even sound horses. As soon as I recalled this incident, I stopped thinking about fibula bones and any time anybody tries to tell me now that I have fibula trouble I just laugh at him.

I've found that stifle trouble isn't usually too hard to clean up if you get at it in time and know what you are doing. The big mistake in treating stifles is that too many of the boys want to work on them in the hollow area around the joint. There's nothing but skin and bone in that hollow area and it doesn't do you any good to treat it there. You have to work out in front of the stifle a couple of inches below that point where the cords and muscles go around the leg. That's where your stifle trouble is and that's where you have to cure it.

Dr. Edward A. Rile, a real good veterinarian from Pennsylvania, taught me this years ago and I still get a chuckle when I see somebody treating stifle trouble by working in the hollow of the joint. I don't inject a stifle either. I take some Kendall's and put it on my hand and rub it into that area around the front of the leg and maybe a couple of inches back on each side. Never take a brush and paint it on. That doesn't provide enough pressure. Rub it in with your hand until it gets hot and the horse squirms. That won't hurt him a bit and is just a sign that you are doing it the way it should be done. That stuff of just rubbing it gently on top won't produce any results.

Horses that are jogged in heavy going are much less prone to stifle trouble than those that are not. I have noticed that if a horse has an inclination to be a little weak in his stifles, that is if he has a tendency to knuckle over behind which is an indication of stifle trouble, that he will improve if you will jog him in heavier going.

I have also noticed that pacers that require a lot of weight behind to get them on gait when you start out with them, those that are wearing sideweight shoes, etc., are less likely to be bothered with stifle trouble at that stage. If these horses are going to become affected in the stifle, it will happen after you remove the weight and have them going in a normal, light shoe. I think the increased weight behind probably helps to keep the stifle muscles stretched tight.

Curbs and splints are common causes of lameness in horses as everybody knows. And I guess like anybody else I've had good luck with curbs and not much with splints. I have never had much curb trouble since the McKay brothers came out with McKay's Maxlin for injecting curbs. I never had a curb come back after I injected it with McKay's and that is about as good a record as you can ask for.

About splints, I don't know. It seems that every time I doctor a splint it doesn't do anything except get bigger. About the best luck I've had is to fire one and hope for the best.

The unsoundnesses that occur during the colt training season are the same in both the north and south. The horses aren't any different. The big difference is that an unsoundness in the north can set you back at a more critical period. What I mean is that if a colt has a weak spot that will eventually develop into a curb or a splint it will usually develop earlier in the south because you are going faster with the horses. In cases like that, you can quit and doctor it and still get going again in time to get to the races. Very often, in the north this same ailment won't come until two months later and then it might slow you down at the most crucial period of your training.

I am not going to bother much with bits and equipment of that nature because Joe O'Brien is discussing them in his chapter, but I do want to offer one thought about driving bits. I prefer a plain snaffle bit for most horses and occasionally you will find that the horse will get a little off center on the bit. When this happens, it usually means that the bit is a little low down and not tight enough in the mouth. The usual sign is an indentation in the gums on one or both sides. In such cases, I wrap a little of that special rubber tape around both sides of the bit and raise it up a little in the mouth. This is usually enough to stop them from getting on one line or the other.

Shoeing is also being considered in chapters written by Johnny Simpson and Frank Ervin and while I will leave the basic techniques to them, I do not think it would be out of order for me to relate a few of the special shoeing and balancing problems that I have run across in my career.

Let me preface these remarks by saying that as a general rule I would prefer a flat (or plain) shoe on a trotter in front rather than a half round. It has always seemed to me that a trotter wearing a flat shoe and a little toe weight in front was a better-balanced proposition than one wearing a half round shoe. But, of course, I have raced plenty of trotters in half round shoes without encountering any problems. A trotter is usually less inclined to hit his shins while wearing half round shoes in front, but I have known some who tapped themselves pretty hard in half round shoes and did not interfere when I switched over to flat shoes and gave them a little more toe and weight. This is opposed to the normal procedure, but if you're going to be a horse trainer you had better learn right away that what appears to be the exception might be a rule in a specific instance.

Earl's Song, a filly that I raced in 2:00 as a 3-year-old for Castleton Farm some years back, taught me that lesson. Earl's Song raced as a 2-year-old in a light half round front shoe and a slightly squared toe that measured 3⅝ inches. She was a darn good 2-year-old and won a stake at Lexington in 2:03⅕ but she had a tendency to hit her shins a little too hard. I knew I ought to do something about it but she was racing so well I didn't want to start experimenting.

When I put her back in training as a 3-year-old she started going very wide behind and kicking my feet out of the stirrups. At the same time, she acted like she wanted to pace. I knew I had to do something so I took her to the shop and put a pad on that ran her toe out to 3⅞. Then I switched from a half round to a heavier flat shoe and added a light quarter boot and a three-ounce toe weight. I squared her toes behind and began to train her. You would have thought that this extra length and weight in front and the change from the half round to the flat shoe would have had her hitting her shins worse than ever, but she was perfect. She went on and won in 2:00 and I know that if I had done that when she was two that she would have trotted close to 2:00 then. But that would have been a very radical change to have made during the course of the racing season and since she was doing quite well I preferred to wait until the following year to experiment.

I remember one year when I was at Pinehurst and Doc Parshall was training King's Counsel as a 2-year-old. That would have been in 1942. King's Counsel had a normal light pacing shoe on in front and wouldn't do a thing for Doc but run and jump in the hobbles. Finally, Doc shod him in front with a three quarter by a quarter half round bar shoe that must have weighed 12 ounces. The horse hit a real pace the next time out and became a great champion.

Waybill, another 2:00 pacer that I raced for Castleton, was also a headache to get shod properly. He didn't have any gait in front and I kept letting that toe grow out in an effort to get him to extend his stride. But the more toe I gave him in front, the more he cross-fired. I went to a horse sale for a week and when I got back he had both front quarters cut about off. I knew then I had to go the other way so I "dehorned" him as we say, that is, I cut his feet down just as short as I could get them in front. He had about 3¼ inches to start, but I kept chopping away at that and I got it way down. Then I shod him in a light half round shoe with a squared toe and at the same time started lengthening his toe behind. That was the only way I could get him to go clear. I finally got him going in a four inch toe behind and, as I said, he went on and took a record of 1:59⅗ shod that way. He was about as manufactured a 2:00 pacer as ever came out.

Mighty Song was another horse that challenged the rule book on shoeing and had me talking to myself for a while. Sep Palin had raced him on the pace for Castleton and had given him a record of 2:01. He was scheduled to be sold the year I went with Castleton, but I had seen him jog on the trot and thought I could make a trotter out of him so we decided to keep him.

The horse was shod a little strange for a pacer in that he wore a 3⅞ toe in front, which was quite a bit longer than normal, with a flat bar shoe that weighed about six ounces. He wore a light half swedge behind and a 3½ inch toe.

I decided, naturally, to follow the usual principle in converting a horse from the pace to the trot which is to add weight in front and take it off behind. I left his front toe at 3⅞ but went to a 5/8ths half-round shoe with a bell boot and three-ounce toe weight. I cut his hind toe down to 3½ and squared it a little. Heck, he wouldn't trot at all. As a matter of fact, every time I stepped him he was about the best-gaited pacer you could want.

I knew I had to go the other way, so I started lightening him up in front, and adding weight behind which isn't the way the rule books says to make a trotter. I took off the bell boots and the toe weights and started cutting the toe down. I wound up with a 3¼ inch toe and a light half-round shoe in front and a 3⅞ toe behind with a full swedge shoe. He was a good-gaited trotter shod that way and won in 2:05 over a half mile track and took a record of 2:00⅗ on a mile track. There are very few horses that want less toe and weight in front and more toe and weight behind in order to trot. It is these exceptions that really test a horse trainer.

Kashaplenty was a mare that presented a challenge to me and I was always pleased that I was able to get a crack at her. I had seen her race at two and three when several trainers had her and while she was a good mare, I can remember saying to myself that I thought she would go a lot more with a shorter toe in front. That fall Mr. and Mrs. Van Lennep bought her for a broodmare but I prevailed on them to let me train her another year. I just wanted to see for myself.

I cut her front feet as far down as I could get them, right down to the white line. They measured a scant 3⅛ and she went in a light half-round shoe with a squared toe. She was 3¾ behind with a full swedge. Not only did she take a record of 1:59⅗ that fall but she also trotted in 2:03 over a half mile track whereas the reputation she had was that she wouldn't go over a half mile track at all.

I can't ever really write about shoeing horses unless I mention an old favorite of mine, a horse named Star Philistine. This is the same horse that took me over the fence at Flint, Michigan, as described in my opening paragraphs. He was a pacer that wore a 10-ounce flat shoe in front with an X-ray pad. That's a lot of weight for a pacer and while he was racing fairly well I thought he could do better. I was just a youngster in those days, but I had an idea that this horse wasn't striding out far enough and the thing that makes a horse stride out farther is weight.

I thought about it a long time and finally I went to Jack Raymond, a famous old blacksmith who was shoeing horses at the time, and asked him to put toe weight spurs on in front. "My gosh," Jack said, "you don't want any more weight on this horse, he's got plenty as it is." My heart sank at that, but I was convinced I was right so I went ahead. I put a four-ounce toe weight on each front foot and the horse went out that day and won the first heat in 2:01⅖ which was his lifetime record. It made me feel pretty good and after that I was never afraid to experiment and to break the rules when I thought the rules had to be broken. My advice to young horsemen is to follow the basic rules as far as possible but not to be afraid to think for themselves and change the rules if necessary. There isn't a good horseman living today who hasn't broken every rule in the shoeing and rigging book when he knew he was right about a particular horse.

Let me add one last thought about shoeing. It is not a bad idea to use a little borium on the front shoes in the winter time if you are training in the north. It gives them a good grip on the track and if properly used is helpful. You can put the borium on sharp or flatten it out. I prefer to flatten it slightly and to put a little dot on each heel. I don't use any on the toes. Occasionally, I will put a little, sharp dot of borium on the outside heel behind. I wouldn't put sharp borium on the inside heel behind since it might catch the coronary band on the opposite foot and cut it.

I guess the time has come now for me to write a little something about track maintenance. The racing season is beginning to bust out of both ends of the calendar these days and more and more horses are being wintered in the north. A lot of people keep asking me how to get a good winter training track.

For the track itself, you need proper drainage and some sand or stone dust and salt to mix in with your clay. In the line of equipment, you should definitely have a Jeep or some vehicle of that type along with a harrow, a float and a snow plow attachment.

The harrow or float can be purchased or even built at a relatively modest cost. You'd have to buy the snow plow attachment but it would be money well spent since you absolutely must get snow off the track. If you could afford it, you probably ought to have a disc and maybe even a grader. But these are items which you can usually rent or borrow if you get in a pinch.

The one surface you don't want is cinders. They freeze and get hard and are plum murder on horses in the winter. Oh, maybe its all right to have a little cinder jog path along the outside rim or something like that, but I always like to keep horses as far away from cinders as I can, especially in the winter time.

I said that you needed either sand or stone dust to mix in with the clay and give you an all-weather surface. Actually, I prefer stone dust and recommend its use. The stone dust will hold up through your clay a little better than sand. When it gets a little muddy, the stone dust will keep the horses from punching through the surface better than sand will.

I actually use sand on the Delaware track but it doesn't have anything to do with winter training. As everybody knows, we get a lot of world's records here and the fact that I mix sand in with the clay is one of the big reasons.

In the summer time when it gets hot and dusty, the stone dust will slow up a track. Sand, on the other hand, will really speed a track up if you put it in gradually and work it in right. That track can look dead but when you put a little water on it you bring it back to life in a hurry.

The sand is the secret of the world's records at Delaware. You get it worked into the clay properly and then you start watering it and it comes alive and provides the spring and the bounce that a track has to have to produce world record miles. At the same time, the sand is also making it virtually an all-weather track.

All of us had that brought home to us in Delaware when Bret Hanover won the 1965 Little Brown Jug in world record time of 1:57 and 1:57⅖. At 10 o'clock that morning the track wasn't anything but a big swamp to look at it on top. But it was solid underneath and I knew that as soon as I scraped that layer of mud off the top I was not only going to have a raceable track but one that would still have a little cushion to it because my sand was working for me and tying in with the clay.

When you scrape a straight clay track, as we had to on Jug Day that year, you will come up with nothing more than a concrete roadway. But all that sand that I had mixed in gradually that year and in previous years came to our rescue. And, like I said, the water brought the sand to life.

Maybe I ought to devote a couple of paragraphs to an explanation of how I get the Delaware track ready for our annual race meeting. Along about the middle of August which is about a month before our meeting, I borrow a grader and set the scarifiers (long metal prongs) down as far as they will go and dig the track up from the hub rail clear out to the fence. The scarifiers are going down about two feet and the dirt comes up in big chunks.

After this I go to work with a disc with a harrow fastened on behind it and start working the track. The disc breaks up those big chunks of dirt and the harrow starts to tie it all back in together again. At the same time, I put on about five or six truck loads of sand and work this in too. I put it on thin and then start watering the track. This starts to tighten her up and in about a month we have the nicest track you'd ever want to see. That's how we get all those world's records.

Getting back to our all-weather training track, the single most important factor is proper drainage. You must have drainage because if you don't, water will start laying in this spot and that spot and another spot and pretty soon all these places will get soft and mucky any time the weather gets above freezing and the track starts to thaw out a little.

The first thing to do is to get yourself a drainage ditch and the easiest and best way to do this is to dig or shape one out just inside the hub rail. Naturally, you have to figure a way for the water to drain out of the ditch and move away from the track, but that is an individual problem that has to be handled differently for each track.

If you pitch your track, or grade it, you may have need for a double drainage ditch, one on the inside and one on the outside. At Delaware, we drain it to the inside for the most part but in the homestretch we drain in both directions. For a moderate operation, I would suggest that you stick with inside drainage and grade your track to provide for it. A lot of training tracks don't have to be as wide as a race track and this makes the grading and drainage problem simpler.

To get a track ready for winter training, you ought to start working it in the fall of the year, say along about in September. This is when you start working your sand or stone dust into it. Because very few people want or need world's records over tracks, I am going to suggest that stone dust be used instead of sand. As I said earlier, stone dust will hold up a little better than sand for winter training.

And when I started to work my stone dust into the track, I would also throw some salt in with it. Pete Langley does this at Sportsman's Park and he has a real good surface all the time. The purpose of the salt is to keep the track from freezing and for this reason it must be put in before the first freeze of the year.

So in the middle of September, you disc your track using a straight disc and cutting perhaps two inches into the surface. Then you go over it and lay a layer of salt about a quarter of an inch thick. This means quite a few tons of salt depending on how wide your track is, but it is important to get it into the surface and to put it on before you apply the stone dust so that it can work in from the bottom.

The next step is to cover the salt with a layer of stone dust about an inch thick. Then you start to work your salt and stone dust in with a harrow and if you do it right you will have about the nicest training track you could ask for.

Stone dust is re-applied whenever you lose your track cushion. Any good horseman can tell when his cushion is going and when he is down to straight clay again. That's the time to come in with more stone dust.

Normally, you might have to come back with additional stone dust about the first of December although, if you have an exceptionally dry fall, you might not need another layer until the first of January. I generally find that after that I will need additional stone dust over my own track about the first of March, and again in the middle of April. It is not usually necessary to add any more stone dust after that. You don't always have to add an inch. Sometimes a half inch is plenty. Actually, it is a visual thing. When the cushion disappears and a horse starts to step through the track, it is time to add stone dust. The depth depends on how long you have let the track go.

If you put salt in a track you can water it all winter and harrow it and get a good cushion on it any time. And, of course, the secret of any race track is the cushion you can get on it. You can't get the proper cushion on a clay track in the winter time. It freezes up and stays hard all the time and there's nothing worse than training a horse over frozen ground.

Years ago I was training at an Ohio fair grounds where they had a cinder track. Along in January most of the other boys started to move their horses along a little and I was young and thought maybe I'd better start moving along too if I wanted to keep up with them. I had a dozen head and I only got one to the races and he was half lame. The reason was that I had been going too much over hard, frozen ground. You just can't train a horse over frozen ground.

If you have stone dust and salt mixed in with clay, you can stand rain, snow, sleet or anything else. After a big snow storm, for instance, you just get out there with your plow and take it off and you'll find that you still have a good track underneath. You might have a little dampness on top of the ground and it might be just a little picky for awhile but that salt in the ground will keep it from freezing. You just can't get a real hard race track if you will keep salt in it.

Once you have established your track, the most important piece of equipment is a harrow. A harrow, as everybody knows, has sharp steel prongs which dig into the track surface and work it up from the bottom. This keeps your track "working," keeps it alive and keeps a cushion on it.

You also use the harrow to keep holes from popping up in your track surface. If a horse starts toeing in someplace, you keep going over it with a harrow and that keeps tightening the dirt and stone dust and prevents the track from pulling out from under a horse when he starts going fast.

A lot of fellows tend to run a harrow too fast over a track. You don't want to go fast, you want to go relatively slow and give those teeth a chance to dig in and do their work. The importance of a harrow is that it keeps changing the surface of the track by bringing new dirt to the top. You have to have that new dirt constantly coming to the surface to maintain the proper condition of the track.

A screen, which is a wire netting, should never be used in place of a harrow. All a screen does is to make a track smooth on top. But it isn't tying the track in from underneath, as a harrow is, and all you have is a rotten race track. There is nothing in the world that will ruin a good race track quicker than constant screening, and floating, and no harrowing.

A screen is a good piece of equipment, but you have to know when to use it. I'll tell you when I like a screen. When I look at a bad sky in the afternoon or read a weather report that indicates a big rain is on the way, I will go over the track with the screen. This closes the track up and the rain will run right off and into your drainage ditch.

You want to be careful about harrowing a track like this too soon. The rule I always like to follow is that I don't harrow a track after a rain until I can walk over it and not have my shoes pull up mud as I walk. As soon as the track passes this test, you can start to harrow it and it shouldn't be any time at all before you have a nice cushion again.

After you've set your track up in the fall and begin training over it, it is probably a good idea to disc it up once more the first time you get a chance. You ought to wait about 30 days but any time after that, providing your track isn't frozen, get out there after a rain and run a disc through it without any weight on it and open it up. That lets the air get to it, tightens the track and freshens it up.

A couple of hours after that, you can usually get on it with a harrow and start developing a real nice cushion again. This also allows the stone dust and salt to tie down in a little more and this is what you're after. You have to tie your race track in from the bottom to the top. A disc is the best way to do this. It's much the best way I ever found to open up a race track.

A training track should be worked with a harrow every day you train over it. I work the Delaware track every day except Sunday. I will harrow it all the way from the hub rail out as far as I am working horses about three times in the forenoon. This maintains the cushion.

I never have to water my track in the winter and there isn't any reason that any northern track should be watered during the winter. There's plenty of moisture in the ground at that time of year. In the spring, when the dust starts to fly you will have to water it and should. But the dust will tell you when the track needs watering.

It really isn't a very difficult or expensive thing to keep a track in good condition for northern training. You do need good drainage. As I said before, that's the most important thing.

But you don't have to have any fancy pitch or grade to your track. And you'll even find that harrow teeth don't wear out as quickly with a combination clay and stone dust track as they will with a clay track. The same thing applies to horseshoes.

It appears to me that I have now covered about everything I had in mind when I started writing this chapter. I could go on, of course, because I've trained horses for more than 40 years and I certainly haven't been able to pack all the thoughts of a lifetime into one chapter of a book. But I do believe I've made some points that might be helpful to young fellows in the sport and maybe even to some who have been in it quite a while. It's been a lot of fun and I've sure enjoyed it.

Thurman Wayne Smart—better known as "Curly" to his harness racing friends from coast to coast —is a pipe-smoking family man who figures he has strayed too far whenever he gets more than 30 miles from the familiar confines of Delaware, Ohio, where he has made his home for the past 35 years. At 63 (born August 29, 1904 at Ostrander, Ohio), he thinks he has been racing too often if he makes more than a hundred starts a year and consequently his name is seldom found these days near the top of the money and race-winning lists. But his reputation for training and driving excellence is such that he is one of the rare few to whom the top professionals them-

selves turn when they need advice on shoeing, balancing or rigging. That he has lost none of his magic touch despite fewer starts each year is demonstrated by the fact that he always compiles one of the leading UDRS (battling average) figures in the nation. He has ranked No. 1 nationally in his UDRS classification on eight different occasions and in one year (1963) he actually won more than half of all the races he started (64 of 126) while compiling a lusty .607 mark. Even that lofty figure wasn't his highest since he "batted" .628 the following year by finishing among the top three 75 times (45 wins, 20 2nds, 10 3rds) in 95 starts. He has notched more than 1,750 official victories (plus hundreds of others before the USTA began keeping such records in 1939) and has earned in excess of $2,500,000. He began driving in 1923 and his fastest mile was behind Gold Worthy in 1:57⅕. He won the inaugural Little Brown Jug with Ensign Hanover in 1946 and scored again in his home town classic with Meadow Rice in 1952. He is a director of the U. S. Trotting Association, and a director and past president of the Ohio Harness Horsemen's Association. In addition, he is also very likely the best track maintenance man in the country and it is he who provides the lightning-fast surface that leads to the annual world record parade over the Delaware track.

12

DRIVING the RACE

WILLIAM R. HAUGHTON

O F all the questions asked of me in my profession as a trainer and driver of harness horses, the most consistent and persistent is "How do I get to be a driver?"

I have heard it from the lips of 10-year-old boys, 60-year-old men and numerous women of indeterminate age. My answer is always the same:

"There is no easy way. You start at the bottom and work your way up."

And when I tell these people "bottom," I mean the very bottom. I mean learning to be a driver by walking hot horses after midnight, mucking out dirty stalls before dawn and performing a thousand and one other tedious and time-consuming tasks.

By themselves, these chores may appear to require nothing more than unskilled labor of the most menial type. But taken together, and in consort with natural ability, they can light the path that leads to a career as a harness horse driver.

I do not know a prominent driver today who was not an expert with a rub rag long before he learned how to handle a whip. In my own organization, I make it a practice to promote from within and such drivers as Al (Apples) Thomas, Clarence Martin, Irvin Roberts and Bill Vaughan were all good grooms long before they became good drivers.

It is interesting, too, to observe that top trainers and drivers feel the same way when their own sons are involved. Three present-day examples that come immediately to mind are Johnny Simpson, Jr., Warren Cameron, and John Patterson, Jr. In each case the father insisted that the son serve a lengthy apprenticeship in the shed row before being permitted to hold a line over a horse in a race.

There is just no substitute for experience gained on the ground to help in the sulky. The late Fred Egan, one of the greatest horsemen who ever lived, told me he began working with horses when he was nine years old but that he never had horses of his own until he was almost 35. He said it was the best thing that ever happened to him because when he did start he knew what the business was all about.

And that is as it should be. Unfortunately, I sometimes think that many of those who inquire about a driving career have the crazy idea that they don't have to know anything at all about horses in order to be a driver; that the only thing necessary is to climb on a sulky and have somebody point them in the right direction.

The truth is that the path of all successful drivers leads through almost identical channels. You become a groom and in the natural course of this employment you jog the horses you are rubbing. At this stage of the game you also possess a fierce determination to succeed and a willingness to work all hours of the day and night.

Then there may come a day when the trainer wants to take a look at the horse from the sideline vantage point and he will say to you, "Take him the first mile." You can be certain that before he says this, he has observed you jogging the horse and is satisfied that you can handle the assignment.

From there you progress to more "first miles," and eventually, if obvious talent is beginning to show through, you will get more training assignments after which the long, slow trail leads through matinee racing, action at the county fairs, appearances in qualifying races, occasional catch drives, a position as a second trainer and finally, if all goes well, a stable of your own.

I have telescoped years into brief paragraphs, but if you should succeed what a wonderful and rewarding career it can be. To me, there are no words adequate enough to describe the emotion you feel when you turn for the word in a classic race like The Hambletonian or The Little Brown Jug. Even now, with more than 25 years of driving experience behind me, I am not immune to that feeling and I hope I never will be.

In this chapter, it is my intention to discuss in a general way the art of driving a harness horse. It has been my good fortune to have won more than 2,500 races in my lifetime and if I can pass on to others some of the knowledge I have gained, I not only will have helped them but I will have helped myself by rendering a service to the sport which has done so much for me.

In addition to determination and willingness to work, which I have already mentioned, the requirements for success are much the same in harness racing as in any other field of athletic endeavor. They include natural ability, intelligence, skill, conditioned reflexes, intuition, common sense, good judgment and self-discipline.

The most important of these, as in any sport, is natural ability. In harness racing, natural ability in driving a horse can be translated primarily into "light hands," a talent peculiar to our sport. I believe great drivers are born and not made and that "light hands" constitute the basic requirement.

This has absolutely nothing to do with how big a man is or how much he weighs. I know little men who are heavy-handed and who will never make it to the top although they possess almost all the other skills. And I know that one of the lightest touches of all belongs to Frank Safford, one of the heaviest men in our sport.

To put it simply, heavy-handed men make hard-mouthed horses and horses with hard mouths cannot and do not respond quickly enough to the demands their drivers make on them in a race. Such a man driving such a horse can lose a fraction of a second of vital time three or four times in a race. When you figure that a full second corresponds roughly to five lengths in a horse race and that almost half of all the races contested are won or lost by a length or less, you can see how important it is to have light hands.

I have run into this myself in taking over a horse that had been handled by a heavy-handed driver. His mouth is tough and hard and he just doesn't respond as he should to my touch. It takes quite a while before I can get this horse to react properly. In the meantime, I will lose races that I should have won.

I am too young to have seen him drive, but they tell me that the late Thomas W. Murphy had perhaps the lightest set of hands of them all and that this accounted in large measure for his fantastic success. I can believe this because I know what a difference a light set of hands makes.

One of the greatest I ever saw in this respect was the late Vic Fleming who was in his prime when I was just a boy. I can see him yet racing at those upper New York State tracks in the late 'thirties, literally driving a horse with two fingers of each hand while they responded almost magically to his feather touch.

Whenever I go out of New York to race as I frequently do, I

always make it a practice to study the drivers I haven't seen before, especially the newer, younger ones. I can almost tell by the way a man sits on the sulky and by his touch on the lines whether he has any future ahead of him.

I can be fooled by a fellow who does both of these things well but who is failing in other aspects of his profession which do not show up in a quick appraisal by a stranger. But this assessment is almost foolproof in the other direction; a boy with a poor seat and a heavy hand just isn't very likely to make the grade.

To sum it up quickly, I think a man ought to have thousands of hours as a groom and have jogged and trained hundreds and hundreds of miles behind all kinds of horses before he even thinks about applying for a driver's license. From that point on his ability or lack of it must speak for him.

Believing this is what it takes to make a driver and that there is no shortcut leading to success, let's go on to the actual racing by considering the basic points and, at the same time, delving into some of the finer arts.

My preparation for any driving assignment always begins with a lesson in reading. After the rule book, the most important piece of literature in a harness horse driver's life is the racing program. Before any race in which I have a horse entered, I go to the program and study the past performance of the other horses.

In my examination of the program, I am interested in general racing patterns of both horses and drivers and specifically, at first glance, in whether there are fast leaving horses in the race. If there are two or three front-running horses inside of me and I have a front-running horse myself, I'm still not going to leave there because it's likely I'll be parked a long, long way before I make it to the top.

There is an exception to this and it's well worth mentioning. I have seen it happen many times. You'll look a race over and see three front runners in there, all on the inside of you and you'll say, "Well, there's going to be a lot of early speed in this one, I'd better lay back a while."

Everybody else, as it turns out, has diagnosed it the same way and they all take back the second the gate leaves. Of course, this is a situation I've seen enough times that I'm always alert for it and when I look over and see the "early speed" boys taking back,

I switch tactics and make a dash for the top. I've won a lot of races that way.

On the other hand, just the reverse can and does occur. You look over a field and decide there's no early speed in the race and that maybe you'd better buzz out of there with your mediocre-leaving trotter from the six or seven hole. Again, everybody has come up with the same thought and they're all blasting out of there.

These two situations require spot judgment and much of the effectiveness of your own decision depends on how quickly you can react to the changing pattern. Reaction has to be almost in-stinctive and I find with myself that it definitely is. Out of the corner of my eye I can determine whether the type of start I an-ticipated is shaping up, whether the "flow" of horses away from the gate is as I thought it would be. If it is not, if the fast leavers are taking back or the slow leavers are suddenly boiling away, you must switch your own gears and adjust promptly. Many a race is won or lost at the start and victory or defeat depends on how you make the adjustment.

In these circumstances, I have noticed also that most top drivers have peripheral vision, that is the ability to size up a situation out of the corner of the eye without turning the head. This is common to top athletes in any sport. It is most noticeable in basketball when a player is driving hard in one direction and suddenly executes an accurate and lightning fast pass to a team-mate who is out of his direct line of vision. Although it is not as obvious, I have also seen it in pro football and baseball. I am sure that all pro football quarterbacks have peripheral vision.

In checking over the program, you give special attention to the drivers. In New York, where I do most of my racing, the vast majority are very good but even the very good ones have certain patterns which they follow quite consistently. After you watch and race with these fellows long enough, you get to know these patterns and try to lay your own plans to take advantage of this knowledge.

For instance, there are a few drivers in the New York area who always want to go to the front and stay there as long as they can. They just won't let anybody go if they can possibly help it. With a fellow like this, your primary job is to beat him to the first turn if you have a horse that will leave out of there at all and especially if you have drawn inside him. This gives you control of the situation when he comes and you can usually hang him out a little bit and then take up a position behind him.

It is often worthwhile to tackle this kind at the very beginning even though he has drawn inside you. If your horse will leave at all, it is sometimes easier to establish an advantageous early position than you might think. The reason is that everybody knows this fellow is going to go out of there and a number of the better drivers intentionally back off a little in the early going because they don't want to fight this fellow on the front end.

I have found that in tackling a fellow like this on the outside that if I can't get past him on the first turn we are usually traveling at such a clip when we head into the backstretch that a hole will open up directly behind him. Because this fellow wants desperately to be on the front end and isn't thinking much about anything else, he isn't nearly as likely to take back and shut you out of the hole.

In a situation like this, you have to watch for a chance to get out again at the half or even earlier. Very often the horse with this type of driver dies in front of you in the late stages and you want to be long gone when that happens. Since this driver isn't going to let anybody go and you know it, it's a good practice to pull out and trail the first horse that challenges him on the outside any place past the three-eighths pole. Then you are in a position to make a strategy decision later as the pattern of the race unfolds.

Then there is the driver who likes to go to the top but is willing and anxious to have somebody cover him up as soon as he gets there. You follow this fellow right on out because you know that even though you can't take the race track from him, he's going to let you go as soon as he makes the top. You can take your own breather as soon as he surrenders the lead, which he will. Even though someone else comes on then and takes the race track from you, you are still well-placed.

You also have to check out the come-from-behind drivers and judge their stock pretty carefully. If you're out on the front end someplace and one of these fellows is buried back in the pack with a particularly fast-finishing horse, you'd better be glancing at your watch and judging the pace right down to a fraction of a second.

Speaking of time in a race, somebody asked me recently whether I still carried a watch since all major tracks now flash the time electronically at each quarter-mile mark where the drivers can see it. I do carry a watch and I use it.

I have found that the electronic timers are not really much help, although they do represent a definite convenience. The trouble is, they flash the time as you *reach* the quarter. That's too late for me. I want to know the time long *before* I reach the quarter—or the half or the three-quarters as the case may be.

Let's say we're down to the eighth in 14 seconds on my watch and the pace shows no sign of abating. That means a quarter in 28 seconds. I know that no matter what else happens in the race I can't afford to be down there that fast with the type of horse I'm driving. So I take back right away.

If I hadn't known exactly how fast that pace was until we reached the quarter and it was flashed on the board, I'd have been in real trouble. But it would have been too late then to have done anything about it.

I believe I can judge pace as well as the next fellow. I know that I could aim at a mile in 2:10 without a watch and not miss it a second either way. But if I aim at a 29-second quarter and get there in 28, I have made a big mistake, much bigger than if my 2:10 mile had gone in 2:09 or 2:11.

I carry my watch in my left hand (Fig. 76). The thong goes around my ring finger and then loops between the index and middle fingers to lay comfortably in my palm. I use my thumb to start and stop the watch at the beginning and end of each mile and to time the eighths and quarters.

Getting back to the come-from-behind driver I was discussing a few paragraphs back, there are times when you have to readjust your own strategy in mid-race to cope with him. That situation might arise on a night when I figured I was best or second best and that the one I had to beat was the combination of a come-from-behind driver and a fast-finishing horse that could really fly the last quarter of a mile, especially if the early pace was cut out to suit him.

Let's say I was in such a race with a group or horses that usually got down to the half around 1:02. But if I noticed in checking the quarter-mile time and glancing at my watch as we headed toward the three-eighths that it looked like a half around

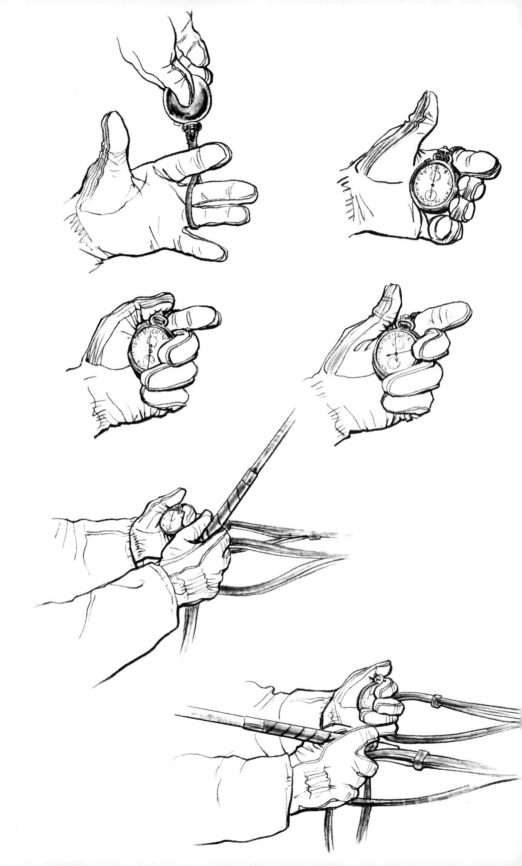

1:04 was shaping up—in an actual race I probably wouldn't have to check the time because I would know instinctively that we were getting down there too slow—I would feel that I had to take some kind of drastic action or lose all chance of winning.

Under these circumstances, I would take out even if a notorious front runner was on top. (Incidentally, a front-running horse isn't necessarily one that takes a strong hold throughout the race in the manner that an absolute "puller" does. A front runner is often content to race at a moderate clip as long as he is on top and will become a "puller" only when another horse tries to take the race track away from him.) I just have to take some of the sting out of that come-from-behind horse and in order to do it I have to quicken the pace in some manner. I would much prefer, of course, that someone else did this job for me while I sat comfortably along the rail and watched the action. But I know from experience that I cannot beat this particular horse and driver unless the pace is stepped up and if nobody else will volunteer I must. I am out there to win every race I drive and if I suspect that I cannot win the way a race is shaping up, then I will take a chance even if it means deviating from my normal driving pattern. This is what I call a calculated risk and I am always willing to take one. At the same time, there is always the chance, however remote, that I might be able to build up enough momentum as I move out to grab the lead from the front-running horse before he can react to my challenge.

If, however, in this same race, I am driving a horse that I know is going to require every break he can get just to finish in

Fig. 76. Proper procedures with respect to watch, whip and driving lines are illustrated on the opposite page. At the upper left, the author demonstrates how the watch is looped around the fingers and, upper right, how it lays in the palm ready for use. The tip of the thumb, center left, is used to depress the stem and start and stop the watch at the beginning and end of the race. The thumb joint, center right, depresses the split timer to catch fractions. At the lower left, the watch is properly positioned in the left hand, the whip is shown in the cocked position in the right hand and the fingers are looped through the hand holds of the driving lines. The hand holds insert between the index and middle fingers with the middle, ring and little fingers positioned within the loop. The illustration at the lower right is similar except that the whip is positioned to lay on the driver's shoulder as illustrated on a larger scale in Fig. 77, bottom. The whip may also be carried in the trailing position as illustrated in Fig. 77, top. The author cautions against holding the whip in the cocked position, lower left, with certain horses that wear an open bridle since it may cause them to fret and worry unnecessarily if they are able to see a whip waving over their back when its use is not intended.

the money, I will not abuse him by taking out and running him down under these circumstances. I have an obligation to the public, to the owner of the horse and to myself to finish as close to first as possible if I cannot win the race. I am not fulfilling this obligation if I drive foolishly. With this type of horse, therefore, I would probably sit still and let somebody else quicken the pace while I waited for an opportunity to improve my position later on. Racing strategy is very often dictated by the type of horse you are driving.

Another type of driver is the one who rarely tries to bust out on top, hunting an immediate hole at the rail instead, but who is clamoring to get out as the field leaves the three-eighths mile mark and heads for the half. This kind can actually be helpful if you have experienced some trouble leaving and wound up parked out yourself. Normally, under these circumstances, you would just have to head for the front end and fight it out. But if you know this fellow is sitting in the three or four hole, your strategy is to mark time on the outside just behind him waiting for him to pull out, which he will invariably do almost as soon as you have passed the three-eighths pole. This will give you cover you didn't figure to have and if you're lucky you'll be able to trail in behind him all the way to the three-quarter pole or even farther. This is not like being in along the rail, but it's not nearly as bad as being parked out without cover the whole mile.

But most of all when I study the driver assignments on the program, I am on the lookout for drivers who are not too capable and who may cause trouble on the race track simply because they are not skillful enough. Unfortunately, there are some of them around and they constitute a real danger especially if they happen to be driving anything but a perfect-mannered horse.

There is a big difference in this business between being game and being foolish. In my opinion, being game means being willing to take a calculated risk under pressure with big money on the line. I have taken these risks and will continue to do so. But I never have done nor will I ever do anything that I consider plainly dangerous as it might affect myself, my horse or my opponents.

The dangerous driver is the one who has a horse that's been trying to make a break for the last quarter of a mile and every driver in the race knows it except the the fellow who's driving him. Or the one who's cutting over from the outside, taking dead aim at your horse's legs and doesn't know either where he's going or what he's doing. These men are foolish and are to be avoided as best as you can.

I think the recent tightening of driver license requirements will help eliminate a great deal of this in the future. Unfortunately, the requirements have not always been as tough as they are now and consequently we still have some pretty risky propositions on the race track with us. The good drivers know who these men are and they give them as wide a berth as possible.

Along this line, I always remember what Billy Muckle told me. Billy Muckle was a sharp old harness horseman who helped break me in at Saratoga Raceway in the early forties. I remember that it had been pretty rough going for a couple of weeks and that I came back to the paddock one night uncertain as to whether I'd been in a horse race or a rodeo. I was young and maybe a little headstrong, but definitely convinced that it was time to start dishing out a little of what I'd been taking; time to prove that I was as game as the next fellow.

I guess I expressed myself in no uncertain terms. Anyway, Billy heard me out without interrupting and then he put his arm around my shoulder and led me off to the side.

"Before you start doing things you'll be sorry for," he said, "I want to remind you that there's a big difference between being game and being foolish. I want you to remember how much the horse is worth and how much the equipment you're using is worth and how much your life is worth. But most of all, I want you to remember that there's another day coming."

So, whenever I see one of these "cowboys" taking dead aim at me, I back off a little rather than get knocked down. I'm game, but I'm not foolish. And I always remember that there's another day coming.

The fact that these "cowboys," as I call them, will cut you down or run you into the fence is only half the black mark I have against them. The other half is that they don't know what to do when they get in trouble.

Even good drivers can get in trouble on a race track. It isn't very difficult when eight horses are locked in tight quarters at a better-than-2:00 clip over a half-mile track. Accidents can and will happen. But the good driver doesn't panic under these circumstances. He knows what to do and he does it instinctively. Hundreds of accidents are avoided every year by good drivers knowing what to do and doing it promptly and efficiently.

Take hooking wheels, for instance, one of the major problems you run into on a half-mile track. A horse is coming up from behind you and maybe you pull out a little quicker than you should or he is in a little tighter than he should be. His left wheel gets hooked in behind your right wheel.

If a poor driver is handling the outside horse, you can almost bet he'll snatch his horse to the right. He's 100% wrong and you're both going down. Or if the poor driver is on the inside, he'll snatch to the left, if he isn't snugged up against the hub rail, with the same result.

The trick is for the driver of the inside horse, the one whose wheel has been hooked, to continue straight ahead and keep his horse moving. The driver of the outside horse must take hold of his horse and gently back him off, keeping him straight at the same time. The wheels will come loose very easily if you will follow this procedure. It can avoid a lot of really nasty spills.

I suppose the most common cause of wrecks is a horse stepping into a wheel. This usually occurs when a driver takes out to go around another horse and doesn't judge the distance carefully enough. Often, he'll be trailing right up tight against the horse in front of him but will be looking back over his shoulder for a horse that is moving on the outside.

He sees this other horse coming, and he jerks, literally jerks, his horse to the right without even thinking about his clearance. The next thing you know he's in your wheel and both of you are down. The secret is to take back just a little bit before you move out and be absolutely certain there is clearance.

This happened to me one time in a big race and it was my fault. I was in The Kentucky Futurity with Galophone and Joe O'Brien was driving Scott Frost. Scott Frost had gone to the top and I was trailing him. At about the half, Home Free, the other half of Joe's entry, came on and Joe let him go to the top.

Just as we were approaching the three-quarter pole, I tried to pull out real quick to see if I couldn't get out with Galophone before Scott Frost could and maybe keep him hemmed in there for a while through the stretch.

Well, I didn't back off and take clearance as I should have and just as I moved Joe moved, too, and my horse stepped right through his wheel. Both of us went down and neither of us finished. That's what I mean by backing a horse off and giving him room enough to clear the wheel when you move out from behind another horse.

That brings up another matter—how close should you trail when you are in behind a horse in a race? Generally, you trail right up close, snugging your horse right up against the horse in front of you. Most horses will relax much better and won't take nearly as much hold if you'll let them get right in close to the horse in front. There is also less wind resistance in this position.

The exception to this is when you're trailing a horse that's known to be bad mannered and will make breaks. I never trail such a horse closer than a half-length. I figure I need that much space to react to anything he might do.

The next time you see a tightly bunched field, except for one position where a horse appears not to be able to keep up with the horse in front of him, take a look at your program and see if maybe the horse that isn't being trailed so closely doesn't have some "x's" in his chart lines. The drivers can read a program, too.

As you know, the "x" on the program indicates a horse breaking stride and this is as good a place as any to write a little about breaking horses.

First of all, if I am in a race and my horse feels as though he's going to make a break, I let everybody know it. I yell as loud as I can. I want to warn everybody and give them a chance to react, especially if it's a hobbled pacer. And I like other drivers to show me the same courtesy. Most of them do it, for their own protection as well as for that of their opponents.

If you know your horse is going to break stride, you are not usually in bad trouble unless he goes down and even then the danger of serious injury is very slight. But where you get into real trouble is if you haven't said anything to alert the boys behind you and you go down and they pile over the top of you.

So I always like them to shout out to me. Then, if I am behind them, I can take out a little and keep an eye on them. If they do make a break, or even if they go down, I have been forewarned and won't pile into them.

It doesn't take any great talent to get a hobbled pacer back on gait after he's made a break. The hobbles will do it for you because the horse doesn't have much choice about how to handle his legs. Just keep a good hold on him until he gets back on gait. A trotter is different and there is a technique involved. As in most other things, knowledge of your horse and his reaction after making a break is important.

The first thing you should do after a trotter makes a break is to move him to the outside to give the other horses clearance on the inside of you. Before you do this, you have to make sure there is room to go out without interfering with someone. Once you have done this, you don't just jerk his head around to get him back on gait. You turn his head gently to the right and then, as the left foot goes forward, you move his head back to the left to get him on that left lead. Then his right foot will have a chance to come down ahead of the left one which is necessary in order for him to regain his gait. Remember, gently to the right or left, depending on which lead you are on, and then gently back to the opposite side. All this time you must have a relatively snug hold on him so that you aren't gaining any ground.

I have also seen horses that will hit back on the trot by themselves if you pull them straight back and then drop their heads suddenly. I am also familiar with some that you just can't get back on the trot unless you stop them dead in their tracks. These are usually the horses that seldom make a break and they just don't know what to do with themselves when it happens. Other trotters are what we call "handy" breakers and can go off stride and get back on again almost before anybody even knows they did it.

I have written quite a bit here about the other horses and drivers in the race but equally important, and perhaps even more so, is that you evaluate the capabilities of your own horse accurately.

You must neither under-estimate nor over-estimate these capabilities. You must know whether he can leave, how much hold he is likely to take both at the gate and when he is covered up, whether he has trouble getting round the turns, whether he can rough it on the outside and how far, how many moves he has, whether he will stand whipping and what type, whether he is likely to bear either in or out under pressure and whether he is brave or faint-hearted.

You would think that any driver would know all these things and more about his horse. All top drivers do. That is one of the reasons they are leading the pack in the driver standings. But you would be surprised at the number who cannot accurately assess the ability of their own horses.

Over the years, I have come to realize that this group of drivers, minority that it is, simply cannot evaluate their own horses much less those that are opposing them in the race. This is hard to believe but it is absolutely true. And a driver who doesn't understand or appreciate the capabilities of his own horse is a definite handicap to that horse.

When you warm a horse up before a race, you are, of course, always checking to see that he "feels" right to you and acts sharp and in good fettle. Since pre-race warmups are being covered by Stanley Dancer and others, I will not go into any detail here except to say that my own pattern has changed over the years. I now warm up my raceway horses just two trips, one to a cart in about 2:40 and the last one to the sulky in about 2:20. I try to go both warmup miles if I can, but I always go the final one because this helps me to determine the immediate pre-race condition and attitude of my horse.

In the last warmup mile I brush my horse about an eighth. I don't believe in brushing a full quarter of a mile and haven't done it for years. A fast eighth will show up any deficiencies that might be going to develop that night—I am speaking of lameness and things like that—and it doesn't take nearly as much out of a horse to go just an eighth at high speed. This final eighth will be from 15 to 16 seconds, depending on the horse.

In the paddock I always make an equipment check before I go with my horse. I want to make sure the lines are buckled, that the check is set right, that the hobbles are on correctly, that all boots are properly buckled and everything in its proper place.

I occasionally miss something and the effects can be disastrous. I recall that one night I didn't discover until we had turned behind the gate that my horse was hitched to the wrong sulky. He was a trotter, one that we just jogged before his race and didn't warm up to a sulky. The boy had brought the wrong bike and it was too small for him. He started hitting it and it scared him so badly that he was down to the half in 1:00⅖ and I was nothing but a passenger. He was a horse that would usually get down to the half in 1:04 so you can imagine where he finished.

I am not afraid to mention something like this because it rarely occurs in my stable but it does demonstrate that mistakes can happen and that they can be costly.

On the other hand, constant attention to detail can pay off. I remember that in the early summer of 1965 I had the filly My Opinion in an $18,000 stake for 2-year-old trotting fillies at Yonkers. She was a filly who was a little pacey and I wore a pair of hinge quarter boots on her. The boy brought her to the paddock without them but I caught the mistake and we went back and got them. She finished second, beaten just a nose and I guarantee she would have been dead last, and probably pacing, without them.

With a horse that wears either a Crit Davis or a Crabb check bit along with a nose band, it is always a good idea to make sure that the nose band is up off the horse's nostrils so that he can breathe properly. All too often a groom in a hurry will let the nose band slide down on the horse's nose when he puts the bridle on and the horse's breathing will be affected during the race.

Another thing to check carefully just before the race is the way the horse's tail is tied. I tie all my horse's tails either with a length of clothesline rope or an elastic bandage. But what you must make certain of is that the groom has made the first loop in the rope or bandage below the dock. The dock is that part of the tail that covers the tail bone and, depending on the horse, runs downward from a foot to a foot and a half from the root of the tail. If the first loop of the rope or bandage is made around the dock and thus over the tail bone, it pinches the horse and makes him uncomfortable. I have seen tail bandages that were much too high. After the loop is made, the tail rope is braided into the hair and then runs straight backward beneath the sulky seat. I like then to loop the tail once or twice around the seat rail and then bring it back up on the seat beneath me. Thus, I am actually sitting on the tail during the race. If the horse is a bad kicker, I will loop the tail around the seat rail a couple of times and then tie it to the rail. The reason that I don't tie any tails down, unless the horse is a kicker, is that I don't like to see a horse lose his driver and still be fastened to the sulky.

Over the years I have heard a lot of discussion, both pro and con, relative to the effect of a driver's weight, if any, on the performance of a horse. You can't go to a race track these days without hearing some conversation about it. I think much of this talk has developed as a result of the outstanding success enjoyed by lightweight drivers like George Sholty (117) and Del Insko (120).

I have my own theory about this and I have always wanted to expound it. I'll never find a better soap box than the one I'm "standing" on now.

Let me start out by saying that I think weight *is* a factor. But let me immediately qualify that by saying I believe it is *where the weight is placed* that counts.

Oh, sure, maybe in terribly heavy going the actual weight of the driver might make a difference. But aside from that possibility, which I will concede without argument simply to by-pass it, I don't think actual weight makes a great deal of difference.

I had that brought home to me one time when I brought a horse down from Monticello to race at Roosevelt. Bill Vaughan, one of my assistant trainers, had been driving him and had won his last start in 2:07. The night I drove him the pattern of the race was almost the same as in his Monticello start and the fractions were almost identical with the mile in exactly 2:07. He got beat a nose. Bill Vaughan weighs almost 200 pounds. I check in at 150. I am certain that if actual weight were a factor that this horse would have raced faster for me than he did for Bill. And there are many other examples just like that one right in my own stable.

No, weight isn't it except in very extreme cases. But I am positive that what does make a difference, and a big difference, is the way the weight is placed in relation to the wheels of the sulky.

To put it briefly, if the weight is behind the wheels, I don't think it makes much difference. But if the weight is directly over the wheels or a little forward of the wheels, I think it makes all the difference in the world and can definitely affect the performance of a horse (Fig. 77).

Before I get deeper into this, perhaps I ought to explain that when I talk about sulky sizes, there are four measurements to keep in mind. They are width, height, wheel diameter and length of shaft. If I ordered a standard sulky from the factory and did not specify any particular dimensions, I would get one that was 50 inches wide and 27 inches high with wheels 28 inches in diameter and a shaft 87 inches long. This sulky, complete with wheels and seat cushion, would weigh 42 pounds, according to Bill Foster of The Houghton Sulky Company. (A training cart, complete with heavy-duty wheels, dash and dust apron would weigh 74 pounds.)

The width of a sulky is measured from the inner edge of the inside axle (or wheel) arch on each side. Sulkies come from the factory in widths of 46, 48, 50, and 52 inches. The average is 50 inches.

The height is measured from the bottom of the center of the cross arch, which is at the center of the sulky seat, to the ground. Factory sizes range from 25 to 30 inches and the average is 27.

Sulky wheels come in two sizes with diameter measurements of 26 and 28 inches. If you went from 28 to 26 inch wheels, you would automatically lower the height of your sulky one inch. You would not be lowering the height two inches, as you might expect, because only half of the diameter measurement of the wheel would be involved.

The length of the sulky shaft is measured on a straight line from the cross arch on either side of the seat, to the tip of the shaft on the same side. The standard shaft length is 87 inches and the range is from 84 inches to 93.

Fig. 77. The illustrations on the opposite page demonstrate the author's feelings relative to the weight of the driver as a possible factor in the performance of the horse. He believes, as discussed in the text, that if the driver's weight is distributed *back* of the sulky wheels and that if the sulky shafts have the proper upward angle, as shown above, then the driver's actual weight makes little or no difference. At the same time, he feels that if a high sulky is required (for reasons of the horse's size or gait) and if this results in the driver's weight riding directly over the wheels and the sulky shafts being virtually on a level instead of pointing upward, as shown below, then weight *is* a factor and can affect a horse's performance. These two pictures are also used to demonstrate proper and improper driving positions. In the drawing below, the hand holds are too far back and the driver's elbows are in against his body. The author calls this type "belly button" drivers and maintains they are unable to exercise proper control over their horses. The proper position is indicated above. Two whip positions are also illustrated. The whip is held in the trailing position above and over the shoulder below.

A high-going trotter might race in a sulky 30 inches high. A wide-going horse, either trotter or pacer, might require a sulky 54 inches wide. To a great degree, sulky measurements are keyed to the size and gait of the particular horse.

I was writing about the placement of weight as a factor in the speed of a horse and perhaps I could explain it better by citing a specific example. Let's say you had a very small trotter, maybe one that stood 14'3 hands, but that was real big-gaited behind. Normally you would use a sulky 26 inches high on a trotter this small but you have to go to a 28-inch bike with this horse because he is so big-gaited that he is hitting up under the seat of the smaller sulky.

In going to a higher sulky you have eliminated the interference problem, but what you have also done by raising the height of the sulky is to lower the angle of the shafts and, in my opinion, created a weight problem. Now, the shafts are almost on a level instead of pointing upward as they should. And when you, the driver, take your seat on the sulky, your weight is directly over the wheels or slightly in front of them. This is dead weight and there is no question in my mind that it is detrimental to the horse and that he will go faster with a lighter driver.

On the other hand, if you have a big, 16-hand horse with a 27-inch sulky, you have your shafts pointed upward at the proper angle and your weight, when you get on this sulky, is *behind* the wheels where it belongs.

If you can raise the angle of your shafts to where the weight of the driver falls well behind the wheels, I don't think it makes much difference how much the driver weighs. I think that horses will go just about as fast for a 200-pound driver as they will for a Sholty or an Insko.

I think you can guess now why I feel the fit of the sulky is a very important thing in my stable. I want that weight back behind the wheels and not on top of them or in front of them. It makes all the difference in the world to me.

A small horse needs a low sulky so that you can get the shafts up and the weight behind the wheels. Of course, what you must watch for here is what I have described earlier—the possibility of his hitting beneath the sulky or hitting the driver's legs with his hocks. Trotters are usually the culprits in these cases; pacers don't usually go that high or that wide. Pacers are more likely to hit the wheels and some of them will take a wider sulky for that reason.

The size of a sulky that a horse requires is determined in workouts and a card bearing the sulky size follows the horse whereever he goes so that he will always have the right sulky to race in.

Occasionally, you run into special problems such as the one posed by Simple Simon, a good raceway horse in my stable. Simon stands barely 14 hands and is very short. We were using a small sulky that was 26 inches high and 48 inches wide, but it was still much too long for Simon with its 87-inch shaft. I talked the situation over with Bill Foster and as a result of our conversation, Bill took a small sulky that Stanley Dancer had used and rebuilt it to Simon's specifications. He lowered the height to 24 inches and narrowed the width to 48 inches. Then he cut the shaft down to 71 inches. I wanted him to make it 70 but he thought 71 was short enough and I settled for that.

The made-to-order sulky stepped up Simple Simon's performance quite a bit. With the longer-shafted sulky, it was as though Simon and I were in different counties, he was so far away from me. I didn't have the control over him that I wanted, but with the shorter shafts I found that not only was I able to control him better but I was also able to steer him into holes that weren't big enough before. And at the same time, by going to the lower height I was able to raise the angle of the shaft and thus shift my weight back behind the wheels where it belonged.

The highest sulky I ever had was a specially-made 32″ bike for a big trotting colt that was getting up under the seat on me. I got him off the seat but the angle of the shafts was not good. Going in that size sulky, my weight was dead weight and I believe a lighter driver could have got more out of him.

Earlier, I touched briefly on the weight of a driver as it applies to a heavy track and conceded that actual weight might make a difference under these circumstances. I would like to pause here and write a little about racing over a muddy track or a very heavy track.

Track surfaces have undergone radical change in recent years and the phrase "all weather" track has come to mean almost exactly what it says. I can't remember the last major track postponement that was caused by weather conditions and you are rarely rained out at any mutuel track these days.

But you do run into some rugged racing conditions with mud and rain and heavy going. These conditions can affect both the performance of horses and your own racing strategy.

For instance, when I am racing in heavy going, I race much more often on the front end than I do over a normal track. There are two reasons for this, one obvious and one not so obvious.

The obvious reason is that visibility is so much much better on the head end. When you race over an off track, chunks of mud and dirt and streams of water are flying at you from all directions. Not only does this hinder your visibility, but pieces of flying debris can and will cause your horse to make a break.

The other thing I have discovered through experience is that a good many horses that have a reputation for stopping will go farther in front on a muddy track. I don't know why this should be, but I can tell you that it is true. You just can't run your horse down to make the front end in a situation like this, but I always give it a little extra try and I have had very good results.

Some horses go better in the mud, others can't go as well and with some it doesn't seem to make any difference at all. I think the gait of the horse is the big factor here.

A big-striding, open-gaited horse won't go through the mud nearly as well as a little short-gaited horse. You'd think maybe the opposite would be true but it isn't. It seems that the big-going horse labors just twice as hard when he hits mud. Such horses, too, usually have big feet and a horse with great big feet just gets bogged down in mud. He usually can't handle it at all.

A medium-sized, choppy, rapid, round-gaited horse, either trotter or pacer, is the best horse for mud. A horse with a "daisy-cutting" gait, that is, one that is just barely getting off the ground, is as bad a risk as the big-striding horse.

A big-going trotter that "dwells" a little, that is, holds his stride a fraction of a second before he puts his foot down in front, is especially vulnerable and the worst of all is a big-going trotter who scrambles a little when he is going, or hits his shins. This kind is terrible in mud.

Except for one horse, I haven't carried any "mud equipment" for a long time. In the old days, before we got our "all weather" tracks, we used to use "dew nails" which are nails with very sharp heads and we would put them on the horse's feet on muddy or slippery tracks to give him traction. We also used to put grabs on horses for the same reason, but I don't even do that any more.

The only exception in my stable in recent years was Duke Rodney who just didn't make it very well on a muddy track. He would slip and slide badly. I used to carry an extra pair of borium-coated shoes for Duke because the borium would help give him a grip on the track when it was muddy or slippery. They helped him a great deal.

A lot of people seem to think that over a muddy track you have to cut the pads out of the feet of horses that wear them. I don't find this to be true and unless the surface is real slippery I leave the pad in. Tom Berry told me one time that a pad will act to keep a horse on top of the surface more and I have found this to be true. A horse wearing a pad doesn't punch down in quite as deep.

Now let's get back to our pre-race check list. One of the first things you check when you climb on the sulky is the fit of the hand holds. Hand holds must be adjusted to suit the individual driver but I have no hesitancy in saying that if there is any question in your own mind, adjust them farther up toward the horse's back. I hate to see anyone driving with the hand holds so far back that they don't have proper control over a horse. If something happened in a race, they'd never have a chance to stop the horse.

Delvin Miller and I have talked about this a great deal and we agree that too many drivers have the hand holds too far back. And we agreed also that if either of us was ever a Presiding Judge and saw one of these "belly button drivers," (Fig. 77) as we call them, we'd tell him either to take them up or get a new driver. A fellow like this has absolutely no control of his horse.

In the post parade, you should stay about a half-length off the horse ahead of you in case he should stop suddenly. And keep alert at all times. A great many horses will stop to empty out during the post parade and I've seen fellows run right up on top of a horse that has stopped. As a matter of fact, once in a while I get a little sleepy and do it myself.

In the post parade, you should also be alert for a horse whirling and turning. Every once in a while a horse will do this and unless you're on the ball and paying attention you can get run into.

After the parade, you score your horse, that is, turn him the right way of the track, with the other horses, and move toward and past the starting line. This is the final warmup preparation and I usually have something I want to check at this time.

If I've got a horse that's "fumbly" going into the first turn or something like that, or especially if I have a horse that is a little sore, I'll score him down real fast in his actual post position to see whether he's going to be all right going into that turn. A good many times a horse like this will make a break while scoring at high speed and if he does, I won't go out of there with him like I normally would. He could go off stride and jam the whole field up. I would definitely be out of the race and I might even cause a bad accident. You can tell by scoring a horse down at high speed whether he's going to be all right or not.

The disposition of the horse I am driving also has something to do with the way I score him down. If my horse is lazy, I like to score him real fast to sharpen him up. If, on the other hand, he is nervous and high strung, I'll score him down real slow to keep him as relaxed as possible prior to the actual race.

Now we are ready to go the gate, but before I proceed any further I want to point out that unless I indicate differently I am talking about half-mile track racing and, specifically, half-mile track racing in New York, that is at Roosevelt and Yonkers Raceways.

I race many places during the course of a season and see all kinds of race tracks with all kinds of shapes, sizes and surfaces. But I do most of my racing in New York and it is from that viewpoint that I will describe actual racing competition.

I also want to point out that the pattern of racing has changed drastically in New York and at all major tracks in the past decade. It used to be that we raced to the quarter pole by which time everybody was pretty well set and usually arrayed in Indian file fashion with the exception of someone who had the misfortune to be parked and had to press on.

From that point on, it was very seldom that you ever saw anybody move before we got to the five-eighths pole and usually we were at the three-quarters before any really exciting action developed. From there on, of course, everybody was on the move.

I think that what has changed the pattern in New York, and, to some extent, at almost all the tracks in the country, is that the competition is so keen and the horses so evenly matched that you find you must be forwardly placed in the latter stages to do any good.

At some tracks, where there are only two or three horses in the race that you figure you have to beat, usually a hole will open up someplace or some other piece of good fortune will develop to compensate for any difficulty you might encounter by not rushing out so fast. But in New York, if you haven't found a place at the rail by the time you reach the eighth pole you're not likely to find one because the fields are so closely matched that every horse in the race can keep on going at that clip until they reach the quarter pole at least.

In New York these days, there is virtually constant movement. You'll see fellows pull out just past the quarter pole right into the turn. And then from the three-eighths pole on it's usually just four on the rail and four on the outside.

So many times I've seen a fellow be on top at the quarter, let one horse go and when they come back to the quarter pole a half mile later, he'd be shuffled clear back to last. It can happen and that's why you have to make frequent decisions and make them fast. You have to decide almost instantaneously whether you are going to go out ahead of somebody, pull out and follow somebody who's coming up alongside, or wait and take your chances.

A lot of this, of course, depends on your horse's ability, as I've mentioned before. You have to know your horse and his capabilities. If your horse can't stand to rough it a good piece on the outside you've just got to sit there and take a chance that later on in the race you can get through on the inside or that a hole will open up somewhere big enough for you to squeeze through.

For the past five years I have been saying that in order for a horse to do any real good in New York he has to be able to rough it for five-eighths of a mile on the outside. This is a fact of life and you have to learn to live with it.

The tactics I am describing apply to half mile track racing. Naturally these tactics will vary; mildly for a five-eighths mile track, greatly for a three-quarter or mile track.

The five-eighths mile track is much easier to drive over than the half-mile track and I definitely prefer it. I wish every track in the country that couldn't build a mile track would go to a five-eighths. It would suit me fine and I know I speak for the vast majority of drivers when I say that.

For instance, you have a much longer stretch before you get to the first turn after the gate leaves and from an outside position you have a much better chance to grab a place along the rail or to make it to the top. And, of course, there is a longer stretch coming home and you don't have to make your move nearly as quickly as you must on a half-mile track. There is also one less turn and the turns are not nearly as sharp and as hard on a horse as they are on a half-mile track. I can think of a dozen advantages and not a single disadvantage.

The mile track is the simplest to drive over. There are only two turns and if you do get parked out you don't lose the ground that you do going around the bends on a half-mile or even a five-eighths mile track. You can almost always remain covered up pretty well until they hit the stretch and then still find racing room because they fan out and there is usually a hole somewhere.

The mile track is, of course, my favorite, but I am not advocating that racing associations start building them. I know they can't because of practical considerations relating to space and other factors. And I am also aware that the racing public doesn't get as close a view or feel as much a part of the program as they do when racing is contested over a smaller track.

The major three-quarter mile track in the country is located at Vernon Downs, between Utica and Syracuse in upper New York State near where I grew up. The start is out of a quarter-mile chute. It is a good track, a fast track and it has a lot of advantages.

I have raced there on many occasions and I do want to offer one observation. I think too many drivers competing at Vernon have a tendency to use their horses too hard the first quarter of a mile.

Coming out of the chute as they do, the horses have more than a quarter of a mile of straightaway before they hit a turn and they are really boiling when they come down through there. It is not uncommon to see 2:06 horses reach the quarter in 29 seconds. Everybody is looking for position and they are taking a lot out of their horses to get it.

If I were racing at Vernon for any extended period, I believe I would let those front-runners go and concentrate on getting in along the rail some place as I came out of the chute. The 2:06 horses that are down to the quarter in :29 also reach the half somewhere between 1:00 and 1:01 and your time to move is when they straighten out in the backstretch, between the half and three quarters.

I'd stay in around the first turn so I wouldn't lose any ground by being out on the bend of the track, but as soon as we were straight, I'd move and move fast. I believe I could make it to the front end most of the time before we hit the next turn which is at the three-quarter pole.

I have seen some of the better drivers doing this at Vernon. In particular, I noticed Al Winger doing it a few years ago and he was very, very successful. He would just sit and wait and make that one big move when he was going in an absolutely straight line down the back stretch. That would be my plan, too.

Now we will go back to the point where we have completed our scoring and are going behind the gate. All horses act a little differently at the gate and you have to know your horses and their habits. Most of them are no trouble at all. They will snuggle right up to the gate without charging it, and will lay their noses against the screen. This is the way I like my horses to be. I want them up on the gate without charging it.

Horses are creatures of habit and if they develop bad post manners early in their careers, it will usually take a long time to change them. That is why it is so important to school 2-year-olds behind a starting gate as early and as often as you can. The sooner you teach them the purpose of the gate, the sooner they will learn to react obediently.

A good post horse means a great deal. When you have a good one, and most major raceway horses are, you can concern yourself with strategy decisions as you roll toward the starting line. But if you have a bad post horse, you have all you can do to get off in line. You can't concentrate as you should on getting a good position or on what the others are doing.

If a horse is inclined to lag at the gate, I will get after him and keep shaking him up. With this kind, I like to give them a couple of good belts with the whip over on the backside just before we get to the gate to wake them up a little.

The other problem horse at the gate is the one who's charging it. These are the ones you have to parade quietly to the post and

Fig. 78. The author demonstrates the proper methods of mounting the racing sulky and training cart. On the left hand page, in the indicated numerical order, he mounts the sulky. Usually, the training cart

would be mounted in exactly the same manner. On the right hand page, he demonstrates an acceptable alternative method of mounting the cart. This method is used with a horse that has a tendency to back up when the driver is attempting to mount. This is not usually necessary with a sulky because there is more leg room, although the sulky must be mounted in this manner if a mud apron is being used. In reverse (reading the numbers backwards) this procedure is followed in dismounting from either cart or sulky. The horse in the photograph is Romulus Hanover.

score down slowly. In other words, just try to keep them from becoming excited from the moment you leave the paddock until the starter says "go." I've had the best luck with this kind by simply turning their heads loose, letting them put their nose against their number on the gate and not fighting their mouth. I've found that the more you fight this kind, the more nervous and upset they get.

I put a horse like this right up against the gate as soon as it begins to move. The gate is going relatively slow from the quarter pole to the eighth pole and usually if you leave one alone he'll settle down and relax and be all right by the time you begin to pick up real speed at the eighth pole.

Now the field has picked up speed, the horses have settled into full stride, the starting line is at hand and the race is underway. There are many things you have to do. There is one important thing you do NOT do. YOU DO NOT TURN YOUR HORSE'S HEAD LOOSE.

I think this is just about the biggest crime that any driver can commit. As far as I'm concerned it's inexcusable.

When I leave out of there I have a hold of my horse and so does every other good driver. This is the place in a race where real trouble can develop and if it does, you absolutely must have control of your horse. You can't have that control if your lines are drooping and you're shooing and shouting for all you're worth.

Anything can happen in that first turn. Even the best-mannered horse in the world can make a mis-step, and if his head is loose he's going to fall down and pile up the field. I've seen so many of the good drivers have a horse make a break and cause no trouble at all for anybody simply because they had their horse under control. On the other hand, I've seen fellows go out of there with loose lines and have seen their horses make breaks that jammed up the whole field. In this respect, I guarantee horses will try harder when you have a hold of them. They have more confidence and they feel more secure when they know you are exercising that control over them. If you turn their heads loose and start hitting them they seem to lose courage as well as confidence. I don't think I've ever seen a real top driver turn a horse's head loose and hit him.

Now I am barreling into the first turn and there is action all around me. If I haven't already, it's time I

*made a decision. First I look for a hole at the rail. If
I am lucky enough to find one, I fall into it and take a
breather for as long as I conveniently can.*

Nine out of ten times there won't be any hole and you have to
decide whether to go to the top or back up. As I said before,
this is where your knowledge of the opposing drivers and horses
comes in handy.

Take a quick look up at the front end. If that's a "pulling"
horse going to the top, (one that his driver can't rate and who
will go as far as he can on the front end) or a driver who you
know won't surrender the lead, take back. Under the circumstances, it's even preferable to go to the end of the line for a
little while if necessary.

I know the "pulling" horse or the front-running driver is going
to run me down and that I am dead for sure if I go with him. In
this circumstance, unless it is a special situation and I have
decided to go out with him as described earlier, I will go all the
way to the end of the line to avoid tangling with him. It's better
to come from a long way off in the last half than to run yourself
completely down in the first half.

*Now I have passed the eighth pole and I have made
my decision or it has been made for me by the actions
of my opponents. I either head for the top, drop in a
hole or go to the end of the line. I have barely reached
this decision, let alone put my plan into operation, before
it's time for another.*

Let's say I was lucky enough to find a hole at the rail and set
up our hypothetical race on that basis. I find myself fourth in
line at the rail as we pass the eighth pole (Fig. 79A). Two horses
are parked out and trying to make the top. The remaining two in
the eight-horse field are trailing me at the rail.

*As I go to the quarter pole I am watching things at the
head end. Just past the quarter, one of the parked horses
makes it to the top. It appears that the other one will
get the lead eventually because the driver who is now
on top is known for wanting to race his horses covered
up as much as possible. But I know he isn't going to let
the other one go before they reach the half.*

*The driver of the horse two places in front of me is
beginning to edge away from the rail although he can-*

*not quite make up his mind whether to take out or not.
I am listening for sounds of activity on the part of the
two that are trailing me.*

*I have plenty of horse and the pace is not too rugged.
I could move now and steal a march on the fellow who
is toying with the idea of coming out up ahead of me.
I could move right on up and get on the outside of the
leader after he makes the top just past the half. But I
know that the horse that is now moving for the top is a
tough one and that he will not let me go when I challenge him. I don't want to tangle with him unless I
have to. The horses behind me are marking time and
I can see a better plan shaping up if the driver two
horses ahead will just move out as he seems to want to.
I must try to encourage him to do so. I must try to flush
him. I do this by pulling my horse slightly out from the
rail and giving every outward indication by voice, gesture and movement, that I am coming on when, in
reality, I am not going to at all unless the other fellow
also moves out.*

*In this instance, I flush my man successfully at about
the three-eighths pole. He hears me (Fig. 79B) and takes
out. As soon as he commits himself, I am out and right
up on his back. And I am not a second too soon because
one of the horses behind me has also moved and I just
did beat him to the punch. He is trailing me on the
outside.*

The changing pattern of half-mile track racing—which all too
often these days results in two, three or even four horses racing
much of the mile in a parked out position—has also been responsible for the new and subtle driving tactic known as flushing.
This is the art of decoying another driver into pulling out ahead
of you and thus providing cover for you as you race on the
outside.

Let's say you are sitting in fourth along the rail and two
horses are driving for the lead on the outside as the field hits
the quarter mile mark. The lead horse is not a front runner and
his driver is not especially known for wanting to race on top
so you can be quite sure that the two horses on the outside are
going to make it to the top within the next few seconds. This will

leave you in the six hole at the rail and this is not a particularly desirable position because the horses behind you are almost certain to be taking out within a matter of seconds.

You would like to take out and go yourself, but you don't want to wind up battling it out with a lead horse that either won't let you go or will carry you a long way at a rugged clip before he does. What I like to do in a situation like this is to make an exaggerated feint indicating to those up ahead by voice, gesture and even by pulling my horse slightly out from the rail that I am about to take out and go on. Usually, one of the drivers up ahead will be fearful that I am coming and that he is about to get boxed in, whereupon he takes out ahead of me and I pull out and follow him. In this manner I have flushed successfully and am sitting in a good position.

In some instances, it is necessary to do more than make an exaggerated feint in order to flush successfully. Depending on who you are trying to flush, you may actually have to pull out and move up alongside the horse ahead of you. In most instances, this will convince the driver you are trying to flush that you really mean business and he will pull out in front of you rather than take the chance of being penned in along the rail. When I flush in this fashion, I am always careful to give the fellow plenty of room to get out ahead of me. Of course, if the man I am trying to flush doesn't respond to this action the results can be disastrous since I will be parked out without cover.

The important thing about flushing is to know your fellow drivers. Some flush very easily and others are quite difficult to flush although I have no intention of giving away trade secrets by naming names. It will be obvious from what I have written that I check very carefully on drivers before I attempt any flushing.

The best place to flush another driver is at about the three-eighths pole or just past it because this is the point where so many of them seem to be most fearful about being boxed in. This is especially true at Yonkers where the short homestretch penalizes a horse that has been boxed in and has to come from far back in the latter stages. Flushing is one of the most important moves a driver can make over a half-mile track and I have won a lot of races by employing the tactic successfully.

Now we reach the half-mile pole. The time is average.

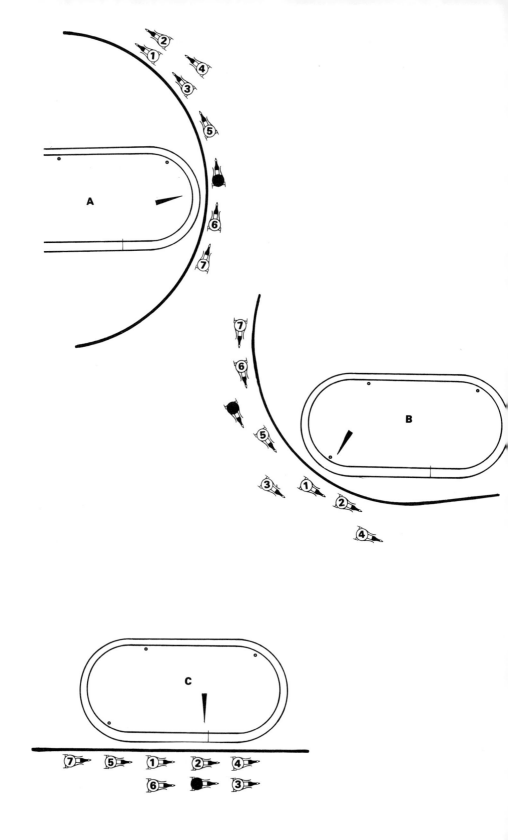

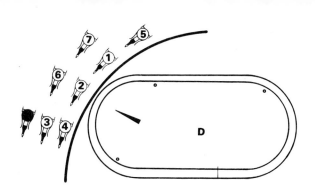

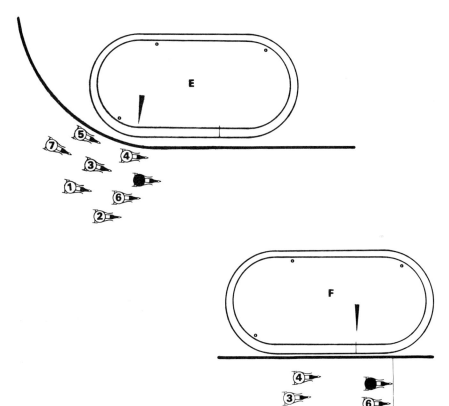

Fig. 79. Action at six key spots in the hypothetical race described in the text is illustrated in this series of drawings. Beginning at the upper left (Fig. 79A), the field is shown at about the eighth pole, just past the three eighths, at the half, around the final turn, in the stretch and at the finish. The author is driving the No. 8 horse which is outlined in black.

The second of the two horses that were parked from the outset has now taken the lead (Fig. 79C). The driver that I flushed successfully and am now trailing moves his horse up to go head and head with the new leader. There is a horse behind me on the outside. There are five horses at the rail and three on the outside. I am in pretty good shape.

I like to trail a horse on the outside. I find it is the ideal place to race the last half on half-mile tracks. Being on the outside and going head and head for the lead is tough on a horse, but for a fellow sitting in behind that outside horse it is much easier. I suppose it is half psychological and half the fact that trailing is not the same as battling a leading horse. But you must be careful when you let a horse go, as I sometimes do, with the idea of taking out and following him. Others have the same idea and if you don't act quickly enough you'll find three or four going by in a row. Then you are in a real jam.

If I am in the three hole and I hear a horse coming on the outside, I always take a look to see if he is alone. If he is, I'll usually let him go and then take out and trail him. But if two or three others are tight on him, I'm forced to take out ahead of him and hope my horse can last the distance. In any event, unless I have a faint-hearted horse or one that is in over his head, I will not sit and wait. I can't afford to in this type of situation.

And one other thing, while we are on this phase of the racing action. If you are forced to move, forced to battle for the lead on the outside of a tough horse that you didn't want to challenge in the first place but were forced to by circumstance, rest your horse all you can. In this situation, I usually make one pass at the horse on top and if he and his driver show me they're not going to let me go, I just sit there. It's a lot easier to sit on the outside than it is to battle for the lead.

I have won races that I shouldn't have simply by employing this tactic. It has always been surprising to me that so many drivers think that just because they are parked outside the leading horse they have to fight for the lead. That's fine if you see that you can take the race track or that the other fellow will let you go. But if not, back off and just ride along for a while.

Again, the ability of your horse is a factor. The average horse (and this type of horse is the lowest of three levels at the New York tracks where I do most of my racing) has one good move in a race. You can use it at the start and shepherd him the rest of the way; you can make it in the middle of the mile and then try to coast home with him or you can save it for the end. But you can only use him once.

He's the kind of horse you have to sit there with and take a chance that a good hole opens when you leave or, if you have used him a little at the start, wait until the tail end and hope that an opening pops up as you roll through the stretch at the finish. Usually, I take this kind back off the gate at the start and save that one move for as late in the race as possible.

The better-than-average horse has two good moves and that makes a big difference. It means you can bust out of there pretty good and still have another move left at the end. Only the really top horses have three moves and it is a pleasure to have one like this. They do not come along very often. Belle Acton could give you three moves and so could Duke Rodney, Charming Barbara, Speedy Count, Duane Hanover, Vicar Hanover, Romulus Hanover and Trader Horn among other horses I have trained and driven.

Now let's get back to our race which we left with me sitting in a trailing position on the outside just past the half. There are five horses along the rail and mine is the middle horse of the three that are parked.

I ease my way around the lower turn and as we head into the backstretch for the last time, I am faced with another decision. I know the horse behind me will move out soon and now I've got to decide whether I want to try to pass the horse in front of me or save ground by staying behind him and taking my chances later on. I will make this decision and act upon it in a matter of split seconds, but all kinds of thoughts are flashing through my mind.

I am most interested in the horse directly in front of me. How strong is he? Will he go on into the stretch or will he suddenly quit and back up into me? If he does the latter and the fellow who is moving from behind has me penned in, I am in trouble. But if I pull to the outside and go three deep around that last turn and through the lane, I need plenty of horse. I've got a good horse and a brave one, but I'm not sure he's that tough.

I take another look at the horse in front of me as we approach the three quarter pole. I'm interested in whether he's being driven all the way or whether he's under a snug hold. I already know from my study of the program, that he is a horse that doesn't like to rough it too much. His driver is shaking the lines over him and asking him for more. I can sense that the horse behind me is starting to edge out and he is the one I really fear. I had better move. (There have been times when I've elected to stay in behind a horse that looked like he was full of trot or pace only to have him die in front of me without any warning at all.)

Now I am three wide around the final turn (Fig. 79D) and while I don't particularly want to be there I can see I made the right move. The horse on the lead is tiring but the horse that was outside of him and in front of me is tiring even more. The horses that were in the two and three hole along the rail are full of trot but they have nowhere to go at the moment. The horse in front of them and the ones outside are backing them up.

I cluck to my horse and he pricks his ears and moves around the two tiring horses on the front end. I am at the top of the stretch and I have the lead (Fig. 79E). But the horse that pulled out from behind me and is now alongside me is going to be tough. The two horses that were locked in along the rail have shaken themselves loose and have moved to the extreme outside. But I can tell that the valuable lengths they lost while they were hemmed in represent too much of a handicap. They will not be a factor. I can tell that the race is between my horse and the one outside me. I go to the whip.

I have to be careful and again I must know my horse. Whipping is an art in itself and you must know when and when not to do it. You can whip too early and your horse will not keep trying long enough. You can whip too late and the horse will not respond quickly enough. There are also horses you cannot whip at all. They will sulk and back up into you. I have some of them in New York and I have the feeling that the public doesn't think I'm giving it 100% when I don't lay a whip to this kind. But when you hit one like this you can be sure he will back up a lot faster than he will go forward.

I have some horses that I try to hit on the flank. Others I try to hit under the belly. Some horses will accept the whip but resent being stung on the flank or under the belly. With these, I try to hit the saddle pad or the sulky shaft.

Every once in a while you run into a strange case. A few years ago I had a mare named Wonderful Time. I discovered that you had to whip her on the left side. If you whipped her on the right side she'd drift in badly and start going crooked in an effort to get away from the whip and wouldn't try real hard. But if you hit her on the left side, she'd go right on, straight down the race track.

I found that I couldn't whip left-handed. I tried it one night and just couldn't handle it at all. I was absolutely helpless. So from then on I'd have to reach over with my right hand and whip her on the left side. As long as I did this, she would respond well and drive straight. But it sure was an awkward way to whip.

When you're whipping a horse with your right hand, you must remember to keep your reins good and tight in the left hand. As I said before, I've never seen a horse try very hard when you just turn the lines loose and start hitting him.

Another thing you have to remember when whipping a horse is to be certain that you have control of him and that he is going straight. If he starts to go crooked, you're going to have to stop whipping, take the lines in both hands and straighten him up again. If you don't you can cause a real bad wreck.

Another device that can be helpful in the late stages of a race is a spur on a whip. A spur is a round, flat piece of metal about a half inch in diameter and the circumference is shaped so that there are points at the outer edges of the circle. It is fastened to the whip about a foot from the butt end and you reach out and roll it on a horse's rump or the butt of his tail. It is on a pivot and moves in a circle, like a wheel, when you use it.

The spur is outlawed in some states but I don't believe that's right because I think a horse is punished much more with a whip than with a spur. The trouble over spurs came about because some fellows were sharpening them on emery wheels and drawing blood. This is unthinkable and should be controlled by rule. But the spur I use is a dull one and you could run it right over your hand and not cut yourself or draw blood.

I have had very good luck using a spur on fillies that resent being hit with a whip. I just run the spur along the butt end of their tail. It doesn't cut them; it just tickles them and I've found that if you'll give them a few roots in the tail with a dull spur they'll take off and go on and try a lot harder.

Now we go back to the race we left in mid-stretch. It is a battle between my horse and the one outside me. I have just gone to the whip. This is a horse that responds to whipping on the sulky shaft and I have the lines in the left hand, whip in the right and am banging away at the shaft. He doesn't feel anything but the noise of the whip against the shaft tells him it is time to do his very best and he is trying.

But he is tired. He has had a tougher journey than the horse on the outside and on paper he does not figure to be quite as good. Now we are in the last 50 yards and he is starting to fall apart on me.

At this point an amateur would throw the lines away, hit him a good clout with the whip and hope for the best. But this is where the professional does just the opposite.

I feel my horse is going so I begin to lift him and work in rhythm with his action. As he strides forward and drops his head, I let the lines go forward with him, although they are still taut and he is still under my tight control. As he begins another stride and his head starts up, I am with him, lifting his head, playing gently on the lines asking for a little more; a little more than I have a right to ask for, a little more than he really has to give.

But he is game and he gives me that little more. Now it is only forty feet to the wire, five horse and sulky lengths, one second on the watch. My moves are automatic and instinctive. My horse is completely out of gas and I must carry him. I can do this. I know how. I have done it thousands of times before.

He strides forward again almost staggering. His head goes down and my hands go with him. When his head reaches its lowest point in what I know will be his final stride, I raise it back, gently yet firmly. I must show him that I am still with him, that I still have confidence in him and I must do it all with my hands. In that vital fraction of a second, I am literally carrying him past the wire.

We cross the finish line (Fig. 79F) and it is a tight one. So tight that I do not know whether I have won or lost. The announcer holds us in front of the stands while they wait for the photo. I have a few seconds to think about being a harness horse driver and of all that is involved from the time you enter the track for a race until you leave it.

Whatever pre-race tension there may have been subsides when the starter says, "Go." As the race unfolds and the patterns develop you respond instinctively to the lessons time and experience have taught. Now you move, now you sit still; now you park this horse, now you let that one go; now you decline a challenge, now you accept one.

And finally it boils down to a battle through the stretch as you and your fellow drivers, immune to sounds around you, take dead aim at the finish line ahead. It is your job to get there first. Sometimes you do it easily; sometimes you have no chance at all. You either have enough horse or you don't. If you do, you win; if you don't, you lose. It is as simple as that.

But then there are those other finishes, the ones that provide the greatest thrill a driver of harness horses can know. These are the times in the final, bitterly-contested stages of a race, that you run out of horse. And when you can take one like this, one that has nothing left to give, and lift him and sustain him and practically carry him across the line a winner, then you can be truly proud of your own contribution. It is the ultimate thrill for a harness horse driver.

My moment of reverie is interrupted by a roar from the crowd. They have posted the winning number. It is mine. I am pleased. I have done my job well.

(Biographical information concerning the author appears on page 109.)

13

CARE of the HORSE

SANDERS RUSSELL

O F all the men associated with the operation of a racing stable and who thereby come in daily contact with an individual horse, there is one who spends more time with the horse and thus is closer to him than any other. That man is the caretaker, or groom as he is usually called. With him, the welfare of the horse is paramount and the hours he spends on the job, whether long or short, a secondary consideration.

In this chapter, I am going to write about the duties of a groom. To some extent, what I will write is intended for men already employed in the profession, for it is a rare groom that cannot improve himself. But for the most part, I will confine myself to the basic techniques because what I have to say is directed primarily at those young men who are not presently employed as grooms but who would like to be.

For it is from these ranks that the top grooms and the leading trainers of the next generation will emerge. As Billy Haughton says in his chapter on driving, all of today's leading reinsmen came up through the caretaker ranks and it will very likely always be that way. The man who does not know a rub cloth from a hoof pick is an unlikely candidate to reach the top ranks of the training and driving profession.

I also know that those who will read this chapter with the most interest and consequently derive the maximum benefit from it are those young men who are naturally industrious and who have a love for and a way with horses.

A "way" with horses is a common ingredient among all top grooms and trainers. It is something a man is usually born with and is seldom acquired. Have you ever noticed, for instance, that some people seem to get along better with dogs than others who appear equally as kind and pleasant? A strange dog will approach a group of people and while he will be naturally suspicious at first, it will not take him long to search out the "animal person" in the crowd and attach himself to him. This is the one man in the group who has an instinctive way with animals and the dog knows it. It is the same way with horses. Horses can tell "animal people" right away.

The value of a good groom and his contribution to the success
of a horse is difficult to measure. But it is a major one, particularly in the career of horses that last a long time and are outstanding. The groom is with the horse practically 24 hours a day
and if he is capable and understanding, the horse is aware of it
and usually repays the devotion in kind.

I think that if I were asked to give advice to a young man who
wanted to be a groom, the first thing I would do would be to try
to make him understand that a horse is a sensitive, intelligent
animal and not a piece of machinery. A horse has feelings just
as we humans do and they can be hurt just as easily.

If a groom is quiet and soothing, he can soon get his horse to
be much the same way. If he starts jerking or snatching the horse
around, it won't be long before the horse becomes timid or re-
sentful, and in either case he will fail to develop the confidence
he should. This can affect the horse's training. Therefore, I feel
the first thing a groom should do is to make an effort to understand his horse. He will get along much better with him that
way than if he just goes ahead with the daily chores without
actually giving the job any more thought than that. If a groom
will start to think and reason a little, and conduct himself in a
quiet manner, he'll be well on the way to success.

The groom should always remember that his orders come
directly from the stable, either through the trainer or the barn
foreman, and that these orders are to be obeyed. These orders,
of course, will vary from stable to stable but it is the groom's job
to follow them to the letter. It is not the groom's job to tell
the trainer how to condition the horse. If the groom thinks he
can do it better, then it is time for him to branch out on his own.

At the same time, it is the groom's duty to call to the attention
of the trainer or barn foreman any change in the horse's normal
disposition or habits. One of the most important things of all is
to go over the horse carefully every day to make certain, for instance, that no boots have begun chafing, that no nails have
pricked the soles of the feet and that the horse is eating and
eliminating properly. These are the things that the trainer can't
do for every horse in his charge and it is up to the groom to be
observant and report his findings to the trainer. Perhaps what he
has observed is minor in nature and does not require remedial

Fig. 80. Much of the equipment with which a caretaker works and some of the tools he uses are illustrated. In the photograph at the left, the tack trunk is the focal point. It is mounted on a platform and two pails, the far one a mud pail, are at the right. Above the trunk are the blankets and coolers with a rake and a fork beside them. The harness is stored in the harness bag hanging at the left. In the photograph at the right are basic items of equipment usually found in the tack trunk. In the front row, from the left, are a pair of hind shin and speedy cut boots, a pair of knee and arm boots and a pair of suspender forks behind which are the actual suspenders. Bell boots and high scalpers are in the center. (This equipment, of course, is for a trotter.) In the back row are a set of cottons (in the box) a set of bandages, a stiff bristle brush and a soft bristle brush, a rubber curry comb behind a body sponge with a tack sponge to the right, a can of talcum powder, a tube of metal polish (in front of the tack sponge), a bar of saddle soap with a hoof pick in front of it and a scraper at the extreme right.

action; but that is for the trainer to decide. The groom's job is to report these findings.

I suppose the proper way to begin this chapter is by reviewing briefly the tools of the caretaking trade. They are many and quite varied. Later on, I will discuss many of them in detail, but for the moment it is probably sufficient to identify and catalog them for future reference.

First of all, there is the equipment used on and worn by the horse (Fig. 80). This will include the harness and, usually, a harness bag for storage as well as the various related items such as bits, boots, bridles and hobbles. There will be a feed tub and two or more pails. One pail will be used exclusively for watering the horse while the others will be used for bathing the horse, cleaning boots and other equipment and for the other jobs that are part of the regular stable procedure.

There will be a tack trunk in which most of the equipment will be stored. Properly, there will be a platform of some type on which the tack trunk will stand. The platform will be a couple of inches off the ground and will keep the bottom of the trunk from becoming wet and possibly rotting out.

In the tack trunk will usually be found a body brush (soft bristles), a mane and tail brush (stiff bristles), a curry comb, occasionally a metal mane and tail comb, and rub cloths, all of which are used in cleaning up the horse. There will also be a scraper, a device which, as the name indicates, is used to scrape water and sweat off the horse's body.

Each trainer has his own opinions regarding some of these items and thus not all of them will be found in all stables. For instance, I do not like a stiff brush or a mane and tail comb. As a matter of fact, I do not permit my grooms ever to use a mane and tail comb and I would prefer that they use their hands rather than a stiff brush in cleaning out manes and tails. Stiff brushes, no matter how expertly used, have a tendency to pull hair out of the mane and tail and I have found that a man's hands are worth more than any brush or comb in cleaning out a horse's mane or tail.

In addition to the rub cloths which are made of linen or cotton and are used in rubbing the horse's body, there will be other assorted cloths which will be used, both wet and dry, for cleaning and polishing equipment. The tack trunk will also contain a number of sponges. These will consist of one or more large, wool body sponges and several smaller sponges called tack sponges which are used, as the name indicates, to wash and clean the tack.

There will usually be a hoof pick (a screwdriver is a good substitute), a pair of scissors, a pair of wire cutters, safety pins, rubber bands, screw eyes and a lock and key for the trunk.

In addition, there will be the various legal medicines which the trainer has approved for use on the horse. This might consist of a bottle of leg brace, a soothing lotion of some type, and some heel salve. Naturally, there will be a bar or can of saddle soap and some leather softener for use in working on the harness and other leather equipment. There will probably be a can of talcum powder, a supply of salt, and a box of oatmeal or a can of white shoe polish to be used in cleaning white felt boots.

Hanging near the tack trunk will be the blankets and coolers, the number depending on the climate in the particular area. Usually there will be at least two coolers and one breezer. The only difference between a cooler and a breezer is that the breezer is lighter. All are made of wool.

For use in cleaning out or bedding the stall, there will be a fork and a muck basket. The number of prongs or tines in the fork will depend on the material being used for bedding the stall. If straw is being used, a 5-tine fork will be about right. If sawdust or shavings are being used, more and closer tines will be required.

For leading the horse and working with him around the stall, there will be a shank and a set of cross ties. The shank is usually made of leather with a chain link section at the snap end. The cross ties are usually chain link and there is a snap on each end. Sometimes they are run through a hollow plastic hose so that a horse will not injure himself if he should get over one.

There are two cross ties and one end of each snaps into a screw eye on the wall of the stall. The other end snaps into the side rings on the halter. They are used to restrict the movement of the horse in the stall.

In addition to one or more sets of cottons and bandages, in which the horse will be "done up and put away," there will also be items of a general nature such as rakes, electric clippers, washing machines and diathermy or other machines which are part of the stable operation and available to the individual groom as necessary.

Now that I have described the equipment which will be used, it is time to start writing about the duties of a groom. There are many duties but one of the first and most important is that of keeping the stall clean. A dirty stall not only reflects adversely on the reputation of the groom but on that of the trainer and owner as well. In addition, a dirty stall is uncomfortable and unhealthy for the horse.

There is no excuse for a dirty stall and the groom who "cuts and covers,"—which is the expression used to describe shaking out dry straw on one side of the stall and throwing it over wet straw on the other side—isn't kidding anybody but himself. He might fool even a good trainer for a day or two, but no longer than that and he would very likely soon find himself looking for other employment.

Most stalls are bedded with straw, although cost and availability, or even the preference of the individual trainer, may result in stalls being bedded with wood sawdust or shavings. I have no complaint with either of the latter, especially if the right type of sawdust is used, and will comment on both later.

Depending on the size and weight of the bales, which will vary, it requires about two bales of straw to bed an average-size stall properly. Starting from scratch, the groom takes his fork and breaks up the flecks of straw and works them into an even bedding over the entire surface. At times, the groom may have to use his hands to break up the straw before he can spread it properly with his fork.

The bedding must be deep enough to be comfortable, to provide a good cushion for the horse when he lies down and to keep him as clean and neat as possible. At the same time, it shouldn't be so deep that it is awkward for the horse to get around in it.

In bedding a stall, one of the first things to learn is to pat the straw gently with each stroke of the fork. In this manner a flat, smooth bed will result and the stall will stay much better than if a fork is used as a rake and pulled through the straw in an effort to level it out.

An intelligent groom will soon learn to bed a stall properly. The main thing is that it should be comfortable and if the stall looks to the groom as though he would be willing to lie down in it himself, it is probably good enough for the horse.

Very often the stall must be mucked out while the horse is in it and special pains must be taken when this is the case (Fig. 81). Some grooms like to tie the horse in the cross ties when they muck out. Others prefer to close the door and permit the horse to move freely about the stall. The method used is usually determined by the reaction of the horse. If the horse is quieter, more contented and easier to work with one way than the other, then that method is employed.

Working with his back to the horse as much as possible, the

Fig. 81. When cleaning out the stall with the horse in the cross-ties, the groom keeps his back to the horse as much as possible to avoid the possibility of injuring the horse with a fork tine. This stall is bedded with sawdust which the author considers an acceptable substitute for straw.

good groom sifts the manure and wet straw out of the clean straw and deposits it in the muck basket. At this time he usually banks the clean straw that he is going to use again around the walls of the stall and leaves the center of the stall open so that it can dry out as much as possible.

At the same time, it is usually best to leave a light covering of straw beneath the horse if he is in the cross ties. It is always good to have a little something for the horse to stand on other than bare ground.

Working around the horse so that the fork tines are never pointed in the direction of the horse's legs, the groom clears the center of the stall and observes its condition. If it appears to be wet, it is a good practice to sprinkle some dry lime which will serve not only to help dry the bottom of the stall but will also eliminate odors and, to some degree, cut down the possibility of infection.

Some horses will get in the habit of relieving themselves in a certain part of the stall and, if this is the case, it is well to devote a little extra attention to this spot. Other horses will develop the habit of pawing in the stall and digging holes, usually near the door but also in other places, depending on the horse and the individual circumstances. When the stall is mucked out, such uneven holes or spots must be smoothed out or refilled.

I have also noticed that some horses will govern their personal habits according to the way their stall is kept. If they are being cared for by a neat, conscientious groom, it seems that they will make a special effort to keep the stall clean. But if the same horse is in the hands of a poor groom who does not keep a neat, tidy stall, the horse will often fall into the same habit.

I think I should say right here that it isn't either necessary or, in some cases, even desirable to use straw as bedding. In many areas, wood sawdust and shavings are used with excellent results. Sometimes peat moss is used, although I don't like it as much as sawdust or shavings.

If you can get good quality shavings or sawdust, either makes fine bedding. I am always happy to get a good grade of green sawdust for bedding. By green sawdust, I mean dust that is fresh from the saw and not kiln-dried. Green dust carries just enough natural moisture to make it very good for a horse's feet. It is hard to beat good pine, oak or cedar sawdust as a proper bedding.

The same holds true of shavings and they, too, should come directly from the saw if at all possible. Actually, I prefer dust to shavings because shavings will get in the mane and tail and it is sometimes quite a chore to get them out without pulling too hard and thus running the risk of pulling out some of the mane or tail.

If I can get the right kind of sawdust, I like it fully as well as I do straw. It makes for a neat, tidy stall and really works out very well. There are cases where straw might be preferable, such as training in an extremely cold climate or something like that, but other than that I do not think there is much difference between straw and a good grade of sawdust.

If a stall is bedded with shavings or sawdust, especially the latter, the stall cleaning chore must be handled a little differently. For instance, a closer-tined fork must be used because the droppings will be more difficult to remove without the "body" that straw provides. At the same time a rake will be used much more

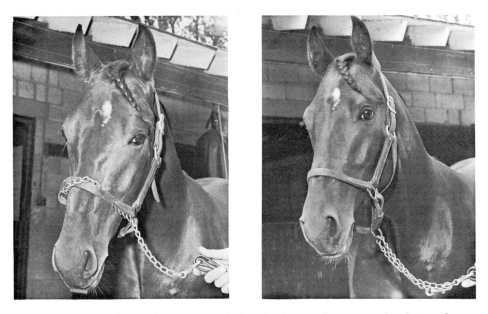

Fig. 82. The usual manner in which a shank is used is to run the chain end through the halter ring on the left side and then over the nose, fastening it into the halter ring on the right side. A variation of this is to twist the chain once around the nose band as illustrated at the left. Another accepable way of using a shank with well-mannered horses is to run the chain end through the bottom ring of the halter, right, and then double it back and snap it into the chain part of the shank near the leather.

often with a sawdust stall than with a straw stall. The stall surface must be smooth and level and the rake is the ideal tool for accomplishing this.

Quite a bit of a groom's time will be spent leading his horse on the end of a shank and this is as good a place as any to describe the proper use of this piece of equipment. Most racing stable shanks are made of leather and have a length of link chain and a snap on one end. A good groom will learn never to abuse the authority which this chain gives him.

The chain end of a shank should be run through the halter ring on the left side, across the bridge of the horse's nose (Fig. 82), and snapped into the halter ring on the right side. By exerting a little pressure on the shank, the groom is able to get the horse's attention and at the same time has a means of handling the horse without punishing him unduly.

The shank chain may be twisted once around the nose band of the halter as a means of keeping it in proper position and to lessen the harshness. I do not think this is usually necessary, although I do not have any strong objection to it. I am unalterably opposed to putting the chain in the horse's mouth or over his gums as I see done from time to time. You are dealing here with the most sensitive part of the horse's anatomy and a chain can cause a sore that will affect the horse's reaction to the driving bit and thus lessen his value as a racing tool.

With most fillies and with some sensitive stallions or geldings that are timid about having something placed over their nose, the chain can be run through the bottom ring of the halter and then doubled back and snapped in at the place where the chain part of the shank begins. This also shortens the length of the chain which is often desirable.

When leading young horses, especially stallions, it is often a good idea for a groom to carry a stump of an old driving whip in his left hand. Something like this will serve to hold the horse's attention and will make some young stallions easier to lead. If such a device is carried, it must be remembered that its primary purpose is as an "attention-getter" and not for punishment. It is a helpful piece of equipment if employed in this manner.

Once the horse has been fed and watered and the stall mucked out, preparations are then begun for the day's work. Depending on the stable schedule, the horse may be walked, jogged, trained or raced on any given day. But whatever the schedule, the first step is always the same. The horse must be cleaned up. This consists of cleaning out the feet, brushing the body and cleaning and straightening the mane and tail. After the horse has been brushed, it is usually a good idea to go over his body with a rub cloth to remove any loose dirt.

Each foot is cleaned carefully (Fig. 83), either with a hoof pick or a screwdriver which, as I have already pointed out, is a good substitute. A pail or basket is placed on the floor close to the foot that is to be cleaned. The foot is picked up and held over the receptacle so that any debris will fall into it and not on the floor of the freshly-cleaned stall. Any clay that drops out of a foot that has been packed the night before will be tossed into the muck basket.

The best way to use a hoof pick or screwdriver is to work first around the rim of the shoe. This cleans the outer edge and

Fig. 83. A hoof pick is used to clean the bottom of the foot. It is important to hold the foot over a receptacle so that dirt and debris do not fall on the stall floor. The same precaution is taken when the foot is being packed with clay.

loosens up the rest of the dirt which will come out easier since it no longer has the inside edge of the shoe to cling to. The proper procedure then is to go through the cleft of the frog with the cleaning tool loosening up any material that may have become packed in these areas.

The next step is to clean the horse's body. Three basic tools are used, two brushes and a curry comb. One brush has soft bristles and is known as a body brush. As the name indicates, it is used on all parts of the body. The second brush has comparatively stiff bristles and is known as a mane and tail brush. It is used on the mane and tail, although, as I have said, I would prefer that a groom use his fingers and a soft brush rather than a stiff brush on the mane and tail. The curry comb, which may be either rubber or metal, is roughly the size of a man's hand and usually has a strap going around it through which the groom inserts his hand. It thus fits in the hand and is used to stir the hair and loosen the skin prior to brushing.

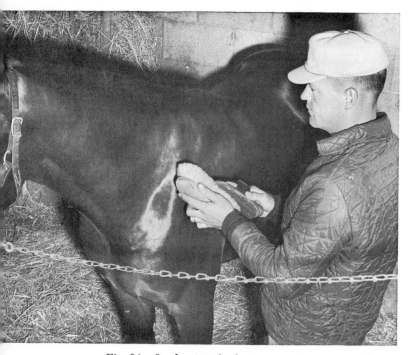

Fig. 84. In cleaning the horse, a good groom uses both a brush and a curry comb as shown here. In the text, the author describes how brush and comb achieve a fast, smooth rhythm when properly used.

I prefer a rubber curry comb because it is softer on a horse and doesn't scratch the skin as easily. But actually, it depends on how it is used as to whether it will cause a horse any discomfort. A good groom can use a metal curry comb and not scratch a hair. An inexperienced groom should always use a rubber comb.

The first thing to be done in cleaning a horse up is to snap him into the cross ties. Work begins around the head and a body brush is used. A curry comb is only used from the neck back. It is too harsh a tool to be used around the head, even if it is a rubber comb.

In using the body brush around the head, or anywhere on the horse's body for that matter, care should always be taken to brush in the direction the hair is growing. This is easily determined by examining the horse's coat and inexperience in this respect will give itself away because there is nothing that will show up on a horse quicker than the hair being brushed the wrong way. Instead of lying flat, hair that has been brushed "against the grain" will stand out and will keep the horse from

having the "slick look" that is always the hallmark of a top caretaker.

The body is brushed next and the proper technique is to go
over a portion of the body with the curry comb stirring up the
hair and working the dirt to the surface and then following
up with the body brush to remove that dirt (Fig. 84).

There are two operations involved, but in actual practice
the experienced groom combines them into one. He works with
the brush in one hand and the curry comb in the other. He
strokes the body with the brush and then brings it across the
face of the comb removing dirt from the brush. After several
strokes he will tap the comb against the side of the stall to
remove excess dirt from it. In changing sides, the groom will
usually switch the brush and comb from one hand to the other
and will soon achieve a rhythm in his work.

Anyone who appreciates rhythm will always enjoy watching
an experienced groom brush a horse in this manner. Almost as
fast as the eye can follow, the brush flashes over a portion of
the coat and the comb follows it in the same motion removing
from the brush the dirt the comb has stirred up.

In brushing the horse, care should always be taken, as I have
said before, to brush with the grain of the hair. No set rule can
be laid down in this respect because the hair will grow in different directions on different parts of the body. But a good
groom will determine these variances the first few times he
works on a horse and it should never give him any trouble
thereafter.

The body is usually brushed first and then the legs. In working on the legs, the body brush is usually all that is required,
although if a horse has caked mud or something like that on
his legs, a stiff brush may be used to help loosen the dirt and
clean the hair.

Once the body has been brushed, the next step is to clean and
straighten the mane and tail. A little extra time should be devoted
to the mane and tail because, to a considerable extent, they
emphasize the beauty of the horse. A naturally "flowing mane and
tail" lends something of a majestic air to the horse and is a matter
of justifiable pride to the owner, trainer and groom involved.

There is a proper technique involved in working on the mane

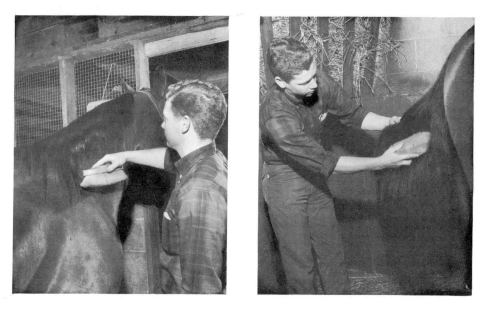

Fig. 85. Proper techniques to be used in brushing the mane and tail are illustrated briefly here and described in detail in the text. The tail should always be brushed with a short stroke out away from the body. The mane should always lay on the right side.

and tail. In brushing the tail (Fig. 85), I recommend standing close to and a little to one side of the horse's rump. The tail is then grasped in the left hand and the brush is held in the right.

Prior to this, however, the groom is expected to go through both mane and tail with his fingers to remove as much trash and other debris as he can before using the brush. Pieces of straw, hay and shavings can be removed quickly and easily in this manner, leaving only the finer debris to be removed by the brush.

In brushing manes and tails, caution must be exercised not to use long, deep, fast strokes. Such tactics will only result in the hair itself pulling out and the horse will soon have a sparse mane and tail. Instead of being one of the best looking horses on the track, he will be one of the poorest.

In working on the tail, it is best to use a short stroke with a pulling motion out away from the tail. This will bring whatever debris there is to the surface enabling it to be removed quickly and effortlessly. If a tail is brushed straight down, the foreign material that is in it will be forced deeper into the hair and will become that much more difficult to remove. The short stroke out and away from the tail removes the debris and at the same time doesn't tangle and pull the hair.

The mane should always lay on the right side (Fig. 85). In some cases, it will become unruly and try to fall over to the left side. In this case, the mane can be done up in braids until it becomes trained to lay the proper way. Under these circumstances the mane brush may be dipped in water and the top of the mane brushed over to the right side to encourage it to fall the right way. The mane is brushed in much the same way the tail is. Straw, shavings and other debris should be removed first by hand and then the brush should be used in completing the job.

The foretop, which is the hair running down the middle of the horse's forehead between his ears, is also brushed at this time. The foretop is sometimes braided (Fig. 86) as a matter of convenience but when this is done the braids should not be left in too long. The reason for this is that a foretop or even a mane that is done up for too long a period can be injurious to the health of the hair. At times it will result in the hair falling out, so all braids should be undone and redone from time to time rather than left in permanently.

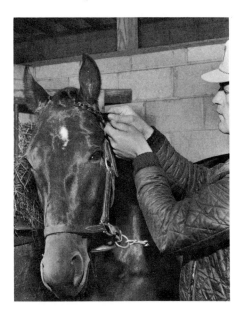

Fig. 86. The foretop is sometimes braided as a matter of convenience. A braided foretop or mane should not be left that way too long since it will sometimes result in the hair falling out.

Between the top of the foretop and the mane itself there is an area about two inches in length (Fig. 87) that should be kept trimmed or clipped. This is where the bridle rests and it is important that there not be any hair in this area in which the bridle might become entangled.

If this job is done carelessly, too much can be taken off the foretop in front or the area can extend too far back toward the mane and the next thing you know you'll have a clipped area six or eight inches long instead of two or three. This detracts from the horse's appearance and gives no practical benefit.

This area is trimmed either with a pair of scissors or an electric clipper. A good groom can usually do this by himself if he has a quiet horse. But an inexperienced groom, or an experienced one who has a nervous horse, should probably request help from one of his fellow workers. The helper can steady the horse's head while the groom in charge does the trimming.

Fig. 87.   An area two inches or more in length between the top of the foretop and the mane, left, should always be kept trimmed or clipped. This is where the bridle rests and there should never be any hair in which the bridle might become entangled. The actual clipping operation is illustrated at the right.

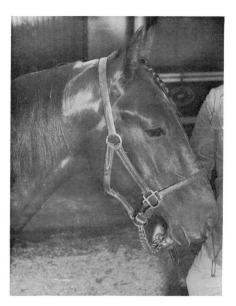 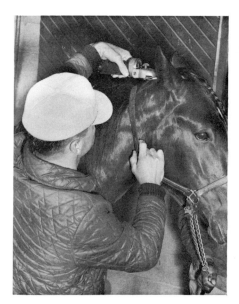

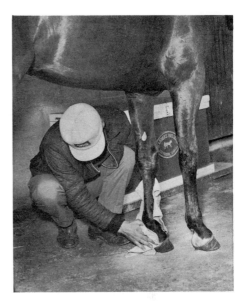

Fig. 88. In the author's opinion, one of the groom's most vital jobs is keeping the horse's heels clean and dry. It is recommended that a cloth, as illustrated, or a soft brush be used.

There is one other area of the horse's body that requires special attention and I think every good groom should learn early in his career that he has not finished his job until he performs this chore. This is the care of the horse's heels (Fig. 88), and I am a stickler for insisting that they be cleaned thoroughly and kept clean and dry at all times.

If this isn't done, you will soon run into sore heels and cracked heels and, ultimately, unsoundness. All that is required is that the heels be kept clean and dry by rubbing them with a cloth or soft brush. A great many grooms have a tendency to overlook this part of their job which is why I want to emphasize its importance. Cracked heels lead to sore horses and then to lame horses. And lame horses aren't any good for owner, trainer or groom.

When the horse has been properly groomed, he is ready for his daily work. On some days there will be nothing but walking or jogging, chores which the groom is called on to handle in most cases. On other days the horse will be trained and on some days he will be raced, either in the afternoon or evening. In any event, let me review what occurs with reference to handling the horse if he is scheduled to go to the track.

The horse is snapped in the cross ties and whatever boots he wears are put on him. These boots were cleaned, scrubbed and powdered after the previous work and close attention should be paid to the way they are put on and adjusted. The groom should look for areas where chafe marks or sore spots may be developing and if he sees any he should report the fact to the trainer or barn foreman. In adjusting the boots, all of which have been described by Joe O'Brien in his chapter, special pains should be taken to follow the recommended procedures and to avoid the pitfalls that Joe has mentioned.

For my own part, I think it will be enough to say that no boot should ever be buckled so tight that it pinches a horse nor so loose that it slides down from its proper position possibly setting up an irritation.

Once the horse is booted, the routine of harnessing begins (Fig. 89). With the horse in the cross ties, a towel or pad is placed on the horse's back where the saddle of the harness will rest. This pad is used to cushion the saddle and to minimize the possibility of chafing.

The harness is hanging outside the stall on a harness hook which is usually attached to a pulley so that the harness may be raised up out of the way when not in use. The harness may or may not be protected by being placed in a harness bag. The harness consists of the breast collar, of which the traces are part, the driving lines, saddle, girth, and crupper or turn back.

The breast collar is separate from the rest of the harness and is put on first. The breast collar, as the name indicates, fits across the breast and has a strap that goes over the shoulder just back of the withers. The breast collar is put on from the left side. The shoulder strap is brought up over the withers and is buckled into the other end of the breast collar on the left side.

The traces, long leather straps that will eventually be fastened to the cart or sulky, are part of the breast collar. While the collar is being adjusted, the traces are folded and tied within themselves and hang near the shoulder as the breast collar is put on. Later, they will be used to hitch the horse and are the part of the harness by which the horse pulls the cart or sulky.

Now the remainder of the harness is placed on the horse's back from the left side. The saddle is placed just back of the pad or towel so that there will be some slack which is necessary in adjusting the crupper. The crupper is a loop at the end of the back strap. The back strap is a leather strap that runs from the saddle to the crupper and connects the two. Taken together the combination of the crupper and back strap is known as the turn back. The horse's tail goes within the loop of the crupper and thus the harness is prevented from sliding forward.

In adjusting the crupper, the groom stands at the left side and toward the rear of the horse and takes the crupper in his left hand and the horse's tail in his right hand. He catches the tail from underneath and his hand encircles it near the base so that the hair will not get tangled up in the crupper. Then he lifts the tail and pushes it through the crupper, at the same time sliding the crupper down so that it falls into place just beneath the base of the tail.

After the crupper is in place, the groom lifts the saddle forward which automatically adjusts the crupper in the desired position beneath the tail. The groom should lift the saddle forward and not slide it. If he slides the saddle forward he will be going against the grain of the hair which is both irritating to the horse and unsightly. The proper place for the saddle after the crupper has been adjusted is just back of the withers.

Once the saddle is in place, care must be taken that the girth, which is the strap that encircles the body, be fastened in line and well forward on the horse. This can be done by going to the right side or very often by using the hand to adjust the girth under the horse while still on the left side. The thing to remember is that the girth strap should be straight up and down and not inclining either forward or backward. If the crupper is tight, the saddle positioned just back of the withers and the girth strap running straight up and down, then the harness may be said to be correctly positioned.

The reason it is important to place the saddle as far forward as possible is that the saddle will never slide forward during jogging, training or racing, only backward. And if it does slide backward a little, it will be going with the hair and will not set up an irritation or a sore spot.

The next step is to tighten the girth. The girth strap hangs on the right side, and is grasped beneath the horse's body, brought to the left side and buckled in whatever hole is the proper one for that particular horse.

After a groom has been working with a horse for a while, he knows what girth strap hole he is using and the hole he uses

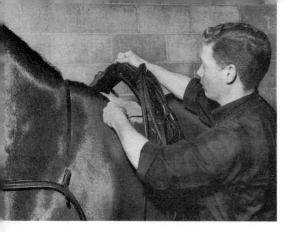

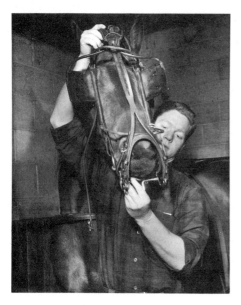

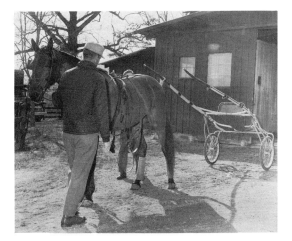

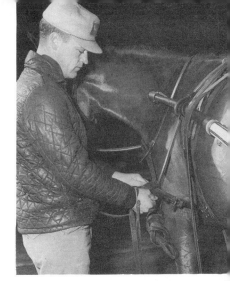

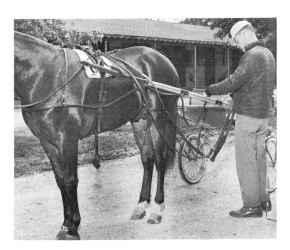

Fig. 89. Some of the steps involved in harnessing the horse for the day's work are illustrated in this series of photographs. Left hand page, upper left, the saddle of the harness is placed on the horse's back. A towel is used to minimize chafing. Upper right, the girth is buckled and adjusted. Center left, the bridle is put on. Center right, the throat latch is fastened and, lower left, is shown properly positioned. On this page, upper left, the training cart is brought into position behind the horse. Upper right, the traces are undone as the first step toward hitching. Center left, the traces are fastened. Center right, the horse is tied down and, lower right, checked up.

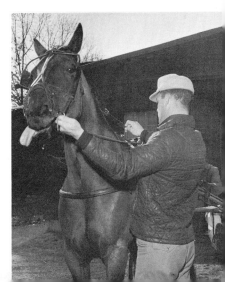

will vary only if there is a change in the horse's physical condition to the degree that he becomes stouter or thinner. But if a groom is working with a new horse, he must take extra pains in this respect.

For instance, some horses will swell up when the girth strap is fastened and directly the girth will be loose. These are the personal idiosyncrasies that some horses have and that grooms must learn in order to do their jobs well. As I will mention later, it is sometimes well to tighten the girth in two stages, once at this point and again later just before the horse is ready to go.

The girth, incidentally, should be adjusted so that it is firm around the horse's body but at the same time it must not be tightened to a point where it is uncomfortable. In this respect, a girth is comparable to a belt that a man might wear. If a man pulled his own belt three notches tighter than he is accustomed to wearing it, he would soon know how a horse feels in a tight girth. This is an area that is often abused. Very many times I have seen powerful grooms pulling a girth much tighter than necessary.

After the girth is fastened, the next step is to put the bridle on the horse. This is done properly with the groom standing at the left side of the horse's head. He takes the crown or top of the bridle in the right hand and holds the two bits, the driving bit and the overcheck bit, close together in the left hand. Then he slips the bits into the horse's mouth, over his tongue, and pulls the bridle over the ears and into place.

Occasionally you will run into horses that are a little touchy around the head and ears. In such cases, it is sometimes a good idea to unfasten the bridle from one side of the driving bit. This will enable the bridle to be slipped over the horse's head without having to fold the ears back abruptly. The bridle can then be buckled back into the bit.

When the bridle is in place, the throat latch, a strap which runs under the throat connecting both sides of the bridle, is fastened. The throat latch should be adjusted quite loosely so that if a horse raises his head a little high or pulls his chin in quite a bit it won't bind against his throat.

The next step is to buckle the lines into the driving bit. The opposite end of each line is for the driver's hands. Unless you are using some special gear such as a four-ring overcheck or

Fig. 90. The hand holds, leather loops attached to the driving lines and through which the driver puts his hands when driving the horse, must be adjusted to the convenience of the individual. The author demonstrates the proper adjustment for him. The adjustment will vary from person to person and should always be checked prior to a workout or race.

a ring martingale, the only openings through which the lines pass, from the bit to the driver's hands, are the terrets. Terrets are similar to screw eyes, only larger, and there is one screwed into each side of the saddle, just below the top. The driving line on each side goes through a terret.

At this time, the hand holds on the line are adjusted in the event that this is necessary. The hand holds are the loops (Fig. 90) through which the driver puts his hands when he drives the horse. They are adjusted according to the convenience of the driver and in different places depending on whether a cart or sulky is being used and whether the driver uses hand holds when the horse is hitched to a cart.

The horse is now harnessed and bridled and all that remains is to hitch him to the cart or sulky. His first trip is usually to the cart so we will hitch this horse to that vehicle. Actually, there is virtually no difference in the method of hitching.

The horse is led from the stall and will be hitched either in the aisleway of the barn or outside if there is no aisleway. Two men are required to hitch a horse properly. One holds the horse at the head while the other gets the cart and brings it forward until it is in position back of the horse. The cart is brought forward and the shafts are passed through the shaft tugs which are small leather loops attached to each side of the saddle. The ends of the shafts are then inserted into the shaft thimbles, sometimes called the point straps, which keep the cart from moving any farther forward.

One end of a shaft thimble is a leather strap which is fastened to the saddle. The other end is made in the shape of a large thimble, thus the name, and the points of the shaft fit into the thimble. The strap itself is adjustable and thus provides a certain degree of leeway in the distance the back of the cart or sulky will be from the horse.

Some trainers want their horses placed relatively far back in the cart or sulky shafts while others want their horses farther forward. The shaft thimble or point strap is adjusted to accommodate the particular trainer's desire in this respect.

The next step in hitching is to fasten the traces. The traces are long leather straps, usually 5/8ths of an inch wide, that come as part of the breast collar. Until now, they had been folded up and tied within themselves and are hanging near the back edge of the breast collar. The reason they have been folded, of course, is so that they will not drag on the ground.

Now they are undone and passed back through the leather loops that are attached at intervals on the inside of the shaft for that purpose. Most carts will have three such loops. The traces are then fastened to a hook at the very back and on the inside of the shaft. There are slots in each trace for this purpose. Since there are more than one of these slots, an adjustment can be made that will position the horse properly in the sulky or cart. But in all cases the traces are fastened to bring the vehicle up to a proper relationship with the saddle and the thimbles. In making this adjustment, caution should be taken to permit enough leeway so that the breast collar does not bind the horse.

The last step in hitching is to fasten the wrap straps which are sometimes called the tie downs. This is also a good time to check the fit of the girth. Because, as I have said, horses have a tendency to "swell up" when the girth is first fastened, some good grooms make it a practice to wait and make the final adjustment of the girth just before they fasten the wrap straps. By this time, most of the harnessing has been completed and the horse is more relaxed than he was in the beginning and less likely to "swell up." One groom can actually tie a horse down, but if a second one is available it is recommended that two do the job. It is easier that way and is the general practice in most stables.

The wrap straps are strong, single straps that are fastened to the girth one on each side and which slide through the loops in the bottom of the girth. Each strap is wrapped securely around one of the cart shafts and buckled, whereupon the horse is said to be "tied down."

The man on the right usually ties down first. He takes the wrap strap on that side in his right hand and loops it once around the shaft in back of the shaft tug, which is the leather loop through which the cart or sulky shaft passes. Then he brings it to the front side of the carrier and wraps it around the shaft, usually twice but occasionally three times depending on the size of the horse. A smaller horse might require more turns around the shaft. The wrap strap is then buckled into place and the horse is properly "tied down" on that side.

It is customary for the wrap strap to encircle the traces on each side. Most good trainers have it done this way because it is an additional safety measure and also keeps the traces from flopping around.

The groom on the left side waits for the first man to complete his chore. The first one will usually say, "Down here," to indicate that he has finished, or perhaps the man on the left side will inquire, "Are you down?" When the reply is in the affirmative, the man on the left "ties down" and the procedure is completed.

If two men are doing this jog and hitching to a sulky rather than a cart, it is a good idea for the one on the right to go to the front of the horse and place both hands on the sulky shafts while the man on the left is completing the tie down as this helps even the shafts for the final adjustment. However, if this procedure is followed, care should be taken not to pull the shafts overly hard thus putting the horse in a vice or an uncomfortable position with regard to his harness and sulky. I have seen this procedure abused on many occasions with the result that the horse has been made uncomfortable and the action of his body restricted.

A proper tie down should hold the shafts good and firm, but it should not be so tight that it binds the horse and makes him uncomfortable. As in so many other areas, common sense is an important factor.

While some experimentation is required with a colt that has just entered training, in actual practice the horse's groom knows exactly how the wrap straps should fit and will tell the groom who is assisting him how they go. For instance, he might advise the other groom to take two wraps around the sulky shaft or perhaps three and then buckle in the third hole or maybe the fourth hole or whatever the case may be.

It is a matter of choice with the trainer whether the loops that are made around the shaft by the wrap strap start or end in front of or behind the shaft tug. As I said, I prefer to make my first loop in back of the tug and tie down in front of it. I feel that this provides a little more reinforcement in front where I would need it most if I had to take a pretty good hold of the horse for some reason. Other trainers, however, tie down from front to back.

It is a good idea at this point to make a final, last minute check of equipment. The good groom will make certain that the boots and harness are buckled, that all buckled straps are through the keepers and that nothing in the way of equipment is hanging loose.

Now the horse is ready to be checked up and there is a right and a wrong way to do it. I have seen grooms who would simply grab the check and pull the horse's head back from the bit and fasten the check. Invariably, this angers the horse and I do not think it is a good idea to get a horse angry just before you are going to jog or train him.

The proper method is to take the end of the check in the right hand while placing the left beneath the horse's chin and at the same time lifting the chin up a little. This provides sufficient clearance for the check to be fastened quickly and effortlessly. If a groom will learn to lift the horse's head and not snap it suddenly backward by pulling on the check itself, the horse will very soon learn to stand quietly to be checked.

The check, which is also called the check rein or overcheck, fastens to the check hook (some of the old timers still call this a "water hook" because it was unfastened when they stopped to give their horse a drink) which is located on the top of the saddle. In connection with checking a horse up, there should be a small, round piece of rubber, roughly the size of but thicker than a fifty-cent piece with a slot in it. This is called a keeper and is always kept in place on the check hook. It is removed just before the check is fastened and then replaced after the horse is checked up. It keeps the overcheck from flipping off and is rather important because there have been a good many races lost just because a horse got his overcheck down. A good groom is always careful to see that the keeper goes on the overcheck hook after the check itself is in place.

Now the horse is completely ready for the day's work and since this is the first trip, the groom will probably jog him until the trainer is ready to go the workout mile. The groom should know the proper way to get on and off the cart as illustrated in Fig. 78 in Billy Haughton's chapter on driving as well as in Fig. 91 in this chapter.

I think one of the important things at this stage is that the horse be permitted to walk off instead of leaving the barn area at the trot or pace. The whole idea is to keep the horse as relaxed as possible so that he will be more pleasant to jog.

The same thing applies to leaving the track and returning to the barn. The horse should always be slowed up a short distance before reaching the barn so that he learns to walk back to it. This tends to relax a horse and he doesn't start fighting either the trainer or the groom. Followed over a long period of time, this practice is a great help in keeping a horse well-mannered and of good disposition.

I am not going to go into great detail regarding the proper way to jog a horse. The best way for a groom to learn this is through observation and actual practice and by following explicitly the instructions of the trainer for whom he is working. All of us have different things we believe in with respect to jogging horses and what suits one of us might not apply to the next one.

I do believe the general rules are the same. All horses should be jogged with both hands on the lines and both feet in the stirrups. Horses should be jogged on the outside rim of the track and caution should be exercised in entering and leaving the track and in making turns of any kind. The jogging rate itself will be established by the trainer and inexperienced grooms will soon learn the proper techniques by jogging with those who have been doing it for many years.

When I mention the differences in practices within stables, the proposition of whether a groom should jog a horse with or without hand holds comes to mind. Some trainers do not permit grooms to jog with hand holds because they think grooms tend to be a little heavy-handed and that their horses might develop into pullers as a result. Hand holds, naturally, enable anyone to put a little more pressure on the bit and thus on the horses's mouth.

Personally, I jog all my own horses with hand holds and like my grooms to do so. I find that it gives them a little more control over the horse and I have never found that it made pullers out of any of them. Nobody hates a puller any worse than I do, but I have never found this to be a cause and thus prefer that my grooms be permitted to exercise this additional degree of control over the horse.

Another thing that falls in this category is the use of kicking straps on 2-year-olds. I don't necessarily feel that they need kicking straps and if I were jogging the horses I probably wouldn't use them except in special cases.

But if a horse is going to be frisky and start kicking and playing, he will probably do it the first time he is out of the stall in the morning and this is when the groom is usually driving him. A groom can't be expected to be quite as adept as a trainer at handling a situation like this and therefore I think it is a good practice to use a kicking strap. It could keep a colt from getting a foot over the shaft and crippling him.

I know there are other trainers who do not share this opinion and that is one of the reasons why I do not intend to go into too much specific detail regarding this phase of a groom's work. He should learn to follow the practices laid down by the trainer he is working for and these will vary.

Let us assume that the horse we have under discussion is being

Fig. 91. The proper steps to follow in switching control of the horse from the driver to groom (or vice versa) are illustrated in this series of photographs. In the upper panel, the driver dismounts and walks toward the horse's head with the lines in his hands while the groom maintains control over the horse. In the center panel, the groom reaches for the lines with his right hand, left, while the driver circles behind him, right, to take control of the horse. There is never a second when either the driver or groom does not have hold of the horse's head. In the lower panel, control of the horse has passed from the groom to the driver, left, whereupon the groom walks back and gets on the cart.

worked and is going to train two or more heats before being cooled out and put away. The groom jogs the horse a couple of miles before the first heat in accordance with the stable schedule and then the trainer takes over and goes the first training mile.

The good groom will be at the draw gate watching his horse and the minute the trainer has finished the mile and starts back with the horse, the groom will be walking out to meet them. As soon as the trainer stops the horse, the groom will take hold of the lines, just back of the bit, with his left hand and will reach back with his right hand and uncheck the horse if he is going to walk him off the track. However, if the groom is going to drive the horse off the track he will not uncheck him until he is back in the barn area and is ready to unhitch.

Special care should be taken when control of the horse is handed from the trainer to the groom or vice versa (Fig. 91). This is something that we all get a little careless about sometimes and very often a little special caution at this stage can keep a horse from getting away or from becoming scared or frightened. In my own stable, if I am taking the horse from the groom I go to the horse's head and have the groom dismount and hand me the lines. The groom then holds the horse's head until I am seated in the cart or sulky. The procedure is reversed if I have just finished driving the horse and the groom is about to take over. In this manner, the horse is never loose or in a position where he can get away.

When he gets back to the barn area, the horse is unhitched in front of the stall and the help of another groom is desirable. The first thing to do is to uncheck the horse after which the traces are unbuckled at the rear of each shaft. In doing this, the groom should either have the lines in his own hands or make certain that his helper does. There is never a time to be careless around a horse whether it is in a stall or on the track. There is always a time when a groom gets a little careless about some routine thing and that is when the horse jumps or shies and injures himself.

After the traces are unhooked, they are pulled through the carrier loops to the front and done up in a knot so that they won't drag on the ground. If the horse is wearing a kicking strap, it should be unfastened next. If the kicking strap is left fastened when you start to remove the cart, it could scare the horse and he might get loose with the cart half fastened to him.

As soon as the traces are unhooked and knotted and the kicking strap unfastened the wrap straps are unbuckled and the cart is backed off the horse. A good groom always backs the cart off the horse; he never leads the horse out of the cart.

The horse is then walked into the stall. If he is wearing a closed bridle, or a blind bridle as it also is called, it is a good idea to remove the bridle before going into the stall. A closed bridle will prevent a horse from seeing the sides of the stall door and he might run into it.

As soon as the horse is in the stall, the driving lines are unbuckled from the bit and hooked into the terret rings on the harness. If the bridle has not already been removed, that is the next step after which the horse's halter is put on and he is snapped into the cross ties.

The breast collar is then unbuckled on the left side and laid back across the saddle of the harness. The girth is then unbuckled and the harness slipped back six or eight inches after which the groom moves back and lifts the horse's tail with his right hand and withdraws the crupper from beneath the tail with the left hand. The harness is then pulled off the left side and hung up.

Once the harness is off, the horse gets a few swallows of cool water, perhaps a half dozen, and the groom goes to work to get his horse ready for the next training mile which is scheduled in approximately forty minutes.

A damp sponge is used to wipe the horse around the face and eyes. If the weather is especially hot, the sponge should be soaked in cold water and rubbed over the head and across the nose where it will cool the horse and freshen the air he is breathing.

The same sponge is then used to go lightly over the horse's body, wiping away excess sweat and harness marks. If the horse happened to be sweating a greal deal, a scraper might be used in addition to or instead of the sponge.

An important thing at this stage is to remember that everything is being done with cold water. Hot water is seldom used on a horse's face or body between heats unless there are special circumstances that required a horse to be steamed out or something like that. Hot water between heats relaxes a horse when it isn't time for him to relax and it opens pores when it isn't time for the pores to be opened.

After this is done, the horse gets a few more swallows of water and then the blanket or cooler is placed on him. Whatever is done in this respect is just enough to keep the horse's body warm and moist. The idea is to keep the horse from drying up or from developing a chill.

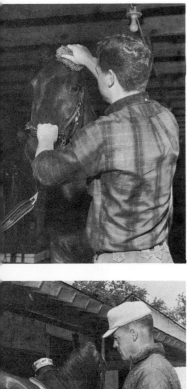

Fig. 92. After a horse is through training or racing, he is returned to his stall where his face and head, upper left, are sponged off with cool water. After that, weather permitting, he is taken outside and first sponged off, upper right, and then scraped, opposite, as described in the text.

There should be enough protection in the way of blanketing so that the muscles stay warm and the horse doesn't take a chill. But you don't want so much cover that the horse starts to sweat and heat up. Good judgment will indicate whether the horse has too much or too little covering.

All boots except quarter boots and scalpers should come off between heats. These boots have to be wiped out clean and perhaps a little talcum powder thrown on the inside surfaces. All body areas where the boots have touched must be checked to make certain that no chafing or soreness of any kind has developed and if something is developing, a little salve or lotion should be applied and a notation made to advise the trainer.

The reason I say that quarter boots and scalpers don't have to be removed between heats is that they are stationary on a horse's foot. All other boots involve areas in which there is movement or flexing of legs or muscles and there is danger of irritation, chafing or infection. All such boots should be kept soft, pliable and clean.

I imagine this is as important a factor as any in judging the ability of a groom. It involves cleanliness and equine hygiene because an irritation of any kind can lead to an infection and affect the horse's health. A sharp groom who watches these things closely and calls their presence to the immediate attention of a trainer is as valuable a man as there is in the organization.

The little things should be reported while they are still little. If they become big before they are reported, it is often too late. A groom who keeps the trainer informed not only is doing his job well, but the trainer begins to have confidence in the groom and if the man shows equal ability in the other phases of his profession, this is the one the trainer starts to think about when there is an opening for advancement. Close attention to this kind of detail, in other words, is one of the best ways for a groom to gain advancement leading toward a possible career as a trainer or driver.

After being stripped, the horse stands in the stall until it is time to hitch him again for the next heat. He is watered probably three times during this interval with perhaps a half dozen swallows each time.

Eventually the horse is harnessed, bridled and hitched up again and goes another training mile. The same routine is followed between all heats and after the last training mile the horse comes back to the barn and it is now the groom's job to unhitch him, cool him out and put him away for the day.

The first step after the race or training session is over is for the horse to be led into the stall and his head sponged off with cool water (Fig. 92) which will freshen him. The next step is for the horse to be stripped down as previously described. This time everything comes off including the scalpers and quarter boots.

Now the horse is ready to be bathed. Warm water should be used. Care should be taken not to use excessively hot water and the water should be tested by hand. It should be about the same temperature as a person would use in taking his own bath. I always recommend that my grooms throw a handful of salt in this water. Salt has certain antiseptic qualities which are highly desirable and I think it is a good idea to include a handful in a pail of bath water.

Usually the horse will be bathed, or showered as it is sometimes referred to, outside the stall, but if it is cold and windy it is done inside the stall. If done in the stall, care should be taken not to slop water around because that means extra work in bedding the stall.

The proper method of bathing a horse is to have one groom hold the horse by the halter while the other bathes him. The groom in charge does this by carrying his pail to the horse's head and starting to work from there. The head and face are carefully sponged off with special attention given to the ears, eyes and nostrils.

The body is sponged off next. The upper part of the body is done first and then the sides, the belly, the inside of the fore and hind legs, and then down all four legs. Once that is completed, the scraper is used to scrape the excess water off the body. The scraper, incidentally, should never be used below the horse's knee or hock.

After that, the horse is returned to the stall and put in the cross ties. The next task is to remove the excess water from both the body and the legs before going on with the cooling out process. Some grooms do this with rub cloths, but the smart groom will wring his sponge very dry and use it to go over the horse's body and legs at this stage. This will save him about two rub rags which would otherwise be soaked.

All the excess water should be wiped out of the hair over the entire surface of the body with special attention paid to the legs. After the excess water has been removed from the horse's coat and his body is beginning to get dry, a rub cloth is then used on both the body and legs.

This is when I like the groom to concentrate on the legs, especially the heels to be certain they are absolutely dry before

the horse is ever walked. I think any horse will cool out better if
he is rubbed until all excess moisture is out of his hair.

There isn't much secret about the proper way to rub a horse
down at this stage. All that is required is a good rub cloth, plenty
of "elbow grease", and a light, airy stroke. When you see a horse
whose coat literally shines and sparkles, it is the primary indication that a good groom is on the job. Rub cloths may be used
more than once without being washed, but it is usually a good
practice to wash them every day by tossing them into a pail
with a little suds or into an electric washing machine which most
stables carry these days. A rub cloth is useful until it wears out
and the only care it requires is to keep it clean and dry.

The next step is to cool the horse out. In the winter, this is
usually done right in the stall. In the summer, it is done by walking the horse outside the stall. The time required depends on
the kind of a day it is and how hot the horse is, that is, the
amount of energy he has expended on that particular day.

Even though the sun may be shining with equal intensity, it
requires a longer period to cool a horse out on a hot, humid
day than on a crisp, clear day. At the same time, it takes longer
after a horse has participated in a strenuous race than after a
light training session. Again, common sense is an important factor.

No matter where he is, what the weather conditions may be
or how strenuous his exercise may have been, the horse should
be blanketed while being cooled out. The number and weight
of the blankets depends on the temperature and the weather
conditions. There are a number of blanket types, the two most
common being the cooler and the breezer. Both are made of
wool. As far as I am concerned, wool is the only satisfactory
material so far produced for a horse blanket. It permits air circulation, dries freely and doesn't get sodden like other material.

A horse usually has at least three blankets, two coolers and a
breezer. He may have more depending on the climate. The only
difference between a cooler and a breezer is that the cooler is
heavier. The number and type of blankets used in cooling a horse
out depends on the weather. In real cold weather, two coolers
and perhaps even a third one will be used. In real hot weather,
perhaps only a breezer will be used. In my own stable, I do not
have any hard and fast rule regarding the amount of covering
used in cooling a horse out. This is a matter of judgment and

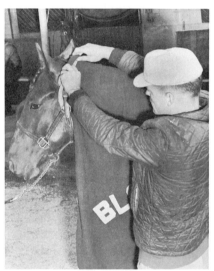

depends to a considerable extent on the weather and climatic conditions. It also depends on the condition of the horse and how strenuous his exercise has been.

The blanket is put on the horse from the forward end. (Fig. 93). Some blankets have a strap at the center in front. This strap fits over and forward of the ears and keeps the blanket from sliding backward. If the blanket doesn't have such a strap, it should be slipped under the top part of the halter and a roll or two taken in it at that point to keep it from sliding backward.

After the blanket is fastened at the top, it is pinned beneath the horse's neck in front. This is done by rolling the blanket beneath the neck and pinning it with a good, big safety pin. The reason for rolling the blanket is to avoid tearing it. A blanket that is pinned without being rolled is much more likely to tear. This is a very common error made in blanketing a horse.

The blanket is then pulled backward toward the horse's tail, but not to the degree that it is made too tight around the head. The reason a blanket is fastened at the front end first is that it will always work backward, never forward, and thus must always be secured in front.

If it is windy, the blanket should also be pinned beneath the horse's body. In extreme cases I have seen blankets pinned at the back to keep the wind from getting at the horse. Clothes pins are very often used instead of safety pins and are an acceptable substitute. A natural advantage is that blankets are much less likely to tear if clothes pins are used.

It is important that the blanket be adjusted so that it is even over the entire body. It is not only unsightly but also unhealthy for the horse to have one corner of the blanket hanging down and the other end up over his back.

The whole idea of blanketing a horse, either while he is being cooled out or when he is at rest in the stall, is to keep his body

Fig. 93. On the opposite page, Donald Holkem, the author's assistant trainer, who appears in many of the photographs in this chapter, demonstrates the proper method of blanketing a horse. The blanket is first laid over the hindquarters, upper left; then brought forward, upper right, to be adjusted at the front end first. The blanket is then slipped under the top part of the halter, left center, and a roll taken in it to keep it from sliding backward. The blanket is fastened beneath the neck with a clothespin, right center, after which it is adjusted in the rear, lower left. At lower right the horse is shown properly blanketed and ready to be walked to be cooled out.

as near to normal temperature as possible and thus from becoming chilled or overheated.

During the cooling out process, the blanket holds the body heat and does not permit the horse to cool out too fast or to develop a quick chill. When the horse is being cooled out in the stall in the winter, two or more blankets might be used at the start and removed at periodic intervals depending on how cold it is. Eventually, a horse is dry and does not require a blanket unless he normally wears a stable sheet while at rest in the stall as part of the routine of that stable. In blanketing a horse, a groom should use the same judgment he does in dressing himself. He wears his own clothes in accordance with weather conditions and so should the horse.

If it is winter and the horse is not being walked to cool out, the groom must rub him dry. He does this by folding back one end of the blanket at a time and rubbing the horse's coat with a rub cloth. About every 10 to fifteen minutes he offers the horse a few swallows of water and reduces the cover by removing a blanket or replacing it with a lighter one. The rule concerning water is, of course, that a hot horse should never have a great quantity of cold water. This can lead to founder and all informed horsemen are aware of this danger. The whole process of watering a horse out is to gradually give him enough water until he is satisfied so that when he is turned loose in a stall he will not consume more than a few swallows at a time.

After two or three of these rubbing sessions, the horse's hair will be thoroughly dry, the body cool to the touch and the horse watered out. This is a sign that the horse is cooled out.

In the summer, the horse is cooled out by being walked. During the time he is being walked, the horse is usually brought back to the stall at least once and usually twice at which time his body is rubbed briskly and he is given a few swallows of water. When the horse is being walked, he wears either a cooler or, if the weather is extremely hot and humid, a breezer. The horse is considered to be cooled out when the hair is thoroughly dry and the body cool to the touch. A good rule of thumb is that the properly cooled out horse looks, feels and acts exactly as he did that morning before his work day began.

The total time involved in putting a horse away—beginning from the moment he returns to the stall after a race or workout until he is cooled out, bandaged and turned loose in the stall—will run from a minimum of an hour and a half to two and a half or more hours if conditions demand it on a real hot, humid day or if the horse had especially strenuous exercise. I would say that the average time for afternoon racing would not be less than two hours. However, I do find that horses racing at night, when the weather is generally cooler, will not usually require that much time. Nevertheless, a horse that is put away in less than an hour and a half after a race has not, in my opinion, been put away properly.

When the horse is cooled out and returned to the stall, the groom should go over his body and legs with a body brush. The horse likes this. It freshens him up and makes him feel good after his exercise. It also improves his appearance.

Now there are two principal jobs remaining before the horse can be "put away" for the day or night. The feet must be packed and the legs bandaged. It may be that the trainer requires that neither of these things be done but it is a rare groom that neither has to pack feet nor bandage his horse's legs.

Before the horse's feet are packed they must be cleaned and washed. A water pail about half full is placed near the foot being worked on and the foot is lifted and held over the pail while it is washed with a sponge.

The feet are packed with clay of a type provided in the stable. This clay may be purchased from the feed man or the supply man and some trainers even have special sources that provide them with a certain type of clay year round. This is a matter of choice with the trainer and in that respect does not concern the groom. The feet are packed daily after the horse has been jogged, worked or raced, depending on what the schedule calls for. Each groom has his own "clay bucket," usually an ordinary water pail set aside for this purpose. There is also a wooden paddle or spatula, similar to the type used to stir paint.

Enough water must be worked into the clay to bring it to the proper consistency. If too much water is added, the resulting mixture will be too loose and will not "hold" in the horse's foot. If too little water is added, the mixture will be too thick and it will be impossible to work it into the foot properly. Experience will determine whether the clay is of the proper consistency. I also recommend that a handful of ordinary coarse table salt be added to this clay mixture. As I said earlier, salt is one of nature's greatest antiseptics and it also tends to hold the moisture and has a cooling, soothing effect on the foot.

In preparing to pack the foot, the groom follows the same policy about keeping the stall clean as he does when he is washing the foot. He places the clay bucket next to the foot he is working on and holds the foot over the bucket. Any clay that falls off the paddle or out of the foot falls back in the bucket.

In packing a foot, the foot is held in one hand and the other hand is used to dip the clay out of the bucket with the paddle. The clay is worked into the foot and the paddle is used to smooth the clay at the edge of the heel and across the sole.

Clay has to be worked pretty stiff or it will fall out of the foot. Sometimes good grooms will use heavy brown paper or something like that on the bottom of the foot to hold the clay in place. This also helps to keep foreign objects from working up into the clay during the night and pushing the clay out.

The importance of keeping a horse's feet soft and moist cannot be over-emphasized. While it is true that horses lie down in the stall, they are actually on their feet most of the time, much more than humans. In addition their "occupation" in life primarily involves the feet and thus they must get special care. The main thing is to keep the feet from becoming hard and brittle. Packing the feet by one means or another is a method of accomplishing this. Incidentally, this is also the ideal time for the application to the heels and coronary bands of whatever lotions and salves are being used.

With the feet properly packed, the major task remaining is for the horse to be done up in bandages (Fig. 94). Not all horses are bandaged and, of those that are, some are bandaged only in front or only behind while others are bandaged all the way around. Bandages are used to lend support to the horse's leg and to facilitate the action of any leg brace, liniment or other preparation being used beneath them. They do not necessarily indicate that the horse is unsound in any way and some horses that are perfectly sound are bandaged all the way around. Others, however, are bandaged because they have shown indications of developing leg trouble and the trainer believes it would be best if protection were provided.

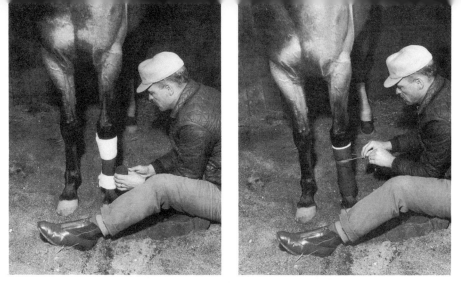

Fig. 94. Some horses are done up in bandages after being cooled out. The proper technique is illustrated in these two steps. At the left, the cotton is in place and the bandage is being rolled on as described in the text. At the right, the bandage is being tied as the final step in the procedure. Bandages should always be tied loosely to avoid possible tendon injury.

Before a leg is bandaged, it should be rubbed down good with a leg brace or other liniment that meets with the trainer's approval. I think that in many instances the rubdown of the leg is just as important as the bandaging itself. There doesn't really have to be anything especially medicinal in a leg brace of this type. It's just to dampen the hair. The groom, acting as a masseur, is the one that helps the horse by the way he rubs the leg. The proper way to massage a leg is to move the hands in the same direction the hair grows. The only exception to this is that it is permissible to rub crossways of the hair around the ankle, especially if a liniment is being used in that area as it usually is. The idea here is to get the liniment rubbed in as deeply as possible and a cross hair motion is permissible. When the area is completely rubbed down, however, the hair should be smoothed out so that it lays flat. On the remainder of the leg, all the motion of the hands is in the direction the hair is growing.

In massaging a horse's leg, a rough touch should not be used. The hands need to be light and flexible. If you are a groom rubbing a horse's leg, just ask yourself if you would appreciate having done to you exactly what you are doing to the horse and in the manner you are doing it. If the answer is "yes," you are probably doing it the right way.

In doing up a horse's legs, cotton and bandages are required. Depending on the trainer, groom and horse, it will usually require from a sheet and a half to three sheets of cotton for each leg.

The way the cotton is wrapped around the leg is not as important as the fact that it be wrapped the same way each time. Cottons set themselves to a leg and may be used a number of times as long as they are clean and don't tear up. The length of time that a groom can use the same cotton often indicates the quality of his work. That is, a good groom, who knows how to roll a cotton and is careful in removing it, will make the cotton last three times as long as the inexperienced or careless groom.

The cotton is rolled around the leg, usually with a right to left motion and extends all the way from the coronary band to just below the knee. The cottons for the front leg are usually interchangeable, as are those for the hind legs. The cotton on the hind legs does not usually come down quite as far as on the front legs.

Once the cotton is in place, the leg is bandaged. A bandage, which usually comes in a three-yard length, runs from around the pastern up to just below the knee or hock. The cotton will protrude slightly at both the top and bottom of the bandage.

I recommend that my grooms start the bandage just above the ankle. They make one turn with the bandage holding it in place, and from that point on the bandage wraps over itself and holds itself in place. A groom should work down with his bandage first and then come up, ending just below the knee or hock.

Each time a turn of the bandage is made it will cover approximately one-third of the bandage used in the previous turn. On the final turn, the bandage is fastened either by string or with a pin. There is a string on the end of the bandage and if that is used to fasten the bandage, caution should be exercised not to tie it too tightly. My rule is that I should be able to get two fingers between the bandage and the string. The knot itself must be tight but the string cannot be, because a tight bandage string can and has corded horses and made them unsound. For this reason, some trainers will not permit strings to be used and insist on pins.

The bandages, which can be plain or ribbed or even made of flannel or wool cloth, should be long enough to cover the horse's leg from pastern to knee or hock and if a groom finds that he is "long" or "short" of bandage it is usually a pretty good sign that he did not do the job right.

Extreme care should be used in putting a bandage on a horse. For instance, the joint area of the leg, such as the ankle, can stand a lot more pressure than the tendon. The bandage should be more firm around the ankle than around the tendon. As a matter of fact, it is always a good idea to make certain that there is sufficient cotton around the tendon so that the bandage won't become too tight in that critical area. I have known instances where the circulation was cut off because a leg was bandaged too tight or the string tied too tight.

At the same time, a bandage should never be applied loosely to a leg. Usually, the primary reason the bandage is being used is to lend some additional support to one or more of the legs and thus it is vital that the bandage provide that support.

After the horse is turned loose in the stall, other attendant duties are ready for consideration, one of which is feeding the horse. But since this subject is being considered at length elsewhere in this book, I will not go into any detail.

The primary concern of a groom in feeding his horse is to make certain that he notes any changes in the horse's feeding habits and reports them to the trainer or the barn foreman and that he follow the simple rule that a horse must clean up his feed. If a horse fails to clean up his feed in a prompt and reasonable time, the feed tub should be removed. A horse should never be permitted to wander about in his stall looking at a feeder with grain in it.

Once the horse has had time to finish his feed, the tub should be removed from the stall, washed thoroughly and hung up outside the stall until it is time for the next meal.

The groom's next chore is to clean and care for his equipment. For this, he will need a supply of saddle soap, metal polish, and possibly some leather softener or Neats Foot Oil to use on the harness if it begins to get a little stiff or dry.

The first step is to take a sponge and put a small amount of saddle soap on it. The sponge is then wet lightly and is used to clean off the harness and boots. Care should be taken to use as little water as possible because excess water will soak into the leather and have a detrimental effect on the natural oil and softness that leather should have. In cleaning leather, a minimum of water and a maximum of elbow grease should be used.

When the leather is clean, it is then gone over with a fresh sponge and a heavier coating of saddle soap or leather softener of some type. This soft dressing or "polish" is what applies the sparkling finish to harness and boots.

The areas of particular concern are the insides of boots where dirt is more apt to collect and from where it is more difficult to remove. Any dirt that remains in boots from one day to the next is bound to cause chafing.

If a horse is wearing white felt boots, it is usually a good idea to sprinkle some oatmeal on the felt part of the boot, rub it in by hand and take a soft brush and brush it out. This removes the darker spots and whitens them. White shoe polish may also be used for this purpose.

After being cleaned and polished, the boots are laid out to dry. Later they will be placed in the tack trunk or hung up on a boot rack. There is one special point relative to boots that I want to make. In an emergency, the harness might be left over to the next day for cleaning, but boots and hobbles absolutely must be cleaned and put away as quickly as possible after being used. As far as I am concerned, there are no exceptions to this rule, and on a number of occasions I have worked at night with my grooms to get this job done.

The harness bits require no special attention other than being dipped in water and rinsed off since they are made of non-rusting metal. Once the harness itself has been cleaned and cared for, it is placed in the harness bag and hung up outside the stall.

Then the cart and sulky are washed down. They are usually hosed off and then gone over with a sponge or cloth and particular attention is paid to the wheel spokes in each vehicle. They must be rubbed dry with a cloth. The sulky is then either set up on its side or hung up by the seat. The cart is never hung up.

After completing these chores, the groom must make a final inspection of the stall. He should check the water pail and top it off if necessary, make certain there is plenty of hay to last through the night and clean the stall if it has been dirtied since he last checked.

In endeavoring to describe the daily routine of a groom, I have confined myself to one groom working with one horse. However, in most stables a groom will have two horses and in some cases he might have even more. His work day will vary with the amount of work his horses are doing but each horse must have the necessary care each day whatever it might be. In describing this routine, I have tried to cover all the details in a way that will be helpful as well as instructive to persons who might not necessarily be well informed in these matters. One important point I would like to make is that a good groom knows what to do and how to do it and doesn't spend a lot of time unnecessarily fussing and fooling around with his horse and interfering with his rest and leisure time. In other words, it isn't good for a horse to be worked on for hours, or to be kept in the cross ties for things that aren't necessary to his well being.

The job of a groom, as I have described it, might seem unduly tedious and tiring. In actual practice, once the groom has learned his job, the work load isn't nearly as heavy as a first impression might indicate. On days when the horse is only walked or jogged lightly and very little equipment is dirtied, the groom has quite a bit of free time to himself. On other days, when the horse is being trained or raced, the hours are longer. But I have found that this usually evens itself up and that while a good groom will always find that he has plenty to do he certainly can't be considered a slave to his job.

A good groom means a great deal to any racing stable. There is no phase of harness racing that is more important than to learn how to take care of a horse properly so that he remains sound, healthy and happy throughout the training and racing season. Like others in my profession who have worked with horses from the groom stage on up through the training and driving phase, I am fully aware of the importance of a good groom and value a competent one. It gives a trainer a feeling of confidence to know that his horse is in the hands of a good groom.

My advice to any young man who wishes to be a groom is that he be industrious, kind to his horse, and keep his eyes and ears open. He can learn a great deal from watching the trainer perform his job and from observing others in the profession perform theirs. If he learns from those who know their own job and has a little ingenuity of his own, he will go forward much faster than he otherwise would and when he does get there he will have a sound foundation from which to work.

Sanders Russell drove his first race in 1915 and in that respect is senior among the drivers who contributed chapters to this book. His great skill, infinite patience and painstaking attention to the intricate details of shoeing and balancing have earned him a deserved reputation as a "trotting horse" man and it is a tossup as to whether he derived his greatest thrill from driving A.C.'s Viking to victory in the 1962 Hambletonian or guiding Fresh Yankee in her world record mile of 1:57⅕ in 1967, more than 50 years after he drove his first race. He was born on April 26, 1900 at Stevenson, Alabama, where he still lives and where the Russell family planted its roots in 1829. His  father was a horse trainer and opened a public stable in 1903. The stable has wintered in the same location and under the same family management ever since. Russell attended his first harness race at the tender age of three and advised his dad, who did not fare well in the first heat of the afternoon, "If you're going to keep finishing last, let's don't race any more." Twelve years later he was in the sulky himself. On official USTA records, he is credited with more than 1,100 victories and in excess of $2,000,000 in earnings, but since those records have been kept only since 1939, he has actually won many more races—at least twice as many—and much more money. His harness racing activities are not confined to the race track alone. He is a long-time director of the U. S. Trotting Association and chairman of its important Classification Committee, and is vice president and director of the Standardbred Owners' Association. He is also a member of the Alabama Sports Hall of Fame, a director of the First National Bank of Stevenson and a steward on the Stevenson Methodist Church Board. His son Walter is a prominent harness racing Judge.

14

TRAINING in NEW ZEALAND

GEORGE B. NOBLE

began writing this chapter while visiting the United States and as I studied the results at American harness racing tracks I sometimes had the strangest feeling that I was not in a foreign country at all but still back home in New Zealand. Staring out at me from racing programs from all over the country were old familiar names like Cardigan Bay, Orbiter, Idaho, Peerswick, Spring Garrison, Terri Lee, Avante, Our Jimmy, Smokeover and Eden Valley just to name a few.

As a matter of fact, I, too, was contributing to this "new look" on the American racing scene by training and driving, first at Santa Anita and then at Washington Park and Liberty Bell Park, the pacers Garcon D'Or and Jay Ar N., bred and owned by Roy McKenzie's Roydon Lodge Stud at Christchurch, New Zealand, for which I have been the manager and head trainer for the past quarter of a century.

It is no secret that more and more of our good Australasian (New Zealand and Australia) horses are coming to this country to race and that many of them are performing quite successfully. And as I moved about in the United States, I had a chance to discuss with curious American horsemen, some of the circumstances surrounding this relatively recent turn of events.

When requested, I not only offered my general views on the subject but also answered a great many questions pertaining to the conditioning, feeding and shoeing of our horses. Therefore, when I was asked to provide a chapter on New Zealand training methods for this book I was delighted to do so because it enabled me to answer more questions in greater detail.

But before I begin I want to be sure to set aside a paragraph to express my gratitude for the splendid way I have been treated on my three visits to the United States. Without exception my friends and I have been greeted warmly by American horsemen and have been made to feel as much at home as is humanly possible considering that 12,000 long miles separate us from our home land. There is no question that people who are mutually devoted to trotters and pacers share a common bond which is even stronger than our common language.

I think there is one other thing that I should comment on and perhaps explain in some detail at the outset so that there will be no confusion later on. Our seasons are exactly opposite those in the United States. We are in the Southern Hemisphere and our hottest months are from December through February and the coldest from June through August. So when I write about doing something in the middle of January that appears to be out of step with an American schedule, you must remember that this is the middle of our summer. I think it would probably be best if I set the months of the year down to show how they compare:

UNITED STATES		NEW ZEALAND
January	(equal to)	July
February		August
March		September
April		October
May		November
June		December
July		January
August		February
September		March
October		April
November		May
December		June

Naturally, this also effects the breeding season and the common birth date of our horses and explains why many New Zealand horses suddenly become a year older when they arrive in this country. The breeding season extends from September first (we are prohibited by rule from breeding a mare prior to that date) through December and the annual birth date for all New Zealand and Australian foals is August first.

A New Zealand horse foaled in August of 1960 and racing in our country in February of 1965 would be four years old. He would not become five until August first. If the same horse were shipped to America in March of 1965 he would automatically become a 5-year-old since the common birth date for horses in America is January first.

That is the principal reason that I doubt you will ever see many of our horses competing in your two and 3-year-old stakes.

A New Zealand foal that arrived at the peak of the foaling season, in October, would have to compete against American horses that had been foaled from January through May of the same year. This is simply too much of a handicap for a young horse to overcome. We do have an occasional New Zealand breeder who breeds his mare on "American time" which would be out of season for us. These breeders are hoping to compete in the American stake and futurity market but I doubt that the practice will become very general because such a foal, by arriving very late according to our breeding calendar, would forfeit any chance of participating on a level basis in the two and 3-year-old stakes in his own country.

In these opening paragraphs you have undoubtedly noted that I have referred to New Zealand much more often than Australia. I think I should explain the geographic circumstances under which I write by saying that I am an Australian by birth but have made New Zealand my home for the past 25 years. I have trained and driven horses in both countries and there is very little difference in the techniques involved. What I will be writing applies for the most part specifically to New Zealand but in almost every instance it would be equally applicable to Australia.

I think many Americans have a tendency to lump New Zealand and Australia together in their thinking but as a matter of fact the two countries are quite separate and distinct with a 1,200 mile expanse of the Tasman Sea stretching between them.

The horses that are now being imported to America in comparatively large numbers come from both countries but the majority come from New Zealand. I firmly believe that the reason for this is that New Zealand has probably the finest pastures in the world and, all other things being equal, probably raises the best physical specimens of horses in the world. I have found New Zealand horses to be stronger, better-footed and sounder than those raised anywhere else.

New Zealand is comparatively tiny in comparison with its neighbor, but I have observed over the span of a lifetime that probably 80% of all the richly-endowed races contested in Australia, both harness races and running races, are won by horses bred and raised in New Zealand. This is a sensational record and when you consider that training methods, types of races, stallion availability and quality of brood mares are roughly the same, there is only one thing left that will account for this phenomenon. That is our New Zealand pastures.

We are blessed in New Zealand with a moderate climate that results in extremes in temperature and weather only in one or two months of the year and at Roydon Lodge, which is roughly in the center of New Zealand, we never have extremes in either direction. There is no snow and freezing temperatures are quite rare. For months on end the balmy climate is reflected in the average temperature of 72 degrees while an average rainfall of 45 inches in my part of the country provides the lushest kind of pasture imaginable.

We also grow outstanding hay. We have cultivated various rye grass crosses and we sow that with red and white clovers and a little timothy and cocksfoot, an all-weather grass with a remarkable recovery growth and which is especially palatable to horses. This all goes to make an outstanding permanent pasture after the hay crop has been made and our horses thrive on it. Alfalfa is also one of our big crops and some horses are fed a great deal of it. However, I have found that New Zealand alfalfa is so rich and tasty that a horse will gorge himself and sometimes become short-winded as a result. For that reason I prefer to feed a good grass mixture instead.

This reference to the lush quality of New Zealand pastures also affords me an opportunity to discuss the reasons why so many of our horses are being imported to America and why they do so well, comparatively speaking.

I believe this probably has something to do with the fact that our horses are jogged much more than American horses and, even more important, that they are turned out so much of the time. Turning a horse out has a beneficial effect on him because it relaxes him in natural surroundings. And a relaxed horse is a better racing tool in my opinion.

I think these two things, along with the fact that New Zealand pastures appear to exercise a definite influence on soundness and stamina, are accountable in large part for the success our horses enjoy. In reaching this conclusion, I have weighed all factors and cannot find anything else that would appear to exert a significant influence.

In studying the matter and attempting to establish a proper

Fig. 95. A field of horses lines up behind the starting barrier at the Timaru Trotting Club in New Zealand. Most of the horses are starting from the "scratch" line but others have been handicapped and have taken up positions an assigned number of yards back of the "scratch" line. Notice how well-behaved the horses are.

perspective, you must remember, first of all, that only the best of our horses ever come to America. We have plenty of bad ones, but you never hear of them. What you are actually doing is skimming the cream of our crop and bringing it over here.

Another thing is that we have never produced one yet that could come here and be the best animal that ever raced in America, although I do believe that Phar Lap, the great runner who was exported from New Zealand many years ago and died in America after his first start, was the best horse I ever saw.

Cardigan Bay, of course, has certainly done some wonderful deeds in America but while we have perhaps one Cardigan Bay in 20 years you have several around that are approaching that class every year.

Breeding is not a factor because most of the horses we export are by American sires or have strong and very close American ties on both sides of the pedigree. Nor do I believe that actual training methods have anything to do with it. Our horses are trained differently, but when they go over to the American system they appear to do just as well. I think a good horse will race well under either American or New Zealand training methods.

I have also heard it said that our horses do well because they do not race as two and 3-year-olds and thus have plenty of fast miles left in them when they arrive in America. I do not hold with that either. While it is true, perhaps, that our youngsters are not raced as hard as yours, most of them that are capable undergo a relatively lengthy campaign in their first two years and we do race our 2-year-olds at both a mile and a quarter and a mile and a half which you do not. It is also true that many of our older New Zealand champions were successful juveniles which is another reason why I am led to doubt the validity of this claim.

Because of the difference in the economic structures of the two countries, it is probably true that at the moment you can get more horse for the same money in New Zealand than you can in America. I read just the other day where an American trainer was leaving to buy horses in New Zealand because every time he tried to buy a decent one in his own country he was asked from $50,000 to $100,000. Despite the fact that Cardigan Bay brought $100,000 and Orbiter $125,000, you can still buy plenty of high class New Zealand horses in the $20,000 to $40,000 range. An American dollar will buy more in our country than it will in the United States.

But, overall, I would have to conclude that the three factors that stand out in my mind are the excellence of our pastures and the two differences in conditioning techniques which result in increased jogging and a great deal of turnout time.

This leads naturally into a discussion of the conditioning methods used in New Zealand (or Australia) and a comparison with American methods. I find that these are the principal differences.

1. Before going to the races, we train our horses three times a week instead of twice.

2. We train only one heat instead of three or four.

3. We train our older horses over a distance of two miles rather than one.

4. We jog our horses much more.

5. We turn our horses out more often and for much longer periods of time than you do or are able to.

Of the five points listed, I do not consider that the first three are significantly different from American methods, although at first glance they might appear to be. As I have already pointed out, I do consider that the last two are. I will explain my reasoning in detail as I go on but right here I want to take just a little time to discuss a couple of factors involving the way we must race our horses and which affect our training methods.

I am sure that the vast majority of New Zealand owners, trainers and drivers would prefer that all races go from a mobile starting gate. Unfortunately, we do not have enough high class horses nor enough races to make this practical.

In the first place, a race meeting in New Zealand is far different from a meeting in America. You race every night while a typical New Zealand meeting will consist of a program on Saturday night, one the following Wednesday night and a third the following Saturday night. Under this system, racing opportunities are quite limited and in order to give horses a chance to compete we have to permit larger fields. It is rare that a race draws fewer than 12 starters and usually there are from 15 to 20.

Since we do not have nearly as many horses available to race as you do, this naturally creates a wide difference of class among horses that are forced to compete against each other. We try to overcome this by handicapping the field. The poorest horses leave from "scratch" while others, depending on their class, will usually start from 12 to 60 yards back of this mark, and there have been instances of horses having been handicapped as much as 120 yards. Under these conditions, a starting gate is worthless and that is why its use in our country has been limited.

Because most races are of the handicap variety, our horses also have to be trained to leave the barrier from a standing start and a good deal of every trainer's time is spent teaching a horse how to do this properly. In New Zealand, fields are very large and the horse has to go away from that barrier and be at the top of his clip in a stride or two and go like nobody's business to get a spot so that he doesn't have to come around the whole field when the money is near.

Many horses never learn to leave fast under these conditions. We call them "poor beginners" and there is nothing quite so frustrating as to know you have a very fast horse and then find that you cannot teach him to get off the mark. American trainers are fortunate that they do not have to contend with this.

This is why the careful New Zealand trainer spends a great

deal of time trying to develop good beginners. It can be done
if you use care, patience and proper common horse sense. The
fellow who trains too many horses and tries to get there the
easy way is always a menace on race day. Not only is his horse
galloping out and losing its own chance but it is likely to interfere with others. In training a horse to go away properly, I
seldom start his training miles from a standing start. I generally
jog up to the starting point and go my training heat. Either
before or after the training period is when I would give him a
few practice starts from a barrier, moving him out as relaxed as
possible so that he won't get excited on race day. Of course,
you would work more on this with a horse that had never
started behind a barrier than you would with an old campaigner
that is accustomed to it and does it well.

This is another of the reasons why our horses race so well
under the American system. The first time they go away behind
a gate it is almost as if they were saying, "Well, how long has
this been going on and why haven't I seen it before?" And since
our horses have been trained to get "off the mark" like a shot
because so many of our races are won or lost at the critical
instant of departure, New Zealand horses are usually exceptionally fast beginners, or "leave fast" as you would say. This is also
why a number of our horses appear so difficult to take up early
and set in a trailing position.

The handicap system which forces standing starts from behind
a barrier is also principally responsible for the fact that our overall times are not as fast as yours. The difference between a standing start and a start behind a gate is worth a certain number
of seconds in anybody's mile any place in the world.

I am not going to go into a detailed description of our starting
system but I should probably mention it in a general way. A
thick elastic strand, about chest high on a horse, is stretched
across the track at the "scratch" line which is the starting line
for the race (Fig. 95). The slower class horses are behind this
barrier. At 12-yard intervals in back of that line, similar strands
are stretched across the track according to the number of handicap marks in use for the particular race. These strands are
fastened to pins which run along the inside rail and when the
starter has the horses aligned properly he pulls a lever, the
barriers fly to the outside and the race is on.

Probably the best way for me to describe New Zealand training methods would be select a hypothetical "cup horse," which is what you would call a top stakes horse, and take him through a racing season. This is a horse that will compete in and is being pointed for the big prize of Australasian racing, The Inter-Dominion Championship for pacers. We also have an Inter-Dominion Championship for trotters but trotters are a minority group and the hypothetical horse I will be training is a pacer.

The Inter-Dominion is the ultimate test of speed, stamina and endurance and consists of a number of qualifying heats followed by the championship final. It is usually raced in late February each year. Crowds of up to 40,000 will see the finals and millions will hear it described over a network of more than 30 radio stations.

The site of the Inter-Dominion changes from year to year with New Zealand and each of several Australian states playing host on a rotating basis. It is held more often in Australia and I shall consider that I am training a New Zealand horse to race in an Inter-Dominion that is to be held in Australia. The distance depends on the size of the track but is about 13 furlongs, a mile and five-eighths. In 1966 it was raced at Harold Park, which is in Sydney, New South Wales, Australia and the final was contested at 13 furlongs and 98 yards, a little over a mile and 5/8ths. Qualifying heats are at varying distances from 1¼ to two miles.

Assuming that my horse has raced in the Inter-Dominion that has just been contested, I will bring him home, let him down and turn him out for about two months. We have year round pastures in New Zealand and the grass is particularly good in the fall of the year which would be the period from March through May. I would let the horse down by jogging him about a fortnight (two weeks) after he arrives home. I would jog him on a lead for about six miles the first few days he was home, would cut back to three miles late in the first week, then to two miles and finally a mile a day the last couple of days before he was turned out.

You will notice that I said, "jog him on the lead." This means that I would be leading him behind another horse I was jogging (Fig. 96). This is a common thing with us and it works very well. Like many of our practices, this one developed as a necessity

Fig. 96. The author jogs one horse, above, and leads two others. This is a common practice in New Zealand. In the lower photograph, he demonstrates the proper method of holding horses that are being led.

because of the chronic labor shortage in our country. We don't ever have enough help and consequently we have to cut corners wherever we can. This is one of the ways we do it.

Employing this method, I will usually jog three horses at a time. One is being driven in harness and the other two are "on the lead." In doing this, one end of a six-foot lead is fastened to the horse's halter and the other end goes in my hand. (Fig. 96) Thus, each of my hands is on the driving lines and the end of a rope lead is held in each. One horse is being led along on the right side and a little behind me and the other on the left side.

Horses learn very quickly to lead this way and we seldom have any trouble. It is especially good for nervous horses or "pullers." A horse like this learns to relax when you are leading horses from him and even a hard pulling horse will jog quietly when he knows a couple are being led from him.

I recall one mare I had that would sweat and get all excited if you tried to jog her in single harness. She wanted to race every time she got the harness on and if you would hobble her up and go with her she was all right. I jogged this mare all the time on the lead and she was never nervous or excitable this way. I had another horse that was a notorious puller even when he was jogging, but if you would lead a couple from him he would quiet down and relax and jog along easily. So this system does have additional advantages besides being a labor saver.

In leading horses this way, I am always careful not to have two stallions on the lead. It doesn't matter whether you are working with stallions or rams or roosters or whatever; if you get two entire males close together you are inviting trouble. When I am jogging horses like this, I always have one end of the lead rope in my hand and never fasten it to the cart or anything like that. You see this done but I cannot recommend it. Occasionally, you will even see as many as five horses being jogged by one man. One is driven, one is tied on each side and two are led. For obvious reasons, I do not do this myself nor do I permit any of my assistants to do it.

I usually jog horses in sets of three with one in harness and the other two being led. But unless I have a problem of some sort relating to a particular horse, I will rotate the three. On each of three successive jogging days, each of the horses will jog in harness one day and be led the other two.

Many of our horses are jogged in grass paddocks and down country lanes (Fig. 97) as well as on the track. One of the reasons for this is that we do a great deal of jogging and this helps to keep our training track clear for horses that are working. It is also very relaxing for a horse not to be going around in the same old circle all the time and I think it keeps him fresh and interested. Even when jogging away from the track like this, one will be driven and one or two led.

This system probably would not work in America because most of your training and jogging is done over crowded race tracks and something like this would not be permitted. But I assure you that it can be done, that it is good for a horse and that anyone who tries it will not have very much trouble teaching horses to do it.

All our horses, incidentally, are jogged without hobbles, boots

Fig. 97. New Zealand horses are often jogged in paddocks and down country lanes rather than on the training track. Here, the author jogs one horse down a quiet country lane and leads another.

or overcheck. Most of them will hit a natural pace and will jog that way. Others will jog on the trot while some will canter or gallop. Most of mine either trot or pace.

This is also as good a place as any to mention that our horses are raced to a sulky (Fig. 98) whose measurements vary considerably from those used in America and which have been detailed by my good friend Billy Haughton in his chapter on race driving. Our sulky is longer, narrower and heavier. Measured from the inside wheel hubs, the width is 37 inches. The height above the ground from the bottom of the center of the seat downward is 29 inches. New Zealand and Australian wheels are almost exclusively 26 inches in diameter. The length of the sulky, measured from the cross arch to the tip of the shaft, is 111 inches. Occasionally, for long-striding horses, we use extensions made of tubular steel which are fitted to the ends of the shaft and which increase the length by several inches. The sulky weighs 47½ pounds. For jogging, we use a vehicle called a jogger which is a little heavier than a sulky and which is fitted with springs under the seat.

During the two or three month period that our horse is turned out prior to entering training for the next year, it is unlikely that he would get any feed aside from what is available in his grass pasture. As I have said, our pastures are exceptionally good at this time of year and in most cases that would be all the horse would need.

If, for some reason, the pasture was not as good as I would like it, I might feed the horse a little hay as well as some chaff. Under these circumstances, I would not feed the horse any grain. The grain he got in the chaff would be sufficient. I think it is a bad thing to give too much grain to a horse that isn't working. It makes his legs fill and causes other kinds of trouble.

You may wonder what I mean when I talk about feeding chaff to horses because the word is used in a different context in my country. In New Zealand, chaff is an excellent horse feed and can be either "wheaten chaff" or "oaten chaff." We get chaff by cutting the stem off at the ground when the wheat or oats has grown almost to the ripening stage. The entire stalk is then bound into sheaves, cured in what we call "stookes" (a stook consists of 10 or 12 sheaves which are stood upright in the field to cure), and then put up in stacks of several tons each (Fig. 99). Later it is cut by machine into small pieces approximately 3/8ths of an inch in length. Both the straw and heads are cut, mixed up and fed together.

After the chaff has been stacked, it is covered with waterproof sheets which are weighted down at the ends to hold them in position. The sheets are used to keep out the winter rains. The chaff is later cut and put up in 80-pound sacks. Some farmers will sprinkle salt on the sheaves as the stack is being built. This not only makes the chaff more palatable but also helps to deter rats and mice from infesting the stack before it is cut for chaff.

Fig. 98. The New Zealand racing sulky is longer, narrower and heavier than its American counterpart. The vital measurements will be found in the text.

Fig. 99. In these two photographs, stacks of oaten hay, still retaining the grain that will later be cut into chaff, are shown at Roydon Lodge Stud near Christchurch, New Zealand. Each stack contains about 20 tons. In the closeup, bottom, the weighted waterproof sheets used to keep out the winter rains are clearly visible. Chaff is a highly palatable roughage made from either oats or wheat. When wheat is used, however, it must be cut while still green but when the grain is forming. Green wheaten chaff is very popular in Australia. The ration of oats or corn is added to the chaff.

Wheat chaff is generally cut a little greener than oats, just as the flower comes on the head of the wheat. The straw is still green when this cutting is made and thus nicely made wheat chaff is very palatable for horses. Because there is less rain in Australia, more wheat chaff is made and fed there than in New Zealand. Actually not very much wheat chaff is made or fed in New Zealand but I like it a great deal and feed it whenever I can get it.

After his turnout period, our horse is brought in from pasture and enters the training routine for the following year. For the sake of discussion, let us say that he had raced in the Inter-Dominion the first week of March after which he was shipped home, let down and turned out the first of April. He ran out in April and May and is now being picked up again on the first of June which corresponds with the first of December, American time.

The horse is scheduled to make his first start late in August and will campaign regularly through the first of December. Along about that time I will bring him home and give him a little breather for a couple of weeks before I settle down to prep him for the Inter-Dominion again. I have prepared a chart (Chart No. 1) on page 734, setting forth exactly how this horse is trained and you are invited to refer to it from time to time.

When I pick my horse up I will commence to jog him and will do nothing except jog him for the first six weeks. During that period he will be jogged daily and the number of miles will be increased from two to about 12. As in your country, Sunday is a day off except under emergency conditions.

Although I say that I would work the horse up to about 12 jog miles, we do not generally jog any particular number of miles but rather for a period of time. We will take a horse out for an hour's jogging or for a half hour or something like that. I have found that a horse moving along at what I call a keen jog will cover about 12 miles in an hour and I have set up my charts to show this.

I have seen and heard of horses being jogged as many as 20 miles, but I think you would find that this would be the very rare exception rather than the rule. I really think that some of our trainers, since they jog by the watch, have an idea that they actually jog more miles than they do. But I think you will find that a horse is being jogged along quite smartly to go 12 miles in an hour. This is what I reckon for my own horses and I think that if it were checked closely you would find that this would be the average rate throughout New Zealand. I would be afraid that if a horse were jogged 20 miles in an hour that he would get pretty leg weary and that the rate would not be good for him except in exceptional circumstances.

In observing American horses jogging, I have noted that they will jog generally a little faster than we do back home, but then you must remember that they are not at the task as long as New Zealand horses are.

In going over the charts I have prepared, you will note immediately that our horses are jogged much more than yours. As I have said, I consider this to be one of the two major differences in our conditioning system. Personally, I think a lot of jogging at a proper rate is a good thing because in my opinion it relaxes the muscles and builds up stamina and resistance to heart strain, especially the latter. Heart strain is something that wrecks plenty of horses. You are not nearly as likely to be troubled with heart strain if a horse has a thorough preparation based on good long periods of jogging. This is one of the principal ways we build what is called "foundation" in both your country and mine. If you rush a horse into fast work without a good period of preparatory jogging and muscle building, you are inviting heart strain.

Incidentally, this matter of heart strain is such an important factor in our thinking that many of our trainers believe in routine cardiographs for horses and will immediately sell a horse whose "heart score" does not measure up. I've used cardiographs and I think they are all right up to a point but I have never quite believed that anyone could predict from a cardiograph whether a horse was going to be any good. There are too many other factors involved, gait and natural speed for example. I have proved this to my own satisfaction.

I supposed you have also heard in America that our horses are jogged the right way of the track and that they are jogged at a gallop. This is true to a certain extent but does not apply to all trainers. I usually jog my horses the wrong way of the track and very seldom gallop them. The jogging techniques I have described are the ones I use and are in general use. However, there are exceptions and they are common enough to merit comment.

The exceptions are usually the result of our labor shortage and arise when a trainer is so short-handed that he simply cannot devote an hour to jogging a single horse. Under these conditions, a trainer might substitute pace work for jogging. This consists of going along at about a 3:00 clip on either the trot or the pace for about four or five miles.

Other trainers prefer to canter their horses and they will go along at a 3:00 clip or faster for the same number of miles. Those who gallop their horses will usually send them along at about a 2:30 clip for two or three miles.

None of these methods is common but all are used. In each instance it is our labor shortage which dictates a departure from the usual jogging routine.

In the first stages of training, I believe in giving a horse hard, keen jogging which, as I have indicated, would be about 12 miles in an hour. But after a horse gets to the races and is racing satisfactorily, I think all jogging should be relaxing. I feel that this type of jogging has a great deal to do with a horse's racing success. I think it relaxes them, keeps them eating and contented and I do believe it helps keep them sound. I think it is much better to jog a horse along slowly than to keep him standing up in a box, or "stall" as you call it in America.

So during the first six weeks of his training, my horse has done nothing but jog. I am busy building up a foundation for the racing ahead. You will note on the chart how the number of jog miles was built up from two a day to 12. When I first started with this horse I probably jogged him along a quiet road or possibly in a grass paddock to keep him away from the excitement of the track until he was thoroughly conditioned. I probably did not take him to the track to be jogged until the third week or when I stepped him up to an hour and its equivalent 12 miles. In almost every instance, he was part of a three-horse jogging team and was jogged in harness one day and led the next two.

In the seventh week of his conditioning program, which is the week of July 13th on the chart, I begin to train the horse. I feel I should pause here and explain our methods in general.

In the first place, as I have already mentioned briefly, we train our horses three times a week instead of two as is the custom in America. I do not think there is any special reason for this and, actually, if you will add up the total number of miles that American horses and New Zealand horses go in one week of training you will come up with the identical number, six.

An American horse is trained three one-mile heats on a Monday and three more one-mile heats on a Thursday. A New Zealand horse is trained one two-mile heat on Tuesday, Thursday and Saturday. It still adds up to a total of six miles trained the right way of the track.

The big difference as I see it is that we train two-mile heats and go many more jog miles than you do. Including our training days, we would jog a horse 54 miles a week as you will observe in studying my schedule. In America, a horse will be jogged perhaps four miles a day on his four "off" days and probably a mile before he goes his first trip on days that he is training three heats. This adds up to a total of 18 jog miles for a typical American horse and is about one-third of what we give our horses. As I said earlier, I believe this is one of the major areas of difference in our two training systems.

The reason we train our horses two miles instead of a mile is that almost all our races are at distances longer than a mile and our horses have to be prepared to go from 1⅝ to two miles. Actually, there is even more to it than that. Since we race under the handicap system, there is very little opportunity to rate your horse as you might like to and you pretty well have to ad lib your strategy according to the way the race develops. If you are starting on a handicap mark 48 yards back, you don't have very much choice except to begin as quickly as possible and hope for an advantageous position, taking advantage of the breaks as they might come along.

When you get 18 horses in a race, there is seldom any opportunity to sit in as a trailer and then pull out at the top of the stretch the final time and make a big run for it as you often can in America in a typical eight-horse field. There just wouldn't be any way in the world you could get through that mass of horses. So we not only have to go a distance with our horses, but we have to do it the hard way. These are some of the reasons we train our horses two-mile heats. Another good reason is that I feel that if we only trained our horses short distances, say a mile, and then went out and raced them two miles, they would get a very bad pain with a long way to go on race day.

On Monday of the week that I am going to turn my horse and begin training, I will jog him the usual hour but on Tuesday I will only jog him a half hour, or six miles, after which I will turn him and go a little easy pace work with him, say two miles in 5:20 with each of the miles in 2:40. This schedule would be repeated on Thursday and Saturday and the regular one-hour jogging would continue on the other "off days," Wednesday and Friday.

During this first week when my horse is being trained at a relatively slow rate, I would probably just turn him on the track after he has gone his six jogging miles and go his two miles in 5:20 without bringing him back to his box. As I have noted, all our horses are jogged without hobbles, boots or overcheck and if he will pace this way when I turn him I will go right on and train him. But if he will not, I will bring him in and gear him up before I work him. Within the next couple of weeks when I begin to go a little faster with him, he will always come back to the box and be geared up before he goes his training miles.

He is usually in the box for ten or twenty minutes while we have our morning tea. During this period he relaxes and usually makes water and relieves himself. Then he is hobbled and geared up, taken back to the track and worked his two miles.

During the second week of his training, the horse would be worked at a 30 clip. Since we train two miles instead of one, we identify the speed according to the "clip" for a mile. Thus a horse working at a 30 clip is going two miles of 2:30 each or one two-mile heat in 5:00.

In the third week after the horse is turned and the ninth week since he has been picked up, he is again trained at a 30 clip and is brushed a little going away and coming home. The brush would be at a 20 clip which is a quarter in 35 seconds. In brushing the first and last quarters in 35 seconds I actually train my horses in about 4:55 since the other quarters are paced roughly at the 30 clip which is a quarter in 37½ seconds. Our horses have to be taught to come home a little faster but we also have to train them to be "fast beginners." The handicap system, as I have explained, really penalizes horses that cannot begin and thus we must teach them the importance of getting away smartly from the barrier.

Our schedule has now taken us through the week of July 27th-August 1st and our horse is down to make his first start three weeks later on Saturday night August 22nd. If he were not going to start until September or October, he would be held about where he is now for a few weeks since I do not believe in working horses at better than a 30 clip (two miles in 5:00) with a brush home except nearing race time. But race time is relatively near now and I must go with the horse.

A decent handicap horse of the type I am training here should be able to race two miles at a rate between 4:10 and 4:15 and I plan to train him in 4:25 before he makes his first start.

During the week of August 3rd I train him on Tuesday and Thursday in 4:44 which is two miles at a 24 clip with brushes of 34 seconds away from the starting line and coming home. On Saturday of that week, two weeks from the day he is to race,

I go two miles in 4:36, each in 2:18 with the first and last quarters in perhaps 33 seconds.

The following week I back him off to 4:44 for his Tuesday workout. On Thursday I go my two miles in 4:42 with a last half in 1:06. On Saturday, a week before the race, I will tie into him a little and go two miles in 4:30 with first mile and a half in 3:25, last half in 1:05 and the last quarter between 31 and 32 seconds.

We are now into the week in which our horse will make his first start and here I change my training schedule. Instead of training the horse on Tuesday and Thursday as I have been doing, I will only train him once that week, on Wednesday.

I will jog him an hour on Monday and Tuesday and then, on Wednesday, I will give him his last and fastest prep of the year going two miles in 4:25. I will go the first mile and a half in 3:20 and come the last half in 1:05 with the last quarter between 30 and 31 seconds.

I would consider that off a prep like this any good handicap horse, one from which you could expect a final quarter in 29 seconds, would be ready to race two miles between 4:15 and 4:20 and go his last quarter as you anticipated. I would jog the horse only a half hour on both Thursday and Friday after this workout and then would be prepared to race him on Saturday.

In New Zealand you are not permitted on the track on race night until your race is called to the post. Therefore, if you want to blow your horse out you must do it in the morning before the track closes. What I will do with this horse is to jog him for about 20 minutes, which would be about four miles, and then work him around a mile and a quarter at a 30 clip which would be about 3:07½ for that distance.

The night of the race I always like to walk my horse and keep him moving as much as possible before his field is called. At most tracks there is usually a walking ring for this purpose in the barn area. If the horse were in a late race, I would probably have him out of the stall several times during the evening for a five or ten minute walk. This helps to relax him and keep his muscles in good shape.

A race is usually called from 15 to 20 minutes before post time. Once they enter the track all horses are required to go in the same direction which is the right way of the track. What I will usually do is jog my horse a lap around the track and then let him breeze along a mile between 2:30 and 2:40. Depending on the horse, I might even go only a half mile with him. However, no matter how far I go I always make sure that I have time to pull him up and let him get his wind back before the race. This is the method I use and, while it is not universal, quite a few trainers do it this way.

Others warm up differently. Some will let their horses walk very quietly until just before it is time to line up and then they will give them one or two sprints of a furlong or a quarter of a mile. Sometimes I will adopt this method myself with a horse that is a slow beginner, one that doesn't accelerate at the start. It is sometimes quite advantageous to give a horse like this a couple of quick sprints just before they line up.

When you do this you will sprint your horse down past the starting point and then pull him up and let him walk most of the way around the track before you sprint him again. If you are sprinting a horse twice, you would only go a furlong instead of a quarter and it would probably be from 16 to 17 seconds.

There are also horses that will become quite excitable when you do anything with them just before the race, whether it is a warmup mile or a sprint. With these, you just walk them along very quietly until it is time to line up.

Incidentally, I should probably mention here that in New Zealand we do race occasionally in a clockwise direction, which is the "wrong way of the track" by American standards. There are not many places where this method is in use but we do race that way at Auckland, which is one of the country's four major tracks.

From my standpoint as a trainer-driver, there is not much difference and I have never noticed any special problems that arose because of it. What is noticeable is that some horses go better in the "wrong" direction while others do not go as well. For instance, I had a very good horse once that always hit a knee quite badly going the regular way, but he was as smooth-gaited as could be going the other way and he always did very well when he raced at Auckland.

In bringing the horse we have under discussion up to the night of his first start, I have intentionally omitted other important phases of the conditioning program in order to preserve continuity. In a little while I will return to pick up the horse and continue his training, but for the moment I think this would be a logical spot to go back and fill in.

First of all, I do want to say that while the conditioning program I have just described is the basic one used by trainers in both New Zealand and Australia, not all of them follow exactly the same pattern. As a matter of fact, I violate the general pattern myself in at least one instance and while I did not include it as part of the general system because it is not a common practice, I think I should mention it here.

I have explained how a horse is jogged a half hour or about six miles and then goes back to his box for about 15 minutes before returning to go his training trip. This is the general practice I follow in the beginning but after I get my horses down to a 20 clip, that is, two miles in 4:40, I like to go an additional easy trip with them.

What I will do is to turn my horse after he has jogged and go a mile and a quarter in 3:07½ or thereabouts which is a 30 clip. If he is a horse that will not hit the pace without hobbles and overcheck, I will take him in and gear him up before going this trip. Then I will bring him back again and let him rest for 10-15 minutes before going his final two-mile workout.

I like to add this first warmup heat because I believe it tones a horse up better for his two-mile work. I think that by using this method my horses train better and stay right longer. However, as I said, this is my own innovation and is not the general practice which is why I did not include it in my description of a routine training program.

Another variation of our training technique is that some of our horses are conditioned partly—and in rare instances almost entirely—at a hand gallop. Some trainers do this routinely in the early stages of a horse's training after he has been away from the races for some time. I do not do it myself unless I am getting ready for early Spring races and we are having a bad winter which has affected our training track and made it virtually impossible to work a horse at any particular speed.

What I will do in a case like this is to send my horse along for two or three miles at an easy swinging gallop instead of hobbling him up and working him. These miles would probably be at a 2:40 clip with a brush at the end and they would substitute nicely for a training journey.

If conditions are very bad and you can't get on the track for any serious work for a week or more, I would send a horse along like this for three miles every day and consider that he had had his jogging as well as his training. It is surprising how well horses will race off a prep like this provided they are seasoned, good-gaited horses. I have done this and have had good results.

Three subjects which are directly related to the conditioning program and which I have not discussed in any detail up to this point are (1) the definite advantage obtained through being able to turn our horses out most of the time (2) the ways in which we cool a horse out and (3) our feeding practices.

In New Zealand, our horses are almost never in a box in the daytime hours. As I have said, we have year round permanent pastures and we take great advantage of them. When a horse is through training and has been cooled out, or when he is through jogging on days he is not being trained, he is turned loose in a yard or a paddock and permitted to run. This is the third of the three reasons why I think our horses do so well in America, the others, as I have noted, being the excellence of our pastures and the additional jog miles we go.

This is also one of the reasons why so many of our horses are gelded, although I suppose the principal reason is that the colonial horse has very little value as a sire. It is a fact, both in New Zealand and Australia, that the magic "imp" behind a stallion's name (meaning that he is imported) makes him more desirable than the local product. And rightly so. Our breed is based almost 100% on American blood.

But it is also true that you can turn a half dozen or more geldings out in the same paddock and that is a very important consideration with us. We put all the geldings in one paddock, all the mares in another and use one or two smaller paddocks for whatever stallions we might have.

I think this is one of the really big advantages our horses have. I know it is not possible to do it in America and I have had a number of your trainers tell me that they wish it were. I believe their horses would do better and race better if they could be turned out.

In my country there are numerous training areas scattered

about in the vicinity of each race track. If you are not close enough to truck your horses from your own farm to the race meeting, you can usually find a paddock nearby or even use the center of the race track. Most horses are trucked to the track to race and then go right back home or to their paddock after the race.

In New Zealand, it is the general rule that all horses are turned out during daylight hours except in the event of very bad weather. Almost everyone is glad to do it and you will seldom find a horse in a stall anywhere in the country, except at night.

The paddocks into which our horses are turned out vary in size from four to 10 acres. Because almost all land in New Zealand is under intensive cultivation, we do have a parasite problem and we deal with it by rotating these turnout paddocks as much as possible.

In addition to one or two smaller paddocks which are set aside for stallions, I like to employ six paddocks for turning out the mares and geldings. All the mares will be turned out in one paddock and all the geldings in another. They will use these two paddocks for three weeks and then the paddocks will be grazed by sheep or cattle while the horses move on to the next two paddocks for three weeks. This rotation is carried on for another three-week period with the other two paddocks so that you are actually using a paddock for horses for three weeks in a row and then resting it from horses for six weeks. I find that this works very well.

Not all trainers have as many paddocks as are available at Roydon Lodge, but all are conscious of the parasite problem and juggle their facilities to whatever extent possible to provide some sort of rotation program.

We also like to have a sand pile in either the yards or the paddocks. There is nothing a horse likes more than a good roll in a sand pile and we always have one available for them.

In conjunction with turning horses out, there is one other thing that I like to do and that I think is very good for horses. That is to keep their feet as moist as possible. One of the ways of doing this is by providing a pond in the paddock (Fig. 100). The Canterbury Plains, of which Christchurch is the principal city, are watered by river water which is carried across the plains in a network of ditches. These ditches are called "water races."

The pond in which the horses are hitched in the illustration is running water. Water from the race runs in one end and out the other and back into the race. In summer, we often hitch horses standing in the water for an hour or so to soften the feet and cool the legs. In addition, horses that are kept in yards often stand in mud holes while they feed from mangers fixed to the fence. These mud holes are easily provided by loosening the soil at the feeder and playing a hose on it occasionally to keep it nicely wet. This also helps keep the feet cool and soft.

After I have finished jogging a horse, I like to walk him an extra mile or so, if time permits, before turning him out for the day. This gives the horse an opportunity to blow out a little, but I can't always do this because of time limitations and, if this is the case, he will be turned out without the walk.

Fig. 100. Horses stand knee-deep in a paddock pond at Roydon Lodge Stud. See text for the author's observations concerning these ponds and their usefulness.

At any rate, after he is through jogging, the horse is covered and turned out. When I say "covered" I mean that he wears a canvas covering (Fig. 101) that is lined with a woolen material. We call it a rug.

The horse will wear the rug most of the time he is turned out. If the weather is cold or chilly, he will wear it all the time. But if it is a real nice day with the temperature in the seventies, I will take the rug off for a few hours in the afternoon. We bring our horses in to feed them and if it is that kind of a day we will remove the rug when the horse comes in for his noon feed and leave it off until he is brought back in for his afternoon feed about 4 p.m. I like them to get a little warm sun on their hides. It is good for them.

If we are having a very hot spell, as we occasionally will, and the temperature gets up in the nineties, we would turn the horse out wearing a light canvas sheet without the lining, which we call a duck sheet. We do this because we have found that a horse can get too much sun, especially our New Zealand horses that are covered a lot. I do not like very hot weather because you will notice that when you turn a horse out on a day like this he develops a listlessness which doesn't ordinarily go with him. I believe horses are subject to sunstrokes, too.

Although our horses are covered and a number of them are turned out together, it is only rarely that you will find a horse that chews his rug or the rug worn by another horse. Like anything else, they become accustomed to it and do not think much about it.

Horses that are turned out also take their own exercise and generally keep themselves in much better condition than horses that are made to stand up in a box night and day. There is no doubt in my mind, that this is one of the major reasons why our horses do so well in America. There is nothing like turning a horse out to keep him fresh and interested. Horses that are turned out like this are seldom still unless it is a very hot day in which case they will relax in the shade. It is too bad that Americans are not in a position to turn horses out like this. It is a great thing.

There are several methods of cooling horses out in New Zealand and Australia and I will try to describe the ones that are most used. Generally speaking, I would say that our horses

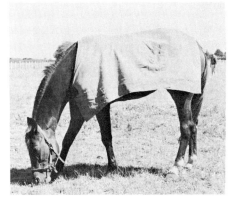

Fig. 101. In the closeup, right and the group picture below, New Zealand horses are shown turned out and wearing their "rugs." A "rug" is a canvas covering lined with a woolen material. These horses are in training, They wear the "rug" most of the time they are turned out.

require less time to cool out than horses in America. I think there are probably two things involved here. On the one hand, I think American trainers are perhaps forced to spend more time cooling out a horse than we are because they have to put the horse back in the stall instead of a paddock. I also think that because of the chronic labor shortage in our country we might not be quite as thorough as we would like.

I usually train horses in sets of four and after they have been worked, they are brought in and the gear removed. Then I like to have them gone over with water from a bucket. I might use a hose and cold water to hose down the legs and belly but over the head and body I prefer tepid water from a bucket and I use this to wash them down with a sponge before scraping them.

After that, I put on a light woolen cover which is thin enough for air to circulate through and then give the horse a few mouthfuls of water. At Roydon Lodge where I train, I have an automatic walker (Fig. 102) on which horses are cooled out. They are fastened to the walker while I train the next team and they walk slowly around for from 30 to 45 minutes, whatever might be required for me to get the next group worked. They are not offered any water during this period but get a few more mouthfuls after we take them off the walker and put the rug on them prior to turning them out.

I have never noticed any ill effects from horses not receiving any water during the period they were behind the walker and although water is available in the turnout paddocks the horses that have just been cooled out do not rush over and gorge themselves. I think the few mouthfuls they get just after they are cooled out are enough. That sort of takes the edge off their appetite for water.

During my career as a trainer and driver, I have also observed other methods of cooling horses out. I suppose there are almost as many different methods as there are trainers.

For instance, one very successful trainer hoses his horses down after they have been worked, scrapes them and leads them for a mile without any covering at all behind another horse that is being jogged. As soon the horse has gone this mile, he is covered with his regular turnout rug and goes to the paddock. These horses never seem to suffer any ill effects.

I know one trainer who brings a horse in from a workout, hoses him down with cold water and covers him right up with a rug rather than the usual thin woolen cover. His theory is that the cold water closes the pores of the skin and prevents the horse from sweating. He maintains that as long as such a horse keeps warm, which he will with the rug over him, and moves about in the paddock no harm will come to him. I have never seen any reason to believe otherwise.

On nights when my own horses are racing, I have to change my cooling out procedure a little because my walker is not available. What I do is hose them down with cold water around the legs and belly and sponge them with tepid water around the head and body. They are then scraped, covered and walked whatever time is available. Once again, the labor situation enters the picture and I usually find that I will walk one about 20 minutes, put him back in the box while I go a race, and then bring him out again when the race is over, maybe 20 minutes later, and walk him another 20 minutes. Usually this will be sufficient to cool the horse out properly. He is given several mouthfuls of water at the start and finish of each of these 20-minute periods.

Depending on whether they were trained or only jogged, our horses are fed either three or four times a day. The first feed is at 5:30 in the morning and the last at seven in the evening. There is also a noon feed which all horses do not get and another feed at four p.m

If a horse is only scheduled to jog on a particular day, he is turned out immediately after he is through jogging and he does not get the noon feed.

But if a horse is trained, he is fed at noon. Adjacent to our stables are about a dozen "yards" which are enclosures about 150 feet square. After a horse is through training and has been cooled out, he is turned into one of these "yards," each of which has a feeder hung on the fence. He gets his noon feed in the "yard" and is then turned out in a paddock until he is brought in for his afternoon feed. Each horse has his own "yard" and is fed individually in it.

The morning feed in my stable consists of about two pounds of oats and a quantity of chaff which I described earlier. I like to give my horses a mash at noon. I consider it better to give them a mash at that time than at night. Usually an assistant feeds at night and he is more likely to give a horse too much and, as you know, a bran mash will sour if not eaten right away.

Fig. 102. The author looks on as horses are cooled out on a automatic walker at Roydon Lodge Stud. Although walkers of a similar type are used in the United States, they have never achieved any degree of popularity. In New Zealand, where a shortage of labor is a big problem, they are used extensively and quite successfully.

The noon mash consists of damp bran, oats and maize, or corn as it is called in America. The corn is kibbled or crushed. The next feed is around four o'clock and consists of about three pounds of mixed grain, oats and maize, and sufficient chaff to make it a good feed. The final feed is at seven in the evening and is the biggest of the day. The horses will get a mixed dry feed of corn and oats and maybe a little crushed wheat or something like that along with a generous supply of hay that will carry them through the night. This is also the feed to which I will add the supplements such as Glucose D powder, crushed linseed meal, pollard and such things which contain the various vitamins and mineral properties and lend a little variety to the diet. Every trainer has a different idea as to the type of supplements he wants to use and some will even add duck eggs and things like that. However, I stick pretty much to the basic supplements I have mentioned.

Now that I have considered some of the fringe factors which I think are especially important as they apply to our conditioning methods, let me go back and pick up the horse that has just made his first start on a Saturday night and has raced two miles in about 4:15, or at that rate if the distance of the race was actually shorter.

Since we do not have racing scheduled every night and yet like to get as many races as we can for our horse, it might well be that at this particular meeting he will be called on to race Saturday, as he has, back on Wednesday and back again on Saturday night. Actually, these are the only three nights of racing for this meeting.

If I have been able to find a paddock or a yard nearby, which I am usually able to do, I will turn my horse out on Sunday and do nothing with him. But if I am unable to do that and am forced to keep him in a box, I will take him out on Sunday morning and jog him about three or four miles in a half hour just as relaxed as he will possibly go.

What I do on Monday, which is two days after his race and two days before his next one, would depend on what kind of a horse he was. If he was a horse that needed a lot of work, I might jog him about 20 minutes and then hobble him up and go two miles in 4:50 evenly rated. I jog him less than usual because with a horse that has raced the previous Saturday night you don't want to be chasing him along at a stiff jog but just letting him go as relaxed as he wanted to. He might only cover three miles in that 20 minutes but that would be enough. If he was a horse that I did not want to do as much with, I would just jog him about a half hour.

On Tuesday morning I would jog him a half hour or 40 minutes quietly, say six miles in 40 minutes letting him relax as much as possible. On Wednesday morning, the day of the race, I would repeat what I had done the previous Saturday morning by jogging him four miles and going a mile and a quarter at about a 30 clip.

On Thursday and Friday I would do nothing but jog him, 30 to 40 minutes quietly each day. On Saturday morning I would give him the usual race-day warmup and race him off that.

Once a horse is up to racing, you don't have to do nearly as much with him as you did while you were bringing him along. Quite a few New Zealand trainers believe in cantering horses a little between races. For instance, they might jog a horse two or three miles and then canter him two or three miles. This is not enough to tax them or strain them and has a tendency to relax them and keep them eating good.

When you have a whole season to go, you have to vary your methods and your training practices. For instance, you might race on a Saturday-Wednesday-Saturday schedule as I have just described and then race the following Saturday night with a long ship in between. You wouldn't want to do too much with your horse that week and since we are dealing with a hypothetical case anyway, let me explain how that would work.

My horse raced on a Saturday night and his next race is the next Saturday night at a track 450 miles away. I let him rest on Sunday and ship him on Monday. On Tuesday and Wednesday I would give him an easy jog each day, say 20 to 30 minutes and only covering three to five miles.

On Thursday I would hobble the horse up after a 20-30 minute jog and go a quiet two miles in 4:50 or 5:00 with no brushing. I do not think it is a good idea to brush horses much between races. You have already built the foundation and now you are just trying to keep him at racing level and keep him sharp. Once in a while you will run into a lazy horse that you will have to liven up a little but this is the exception rather than the rule.

If a horse is properly prepared he doesn't need any brushing or excitement between races. He trains better and lasts longer this way.

I think the big thing here is in relaxing your horse and keeping him thinking it is fun rather than work. It just isn't possible to keep a horse at the top of his form for long periods. I think you have to have periods of relaxation whenever you can get them in.

On Friday, the day before the race I was writing about, I would jog the horse quietly for about a half hour and then would warm him up the usual way on Saturday morning.

If this horse were scheduled to race again the following Saturday night, I would jog him as indicated on the training chart every day except Wednesday. On that day I would go one two-mile heat in 4:50 and would consider that this was plenty to keep him sharp. As I said, I would not brush him unless I had some special reason to do so.

On my jogging days, I would be getting from seven to eight miles per session into the horse. If he were a keen jogger and wanted to step along, a period of about 30 minutes might be involved. But if he were a relatively slow jogger, it might take 40 minutes for the same number of miles. I am interested here in the number of miles not the time involved.

A schedule that calls for a top horse to race on a Saturday night and back again exactly a week later is identical very often to the pattern in America. I have just described how I would train a horse to race in New Zealand and since I recently trained two New Zealand horses in the United States let me explain how I conditioned them to race on Saturday and back again a week later.

I jogged each horse about a half hour on Monday and Tuesday, about six miles each day, and worked them three heats in 2:30, 2:20 and 2:15 on Wednesday after jogging them three miles. They would jog normally on Thursday and Friday and on race night would warm up two trips in 2:30 and 2:20.

I think the main thing my horses missed was being turned out and in order to try to compensate a little for this I walked them for at least a half hour every afternoon.

I found that both Jay Ayr N. and Garcon D'Or trained well under this system. I noticed that Jay Ayr N. wanted to jog along faster than our usual rate. The reason for this was that he was accustomed to having horses led off him or being led himself and he seemed to think that whenever he was in single-handed harness he should be going faster.

As I said at the beginning, there isn't really much difference in the actual training miles except that we are prepping for longer distances. The difference lies in the amount of jogging we give our horses and the fact that they are turned out so much more of the time.

The training and racing schedule I have been describing has taken me through the middle of September. From that time until the first of December there would be very little variance so I am going to skip over it and get back to the original idea that I am conditioning a horse to compete in the Inter-Dominion Championship which is being held in Australia the last week of February.

On December first, at the conclusion of the N.Z. Cup November Carnival, I would figure that it was time to freshen my horse up a little for the big race ahead. And the Inter-Dominion is a big race and difficult to win. I have been training horses since before it was inaugurated in 1936 and have only won it once. At that, I dead-heated in the finals with the great New Zealand mare Robin Dundee. I was driving Jay Ar N., one of the horses I trained in America. But I don't feel too badly about that record because only one driver, my New Zealand friend Maurice Holmes, has ever won it more than once (1938 and 1951). It is a difficult and challenging task and considering the fact that it is run under handicap conditions, even great horses have trouble winning it.

With that in mind, I bring my horse home from the races and turn him out for a period of two weeks early in December. If he is a gross horse, I might consider jogging him a half hour a day but normally the horse would simply run out all day and be brought in late in the evening. It is early summer in New Zealand now and the pastures are excellent and the horse is enjoying himself.

You can refer to the chart for the daily routine to be followed thereafter. Through the last two weeks of December I would jog the horse 40 minutes a day for the first few days and then an hour a day. Then I would go ahead with a training period similar to the one I used earlier in the year when I was prepping him to return to the races.

The difference here is that I would not drag the schedule out with so much jogging. The horse still has a solid foundation and doesn't need as much. Instead, I would sharpen him up with a good stiff one now and then, say once a week. A good stiff workout is one that would be two miles anywhere from 4:20 to 4:25. The horse will have to go at a 4:10 to 4:12 rate to win the Inter-Dominion and he has to be on his toes.

Since I am in New Zealand, I have to leave room for a week that will be lost in shipping and also keep in mind that I will pretty well have to have the horse sharpened up before he arrives in Australia.

I would ship to Australia about the first week of February and would then have three full weeks before the first of three qualifying heats which I have set down on the chart to be February 28th. I would hope that I could get a start for my horse but if not I would have to keep him sharp with some pretty good work.

With the first Inter-Dominion qualifying heat three weeks off, I would train my horse lightly on Tuesday and Thursday, not faster than 4:50 and then give him a moderate work of 4:35 on Saturday (week of February 8th). The following week I would go fairly easy on Tuesday and Thursday, 4:45 each day, and give him a stiff run on Saturday. That would be two miles in 4:20 with a pretty good front and last end. I would let him bowl along the first quarter around :32 and the last half mile around 1:02 with a last quarter in 30 seconds. The week of the race I would train him only once, on Wednesday, and would go two miles in 4:30 evenly rated. I would warm up as usual the morning of race day.

I figure that would set him up pretty sharp. If he were a good, game horse that had extreme speed, could cope with all the traffic problems, handle any kind of a race track, leave like a shot, race on the outside three and four wide for almost the entire distance and finish with a burst of speed, I would think I might have a chance to do some good. That's how tough the Inter-Dominion is!

Having discussed quite thoroughly the conditioning program for an older New Zealand horse by completing an annual cycle from one Inter-Dominion to the next, it might be of interest now if I reviewed the general methods used in training 2-year-olds. I have set this out on Chart No. 2 on page 736.

In New Zealand and Australia, 2-year-olds are not started as early or raced as often as in America. A 2-year-old would not normally make his first start until January or February, which corresponds to July or August in America, and an average youngster would not make more than ten starts in his 2-year-old season. The interval between his races would be closer to two weeks than the usual one week in America.

However, whereas no American 2-year-old may race at a distance beyond a mile, most of our feature races for youngsters are at a mile and a quarter and the most important race of the season, The Sapling Stakes, is at a mile and a half. This race is contested in June which is comparable to December in America. There are some races at the mile distance early in the season. There is no heat racing.

Foals arrive in New Zealand between August and December and along about Christmas week in December of their yearling form, it is our practice at Roydon Lodge to send them to a "horse breaker" for a period of about six weeks. This man, who is an expert in his particular field, breaks the yearlings and manners them. They are then returned to the farm and turned out until winter sets in at which time we pick them up and begin to jog them much as you do in America.

Our winter begins in late May. I pick the yearlings up then (they will become 2-year-olds on August 1st) and start them off jogging 20 minutes during which time I would cover three or four miles. I would do this six days a week. After a couple of weeks I would work them up to six to eight miles a day which would be about 40 minutes. This continues until about the first of August. It is my feeling that in jogging 2-year-olds through the winter, a period of about two months, they are getting thoroughly legged up and gentled and being made ready to stand a good period of training when you have to get going with them.

Along in August, or sometimes in early September depending on how the weather breaks, we start to go a few training miles with them. We are aiming for a first start in January or February and we are thus able to give them quite a good prep before we call on them to do any real fast work. I have set the chart up to go my first training miles the first week of August and race in the middle of January.

In general terms, the training schedule for a 2-year-old is roughly the same as for an older horse except that the task assigned a youngster is never as long or as severe. I would never train a 2-year-old two miles, for instance, nor would I ever brush one as fast as an aged horse.

The first day I trained a 2-year-old I would jog him two or three miles instead of the customary six to eight and would then turn him and go a mile in 3:00. I would do this a couple of times the first week and the second time I would brush him a little at the end of the mile.

At the beginning of the second week, the colt would go on a regular schedule of being trained three times a week and I would reduce his mile to 2:50 that week. Depending on the colt and the time at your disposal you might work this mile without leaving the track after jogging him or you might let him stand up for ten or 15 minutes between his jogging miles and his training mile. I like to spend a lot of time with colts and for that reason we scheduled them to train on the days the older horses are jogging. If the older horses were being trained on Tuesdays, Thursdays and Saturdays, the youngsters would be on a Monday-Wednesday-Friday schedule.

I would continue to train the 2-year-old evenly-rated one-mile heats until the last week of September by which time I would have him down to 2:35 as the chart shows. Then for a period of a month I would continue to train one mile on Monday and Wednesday but would step him up to two one-mile heats on Friday. Late in October I would start training two heats on each work day and the following week I would begin to extend the training distance.

I would go my first mile in 2:40 (this "40 clip" is always my rate for the first training mile with a 2-year-old) and then would train him a mile and a quarter at a 30 clip which is 3:07½. I think you can follow the remainder of my training program quite easily on the chart. I gradually bring the colt along until he is asked for a mile and a quarter in 2:55 about a week or two before he races.

I would only train him once the last week and that would

be three days before he raced at which time I would train him a mile in 2:12 with last half in 1:04 evenly rated. Off this, I would expect that my colt could show a mile rate between 2:07 and 2:08 from a standing start. This is a pretty good clip for a 2-year-old from a stand, but the good ones can do it.

Now my colt is at the races and doing quite well. What I have in mind is to win the big race of the season which, as I said before, is The Sapling Stakes to be raced in June at a distance of a mile and a half. This is a pretty stiff task for a 2-year-old, and I have to think about conditioning him for it.

What I will do is to start training him mile and a half heats beginning about the middle of March. I am not going to chart this phase of the program but will describe it in general.

I am still training my colt three times a week and his first mile is always in 2:40. When I start going a mile and a half it will be in 3:40 with the mile in 2:30 and the last half in 1:10. These two training heats, 2:40 and 3:40, will be just about the same on every Monday and Wednesday with Friday reserved for going at a faster rate, or what you would call your "fast work" day.

Actually, I would be dropping him from the 3:40 rate very slowly and probably would not get down to 3:30 until a couple of weeks before the stake at which time I would go a mile and a half at that rate with the last half around 1:06.

If he is scheduled to start in The Sapling on a Saturday, I would only train him once that week, on Wednesday, and after going my 2:40 mile would set him along pretty good with a mile and a half in 3:25 and the last half in 1:04. He would race off that.

I think I have now explained in considerable detail the general training and conditioning methods used in my country. The only other area in which I might properly offer comment of interest is that of shoeing and before I sign off there are a couple of points with respect to that important phase that I should probably mention.

For the most part, we shoe trotters much as you do in America. But with regard to pacers there are two things we do differently and I think they are of sufficient general interest to warrant discussion.

As to toe and angle, we shoe our pacers just the opposite of the way you do. Our pacers will wear a longer toe behind than in front. Your pacers usually wear a longer toe in front. We will also have a higher angle in front whereas your angle is usually higher behind.

A New Zealand pacer might go with a 3⅜-inch toe and a 52-degree angle in front. Behind he might wear a 3½-inch toe and a 50-degree angle. The same horse, shod by an American, might wear a 3½-inch toe and a 50-degree angle in front and a 3⅜-inch toe and a 54-degree angle behind.

I have found that in gaiting pacing youngsters their feet are naturally like that and that is how I have them trimmed. I find that pacers are less likely to cross fire if they carry a little longer toe and a little lower angle behind. Generally speaking, a hind toe will be an eighth of an inch longer and the angle two degrees lower than in front.

The other thing I have found is that it seems to suit pacers a little better to be trimmed a little lower on the outside of both the front and hind feet. This also is directly opposite of what is usually done in America where the general practice is to trim them a little lower on the inside behind to widen out their gait and get them away from cross firing. I have not found this to be true and in New Zealand cross firing pacers are quite rare. In a field of 20 New Zealand pacers, you probably wouldn't see more than two wearing quarter boots.

I think the reason for this is that the center of gravity of the horse's body as it travels at speed is supported diagonally trotting and laterally pacing. In the case of the pacer, for instance, the feet must strike the ground directly under the line of the center of gravity of the body and simultaneously. Therefore, it seems to me that a pacer that is trimmed a little low on the outside would be much more comfortable in motion than if his feet were trimmed lower on the inside.

I began to arrive at these conclusions many years ago after studying the methods of an old blacksmith friend of mine who was an outstanding craftsman. If he was having trouble gaiting horses, he would take their shoes off and let them run until they developed a natural foot. He found that pacers would naturally wear down the outside of both front and hind feet. I have followed that theory for a number of years now and I rarely have a cross firing pacer. In fact, I do not have any pacers racing either in New Zealand or America that wear quarter boots.

All of what I have written in the last three paragraphs is exactly opposite for the trotter who, I have found, goes better if trimmed just a little lower on the inside front and back.

Other than that, there is no difference in the shoeing techniques in our two countries. We do not use very many calks, grabs or trailers. Our shoes are basically made of English steel, although we do use some aluminum ones. The English steel is "fullered," that it is has a groove down the center of the entire shoe and is what you would call a full swedge shoe. We make half swedge shoes from these fullered rods by heating the rod red hot and running what will be the inside part of the shoe through a half-round mold before shaping it.

This concludes my presentation. I am hopeful that what I have written will serve to better acquaint my American friends with the general training and conditioning practices in use in my country while at the same time possibly clearing up some of the misconceptions that may have existed until now. I do not pretend to speak for all New Zealand and Australian trainers any more than any one American trainer would be willing to set himself up as the sole spokesman for all horsemen in his country. There is too wide a difference of opinion on too many subjects, even among the very top trainers, for this to be either possible or desirable.

But I do feel that the thoughts I have offered are practical and generally representative of the thinking in my part of the world. The opinions I have expressed have been developed, tested and proved out to my own satisfaction over a period of almost 50 years. I hope they will be accepted in the spirit in which they have been offered—as a small and personal gesture intended to acquaint harness horsemen in one country with the training methods in use in another.

CHART NO. 1 — TRAINING SCHEDULE

New Zealand Cup (Stakes) Horse

DATE Week of	MONDAY	TUESDAY	WEDNESDAY	THURSDAY	FRIDAY	SATURDAY
June 1	J-2 (10 min)	J-2	J-2	J-3 (15 min)	J-3	J-3
June 8	J-4 (20 min)	J-4	J-4	J-6 (30 min)	J-6	J-6
June 15	J-8 (40 min)	J-8	J-8	J-10 (50 min)	J-10	J-10
June 22	J-12 (one hour)	J-12	J-12	J-12	J-12	J-12
June 29	J-12	J-12	J-12	J-12	J-12	J-12
July 6	J-12	J-12	J-12	J-12	J-12	J-12
July 13	J-12	J-6 2m in 5:20E	J-12	J-6 2m in 5:20E	J-12	J-6 2m in 5:20E
July 20	J-12	J-6 2m in 5:00E	J-12	J-6 2m in 5:00E	J-12	J-6 2m in 5:00E
July 27	J-12	J-6 2m in 4:55 1st ¼ :35 last ¼ :35 other ¼'s :37½	J-12	J-6 2m in 4:55 1st ¼ :35 last ¼ :35 other ¼'s :37½	J-12	J-6 2m in 4:55 1st ¼ :35 last ¼ :35 other ¼'s :37½
Aug. 3	J-12	J-6 2m in 4:44 each mile in 2:22 1st & last ¼'s in :34	J-12	J-6 2m in 4:44 each mile in 2:22 1st & last ¼'s in :34	J-12	J-6 2m in 4:36 each mile in 2:18 1st & last ¼'s in :33
Aug. 10	J-12	J-6 2m in 4:44 each mile in 2:22 1st & last ¼'s in :34	J-12	J-6 2m in 4:42 1st in 2:24 2nd in 2:18 last half 1:06E	J-12	J-6 2m in 4:30 1st 1½ in 3:25 last ½ in 1:05 last ¼ :31-:32
Aug. 17	J-12	J-12	J-6 2m in 4:25 1st 1½ in 3:20 last ½ 1:05 last ¼ :30-:31	J-6	J-6	J-4 1¼ in 3:07½ RACE
Aug. 24	J-6 (30-40 min)	J-6 (30-40 min)	J-4 1¼ in 3:07½ RACE	J-6 (30-40 min)	J-6 (30-40 min)	J-4 1¼ in 3:07½ RACE
Aug. 31	SHIP	J-3-5 (20-30 min)	J-3-5 (20-30 min)	J-4-5 (20-30 min) 2m in 4:50E	J-6 (30-40 min)	J-4 1¼ in 3:07½ RACE
Sept. 7	J-7-8 (30-40 min)	J-7-8 (30-40 min)	J-4 2m in 4:50E	J-7-8 (30-40 min)	J-7-8 (30-40 min)	J-4 1¼ in 3:07½ RACE

To prepare for Inter-Dominion, race through November 30. Bring horse home and turn out for first two weeks of December, or, if horse is carrying too much flesh, jog 5-6 miles daily, about a half hour.

| Dec. 14 | J-8 | J-8 | J-8 | J-12 | J-12 | J-12 |

CHART No. 1 Continued

DATE Week of	MONDAY	TUESDAY	WEDNESDAY	THURSDAY	FRIDAY	SATURDAY
Dec. 21	J-12	J-12	J-12	J-12	J-12	J-12
Dec. 28	J-8-12 (40-60 min)	2m in 4:50E	J-8-12	2m in 4:50E	J-8-12	J-4 2m in 4:47 1st 2:25 2nd 2:22-1:10
Jan. 4	J-8-12	2m in 4:50E	J-8-12	2m in 4:50E	J-8-12	2m in 4:42 1st 2:25 2nd 2:17-1:05
Jan. 11	J-8-12	J-4 2m in 4:45E	J-8-12	J-4 2m in 4:45E	J-8-12	J-4 2m in 4:40 1st 2:25 2nd 2:15-1:03-:31
Jan. 18	J-8-12	J-4 2m in 4:45E	J-8-12	J-4 2m in 4:45E	J-8-12	J-4 2m in 4:25 1st 2:15 2nd 2:10-:30
Jan. 25	J-8-12	J-4 2m in 4:45E	J-8-12	J-4 2m in 4:45E	J-8-12	J-4 2m in 4:20 1st 2:12 2nd 2:08-:30
Feb. 1	Week off for shipping to Australia					
Feb. 8	J-8-12	J-4 2m in 4:50E	J-8-12	J-4 2m in 4:50E	J-8-12	J-4 2m in 4:35 1st 2:20 2nd 2:15-1:05-:32
Feb. 15	J-8-12	J-4 2m in 4:45E	J-8-12	J-4 2m in 4:45E	J-8-12	J-4 2m in 4:20 1st :32-2:12 2nd 2:08-1:02-:30
Feb. 22	J-8-12	J-8-12	2m in 4:30E	J-8-12	J-8-12	J-4 1¼ in 3:07½ RACE

J—Jog. E—Evenly rated. 2M—Two miles.

CHART NO. 2   TRAINING SCHEDULE

New Zealand 2-year-old

DATE Week of	MONDAY	TUESDAY	WEDNESDAY	THURSDAY	FRIDAY	SATURDAY
June 1	J-3 (20 min)	J-3	J-3	J-3	J-3	J-3
June 8	J-4 (25 min)	J-4	J-4	J-4	J-4	J-4
June 15	J-6 (30 min)	J-6	J-6	J-6	J-6	J-6
June 22	J-8 (40 min)	J-8	J-8	J-8	J-8	J-8
June 29	J-8	J-8	J-8	J-8	J-8	J-8
July 6	J-8	J-8	J-8	J-8	J-8	J-8
July 13	J-8	J-8	J-8	J-8	J-8	J-8
July 20	J-8	J-8	J-8	J-8	J-8	J-8
July 27	J-8	J-8	J-8	J-8	J-8	J-8
Aug. 3	J-3 (15-20 min) 3:00	J-8	J-8	J-8	J-3 3:00	J-8
Aug. 10	J-3 3:00	J-8	J-3 3:00	J-8	J-3 2:50	J-8
Aug. 17	J-3 3:00	J-8	J-3 3:00	J-8	J-3 2:50	J-8
Aug. 24	J-3 2:40	J-8	J-3 2:40	J-8	J-3 2:40	J-8
Aug. 31	J-3 2:40	J-8	J-3 2:40	J-8	J-3 2:40	J-8
Sept. 7	J-3 2:40	J-8	J-3 2:40	J-8	J-3 2:35	J-8
Sept. 14	J-3 2:35	J-8	J-3 2:35	J-8	J-3 2:25	J-8
Sept. 21	J-3 2:35	J-8	J-3 2:35	J-8	J-3 2:40 2:35	J-8
Sept. 28	J-3 2:35	J-8	J-3 2:35	J-8	J-3 2:40 2:35	J-8
Oct. 5	J-3 2:35	J-8	J-3 2:35	J-8	J-3 2:40 2:30-:35	J-8
Oct. 12	J-3 2:35	J-8	J-3 2:35	J-8	2:40 2:30-:35	J-8
Oct. 19	J-3 2:40 2:30	J-8	J-3 2:40 2:30	J-8	J-3 2:40 2:25-:35	J-8
Oct. 26	J-3 2:40 1¼ in 3:07½	J-8	J-3 2:40 1¼ in 3:07½	J-8	J-3 2:40 1¼ in 3:07½	J-8

DATE Week of	MONDAY	TUESDAY	WEDNESDAY	THURSDAY	FRIDAY	SATURDAY
Nov. 2	J-3 2:40 1¼ in 3:07½	J-8	J-3 2:40 1¼ in 3:07½	J-8	J-3 2:40 1¼ in 3:07½	J-8
Nov. 9	J-3 2:40 1¼ in 3:07½	J-8	J-3 2:40 1¼ in 3:07½	J-8	J-3 2:40 1¼ in 3:07½	J-8
Nov. 16	J-3 2:40 1¼ in 3:07½	J-8	J-3 2:40 1¼ in 3:07½	J-8	J-3 2:40 1¼ in 3:05 2:30-:35	J-8
Nov. 23	J-3 2:40 1¼ in 3:07½	J-8	J-3 2:40 1¼ in 3:07½	J-8	J-3 2:40 1¼ in 3:05 2:30-:35	J-8
Nov. 30	J-3 2:40 1¼ in 3:00	J-8	J-3 2:40 1¼ in 3:00	J-8	J-3 2:40 1¼ in 3:00 2:26-:34	J-8
Dec. 7	J-3 2:40 1¼ in 3:00	J-8	J-3 2:40 1¼ in 3:00	J-8	J-3 2:40 1¼ in 3:00 2:26-:34	J-8
Dec. 14	J-3 2:40 1¼ in 3:00	J-8	J-3 2:40 1¼ in 3:00	J-8	J-3 2:40 1¼ in 3:00 2:26-:34	J-8
Dec. 21	J-3 2:40 1¼ in 3:00	J-8	J-3 2:40 1¼ in 3:00	J-8	J-3 2:40 1¼ in 3:00 2:26-:34	J-8
Dec. 28	J-3 2:40 1¼ in 3:00	J-8	J-3 2:40 1¼ in 3:00	J-8	J-3 2:40 1¼ in 2:55 1st half 1:05E ¾ in 1:50 last half 1:05E	J-8
Jan. 4	J-3 2:40 1¼ in 3:00	J-8	J-3 2:40 1¼ in 3:00	J-8	J-3 2:40 1¼ in 2:55 1st half 1:05E ¾ in 1:50 last half 1:05E	J-8
Jan. 11	J-8	J-8	J-4 2:40 2:12-1:04-:32	J-8	J-8	J-3 2:25 RACE

George B. Noble is one of the best-known and most respected horsemen in Australasia and since 1941 has been the manager and head trainer for the famed Roydon Lodge Stud, the "Hanover of the Southern Hemisphere" whose racing stable has led the New Zealand money-winning list in nine of the past 12 years. Noble was born on July 13, 1900 at Cootamundra, New South Wales, Australia, the son of a horseman-farmer who operated a small Standardbred stock farm. Young Noble worked with horses from an early age and drove his first winner when he was 18. He decided, however, to forsake harness racing for a career as an architect and did so until 1930  when the depression led him back into the sport. He soon became one of the top trainers in Australia and in the next decade developed many champions including the trotting mare White Globe and the pacer Bob Tingle. In 1941, Sir John McKenzie, owner of Roydon Lodge, offered him the job as head trainer and manager of that vast operation (where the foundation sires Light Brigade and U. Scott stood) and he left Australia for New Zealand. Under Noble's direction —first for Sir John and then for the latter's son, Roy—Roydon Lodge horses have dominated New Zealand racing. Some of the Cup (stakes class) horses he has campaigned are Highland Aire, Highland Kilt, Fantom, Bronze Eagle, Arania (who took a record of 1:57 in the United States) Jay Ar N. and Garcon D'Or. He reached the mandatory retirement age as a driver (65) in 1965 and celebrated by winning his first Inter-Dominion Championship (dead-heating Robin Dundee with Jay Ahr) and leading the New Zealand trainer's list. He is still permitted to train and has headed the trainer's list in six of the past nine years. He has also brought his architect's background into harness racing by designing race tracks at Wellington (a 4½ furlong track where Cardigan Bay went in 1:56⅕) and Cambridge (where Orbiter N won in 1:58⅘).

15

STABLE MANAGEMENT

DELVIN MILLER

T HE time is gone in harness racing when a man can be said to have achieved complete success simply because he knows how to hang up a horse and drive one. The rapid expansion of our sport which has, in recent years, seen the advent of the two million dollar horse and the billion dollar national handle has brought with it increased responsibilities relating to proper stable management.

In a day and age when a driver races in New York on Friday night and in California on Saturday afternoon; when he has divisions of his stable and/or individual horses scattered at a half dozen tracks; when he is buried by long distance phone calls and constantly besieged by complicated inquiries relating to workmen's compensation, social security and state and federal income tax matters, then managerial ability becomes a function that ranks on a par with training and driving skills.

I am well aware that there are not many horsemen whose schedule is as hectic as that described in the preceding paragraph, although we do have a few. But at the same time, every trainer worth his salt knows that management problems, no matter how large or small his stable may be, have expanded in recent years and that they promise to grow more complicated before they become simpler.

Consequently, efficient, business-like stable management is an absolute must in harness racing today. In this chapter, therefore, I intend to discuss the problems involved in stable management, principally by explaining how I developed the system under which I operate my own racing stable. At the same time, I plan to borrow ideas successfully introduced by others and to include them in my presentation.

Everyone knows that I do not race nearly as many horses as I used to, but there was a time when my stable was among the largest in the country. It was during this period—dating roughly from the late forties to the late fifties—that I was faced with many of the managerial problems that are confronting young trainers of today. I discovered that it was no longer practical to operate with my office under my hat and a little black notebook in my breast pocket. Therefore, I undertook to establish for my own stable what I considered to be good business practices and procedures, both in the operation of the racing stable itself and in other matters relating to the rapidly-expanding fields of office bookkeeping and taxation.

In doing this, I found that the most important thing was to hire good help. Since I had always followed this policy with respect to second trainers—Jimmy Arthur was my chief aide for 25 years until I cut down to the point where it was no longer feasible for him to remain whereupon he took off successfully on his own—I knew that I had to do the same thing in the other fields.

When I discovered that the field of race horse taxation was beginning to get very complicated, I sought out the best man I could find. That was Neil Engle who not only set up my own books, but who laid down general guidelines that have been picked up and copied by other trainers. When I saw that I had to have a bookkeeper to handle the day-to-day details, I hired Joe Burke who has been with me for the past 20 years. His contribution to the success of my operation has been a tremendous one.

All this boils down to one thing. If a trainer hires the right kind of assistants, whether they be second trainers, tax men or bookkeepers, he is then free to concentrate on the one subject he knows best—the actual training and driving of the horses which, basically, is what he is being paid to do. But if he hires dead beats, either because he is trying to go cheap or because he is ill-advised, he is heading for trouble. No man can train and drive horses properly if he has to waste a lot of time on other matters.

This chapter is directed primarily, of course, to trainers because I am passing on knowledge that I acquired as a trainer and that I hope will be of benefit to other trainers. But at the same time, I think all owners should read the chapter as well. Not only will what I write give owners an insight into the complicated operation of a racing stable, but I also plan to discuss the ways in which a new owner should and should not get into the sport and, in quite specific terms, what it costs to race a horse.

I think that probably the logical place to start is with the second trainer, or assistant trainer as he is also known. I have been blessed with a number of very good ones including, in addition to Jimmy Arthur, fellows like Bob Whitehill, Harry Harvey, Ned Bower, Houston Stone, Jimmy Jordan, Foster Walker and my present assistant, Aime Choquette.

In very small stables, there is no necessity for a second trainer. In very large stables, there will be several and in some stables— Billy Haughton is the prime example—there will actually be divisions at various tracks with an assistant trainer in complete charge at each place. These men, of course, are a cut above the routine second trainer and are paid accordingly.

In my opinion, a trainer can handle 10 horses and perhaps even 12 without an assistant if he gets to the barn very early every morning and stays very late. But if you have more than a dozen to train, it is pretty hard to get along without an assistant.

The value of an assistant lies in the fact that he can help you train whereas a groom usually cannot. If you have to do all the training by yourself, you are stretching your own time pretty thin and dragging things out for the grooms who cannot get the major share of their work done until you are through.

This is especially true if you have any appreciable number of colts (a word that horsemen invariably use in describing 2-year-olds of either sex) in your stable. It is desirable that a capable horseman drive the colts and also quite important that they be worked in company. You cannot do this properly unless you have a qualified assistant.

If you are operating a small stable and feel you need an assistant but actually cannot afford one, it is usually a good idea to hire one very good groom, pay him a little extra money and make him your straw boss. Many good grooms who want to become trainers and drivers would accept employment of this type quicker than they would a position as a routine groom at higher wages in a large stable. Sometimes you can come up with a good man, who would actually be a hybrid between a groom and an assistant trainer, by offering this type of employment.

A good second trainer has many duties. He is in charge when the head trainer is not around and he should have the authority to hire and fire caretakers. He should be well-groomed, neat and pleasant to the owners and visitors who come to the barn. He is expected to talk with the owners and tell them about their horses, but he is not expected to second guess the head trainer.

One of the hardest lessons for young second trainers to learn is that they must remain a trifle aloof from the help. An assistant trainer who goes out on the town with the men and plays cards with them in the stable area cannot and will not command their respect. He has to listen to and sympathize with their problems, but he also has to be stern. In other words, he represents management.

The assistant trainer has to be qualified to go out on his own with a group of horses from time to time. He has to be able to take over just as if it was his own stable. If he has trouble with a horse, he should call the head trainer for advice and if he is not qualified to drive or if there is a particular horse that he cannot drive he has to arrange for a substitute.

When I hire an assistant trainer, I usually spend some time with him describing what I expect of him. This applies not only to his work on the track but, to an even more pronounced degree, his work around the barn area before and after the daily training routine is completed. The head trainer is usually on the job early in the morning but often he has to leave in the afternoon and this is when the assistant earns some of his money by keeping things in the stable in tip-top condition.

For instance, I consider good housekeeping a by-word in my stable and my assistant trainers are responsible that everything is in good shape. I want the trunks and harness bags lined up and shining. I make it a point to measure the alignment of trunks so that they are lined up in a neat row. About once a week, I insist on a check of the trunks for neatness and at the same time the tack and equipment is inspected to be certain it is clean and in good repair. Also once a week, the trunks are moved out and the floor cleaned around and beneath them. You would be surprised how many dirty boots and how much missing tack will be discovered.

The assistant trainer is also expected to make certain that no groom leaves before he has cleaned all the tack and harness that has been used that day. He must also be sure that the carts and sulkies have been washed and properly taken care of. Once a week he should check wheel bearings on both carts and sulkies.

This is a very important assignment that many trainers are

not even aware of, let alone their assistants. I venture to say that there are horses racing today, even world champions, whose cart and sulky wheels have never been checked for balance from spring until fall.

In order to obtain maximum efficiency from a wheel, the ball bearings should be free and loose within their casing. Except where there are sealed bearings, dirt and dust can collect within the casing and affect the efficiency of the wheel.

The proper way to test this is to lift the sulky wheel off the ground and spin it. If it is properly balanced, the valve will eventually stop directly at the bottom of the wheel. If it does not, then the wheel is not balanced and a cleaning is indicated.

In the old days, the good grooms would take the sulky wheels apart the day before a race, clean the bearings and put in new oil or grease. This doesn't make a great deal of difference, I will admit, but it is the little things that count and if a sulky wheel isn't moving as freely as it should, there has to be an adverse effect on the horse, no matter how slight. It could make the difference in a race between two otherwise absolutely equal horses.

The trainer also passes on to the grooms, through his assistant, the manner in which each horse is to be jogged. Some horses need to be jogged stiffer than others and the jogging schedule will vary depending on whether the horse is being trained and how many days it has been since he was last trained. It is up to the second trainer to see that this is done properly. The foreign horses have proved to us that a good jogging routine is essential and I think this is an area that is overlooked in some of our stables.

The trainer should always specify exactly how many miles a horse is to be jogged and how stiff the jog is to be. It is up to the assistant to see that these instructions are carried out. A lot of grooms have a tendency to let a horse mope along whereas most of them need to be jogged at a fairly stiff rate in order to keep their muscles in good shape. In addition, some grooms will jog along at a very slow rate to keep the horse from getting warm so that there is less work involved in putting him away. This is wrong and it is up to the assistant trainer to see that it doesn't happen.

The assistant trainer is also responsible for a daily check on the feeding habits of the horses. He gets his orders from the trainer and sees that they are carried out. Grooms have a tendency to over or under-feed and the assistant should jump right on one who does this. He should also see that the horses are being fed from clean tubs. We all like to eat from clean dinner plates and a horse is entitled to the same consideration.

The assistant trainer should also be the man with the key to the supply room since he is available at the stable more than the head trainer. If you don't keep the supply room locked and the key in the possession of one responsible man, you will find two things happening: wasteful grooms will be taking a lot more than they actually need for their purposes and grooms will be failing to report what they took from the supply room and as a result no one will be billed for these supplies at the end of the month. The trainer will wind up paying for them out of his own pocket and this is a poor way to do business.

When a horse is in training he will spend a great many hours in the blacksmith shop. It is important that the trainer be there when horses are shod unless he has an assistant who is competent enough to handle this assignment. Even then, I think the head trainer should make it a point to be on hand, at least when a change in the type of shoe is being made. Many a race is won or lost in the blacksmith shop.

Incidentally, before I go on, let me point out that while a man who shoes horses is known as and commonly referred to as a blacksmith, there is a technical distinction involved that I would like to place in the record. A blacksmith is a man who can and does shoe horses but whose basic work is with iron products of all types. He shoes horses only as a sideline. A horseshoer on the other hand is a blacksmith who does nothing except shoe horses and who is an artist in this respect. This is why you will hear many of the leading trainers talk about a horseshoer rather than a blacksmith. It is a fine distinction but one that I consider important. It is comparable to a doctor (blacksmith) who specializes in children (horses) and thus is known as a pediatrician (horseshoer).

At a race track, a horseshoer is like a doctor. You don't just rush into his "office" unless it is an emergency. Otherwise, you make an appointment. The assistant should make these appointments after consulting with the head trainer and they should be made so that the groom is always available to take the horse to the shop. Since a groom usually has two horses, it is important that the appointment be made for a time when his other horse is not training or racing. A horse will stand a lot better in the shop and be much more content if his regular groom is with him. Then, too, in the summer the groom can help keep the flies off the horse. Flies are a real bother when a horse is being shod.

While I do not always stand around during the entire shoeing process, I like to be there when the shoe comes off to examine the foot along with the horseshoer, checking for corns, bruises, quarter cracks and things like that. There is nothing truer than the adage, "No foot, no horse," and sometimes you can spot a danger sign when a shoe comes off and take immediate action to counteract it. If the assistant trainer is especially competent, it is perfectly all right for him to represent the trainer in the shop, but shoeing is a tricky process and deserves the attention of a knowing person. I have known occasions where a horse has been shod at least four times in a row without either the head trainer or his assistant being there. I have a great deal of confidence in our horseshoers, but I can't believe this is right.

Another thing I try to do is to arrange my shoeing appointments so that they fall just before a horse is scheduled to race, perhaps a day or two in advance. This assures me that my horse has new shoes, or that the old ones have been re-set, and that there is less likelihood that he will lose one in the race. The exception to this is that when I am dealing with a horse that is a little peculiar about his shoes and will notice any slight change in the length of his toe, I will have him shod immediately after the race instead of before it. This usually involves a trotter that might miss as little as a sixteenth of an inch off his toe and make a break for that reason. By the time this horse is ready to race again, he has no problem. However, I always make a special check of this horse's shoes before he goes to the track on race day to make certain that a shoe is not loose or anything like that.

In any event, every shoe should be checked carefully within six hours of the time the horse is scheduled to race to make certain that every nail is absolutely tight. Occasionally, in an inspection of this type, you will notice the head of a nail that looks as though it might be going to break off and you can take the horse to the shop and have this nail re-set prior to the race.

When a horse leaves the home base and goes on the road, a large envelope containing all his vital statistics goes with him. The groom carries this envelope with him until the horse arrives at his destination at which time it is placed in the tack trunk. In this envelope will be the Eligibility Certificate, Health Certificate, a list of the horse's equipment, his shoeing and equipment card and a list of the dates on which he is scheduled to race (if he is a stake horse) as well as a notation relative to declaration time and the amount of the starting fee.

Usually, the assistant trainer will handle details of this sort if the head trainer is not available or in some instances, depending on the size of the stable, even if the head trainer is available. But occasionally a horse will be sent somewhere for a stake engagement with only the groom accompanying him. It is important that a good groom be given this assignment. For in addition to jogging the horse and getting someone to train him if he cannot do that himself, he must also enter the horse and handle all the other details. That is why it is important that every possible bit of information pertaining to the horse be placed in the envelope.

A horse like this might be on the road for as long as three or four weeks with the trainer arriving only on race day to handle the driving assignment. This is a good opportunity to determine whether a groom has the makings of a trainer. He has had an opportunity to train the horse between starts and I usually let the groom warm up the horse the first mile on race day. I can usually tell then by the horse's condition and reaction how well the groom is doing and whether it looks as though he has any future as a trainer.

These are also the grooms that should get a little extra bonus at the end of the season. I pay a bonus in my stable and advise new owners at the beginning of the year that I do since it is chargeable to them. I base the amount of the bonus on a man's contribution to the stable rather than on the earnings of his horses. This is because the top grooms will not necessarily have the best horses and I do not think I should penalize a groom who is doing an excellent job with a horse of moderate ability simply because that horse isn't winning as much money as some of the others.

The success of any business operation—and as I have already indicated a racing stable is a big business these days—is dependent to a great extent on the maintenance of accurate, meaningful records. In this section, I am going to review the methods I use to keep my owners and employees informed as to what is going on in my stable. In doing so, I am going to reproduce actual forms that I use or whose use I recommend. Not all of these forms are distributed to everyone—there would be no reason, for instance, to send my accountant a copy of a horse's shoeing record—but each form serves a specific purpose and is useful to one or more persons associated with the stable. Trainers who wish to use any of these forms may obtain them without charge by writing to the USTA.

One of the most important things is to keep the owner advised as to the progress of his horse or even the lack of such progress if that be the case. When a horse is in training and has not yet gone to the races, I think the least any trainer can do is to append a note to the monthly bill detailing the progress of the horse, especially if it is a 2-year-old. Frankly, I do not like this way of doing it and I do not recommend it because I think it creates a poor atmosphere between owner and trainer if the only time the owner hears anything about his horse is when the trainer wants money, which is what it boils down to. For that reason, I prefer to drop a line to each owner at least once a month and not at the time the bill goes out. This is where a secretary can be very helpful. A good one can ask the trainer for a few general words about the horse and convert them into a message to the owner. Believe me, I am all in favor of this and would do it on a weekly basis if I could because I believe an owner is fully entitled to know what is going on with regard to his horse. This is not so vital with reference to an old horse whose form and ability have been amply demonstrated in the past, but is especially important when 2-year-olds are involved. Every owner likes to think he has the next Bret Hanover in training and eagerly awaits word, any word, from the trainer.

It is just as important to advise an owner that his horse isn't doing well as it is to tell him that you think he has a coming champion. The owner is entitled to a trainer's best professional judgment and if he is making heavy stake payments on a colt

```
HORSE   MEADOW A.

WEEK OF   April 15th


    Monday 2:50, 2:35, 2:18 -1:06-:32

    Tuesday      Jog 3 miles

    Wednesday      Jog 4 miles

    Thursday  2:50, 2:35, 2:25

    Friday      Jog 3 miles

    Saturday      Jog 4 miles


COMMENT  Trained very well this

week.  Acted like he could go more

on Monday, but 2:18 is fast enough

for now.

SIGNED      Delvin Miller
```

Fig. 103. Each Saturday during the training season, the author mails to the owner of each 2-year-old in his stable a post card report like this which records the colt's training for the week just ended along with comment regarding his progress.

he should know exactly what the trainer thinks of that horse's chances. Of course, even the best trainers can't pick out the champions in January, but there are some horses whose progress is so slow and whose gait is so poor that it is obvious they are not going to make colt performers. These are the ones the trainer should tell the owner about promptly.

I have devised a little postcard report from (Fig. 103) that a trainer can use to keep an owner up to date on the progress of his colt. It is mailed out each Saturday afternoon so that on the following Monday morning the owner knows exactly what the horse did the preceding week along with any comment the trainer cares to make. This is intended basically for 2-year-olds, but it can also be used for older horses to give the owner an idea of how far along the horse is in his training program.

Believe me, an owner likes to get such information and, what is more, he is entitled to it. I don't think there's anything worse for an owner's morale than to lay out a healthy sum of money for a horse and then to have the horse disappear in the wilds of some large stable with no indication at all of how he is doing.

I also feel that it doesn't hurt for the trainer to pick up the telephone a couple of times a month and talk to the owner about his horses if he is not adept at letter writing or if he doesn't care to adopt the weekly postcard system. An owner is usually more than willing to accept a collect call in a case like this and I would rather do that to report something good to an owner than to have him start thinking, as many do, that the only time the trainer calls is when something bad has happened to the horse.

Once the racing season begins, the owner should be advised, either by mail, or by phone, if he prefers it that way, when the horse is going to start and, after he races, what he did. For this purpose, I use a post card (Fig. 104) which I mail to the owner both before and after the race.

It provides the pertinent information and I leave space at the bottom for any message of interest concerning the horse or the race. I also make it a practice wherever possible to send

---

_____DUKE'S SON_____ will/did race __April 4th_____

at __TROPICAL PARK_____in the __8th__ race, Post Position __4__

Purse _$2,500_____Finished _2nd___ in _2:00 3/5_ Driver _D. Miller_____

Earned $625_____Type of Race __Invitational_____Track Cond. _fast____

Comments __Raced good. Lost by head in photo. Took him__

__out at the half and he was parked out and raced gamely__

__the rest of the way.__

Signed ____*Delvin Miller*____

Fig. 104. Before and after most races, depending on where the owner is, the author mails a post card indicating either when the horse is scheduled to race or, as in this case, details of a race in which the horse has already participated.

OWNER INFORMATION SHEET

Name __John Jones__

Address __275 Main Street__

__Anytown, U.S.A.__

Telephones __865-209-3514__   __865-203-9581__
                    Home   Business

USTA M'ship Number ___86414___

Social Security Number __175-01-2568__

Claiming Authorization for __Meadow A.,__
__Meadow C., Meadow J.__

STATE LICENSE NUMBERS

Cal. __12345__ Del. __9101__ Fla. __6789__

Ill. __678__ Ky. __234__ Me. __0123__

Md. __9102__ Mass. __5678__ Mich. __456__

N. H. __345__ N. J. __910__ N. Y. __7890__

Ohio __678__ Pa. __2345__ Vt. __1234__

OWNS HORSES IN PARTNERSHIP WITH

__Ed Smith__

__Bill Forbes__

__Larry Johnson__

Fig. 105. These are the front and reverse sides of an Owner Information Sheet which the author maintains for each person who has horses in his stable.

HORSES OWNED

	Name	Partner	Where & When Purchased
1.	Meadow A		65 Harrisburg sale
2.	Meadow B	Forbes	65 Lexington sale
3.	Meadow C		Homebred
4.	Meadow D	Smith	Privately - 7/65
5.	Meadow E	Smith & Forbes	Privately - 8/66
6.	Meadow F		Homebred
7.	Meadow G	Johnson	65 Harrisburg sale
8.	Meadow H		Homebred
9.	Meadow I		Homebred
10.	Meadow J		Homebred
11.	Meadow K		Homebred
12.			
13.			
14.			
15.			
16.			

the owner a copy of the program for the night his horse raced
as well as a copy of the following night's program which usually
carries the charts for the previous night. If a horse is off somewhere in the care of a groom, the groom is charged with this
responsibility.

I do not mail any post-race information to local owners who
live near the track because they will know the results as soon
as I will. However, I do make it a point to call them when
their horse gets in a race because that is usually three days in
advance and the entries are not published in the daily news-
papers until the day of the race. I send an overnight sheet,
which lists the entries, to all owners as soon as it is printed.

In the conduct of my business, I find that it is very important
that I have at my fingertips a sheet containing all information
relative to an owner (Fig. 105). This is one of the sheets that I
have printed up in a size that will fit into a small loose leaf notebook that I always carry with me. In addition, a copy remains
in the office and each assistant trainer has one.

You would be surprised at the number of times I am called
on to provide one or more of the specific items on this sheet.
All of us are working to obtain a Universal Identification Card
for all owners, trainers and drivers. But until we do, we will be
faced with the proposition that we have to deal with different
license numbers as we move from state to state. This sheet is
a handy reference for those numbers and if I do not have a
number for a certain state, it means that my owner has not
acquired a license in that state and that he should.

What I try to do in this respect is to sit down at the beginning
of the year and go over an owner's horses in an effort to determine where they will be racing during the season. Then
I advise him which licenses to apply for. It is a darn good policy
to have these licenses in advance because there have been
instances where horses were not allowed to start in certain states
because the owner was not licensed.

In addition to the obvious things such as addresses and telephone numbers, this card also has the owner's USTA identification number, and his Social Security number which is a "must"
now on the trainer's records since so many things are keyed to it.

It also indicates those persons with whom this owner has
horses in partnership. This information is necessary in certain

states because of rules regarding entries. A list of the owner's horses appears on the back of this sheet.

I also recommend the use of a general purpose summary sheet (Fig. 106) that chronicles every start a horse makes. From

YEAR __1967__   NAME OF HORSE __MEADOW A.__   OWNER __John Jones__

DATE	PLACE	FIN.	TIME	DRIVER	PURSE	EARNINGS	TOTAL EARNINGS	10%	10% TOTAL	CHARGES	NET
2/11	A.B.	2	2:08	Smith	$1,000	$ 250	---	$ 25	$ 25	$525/ 525	(300)
2/18	A.B.	4	2:07	Smith	1,000	80	$ 330	8	33	---/ 525	(228)
3/4	C.D.	8	2:05	Smith	1,000	----	----	----	----	422/ 947	(650)
3/15	C.D.	1	$2:07^2$	Smith	1,000	500	830	50	83	---/ 947	(200)
3/22	C.D.	3	$2:06^3$	Roberts	1,500	180	1,010	18	101	---/ 947	(28)
3/29	C.D.	7	2:04	Smith	1,500		1,010			---/ 947	(28)
4/8	E.F.	6	$2:05^2$	Smith	1,500	----	----	----	----	500/1,447	(528)
4/16	G.H.	2	$2:06^1$	Smith	2,000	500	1,510	50	151	---/1,447	(78)
4/23	G.H.	1	$2:05^4$	Smith	2,000	1,000	2,510	100	251	---/1,447	822
5/7	G.H.	1	$2:05^2$	Edwards	3,000	1,000	3,510	100	351	485/1,932	1,237
5/14	J.K.	6	2:04	Smith	3,000	----	----	---	---	---/1,932	1,237
5/20	J.K.	4	$2:04^3$	Edwards	3,000	240	3,750	24	375	---/1,932	1,453
6/2	L.M.	3	$2:08^1$	Smith	3,000	360	4,110	36	411	625/2,557	1,152
6/9	J.K.	2	$2:04^2$	Smith	3,000	750	4,860	75	486	---/2,557	1,827
6/17	J.K.	1	$2:04^1$	Smith	3,000	1,500	6,360	150	636	---/2,557	3,177
6/26	O.P.	8	$2:03^2$	Smith	4,000	----	----	----	---	---/2,557	3,177
7/5	O.P.	5	$2:03^4$	Smith	4,000	200	6,560	20	656	480/3,037	2,877
7/12	O.P.	2	2:04	Roberts	4,000	1,000	7,560	100	756	---/3,037	3,777
7/20	Q.R.	1	$2:03^4$	Smith	4,500	2,250	9,810	225	981	---/3,037	5,802
7/27	Q.R.	3	$2:02^3$	Smith	5,000	600	10,410	60	1,041	---/3,037	6,342
8/7	O.P.	1	2:04	Smith	5,000	2,500	12,910	250	1,291	535/3,572	8,057
8/16	Q.R.	4	$2:02^2$	Smith	7,000	560	13,470	56	1,347	---/3,572	8,561
8/23	S.T.	2	2:03	Smith	7,000	1,750	15,220	175	1,522	---/3,572	10,136
9/1	S.T.	5	$2:01^4$	Smith	7,000	350	15,570	35	1,557	450/4,022	10,001
9/10	U.V.	2	2:02	Johnson	7,000	1,750	17,320	175	1,732	---/4,022	11,576
9/18	U.W.	1	$2:02^1$	Smith	8,000	4,000	21,320	400	2,132	---/4,022	15,176
9/25	W.X.	1	$2:01^3$	Smith	8,000	4,000	25,320	400	2,532	---/4,022	18,766
10/4	Y.Z.	3	2:01	Smith	10,000	1,200	26,520	120	2,652	520/4,542	19,326
	SUMMARY		28-8-6-4				$26,520		$ 2,652	$ 4,542	$ 19,326

OWNER SITUATION SHEET

NAME_____John Jones_____

| | Monthly | | Cumulative | | |
	Winnings	Expenses	Winnings	Expenses	Status
January	$ 1,650	$ 11,892	$	$	$ (10,242)
February	2,200	10,240	3,850	22,132	(18,282)
March	3,160	9,450	7,010	31,582	(24,572)
April	2,640	10,300	9,650	41,822	(32,232)
May	4,200	11,285	13,850	53,107	(39,257)
June	7,800	12,632	21,650	65,739	(44,089)
July	21,450	14,009	43,100	79,448	(46,348)
August	33,600	16,120	76,700	95,868	(19,168)
September	28,400	15,299	105,100	110,887	(5,787)
October	36,400	14,890	141,500	125,777	15,732
November	25,240	8,675	166,740	134,452	32,288
December	8,400	9,860	175,140	144,312	30,828

Fig. 106-1

SPECIAL NOTES AND COMMENTS

Meadow C claimed March 8th for $6,000

Sold 6 head at Fall sales for $84,000

Purchased 4 yearlings at Fall sales for $38,000

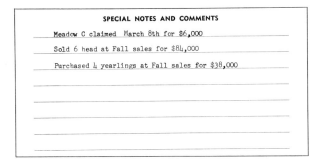

CLASSIFICATION SHEET

HORSE___Meadow II_____AGE__4___GAIT__trot_____SEX_mare_

MONEY WON PREVIOUS YEAR $26,312 _ LIFETIME $41,815 _ DASHES WON PREVIOUS YEAR 8

CURRENT YEAR RECORD

| | | | MONEY WON | | | |
Track	Date	Finish	This Start	This Meeting	This Year	Lifetime
A.B.	2/15	3	1,000	1,000	1,000	42,815
A.B.	2/26	1	3,000	4,000	4,000	45,815
A.B.	3/9	6	---	4,000	4,000	45,815
A.B.	3/16	2	1,000	5,000	5,000	46,815
C.D.	3/23	1	3,000	3,000	8,000	49,815
C.D.	3/30	7	---	3,000	8,000	49,815
C.D.	4/7	4	480	3,480	8,480	50,295
C.D.	4/14	2	1,250	4,730	9,730	51,545

Fig. 106-2

Fig. 106. Each horse in the author's stable has a sheet like the one at the left which chronicles each of his racing starts in the form illustrated. From this sheet, and from others for horses owned by the same person, an Owner Situation Sheet (Fig. 106–1, front and back) is prepared. This form enables the trainer to keep abreast of the owner's profit or loss status and is also used to record purchases and sales. Fig. 106–2 is another spinoff form from Fig. 106. This one is a Classification Sheet which carries information that enables the trainer to enter the horse properly in conditioned races.

it, I am able to spin off two additional sheets (Figs. 106-1 and 106-2) that I have made up in notebook size and carry with me.

I believe the summary sheet itself is self-explanatory It provides at a glance all that I need to know about a horse in my stable. Its form can and does vary with the individual trainer, but I think this one carries all necessary information.

The situation sheet (Fig. 106-1) is an interesting and informative one and it is a good idea for a trainer to keep a record like this. While the summary sheet relates only to one horse, the situation sheet applies to all the horses owned by any one patron of my stable. I update it each month at which time I add up all the winnings of that owner's horses, deduct the expenses and come up with a "situation" figure for the owner.

The value of this form is that it permits me to see at a glance how an owner stands financially. Perhaps I am training a horse that is a little off but that I think I could get back to the races and do some good with later on if I kept going. If the situation sheet for that owner shows me that he is having a rough year, I would be more inclined to turn the horse out and cut down the expenses. The same holds with relation to buying or selling. If an owner is doing well, I might suggest that he purchase a horse that I know is for sale and that I think is worth the money. If he is doing poorly, I might recommend that he sell a horse that I know can bail him out pretty good. Toward the end of the year, I sit down with an owner and go over this sheet with him. At this time, we discuss his general situation and try to determine whether it is necessary for him, for tax reasons or otherwise, to establish a better cash position for his operation.

The other form is the classification sheet (Fig. 106-2) which is also made up in notebook size. With conditioned racing in effect at most major tracks today, it is imperative that the trainer know to which events his horse is eligible. You would be amazed at the number of trainers who are unable to interpret a condition sheet properly and therefore do not enter their horses to the best advantage.

All that is really required is having the right information available on a day-to-day basis and that is what this card does. Most conditions are based on money or race winnings, either for the current year, the previous year (during the early part of the

Note: Mail to Stable Office every Sunday Morning.		DELVIN MILLER STABLE					Week Ending July 31, 1965
Name of Horse	Driver	Day	Fin.	Purse	Money Won	Groom	Place
Tarport Lib	Miller	26	1	$18,910	$9,455	Allen	Liberty Bell Park
Meadow Gladys	Miller	26	6	4,000	----	Erasmie	Liberty Bell
Meadow Janice	Arthur	28	2	16,860	4,215	Sepanick	Liberty Bell
Meadow Lenco	Miller	29	5	16,785	839	Armeno	Liberty Bell
Tarport Paul	Miller	29	1	16,785	8,392	Sanderson	Liberty Bell
Tarport King	Arthur	31	5	12,450	622	Smith	Liberty Bell

COMMENTS: (List Horses shipped, Date, Destination, Groom, Trucker)

Bernadet Hanover (Erasmie) to the Meadows July 28 via Sayre Trucking

Meadow Lenco (Armeno), Meadow Janice (Sepanick), Tarport Lib (Allen), Tarport Paul(Sanderson),

to Yonkers July 30 via Sayre

Tarport King to the Meadows August 1st via Sayre

Meadow Gladys to Jimmy Arthur Stable August 1st

Date: August 2nd   Trainer   Aime Choquette

Fig. 107. When horses in the author's stable are "on the road," a report concerning them is sent in to the home office at the end of each week. This is an actual form as it was mailed to the author's bookkeeper in 1965.

season) or during the current meeting. A trainer who has this information available in a small notebook is better prepared to enter his horses.

My sheet identifies the horse and lists age, gait and sex since

DAILY STABLE CHART

HORSE __FLORAL HANOVER__   AGE, GAIT & SEX __3, filly, trot__ TATTOO __2212D__

SIRE __Star's Pride__   DAM __Florella Hanover__   TRAINER __Del Miller__

ARRIVED __November 14__   DEPARTED_____   ELIGIBILITY CERT. { SENT FOR __Dec. 28__ / RECEIVED __Jan. 7__

Month Feb.	Temp.	Training and Racing Schedule					Special Notes
		Type	Miles	Time	Time	Time	
1	99.4	J	5				Plays when jogging, use bell
2	100	J	5				boots to jog in.
3	99.4	J	5				Jogged brisk last two miles
4	99.3	J	5				
5	100.1			Walked	20 minutes		
6	99.4	J	4				
7	100.2	W	J3-W1	2:55			Jogged 3 - came back for single
8	99.3	J	3				*Headpole on right side
9	99.4	J	5				Headpole on right side
10	100	W	J3-W1	2:53			Jogged 3 - turned & went single
11	100.1	J	5				
12	100.2			Walked	20 minutes		
13	99.4	J	4				
14	99.4	W	J2	2:50	2:48		Repeated for first time
15	100	J	3				Re-shod
16	100.1	J	4				Took fecal examination
17	100	W	J2	2:52	2:45		New hind shin boots
18	99.4	J	5				Fecal exam - no worms
19	100.1			Walked	20 minutes		
20	99.4	J	4				Teeth dressed
21	100	W	J2	2:49	2:42		
22	100.1	J	3				**With shadow roll
23	100.2	J	4				With shadow roll
24	99.4	W	J2	2:51	2:44		With shadow roll
25	99.4	J	5				With shadow roll
26	100			Walked	20 minutes		
27	100	J	4				Jogged 2 behind gate (perfect)
28	99.4	W	J2	2:50	2:39		Trained by Pres Jenuine
29							
30							
31							

J — Jog   W — Work   R — Race

*Wore headpole on right side on half mile track last year. I put it on in training once in a while so she will remember it.
**She jumped over paper late last year. Suspect might need shadow roll. Want to get her used to it just in case. She was fine.

Fig. 108. A daily stable chart is maintained for each horse in the author's stable. This is the actual chart for the filly Floral Hanover for the month of February 1967.

some conditions are written to accommodate these factors. There also appear at the top of the sheet the horse's lifetime earnings at the start of the year and the amount of money and the number of dashes he won the preceding year. Beneath that, I enter his current year starts as they are made indicating the track, date, finish and money winnings. The money-winning figures are for four separate categories, the last three of which—this meeting, this year and lifetime—can be and often are the sole basis of conditioned races. Additional lines appear on the reverse side of the sheet.

In almost all instances, I can immediately determine the eligibility of my horse by glancing at the card. Even when the conditions become more complex—such as a race for a horse with average earnings of $1,000 in his last six starts or for a winner or non-winner of so much in his last three starts—I have enough information on the sheet to determine eligibility with a minimum of fuss and bother.

In order to coordinate the activities of that portion of my stable that may be on the road and away from the home base, which I usually maintain at a pari-mutuel track, I have a special report sheet (Fig. 107) that is sent to the office every Sunday morning. It details the activities of all horses during the preceding week showing where and when they raced, where they finished, the purse and what amount of it the horse won, and the name of the driver and the groom.

In addition, I leave plenty of space at the bottom for the man who is charged with this responsibility, usually an assistant trainer, to list other items. Details relating to trucking arrangements, etc., are indicated so that they may be checked out by the bookkeeper when the charges are submitted. This sheet is made up in carbon-duplicate form. The man on the road retains the extra copy.

The remainder of the charts apply to individual horses and all except one are maintained in a large loose-leaf folder.

The first of these, the Daily Stable Chart (Fig. 108) is, perhaps, the most important record of all in that it details the day-by-day history of the horse. Each chart covers one month in the horse's career and tells me what the horse did every day of that month. I have filled out a sample form for the month of February in order that the reader will get an idea of how the chart works.

Both sides of the sheet are used as is the case with most of my charts.

The information at the top of the sheet is routine but includes two important pieces of information that should always be available. One is the USTA tattoo number (every horse is assigned such a number whether he is tattooed or not) and the other is a notation as to when the USTA Eligibility Certificate was sent for and when it was received.

Some trainers are very lax in this latter respect in that they wait until the last minute before they are shipping out to the races to apply for an Eligibility Certificate. Then, if it is determined that some little thing is out of order, such as the failure of an owner to have filled out his USTA membership application properly, the certificate is held up and the horse cannot be raced. This is why I always apply for my certificates early and make a notation on the daily chart as to when I did apply and when the papers arrived. The service from the USTA is very fast and Eligibility Certificates can be had virtually overnight if everything else in relation to them has been handled properly.

In the work section, I always enter the horse's temperature. There is nothing that will tell you quicker that a horse is coming down with something than a rising temperature. I have found that if you do not have a place to enter the temperature daily, the help will start to get lax about doing it and the next thing you know a week will go by without a temperature being taken. But when they know that there is a place for it to be entered each day and that I will be looking for it, it is done routinely and without fail.

To the right of the temperature column, I indicate by a capital letter what was done with the horse that day. He may have been trained (T), jogged (J), raced (R), walked (W), or shipped (S). In the next columns, I enter exactly what was done with the horse. If he was trained, I note how fast the miles were and if the quarters were anything but evenly-rated I indicate that as well. I reserve the right hand column for special notes such as equipment changes or the fact that the horse was re-shod or re-set.

Every horse in my stable has an equipment card or sheet (Fig. 109) that accompanies him wherever he goes. The purpose of an equipment card is to be certain that everyone associated

EQUIPMENT SHEET FOR ___DUKE'S SON___ GAIT ___PACER___

ITEM	DESCRIPTION
DRIVING BIT	Plain Snaffle
CHECK BIT	Speedway
BRIDLE	Open
OVERCHECK	PLAIN __x__ 4-RING ___
HEAD HALTER	PLAIN __x__ FIGURE 8 ___ NOSE BAND ___
SHADOW ROLL	YES ___ NO __x__
SHADOW BLIND	YES ___ NO __x__
MURPHY BLIND	RIGHT EYE ___ LEFT EYE ___
LIP CORD	YES ___ NO __x__
TONGUE STRAP	YES ___ NO __x__
HEAD POLE	LEFT ___ RIGHT ___ BOTH ___
GAITING STRAP	LEFT SIDE ___ RIGHT SIDE __x__ (HMT only and close to stirrup)
MARTINGALE	STANDARD ___ COMBINATION ___ RING ___
HOBBLES	TYPE _plastic_ LENGTH __60"__
SULKY SIZE	_52-28_

FRONT LEGS

ELBOW BOOTS	FELT ___ LEATHER ___
ARM BOOTS	YES ___ NO ___
KNEE BOOTS	PLAIN __x__ HALF ARM ___ FELT ___ LEATHER ___ (HMT only)
SHIN & TENDON BOOTS	FELT ___ LEATHER ___
ANKLE BOOTS	FELT ___ LEATHER ___ JOGGING ONLY ___
SCALPERS	LOW ___ HIGH ___
QUARTER BOOTS	LEATHER ___ FELT ___ RUBBER __x__ HINGED ___ (Jogging only)
BELL BOOTS	PLAIN ___ RIBBED ___
TOE WEIGHTS	2 OZ. ___ 3 OZ. ___ 4 OZ. ___
BRACE BANDAGES	YES ___ NO ___

HIND LEGS

SHIN BOOTS	YES ___ NO ___ FULL HOCK ___ HALF HOCK ___
ANKLE & SPEEDY CUT BOOTS	YES ___ NO ___
CORONET BOOTS	RUBBER ___ LEATHER ___
SCALPER	RUBBER ___ LEATHER ___ HIGH ___ LOW ___
BRACE BANDAGES	YES ___ NO ___

SHOEING

FRONT	TYPE _full swedge+bar_	TOE _3 5/8"_	ANGLE _48°_
HIND	TYPE _full swedge_	TOE _3 5/8"_	ANGLE _54°_

Fig. 109. An equipment sheet of this type accompanies each horse in the author's stable. It is usually taped to the inside of the tack trunk lid. This sheet is also available in smaller, loose leaf form.

SHOEING CARD

NAME _FLORAL HANOVER_ YEAR _1967_

Date	Front Feet		Hind Feet		Type of Shoe			
	Length	Angle	Length	Angle	Front Feet		Hind Feet	
1/2	3½	51	3⅜	55	HALF INCH - HALF ROUND	N	HALF ROUND-HALF SWEDGE	N
1/24	3½	50	3⅜	55	SAME	R	SAME	R
2/15	3½	49	3⅜	55	SAME	N	PLUS OUTSIDE HEEL CALK	N
3/4	3½ˢ	49	3⅜	55	SAME PLUS RIM PAD	N	SAME	R
3/20	3½ˢ	49	3⅜	55	SAME	R	SAME	R
4/6	3½ˢ	49	3⅜	55	SAME	N	SAME	N
4/22	3½ˢ	49	3⅜	55	SAME	N	SAME	R

Fig. 110. This is a shoeing card as maintained for each horse trained by the author. The lower case "s" in the second column indicates that the toe length measurement is "scant," that is, slightly less than 3½ inches but more than 3¼ inches. The symbols "N" and "R" under shoe types are used to differentiate between new shoes (N) and re-set shoes (R).

with the horse knows exactly what the horse wears. Many a race is lost by a horse wearing improper equipment and the question I ask myself before I finally put my o.k. on an equipment card is whether anybody in the world could rig the horse properly if neither I nor my assistant trainer nor the groom were there. If I can look the card over and answer "Yes," to that question I am satisfied.

I have filled in a card as it might look for a horse in my stable. Information relative to shoeing including type, length of toe and angle is also included on the equipment card. This information may be prepared on loose-leaf paper and placed in a notebook, but it is also a good idea to have it printed up on stiff cardboard and taped to the inside of the tack trunk lid when the horse goes on the road. In this manner, it is less likely to become lost.

Shoeing information is also maintained on a shoeing card that I carry in my note book. Every time the horse goes to the blacksmith shop, the exact measurements are entered on the card and thus I always know exactly what they should be. If I decide to make a change, I indicate that on the succeeding entry. I have filled out a typical shoeing card (Fig. 110).

Every stake horse in my stable also has what I call a route sheet (Fig. 111). This is not necessary in a stable made up mostly

ROUTE SHEET

HORSE __KEYSTONE SPARTAN__   YEAR __1967__

WEEK OF	DAY	DATE	EVENT & TRACK	PURSE	DECLARE	ST. FEE
Aug. 6	Thurs.	Aug. 10	Arden Stake Meadows	$12,500E	9 A.M. 8/7	$ 300
Aug. 13	Wed.	Aug. 16	Greyhound Springfield	23,000E	9 A.M. 8/14	250
	Fri.	Aug. 18	Carlisle Stake Carlisle	7,000E	12 noon 8/16	100
Aug. 20	Tues.	Aug. 22	American-National Sportsman's	12,500	9 A.M. 8/18	250
	Thurs.	Aug. 24	George Wilkes Brandywine	14,200E	9 A.M. 8/21	150
Aug. 27	Tues.	Aug. 29	Castleton Stake Du Quoin	24,000E	10 A.M. 8/27	200
Sept. 3	Mon.	Sept. 4	Hoosier Indianapolis	11,000E	10 A.M. 9/2	100
	Mon.	Sept. 4	Horseman Indianapolis	50,000E	10 A.M. 9/2	500
Sept. 10	Mon.	Sept. 11	Sep Palin Hazel Park	6,000E	9 A.M.9/7	35
Sept. 17	Wed.	Sept. 20	Ohio Standardbred Delaware	14,000E	10 A.M.9/18	None
Sept. 24	Wed.	Sept. 27	Bloomsburg Stk. Bloomsburg	10,000E	10 A.M.9/25	100
	Thurs.	Sept. 28	Transylvania Lexington	7,500E	9 A.M. 9/26	100
Oct. 1	Wed.	Oct. 4	The Saul Camp Lexington	9,000E	9 A.M. 10/2	100
Oct. 8	Wed.	Oct. 11	Hanover Colt Liberty Bell	28,500E	9 A.M. 10/7	200
	Fri.	Oct. 13	*Roosevelt Futy. R. R.	55,000E	9 A.M. 10/7	1,000
Oct. 15	Tues.	Oct. 17	Roosevelt Futy. R. R.	55,000E	9 A.M. 10/7	1,000
Oct. 22	Sat.	Oct. 28	The Scotland Yonkers	75,000	9 A.M. 10/25	500
Oct. 29	Sat.	Nov. 4	The Harriman Yonkers	100,000	9 A.M. 11/1	2,000
Nov. 5						
Nov. 12						
Nov. 19						
Nov. 26						
Dec. 3						

* Qualifying race if necessary

Fig. 111. A route sheet is prepared for heavily-staked two- and 3-year-olds. Both sides of the sheet are used. This is the reverse side of the actual 1967 route sheet for the 2-year-old trotter Keystone Spartan.

of raceway horses, but I consider it a must in a stable like mine that consists principally of two and 3-year-olds competing on the Grand Circuit. The route sheet tells me where each horse is entered each week along with other detailed information relative to the event.

Most of the time there will only be one event a week for a horse because I try not to double-stake too often, that is, name and pay twice when I know that I can only compete in one event. But sometimes, early in the season, I will double-stake if the sustaining fee is not too costly because my horse might be just coming on and I wouldn't want to tackle the bearcats at that stage. This is known as "out-shipping" your competitors.

It used to be that it was difficult not to double-stake because there were a great many conflicting events and the dates were not announced until after some sustaining fees had been paid. But in recent years the USTA and HTA (Harness Tracks of America) have made a cooperative effort to eliminate this and they have been very successful. The two organizations publish a superb stakes guide that lists all major events and is published early enough (usually the last week of December) that a trainer can avoid double-staking completely if he wants to.

As the reader well knows by now, this is a highly technical book aimed at converting into specific knowledge general information already possessed by would-be trainers and drivers and campaigning owners. I venture to say that in this respect it will serve for many years as the basic hand book of the sport and will become a well thumbed addition to any horse owner's library.

Because it is so technical, most of the book will be extremely heavy going for anyone who has no knowledge whatsoever of harness racing. This particular section, however, will not be because I am going to write it exclusively for those people who do not know a head halter from a hobble carrier but who, for one reason or another, think they might like to become a part of what I think is the greatest sport in the world. If you have ever wanted to own a harness horse and have wondered how to go about it and what it costs, this section is for you.

There are three basic ways of acquiring a horse. It can be done by buying one directly from the owner, a straight man-to-man business transaction. This is known as a private sale. It can be done by buying a horse at public auction. This is where most of the yearlings (horses that are a year old and whose racing potential is thus completely unknown) change hands each year, although a great many older horses are also sold in this manner. It can also be done by claiming a horse that is already racing, although in most states a person must already own a horse campaigning at the particular track in order to be eligible to make a claim.

In a private transaction, the owner sets a price and the prospective purchaser either meets it, turns it down or negotiates for more favorable terms. Many horses change hands in this manner and on my own and as an agent for some of my owners I have bought and sold a great many such horses over the years.

Very often, the highest priced horses are the best bargains. The most I ever got for a horse was the $500,000 Hanover Shoe Farms paid me for Adios when that great stallion was 15. I think everybody in harness racing will agree that he was just about the cheapest horse ever sold. Max Hempt and I each bought a one-third interest in Adios later on and he made money for anyone who ever had anything to do with him.

The highest price I ever sold a race horse for was the $150,000 received by Hugh Grant, one of my owners, when I sold his Meadow Skipper to Norman Woolworth. But Meadow Skipper went on and won in 1:55⅕ and earned $428,057 for Norman and was one of the best and fastest horses of all time. He, too, was a bargain.

At the same time, I have sold horses for as little as $200 which were, in comparative terms, just as successful. I have also sold horses that did not measure up to the potential I thought they had as well as some I did not think had very much potential and later verified my judgment.

But in every instance, I followed a policy I adopted over 30 years ago and that I think is a good one. If a horse I am selling has any known faults, I point them out to the prospective purchaser. And if I don't think a horse amounts to very much at all, I will say that. But I will also have that horse priced accordingly. I think the big mistake that many sellers make is that they over-price their horses, either because they cannot properly evaluate the animal or because they are afraid that the horse will do good in new hands.

I am exactly the opposite about that. I like a horse that I sell to do good for the new owner. Nobody was more thrilled than I was when Howard Beissinger won in 1:56⅖ with Tarport Lib as a 3-year-old and made her the fastest pacing mare in the history of the sport. I had consigned Tarport Lib, who was owned by Mr. Grant, to the Harrisburg auction at the end of her 2-year-old form and told all my friends that I thought she would make a great, great mare for someone. Howard bought her for $42,000 and I am sure her owners wouldn't sell her now for twice that amount.

The question then arises as to how much a horse is worth at private sale. I have a rule of thumb that, with certain variations, I follow in this respect. Generally speaking, a race horse is worth what he can reasonably expect to earn in one season. This will not be a net return to the owner of his invested capital in one year because he has to figure the training expenses. In actual fact, what it usually boils down to is that the purchaser should be able to anticipate recovering his investment and showing a profit, with all expenses paid, in something less than two years.

Now let's take a look at some of the variations of that rule. In the first place, it is obvious that if the horse has potential as a breeding animal when his racing days are over, then the purchaser can take that into account. Just as obviously, a gelding, which has no breeding potential, has to be figured strictly as a racing proposition and purchased as such. An entire horse that is fast enough and well enough bred to enter the stallion ranks later on conceivably could, and usually does, bring in excess of the one-year earnings formula. But you must remember that very few race horses have actual stallion value. The ones that do are those that usually sell in the $100,000 and up range. But while very few stallions make the grade in the breeding ranks, a great many mares do. Therefore, in buying a mare, especially a well-bred one, a certain upward revision of the one-year-earnings formula is permissible.

The formula must also be adjusted to compensate for specific racing circumstances that exist while the purchase is being contemplated and which might not exist a year later.

In favor of the purchaser, is a situation wherein the horse has been racing that year at a smaller pari-mutuel track, or even at the county fairs, where the purse structure is low in comparison to the horse's ability. For instance, a horse might be able to pace in 2:03 over a five-eighths mile track and 2:05 over a half mile track and be racing for purses ranging from $500 to $1,200. At the larger tracks with the bigger purses, this same horse might be able to race for purses ranging from $2,500 to $4,000. By my formula, it would be necessary to convert this horses's earnings potential to what it would be at the bigger tracks—providing the new owner planned to race him at those tracks—in determining his worth.

On the other hand, there are cases wherein horses are not worth as much as their current earnings might indicate. Falling in this category are horses that are presently competing in stake events that are limited to the get of certain sires and to which many of the better horses are ineligible, and horses which are eligible in the current year to a certain series of races, such as the Atlantic Seaboard Series or the Can-Am Series. In each of these cases, the value of the horse must be based not on what he is making that year but what his *potential* is the following year when he is no longer eligible for this type of protection and must compete on an equal basis with all horses.

In addition, when purchasing a horse at the end of his 3-year-old form, you want to be sure that you rate his prior earnings accurately. For instance, a horse might have been lucky and have won a couple of stakes at three which would increase his earnings beyond his actual race track ability. This would show up in the early part of the following year when the horse was entered in conditioned money-winning classes based on prior year earnings and which might tend to put that horse in over his head for the first couple of months.

Adjustments must be made for such horses, but I think you will find that the best rating formula is that a gelding, or a horse that does not have any obvious stallion potential, or an ordinarily bred mare is worth what he or she can reasonably be expected to earn in a single year.

Frankly, I would rather advise an owner to purchase a trotter instead of a pacer. I know that there are not as many races for trotters but I also know that a good trotter can get more starts and win more money, on a comparative basis, than a pacer that can go just as fast or even considerably faster.

This same formula should be employed in purchasing horses of racing age at public auction. But for obvious reasons it cannot be used in purchasing yearlings, horses that have never been trained, let alone raced, and a different approach must be made.

The annual yearling sales have great appeal to everyone in harness racing because the element of chance is so directly involved. This is the one area in which it can definitely be said that there is no truth to the adage, "the higher the price the better the horse."

As in anything else, your chances generally improve in relation to the price you pay since the higher-priced horses obviously will have the best pedigrees and the finest conformation. The reason this is true is that it is virtually all you have to go on in making your selection. Some farms lead their yearlings alongside ponies so that trainers and owners can get an idea of how they are gaited and a few consignors, including me, actually hitch their yearlings to cart before the sale. But even this provides only a smattering of information for the prospective purchaser and no indication whatsoever of how much heart, determination or extreme speed the horse has.

In some instances, the highest priced yearling is the best. In one year, Bret Hanover was sold for $50,000 and Noble Victory for $33,000. They were the best. But a year later Romeo Hanover sold for $8,700, Carlisle for $5,500, Polaris for $7,000 and Kerry Way for $16,000. Each of them won in excess of $100,000 at two and three.

One year somebody was complimenting Stanley Dancer on the success he had had with a number of high-priced yearlings. "Yes," said Stanley, "I paid $66,000 for a yearling pacer last fall and I wound up getting beat in the richest 2-year-old race the following year (The $100,000 Lawrence B. Sheppard Pace) by Nardin's Byrd, a colt that Billy Haughton bought for $2,500."

This is the essence of the appeal the yearling market has for the small owner. It is the one area in which he can successfully compete with the richer owners. In the long run, breeding and conformation will pay off, but if the small owner or the new owner is lucky, very lucky, he can come up with a Romeo Hanover or a Carlisle or a Nardin's Byrd and beat the world.

Let me wind up my discussion of the ways by which a horse may be acquired by explaining claiming races. These are relatively new to harness racing and did not take hold until the early 1960's. For years, prior to that, owners of harness horses seemed to be opposed to claiming races and were reluctant to enter their horses in them. That reluctance seems to have been overcome now and claiming races are common-place at almost all tracks.

A claiming race is one in which the horse is entered to be claimed for a certain amount ranging from as little as $500 at some of the small tracks to as much as $35,000 at the larger ones. The general range would be from $2,500 to $10,000.

A claim for a horse is deposited in the claiming box at the track prior to the actual race. For the indicated price, the horse then becomes the property of the person who puts in the claim. The money won in the race goes to the previous owner, but the horse is technically the property of the new owner from the moment the race starts and if he drops dead in the race the one who claimed him is the loser since he has already paid for him.

As I said, a brand new owner cannot usually break into the sport in this manner because only those racing horses at the meeting are eligible to claim a horse. The major exception to this rule, as I write this, is Illinois where anyone may make a claim.

Now, as a person interested in harness racing, you know as a result of having read this how to acquire a horse. But what do you do then? What you do, of course, is just what you would do if you were considering going into any other business about which you had no basic knowledge; you would seek advice, competent advice.

This advice should come preferably from a trainer since sooner or later you will have to become involved directly with one. For this, you need entree to a trainer. You may gain this entree either through a friend who is already in harness racing, or by calling an official at a track in your area, such as the race secretary, or by writing (a letter is better than a telephone call) to a trainer whose name you have noticed in the driver's standings on the track program or in a newspaper.

This is also where a new owner can get into trouble. Unfortunately, we do have some trainers in our sport whose glib tongues and pleasant personalities mask their shortcomings as conditioners of horses and representatives of owners. I have seen new owners fall into these traps which are baited with false or misleading quotations as to cost and glowing descriptions of an easy path to riches. There is no such thing as going the cheap way and being successful nor is there any easy road to riches. These owners learn their lessons the hard way and quickly depart the sport. I am sure that many of them, in proper hands, could have become wonderful owners. Trainers of this type will also "locate" a horse for a new owner and then charge him a fantastic mark up in making the purchase. There are not many trainers like this, but they do exist.

The best way to get a trainer is to be turned down by one of the top men who has so many horses that he cannot accept any more and to ask him to recommend someone for you. I know that Stanley Dancer and Billy Haughton do this routinely and I also do it.

I have been cutting back on my own stable in recent years but I still get many inquiries from persons who want me to train horses for them. I have to turn them down, but I am always glad to recommend someone else that I know is dependable, talented, and conscientious. I know a number of good young trainers scattered at various tracks throughout the country and I also know many experienced trainers whose names are not nationally known but who are high class horsemen. Depending on the area in which the new owner wants to race, I am always glad to recommend someone. I am careful who I recommend in these cases because I think every new owner is a big plus for harness racing and I want to see him get started right. If you have a problem in this regard, you can write to me at The Meadows, Washington, Pa. and I will be glad to advise you to the best of my ability.

Now let's proceed by assuming that the new owner has become associated with a good trainer and that they are about to make their first purchase. The trainer will first determine approximately how much money the owner wishes to invest and advise him as to the procedures involved in acquiring a horse and which I have already discussed.

I would say that the best way for a new owner to break into harness racing is to buy a ready-made horse that could be expected to race regularly. By this, I do not mean an especially high class horse, but rather one that possessed moderate ability and that was sound and could be counted on to race week after week. In this manner, the new owner can get his feet on the ground while he finds out what harness racing is all about. Then, as he gains knowledge of the sport and confidence in his trainer, he can expand according to his inclination and financial ability.

At the larger tracks, I would say that a horse of the type I have in mind would cost somewhere between $7,500 and $12,500. The ability of this horse would have been pretty well established and the program would show that he could go somewhere between 2:04 and 2:06 on a half mile track if he was a pacer and between 2:05 and 2:07 if he was a trotter. At a smaller track, the price range might be from $3,000 to $5,000 for a horse that could compete in the better classes.

With this as a starting point, the owner can then decide for himself, or be guided by the advice of his trainer, as to the future course to follow. Perhaps within a year they might want to take a rattle at the yearling sales or they might expand their operation the same year by picking up a useful claimer. I feel that the first year an owner is in the sport should be used to help him get his feet on the ground; a year in which expenses should be held to a minimum while the various ramifications of owning a horse are explored.

When an owner buys his first horse, he also finds out something about the United States Trotting Association. This vast organization is the parent body of harness racing throughout the United States and the Maritime provinces of Canada and is headquartered at Columbus, Ohio.

Every person who races a harness horse must be in membership with the USTA. Present membership exceeds 25,000. In addition to individuals, all race tracks are either USTA members or have a service contract with the association.

The results of every race, including those at hundreds of county fairs, flow daily into the USTA headquarters where they are processed by computer and become the only permanent record of the sport. Each year the USTA publishes both the Year

Book, which lists every race contested the previous year, and the Sires & Dams Book, the Association registry, which chronicles the performance and production of stallions and mares.

The USTA formulates national racing rules which are enforced in conjunction with the various State Racing Commissions. It licenses drivers, trainers, and officials such as judges, starters, race secretaries and clerks of course. In short, the USTA is harness racing and without it the sport would undoubtedly fall back into the chaos that existed in the late 1930's when three governing bodies with conflicting rules were attempting to administer the sport. It was to eliminate this chaos that the USTA was organized in 1938.

In addition to its other functions, the USTA also issues an annual Eligibility Certificate for every horse. Without this certificate, a horse cannot race. The certificate chronicles the racing performances of the horse and goes with him from track to track. It is filled out after every start and thus up-to-the-minute information is always available on any horse. Incidentally, if an owner is considering the purchase of a horse, he should always ask to see the Eligibility Certificate for the current year and have his trainer review it with him. It gives complete information relative to every start the horse has made and is a useful tool in deciding whether to make a purchase.

There is one other thing that a prospective owner should bear in mind when he is considering purchasing a horse. If he can't stand a fingerprint check he might as well not try to become an owner. State agencies require that applicants for an owner's license be finger-printed and they and the USTA are very strict, as they should be, in refusing to license undesirables.

The next question naturally arising—and the most important of all to many new owners—is, "How much does all this cost?"

Here, and to the best of my knowledge for the first time anywhere, I will show exactly what it costs to train and race a horse and explain in detail each and every item on a trainer's monthly bill.

But since we are assuming that the owner reading this section is brand new in the sport and owns no equipment whatsoever, I think it would be well if I reviewed first what it costs to outfit a horse. I have, therefore, prepared the chart on the following page which lists the items of equipment that a horse should have.

BASIC EQUIPMENT LIST

VEHICLES
*Sulky	$400.00	
*Jog Cart	350.00	
	$750.00	$750.00

GENERAL EQUIPMENT
*Harness with bridle	$165.00
Head Halter	8.25
*Trunk	85.00
*Trunk Cover	12.50
Stall Screen	20.00
*Harness Bag	14.00
*Harness Hook	5.00
*Refuse Basket	12.00
Feed Tub	10.00
Water Pail	4.00
*Wash Pail	4.00
*Lead Shank	6.00
Cross Ties	2.00
Salt Rack	1.25
*Foot Pick	.50
Stall Bandages, 2 sets	8.00
Brace Bandages, set	5.00
	$362.50 $1,112.50

BLANKETS
3 Coolers @ $16.00	$48.00	
1 Breezer	12.00	
2 Stable Sheets @ $12.00	24.00	
1 Baker Blanket (in North)	25.00	
1 Fly Sheet	9.00	
	$118.00 $1,230.50	

BRUSHES AND SPONGES
*Body Brush	$2.50
*Mane & Tail Brush	2.00
*Curry Comb	.75
*Body Sponge	4.00
*Tack Sponge	1.00
*Scraper	.75
	$11.00 $1,241.50

PACING EQUIPMENT
Hobbles	$70.00
Knee Boots	40.00
*Shadow Roll	7.00
Scalpers	4.00
*Bell Boots	4.00
	$125.00
TOTAL FOR PACER	$1,366.50

TROTTING EQUIPMENT
Hind Shin Boots	$40.00
Quarter Boots	5.00
*Scalpers	4.00
*Bell Boots	4.00
	$53.00
TOTAL FOR TROTTER:	$1,294.50

In addition, there are many other items of racing equipment that may or may not be needed. Some of these and their prices are: *Head Pole ($18.00), Elbow Boots ($45.00), Tendon Boots ($30.00), Toe Weights ($3.00), *Gaiting Strap ($15.00), Stud Support ($12.75), *Surcingle ($12.50), *Blinker Hood ($7.95), and Standing Martingale ($5.25).

If an owner has two raceway horses that will be stabled together throughout the year, all equipment indicated by the asterisk (*) above can be used for both horses (bearing in mind that the harness itself can be used by both horses but that separate bridles are required), thus affecting a considerable saving. Extra blanket items would have to be purchased for each horse according to the list above except that one additional cooler instead of three would be enough. Each horse should have his own hobbles and boots except for scalpers and bell boots. As far as vehicles are concerned, one sulky will be enough for as many as four horses and one jog cart sufficient for two.

The prices are those that were in effect in 1967 and as to the individual items are neither the highest nor the lowest prices charged. I have prepared the chart from my own records and the prices are those that I would pay if I were outfitting a horse with first class equipment.

It must also be borne in mind that some equipment can and probably will be purchased second hand. The trainer, for instance, might have a trunk that another owner wants to dispose of and which would be available at a discounted price because it has been used. If the trunk is in good condition, it would be perfectly all right to purchase it instead of buying a new one. Generally speaking, I cannot say the same of harness and boots because I prefer that such equipment be new. But even this is not always the case because there are times when you would be able to buy slightly used harness at a price that was discounted enough to make it worthwhile.

You will note that it costs in the neighborhood of $1,300 to properly equip a horse. I think the list is pretty well self-explanatory and I am not going to bother to explain the individual items. There are others that can be purchased, but I think that this list is quite complete.

There is a slight cost difference in outfitting a horse depending on whether he is a trotter or a pacer. A pacer, for instance, requires a set of hobbles at approximately $70 whereas a trotter does not. A trotter, on the other hand, almost always needs hind shin boots at about $40 while a pacer does not. I have separated the trotter and pacer in the last two categories on the equipment list and have assigned to each the basic equipment usually required. In addition, I have added a number of items at the bottom that may or may not be required depending on the individual horse.

All equipment purchased for a specific owner should immediately be identified by labeling, either by using strip tapes or indelible pencil or something like that. This is the practice in major stables and it is a good one. There is nothing more discouraging for an owner than to lay out $1,000 for equipment, sell the horse after a year and find out he only has equipment worth $400 credited to him. In this respect, an owner should receive an itemized list at the beginning of each year showing what equipment he owns and what changes have been made— that is, new equipment purchased or old equipment damaged or destroyed—during the preceding year.

Some equipment will last a long time and some should be replaced at frequent intervals. For instance, I never like to use a set of hobbles on a race horse for more than a year. What I usually do is buy a new set for the race horse and use the old ones on colts, that is, young horses that haven't been to the races yet. I figure the useful life of a set of hobbles is one full year at the races and one full training season for colts. After that, I try to get rid of them. I know that hobbles will last two or three years, but I don't like to take a chance on their breaking. It could happen in a big race and it just isn't worth the risk.

Sometimes the hobble hangers, the straps that hold the hobbles up, won't last a year, especially with a horse that sweats a lot. I keep checking this and if I notice that the hangers appear to be getting weak I will replace them.

The life of other items of equipment depends on the individual horse and, to a surprising degree, on the competency of the care-taker. In particular, the life of a set of harness is dependent on this latter factor. With a good groom, a set of harness will last three or four years with only the driving lines having to be replaced. But with a groom who isn't careful and doesn't clean his harness properly each time it is used, a set will last barely a year. The same applies to the various boots that the horse might wear.

Actually, equipment wears out quicker now than it used to. The quality is just as good, but our horses are racing now in all kinds of weather in all seasons of the year and rain, mud, snow and cold take a heavy toll.

For the purpose of determining as accurately as possible the cost of racing a horse for a full year, I have worked from my own bills and from a number of others that have been made available to me by other trainers. From them, I have prepared two detail charts which I have broken down to indicate typical monthly charges.

CHART NO. 1
COST OF TRAINING

This chart indicates what it would cost to campaign a raceway horse in the New York area. The horse was in training on January 1st, went to the races on February 15th and remained there through October 31st. He was then turned out until December 15th and was picked up on that date to begin training for the following year.

EXPENSE	JANUARY	FEBRUARY	MARCH	APRIL	MAY	JUNE	JULY	AUGUST	SEPTEMBER	OCTOBER	NOVEMBER	DECEMBER	TOTAL
Training @ $4.00 per day	$124.00	$112.00	$124.00	$120.00	$124.00	$120.00	$124.00	$124.00	$120.00	$124.00	----	$ 68.00	$1,284.00
Stall Rent @ $1.00 per day	31.00	15.00	---	---	---	---	---	---	---	---	---	17.00	63.00
Feed @ $3.00 per day	93.00	84.00	93.00	90.00	93.00	90.00	93.00	93.00	90.00	93.00	---	51.00	963.00
Groom @ $90.00 per week	199.33	180.04	199.33	192.90	199.33	192.90	199.33	199.33	192.90	199.33	---	109.31	2,064.03
Paddock Expense	---	20.00	40.00	20.00	10.00	40.00	30.00	40.00	30.00	60.00	---	---	290.00
Comp. Insurance @ 5%	9.96	10.00	11.97	10.64	10.47	11.65	11.46	11.97	11.15	12.96	---	5.47	117.70
Federal Taxes @ 5%	9.96	10.00	11.97	10.64	10.47	11.65	11.46	11.97	11.15	12.96	---	5.47	117.70
State Taxes @ 2½%	4.97	5.00	5.97	5.33	5.24	5.83	5.73	5.97	5.58	6.49	---	2.74	58.85
Public Liability @ 7¢ per day	2.17	1.96	2.17	2.10	2.17	2.10	2.17	2.17	2.10	2.17	2.10	2.17	25.55
Shoeing Charges	40.00	40.00	36.00	48.00	48.00	64.80	40.00	60.00	40.00	71.00		22.00	509.80
Trucking Charges	---	17.30	---	---	13.50	---	---	15.75	---	---	20.95	---	67.50
Veterinary Charges	19.00	18.00	17.00	---	7.00	---	---	---	5.00	29.00	---	17.00	112.00
Harness & Repairs	5.25	15.25	5.95	---	8.50	4.50	---	15.40	---	5.95	2.55	---	63.35
Supplies	7.60	8.30	2.42	1.95	.85	.50	3.35	5.00	.50	5.75	1.25	---	37.47
Administrative Charges	5.00	5.00	5.00	5.00	5.00	5.00	5.00	5.00	5.00	5.00	5.00	5.00	60.00
Turnout Charge	---	---	---	---	---	---	---	---	---	---	100.00	46.62	146.62
TOTAL	$551.24	$541.85	$554.78	$506.56	$537.53	$548.93	$525.50	$589.56	$513.38	$627.61	$131.85	$351.78	$5,980.57

CHART NO. 2
COST OF TRAINING

This chart indicates what it would cost to campaign a raceway horse at a smaller pari-mutuel track. The horse entered training on February 1st, went to the races on May 1st and remained there through October 31st. He was then turned out for the remainder of the season.

EXPENSE	JANUARY	FEBRUARY	MARCH	APRIL	MAY	JUNE	JULY	AUGUST	SEPTEMBER	OCTOBER	NOVEMBER	DECEMBER	TOTAL
Training @ $2 per day to May 1st $3 per day thereafter	---	$ 56.00	$ 62.00	$ 60.00	$ 93.00	$ 90.00	$ 93.00	$ 93.00	$ 90.00	$ 93.00	---	---	$ 730.00
Stall Rent @ $10 per month	---	10.00	10.00	10.00	---	---	---	---	---	---	---	---	30.00
Feed @ $50 per month	---	50.00	50.00	50.00	50.00	50.00	50.00	50.00	50.00	50.00	---	---	450.00
Groom @ $65 per week	---	65.03	143.99	139.35	143.99	139.35	143.99	143.99	139.35	143.99	---	---	1,202.97
Paddock Expense	---	---	---	---	20.00	20.00	25.00	20.00	20.00	15.00	---	---	120.00
Comp. Insurance @ 5%	---	3.25	7.20	6.97	8.19	7.97	8.44	8.19	7.97	7.95	---	---	66.15
Federal Taxes @ 5%	---	3.25	7.20	6.97	8.19	7.97	8.44	8.19	7.97	7.95	---	---	66.15
State Taxes @ 2½%	---	1.63	3.60	3.49	4.09	3.98	4.22	4.09	3.98	3.98	---	---	33.07
Public Liability @ 7¢ per day	---	1.96	2.17	2.10	2.17	2.10	2.17	2.17	2.10	2.17	---	---	19.11
Shoeing Charges	---	12.00	6.00	12.00	24.00	12.00	18.00	26.00	12.00	12.00	---	---	134.00
Trucking Charges	---	---	---	---	14.50	---	---	---	---	---	13.00	---	27.50
Veterinary Charges	---	8.00	10.00	5.00	10.00	---	6.00	12.00	10.00	5.00	---	---	66.00
Harness & Repairs	---	12.00	3.00	---	2.50	4.50	2.00	---	4.00	---	---	---	28.00
Supplies	---	4.50	2.00	3.50	6.00	5.00	3.00	2.00	2.00	3.50	---	---	31.50
Administrative Charges													
Turnout Charge	50.00	---	---	---	---	---	---	---	---	---	50.00	50.00	150.00
TOTAL	50.00	227.61	307.16	299.38	386.63	342.87	364.26	369.63	349.37	344.54	63.00	50.00	$3,154.45

CHART NO. 3

COST OF TRAINING AND RACING A 2-YEAR-OLD STAKE COLT

In this presentation, two types of 2-year-old stakes colts are considered. One is in the same stable as the raceway horse in Chart No. 1 and will make a Grand Circuit stakes tour in the hands of one of the country's leading trainers. The other 2-year-old is in the same stable as the raceway horse in Chart No. 2 and will race in stakes and/or early closers at the smaller tracks and county fairs. The basic charges --- training, stall rent, feed, groom and turnout --- are the same for both horses in each of the two categories, but there will be a minor variance in the amounts because of the length of time the horses were in the training stable and/or at the home base before they went to the races. The 2-year-old in the Chart No. 1 comparison was in training on January 1st and raced through the end of October. The 2-year-old in the Chart No. 2 comparison was also in training on January 1st but he only raced through the end of September. The dates and charges are in keeping with national averages for each type of colt.

	WITH CHART NO. 1 AS BASE		WITH CHART NO. 2 AS BASE	
EXPENSE	RACEWAY HORSE	STAKE 2-YEAR-OLD	RACEWAY HORSE	STAKE 2-YEAR-OLD
TRAINING	$ 1,284.00	$ 1,216.00	$ 730.00	$ 701.00
STALL RENT	63.00	120.00	40.00	50.00
FEED	963.00	912.00	450.00	450.00
GROOM	2,064.03	1,954.92	1,202.97	1,178.56
PADDOCK	290.00	180.00	120.00	70.00
ALL TAXES	294.25	267.49	165.37	160.00
LIABILITY INSURANCE	25.55	25.55	19.11	19.11
SHOEING	509.80	428.00	134.00	110.00
TRUCKING	67.50	67.50	27.50	27.50
VETERINARY	112.00	303.50	66.00	140.00
HARNESS & REPAIRS	63.35	113.40	28.00	65.40
SUPPLIES	37.47	247.85	31.50	84.50
ADMINISTRATION	60.00	60.00	---	---
TURNOUT	146.62	200.00	150.00	150.00
TOTAL	$ 5,980.57	$ 6,096.21	$ 3,164.45	$3,206.07

POTENTIAL ADDITIONAL CHARGES FOR STAKE COLT

	RACEWAY HORSE	STAKE 2-YEAR-OLD	RACEWAY HORSE	STAKE 2-YEAR-OLD
2-YEAR-OLD SUSTAINING FEES	---	$2,285	---	$ 400
TO SUSTAIN FOR 3 & 4-YEAR-OLD EVENTS	---	750	---	---
TOTAL SUSTAINING FEES	---	$3,035	---	400
STARTING FEES	---	5,500	---	400
TOTAL SUSTAINING & STARTING FEES	---	8,535.00	---	800.00
ADDITIONAL TRUCKING	---	1,000.00	---	250.00
TRAINER TRAVEL EXPENSE	---	1,000.00	---	---
TOTAL	$ 5,980.57	$16,631.21	$ 3,164.45	$ 4,156.07

STAKES PROGRAMS FOR 2-YEAR-OLDS

	VERY HEAVY	COMPLETE	MODERATE	PROTECTIVE	COUNTY FAIR	FILLY
NUMBER OF 2YO STAKES	20	14	10	5	12	11
SUSTAINING FEES	$ 2,770	$ 2,285	$ 1,560	$ 765	$ 400	$ 1,150
SUSTAIN FOR OLDER EVENTS	900	750	500	500	---	500
TOTAL SUSTAINING COST	3,670	3,035	2,060	1,265	400	1,650
STARTING FEES	7,200	5,500	2,550	4,700	400	2,700
TOTAL	$ 10,870	$ 8,535	$ 4,610	$ 5,965	$ 800	$ 4,350
EST. VALUE, 2YO EVENTS	$ 480,000	$ 375,000	$ 175,000	$ 200,000	$ 70,000	175,000
*EST. VALUE, OLDER EVENTS	1,000,000	800,000	485,000	780,000	30,000	725,000
TOTAL	$1,480,000	1,275,000	660,000	980,000	100,000	$ 900,000

* Additional sustaining fees and starting payments must be made as 3 and/or 4-year-olds.

These charts are for raceway horses which compete only in overnight events at the pari-mutuel tracks. Using them as a base, I will also show the cost of racing a 2-year-old stake colt on the Grand Circuit and one at the county fair level.

In compiling the charts, I have attempted to retain a consensus pattern and thus have not followed the exact billing procedures of any one trainer. Some trainers will have charges that do not appear on my charts while others will not charge for everything that I have indicated. But, overall, I think an owner can assume that these are representative cost figures.

Chart No. 1 is for a raceway horse that is being campaigned at the metropolitan New York tracks by one of the leading trainers. It indicates, and accurately I feel, that it costs approximately $6,000 to maintain such a horse for a full year. The horse is in training on January 1st, goes to the races on February 15th and remains there until October 31st. He is then turned out at the trainer's farm until December 15th at which time he re-enters training for the following year.

Chart No. 2 represents the cost of training a horse at one of the smaller tracks where the purses are not as large and labor costs cheaper. The horse enters training on February 1st and races from May 1st until October 31st after which he is turned out for the balance of the year. The cost is approximately $3,200.

Depending on the geographic area and the purse structure at the track, other annual charges for raceway horses would fall somewhere between these two figures. It should not cost more than $6,000 to train a raceway horse and while it is possible to have one trained for less than $3,000, I feel that this would be the exception rather than the rule.

I have also prepared an additional chart (No. 3) for stake colts although I have not repeated the detailed monthly charges that appear on the other two. Instead, I have worked with the raceway horses as a base and have attempted to show the additional charges that a 2-year-old stake colt (the figures would be much the same for a 3-year-old) might reasonably be expected to incur. I will comment on these charges as I review the individual catagories although it is obvious from glancing at the chart that the major difference lies in the cost of making sustaining and starting payments in stake races. The cost of training a 2-year-old that is in the hands of a top colt trainer and makes a full Grand Circuit campaign can run as high as $15,000 or even more.

In addition to the costs I have indicated on the charts, the trainer also receives ten percent of the horse's gross earnings. The stable may also pay an annual bonus to its caretakers, but this practice varies so widely that I have not included it as a routine charge. Nor have I included a charge for insuring horses since there does not seem to be any definite pattern in this respect. Full mortality insurance on a race horse is about four percent.

Now that I have established the format, let me devote some time to a discussion of the individual charges as they appear on the charts.

TRAINING FEE—In most cases, the cost of training a horse is based on a specific daily rate. However, there are trainers, including me, who charge an overall daily rate that includes the cost of training, groom and feed. In my own case, the present charge is $13 a day when the groom is taking care of the usual two horses.

Since the daily charge for training only is the more common of the two billing methods, I have used it on the charts. For the horse campaigning at the leading raceways and in the hands of a top trainer, the charge is $4 a day. I do not believe any trainer charges more than this. Quite a few charge less including the one (Chart 2) who is campaigning our horse at the smaller track. He charges $2 a day until the horse gets to the races (February, March and April) whereupon the charge is increased to $3 a day.

It used to be that most trainers used this method, charging less before the horse went to the races, or at least during the period that the horse was in training but only being jogged, and more when the racing season opened. However, I have observed that the leading trainers have begun to make a flat charge the year round and I have indicated this on Chart No. 1.

From this charge, the trainer pays his assistants and part of his overhead. It has been my experience, and most trainers tell me the same thing, that a trainer does not actually make any money from this basic charge. It is usually eaten up in the form of salaries for assistant trainers and by paying grooms for whom there are no horses available but who are good enough to be kept on the payroll throughout the year. A trainer cannot afford to let a good groom go just because he doesn't have a horse available for him and sometimes he has to pay him out of his own pocket.

The trainer actually makes his profit out of the ten percent he charges on the purse money won and I have alway found that owners are happy to pay this because it means that their horses are making money.

STALL RENT—This is an item that appears on almost every training bill in one form or another until the horse gets to the races. I have set Chart No. 1 up to show that the trainer has his own operation and charges $1 a day for use of his stalls and track facilities. The other trainer, who is probably conditioning his horses at a county fair track somewhere, charges $10 a month.

Even if you train at one of the larger public training areas, stall rent is involved. I train at Pompano Park in Florida and pay $120 a season for each horse. I bill this to the owners. There is no charge for stall rent at the race tracks once the racing season begins. Some race tracks permit winter training and usually make a charge. At The Meadows, the track at Washington, Pa., with which I am associated as President, the winter-training charge is 50 cents a day.

FEED—All trainers charge for feed. As with everything else, the amount depends on the trainer and his location as well as the quality of feed he buys. The $3 daily charge on Chart No. 1 is a fairly high one, but I find that more leading trainers are using this figure than any other so I have listed it that way. Our other trainer charges $50 a month for feed but he is located in an area where he does not have to pay high freight charges.

CARETAKER—The cost of caring for a horse has gone up in recent years. It used to be that a good groom could be hired for from $40 to $60 a week but that is no longer possible now at any of the large racing centers close to the big cities.

On Chart No. 1, I have put the groom in at $90 a week. On Chart No. 2, I have figured the cost at $65 a week. I pay grooms from $70 to $100 a week and I find that the going rate for a good groom in a top stable is $90. For this salary, the groom is expected to take care of two horses throughout the year and this is indicated on the charts where the charge for the groom actually represents half his weekly pay. Another horse is charged with the other half.

Some trainers will assign three or even four horses to a caretaker and thus reduce the charge to the owner. However, it is my opinion that a good groom has his hands full taking care of two horses properly and that he should not be assigned more except in an emergency.

There is an exception to this general rule. When horses first go into training and are only being jogged, or when yearlings arrive to be broken, a good groom can take care of three and even four without too much trouble. I do this in my own stable and recommend it. But once horses are turned and begin to go training miles, two to a groom is usually plenty.

I have taken this into account on Chart No. 2. This raceway horse was only jogged in February, the first month he was in training, and the groom had four horses at the time. The charge is reduced accordingly on the chart. The 2-year-old in the same stable (Chart No. 3) was in training during the month of January but he was not being repeated (trained more than one heat on any one day) and thus his groom also had four horses at a reduced charge to the owner. The 2-year-old, however, started to repeat in February and from then on his groom had only one other horse. It might not seem necessary to make these minor distinctions but since I am attempting here to portray actual situations and thus develop realistic cost figures I am presenting them exactly as they would probably occur.

Very often, when a top horse is involved, he will have a caretaker assigned specifically to him and that caretaker will not have another horse. The owner of this horse is then billed for the groom's entire wage instead of half of it. This horse is usually the type that is making plenty of money. Since this is the exception rather than the rule, I have not indicated it in either of my basic charts.

TAXES AND INSURANCE—Just as in every other business these days, the federal and state governments are standing by to take their share. Workman's compensation insurance must be purchased and the employer's percentage of social security and state and federal unemployment taxes must be paid.

I have listed compensation insurance on all charts at five percent. The rate varies depending on the employer's rating. It can be higher or lower than five percent but I feel that figure is about average.

Federal taxes include social security and federal unemployment insurance. As I write this they amount to about five percent and I have charged them at that figure. The social security tax will continue to rise and as it does, the chargeable rate will increase. I have listed the state unemployment tax at 2½ percent. This figure varies widely from state to state and all I have tried to do is to hit a happy medium.

I have also listed a public liability insurance charge of seven cents a day. Not all trainers carry this insurance, but it is a good idea to do so and I recommend it.

PADDOCK EXPENSE—In most areas of the country, it is now customary to pay a caretaker a "paddock fee" whenever he goes to the paddock with his own horse on race day or when he goes as a helper for another caretaker. Although it is not always possible, it is best if two caretakers are on hand whenever a horse races. Uusally, the regular caretaker and one from the same stable who does not have a horse racing that day or night work as a team.

The "paddock" rate at the larger tracks is $5 a man and at the smaller tracks $2.50 a man. These charges are indicated on all charts and since they represent income to the groom, the standard tax and insurance payments must be made.

SHOEING—Shoeing charges depend on rates charged by horseshoers and on the type of shoe involved. A bar shoe or one with calks or a set of pads results in a higher charge. After studying various bills, I have determined that the usual charge for re-setting shoes (removing the shoe, trimming the foot and replacing the same shoe) runs from $4 to $8 and the charge for a new set of shoes from $12 to $20.

It actually costs about the same to shoe a raceway horse or a stake horse. The difference in the charges shown on Chart No. 3 reflects the fact that the raceway horses were at the races longer and made more starts. It cost less to shoe raceway horses at the smaller track because blacksmith charges were not as high and the horse did not race as long.

TRUCKING—Trucking rates are set by law and there is not much variance. The "traveling" horse is the one that eats up the money in this respect and you will note that while the trucking charges for the two raceway horses were very moderate, the stake horses who were moving from track to track, had larger charges even at the county fair level. I estimated from the bills submitted to me that it would cost an additional $1,000 to ship a Grand Circuit colt and another $250 to ship the county fair colt in his home state. The $1,000 charge could have been even higher if the colt was flown from one track to another to meet an engagement. The trucking charges shown on Charts Nos. 1 and 2 are absolute minimums in that one horse spent the entire season at the same track while the other raced only at two tracks. A raceway horse would naturally incur higher charges if he moved from track to track.

In shipping horses, the thing you always strive for is to make sure your horse goes as part of a load and thus is on a "convenience" basis. In this manner, the set transportation rate for the entire load is divided among the horses on the truck. If yours is the only horse on a load, you can let yourself in for a whopping charge. There are none of these on my charts. All shipping was done on a "convenience" basis which is not difficult to arrange when a number of horses are moving from one track to another.

VETERINARY CHARGES—On Chart No. 1, the veterinary charge for the year is $112. This can be considered to be an average annual charge in New York-Pennsylvania area for a horse that was neither sick nor lame during the year. The veterinary charge for the raceway horse at the smaller track is roughly half that amount.

The stake horse is a little different proposition because younger horses are more likely to develop a sickness of some sort or to go lame. This is reflected in the charges for our stake colts who, while never lame or sick enough to miss a race, did require some additional treatment during the season. Their bills amounted to $303.50 and $140 as indicated on Chart No. 3.

And let me add right here that I think it is very important that a trainer identify the exact nature of each veterinary charge on the monthly bill. There is nothing that will scare an owner more than a big veterinary bill without an accompanying explanation. Actually, I make it a point to call the owner if I find it necessary to summon the vet for anything more than a routine visit. If his horse is sick or lame, the owner is entitled to know it immediately.

HARNESS AND REPAIRS—In itemizing these charges on the charts, I have taken into consideration the fact that this is a new owner and that I have purchased new or good second hand equipment for his horse at the beginning of the year. Therefore, in reviewing the bills from which I worked, I eliminated most charges for new equipment and listed only those items that could reasonably be expected to be charged against any horse in the course of a racing season. The range of these annual charges on the three charts was from $28 to $113.40.

Since my charts do not show what the specific charges represented, it would probably be a good idea if I listed some of those that were incorporated into the annual bills. A random selection is as follows:

One pair scalpers ($3.95), repair gaiting strap ($1.50), line quarter boots with rubber ($4.00), hobble hangers ($12.50), new suspender on knee boot ($2.00), repair knee boot ($ .75), strap on bike seat ($1.75), wrap bit ($1.50), two inner tubes ($4.00), repair scalpers ($1.50), shadow roll ($7.00) and repair training cart ($35.00).

I cannot say that the last charge is a routine one but every once in a while a colt will tear up a cart and when he does it has to be repaired and the owner is billed for it. This item or a similar one appeared on three of the bills that were submitted to me so I thought I would include it in my consensus program on the grounds that it is not entirely rare.

Incidentally, some trainers who operate public stables actually prefer that the owners do not provide three basic pieces of equipment, the sulky, jog cart and tack trunk. They have these painted in their own stable colors and rent them to the owners. One leading trainer makes a daily rental charge of 50 cents. There seems to be a trend in this direction and it does not appear to be a bad idea at all.

SUPPLIES—These are the little things such as cotton, bandages, liniments etc. which are part of any stable operation. Some trainers also have a basic daily rate for such minor supplies and one charges 20 cents a day for use of cottons and mud, which he provides.

Again, I think that probably the easiest way to demonstrate the nature of these charges is to list a selection at random:

Set of cottons ($3.95), tack sponge ($ .75), painting equipment ($2.65), two tapes ($ .70), oatmeal ($ .25), two rub towels ($2.00), safety pins ($ .60), Creolin ($3.00), Hooftone

($6.00), coronary paste ($9.00), hobble chafe ($3.50), poultice powder ($3.00), kidney medicine ($ .50) and Epsom salts ($ .50).

The supply bill for the Grand Circuit stake colt ($247.85), who is usually getting a costly tonic of one kind or another, is much higher (Chart No. 3) than any of the others.

ADMINISTRATIVE CHARGE—Some trainers add an administrative charge to each horse's monthly bill to cover overhead, such as secretarial work, which cannot otherwise be recovered by the trainer. The charge is usually made only by trainers with large public stables and it varies from $2 to $5 a month per horse. I have set it up at $5 for Chart No. 1 but have not made it a chargeable item on Chart No. 2.

TURNOUT CHARGE—When horses are not in training they are turned out. The usual charge is $100 a month which is what I have used although it varies depending on the locale and sex of the horse. Turnout rates are much cheaper in rural areas where farms are plentiful and the rate is also usually less in the case of mares and geldings that can be turned out in groups. Stallions require individual paddocks and the turnout rate for them is often in excess of $100 a month.

All charges for training, care and feed cease when the horse is turned out and turnout dates should be recorded accurately by the trainer. I have known instances of an owner being charged training rates for a horse that was turned out. Since this is not an actual training charge, I could have left it off my chart, but in order to reflect accurately the cost for a full year I included it. I set the charge up at $100 a month on Chart No. 1 and $50 a month on Chart No. 2. The Chart No. 1 horse is turned out at the trainer's farm, thus the public liability insurance charge continues. The Chart No. 2 horse is turned out elsewhere and the liability charge is dropped.

TRAVEL EXPENSE—The charges for travel expenses vary from trainer to trainer, but it is customary for them to be made provided that the trainer must leave his home base (the place where most of his horses are stabled) to race elsewhere. This charge is not usually made in the case of raceway horses but it can result in a considerable amount where stake horses are involved and the trainer must fly somewhere each week to race the horse. In this respect, Chart No. 3 shows an expense item of $1,000 for the Grand Circuit 2-year-old that is on the road most of the summer.

I will not bother to detail these expenses, but, in general, they consist of transportation charges from the trainer's home base to wherever the horse is racing. I have included motel bills but not meals and incidental expenses which I do not feel are normally chargeable. When a trainer goes to another track and races more than one horse, the travel expenses are pro-rated against all horses involved.

STAKE PAYMENTS AND STARTING FEES—It is quite obvious in studying the charts that the related items of stake payments and starting fees constitute the major difference between the cost of campaigning a raceway horse and a stake colt. There are no stake charges against either of the raceway horses while for the stake colt they can spiral beyond $10,000 in extreme cases. In addition, the cost of training and racing is further swelled by additional charges for transportation and travel expense which go hand in hand with campaigning a stake colt.

There is no question that these stake fees really eat up an owner's money. But while there are more stakes today than ever before and thus larger sustaining and starting fees, we are also racing for a great deal more money and thus the percentage paid by any individual owner is proportionately less than it was when I started racing horses.

As chairman of the USTA Stakes & Futurities Committee, I am constantly working to get these payments lowered and to have the tracks contribute more money. I think our committee has made appreciable progress in a number of respects but there is no disguising the fact that stake payments and starting fees are still a very heavy burden for an owner to carry.

In a sense, stake payments represent a form of insurance. An owner pays a fee (sustaining payment) and in so doing takes out an insurance policy guaranteeing that his colt will be eligible to compete in a rich race when it is eventually contested. In the 2-year-old division, many of these payments are due between January and April and thus before the trainer has any real idea how good his colt is. For that reason, large numbers of horses are kept eligible while the trainers and owners cross their fingers and hope for the best. As later payments become due and the colts begin to sort themselves out as to ability, sustaining payments are made on fewer and fewer. Those who start in any given stake are the cream of the crop.

In order that an owner may have an idea of what it costs to stake a horse and how much money that horse can compete for, I have prepared Chart No. 4 consisting of six different stakes programs for 2-year-olds. In order, this chart lists stakes schedules that are very heavy, complete, moderate, protective, and county fair, plus one for a filly.

Our Grand Circuit stake colt whose training costs are detailed on Chart No. 3 has the "complete" stakes schedule as outlined in the second column on Chart No. 4. I have made payments on this colt in 14 of the leading 2-year-old stakes worth an estimated $375,000 and at the same time have made sustaining payments while he was still a 2-year-old for three and four-year-old events that will make him eligible to an additional $800,000 in purse money.

All this cost the owner $3,035 before either he or I knew very much about the colt. All we knew at the time that most of these payments were made was that he was sound and training as well as could be expected.

If this colt gets to the races, it will be necessary to pay the starting fees in the various events. These amount to $5,500 but to be honest about it, the starting payments aren't nearly as hard to make as the earlier sustaining payments. I never start a stake colt unless I think he has a chance of winning money and the payment of a large number of starting fees usually indicates that the horse is showing a profit.

My other 2-year-old that is being trained in conjunction with the raceway horse whose expenses are outlined on Chart No. 2 also has a stakes schedule. But instead of going on the Grand Circuit he is campaigning in county fair stakes and early closers and in one or two moderate pari-mutuel track stakes in his own state.

Because a great many states these days have fine state aid programs for young horses, this colt is able to race a complete stakes schedule at a moderate cost. I checked some of these state aid programs and found that I could stake the 2-year-old for about $400 in sustaining fees and an additional $400 in starting fees. This outlay would give my colt a dozen races, ten at the fairs and two at pari-mutuel tracks. He would be eligible to about

$70,000 worth of races at two and a total of $100,000 in all. These state aid programs are great for 2-year-olds.

Now let's refer again to Chart No. 4 and review some of the other ways a colt may be staked. In the first column we have a colt that is very heavily engaged. He has been kept eligible to 20 2-year-old stakes which is an extremely large number. Only one or two trainers in the country will pay up in this many stakes. This colt is not only eligible to the principal raceway stakes but is making a complete tour of the Grand Circuit including stops at such places as Springfield and Du Quoin, Ill.; Indianapolis; Delaware, Ohio; and Lexington. It costs $3,670 to make the sustaining payments and if the colt starts in every stake to which he is eligible, the starting fees will amount to $7,200 for a grand total of $10,870.

Of the total amount of the sustaining payments, $2,770 went for stakes which have 2-year-old divisions. Some of these stakes also have three and 4-year-old divisions and the colt is still eligible to them.

The remaining $900 was paid to keep the colt eligible to races for horses older than two but which require a sustaining payment on 2-year-olds. Falling in this category are such classic races as The Hambletonian, The Messenger, The Dexter, The Little Brown Jug, The Colonial, The Kentucky Futurity, The Adios and The Realization.

The very heavily staked horse thus will be eligible to 2-year-old races worth about $500,000 and three and 4-year-old races worth a million dollars. This is a big jackpot and is the reason why owners are willing to make these heavy payments to guarantee eligibility.

The second column on Chart No. 4 is for the colt that I call "completely" staked and is the one I have used to illustrate the cost of racing a stake colt on Chart No. 3 and which I have explained previously. It provides for a total of $1,275,000 to race for.

The third column is for a colt that is staked moderately in 10 events which are selected with a view toward keeping him away from the top stakes and the top stake colt performers. This is the colt that gives an early indication that he might make a useful second rate stake horse. It cost $1,560 to keep him eligible to the 2-year-old events and I name him in a few of the better 3-year-old classics at an outlay of $500 just in case he turns out to be more horse than I think he is.

The fourth column is what I call a "protective" staking program. I am working here with a colt that indicates that he might come on as a 3-year-old much more than at two. Or perhaps he is a little off early in the season and I am fearful of doing too much with him at two.

What I do is select five stakes that have the best three and 4-year-old divisions and then add a couple from the list of events for three and 4-year-olds only. It costs me $1,265 to do this but at the same time I have set my colt up to compete in races worth $200,000 at two and almost $800,000 at three and four. If my colt comes on, he has about a million dollars worth of stakes on his schedule at a minimum cost.

I have already explained the next column which is for the county fair stake colt and I have also taken the liberty of setting up a column for a filly. I have named her principally in stakes that have filly divisions but have protected her by paying her up at two in a couple of the richer three and 4-year-old events just in case she is another Countess Adios or an Armbro Flight. It costs me only $1,650 to make the 2-year-old sustaining payments and she has a potential of $900,000 to shoot at.

It must also be borne in mind that additional sustaining payments as well as the starting fees must be made at three and four in those events conditioned for horses of those ages. But once I get a colt past his 2-year-old form, I have a pretty good idea of his potential and can make sustaining payments with more confidence than I could when he was an untried youngster.

I have also listed the 2-year-old starting fees on Chart No. 4 and they amount to a great deal. But, as I said before, a colt on whom the starting payments are being made is almost always making money.

While I have referred specifically in this section to payments in stakes and futurities, I should also mention that there is another type of race that falls in this category and which is known as an early closer. The only real difference between a stake, a futurity, and an early closer is the year in which nominations are taken. Nominations for futurities are taken the year the horse is born; in stakes, the year the horse is a yearling and, in early closers, the year of the race. I have included some early closers among the races for my 2-year-old stake horses.

The extra money an owner pays to keep a 2-year-old eligible to the rich stake races can, naturally, pay big dividends. The annual earnings potential of any proven raceway horse can usually be predicted in advance to a reasonably accurate degree. The stake horse, on the other hand, is an unknown quantity when he enters training as a 2-year-old. He could be an absolute dud or he could "shoot the moon," as the saying goes. It is the dream that the untried 2-year-old on which sustaining payments are being made might be harness racing's next Bret Hanover that encourages owners to meet these stiff tariffs.

In closing out this section, I think I should point out that it is usually advisable for the trainer to make the stake payments rather than the owner. The trainer has a much better idea of the caliber of the horse and usually has a general racing schedule outlined in his mind, if not on paper, for this colt and others in his stable. In addition, owners have a tendency to make payments earlier than they should (I always wait until the actual due date to pay because you can never tell when a horse might go lame or even drop dead) and to double-stake their horse, that is name them to events scheduled at different tracks the same week. I think the trainer should consult with the owner but that, as in most other cases, the owner should be guided by the trainer's advice and let him handle the details.

Billing owners for stake payments also creates a problem for some trainers. It takes many thousands of dollars to make these payments and some trainers, especially those with relatively small stables, don't have that kind of cash on hand. To tell the truth, it also creates a hardship on trainers with large stables because they have so much more to pay out. When I operated a large stable, I had a policy of either billing my owners two weeks in advance of the actual due date or immediately after making the payments, all of which fall due by rule on the 15th of the month. If I billed in advance and later found that it was not necessary or desirable to enter a colt, I would give the owner credit on his next bill.

I hope that in discussing the ways and means of acquiring a horse and the various costs involved that I have been able to clarify this phase of harness racing for newcomers to the sport. In the final analysis, a new owner should tread very lightly until he gets his feet planted firmly on the ground and should seek and follow the advice of a reputable trainer until he has sufficient experience to make major decisions on his own.

(Biographical information concerning the author appears on page 141.)

16

LAMENESS
in the STANDARDBRED

DR. EDWIN A. CHURCHILL

I think lameness in the trotter and pacer is one of the more important considerations with respect to training and racing because very few horses and particularly very few good or fast horses get through a racing season without becoming lame to some degree somewhere.

Considering the present high cost of racing, we would be able to make it much more profitable for the owner if we were able to control lameness. We would have more starts per season per horse and therefore more income per season per horse with all owners profiting as a result. There is no way of knowing how many potential world champions have never even raced because they went lame before they even reached the races. But you may be sure that there have been many.

In order to stimulate thought in the direction of lameness in the trotter and pacer, I am going to consider a number of the various lamenesses along with their causes, symptoms and treatments in the hope that someone will benefit from what I write and thereby enjoy greater good fortune in racing.

My remarks will be confined specifically to the Standardbred and I should point out in the beginning that lamenesses in the trotter and pacer are often peculiar to the breed and not necessarily common in other race horse breeds such as Thoroughbreds and Quarter horses.

First of all, I think we should understand why this is so. Let me lead into that by discussing briefly the basic characteristics of the trotting and running horse breeds, both generally and in this specific respect.

The Thoroughbred horse has been bred over many centuries and next to the Arabian is the oldest popular breed still in existence today. The Thoroughbred has been evolved through selective breeding, largely through the use of fast horses for breeding purposes and therefore we have produced a breed that is constantly breaking track records. The modern Thoroughbred, as bred in the United States, is a racy looking individual with very fine quality, fine bone, fine features, prominent eyes, and a very fine hair coat. He appears to be leggy, or rather he appears to have long legs in comparison to the Standardbred. He has a fairly long barrel and considerable length from the point of his hips to his pin bones. The modern Standardbred does not show the quality that the Thoroughbred does only because the Standardbred is not an old enough breed. Many Standardbred families still show very prominently the effects of the cold blood which was introduced into the breed along with the gait. At the same time, the better Standardbred families today are showing many quality horses. By that, I mean horses that are fine-haired and fine-boned and have fine features. Along with these qualities, the better families are also producing speed. Through selective breeding, we will eventually produce a uniform horse with all the quality of the Thoroughbred as well as great speed.

The lamenesses of the Thoroughbred are confined largely to the front quarters because at top speed the Thoroughbred puts most of the stress on these quarters. This is brought about by the fact that a Thoroughbred pushes off the ground with both hind legs at the same time and lands on his front legs one at a time after a long stride through the air. At this instant, the front legs receive individually the entire weight of the horse plus the jockey and are therefore exposed to greater stress than the hind legs. A Thoroughbred can become lame behind but before this happens the front quarters are usually involved.

Both trotters and pacers, on the other hand, push off the ground with one hind leg at a time. Therefore, that individual hind leg, in an attempt to propel the entire horse, is necessarily exposed to greater stress than the same leg on the Thoroughbred who pushes off the ground with both hind legs. The Standardbred thus is subject to become lame in the hind quarters just as frequently as he does in the front quarters because weight and stress are pretty much individually distributed.

PREDISPOSING CAUSES OF LAMENESS

One of the most important predisposing causes of lameness is conformation. It is almost impossible to purchase a horse that has ideal conformation. In most cases, we are forced to accept a horse that has more good features than bad. It is frequently the bad features that lead to eventual lameness and poor performance on the race track. I will not attempt to describe an ideal horse because I think all of us have a different idea of what such a horse should look like. As I discuss certain conformation features, the reader may refer to Billy Haughton's illustration of the typical Standardbred, (Fig. 6).

I do think, first of all that we should strive to purchase an animal that has good feet as we are all aware of the saying "No foot, no horse." By a good foot, (Fig. 112) I do not necessarily mean a large foot but one that is in line with the rest of the horse's size. It should be well shaped with a large degree of concavity of the sole, a good wide frog, broad at the heels and of good quality. Good quality means that the foot should not be shelly or hard but should give freely to thumb pressure in the heel and around the coronary area. Even good feet will become deformed during a racing season through constant shoeing, bruising, and/or cutting (such as cross-firing or forging) so it is most important that we start with a good foot if the horse is to be raced for any length of time.

The pastern should be of medium length, neither too long nor too short. A short pastern is usually a very straight pastern and is frequently associated with horses that have very little action in the front legs. A long pastern puts excessive strain on the tendons and suspensory ligament and is frequently associated with horses with extreme action of the front legs and with bowed tendons and other serious lamenesses.

The ankle joint should be flat in front and not too prominent although there should be sufficient depth from front to back to allow for strong attachments of the suspensory ligament and adequate room for the tendons which run between the sesamoid bones in the back of the ankle.

The shin bone should be deep and flat. The suspensory ligament should be well outlined and the tendons should also be well outlined and straight, and not cut in under the knee.

The knee should be flat on the front, should be in proportion to the horse's size and, as viewed from the side, should be in line with the shin bone so that the horse is neither buck-kneed (Fig. 10-3) nor calf-kneed (Fig. 10-4). If one or the other of these latter defects cannot be avoided, it is preferable to take the horse that is slightly over in the knees, or buck-kneed rather than the calf-kneed horse because of the stress the knee receives during racing. A calf-kneed horse will very frequently develop arthritis of the knee joint and is subject to chip fractures involving the small bones of the knee. In both the trotter and the pacer, the knee joint receives its greatest stress when the front foot hits the ground. With the buck-kneed horse that is over in the knee, the muscles of the leg receive most of the shock and stress rather than the joint itself. With a calf-kneed horse, the knee joint itself receives the greatest amount of stress because the knee tends to turn backward under the horse's body in a direction opposite to its normal motion. This backward action compresses the bones on the front side of the joint surface causing damage to the cartilage and, frequently, chip fractures in this area. With respect to a calf-kneed horse, I don't think there is any difference in the gait of the trotter or the pacer that would lead anyone to believe that there is a lesser impact in one as opposed to the other.

The shoulder area should be wide and deep with as much angle as possible to the length of the shoulder blade. The greater the length and angle, the more muscle there will be to act both as a shock absorber and as a source of propulsion for the front legs.

The hind leg should be in line with the pelvis so that a plumb line dropped from the pin bone would approximately parallel the rear tendons. The hocks should be in proportion to the horse's bone structure and neither too fine nor too coarse. Naturally, the hind legs should point straight ahead so as to preclude a cow-hocked condition (Fig. 13-6) (horses that stand toed-out behind are said to be cow-hocked) and if the back line of the tendons is perpendicular this precludes a sickle-hocked condition (Fig. 13-2). (A sickle-hocked horse is one whose hind legs extend forward from a perpendicular line from the hock to the ground). Horses that are cow-hocked and/or sickle-hocked usually have a gait that tends to put excessive strain on the upper portions of the leg as well as the hock itself.

The stifle area should be well muscled and have a good angle from the hock to the stifle and from the stifle to the pelvis. The stifle area receives extreme stress during high speed and is one of the most important areas in the discussion of lameness in the Standardbred.

Even the body structure may predispose a horse to lameness if he carries excessive weight and thereby subjects the legs to unnecessary stress due to poundage alone. Also, the head and neck area must be long enough to balance the horse either trotting or pacing. Balance is all-important in the Standardbred and without it either the front or rear quarters are bound to be subjected to more than their normal share of work.

TEMPERAMENT—Temperament is not extremely important as a cause of lameness except among horses that are bad-tempered in the stall and kick excessively thereby causing bruises to bones or other tissue that may lead to more serious troubles on the race track. A horse that pulls while being jogged or trained ordinarily subjects himself to unnecessary stress and thereby may predispose to any type of lameness. Horses that are very nervous are frequently predisposed to tying up or to other muscular ailments involving the nervous system and should be discriminated against.

GAIT—The gait of a horse is all-important as a predisposing cause of lameness and I do not think it requires any detailed explanation. Certainly, for example, a horse that goes high and hits the ground hard is more predisposed to bruises or other ruptures of tissue than the horse that has moderate action with a smoother gait that allows him to slide a little when his feet hit the track. Among trotters, the horses that are most apt to become lame because of a faulty gait are those that go high in front or are sprawly-gaited behind with the hind legs opening up to overlap the front to an extreme degree.

A trotter that has excessive action in front ordinarily hits the ground with sufficient concussion to cause eventual lameness in the front leg. A horse that trots extremely wide behind puts excessive strain on the stifle area and in most cases the trainer tries to shoe the horse to compensate for the gait. When a horse is shod to compensate for a wide gait behind, it ordinarily stops a natural motion of the foot when it hits the track and puts excessive strain on the suspensory ligament in the lower portion of the leg as well as on the stifle ligaments. In addition, the horse wastes a lot of energy because a great deal of his effort is spent maintaining this wide gait instead of pushing with the hind legs and using his muscles to propel himself forward. In other words, at such a gait there's too much lost motion to each hind leg.

All of this has equal application to a pacer except that it is desirable to have a pacer go just a little wide behind because it helps him to maintain his balance and roll with his body. Since a pacer pushes with both legs on the same side at the same time, he can only keep his balance and maintain speed if his weight is directly over these legs at the moment he pushes with them. If his gait is not wide enough, he cannot propel the weight of his body to any great degree. A wider gait also makes a pacer much less likely to cross-fire or to interfere with his knees.

SHOEING—Horses are shod for two reasons. The first is to provide some protection for the hoof from concussion and from excessive wear due to abrasive race track surfaces. The second is to complement the horse's gait as much as possible. A horse with an absolutely normal foot requires only a light shoe with no special ground surface. On the other hand, a horse with a flat sole is frequently helped by using a pad to reduce concussion and excessive bruising of the sole surface. How any one horse should be shod depends on that individual and cannot be described as applying to all horses. When it comes to complementing a horse's gait by shoeing, the most important thing to remember is that if a horse is good-gaited he should be shod just as plain as possible and consistent with the race track surface. A pacer that requires shoeing to correct cross-firing or a trotter that requires special shoeing to clear the hind shins, is much more predisposed to lameness because his feet are being stopped or accelerated unnaturally. For example, if we try to shoe a trotter off his hind shins by squaring the front toes, and thus speeding up his action in front, the horse may become shoulder weary from snatching his front feet off the ground before they are ready to leave the ground. Likewise, if we put swedges or swedges and bars on this horse behind, we are stopping his hind legs when they hit the ground and putting excessive strain on the hock and stifle area.

Corrective shoeing is much more apt to produce lameness in a young horse than in an old horse. Therefore, young horses, two and 3-year-olds, should be given every opportunity to develop a natural gait rather than an artificial one as a result of shoeing. Older horses can be shod with more severe devices, such as borium and grabs, without nearly as much risk of causing lameness. The older horse is more developed while the bones of the young horse are not set and his ligaments and muscle structure are not developed to the same degree. Although the race track records would not indicate it, we still haven't developed a super breed that can stand excessive strain as two and 3-year-olds. A horse still continues to grow to his 5-year-old year and while many of our colts develop at an early age, they continue to mature until they are five. All young horses that require special shoeing should be given an opportunity as often as possible to show whether this shoeing is still necessary because it will frequently be found that after a horse develops a gait and attains racing capacity he can be shod with a plainer shoe.

RACE TRACK SURFACES—One of the most frequent causes of lameness in the harness horse today is the type of track surface he races over. The ideal track is one that has resiliency and spring to its base and yet has enough cushion so that the horse's feet and legs do not have to be the sole source of shock absorption. We have many types of race tracks in use today. The types of lamenesses that are produced over these tracks vary with the type of surface. The race track that has a very hard surface predisposes the horse to bruises of the feet and to all sorts of bony bruises in all sections of the leg. Once a horse's foot becomes bruised or sore from traveling over a hard race track, he will alter his gait to try to protect his feet and as soon as he does this he puts excessive strain on other structures of the leg. One of the most prominent examples of the disadvantage of a hard race track is the great number of splints that are produced on horses of all ages as a result of trying to protect themselves while traveling with sore feet. For example, a horse that develops a severe bruise on the outside quarter of the right front foot will alter his gait so that he will try to land on the inside quarter of that foot. In so doing, he will change the center of gravity of his body over the leg so that a greater amount of weight is being borne by the structures on the inside of the leg. As a result, the suspensory area and the splint bone on the outside of the right front leg are exposed to extreme tension, and very often the splint bone will pull loose from its attachment to the shin and a large splint will result.

The hard race track surface also exaggerates the action of any corrective shoe. I think it is very obvious that a horse wearing full swedge shoes is going to come to a quicker stop on a hard surface than he will on a soft surface where the swedges cannot develop the same degree of friction. This is particularly true of horses that wear swedges on the hind feet and the quick stopping action of such shoes is the frequent cause of stifle lameness on hard race tracks. Another effect of the hard race track is the obvious fact that without proper protection from concussion a horse is much more apt to sustain a foot bone fracture. This applies especially to a horse that has a fairly large foot. Also, the incidence of all other types of fractures is increased over the hard track. For instance, a horse that is developing sore heels as a result of bruising will try to catch his weight on the toe area of the foot and as a result puts excessive strain on the suspensory ligament which in turn causes a chip fracture of the sesamoid bone. Any horse that becomes sore-footed in front will become sore in his shoulders if the bruises are not corrected and any horse that is sore in his shoulders is much more subject to fractures of the pastern because he lands toe-first instead of heel-first or flat-footed as he should. When a horse lands toe-first and the toe does not slide and allow the rest of the foot to come in contact with the ground, it is somewhat like shooting an arrow into the ground in that the concussion of impact goes directly up the pastern and ordinarily causes a fracture of the long pastern bone.

This is as good a place as any to insert a paragraph relative to the manner in which a horse's foot comes in contact with the ground when he is racing. Among sound horses, about nine out of ten will hit the ground heel first. The other one will hit the ground flat-footed. The only time a horse's foot hits the ground toe-first is when he is unsound. A trotter is much more apt to hit flat-footed than a pacer and the more front leg action a horse has the more likely he is to hit flat-footed. The foot of a horse that hits heel-first will ordinarily slide along the surface of the track to some degree. Trotters usually slide more than pacers although long-gaited pacers will also slide when they hit. A horse that hits toe-first in front is usually doing so because he is sore in the shoulder and is not completing extension of the leg before the foot hits the ground. Under these circumstances, the toe will hit first. A horse that hits toe-first behind is usually sore in the hock or stifle and here again is not extending the leg fully before the foot hits the ground.

Hard race track surfaces are desirable from the standpoint of providing all-weather racing, but they increase the incidence of lameness so much that I don't believe they are worthwhile at the expense of the horse's soundness. It is true that there are some types of lameness that are easier to treat when a horse is racing or training over a hard race track but most types are easier to deal with when the horse is racing over a track that has adequate cushion.

A soft race track is not desirable either. A track that has too much cushion or breaks away with the horse's feet can also cause many types of lameness although most of these lamenesses are not as severe or as permanent as those produced over hard going. The only ordinarily serious lameness that occurs because a track is too soft is a tendon injury or bowed tendons, although any old ligament injury can also be aggravated as a result of the track breaking away. It is very hard on a horse to switch from a hard or good-surfaced track to a deep-surfaced track because his muscles are not conditioned to that kind of going. A horse transferring from a deep track to a hard track is much more apt to race to his true from.

I think it would be ideal if we could condition our horses over different types of race tracks. I believe that if, in the fall of the year when we start training a horse, we would start jogging him and conduct our slow training over a deep track, we would produce a much better conditioned horse than we do by going the same number of jog miles and training miles over a relatively hard-surfaced track. A horse that jogs over soft going develops his muscles to a much greater degree. I think this is especially true in conditioning young horses when their muscles are just developing and I have frequently noticed that horses trained on soft tracks and then moved to a good race track for final conditioning and racing develop many fewer cases of lameness than those trained over tracks ordinarily termed good. I think the reason for this is that the soft track develops a greater amount of muscular ability, much like the baseball player who swings three bats before he steps up to the plate with one. As a specific example of race tracks, I have noticed that Stanley Dancer's horses that are trained over a relatively deep track in the winter time, very seldom develop any stifle lameness during the racing season that follows. On the other hand, I have noticed that horses winter-trained on race tracks with good firm surfaces do not usually achieve proper muscular development and frequently develop stifle lamenesses during the ensuing racing season. I have noted one exception to this, a specific case where a particular trainer inadvertently compensated for the lack of muscular development by over-training his horses during the winter. In this manner, he avoided stifle lameness when he went to the races. However, I don't recommend that horses be over-trained in the winter just to avoid stifle lameness.

FATIGUE—One of the most if not *the* most important pre-disposing causes of lameness is fatigue of the muscle and skeletal structure. Perhaps some of you have indulged in sports to the extent that you have experienced the same degree of fatigue that a horse does when he races. Those of you that have, know what I mean. If you are running a race, in the last portion of the race your legs actually become numb and you don't have any conscious feeling of your feet touching the ground. The ligaments and muscles of the horse's legs are designed by nature to act as natural shock absorbers when the legs make contact with the ground much like one of us jogging along on our toes, to cite an exaggerated example. When we are not tired, the muscles themselves take up all the shock and bear all the weight of the body. The same thing is true of the horse. However, when we run fast enough and get tired enough so that we no longer land on our toes and take up all the shock with the muscles of our legs, we then start hitting heel first and thereby lose not only speed and balance, but also become unsteady on our feet. The same thing happens to a horse. In the first part of the race, his muscles are fresh and easily able to withstand the stress. In the last part, when the horse begins to get tired, he loses the shock absorber action of the muscle structure and is forced to rely instead on the shock absorber action of the suspensory ligaments themselves as well as all the other ligaments of the leg. This is when the horse is most apt to break down in a race and I am sure that everyone is aware that most fractures and other serious injuries occur between the three-quarter pole and the wire. Therefore, it is extremely important that horses be trained sufficiently so that they do not experience extreme fatigue during a race. At the same time, it must be remembered that over-training as well as under-training can result in a horse becoming fatigued. All horses do not train alike nor do all horses require the same amount of work to get ready to race. Each trainer must decide what he must do with each individual horse. Too many horses are trained the same way, which means that some are under-trained and some are over-trained.

LENGTH OF RACING SEASON—We have now entered a harness racing era in which racing is possible on a year-round basis. We do not yet know all the effects this will have as far as lameness is concerned, although I think it is fairly obvious that the more starts a horse makes or the longer he stays in training the more susceptible he naturally will be to some sort of lameness. I don't think any horse can compete 12 months a year and race to his full potential. Just what the increase in the length of the racing season will mean is hard to evaluate at this time. It would appear, however, that we are going to have to adopt systems of racing similar to those used by the Thoroughbred people. They maintain some horses at the race track, some in training at the farm and have others turned out. These horses are rotated at varying intervals thus assuring a fresh supply of ready-to-race horses. This system obviously cannot be applied to the younger two and 3-year-old horses that have to make stake engagements on specific dates and which will still be pointed for the stakes.

VISUAL EXAMINATION FOR LAMENESS

One of the most difficult of all chores for young veterinarians as well as young and inexperienced horsemen is to determine exactly where a horse is lame. I think it might be worthwhile here to devote a little space to a discussion of this matter. In the first place, it is not always possible, even for one who has experience around horses, to determine exactly where a horse is lame at first glance. One must educate himself in the various methods of observation in attempting to determine the seat of any lameness.

First, you must look the horse over completely on the race track in an effort to acquaint yourself with his general attitude and the way he carries his head, neck, body, and even his tail. It is best to examine a horse without too many hindrances, such as head poles, gaiting straps and other devices calculated to make a horse carry himself straight in spite of the way he wants to go. I usually look at the head first and see which way the horse wants to carry it; whether his head is down, or is nodding with each step and whether his check is loose or tight. I observe

whether he turns his head to one side or the other and if so
whether he has a comfortable or a rather grim look about his eyes
as he grasps the bit. In other words, you have to develop an
impression of the horse's feelings in relation to what he is doing.
Is the horse aggravated or angry or is he just feeling sorry for
himself or doesn't he care? Also, notice his back. Is it stiff? Is
his back straight? Is the tail held straight up and down or is there
a kink in it?

After making a superficial examination of this type, it should
require only a few seconds to reach the following conclusions: A
horse that turns his head in toward the rail when he is going the
right way of the track is usually on the left line and bearing out.
This would normally indicate to me that the horse was lame on
the left side, either in front or behind or both. However, it may
also indicate that the horse is attempting to extend his right
front leg. If this proved to be the case, the right front leg would
be involved in some area that would in itself involve the extension
of the leg such as ringbone, or knee or shoulder lameness. This
latter situation is analogous to a pitcher throwing a baseball. He
cannot achieve the proper extension of his pitching arm unless
he turns his head away from that arm. It is the same with a
horse. In order to extend the front leg as far as possible, he must
turn his head away from that leg in order to achieve the proper
extension. With a sound horse, this movement is barely noticeable. But in cases of lameness involving the extensor area of the
front leg, the horse atempts to compensate for this limitation of
natural extension by turning his head noticeably away from that
leg. All of the situations described in this paragraph are exactly
reversed if the horse is bearing in and thus turning his head out
and away from the rail.

A horse that carries his head down as far as possible between
his front legs and therefore tightens his check like a banjo string
is ordinarily lame in the front end somewhere. This symptom
can be evaluated along with the others.

The attitude of the horse's back is important as is its position in
relation to the shafts. A horse is much more crooked in the shafts
and his tail has a kink in it much more often if he is lame behind.
A horse that rides the right shaft is usually sore in the left hind
leg and, conversely, a horse that rides the left shaft is usually
lame in the right hind leg. Never rule out the possibility that

the horse may be lame both in front and behind at the same time.

After noting the general attitudes I have described, then the individual parts of the horse must be observed. Look at either the front legs or the hind legs by themselves. Do not allow your vision to wander to the other end of the horse at any time. Watch the legs from the elbows down in front and from the stifles down behind. Do not attempt to look at the entire horse at one time.

A horse that is lame in front will catch his weight on the good leg, not the bad leg. He will hit the ground harder and his head will come down when the good leg hits the ground. On a hard race track, you can frequently close your eyes and tell by the sound of the feet hitting the ground which leg the horse is lame on.

After determining which is the bad leg, the stride should be evaluated carefully as an aid in pinpointing the area of lameness. As the horse goes by, try to measure in your mind the distance between the legs as he takes each stride. Is he going short, in which case his extension is affected, or is he taking an equal stride with both legs and simply evidencing more pain when one leg strikes the ground? The reason for this is that anything that would interfere with extension would more or less point to a certain group of lamenesses.

It is also necessary to determine what part of the foot on the affected leg is hitting the ground first. In order to be able to do this accurately, you should be familiar with the horse's natural gait. Each horse is gaited differently depending on shoeing and natural way of going. Some horses hit heel first and hit the ground very hard. Some horses land flat with the foot sliding as much as six inches after it hits ground. The way the horse is landing on the good leg will usually indicate his natural inclination in this respect. With this in mind in your visual examination, you must now look only at the horse's feet as they hit the ground. On a firm race track, the foot that hits the ground toe first is going to kick up a spray of dirt. The foot that hits the ground heel first or flat is not going to kick up any dirt.

When the lameness is in front, the horse that hits toe first on the lame leg may ordinarily be assumed to be affected somewhere on the back surface of the leg between the foot and the knee. Since most lamenesses occur in the foot, your examination would be for navicular disease, sidebones or anything up the back of the pastern as well as sesamoids, suspensory and tendons. Keep in mind at this time that a horse that is lame in the shoulder or knee and traveling slowly will hit toe first because the foot hits the ground before the horse has a chance to fully extend it into its normal landing position.

Now watch the rear end of the horse from a side view. You look at nothing but the hind legs from the stifle down. Here again you must determine which leg is hitting the ground hardest and whether either or both feet are hitting the ground toe first or heel first. Is the horse bending the right hock the same as the left? Does the foot cover the same arc over the ground? Is the foot traveling as high over the ground with one leg as with the other? How much dirt is being kicked up by one toe as opposed to the other? Deviations in any of these respects furnish clues relative to the area of lameness.

By viewing the hind legs from the side, it may be determined whether the horse is bearing his weight entirely on his toes or on one toe. Is he bending or flexing the hock the same in both legs? On the affected side he usually carries the leg fairly stiff, landing on the toe if a hock is involved.

Now look at the horse coming toward you. Observe how he carries his front legs in relation to the perpendicular lines of his body. Now watch him go away from you and pay attention to the way he carries his hind legs in relation to the perpendicular.

Any outward deviation of the front leg may indicate knee or shoulder lameness. Any outward or inward deviation of the hind leg may indicate stifle or whirlbone lameness. All these considerations must be taken into account when you are trying to determine where a horse is lame or in which leg he may be lame.

It must be remembered that when a pacer appears to be lame in one hind leg he will also appear to be lame to some degree in the front leg on the same side. The opposite is true of a trotter. When the trotter is lame, for example, in the right hind he will also appear to be lame in the left front. This is because both extending members must extend to the same degree at any one time. Otherwise, the horse is either going to fall apart in the middle or will get all up in a heap in the middle.

Although I could go on and write 10,000 words on just what to look for, there is no substitute for sitting on the knocker's bench and watching horse after horse go by. Experience is the only real teacher.

EXPLANATION OF TERMINOLOGY

Throughout this chapter, I am going to make a special effort to avoid technical language and use words that are readily understandable to both owners and trainers. At the same time, since it will be necessary to refer occasionally to certain routine veterinary terms and procedures, I think it would be well at this point to enter in the record an explanation of a few of the more prominent ones.

For instance, when veterinarians talk about blocking or nerve-blocking, they are actually referring to a procedure employed as an aid in diagnosis relative to the specific area of lameness. Blocking is a method of diagnosis in which an anesthetic is injected over a nerve trunk that supplies a specific area of the leg. By anesthetizing (or freezing, as it is sometimes called) a particular area, it can be determined whether that area is involved in the lameness. It is obvious that if the area that is causing the lameness is anesthetized, the symptoms should disappear when the horse is worked immediately thereafter. In this manner, it is often possible to make a specific diagnosis.

We don't always inject a nerve trunk. Occasionally, we anesthetize a local area such as the inner face of the hock, or we might infiltrate an entire joint such as the upper or lower compartment of the knee or the hock joint itself. In other cases, a specific existing pathologic condition such as a splint may be blocked in an effort to determine whether the splint itself or some other unseen condition is responsible for the visible symptoms of lameness.

A steroid injection refers to the injection of any one of a tremendous number of cortisone or cortisone-derived products which are in themselves classified as anti-inflammatory drugs. The specific action of these products is to decrease the inflammation in the area into which they are injected. As a result, pain is also decreased. This does not mean that the lameness is cured but rather that there is an alleviation of the pain symptoms.

Another reference throughout the chapter will be to the injection of counter-irritants. Counter-irritants are substances that cause irritation upon injection into a specific area. The reason for such an injection is to increase the blood flow to the part injected and as a result of this increase to effect a cure or healing process which in the end is directly proportional to the blood supply involved.

Blistering is a process whereby an irritant is applied to the surface of a specific area of an extremity of the horse in an artificial attempt to increase the blood volume supplying that particular part. If a blister such as iodine or one of its derivitives is applied, the irritation produced on the surface of the skin will cause an enlargement or engorgement of the blood vessels of the surrounding area. It is this supplemental blood supply or increased blood volume to the local area that in effect cures or allows nature to cure or heal the pathology involved. Thus, a blister is the external equivalent of an internally injected counter-irritant.

Firing is the name given to the use of a red hot needle or other device in an effort to produce irritation on the surface of the skin and thus increase the blood supply to that area and hasten healing. In the case of firing, many small penetrations are made on the skin in an effort to produce irritation in a local area. The inflammation can be further increased by the application of a blister over the firing immediately after the firing is completed.

Firing is generally categorized into two types, point-firing, also called pin-firing, and feather-firing. In point-firing, the firing iron actually makes small, round holes and thus penetrates the skin and tissues involved. Feather-firing consists of lines being drawn on the skin by a red-hot, knife-like blade. In my opinion, point or pin-firing is by far the most effective. You cannot feather-fire a horse through the skin because the skin will die as a result of interruption of normal blood supply. By placing holes through the skin at regular intervals, as is the case in point-firing, the skin integrity can be maintained and much more good can be accomplished. The same principles are applied in firing and blistering, but firing is the more severe.

AREAS OF SPECIFIC LAMENESS

FOOT BRUISES—Bruises of the foot appear most often in the sole area (Fig. 112) and are usually caused by the pounding of the foot on hard race tracks or by improper shoeing. The improper shoeing applies to those cases where the shoe makes con-

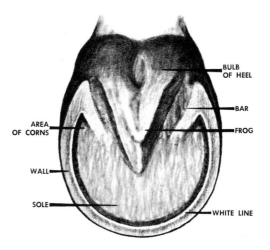

Fig. 112. The bottom of a normal front foot with the principal parts identified.

BULB OF HEEL

BAR

FROG

AREA OF CORNS

WALL

SOLE

WHITE LINE

tact with the sole over too great an area, that is, where the sole is flat instead of concave. A bruise is actually a hemorrhage of the blood vessels between the horny layer of the sole and the fleshy sole underneath. In the initial stages, it is not usually visible in the sole. Symptoms vary widely depending on the severity of the bruise and the extent of the area involved. The usual symptoms are varying degrees of lameness in the leg in addition to fever in the foot as determined by feeling the foot itself or by enlargement of the artery which runs down the inside of the tendons between the knee and ankle. In the beginning, the most common method of determining whether a bruise exists is by using hoof testers or by otherwise putting pressure on the sole and observing whether the horse reacts to this pressure in any given area. A hoof tester is a large forceps-like instrument designed to put pressure on small areas of the hoof.

After a certain length of time, usually from two to four weeks, a bruise becomes visible as it grows down to the sole from the fleshy layers underneath in the form of a reddish discoloration of the horn. A bruise is actually a pocket of blood between the horn and the flesh and the blood is absorbed by the horny sole as it grows out causing its discoloration. A foot bruise that becomes chronic is always a source of concern since an old bruise will continue to hemorrhage from time to time because the blood vessels themselves have been partially destroyed as a result of the original hemorrhage. In an acute case of a bruised foot, it may be difficult to determine whether it is a simple bruise and hemorrhage, or whether there is an infection of that area of the foot. In the case of a bruise, the inflammation subsides rapidly with adequate treatment, whereas in the case of an infection the lameness not only persists but increases over a short period of time. The infection, which is known as a gravel, will soon make its way through the sole or through the coronary area of the hoof.

Bruises are treated by reducing the fever in the foot by tubbing the horse religiously and, after the initial inflammation has subsided, by giving the horse adequate protection in the form of a special shoe or pad. The only way to prevent a foot from becoming bruised is to be aware of the type of track the horse is training and racing over and by using pads to help minimize concussion if the track is too hard. This is particularily true of horses that are inclined to have flat soles or large feet.

CORNS—A corn (Fig. 112) is a chronic bruise in a specific area, that area being the point between the outside wall and the bar where they meet at the heel. A corn starts as a bruise and continues over a long period of time until the discoloration reaches the outside of the sole. Then the soft tissue of the sole continues to prolifierate or grow underneath the sole to the extent that it may erupt through the sole itself in the form of a soft, weeping, or bleeding tuft of tissue. Corns cause varying degrees of lameness but are not ordinarily considered a very serious condition, provided that care is given them when the horse is shod. Corns are a fairly obvious condition that usually do not require veterinary attention since they are visible on the outside at the time of shoeing. Most blacksmiths have their own favorite remedy for corns. Treatment of corns varies from trainer to trainer and from blacksmith to blacksmith. In most cases, the treatment consists of cauterization either by hot iron or by iodine crystals and turpentine or some other corrosive solution which burns the soft tissue involved and causes it to heal over and dry up. However, once a horse develops a corn he will be subject to them from that time on, particularly if the corns are allowed to become very large. There is no way of preventing corns if the conformation of the horse's hoof is such that he receives excessive concussion when the hoof hits the ground. Corns are most frequently seen in those horses that have a flat sole and a rather wide frog with a very angular slope to the bar of the hoof.

GRAVEL—Gravel is the term used to describe any infection that gains entrance to the hoof. It can develop as a result of thrush (a specific infection usually involving only the sole or frog of the hoof) in the sole of the foot but most often comes about through a separation of the sole from the wall somewhere along the white line (Fig. 112). A gravel causes a horse to become slightly lame at first and then, as the infection progresses from the sole surface under the wall toward the coronary band, the lameness increases greatly and frequently to a point where the horse will not walk on the foot. A gravel that covers a large area can cause symptoms of lameness just as acute as a fracture of one of the main bones of the foot. The gravel is actually a separation of the horny layer of the wall from the fleshy layer by an accumulation of pus which cannot find its way out of the area. A gravel can be distinguished from a fracture or other type of inflammation of the hoof or foot by the nature in which it progresses. The horse is usually only slightly lame in the beginning but over a period of 24 hours becomes very lame. During this period, the artery supplying the foot becomes greatly enlarged and the leg may fill slightly from the ankle to the hoof. In addition, heat and/or pain develops along the coronary area and becomes very acute. There are some cases where a gravel will take as long as a week before it can be brought to the surface at the coronary band. In most cases, however, the entire lameness transpires within one to three days.

Treatment consists of soaking the affected foot in a foot bath of hot Epsom Salts with the water just as hot as the hand can stand. Usually, after one or two one-hour periods of soaking, the gravel will break out at the coronary area and the horse will again be sound within a 24-hour period. A gravel can only be prevented by conscientious searching of the foot by the blacksmith at the time of shoeing. All discolored areas of the sole and along the wall and white line should be investigated with the hoof knife to make sure that a gravel is not starting or that the wall is not beginning to separate from the sole to a point where dirt or other foreign material can be packed up into the crack.

QUARTER CRACKS AND BAR CRACKS—A quarter crack is a crack in the wall of the hoof extending from the outside surface through and into the fleshy portion (Fig. 37). The crack may extend any distance from the ground surface all the way up to the coronary band or any portion thereof or may begin at the top and work downward in the same manner. A bar crack is a crack in the bar of the hoof extending from the outer surface into the fleshy portion of the hoof. Quarter cracks occur much more frequently than bar cracks.

There are many causes of quarter cracks and bar cracks. Probably the most consistent cause is the race track itself. In the last few years there has been a noticeable trend toward the installation of so-called all-weather tracks and as a result these tracks are becoming more and more firm. This firmness or hardness makes it much more difficult to preserve adequate feet on our horses. Any horse that has any defect in the hoof itself is apt to develop a quarter crack and go lame as a direct result of concussion.

In addition, we have many, many horses racing today that at one time or another have had a minor case of laminitis (founder) which has left the foot permanently affected. These feet ordinarily carry varying degrees of fever all the time and as a result they usually dry out and become hard. Such feet are always susceptible to quarter cracks and bar cracks.

There are also certain families—and this is particularly noticeable among some of the more prominent families racing today— that tend naturally to have hard, shelly feet. These horses are more susceptible to quarter and bar cracks. Likewise, we have other families that normally run to contracted heels (quarters) and carry this type of foot as a natural foot. And any foot in which the heels are contracted or pinched in, thereby causing considerable bending or bowing of the heel itself, is much more susceptible to quarter and bar cracks.

There are also horses that at one time or another have sustained an injury to the coronary band and as a result the wall of the hoof does not grow in the normal fashion but with somewhat of a fissure running down the side. Under the stress of a hard race track, such feet are apt to split through this fissure and thereby produce a quarter crack.

Horses that develop quarter cracks and bar cracks ordinarily go lame very suddenly, that is, the moment the crack occurs and occasionally before it is visible. Bar cracks and quarter cracks are usually self-evident and both types will ordinarily bleed when a horse is worked, thus rendering the diagnosis that much easier. However, in some cases I have observed that a horse will be lame for a matter of days or even weeks before a quarter crack appears. Apparently, in these cases, the crack develops on the inside of the hoof layer next to the fleshy laminae resulting in hemorrhage, pressure from which brings about lameness. This condition can exist for some time before the crack breaks completely through the horny layer on the hoof. Therefore, in cases of this type, the diagnosis of quarter cracks is delayed because we cannot find the crack and may suspect a bruised quarter or a bruised bar and treat it as such until the crack itself becomes apparent.

The treatment of quarter cracks has become revolutionized in the last few years. Formerly, the only treatment available was to cut the quarter crack completely out and give the foot or quarter adequate protection by shoeing the horse with a bar shoe and relieving all the pressure on the affected quarter or bar. We have in addition today a method of patching the quarter crack by applying a heavy layer of synthetic rubber over it. The patch is actually glued to the hoof surface itself thereby giving the quarter enough support to prevent the crack from spreading or at least preventing the quarter itself from becoming loose. Many horses have raced successfully while wearing patches. There are, however, limitations to these patches and in a number of the more severe cases it is still necessary to resort to the old treatment of cutting out the crack and growing a whole new quarter.

A great many of the quarter cracks and bar cracks that reappear today could be prevented if adequate attention was given to the horse's feet before the condition occurred. For instance, once a horse has developed contracted heels everything possible should be done to spread the heel and regain normal conformation through the application of adequate frog pressure in shoeing and by trimming the foot so as to keep the heel spread. In addition, everything should be done to keep a horse's hoof growing at a normal rate. In order to do this, moisture must be applied to the foot in some form on a regular basis. If necessary, medication should be applied to the coronary band to make the feet grow at a normal rate.

CONTRACTED HEELS—Contracted heels, in addition to being a cause of quarter cracks and bar cracks, are in themselves a cause of lameness. I mentioned earlier that some families have them as a normal conformation defect, but I should also point out that contracted heels are frequently acquired. They can develop as a result of improper shoeing or from a horse carrying too much foot, among other things. In addition, there are certain forms of lameness, such as navicular disease, that will produce contracted heels. Whether hereditary or acquired, contracted heels are the source of many cases of lameness. They can lead to more serious lamenesses if not corrected promptly.

A horse with contracted heels (Fig. 113) is usually a horse with sore heels. The soreness or lameness is much more pronounced on a hard race track than in the mud or on a race track

Fig. 113. A contracted hoof illustrating pinched heels, curved bars and a long, narrow frog. A normal foot is illustrated in Fig. 112 on page 811.

with a deep cushion. In the early stages, a horse will usually show the symptoms when first brought out on the track but will warm out of the lameness after going a short distance.

Contracted heels are self evident and one need only look at the shape of the foot to make the diagnosis. The degree of lameness is in direct relationship to the degree of soreness displayed when hoof testers are applied to the heel or frog. Also, a horse with contracted heels ordinarily carries a good bit of fever in the foot. If there is any question as to whether the contracted heels are bothering a horse, the nerve that supplies the heel should be blocked and the horse worked in order to determine the difference in gait.

Contracted heels are most effectively treated during the off-season when the quarters and heel portion of the hoof can be rasped down to a paper thin consistency. This lets the hoof spread readily with normal frog pressure. It is not practical to thin the walls during the racing season and contracted heels are spread only with difficulty at that time since it is necessary to apply a good bit of frog pressure to spread the foot without first thinning the walls of the quarters. It may be done, however, if the foot is kept soft enough, usually by tubbing or poulticing. If frog pressure is too much for the horse and he cannot tolerate it without going lame, sometimes the quarter or heel may be spread by applying a bar shoe without frog pressure by beveling the branches from the last nail hole back. Here again, the foot must be kept very soft and pliable during the period that the spreading is being attempted. Unfortunately, it is not uncommon to spend months spreading the heels only to find that when the horse is shod normally once or twice that the heels resume their old contracted appearance. Every effort should be made to control contracted heels, however, since they can lead to many more serious lamenesses such as bowed tendons, to name but one.

NAVICULAR DISEASE—Navicular disease is another condition of the foot that causes lameness. It takes its name from the navicular bone (Fig. 114), an ovoid, flat bone that lies transversely almost at the juncture of the second and third bones of the pastern. It lies directly under the middle portion of the frog in relation to the hoof capsule.

The cause of navicular disease is not always completely understood. It is known that over a long period of time contracted heels can cause navicular disease and that some horses seem to be born with the disease leading to the logical conclusion that certain families carry the condition hereditarily.

In other cases, it must be assumed that navicular disease is a direct result of concussion as the hoof meets the race track through many miles of training and racing. A horse can have navicular disease for a long time before it becomes apparent to the trainer. Most horses with navicular disease will start out a little stiff in the morning but after going anywhere from a quarter of a mile to two miles will be perfectly sound. This can go on for as long as several years before the horse finally doesn't warm out of the lameness and becomes perpetually lame or, at best, perpetually stiff-gaited.

A horse with navicular disease leaves the impression that he is feeling his way along with his front feet more or less in the attitude of a horse creeping along on glazed ice and being afraid of slipping or falling. He also stumbles frequently and has very little action in front. X-rays are frequently used to determine the presence of navicular disease but the most valuable aid in making a diagnosis is a block of the heel nerve to determine the difference in the horse's gait.

Navicular disease is a progressive disease. In the early stages, only the navicular bursa is involved. Then the navicular bone itself becomes involved and finally the entire pedal joint. When the disease reaches the latter stage, there is little to be done.

When only the bursa or the bursa and bone are involved, the horse can usually be helped considerably by raising the angle of the foot as many degrees as practical and squaring the toe to help him break over more easily and thus relieve some of the tension on the bone. The heel nerves may also be removed, rendering the horse sound for a variable period of time. When the disease has reached the terminal stage with involvement of the entire pedal joint, nothing can be done to make the horse useful again.

SIDE BONES—Side bones (Fig. 115) is actually another name for ossification of the lateral cartilages of the coffin bone which is the os pedis or main bone of the foot. There are several schools of thought as to the origin of side bones although it is largely agreed that it is primarily an hereditary lameness. Actually, a horse is not born with side bones but the tendency to develop them is thought to be an hereditary factor. Conformation of the foot enters into the picture inasmuch as the bell shaped foot—one with a considerable flare to the toe and side walls—is the type that is ordinarily conducive to the formation of side bones. It is also possible, and even probable that concussion or repeated trauma of the cartilages of the foot as a result of going over a hard race track may be an influencing factor.

Most horses with side bones go lame over a relatively long period of time. At first, the horse just doesn't act quite right. He may get a little heavy-headed and start putting his head down into

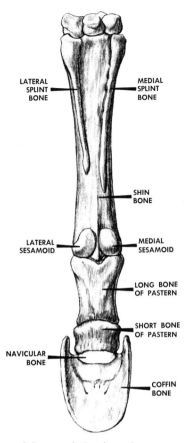

LATERAL SPLINT BONE

MEDIAL SPLINT BONE

SHIN BONE

LATERAL SESAMOID

MEDIAL SESAMOID

LONG BONE OF PASTERN

SHORT BONE OF PASTERN

NAVICULAR BONE

COFFIN BONE

Fig. 114. The principal bones of the front leg, as viewed from behind, are illustrated and identified.

the check excessively. Other than that, very little lameness is noted until the horse actually starts to get rough. Most of the time this happens on the turns. The formation of side bones makes the pain much greater when the horse has the weight on one side of the foot no matter which side it is. Therefore, a horse with side bones will frequently trot or pace in a straight line very satisfactorily only to nod or show extreme lameness when starting into a turn and for the entire length of the turn.

A horse will also get on one line to some degree as a result of side bone formation. This is usually one of the first symptoms the trainer will notice when side bones start to form. Of course, there is also some heat in the foot at this time. However, it may be variable and very hard to detect in early cases, and soreness over the lateral cartilages may or may not be present.

Actually, the only reliable means of diagnosis in the early stages is by X-ray. In advanced stages, the symptoms are much more pronounced. As a result of the side bones being present over a long period, the quarters will start to contract and sometimes become very flat and contracted. The cartilages themselves become hard to thumb pressure and lose the normal flexibility that is usually noted when the tops of the lateral cartilages are compressed between the thumbs.

Side bones seem to develop in some horses rather rapidly while in others the disease is dragged out over a long period of time, perhaps as long as two or three years. There is very little that can be done to help a horse that has side bones other than to try to maintain a normal shape to the foot and to try and reduce the fever.

Shoeing is of some benefit. To shoe a horse with side bones, a wide web shoe is recommended to give the horse plenty of support and rim pads or a full pad should be used. Frog pressure in any form should be avoided. The horse should also be tubbed daily to relieve the formation of fever in the foot. The side bones themselves are actually a part of the main bone of the foot and therefore cannot be satisfactorily removed. Most horses that have side bones will race much better over a five-eighths, three-quarter or mile track due to the fact that they do not have to go around the sharp turns of the half-mile track. There are a great number of horses with sidebones that race satisfactorily since it is a relatively common condition in Standardbreds. Personally, I would discriminate against a broodmare that I knew had side bones.

RINGBONE—Ringbone is another lameness of the Standardbred but fortunately it is fairly uncommon. Ringbone (Fig. 115) can occur in two different places on the pastern. The first, or low ringbone occurs approximately at the level of the coronary band while the high ringbone occurs above the pastern joint or approximately half way between the coronary band and the ankle. Ringbone is also thought to be an hereditary condition. However, I am relatively sure that most of the ringbone we see at the race track today is of traumatic origin. That is, most horses that develop ringbone do so as a result of the bone being bruised or struck repeatedly as in the case of a cross-firing pacer.

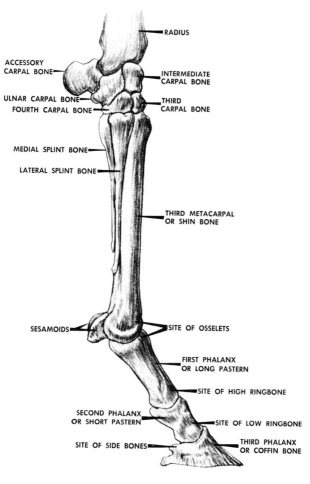

RADIUS

ACCESSORY
CARPAL BONE

INTERMEDIATE
CARPAL BONE

ULNAR CARPAL BONE
FOURTH CARPAL BONE

THIRD
CARPAL BONE

MEDIAL SPLINT BONE

LATERAL SPLINT BONE

THIRD METACARPAL
OR SHIN BONE

SESAMOIDS

SITE OF OSSELETS

FIRST PHALANX
OR LONG PASTERN

SITE OF HIGH RINGBONE

SECOND PHALANX
OR SHORT PASTERN

SITE OF LOW RINGBONE

SITE OF SIDE BONES

THIRD PHALANX
OR COFFIN BONE

Fig. 115. This is a side view of the right front leg with the principal bones identified.

A ringbone does not have a truly diagnostic symptom. The symptoms are quite varied and depend on the location and what structures are involved. A ringbone that involves only the ligaments of the pastern joint may cause lameness only when a horse is going around the turn whereas a ringbone that involves the front surface of the pastern will cause lameness constantly due to its interference with the tendon that is responsible for extension of the foot.

Most ringbones are self-evident and diagnosis is usually based on visual examination plus local fever and X-ray. A ringbone is actually an inflammation of the periosteum or covering of the bone which in turn causes decalcification in some areas of the bone and calcification, or building up of calcium, in other areas of the same bone. On X-ray film, a great many ringbones look like a moth-eaten piece of cloth.

A ringbone should be treated as early as possible after diagnosis has been made. The longer a ringbone is allowed to progress and the longer a horse is raced with a ringbone, the worse the condition becomes and the longer it takes the animal to recover. Early ringbone is frequently treated successfully by firing and blistering along with extended rest. If a ringbone is allowed to progress to a point where it involves the margin of the joint or the joint surface itself, it is almost incurable as far as racing is concerned since the joint then will become stiff and the animal will lose the proper action of the limb.

A ringbone derives its name from the fact that in advanced cases the periostitis or inflammation of the bone extends around the entire circumference and therefore produces an enlargement which goes all the way around the pastern. However, a ringbone need not involve all of this area and a relatively small involvement on one side of the leg or the other can correctly be called a ringbone.

OSSELETS—An osselet (Fig. 115) is a bony proliferation involving the perimeter of the ankle or fetlock joint. In the Standardbred, an osselet is for the most part self-limiting. That is, it will grow to a certain stage and then solidify and become dormant. This is not true among Thoroughbreds where an osselet constitutes a permanent source of trouble, basically because of breed susceptibility. Conformation is probably the principal cause of osselets. It is very noticeable that horses that stand straight in front are much more apt to have osselet trouble.

In the initial stages, an osselet does not involve the joint surface itself but rather the margin of the joint surface both of the shin bone and of the long bone of the pastern. As a result of the inflammation of the joint margins, calcium is built up in the area and this causes a lipping or protrusion of the surface of the joint. This calcium or new bone formation causes an inflammation of the entire joint area which in turn causes the animal pain. A horse suffering with osselets does not have any particular or diagnostic way of traveling on the race track. Ordinarily, the horse just acts tender in front usually more so in one leg than the other and tends to travel away from the affected side. As I stated previously, osselets are usually self-limiting and, if given proper rest, usually in combination with firing or blistering, will ordinarily solidify and become dormant.

Making a diagnosis of osselets is not difficult since the swelling and fever in the area are self-evident. Indeed, a well-developed set of osselets can be diagnosed from a distance of many feet. Since most cases appear in young horses, that is, two and 3-year-olds, the treatment is usually one of turning the horse out for extended rest in combination with firing, blistering or both.

If the osselets are not too extensive, it is possible to keep some horses racing by the judicious use of steroids injected over the osselet and into the ankle joint itself. Since the average horse will usually exhibit the presence of osselets well in advance of the time he shows any lameness, most osselets are treated during the racing and training program by the use of leg paints. Probably the majority of osselets are cured over a period of time with the horse actually in training.

In advanced cases, usually observed in older horses where the calcium has built up on the joint margins to a point where the ankles are relatively large and the osselets very, very noticeable even from a distance, the ankle joint itself loses some percentage of its flexibility and extension. When you lift the leg off the ground and hold the lower part in your hands, the joint is very stiff and it is impossible to flex it to the same degree as in the normal horse. Also, when the horse is in motion and the foot hits the ground, the ankle loses its normal ability to sink toward the ground and help cushion the shock of concussion. This normal sinking action of the ankle joint can be observed in any moving picture and most still shots. Naturally, this loss of motion contributes to the continual irritation of the joint which in turn causes the horse to be chronically lame on osselets. In such cases, it is usually recommended that the horse wear a very short toe or even a half-round shoe with a squared toe to break him over quicker and compensate for the ankle joint's lack of natural motion. A horse with advanced osselets is also subject to chip fractures of the joint margin which can also contribute to the lameness.

SESAMOIDITIS—Sesamoiditis is the name given to the condition defined as an inflammation of the sesamoid bones and is a very serious and usually very chronic lameness. The sesamoid bones (Figs. 114 and 115) are the two small bones that lie on each side and directly behind the ankle or fetlock joint and between which the main flexor tendons run. In addition, the sesamoids also have the all-important function of providing a source of support for the suspensory ligament. Any inflammation of a sesamoid bone, therefore, can also directly involve the suspensory attachment and thereby cause very serious trouble.

Sesamoiditis is usually caused by bruising or some sort of injury to the sesamoid bone itself. To cite extreme ranges, this might come about as a result of a pacer cross-firing or develop as a result of a horse being kicked while in pasture. In some cases, it is even seen in young horses where no evidence of injury has ever been observed indicating an hereditary factor. Special care must be taken when examining a yearling to make certain that the sesamoid bones are absolutely clean. An enlarged sesamoid on a yearling almost always indicates future trouble.

The reason that sesamoiditis is such a problem is that the sesamoid bones have a very limited blood supply and no periosteum, which is the normal protective covering surrounding most other bones. As a result, when a sesamoid bone is injured or bruised it does not possess the same ability to heal as other bones do. Blood is the essential ingredient for healing all tissue and where there is no blood or where insufficient blood is available, complete healing does not result but, rather, there occurs a partial healing which is easily aggravated by any stress or strain.

What actually happens in the case of sesamoiditis is that the inflammation causes a decalcification in some areas of the bone and a calcification in other areas. On X-ray, the decalcified area would be indicated by giving the appearance that the bone was moth-eaten or had small channels running through it. At the same time, the X-ray might show calcium deposits on the surface of the bone, particularly in the areas of the suspensory ligament attachments. Both decalcification and calcification cause considerable interference with the areas of attachment of the ligaments. Naturally, when decalcification of the sesamoid occurs, the area of attachment of the suspensory ligament upon it is destroyed resulting in a thickening of the suspensory as it enlarges in an effort to regain contact with the bone. As a result, a primary lameness of the suspensory will often develop. A large percentage of suspensory lameness cases actually originate as cases of sesamoiditis.

The symptoms of sesamoiditis are for the most part self-evident. There is a swelling or enlargement in the area of the sesamoids and usually an accompanying thickening of the suspensory ligament on the side that is involved or on both sides if both sides are involved. There is heat and pronounced soreness when the area of the suspensory attachment is pressed with the thumbs and the horse resents flexion of the ankle joint.

Depending on the degree of involvement, some horses with sesamoiditis are raceable. However, most horses with advanced sesamoiditis are chronically sore and are only raceable periodically. Sesamoiditis responds to some degree to steroid injection, to keeping the affected area warm by means of a sweat under plastic or cotton and bandages, and to a light training schedule. Most affected horses cannot be trained to the same extent as a normal horse and it is not unusual to find that they are not trained at all between races.

In many cases of sesamoiditis in 2-year-olds, all or most of the sesamoid bones are involved to some extent. In such cases, it is unreasonable to assume that the horse suffered injury to all eight sesamoids. It is therefore likely that the condition came about as a result of improper bone formation in the first place.

Sesamoid bone fractures are very common in the Standardbred. Most involve the sesamoids of the hind leg (the front leg in Thoroughbreds) and the upper one-quarter or one-third or even a smaller portion of the bone. These small chips or pieces can be removed successfully and the horse can be returned to racing in four to six months' time. Fractures involving the lower portion of the sesamoid bone cannot be removed successfully as of this writing. About the best that can be done is to watch such horses carefully and if resorption of the chip occurs the horse can be put back in training. If resorption does not occur, the horse is used for breeding purposes if possible.

Long range treatment of chronic sesamoiditis is for the most part a hopeless situation since, in spite of the fact that the horse can be gotten sound and all the symptoms of lameness can disappear, it is a matter of record that as soon as the animal is put back in serious training all the symptoms recur and the condition continues to persist.

SUSPENSORY LIGAMENT—Suspensory ligament lameness

is one of the most common observed in the racing Standardbred. This is because the suspensory ligament (Fig. 116) is one of the main supporting structures of the horse's leg and is subjected to great stress at all times. The horse has a suspensory ligament in each of his four legs, all of which are essentially the same structurally. The suspensory ligament is a hard band of elastic tissue approximately an inch and a half wide at the top and about three-eighths of an inch thick. It attaches to the back of the shin bone just below the knee, continues down about two-thirds of the distance to the ankle and then splits into two parts looking somewhat like an inverted Y. Each of the two segments below the bifurcation attach to the top and side of the sesamoid bone on its own side. Then a smaller remnant of the suspensory continues downward and forward to attach on the lower part of the first bone of the pastern.

The suspensory ligament has no muscular power but it acts as a shock absorber for the leg. The tendons and the muscles that support the tendons also act as shock absorbers. When a horse gets tired, especially toward the end of the mile, he loses the resiliency in his muscles and the suspensory ligament is subjected to even more than its normal share of shock, concussion and shock-absorbing action. Therefore, a suspensory lameness can occur as a result of a horse being fatigued or over-tired, as a result of a horse bearing excessive weight on one leg while trying to favor another, or as a result of a horse trying to keep off or rest certain other structures of the same leg. For example, if a horse has a sore heel he would naturally tend to carry most of the weight on the toe of the foot. In so doing, he puts an added strain on the suspensory ligament and this can lead to a suspensory tear or pull.

The suspensory tear or sprain can occur in any portion of the ligament. Those occurring high up, near the suspensory ligament's origin under the knee, are usually referred to as check ligament lamenesses although they do not actually involve the check ligament. These so-called check ligament lamenesses are very common in young horses and are observed primarily in 2-year-olds although older horses develop them frequently.

This type of lameness is a very serious proposition. What actually happens is that the fine, tiny fibers of the suspensory ligament that constitute the upper attachment of the ligament to the shin bone and which fit into little pin holes on the surface of the bone are torn loose. When the suspensory eventually heals, the tiny fibers do not go back into these small openings but adhere to the bone surface instead. This results in a very weak attachment and consequently check ligament lamenesses are prone to recur time and again as this attachment breaks loose. It is not uncommon for horses with check ligament trouble to be persistently lame for months at a time.

Suspensory lamenesses involving the middle portion of the ligament are frequently associated with splints or calcification of the splint bone with the calcium deposit extending underneath the suspensory ligament and thereby causing pressure and inflammation.

A suspensory sprain in the area of the bifurcation—where the suspensory divides—is also a very serious proposition since every time the leg hits the ground and the ankle sinks down toward the ground it acts as a spreader between the two branches of the suspensory. This action is very painful and pretty much the same as trying to pry two of your fingers apart. Such action, of course, causes a sprain or suspensory tear to be continuous and prevents it from healing properly.

Suspensory sprains or enlargements in the ankle area will usually heal fairly well if they do not involve the sesamoid bones. However, a large percentage of this type of suspensory trouble does involve the sesamoids and X-rays are usually necessary before a long range prognosis can be made.

Suspensory involvement below the ankle usually heals with little consequence although occasionally there is some calcification or bony growth in the area where the suspensory ligament attaches to the long bone of the pastern.

Making a diagnosis of suspensory lameness is not ordinarily very difficult since the trouble is usually apparent to the naked eye. However, each case of suspensory lameness must be carefully evaluated on its own merits before any reasonable prognosis can be made. There are some cases that are of little consequence and the horse is back in racing condition within a few weeks. On the other hand, there are many cases where the horse can never race satisfactorily again.

The treatment of suspensory lameness is variable. It depends on the area of the suspensory involved and the degree of involvement. It must be remembered that the suspensory ligament does not have a large blood supply and thus it requires a considerable time for the ligament to heal following an injury. It takes a minimum of six weeks for an ordinary suspensory pull to heal completely. It may take up to a year or even more for a very severe tear. Ninety percent of the so-called check ligament lamenesses never do heal satisfactorily. A horse with a check ligament lameness must be considered a permanent cripple until proven otherwise.

Treatment ranges from a mild leg paint and a few weeks' time in the case of a minor sprain to as long as a year or more away from the race track and a considerable amount of treatment in the form of firing, blistering, etc., in more serious cases.

I do not believe that very many horses actually have weak suspensories as such. I think most suspensory lamenesses are brought about through injudicious training in the case of many 2-year-olds, racing 2-year-olds on muddy, slippery tracks and racing any aged horse that is actually too lame to race thereby putting added pressure on the ligament.

A thickening of the suspensory ligament can also lead to other problems. Many times, following a tear which results in the thickening of the suspensory ligament, the splint bone adjoining the suspensory is pushed so far out of its natural position that the bottom inch or two will snap off resulting in further complications. Actually, this condition can work both ways. A primary fracture of the splint bone can also cause the suspensory to thicken just as a thickened suspensory can cause a fracture of the splint bone. Fractured splint bones will be discussed later.

Before determining the action to be taken relative to any case of suspensory lameness, a complete X-ray study should be made to determine if there are any influencing factors involved. In this manner, a lot of time and money can be saved by not trying to persevere with a horse that is obviously going to be chronicly lame. Naturally, if a horse tears a suspensory ligament as a result of being lame in the opposite leg, it is necessary to evaluate the lameness in that leg in trying to determine whether a cure can be accomplished.

Suspensory lameness in the front leg, although a serious proposition, does not alter the speed of a horse nearly as much as a suspensory involvement of the hind leg since the hind leg is

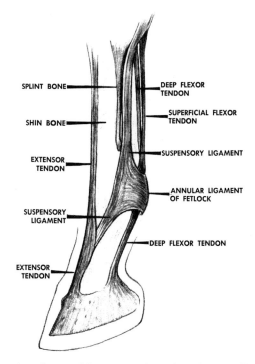

SPLINT BONE

SHIN BONE

EXTENSOR
TENDON

SUSPENSORY
LIGAMENT

EXTENSOR
TENDON

DEEP FLEXOR
TENDON

SUPERFICIAL FLEXOR
TENDON

SUSPENSORY LIGAMENT

ANNULAR LIGAMENT
OF FETLOCK

DEEP FLEXOR TENDON

Fig. 116. The principal tendons and ligaments of the front leg are illustrated and identified.

the source of the horse's driving power. This is particularly true of a high suspensory or so-called check ligament involvement. A check ligament involvement in a hind leg always causes a horse to lose a considerable amount of his normal speed.

BOWED TENDONS—A discussion of bowed tendons is of such scope and importance that it could easily involve the writing of a special chapter. First of all, we must keep in mind that when we are talking about bowed tendons we are actually talking about two different tendons. Either one or both can be damaged.

The flexor tendons of a horse—the only ones that are involved in bowed tendons—are considered extensions of muscular tissue and go down the back or flexor surface of the leg (Fig. 116) attaching to various bony structures, thereby producing the normal flexion of the joints which is necessary to a normal gait. In this section, we will not be discussing the extensor tendons which run down the front of the leg and control extension or length of stride.

The tendon tissue itself is highly elastic, more elastic actually than the suspensory ligament, and is composed of tiny bands of white fibrous tissue. These bands are very, very tough and whenever they are required to make a turn of direction over a bony prominence they are encased in a thick fibrous envelope known as a tendon sheath. There are two such sheaths on each leg and they contain fluid which allows the tendon to ride over the bony prominence without any adhesions or restrictions of motion. In some cases, these sheaths are torn accidentally and a swelling and lameness develops that can be confused to some degree with actual tendon injury. Tears in the sheath may also be associated with actual tendon injury and both conditions may exist at the same time.

In the area just below the knee, the flexor tendons are superimposed upon one another. The one nearest the skin is called the superficial flexor tendon and the one beneath it is called the deep flexor tendon. The superficial flexor continues as far down as the ankle where it forms a ring and attaches to the bony structures of the pastern. The deep flexor tendon continues downward from the ankle, actually going through the ring formed by the superficial flexor and fastens to the bottom of the coffin bone right under the frog. It lies between the superficial flexor and the suspensory ligament as far down as the ankle and from the ankle to the hoof, it lies directly behind the bone of the pastern.

The flexor sheath behind the knee extends below the knee for approximately two to three inches, depending on the size of the horse. The flexor sheath in back of the ankle and pastern starts about two or three inches above the ankle and extends through the back of the ankle all the way down to about the level of the coronary band.

A bowed tendon can be caused by any one of a number of things. The conformation of the horse is one of the all-important factors since the way a horse stands frequently has to do with the development of a bow. A horse that has a long shin bone and a long, angular pastern is much more predisposed to a bow than a horse that is short from the knee to the ground and has a short pastern. A horse that stands over in the knee is less likely to have a bow than a horse that stands back in the knees or is calf-kneed. A spindly-legged or fine-boned horse is more apt to have a tendon problem than the horse with adequate bone or even a heavy-legged horse.

Heredity is another factor involved in bowed tendons. I am sure that all of us know certain broodmares whose offspring have tendon problems year after year. Sometimes this is difficult to blame on conformation alone. It is also interesting to note in passing that while all of us can think of a great number of mares who have produced a large number of foals that eventually bowed how many popular sires can you think of who produce a large number of tendon problems in their foals? It would appear to me that in the bowed tendon area the influence of the mare, at least on the surface, seems to be greater than that of the sire.

Bowed tendons can also be produced by a number of outside influences, such as a horse hitting the tendon accidentally, or the tendon being corded by a bandage or an improperly fitting boot. Polo boots are probably the worst offenders, particularly in wet weather, since they frequently absorb moisture and, due to the weight involved, will slide down the leg and cord the tendon.

The symptoms of a bowed tendon are largely self-evident. The horse may or may not be lame depending on the severity of the injury. But in most cases there is some swelling or deviation of the normal outline of the tendon. This is usually apparent to the eye when viewing the horse from either side. If the injury to the tendon is a minor one, there may not be enough swelling or deviation for it to be noticeable to the naked eye. However, in these cases, a careful examination, using the thumb and forefingers to exert slight pressure on the tendon, will reveal the tender area and the location of the tendon damage.

The area of involvement may vary considerably. The damage may take place directly below the knee or on the extreme lower part of the leg just above the hoof. It can also occur anywhere between these two points. Generally, horsemen classify bowed tendons as high bows or low bows. The high bows refer to those involving the tendon from the middle of the tendon as far up as the knee and the low bows are those extending from the ankle down the back of the pastern.

From the anatomical description, it should be apparent that a tendon is a structure that is almost always in motion to some degree. Therefore, it goes practically without saying that any tendon injury is a serious one since it is an all-important structure in the locomotion of the horse.

It is vitally important that when a tendon does heal after an injury that it not be restricted in its motion since the adhesions that form will almost always cause a recurrence of the original injury when they are torn loose due to subsequent fast work or racing stress.

It is, therefore, my opinion that if a tendon can be healed with a horse in some sort of mild exercise the resulting healing will be much stronger and much more lasting than a healing that was effected while the horse was at complete rest. The most succesful bowed tendon cases I have ever treated have been those in which the horse was treated while in a mild form of training, such as jogging. Of course, it is quite obvious that in cases of a severe tendon injury where the horse is quite lame and unable to jog or exercise, this form of treatment cannot be followed.

The treatment of bowed tendons is a very complex consideration. The first thing to decide, if possible, is how the injury occurred because it is upon this information that most of the treatment will be based. If it can be established that a bowed tendon was caused from a boot or from a horse hitting himself or from any other outside influence, the prospects for recovery are ever so much greater than they are for those that occur as a result of a weak tendon structure due to conformation. The tendon that is accidentally injured usually does not cause quite as much lameness or involve nearly as much area as the one in which conformation is the basic cause. Frequently, in these latter cases, the entire tendon is involved.

The treatment depends to some degree on the individual horse. It is important that everyone concerned—trainer, owner and veterinarian—know and agree in advance what the future may be considered to hold for this horse. That is, if it is a young horse with great racing potential as a two and 3-year-old, it is necessary that treatment be initiated at once so as to get the horse back on the road to recovery. But if it is just an ordinary young horse with no great potential, chances are it is more economical to turn the horse out and treat him at home until such time as he may resume training. In the case of the top horse with stake engagements to meet, accidental injuries are treated while the horse continues in light training or at least while being jogged. This keeps the tendons moving and at the same time does not put excessive strain on them while allowing them to heal. The actual act of exercise increases the blood supply to the leg which is necessary for a normal healing. Therefore, in the case of a tendon rap or a corded tendon, the tendon is treated first by removing the heat and swelling in the local area and then by applying a counter-irritant in the form of a paint or a light blister until such time as the tendon loses its sensitivity or soreness whereupon the horse can resume training. In the case of an accidental injury, this may very often be accomplished in a period of from four to six weeks. Many good horses have had such accidents right in the middle of the racing season and have come back to regain their original form and race very well. It is, therefore, important that it be decided just what type of tendon injury has occurred since it is entirely possible for a real good horse to be turned out unnecessarily for the balance of the season.

When these injuries first occur, they nearly all look alike and it cannot be determined from examination alone just what did happen. A good bit of the information has to be obtained from the trainer or driver of the horse at the time the injury was sustained.

I should also mention that tendon injuries can occur from catching weight on a particular leg as a result of being sore on the opposite member. This is also a very frequent cause of bowed tendons. For example, a horse that is lame in the right knee may bow the left tendon as a result of compensating for weight adjustment. It goes without saying in these cases that successful treatment of the bowed tendon on the left side is entirely dependent on successful treatment of the knee trouble on the right side.

If there is considerable distortion of a tendon following an injury, whether it be accidental or otherwise, it is frequently advisable to apply a cast in an effort to reduce the distortion and straighten up the tendon. The application of a cast has a remarkable effect on reducing the inflammation and the amount of tissue that is formed around the original injury. A tendon that is cast immediately following an injury and allowed to heal partly in a cast will usually have much less deformity after healing takes place than a tendon that is not cast.

In a case where a horse is to be jogged following a tendon injury, a fairly soft cast is applied, one that can be worn comfortably by the horse while he is jogged. It is usually necessary to renew a cast on a weekly basis since it has a tendency to work loose in addition to the fact that the natural reduction of swelling also causes the cast to become loose in about the same length of time.

In cases where a tendon injury involves a horse that has a limited value on the race track, other methods of treatment may be employed. It has been popular for the past several years to inject a tendon with steroids immediately following an injury in an effort to artificially reduce the fever, pain and swelling and to allow the horse to remain raceable. In cases of accidental injury, this method is fairly successful and many horses that have been so treated continue racing on a regular basis without any ill effects.

I do not advise that such treatment be employed on a top horse with great racing potential because the horse is much more likely to re-injure the tendon. It can be a dangerous procedure because further injuries to a tendon will prolong the eventual healing, if, indeed, healing will ever occur. For that reason, I think it is a good idea for the owner, trainer and veterinarian to have a conference and decide just what plan of action should be followed so that the veterinarian can be guided by the wishes of the other two. At the same time, he can advise them of the hazards involved in the treatment, if any exist with respect to the particular case.

If a horse bows a tendon as a result of conformation, it is almost impossible to bring him back to the races in a relatively short period of time since the same conditions will exist again when the horse reaches the same stage in his training. The only hope for such a horse is that he become mature enough and that his legs become solid enough to enable him to resume training at a later age.

In the last several years, horses of this type have been subjected to many experimental surgical procedures which, as of now, have not proven to be of much merit. It is true that there have been a few horses that have been operated on for bowed tendons and have resumed racing with some success, but this is the exception rather than the rule. As of this writing, it is impossible for a veterinarian to employ surgical interference on a bowed tendon on anything except an experimental basis.

I should also point out that a bowed tendon in a trotter is a much more serious proposition than in a pacer. A pacer can pace relatively well with a bowed tendon after it is healed even though the tendon may be restricted in motion to some degree due to adhesions. A trotter must reach and fold almost perfectly with all four legs in order to stay on gait and to keep from hitting himself and making a break. A pacer on the other hand, can pace satisfactorily even while quite stiff-legged despite the fact that he does not have absolutely proper extension of one of his legs. Because of the way they handle themselves according to the nature of the respective gaits, this is true of most lamenesses involving trotters and pacers.

It should also be borne in mind that a tendon injury takes many months to heal completely and the more tendon tissue involved the longer the healing process takes. In the case of a tendon that bows over a relatively large area, it may require as long as two years for the tissue to return to normal. This has been proven by tissue sections taken from tendons at many stages of recovery and it explains the reason why bowed tendons are treated so unsuccessfully in so many cases. When tendon fibers rupture, they do not regenerate as tendon fibers. The space that the tendon fiber once took up in the tendon is replaced by scar tissue alone.

Since the blood supply in a tendon is very limited, the process of replacing the hemorrhage and damaged tendon by scar tissue takes an extremely long time. As a result of this long, continued irritation, most injured tendons have a tendency to thicken in the early stages of healing as nature goes about her task of trying to provide more blood and additional support to the injured area. As the healing process continues, the tendon will gradually assume a more normal outline but will still retain something of its typical bowed appearance.

SPLINTS—A splint is defined technically as any bony growth that involves the splint bone and/or the shin bone of the horse between the knee and ankle.

Many thousands of years ago, the horse was a three-toed animal but through evolution has became a one-toed animal. The horse now walks on the tip of the original middle toe while the other two have regressed to a point where they are not visible outwardly but still remain from the knee down as vestiges in the form of splint bones. Thus, every horse has eight splint bones, two on each leg.

Splint bones have no useful value aside from the fact that they provide a channel for the suspensory ligaments on the back of the shin. They attach into the base of the knee joint and run down the inside and outside borders on the back side of the shin (Fig. 114). A splint bone is attached only at the top to another bone. It is completely free of the shin bone except for a hard fibrous ligament that runs between the two bones. The splint bone extends from the knee downward to a point approximately three inches above the ankle. It is tapered in shape being more or less triangular at the top and measuring about an inch on all three sides. As it goes down the back of the leg it becomes thinner and thinner until at the bottom it may be only a sixteenth of an inch thick and perhaps a quarter of an inch wide. At the very lower end of the splint bone there is usually a bony prominence that may be visible but which is not a splint and should not be confused with one.

Splints occur in all age groups but are most common in younger horses. This has led some of us to believe that, at least in part, splints may be the result of some upset in the mineral metabolism of the horse. This is not, however, the only cause of splints and among other causes there may be listed any bone bruise in the area of the splint bone or shin and faulty conformation of the splint bone resulting in a very loose attachment between it and the shin bone. In addition, anything that causes a horse to redistribute his weight in an unnatural manner is a predisposing cause of splints. In many if not most cases, the actual cause of any one individual splint is probably unknown.

Splints may be observed on foals just a few weeks of age that have really had no opportunity either to have sustained an injury or to have had their mineral metabolism upset. New splints are occasionally observed on 13 and 14-year-old horses as a result of foot problems, primarily from traveling over a hard race track. In between these extremes, we have all sorts of splints, the origin of which we cannot explain but which, in most cases, may be treated successfully and with uniformly good results.

A splint is very frequently difficult to diagnose until it actually pops out or appears on the surface of the bone. Until then, the horse may exhibit nothing more than ordinary symptoms of periodic lameness. He may just be on one line a little or turning his head to some slight degree; he may have lost a little of his sting in a race or show any of a number of other varied symptoms that cannot be related specifically to a splint. In this stage of development, a splint may be diagnosed only by very, very careful examination of the legs, putting pressure on all areas of the splint bone and trying to find a sore spot which may be expected in time to develop into a splint.

A splint may be in the process of development over a period of from three to four months without ever showing as a splint. I am certain that splints are to be blamed for many things that a horse does that we do not relate to splints as the causative agent at that stage. Conversely, there are many splints that appear during the racing season that do not seem to interfere with either performance or gait. These splints will actually enlarge and be very sore to the touch but they will not interfere in any way with the horse's soundness or racing ability.

Because of the location of the horse's center of gravity, a vast majority of splints, probably 97 out of 100, involve the inside of the leg. A splint that is high up on the splint bone is called a high splint and one that involves the articulation or movement of the knee joint is called a knee splint. There is no special terminology for one that involves any of the remainder of the splint bone. A splint that involves the shin bone alone is called a shin splint (Fig. 11A) and there is a certain type of shin splint that is quite serious and that I will write about a little later on. About 80% of all splints involve both the splint bone and the shin bone, there being an overlapping of the bony tissue. The other 20% may involve either the splint bone or the shin bone by itself.

A knee splint (Fig. 11D) is a very serious type of lameness. It usually occurs in coarse, heavy-boned horses and very often takes the appearance of and is mistakenly diagnosed in the early stages as actual knee lameness. The horse does not extend the leg properly and also swings the leg in an arc to the outside making it appear as if he were trying to straddle an object with his front leg. The horse usually warms out of the lameness to some extent but in most cases is very unhandy in the turns.

So similar in the early stages are the symptoms of a knee splint and actual knee lameness that when the lower compartment of the knee is blocked, a horse with a knee splint will also respond very well thereby further confusing the diagnosis. Most horses with a knee splint will trot or pace the stretches without too much difficulty after they have been properly warmed up but when they reach a turn and are called upon to redistribute their weight the pain becomes unbearable and they will either bear in or out very badly or make breaks. This difficulty in getting around turns is much more characteristic of a knee splint than of just plain knee lameness and is one of the principal means of differentiating between the two.

An ordinary splint will produce all sorts of symptoms of lameness which are not specific and cannot be discussed here with any degree of benefit to the lay reader. A shin splint, if it is accidental in nature and results from a bone bruise, is not a serious thing. The shin bone will remain sore for a short period of time but the lesion will heal and cause no permanent problems. However, there is a special type of shin splint that results from excessive strain on the cortex or hard structure of the shin bone itself and causes an extremely painful type of lameness. The shin bone is involved almost in its entirety although the deformity of the splint, that is the area of swelling, may only show over a rather limited area. Some authors have described this condition as being almost analogous to a fracture of the shin bone and, indeed, such horses are so lame that one would think they did have a fracture were not the shin splint evident. A shin splint that involves the cortex of the bone may be differentiated from the ordinary shin splint by the degree of lameness exhibited.

Shin splints occur only in young horses. I have never seen one on a horse over three years of age. They are probably associated to some degree with mineral metabolism since they appear to be very, very difficult to heal, some remaining sore for two or more years. This, of course, is not normal even for a fractured bone and that is why we veterinarians feel there are metabolic processes involved.

The size of a splint has no relation to its potential to cause trouble or to the severity of the lameness it may produce. Most large splints involve areas of the shin bone and are superficial enough so that they can be easily treated and their sensitivity controlled without too much difficulty. Some of the worst splints, as far as diagnosis and treatment are concerned, are the very tiny splints no larger than half a pea, say the size of a grain of wheat, that lie between the splint bone and the shin bone or sometimes on the inside of the splint bone itself.

In the examination of a splint bone, it should be pointed out that you cannot examine a horse satisfactorily while he is standing on the leg. The leg must be picked up and the fingers introduced between the suspensory ligament and the splint bone in order to examine the splint bone thoroughly. The reason for this is that when a horse is standing on the leg the suspensory pretty well covers up the splint bone and makes it unavailable for examination.

A splint that is not readily detectable or a splint that has not actually started to produce calcium is sometimes referred to as a blind splint. These are frequently diagnosed by X-ray examination and the areas of the splint bone or shin bone or both that are involved will show small areas of soft calcium or in some cases decalcification. Even though they will eventually produce a splint of some size, they are still referred to as blind splints.

There are some splints that actually invade the area underneath the suspensory ligament (Fig. 11E) and, indeed, there are some that actually go from one side of the leg to the other underneath the suspensory. These splints are, of course, very serious and interfere with the normal action of the suspensory ligament and therefore cause very severe lameness. The average splint, however, does not cause lameness as a result of interference with another structure or interference with locomotion. Horses usually are lame on splints because of the pain they feel when the leg hits the ground as a result of concussion between the leg and the ground surface.

Splints are occasionally observed on the hind legs and may be a cause of lameness there. Most hind leg splints are observed in trotters or pacers that interfere with themselves to some extent behind and are the direct result of bone bruises arising out of this interference. Most of these bruises occur when the horse is jogging and not while he is working, although in the case of a trotter that hits his shin pretty hard the bone bruise can occur at work time also. The reason for this is that many horses are not jogged with shin boots or other protection such as brace bandages behind and the result is that they are actually more susceptible to such injuries while jogging than while working.

The treatment of any individual splint depends on the age of the horse, how long the splint has been present and the horse's proposed racing program.

On yearlings and 2-year-olds, I do not think it is wise to treat splints at all unless they begin to cause trouble. Ninety percent or more of the splints that we see at the yearling auctions heal by themselves without any firing or blistering or other forms of treatment.

When a horse develops a splint, care should be taken not to treat it too quickly or too severely. At the time a splint occurs or develops on the horse, the bone is in a stage of acute inflammation. Any irritation applied at this time will further increase the size of splint and the amount of inflammation and will prolong healing time. A new splint should be carefully observed and cooled out by use of cold water, poultices, etc., until such time that it can be treated with paints, blisters or a firing iron.

Generally speaking, the more superficial the splint the more successfully it can be treated because of its accessibility to medication such as blisters or paints as well as to injection of steroids if that be the treatment of choice. Many splints are injected with steroids if it is important that the horse be raced in the immediate future. This is particularly true of stake horses facing up to the most important races of their career.

Injection of steroids into and around a splint is not necessarily considered a form of curative treatment but it frequently turns out that way. Probably a third to a half of all splints injected may be controlled in this manner and over a period of time the splint will heal and repeated injections are no longer necessary.

Most superficial splints can be treated successfully by painting, blistering or firing provided adequate time is allowed for the splint to heal. The larger the area involved, of course, the longer the time involved in the healing process. The average splint requires approximately 30 days for successful treatment to be completed. If a splint is blind or is not readily accessible from the surface of the skin, the treatment is necessarily more drastic and, of course, takes a longer period of time.

Blind splints are usually treated by blistering first in an effort to bring the splint to the surface or to encourage calcium formation in the area. After the splint appears, the ordinary methods of blistering and/or firing are employed.

Knee splints are difficult to treat because they are easily aggravated and reactivated due to training and racing. Their progress can only be followed by repeated X-ray examination.

Shin splints that involve the cortex of the bone are usually treated by repeated blisters or by firing and blistering and these require extended lengths of time for complete healing to take place. Most horses, if not all horses involved with this type of shin splint, are turned out at least for the balance of the racing season.

Splints are occasionally treated by the implantation of radium pellets beneath the skin and over the area of the splint. They may also be treated by the direct application of gamma rays in the form of radium, or X-rays in the form of direct exposure to radiation. While splints are occasionally treated in this manner, I have found that over a long period of time results are not uniform and therefore the treatment is not very popular. Treatment by radiation in any of its forms results in temporary desensitivity of the treated area and enables the animal to race successfully for a limited time. In most cases, however, sensitivity will return and the splint will become reactivated and require other treatment to effect its cure.

Lameness is occasionally produced in the trotter and the pacer as a result of a fractured splint bone. The splint bone, as described earlier, is quite thin and narrow at the end nearest the ankle and it is not uncommon for an inch to two of the bone to break off at the bottom. The primary cause of such fractures is accidental injury in the form of hitting a wheel or a horse interfering with himself. Concussion, that is the shock of the leg hitting the ground at high speed, may also be sufficient to fracture the splint bone under certain conditions and one of the most frequent of all causes is a deformity of the suspensory ligament. When the suspensory becomes thickened and deformed, it pushes the splint bone out of its normal alignment with the shin bone and actually causes the splint bone to bow outward which has pretty much the same effect as pulling on the wishbone of a chicken. The splint bone will only bend so far and then it will break. Indeed, it can almost be foretold that a great number of horses will eventually have splint bone fractures as a result of a suspensory deformity.

If a horse is continued in training after a splint bone fracture, nature, in her endeavor to heal the bone and effect a union between the two pieces, builds up a bony callus around the fractured area. This callus usually causes a good deal of trouble in the race horse. It ordinarily lies underneath the suspensory ligament and aggravates the suspensory much in the same fashion as a pebble in a person's shoe. Eventually, the entire leg becomes sore and inflamed. If the callus around the fracture does not lie under the suspensory ligament, the horse will not be lame and can continue to race without any trouble.

Many horses are operated on for removal of the broken fragment of the splint bone but, unfortunately, only a relatively small percentage of these operations are completely successful. The principal reason for this is that most splint bone operations are not performed until long after the fracture has occurred and until after callus formation has taken place. When the splint bone is removed at this time, it can rarely be done without causing damage to the suspensory ligament and to its blood supply.

In order to remove the splint bone successfully, the operation should be performed before the callus has formed and before any excessive damage has been done to the suspensory ligament. A fractured splint bone may be successfully removed for approximately two weeks following its fracture and thereafter it should only be removed when all other treatment has failed.

We are frequently faced with the fact that a fractured splint bone has already started to heal and in such cases there isn't much that can be done about it except to allow the healing to take place completely before attempting to go on with the horse. This is a necessary procedure since it is too late to take the bone out and the horse is either too lame or the suspensory too aggravated to allow further racing.

The important thing to remember in this respect is that if the condition is diagnosed in time and the horse allowed sufficient rest immediately after sustaining a broken splint bone its removal is, in most cases, neither necessary nor desirable. If a horse is permitted to rest, the bone will knit and heal properly and no excessive callus will form because nature will have time to do her work without outside interference. Therefore, when the horse returns to racing there won't be an infringement on the suspensory, or at least there should not be. But if a horse has raced for any length of time after such a fracture, nature cannot properly heal the break and a callus forms as described. The callus enlarges as a result of the irritation that occurs each time the horse's foot hits the ground and the suspensory is affected. These are the ones that go bad.

KNEE LAMENESS—Of all the race track lamenesses, the one that has grown at the most rapid rate in recent years is knee

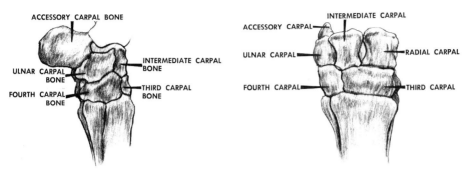

Fig. 117. Two views of the knee are illustrated and the principal bones identified. The view at the left is from the side and at the right, from the front.

lameness. Twenty-five years ago, knee lameness was a rarity in the Standardbred. Today, it is close to being the most common lameness involving the front leg. I am at a loss to explain technically why this should be but I would guess that there are three principal reasons for it. For one thing, today's tracks are much harder and the concussion effect of a horse's foot much greater than it was 25 years ago. For another, horses tracing to a couple of our fastest and most precocious sire families seem to be predisposed to knee lameness. And I am likewise sure that another contributing factor is the much larger number of 2-year-olds being trained today along with the fact that some of them are being called upon for maximum efforts as early as the month of May.

The knee or carpal joint is a complex joint that can be compared anatomically to the wrist of a human being. It is composed of two rows of small bones (Fig. 117) that rub against each other and which are attached to each other by a series of ligaments. Technically speaking, the knee joint actually consists of two joints, each of the two rows of bones being a separate joint operating independently of the other. These two rows are known as the upper and lower compartments of the knee joint. Each has its own moveable and stationary parts and there is no communication between the compartments. There are four bones in each compartment and lameness may develop in either or both compartments simultaneously.

As a result of the complexity of the joint, there are a number of areas where lameness may exist and where disease processes can take place. While injuries can and do occur in both compartments, most injuries involving the Standardbred are in the lower compartment.

The knee joint itself is meant to be flexed to its fullest possible extent, but is not meant to be extended beyond the perpendicular. That is, when the foot hits the ground at full speed or what would normally be considered full speed in an average horse, the knee should not be inverted to the rear beyond its normal perpendicular position in relation to the forearm and shin bone.

Such, however, is not always the case and can be demonstrated in moving pictures and in some still pictures which show conclusively that the knee is no longer perpendicular but is actually inverted due to the extreme pressures of speed, concussion, and weight of the horse.

When the knee joint is over-extended in this manner, it is only reasonable to assume that the cartilaginous margins of the small bones that comprise the knee joint are squeezed or pinched together repeatedly, step after step. As a result of this repeated compression, an inflammation of the cartilage results and this in turn leads to arthritis and other deformities of the knee joint.

The injury to the cartilage in the small bones of the knee is not limited solely to compression of the normal tissue and the chronic inflammation that results. Indeed, in many cases, chips or small fragments of bone are broken away from the face of the small bones of the knee and constitute hazards to the normal motion of the joint.

The knee joint has a relatively poor blood supply and this is especially true with respect to the cartilage surrounding the surfaces of the small bones. Once cartilage is damaged, it takes much longer for it to repair than it would for bone or other tissue located in a place of adequate blood supply. In fact, the cartilage in the knee not only takes a long time to heal but frequently never does heal, since it is often completely deprived of blood as a result of chronic irritation and ulcer formation on the surface of the bone. Therefore, any lameness involving the knee is very serious. It is essential for the knee to be relatively normal in order for the horse to race properly and for the knee to be normal it sometimes requires an extremely long period to effect a real cure of any chronic arthritis that may be present. Many horses never do recover completely from knee lameness but will race in spite of their problems.

In the very early stages, knee lameness is rather difficult to diagnose because the horse is neither lame enough nor does he stay lame long enough to really observe much on the race track. During this period the horse may come out of the stall in the morning in a fashion that we call "swimmy" legged, which actually means that he carries both front legs, or at least the affected front leg, away from the body as if he were trying to straddle an object between them. Of course, if both knees are involved he carries both legs the same way.

Actually, what the horse does is that instead of flexing the knee and picking the leg up and putting it down in front of him in the normal manner, he attempts to slide the leg to the side and forward in an arc so that he doesn't have to bend the knee in order to get his foot to the same location. This rolling type of walk or gait when the horse first comes out of the barn in the morning should be regarded with suspicion since it would indicate that there is something wrong with his manner of extension and in most cases it will turn out to be a knee problem. (It must also be remembered that a horse can and will show the same symptoms if he has a shoulder problem).

A horse may come out of the barn and walk in this manner for a hundred yards and then warm quickly out of it and show nothing for the balance of the day during his jogging and training. For this reason, trainers are frequently not observant enough to pick up this signal in the initial stages which is why many cases of knee lameness get beyond them before they realize exactly what is going on. This is particularly true in large stables where trainers station themselves at the race track and wait for the grooms to bring the horses to the track to be trained. Many of these horses leave the barn in questionable fashion but are sound by the time the trainer takes over at the track.

From this stage, the lameness advances until the horse may require any distance from a quarter of a mile to three miles of jogging to warm out of it. Finally, of course, the horse does not warm out of the lameness at all but shows it in his training miles. In the young horse, I am sure that several weeks pass from the time the first signs appear until the horse becomes untrainable. This is true despite the fact that in most cases the trainer has only been aware for a few days that the horse has been lame. In my opinion, it is very important to make a diagnosis of knee lameness as early as possible so that steps can be taken to prevent permanent damage to the knee joint which will ruin the horse for all time. This is particularly true of 2-year-olds.

After a horse has an inflammation in the knee for a few days, a certain puffiness or distension of the joint capsule, caused by fluid from within the joint, will develop. If the knee is carefully examined, this may be noticeable to the eye but is more likely to be picked up by palpation (touch) alone. The examination is made both with the leg on the ground and the knee straight and then with the leg held off the ground and the knee flexed. In the former examination, increased tension can usually be detected when the thumb is used to put pressure on the joint capsules of both compartments. With the knee in a flexed position, pressure can be applied to the margins of the joint and soreness in these areas can be detected by thumb or finger pressure. As the inflammation of the joint (or arthritis) progresses, the knee may become deformed with excessive fluid formation in the joint capsule and the horse may even be sore enough to resist flexion of the knee joint.

About a month after the horse first goes lame, calcium deposits may be detected on X-ray along the joint margins. These calcium deposits not only interfere with the normal motion of the knee joint but can also be fractured much in the manner that normal bones are. The longer the acute arthritis exists the more deformity will occur. The more deformity that occurs the less likelihood there is of a successful racing career for that horse. Therefore, it is very important that knee problems be diagnosed early. Deformity of the joint should be avoided wherever possible in order to preserve the horse's racing potential.

I have previously discussed conformation defects of the knee which consist basically of the horse being calf-kneed (back on the knee) or buck-kneed (over on the knee) (Fig. 10). The calf-kneed horse is quite subject to knee lameness but a buck-kneed horse very seldom is.

In this connection, I would like to comment on an alleged defect which is not really one at all. At yearling sales we frequently observe horses that have a slight indentation from side to side on the front surface of the knee just below the upper margin of the knee joint. I have heard it said that such horses should be avoided but actually this indentation does not denote any knee problem either present or future. All it indicates is that the animal is immature. The knee will eventually fill out and present a flat surface.

I have also noticed that certain trotters and pacers seem to use their front legs as a source of locomotive power much more than others and that such horses seem more prone to knee trouble. Close observation of horses in training and racing will show that most horses use the hind legs as the primary source of driving power when they are going at speed. But there are horses with a more synchronized gait that seem to be using the front and hind legs alike to develop their speed. It has always been my opinion that horses that use both front and hind legs to develop speed are better-gaited horses and usually develop more speed as a result. Unfortunately, experience has also taught me that horses that do use the front legs as a source of driving power, particularly pacers, are more prone to knee problems. This may be the result of greater effort on the part of the individual leg. It has also been my observation that pacers that seem to have a lot of driving power derived from the front legs are often best shod with a full swedge shoe in front while trotters in the same category are frequently best shod with a grab or at least a crease in the toe.

The treatment of knee lamenesses can be categorized according to the age of the horse and the length of time the condition has existed. In my opinion, all 2-year-olds that develop a knee lameness should be taken out of training and treated with rest and/or blisters or whatever else is necessary until such time as the knee is completely healed and free of any inflammation or fever before training is resumed. In most cases, this means that the horse must be turned out for the balance of the 2-year-old year.

When you are dealing with a horse that is three or older and that has sustained a recurrence of a knee problem, the best procedure seems to be to keep the horse in light training, such as jogging, while blistering the knee and using a paint on it and maintaining a scurf or blister over a period of from four to six weeks. Thereafter, serious training may be resumed.

Many horses with chronic cases of knee lameness are kept raceable by a steady application of a paint or mild blister over the entire period of the racing season. In fact, I know some horses that were raceable for a number of years as long as their knees were being painted regularly and that became useless for racing if the painting or blistering was discontinued for any length of time. In cases where relatively cheap horses are involved and the future racing career of the horse is not bright in any case, injections of the knee joint with steroids can be employed, usually with moderate success. Many of these horses will race successfully over a period of several months as long as they receive periodic injections. In most cases, the horse eventually becomes more or less immune to the injections but while he is being injected, he has earning potential and many horses earn considerable amounts of money in this fashion.

In almost every case of lameness involving the knee, I think complete X-ray examination of the joint is indicated so that the proper prognosis can be made and treatment begun before too much time has elapsed.

Naturally, in cases where bone chips have been broken off the joint margin, results are not going to be nearly as good as in cases where chips are absent. If the bone chip is of any great size, surgical removal is probably the best plan of treatment. However, if the chip is very small, it will often absorb and completely disappear within a few months.

In the event that steroids have been employed and/or the knees painted and blistered with no results, it is obvious that more time must be taken in order to effect a cure. In these cases, I think it is beneficial to turn the horse out for several months in toe-weight shoes which will produce extreme flexion of the knees during normal exercise and allow the joints to heal while the knee is being flexed in an extreme fashion on a regular basis. The turnout period would probably be for from four to six months.

Knees that heal under these circumstances usually heal more permanently and more durably. After the horse has been turned out for several months in the toe-weight shoes and all the fever, swelling and other evidence of inflammation have disappeared, the knee may be fired and blistered or otherwise treated until X-rays indicate that healing is complete or as complete as can be expected.

SHOULDER LAMENESS—Lameness involving the shoulder is, in most cases, a secondary lameness. That is to say, when a horse is lame in the shoulder, it usually indicates that he is lame somewhere else as well and has become lame in the shoulder only because he is trying to protect himself from the primary lameness. The other area need not necessarily be in the same leg. It can be in the opposite front leg or it can be in the hind leg on the same side.

The shoulder of a horse involves a lot of territory. As a matter of fact, in the average horse an area roughly 30 inches in length can properly be described as the shoulder (Fig. 6). So when we talk about shoulder lameness we are actually or potentially talking about several different types that can occur at one or more places over a relatively large surface.

There is one primary shoulder lameness that is known as bicipital bursitis. This is the same type of bursitis that all too often affects the shoulder of a human being. In the horse, it involves the bursa right on the point of the shoulder. It is the spot where the tendons of the shoulder muscles run over the point of the shoulder and attach to the bone of the arm. The bursa becomes inflamed and sore for the same reason that it does in human beings. That is, it can be injured as a result of being hit or it can become inflamed as a result of internal disease. Many cases of bursitis in horses follow epidemics of influenza and other respiratory or viral diseases.

The shoulder lameness that we see most frequently in the Standardbred is actually a myositis involving the shoulder muscles, that is, an inflammation of the muscle structure of the shoulder itself. It comes about from the horse catching weight on the affected side as a result of lameness in the opposite front leg or as a result of the horse becoming muscle-weary or leg-weary from trying to compensate for a lameness behind on the same side. The latter occurs more often with hobbled pacers although it can also happen with trotters. When a hobbled pacer is lame in the stifle, he breaks over late with the affected hind leg and more or less drags the leg. When he does this, the hind leg does not start forward at the time it should and the front leg is forced to pull the hind leg forward using the hobble as a point of attachment between the two legs. Therefore, in addition to doing their own work, the shoulder muscles are also doing the work of the muscles on the front of the hind leg. Consequently, the overworked shoulder muscles become weary, fatigued and inflamed.

Under these circumstances, the horse will develop a rolling action with the front leg quite like that described in the preceding section on knee lamenesses. Instead of picking the front leg up and extending it forward as he should, the horse, in his attempt to rest the shoulder muscles, rotates the leg outward and forward in an arc which produces a kind of swimming motion.

There is another type of shoulder lameness that is not very common but which is a very serious proposition when it does occur. It is observed most often in yearlings and other young horses but also appears occasionally in older horses that have been turned out for some length of time or in a horse that has been involved in a wreck. In one way or another, the horse has fallen or thrown himself either in playing or as a result of an accident and has suffered a neck injury. When this happens, the nerve that supplies some areas of the shoulder is pinched and the horse has a stilted gait on the involved side. Either in the case of yearlings or horses that have been turned out, the lameness shows up the instant the horse is hooked up. This type of shoulder lameness is difficult if not impossible to treat.

To examine a horse for shoulder lameness, it is necessary to examine the shoulder thoroughly with the fingers and then to pick the leg up, flex the knee and pull the entire leg outward away from the body. This puts tension on the top of the shoulder. The leg may also be pulled backward, holding it by the ankle with the knee in a flexed position. This puts pressure on the bursa on the front of the shoulder. In addition, the entire leg can be lifted by standing in front of the horse and grasping the leg by the foot and just below the knee and pulling the leg upward as hard as possible, thereby flexing the point of the shoulder and putting strain on the top of the shoulder as well. A horse will occasionally react dramatically to this type of test. One or more of these tests will indicate the area of lameness.

The usual treatment for primary shoulder lameness consists of injecting the area around the bursa and the bursa itself with a counter-irritant, usually an iodine preparation. In cases where the lameness is not serious and of recent origin, steroids may be injected with equally good results. When the shoulder lameness is actually a myositis—a secondary lameness resulting in an inflammation of the shoulder muscle—the first thing to do is to try to evaluate the myositis in the light of the other lameness that is probably present. This means observing the horse on the track to determine whether he is lame in the opposite front leg, in the hind leg on the same side or somewhere else in the affected leg. This is not usually a difficult determination and involves nothing more than a careful examination of the horse.

For example, when examining a horse that appears to be lame in the shoulder, if you also notice that the tendon on that leg has an old bow it would be proper to assume until proven otherwise that the old bow has caused the shoulder to become sore as a result of favoring the bow to some extent. The same may be said for an old osselet or an old knee fracture or anything else that might impair the normal locomotion of the leg.

It is obvious that if the horse is lame in the opposite front member that the lameness on that side must be diagnosed and relieved before the shoulder myositis can be cleared up. It is equally obvious that in the case of the hobbled pacer I previously described that in order to relieve the shoulder myositis the hobbles must be removed and left off until the stifle condition has been treated and cleared up. If any length of time is required to clear up the lameness, the hobbles should be used very sparingly if the horse is still in training. The best thing is to use the hobbles only for the last training trip or in an actual race. If the horse simply cannot be trained without the hobbles, then they should be let out as far as possible.

In the treatment of the sore shoulder muscles themselves, liniments, steaming applications, etc., may be applied directly to the area in an effort to stimulate the circulation and relieve the muscle soreness. A steamer (a thick blanket designed to fit over the shoulder area) may be applied to the horse if the weather is cold enough for him to wear it without becoming itchy. In other cases, the muscles themselves may be injected with a mild counter-irritant or with steroids. In cases where it appears that the lameness is the result of a previous nerve injury in the neck area, or perhaps due to adhesions of the muscles or the tendons of the muscle of the shoulder, excessive weight may be applied to the affected leg in an effort to make the shoulder muscles develop and compensate for the weakness. Occasionally, we will find a horse that will race in this manner with more weight on one front foot than on the other. Usually, the extra weight is in the form of quarter boots, toe weights, or similar devices, rather than in the shoe itself.

HIND LEG LAMENESS

Lamenesses involving the hind leg (Fig. 118) probably account for fully half of all those observed at harness racing tracks and in my opinion are equally as important as those involving the front leg. Trotters and pacers develop hind leg lamenesses with equal frequency.

In general, all the subjects I have already discussed relative to the foot, pastern, ankle, suspensory ligaments and tendons of the front leg apply just about as well to the same areas of the hind leg since the anatomical structures and the principles involved are essentially the same.

BRUISED SHINS—Bruised hind shins are observed most frequently, of course, among trotters and are a result of the trotter hitting his hind shins with his front feet. This may occur because the horse is bad-gaited or may develop when a horse is favoring one hind leg or the other and, in an effort to protect himself by redistributing his weight, is interfering and bruising a shin. I think it is readily apparent that a horse that is, for example, lame in the left hind leg and taking a short step with that leg, has to compensate by taking a longer step with the right hind leg. The two members have to get over the same ground in some fashion and if one leg is going short, the other leg has to compensate by going long. Because it is striding longer to compensate for the trouble on the opposite side, the right hind leg is very apt to interfere with the right front leg and a bruised right hind shin can usually be expected. This can occur even in the presence of ordinarily adequate protective equipment such as shin boots or brace bandages or both because a horse traveling at high speed can hit his shin hard enough so that any protection on the leg may be inadequate.

A horse may also hit a shin behind as a result of being late with the front leg on the same side. For example, a trotter that is lame in the knee or shoulder or any other place that interferes with the extension of the front leg is going to be late with that leg and therefore the hind leg on the same side is more apt to catch up and interfere with the front leg.

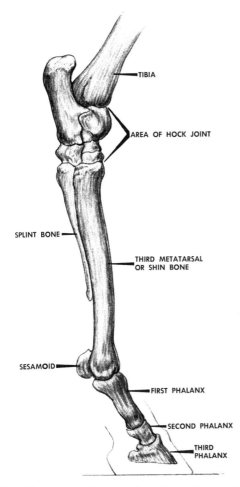

TIBIA

AREA OF HOCK JOINT

SPLINT BONE

THIRD METATARSAL
OR SHIN BONE

SESAMOID

FIRST PHALANX

SECOND PHALANX

THIRD
PHALANX

Fig. 118. The principal bones of the hind leg are illustrated and identified.

If a shin is hit hard enough, it will cause a hemorrhage to develop either between the skin and the bone, or between the bone covering, or periosteum, and the cortex which is the hard substance of the bone as opposed to the marrow or soft structure.

When the hemorrhage occurs between the skin and the bone, it will be absorbed within a reasonable period and the tissue will return to normal provided the cause of the shin-hitting is removed. Naturally, if the shin is repeatedly struck and damaged, no improvement in the local area can be expected.

When the hemorrhage occurs between the bone covering and the bone itself, the injury is much more serious and will be of much longer duration. Absorption of a hemorrhage underneath the bone cover takes considerable time and is usually accompanied by a bony proliferation on the surface of the bone as a result of the inflammation. This may cause the horse to remain sore in the shins over a period of many weeks or months. Therefore, as soon as it becomes apparent that a horse is going to hit his shins, prompt measures should be taken to get him off his shins either by shoeing or otherwise.

Hemorrhages, whether under the skin or under the bone cover, will be absorbed more readily by the injection of enzymes. The application of poultices and other antiphlogistics also constitutes proper treatment.

A horse with a chronically bruised shin usually does not race very well because the shin is so sore that whenever the horse touches the area, even with a boot or brace bandage in place, it will cause him excessive pain and he will make a break.

Some pacers also hit their shins behind but this is an unusual situation and is usually remedied by the application of brace bandages or shin boots. I don't believe I have ever seen a pacer that hit hard enough behind to cause a hemorrhage or a chronically bruised shin.

CHECK LIGAMENT—Check ligament lameness—and once again I am writing about what horsemen call check ligament lameness but which is actually a high suspensory ligament lameness—was described briefly in relation to the front leg and essentially the same conditions exist on the hind leg. Most check ligament lamenesses behind are caused by a horse slipping in the mud or on a type of race track that breaks away, resulting in a ligament tear. It can also develop as a result of excessive strain on the leg such as carrying the weight of the rear end when the opposite hind member is sore.

Most check ligament lamenesses do not occur suddenly in the sense that they are here today but were not there yesterday. In most cases, check ligament soreness develops over a period of time and may be confused with other lamenesses behind in its initial stages. Therefore, it is very important that when first examining a horse that is lame in the hind leg that the check ligament area be palpated thoroughly and the upper portion of the suspensory itself squeezed and exposed to pressure over its entire area in an effort to determine if any degree of soreness is present. Many times, soreness will show as a result of this type of examination long before any swelling or deformity of the ligament itself is evident. This is very important because once the suspensory ligament has torn completely loose from the hind leg at its upper attachment it never heals as strong as it was originally. And since the hind leg is the main source of driving power, this means that the horse will never develop the same speed again.

Actually only about 10 percent of all horses that suffer complete suspensory ligament tears of the hind leg ever return to the race track. Those that do are usually three or four classes below what they were before the injury occured. Therefore, it is important that if a horse is going to develop a check ligament problem that the difficulty be diagnosed and treated before the suspensory is torn loose and the animal rendered useless as is very often the case.

When swelling does appear as a result of check ligament soreness, it occurs just below the hock over the suspensory area and can easily be detected by running the thumb and forefinger over the suspensory area comparing one hind leg with the other. In most cases, the treatment consists of blistering, painting or firing and rest.

CURBS—A curb (Fig. 14) is actually a rupture of the calcaneo-cuboidal ligament on the back of the hock joint. This ligament attaches the calcaneus bone to the cuboidal bone of the hock or tarsus joint. It is only about an inch and a half long and is on a level with the chestnut in the average horse. When it ruptures, there is an accompanying rupture of the blood vessels which lie adjacent to the ligament and usually an attendant hemorrhage which causes considerable swelling and filling in the area. The subsequent curb itself is usually evident starting about an inch and a half below the point of the hock and extending downward from six to eight inches.

There are a number of causes of curbs. One of the principal causes is faulty conformation. Horses that are cow-hocked or sickle-hocked are prime candidates for curbs and, indeed, in such cases it may be predicted well in advance that a curb will develop in an early stage of training and long before the horse has ever had an opportunity to demonstrate his potential speed.

But curbs also occur with regular frequency in horses that have normal conformation of the hind leg and hock. As with most other lamenesses, stress and strain are causes as well as the shifting of weight to accommodate the effect of another lameness. Very often, if a horse is lame from another cause on one hind leg he will develop a curb on the opposite leg from catching the weight on the good leg and straining it. In addition, at certain periods of their training—roughly in the 2:25 to 2:35 area—young horses are predisposed to stifle lameness as a result of muscular immaturity. This usually comes about because the horse is being asked to carry his speed farther than he is prepared to at the moment. When this happens and the stifle becomes inflamed, the horse begins carrying most of his weight on the toe. As a result, the tension on the back surface of the leg is greatly increased, extensive pressure is placed on the hock ligament and a curb develops.

It has been my observation that a colt that has undergone a real solid prep enabling him to develop his muscles properly is much less likely to develop a curb. I think the muscular ability is, in many ways, responsible for the making or breaking of a colt at certain points in his training. In this respect, I think that another mistake that some trainers make is that they want to rush a colt along too fast after he has had a setback of some type. If a colt is laid up for two or three weeks, I don't think the trainer should try to hurry that colt along just to catch up with the others in the stable. Rushing a colt along in this fashion is one of the easiest ways in the world to produce a curb.

Once a curb develops, it is pretty much self-evident and almost anyone can make a diagnosis. Care should be taken, however, in the treatment of a curb. Most curbs that are treated unsuccessfully, that is, those that are not gotten sound within a period of from four to six weeks, are those that were treated too quickly following the injury. Earlier, I mentioned that when a curb pops there is a considerable amount of hemorrhage in the area. If a blister is applied or the curb fired before the hemorrhage has had an opportunity to be absorbed, the entire healing process will be delayed because the area will become more or less stagnant, the counter-irritation will not be effective and healing will take two or three times as long as it should. For this reason, when a curb appears it should be massaged or rubbed with any non-irritating substance until most of the swelling and the soft, juicy feeling that it normally has disappears. This may require from two to ten days and only then should the curb be blistered or fired.

It requires about thirty days for the average curb to heal and this usually means that it is going to cost about thirty days of training time. Some horses will be laid off less than that and some longer but I believe thirty days is about average. It is my practice in cases where the curb requires blistering only to recommend that the horse be completely rested for about two weeks after which he may be jogged for two weeks before training is resumed. In cases where firing is necessary, I think the colt should have three weeks of complete rest before jogging is resumed and then be jogged for an additional two or three weeks before returning to regular training.

In determining whether to fire or blister a curb, I am guided by the severity of the curb, the amount of area involved, the conformation of the horse and his planned schedule and racing potential. I have more confidence in the permanency of firing as a treatment for curbs, but the circumstances involving the individual horse would probably be the over-riding factor in making the decision.

If it was early in the year and I was treating a top colt that was going to have a race against the top colts throughout the season, I would rather that he was laid up a little longer at that stage and thus more certain to race the entire season. For that reason, I would probably fire him instead of blistering him because a curb that has been blistered is more likely to break loose again at a later date, perhaps during the height of the season when time on the shelf is costly time. The exception is that if the curb was a very small one I would probably be satisfied to blister it.

HOCK LAMENESS—The hock is a fairly complex joint and is responsible for a great deal of hind leg lameness. The hock joint (Fig. 119) is comparable to the ankle of a human being and while it is composed of many small bones bound together by numerous ligaments, it has only one complete joint capsule and one moveable surface. Lameness can originate in any of these numerous bones and ligaments. Horsemen are generally acquainted with such terms as spavin, bog spavin, capped hock and thoroughpin all of which refer to specific conditions involving various areas of the hock.

A spavin (also known as a bone spavin, jack spavin or jack) is the name given to a bony proliferation that involves the hock joint (Fig. 14), usually on the inside just below the chestnut in the area where the splint bone attaches to the bottom of the hock on the inside of the leg. Throughout this section I will refer to this type of spavin as a jack spavin in order to avoid confusion.

A jack spavin involves the area of the hock that does not move in the sense that we think of a joint moving. When a jack spavin gets bad enough and involves a large enough area, these bones will become adherent. When they do, there is a complete lack of motion in the area and as a result there is no pain.

A bog spavin (Fig. 14) is a distention of the joint capsule of the hock joint and is evidenced by a swelling on the front of the hock toward the inside in addition to two swellings on the back of the hock, one inside and one outside at about the level of the point of the hock.

A blood spavin is something of a misnomer in that it is a normal condition and does not usually contribute to or cause any lameness in the hock area. Actually, what horsemen refer to as a blood spavin is really nothing more than the normal prominence of the saphenous vein which is the large vein running up from the bottom of the leg and crossing the front surface of the hock at its innermost corner. This results in a prominence in this area and it is identified and entered in the record here only as a reference point in that unknowing people will occasionally look at it and think it is a serious fault of some kind.

A thoroughpin is a distention of the flexor sheath just above the hock joint which results in an enlargement just above and in front of the point of the hock. This swelling may be moved from one side of the hock to the other by manipulation with the fingers.

A capped hock (Fig. 14) is a distention of the bursa and is located directly on the point of the hock. It occurs as a result of injury, such as the horse kicking in a van or stall.

In addition to these specific conditions, there is also plain, ordinary inflammation of the hock joint or arthritis, which can occur in any area or on any surface of the joint. Therefore, when we talk about hock lameness we may actually be referring to any one of a number of specific conditions including arthritis.

A capped hock very seldom causes lameness. It may cause a horse to be stiff for the first few steps but after he hits the track

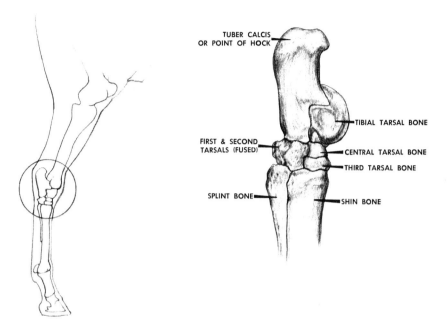

Fig. 119. The hock joint is illustrated at the right and the principal parts identified. The circled area in the illustration at the left pinpoints the location of the hock joint with respect to the hind leg.

it will very seldom interfere with his ability to train or race. All the other conditions except the blood spavin are responsible for lameness to some degree.

The thoroughpin, although it involves the general area of the hock, will not be considered as a hock lameness because it does not involve structures that are directly associated with the hock joint. Being a distention of the tendon sheath, a thoroughpin constitutes nothing more than a torn tendon sheath that will heal with time and may be reduced in size by draining the fluid and injecting the cavity with steroids. Thoroughpins are not of much consequence in a race horse; they are mostly a headache to people in the show horse business who do not want the thoroughpin to show in a conformation class. A thoroughpin will cause lameness when it first occurs, that is, when the tendon sheath first tears. After the sheath heals, the swelling may remain but can be controlled as described.

The symptoms of hock lameness are varied and are very difficult to describe in a manner that everyone will understand. In about 90% of the lamenesses involving the hock, the horse has a tendency to bear weight on the toe portion of the foot. One of the first signs of impending hock trouble is the fact that a horse will start to wear the toe portion of his shoe without wearing the heel. It will also be noticed that not only the toe but the outside of the toe and/or the outside branch of the shoe will be worn more than the inside branch. Therefore, the first thing to do if there is any question that hock lameness may be involved is to determine how the horse is wearing his hind shoes.

The reason for this is that the horse with a hock lameness will break over on the inside toe when the foot leaves the ground. That is, the line of flight of the foot as it leaves the ground carries the foot underneath the horse toward the opposite hind leg and then back out toward the outside of the body. When the foot is handled in this fashion, the toe portion of the foot and the outside branch of the shoe hit first and thus there is excessive wear in these areas. The horse handles himself this way, of course, in an effort to relieve the soreness.

When you are riding in a cart or sulky behind a horse with hock lameness, he will usually carry his hind quarters toward the opposite shaft as well as carrying the affected leg underneath the body and putting it down on the outside of the front foot on the affected side. In addition to carrying the hind quarters in this manner, many such horses will actually bend their spines at a point just in front of the pelvis so that instead of the back being gradually crooked along its entire length, the pelvis itself seems to be hinged just in front of the pelvic area. The horse does this in an effort to rest the area of the whirlbone (to be discussed later) which is inevitably sore in the case of hock lameness. There has never been a horse with hock lameness that did not also have whirlbone lameness. Therefore, in the majority of cases of hock lameness, at least a suspicion of the area involved may be obtained by watching the horse's appearance as he jogs or trains and by examining his hind shoes to see how he is wearing them.

Examination of the horse to determine whether a hock lameness actually exists can be difficult and misleading. For instance, although a bog spavin or distension of the joint capsule may exist in the absence of any other pathology, the fact that the joint is distended doesn't necessarily mean that it is involved and this can serve to confuse the diagnosis. Likewise, the fact that the bony structure of the hock appears to be normal, that is, there is no visible jack spavin, certainly does not rule out the possibility of the existence of a jack spavin or, for that matter, of the existence of arthritis in the entire joint.

When a hock lameness is suspected, the first thing to do is to try to determine as accurately as possible which specific area, if any, is involved. This is usually accomplished by blocking areas of the hock joint. First, an anesthetic is introduced directly into the joint capsule which will anesthetize the area of the bog spavin as well as any arthritic changes in the moveable portion of the hock joint. If the area of involvement has then been blocked, the horse will be much improved if not completely sound when jogged or worked immediately thereafter.

The introduction of anesthesia into the joint capsule does not anesthetize the area of the jack spavin. This must be done by means of a separate injection under the skin on the inside of the hock and in doing this you must also be certain to block the cunean bursa, a small bursa on the inside of the hock that is frequently involved when a jack spavin is present. After this block has taken effect, the horse is again tested on the track and the results evaluated. In most cases, after blocking either the joint capsule and/or the jack spavin area, improvement will be noted on the track after one or the other of the injections. And once the area of involvement has been isolated, an extensive X-ray study should be made to determine just what pathology does exist and what the chances of treatment may be. It must be remembered that in the area of the jack spavin which is very frequently involved, you will very seldom notice any deformity on external examination of the leg itself.

As a matter of record, there is one area of the hock, the lower portion next to the shin bone on the front surface, that cannot be blocked satisfactorily except by nerve trunk blocks, in which case the horse cannot be worked because he may hurt himself. Therefore, it is only rarely that this type of block is used as a method of diagnosis.

X-rays may show little or no pathology present in the very beginning of some cases of hock lameness. Most times the lameness has to be present for a period of from four to six weeks for much pathology to show up on X-ray. In the absence of such X-ray evidence but with the knowledge that blocking does cause the horse to go sound, appropriate treatment can still be instituted to keep the horse in racing condition or to try to effect a complete cure depending upon what type horse is involved. In the case of a well-bred stake colt, it is usually advisable to try to effect a permanent cure and not take a chance on local injection of steroids or counter-irritants to offset the inflammation. If the horse involved is just an ordinary raceway horse, then in most cases an attempt is made to keep the horse raceable by injecting him locally.

In cases of joint involvement, X-rays should be taken periodically to determine the exact condition of the joint, particularly when steroids are used since deterioration of the joint may take place. Should this happen, the only recourse is to notify the owner that the end of the horse's race track usefulness is at hand.

Complete deterioration in the hock is not very common. In most cases, hock lamenesses will heal themselves if given sufficient time—say 12 to 18 months—and the horse will be able to race. Most horses with minor hock problems eventually compensate for them in their gait and, indeed, many go on to race satisfactorily, if not brilliantly, a year or two after the hock lameness has started.

In cases where the hock problem is one of arthritis and the animal involved is a stake horse, it may not be desirable to inject steroids into the hock joint continually over a long period of time. If the horse is a valuable one, he should be turned out instead and allowed to rest while a series of blisters is applied in an effort to effect a cure in a less hazardous fashion.

In cases where jack spavins continue to grow and proliferate on the inside of the hock, it is frequently advisable to cut the cunean tendon where it fastens on the top of the splint bone to relieve tension on the area and thereby relieve pain. This operation is most effective in those cases where a horse places an exceptional amount of weight on his toe; where he walks out of the barn virtually without touching his heel to the ground. In such cases, the horse will get immediate relief and is frequently sound the day following the operation. This operation is usually followed by later firing and blistering although when it is performed in the middle of a racing season it is not uncommon for the horse to continue to race successfully until the fall of the year without any further treatment.

The cutting of the cunean tendon is a relatively minor procedure and ordinarily does not adversely affect the horse in any way. Actually, it consists of cutting only one tendon of the muscle involved, there being another tendon of insertion on the face of the hock that is not cut and whose function is not impaired. Therefore, there is no interruption of muscular activity and consequently no adverse change in the horse's gait.

The most important thing in the handling of hock lamenesses is to be relatively conservative in the way of treatment. It is important to give the horse a chance to compensate and Mother Nature a chance to lend a helping hand. All too often, the hock is injected or surgery performed unnecessarily, As a result of this aggressive therapy, undesirable reactions are produced and very often more harm is done than good.

Another point that I think should be made is that the diagnosis of hock lameness cannot be made on the basis of X-rays alone. You can X-ray almost any horse over three years of age at any race track, and find areas of involvement in his hocks whether or not he has ever been lame there. Therefore, the fact that some trouble does show up on X-ray does not necessarily mean that it is causing the horse any grief. It is impossible to make an intelligent diagnosis without blocking the area involved.

The most serious lamenesses of the hock are those involving the articular surface, that is, the moving surfaces of the joint, such as arthritis. This would also include bone chips which are not too common in a hock but which are occasionally present, and idiopathic arthritis, or arthritis resulting from excessive race track wear.

STIFLE LAMENESS—Stifle lameness is one of the more common lamenesses involving the Standardbred. It occurs much more frequently in pacers than in trotters, but almost every horse will become affected to some degree, however minor, some time during his racing career.

The stifle joint (Fig. 120) is an extremely large joint with a very large area of articulation, that is, a large area of joint surface. The stifle is the joint of the hind leg located approximately at the level where the horse's belly meets the hind leg. The angle of the joint points forward and it is the extension of the stifle joint by the large muscles of the hind leg that actually propels the horse and thus induces speed.

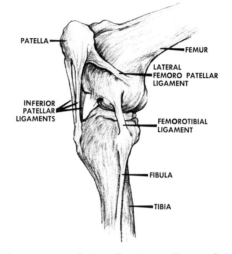

Fig. 120.   The structure of the stifle joint is illustrated and the principal parts identified.

In relation to the human being, the stifle joint—although placed much higher on the side of the horse—is the joint that connects the femur or thigh bone with the tibia or leg bone and thus is comparable to the knee. There is a patella or knee cap on the stifle just as there is on the knee of a human being.

Because of the large area it involves, the stifle joint is held in position by a number of very long ligaments. There are 14 in all positioned in four groups of six, three, three and two. Except on its front surface, the stifle joint is surrounded by heavy muscle and the efficiency of the joint is directly proportional to the efficiency of these muscles.

As a result of the large area that the joint covers and the length of the ligaments involved, ligament problems are the principal sources of trouble when stifle lameness occurs. Torn or partially torn ligaments or strained ligaments account for most of the stifle lameness seen at race tracks.

One of the main ligaments involves the head of the fibula bone where it attaches to the tibia. The fibula bone lies on the outside of the tibia just below the level of the stifle joint on the outside of the hind leg (Fig. 120). Most of you will recall that about 10 years ago there was a sudden outbreak of interest in the fibula bone in conjunction with stifle lameness and that many horses were laid up for long periods of time because X-rays indicated that they had fractured fibula bones. It has since been resolved that the fibula bone does not fracture as frequently as was formerly believed and that what were considered fractures at that time were actually incomplete bone formations. It is generally agreed now that the fibula bone is actually responsible for very few cases of stifle lameness. That is not to say that the ligament that inserts on the fibula bone is not responsible, but only that the fibula bone itself is not.

In my opinion, the cause of stifle lameness is inadequate conditioning. By that I don't necessarily mean that we should intensify our training programs but rather that I believe proper conditioning of a horse, especially in the early stages of the training program, has a great deal to do with his avoiding stifle lameness during the racing season.

I mentioned previously that hard tracks or so-called good race tracks were conducive to stifle lameness. I believe this to be true because a hard race track, the billiard table type, is not a challenge to the muscles of the stifle. To build up the stifle muscles adequately, the horse has to be exercised over a soft type of race track where there is enough pull and enough drag on the hind leg to cause the stifle muscles to develop to their fullest potential. Once these muscles have developed, then I believe they can be maintained over a good race track.

Stifle lamenesses, of course, can occur accidently as in cases where the track breaks away. Stifle ligaments are frequently strained as a result and lameness develops. Stifle ligament soreness can also result from a horse's foot stopping too quickly after it hits the ground during flight. This is frequently observed in cases where horses are shod with swedges, calks, grabs or other devices that tend to hold a horse to the track and stop any natural sliding action. It is also seen on the Tartan brand track where the foot tends to stick to the surface rather than to slide, although Del Miller seems to have done away with this at his track by adding a thin layer of sand to the surface.

The symptoms of stifle lameness are relatively characteristic and identifiable although here again somewhat difficult to describe. A horse with stifle lameness will break over on the outside toe of the foot and carry the leg away from the body in a lateral arc after which it will swing back in and land underneath the body. This is a very accurate way for a trainer to differentiate between a stifle problem and a hock problem because the horse arcs the affected hind leg to the outside if the stifle is bothering him and to the inside if it is the hock. This can be determined with a great degree of accuracy just by watching the horse closely as he jogs along at a medium gait. At the same time, additional evidence is provided by the wear on the hind shoe since the inside branch will show more wear if it is stifle trouble and the outside branch if it is hock trouble.

The reason the horse arcs his leg to the outside is that he does not want to flex the stifle joint because this causes pain in the stifle ligaments and muscles. In an effort not to flex the joint, he carries the leg more or less stiff but in an arc so that the toe will not touch the ground. And to prevent the toe from touching the ground he must carry the leg away from the body in order to get it back out in front of the pelvis again where it belongs. He will also carry his hind quarters toward the shaft opposite the affected leg, but unlike the horse with hock trouble he does not either tilt his pelvis or twist his back just in front of the pelvis.

It is much easier for a horse to trot with a sore stifle than it is to pace. For that reason, many pacers are hard to get on gait after they have developed stifle lameness and will insist on wanting to trot even in the hobbles. This is a sure sign of stifle trouble. Any horse that is lamer pacing than he is trotting usually has a stifle problem.

When examined in the stifle area, some horses will exhibit pain when the ligaments are pressed with the fingers. But it is difficult to arrive at an accurate diagnosis in this fashion since many horses are naturally a little touchy when pressed in this area and resent being examined, lame or not.

Some inference can be gained by determining the amount of fluid in the stifle joint. In many cases of chronic stifle lameness, the joint is distended with fluid and is easily recognized as a distended joint under careful examination. But the cardinal symptom of stifle lameness is the associated soreness of the gluteal muscle in the area between the point of the hip and the backbone. Almost every horse with stifle lameness will exhibit a soreness of the muscles in this area when they are pressed with the fingers or palm of the hand. This a very significant symptom and a horse should be examined for it routinely. The reason the muscles of the back become sore is because the horse is trying to compensate for the stifle lameness by carrying his back in a very stiff, rigid position. This makes the muscles sore and inflamed in that particular area.

As I previously stated, the ligaments involving the stifle joint are the chief sources of pain in stifle lameness. There are a great number of ligaments involved, 14 to be exact, and any one of them or any group of them can become sore at any one time. The stifle joint itself, that is, the joint surface, is very seldom involved in any lameness with two general exceptions: (1) cases of injury where a horse has been in an accident and the joint or a portion of the joint has been fractured and (2) where the lameness may follow an old case of joint infection, most of which occur when the animal is just a foal but which may remain dormant and go unnoticed until the horse actually reaches the race track. I have seen a couple of cases of latent joint infections that were injected with cortisone and proceeded to deteriorate very rapidly necessitating eventual destruction of the horse.

If at all possible, the treatment of stifle lameness should be one of prevention rather than of cure. In my opinion, as I have now said a number of times, a horse that is properly trained and muscled, will rarely develop stifle trouble during the racing season. In order to produce the proper muscling effect on the stifle, I think it is essential that the horse get adequate work, slow work over soft going, in order to be able to compensate for the extreme pressures applied to the stifle ligaments during the normal racing year. If, however, stifle lameness does occur, it may be alleviated completely or helped immeasureably by local injections of either steroids or counter-irritants, these working in exactly opposite fashions. The steroids relieve the pain and allow the joint to function in its normal fashion. The counter-irritants cause an increase of blood supply to the area and this actually heals the damage done to the ligaments and returns them to their normal function. There are some horses that have chronic stifle problems requiring periodic injections to keep them racing satisfactorily. In other cases, the applications of liniments or liniment-like rubbing agents may be all that is necessary to keep the circulation in the stifle area stimulated and the horse in a sound racing condition.

It might also be worthwhile to mention one other affiliated condition that is occasionally seen in young horses wherein the stifle joint becomes misaligned due to a shift in the so-called tibial crest, or at least a shift in the alignment of the stifle joint due to the immaturity of the horse. This is not exactly a rare condition but it does not happen with any great frequency. When it does occur, the only thing that can be done is to turn the horse out until the stifle attains its normal growth. Occasionally, the head of the fibula bone will rotate allowing the colateral ligament of the stifle joint to become loose and sore and in these cases it is necessary to inject a counter-irritant underneath the head of the fibula bone in an effort to stabilize it and fuse it to the tibia so that it can no longer move about.

With trotters and pacers alike, I think it is essential to increase the exercise of any horse that shows any stifle soreness or weakness. This increase in exercise should be on a gradual basis. Usually, I advise increasing the jog miles at least one per day and the training miles at least one per workout. It is important to remember that it is not the fast miles that are increased but the slow ones in an effort to get the horse back into condition so that the stifles will remain sound.

In the case of a pacer that is dragging his hind leg in the hobbles, it is quite necessary to work the horse free-legged if this is at all possible or to work him with the hobbles just as loose as possible so that he can drag the affected leg without getting a shoulder sore on the same side. I have already explained this in my discussion of shoulder lameness. After the horse becomes sound, the hobbles may be taken up to their optimum length. In my opinion, working a horse free-legged helps to keep his stifles in condition because it requires a horse to have better control over his legs during flight. I believe that if a horse is coached and very carefully permitted to train free-legged, his stifles, in particular, will remain sounder than they will with the horse that must continually jog and train in the hobbles. This applies to all pacers of all ages.

WHIRLBONE LAMENESS—Actually, there is no such thing as whirlbone lameness since a horse doesn't have a whirlbone, nor does he even have a whirl of hair in the area where the lameness occurs. The name probably came about because some groom decided a hundred or more years ago that it was much easier to say his horse had whirlbone trouble than to try to describe it is as trochanteric bursitis. This is the technically accurate name for what all horsemen call whirlbone lameness.

The trochanteric bursa lies on the back side and at the top of the femur or thigh bone, not far from the ball and socket joint of the hip. This bursa acts as a pulley over which the main tendon of the middle gluteal muscle runs. This muscle is responsible for straightening the hip joint and the hind leg and as one of the main propellant muscles of the pelvis is very much involved in gait and speed.

When the trochanteric bursa becomes sore and inflamed, it affects this important muscle that rides over it. This is the reason that horses with whirlbone trouble go so lopsided. It is difficult for them to develop propulsion with the affected leg and it is also very painful.

Whirlbone lameness behind is similar to shoulder lameness in front in the sense that it is only rarely that either is a primary lameness. A horse very seldom develops a sore whirlbone without first being sore in some other area. Ninety percent, if not more, of all cases of whirlbone lameness are also cases of hock lameness. The remainder are horses that are lame in the front end and over-extending the hind leg in an effort to compensate weight-wise, or lame below the hock, chiefly in the suspensory or sesamoid areas.

When it becomes evident on examination that the whirlbone is sore, then the hock is automatically suspect as the original source of the whirlbone trouble even though the hock appears to be clean. Whirlbone soreness is very often evident long before the hock lameness shows sufficiently to be readily diagnosed and thus provides an almost certain clue that the hock is involved. The method of travel for a horse with whirlbone lameness is the same as described under hock lameness, the symptoms for one being exactly the symptoms for the other.

To put this in its proper perspective with relationship to whirl-bone lameness, let us assume that the horse does have hock trouble of one kind or another. Almost the first thing he does, even before any obvious symptoms appear, is to begin landing on the toe of the affected leg as previously described. The immediate effect of this unnatural way of going is to cause an excessive strain on the gluteal muscles and the trochanteric bursa or whirlbone. In almost all cases, this secondary lameness reveals itself long before the hock lameness becomes evident and points to the hock as the source of primary lameness.

A whirlbone lameness is usually treated by steroid or counter-irritant injections. It is also routine to treat the whirlbone when-ever the hock is treated, since the two are so closely associated, and it is not a bad idea to treat the whirlbone when any other hind leg lameness exists since a secondary involvement of the whirlbone will frequently develop.

BONE FRACTURES

Fractured bones are not actually very common among race horses although they do occur with rather alarming frequency at certain tracks. It appears to me that most fractures occur at tracks where the racing surface is very hard.

Fractures are not ordinarily too difficult to diagnose. In most cases, the horse shows an extreme amount of pain and by diligent examination a reasonable diagnosis can usually be made even without X-rays. However, there are some cases where the fracture is very difficult to demonstrate even after repeated X-ray examinations. Indeed, it frequently happens that a fracture line is so irregular and so devious in its course and there is so little separation of the bone fragments that the fracture line cannot be demonstrated on an X-ray for two or three weeks. After that, the fracture has a tendency to separate and the line becomes wider and therefore more apparent on X-ray. This is a rather common thing, particularly in fractures involving individual bones of the hock and knee and occasionally the coffin bone. Most other bones do not fracture in a fashion that makes them difficult to demonstrate on X-ray.

Another feature of fractures that must be kept in mind is that satisfactory bone healing is directly related to the amount of periosteum or bone covering. To put it in plain words, if you're going to fracture a bone you'd better fracture a large one because it will heal much more solidly. A fracture of the pastern or shin bone will heal much more satisfactorily than will a fractured sesamoid bone or a bone in the knee or hock, or the coffin bone which has a very poor periostial development. For obvious reasons, fractures that involve a joint are much more serious than those that do not.

In certain cases, such as fractures of a sesamoid bone, fragments may be removed satisfactorily. The same is true in cases of small chip fractures of the knee or hock. Certain fractures involving, for example, the third carpal bone of the knee lend themselves well to the placement of a screw in the affected bone and good results are frequently obtained by screwing the piece back into its original alignment. Fractures of the long bones, such as the shin or pastern, occasionally are shatter type fractures which must be pinned in order to maintain good alignment. This can be done satisfactorily although it requires expert attention.

Open reductions and splint applications in the horse have not yet been developed to a point of every day usage. However, I would encourage anyone with a horse that has a fracture to at least try to repair it because sometimes miraculous results are obtained when a minimum result was expected.

Treatment of most fractures, of course, consists of nothing more than complete rest until healing has taken place. Many horses sustain bone fractures and later return to the races with no loss of ability.

CLOSING NOTES

In closing this discussion on lamenesses, it must be pointed out that there are some conditions that relate to the soundness of the horse that cannot either be pinpointed or specifically explained in a few words or even a few paragraphs.

For example, there are conditions of metabolism, particularly those involving some of the endocrine glands, that can upset the horse's mineral metabolism and thereby influence his muscular action. Another prime example is that of the general muscular soreness which is exhibited in some horses following attacks of influenza. The horse seems to be tight all over for a number of weeks following the attack and this is attributable to a toxic type of metabolism resulting directly from the viral attack.

There are many such examples that could be cited in this connection but they require specific tests and specific knowledge of the individual horse. General statements regarding these conditions would serve no useful purpose in this discussion because of the large number of variables involved.

For the same reason, I have not discussed a number of lamenesses that may develop from specific conditions involving the general nervous system such as brain tumors, lesions of the spinal cord, and lesions involving the spine itself which in turn involve the spinal cord. Nor have I discussed the diseases of the blood vessels which may involve the blood supply to a certain group of muscles necessary in the normal locomotion of the horse and which under certain conditions may produce extreme lameness.

Instead, I have concentrated on presenting in understandable language a basic resume of every-day lamenesses with which campaigning harness horsemen are likely to come in contact. To the best of my knowledge, this is the first time that a presentation of this type and scope has ever been made specifically for harness horsemen. If, in doing this, I have enabled any trainer or owner to increase his knowledge with respect to lamenesses that affect the trotter and pacer, then I have accomplished what I set out to do.

Dr. Edwin A. Churchill, one of the country's most prominent veterinarians, was born in Phillipsburg, N. J. on June 22, 1918. As a youngster he worked as a groom in a nearby riding stable and later leaned on that experience to operate a riding academy in the Poconos, using the money to put himself through the University of Pennsylvania Veterinary School. After graduation in 1941, he entered general practice in Maryland, returning to the University three years later as an assistant professor of Surgery and Obstetrics, specializing in horses. In 1947, he became director of the University's Large Animal Clinic and, as an associate professor, head of the Department

of Surgery and Obstetrics. He was the youngest man ever to head the department. In 1950 he returned to private practice and located in Centreville, Md. where he still resides. He worked primarily with harness horses on the Maryland-Delaware circuit and established his own Springbrook Farm where he has stood several stallions including Adios Senator and Rodilo. He sold his private practice in 1966 and accepted a position as Farm Director and veterinarian for Mrs. Richard C. duPont's Woodstock Farm and Bohemia Racing Stable, one of the most prominent (Mrs. duPont owns the great Kelso) in Thoroughbred circles. He still maintains a limited Standardbred practice on a consulting basis, serves as the veterinarian for The Standardbred Horse Sales Company of Harrisburg, Pa., and is a familiar and popular figure at eastern harness racing tracks. He is a fellow and founding member of the American College of Veterinary Surgeons and one of the founders and former president (1958) of the American Association of Equine Practitioners. While at the University of Pennsylvania, he attained national prominence as the first man to introduce joint surgery on horses, the first to remove sesamoid bone chips and the first to remove fractured splint bones.

17

NUTRITION and FEEDING
Part I—NUTRITION

DR. WILLIAM J. TYZNIK

TRADITIONALLY the horse has been considered a "hay burner." This belief has developed from the fact that many horses can and do subsist on hay of reasonably good quality. The horse is somewhat unique among domestic animals in that he is monogastric with a facility to digest and utilize considerable amounts of roughage. This is due to the fact that the cecum or "blind gut" has a population of microorganisms that have the ability to break down cellulose in roughages. Unfortunately more credit has been given to this organ because of the lack of sound information concerning this part of the anatomy of the horse. This lack of information has developed many mistruths and mysticisms about the horse. Any number of comparisons can be found between cattle and horses. The similarity may be present to some degree, however it is far from complete. The capacity of the digestive tract of a horse is considerably smaller than that of the cow.

In addition, the cow has a much greater facility to digest—through the aid of a much greater microbial population—than the horse. The cow has a facility for remastication of rough fibers whereas the horse does not. All animals chew their food for the simple reason of swallowing. The horse is no exception. Therefore any feedstuff that is coated with fibrous material will be readily swallowed and once it passes the mouth it will usually pass through the gut with little change because no enzyme or bacteria break the lignin which surrounds the seeds of plants and stalk of mature forages. This may explain why the feces of horses usually contain considerable amounts of fiber as compared to other species.

Considering the digestive systems of animals, the horse seems to fall somewhere between the ruminant and the monogastric. He is far from the efficient utilizer of roughages that the cow is, but much better than the pig. This fact is further shown by the blood glucose level of the horse which is intermediate between the cow and the pig. We might assume, therefore, that we have an animal that combines the nutritional requirements of these divergent species and seems to strike somewhat of an average.

We must however always keep in mind that the horse is an animal and as such has all of the physiological and biochemical processes that occur in other animals. Although some of the end products of digestion may be somewhat different, the end result in metabolism of energy, protein, vitamins and minerals is relatively the same. In general, we must consider the horse an animal set around a digestive system somewhat different from other animals.

Nutrition is the process whereby substances in food or feedstuffs are broken down, absorbed and rebuilt into components of the animal. This process must involve all of the functions related directly and indirectly to metabolism. As we are all aware, animals doing different things require different amounts of nutrients but the fact remains that all nutrients are required for all animals at all times. In addition to the presence of nutrients, we must concern ourselves with the relative proportions of nutrients or ratios of one nutrient to the other. Every year more is being learned about the highly significant effect of nutrient interrelationships. In other words, we are becoming more aware of the fact that additional amounts of a nutrient may be as detrimental as a deficiency of a nutrient by causing nutritional deficiencies which are not simple but severely complicated. Some nutrients, especially in the form of minerals, which have been considered toxic for many years are now exhibiting not only a role that is essential, but one that seems to be extremely critical.

The time has come when nutritionally adequate and balanced rations for horses must be considered. All things in the development of a horse are not a result of nutrition. The potential of a horse must be present and if the animal is well fed and well managed, we can expect to realize this potential.

The beginning of nutrition is the palatability of a feed. Many horses are spoiled simply because of the owner. On the other hand, any number of nutrients in a bag are of little value to the horse.

Feed digestion by the horse is the beginning of nutrient release. A fact that is difficult to comprehend by most people is that food in the digestive tract of an animal is no better than the material remaining in the bin. The gut must be considered as a tube through which the feed passes to be broken down. Most plant material is covered with a hard woody coat known as lignin. This material cannot be broken down or digested by any enzyme or bacteria. The teeth of the animal are highly critical for breaking this hull to provide an entry for the digestive juices to function in releasing nutrients. Animals chew to facilitate swallowing. The small hard seeds can be swallowed easily without chewing. Therefore it is imperative that the hull be broken by some mechanical means before being fed to the horse.

After swallowing has taken place, digestive processes begin. The break-down of easily digested carbohydrates and proteins begins in the stomach of the horse to be continued in the small intestine. Beyond this point fermentation takes over in the colon and the cecum or blind gut. Much more credit seems to have been attributed to the function of the cecum than seems justified. The cecum of a 1200-pound horse will have a capacity of about 7-10 gallons; the colon has considerably more capacity. Although populations of microorganisms in rather large quantities are present in these organs, their absolute functions have not been established. If we transpose from the ruminant animal, we may assume that cellulose is digested or broken down in these organs. The efficiency with which it is broken down does not appear to be as good as that of the ruminant. Another function attributed to the cecal microorganisms is that of B-complex vitamin synthesis as well as possible protein synthesis.

We must take into account the location of the cecum in relation to the rest of the digestive tract. Unlike the ruminant in which the fermentation precedes true digestion and absorption, the fermentation "vat" of the equine succeeds the absorption area— the small intestine. If the cecum and colon have only limited absorption, which may be the case, a different approach to his nutrition must be considered.

Studies indicate that the rate of passage from the stomach to the cecum occurs in about three hours which does not permit a great deal of time for a great deal of digestion. Much research needs to be done to find answers for this myriad of questions.

Since horses are animals and in general react as other animals do metabolically, we need not wait until research findings with the equine provide us with exact figures. Data from other animals can be extrapolated to the horse until such time as data are available. This has been a common practice over the years with reasonable success in other species. There probably is no live-stock area as riddled by old wives' tales as the equine nutrition area. The lack of information is a possible reason for this problem. In this section we shall discuss the various nutrients and their fundamental function in nutrition with the hope of alleviating some of the misconceptions.

Water is rarely considered as a nutrient but it happens to be the one nutrient needed and consumed in largest quantity by all animals. The horse is literally living in water since every tissue is surrounded by water. The blood contains about 90% water—muscle 70-75%—fat 40%, bone 25% and the enamel of the teeth which is the hardest and driest part of the animal body contains 5% water. The many functions of water add to the appreciation of water as a nutrient. Starting at the mouth, food must be lubricated with saliva before swallowing after which digestion occurs in a liquid media followed by absorption in solution or suspension. After the nutrients are absorbed into the blood system, they are transported in a water medium to the various cells in the body. Another more apparent function is that of cooling the body, as the temperature and/or activity of the horse increases, the rate of perspiration increases. Cooling is accomplished by the evaporation of the water from the skin. The horse cannot tolerate much of an increase in body temperature. It is therefore imperative that a horse sweat freely to keep cool and comfortable. If perspiration is not adequate, the only other method of cooling is by increased breathing rate which increases the evaporation of water from the lung surface. Obviously as the water loss increases by perspiration, it must be replaced in the body.

Excretion of materials from the body also requires considerable amounts of water. All nutrients that have been absorbed from the digestive tract and served their function in the body must be eliminated from the body or toxicities will result. Certain nutrient classes, if fed in excess, such as mineral and protein, are also excreted in the urine, thus increasing the demand for water. We are all familiar with the effect of eating large quantities of salt and its effect on thirst. The sensation of thirst in man or in animals comes from dehydration or the loss of water from cells.

Lactation in the case of the mare requires rather large quantities since the water content of milk is about 85-86%. Other more subtle but equally important functions are eyesight, hearing, cushioning, reproduction and maintenance of form.

Water should be supplied to all animals at all times on a free choice basis. The only exception to this generalization is when a horse has been overheated from working. It is almost an imposition to water a horse once or twice daily and expect him to do well under any circumstances. Water should be clean and cool. Temperatures should range between 45° and 65° fahrenheit. Horses should never be forced to drink from pot holes in the field or from any other stagnant sources. Too often water tanks used on brood mare farms are so poorly managed that algae becomes so dense that horses have to paw their way to the water. An excellent rule of thumb for water containers is to keep them clean enough so that you are willing to drink from them. Fresh flowing streams may be used if one can be assured that disease contamination is not occurring upstream. Many infections can be water borne and infect an entire herd like an outbreak of a prairie fire. Automatic waterers are now available that will provide adequate supplies of fresh water at a minimal outlay and labor. There is no need to provide water in the form of a mash or slop since readily accessible sources will serve the horse well.

Often figures are listed for the consumption of water but the range will be affected by things such as size and activity of the horse as well as the ration the horse consumes. Rations high in mineral or protein will increase water intake as was indicated earlier. Horsemen have come to associate frequency of urination with kidney damage—the kidney is designed as a filtration mechanism and does not become damaged from putting fluids through it.

A horse will consume between 5-15 gallons of water daily. A horse on pasture will usually drink less water than one on dry hay for obvious reasons. Some people believe that a horse should be given water after feeding while others believe it should be provided before feeding. The fact remains if a horse is thirsty he will not eat and vice versa. The horse should be provided water when he wants it at some distance from his feed box to avoid messing up the water by some horses.

The next most widely consumed group of nutrients are those that provide energy to the horse. Energy is measured and expressed in four basic units, British Thermal Units (BTU), Total Digestible Nutrients (TDN), therms or calories. The terms most widely applied to animals are either therms, TDN or calories. Energy is required for a variety of purposes such as work, lactation, heat, cooling, etc. The nutrient classes that yield energy to the animal are carbohydrates, fats and proteins.

The carbohydrates are composed of carbon, hydrogen and oxygen with the hydrogen and oxygen found in the same proportions as in water and yield four calories of energy per gram when they are metabolized in the body. The simplest carbohydrate of significance to the animal are the monosaccharides and especially the six carbon sugars. Glucose or dextrose is the common form of blood sugar and and is responsible for carrying energy to all parts of the body. Fructose or fruit sugar is the sweetest of sugars and is found in honey or ripe fruits. Galactose is found as part of milk sugar and is somewhat less soluble in water than are the other two. The monosaccharides are the only form of carbohydrate found in the bloodstream of animals but are not fed in the diet as such. The blood glucose level can be raised in the horse by injecting dextrose but it will soon drop to the normal of about 70 or 80 mg. per 100 grams of blood. The return to normal is rather rapid occurring in about five minutes. Normal levels are maintained by release of glucose from glycogen stores (animal starch) found in small quantity in the liver and muscle.

The next most complex carbohydrates are the disaccharides or double sugars. They are made of two simple sugars chemically bounded together. The most common of these is sucrose which comes from a variety of sources, but most widely from cane or sugar beets. Practically, sucrose is fed to horses in the form of molasses. Sucrose is sweet to the taste and readily dissolved and digested. Maltose, commonly known as malt sugar, is not widely fed but is a breakdown of starch in the digestive process. Upon digestion, each maltose molecule yields two molecules of glucose or blood sugar. The last of the disaccharides that has significance is lactose which occurs naturally in milk of all mammals. Young animals have an enzyme which breaks lactose to its component sugars (glucose and galactose). The mature animal is not as capable of using this sugar as is the young animal. The relative insolubility of lactose, due to the presence of galactose, has a tendency of being laxative in nature when fed in excess of 5-10 percent of the diet. On the other hand, young foals do not seem capable of utilizing sucrose in any significant quantity.

As the number of simple sugars increase, the carbohydrates become more complex and less soluble. Many simple sugars chemically bound to each other are known as polysaccharides. The polysaccharides of concern to us in feeding horses are starch and cellulose. Starch is comprised of long chains of glucose molecules hooked together. All animals have the ability to break starch into the component simple sugars. The enzyme responsible is amylase which is secreted by the pancreas into the small intestine. Conveniently for horsemen, plants store their reserve energy in the form of starch. The only difference in starch from various grain is in the size of granule. Chemically they are all the same so that it makes absolutely no difference which starch is fed to animals since they all yield the same amount of energy. Cereal grains are the primary source of starch as a supplementary energy supply. Differences are present between various cereal grains as to the amount of starch and therefore the amount of energy present. Most grains are sold by the bushel which is a volume measure. The varying weights indicate the wide variation of energy present.

The following is a list of the common grains and their bushel weights:

Shelled corn	56 lbs.
Oats	32 lbs.
Barley	48 lbs.
Wheat	60 lbs.
Rye	56 lbs.

Traditionally, oats have been a cereal grain of choice for horses. It is a highly palatable grain but also one that has a tendency toward great variation due to hull. Oats in the northern United States and Canada are oats that may have bushel weights up to 46 to 48 lbs. whereas oats grown further south become lighter in weight with some testing as low as 24 pounds per bushel. The low weight is indicative of low energy content.

Corn is the most widely grown cereal grain in the United

States and is a highly palatable and nutritious feed for horses. Caution must be exercised when horses are being converted from oats to corn because corn will weigh almost twice as much as oats for the same volume. Many accusations have been made against corn such as that it is too fattening and too hot. Both of these statements indicate misuse of corn. If the same weight rather than volume of corn replaces oats, little difficulty will result.

Barley is widely used in the western part of the United States and other parts of the world. Barley is an excellent feed with considerably less variation than is found in oats. The protein level is somewhat higher than corn or oats although the quality of cereal grain protein is questionable.

Wheat is not widely used because of cost and its extremely high energy level and rapid digestibility which has a tendency to produce severe digestive disturbances. Not more than 20-25% of the grain ration should be wheat and then extreme caution should be exercised in feeding. Wheat is probably the most dangerous of the cereal grains because it can be so easily overfed.

Rye should not be fed to horses because it is highly unpalatable and may contain ergot—a fungus which will cause abortions and may cause death.

The only purpose of feeding grain to horses is to increase energy intake. If too little is fed, horses will lose weight whereas if too much grain is fed, horses will become too fat—no specific grain will make horses fatter than any other, so long as the level of grain feeding is properly regulated.

Cellulose is a carbohydrate that cannot be digested by any animal. This does not mean they cannot use it. The horse like the cow, has a large population of bacteria in the intestinal tract which ferment the cellulose to fatty acids—acetic acid, propionic acid and butyric acid. In ruminants, all of these acids can and are used for energy when metabolized. The exact method whereby this material is used in the horse is not known but they do provide energy. Because the cecum is located at the end of the absorptive area, serious questions are being raised concerning the efficiency with which absorption occurs. Cellulose is the primary structural units of forage plants, therefore the horse consumes relatively large quantities of cellulose which the horse can apparently use relatively well. Unfortunately, as plant materials mature, much of the cellulose is replaced by lignin which is a hard, woody, completely undigestible material. The horse does not have the facility to rechew his food after swallowing, thus making the lignified coating more of a disadvantage in that any nutrients that may be trapped by the lignin cannot be released even though chemical analysis may show considerably more nutrient value.

Fats are not used to any degree by horses and are probably not required except for the essential fatty acids which are found in unsaturated fats such as corn or soybean oil. The apparent function of these fatty acids (linoleic, linolenic or arachadonic) is in the maintenance of skin and coat condition. Few things will add "bloom" to a horse more quickly than a tablespoon of corn oil added to the ration once daily. Addition of fats to rations of horses is not only unnecessary, but may be detrimental because severe digestive disturbances result due to the very low tolerances a horse has for fat.

Protein is one of the nutrients that has several functions in the animal body. The least known of these is its use in providing energy—the yield of energy from protein is identical to that of carbohydrates. Using protein for energy is highly inefficient and quite costly. Proteins differ chemically from all the preceding nutrients in that they contain nitrogen in addition to carbon, hydrogen and oxygen. Proteins are composed of some 23 or 24 amino acids which are to proteins what letters are to words. Proteins are large compounds and are also quite complex. One needs only to look at the number of words made from 26 letters to appreciate the vast array of different proteins that are found in nature. The functions of protein are quite numerous in the animal body. Proteins comprise muscle, skin, blood cells, enzymes, lining of the digestive system, hair, hooves, milk, organs, etc. The varied functions give varied deficiency symptoms in animals. The most profound of these is growth, followed by lactation, anemia, etc.

When a young horse is expected to grow and train or race he has a considerably higher protein requirement than is required for simply maintaining a mature horse. The equine young is the only known species that is expected to grow well and work hard as a juvenile and get the lowest protein level of any known species. No other animal has ever been expected to grow well on a 10% protein ration.

There has been and still is an unwarranted fear of protein in horse rations. There is no known harmful effect from feeding high levels of protein to horses of any age. Horses that consume relatively large quantities of protein will consume more water and urinate more frequently. The increased water consumption is simply used for diluting urea which results from the excess nitrogen being excreted from the body. Just because a horse is urinating more frequently does not indicate that his kidneys have been adversely affected. The only real objection to over-feeding protein to horses is the cost incurred by wasteful use of protein. Everyone is aware of the smell of ammonia that is present around horse barns that are not particularly well taken care of. The ammonia results from the microbial breakdown of urea after excretion. The type of hay fed will usually set the stage for the level of protein that must be incorporated into the grain ration. As a general rule, growing, working or lactating horses should have about 16% crude protein in the grain portion of the ration. On the other hand, mature, idle horses can subsist on little or no protein in addition to normal grains and hay.

The level of protein is not in itself the most significant part of protein. Chemical analysis of protein is determined by measuring the nitrogen in a substance and multiplying the percent of nitrogen by 6.25. As one can readily see, this procedure does not indicate digestibility of the protein. Superimpose on the digestibility the quality which is determined by the number and assortment of essential amino acids and you can honestly appraise protein value. Currently, data are not available that would tell us what proteins are of value to the horse, but data are available for other species. Generally, the best protein for any animal is that which most nearly approaches the protein in his own body. It thus seems desirable to provide the best protein that can be obtained at least cost. Linseed meal has been a protein supplement of choice among horsemen and yet it is one of the poorest supplements as far as protein is concerned for two reasons; (1) relatively low digestibility (2) relatively poor quality. Linseed meal will impart a certain amount of bloom to a horse which will be present anyway if the horse is nutritionally well fed. Cottonseed meal may have one difficulty—it contains gossypol which may be toxic to the horse. Degossypolized cottonseed can at present be obtained and this material would be completely safe. Milk by-products such as powdered milk or whey are not worth the extra cost involved in providing them.

The most widely available protein supplement and a very high quality supplement is soybean meal. Supplement obtained from cereal grains such as corn gluten feed or corn gluten meal are not the most desirable since they would be lacking in many of the same amino acids that are lacking in other cereal grains.

Much good quality and readily available protein can be obtained from good forages. The quality of protein as well as the digestibility of the protein in forages does not differ a great deal so long as the forage is used at an immature state of development.

The significance of protein availability and quality is greater for the young, rapidly developing animal than it is for the mature idle horse.

The use of urea as a protein replacement for horses is not understood. Limited amounts (up to 1% of the grain mixture) do not seem to be harmful, but it is unknown whether the horse can use urea in protein synthesis.

An excess of protein would be much more desirable than a deficiency of it because the horse can use excesses for energy with no adverse affect. A slight protein deficiency will interfere with proper growth and development.

The last group of organic nutrients is the vitamins. Vitamins are nutrients that contribute to the animal by aiding in the utilization of other nutrients but are not used in body structure.

Vitamins are separated into two major divisions on the basis of solubility—the fat soluble vitamins A, D, E and K, and the water soluble vitamins which are the B-complex and Vitamin C.

Vitamin A is currently one of the most widely supplemental vitamins in the rations of horses. Under natural conditions the horse consumes very little preformed Vitamin A because very small quantities are produced by plants. The substance carotene and more specifically, betacarotene provides the major source of Vitamin A to the horse. Carotene must be converted to Vitamin A by the animal before it can be used in metabolism. This conversion occurs for the most part in the wall of the small intestine and to a lesser degree in the liver. Carotene is yellow in color, whereas Vitamin A is colorless. The best naturally occurring sources of carotene are green growing forages—the yellow color is masked by the green chlorophyll and is thus not visible. The only cereal grain that contains any carotene is yellow corn but the level is so very low that it can hardly be considered as an important source in meeting the animal's requirement. Both Vitamin A and carotene are unstable to heat and light. About 80% of all the carotene in hay will be destroyed by the sun in 24 hours of field curing hay. Under these conditions more than adequate amounts of carotene should be present to maintain an animal well. Additional destruction of Vitamin A or carotene occurs as hay is stored in conventional hay mows. Greater losses take place in hot weather than in cold weather, but under any conditions one should not plan on obtaining Vitamin A from barn stored hay after a six-month storage period. There are a number of readily available sources of supplement Vitamin A and carotene on the market today which are relatively cheap. Dehydrated alfalfa meal with a guarantee of 100,000 international units of Vitamin A per pound of alfalfa is an excellent source. Many vitamin houses produce crystalline preformed Vitamin A in the form of Vitamin A acetate or Vitamin A palenitate at a very reasonable cost per unit of Vitamin A.

Unfortunately, the ready availability of this vitamin has brought about a promiscuous use of the vitamin even though it may not be needed. The absolute requirement of Vitamin A for the horse is not known, but it seems to hover somewhere in the area of 20,000 to 50,000 international units per horse per day.

The primary function of Vitamin A in animals is the maintenance of epithelial tissues which is that tissue which covers the outside of the animal, or those parts which are open to the outside. This would involve such things as the skin, eye, respiratory tract, digestive tract, and reproductive tract. The epithelial tissue in these areas provide an excellent barrier to infectious organisms that are always present and awaiting entry into the body. The first effect of Vitamin A deficiency in many animals is night blindness in which the animal has difficulty in adjusting from bright light to dim light. Poor condition of hide and coat, frequent digestive disturbances such as diarrhea as well as susceptibility to respiratory difficulty characterized by frequent colds and pneumonia can occur. Certain skeletal deformities may also result.

Reproductive failure may result from infections of the uterus and vagina of the mare. Vitamin A deficiency does not cause infection, but rather is a predisposing factor to it.

Caution should be exercised so that over-supplementation does not occur. High levels (100,000 I.U. or more) of preformed Vitamin A over extended periods may cause a toxicity which results in many of the same conditions as are found in a deficiency.

Nature has provided the animal with a safety factor in that the horse has the ability to store vitamins in the body, primarily in the liver, for a period of three to six months. Because of the storage facility one could expect problems at the end of winter feeding or midway in the racing season if the horse is provided with a ration consisting of poor hay and oats. Hay with a green color and less than a year old should provide adequate quantities. The level of Vitamin A in the mare's milk will be determined by the amount of Vitamin A she consumes in her ration. In most cases vitamin deficiency in a mare will be first noticed in her foal. Foals born of mares deficient in Vitamin A will be weak or dead at birth.

The second most widely used fat soluble vitamin is Vitamin D which is involved with the absorption and deposition of calcium and phosphorous in the skeletal structure.

Two natural sources of Vitamin D are available. The first is irradiation of the animal body by the ultra violet rays of the sun which convert cholesterol substances to Vitamin D. Because of this action, a horse that is out of doors several hours a day will obtain all of the Vitamin D that he requires.

The other source of Vitamin D is from plant material that has been cut and field cured. There is no vitamin present in green growing forages; it is only after cutting or field curing that ergosteral (the plant corollary of the animal source) is converted to Vitamin D. If ergosteral is consumed as such it does not seem to have any nutritional significance.

Vitamin D deficiencies are characterized by skeletal malformation. The most apparent difficulty occurs in the rapidly growing young foal that is housed during the bright sunny part of the day. The milk of all mammals is essentially devoid of Vitamin D. It is thus imperative that the young foal either be given supplemental Vitamin D or be turned outside to be irradiated—usually less difficulty will be experienced when animals are outdoors rather than meeting the requirement by supplementation.

Rickets is the name applied to bone deformity that develops from a Vitamin D deficiency and can be readily identified by swelling or enlargement of joints such as the knee or hock, a humped back, constriction of the heart girth or chest, and eventually severe bowing of the long bones. In cases where young foals and their mares are kept indoors, it is highly desirable to provide supplements to the foal.

More difficulty seems to result from over supplementation of Vitamin D than from a lack of it. Vitamin D toxicity results in excessive calcification of joints as well as soft tissue such as the blood system, spleen, etc. The required Vitamin D level for horses is estimated at 200 to 500 international units per 100 lbs. of body weight or about one tenth the level of Vitamin A. Excessive Vitamin D feeding to the mare may cause calcification of soft tissue in the unborn foal which results in a dead foal or one that will die shortly after birth because of occlusion of the aorta caused by calcium deposition in this organ.

Vitamin E has been erroneously associated with reproduction. This came about because the original research work was done with rats and Vitamin E did have an effect on their reproduction. On that basis, it was assumed that Vitamin E would affect other species similarly. However, recent work has demonstrated that Vitamin E has no effect on reproduction in other species including the horse. A great deal of work has been reported stating that Vitamin E is in some way involved with the maintenance of muscles. This has been shown to be the case in all animals studied. There may be a relationship between muscle soreness and Vitamin E in the young horse in training.

Natural Vitamin E is extremely unstable to oxygen and will be destroyed in a few weeks of storage. The germs of cereal grains, especially of wheat, are some of the best sources of Vitamin E available in nature. Presently, high potency tocopherols can be obtained which are much less costly than the natural Vitamin E. Toxicity does not seem to develop from an excess of tocopherol or Vitamin E as is the case with other fat soluble vitamins.

Vitamin K is the last of the fat soluble vitamins. The primary function of Vitamin K is to aid in the clotting of blood. Under normal conditions most animals have adequate gut synthesis of this vitamin. The only possible way in which a Vitamin K deficiency can be produced would be by feeding high levels of sulfa drugs and/or antibiotics or by feeding an interfering substance such as dicoumarin that occurs in molded sweet clover hay. It is doubtful that any Vitamin K additions are necessary on normal diets. Dietary sources are green forage and a synthetic compound, menadion, which has Vitamin K activity.

The relatively large group of B-complex vitamins have a number of similar deficiency symptoms. The most notable of these is a loss of appetite which results in a loss of weight and vitality. Many horses are expected to work hard on a ration of oats and timothy both of which are desperately deficient in most of the B-complex vitamins. This may explain part of the reason horses seem to get "track sour" midway through the racing season. The horse does synthesize, through the aid of bacteria in his gut, considerable quantities of the B vitamins, but absorption seems to be in the neighborhood of 25%. The available data have been obtained from mature idle horses that do not have any stresses of consequence.

Many of the B-complex vitamins are directly involved with the metabolism of carbohydrates in the yield of energy. Thus as the energy expenditure increases, more carbohydrates are needed, which results in a greater need for the B-complex vitamins. The traditional horse rations do not provide very much of the requirement during the stress of racing. If the carbohydrates cannot be metabolized, intermediate compounds accumulate and become toxic to the animal which in turn puts the animal off feed. A horse that becomes track sour is frequently turned out and comes back on feed. This happens for two reasons. The first is that energy demands have been reduced and the second—the hay and/or grass are higher in the content of B-complex vitamins.

Some of the more specfic vitamins and their functions are as follows. Thiamine or Vitamin B, is probably the first deficiency of this group that would become apparent. The deficiency is characterized by loss of appetite and loss of body weight. As the deficiency becomes more pronounced, there may also be loss of gait. Infertility in both sexes may result from thiamine deficiency. Sources of thiamine are the bran of cereal grains such as wheat and green forage or good hay. Oats have very limited quantities of thiamine.

Riboflavin or Vitamin B_2 deficiencies have been reported in horses from time to time. Riboflavin deficiency as a predisposing factor to moon blindness has been indicated. The best available data indicate that 2.0 milligrams of riboflavin per 100 lbs. of body weight daily will meet the requirement.

Niacin is no doubt synthesized in the gut of horses. No data are available to prove that the horse can adequately convert tryptophane to niacin. About 10 mg. of niacin per 100 lbs. daily seems to be quite adequate.

Pantothenic acid seems to be synthesized in adequate quantity by the horse.

Vitamin B_{12} which has been more widely misused in horses than any other single nutrient, does not seem to carry the value assessed to it. What little work has been done with B_{12} in horses indicates that the horse either synthesizes adequate quantities or has a very low requirement for this vitamin.

Ascorbic acid, or Vitamin C, has been considered non-essential for the horse as a dietary ingredient. In animals where Vitamin C is shown to be essential, a deficiency results in weakening of blood capillaries—this may be related to bleeders in race horses although no known data are available on a controlled basis to establish a requirement.

Salt is the one mineral that is probably more widely provided to horses than any other single mineral. This is not only desirable, but imperative since salt is required in so many functions of the animal body. Salt is also lost from the body in such relatively large quantities. The more the horse perspires, the more salt is lost, thus more is needed. Because of the rather large variation among horses and the activity of them, it does not seem reasonable that anyone can measure and give any animal the correct amount of salt on a day to day basis. Since the variables exist, it is much more realistic to allow the horse free access to salt at all times, either in block form or in granular form. More difficulties will present themselves from underfeeding salt than from over feeding it. Force feeding salt is not advocated because an excess will decrease feed consumption. A maximum of 1% salt should be incorporated into the grain portion of the ration.

Calcium and phosphorous are the two minerals by which the horse is most adversely affected. The majority of these minerals are found in the skeleton of the horse and are thus associated with bone development. A deficiency in either of these minerals can result in rickets in the young horse or more subtle deformities may occur in the skeleton and supporting structures. The young horse is forced to put considerable stress on his skeleton at a very early age, which makes it doubly important to make certain that every opportunity has been provided for proper skeletal development.

In addition to the skeleton, phosphorous particularly is involved with many other functions such as energy transfer, etc. in the body.

The ratio of calcium to phosphorous is also of major importance. The most desirable ratio seems to be 1.4 to 1.0 with a level of 30-40 grams of phosphorous required daily. Another complicating problem in establishing levels is the question of availability of the minerals from plant sources. Interfering substances such as oxalates and phytates may bind significant quantities of these minerals so that chemical analysis may not give a true value of content.

Eating of wood and other foreign materials may indicate that inorganic sources of calcium, and phosphorous must be provided. Realistically one would be ahead if the calcium-phosphorous ratio were calculated on a 1:1 basis which would in part allow for this discrepancy. Many products are currently available which provide both calcium and phosphorous in ratios ranging from 2:1 to 1:1. Some of these are dicalcium phosphate and defluorinated rock phosphates. If a horse is receiving legume hay or a mixed hay, the probability of additional calcium other than found in the phosphorous supplements listed above will not be required.

A horse receiving mature timothy or comparable roughage would need to have additional calcium as well. Steamed bone meal which has been a standard phosphorous supplement is one of the less desirable in relation to the cost of a unit of phosphorous.

Magnesium is becoming a mineral of concern in areas such as Ohio, the Virginias and Kentucky. This is probably due to the lack of magnesium addition to soil accompanied by leaking of this mineral from soils. Magnesium is known to bind calcium and make it unavailable but this is true of so many minerals. In certain areas it seems as though the pendulum has swung too far, thus creating the problem. In areas where problems of tetany have been observed, 1% magnesium sulfate can be added to the salt mixture to avoid the problem.

The rather vast array of trace elements has not been studied in the horse; indeed they have not been studied to any great extent in other animals. Probably more significant than the absolute quantity of any trace element is the relationship between the minerals.

Iodine deficiency is probably the most widely appreciated. This mineral is found in low quantity around large bodies of fresh water such as the Great Lakes region of the United States. Deficiency is characterized by goiter (an enlargement of the thyroid gland) and some indication exists that foals born of mares with insufficient iodine may be more susceptible to navel ill, which is a general systemic infection. Iodized salt has done an excellent job in preventing or eliminating the problem.

Copper and iron are both involved with red blood cell production. A deficiency results in one of the anemias. Anemia due to iron or copper deficiency is more prevalent in young foals that are not given access to food other than milk for extended periods of time. If foals are permitted on soil, the possibility of anemia from deficiencies is most unlikely. Cobalt requirements for horses seem to be extremely low and supplementation at the present time does not seem necessary.

Manganese has been associated with reproduction in cattle and swine but no data are available for the horse.

Selenium is a relative newcomer to the ranks of essential minerals. Indications from the field are that selenium may have an effect in preventing the "tying up" syndrome in horses—no data of a controlled nature are available. Certain feeds such as linseed meal and certain wheat brans contain relatively high levels of selenium.

The other trace elements, namely fluorine, zinc and sulfur, are required by other animals and probably by horses, but no data for the horse are available.

In general, excellent mineral nutrition can be arrived at by providing trace mineralized salt and dicalcium phosphate (or some other phosphorous supplement) in separate containers. The horse should have access to these materials at all times. Under certain conditions a container of limestone may also be provided.

Hay and pastures for horses have been given much less attention than they deserve. If the forage provided for horses is of the best quality available, many of the ration problems will resolve themselves.

Unfortunately, horses are expected to do well on mature, undigestible hay. Dairy men and sheep men have known for some time that excellent quality hay is imperative to the building of sound rations. The type of hay, whether it be grass or legume, is not nearly as important as the age at which the hay was harvested. Good indicators of hay quality are as follows:

1. Leafiness
2. Fineness of stem
3. Free of must, mold or dust
4. Velvety to the touch
5. Green in color which gives an indication of Vitamin A or carotene content
6. The heads of timothy should not be more than 1 to 1½ inches in length.

The problem of "hay belly" is more likely due to feeding of poor quality hay that does not move through the digestive tract quickly and results in distention of the abdomen. The feeding of pelleted hay (½ to 1 inch in diameter) alleviates the problem because the hay is fine enough to pass through the system. Mixtures of grasses and legumes are fully as nutritional as either separately and have an advantage of yielding more per acre for the most part. Red clover hay may cause "slobbers," which is severe salivation and poor consumption of hay. New hay can be fed safely if it has gone through the sweating process.

The standard pasture for horses has been blue grass. The only real justification for blue grass seems to be that it grows readily in the traditional horse areas of the United States. Unless irrigation, fertilization and good management of blue grass pasture is practiced, the productivity is not as great as many other forage plants that can be grown. Currently, sorghum hybrids have been introduced as temporary or annual pastures. These forages can be used to advantage if caution is exercised. The sorghum or sudan grasses contain hydroxyanic or prussic acid, which is toxic to horses if consumed in quantity. The plants have a high concentration of this toxin which is highest in very young or stunted plants. Horses should not be grazed until the forage is 18 to 20 inches tall. By this time the acid has been quite well diluted. A disease known as cystitis will result if the forage is improperly used.

Horses that are mature and expected to do little or no work can be maintained very well on hay or pasture alone with no supplemental grain feeding.

Pelleted feeds have become rather prevalent today and much misunderstanding exists as to their merits. The complete ration including the roughage and the grain is an excellent feed for horses so long as the forage used is of good quality. The pellet should be no less than ½ inch in diameter to avoid wood chewing by the horse. The use of this type of ration may present difficulty if the same ration is used for idle and working horses. A ration produced for the idle horse is more versatile since energy can be added more easily than it can be removed. Another consideration that must be kept in mind is the fact that most complete horse feeds carry between 50-60% roughage of some type. The cost of rations must be calculated on this basis. The processing of rations does have a cost attached to it. The real decision that must be made is how much can you afford to pay for roughage in this form.

The grain pellet should more realistically be 1/4 to 5/16 inches in diameter so as to expedite mixing with additional grain if necessary.

The advantages of pellets are that each bite of feed is as fully balanced as every other. Pellets eliminate separation of ingredients to different size and specific gravity. Pellets eliminate dust and waste since a horse can readily pick up a pellet which he cannot do with a ground feed. The storage requirements of pellets are only two-thirds as great as for the same feed in a ground mixture.

Just a word about feed preparation. The only reason for grinding grain for horses is to break the hull of cereal grains that horses may not chew readily. If the hull is cracked or broken, the grains will be digested. On occasion a gluttonous horse will bolt his feed which means he will not chew it. Crimping of grains or placing a few stones in the feed box the size of baseballs to softballs will force a horse to pick his grain from between the stones thus slowing him down and making him chew more thoroughly.

Finely divided grains, such as result from preparation with a hammer mill, are not desirable because of dustiness and difficulty in consumption. Feeds that are finely ground do not conserve energy of chewing but will decrease consumption unless relatively large quantities of molasses are used to stick the dust particles together which will eliminate the dust and increase palatability.

The cooking, soaking or sprouting of grains seems to be nothing more than an increase in labor with no return for the effort. Little controlled work is available to indicate advantages for these treatments. The use of bran mash in feeding a horse does provide a means for getting water into a horse but he will usually drink enough water if it is clean and always available. On occasion, such as at foaling time, the mare may not drink adequate amounts of water to replace the fluids lost during parturition in which case a bran mash may be desirable. The feeding of mash should be an occasional rather than a common occurrence.

The sprouting of grain has been proposed and used from time to time. The objection to this method of grain handling is twofold; the first is initial and subsequent maintenance cost of equipment and the second is labor involved in handling the material. The net gain in nutrients will not pay for the foregoing cost. There do not seem to be any special nutritional advantages that cannot be obtained from conventional methods of feeding.

Feeding the foal is a most critical part of developing horses to their inherited potential of growth. Since horses usually work

HORSE FEEDING SUMMARY

First and foremost the horse should always be provided unlimited fresh, cool, clean water. An exception to this rule is when the horse has been worked hard and has been overheated. After cooling out he can be allowed all of the water he wishes.

Energy can be provided from hay or grains, or both. If hay is of poor quality and the horse cannot maintain his weight, grains must be fed. We must keep in mind that horses that are losing weight consume too little energy whereas those that are gaining weight consume too much.

Because most horses are fed by measure, the weight of various grains per volume must be taken into account. Most grains are measured in bushels. Each bushel contains 16 quarts. The following table gives bushel weights and energy value per pound of common grains as compared to corn:

	Value	*Wt. Per Bushel*
Corn	100%	56 pounds
Oats	60-90%	32-46 pounds
Barley	85%	48 pounds
Wheat	100-110%	60 pounds
Molasses	80%	

As one can readily see, the same volume of different grains will give widely different results. Caution must be exercised in the use of feeds such as corn when it replaces rations made of wheat bran, light oats, etc., or severe digestive disturbances will result.

Sweet feeds, providing that they consist of good quality ingredients, are nutritionally sound but do not contribute any "tonic effect."

Soybean meal should be added to the ration of most horses to make a 16% crude protein grain mix for racing, growing, or lactating horses. Mature horses can be maintained on medium quality hay if the horse is idle.

The capacity of the horse will determine how much to feed—most horses consume about 2½-3 percent of their body weight in feed daily, thus a 1000-pound horse would consume 22-30 lbs. of dry feed daily which would be split between hay and grain.

Any major ration change should be made gradually to allow for adjustment by the horse. Trace mineral salt and dicalcium phosphate should be provided on a free choice basis at all times.

The following grain combinations will provide a 16% crude protein mixture:

1500# Shelled corn		800# Corn		1700# Oats
500# Soybean meal	or	800# Oats	or	300# Soybean meal
		400# Soybean meal		

The B-complex vitamins which play an important role in appetite, can be provided by adding four or five pounds of brewer's yeast per ton or one to two teaspoons per horse daily. Vitamins A and D can be purchased economically in pure form but may not be needed.

harder as 2-year-olds than at any other time it would appear that they should be grown as rapidly as possible to mature size. The most rapid and economical development in the equine occurs at the very early stages of development. No other animal is expected to grow as rapidly on so little nutrient—is it any wonder that so many horses fail to perform well?

Mares are not purchased for brood mares on the basis of milk production which makes it doubly important to give serious consideration to supplemental feed at an early age. Most foals should be introduced to some form of dry feed by at least seven to ten days of age. Any number of feeds can be used for this purpose. Either a purchased feed for foals or hulled, rolled oats can be used at the beginning. At the very early stages, the management of the horse is much more critical than the actual feed. The only prerequisites of the feed are that it be digestible and reasonably palatable. Rolled oats fit this description. Since most foals are stabled with their mares, it is a simple matter to put a handful of feed into the mouth of the foal at the time the mare is being fed. In addition, fresh feed should be provided for the foal where the mare cannot get it and the foal can still eat peacefully and undisturbed. In about two weeks the foal will be eating and at a period of six to eight weeks he will consume feed in quantity. All remaining feed for the foal should be removed daily to avoid staleness. When consumption is appreciable, the grain ration can be converted to that which the mare is consuming (16% protein concentrate).

In most cases, the mare is not producing very well after three or four months of lactation so that the grain would be better fed to the foal to stimulate growth. Any mare that does not lose some body weight while nursing her foal is probably being overfed. Foals that have been introduced to grain feeding at an early age can be turned into pasture with their mares. A creep feeder, which is simply an area where the foals can go and eat at will but the mares cannot, should be placed there. All creep feeders should be built for the convenience and accessibility of the foal. This may be in a shady area, watering area, etc., where the mares have a tendency to congregate. The eating habits of foals are established at a rather early age. The type of grain, etc, that a foal starts with will no doubt determine what he will like to eat later.

All grains should be cracked or crimped for the horse until he is nine months to one year of age. Fine grinding is highly undesirable because of dust and difficulty in consumption.

From time to time, mares either do not have a milk supply, will not accept their foal or for some reason are incapable of caring for foals. Hopefully the foal will have had access to colostrum or the first milk of the mare. As fine a milk substitute as can be found is canned baby formula. This food can be used for the first two or three weeks. As can be readily appreciated, this material is well fortified with minerals, vitamins, etc., and is in fact a complete food.

Most brood mares are seriously overfed during their gestation. The first two-thirds of the gestation period requires little more nutrient than that required for maintenance. Any increases in dietary intake should occur during the last trimester when two-thirds of the fetal growth occurs. Too often, only vitamin supplementation is increased when the entire requirement for all nutrients should be increased proportionately. If a mare is fat when she approaches the third trimester, feed should not be decreased at this point. It would be more desirable to keep the mare in a gaining state and adequate exercise be provided. The ration for the first period, as well as after weaning, can be comprised of only good hay and/or pasture with no additional grain or vitamin supplements.

The requirements of a stallion may have to be increased just prior to and during the heavy breeding season. No evidence is present to indicate that sperm will be more viable if the stallion is fat or if he is trim. If we can transpose from other species of animals, the most important nutritional factor is a well balanced diet fed to the condition of the horse. There is really no need to increase protein or vitamin supplements for a stallion during the breeding season. A stallion in heavy service will lose some weight. The loss in weight should indicate that more concentrate needs to be fed.

No one method of feeding horses is the best method since many horses are raised and raced by many horsemen. This in itself should indicate that more or less adequate rations can be formulated using a myriad of different ingredients. As research shows the way to better nutrition, I am sure horses will be better for it.

Selected References:

Alexander, F. "Digestion in the Horse," *Progress in Nutrition and Allied Science*, London, Eng., Oliver and Boyd (1963) 259.

Carrol, F. D., Goss, H. and Howell, C. E. "The synthesis of B-complex vitamins in the horse," *J. of Anim. Sci.*, 8 (1949) 290.

Cunha, T. J. "Equine Nutrition," *Mod. Vet. Prac.* 45, No. 5 (1964) 139.

Earle, I. P. "Grassland Crops as Feed For Horses," *Yearbook of Agriculture* 1948, 86.

"National Research Council, Nutrient Requirements of Horses" Washington D.C. National Research Council, 912 (1961).

Nelson, A. W. "Nutrient Requirements of the Light Horse," American Quarter Horse Association, Amarillo, Texas (1961).

Olsson, N. and Rurudvere, A., The Nutrition of the Horse, Nutrition Abstracts and Reviews, 25 (1955).

Dr. William J. Tyznik is a professor in the department of Animal Science at the Ohio State University, Columbus, Ohio. He is nationally known for his contribution to teaching in the fields of animal science and nutrition and serves as chairman of the Equine Nutrition Committee of the National Academy of Science. He is a consultant to two feed and grain companies, has written a number of articles for professional journals, conducts a monthly column on nutrition and feeding in *Hoof Beats*, official publication of the U. S. Trotting Association and has also written for *The Blood Horse*, a running horse publication. Dr. Tyznik was born in Milwaukee, Wisc., on April 26,  1927 and was educated at the University of Wisconsin where he earned his bachelor of science degree (with honors) in 1948, his master of science degree in 1949 and his Ph.D. in 1951. He joined the Ohio State faculty that year as an assistant professor, became an associate professor in 1955 and a full professor in 1959. He is a member of the American Society of Animal Science and serves on its national committee on undergraduate teaching. He is a member of the American Dairy Science Association and chairman of a National Academy of Science committee which is seeking to establish nutrient requirements for horses. At Ohio State, he has earned the Alfred J. Wright award for distinguished service as a teacher and student advisor, was chosen in 1954 as the first "Professor of The Year" in the College of Agriculture and in 1959 was one of 42 men in the country nominated for the Outstanding Teacher Award of the American Society of Animal Production. He is listed in American Men of Science.

NUTRITION and FEEDING
Part II—FEEDING

DELVIN MILLER

T HIS chapter is being presented in two parts, and before I begin my own contribution I want to compliment Dr. Tyznik on the fine job he has already done in writing about fundamental horse nutrition. I have been reading Dr. Tyznik's interesting articles in *Hoof Beats* magazine for a number of years and I have always had a great deal of respect for his knowledge and his sound, intelligent approach to this somewhat controversial subject.

I use the word "controversial" because it seems I am always running across people who have weird ideas about the proper way to feed a horse. And when I try to explain patiently that the best way to feed a horse is to imitate nature as closely as possible, they act as though I am trying to discourage them from opening up new feeding horizons.

I was the first man in the world to put down a Tartan synthetic race track, and for that reason alone I do not think anyone can ever accuse me of being afraid to take a gamble. It is the same with feeding. If anyone can show me anything new that looks like it might be an improvement over what we have, I am willing to try it. So far they haven't; and that is the reason I stick with the basic ingredients of top hay and oats and advise everybody who seeks my opinion to do the same.

But if a simple reference to top hay and oats constituted absolutely all there is to the proper feeding of race horses, I could stop right now and wouldn't have to add another word to this chapter. There is, however, quite a bit more to it than that. There are plenty of "do's" and "don'ts" involved as well as other fringe area subjects about which I feel I can offer advice that might prove helpful. That is what I hope to accomplish in devoting the next few pages to a discussion of the actual feeding of a race horse in training.

For instance, one of the phases of feeding that in my opinion is either neglected altogether or glossed over much too lightly is the human element. By that I mean the importance of having a good groom. I have seen good grooms literally work miracles with poor doers, that is, horses that for one reason or another simply won't eat the way they should. In every racing stable of any size, there are always a few grooms who are particularly adept at this. They have a way with animals and animals react instinctively toward them. A good trainer knows who these grooms are and my advice is that these talents should not be wasted, and that men like this be put on the horses that are not eating the way they should. Very often you will find that this solves the problem of the poor doer and does it better than any special feed or feeding technique ever will or can.

Having emphasized the importance of good oats, hay and grooms, let me talk about feeding horses in detail, beginning from the time they arrive in a trainer's stable as a yearling, usually some time late in the year.

Many of these colts have been purchased out of auction sales and you will usually find they tend to carry quite a bit of soft fat. Horsemen have preached for years that stock farms should market ready-to-race yearlings that are not "hot-housed" and not stuffed with feed during the last few months before their sale. But it is also a fact that most owners and trainers, despite what their natural inclination might be, seem to prefer slick, stout yearlings that actually have been overfed. Apparently this is an occupational hazard of the yearling selection business and it is doubtful that it will ever change.

The first thing I do with a yearling like this is cut him back to two feeds a day, each consisting of from two to three quarts of dry feed, usually oats. If a horse is very fat, or if I am having trouble getting him broken, I may cut this ration back to one or two quarts. On the other hand, I will occasionally get a yearling that is in poor flesh and I will feed him three times a day, four quarts each time. Bear in mind also that the amount of feed is almost always in proportion to the amount of work the horse is getting.

If a horse is not emptying out as he should and I feel he needs a little laxative, I will add a little wheat bran to the ration, usually in the evening. The proportion will probably be on a 2-1 basis, three quarts of dry feed to a quart and a half of bran. I add water and feed this as a hot wet mix if I am training in the north and as a dry mix in the south where the climate is warmer. When it is cold, it does not hurt to warm a horse's feed in this manner. In many ways horses are like human beings, and all of us know that it's a good feeling to be served a piping hot meal on a real cold day.

Eddie Neloy, one of the very best running horse trainers—as I write this, he has Buckpasser and a host of other top horses—gives his horses a hot, cooked feed every evening the year round, and their physical condition is as good as any I have ever observed anywhere in the world. He has been following this practice for years with excellent results.

I feed bran to horses only when I feel they need a laxative. Depending on the individual, I feed it to some horses all the time, some horses occasionally and some not at all. If you do not want to feed bran for one reason or another, you can feed alfalfa instead. Alfalfa is very helpful in such cases. When I feed bran, I always make sure to add a good, heavy tablespoonful of salt which helps to flavor the mixture. I do this whether it is a wet or dry feed. I always make sure the salt is mixed in very well.

The usual routine is for horses to be fed three times a day. As soon as I have my yearlings straightened away and have worked some of the fat off them, which is usually around February 1 of their 2-year-old form, I switch them over from two to three feeds a day. My older horses, of course, are already being fed three times a day, since they are in active training. My general practice is to feed three quarts of grain in the morning, three to four quarts around noon and four quarts in the evening. If you are feeding a supplement, you naturally cut back on the amount of grain being fed according to how much supplement you are using.

You will also find that as a rule fillies will eat less than colts. Usually, you can give a filly from a half-quart to a quart less than a colt at each feed. However, you must not adhere too strictly to this rule because you will often find that some fillies will eat as much as the colts and once in a while you will run across one that eats more. Again, you must keep in mind that all horses are individuals and must be treated as such.

The feeding practices I have outlined in the last two paragraphs are completely dependent on a rule of thumb I have followed all my life and that I think any good horseman will agree with: a horse should be fed exactly as much at each feed as he will clean up and still be the least bit hungry. If you will remember that rule, you will have passed one of the most important hurdles in the feeding of race horses or any other kind of horses.

Let's say that the horse doesn't eat the three quarts of grain that make up his morning feed. The first thing I will do is to make sure the horse isn't sick by noting his general condition and his eyes and by taking his temperature. If he isn't showing any adverse symptoms and appears normal in every way, I won't do anything at all and will feed the same ration the next two mornings. But if the horse does not clean up those two feeds, I will consider that he simply doesn't need or want as much feed and I will cut him back.

I will go to a 2½-quart ration the next morning and observe the horse closely. If he finishes it off and continues to do so, I will keep feeding him that amount. If he still leaves a little, I will back the ration off again until I reach the point where he cleans it up. After a month or so, I might try to build the ration back up to what I consider the normal three quarts. If I had cut him back to two quarts, I would offer him 2½ quarts one morning a month later and see what happened. Very often the horse will finish the ration this time and I will try to work it up to three in the next week or so. But I will always stop and retrace my steps when I reach the point where he is leaving some.

This also works in the opposite direction. If I think a horse could stand a little more, I will start increasing the ration by maybe a half-quart at each feed or perhaps a half-quart once a day. If he cleans that up, I will increase it still more until he starts to leave a little. Meadow Rice, for instance, was a horse that would eat all day. He would get 12-14 quarts of grain a day and would still be looking for more. You will usually find that these are the horses that either require a lot of work or that are being worked harder for some other reason. But that is not always the case because some horses that require only light work will eat more feed than you think they should. That is all right and if they aren't getting too fat, let them have what they want.

There is one other thing I do with horses that are slow or "picky" feeders that I think is worth mentioning. I will often delay the feeding of these horses until after the others have been fed. In many instances this will get the slow feeder worked up a little and he will be more inclined to go after his feed when he does get it. Of course, if this horse starts banging himself against the side of the stall because he isn't fed on time, you'll have to put him back on the regular schedule. I would much rather take my chances with a slow feeder than with an injured or crippled horse.

I think it is important that horses be fed at the same time every day. If you are late in feeding, horses will get nervous and upset and start pawing around the door. This is not a desirable situation because a horse can injure himself if he gets too excited, so every effort should be made to feed at the identical time every day. In addition, with the exception of a possible slow feeder that you might be feeding late intentionally, all horses should be fed at one time. This means the grooms have to be on the job and all putting the feed in at once. If a groom is late feeding his horses, they will get very upset and can injure themselves.

Feeding times will vary according to the individual trainer, but I recommend that the morning feed be scheduled for 6 a.m., followed by a noon feed between 11:30 and 12:00 and an evening feed at 5:30 p.m. I make it a practice to cut back on the amount of the feed on days when a horse is not being exercised. For instance, I recommend a half to three-quarter ration on Sunday and that also applies to rainy days when a horse cannot train or jog as planned, as well as on days when a horse might be sick and laid up. A normal feed ration is for a horse that is getting his usual exercise every day. If that exercise is interrupted, the ration is cut back.

I should mention here that you should not cut back the daily ration of a horse that is getting plenty of work but still looks too fat. You will find that a horse like that will lose some of the extra weight when he works hard or races on a very hot day. As a matter of fact, it is much better to go into the racing season with a little excess flesh on your horse. He will work it off soon enough during the long campaigns that are the rule these days.

Hay is the basic ingredient of the race horse diet. A horse will get more of that in his lifetime than anything else and common sense tells you that it should be the highest quality you can buy. A horse will eat from 15 to 20 pounds of hay a day and if you are going to feed poor hay you might as well not feed any at all.

It is important that hay be properly cured and dried and that a trainer be able to recognize good hay when he sees it. Hay should not be too dry when cut and it should not be cured too dry. I recommend very strongly that whenever possible you feed hay that has been cured in a dryer. Hay dryers are expensive, but I bought one for my farm at Meadow Lands, Pa., and it has been well worth the money. In my opinion, hay that has gone through a dryer is the best there is and it is a means by which man finds himself able to control an important part of its production by eliminating the possibility of it being rained on when down in the field. If you can't feed hay that has been through a dryer, make certain that what you do buy has been put up at the proper time.

I prefer a mixed high-grade timothy and clover hay with the clover running perhaps 40%. I also feed a timothy and alfalfa mixture of the same proportion. I like alfalfa and feed it all year long when I can get it. When I am feeding a timothy-clover mixture and can still get good alfalfa hay I will put about a pound of alfalfa in the rack for every six pounds of the mixed hay and figure I am feeding the very best hay ration possible.

From time to time I receive inquiries from people who want to know if it is desirable to feed alfalfa alone all year round. My answer always is and always has been "Yes." There is an old wives' tale that alfalfa has a detrimental effect on a horse's kidneys but, as with most "rules" of this type, it is an exaggeration.

The important thing is that you have to use a little restraint in feeding alfalfa as opposed to a mixed hay. You do not feed as much and I recommend perhaps two-thirds of the normal hay ration daily.

When I worked for Mr. W. N. Reynolds and we raised all our yearlings in North Carolina we fed lespedeza hay exclusively. Lespedeza is high in protein and very similar to alfalfa. Horses like Tar Heel and Solicitor were raised on a good grade of this hay and their records helped prove to me that a horse could be raised and raced on alfalfa or lespedeza alone. Up to the time I started to feed Mr. Reynolds' home-grown lespedeza, he had been importing hay from the north for years thinking lespedeza was not good for horses.

There are two things that work against feeding alfalfa all year round. For one thing, it is not always available and, secondly, the cost is prohibitive in some areas. While I have said that I always feed the best available hay to my horses, I certainly would not pay a premium price for alfalfa if I could get an outstanding timothy-clover mix much cheaper. The same situation might be reversed in the far west where a top grade of alfalfa can sometimes be obtained at a more reasonable price than a top grade of mixed hay. In that case, I would feed alfalfa and be happy that I had it.

A horse trainer should never let the feed man deliver a load of stale, musty hay. If you will make a feed man take back a load like this, it probably won't happen again. Most feed men are reliable but even the best of them will sometimes wind up with a load of marginal hay that they have to dispose of. If you are a trainer that has been constantly emphasizing that you want only quality hay, they are more likely to pass you by when they think about who might accept a load of this type. You must also check out your storage space and make sure your hay is kept in a dry place and above any dampness. Dampness will ruin good hay quicker than anything else and horses recognize the difference right away and either will not eat it or will only nibble at it.

A great deal of the hay that is fed to horses in my racing stable is raised on my farm at Meadow Lands or at nearby farms with which I am familiar. This is especially true when the stable moves north in the spring. At Meadow Lands, we have soil tests made of our hay fields and add the exact amount of lime or fertilizer that is recommended. Incidentally, most fertilizer companies will test your soil without charge and provide a free analysis made by a state laboratory. You can also arrange to have this done through your county agent.

Hay grown on properly fertilized land and run through a hay

dryer is the best in the world and there is simply no way to beat it.

I am just as "choosey" about oats as I am about hay. I insist on oats that weigh a minimum of 40 pounds to the bushel, have been recleaned—that is run through the cleaning process twice— and have had all foreign substances removed, preferably through magnetization. You would be surprised to see the debris that the magnets pick up such as old nails, wire, pieces of steel, etc.

For years I have been feeding Jockey Oats processed in Minnesota and I think they are the best available. They will usually run around 42 pounds to the bushel and I have checked them out to weigh as much as 45-46. This is a rich oat and if you have been feeding a lighter brand and switch over you should probably cut your ration back a trifle until the horses get used to it.

I usually feed whole oats but I would prefer to feed them crushed or crimped if possible. Crimped oats are those which have had the tails cut off and crushed oats are as the name implies. The advantage of crimped or crushed oats is that horses get the full benefit of the grain itself which is contained inside the oat husk.

Whole oats will sometimes pass completely through a horse's digestive tract with the husk unbroken. Naturally, the horse derives absolutely no nutritional benefit in a situation like this since the grain itself, or kernel, is enclosed within the husk or shell. I always make it a practice to check a horse's droppings to see if whole oats are passing through. If they appear in any appreciable number I go to crimped or crushed oats. I do not like to purchase oats that have already been crimped or crushed as they may have been crimped a long time back and they sometimes get stale quicker than the whole oats.

One of the worst things you can do with a horse is to feed him a cheap grade of uncleaned oats. They are on the market and you can buy them for practically nothing in comparison with the price for top oats. But they will only weigh about 30 pounds to the bushel and they will be dusty and infested with foreign substances. They are mostly all husk and no kernel and the nutritional effect is what you would expect, practically nil.

Proper storage is just as important for oats as for hay. If the grain is in sacks, it must be kept off the floor. If it is placed in a bin, the bin should be cleaned out about every two weeks. What you run into if you don't do this is that new quantities of oats, or whatever grain it may be, are poured right on top of the old grain. If you do this, you never get to see the bottom of the bin to determine whether there are any holes that mice or rats might get through. At the same time, if you will do this the proper way, you will not have old musty grain working its way up and getting mixed in with new feed.

I have no particular quarrel with the various packaged feeds, supplements and pellets that are presently on the market. As a matter of fact, I usually use a supplement, Stamm, with the oats I feed. But I do want to caution that unless you are completely familiar with the product, the reputation of the people putting it out and know something of the source of the grains being used, you are probably better off to forget it. I think some of these manufacturers have a tendency to load up on some of the cheaper grains at the expense of the more costly oats and for that reason I prefer to stick with a ration of top hay and oats which, in the long run, will not cost nearly as much. If you are satisfied with something like Stamm with the right kind of ingredients, then it can easily be substituted for a part of your oats.

It seems to me that too many trainers and owners seem to think that simply because a new feed comes out with a lot of high sounding ingredients and glowing representations regarding vitamins and minerals that they have to have it in order to keep up with the fellow next door. It is my opinion that horse owners are paying a great deal of money every year for special feeds they just don't need.

If you do feed a supplement, it is important that it be mixed in thoroughly with the grain you are feeding. Do not just put the oats, or whatever grain you are using, in the bottom of the tub and throw the supplement over the top. Instruct the groom to mix the ingredients thoroughly, usually by picking the feed up in his hands several times and running it through them. The same holds true any time you are feeding two or more ingredients of any kind in the same ration.

While I am willing to leave the door open a little regarding these packaged feeds, I have no hesitancy whatsoever in declaring that one of the biggest wastes of an owner's money is that which is spent on the various mineral and vitamin shots. When they first came out many years ago, I was as enthusiastic as the next fellow and tried them immediately. For what it might be worth, it is my considered opinion that they have no value at all and I cannot honestly say that I know of a single instance where they did a horse any good. Such horses as Tar Heel, Solicitor, Harlan Dean, Direct Rhythm, Stenographer, Countess Adios, Dottie's Pick, Meadow Farr and Meadow Rice, all two-minute performers, rarely if ever had vitamin shots or minerals and neither did Adios when he was in stud at Meadowlands. If my horses get run down during the racing season I call a veterinarian and he can give the horse the necessary vitamins.

I believe that hay, oats, salt and maybe a sprinkling of a good pellet supplement from a reliable manufacturer, and a piece of sod thrown in the stall every once in a while, will give a horse all the vitamins and minerals he needs. And if a horse gets a little run down, I much prefer a good tonic that a veterinarian can recommend.

Many years ago I asked the late Doc Parshall, whom I regard as one of the very best and maybe the greatest horseman of all time, what kind of minerals he fed his horses. "Good hay and good oats are the best minerals available," he told me, and I believe it to this day.

I also feed a little ear corn occasionally, especially if a horse has bad teeth or very sharp teeth. Under these circumstances, I will give him an ear or more in a ration. I think it helps this kind of horse and ear corn is also beneficial for horses that have caps that are ready to come off their teeth. It helps get them off.

In addition to feed, horses should always have all the fresh water they want. A horse will usually eat a few bites of feed or hay and then go to the water bucket. Water makes the feed more palatable. A normal horse will consume probably 8-12 gallons of water a day and his intake will be more if it is very hot. It is especially important that the water bucket be filled at night because very often that bucket has to carry the horse until the following morning. You will find that most good grooms will top off the water bucket just before they turn in for the night.

A good groom, as I have said, plays a vital part in establishing proper feeding habits for a horse and can be most helpful in handling poor doers. Since poor doers represent the principal problem that will be encountered with respect to feeding race horses, let me write a bit about them.

There are many reasons why a horse won't eat properly, and this should not be surprising because we run into the same thing with human beings. Every nutritionist stresses the importance of a human being eating a good breakfast. But there are still a great many people who eat no breakfast at all. There are others who want a heavy lunch or will insist on a hot lunch, while a quick sandwich will do just as well for the fellow at the next desk. Some people will eat big meals regularly and not gain an ounce of weight. Others, eating the same meals, will gain rapidly and get fat.

It is the same with horses and when you consider that we are feeding them according to a schedule that we have adopted and that we give them very little choice in the matter of how often they will eat or what and how much, you can see that it is not surprising that we run into problems occasionally. So it is a good idea to always keep in mind when you are training and feeding horses that no two are alike. They are all different individuals just as people are.

The big problem, of course, is the nervous, fussy horse that just picks at his feed. In a half hour, which is the longest period of time required for a normal horse to clean up his feed, this horse will only have taken two or three mouthfuls.

This is the kind you have to pamper, and if you have a groom that is especially good at babying a horse, you should switch him over to this one if you possibly can. The rule to keep in mind is that the horse should never have more than he will clean up at one time and I stick to the rule even if I am dealing with a horse that won't eat more than half a quart at a time and I wind up having to feed him seven or eight times a day.

Some horses will eat their grain normally but otherwise appear nervous and want to have their heads out over the top of the stall door all the time. They simply won't stand back in a corner and eat their hay out of the rack or off the floor. If this reaches the stage where the horse is not eating enough hay, I suggest that you take a rope hay rack, fill it and tie it close to the door, either on the inside or the outside. I have found that a horse will eat plenty of hay that way. He will take a bite of hay and look around awhile and then take another bite or two. He will do this as long as the hay is right there and easily accessible. Horses like this will usually eat out of the regular rack at night.

Other horses won't eat their grain out of a tub, bin or container of any kind. I have found that you have to use a little psychology in cases like this. I put the ration in the corner of the stall and cover it with a little straw. The horse thinks he is "stealing" the grain and will eat it. I have also run across horses that wouldn't eat except off the top of a tack box and others that had to have a goat in their stall to share their feed with them before they would eat.

Don't despair when you run into one like this because there isn't a feed problem in the world that can't be solved. What I do is try to figure what the horse is thinking and then come up with something that is designed to handle that particular kind of situation. The thing you want to avoid is forcing the horse to adopt a schedule that doesn't suit him.

Horses that are problem feeders aren't anything new. They've been with us ever since we domesticated the horse and always will be. Lou Dillon, the first two-minute trotter, who took a record of 1:58½ back in 1903, was a poor doer and I think the story of how Millard Sanders, her trainer, overcame the problem is still worth repeating in any discussion of feeding methods.

Lou Dillon was a high-strung, nervous mare who would not eat when she was in serious training. She did not have a record at the beginning of the 1903 season, but Sanders thought she had 2:00 potential. As he proceeded to dig into her early that year, she became more nervous and more high-strung and it finally reached the point where she would not eat a quart of oats in 24 hours. She was losing weight rapidly.

Sanders knew he had to do something and decided to conduct an experiment in an effort to get the mare to eat. He went to the market one morning and purchased small quantities of every vegetable, fruit and cereal he could find. He returned to the barn with three or four different kinds of cereals as well as apples, peaches, pears, potatoes, turnips and carrots. Then he spread a blanket in a corner of Lou Dillon's stall and placed a sample of each of the ingredients in a separate pile.

Lou Dillon nosed the food and when she came to the carrots she cleaned them up. Then she smelled everything else and turned away.

Sanders was overjoyed. He immediately purchased a half bushel of fresh carrots and a coarse vegetable grater and grated two quarts of carrots which he mixed with two quarts of oats. Lou Dillon cleaned up the feed tub and looked for more. From that moment on, her daily ration consisted of three quarts of grated carrots mixed with two quarts of oats fed four times a day. She gained in flesh and went on to become a great champion, taking her record later that year. She probably would not have achieved that peak if Sanders had not conducted his experiment and found something she liked.

You would be surprised at the things horses will eat and enjoy and that are good for them. In Lou Dillon's case it was carrots. From my own standpoint, I can report that Adios enjoyed apples and ate them all the time. There was an apple tree in his paddock at my farm and when the fruit ripened and fell Adios would eat the apples right off the ground. He didn't have a feeding problem so there was no necessity of adding them to his daily ration. But if there had been, I know I could have fed him apples and overcome it.

Delicate feeders are also the horses that are most likely to resent any kind of change in the quality of the feed or the cleanliness of the feed box. Oats that aren't up to snuff or hay that isn't quite as good as the horse is accustomed to will knock him off his feed. If this happens to two or three horses at once, you can be quite sure there is something wrong with the feed and you had better check it out right away.

You will also find that some horses are good feeders in the winter but won't eat in the daytime during the summer months when it is so hot. With horses like this, you have to adjust your schedule and probably add a feeding at nine or ten in the evening.

There are also horses that will eat better at night at any time of the year. I have known horses that would eat six quarts of grain at night and would just pick at their ration during the day. When I run across a horse like this, I immediately start to cut back on his daytime ration and give him at least one strong feed at night.

With respect to delicate feeders, you should also be careful about making sudden changes in the type of feed you are using. If you decide to go from oats to a pellet feed, for instance, I suggest that you not do it overnight. Rather, I think it would be better if you start out by scattering a few pellets in with the oat ration and then gradually increase the number of pellets and decrease the amount of oats. Eventually you will have an all-pellet ration, if that is what you are after, with no oats.

Occasionally, you will find if you go to pellets and mix them in with the oats the horse will separate the pellets, push them aside and not eat them. If this is the case, you should not go to more pellets right away but should wait until the horse has become accustomed to them and starts eating them, which he usually will do within a week.

However, you will occasionally run across a horse that will continue to push the pellets aside and will not eat them. In a situation like this, I would probably take the grain away for one feed each day for a while and feed the horse a pellet ration only. It shouldn't be very long before a horse starts eating the pellets if you do it this way.

A sudden change in feed can also result in colic. This is more pronounced when the new crop of hay comes in and horses suddenly switch over from comparatively dry hay to new, green hay. What I like to do to take the edge off this is to start giving horses a few bites of green grass when it first appears in the spring. If there is any way you are able to do this and keep it fairly routine for a month or so, the switchover in hay crops will not be nearly as noticeable to the horse and colic is much less likely to result.

This is a good place to make the point that a horse that has colic should never be fed until after the veterinarian arrives to treat him. Colic, as I guess everybody knows, is comparable to a stomach-ache in humans, and it just isn't a good practice to feed a horse that is showing these symptoms. As a matter of fact, it is a standing rule in my stable that a sick horse of any kind is never fed until the veterinarian has a chance to look him over.

In addition to horses that are slow feeders, you will also run across some that have a tendency to bolt their food, just as some human beings will. This is no better for a horse than it is for a person and should be corrected. What I do is feed these horses out of a "slow feeder," which is a special feed tub that has a network of bars built across the bottom level. A horse has to work to get his feed out of one of these tubs and his eating time is slowed down. If you don't have a "slow feeder" you can accomplish the same purpose by putting two or three small salt blocks or a few round, small stones in his feed. This will force him to slow down and pick his way around to get at the feed. Make sure, of course, that the stones you use are big enough that the horse will not put them in his mouth and possibly swallow them. I am talking here about stones, not pebbles.

I insist that all my horses be fed either from a galvanized tub or from one of those plastic tubs that are now in use. Either can and should be washed out thoroughly after every feeding so that they don't start smelling sour. This applies when horses are in winter training as well as when they are at the race tracks. A built-in wooden feed box just can't be kept clean and if a horse smells an odor he doesn't like in the feed tub he won't eat. This is very easy to avoid by always using a freshly-scrubbed tub.

In addition to oats, hay and water, the other basic ingredient that all horses must have is salt. I always keep a salt block or some loose salt in the stall. I prefer loose salt because horses will eat more of it that way. You have to keep in mind that a horse's tongue is not as hard as a cow's and for that reason most horses will prefer the loose salt over the block. However, the manufacturers are now putting out a "soft" block that I like and use quite a bit. I am very strict about salt being available to my horses at all times and I am especially watchful during hot weather periods.

The feeding of horses should always be kept as close to nature as possible and nature's way is to provide plenty of fresh, green grass. Unfortunately, there isn't much grass around race tracks these days but whenever I find any I make use of it. I remember how Fred Egan and some of the others used to graze their horses at the end of a shank in the center field at Goshen Mile Track years ago and it certainly was a wonderful sight. You can't imagine what something like that does for a horse. Not only for the feed value of the fresh grass, but just as much for the idea of the horse getting out of the stall and stretching his legs a little. If there is any chance at all that you can get your horse out and graze him near a race track, even if it's only for five or ten minutes, by all means do it. There is nothing more relaxing in the world.

In the old days we had grooms who would get in their car and drive a couple of miles, or even walk a couple of miles, just to find some nice clover grass they could bring back for their horses. There aren't many like that around any more and not enough trainers who would encourage the grooms to do it if they wanted to. But it still can be done around a lot of race tracks and I recommend it wherever possible.

That brings me to another thing I mentioned briefly earlier and which ties in with grazing. If you have ever noticed horses grazing, you have observed that they will dig right down into the sod, get into it as deep as they can. This is their way of getting minerals. The sod is full of minerals that are very beneficial to a horse. Again, this is nature's way.

A good, smart groom will go out every once in a while and dig up a big chunk of sod for his horse. He'll toss it in the stall and the horse will nibble at it, extracting minerals. It is more beneficial, of course, if this sod comes from a piece of ground that has been well fertilized, but any kind is better than none at all. I like to see a chunk of sod in every horse's stall every few days.

Probably the best way to close out this section is to describe what I do in the way of feeding on race day. For one thing, I don't feed as much hay the night before a race. I cut down on the quantity in the rack. If the horse is going to race in the afternoon and is scheduled to start warming up at noon, I will give him his noon feed about 10:45 a.m. I will also cut the quantity back and feed perhaps two quarts instead of the usual three or four. I will sometimes muzzle a horse to keep him from eating too much hay on race day. I think hay has a tendency to lay in a horse's digestive tract and make him loggy. A heavy feeder should be jogged the morning of the day he is going to be raced, especially if it is a Monday since he did not get any exercise on Sunday.

If a horse is racing at night, as most of them are these days, I would feed him two hours before his first warmup heat was scheduled. This would be a lighter-than-usual ration because I do not like to feed a horse too much just before he races. I would compensate for this by increasing his noon feed by about 25%. It is also important that a horse not be fed for at least a half hour after he is completely cooled out. When my horses race at night, I give them a short feed after the race, something like a couple quarts of grain, or perhaps a hot mash in cold weather or a cold mash in hot weather.

Our horses are shipped around a great deal these days and it is important that they be fed when they are being trucked from one track to another. I don't try to feed mine any grain but I like to have a hay net filled with good hay placed before them. Any horse, and especially a nervous one, will ship a lot better if there is hay available that he can nibble on during the trip.

If you are hauling your own horse and you stop to gas up or something like that, it is a good idea to give your horse a little walk if possible, but if you can't do that, you should be sure to offer him water. If you ship a horse a relatively long distance without giving him any water, especially in warm weather, he will usually be all heated up when he gets off the truck and will down a couple of quick buckets if you aren't careful. This could lead to founder, and I know that it has in a couple of instances. While horses should be watered during shipment, they shouldn't get too much at one time when they come off the truck.

In closing, I think it appropriate to point out that almost invariably the men who are training and driving the best horses are the ones who are feeding the best. Maybe you can get away as much as a dollar a day cheaper if you scrounge on feed, but it will be disastrous in the end. Your horses won't look as good and, even more important, they won't race as well. So you are just kidding yourself when you don't feed the best hay and the best oats. If you will remember that, and exercise a little common sense when you run across a feeding problem, your horses will look in better flesh and you will train and drive more winners.

Although we have not made the progress that some of the other animal breeds have, there is more research being done now than ever before relative to the horse's digestive system and we can expect that new feeds and new varieties of present feeds will be developed. Until that time, I recommend that you follow the advice offered by Dr. Tyznik and the general rules which I have laid down in this chapter. If you do, you will be feeding well.

I think that sometimes we feel we are not making the progress we should in this field, but as I look back, it is clear to me that we are better off than we were 30 or 40 years ago. I know we are feeding better than the old timers did because our horses maintain a lot more weight and look better. This is also tied in with better parasite control, but there is no question that we are racing a healthier, stronger horse than did our predecessors in harness racing.

(Biographical information concerning the author appears on page 141.)

18

STOCK FARM MANAGEMENT

HARRY M. HARVEY

A horse farm operates something like the heart of a living person. It never stops functioning entirely. In each case, there are times when the rate of activity slows down a little, but there is never a single second when everything comes to an absolute halt. For that reason, stock farm management is a never-ending cycle and no matter what the economists say about the proximity of the four-day work week, horse farming will never conform to the pattern.

The accepted eight-hour industrial work day thus has little application to the life of a stock farm manager whose daily tour of duty may begin shortly after midnight with a foaling mare in trouble and wind up almost 24 hours later with a large stack of book work. In between, there were mares to be teased and bred, foals to be wormed, shots to be given, hay to be made and pastures to be mowed. It is a profession that smacks of variety and variety is one of the things that makes it so interesting.

I have been either a farmer or a horseman or a combination of both all my life so I am accustomed to the vagaries of the hours, work and weather and think nothing of them. I am certain the same holds true for any dedicated person involved in stock farm management and for whom the long hours and hard work are more than compensated for every time a healthy, newborn foal struggles to its feet or whenever nature unfolds another of her never-ending wonders that comprise all the facets of farming.

When I was approached to write a chapter for this book, my first reaction was that there was no possible way that all the aspects of stock farm management could be covered adequately in the limited space available. I know that a more thorough job could be done by writing a book instead of a chapter but at the same time I know that I can draw from my own experience to sketch out the rough framework of a successful stock farm operation and thus provide basic background information for those whose knowledge of the subject is limited. In the pages that follow, I intend to do that to the best of my ability.

I should say at the beginning that I will be writing generally from the standpoint of a farm operation that is located in the northern half of the United States. All my experience has been in this section, mostly in western Pennsylvania at Del Miller's Meadowlands Farm and my own Loch Arden Farm where the winters are quite cold but not uncomfortably severe and the summers hot and fairly dry.

My starting point has nothing to do with horses as such and yet it is of vital importance. The starting point is land; good land that grows plenty of grass for grazing and good hay. Quality grass and hay are basic to a successful stock farm operation.

If we can assume that a foal remains at the place of his conception and birth until November first of his yearling form, then, depending on when he was foaled, he has spent the first 28 to 33 months of his existence (11 in utero and 17 to 22 at his dam's side and on his own thereafter) on the same land. From the standpoint of basic nutritional values and exposure to parasites which affect rate of growth and development of bone and muscle, these are the most important months of a horse's life. If the land feeds him and his mother well, he will grow and develop as nature intended. But if the land is poor, the horse's physical condition will be affected adversely both before and after birth.

Actually, good pasture land for horses involves a great deal more than the basic quality of the soil itself. To a very great degree, geographic limitations can dictate the soil type on which horses must be raised. But many types of soil are capable of being converted into good pasture land through good management practices. Among the factors involved and which I will discuss are proper seeding, mowing, liming, fertilization, water supply and drainage.

As to soil types, it has been my experience that a well-drained loam soil that is comparatively free of rocks is ideal. I prefer a good loam soil to a clay soil. Clay soil tends to harden quickly in dry weather and, in addition, does not utilize fertilizer efficiently.

If there is any question as to the quality and makeup of the soil, the U.S. Soil Conservation Service may be consulted. The SCS has on file maps which show the soil type on all the farms in its district. If the soil has not been typed, the SCS will arrange to do it. Certain soil conservation practices, such as renewing grass stands and developing springs to insure adequate water supply, may be arranged on a cost-sharing basis with the Federal Government.

I also think that horse farmers should take advantage of the free services offered by the county agent who is usually a knowledgeable, college-educated expert on farming matters. These agents will offer advice that will save time and money. Whether we do it ourselves or take advantage of the governmental services, we should always be trying to improve the quality of our land. No more is being made and people are multiplying.

I prefer a gently undulating land that is dotted with good shade trees (Fig. 121). Rolling land seems to produce better grazing areas and there is no question that young horses benefit from the exercise they get over this type of land. Even an occasional good-sized hill is not objectionable in that it helps to condition young horses for the rigors of training that lie ahead.

An adequate water supply is one of the most important considerations on any stock farm. If your farm is located close enough to a city water supply, it is probably the best and cheapest source of water. This does away with maintenance problems, which can become a headache if you have your own system, and assures that there will always be plenty of water. A great deal of water is required to satisfy the needs of horses and resident employees. An average horse will consume 10 gallons of water a day and when you start multiplying that by a large number of animals it soon becomes obvious that it is not a minor consideration.

Drilled wells are common on horse farms but they are sometimes quite expensive because the water level is so deep. Very often, a water source close to the surface can be tiled and dammed and converted into a natural spring. Any time you walk around your land in dry weather and notice wet areas, you can almost be certain that you can dig down three or four feet and pick up the water nearer its source. This can be collected by tiling the water into a drop-box—usually a round, concrete tank holding about 25 gallons and in which the sediment drops to the bottom—and from there it can be piped to a watering trough on a lower level. By doing this, you gain a good water supply and put more land to beneficial use.

Fig. 121. Gently undulating land dotted with shade trees as illustrated in the upper photograph is the type the author recommends for raising horses. Shade trees and a farm pond are the highlights of the lower photograph made at his Loch Arden Farm.

In considering a farm water system, be certain that the water line is sufficiently large to take care of whatever expansion plans you may have in mind. If, for instance, you installed a one-inch system you might find it inadequate for your needs as you enlarge your operation. It is better, therefore, to start off with a pipeline a little larger than your present needs might indicate. The underground pipeline that I would prefer for any large scale stock farm would consist of a four-inch line from the source to major buildings, and a two-inch line to the secondary buildings. Within barns and other buildings, a one-inch pipe is adequate.

Each field should have its own watering trough. Usually, it is sufficient to run a three-quarter inch pipe to watering troughs. There are many types of watering troughs but I have always used the conventional galvanized tank (Fig. 122) and recommend it. These tanks have rounded ends, are two feet wide, two feet high and come in varying lengths ranging from four to ten feet. The length of the tank would depend to some degree on the number of horses in the field. I have found that an eight-foot tank will usually take care of 20 horses. All piping should be underground. Although it is much easier to tap a line in on the side of the tank, doing so creates a danger to horses and should be avoided.

One of the biggest mistakes people make with respect to the establishment of a horse farm is that they want to get their horses on the land before it is actually ready for occupancy. The secret of maintaining a good pasture over long period of time lies in having a good turf underfoot. It is difficult to build up this turf on land that is being grazed by horses. The reason for this is that horses have a naturally peculiar grazing habit in that they will group together and graze one spot taking everything out of that area, including some of the roots, while ignoring an equally good area close by that soon becomes a rank growth of high grass and weeds. The spots that are grazed heavily soon become bare and the soil in that area tends to erode.

In order to maintain the proper perspective, let us assume that we have just purchased a farm on which we intend to raise horses. We are satisfied with the quality of the soil and an adequate water supply is available. The land has been producing routine farm crops—corn, wheat, barley, beans, etc.—and we are going to convert it into a horse farm.

Fig. 122. Galvanized water tanks of this type are used and recommended by the author. In the background are two types of fence discussed in the text; a wire fence with a barb on top at the left and a four-board wooden fence at the right.

I think the first thing is for the owner to avoid putting horses on the land for at least 18 months. The establishment of the proper turf is vital and if horses are permitted to graze new land too soon, as I explained above, they can easily ruin it for the next several years.

If you are working with comparatively hilly land, this would also be the time that you would put in one or more diversion ditches or terraces as I prefer to call this particular type of installation. These terraces will help to prevent erosion. They should be put in according to the advice of soil conservation personnel who are familiar with the proper methods.

Diversion terraces are put in about halfway down the slope (Fig. 123). A bulldozer is used to peel back the top soil and then to tear up a strip of ground approximately 20 feet wide. The sub soil is then pushed down the hill into a mound which resembles a dam and which will have much the same effect. The top soil is then bulldozed back on the terrace and the area is seeded along with the remainder of the pasture.

While a bulldozer is on the property, it is also a good time to clean out fence rows, cut down steep stream banks, and eliminate other hazards to horses before seeding.

The next step is to properly lime and fertilize the fields and before this is done it is very important that time be spent discing, cross-harrowing and leveling the land. A good smooth pasture is one of the most vital factors in developing superior grazing land. Liming and fertilizing are done in accordance with the results of soil tests which are usually made by a soil consulting service and then analyzed free of charge by the State Extension Service laboratory. Representatives of commercial fertilizer companies will also make these tests without charge.

Lime is vital to horses. It contains calcium; calcium builds bone and is one of the reasons why so many good horses are raised on land that has a natural limestone base such as is found in Kentucky, parts of Pennsylvania and in certain other states. When soil is tested, it is given a PH rating which indicates whether the soil is acid or alkaline. PH is a numerical scale ranging from one to fourteen with 7.0 being neutral. Technically, the PH scale deals with hydrogen ions.

A PH of 7.0 or higher indicates that the soil is alkaline or sweet. A reading below 7.0 indicates that the soil is acid or sour. In order to utilize fertilizer efficiently, grazing land for horses should carry a PH level of from 6.7 to 7.0.

I think lime is much more effective if it is tilled into the soil in some way, either by plowing or deep discing. Lime is needed at the roots and thus does the root structure of both grasses and legumes much more good if it is tilled in. If it is spread on the surface and permitted to be assimilated into the soil naturally,

Fig. 123.   This is a newly-seeded diversion terrace. The section between the two white lines is the "dam" part which prevents the water from flowing down the hill to the left. The water flows down from above until it reaches the terrace whereupon it is gradually diverted around the curve of the hill. In the process, most of the water is actually absorbed by the soil.

it will only achieve a depth of about a half inch a year and a good deal of it could be lost by erosion before it had a chance to do its work.

Depending on the result of the soil test and the PH level you wish to attain, you might spread anywhere from a ton and a half to four tons to the acre. This application would be good for four years. This is done preferably in the fall of the year which is the best time to begin to establish a stand of grass if the weather is not too dry. The most desirable time to begin the operations we are discussing now is the last week of August or the first week of September.

The next step is to fertilize the land. This, again, is done in accordance with the results of the soil tests. The three basic ingredients in any fertilizer mixture are nitrogen, phosphorus (phosphate) and potassium (potash). All serve a specific useful purpose in promoting the growth and health of grass and the quantities of each depends on the soil test.

A 10-10-10 mixture, for instance, would consist of equal parts of all three elements. But if the soil test indicated plenty of nitrogen and a shortage of the other two elements, the recommended mixture might be 0-20-20. If the test showed no shortage of nitrogen but a need for more phosphate than potash, the mixture might be 0-20-10.

Since nitrogen helps promote quick growth, it is more likely to be used in conjunction with a fall seeding because the growth rate is less at that time of year than in the spring. Our mixture, therefore, might be a 5-10-10.

In testing the soil, incidentally, a representative number of samples should be taken from each field. It is very possible that the requirements for one side of a farm would be different than for the other side. I have actually seen variations in the same 50-acre pasture field and if this is quite widespread and it is neither practical nor economical to change the mixture often, an "average" mixture for all fields should probably be decided upon. Of course, if the variation is very great, separate mixtures should be used.

Fertilizer is applied after the land has been limed and then well-tilled by discing and cross-discing. Fertilizer is more effectively applied right on the surface immediately after the field has been limed and disced. You can apply fertilizer yourself by rigging up some kind of a spreader on the back of a truck, but it is much more efficient to have it done by a fertilizer company using its own trucks which have been adapted for this purpose. In this manner, you can also purchase the fertilizer in bulk rates. According to the recommendations of the soil testing agency you might spread from 200 to 600 pounds per acre. I have found that in western Pennsylvania fertilizer costs average about $20 per acre.

Within the last few years, liquid fertilizer sprayed on by tank truck, or even by airplane, has been used very effectively. If there is a distributor in the area, it may be well to look into this form of fertilization since it can often be done more economically.

Once you have achieved the proper soil condition, fields should be fertilized at least every two years and preferably every year, especially if they are heavily populated. Liming is usually repeated every four to five years depending on the PH. Fields may be treated either in the spring or the fall. Fall treatment is preferred because if there is a wet spring it will be a long time before the land is dry enough to stand the weight of a heavily-loaded lime or fertilizer truck. One word of caution: *never* turn a horse out on a freshly-fertilized field. No matter what anybody tells you, it is possible for a horse to be poisoned. My practice is to keep stock off a newly-fertilized field until after the first heavy rain. Lime is not nearly as dangerous, but I also make it a practice not to turn horses out on a newly-limed field until after a good rain.

Now it is time to seed and we will use a grass-clover-cover crop mixture that has been selected in advance since fertilizer requirements will vary according to the seed being used. There are a lot of grasses available for horses, but the basic one is blue grass. I am going to recommend it and refer basically only to it in my discussion. Blue grass matures early, grows rapidly and is very nutritious. As a matter of fact, there are more nutrients per ton in blue grass than in any other pasture grass that has been tested for horses. One of its few shortcomings is that in certain sections of the country where the summers are especially hot and dry it has a tendency to burn off and you don't get very much feed value from it during that period. However, one of the great advantages of blue grass is that it has a remarkable recovery factor and after a couple of good autumn rains it will make a big comeback and is usually quite luxurious in September and October. All in all, I have found that it is much the best grass for horses.

On new fields, I would recommend sowing a mixture consisting of 15 pounds per acre of blue grass, five pounds of white clover and a bushel of either rye or oats as a cover crop. You won't necessarily notice the clover in the beginning, but it will come and it does add a certain palatibility to any pasture field. I have noticed that on western Pennsylvania fields that are already in pasture on well-cultivated land you will get a lot of volunteer blue grass as well as a good stand of white dutch clover.

On diversion terraces and in other places where traffic is quite heavy—around gates, watering troughs, and feeding places—it is usually a good idea to seed a grass that is more rugged than blue grass and that will stand wear and erosion better. I prefer to use Kentucky Fescue 31 or something of that nature. Actually, it is nearly impossible to establish good sod in these areas and if concrete was cheaper I would pave them.

If you are going to seed only a small area, it can be done with a broadcast seeder. A man walks along with this type of seeder and turns a crank which spreads the seed out onto the soil. However, if you are going to seed an entire farm, as we are, you should have a drill type seeder which is hitched to a tractor and can seed an eight-foot width at one time.

Once the seed has been planted, you should go over the land with a cultipacker which breaks up any remaining dirt clods and firms the soil. This will leave the seed close to the surface where it belongs but at the same time it will provide some basic protection to the newly-planted grass. After doing this, I prefer to mulch all hilly land which is the most prone to erosion. This is accomplished by using a manure spreader and setting it for a very light covering of straw and manure. If you put too much on, you will do more harm than good. An ideal covering is one in which you can see about half the soil. I have seen flash storms wash a new seeding down a hillside in a big hurry. A light covering of straw and manure will do much to prevent this kind of erosion.

We have now seeded in September land that we are going to put into active use a year from the following spring. We might be able to get a little limited use from it next fall, a year from now, but if at all possible we should wait the full 18 months. This will assure a real turf sod and the additional waiting time will be more than compensated for by the quality of the pasture.

This seeding could actually be done either in the spring or fall and obviously if you purchased a farm during the winter months you would try to get a spring planting simply as a time saver if for no other reason. One of the advantages of planting in the fall is that if the grass doesn't take because you've had a hard winter with a lot of freezing and thawing, you can come right back and plant again in the spring without losing a summer's growth. But if a spring planting goes bad, you have lost an entire growing season. I have found, too, that grass will take better if planted in the fall because of the cooler weather. Hot weather, especially without a normal amount of rainfall, will kill a new grass seeding quicker than anything.

If there is a normal amount of rainfall after the land has been seeded, it won't be long before the cover crop begins to make its appearance. The reason a cover crop was sowed along with the grass seed and clover was to provide the young grass seedlings with a certain amount of shade in the early growth stages so that they would not be burned out by the sun before they could take hold and prosper on their own. In addition, the cover crop roots tend to stabilize the soil and thus help to slow down erosion when the seeding has been made on a hillside or on rolling land.

I have been writing about seeding a brand new field, but I want to point out that if you buy a farm it will not always be necessary to seed the entire farm. Some fields may already be in grass and if these fields are treated in accordance with the lime and fertilizer recommendation obtained from a soil test, they will prove entirely satisfactorily to the new operation. If the PH is at an acceptable 6.7 level and you fertilize such a field properly, you will find volunteer blue grass and white clover springing up and within a couple of years a fair stand of grass will have been converted into a good stand.

Once the cover crop reaches six to eight inches, it should be mowed to a height of about two inches. The purpose of the cover crop is to provide a measure of protection for the new grass, not to blot out the sun completely or to compete with the grass seed for soil nutrients. This is why it is mowed back and in so doing we also provide a natural mulch which is helpful.

As long as I have introduced the subject of mowing, I might as well continue on and discuss it at some length. All pastures should be mowed during the growing season. This usually extends from April through June in most areas and again from about the middle of September through the middle of October.

There are three basic types of mowers, the rotary mower, which is the most common type used on horse farms, the flail mower and the cutter bar mower.

A rotary mower is very good but it has one bad feature. If you let the grass go too long before mowing, the rotary mower has a tendency to windrow, that is, it doesn't spread the grass evenly over the width of the cut and about every eight feet you will find a strip of dead and decaying grass. I prefer the flail type mower because it doesn't windrow. A flail mower has a series of flails on a reel and as these reels go over the ground they cut and mulch uniformly without windrowing. A cutter bar mower is more routinely used for cutting hay fields rather than mowing pastures.

Windrows can be dangerous on horse farms. There are a lot of things we don't know about botulism but we do know that it can be caused by molds. If you will examine a windrow—a normal windrow might be an inch thick and eight inches wide— two weeks after the grass has been cut, you will find that there is a lot of mold around the edges. It is possible for a horse to develop gastronomic difficulties from grazing around decaying grass of this type.

There are different schools of thought on trimming pastures. I like to see grass mowed just as soon as it is dry enough to get on in the spring, when it is approximately four to six inches high. By mowing early, you strengthen the stand in that you encourage the roots to grow faster.

In the early stages of the most rapid growth, perhaps from mid-April to mid-May, you can clip pastures as low as two inches. As you get closer to summer and the growth starts to slow up, especially if it looks like it might be a dry summer, it is a good idea to cut back on the mowing or even stop mowing

Fig.124. A flail type mower with a chain harrow fastened on behind is shown in operation. The author recommends this procedure as described in the text.

altogether. You might get a few weeds this way, but that is preferable to continued mowing up to the time the soil hardens. Leaving a stand sufficient to shade the soil is a good idea under these circumstances.

Pasture fields should be harrowed as well as mowed. For this purpose I recommend an Australian harrow or a chain harrow hitched behind the mower (Fig. 124). The harrow breaks up the clods and also scatters windrows if you have them. Harrowing pasture fields in this manner is especially desirable in the fall but it is a good idea to do it in the spring as well. If it is convenient, it is never a bad idea to hitch a harrow behind a mower.

Of course, there is nothing that will do a pasture more good than a controlled rotation program. I realize that this cannot be done on many horse farms, but I know that if it could we would all raise better horses. It would help the parasite problem tremendously and would also enable our land to recover from the depletion it undergoes as a result of constant grazing.

If I had my own farm and all the money in the world, I would divide it up into three-acre paddocks which I would rotate. I would put half the paddocks in use and graze six horses in each paddock permitting them to remain there until heavily-grazed areas began to appear. Depending on the growing season, this period might be as brief as two weeks or as long as two months. Then I would move the horses to a fresh paddock while the one they had been in was rested. I would assume that the vacated paddock would be ready for horses again when the growth reached four inches.

My next choice would be a series of 12 to 15-acre fields for which I would follow the same rotation procedure. In other words, I would adopt a system that would utilize the smallest sized field that would enable me to practice practical rotation.

Rotation not only upgrades the quality of the grass, but it is the best thing in the world for combating parasite infestation. We might as well face it, parasites are a constant problem and anything we can do to eliminate them from the horse's intestinal tract is a big plus. The primary way that horses are contaminated is through other horses. If you can take horses off a field and drag and clip that field and rest it, you are breaking up or at least slowing down the worm cycle.

It is a good idea to permit cattle to graze on land that you are building up for horses. For one thing, cattle are uniform grazers and are much less likely to create bare spots in a field. In addition, cow droppings have more value as fertilizer than horse droppings. A chain harrow should be used to scatter the droppings. The reasons, incidentally, that horses create bare spots while cows do not are (a) that cows cut the grass off when they graze while horses have a tendency to pull it out and (b) that cows will eat rough stands of grass whereas horses concentrate on specific areas and are thus more likely to crop it too close in those areas while ignoring others. A cow, of course, will eat about twice as much as a horse in a day. So I would recommend that if you plant a new grass stand in the fall, that you permit cattle to graze it moderately the following summer.

However, I do not recommend that cattle and horses graze the same field. This has been done and I guess it is all right, but I wouldn't do it myself. There is a certain natural antagonism which is compounded if there are mares and foals in the field. Cattle will also get into creeps (pens in which foals are fed and which I will discuss later) and this is not a satisfactory situation.

I have never handled sheep and don't know very much about them except that they are very efficient grazers, constitute a major parasite problem and are a high care species. I know that if I were going to use sheep that I would make certain that I had a good shepherd working for me.

Many horse farms will also raise a hay crop in conjunction with its pasture land operation. You can raise straight timothy hay, a mixture of clover and timothy or alfalfa. At Meadowlands we raised a good grade of alfalfa and fed it to the horses constantly with no ill effects. It has been an old wives' tale for years that alfalfa is not the ideal feed for horses because it loosens them up too much. But I have not found this to be true and I think it is one of the very best hay types that can be fed. Del Miller and I have discussed this many times and we always noticed that our stock did much better on alfalfa than on grass hays. At the same time, a properly cured grass hay will do very well. In western Pennsylvania, a certain amount of volunteer orchard grass will invade an alfalfa stand early in the year. Orchard grass is all right for horses but it is not nearly as good as alfalfa and I always try to cut it early, about the first of June. The feed value of orchard grass is very low after it ripens.

One of the reasons that we raised alfalfa at Meadowlands was that the grass hays had a tendency to burn off in dry summers and alfalfa, with its deeper roots, proved to be much more drought and heat resistant than other types. We would always get two and usually three crops from our alfalfa fields. My policy at Meadowlands was to make two or three cuttings and then to permit horses to graze the fields. Their condition improved and at the same time this practice enabled me to rest a pasture field.

It is a good idea to take horses off an alfalfa field after the first frost. Horses, unlike cattle, aren't susceptible to bloat but I have observed horses that encountered a little digestive trouble after grazing alfalfa that had been touched by frost. This is a case of better safe than sorry. By taking the horses off a little early, you also give the field a chance to come back somewhat before winter sets in.

If you have some land with rough grass on it, and don't want to use that field for grazing, it is better to mow the field instead of taking the crop off. The debris that is left will decay and help build up organic matter and is much the same as if you spread manure over the entire field. An application of super phosphate will speed up the decaying process and further aid the field.

I'm kind of a nut about trees and I want to write a little something about them. I think trees are great for horse farms. If you have recently purchased a horse farm and want to establish some shade, it is best to contact a nursery and order some trees with a little size that can be planted in the fall of the year. They should be properly burlaped and balled when being transported. If you will spend as much time cultivating the trees as you do the grass, you will have some good shade in a comparatively short period of time. But if trees are just dumped into the ground and not taken care of they are a bad investment.

I prefer maple trees for a horse farm. I know they are slower growing but there is something majestic about them. If you want something that will grow in a hurry, the Lombardy Poplar is the best choice in the northeast. They grow fast and are very good along borders and fence lines. They will die out in from 20 to 30 years, but they will give you the best growth rate during that period. Poplars should be planted away from sewer and water lines. All trees planted along fence rows should be kept well back from the fences so that horses cannot reach over and chew them.

Trees must be protected or horses will eat the bark off and the trees will die. There's something about a tree that attracts a horse. When a horse becomes bored, he will go to a tree and start eating the bark. A man told me once that horses ate trees because they were "after the grain in the wood." I don't know whether this is true or exactly what they are after but I know they will damage trees. It is very possible that the horse lacks a mineral that is available in the wood and not in the soil. There are commercial products on the market that can be sprayed or painted on trees that will keep horses away from them. I recommend that this be done or that another method of preservation be used. There just isn't any reason for a good tree to be lost.

I find that the best means of keeping a horse away from a tree is to spot it with Ebanol, a commercial product that has a tar base. I dab Ebanol on the tree approximately six inches apart

Fig. 125. As a means of keeping horses from chewing trees, the author dabs the bark with Ebanol roughly on six-inch centers as illustrated.

on centers (Fig. 125). A tree, especially a young tree, should not be completely painted. When you do paint completely, you inhibit natural bark growth. I have seen a good many trees killed this way. My preferred treatment is to dab with Ebanol at six to eight month intervals.

If you have a clump of trees, you should build a wooden fence around them to keep the horses out. The same applies if you have two trees that are fairly close together. It is also important to remove overhanging limbs, so that horses cannot get at them and to fence any tree that has a low crotch in which a horse might get hung up.

You can protect trees with a fine mesh wire, but I have found that sooner or later horses will rub against the wire long enough to loosen it up and create a hazard that could result in injury. All trees should be pruned every three or four years, preferably in the fall or winter.

As a rule, tree leaves and bark are not poisonous to horses with one major exception. In the northeast, the wild cherry tree is poisonous at a certain stage of wilt. If you have a storm and tree branches fall around the farm, as they will, it is always a good idea to go around the next day and collect them. The branch of the wild cherry tree is very high in cyanic acid and can be fatal to horses at the wilt stage.

Many farms have telephone poles or electric power lines going through them and even though these may be a sign of progress they certainly don't add anything to the scenery. They are necessary evils however, and must be dealt with.

Most new poles have been pressure treated in creosote or some

Fig. 126. Various types of fences, as described in the text, are illustrated. Upper left, four-board wooden fence; upper right, multiflora fence; lower left, wire with a board on top; lower right, wire with a barb on top.

other similar substance and horses will not bother with them. They will chew at some of the older poles and I paint these solidly with a coat of Ebanol. The major thing you have to be concerned with is the guy lines that are used in conjunction with some poles. If you will request it of the utility company, they will provide a livestock shield for the guy lines that will protect the stock from injury.

If the terrain and water supply lend themselves conveniently to it, it is a good idea to put in one or more farm ponds. In addition to their natural beauty and the fact that they can provide decent fishing if properly stocked, farm ponds also provide a good source of water in the event of fire. A properly-constructed pond also prevents a fast runoff of water which is the principal cause of soil erosion. Theoretically, stock should be fenced out of ponds. Information regarding types of farm ponds and their cost may be obtained from the Soil Conservation Service. A typical farm pond is illustrated in Fig. 121.

Now that we have our new farm laid out, seeded, fertilized and limed and have planted our trees, and built ponds we have to think about fencing. There are three basic types of fences: board fences, wire fence, and wire fence with a board on top (Fig. 126).

No matter which type you use, you will have to have fence posts so let me discuss them first. As far as I am concerned, a locust post is the best. I like locust because it is sturdy, holds nails or staples well and is rot resistant. Untreated locust posts can be in the ground for up to 30 years without rotting out. It is uncommon to find this in any other untreated post.

Unfortunately, it is becoming increasingly difficult because of the high cost of labor to obtain an adequate supply of good locust posts. As a substitute, I have recently been purchasing a pressure treated pine post that I consider second best to locust.

A fence post (Fig. 127) should be eight feet long, straight, and have a top diameter of from four to five inches. Untreated posts

Fig. 127. The manner in which board joints are broken to give a fence greater strength is illustrated at the left. The top board and the third one down have broken joints butting in the center of the post as described in the text. The second and fourth boards are butted on adjacent posts. This photograph also illustrates the manner in which the post is slabbed to accommodate the fence boards. In the photograph at the right is a cap board which is nailed over the joints to give the fence even more strength.

should be skinned prior to use, that is the bark should be removed. If you are installing board fence, the side that the board is to be nailed to should be slabbed or faced at the saw mill. This leaves a flat surface approximately three inches across and provides a good nailing surface for the boards.

Fence posts should be sunk to a depth of three feet, which will leave approximately five feet above ground. The top line of the fence itself will usually be from 53 to 55 inches high with the posts extending slightly higher than that. I have tried to sink posts with a power driver but it has never worked very well. I have found that even though it is time consuming the best way is to use an auger and drill a hole three feet deep. Then the hole is cleaned out, the post placed in it and the dirt tamped back in around it. It is important that the dirt around the post be tamped firmly in place. If a post is properly set, no dirt will remain after the tamping is complete. A transit can be used to line up posts but an experienced man can do it by eye. A piece of wire or strong cord can also be used.

If you are going to install a board fence, I recommend oak boards. The proper size for a fence board is one by six, that is, one inch thick and six inches wide. Any larger is superfluous and any smaller is not strong enough. You can build three, four or five-board fence. In my opinion, a five-board fence is unnecessary and uneconomical and a three-board does not provide enough coverage. I recommend a four-board fence. On a three-board fence, if the top board is high enough then the bottom board is too high to prevent foals from rolling under the fence if they lay down alongside it as they will.

Whether the boards are nailed on the inside or outside of the fence post is somewhat controversial depending on what part of the country you happen to be in and at the same time is relatively immaterial in my opinion. A fence will be stronger and a little safer if the boards are nailed on the inside. By the same token, the fence looks better if the boards are on the outside and I have never known of a horse to be injured through contact with a fence post on the inside.

In building a board fence, the posts should be eight feet apart measuring from the center of one post to the center of the next. Posts that are 12 or 16 feet apart will not support a board fence properly. In purchasing boards, you should order most of them in 16-foot lengths so that you can break joints in the installation and thus provide greater strength. That is, on any one post (Fig. 127), ends of two of the four boards and centers of the other two will be nailed. Regular nails are used with locust posts but with pressure treated posts a lag nail, which grips the wood better, is necessary.

In a four-board fence, the bottom board will be from five to seven inches off the ground and there will be eight inches between boards. That will bring the top of the top board from 53 to 55 inches off the ground. The reason for the slight variation at the bottom lies in accommodating the topography of the land. Very little land is entirely flat and an occasional adjustment must be made in this respect. These adjustments are made at the bottom rather than the top. In other words, a board fence is built from the top down.

A four-foot oak face board, also called a cap board, covers the board joints on every post. This board runs downward from the top of the post and gives the fence extra strength. This also lends additional support to the nailed surfaces in the event a horse hits the fence. Surfaces beneath the face board should be painted before the face board is nailed in place. If not, this area of the fence will be the first to rot out.

After the fence has been completed, I always have my men go along the row with a power saw and cut the posts off three inches above the top board. This cut is made on a slight angle so that snow and water will not lay on top of the post and help rot it out. It is also a good idea to go over all posts with a power saw cutting off any protrusions. This should actually be done before the boards are nailed up.

All board fences should be painted. It is strictly a matter of opinion, but I prefer black over white. Black has much better longevity. Another thing is that when you have to repaint the fence you don't have to do a lot of scraping as you do with white paint. You simply paint over the top. Scraping paint is a high cost maintenance factor. I paint my fences with Ebanol, the same product I use on trees, although there are other good products available at comparative prices.

I have found that the best way to paint fences is to use a wide brush. I have done some spray painting but have found it an inefficient method. Fences should be painted in the summer when the Ebanol, or whatever product you are using, flows more freely. The fence should also be good and dry before you put any paint on it or you won't get the desired penetration. For this reason, do not paint fences early in the morning when the dew is on. You simply don't get the penetration you should.

If you can stand the sight of an unpainted fence, it is actually a good idea to let a new board fence stand for a year before painting it. If the boards are fresh from the saw mill and the posts are freshly cut, you'll get a lot of checking and cracking if you paint them right away that you won't get if you wait a year. It is also important to bear in mind that it is impractical to try to paint a treated post white. The dark color will eventually bleed through.

A wire fence (Fig. 126) costs about half as much as a board fence and is highly satisfactory. I recommend a nine gauge wire that is 42 inches high for making wire fence. Technically, this is known as a woven wire fence, but for the sake of brevity, I will refer to it throughout simply as a wire fence. I used round, pressure-treated posts. If you use this type of post, you have to use a special staple with lags in it to prevent the staples from pulling out. I set my wire fence posts 12 feet apart on centers, although if you have any idea that you might want to substitute board fence later, the posts should be set eight feet apart.

In putting in wire fence, you will notice that the sections on one side are closer together than on the other. The small sections go at the bottom and the wider sections at the top. You will also notice that there is a slight ripple in the wire. The ripple compensates for the contraction and expansion that occurs in winter and summer. Therefore, these ripples should not be straightened out because they represent a safety factor.

One of the most practical fences for a stock farm is a wire fence with a single board on top (Fig. 126). This combines the safety features of the board fence and the economical features of the wire fence. However, if you are going to use wire with a board on top, it is better to set the posts eight feet apart instead of 12 because the boards have a tendency to buckle if you go over eight.

Brace and corner posts assemblies are the keys to successful wire fence construction. A brace assembly consists of two eight-foot posts with six inch diameters at the top set six feet apart.

Fig. 128. In the photograph at the left, a proper corner post brace assembly as described in the text is illustrated. At the right is a closeup of a brace post showing the device used by the author to anchor the ends of the pipe to the post. The flat portion of the anchor is lagged to the fence post with long screws and the cylindrical portion receives the pipe. For purposes of illustration, an actual anchor has been placed temporarily on the post to demonstrate how it functions. The anchors that are being used at top and bottom are invisible except for the sides since they are positioned within the pipes.

Such a combination is set about every 250 feet when a wire fence is being run along a straight line. A corner assembly consists of five similar posts, one at the corner of the fence and two on either side of it at six-foot intervals. The proper installation of a brace and corner post assembly is illustrated in Fig 128.

I must also confess at this point that if I do not use a board I am sometimes guilty of using a strand of barbed wire at the top of a wire fence. If you use plain wire fences without something on top, you will usually find that horses will start riding the fence and cause the wire to sag. I have found that a single strand of barbed wire 55 inches off the ground will stop this habit. I have never observed a horse that I thought had been injured on a barb that was placed this high and well maintained. A barb is especially useful if two fields of horses are separated by a single wire fence. There seems to be a natural antagonism, for instance, between barren mares in facing fields and they sometimes like to challenge each other. A barb tends to discourage this. I have seen horses that were injured either by kicking

Fig. 129. If an electric fence is being used with horses, the author recommends this type of installation in which plywood arms bearing the wire are extended two feet beyond the fence on each side.

through a fence while trying to get at other horses or that have fallen and got a foot caught. A barb tends to keep horses away from fence lines.

I have had some experience with electric fences but have never enjoyed too much success with them. For some reason, a horse doesn't seem to respect an electric fence the way a cow does. I think that in order to have any kind of an efficient electric fence you have to use two strands of wire. This wire is smooth and that in itself constitutes a danger point because horses have a tendency to get into smooth, fine wire and they can be severely injured.

If you are going to use an electric wire fence, the best way to do it is to use plywood braces extending out from the post as illustrated in Fig 129. These braces keep the horses farther apart due to their extensions on each side of the fence.

A multiflora fence also serves very well on a horse farm. Multiflora is a thorny bush of the rose family that grows to a height of eight feet and a width of approximately six feet. It takes from six to eight years to properly develop a multiflora fence. Livestock should be kept away from it while it is still growing and it should be properly cultivated during the first couple of years. When it attains full growth, a multiflora fence not only prevents horses from coming in contact with each other in adjoining fields, but it is also the only type of fence that I have never seen a horse challenge. Personally, I find it ideal and wish I had more of it.

In addition to being a good fence (Fig. 126), it is also a haven for wildlife and a natural windbreak for any type of livestock.

In constructing any kind of fence, it is a good idea to board up the corners, if that is at all convenient. Horses tend to congregate in right angle corners and if you have a mean yearling or mare in a field they will soon learn that the best place to get at another horse is in such a corner. If you do away with corners, you also do away with this type of thing.

A corner is also a good place to plant a nice shade tree. What I like to do is to go back about 16 feet from the corner on each side and run a board fence setup across the angle (Fig. 130). This is a large enough area for a nice-sized tree and if you do that you are killing two birds with one stone: eliminating a danger area and creating shade.

In fencing paddocks, I think there should be minimum 12-foot aisleway between paddocks for mares or yearlings and a minimum of 24 feet between paddocks for stallions. For the sake of the record, I should probably point out here the obvious fact that two stallions will fight if they get together. As to boarding a paddock, it is my experience that any paddock that will hold a mare will hold most studs. Therefore, a four-board

Fig. 130. This photograph indicates the manner in which a shade tree is fenced off in the corner of a field. The fence serves the dual purpose of eliminating a sharp corner and providing protection for the tree.

Fig. 131. The author stands beside a wooden pasture gate of the type he recommends. Wherever possible, gates should open inward and to the left as this one does.

paddock is usually enough for stallions, although some farm managers insist on five or six board paddocks six feet high. I do not believe this is necessary although I would not quarrel with anyone who built his stud paddocks this way. It sure is safe!

Pasture gates (Fig. 131) may either be purchased or built. The three basic types are aluminum, galvanized iron and wood. I prefer wooden gates but if you use this type you have to protect the top edge or horses will chew it. I cover the top edge with a five-eighths inch strip of metal. If aluminum gates are used, all sharp edges should be covered. If the terrain permits, all gates should swing inward and to the left.

In winding up this discussion of fencing, let me say that it is a good idea to keep a supply of boards and posts on hand. Not only will replacements be necessary from time to time, but a dried locust post will last longer and take a nail better than one that is green, while a fence board, although harder to nail, will take paint better if it has aged for a while.

As long as I am talking about construction, let me continue in that vein by discussing creeps for suckling foals.

A creep (Fig. 132) is an enclosure in which sucklings (foals nursing at their dam's side and not yet weaned) feed and to which the mothers of the foals are denied admission. Growing foals require more nutrition than is provided through nursing their dams and this is made available at all farms in the form of oats and/or supplementary feeds. A foal will often start eating from his mother's feed tub when he is as young as two weeks old and will almost always be doing so within a month after birth. Because the mother would consume most of the feed that you set aside for the foal unless she were prohibited in some manner, it is necessary to establish a method of feeding a foal by himself. When mare and foal are in a stall, this can be accomplished by tying the mare on one side of the stall and permitting the foal to feed on the other side. But when the weather grows warmer and the mares and their foals are turned out night and day, it becomes necessary to adopt another system. This is known as creep feeding.

At Meadowlands, our creeps were a uniform 32 feet long and 16 feet wide. Posts were set eight feet apart, five on the long side and three on the short side with the posts on the corners serving both sides. The posts extend 46 inches out of the ground and are topped on all sides by a hollow steel pipe two inches in diameter. This makes the overall height of the creep 48 inches. To keep the pipes attached to the tops of the posts, I used perforated metal plumber's tape which comes with a series of holes in it. This tape extends over the pipe and down the sides of the post. Lag screws are inserted in the metal tape to hold it in position and I have found this type of tape holds pipe to post better than anything else.

Fig. 132. A creep, shown here, is a device which permits foals to feed (by walking beneath the pipe rails) while denying access to the mares. A feed bunk, as described in the text, is placed inside the creep.

Of course, no matter how low you build your creep, you will always have the problem of a mare getting beneath it and eating with the foals. Certain mares would manage to do this if you lowered the creep height to 36 inches. About the only thing you can do in a case like this is to take the mare out of the field and put her and her foal in a paddock with a special type creep that only the foal can get into. For this purpose, I recommend a cattle type creep which has an adjustable board so that the width can be varied to permit entry to the foal while denying it to the mare.

Inside the standard creep are either one or two feed troughs or bunks. Each is 12 feet long, four feet wide and six inches deep. If two are being used, they are placed end to end within the creep and thus there is feeding space measuring 4x24 within an enclosure that is 16x32. The legs of the feed bunks consist of 4x4 posts at the corners and 2x6 rails on each side for rigidity. Foals usually don't chew very much on creep wood and if you are using a hard wood—oak is preferred—you will find that you will not have any problem in this respect.

I recommend a masonite material in the bottom of the bunk placed over the top of tongue and groove flooring. We use a small piece of quarter round in the corners to keep debris from collecting. This makes the bunk much more sanitary. In addition, we have a one-inch rubber plug in the bottom of the bunk so that it may be drained conveniently after a storm. The height of the feed bunk itself should be from 36 to 40 inches measured from the top edge of the bunk border to the ground.

At one end of the feed bunk, I like to run a partition the width of the bunk about six inches from the end. I split this in two by means of another partition running in the opposite direction and put salt in one half and a mineral mixture of some sort in the other half.

Creeps should be placed in that portion of any pasture field where the mares have a tendency to spend the most time. For some reason, mares will prefer to loaf in one general area of a field and if the creep is located in this area, the foals will visit it while their mothers are nearby. At some farms, a quantity of ear corn or hay is thrown around the perimeter of the creep area to attract the mares to it. I do not do this because it has always been my policy to bring the mares in once a day throughout the year and give them a separate feed, but where the mares are not otherwise fed after turnout time it is a good idea.

Now that we have our farm in shape, we come to the proposition of mating mare to stallion to produce the end product of any stock farm, the foal. For two reasons, I intend to treat the subject in a very general way without getting too technical and without trying to lay down any hard and fast rules.

One reason is that I will be writing about a very complicated subject that has been the topic of numerous technical books that can be referred to by any reader who is genuinely interested in the process of breeding horses. In this chapter, I would much rather keep my discussion on a non-technical level and thus make it as understandable as possible even though the reader has no knowledge whatsoever of a stock farm operation.

The other reason is that anybody who sets himself up as an authority by saying that "this is what a mare will do and this is what a mare will not do" is asking for trouble. I think it is safe to say that the only thing consistent about a brood mare is her inconsistency. Because of that, I am going to be very careful and am warning in advance, in the unlikely event that I fail to qualify myself somewhere along the line, that we are dealing in generalities and must consider the subject wholly in that manner. Breeding is an inexact science.

First of all, I think we should understand a little something about the endocrine system of the mare. Generally speaking, a mare will be receptive to a stallion every 18 days if she is not in foal. But there again, a qualification is in order. I have known mares that have gone months at a time without ever being in shape to take the stallion. And I am not writing here about the "liars," mares that are outwardly unwilling but inwardly willing and which I will discuss later. I am talking about mares that simply haven't reached a normal breeding condition. On the other hand, I have seen mares that would have taken the stallion any day for as long as two months. Is it becoming clearer now why I hesitate to lay down rules that govern brood mares?

The endocrine system is tied to the pituitary gland which relays the messages that sets the system in motion. Cut down to its bare essentials, it works like this: a follicle rises on one of the mare's two ovaries. At first it is small and hard, much like a pea, but during a period that ranges from three to seven days it grows larger and softer until it reaches the size of a hen's egg or even larger and finally ovulates or separates from the ovary. Within the follicle is contained the egg or ova. Upon ovulation, the egg passes down into the fallopian tube where a sperm from the male, if present, will fertilize it and create new life.

Meanwhile, there have been other indications that the mare is in condition to conceive. The cervix, or os, the entrance to the uterus or womb, grows larger and changes in color from a dull white to a pinkish red. The cervix opens up, the vagina leading to it becomes lubricated and the stallion enters through the vagina to the cervix. His sperm is deposited there and makes its way toward the fallopian tube and the egg. There are millions of sperm. Only one penetrates the egg. When this happens, conception takes place.

During this period, the mare herself usually, and I repeat "usually," shows outward symptoms of being receptive to the stallion. Instead of pinning her ears back and lashing at him as she would do if she were not in season, she pricks her ears and expresses interest in him. Her vulva relaxes and blinks and she raises her tail.

If all of these symptoms occur, if the timing is exactly right, if the sperm does not die before it reaches the egg, and if the egg is in position and ready to be impregnated when the sperm is swimming about searching for it, then conception will occur. In the absence of any of these factors, conception is unlikely to occur and the process will have to be repeated.

The normal mare comes in to the horse and remains in from three to seven days depending on the time of the year. In the early part of the breeding season, in February and March, the normal mare will remain in about seven days. Later in the season, along about June, when the weather grows real hot, a normal period may last as briefly as three days although this is uncommon. The normal mare having a seven-day period will ovulate on about the fifth day. If the mare does not get in foal from that breeding and if she is routinely normal, she will be back in again 18 days after she goes out of season which will be within about two days after ovulation. The process is then repeated until the mare either gets in foal or the end of the breeding season arrives.

In view of all this, it is obvious that it is important to the stock farm manager to know when his mares are in season and when they are not since he cannot breed them unless they are. In order to establish this, he "teases" the mares, that is he exposes them to the male of the species to which they will, the book says, respond if they are in season and ready to be bred.

The regular stallions, however, are not used to tease mares. For when a mare is not in season, she will lash out at the male and attempt to do bodily harm to him for the liberties he is trying to take. No valuable stallion could be exposed to this danger on a day-to-day basis. Therefore, the farm manager employs the services of what are known as "teasers." These are stallions that have no worth as breeding animals but which are among the most important horses on the farm. They can be Standardbreds or cold-blooded horses or even ponies. The teaser approaches the mare and from the symptoms she exhibits or fails to exhibit the man handling the teaser can report that a particular mare is either in season (she will accept the stallion) or out of season (she will not accept him).

A good teaser is difficult to find and extremely valuable to a stock farm. A top teaser is capable of handling as many as 100 mares a day and he will be just as charged up for the last one as he is for the first. Very few horses make good teasers. They either become too excited and too difficult to control or will tease a few mares satisfactorily and then begin to take little or no interest in their job when they discover they are not going to be the groom at any of the weddings they are arranging.

If a teaser is too rank and is continually charging at his mares, the mares will become timid in his presence and will resist him whether in season or not. If a teaser is otherwise good but has a bad habit of trying to bite the mare on the flank or elsewhere, he should be muzzled. It is also a good idea for a teaser to be controlled either by means of a chiffney bit or by a lead shank with the chain end running under the jaw.

Equally as important as the teaser himself is the man who is handling the teaser. This must be an experienced horseman, for not only must he be able to exercise control over the teaser but he must also know the mares and their habits. It seems that some men have a knack for this sort of thing and I have found that these are the ones who have great patience and are gentle with the mare as far as handling the teaser is concerned.

Fig. 133. Three methods of teasing mares are illustrated. At the upper left, the mare is being teased in a teasing chute; at the upper right in a stall and, opposite, in the field.

There are different methods of teasing mares (Fig. 133). For a long time we used a teasing bar at Meadowlands and since this is the most common method, I will review it briefly. The mare is led into a chute that is open on both ends and approximately 10 feet long and four feet high. The chute is double boarded because it will take some strong pounding from angry mares. The man handling the teaser steps back a safe distance from the chute while the mare is led in by an attendant. The mare is held in position in the chute and the teaser is led toward her. The teaser usually approaches at the mare's head and exchanges sounds with her. This will give the man handling the teaser an indication of whether it is necessary or worthwhile to proceed further. If the mare resists completely and starts kicking, it is a pretty good sign that she is not in season.

Nevertheless, this is not always sufficient since many mares indicate in the first few seconds or even minutes that they are definitely out but will then begin to relax under the constant, gentle pressure of a good teaser and subsequently show well. If it is questionable whether the mare is in, the teaser is permitted to nuzzle at her flanks and to approach gradually toward the rear. It is important, however, that the chute be kept between the teaser and the mare at all times. After a thorough session of this type, usually requiring a couple of minutes, the man handling the teaser is satisfied that the mare is either in or out and so notes on the report sheet he carries.

One of the weaknesses of this system is that it requires a great deal of time for the mares to be caught and led individually through the teasing chute. In addition, I have found that there are certain mares that will simply "hobby horse." That is, they will start jumping up and down in the chute as soon as they see the teaser whether they are in season or out. I came to the conclusion some time ago that this system by itself was not the best.

I now prefer to tease mares in their stalls. All stalls at Meadowlands had a grill front and it was possible for the teaser and mare to get their noses together without any danger of their becoming too familiar. I have found that mares will respond better in this manner and if they are in season they will come right up to the grill and exhibit obvious symptoms. Of course, if a mare has a foal at her side and indicates that she is not in season, you do not want to fool with her too long. She might accidentally kick the foal, although I can honestly say that we never had a foal injured in this manner at Meadowlands.

If there is a question about a mare that is being teased this way, we will take her out of the stall and try her in the teasing chute. If necessary, she will be twitched. A twitch is a stick about four feet long either rectangular in shape or round like a broomstick handle. The stick has a hole drilled through it about an inch from the top. A length of clothesline cord is hooped through the hole and tied. The loop is then placed over the mare's nose and twisted until it is tight by using the stick as a lever. A twitch will calm some mares down and result in their showing to the teaser when they would not ordinarily do so.

Some farm managers prefer to tease out in the pasture field, maintaining that this keeps things closer to nature and that mares will show better in these surroundings. My experience with this type of teasing has not been very successful. I have found that transient mares that are new to the system, or mares that are dead out and mean about it will charge the teaser and set up a fearful commotion that affects mares that normally might want to show. However, I also know that if you could work under such circumstances with a good teaser and eliminate the bad acting mares that cause the trouble that you could do a good job. It depends on how you are set up at your own farm as to whether this is a practical consideration. As I will explain in more detail later, I suggest teasing three times a week, every other day with Sunday off and using varying methods.

If all mares showed to the teaser when they were in, and were definitely out when they exhibited negative symptoms, the job of the stock farm manager would be a comparatively simple one. All it would consist of then would be acting as a booking agent and making a list of which mares were to be bred on what days. Unfortunately, this is not the case and very often a mare that is in tip-top breeding condition internally and who would accept the stallion readily if sent to the breeding shed will react violently and in a positively vicious manner toward the teaser. A little earlier I mentioned "liars" which is what we call this type of mare. They are said to be "lying to the teaser."

Some mares "lie" only occasionally or rarely. Others lie constantly and I know a few mares that have never shown anything to a teaser in their entire lives. Some mares will show to a certain teaser but not to another one. Others will show to another mare out in the field but not to a teaser. There are all kinds and they complicate the farm manager's job.

The reason that mares react this way is unknown. There is no question that some mares will not show because they have a foal at their side. In cases like this, the maternal instinct is stronger than the sexual instinct. Early weaning of the foals of such mares will often return them to a normal cycle and enable them to get in foal.

How can you tell if a mare is in season if she will not show to a teaser? The only surefire way is for the veterinarian to make

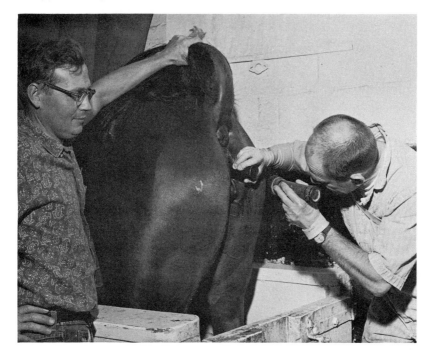

Fig. 134. Dr. Joseph Campbell is shown examining a mare by means of a plastic fiber speculum of the type the author recommends.

an internal examination. He can determine if the cervix is open and check for the presence of a ripe follicle. With both conditions being favorable, the mare has a very good chance of conceiving, when bred to the stallion, no matter what symptoms she is or is not showing to the teaser. The examination of the cervix is made by using a speculum. There are two types of speculums in popular use. One is the Caslick, the basic, stainless steel instrument that all veterinarians carry with them. The other type, and the one that I recommend, is a round tube made of plastic fiber. It is about 18 inches long and an inch and a half in diameter. Both types are inserted in the vagina and the cervix observed (Fig. 134). A flashlight may be employed to afford a better view.

When a mare is not in season, the cervix is a small, white, button-shaped affair that lies at the entrance to the uterus. But when the mare is in, the cervix expands, changes color and opens up affording the stallion's sperm free passage into the uterus. The appearance of the cervix of a mare that is in full season looks more like a large red rose than anything else. At the same time, the vagina of a mare that is in season will usually be well-lubricated and the evidence of this will be observed on the speculum when it is removed.

In using any kind of speculum, you must always bear in mind that maintenance of proper sanitary conditions is of the utmost importance. It is my opinion that improper use and/or sterilization of speculums is one of the primary causes of infection in mares. And, as we all know, infection is the surest way in the world to keep a mare from getting in foal.

When you are probing around in the vagina of a mare that is not in season, you must remember that nature did not intend that this be done. In the wild state, it could not happen because a mare that was not in season would not accept the stallion and thus no penetration of this type could be effected. But man, in his desire to improve on nature, has taken liberties with many of her laws and unless he takes great precautions he is likely to suffer as a result.

I make it a practice never to use a spec (all farm personnel call them by this name) on more than one mare before putting it in an autoclave and sterlizing it. There is a special paper envelope that can be purchased and after the spec is used it is inserted in this envelope and placed in the autoclave. The paper envelope has a purple line on it that indicates when the spec has been properly sterilized and is ready for use again. The paper is removed just before the spec is inserted in the mare and thus the greatest possible sanitary precautions are being taken.

In examining a mare by spec, the vulva is washed with paper towels dipped in a solution of warm water and viscogin, a disinfectant soap. The paper towels represent a slight additional cost but they aren't as expensive as cotton and do the job just as well. The spec itself should be liberally coated with KY jelly or some similiar lubricating agent. It is very easy to bruise a mare that is not in season and this jelly helps protect the mucosa of the vagina.

In checking a mare on the spec, the cervix is rated by means of a scoring system that ranges from one (dead out) to four (in full season). These notations are kept on record sheets and it is important to remember that some mares will be in full season without ever reaching a No. 4 stage. They don't quite achieve that red rose appearance, but they are just as breedable.

This is one of the reasons why records are so important on a stock farm. A manager who has access to good records can make wise decisions that will benefit the overall operation of the farm and result in a higher percentage of mares getting in foal. A manager who is "guessing" is a liability to his farm. I think a competent stock farm manager should get 80% of his mares in foal every year.

I will write more later about record keeping but for the time being I want to continue on the subject of mares that are not showing to the teaser and whose heat periods must be detected by other methods.

Just because you spec a mare and find her in season, doesn't necessarily mean that she is ready to conceive. For no mare can conceive without ovulation, the releasing of the egg to be impregnated by the male sperm. A mare may also be examined internally to determine her status with reference to this particular factor.

A veterinarian makes this examination by inserting his hand into the rectum and palpating each of the two ovaries in turn. If there are no follicles developing on either ovary, the mare just isn't going to conceive no matter what she is showing to the horse or on the speculum.

This type of mare is one of the banes of a farm manager's existence. A mare will come in to the horse, and show beautifully on the spec but an examination of the ovaries will indicate an absence of follicular activity. You can breed this mare until the cows come home and never get her in foal.

This situation may be observed in any mare at any time of the year but it is most pronounced early in the season and with maiden mares. These mares will come in to the horse along about the start of the breeding season and will show to the teaser for as long as six to eight weeks. I will offer a small word of advice concerning them: Forget about them. It is a waste of your time and the stallion's sperm to breed them. They will eventually go out of season and will then come back in normally and usually get right in foal.

Maiden mares, incidentally, are said to be problem mares on stock farms but I cannot say that this is true. I have observed that aside from the habit I have just discussed and which, actually, is confined to a relatively small percentage, maidens are good breeders and get in foal quite easily. The thing about maiden mares is to go a little easy with them in teasing and in introducing them to the other aspects of the farm routine. If you don't get them upset or excited most of them will fall right into the pattern and not cause much trouble at all. They should also be given a little better barn care.

Now let me go back and comment at greater length on the palpation of ovaries which has developed into something of a science on certain farms in recent years. I have participated in palpation programs and it is my observation that it is an extremely useful tool when taken in conjunction with all the other factors that are involved in breeding.

It is not a panacea for breeding troubles in the sense that it provides absolute assurance that a mare will get in foal when properly bred off a palpation program. Any mare that comes in to the horse and goes through a normal five to seven-day cycle and is bred on the third and fifth days has just as much chance of getting in foal as one that is palpated and bred only once during the same period. The big advantage of a properly-managed palpation program is not that it assures you of getting more mares in foal, but rather that it keeps mares out of the breeding shed that don't belong there and thus saves a farm manager a lot of time and effort. In addition, it permits a manager to exercise a little discretion as to which mare will be bred on which day.

A mare that is going to be in season for seven days will usually ovulate about the fifth day since a normal mare will remain in season for about two days after she ovulates. A good veterinarian can palpate a ripe follicle and usually tell within a range of 24 hours when the follicle is going to rupture. I like to breed mares as close to ovulation as possible. I would prefer to do it within six hours of ovulation but that obviously cannot be arranged conveniently.

The experts seem to agree that the closer a mare is bred to ovulation the better her chances of conception are. However, I have known of mares that got in foal off a breeding that took place six days prior to ovulation. I would think that breeding 48 hours ahead of ovulation would be satisfactory in most instances and that breeding within 24 hours would be optimum considering that it is difficult to figure it closer than that. Some follicles will go off quicker than the veterinarian expects while others will hang on longer. My records show that once a mare has ovulated it doesn't do much good to breed her although I do know of isolated instances in which such mares have conceived.

Now let me go back and start to tie all this in chronologically. We are going to start our breeding season on or about February 15th and be pretty well finished by July first, although a few mares will be bred later than that. The reason we do not start breeding until February 15th is that the gestation period for a brood mare is about 11 months—I figure it at 11 months and three days for the average mare—and we do not want a foal to arrive prior to January first. Since the universal birthday for all horses is the first day of the year, a foal that arrived the last week of December would be a year old by the calendar when he was actually only a few days old.

The breeding season used to end the last week of June and even a little earlier than that on some farms. But in recent years there has been a tendency to breed on into July in an effort to get as many mares as possible in foal. The only thing wrong with this is that the resulting foals are quite a bit younger than the majority born in that particular year and some of them will be called on to race as 2-year-olds when they are not even that old by calendar count. It is more natural for horses to breed in the warmer months, since in the wild state nature would see to it that mares did not foal in the heart of winter when there would be little likelihood of the foal surviving. We have actually changed nature's calendar by breeding in February and March which is one of the reasons why the bulk of barren mares are not prime breeding candidates until the month of April or later.

If I had my way, all mares would be bred in May and June with all foals arriving in April and May. But the commercial aspects of the present-day breeding picture mitigate against holding off the breeding program that long. Owners seem to think that there is a great advantage in having early foals—those that arrive in January and February—so there is constant pressure on the farm manager to breed early and often. As far as I am concerned, the May foal is just as good as the January foal and I recall from my own experience at Meadowlands that Barbara Direct was bred to Adios the first week of July to produce the fastest 2-year-old of all time, Bullet Hanover, p, 2, 1:57, who arrived on June 7th.

On January first all the mares on the farm are in barns, barren mares as well as mares due to foal. On some farms, barren mares—and even late foaling mares in some isolated instances —are out all year round with only a shed of some type for shelter. There is nothing wrong with this but since I do not follow the practice at Meadowlands I am not going to consider it a part of the program that I am discussing.

Our foaling mares have been gathered together in barns according to their due dates. If we assume that the foaling barn has 24 stalls, the first 24 mares due to foal are quartered in this barn. As they foal, they are moved to another barn when their foal is about two weeks old and their place is taken by the mare whose foaling date is next closest.

In moving mares into the foaling barn, it is a good idea not only to check the outward symptoms of approaching birth but also to have a record of the mare's foaling history from previous years. Most mares follow the same pattern year after year. Some foal earlier than the projected due date and some foal later. It is a good idea to move mares who have an early foaling history into the foaling barn a little sooner than the calendar might call for.

Roughly speaking, a normal foal can arrive two weeks early or two weeks late. Three weeks on either side of the due date is uncommon but not at all unheard of. Four weeks on either side is a rarity, although I have known mares that carried their foal for more than a year.

I do not plan to devote a great deal of space to the actual foaling procedure but this appears to be as good a place as any to discuss a few basic premises which I think are worth mentioning. When a brood mare foals, it represents the culmination of all the work and effort on a stock farm and thus occupies a position of unique prominence. If a mare foals normally, she will not require help from anyone. If she needs help, she needs it in a hurry and from a skilled veterinarian. That is why the farm manager should always have a phone number that will enable him to locate his veterinarian on very short notice. The difference of a few minutes is often the difference between a live foal and a dead one when a difficult delivery is involved.

The first sign of approaching parturition is usually a filling of the udder as nature begins to make her preparations for the arrival of the foal. This is known as "making bag" and usually begins about three weeks before foaling. About two weeks before foaling, the muscles on each side and below the tailhead start to relax and this becomes quite pronounced just prior to foaling. From 12 to 72 hours before foaling, the normal mare "waxes up," that is, a small quantity of milk is visible on the end of each teat. But, as in all cases involving brood mares, the signs sometimes fail or are not as clear as the "book" says they should be.

For instance, an occasional mare will foal without making any bag at all. This is rare but I have seen it happen and when it does it usually involves a maiden mare. I have also seen mares that will actually milk for several days prior to foaling. The point I am making is that a farm manager should never count on absolute signs or the lack of them.

A mare should be permitted to foal in a large, roomy stall. If she is in a small stall, it is possible that she might lie down against a wall or in a corner and not have sufficient room to foal properly. Mares usually foal while lying on their side.

A few hours prior to foaling, a normal mare will have a fully distended udder with wax on the end of the teats, will be restless, sweating and possibly switching her tail, turning her head back toward her flanks and urinating frequently. In the last hour, she will be up and down in the stall a number of times. At this stage, the mare should be left alone although observed carefully from a comparative distance.

The foal arrives in a thin membrane sack called the placenta which is actually the lining of the uterus. In a normal delivery, the front feet appear first, heels down, with the head positioned between them and a little farther back. If the foal is not presented in this position, the veterinarian should be summoned immediately. Often, it is simply a case of one leg being tucked back, a problem that can be handled in relatively routine fashion by an experienced veterinarian. On some occasions, the delivery is much more complicated but I do not believe that any good purpose would be served by my discussing such situations here. Let me just say that it is nothing for an amateur to become involved with.

The foal almost always breaks through the surrounding membrane at the moment of birth. But if it should fail to do so for some reason, the membrane should be pulled away from around the face at the start of the birth process to avoid the possibility of drowning. A normal mare retains a portion of the placenta after birth but usually casts it off within three hours after foaling. If she has not "cleaned" (the expression used to describe the casting off of the remnants of the placenta) within that time a veterinarian should be called. Infection can develop if a mare fails to "clean" properly.

At birth, the foal is still joined to the placenta by the umbilical cord which normally separates by itself shortly thereafter. If the cord does not separate at birth, it should not be cut for several minutes after foaling in order that the blood in the afterbirth may be transferred completely to the foal. After the cord is separated, the navel is treated with a strong iodine solution.

A normal foal should stand and nurse within two hours after birth. Some foals will have a little trouble finding the milk supply at first and may be guided to it. If a foal has not nursed within that period but appears normal in every other respect, it should be fed a quantity of its mother's milk via syringe. If it is normal, it will usually begin nursing on its own within the next half hour. If it does not or if it appears abnormal in any respect, the veterinarian should be called.

The first milk that a mare gives after a foal is born is known as colostrum. It contains antibodies, is high in protein content, rich in Vitamin A and contains a natural purgative. It is vital that the foal receive it. The colostrum usually lasts for about 36 hours. This, again, is nature's way of providing something a little special to help during the first critical days of life.

Occasionally, you will run across a "jaundice" foal. This is a condition that is somewhat, although not exactly, comparable to the RH factor in humans. The foal's blood type is such that his blood cells are destroyed when he ingests the mare's colostrum. The symptoms are general weakness and usually a yellowish tinge around the eyes and gums. It is usually fatal unless diagnosed promptly.

The thing to do with a jaundice foal is to muzzle him so that he cannot ingest the colostrum. He should not be permitted to nurse the mare for three days unless a veterinarian checks the mare's milk earlier than that and advises that the colostrum is gone and that it is safe for the foal to begin nursing. If a mare is known to have had a previous jaundice foal, it is a good idea to muzzle the foal at birth. Blood types of stallion and mare may be matched to determine if a jaundice foal may be expected, although this is not always practical or possible. I am sure that a number of foals are lost each year because there is a lack of awareness of how to cope with the situation.

For some reason, most mares foal at night and the most popular hours are from 10 p.m. to two a.m. That is why it is important to have a night watchman if any large number of mares is involved. Usually the night watchman's duty is just that; to watch. His main job is to ascertain whether the mare is having a normal delivery and, if not, to call the veterinarian promptly. His other duties are routine and in conjunction with the foaling process include cleaning the stall out thoroughly and washing the mare's udder immediately after birth.

The morning after they are born foals are routinely given a warm water enema to which soap is added, three cc's of combiotic (penicillin and streptomycin) and a tetanus anti-toxin shot.

Occasionally, a stock farm manager will wind up with an orphan foal and will have to raise it "on the bottle." I dislike having to do this because it is quite a nuisance and I will try to get the foal on another mare if I possibly can. Nurse mares may be rented for this purpose but if a foster mother is to become involved, it is much more likely that it will be one on your own farm that has lost her foal. The ideal type is the mare that has just lost her own foal at birth and is anxious to have one. In a case like this, I have even taken the placenta that came with the lost foal and actually wrapped it around the orphan foal for whom I am trying to find a mother. I am certain that mares are guided basically by smell and the placenta of her own foal wrapped around the orphan will usually convince her that it is her own. Normally, of course, a mare will not permit any foal except her own to nurse her although, as in everything else, there are exceptions.

If I do not have a nurse mare and cannot acquire one, I will, of course, raise the orphan by hand. For a new-born foal, I prepare a basic formula made up of 20 ounces of cow's milk, 12 ounces of lime water and two ounces of white granulated sugar. For the first few days, this formula is fed at the rate of four ounces per feed every four hours around the clock. The amount of formula per feeding is increased gradually and after three days the foal is usually up to eight ounces. Eventually, a normal, healthy foal will get up to a quart of formula, or 32 ounces, at a single feed but by this time the number of feedings has been cut back to three a day. A foal will go on like this for perhaps two and a half months until he is on a substantial enough grain diet to sustain him. Strangely, orphan foals are more difficult to get established on a grain diet and lot of special care and attention is required. These foals also require adequate amounts of vitamins and it is advisable to discuss the matter with your veterinarian and follow his advice.

Now let me get back to the preparations for the breeding season which include the establishment of a separate chart (Fig. 135) for each mare. Space is provided on this chart for a separate entry for each day of the breeding season. The chart is in notebook form and I either carry it with me or have it at my fingertips in the office. During the breeding season, it is the farm manager's "bible." I always take it home with me at night because I get a lot of calls from anxious owners and by referring to the notebook I am able to advise them of the exact status of their mares.

On this chart, I enter a symbol when the mare shows to the horse and indicate how long she stayed in season and when she was bred or impregnated. I also have symbols that indicate whether she actually showed to the horse or was picked up on a spec examination or by some other means. If she is a spec mare, the code number from one to four indicating the condition of the cervix with respect to breeding potential is entered. By the same token, if the mare's ovaries are being palpated, a symbol is used to indicate the condition of the follicle. An S.H.R. rating indicates that the mare has a small hard follicle on the right ovary and is some time off from ovulation. An L.S.L. rating indicates that she has a large, soft follicle, is about to ovulate off the left ovary and thus is a prime candidate to be bred that day.

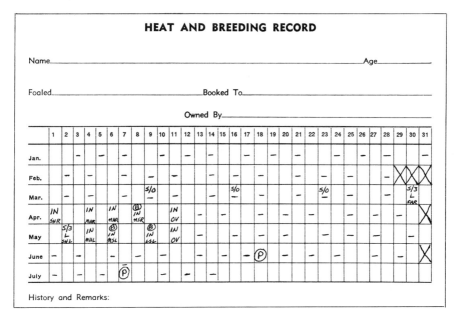

Fig. 135. Good record keeping is essential to the successful operation of any stock farm. Here is one type of record-keeping form that is used to chronicle the day-to-day activity of a brood mare during the breeding season. The mare is teased each Monday, Wednesday and Friday beginning the first of the year and a dash (−) is used to indicate that she is not showing to the horse. This mare did not show through January, February and most of March. The speculum was used on March 9th, 16th and 23rd to determine whether she might be in season even though she was not showing to the horse but she was not in as indicated by the s/o symbol on those days. The mare showed a little (L) to the horse on March 30th and was just in on the spec (S/3) on that day. She was examined rectally and found to have a small, hard follicle on the right ovary (shr). She showed to the horse (IN) on April 1st and the follicle progressed from medium hard (April 4th and 6th) to medium soft on April 8th. She was bred on the 8th, a Friday. She was still in season but had ovulated on the following Monday and showed out on Wednesday. She was teased thrice weekly thereafter and showed signs of coming back in season on May 2nd. She showed in slightly (S/3) on that day and had a small hard follicle on the left ovary. The mare showed to the horse on May 4th and was bred on Friday, May 6th when the follicle reached the medium soft stage. On the following Monday, the mare was still in, the follicle was large and soft and she was bred again. She had ovulated on May 11th and was out to the teaser on the 13th. She did not come back thereafter and was examined for pregnancy and was found in foal on June 18th. The pregnancy was re-checked and confirmed on July seventh. She was teased through July 14th, the end of the breeding season.

Other farms use a similar system but set it up in chart form with a separate sheet set aside for each stallion. All the breeding season dates are included on the chart and the mares that are booked to that stallion are listed alphabetically. The chart is fastened to the wall in such a manner that a clerk or the manager may stand in front of it and make the proper entries each day. In using this system, it is customary for the condition of the mare to be indicated on a particular date by using a standard pencil eraser which is rubbed against a colored stamp pad and the proper symbol entered on the date line. A blue mark indicates that the mare is in season but that she is not yet in breeding condition which will be indicated by a red mark at the proper time. In this manner, the entire season for a particular mare stretches across one line of a chart and may be observed in its entirety.

At some farms, barren mares are teased throughout the year but I do not advocate teasing them in the winter months prior to the start of the breeding season. If I notice them horsing in the field or something like that, I will make a note on my chart but otherwise I let them go until about January 15th, a month prior to the start of the breeding season. I think mares tend to become antagonistic if they are teased constantly and I like to give them a breather. If I have a problem mare, I will have the veterinarian work on her in the fall and then let her go until mid-January.

At this time of year, I also like to collect all my "problem" mares in one barn. These are all barren mares, of course, because if they were in foal they wouldn't be problem mares. They include mares that don't show to the teaser, mares that have been infected and mares that haven't got in foal for one reason or another for two consecutive years. In this manner, I am able to concentrate my efforts on these mares and do little extra things for them such as providing the most effective teasing horse for that barn. If the teaser is quartered in the same barn, as is often the case, it is a good idea to switch the mares into different stalls from time to time putting the mare that shows the least or the one that you are especially watchful for in the stall next to or across from the teaser. Constant exposure to a teaser in this manner will cause some mares to let down and show.

With the mares properly barned, routine teasing is begun. As I mentioned earlier, we tease three days a week, Monday, Wednesday and Friday. I do not think it is necessary to tease more often than that unless you are concerned with a specific mare that has been giving you trouble. It is a rare mare indeed that will come in on Saturday and be out by Monday, which is the next teasing day and the longest period during which mares are not teased.

When a mare shows in to the horse on Monday morning—for our purposes we will tease in the morning and breed right after lunch—the fact is noted on her chart. The teasing man is consulted as to whether he thinks she will go over until Wednesday and if she will I usually let her go. I do not think it is necessary to breed a mare prior to the third day she is in season and with most mares and you can safely wait until the fourth day.

In actual practice, I will usually breed the mare on her third day and back on her fifth day. If she is normal, she should go out within two days thereafter. Of course, if I am checking this mare's ovaries I can feel safer about letting her go to the fourth or fifth day without being bred on the third day when I know that the follicle is not going to rupture before then. On many occasions, a mare will be in normally as long as ten days, especially during the early weeks of the breeding season, and if I am following her by ovarian palpation I may not breed her until the ninth day.

After a mare has been bred and gone out of season, I will usually let her go for about 10 days before I begin teasing her again. There is little likelihood that she will be back in sooner than that and if she does come in it is usually because her hormone balance is upset in some way and she would not be a good candidate to get in foal anyway. If she did, she is the type that might very likely have twins.

When I start teasing this mare again, I am especially watchful of her—or I instruct the teasing man to be—at about 18 days after she went out. This is when a normal mare will come back if she is not in foal and it is helpful if the man who is teasing the mare knows this. There is one thing you must be careful about with mares that are on the 18-day cycle. Because of the nature of the endocrine system, some mares that are in foal will "flash" to the teaser at about this time and only an expert can detect that she is "flashing" (indicating symptoms of horsing but not actually being in season) and not actually showing. Of course, if you brought such a mare to the breeding shed, you would soon find out that she was not horsing. She would clean house. This is where speculum and ovarian examinations come in handy.

And here is one other little note that I will leave with you in passing. There actually are mares that will show to the teaser and will take the stallion when they are in foal. Unless you check with a spec or by reaching a plastic-gloved hand into the vagina and feeling the cervix to determine whether it is open or closed you could actually breed this mare. The act of penetration by the stallion could open the seal on the cervix and cause the mare to abort. However, I have known mares that have been bred when they were in foal and which later delivered a normal foal. There is no question either that this can be an inherited trait. Very few mares ever do this but two that I know are the mother-daughter combination of Norette Hanover and Barbara Jones.

If a mare does not show back to the teaser for about 40 days after she went out of season, she may be examined for pregnancy. This may be done through a laboratory test of the mare's blood but the quickest and most convenient way is for her to be examined by a skilled veterinarian. The veterinarian reaches his hand into the rectum and palpates the horns of the uterus. If the mare is in foal, there will be a bulge ranging in size at this stage from that of a lime to an orange. A good rule of thumb is that a young or maiden mare, those that generally have more tone to the uterus, may be examined on the 38th day and an older mare or a foaling mare on the 44th day after being bred. Pregnancies may be diagnosed in either horn and an important thing to remember—and something that even some young veterinarians do not know—is that a pregnancy can occur in the bifurcation which is where the horns of the uterus come together. That area should be palpated as well as the horns.

A skilled veterinarian can pick up a mare in foal as early as 30 days and there are vets who make a positive diagnosis at that time. I feel, however, that it is safer to wait for 40 days on the average as I have already explained. Another thing about examining mares for pregnancy is that there are some that have natural deviations in the shape of one of the horns that will make the vet think the mare is in foal unless he is familiar with her. Every farm will have one or more mares like this and it is a good idea to make a note to that effect and advise the veterinarian of it when he makes his examination.

Some mares have a history of aborting fairly early in term and in known cases, of this type, I give the mare a series of Progesterone (pregnant mare serum) shots a month apart until 60 days before her due date, as an aid in holding the foal. I know mares that could not carry a foal full term under any circumstances without this artificial assistance. Progesterone should be administered only under the direction of a veterinarian.

If the mare proves to be in foal, she should continue to be teased about twice a week to guard against the possibility of an early abortion going undetected. If possible, I would like to have her re-checked to confirm the pregnancy at 60 days. Early abortion mares are occasionally picked up in this manner.

That takes care of the mare that proves in foal, but that is not the one that worries farm managers. The ones that bother us are the ones the veterinarian palpates thoroughly without finding any evidence to indicate they are in foal. This type is the "liar" and the trouble mare because it is presumed that if she is not in foal she must have horsed sometime during the intervening period and went undetected. However, this is not always true because I know mares that have been followed religiously both by spec and ovarian examination at twice weekly intervals from the time they went out of season after they were bred until they had 40 days on them and never once detected any sign of their being in season or even close to it. Therefore, it is my opinion that certain mares do not get in foal but think they are and conduct themselves like pregnant mares in every respect. These are what the veterinarians call spurious or false conceptions. For years this was thought to be nothing more than an excuse used by vets and farm managers to explain a mare they failed to catch horsing. But my experience in following them closely indicates that it does happen.

This is interesting, but of no help in solving our basic problem of getting this mare in foal. She was bred on February 24th, went out on the 26th and was examined and found barren on April 7th. It is still fairly early in the season, but we have to make a fresh start and we don't want to lose any time.

The first thing to do when the vet says "barren," is to examine the mare on the spec. I cannot count the number of times I have done this and found the mare to be in full bloom after having showed beautifully to the teaser six weeks earlier and having tried to kick him out of the county when she was tried 15 minutes before her pregnancy examination. Don't ask me what makes mares act this way. If I knew, I would have the game licked because I would never let it happen. But it does occur time and time again and you grow accustomed to it after a while, although you never learn to accept it cheerfully.

If the mare is in season on spec exam, the veterinarian can check the ovaries and if she has a prime follicle, all is well and good. You take her back to the shed and breed her. But if the mare shows out to the spec with the classic small, white, button-like and obviously sealed cervix, you have to think again.

Incidentally, you will notice here that I didn't note this mare's ovaries to determine their condition, although the vet probably went over them routinely before removing his hand while making the pregnancy examination. The reason we don't pay too much attention unless the mare is in on the spec is that follicles will occasionally appear, mature and even rupture when mares are in foal, although this is not normally the case. So this is not always a sure sign that the mare is ready to be bred. And while I am on that subject, let me say that a really experienced veterinarian not only can examine the ovaries and the horns of the uterus, but he can also reach down and feel the cervix and tell to a remarkable degree of accuracy whether it is closed or open. I know that this is done routinely at Hanover Shoe Farms by Dr. Garner Greenhoff, one of the country's leading veterinarians, who is so accurate that the speculum is rarely employed and the danger of infection therefrom practically eliminated. But a man has to be a real expert to make an absolute diagnosis of this type.

The first thing I do after finding my mare barren and not in season is to put her down for a pregnancy re-check from five to seven days later. On occasion, the swelling in the horn will not be of sufficient size for even an experienced vet to pick it up at 40 days. But at 45 to 50 days there should be no trouble and if she is still barren at 50 you can figure that she is really barren about 999 times out a thousand.

After my mare checks out barren on the second examination, I continue to tease her for a few more days and then somewhere between her 50th and 60th day—between April 17th and April

27th in this case—I will try to bring her in season artificially. There are shots that can be given mares to accomplish this purpose, but I prefer to use the old reliable saline douche. A mare will usually come in season from three to seven days after being salined.

Saline should be administered by a veterinarian. Usually, he adds a small quantity of antibiotics to 500 cc's of physiological salt solution which is gravity-fed from a bottle through a pipette into the uterus. This produces an irritation which more often than not starts a heat cycle in the mare. Sometimes this cycle is an abnormal one, but, if so, it is usually followed by a normal one soon thereafter. The manner in which saline works on the endocrine system is still not completely understood.

If a mare does not respond to a saline treatment within 10 days, I will give her another one. I have had some mares that have taken as many as three saline treatments before they came in.

Although a saline douche is not technically a hormone treatment, it falls in the general category and this might be a good place to discuss hormones and my feeling toward them. Generally speaking, I am opposed to giving mares a lot of hormone shots. I think that if you adopt this kind of a program on a routine basis that you can do a great deal of harm by upsetting the mare's endocrine system. I have seen mares get completely out of whack through the promiscuous use of hormones.

In this respect, I am writing specifically about follicle stimulating hormones (FSH) and such things. FSH is used to produce a follicle on a mare that is showing good to the horse but that has no ovarian activity. I have never had any luck with FSH and abandoned it long ago.

I do use Progesterone, as I have already explained, on mares that have shown a tendency to abort early in term, but I do not use it to knock mares out of season. When a mare horses for a month or six weeks in a row, some farm managers like to knock them out with Progesterone. I do not think this is a good idea and don't do it. Actually, even those mares that horse for long periods will eventually go out and come back normally. I think these long periods of horsing that some mares go through early in the year is nothing more than nature's way of keeping them from being bred until the weather changes for the better. There is nothing like a spell of good hot weather and good green grass to tone a mare up and get her endocrine system operating properly.

There is one hormone that I have used with success and which I recommend for those following an ovarian palpation program. This is Chorionic Gonodatrophin. It is a lutenizing hormone and it will encourage the release of a hanging follicle. Through experience, I have learned that one of the most common things that a brood mare will do is to go through an absolutely normal heat cycle except that she does not release her follicle. The follicle becomes large and thin and gives every indication that it will rupture. But it does not. In cases like this, I have found that a shot of Chorionic Gonodatrophin will almost always cause the follicle to rupture. I have found also that it is the same mare that will do the same thing the next time around. In other words, this is her definite pattern which is unnatural and which can be helped by giving her a hormone shot. Incidentally, a lutenizing shot should never be given until a follicle has reached full growth and is actually hanging and ready to release.

Although the condition is not technically the same, it ties in with another type of mare that has a somewhat similar problem in that she is not confluent. A mare is confluent when the growth and development of the follicle coincides with the action of the cervix as it expands and opens indicating the peak efficiency of the endocrine system.

I have found that some mares do not coincide and thus are not confluent. For instance, when the follicle is about to rupture, the cervix is barely open and the mare will just about take the horse and no more. On the other side of the coin, the cervix will be in peak condition but the follicle will be several days off. The best you can do with mares like this is to breed them when the cervix is right and hope for the best.

There is one other interesting thing that ties in with ovarian activity and which I ought to mention. That is the fact that mares will frequently raise two follicles on the same ovary or one on each ovary during a single heat period. When we first started palpating mares, I was very careful about breeding this type because I was afraid of getting twins. I would usually let the first follicle pop off and try to breed on the second one. But

I found that in too many instances either the second follicle would not mature or the mare would go out of season before it did.

Later that same season, when we were getting to the time of the year when it was then or never for getting a mare in foal, I bred these mares rather promiscuously. To my surprise, I found that I didn't get any twins. From that time on, I have not been too concerned with double follicles, although if they are about the same size and both are obviously going to pop within 24 hours of each other, I will let the first one go before breeding the mare.

There was a study made a few years ago in which about 50 twin follicle mares were bred and checked closely thereafter. Twenty-two of these mares were found pregnant and each produced a single foal. Twenty-seven failed to get in foal and were rebred. One mare had twins. So I would say that if only one of 50 twin follicle mares is going to have twins, it is better to breed all of them and take your chances than to let them go. Incidentally, in that same study two other mares that were bred off a single follicle produced twins the following year. Apparently the single follicle contained two eggs and both were impregnated.

Another thing that I like to do to keep my mares in good breeding condition is to suture them (Fig. 136). I am a strong advocate of suturing because it not only guards against infection but it also prevents a certain amount of air irritation of the vaginal tract and cervix. Suturing is the sewing together of the lips of the vulva for approximately two-thirds of its length from the top down.

The anatomical makeup of a mare is such that it is a very simple matter for her to contaminate the vaginal tract when she defects. This is especially true of a mare whose vulva tips forward naturally or assumes that attitude as she grows older and which is a common occurrence. In selecting yearling fillies, I think it is a good idea to lift the tail and take a look at the tilt of the vulva. I wouldn't go so far as to say that a filly should be rejected on this account, but she is a better breeding proposition if the vulva runs straight up and down.

Naturally, mares that have been sutured constitute a problem in the breeding shed since a tight suture renders it difficult for

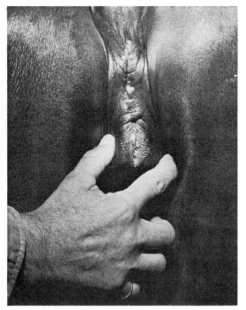

Fig. 136. This is an example of a tight suture in which all except the lower two inches of a mare's vulva is sewed up. This mare's vulva is inclined at such an angle that she could easily become infected if she were not sutured.

the stallion to enter the mare without tearing the suture. The ideal thing, of course, is to impregnate such mares instead of putting the stallion on them, but this cannot always be done. If this is not possible, a retention stitch should be taken at the top of the suture to hold it in place while the mare is being bred. This stitch is taken with umbilical tape using a curved needle and is removed immediately after breeding.

Foaling mares are teased along with all other mares beginning on the eighth day after they have foaled. All mares have what is commonly called a 9-day or foal heat period. They will come in to the stallion or can be picked up via spec or ovarian exam somewhere between the 9th and 13th day after they foal. Because they have foaled so recently and the maternal instinct is so strong at this stage, some mares will not show to the teaser. But 99 out of 100 will have a foal heat period and can be bred.

It used to be that these mares were bred routinely on the 9th day after foaling but I have found that ovarian palpation indicates that many of these mares are much better on the 12th day than the ninth. The trouble with waiting for the 12th day without an accompanying ovarian palpation program is that quite a few will ovulate prior to that. Therefore, if you are not checking ovaries, it is best to breed on the 9th or 10th day in accordance with how the mare is showing to the teaser and/or on the spec.

There is some controversy surrounding the advisability of breeding a mare in her foal heat period. Many of the old timers felt that it was much better to let mares go during this period and catch them 18 to 21 days later or 27 to 30 days after foaling. But in this day and age of high-powered commercial breeding it is the rare farm manager who will intentionally pass the foal heat period unless the mare was injured in foaling or is otherwise incapacitated.

It has been my experience that a good program will result in three out of eight mares becoming pregnant from foal heat breeding. This is a 37.5% figure and is much too high to be laughed off. This percentage varies with the season of the year from a low of one out of four (25%) early in the season to one out of two (50%) that foal in May and June. I do not think the foal heat should be passed without breeding unless there is a good reason for passing the mare. We examine the placentas (the membrane in which the foal is enclosed prior to birth) for tears and also weigh them routinely. If they are over 14 pounds the mare is passed. A heavy placenta indicates infection. Cervical bruises, caused by foaling and retained placentas, are the common causes of passing a mare in her foal heat period.

So far I have talked about teasing mares and getting them in foal while by-passing the actual breeding operation. I did that intentionally in order to provide continuity but now it is time to go back and pick things up at the breeding shed.

The mare is usually brought to the breeding shed without her foal. However, if I am dealing with a highly nervous mare who misses her foal, I will bring it along and have a man hold the foal in one corner of the shed where the mare can see it.

When the mare is led in, she is placed in a chute approximately eight feet long and three feet wide. The back wall of the shed serves as one side of the chute. There is a small door at the back end of the chute which is closed behind the mare after she enters. This door is not high enough to interfere with the next process which consists of wrapping the mare's tail with a derby bandage or gauze and washing her off. The vulva and surrounding area are washed with Viscogen and water using paper towels. In most cases, some KY lubricating jelly is applied to the external genitilia, also with a paper towel. This is especially necessary with maiden mares and mares that are sutured. As I said earlier, a retention stitch is taken if it is a sutured mare that is being bred.

After the mare is prepared, I like to tease her briefly in the chute as a last minute check to confirm all other examinations and observations and to get the mare accustomed to the idea that she is about to be bred. I use a Shetland pony for this purpose most of the time. In some cases, I will put a shield over the hind quarters of the mare and actually let the teaser mount her. I do this with highly nervous mares, usually maidens, who act as though they might resent the stallion even though they are fit for breeding. After a teaser mounts a mare once or twice in this fashion, she will usually lose her fear.

After the mare has been teased, she is led out of the chute and is placed so that she is facing the side of it (Fig. 137). The attendant stands inside the chute and thus is provided a measure of protection in the event the mare starts acting up. I prefer to use breeding hobbles on all mares routinely. They don't hurt a mare and represent a safety factor. Most mares don't need them but you do get the odd mare that will kick a stud even when she is in full season and it just isn't worth the risk. A stud with a broken leg is a big minus for a breeding farm. Mares in the breeding shed wear a halter with a loose chain under the jaw. A shank is attached to the halter ring and the attendant holds it. This provides additional control if needed.

I only twitch mares when they indicate that additional control might be required. If I am going to use a twitch, I will not put it on until the stallion is ready to mount. There is no sense in having a mare stand around with an uncomfortable twitch on when you don't need it. It is a good idea to get the tail out of the way in the breeding shed and I prefer to use a clothesline rope, tying one end around the tail, near the base, and the other around the right hand side of the breast strap of the hobbles.

With the mare in this position, the stallion is led into the shed. He knows what he is there for and he is usually ready. Some horses are gentle breeders and may be controlled in the breeding shed with nothing more than a lead shank. Others are more vigorous and require greater control. I use a chiffney bit on some stallions and a chain under the jaw of others, I would rather

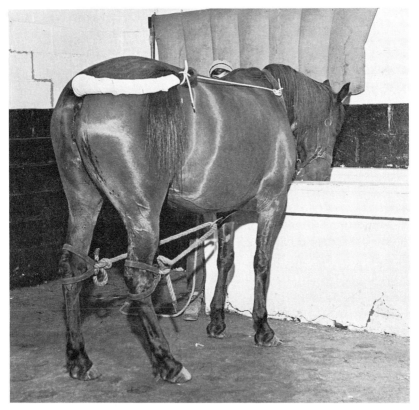

Fig. 137. The mare in this photograph has been properly prepared and positioned for breeding. She is hobbled, her tail is bandaged, tied and pulled to the side; she wears an extra halter with a chin chain and she stands facing the teasing chute.

use a chain under the jaw than over the nose and a bit rather than any kind of chain.

When the stallion indicates he is ready to breed, he is washed off with a Viscogen powder and warm water solution and rinsed with clear water. Cotton is used for this purpose. If a breeding bag is being used, it is put on at this time and a small amount of lubricant jelly is applied to the outside of the bag.

The stallion is then led up to the mare. Some stallions are eager and aggressive and complete the sexual act almost at once. Others, whose libido is not as high, are more deliberate and will want to spend some time acting as their own teaser before they breed. Still others will mount the mare several times before completing the act.

It is advantageous, of course, if the stud is a prompt, sure breeder. Adios was this way. He approached his mares in a businesslike manner and performed his function promptly and usually on the first mount. But I have had other horses that had different habits and were not as easy to control. A horse like Adios is a good one to have around the breeding shed for more than the obvious reason of the kind of foals he is going to sire. He keeps the action moving along. Horses that take a long time to breed can slow up the operation of any farm. But in most cases there is nothing you can do about it except wait.

As the mare is being bred, it is necessary to observe some stallions closely in order to determine whether they have actually ejaculated and thus completed the sex act. Some studs will give every outward indication of having bred the mare when actually they haven't at all. The best way to determine this is to catch a brief sample as the stallion comes off the mare and check it under a microscope. If there are actual sperm in the sample, the mare has been bred; if not, the stallion has been kidding you. Even experts can be fooled this way. Aside from checking semen in this manner, the best way is to watch the tail because all horses will "flag" (move the tail sharply up and down) when they ejaculate. However, even though most horses flag obviously it is barely noticeable with others, and these are the ones that must be observed very closely.

Artificial insemination has become a big thing in breeding harness horses, and since it is tied in directly with the breeding shed operation, I feel I should comment on it at this point. There are two ways to collect semen for impregnation. The first is to use a breeding bag and the other is to collect a dismount sample as the horse gets off the mare after having bred her.

The ideal way, of course, is to use a breeding bag. These bags are made of very thin gauge rubber and most horses do not even know they have them on although there are horses that resent them. It is a good idea to place an elastic band around the top of the breeding bag so that it will not slip off while the stallion is breeding the mare.

After the semen is collected in the breeding bag, it is transferred to a warmed glass or plastic receptacle. Several layers of gauze should be stretched across the top of the receptacle so that non-essential portion of the ejaculate will be strained. The semen should be kept out of the light as much as possible.

The insemination is made by means of a plastic pipette (a long hollow tube) and a unit which connects it to a standard syringe. The semen is first drawn into the syringe from the receptacle and then the pipette is connected. The forward end of the pipette is held in the fingers of the plastic-gloved and lubricated right arm of the inseminator and inserted through the vagina and cervix directly into the uterus. The semen in the syringe is then forced through the pipette into the uterus where it immediately begins to seek out the egg. The pipette and glove are used on one mare only and then discarded.

A normal stallion will deliver about 75 cc's of semen although the range can extend from a high of about 125 or even more to a low of about 30. I think that a minimum of 10 cc's should be figured on for an individual mare although I know of at least one mare that got in foal and had a normal foal while receiving only one cc of semen. Ordinarily, about seven mares can be inseminated from the ejaculate of a normal stallion. If a horse produces a very small quantity of semen, a veterinarian may employ an extender, a liquid mixture, to increase the quantity and, hopefully, prolong the life of the sperm.

The secret of inseminating a mare successfully lies in working slowly and smoothly. It is possible to damage the cervix if you are too hasty. A bruise in this area can easily cause infection.

When artificial insemination first became popular, it was customary to fill a capsule with semen and insert it into the uterus. The capsule eventually melted freeing the semen for its work. The pipette system is much more efficient and capsules are rarely used these days. Although artificial insemination is permitted, semen may not be transported off the premises.

Upon completion of the breeding act, the stallion dismounts and is backed off by the stud groom to a far corner of the shed where he is washed down in a solution of warm water with Novalsan added. The mare is kept under restraint as long as the stallion is in the shed. As soon as he leaves, the breeding hobbles are removed and the mare is taken out of the shed. The process is then repeated for as many stallions and mares as are involved that day.

A stallion can breed once a day without any trouble. It is customary at Meadowlands and at most other farms to breed six days a week with Sunday an off day unless there is a mare that absolutely will not hold off until Monday and has not yet been bred during that heat period. During the heart of the season—in late May and early June— a vigorous stallion in good condition may be used twice a day a couple of days a week. With the advent of artificial insemination, this is rarely necessary. If I find that for some reason I have to use a stud twice a day, I will do it early in the morning and late in the evening. I will also try to give a stallion a day off after he has been doubled, as it is called. This is much more of a problem with Thoroughbred breeders who are not permitted the luxury of insemination.

As long as I am writing about the stallion, let me continue in that vein by discussing conditioning techniques. Since breeding represents nothing more than a continuation of physical exercise, a stallion is in better shape to stand the taxing qualities of a long breeding season if he is in good physical condition.

I think all stallions should be exercised with the exception of those that are highly nervous and on the move much of the time, either in the stall or paddock. These stallions take enough exercise on their own and do not need any special work. On the other hand, lethargic stallions, and there are a great many of them, require a supplemented exercise program. I prefer to accomplish this through riding them rather than by driving, although either is satisfactory. The reason I ride the studs is that it saves time. It doesn't take as long to saddle up as it does to harness up and there is less work to do afterward.

A couple of miles a day at a good brisk jog or until the horse starts to break out slightly is enough. At Meadowlands we rode a great many of the stallions including Adios and they all enjoyed it. Horses that are being exercised are shod all the way around and during the winter months it is a good idea to put a spot of borium on the shoes to keep them from slipping. Horses that are exercised are not usually turned out on those days. Horses that are not being exercised are turned out after the morning feed and picked up at noon. This schedule is variable and the turnout time may be increased for some stallions.

This leads naturally into the feeding program for the stallion and I will enlarge on that by devoting the next few pages to a discussion of general feeding programs for all types of horses— weanlings, yearlings and brood mares as well as stallions.

With regard to stallions, let me say first of all that I think far more are overfed than underfed. This is especially true after the breeding season ends. I think owners have a tendency, perhaps understandable, to want their stallions looking slick and fat. Slick is all right but fat is not. A stallion should never be permitted to get fat, especially during the breeding season when he is at daily work.

I think the prime reason that some stallions tend to get fat is that they are fed too much hay. In my opinion, 20 pounds of hay a day is enough for any stallion. I prefer a good grade of timothy hay to a legume hay such as pure alfalfa. Alfalfa is a fattening feed and a good grade of timothy is better for a stallion. A farm manager's daily observation is better than a feed program that does not vary from month to month. When four or five ribs start showing, the horse is too thin and should be fed more. When a horse looks fat, his feed should be cut back.

I use my eye in feeding horses but otherwise I follow a fairly regular schedule for the stallions which varies according to the time of the year. They get more during the breeding season and less at other times.

Let me start out by saying that all stallions get about 20 pounds of hay a day plus grain and supplements. Using a calendar basis we will begin with August which is a non-breeding season month. The stallion is being fed twice daily, once in the morning and once at night. At each feed he gets three quarts of good oats plus a supplement of some type.

This ration continues until February which marks the beginning of the breeding season and at this stage the daily oat ration is stepped up. The daily feed might now consist of two meals, each made up of four quarts of oats plus a recommended amount of a good supplement added to the evening feed. The recommended amount of supplement might be from three to 16 ounces.

Along about the first of April, as we approach the heart of the breeding season, I go to three meals a day for the stallions, if their condition indicates it is necessary, by adding a noon feed consisting of two quarts of oats. The morning and evening feeds remain the same and thus the stallion is getting 10 quarts of oats a day plus the supplement. Some stallions will get up as high as 16 quarts a day, But I think you would find that 10 would be more normal.

One of the things we are aiming at with stallions is to keep away from a high protein diet. We don't know nearly as much about nutrition as we should but it is generally agreed that excessive protein intake is detrimental to the proper production of sperm.

At the end of the breeding season we revert to the formula that was in effect the previous August and start the cycle over.

I think it goes without saying that a stallion should have access to plenty of water and I recommend that bowls with an automatically-controlled water supply be placed in every stall. Likewise, at least one salt block as well as a supply of loose salt should be made available in the stall. If you are going to use only one salt block, plain white salt is best. If you want to add another block of mineralized or iodized salt it is all right. It has been determined that the sodium chloride content of loose salt is very beneficial to the digestive process of a horse which is why I always place some in the stall, either on a ledge or in a corner niche. A horse can handle loose salt much easier than block salt.

Brood mares are fed according to condition, time of year and status. Condition means that a thin mare is fed more than a fat mare; time of year means that a mare is fed more in the winter than in the summer; status means that a mare that is due to foal or that has foaled is fed more than a barren mare.

A barren mare is fed twice a day when she is stalled. She will get three quarts of oats morning and evening with a supplement added to each feed. She will also get two or three ears of yellow corn during the winter months—November through March—and all the hay she can eat. A mare will eat up to 30 pounds of hay a day and that is not too much if she does not get fat. If she does, cut back on the hay. I feed yellow ear corn rather than white or red because Vitamin A content is higher in the yellow corn. You can easily tell if a mare is too thin or too fat and thus increase or decrease her ration. During the summer months when they are on pasture, barren mares do not get any additional feed as long as they are in a good field. Bear in mind that it is better for a barren mare to be a little thin than a little fat. Fat mares are not good candidates to get in foal. To me, the condition of the hair is a good barometer of the mare's physical state. A normal mare in good condition will begin to shed her winter coat by mid-March and will have a slick hair coat by mid-April.

You will also find that mares with foals at their sides will tend to lose weight late in the year as the pastures dry up and lose some of their nutrient value. This is one reason that mares that foal early should be weaned early. It is not usually very long after a foal has been weaned that the mare starts to pick up weight again.

The process of weaning is the act of separating mare and foal permanently. I wean all foals after they are five and before they are six months old. By this time, a lot of mares have started to dry up and the foals are consuming from three to five quarts of dry feed per day. Some mares will even wean their own foals before the farm manager gets around to it. I usually wean my first group around the end of August and the final group in mid-November. It is better for the foals to make the separation while the weather is still good since there is a certain amount of stress involved.

I wean by the sign of the Zodiac and while I know that this is probably not a vital factor I have always done it and have been satisfied with the results. There are 12 Zodiac signs covering the various parts of the human body and running from head to feet. According to this system, the best time to wean is when the sign is in the feet and the poorest time is when the sign is in the head. I wean only when the sign is below the knees. Only two signs, legs and feet, are below the knees. Each sign lasts from two to three days and a complete Zodiac cycle consists of 28 days. Thus there are four or five days in a month when the sign is "below the knees" and this is the period during which I wean my monthly batch.

In preparation for weaning, the mare and foal are brought into a stall. The markings of the foal are checked closely and if the foal's foot is to be branded or if another means of permanent identification is to be employed, it is done at this time. Then the mare is taken from the stall and to a field as far from the foal as possible. The mare and foal should not be able to hear each other.

After weaning, I like to leave the foals in stalls for a couple of days until they get used to being without their mothers. In doing this, I try to put two foals in a single stall so that they will be company for each other. The mares should be milked out by hand every other day for a week and as little as necessary thereafter. It is during this stage that you must be especially watchful for mastitis.

After they have spent a couple of days in the stall, the weanlings (they are no longer called sucklings) should be turned out and a special effort should be made to see that they get the choicest possible hay since pasture fields are not at their best at this time of year. Colts and fillies should be separated after the last batch of foals has been weaned.

Now let me return and pick up the in-foal mare at the time her previous foal is weaned. As we now know, this is anywhere from the last week of August until mid-November and during that period the mare remains out on pasture. However, if I see that a mare is not doing well on pasture during the late summer and early fall, I will pick her up and feed her daily as during the winter months.

When the in-foal mares are barned for the winter—usually in mid-November but sometimes a little earlier or later depending on the weather—one of the first things to do is to re-check pregnancies. It is a matter of record that anywhere from three to seven percent of those that have previously been pronounced in foal will come up barren. Every stock farm manager feels bitterly about this because he has counted the mare "in the bank" to produce a foal the following year. But it is a percentage you have to learn to live with and there isn't much that can be done about it. Occasionally, it will develop as a result of a spurious pregnancy that fooled both the mare and the veterinarian, but in most instances, it is a matter of early abortion that occurred sometime after the 60th day. Such mares do not indicate any abortive symptoms and the fetus is usually too small to be found. The November re-check is made because it is much better to find out then than to wait and discover it the following March. Possibly, the mare has an infection which caused the abortion and should be treated. Such treatment should be instituted in November rather than March.

Many of the mares that we now have in barns are entering the last third of their pregnancy and it is during this period that the fetus grows at the fastest rate and that the mare needs the most in the way of nutrition.

I feed foaling mares twice a day plus all the hay they will eat. Like barren mares, they will consume up to 30 pounds of hay a day. In addition, they will receive three quarts of oats and a supplement at both the morning and evening feed until they reach the last four months of pregnancy at which time the grain ration is stepped up to four quarts per feed. Yellow ear corn is added to the evening feed. Needless to say, the hay fed to foaling mares should be of the highest quality. I prefer alfalfa and feed it routinely. Naturally, a mare that still appears too thin under this program will have her ration increased. One that is too fat will get less. If a mare doesn't do well, have her blood and teeth checked.

As soon as the mare foals or shortly thereafter, her grain ration is increased to 10 quarts a day, five at each feed. She still gets a supplement with each feed and her corn ration is not cut off as the season advances as it is for the barren mare.

When mares with foals at side are turned out for the summer, I always make it a practice to bring them in and feed them each morning. I realize that this is extra work and that a lot of farms don't do it, but I have always felt it was necessary. In addition to keeping the mare in good condition, it also gives us an opportunity to work around the foals a little bit and to teach them to lead, etc. At this time these mares get six quarts of oats and a supplement and remain in the stall a couple of hours, long enough for them to eat a good bit of hay. Ideally, in summer it is best to leave mares and foals in the barn during the heat of the day and turn them out in late afternoon.

From stallions and brood mares we go on to the feeding of foals with three categories under consideration—the suckling foal that is nursing his dam, the weanling and the yearling.

First of all, it should be recognized that the production of a big, strong, healthy foal depends to a great extent on the milk-producing ability of the dam. Year after year, the mares that are the best milkers produce the biggest and best-looking foals. You cannot do much to increase the milk production other than good feeding. Some mares simply produce more milk than others and I am sure that to some degree it is an hereditary thing. It is interesting to note that it is not always the biggest, fattest mares

Fig. 138. In the early stages, as described in the text, the author permits the mare and foal to feed from the same box.

that produce the most milk. Some very small, relatively thin mares are excellent milk producers.

A foal will start looking for feed to supplement his natural milk diet at about a month of age as previously explained. At some farms, it is the practice to provide a special feed box for the foal when he is about six weeks old. I have never followed that practice but instead have given the mare some extra grain and permitted the foal to feed out of the same box with her (Fig. 138). This has worked quite satisfactorily as far as I am concerned. The main thing is to have the feed box big enough so that the foal can have access to it.

For that reason, I prefer to have a permanent feed box built into the stall instead of feeding from a feed tub. This feed box or bunk is built into a corner of the stall and is approximately 40 inches off the ground. It consists of a piece of two by eight plank which forms the hypotenuse of a triangle in which the right angle is the one formed by the two walls of the stall coming together. The hypotenuse board is from 32 to 36 inches long and thus there is plenty of room for both mare and foal to stand side by side. The bottom of the feed box is made of masonite or galvanized metal.

I am going to mention stalls and barns only briefly in passing and this seems a logical place to do it. Horse barns are like houses; the habitation depends on the exchequer. Basically, I recommend a 24-stall barn. A barn this size is not too large and at the same time I feel a man can take care of that many mares. Adequate ventilation is of prime importance and if you are building a barn it is probably best to consult an expert on this phase of it.

Ideally, a brood mare stall should be 12x12 with at least eight feet of head room. The lower four feet of the stall should have a smooth interior surface, preferably oak. Every stall should have an awning type window measuring three feet by two. The floor should be clay and a grill type front with a sliding door is desirable. I also prefer to have automatic water in each stall for obvious reasons of convenience. I also favor hay racks although I know that some farm managers feed hay off the floor. My experience has been that a mare will mess up a lot of hay in a year if you feed it off the floor. The feed bunk is placed in the corner of the stall as described above. I think the aisleway of the barn should be 12 feet wide and paved with some type of non-slip material. There are several such products on the market.

Getting back to feeding, the grain consumption of a foal will be quite small in the beginning but at the age of two months a foal will probably be consuming about a quart of grain a day from the feed box he shares with his mother. From that stage on, the foal will take increasing amounts of grain and separate feeding facilities must be made available. This is accomplished by means of a creep as previously described.

There are a vast number of creep feeds available but I have always stuck to the basic items of good oats and a supplement. For purposes of discussion here, I am going to assume that we are feeding a pint of supplement to two quarts of oats. At the age of two months, a foal will be started on creep feeding on a ration of a quart of oats per day and a half pint of supplement. Thus, if there are 12 foals in a field, 12 quarts of oats and three quarts of supplement will be mixed together and placed in the feed bunks each morning.

Incidentally, the quality of oats is very important. For many years I fed a top grade of oats which I purchased in carload quantities from the mid-west. They would weigh from 42 to 45 pounds to the bushel, and had been recleaned and of uniform quality. I found that this type of oats had much more feed value than local oats and that the cost of energy was less than if I fed a larger quantity of lesser quality. I have also used and can recommend a good grade of crushed oats. The important thing is to have them freshly crushed because a considerable amount of feed value is lost during storage. To my way of thinking, no farm should ever stand short on the quality of the hay and oats it feeds. These are the basic ingredients of the horse's diet and they should be the best that can be obtained.

The rule of thumb in feeding young horses is to feed what they will clean up. When you start feeding a dozen sucklings 15 quarts a day (12 quarts of oats and three quarts of a supplement) watch the results very carefully the first few days. If you feed in the morning and check the feed bunk out in the afternoon, there should be just a little feed left. If there is a great deal left, you are probably feeding too much and should cut the ration back until the foals catch up to it. If the feed bunk is cleaned up to the last kernel on three consecutive days, you can assume that the ration is not enough.

With the specific group of 12 that I am working with, I would move the ration up or down 2½ quarts when I changed it. That would represent two quarts of oats and a pint of supplement. I would then watch carefully and adjust the amount of feed to the manner in which it was being cleaned up.

Once you get the basic starting ration established, any future change would obviously be on the upward side since the foals require more feed as they grow older. The rule of thumb is that each time the feed bunk comes up completely clean for three days in a row it is time to increase the ration. Make the increase a small one each time to permit the foals to adjust to it.

The foal is weaned or separated from its mother in late summer or early fall as previously described and a new feeding process begins. Now the foals are on their own and do not have their mother's milk to supplement their diets. They must be given access to hay and minerals as well as oats. They are also turned out in a field with loose housing (discussed elsewhere) and are strictly on their own. A good grade calcium-phosphorous preparation should be available free choice. For several years I have made free choice minerals available with no ill effects. Young horses need a large amount of calcium to build bone. They get a great deal from hay but the experts seem to think they need even more than that.

I prefer to have at least two acres of pasture for each horse. I like a 25-acre field for 12 weanlings. Actually, except for the quantity of the feed, there is no difference in the way that weanlings and yearlings are fed since the only change they undergo is the technical one of becoming yearlings on January first.

When first weaned, foals will consume an average of six quarts of oats per day plus a quart of whatever supplement is being used. They are now fed twice a day at 8 a.m. and 4 p.m. with half the feed set out each time. I make it a practice to watch the feeding habits of the foals very carefully at this stage, principally to make certain that they are not getting too much. If the feed bunk is not cleaned up within an hour after feeding, the ration is cut back slightly until it is cleaned up promptly. Free choice salt is also available plus two or three different kinds of minerals to supplement the diet. In addition, high quality legume hay is fed in the hay racks. I prefer to feed a second or third cutting hay. You will find that by feeding high quality legume hay that it is very easy to get into a high protein diet. The experts seem to think that a growing horse doesn't need more than 14% protein so if you are feeding high quality legume hay it is probably a good idea to cut back on the supplement since most of them are also high in protein.

In figuring feeding space for yearlings, I find that two feet should be allowed for each horse. Thus, 12 yearlings would be fed in a bunk that was 24 feet long. I also watch the habits of the weanlings closely when they are first turned out. If there is a bully in the crowd I pull him out of that group and put him in with some other colts that he is less likely to dominate. Weanlings and yearlings that are together all the time will not have much of this kind of trouble. As a rule, it is only when you put another colt, a stranger, in with them that it will develop. The new colt is like a new kid in the neighborhood. The "regulars" have to try him a little to see how tough he is.

Generally speaking, weanlings are separated according to age (as well as sex, of course) and thus some fields will have older foals than others. The older foals will get more feed through most of the winter and spring months although the ration for all groups will tend to even out in late summer.

From a starting point of six quarts of oats a day just after they are weaned, young horses will work themselves up to about 10 to 12 quarts a day in the summer of their yearling form. This is in addition to whatever supplement you are feeding plus grass, hay, salt, minerals and plenty of water.

The thing I have noticed about feeding yearlings is that they don't eat enough hay. I think we could raise a better animal cheaper if we could increase the hay consumption. Part of this, of course, is due to the fact that horses will tend to ignore hay, even high quality hay, when there is good green grass. But there is so much good in hay that I think horses ought to eat more of it. I have gone to the extreme of lighting the hay rack at night to try to bring it to their attention. I have also used additives but I haven't found any happy solution.

I think that takes care of feeding and since I finished by writing about yearlings, let me continue by discussing the housing accommodations for horses of that age. What I will say here applies, of course, from the time foals are weaned the previous fall so even though I will be referring to yearling facilities, the period involved also includes a portion of the weanling form.

I am a strong advocate of loose housing for yearlings. In years past, it was a relatively routine custom for yearlings to be stalled at night from October through the middle of April after which they were turned out night and day. During the winter and spring months, the yearlings went out at about 7:30 a.m. and came in about 4 p.m.

But any time you can give a horse free choice, you are keeping in step with nature and I believe now that most major farms have gone to loose housing and are satisfied with it. I know I am.

As I wrote earlier, I like to use a 25-acre field for 12 yearlings. I prefer a well-made shed shelter of some type with free access for the yearlings (Fig. 139). You will find that you can just about predict when they will congregate in the shelter unless it is feeding time. They do not like ice storms, bitter cold weather with an accompanying high wind or extremely hot weather. They will go in the shed during these periods but otherwise will spend most of their time out in the field. Snow does not bother them nor does cold unless accompanied by wind. In the summer they will remain out all night and through most of the morning and then will retreat to the comfort of the shed when it

Fig. 139. A yearling shed with a run-in yard is shown at the upper left. At the upper right is a view of the inside of the shed indicating the manner in which a corner is properly boarded up to eliminate a sharp corner and minimize the chance of injury. At the lower left is a rubber bumper as used on gates and doorways of yearling housing facilities, also to minimize the possibility of injury. At the lower right is an interior view of the shed showing how the feed bunks are placed directly beneath the hay racks. (The hay rack at the right is not visible in the picture.) Between the hay racks are two automatic watering troughs as illustrated. The owl in the picture (near the top edge of the hay rack at the left) is plastic. The author finds it useful in keeping birds out of the shed and recommends that it be moved about occasionally and held in place by an overhead wire so that it will wave in the wind.

gets very hot and the flies become bothersome.

If I were building a new shelter for yearlings, I would construct a three-sided shed with the open side facing the south. It would be 48 feet wide and 24 feet deep. The feed bunk would be built against the back wall and would be 24 feet long and two feet wide. It would be 42 inches off the ground and a hay rack with metal pipe slats would run its entire length. Thus, any hay that dropped out of the rack would fall into the feed bunk. Some new hay, incidentally, should be added to the hay rack every day to keep it as fresh as possible. If you throw in a lot of hay and fill the rack up completely the hay will tend to become dusty. You should shake the hay when you put it in the rack.

Most watering facilities that are built in sheds are placed at one end of the feed bunk. However, I would place my water bowl in the center of the feed bunk and thus would have two 12-foot bunk sections on each side of the watering trough. The water should be thermostatically heat-controlled so that it will not freeze over in the winter. Some farms put their troughs out in the middle of the pasture field but I prefer them in the shed. Even outside troughs can be fitted with heating elements when they are built so that they will not freeze over. There is an extra cost involved in doing this and, of course, your electricity charges will be higher. But if you have ever worked closely with watering troughs that freeze over on a winter morning and thus require a lengthy session with an axe to make water available to the horses, you would not quarrel much about the cost of a heating element.

There are two reasons why I like troughs in the sheds rather than in the field. One is that an inside water source is not exposed to the weather and the other, which is more important, is that yearlings seem to like to drink while they eat. They will feed a short time and then go over to the watering trough and drink before returning to the feed bunk. The watering troughs should be cleaned out twice a week without fail.

The loafing sheds can be bedded either with straw or shavings. Shavings are quite good as long as they are renewed often and not allowed to become dusty. Personally, I prefer straw but in either case the shed should be gone over twice a week and the wet straw or shavings removed and the bedding freshened up.

It is also important to keep the ground filled in and level. It has a tendency to ditch out in front of the feed bunks as a result of the colts eating there. If you don't put down new clay at least once a year you will find that the colts will be standing six inches lower than you had planned and reaching up for their feed instead of down.

The sidewalls should be at least eight feet high and preferably 10 to provide adequate head room. Windows should be of the awning type so that they can be left open during a storm without running the danger of rain water being blown into the shed and getting on the feed.

The square corners of the shed should be boarded across and thus eliminated. I would come out six feet from each corner and then run a series of boards one on top of the other across to a point six feet from the same corner on the diagonal wall.

Rubber bumpers should be installed on all posts and doorways (in the event you are using a doorway instead of leaving the entire front of the shed open) or on the corners if it is an open front construction. Boat bumpers may be fastened to the doorways or wall ends. At Meadowlands I was fortunate in this respect in that there is a nearby factory that manufactures industrial rubber rolls. They pull the cores out of these rolls and this leaves a cylinder about six inches in diameter with the rubber circumference about an inch thick. Metal brackets and lag screws are used to fasten them. This is the type of protective device that will keep a colt from getting a hip knocked down. Sometimes, either while at play or if frightened, yearlings will rush pell mell in or out of a shed. When this happens it is almost certain that a couple of colts are going to be crowded against the edge of a shed or door opening. These rubber bumpers will usually prevent injury in such cases.

A permanent stall or work room should be constructed at one end of the shed and a doorway should lead from it into a catch pen or yard that is backed up to one side of the shed. The stall should be about 10x10 and the yard should be about 60x60 and enclosed by a four-board fence.

It is frequently necessary to catch the yearlings in order to trim, worm, treat or give shots. Usually, you can handle this in a yard, but I have found that after you catch the first two or three and work on them, the rest will get foxy and avoid you in an enclosure that big—or at least make you work hard to catch them. If you have a stall that you can run one or two into, you will find this task much easier.

The feed storage area should run across the same side of the shed the work stall is on and take up the remainder of the room. Thus, it would also be a 10x10 structure. Hay, oats and straw will be stored here. The oats bin should be metal lined so that mice cannot gain entry and there should be an opening near the top and on the outside so that oats can be augered out of a truck and into the bin.

Some people seem to think that yearlings that run out in an open shed are more difficult to handle, but I have not found this to be true. Actually, there are so many things, that have to be done with yearlings that they are handled quite often. They have to be trimmed and wormed at frequent intervals and they also receive shots and must be branded. In branding a foal, a number that is the same as the one carried on the foot of the foal's dam is branded on the front of one of the front feet with a hot iron at weaning time. It is a painless procedure and is repeated as the foot grows out and the original brand with it.

Trimming the feet is one of the most important things involved in the raising of young horses and I am quite strict about it. A foal should be trimmed for the first time when he reaches eight weeks of age and every four to six weeks thereafter until he leaves the farm. There are certain foals that must be trimmed earlier than eight weeks and more often than the standard four to six-week interval. But a good farm manager will spot these colts and arrange a special schedule for them. The main thing in trimming is to keep the foot level and the heel cut down. Many of the bad feet we see on race tracks had their origin in poor trimming practices at the farm where the horses were raised.

One of the advantages of housing yearlings in comparatively small fields is that it enables you to set up some kind of pasture rotation. I would much rather use two 25-acre fields and rotate them every month than one 50-acre field. This is because the rotation permits the grass to recoup in the vacated pasture and is a big help in combating the parasite problem.

Parasites are a continuing annoyance to farm managers and they are still with us despite all the new and revolutionary drugs that are on the market. There are three basic types of parasites with which a horse farm manager must be concerned. They are ascarids, (round or white worms) strongyles, (blood worms) and bots (stomach worms). As I write about them and the treatment for each, please bear in mind that the drugs I mention are those that I am using as I write this. New drugs come out every year and I change if I find something that I think will do the job better. They are making great progress in this field and I am sure that one day they will conquer the parasite problem completely. But meantime, a constant battle has to be fought to keep foals free from parasites.

Strongyles are blood worms (the one that principally affects horses is known as Vulgaris S.) that penetrate the capillary system and often the mesentery which is a section of the digestive system. If the concentration of larvae becomes too great in any one section of the mesentery or intestinal wall, a fatal rupture will often occur. If the concentration is not large enough to cause a rupture, a condition will develop that lessens the effect of nutrients in this area and the horse will not be able to derive as much nourishment from his food as he should. Occasionally, you will get a concentration that will not cause a rupture but which will form an anuerism that lodges in the aorta or other part of the circulatory system causing hemorrhage and death.

The current drug that I am using to combat strongyles is Equizol. I have found that it is the most effective of the commercial drugs on the market. But to demonstrate how things can change quickly in this field, they already have a new drug which is rated superior to Equizol even though it isn't on the commercial market yet. It is called Dichlorvos and has been tested and proven effective for all parasites in horses. It has been used successfully in the swine industry for the past three years and was recently released for use on dogs. It is a nitrate drug and the only reason that it hasn't been released for horses is that they have not yet finalized the tolerance rate for the horse.

Ascarids are the long white worms (also called round worms) that a horse passes in his stool. They become most noticeable in late summer with colts that haven't been properly wormed. They run from four to five inches in length and the primary damage they cause is to the intestinal wall. Fecal samples should be checked to get ascarid count. The sample is run through a sugar and water solution, whirled briefly in a centrifuge and then checked under a microscope and rated. Most laboratories will give you a one, two, three or four plus rating. That is, a "one plus" rating would indicate four ascarid eggs in the field of view on a miscroscope at ten power. Sixteen eggs would be a four plus rating. Any horse whose fecal sample registers more than one plus is in need of worming and everything over three plus is heavily contaminated. If you have a heavily-contaminated group of yearlings, you won't need a laboratory report. They will be pot-bellied and have poor hair coats. The current drug of choice for ascarids is Dyrex. I have found it to be very effective against them.

The third parasite is the bot worm. Bots are short, round worms that actually cling to the intestinal wall. They can cause a blockage of the intestine and death and are a very persistent and tenacious form of parasite. Bot flies go through a continuous life cycle. They are voided by the horse and hatch out in the hot summer months of July and August. You can observe them then as little fly-speck eggs clinging to the throat and the inside of the front legs of mares. They are annoying and the mares lick at them and ingest them whereupon they enter the horse and begin another cycle. It takes about six months for them to hatch. Horses are treated for bots usually once a year in December. An early winter month is selected because the first frost has killed the bot fllies that are still living outside the horse and the larvae on the inside may now be treated without fear of additional ingestation until the following summer. The drug of choice right now is Anthon.

Now let me go back and pick up the foals as they are born and develop a proper worming program for them. In actual practice, the farm manager should consult his veterinarian and work out a schedule with him.

Foals are first wormed when they are from six to eight weeks old. They receive a piperate solution administered by a dose syringe. This works against strongyles and ascarids. While they are on the mares, this treatment is repeated every six weeks. Equizol can be added to the piperate as they get older. After the foals are weaned, they go on a regular schedule of Equizol for strongyles and Dyrex for ascarids.

The weanlings get their first dose of Dyrex about the middle of November. Dyrex comes in bolus form and in two sizes, one for weanlings weighing approximately 300 pounds and a larger one for those weighing approximately 500 pounds. Most weanlings will get the larger bolus. This is usually administered with a balling gun and preferably by a veterinarian. If a veterinarian is not available, I would suggest that the bolus be wrapped in a tissue and inserted on the back of the tongue either by using a rubber glove or a balling gun, whichever the farm manager might be more proficient with. It is a good idea to "draw" the weanlings—that is cause them to miss one feed—before worming. You can also expect that they will appear a little off for the next couple of days since any drug as effective as Dyrex can be expected to have a certain amount of toxicity.

After the first heavy frost, the weanlings are wormed once with Anthon for bot control. Normally, bots aren't too much of a problem in weanlings although you do observe some. They have not had a real chance to ingest the bots into their system the way older horses have. Yearlings are seldom present to be treated for bots since they have usually left the farm to go into training before it is time to worm them. One thing I do with all yearlings leaving the farm is to shave the bot eggs from their legs. This helps immeasureably. I also do this with all yearlings that are brought up to be broken or sent to the sales.

On or about January first, the yearlings (our weanling crop is now a year older) receive another dose of Dyrex. From six to eight weeks after that they receive Equizol on their feed and continue to receive it once every six weeks thereafter. Equizol comes in a sugar base and is very palatable. It may be sprinkled on top of the feed or mixed in with it. I prefer to sprinkle it on top. The dosage is indicated on the instructions but I usually give about 10 percent more than the instructions call for. I have never noted any harmful effects.

Along about the first of April, I will give the yearlings another dose of Dyrex to control ascarids unless my fecal samples show that I have practically no contamination in which case I will pass it up. The only worming the yearlings get during the summer months is Equizol for strongyles on their feed once every six weeks.

You must also establish a vigilant worming program for mares since many of them are permanent residents of the farm and are thus more prone to become contaminated. Mares are susceptible to strongyles and bots but rarely to ascarids. For that reason, I do not worm the mares for ascarids unless fecal checks indicate that there is trouble.

Mares are wormed periodically with Equizol much as the weanlings and yearlings are. That is, they receive a dose on their feed once every six weeks except when they have been wormed for bots and up until a month before they foal. It is best not to use any more of a harsh drug than necessary on a mare that is in foal, but it has been my experience that mares can safely be wormed with Equizol up until 30 days before their due date.

In early December, all mares are wormed for bots with Anthon. This is a palatable drug contained in a sugar base and all mares will take it quite readily on their feed. After they have been wormed for bots, it is a good practice to take a fecal check about two weeks later and give another dose to mares that still show a relatively high contamination.

Mares that are turned out during the summer are brought in and wormed with Equizol by dose syringe. When this is done, sufficient water is added to the drug to assure a relatively thick consistency. Mares who refuse to take Equizol on their grain are also wormed in this manner.

Because they have their own paddocks and thus are not exposed to the degree of contamination that other horses are, stallions do not pose a major problem as far as worming is concerned. My program consists of checking fecal samples and worming routinely with the various drugs of choice as the fecal counts indicate. Actually, the stallions do not get much more than an occasional dose of Equizol on their feed. I never worm stallions during the breeding season for fear that it might lower their libido or otherwise upset them.

I think the main thing about any worming program is to be aware that a parasite problem does exist and that it has to be faced up to and dealt with. Horses come to a major breeding farm such as Meadowlands from a number of different farms scattered throughout the country and these mingling horses tend to contaminate each other. It is the contamination by other horses that brings about the high worm count on farms.

Another important thing is to keep abreast of the latest developments in the field. There are always some new and effective drugs coming out. I try to be aware of the experimental work that is going on and as soon as these drugs have been through the mill and released, I try them if they have been recommended by the Animal Pathology Department of the University of Kentucky. In a sense, parasites are like flies in that they eventually develop a tolerance to certain drugs the way flies became tolerant to DDT. When this happens you have to go to a new drug.

At this point, I feel I have covered the basic phases of stock farm management and thus will bring this chapter to a close even though it is quite evident that space limitations have prevented me from going into as much detail as I might have liked. What I have written is intended to be helpful and I hope I have achieved that goal. If I have helped anyone to tend his soil better, to build a better fence, to practice hygienic breeding methods or to produce a properly-raised foal that is capable of realizing his utmost potential at the race track, then I will consider that my time has been well-spent.

Harry M. Harvey has been a "farm boy" all his life and is proud of it. One of 11 children, he was born October 22, 1923 on a farm near Duxbury, Vt., where his father ran a large-scale dairy operation and dealt in draft horses. He was a "working farmer" almost from the time he could walk and had decided before he reached his teens that he wanted to become a horse trainer and then a horse farmer. Having set that goal, he continued working with his father after graduation from high school while undertaking a systematic campaign to obtain employment with the late Thomas S. Berry, a famous Grand Circuit trainer. He fired off letter after letter to Berry  describing his farm background, his love of horses and his willingness to work 24 hours a day. "I finally hired him as a groom," Berry said in later years, "just to stop those letters." That was in 1947 and Harvey rose rapidly through the ranks. He became Berry's stable foreman in 1948 and assistant trainer in 1949. He drove his first race that year. In 1951 he went with Del Miller as an assistant trainer and climaxed his driving career by piloting Helicopter to victory in the 1953 Hambletonian. He was then and still is the youngest driver (29) ever to win the trotting classic. But despite his success in the sulky, he knew he wouldn't be completely happy until he got back to farming and jumped at the chance when, in late 1954, Miller asked him to become superintendent at Meadowlands Farm, Meadow Lands, Pa. He remained there a dozen years, supervising the breeding activities of Adios, among other stallions. After Adios died in 1965, Miller began to cut back his operation and Harvey moved to his own nearby Loch Arden Farm where he stands Majestic Hanover, Express Rodney and Vicar Hanover. He still drives occasionally at both fairs and mutuel tracks.

Appendix

A number of tabulated pedigrees as well as two special charts that trace the lineage of certain foreign horses are presented on the following pages. One chart traces the male line descent of the French trotting breed and is accompanied by tabulated pedigrees of the two leading French trotters, Roquepine and Toscan. The other chart traces the male line descent of 2:00 horses in Australia and New Zealand. The basic pedigree section includes 66 of general interest plus another 16 for foundation mares from the seven maternal families that have produced the most 2:00 performers.

Most pedigrees have been carried to the fourth generation of 16 ancestors. For obvious reasons of space, it has not been possible to include all pedigrees of interest. In the basic section, the intent is to portray as clearly as possible the lines of sire family descent from Hambletonian and to illustrate specific types of crosses that have produced superior trotters and pacers. The four sire lines stemming from Hambletonian are laid out in family groups and reference is made to indicate other horses in this section that are members of the same male line family.

Not all major foundation sires were included as individual pedigree subjects. Peter Volo and Peter Scott, for instance, two legitimate giants of the breed, were left out because it was assumed that sufficient of their pedigrees appeared in those of their sons that are carried. In this manner, it was possible to avoid a great deal of repetition, although a certain amount will still be apparent as might be expected of a breed that is linked so recently to so very few foundation sires.

Examples of crosses that highlight the close-up blood of a common ancestor have also been included along with a selection of basic crosses employed to produce pacers. Similar examples for trotters are not included since all descend from Peter The Great or Axworthy and thus any modern American trotter whose pedigree is carried in this appendix is, in one way or another, a representative of this cross.

Many more great females could also have been included in the maternal family section. Indeed, many more actual families could have been charted. But, again, the intent is to demonstrate basic channels of leading families and this policy has been adhered to.

A special feature of the appendix is a master list of sires (see next page) that has been compiled, arranged alphabetically and numbered. By referring to this list, horses appearing in any of the pedigrees, except Messenger, Hambletonian (whose pedigrees appear in Chapter 1) and the two French horses, may be traced back to the last identifiable male line ancestor.

In every pedigree, the name of each horse in the last tabulated generation is followed by a number which refers to the same number on the master list. For example, in the pedigree of Axtell (No. 1), Abdallah's name (top right) is followed by the number 19. On the master list, No. 19 is American Mambrino, the sire of Abdallah. The number following American Mambrino's name (234) is that of his sire, No. 234 on the master list, Messenger. In this manner, almost any horse appearing in the fourth generation may be traced all the way back in the male line to the Darley Arabian or one of the other foundation sires, the Godolphin Arabian or the Byerly Turk. Where there is no number following the name of a fourth generation horse or after the name of a horse on the master list, it means that the sire of that horse either is unknown or that his breeding is not officially documented.

In a few instances, it has been necessary to place two numbers after the name of a horse both in pedigrees and on the master list. This is because some horses have the same name and the same sire. There are, for instance, three Cassius M. Clay Jr.'s, all by Cassius M. Clay. Where this occurs, the actual registry number of the horse, which distinguishes him from another of the same name, appears in parenthesis directly after his name and the reference number to his sire follows that. The names of all purely Thoroughbred horses appear in bold face type.

1. Abbedale 322
2. Abdallah 19
3. Aberdeen 166
4. Adam's Stump 315
5. Adioo Guy 161
6. Advertizer 120
7. Alcade 220
8. Alcantara 146
9. Alcyone 146
10. Alexander's Abdallah 166
11. Allerton 186
12. Allie Gaines 13
13. Almont 10
14. Almont Jr. 13
15. Almont Lightning 13
16. Al Stanley 330
17. American Clay 81
18. **American Eclipse** 115
19. **American Mambrino** 234
20. Anderson Wilkes 250
21. Andrew Jackson 366
22. Andrus's Hambletonian 199
23. Archdale 132
24. Argot Hal 67
25. Arion McKinney 229
26. Artillery 166
27. Ashland Wilkes 278
28. Atlantic Express 47
29. **Australian** 354
30. A. W. Richmond 59
31. Axtell 359
32. Axworthy 31
33. Azoff 265
34. Bald Hornet —
35. Bald Stockings 252
36. Baron Brooke 201
37. Baron Dillon 40
38. Barongale 39
39. Baronmore 40
40. Baron Wilkes 146
41. **Bartlett's Childers** 97
42. Bay Chief 220
43. Bay Kentucky Hunter 203
44. Bay Tom —
45. Bay Tom Jr. 44
46. **Bedford** 113
47. Bellini 26
48. Belmont 10
49. Belwin 229
50. **Beningbrough** 206
51. Berkshire Chimes 83
52. **Berthune** 291
53. Betterton 146
54. Bingara 55
55. Bingen 228
56. Bingen Silk 55
57. **Birmingham** 310
58. **Bishop's Hambletonian** 234
59. Blackbird 76
60. Blackhawk Telegraph 343
61. **Blank** 150
62. **Blaze** 136
63. Blood's Blackhawk 343
64. **Blucher** 115
65. **Boston** 329
66. **Bourbon** 300
67. Brown Hal 147
68. Brown Highlander —
69. Brown Highlander II 297
70. Bryson 294
71. **Buzzard** 363
72. **Byerly Turk** —
73. **Cade** 150
74. Caliban 226
75. Calumet Chuck 339
76. Camden 288
77. **Camel** 355
78. Cassius M. Clay 174
79. Cassius M. Clay Jr. (20) 78
80. Cassius M. Clay Jr. (21) 78
81. Cassius M. Clay Jr. (22) 78
82. **Catton** 153
83. Chimes 120
84. Chitwood 246
85. **Citizen** 61
86. Clark Chief 220
87. Clark Chief Jr. 86
88. Clay Pilot 79
89. Coaster 74
90. Colbert 250
91. Colonel Gentry 198
92. **Colossus** 302
93. **Comus** —
94. **Conductor** —
95. Conductor 120
96. **Croft's Partner** 189
97. **Darley Arabian** —
98. Delmonico 162
99. **Dick Andrews** 192
100. Dictator 166
101. Dillon Axworthy 32
102. Dillon Volo 266
103. **Diomed** 135
104. Direct 107
105. Direct Hal 104
106. Direct Line 107
107. Director 100
108. Directum Kelly 104
109. Don Pizzaro 139
110. Downing's Bay Messenger 170
111. Downing's Vermont 343
112. Driver 287
113. **Dungannon** 117
114. Duplex 45
115. **Duroc** 103
116. Duvall's Mambrino 220
117. Eclipse 227
118. Edward Everett 166
119. Edwin Forest 43
120. Electioneer 166
121. Electricity 120
122. **Emilius** 253
123. Empire Direct 105
124. **Endorser** 348

125. **Engineer** 281
126. Engineer 234
127. Engineer 2nd 126
128. **English Mambrino** 125
129. Erector 107
130. Ericsson 220
131. Etawah 16
132. Expedition 120
133. **Express** 124
134. Fireaway 112
135. **Florizel** 175
136. **Flying Childers** 97
137. Flying Cloud 343
138. **Gallatin** 46
139. Gambetta Wilkes 146
140. **Gano** 18
141. Gay Boy 11
142. General Taylor —
143. General Watts 32
144. General Withers 13
145. George M. Patchen 78
146. George Wilkes 166
147. Gibson's Tom Hal 207
148. Gill's Vermont 111
149. **Glencoe** 316
150. **Godolphin Arabian** —
151. **Gohanna** 233
152. Goldsmith's Abdallah 347
153. **Golumpus** 151
154. Governor Sprague 280
155. **Grand Bashaw** —
156. Grand Sentinel 286
157. Grattan 358
158. Grattan Royal 157
159. Green's Bashaw 344
160. Guy Axworthy 32
161. Guy Dillon 293
162. Guy Miller 166
163. Guy Wilkes 146
164. Hal Dale 1
165. Hal Pizzaro 109
166. Hambletonian 2
167. Hamlin Patchen 145
168. Happy Medium 166
169. Harold 166
170. Harpinus 58
171. Harry Clay 79
172. Heir At Law 222
173. **Henry** 295
174. Henry Clay 21
175. **Herod** 319
176. **Highflyer** 175
177. High Private 347
178. Homer 220
179. **Howard's Sir Charles** 295
180. **Humphry Clickner** 93
181. Hunt's Commodore 19
182. **Hurrah** 243
183. Imp. Bellfounder 309
184. **Imp. Trustee** 82
185. **Jack Hawkins** 65
186. Jay Bird 146
187. Jersey B. B. 188
188. Jersey Wilkes 146
189. **Jigg** 72
190. J. J. Audubon 9
191. J. Malcolm Forbes 55
192. **Joe Andrews** 117
193. Joe Bowers —
194. Joe Dodge 55
195. Joe Patchen 259
196. Joe Young 306
197. John Eaton —
198. John R. Gentry 27
199. Judson's Hambletonian 58
200. Jupiter 215
201. Justice Brooke 38
202. Justin Morgan —
203. Kentucky Hunter 352
204. Kentucky Prince 86
205. King Clay 171
206. **King Fergus** 117
207. Kittrell's Tom Hal 35
208. Lafayette —
209. **Lear's Sir William** 179
210. Lee Axworthy 160
211. Lee Tide 210
212. Lee Worthy 210
213. **Leviathan** 240
214. Logan 166
215. Long Island Blackhawk **21**
216. Lumps 146
217. Major Edsall 10
218. Malcolm Forbes 55
219. Mambrino Boy 224
220. Mambrino Chief 225
221. Mambrino Chief Jr. 220
222. Mambrino King 224
223. Mambrino Messenger 225
224. Mambrino Patchen 220
225. Mambrino Paymaster 19
226. Mambrino Pilot 220
227. **Marske** 304
228. May King 120
229. McKinney 9
230. McNitt Horse —
231. **Melbourne** 180
232. Mendocino 120
233. **Mercury** 243
234. **Messenger** 128
235. Moko 40
236. Montjoy 144
237. Morgan Axworthy 32
238. Morse Horse 230
239. Mr. McElwyn 160
240. **Muley** 253
241. Napoleon Direct 351
242. Nervolo 90
243. **Newminster** 336
244. Norman 238
245. North American —
246. Nutwood 48
247. Nutwood Wilkes 163
248. Octaroon —

249. Old Pilot —
250. Onward 146
251. Oratorio 358
252. Original Tom Hal —
253. **Orville** 50
254. **Pacolet** 85
255. Pactolus 261
256. Paddy Burns —
257. Pancoast 362
258. Parkville 120
259. Patchen Wilkes 146
260. Patriot 64
261. Patronage 257
262. Peter McKlyo 265
263. Peter Scott 265
264. Peter The Brewer 265
265. Peter The Great 269
266. Peter Volo 265
267. Piedmont 13
268. Pilot Jr. 249
269. Pilot Medium 168
270. Pistachio 48
271. **Pot-8-os** 117
272. Prescott 169
273. Pretender 134
274. Prince Pulaski —
275. Prince Pulaski Jr. 274
276. Prodigal 257
277. **Rattler** 289
278. Red Wilkes 146
279. **Revenue** 184
280. Rhode Island 356
281. **Sampson** 62
282. San Francisco 370
283. Santa Claus 313
284. **Seeley's American Star** 311
285. **Selim** 71
286. Sentinel 347
287. Shales 62
288. Shark —
289. **Shark** 227
290. Sherman Morgan 202
291. **Sidi Hamet** 346
292. Sidney 283
293. Sidney Dillon 292
294. Simmons 146
295. **Sir Archy** 103
296. **Sir Charles** 295
297. Sir Patrick Highlander 68
298. **Sir Richard Tonson** 254
299. Sir William —
300. **Sorcerer** 341
301. **Sour Crout** 176
302. **Sovereign** 122
303. Spencer 211
304. **Squirt** 41
305. Star Almont 13
306. Star of the West 137
307. Steinway 313
308. Steven's Bald Chief 42
309. Steven's Bellfounder 273
310. **Stockholder** 295
311. **Stockholm's American Star** 115
312. **St. Patrick** —
313. Strathmore 166
314. Strideaway 60
315. **Stump The Dealer** 329
316. **Sultan** 285
317. Sultan 327
318. **Sumter** 295
319. **Tartar** 96
320. Tattler 268
321. Taylor Messenger 142
322. The Abbe 83
323. The Bondsman 40
324. The De Forest 31
325. The Harvester 350
326. The Laurel Hall 265
327. The Moor 88
328. The Viceroy 222
329. **Timoleon** 295
330. Todd 55
331. Toddington 235
332. Tom Crowder 249
333. Tom Kendle 129
334. Tom Wonder 332
335. **Top Gallant** 138
336. **Touchstone** 77
337. Tramp 214
338. **Tramp** 99
339. Truax 160
340. Truman's Brother 120
341. **Trumpator** 94
342. Venture 34
343. Vermont Blackhawk 290
344. Vernol's Blackhawk 215
345. Vice Commodore 55
346. **Virginian** 295
347. Volunteer 166
348. **Wagner** 296
349. **Waller** 182
350. Walnut Hall 95
351. Walter Direct 105
352. **Watkin's Highlander** —
353. **Waxy** 271
354. **West Australian** 231
355. **Whalebone** 353
356. Whitehall 245
357. **Wild Bill** 295
358. Wilkes Boy 146
359. William L. 146
360. Williams' Mambrino 130
361. Wilton 146
362. Woodford Mambrino 220
363. **Woodpecker** 175
364. Worthier 6
365. Yellow Jacket —
366. Young Bashaw 155
367. Young Conquerer 208
368. Young Jim 146
369. Young Patriot 260
370. Zombro 229

See also Nos. 25, 40, 44, 47, 49, 51, 59, 63, 65, 70, 72, 76, 77, 78

No. 1

Axtell, b h, (1886) 3, 2:12m

Hambletonian	Abdallah	19
George Wilkes	Chas. Kent Mare	183
Dolly Spanker	Unknown	
William L.	Unknown	
M'brino Patchen	Mambrino Chief	225
Lady Bunker	Mare by	140
Lady Dunn	American Star	284
AXTELL	Roberts Mare	—
M'brino Patchen	Mambrino Chief	225
Mambrino Boy	Mare by	140
Roving Nelly	C. M. Clay Jr. (22)	78
Lou	Mare by	52
Mambrino Royal	Mambrino Pilot	220
Bird Mitchell	Unknown	
Unknown	Unknown	
	Unknown	

No. 2

Dean Hanover, b h, (1934), 3, TT1:58½m

Axtell	William L.	146
Axworthy	Lou	219
Marguerite	Kentucky Prince	86
Dillon Axworthy	Young Daisy	314
Sidney Dillon	Sidney	283
Adioo Dillon	Venus	—
Adioo	Guy Wilkes	146
DEAN HANOVER	By By	133
Bellini	Artillery	166
Atlantic Express	Merry Clay	171
Expressive	Electioneer	166
Palestrina	Esther	133
Bingen	May King	120
Pilatka	Young Miss	368
Hatteras	Wilkes Boy	146
	Kincora	220

No. 3

Mr. McElwyn, b h, (1921) 5, TT1:59¼m

Axtell	William L.	146
Axworthy	Lou	219
Marguerite	Kentucky Prince	86
Guy Axworthy	Young Daisy	314
Guy Wilkes	George Wilkes	166
Lillian Wilkes	Lady Bunker	224
Flora	Unknown	
MR. McELWYN	Unknown	
Pilot Medium	Happy Medium	166
Peter the Great	Tackey	268
Santos	Grand Sentinel	286
Widow Maggie	Shadow	248
Onward	George Wilkes	166
Maggie Onward	Dolly	220
The Widow	Wilton	146
	Maggie H.	178

No. 4

Florican, b h, (1947) 5, 1:57⅖m

Guy Axworthy	Axworthy	31
Guy McKinney	Lillian Wilkes	163
Qu'nly M'Kinney	McKinney	9
Spud Hanover	Princess Royal	83
Peter the Great	Pilot Medium	168
Evelyn the Great	Santos	156
Miss De Forest	The De Forest	31
FLORICAN	Red Hose	108
Lee Tide	Lee Axworthy	160
Spencer	Emily Ellen	330
Petrex	Peter the Great	269
Florimel	Extasy	40
Mr. McElwyn	Guy Axworthy	32
Carolyn	Widow Maggie	265
Harvest Gale	The Harvester	350
	Morning Gale	39

No. 5

Hickory Smoke, b h, (1954) 4, TT1:58⅖m

Truax	Guy Axworthy	32
Calumet Chuck	Hollyrood Nimble	194
Sumatra	Belwin	229
Titan Hanover	Sienna	265
Peter the Brewer	Peter the Great	269
Tisma Hanover	Zombrewer	370
Justissima	Justice Brooke	38
HICKORY SMOKE	Clarie Toddington	331
Dillon Axworthy	Axworthy	31
Dean Hanover	Adioo Dillon	293
Palestrina	Atlantic Express	47
Misty Hanover	Pilatka	55
Mr. McElwyn	Guy Axworthy	32
Twilight Hanover	Widow Maggie	265
Rose Scott	Peter Scott	265
	Roya McKinney	229

No. 6

True Duane, br h, (1963) p, 3, 1:56⅘m

Nibble Hanover	Calumet Chuck	339
Knight Dream	Justissima	201
Lydia Knight	Peter the Brewer	265
Duane Hanover	Guy Rosa	160
Dillon Axworthy	Axworthy	31
Dorsh Hanover	Adioo Dillon	293
Great Medium	Peter the Great	269
TRUE DUANE	Dorsh Medium	278
Abbedale	The Abbe	83
Chief Abbedale	Daisydale D.	23
Marion Candler	Napoleon Direct	351
Truella Chief	Cherry Gentry	91
Truax	Guy Axworthy	32
Truella	Hollyrood Nimble	194
Petrella	Peter the Great	269
	Barella	54

MALE LINE DESCENT OF THE PETER THE GREAT (HAPPY MEDIUM) FAMILY

See also Nos. 26 through 36, 41, 45, 48, 50, 52, 53, 56, 58, 69, 73

No. 7

Peter the Great, b h, (1895) 4, 2:07¼ m

Hambletonian	Abdallah	19
Happy Medium	Chas. Kent Mare	183
Princess	Andrus's Ham'tn	199
Pilot Medium	Unknown	
Pilot Jr.	Old Pilot	—
Tackey	Nancy Hope	—
Jenny Lind	Unknown	
PETER THE GREAT	Unknown	
Sentinel	Hambletonian	2
Grand Sentinel	Lady Patriot	369
Maid of Lex'ton	Mambrino Pilot	220
Santos	**Brownlock**	213
Octaroon	Unknown	
Shadow	Unknown	
Dixie	Creole	—
	Barker Mare	—

No. 8

Scotland, bl h, (1925) 5, TT1:59¼ m

Pilot Medium	Happy Medium	166
Peter the Great	Tackey	268
Santos	Grand Sentinel	286
Peter Scott	Shadow	248
Bryson	Simmons	146
Jenny Scott	Lena	87
Aetna	Aberdeen	166
SCOTLAND	Etona	13
Alcyone	George Wilkes	166
McKinney	Alma Mater	224
Rosa Sprague	Gov. Sprague	280
Roya McKinney	Rose Kenny	223
Chimes	Electioneer	166
Princess Royal	Beautiful Bells	327
Estabella	Alcantara	146
	Annabel	146

No. 9

Volomite, br h, (1926 3, 2:03¼ m

Pilot Medium	Happy Medium	166
Peter the Great	Tackey	268
Santos	Grand Sentinel	286
Peter Volo	Shadow	248
Nervolo	Colbert	250
Nervolo Belle	Nelly D.	12
Josephine Knight	Betterton	146
VOLOMITE	Mambrino Beauty	222
Zombro	McKinney	9
San Francisco	Whisper	15
Oniska	Nutwood Wilkes	163
Cita Frisco	Bay Line	106
Mendocino	Electioneer	166
Mendocita	Mano	267
Esther	**Express**	124
	Colisseum	302

No. 10

Speedster, b h, (1954) 4, 1:59⅘ m

Scotland	Peter Scott	265
Spencer Scott	Roya McKinney	229
May Spencer	Spencer	211
Rodney	Guyellen	160
Protector	Peter Volo	265
Earl's Pr. Martha	Margaret Arion	160
Mignon	Lee Axworthy	160
SPEEDSTER	Mary Thomas S.	330
Dillon Axworthy	Axworthy	31
Dean Hanover	Adioo Dillon	293
Palestrina	Atlantic Express	47
Mimi Hanover	Pilatka	55
Guy McKinney	Guy Axworthy	32
Hanover Maid	Queenly McKinney	229
Lexington Maid	Peter Volo	265
	Fruity Worthy	32

No. 11

Star's Pride, br h, (1947) 5, 1:57⅕ m

Peter Volo	Peter the Great	269
Volomite	Nervolo Belle	242
Cita Frisco	San Francisco	370
Worthy Boy	Mendocita	232
Peter the Brewer	Peter the Great	269
Warwell Worthy	Zombrewer	370
Alma Lee	Lee Worthy	210
STAR'S PRIDE	Jane Revere	160
Guy Axworthy	Axworthy	31
Mr. McElwyn	Lillian Wilkes	163
Widow Maggie	Peter the Great	269
Stardrift	Maggie Onward	250
San Francisco	Zombro	229
Dillcisco	Oniska	247
Dilworthy	Axworthy	31
	Dillon's Last	37

No. 12

Blaze Hanover, ch h, (1957) 3, 1:59⅘ m

Peter Scott	Peter the Great	269
Scotland	Jenny Scott	70
Roya McKinney	McKinney	9
Hoot Mon	Princess Royal	83
Guy Abbey	Guy Axworthy	32
Missey	Abbacy	322
Tilly Tonka	Spencer	211
BLAZE HANOVER	Minnetonka	49
Guy Axworthy	Axworthy	31
Mr. McElwyn	Lillian Wilkes	163
Widow Maggie	Peter the Great	269
Beverly Hanover	Maggie Onward	250
Peter Volo	Peter the Great	269
Hanover's Bertha	Nervolo Belle	242
Miss B'tha Dillon	Dillon Axworthy	32
	Miss Bertha C	39

MALE LINE DESCENT OF THE ABBE (ELECTIONEER) FAMILY

See also Nos. 37, 38, 39, 42, 43, 46, 55, 60, 62, 64, 68, 75, 80

No. 13
Chimes, br h, (1884) 3, 2:30¾

	Abdallah	Mambrino 234
Hambletonian		Amazonia —
	Chas. Kent Mare	Bellfounder 309
Electioneer		One Eye 58
	Harry Clay	C. M. Clay Jr. (20) 78
Green Mt. Maid		Mare by 183
	Shanghai Mary	Unknown
CHIMES		Unknown
	Clay Pilot	C. M. Clay Jr. (20) 78
The Moor		Mare by 268
	Belle of Wabash	Unknown
Beautiful Bells		Unknown
	Stv'n's Bald Chief	Bay Chief 220
Minnehaha		Dolly Spanker 181
	Nettie Clay	C. M. Clay Jr. (22) 78
		Col. Morgan Mare 2

No. 14
Abbedale, bl h, (1917) p, 2:01¼ m

	Electioneer	Hambletonian 2
Chimes		Green Mt. Maid 171
	Beautiful Bells	The Moor 88
The Abbe		Minnehaha 308
	Mambrino King	Mambrino Patchen 220
Nettie King		Mare by 119
	Nettie Murphy	Hamlin Patchen 145
ABBEDALE		Unknown
	Expedition	Electioneer 166
Archdale		Lady Russell 169
	Aline	Allie West 13
Daisydale D.		Coquette 17
	Pactolus	Patronage 257
Mrs. Tmolus		Buda 337
	Flaxey	Unknown
		Unknown

No. 15
Gene Abbe, b h, (1944) p, TT2:00⅗ m

	Chimes	Electioneer 166
The Abbe		Beautiful Bells 327
	Nettie King	Mambrino King 224
Bert Abbe		Nettie Murphy 167
	Mack H.	John A. McKerron 247
Miss Ella H		Wainscot 250
	Nelly Patch	Dan Patch 195
GENE ABBE		Dun Daisy 342
	Cochato	Todd 55
Martinos		Caslanea 270
	Queen Audubon	Audubon Boy 190
Rose Marie		Miss Nutonia 246
	Coastman	Bourbon Wilkes 146
Lady Permilia		Abatross 89
	Virginia Alta	Anderson Wilkes 250
		True Lady 340

No. 16
Good Time, b h, (1946) p, 5, 1:57⅘ m

	The Abbe	Chimes 120
Abbedale		Nettie King 222
	Daisydale D.	Archdale 132
Hal Dale		Mrs. Tmolus 255
	Argot Hal	Brown Hal 147
Margaret Hal		Lady Wildflower 114
	Margaret Polk	John R. Gentry 27
GOOD TIME		Stella Hal 147
	Peter Volo	Peter the Great 269
Volomite		Nervolo Belle 242
	Cita Frisco	San Francisco 370
On Time		Mendocita 232
	Guy Axworthy	Axworthy 31
Nedda Guy		Lillian Wilkes 163
	Nedda	Atlantic Express 47
		Pleasant Thoughts 276

THE MAMBRINO LINE

No. 17
Mambrino King, ch h, (1872)

	Mam. Paymaster	Mambrino 234
Mambrino Chief		Unknown
	Unknown	Unknown
Mambrino Patchen		Unknown
	Gano	American Eclipse 115
Mare by		Betsey Richards 295
	Mare by	Son of 299
MAMBRINO KING		Unknown
	Bay Ky. Hunter	Kentucky Hunter 352
Edwin Forest		Unknown
	Unknown	Unknown
Mare by		Unknown
	Birmingham	Stockholder 295
Mare by		Black Sophia 335
	Mare by	Bertrand 295
		Mare by 318

THE CLAY LINE

No. 18
Cassius M. Clay Jr. 22, br h, (1842)

	Andrew Jackson	Young Bashaw 155
Henry Clay		Unknown
	Lady Surrey	Unknown
Cassius M. Clay		Unknown
	Unknown	Unknown
Jersey Kate		Unknown
	Unknown	Unknown
CASSIUS M. CLAY JR.		Unknown
	Mambrino	Messenger 128
Abdallah		Mare by 301
	Amazonia	Unknown
Mare by		Unknown
	Lawr'ce's Eclipse	American Eclipse 115
Mare by		Unknown
	Hadley Mare	Messenger 128
		Unknown

1009

MALE LINE DESCENT OF THE DIRECT (DICTATOR) FAMILY

See also Nos. 57, 61, 66

No. 19
Director, bl h, (1877) 2:17

```
                    Mambrino          234
        Abdallah
                    Amazonia          —
Hambletonian
                    Bellfounder       309
        Chas. Kent Mare
                    One Eye           58
Dictator
                    St'klm's Am. Star 115
        Seeley's Am. Star
                    Sally Slouch      173
Clara
                    Unknown
        McKinstry Mare
                    Unknown
DIRECTOR
                    Mambrino          234
        Mam. Paymaster
                    Unknown
Mambrino Chief
                    Unknown
        Unknown
                    Unknown
Dolly
                    Unknown
        Unknown
                    Unknown
Unknown
                    Unknown
        Unknown
                    Unknown
```

No. 20
Walter Direct b h, (1900) p, 2:05¾ m

```
                    Dictator          166
        Director
                    Dolly             220
Direct
                    Echo              166
        Echora
                    Young Mare        65
Direct Hal
                    Tom Hal           35
        Gibson's TomHal
                    Julia Johnson     4
Bessie Hal
                    Prince Pulaski    —
        Princess
                    Vidette           14
WALTER DIRECT
                    Unknown
        Prince Pulaski
                    Unknown
Prince Pulaski Jr.
                    Gibson's Tom Hal  207
        Molly
                    Lady Ottis        177
Ella Brown
                    Unknown
        Joe Bowers
                    Unknown
Fanny Brown
                    Unknown
        Unknown
                    Unknown
```

No. 21
Billy Direct, b h, (1934) p, 4, TT1:55m

```
                    Direct            107
        Direct Hal
                    Bessie Hal        147
Walter Direct
                    Prince Pulaski Jr. 274
        Ella Brown
                    Fanny Brown       193
Napoleon Direct
                    Erector           107
        Tom Kendle
                    Winnie Davis      258
Lady Erectress
                    Hal Pizarro       109
        Nelly Zarro
                    Mare by           44
BILLY DIRECT
                    May King          120
        Bingen
                    Young Miss        368
Malcolm Forbes
                    Happy Medium      166
        Nancy Hanks
                    Nancy Lee         100
Gay Forbes
                    Chimes            120
        Berkshire Chimes
                    Berkshire Belle   9
Gay Girl Chimes
                    Gay Boy           11
        Miss Gay Girl
                    Electric Belle    121
```

No. 22
Thorpe Hanover, br h, (1955) p, 3, TT1:58⅔m

```
                    Walter Direct     105
        Napoleon Direct
                    Lady Erectress    333
Billy  Direct
                    Malcolm Forbes    55
        Gay Forbes
                    Gay Girl Chimes   51
Tar Heel
                    Peter Volo        265
        Volomite
                    Cita Frisco       282
Leta Long
                    Mr. McElwyn       160
        Rosette
                    Rose Scott        263
THORPE HANOVER
                    Axworthy          31
        Guy Axworthy
                    Lillian Wilkes    163
Guy Abbey
                    The Abbe          83
        Abbacy
                    Regal McKinney    229
The Old Maid
                    Lee Tide          210
        Spencer
                    Petrex            265
Spinster
                    Belwin            229
        Minnetonka
                    The Miss Stokes   265
```

THE TENNESSEE HAL LINE

No. 23
Star Pointer, b h, (1889) p, TT1:59¼m

```
                    Bald Stockings    252
        Kitr'l's Tom Hal
                    Unknown
Gibson's Tom Hal
                    Adam's Stump      315
        Julia Johnson
                    Julia             —
Brown Hal
                    Ty'ler's Hen. Hal 207
        John Netherland
                    Unknown
Lizzie
                    John Hal          197
        Blackie
                    Old March         367
STAR POINTER
                    Kittrell's Tom Hal 35
        Knight's TomHal
                    Unknown
Knight's Snow Heels
                    Buckett's Glencoe 149
        Mare by
                    Unknown
Sweepstakes
                    Sugg's Stump      315
        Traveler
                    Unknown
Kit
                    Unknown
        Unknown
                    Unknown
```

THE McKINNEY LINE

No. 24
Belwin, b h, (1910) 4, TT2:06¾m

```
                    Hambletonian      2
        George Wilkes
                    Dolly Spanker     —
Alcyone
                    Mam. Patchen      220
        Alma Mater
                    Estella           29
McKinney
                    Rhode Island      356
        Gov. Sprague
                    Belle Brandon     166
Rosa Sprague
                    Mam. Messenger    225
        Rose Kenny
                    Mare by           220
BELWIN
                    Electioneer       166
        Advertiser
                    Lula Wilkes       146
Adbell
                    The Moor          88
        Beautiful Bells
                    Minnehaha         308
Belle Winnie
                    Hambletonian      2
        Electioneer
                    Green Mt. Boy     171
Gertrude Russell
                    Planet            279
        Dame Winnie
                    Liz Mardis        149
```

No. 25
Greyhound, gr g, (1932) 6, TT1:58¼m

		Axworthy	Axtell	359
	Guy Axworthy		Marguerite	204
		Lillian Wilkes	Guy Wilkes	146
Guy Abbey			Flora	—
	The Abbe		Chimes	120
			Nettie King	222
	Abbacy		McKinney	9
	Regal McKinney		Princess Royal	83
GREYHOUND			Happy Medium	166
	Pilot Medium		Tackey	268
Peter the Great			Grand Sentinel	286
	Santos		Shadow	248
Elizabeth			McKinney	9
	Zombro		Whisper	15
Zombrewer			Montjoy	144
Mary Bales			**Molly J.**	349

No. 26
Noble Victory, br h, (1962 4, 1:55⅗m

		Peter Volo	Peter the Great	269
	Volomite		Nervolo Belle	242
		Cita Frisco	San Francisco	370
Victory Song			Mendocita	232
		Nelson Dillon	Dillon Axworthy	32
	Evensong		Miss Pierette	265
	Taffolet		Guy Axworthy	32
NOBLE VICTORY			Taffeta Silk	235
	Worthy Boy		Volomite	266
	Star's Pride		Warwell Worthy	264
	Stardrift		Mr. McElwyn	160
Emily's Pride			Dillcisco	282
	Scotland		Peter Scott	265
	Emily Scott		Roya McKinney	229
	May Spencer		Spencer	211
			Guyellen	32

No. 27
Matastar, b h, (1958) 4, TT1:55⅘m

		Volomite	Peter Volo	265
	Worthy Boy		Cita Frisco	282
		Warwell Worthy	Peter the Brewer	265
Star's Pride			Alma Lee	212
		Mr. McElwyn	Guy Axworthy	32
	Stardrift		Widow Maggie	265
	Dillcisco		San Francisco	370
MATASTAR			Dilworthy	32
	Guy McKinney		Guy Axworthy	32
	Spud Hanover		Queenly McKinney	229
	Evelyn TheGreat		Peter the Great	269
Honey Flower			Miss De Forest	324
	Spencer		Lee Tide	210
	Florimel		Petrex	265
	Carolyn		Mr. McElwyn	160
			Harvest Gale	325

No. 28
Scott Frost, b h, (1952) 4, 1:58⅗m

		Peter Scott	Peter the Great	269
	Scotland		Jenny Scott	70
		Roya McKinney	McKinney	9
Hoot Mon			Princess Royal	83
		Guy Abbey	Guy Axworthy	32
	Missey		Abbacy	322
	Tilly Tonka		Spencer	211
SCOTT FROST			Minnetonka	49
	Lee Tide		Lee Axworthy	160
	Spencer		Emily Ellen	330
	Petrex		Peter the Great	269
Nora			Extasy	40
	Peter the Brewer		Peter the Great	269
	Belvedere		Zombrewer	370
	Jane Revere		Guy Axworthy	32
			Volga E.	265

No. 29
Rosalind, b m, (1933) 5, TT1:56¾m

		Peter the Great	Pilot Medium	168
	Peter Scott		Santos	268
		Jenny Scott	Bryson	294
Scotland			Aetna	3
		McKinney	Alcyone	146
	Roya McKinney		Rosa Sprague	154
	Princess Royal		Chimes	120
ROSALIND			Estabella	8
	Lee Axworthy		Guy Axworthy	32
	Lee Worthy		Gaiety Lee	55
	Emma Smith		Morgan Axworthy	32
Alma Lee			Mary Tudor	364
	Guy Axworthy		Axworthy	31
	Jane Revere		Lillian Wilkes	163
	Volga E.		Peter the Great	265
			Nervolo Belle	242

No. 30
Armbro Flight, br m, (1962) 3, 1:59m

		Volomite	Peter Volo	265
	Worthy Boy		Cita Frisco	282
		Warwell Worthy	Peter the Brewer	265
Star's Pride			Alma Lee	212
		Mr. McElwyn	Guy Axworthy	32
	Stardrift		Widow Maggie	265
	Dillcisco		San Francisco	370
ARMBRO FLIGHT			Dilworthy	32
	Scotland		Peter Scott	265
	Hoot Mon		Roya McKinney	229
	Missey		Guy Abbey	160
Helicopter			Tilly Tonka	303
	Lawrence Han'vr		Peter Volo	265
	Tronia Hanover		Miss Bertha Dillon	101
	Twilight Han'vr		Mr. McElwyn	160
			Rose Scott	263

No. 31

Ayres, b h, (1961) 3, 1:56⅘m

AYRES

Star's Pride	Worthy Boy	Volomite	Peter Volo	265
			Cita Frisco	282
		Warwell Worthy	Peter the Brewer	265
			Alma Lee	212
	Stardrift	Mr. McElwyn	Guy Axworthy	32
			Widow Maggie	265
		Dillcisco	San Francisco	370
			Dilworthy	32
Arpege	Hoot Mon	Scotland	Peter Scott	265
			Roya McKinney	229
		Missey	Guy Abbey	160
			Tilly Tonka	303
	Goddess Hanover	Dean Hanover	Dillon Axworthy	32
			Palestrina	28
		Little Lie	Mr. McElwyn	160
			Great Patch	265

No. 32

Speedy Scot, b h, (1960) 3, 1:56⅘m

SPEEDY SCOT

Speedster	Rodney	Spencer Scott	Scotland	263
			May Spencer	303
		Earl's Pr. Martha	Protector	266
			Mignon	210
	Mimi Hanover	Dean Hanover	Dillon Axworthy	32
			Palestrina	28
		Hanover Maid	Guy McKinney	160
			Lexington Maid	266
Scotch Love	Victory Song	Volomite	Peter Volo	265
			Cita Frisco	282
		Evensong	Nelson Dillon	101
			Taffolet	160
	Selka Scot	Scotland	Peter Scott	265
			Roya McKinney	229
		Selka Guy	Guy Axworthy	32
			Selka	265

No. 33

Nevele Pride, b h, (1965) 2, 1:58⅖m

NEVELE PRIDE

Star's Pride	Worthy Boy	Volomite	Peter Volo	265
			Cita Frisco	282
		Warwell Worthy	Peter The Brewer	265
			Alma Lee	212
	Stardrift	Mr. McElwyn	Guy Axworthy	32
			Widow Maggie	265
		Dillcisco	San Francisco	370
			Dilworthy	32
Thankful	Hoot Mon	Scotland	Peter Scott	265
			Roya McKinney	229
		Missey	Guy Abbey	160
			Tilly Tonka	303
	Magnolia Hanover	Dean Hanover	Dillon Axworthy	32
			Palestrina	28
		Melba Hanover	Calumet Chuck	339
			Isotta	265

No. 34

Impish, b m, (1959) 2, 1:58⅗m

IMPISH

The Intruder	Scotland	Peter Scott	Peter the Great	269
			Jenny Scott	70
		Roya McKinney	McKinney	9
			Princess Royal	83
	Mighty Margaret	Volomite	Peter Volo	265
			Cita Frisco	282
		Mgt. Castleton	Guy Castleton	160
			Margaret Parrish	345
Ilo Hanover	Nibble Hanover	Calumet Chuck	Truax	160
			Sumatra	49
		Justissima	Justice Brooke	38
			Clarie Toddington	331
	Isabel Hanover	Dillon Axworthy	Axworthy	31
			Adioo Dillon	293
		Isotta	Peter the Great	269
			The Zombro Belle	370

No. 35

Rodney, b h, (1944) 5, TT1:57⅖m

RODNEY

Spencer Scott	Scotland	Peter Scott	Peter the Great	269
			Jenny Scott	70
		Roya McKinney	McKinney	9
			Princess Royal	83
	May Spencer	Spencer	Lee Tide	210
			Petrex	265
		Guyellen	Guy Axworthy	160
			Emily Ellen	330
Earl's Princess Martha	Protector	Peter Volo	Peter the Great	269
			Nervolo Belle	242
		Margaret Arion	Guy Axworthy	32
			Margaret Parrish	345
	Mignon	Lee Axworthy	Guy Axworthy	32
			Gaiety Lee	55
		Mary Thomas S.	Todd	55
			Olga	216

No. 36

Hoot Mon, bl h, (1944) 3, 2:00m

HOOT MON

Scotland	Peter Scott	Peter the Great	Pilot Medium	168
			Santos	156
		Jenny Scott	Bryson	294
			Aetna	3
	Roya McKinney	McKinney	Alcyone	146
			Rosa Sprague	154
		Princess Royal	Chimes	120
			Estabella	8
Missey	Guy Abbey	Guy Axworthy	Axworthy	31
			Lillian Wilkes	163
		Abbacy	The Abbe	83
			Regal McKinney	229
	Tilly Tonka	Spencer	Lee Tide	210
			Petrex	265
		Minnetonka	Belwin	229
			The Miss Stokes	265

No. 37
Adios, b h, (1940) p, 5, TT1:57½m

ADIOS

Hal Dale	Abbedale	The Abbe	Chimes	120
			Nettie King	222
		Daisydale D.	Archdale	132
			Mrs. Tmolus	255
	Margaret Hal	Argot Hal	Brown Hal	147
			Lady Wildflower	114
		Margaret Polk	John R. Gentry	27
			Stella Hal	147
Adioo Volo	Adioo Guy	Guy Dillon	Sidney Dillon	292
			By Guy	163
		Adioo	Guy Wilkes	146
			By By	246
	Sigrid Volo	Peter Volo	Peter the Great	269
			Nervolo Belle	242
		Polly Parrot	Jersey B. B.	188
			Lady Maud C.	84

No. 38
Bret Hanover, br h, (1962) p, 4, TT1:53⅗m

BRET HANOVER

Adios	Hal Dale	Abbedale	The Abbe	83
			Daisydale D.	23
		Margaret Hal	Argot Hal	67
			Margaret Polk	198
	Adioo Volo	Adioo Guy	Guy Dillon	293
			Adioo	163
		Sigrid Volo	Peter Volo	265
			Polly Parrot	187
Brenna Hanover	Tar Heel	Billy Direct	Napoleon Direct	351
			Gay Forbes	218
		Leta Long	Volomite	266
			Rosette	239
	Beryl Hanover	Nibble Hanover	Calumet Chuck	339
			Justissima	201
		Laura Hanover	The Laurel Hall	265
			Miss B'tha W'thy	212

No. 39
Bullet Hanover, b h, (1957) p, 3, TT1:55⅗m

BULLET HANOVER

Adios	Hal Dale	Abbedale	The Abbe	83
			Daisydale D.	23
		Margaret Hal	Argot Hal	67
			Margaret Polk	198
	Adioo Volo	Adioo Guy	Guy Dillon	293
			Adioo	163
		Sigrid Volo	Peter Volo	265
			Polly Parrot	187
Barbara Direct	Billy Direct	Napoleon Direct	Walter Direct	105
			Lady Erectress	333
		Gay Forbes	Malcolm Forbes	55
			Gay Girl Chimes	51
	Norette Hanover	Peter the Brewer	Peter the Great	269
			Zombrewer	370
		Helen Hanover	Dillon Volo	266
			Helen Dillon	101

No. 40
Dan Patch, br h, (1896) p, 9, TT1:55¼m

DAN PATCH

Joe Patchen	Patchen Wilkes	George Wilkes	Hambletonian	2
			Dolly Spanker	—
		Kitty Patchen	Mambrino Patchen	220
			Betty Brown	224
	Josephine Young	Joe Young	Star of the West	137
			Lady Gregory	159
		Unknown	Unknown	
			Unknown	
Zelica	Wilkesberry	Young Jim	George Wilkes	166
			Lear Mare	209
		Madam Adams	American Clay	81
			Lady Adams	80
	Abdallah Belle	Pacing Abdallah	Alex's Abdallah	166
			Lydia Talbot	321
		Fanny	Well's Yellow J'kt	365
			Unknown	

No. 41
Bye Bye Byrd, b h, (1955) p, 5, TT1:56⅛m

BYE BYE BYRD

Poplar Byrd	Volomite	Peter Volo	Peter the Great	269
			Nervolo Belle	242
		Cita Frisco	San Francisco	282
			Mendocita	232
	Ann Vonian	Grattan at Law	Grattan Royal	157
			Daisy at Law	172
		Margaret Vonian	Favonian	191
			Mgt. C. Brook	36
Evalina Hanover	Billy Direct	Napoleon Direct	Walter Direct	105
			Lady Erectress	333
		Gay Forbes	Malcolm Forbes	55
			Gay Girl Chimes	51
	Adieu	Hal Dale	Abbedale	322
			Margaret Hal	24
		Adioo Volo	Adioo Guy	161
			Sigrid Volo	266

No. 42
Adios Harry, br h, (1951) p, 4, 1:55m

ADIOS HARRY

Adios	Hal Dale	Abbedale	The Abbe	83
			Daisydale D.	23
		Margaret Hal	Argot Hal	67
			Margaret Polk	198
	Adioo Volo	Adioo Guy	Guy Dillon	293
			Adioo	163
		Sigrid Volo	Peter Volo	265
			Polly Parrot	187
Helen Win	Mc I Win	Mr. McElwyn	Guy Axworthy	32
			Widow Maggie	265
		Olivia Worthy	Axworthy	31
			Ollis McKinney	229
	Helen R.	Harvest Wind	The Harvester	350
			Lucile Marlowe	276
		Virginia Humbug	Cochato	330
			Baroness Maid	40

No. 43

Romeo Hanover, ch h, (1963) p, 3, 1:56⅕f

		Abbedale	322
	Hal Dale	Margaret Hal	24
Adios		Adioo Guy	161
	Adioo Volo	Sigrid Volo	266
Dancer Hanover		Guy Axworthy	32
	Guy Abbey	Abbacy	322
The Old Maid		Spencer	211
	Spinster	Minnetonka	49
ROMEO HANOVER		Napoleon Direct	351
	Billy Direct	Gay Forbes	218
Tar Heel		Volomite	266
	Leta Long	Rosette	239
Romola Hanover		Abbedale	322
	Hal Dale	Margaret Hal	24
Romola Hal		The Senator	265
	Romola	May Dodge	194

No. 44

Elma, br m, (1960) 3, TT1:58⅘m

		Truax	160
	Calumet Chuck	Sumatra	49
Titan Hanover		Peter the Brewer	265
	Tronia Hanover	Justissima	201
Hickory Smoke		Dillon Axworthy	32
	Dean Hanover	Palestrina	28
Misty Hanover		Mr. McElwyn	160
	Twilight Han'vr	Rose Scott	263
ELMA		Peter Scott	265
	Scotland	Roya McKinney	229
Hoot Mon		Guy Abbey	160
	Missey	Tilly Tonka	303
Cassin Hanover		Dillon Axworthy	32
	Dean Hanover	Palestrina	28
Goddess Hanover		Mr. McElwyn	160
	Little Lie	Great Patch	265

No. 45

Hickory Pride, br h, (1956) 5, TT1:59⅖m

		Peter Volo	265
	Volomite	Cita Frisco	282
Worthy Boy		Peter the Brewer	265
	Warwell Worthy	Alma Lee	212
Star's Pride		Guy Axworthy	32
	Mr. McElwyn	Widow Maggie	265
Stardrift		San Francisco	370
	Dillcisco	Dilworthy	32
HICKORY PRIDE		Axworthy	31
	Dillon Axworthy	Adioo Dillon	293
Dean Hanover		Atlantic Express	47
	Palestrina	Pilatka	55
Misty Hanover		Guy Axworthy	32
	Mr. McElwyn	Widow Maggie	265
Twilight Hanover		Peter Scott	265
	Rose Scott	Roya McKinney	229

No. 46

Race Time, b h, (1961) p, 3, 1:57m

		The Abbe	83
	Abbedale	Daisydale D.	23
Hal Dale		Argot Hal	67
	Margaret Hal	Margaret Polk	198
Good Time		Peter Volo	265
	Volomite	Cita Frisco	282
On Time		Guy Axworthy	32
	Nedda Guy	Nedda	28
RACE TIME		Peter Volo	265
	Volomite	Cita Frisco	282
Worthy Boy		Peter the Brewer	265
	Warwell Worthy	Alma Lee	212
Breath O' Spring		Peter Scott	265
	Scotland	Roya McKinney	229
Lady Scotland		Spencer	211
	Spinster	Minnetonka	49

No. 47

Evensong, b m, (1925) 2, TT2:09¾m

		Axtell	359
	Axworthy	Marguerite	204
Dillon Axworthy		Sidney Dillon	292
	Adioo Dillon	Adioo	163
Nelson Dillon		Pilot Medium	168
	Peter the Great	Santos	156
Miss Pierette		Guy Wilkes	146
	Mdm. Thompson	Eva	317
EVENSONG		Axtell	359
	Axworthy	Marguerite	204
Guy Axworthy		Guy Wilkes	32
	Lillian Wilkes	Flora	—
Taffolet		Baron Wilkes	146
	Moko	Queen Ethel	313
Taffeta Silk		Prodigal	257
	Sybil Knight	The Red Silk	40

No. 48

Maggie Counsel, bl m, (1945)

		Peter the Great	269
	Peter Volo	Nervolo Belle	242
Volomite		San Francisco	282
	Cita Frisco	Mendocita	232
Chief Counsel		Axworthy	31
	Guy Axworthy	Lillian Wilkes	163
Margaret Spangler		Oratorio	358
	Maggie Winder	Clara Direct	104
MAGGIE COUNSEL		Pilot Medium	168
	Peter the Great	Santos	156
Peter Scott		Bryson	294
	Jenny Scott	Aetna	3
La Reine		Axworthy	359
	Guy Axworthy	Lillian Wilkes	163
La Roya		McKinney	9
	Roya McKinney	Princess Royal	83

CROSSES CLOSER THAN 3x3 TO A COMMON ANCESTOR

No. 49

Crusader, b h, (1964) p, 2, 2:00⅖ m

CRUSADER
- Torrid
  - Knight Dream
    - Nibble Hanover
      - Calumet Chuck 339
      - Justissima 201
    - Lydia Knight
      - Peter the Brewer 265
      - Guy Rosa 32
  - Torresdale
    - Abbedale
      - The Abbe 83
      - Daisydale D. 23
    - Calumet Cream
      - Truax 160
      - Zombrewer 370
- Miss M. B.
  - Torpid
    - Knight Dream
      - Nibble Hanover 75
      - Lydia Knight 264
    - Torresdale
      - Abbedale 322
      - Calumet Cream 339
  - Breeze On Hal
    - Hal Dale
      - Abbedale 322
      - Margaret Hal 24
    - March Breeze
      - Billy Direct 241
      - Primrose Polly 266

No. 50

Gang Awa, ch h, (1955) 2, 2:03⅗ m

GANG AWA
- Hoot Mon
  - Scotland
    - Peter Scott
      - Peter the Great 269
      - Jenny Scott 70
    - Roya McKinney
      - McKinney 9
      - Princess Royal 83
  - Missey
    - Guy Abbey
      - Guy Axworthy 32
      - Abbacy 322
    - Tilly Tonka
      - Spencer 211
      - Minnetonka 49
- Miss Tilly
  - Nibble Hanover
    - Calumet Chuck
      - Truax 160
      - Sumatra 49
    - Justissima
      - Justice Brooke 38
      - Clarie Toddington 331
  - Tilly Tonka
    - Spencer
      - Lee Tide 210
      - Petrex 265
    - Minnetonka
      - Belwin 229
      - The Miss Stokes 265

No. 51

Alma Lee, b m, (1925) 4, 2:04¾ m

ALMA LEE
- Lee Worthy
  - Lee Axworthy
    - Guy Axworthy
      - Axworthy 31
      - Lillian Wilkes 163
    - Gaiety Lee
      - Bingen 228
      - The Gaiety Girl 278
  - Emma Smith
    - Morgan Axw'thy
      - Axworthy 31
      - Kinglyne 228
    - Mary Tudor
      - Worthier 6
      - Rusella 169
- Jane Revere
  - Guy Axworthy
    - Axworthy
      - Axtell 359
      - Marguerite 204
    - Lillian Wilkes
      - Guy Wilkes 146
      - Flora —
  - Volga E.
    - Peter the Great
      - Pilot Medium 168
      - Santos 156
    - Nervolo Belle
      - Nervolo 90
      - Josephine Knight 53

No. 52

Helen Hanover, b m, (1927) 3, 2:04¾ m

HELEN HANOVER
- Dillon Volo
  - Peter Volo
    - Peter the Great
      - Pilot Medium 168
      - Santos 156
    - Nervolo Belle
      - Nervolo 90
      - Josephine Knight 53
  - Miss Bertha Dillon
    - Dillon Axworthy
      - Axworthy 31
      - Adioo Dillon 293
    - Miss Bertha C.
      - Baronmore 40
      - Marble 205
- Helen Dillon
  - Dillon Axworthy
    - Axworthy
      - Axtell 359
      - Marguerite 204
    - Adioo Dillon
      - Sidney Dillon 292
      - Adioo 163
  - Miss Pierette
    - Peter the Great
      - Pilot Medium 168
      - Santos 156
    - Mdm. Thompson
      - Guy Wilkes 146
      - Eva 317

FORMER CHAMPION TROTTER

No. 53

Peter Manning, b g, (1916) p, TT1:56¾ m

PETER MANNING
- Azoff
  - Peter the Great
    - Pilot Medium
      - Happy Medium 166
      - Tackey 268
    - Santos
      - Grand Sentinel 286
      - Shadow 248
  - Dolly Worthy
    - Axworthy
      - Axtell 359
      - Marguerite 204
    - Dolly Phoebe
      - Hamb'n Wilkes 146
      - Dolly Smith 221
- Glendora G.
  - Emmett Grattan
    - Grattan
      - Wilkes Boy 146
      - Annie Almont 14
    - Maggie McGr'gr
      - Robert McGregor 217
      - Maggie Medium 168
  - Wallie Moore
    - Gambetta Wilkes
      - George Wilkes 166
      - Jewell 148
    - Bellfield
      - Enfield 166
      - Lady Belmont 48

THE FIRST TWO-MINUTE TROTTER

No. 54

Lou Dillon, ch m, (1898) 5, TT1:58½ m

LOU DILLON
- Sidney Dillon
  - Sidney
    - Santa Claus
      - Strathmore 166
      - Lady Thorne, Jr. 360
    - Sweetness
      - Volunteer 166
      - Lady Merritt 118
  - Venus
    - Unknown
      - Unknown
      - Unknown
    - Unknown
      - Unknown
      - Unknown
- Lou Milton
  - Milton Medium
    - Happy Medium
      - Hambletonian 2
      - Princess 22
    - Mare by
      - Sackett's Hamb'n 166
      - Unknown
  - Fly
    - Unknown
      - Unknown
      - Unknown
    - Unknown
      - Unknown
      - Unknown

EXAMPLES OF VARIOUS TYPES OF PACING CROSSES

ABBEDALE SIRE ON VOLOMITE MARE

No. 55

Meadow Skipper, br h, (1960) p, 3, 1:55⅕ m

- **MEADOW SKIPPER**
  - Dale Frost
    - Hal Dale
      - Abbedale — The Abbe 83; Daisydale D. 23
      - Margaret Hal — Argot Hal 67; Margaret Polk 198
    - Raider
      - Galloway — Peter Volo 265; Nelda Dillon 101
      - Bethel — David Guy 160; Annotation 33
  - Countess Vivian
    - King's Counsel
      - Volomite — Peter Volo 265; Cita Frisco 282
      - Mgt. Spangler — Guy Axworthy 32; Maggie Winder 251
    - Filly Direct
      - Billy Direct — Napoleon Direct 351; Gay Forbes 218
      - Calumet Edna — Peter the Brewer 265; Broncho Queen 123

VOLOMITE SIRE ON ABBEDALE MARE

No. 56

Overtrick, b h, (1960) p, 3, 1:57⅕ h

- **OVERTRICK**
  - Solicitor
    - King's Counsel
      - Volomite — Peter Volo 265; Cita Frisco 282
      - Mgt. Spangler — Guy Axworthy 32; Maggie Winder 251
    - Jane Reynolds
      - Scotland — Peter Scott 265; Roya McKinney 229
      - Jane Revere — Guy Axworthy 32; Volga E. 265
  - Overbid
    - Hal Dale
      - Abbedale — The Abbe 83; Daisydale D. 23
      - Margaret Hal — Argot Hal 67; Margaret Polk 198
    - Barbara Direct
      - Billy Direct — Napoleon Direct 351; Gay Forbes 218
      - Norette Hanover — Peter the Brewer 265; Helen Hanover 102

DIRECT SIRE ON VOLOMITE MARE

No. 57

Tar Heel, bl h, (1948) p, 4, TT1:57 m

- **TAR HEEL**
  - Billy Direct
    - Napoleon Direct
      - Walter Direct — Direct Hal 104; Ella Brown 275
      - Lady Erectress — Tom Kendle 129; Nelly Zarro 165
    - Gay Forbes
      - Malcolm Forbes — Bingen 228; Nancy Hanks 168
      - Gay Girl Chimes — Berkshire Chimes 83; Miss Gay Girl 141
  - Leta Long
    - Volomite
      - Peter Volo — Peter the Great 269; Nervolo Belle 242
      - Cita Frisco — San Francisco 370; Mendocita 232
    - Rosette
      - Mr. McElwyn — Guy Axworthy 32; Widow Maggie 265
      - Rose Scott — Peter Scott 265; Roya McKinney 229

VOLOMITE SIRE ON DIRECT MARE

No. 58

Sampson Direct, br m, (1957) p, 4, TT1:56 m

- **SAMPSON DIRECT**
  - Sampson Hanover
    - Volomite
      - Peter Volo — Peter the Great 269; Nervolo Belle 242
      - Cita Frisco — San Francisco 370; Mendocita 232
    - Irene Hanover
      - Dillon Axworthy — Axworthy 31; Adioo Dillon 293
      - Isotta — Peter the Great 269; The Zombro Belle 370
  - Dottie Rosecroft
    - Billy Direct
      - Napoleon Direct — Walter Direct 105; Lady Erectress 333
      - Gay Forbes — Malcolm Forbes 55; Gay Girl Chimes 51
    - Beams Hanover
      - Calumet Chuck — Truax 160; Sumatra 49
      - Lexington Maid — Peter Volo 265; Fruity Worthy 32

AXWORTHY SIRE ON AXWORTHY MARE

No. 59

Duane Hanover, b h, (1952) p, 4, 1:58 m

- **DUANE HANOVER**
  - Knight Dream
    - Nibble Hanover
      - Calumet Chuck — Truax 160; Sumatra 49
      - Justissima — Justice Brooke 38; Clarie Toddington 331
    - Lydia Knight
      - Peter the Br'wer — Peter the Great 269; Zombrewer 370
      - Guy Rosa — Guy Axworthy 32; Rosa Lake 323
  - Dorsh Hanover
    - Dillon Axworthy
      - Axworthy — Axtell 359; Marguerite 204
      - Adioo Dillon — Sidney Dillon 292; Adioo 163
    - Great Medium
      - Peter the Great — Pilot Medium 168; Santos 156
      - Dorsh Medium — Red Medium 278; Vicanora 328

ABBEDALE SIRE ON ABBEDALE MARE

No. 60

Adios Vic, b h, (1962) p 3, 1:56¾ m

- **ADIOS VIC**
  - Adios
    - Hal Dale
      - Abbedale — The Abbe 83; Daisydale D. 23
      - Margaret Hal — Argot Hal 67; Margaret Polk 198
    - Adioo Volo
      - Adioo Guy — Guy Dillon 293; Adioo 163
      - Sigrid Volo — Peter Volo 265; Polly Parrot 187
  - Miss Creedabelle
    - Jimmy Creed
      - Frisco Forbes — Frisco Dale 164; Elizabeth L. 191
      - Virginia Grattan — Silent Grattan 158; Myrtle McKlyo 262
    - Belle Grattan
      - Dexter Worthy — Full Worthy 160; Daisy Grattan 158
      - Iola Grattan — Grattan Royal 157; Iola Hal 24

DIRECT SIRE ON ABBEDALE MARE

No. 61

Tarport Lib, b m, (1963) p, 3, 1:56⅖m

Sire / Dam				No.
Thorpe Hanover	Tar Heel	Billy Direct	Napoleon Direct	351
			Gay Forbes	218
		Leta Long	Volomite	266
			Rosette	239
	The Old Maid	Guy Abbey	Guy Axworthy	32
			Abbacy	322
		Spinster	Spencer	211
			Minnetonka	49
TARPORT LIB				
Adios Betty	Adios	Hal Dale	Abbedale	322
			Margaret Hal	24
		Adioo Volo	Adioo Guy	161
			Sigrid Volo	266
	Shy Ann	Cardinal Prince	Peter Potempkin	265
			Lillian L.	56
		Bid Hanover	Sandy Flash	266
			Betty Blythe	237

ABBEDALE SIRE ON DIRECT MARE

No. 62

Adios Butler, b h, (1956) p, 4, TT1:54⅗m

Sire / Dam				No.
Adios	Hal Dale	Abbedale	The Abbe	83
			Daisydale D.	23
		Margaret Hal	Argot Hal	67
			Margaret Polk	198
	Adioo Volo	Adioo Guy	Guy Dillon	293
			Adioo	163
		Sigrid Volo	Peter Volo	265
			Polly Parrot	187
ADIOS BUTLER				
Debby Hanover	Billy Direct	Napoleon Direct	Walter Direct	105
			Lady Erectress	333
		Gay Forbes	Malcolm Forbes	55
			Gay Girl Chimes	51
	Bonnie Butler	Volomite	Peter Volo	265
			Cita Frisco	282
		Ruth Abbe	Abbe Guy	322
			Ruth McKinney	25

AXWORTHY SIRE ON ABBEDALE MARE

No. 63

Torpid, b h, (1954) p, 2, 1:58m

Sire / Dam				No.
Knight Dream	Nibble Hanover	Calumet Chuck	Truax	160
			Sumatra	49
		Justissima	Justice Brooke	38
			Clarie Toddington	331
	Lydia Knight	Peter the Br'wer	Peter the Great	269
			Zombrewer	370
		Guy Rosa	Guy Axworthy	32
			Rosa Lake	323
TORPID				
Torresdale	Abbedale	The Abbe	Chimes	120
			Nettie King	222
		Daisydale D.	Archdale	132
			Mrs. Tmolus	255
	Calumet Cream	Truax	Guy Axworthy	32
			Hollyrood Nimble	194
		Zombrewer	Peter the Brewer	265
			Mary Bales	236

ABBEDALE SIRE ON AXWORTHY MARE

No. 64

Best of All, b h, (1964) p, 3, 1:57m

Sire / Dam				No.
Good Time	Hal Dale	Abbedale	The Abbe	83
			Daisydale D.	23
		Margaret Hal	Argot Hal	67
			Margaret Polk	198
	On Time	Volomite	Peter Volo	265
			Cita Frisco	282
		Nedda Guy	Guy Axworthy	32
			Nedda	28
BEST OF ALL				
Besta Hanover	Knight Dream	Nibble Hanover	Calumet Chuck	339
			Justissima	201
		Lydia Knight	Peter the Brewer	265
			Guy Rosa	160
	Bertha Hanover	Guy McKinney	Guy Axworthy	32
			Queenly McKinney	229
		Miss B'tha Dillon	Dillon Axworthy	32
			Miss Bertha C.	39

AXWORTHY SIRE ON DIRECT MARE

No. 65

Vicar Hanover, b h, (1961), p, 3, 1:59⅕f

Sire / Dam				No.
Torpid	Knight Dream	Nibble Hanover	Calumet Chuck	339
			Justissima	201
		Lydia Knight	Peter the Brewer	265
			Guy Rosa	160
	Torresdale	Abbedale	The Abbe	83
			Daisydale D.	23
		Calumet Cream	Truax	160
			Zombrewer	370
VICAR HANOVER				
Valentine Day	Tar Heel	Billy Direct	Napoleon Direct	351
			Gay Forbes	218
		Leta Long	Volomite	266
			Rosette	239
	Holiday Hanover	Nibble Hanover	Calumet Chuck	339
			Justissima	201
		Gail Hanover	Mr. McElwyn	160
			Volga Hanover	101

DIRECT SIRE ON AXWORTHY MARE

No. 66

Direct Rhythm b, h, (1948) p, 4, TT1:56⅕m

Sire / Dam				No.
Billy Direct	Napoleon Direct	Walter Direct	Direct Hal	104
			Ella Brown	275
		Lady Erectress	Tom Kendle	129
			Nelly Zarro	165
	Gay Forbes	Malcolm Forbes	Bingen	228
			Nancy Hanks	168
		GayGirl Chimes	Berkshire Chimes	83
			Miss Gay Girl	141
DIRECT RHYTHM				
Rhythm	Guy Abbey	Guy Axworthy	Axworthy	31
			Lillian Wilkes	163
		Abbacy	The Abbe	83
			Regal McKinney	229
	Lyric	Peter Volo	Peter the Great	269
			Nervolo Belle	242
		Zombelle	Guy Axworthy	32
			Belle Zombro	370

MATERNAL FAMILIES

Through the end of the 1966 season, a total of 829 horses had been credited with officially recorded miles in 2:00 or faster in this country and Canada. These horses were by a wide assortment of sires—Adios led the list with 75—and sprang from an even wider assortment of maternal families. The maternal family is determined by tracing the performer from dam to dam to dam on the bottom line of the pedigree to a single tap root mare just as the sire family is traced from sire to sire to sire on the top line. Although no complete study has ever been done, it is known that there are more than 200 distinct maternal line sources which will, of course, shake down to fewer and fewer with each succeeding generation. The strength of certain maternal families is already quite evident to the extent that 34 families (each with 5 or more 2:00 credits) have produced 490 of the 2:00 horses which breaks down to a percentage of 59.1. Even among this elite group there is a sharp class distinction in that seven of the families tower over all the others. These seven have produced 241 2:00 horses, 29.1% of the total. The seven maternal families that led in the production of 2:00 horses through the end of 1966 were as follows:

	PERFORMERS		
FAMILY	Trot	Pace	TOTAL
Jessie Pepper	9	35	44
Eva (Thompson Sisters)	6	35	41
Medio (Miss Bertha C.)	13	25	38
Kathleen (Ethelwyn)	9	23	32
Mamie	15	17	32
Nervolo Belle	9	21	30
Midnight (Emily Ellen)	8	16	24
	69	172	241

On the pages that follow are presented tabulated pedigrees of the tap root mares of these seven families along with either one or two additional mares for each, selected with a view toward indicating the direction the family has taken. Like the sires that made the breed, many of the mares have blank spaces in their pedigrees. This does not mean that the unknown ancestors lacked quality, only that their pedigrees could not be verified. And if these pedigrees did contain "weak links," the mares, like the sires, have managed to rise above it and prosper.

No. 67

Jessie Pepper, br m, (1861)

JESSIE PEPPER	Mambrino Chief	Mambrino Paymaster	**Mambrino**	**Messenger**	128
				Mare by	301
			Unknown	Unknown	
				Unknown	
		Eldridge Mare	Unknown	Unknown	
				Unknown	
			Unknown	Unknown	
				Unknown	
	Mare by	Sidi Hamet	**Virginian**	**Sir Archy**	103
				Unknown	
			Lady Burton	**Sir Archy**	103
				Unknown	
		Wickliffe Mare	Unknown	Unknown	
				Unknown	
			Unknown	Unknown	
				Unknown	

No. 68

Princess Royal, br m, (1890) 2, 2:20m

PRINCESS ROYAL	Chimes	Electioneer	Hambletonian	Abdallah	19
				Chas. Kent Mare	183
			Green Mt. Maid	Harry Clay	79
				Shanghai Mary	—
		Beautiful Bells	The Moor	Clay Pilot	79
				Belle of Wabash	—
			Minnehaha	Steven's Bald Chief	42
				Netty Clay	81
	Estabella	Alcantara	George Wilkes	Hambletonian	2
				Dolly Spanker	—
			Alma Mater	Mambrino Patchen	220
				Estella	
		Annabel	George Wilkes	Hambletonian	2
				Dolly Spanker	—
			Jessie Pepper	Mambrino Chief	225
				Mare by	291

THE JESSIE PEPPER FAMILY

The leading family of 2:00 performers is that of Jessie Pepper, a mare with a strong Thoroughbred background that is verified in part and unverified but undoubtedly present in other parts. Through the inbred George Wilkes mare Estabella, the basic line leads to Princess Royal, she the dam of the famed McKinney sisters by the stallion McKinney, Roya McKinney (the first mare to produce three in 2:00–Scotland, Highland Scott and Rose Scott, all by Peter Scott) Regal McKinney and Queenly McKinney.

The five fastest trotters in the family are: Hickory Smoke, 4, TT1:58⅖m, Guy McKinney, 4, TT1:58¾m, Armbro Flight, 3, 1:59m, Scotland, 5, TT1:59¼m, and Hickory Pride, 5, TT1:59⅖m.

The five fastest pacers are: Mighty Tar Heel, p, 5, 1:56⅗m, Tar Heel, p, 4, TT1:57m, Keystoner, p, 6, 1:57⅘m, Lang Hanover, p, 3, 1:57⅘m, Meadow Rice, p, 3, 1:58⅕m, and Queen's Adios, p, 4, 1:58⅕m.

See also pedigrees Nos. 5, 8, 30, 45, 48 and 57.

<table>
<tr><td colspan="3">No. 69</td></tr>
</table>

No. 69 — Medio, ch m, (1887)		
Hambletonian	Abdallah	19
Happy Medium	Chas. Kent Mare	183
Princess	Andrus's H'tonian	199
Cooper Medium	Unknown	
Mam. Champion	Mambrino Chief	225
Queen	Champion	—
Mag Cooper	Ashland	220
MEDIO	Unknown	
Mam. Patchen	Mambrino Chief	225
Mambrino King	Mare by	140
Mare by	Edwin Forest	43
Topsey	Mare by	57
Unknown	Unknown	
Unknown	Unknown	
Unknown	Unknown	
Unknown	Unknown	

No. 70 — Miss Bertha Dillon, ch m, (1914) 4, 2:02½m		
Axtell	William L.	146
Axworthy	Lou	219
Marguerite	Kentucky Prince	86
Dillon Axworthy	Young Daisy	314
Sidney Dillon	Sidney	283
Adioo Dillon	Venus	—
Adioo	Guy Wilkes	146
MISS BERTHA DILLON	By By	246
Baron Wilkes	George Wilkes	166
Baronmore	Belle Patchen	224
May Wagner	Strathmore	166
Miss Bertha C.	Mary S.	8
King Clay	Harry Clay	79
Marble	Modesty	334
Medio	Cooper Medium	168
	Topsey	222

THE MISS BERTHA C. FAMILY

This family descends from Medio but owes almost all its success to Miss Bertha Dillon and her daughters. The family has a distinct Hanover Shoe Farms flavor and probably should be called the Hanover family as it already is by some authorities. The key mares in the modern era were the famed 2:00 sisters, Hanover's Bertha, Miss Bertha Hanover and Charlotte Hanover (by Peter Volo-Miss Bertha Dillon) as well as a number of their sisters and half sisters with lesser race track records.

The five fastest trotters in the family are: Spicy Song, 4, TT1:57⅘m, Worth Seein, 3, TT1:58m, Caleb, 3, 1:58⅕m, Dashing Rodney, 4, TT1:58⅘m, Clever Hanover, 6, 1:59½m, Hanover's Bertha, 3, TT1:59½m, and Charlotte Hanover 3, TT1:59½m.

The five fastest pacers are: Bret Hanover, p, 4, TT1:53⅗m, Best of All p, 3, 1:57m, Bonjour Hanover, p, 3, 1:57m, Coffee Break, p, 3, 1:57m, and Cold Front, p, 5, 1:57⅕m.

See also pedigrees Nos. 12, 38 and 64.

No. 71

Eva, b m, (1879) 2:23½ m

EVA			
Sultan	The Moor	Clay Pilot	C. M. Clay Jr. (20) 78
			Mare by 268
		Belle of Wabash	Unknown
			Unknown
	Sultana	Delmonico	Guy Miller 166
			Adams Mare 166
		Celeste	Mambrino Chief 225
			Big Norah 110
Minnehaha	Steven's Bald Chief	Bay Chief	Mambrino Chief 225
			Keokuk Mare —
		Dolly Spanker	Hunt's Commodore 19
			Mare by 69
	Netty Clay	C.M. Clay Jr.(22)	Cassius M. Clay (18) 78
			Mare by 2
		Mare by	Abdallah 19
			Mare by 126

No. 72

Tillie Thompson, b m, (1890)

TILLIE THOMPSON			
Guy Wilkes	George Wilkes	Hambletonian	Abdallah 19
			Chas. Kent Mare 183
		Dolly Spanker	Unknown
			Unknown
	Lady Bunker	Mam. Patchen	Mambrino Chief 225
			Mare by 140
		Lady Dunn	American Star 311
			Roberts Mare —
Eva	Sultan	The Moor	Clay Pilot 79
			Belle of Wabash —
		Sultana	Delmonico 162
			Celeste 220
	Minnehaha	Stv'n's Bald Chief	Bay Chief 220
			Dolly Spanker 181
		Netty Clay	C. M. Clay Jr. (22) 78
			Mare by 2

No. 73

Miss Pierette, bl m, (1912) 3, TT2:09¾ m

MISS PIERETTE			
Peter the Great	Pilot Medium	Happy Medium	Hambletonian 2
			Princess 22
		Tackey	Pilot Jr. 249
			Jenny Lind —
	Santos	Grand Sentinel	Sentinel 347
			Maid of Lexington 226
		Shadow	Octaroon —
			Dixie —
Madam Thompson	Guy Wilkes	George Wilkes	Hambletonian 2
			Dolly Spanker —
		Lady Bunker	Mambrino Patchen 220
			Lady Dunn 284
	Eva	Sultan	The Moor 88
			Sultana 98
		Minnehaha	Steven's Bald Chief 42
			Netty Clay 137

THE EVA FAMILY

The Eva family is also known as the Thompson Sisters family. It descends from a mare that was a three-quarter sister to the dam of Chimes (he was by Electioneer out of Beautiful Bells by The Moor-Minnehaha), one of the key horses of the Hal Dale-Adios sire line. The principal sources of descent are through Tillie Thompson and Madam Thompson, both of whom appear in the accompanying pedigrees.

The five fastest trotters in the family are: Sprite Rodney, 3, TT1:58⅖ m, Tilly Brooke, 6, 1:59h, Diller Hanover, 3, TT1:59⅖ m, Sara Black, 3, 2:00m, Something Special, 5, 2:00m, and Hoot Mon, 3, 2:00m.

The five fastest pacers are: Bullet Hanover, p, 3, TT1:55⅗ m, Dancer Hanover, p, 4, TT1:56⅘ m, Race Time, p, 3, 1:57m, Right Time, p, 4, 1:57⅕ m, and Overtrick, p, 3, 1:57⅕ h.

See also pedigrees Nos. 13, 22, 36, 39, 46, 50, 52 and 56.

No. 74

Midnight, gr m, (1865)

MIDNIGHT	Pilot Jr.	Old Pilot	Unknown	Unknown	
				Unknown	
			Unknown	Unknown	
				Unknown	
		Nancy Pope	Unknown	Unknown	
				Unknown	
			Nancy Taylor	Unknown	
				Unknown	
	Twilight	**Lexington**	**Boston**	**Timoleon**	295
				Mare by	135
			Alice Carneal	**Sarpedon**	122
				Rowena	295
		Daylight	**Glencoe**	**Sultan**	285
				Trampoline	338
			Darkness	**Wagner**	296
				Lady Gray	298

No. 75

Emily Ellen, bl m, (1907) 3, 2:09¼m

EMILY ELLEN	Todd	Bingen	May King	Electioneer	166
				May Queen	244
			Young Miss	Young Jim	146
				Miss Mambrino	278
		Fanella	Arion	Electioneer	166
				Manette	246
			Directress	Director	100
				Aloha	30
	Morning Bells	Bow Bells	Electioneer	Hambletonian	2
				Green Mt. Maid	171
			Beautiful Bells	The Moor	88
				Minnehaha	308
		Rosy Morn	Alcantara	George Wilkes	166
				Alma Mater	224
			Noontide	Harold	166
				Midnight	268

No. 76

Little Lie, b m, (1936) 2:01¼m

LITTLE LIE	Mr. McElwyn	Guy Axworthy	Axworthy	Axtell	359
				Marguerite	204
			Lillian Wilkes	Guy Wilkes	146
				Flora	—
		Widow Maggie	Peter the Great	Pilot Medium	168
				Santos	156
			Maggie Onward	Onward	146
				The Widow	361
	Great Patch	Peter the Great	Pilot Medium	Happy Medium	166
				Tackey	268
			Santos	Grand Sentinel	286
				Shadow	248
		Fan Patch	Joe Patchen	Patchen Wilkes	146
				Josephine Young	196
			Polly Pry	Prince George	204
				Lady Kerner	272

THE MIDNIGHT FAMILY

This maternal family is unique in two respects. The foundation mare, Midnight, was out of a fashionably-bred Thoroughbred mare and thus was half Thoroughbred herself. In addition, it is one of the few maternal families that has two distinct modern branches. One of these is through Emily Ellen and the other through Little Lie. Lady Kerner, the fourth dam of Little Lie, is out of Midnight and thus is a half sister to Noontide in the Emily Ellen pedigree.

The five fastest trotters in the family are: Noble Victory, 4, 1:55⅗m, Ayres, 3, 1:56⅘m, Spencer Scott, 4, TT1:57¼m, Emily's Pride, 3, TT1:58m, and Elma, 3, TT1:58⅘m.

The five fastest pacers are: Diamond Hal, p, 4, 1:57⅖m, Thor Hanover p, 4, 1:57⅘m, Stand By, p, 3, TT1:58m, Merrie Gesture, p, 3, TT1:58m, and Jeremiah Hanover, p, 4, 1:58⅕m.

See also pedigrees Nos. 26, 31 and 44.

No. 77

Nervolo Belle, br m, (1906)

Nervolo	Colbert	Onward	George Wilkes 166
			Dolly 220
		Queen B.	Kearsarge 256
			Jenny 116
	Nelly D.	Allie Gaines	Almont 10
			Maggie Gaines 63
		Jenny	Alexander 152
			Nelly Orvis —
NERVOLO BELLE			
Josephine Knight	Betterton	George Wilkes	Hambletonian 2
			Dolly Spanker —
		Mother Lumps	Pearsall 200
			Lady Irwin 166
	Mambrino King		Mambrino Patchen 220
			Mare by 119
	Mambrino Beauty	Mare by	Allie West 13
			Mare by 7

No. 78

Jane Revere, b m, (1920) 2, 2:05¾ m

Guy Axworthy	Axworthy	Axtell	William L. 146
			Lou 219
		Marguerite	Kentucky Prince 86
			Young Daisy 314
	Lillian Wilkes	Guy Wilkes	George Wilkes 166
			Lady Bunker 224
		Flora	Unknown
			Unknown
JANE REVERE			
Volga E.	Peter the Great	Pilot Medium	Happy Medium 166
			Tackey 268
		Santos	Grand Sentinel 286
			Shadow 248
	Nervolo		Colbert 250
			Nelly D. 12
	Nervolo Belle		Betterton 146
		Josephine Knight	Mambrino Beauty 222

THE NERVOLO BELLE FAMILY

This family is one of the very few and the only one among the leading families that has the dam and full sister to a great sire as tap root mares. Nervolo Belle is the dam of the great sire Peter Volo and her daughter Volga E. is a full sister to that horse. Jane Revere, through her daughters Alma Lee and Belvedere, is the third dam of Worthy Boy and Scott Frost and the second dam of Rosalind.

The five fastest trotters in the family are: Rosalind, 5, TT1:56¾ m, Fisherman, 6, TT1:58m, Scott Frost, 4, TT1:58⅗ m, Lowe Hanover, 3, TT1:59m, Vamp Hanover, 4, 1:59⅖ m, and Hoot Frost 4, 1:59⅖ m.

The five fastest pacers are: Timely Beauty, p, 2, TT1:57⅕ m, Solicitor, p, 3, TT1:57⅖, Honor's Truax, p, 6, TT1:58⅖ m, Vogel Hanover, p, 4, 1:58⅗ m, and Lehigh Hanover, p, 3, 1:58⅘ h.

See also pedigrees Nos. 28, 29, 51 and 65.

<table>
<tr><td colspan="3">No. 79</td></tr>
</table>

No. 79

Mamie, br m, (1880)

		Alex's Abdallah	Hambletonian	2
	Almont		Katy Darling	—
		Mare by	Mambrino Chief	225
Star Almont			Mare by	268
	Blood's Bl'khawk		Vt. Black Hawk	290
	Maggie Gaines		Unknown	
		Unknown	Unknown	
MAMIE			Unknown	
		Unknown	Unknown	
	Long's American Boy		Unknown	
		Unknown	Unknown	
Kit			Unknown	
		Roger's Hi'lander	Unknown	
	Gardner Mare		Unknown	
		Unknown	Unknown	
			Unknown	

No. 80

Margaret Parrish, b m, (1908) 4, TT2:06¼m

		May King	Electioneer	166
	Bingen		May Queen	244
		Young Miss	Young Jim	146
Vice Commodore			Miss Mambrino	278
		Arion	Electioneer	166
	Narion		Manette	246
		Nancy Hanks	Happy Medium	166
MARGARET PARRISH			Nancy Lee	100
		Electioneer	Hambletonian	2
	Arion		Green Mt. Maid	171
		Manette	Nutwood	48
Lady Leyburn			Emblem	320
		Wilton	George Wilkes	166
	Margaret Leyburn		Alley	166
		Rose Leyburn	Onward	146
			Mamie	305

THE MAMIE FAMILY

The Mamie family has for 75 years been tied in with and contributed to the success of Walnut Hall Farm. It has produced many of the great horses of the breed and the basic maternal line runs through two daughters of Margaret Parrish—Margaret Castleton by Guy Castleton and Margaret Arion by Guy Axworthy.

The five fastest trotters in the family are: Prince Victor, 5, 1:58⅕m, Silver Song, 6, 1:58⅖m, The Intruder, 3, TT1:59⅕m, Margaret Castleton, 4, TT1:59¼m, Protector, 3, 1:59¼m, and The Marchioness, 3, TT1:59¼m.

The five fastest pacers are: Combat Time, p, 3, TT1:57m, Henry T. Adios, p, 6, 1:57m, Milford Hanover, p, 5, TT1:57⅕m, Cape Horn, p, 5, TT1:57⅘m, and Dudley Hanover, p, 5, TT1:57⅘m.

Ethelwyn, b m, (1882) 2:33

		Abdallah	Mambrino	234
	Hambletonian		Amazonia	—
		Chas. Kent Mare	Bellfounder	309
Harold			One Eye	58
		Abdallah	Mambrino	234
	Enchantress		Amazonia	—
		Mare by	Bellfounder	309
ETHELWYN			Unknown	
		Pilot	Unknown	
	Pilot Jr.		Unknown	
		Nancy Pope	Unknown	
Kathleen			Unknown	
		Sovereign	Emilius	253
	Little Miss		Fleur-de-lis	66
		Little Mistress	Shamrock	312
			Glance	357

Nedda, b m, (1915) 7, TT1:58¼m

		Artillery	Hambletonian	2
	Bellini		Well's Star	284
		Merry Clay	Harry Clay	79
Atlantic Express			Ethelberta	169
		Electioneer	Hambletonian	2
	Expressive		Green Mt. Maid	171
		Esther	Express	124
NEDDA			Colisseum	92
		Pancoast	Woodford Mam.	220
	Prodigal		Vicara	169
		Beatrice	Cuyler	166
Pleasant Thought			Mary Mambrino	224
		Baron Wilkes	George Wilkes	166
	Extasy		Belle Patchen	224
		Ethelwyn	Harold	166
			Kathleen	268

THE ETHELWYN FAMILY

This family is grounded in lines similar to those of the Midnight family. The tap root mare, in this case Kathleen, the dam of Ethelwyn, is by Pilot Jr. out of a Thoroughbred mare just as Midnight was. The parallel is even more striking in view of the fact that Ethelwyn herself was by Harold, the inbred son of Hambletonian, as was Noontide, the daughter of Midnight that founded the Emily Ellen branch of that family. Nedda, whose sire has a Thoroughbred second dam, is a key mare in the family with the principal speed lines running though Pleasant Thought and her half sisters, Petrex by Peter The Great and Ethel Volo by Binvolo.

The five fastest trotters in the family are: Nedda, 7, TT1:58¼m, Safe Mission, 3, 1:59⅕m, Stenographer, 3, TT1:59⅕m, McLin Hanover, 4, 1:59¼m, and Bill Gallon, 3, TT1:59½m.

The five fastest pacers are: Dottie's Pick, p, 4, TT1:56⅘m, Good Time, p, 5, 1:57⅘m, Meadow Battles, p, 3, 1:58⅕m, Stormy Dream, p, 6, 1:58⅖m, Muncy Hanover, p, 3, 1:58⅗h, and Meadow Russ, p, 3, 1:58⅗m.

See also pedigree No. 16.

2:00 HORSES IN AUSTRALIA AND NEW ZEALAND

Seventeen horses, all pacers, have acquired records of 2:00 or faster in Australia and New Zealand through the 1966-67 racing season. They are listed on the chart below which also indicates their descent from Hambletonian. Ribands, James Scott and Avian Derby were bred in Australia and took their records in that country. Lawn Derby was bred in Australia but took his record in New Zealand. All others were bred and took 2:00 records in New Zealand. Highland Fling and Robin Dundee are the only horses credited with more than one 2:00 mile. Highland Fling had four, all in New Zealand, Robin Dundee had two, one in each country, and her fastest record, taken in Australia, is listed. The listed years are the ones in which the indicated records were taken.

- HAMBLETONIAN
  - Happy Medium
    - Pilot Medium
      - Peter the Great
        - Peter Volo
          - Volomite
            - Light Brigade
              - Fallacy
                - False Step p, 4, 2:00 (1957)
        - Peter Scott
          - Scotland
            - U. Scott
              - Highland Fling p, 6, T1:57⅘ (1948)
              - Caduceus p, 9, T1:57⅗ (1959)
              - Orbiter N p, 6, 1:58⅘ (1966)
              - Noble Scott
                - James Scott, p, 8, T1:59⅕ (1962)
  - Strathmore
    - Steinway
      - Charles Derby
        - Owyhee
          - Mambrino Derby
            - Globe Derby
              - Robert Derby
                - Lawn Derby p, 8, T1:59⅖ (1938)
                  - Ribands p, 5, T1:58 7/10 (1954)
                  - Avian Derby p, 7, T2:00 (1952)
              - Logan Derby
                - Johnny Globe p, 6, T1:59⅘ (1953)
                  - Lordship p, 8, 1:58⅗ (1967)
              - Springfield Globe
                - Tactician p, 12, 1:59⅘ (1957)
  - Dictator
    - Director
      - Direct
        - Direct Hal
          - Walter Direct
            - Napoleon Direct
              - Billy Direct
                - Smokey Hanover
                  - Elegant Hanover p, 6, 2:00 (1967)
  - Electioneer
    - May King
      - Bingen
        - Nelson Bingen
          - Nelson Derby
            - Haughty p, 9, 1:59⅗ (1944)
    - Chimes
      - The Abbe
        - Abbedale
          - Chief Abbedale
            - Newport Chief
              - Tobias p, 4, 1:59⅘ (1967)
  - George Wilkes
    - Wilkes Boy
      - Grattan
        - Grattan Royal
          - Grattan Loyal
            - Gold Bar p, 5, T1:59⅗ (1942)
    - William L.
      - Axtell
        - Axworthy
          - Guy Axworthy
            - Truax
              - Tryax
                - Hal Tryax
                  - Cardigan Bay p, 7, 1:56⅕ (1963)
                  - Robin Dundee p, 9, 1:59 (1967)

Roquepine, b m, (1961)

ROQUEPINE	Atus II	Hernani III	Ontario	Bemecourt
				Tunisie
			Odessa	Fauchon II
				Tenebreuse
		Juignettes	Cormantrail	Quarteron
				Oriflamme
			Quarantaine	Kalmouk
				Une Divorcee
	Jalna IV	Kairos	The Gt. McKin'y	Arion McKinney
				Virginia Dangler
			Uranie	Intermede
				Pastourelle
		Sa Bourbonnaise	Karoly II	Trianon
				Braila
			Beresina II	Nenni
				Palatine

Toscan, b h, (1963)

TOSCAN	Kerjacques	Quinio	Hernani III	Ontario
				Odessa
			Germaine	Phoenix
				Lysistrata
		Arlette III	Loudeac	Bolero
				Bonne Fortune
			Maggy II	Fidus
				Dedette II
	Toscane B.	Junior du Verdier	Salam	Kalmouk
				In Salah
			Delpe du V'dier	Tigrane
				Oublieuse
		Baronne	Intermede	Bemecourt
				Belle Poule
			Duchesse	Jaguar III
				Turlurette

The two pedigrees on this page are those of the leading French trotters of the day, the great mare Roquepine and the fast young horse Toscan. From an American standpoint, the bloodlines are unique in that Toscan has no American crosses and Roquepine has only two. The sire of Roquepine's dam, Kairos, is by the American-bred The Great McKinney. Much farther back is another cross through Braila to the American mare Helen Leyburn (by Onward out of the foundation mare Mamie) who was exported to France more than 50 years ago. The names of all horses in the fourth generation of these pedigrees either appear in the French lineage chart on the next page or, with exceptions to be indicated, may be traced in the tail-male line to a horse on that chart as follows:

Fauchon II, Oriflamme, Trianon, Odessa and Fidus trace to Intermede; Tunisie, Quarteron, Nenni and Belle Poule to James Watt; Pastourelle, Lysistrata, Bonne Fortune, and Oublieuse to Bemecourt; Bolero to Koenigsburg; Palatine to Cherbourg; Dedette II to Ontario; Turlurette to Phaeton and Tigrane to Beaumanoir.

The exceptions are (1) the American horses Arion McKinney and Virginia Dangler (by Peter The Great) in Roquepine's fourth generation and (2) Tenebreuse, Braila and Une Divorcee for Roquepine and In Salah and Jaguar III for Toscan, who trace in tail-male to a horse named Lavater who is also the sire of the dam of the foundation stallion Fuschia. Lavater's sire is given officially as *either* Y (that is his full name) *or* Crocus. Y was by the Norfolk Phenomenon, the famous Norfolk trotter who traces to the Darley Arabian through Blaze, while Crocus also traces back to the Darley Arabian through 12 additional crosses.

THE PRINCIPAL LINES OF DESCENT OF THE FRENCH TROTTING BREED

The charts on this page set forth the male lines of descent of the French trotting breed, one of only two in the world (the other is the Russian Orloff) that does not trace directly back to Hambletonian in all tail-male lines. For comparative purposes, the French lines that do trace to Hambletonian—through the imported American stallions Sam Williams, The Great McKinney and Net Worth—are illustrated in the chart headed by Flying Childers at the lower right. The most prominent French sire line, opposite, traces to the Godolphin Arabian who, along with the Darley Arabian and the Byerly Turk, established the three lines of descent of the Thoroughbred horse. The last completely Thoroughbred horse in this French line is Old Rattler. His son Rattler was a half-breed, or "demi-sang," as the French call such horses. The other non-Hambletonian line, lower left, traces to the Darley Arabian through Eclipse—from whom virtually all the great runners of the current Thoroughbred era descend—and thence through Bartlett's Childers, a full brother to Flying Childers, the horse that established the Messenger-Hambletonian line. The last completely Thoroughbred horse in this line is Galoar, whose son The Heir of Linne was only half-Thoroughbred. The French consider their foundation sires (comparable to Hambletonian in the United States) to have been Fuschia, Normand and Phaeton. In a few instances, famous female horses have been included in the charts, and they are indicated by the asterisk (°). French breeding is also discussed in Chapter 1.

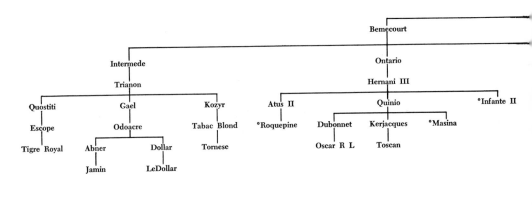

DARLEY ARABIAN

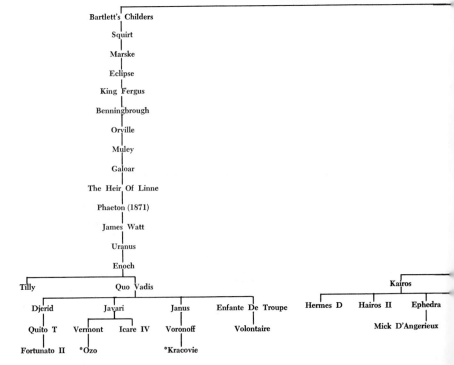

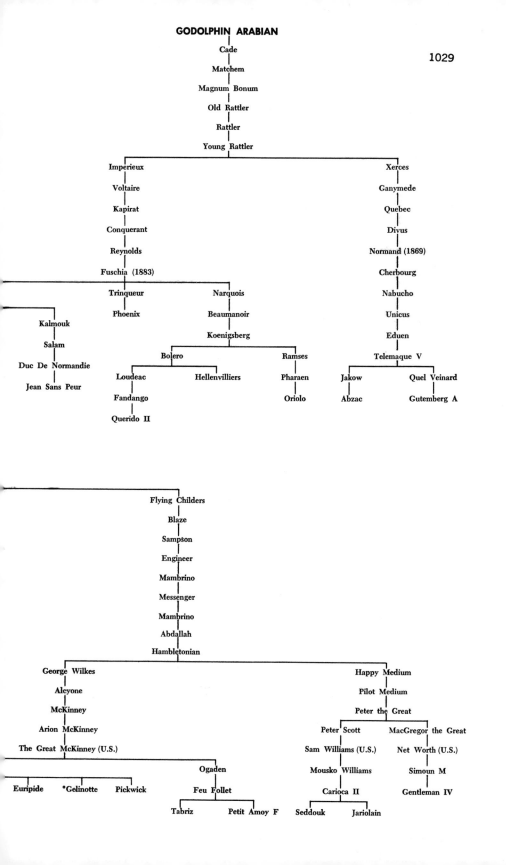

GODOLPHIN ARABIAN
Cade
Matchem
Magnum Bonum
Old Rattler
Rattler
Young Rattler

Imperieux — Xerces

Imperieux
Voltaire
Kapirat
Conquerant
Reynolds
Fuschia (1883)

Trinqueur — Narquois

Kalmouk
Salam
Duc De Normandie
Jean Sans Peur

Trinqueur → Phoenix
Narquois → Beaumanoir → Koenigsberg

Bolero — Ramses

Bolero → Loudeac — Hellenvilliers
Loudeac → Fandango → Querido II
Ramses → Pharaen → Oriolo

Xerces
Ganymede
Quebec
Divus
Normand (1869)
Cherbourg
Nabucho
Unicus
Eduen
Telemaque V

Jakow — Quel Veinard
Jakow → Abzac
Quel Veinard → Gutemberg A

Flying Childers
Blaze
Sampson
Engineer
Mambrino
Messenger
Mambrino
Abdallah
Hambletonian

George Wilkes — Happy Medium

George Wilkes
Alcyone
McKinney
Arion McKinney
The Great McKinney (U.S.)

Happy Medium
Pilot Medium
Peter the Great

Peter Scott — MacGregor the Great
Peter Scott → Sam Williams (U.S.) → Mousko Williams → Carioca II → Seddouk — Jariolain
MacGregor the Great → Net Worth (U.S.) → Simoun M → Gentleman IV

Euripide   *Gelinotte   Pickwick   Ogaden
Ogaden → Feu Follet → Tabriz — Petit Amoy F

Index

X

Y

Z